Shanghai Delta

This is China's richest part. Jiangsu long led the provinces in both industrial and agricultural production mainly because of "Sunan," i.e., the counties put under Suzhou, Wuxi, Changzhou, and Nantong. The Shanghai delta also includes the ten counties shown under the metropolis, plus Zhejiang counties under Hangzhou, Jiaxing, Huzhou, Shaoxing, Ningbo, and Zhoushan. Shanghai was populated from the delta; many of its families retain ties there, and these grew in economic importance during the 1970s and 1980s. But about a quarter of Shanghai's families come from Subei— i.e., all Jiangsu north of Sunan. No map legend can do justice to the lakes, gardens, poems, wines, or operas the flat delta bred. People meet in autumn at teahouses to enjoy chrysanthemums and freshwater crabs, discussing art and politics as well as business. Many small canals, not shown on the map, join all parts of this area.

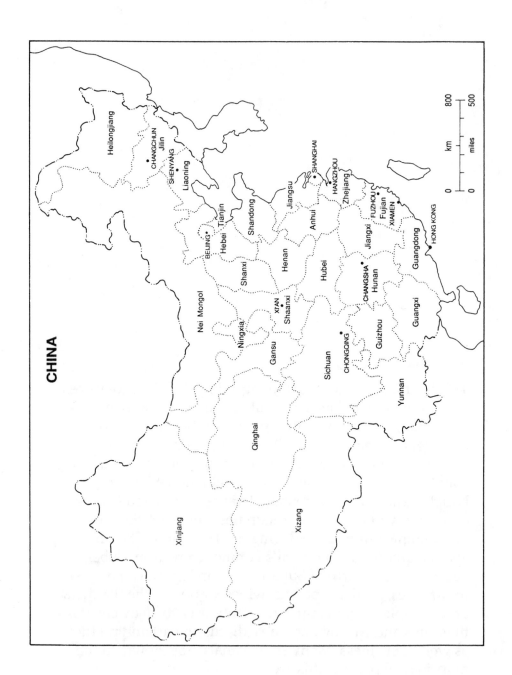

UNSTATELY POWER

VOLUME II
Local Causes of China's Intellectual, Legal, and Governmental Reforms

LYNN T. WHITE, III

Written under the auspices of
the Center of International Studies, Princeton University
and
the Centre of Asian Studies, University of Hong Kong

An East Gate Book

M.E. Sharpe
Armonk, New York
London, England

An East Gate Book

Library of Congress Cataloging-in-Publication Data

White, Lynn T.
Unstately power. Local causes of China's intellectual, legal and
governmental reforms / Lynn T. White III.
p.   cm.
Includes bibliographical references and index.
"An East Gate book."
ISBN 0-7656-0148-6 (cloth : alk. paper)   ISBN 0-7656-0149-4 (pbk. : alk. paper)
1. Political planning—China.   2. Power (Social sciences)—China.
3. Politics and culture—China.   4. Law reform—China.   I. Title.
JQ1509.5.P64W55   1997
306.2—dc21
97-26805
CIP

Printed in the United States of America

The paper used in this publication meets the minimum requirements of
American National Standard for Information Sciences—
Permanence of Paper for Printed Library Materials,
ANSI Z 39.48-1984.

EB (c)   10   9   8   7   6   5   4   3   2   1
EB (p)   10   9   8   7   6   5   4   3   2   1

For my family

Heaven sees as my people see. Heaven hears as my people hear.
—*The Book of Documents* (*Shu Jing*)

We rely largely on men for our evidence about women, on conformists for our
evidence about deviants, and on élites for our evidence about non-élites. . . .
How, why, and in what ways did bias work? Precisely how did it affect
interpretation, and how can it be used against itself? The study of group
ideology, of *mentalité*, is not the opposite of empirical revision, but its
necessary partner.

— James Belich

Unstately Power: Local Causes of China's Intellectual, Legal, and Governmental Reforms

Contents

Conclusion: China Changes 611

Abbreviations

BR	*Beijing Review*
CCP	Chinese Communist Party
CD	*China Daily,* Beijing
CNA	*China News Analysis,* Hong Kong (Taiwan)
CPSU	Communist Party of the Soviet Union
CR	Cultural Revolution
CYL	Communist Youth League
DGB	*Dagong bao* (L'Impartial), Shanghai, Tianjin, or Hong Kong
ECMM	*Extracts from China Mainland Magazines,* Hong Kong
EE	*Eastern Express*, Hong Kong
FBIS	*Foreign Broadcast Information Service,* Washington
FDXB	*Fudan xuebao* (Fudan Academic Journal), Shanghai
FEER	*Far Eastern Economic Review*, Hong Kong
GMRB	*Guangming ribao* (Bright Daily), Beijing
GRRB	*Gongren ribao* (Workers' Daily), Beijing
HQ	*Hongqi* (Red Flag), Beijing
JFRB	*Jiefang ribao* (Liberation Daily), Shanghai
JJRB	*Jingji ribao* (Economic Daily), Beijing
JJYJ	*Jingji yanjiu* (Economic Research), Beijing
JPRS	*Joint Publications Research Service*, Washington
KMT	Kuomintang (Nationalist Party; a.k.a. Guomindang)
LDB	*Laodong bao* (Labor News), Shanghai or Beijing
LSYFZ	*Lüshi yu fazhi* (Lawyer and Law), Hangzhou
LW	*Liaowang* (Outlook), Beijing
MFN	Most-favored nation (whose exports enjoy low tariffs)
MZGBDS	*Meizhou guangbo dianshi* (Radio and TV Weekly), Shanghai
NCNA	*New China News Agency*, Shanghai unless noted
PLA	People's Liberation Army
Post	*South China Morning Post,* Hong Kong

PRC   People's Republic of China
PSB   Public Security Bureau
QNB   *Qingnian bao* (Youth News), Shanghai and Beijing
RMRB   *Renmin ribao* (People's Daily), Beijing
RMRBHWB   *Renmin ribao haiwai ban* (*RMRB* Overseas Edition), Beijing
SASS   Shanghai Academy of Social Sciences
SCMM   *Selections of China Mainland Magazines*, Hong Kong
SCMP   *Survey of China Mainland Press*, Hong Kong
SF   *Shanghai Focus* (*China Daily* weekly supplement), Shanghai
SHGG   *Shanghai gaige* (Shanghai Reforms)
SHGYJJB   *Shanghai gongye jingji bao* (Shanghai Industrial Economy)
SHHJKX   *Shanghai huanjing kexue* (Shanghai Environmental Sciences)
SHJJ   *Shanghai jingji* (Shanghai Economy)
SHJJDB   *Shanghai jingji daobao* (Shanghai Economic Herald)
SHJJNJ##   *Shanghai jingji nianjian, 19##* (Shanghai Economic Yearbook, 19##)
SHJJYJ   *Shanghai jingji yanjiu* (Shanghai Economic Research)
SHKXB   *Shehui kexue bao* (Social Science News), Shanghai
SHTJNJ##   *Shanghai tongji nianjian,* 19## (Shanghai Statistical Yearbook, 19##)
SHWB   *Shanghai wanbao* (Shanghai Evening News)
SHWL   *Shanghai wenlun* (Shanghai Literary Theory)
SHWXJ   *Shanghai wenxue jiao* (Shanghai Literary Corner)
SHXW   *Shanghai xinwen* (Shanghai News)
SJJJDB   *Shijie jingji daobao* (World Economic Herald), Shanghai
WHB   *Wenhui bao* (Wenhui News), Shanghai [or Hong Kong, if noted]
WHZY   *Wenhui zhi you* (Friend of Wenhui), Shanghai
XDRB   *Xingdao ribao* (Sing Tao Daily), Hong Kong
XMWB   *Xinmin wanbao* (Xinmin Evening News), Shanghai
XWB   *Xinwen bao* (News Report), Shanghai
XWJZ   *Xinwen jizhe* (Journalist), Shanghai
XWRB   *Xinwen ribao* (News Daily), Shanghai
ZGQN   *Zhongguo qingnian* (China Youth), Beijing
ZGQNB   *Zhongguo qingnian bao* (China Youth News), Beijing
ZGTJNJ##   *Zhongguo tongji nianjian, 19##* (Chinese Statistical Yearbook, 19##)
ZW   *Zhanwang* (Prospect), Beijing

Romanizations

This book generally romanizes Chinese in pinyin. This system may at first seem odd to English readers, because it uses frequent q's, x's, z's, and zh's with unexpected sounds. It is even more counterintuitive than the Wade-Giles system, the older alternative that was developed by British diplomats and missionaries. Pinyin has become standard in the People's Republic of China and in most publications. It is used in this book except for terms (and abbreviations such as KMT) associated with the Nationalist government or Taiwan. A brief table can help readers gain confidence about saying names in pinyin. The system is difficult mainly because of five consonants, listed below, that can be practiced.

The basic unit of this language is the syllable (which is always written with a single character). When you see a romanization, it should generally be either one or two syllables long. (If it is two, the division will usually be obvious in the lettering.) Pronounce each syllable as a unity; do not extend dipthongs so that they sound like two syllables.

Chinese, like any other tongue, has a distinctive sound system. Exact equivalences to English are difficult to reproduce on a printed list, but the aim here is only to give readers who specialize in other languages a sufficient accuracy so that they can be brave when referring to Chinese words in speech. On the next page are only the letters that most differ from what English readers expect. The first five are consonants, always occurring at the beginnings of syllables. After these, four syllable endings are also listed. A reader who follows this table—and says all other pinyin as if it were English—can feel confident the pronunciation will not be very far wrong.

Pinyin = Sound

five sounds to start syllables:

c-	= ts-
q-	= ch-
x-	= sh-
z-	= dz-
zh-	= j-

four sounds to end syllables:

-ian	= -ien
-ong	= -ung
-ui	= -way
-i	= -ee (sometimes -r, or -uh)*

Pronounce all other letters as in English. Assume most romanized words have two syllables. The most problematic symbol in this system is *-i*. A viable policy for most readers is to ignore its irregularities, although these are described in a note below.

---

*The pinyin *-i* varies in sound. Usually pronounce it as "-ee." But it is like "-r" after the initial consonants *ch*-, *r*-, *sh*-, and *zh*-. It is a deep "-uh" after *c*-, *s*-, and *z*-. This *-i* is the main technical flaw of pinyin, the most frequent case in which a single printed symbol does not map uniquely to a single sound. Because some have praised pinyin for its distinction between palitals and retroflexes, the pinyin blitheness about *-i* is odd. English readers who do not know Chinese can learn sounds for the *c*-, *q*-, *x*-, and *zh*- initials that seem most fearsome; then they can respectably neglect any further problems.

A Note about Wordings

Since this book is in English, its terms are chosen to approximate their usual meanings for many English-language readers. "Public prosecutor" is sometimes used here instead of "procurator" (*jiancha yuan*). When China's administrative jurisdictions are discussed here, for example, the four "directly ruled municipalities" (*zhixia shi*; Shanghai, Beijing, Tianjin, and Chongqing) are called "provinces" along with the other provinces and "autonomous regions" (*zizhi qu*, such as Tibet), because they all operate similarly as branches of the central government. "High school" is preferred to "upper middle school" (*gaozhong*), and "junior high" to "lower middle" (*chuzhong*). Sometimes the term "State Cabinet" is inserted in the text near "State Council," when it is clear they refer to the same body, in an attempt to approximate for common readers what that body is. No solution to these problems is perfect, but this approach may help to demystify terms, despite real differences in national institutions. New China hands will know the referents anyway.

Tables

Percentages in this book are usually rounded from the sources.

Plates

(Plates follow page 170)

Preface and Acknowledgments

Most writers date China's reforms from 1978 and suggest these momentous changes were caused by the policies of high state leaders under Deng Xiaoping. The book in your hands is the second volume of a two-part series, whose first half is titled *Unstately Power: Local Causes of China's Economic Reforms*. It provides evidence that the syndrome now called "reforms" began in the early 1970s. Agricultural extension by the late 1960s freed great amounts of labor from the land. Rich Chinese rural areas, notably Shanghai's suburbs and adjacent parts of the Shanghainese flatland, experienced very quick mechanization of farm work during the late 1960s, the most tumultuous years of the Cultural Revolution. After 1970, rural leaders in these relatively prosperous areas founded or revived local factories outside the effective purview of central state control. This was the start of reforms.

Many of these rural leaders were avowed "state cadres," but the unintended effects of their actions helped their local constituencies far more than they helped Beijing. Local enterprises, which the central bureaucracy could not monitor, took materials and markets away from state industries. Socialist control of input prices and commodity flows gradually eroded, until it mostly collapsed in the mid-1980s. Shortages and inflation bedeviled the economy, the state ran deficits, management decentralized, local banks proliferated, and unregistered immigration to cities soared.

These changes, which have ended the institutions that China's revolutionaries created under Mao, do not owe their origins solely to economic or material causes. The current volume explores other kinds of evidence for the onset of reforms: in the ideas and religions of small groups, in arts that range from quasi-political films to pop rock music, in the diversification of laws and of China's coercive institutions, and in transformations of the structure of actual power. "Reforms" are treated in this research as a syndrome of changes that mutually reinforce each other in many functional fields. They emerge not just from the intended policies and unintended situations of the state, but also from the notions and contexts of individuals or small groups— whose power, uncivil and inarticulate though it often is, can be considered alongside official influences as factors that made the reforms. Together, these reforms are changing the wealth and freedoms of the largest national group on earth.

The author's debts are many, and the earlier volume provides a long list of institutions and people to whom he owes great thanks for help with this project. Because the plates appear in this book, special thanks are due here to Joan Lebold Cohen for permission to use three pictures from her pioneering book about *The New Chinese Painting, 1949–1986* (New York: H. N. Abrams, 1987). I am also thankful to the artists Guan Xiaobin, Jier Gebang, and Xu Mangyao, and to the Hanart TZ Gallery of Hong Kong for permission to reproduce a painting by Li Shan. The author's debt to institutions is so heavy that they should again be listed here: the Centre of Asian Studies of Hong Kong University and its Director Wong Siu-lun and Deputy Director Elizabeth Sinn, the Center of International Studies and Woodrow Wilson School of Princeton University, the Shanghai Academy of Social Sciences, the Institute of International Relations of National Chengchi University and the Academia Sinica on Taiwan, Universities Service Centre at the Chinese University of Hong Kong— and for financial help, the Harry Frank Guggenheim Foundation, the Chiang Ching-kuo Foundation, and Princeton University. Warm thanks go also to colleagues at M. E. Sharpe, notably Doug Merwin, Patricia Loo, and Angela Piliouras for squiring the manuscript to publication, and now also to Nancy Hearst and Doris Mount for proofreading, and Joan Zurell and Bryan Lammers for typesetting. The very long list of individuals to whom further specific debts are owed appears in the first volume, and here there is only space to thank them collectively. The author is solely responsible for all mistakes in this book. He is immensely grateful to his family and to all the other blameless people and institutions without whose help this research would never have appeared.

Lynn T. White III
Princeton, New Jersey
April 1997

UNSTATELY POWER

Part 2

Legitimation:
Local Seers Reform Political
Truth—Commitment After Campaigns

Dao ke dao, fei chang dao; ming ke ming, fei chang ming.
The way that can be described is not the natural way;
the name that can be named is not the true name.

—Dao de jing[1]

"The Chinese have a propensity to ascribe reality to symbols," according to Lucian Pye. "Words and slogans often pass in their minds for established facts or accomplishments. The result is that there is often a very large make-believe dimension to Chinese politics."[2] This is certainly not unique to China; but wherever it occurs, social scientists can distinguish things from signs and see that both affect behavior. One kind of writing about politics or history tends to explain actions primarily according to their contexts, while another type gives pride of place to the styles and cultures of the actors. These methods are both analytical; they complement rather than exclude each other. They are like what they generate: predicate hypotheses, whose use is proven in practice rather than before research. Politics is not, after all, just a matter of allocation. It is that, and also a form of theater.[3]

Symbolic, Causal, Partial Explanations

Some analysts who study symbols seem oddly nonchalant about their origins. What makes stories interesting? Why do people manufacture some fictions but not others? Geertz quotes Auden's claim that "poetry makes nothing happen."[4] But evidence, such as will be presented below, shows this is untrue. Symbols spur reactions among their perceivers, no less in social life than in art.[5] Symbols have functions, their expression can make things happen, and it is possible to speak about ideal and behavioral causes together.

To ignore normative causes is not to be modest or careful; it is simply to ignore scientific data. Such an effort can be self-defeating for those concerned about the ethical dangers of ethnocentrism, because it neglects kinds of information needed to explore causations for solving many moral questions.[6] Professionalizing stances in recent academic debates have obscured this. James Scott distinguishes "objective facts" from "social facts."[7] There must be some objectivity about the social facts, however, because they are communicated. They can be objective without being mutually consistent. Mental habits and conscious values constrain behavior, just as concrete things do. They can be causes.

Positing causes is always theoretical. No conclusion to a debate about causation, correlation, and proof can make an adjective or predicate explanation solid, like a noun or subject. An event is not the account of it. Many theorists argue that only a deductive method can explain an action causally. Proponents of both "natural science" and "human science" in social studies have said this. Those who approach social action through cultural symbols say they cannot offer causal explanations. Those who approach it through deductive hypotheses say they alone can identify causes. This assertion has been repeated very often by many fine scholars, but that does not make it right. Robert Darnton, a culturalist historian, makes a better and different point when he offers texts that "cannot be taken to typify eighteenth-century thought but that provide ways of entering into it."[8] This kind of intellectual reserve could also be adopted by deductive thinkers, whose proven hypotheses also just "enter into" facts rather than explaining all the variance among them.

Both approaches can seek causes, or both can also look at noncausal attributions. The only difference between these researchers is whether they begin with greater faithfulness to articulating actors' meanings or their own. Political science, in particular, is strongest when using these complementary methods together. An interpreter-analyst can move between texts and contexts, to see the light they throw on each other. Exploring the ways in which seminal or "radial" symbols are used, as people interact with external situations, is a sensible method to find such links.

Since logics are merely analytical, dependent for their usefulness on the cases to which they are applied, there is no problem in the fact that different logics may be needed to deal with symbolic "controlling factors" and incidental "conditioning factors." George Lakoff distinguishes the "objective" categories of classical logic from "experiential" categories that linguists and psychologists have observed people using. The latter are inseparable from experiences and embodied in the image-making "wetware" of our brains. Objective categories obtain their meanings from "correspondences to things in the external world" that can be shown in replicable tests. Experienced categories get their meanings from similes of many sorts, which are replicated with great regularity among people.[9] But neither category excludes the other. The only problem is to use each for what it can do.

In studies of Chinese politics, symbols (especially symbols of hierarchy) have often been useful in explaining what happens. The Chinese state has long employed nonconcrete, noncoercive tools to buttress its influence; this helps explain why it has lasted for millennia. Prasenjit Duara, an analyst willing to talk about symbols, sees the state as part of a "cultural nexus of power." But the Chinese state "did not exist only in its cultural form." He calls it "a collection of normative and symbolic representations, interlaced with Confucian ideals, though by no means exhausted by them. In this manifestation, the state functioned first and foremost as a series of legitimation strategies: controlling the distribution of rank and honors, performing paradigmatic rituals, and inscribing its hegemony on popular symbols."[10] Duara claims that in the twentieth century, the Chinese state "gradually relinquished and destroyed certain important channels of communication within this nexus, without being able to create working alternatives."[11] This whole discourse identifies a kind of evidence, normative and mainly about small groups, that is a partial determinant of the Chinese state's power.

The following text will discuss "reforms" in art or religion, not just because it is fashionable to be interdisciplinary, but because these reforms are normative and individual, not just situational and collective. Some readers may object to talk about reforms of aesthetics or beliefs, noting that most such changes are individual or familial or local and do not come from state leaders. But an argument here is that in many fields, even in politics and economics, reforms are also local. The state has no monopoly on initiating change. Much use of the word "reforms" unnecessarily restricts them to policies proclaimed for a whole society by high politicians. The behavioral definition of reforms in this book sees them as a syndrome of influences, some state and some local, some intentional and some circumstantial. With that definition, it is not just possible but also necessary to talk about reforms in small-group normative fields such as religion or art, since these affect what people do.

Reforms of political truth that have recently emerged in China have, of course, been contested. Reformist or protoliberal "foxes" have alternated with conservative "lions" in defining looser or stricter norms for ideology, religion, media, and art. The kind of authority that has spurred the waves of quickest change has often been associated with deceased heroes, such as Zhou Enlai or Hu Yaobang, who proved to be politically less ambiguous after death than they were in life. The adulation that Zhou received upon his passing in 1976, or Hu Yaobang in 1989, was not patrimonial or rationalistic; it was charismatic. Very few of the demonstrators in each case knew the deceased leader personally. They were no more in patron-client networks under Zhou or Hu, or reformer Zhao

Ziyang, than under any other high leader. What the followers did may have had factionalist results, but the debate was about leadership and policies. It was based on a sense that the dead prophet had been right and had known what principles to apply for China's benefit. Such rallies based on charismatic authority are of course not workaday institutions. Deng Xiaoping, lasting longer, alternately donned or doffed this charisma, depending at each time on his latest actions, although most Chinese most of the time credited him as a reformer. Leaders make images for themselves. State personalities are important for politics as symbols, not just as policy makers.

The Monkey King, hero of *Journey to the West,* was, like Hu or Zhao, a political icon of reform. Basic political-cultural confusion after the Cultural Revolution was widely symbolized by an episode from this old novel. The heroic monkey, Sun Wukong, seeking Buddhist scriptures in India, was challenged by a demon disguised to look exactly like himself. Even most of the gods could not tell the two apart, and the success of the pilgrimage (which in the 1980s always meant the drive for modernization) was threatened by the impostor. This story of "the true and false monkey" became a sermon on the ambiguities of distinguishing good leaders from bad.[12] (The true monkey, of course, won out in the end, but only after tremulous moments for himself and his cause.) Such a lively but complex presentation would have been impossible to publicize before the revolution began its decline. By the 1980s, it was very popular and available in books, magazines, movies, and cartoons, apparently because it caught the ambiguities and intentions of China's broad-based political quest at that time.

Individual vs. Collective Sources of Values

Popular ideas about the relationship between large collectives and individuals altered somewhat during reforms. This was particularly evident in changing concepts of public corruption—what was dirty and what was clean. The trend in these notions as the revolution receded was demonstrably opposite from what it had been as the revolution rose. One of its aspects was some assertion of the legitimate separateness of individuals and of families.[13] A local Shanghai symbol of these noncollective, even antisocial, interests was the Great World (*Da Shijie*) amusement center on Tibet Road in the city center. This place had been founded in 1917 by a Chinese associated with foreign interests. Gambling, prostitution, and other socially dubious activities took place either inside its large building or nearby; but Great World also catered to families, presented movies, and held games. It was a permanent carnival. After Liberation, this center was too popular locally to close down, so it became the People's Amusement Park (*Renmin Youle Chang*), and its activities were far more decorous. It remained anathema to radicals during the Cultural Revolution, when its doors were shut.

It opened again in October 1974—before the fall of the Gang of Four—as the Shanghai Youth Palace (*Shanghai Qingnian Gong*). In January 1987, Shanghai's government and Party leaders came in person to help celebrate the resumption by Great World of its original name.[14] This entertainment center is now used for movies, acrobatic performances, dance troupes, singing groups, and the like. It also has booths for magicians and an old set of image-distorting mirrors.[15] Ideological collectivists had to treat Great World circumspectly, because of its obvious popularity. But this place served the interests of individuals and families, not larger groups.

The revival of free markets, along with public exhortations from high leaders that individuals could get rich, clearly undermined the egalitarian and communitarian claims the CCP had once made. By 1980, Party propaganda was encouraging people to "create a name for themselves," even though such activities had often been castigated as "individualist" after the 1957 Antirightist Campaign.[16] Since this change benefited local power networks, it is reasonable to think they at least connived in it. Writers often implicitly assume that Chinese morality comes only from the state. A sociologist has, for example, written: "When societal changes outpace the emergence of clearly defined statements of what is acceptable behavior in a given context, social transactions become problematic because people do not know what behavior to expect of others."[17] This certainly describes China in the 1970s and 1980s. But who effectively defines morality?

Just after the successful revolution, the revolutionaries could largely do so. Later, ambiguity became the norm—and not just in the Chinese case. From Carlo Levi and Eric Hobsbawm to James Scott, many diverse writers about different countries have shown the vibrancy of nonstate norms of right and wrong. These writers may for the sake of simplicity sometimes write as if nonstate moralities are as consistent as the state ethics they oppose. Actually, neither governments nor societies are so monolithic. In the contemporary China countryside, for example, new entrepreneurial wealth and sharp practices have been accepted by some peasants while being rejected by others. Unofficial cultures have no need to be consistent, any more than official cultures are; and anthropologists often show these cultures' internal diversity.[18]

On some occasions during reforms, people in Shanghai suggested openly that collective norms were not universally better than personal values. Rarer, because more dangerous, were public expressions that the state is not always competent to represent the collective. The *World Economic Herald* in mid-1988 nonetheless carried an article whose title argued that "statism" was "the root cause of all faults in the old system."[19] No one source for ideological claims will provide full coverage of people's thinking. But normal ideas about politics can be found from many sources. Evidence is available about their effects on China's politics in the era of reforms.

Chapter 2.1

Reform of Ideology

If modern international culture does indeed become the first force in history to dissolve China's notion of its moral uniqueness, that process will, at a minimum, take decades or centuries to finish.

—Perry Link[20]

The convenient working distinction between cultural texts that are social and political and those that are not becomes something worse than an error: namely, a symptom and a reinforcement of the reification and privatization of contemporary life. . . . The only effective liberation from such constraint begins with the recognition that there is nothing that is not social and historical—indeed, that everything is "in the last analysis" political.

—Fredric Jameson[21]

What is ideology? It is something about collective groups, not just individuals alone; but individuals are the ones who might believe it. Marx saw much of it as "false consciousness," the normative tool by which a class of rulers achieves its own results in concrete situations, a mystique to hoodwink the oppressed (or in a temporary socialist-vanguard form, to lead them to liberation). It has often served such roles, whether that makes it false or not. Then Weber treated ideological doctrines largely as systems of philosophical concepts that relate people to concrete situations and can make people cohere in large groups. Mannheim can be said to have specified these two approaches functionally, showing how "ideology" (either lies or truths) serves to stabilize a system within its boundaries,

9

or else to justify a partial group's "utopian" invasion across its boundaries to change the rest.[22] An ideology is a set of norms with a claim to truth that helps its advocates advance their social interests, on behalf of either a large group or a small one.

Ideology, whenever it is used, is also a fact. As Mosca wrote, "One of the most constant human tendencies is the tendency to justify an existing form of government by some rational theory or some supernatural belief."[23] Any creed of this sort could be tested for its content and consistency as philosophy, and that might offer some predictions about its credibility. A more pragmatic, and concurrent, approach to assessing its truth is that of a social scientist assessing its uses.

This kind of pragmatism is not just academic theorizing. It was also the first trend in the explicit reform of CCP ideology after the Cultural Revolution. On April 1, 1972, the Party's theoretical journal *Red Flag* published an article entitled "Correctly Understand and Manage the Link Between Politics and Vocational Work." The problem, as presented by this article, was that politics had been seen as separated from, and far above, the practical problems that individuals and small groups had. Although Cultural Revolution doctrine had decreed redness as more important than expertise, *Red Flag* now claimed that "it is against Mao's revolutionary line to neglect the importance of vocational work. Everyone should try to gain professional skills for the revolution."

Then a June 12, 1972, *People's Daily* article called for a "sensible wage structure," i.e., higher wages for people who worked hard. It criticized "egalitarianism." In July, an American-trained physicist was authorized to draft a "plan for the development of science." In September 1972 he published an article in *Bright Daily* stressing the practical need for pure research.[24] Articles of this kind sporadically appeared during the early 1970s—and radical peans to the eternal glory of proletarian class heroes sporadically appeared against them. This pattern continued into the 1990s, although the praxis-oriented ideologists gradually became bolder, and those nostalgic for communitarian revolution on average became older.

The variety of officially propagated ideologies altered in the early 1970s, but change in this field came more slowly than in other areas such as rural industrialization or foreign trade. The quicker reform of situations than of norms is a general fact. The Gang of Four, while it was powerful in Shanghai, sponsored many campaigns that slowed reforms in this field. Not until April 1977 did several PRC newspapers, including Nanjing's *New China Daily,* raise a series of questions criticizing the radical ideology that had been articulated by Zhang Chunqiao.[25] Zhang had said, "If you want socialist grass, don't begin with capitalist sprouts."[26] But these papers now asked about the relevance of socialism to production, capital accumulation, and technical expertise. The paper said that mere ideological orthodoxy, the right "sprouts," would not provide modernization. It is hardly surprising that by the mid-1970s many Chinese who had participated in the Cultural Revolution, whose egalitarian ideals had been attractive, should ask themselves what had gone wrong. In the early 1970s just implicitly, and in later reforms very directly, a more pragmatic view of human action became popular. Many began to think that the results of action do not spring from intentions alone, but that even political will can be affected by circumstances.

A middle-school teacher from Chongming Island, Shanghai, could publish questions, by late 1977, on whether the history of the Party had been written accurately. He noted, for example, that the usual account of the First CCP Congress, which met at Shanghai in 1921, should be considered moot, because it conventionally reported that just twelve leaders attended, representing fifty Party members throughout the country. But during the Cultural Revolution, some history books had reported seventy CCP members then—though most recent research suggested the number was only forty, and that thirteen delegates were at the congress.[27] Moreover, the lists of particular people attending the First CCP Congress varied over time. In general, history books named only "Mao Zedong, Dong Biwu, Chen Tanqiu, He Shuheng, etc." But this "etc." might, the writer thought, be spelled out—it actually included Zhang Guotao (who later defected) and several whose later careers had not made them famous.[28] This writer called for an "objective, materialist, and factual" approach to the writing of Party history. He excoriated past excesses—for example, the Cultural Revolution claims for Lin Biao's importance in the Nanchang Uprising of August 1, 1927, when Lin was a lowly platoon leader and when, as PLA tradition had it, that army was established. This was not purely scholastic discussion. It was scarcely less important to ardent Chinese Communists than are, for example, debates about the historicity of Christ to literalist Christians. Many in China thought it was especially important to know which particular leaders had founded the CCP. Such questions could, however, broach more rationalist faiths.

A Shanghai critic in the 1980s took much of Chinese historical writing to task because it tended to describe the past as uniformly bad and the present as uniformly good. This habit "distorted the nature of history" and was castigated as unconvincing.[29] Subtle historiography would judge more slowly, in this view. Yet such an interest in ideology, if taken far, reduced it to science. This would be agreeable to any social scientist; but as Karl Mannheim made clear, ideology actually has a more restricted, less universal role.[30] It is a set of truths and lies designed to legitimate a political elite. Ideology as a serious search for scientific truth would be useful as a claim only to rulers who could let the conclusions depend on found facts. That is exactly the claim that China's reformists made, but they had no advance way to assess its consequences.

Approaching this large subject, it makes some sense to begin with official ideas in their various forms, and then to discuss alternatives that have emerged in unofficial groups. The analysis of official conservative and reform ideologies, presented below, can be organized around four practical questions: First, what do the official ideologies legitimate? In other words, what claims to compliance or to leadership talent do they ordinarily make? Second, what scope of topics do officially correct ideas presume to cover? Is this scope broad, comprehending everything from art to cosmology, or is it restricted? Third, with what intensity are people generally expected to believe the official ideology? Is firm credence taken to be a life-or-death matter, or is it instead seen as just one aspect of belief, which may be assimilated to or affected by others? Fourth and finally, what audiences are particularly addressed by public statements of ideology? Is everyone supposed to care equally about the content of such ideas, or are they aimed in practice at more limited assemblies of listeners?

What Do Reform China's Official Ideologies Legitimate?

Party leaders after the Cultural Revolution knew their organization had a problem with legitimacy (*weixin*). For many years before reforms, public propaganda about the CCP's solicitude for disadvantaged people had alternated with a stress on the charismatic virtue of the supreme ruler, Mao Zedong. By the early 1970s, widespread violence had eroded the first claim. By the late 1970s, personality cults slowly went out of style. Under Chairman Hua as under Chairman Mao, portraits of the national leader were requisite at the fronts of meeting halls and theaters, but a few years later, they were often replaced by abstract hammers and sickles. In 1980, a series of directives discouraged their use.[31]

As the personal charisma of the CCP's main builder, Mao, was more weakly replaced by that of others, the Party sought new bases to legitimate its collective rule. The Four Basic Principles (*sixiang jiben yuanze*) were first enunciated to tame the Democracy Wall movement of 1979. They called for faithful support of socialism, the proletarian dictatorship, Party leadership, and Marxism–Leninism–Mao Zedong Thought. Their operational meaning was far less abstract: They were simply a call for obedience to the established CCP authorities. This was a classic political platform for Paretan lions. A PRC political scientist explicitly identified these Four Basic Principles with an older concept, Chinese "national essence."[32] The equation is dubious, but patriotism became the Party elite's safest refuge.

Public Results or Party Leaders as Objects of Legitimation

Legitimate rule was thus linked to national results, of which the most obvious was the reform era's economic boom. Equating prosperity with nationalism, then nationalism with socialism, and then socialism with leadership by the CCP's particular elite made a sufficiently clear claim—and a successful one for many years. But there was risk for the Party if the nation did not continue to prosper. At a meeting with the last Communist premier of Poland in 1985, Deng Xiaoping sermonized, "If we make our work a success, we will be able to show the superiority of socialism over capitalism. Otherwise, we will not be qualified to talk about the superiority of socialism, let alone our ideal of reaching the stage of Communist society."

As Party conservatives pointed out, this formula legitimated prosperity more than CCP rule. The conservative who chaired the Standing Committee of the National People's Congress, Peng Zhen, spoke on November 25, 1985, of the need to believe implicitly and steadfastly in Communism. He said that "some people" felt homilies about establishing an ideal Communist society were "mouthing lofty phrases, big words, and empty talk." Peng said Party members should not only have "a Communist world view," they should also be clear on "the question of whether they have faithfully carried out the solemn vow made upon entering the Party, and whether they can be considered qualified Party members."[33] Sure faith in Leninist discipline was the touchstone of legitimacy that Peng Zhen proposed, and it was clearly different from that advocated at the same time by Deng Xiaoping.

Lenin himself came in for open, published criticism in two 1988 issues of Shanghai's *Wenhui News,* at the hands of author Wang Ruoshui.[34] This was the first PRC attack against the founder of Bolshevik organization. Wang hoped that by rejecting some of Lenin's organizational techniques, China could develop a more human form of Marxism, to oppose "alienation" in socialist as well as capitalist systems. This extreme reformist view of legitimacy put a social test to the Party's claim for obedience, going far beyond the success of market policies to the protection of individuals as most early socialists had envisaged.

After the Tiananmen massacre, this zigzag reform continued, veering toward the conservative side. The reactionary pitch by the 1990s was explicitly romantic and nostalgic. The *People's Daily* praised Mao as "the symbol of a bygone era," when "cadres were uncorrupt, and the people were harmonious and loved each other."[35] With a blithe amnesia about certain events in Mao's time that had actually discouraged harmony and love, sentimental conservatives advertised Mao as a man of compassion for the needy, stability for the economy, honesty among bureaucrats, and frugality in management. These conservatives had a powerful political appeal, which attracted people because of the tumult of reforms. When the market threatened careers and disturbed people personally, Mao was remembered more warmly. The disoriented wanted their sun in the east again. When they urged respect for old communalist values under the banner of Mao, many and others agreed. Above all, Mao represented the legitimacy of Party rule. As a 1991 source said simply: "To downplay Mao Zedong Thought is to negate the Party."[36]

Central vs. Local Leaders as Objects of Legitimation

The same zigzag pattern shows in alternating public demands for obedience to more-central or more-local leaders. In Mao's time, the main means for spreading the centralist claim throughout society was the political campaign. By mid-reforms, specifically in 1980, such movements were used for a revised purpose:

local elections. These were supposed to link local leaders more surely to their constituents—and in the long run, the electoral institution will probably do that in China, as it has in other countries where it has been tried. But in the short run, such leaders had other sources of support in local hierarchies. The movement for elections came from high reformers.

"Campaigns debilitated rule," Barrett McCormack argues specifically as regards the official movement for the 1980 elections. So "the campaign to strengthen laws and institutions can be seen as an attempt by the party center to increase its administrative capacity."[37] Some liberal-appearing policies of the Leninist state, such as those calling for local elections, were often implemented in practice toward statist ends. They supported campaigns for better linkages between state and people; but another aim was to instill a more extensive popular obedience. The long-term results are much less clear, because people might later begin to take elections seriously.

These policies of the 1980s, trying to coordinate local interests while restoring the revolutionary hegemony of the 1950s, confirmed order in noncentral networks, not just under the coordinated state. "The reforms can be viewed as a Leninist revival," McCormack claims, both in general and with regard to local elections.[38] Some at the center surely intended them as such, and the state can almost always intervene successfully at any specific time and place to achieve what it wants just then and there. But by the 1980s, local leaders (especially in rural areas far from capitals) gave evidence of having diverse intentions. The Leninist state, theoretically so strong, very often did not get its way. Over the long haul and in many places, the practice of elections could loosen its internal discipline.

Campaigns in previous years had strengthened clientelist ties, but they also let the state accumulate capital for more diversified communications and specialized economic infrastructure—and in the long run, this weakens patrimonial patterns. A difficulty with much of the available literature about CCP campaigns is that it judges them almost exclusively according to their intentions and immediate reported results, not according to the long-term and unintended results. The former are understandably statist; the latter are often not.

Ideological propaganda, which central state leaders design to benefit themselves, can be received by diverse audiences as legitimating local leaderships separately. Anthropologist Stevan Sangren describes all Chinese voluntary organizations as variations on a common theme. Lineage halls and temples set the hierarchic style for most other rural organizations, all of which have great formal similarities in both structure and ideology.[39] Disciplined hierarchy, though urged by the state, does not always benefit the state. Unorganized or officially illegitimate mass movements could hardly threaten central authorities quickly, but regional and local networks influenced by them can do so slowly. The nearly constant tattoo about the need for discipline in China may strengthen noncentral leaders too.

The Shanghai delta is one of the best-organized parts of China, and statist norms are readily used by local governments there even when they may weaken the state. Collective enterprises in and near Shanghai have been popularly conceived more like state enterprises than have collectives in many other parts of the country. In Guangdong under reforms, the term "cadre" (*ganbu*) usually refers to state enterprise officials proper, but in Shanghai, collectives' leaders are also called "cadres." In exchange for bows to state propriety, leaders are often free to do whatever they wish in the interests of their own local structures.

Personal vs. Collective Interests in CCP Talent Recruitment

Individual leaders need the confidence to do their jobs, and a major function of ideology is to guide them not just to coordinate decisions but to make them. Common ideas are crucial criteria for recruiting leaders (as will be discussed in the part of this book that deals with collective governance), but they also help individuals justify decisions to themselves and in small groups. A claim to truth is an aspect of recruitment. Ideology is supposed to inspire young leaders to want the jobs that are available. Common bonds that come from fellow feeling in small groups often influence the way these groups affect larger politics.

The Cultural Revolution, in which most Party leaders had been attacked, weakened the CCP's ability to enlist new blood. Many talented youths had been sent out of Shanghai, for example, and rightly or wrongly they felt that an injustice had been done to them. The interest in Party membership among the formerly sent-down youths who returned to Shanghai (as most had done by the middle of the 1980s) was reportedly not great. Even among youths from workers' families, the CCP faced far more apathy in the 1980s than it had, for example, in the 1950s. At the Shanghai First Steel Mill, which employed many workers with impeccable proletarian backgrounds, the portion of all staff under age 28 who applied to join the Party in 1981 was only 3.8 percent.[40] Even among Communist Youth League members there, only one-tenth bothered to apply. This low rate was attributed to the youths' lack of "ability to distinguish between the Party and improper tendencies within the Party." Membership no longer helped careers enough to be worth the considerable commitment of time.

Youths in late reform years held off from joining the Party for many reasons. Some reportedly feared a possible change of regime later, in a post-Communist era, that could make a CCP application in their files become a "political blemish" (*zhengzhi wudian*). As Andrew Nathan has written, "Society was beginning to penetrate the party. . . . Independent people found it useful to join the party and to get party sponsorship for their initiatives. Each side pretended to play the other's game, and each thought it was winning."[41] The private motives of students were obvious when they approached political instructors to ask for estimates on "how many years of benefit we can receive by applying to join the Party now."[42]

Communist Party membership thus became for many a career move, not a commitment of faith. When Shanghai university students were asked, in a relatively careful 1988 survey, why some of their friends wanted to join the Party, about seven-tenths responded either that the applicants thought CCP membership would help them further their educations or that "they want a 'Party card,'" which they can use as capital to receive future benefits."[43] Stanley Rosen shows a "decollectivization of morality" among Chinese youths: "With the students no longer 'true believers' and a reward structure no longer so fully under the control of the state, political activism in support of regime values is now rare."[44] Ideologies of hierarchy remained robust in China, but specific enthusiasm for the hierarchy of the PRC state was harder to muster.

What Scope of Things Does Ideology Claim to Cover?

Official Chinese have long thought that good rulers become so by having correct philosophy. To do the sensitive business of government well, rulers are supposed to know essentially everything, even though details can be left to subordinates. The *claim* to have such a total vision of the world is seen as needed for legitimacy. This view of things justifies hierarchy, because few can be taught enough of the relevant wisdom. It confirms the charisma of top leaders, whose opinions on all kinds of sundry topics are widely mentioned in China as if they had special profundity in all fields. The "thoughts" of political leaders have been supposed useful in tasks that range from writing music to building tractors. This penchant was not quite as evident in Deng's time as it was in Mao's—and that change shows some reforms—but politicians still present themselves as surprisingly knowledgeable in China.

The summa of political wisdom under Deng Xiaoping became the motto that "practice is the sole criterion to test truth."[45] This pragmatic slogan seems sensible to rationalists, and it also sounds generally consistent with Marxist scientific materialism. It was proposed in the late 1970s as a counter to espousals by Hua Guofeng of Mao's voluntarism, based largely on CCP epiphanies such as the Long March.[46] One observer has called this method "naive inductionism."[47] Despite references to Mao's 1937 essay "On Practice," the revival of the "truth through practice" motto in the late 1970s was not just to affirm the importance of science. It was also to claim legitimacy for reformist politicians pushing the modernization program, as against conservatives concerned about the integrity of their elite. The import of the slogan was that Deng Xiaoping claimed power on the basis of faith that science could do much for China's national strength.

"Science" is a singularly unspecific ideological claim. Antisuperstitious and ex-romantic ideologies have been evident in the elites of many regimes after periods of intense political centralization. In England after Cromwell, veneration for saints had been replaced by other pious attitudes, but the status of the clergy did not fully come back with the king; large parts of the elite did not treat the clergy as they had in pre-Commonwealth times. In France after the height of revolution, Enlightenment rationalization had come to stay not just in urban salons, but also in much larger groups. It structured Napoleonic and late-Bourbon institutions far more than those of the *ancien régime*. In Russia, even the parts of the elite that still believe in Orthodoxy have been deeply affected by Westernizers, including Lenin, as Solzhenitsyn has never missed an opportunity to complain. Similarly in China, although the revival of peasant piety since the 1970s has somewhat affected elite attitudes, May 4 rationalist traditions have a very strong continuing influence on government. Science, unspecific though it is, has always been near the center of this ideology.

A scientistic ideology controls most people in the modern era, according to Jürgen Habermas, as citizens have tended to believe in "the rationality of domination." This becomes an "ideology for the new politics, which is adapted to technical problems and brackets out practical questions."[48] Future difficulties can be predicted for this ideology, but Chinese intellectuals have cottoned to it with great gusto. "Scientism" was a fad toward the beginning of this century, and over time it has had increasing political results.[49] Technocratic ideology, justifying rule on the basis of scientism, is the faith that most Chinese thinkers imagine to have a future.

Article 24 of the 1982 PRC constitution speaks of science in moral terms: "The state advocates the civic virtues of love of the motherland, of the people, of labor, of science, and of socialism. . . . It combats capitalist, feudal, and other decadent ideas."[50] Science became the equivalent of what Americans call "motherhood and apple pie," the ideology nobody could rightly reject. "Science," whose methods are in practice many, was indiscriminately grouped with "love of the motherland," which any serious Chinese contenders for state power naturally had to claim, and also with "socialism," which the Communists claimed to monopolize despite many actually nonsocialist policies during reforms. Yet Chineseness and socialism were not global. Science could be imagined so. The universalist claim to truth was important for Chinese rulers, and making it in terms of "science" undergirded rule by a relatively competent group of Chinese administrators.

What can be translated as "the study of science" (*kexue xue,* a redundant phrase that even a PRC interviewee thought sounded odd, despite its occasional use) is a recognized academic discipline in China, whose topics of research are treated differently if at all in the West. This field is not the history of science, although another interviewee said it studies "the laws and customs of scientific development." There is a great tendency among Chinese intellectuals (and some elsewhere) to presume that these are quite standard, predictable, and regular. Such habits may come from Confucian precedents, as much as from Bacon or Marx. In any case, they undergird an ideology for rule by those educated in science.

A virtue of science as a political legitimator is its wide scope, but the corresponding main problem is that political leaders do not necessarily make good scientists, or vice versa. The presumption that so much unity is natural in the world amounts to an imposition on individual thinkers and events. Marxist physics is supposed to be dialectical. Some conservative theoreticians took this to imply, first, that matter had to be "infinitely divisible," so that even extreme subatomic specks could contain "contradictory opposites." And at the other end of the scale, for the sake of dialectical symmetry these conservative theorists insisted the universe must be infinitely large.

Quantum mechanics, however, challenges the first of these two related ideas, because it adds the wrinkle of indeterminacy: If some characteristics of an atomic situation are known, then others can be known only within probable limits. This was anathema to the definite, clear, Enlightenment view that conservatives thought they found in Marx. The second Marxist idea, asserting the infinite size of the cosmos, is similarly challenged by the "big bang" consensus. This theory depicts an expanding but finite universe, which had a finite beginning. Fang Lizhi is disliked by the conservatives for his astrophysics, not just for his politics, because he gives evidence against the cosmological hunches attributed to Marx.

For the Paretan lions, this scientific discussion was really about political legitimacy. Astronomers such as Fang stressed the obtuseness of sticking to a theory against which there was a good deal of empirical evidence. But conservatives, such as Shen Xiaofeng, He Zuoxiu, or Yin Dengxiang, stressed that such evidence was not clear. They assumed that Marxism had to include cosmology; and Marxism had to be right, after all, so that the Communist Party should rule China.[51]

The functional uses of ideology become all too apparent in the hands of intellectuals. Personal clashes sullied debates between thinkers who tried to exclude each other's ideas. He Zuoxiu reportedly had tried to prevent Fang Lizhi's 1983 appointment to a university vice presidency, and perhaps again in 1987 to the Beijing Observatory. The director of that institution, showing his conservative credentials, opined that observational astronomy disfavors the idea of a finite or bounded universe.[52] It is telling that anybody should presume, even in a period when Chinese values are in such flux, that the stars must mesh with politics. Severing this tie between nature and power still presents a cultural problem especially for conservatives, who take "science" as a necessary buttress of a ruling elite.[53]

Sociobiology has been particularly controversial during the reforms, because some sociobiologists stress links between the "selfish" preservation of individual genes and motives for altruism.[54] Any suggestion that virtue could come from a source other than a well-ordered large collective comes in for immediate criticism from people who want to do the political ordering. So the Party's theoretical journal attacked sociobiological ideas, which contrast with Confucian hopes for the efficacy of moral education as much as they contrast with Communist notions. Nonsocial generators of any human motive, especially altruism and especially if distributed throughout the human species, might be a challenge to intellectuals' claims that they are needed to run the state, and perhaps the cosmos too. To make full claims to rule, politicians often find themselves maintaining they know about a wider range of things than is really in their competence. The scope of both the reactionary and reformist ideologies in China recently has remained very broad, because of their common scientism.

What Intensity of Belief Does Ideology Command?

This does not mean that people all ardently believe what politicians tell them. Both conservative and reform ideologies continued to claim wide scope, but surveys suggest another fact: The intensity of popular credence in them dropped. When categorizing regime types, political scientists seem largely to agree that several kinds of indices are crucial: "Participation," or the extent to which the adult population is involved in politics, and "contest," or the extent to which potential leaders can express their views, are (if extensive) the two defining traits of a democracy, but the near absence of either can also be used to classify other regime types. Distinguishing totalitarianism from authoritarianism, Juan Linz introduces a third dimension, and it is ideological: the extent to which a regime's justifying ideas are exclusive-atavistic or, instead, more tolerant. This may partly correlate with the degree of legitimate contest in a political system, so it may not be entirely new, but it apparently also measures whether a regime finds a sustainable balance between "lions" and "foxes," or between the "pure ideology" that can make a regime sufficiently stable and the "practical ideology" that can make it flexible.

Shanghai in particular, because the Gang of Four was based there, has acquired a reputation as a center of radicalism.[55] This and other China coast cities, however, have a deeply conservative tradition that is also strong. Ideologically inspired violence in the Taiping Rebellion and later phases of the Chinese Revolution, from which rich inland families fled to Shanghai, made this city's culture also antiradical. Fearsome campaigns by the CCP after 1949 only strengthened this trend, and some of Shanghai's ostensible leftism during the Cultural Revolution was a reaction against the revolution these campaigns brought. Net immigration to the city was highest at times of rebellion, and the people who came were supremely interested in protecting themselves and their wealth.

If a cultural symbol of this conservatism is sought, it can be found in the architecture of the most prosperous China coast cities. Protection against robbers has been a standard urban interest.[56] But perhaps nowhere else in the modern world have such elaborate schemes of window bars, building entrance codes, and burglar alarms pervaded residences at middle-income levels as in the relatively safe cities of the China coast. The emphasis on "units" (*danwei*), for residence as well as work, before 1949 and since then, has helped finance this culture of urban screens. Some Shanghai traditions are communitarian, but others are distinctly against large collectives and protective of small ones.

Many in China's most bourgeois city understandably welcomed the 1978 abandonment of the slogan "Taking class struggle as the key link."[57] What had happened earlier bore scant relation to classes in the original sense, and struggles at the local level in most places (though not against and among intellectuals) had been decreasing irregularly for most of a decade. Still, "class struggle" was an ideological shibboleth many in Shanghai were glad to see go. The notion reappeared later, but never with the virulence of the 1950s and 1960s. The Cultural Revolution at least temporarily gave collective politics, especially collective norms, a bad name.

When an editor of the *Wenhui News* was asked why the circulation of his paper had risen more slowly than that of the *Xinmin Evening News,* he cited two broad and revealing reasons: Politics became a decreasing focus of popular interest during the reforms. Also, there was an increase (by more than one million) in the number of Shanghai retired people, and the editor said they were less interested in political issues because their careers had ended—but they had a great deal of free time to read newspapers, and the less political *Xinmin Evening News* met their interests better than his own paper did. Many in Shanghai during reforms were openly wary of politics, and they were no longer quick converts to any collective philosophy.

Even the top state leaders during reforms occasionally expressed their aversion to excessive ideology. CCP general secretary Hu Yaobang confessed in 1983 that he found *Red Flag,* the main theoretical journal of the Party he headed, "boring." His successor Zhao Ziyang once remarked that he "never read" *Red Flag.*[58] Until its abolition, many of its staff were conservatives; but the problem was with theory, not just reaction. Zhao more pragmatically espoused "crossing the stream by feeling for the stones."[59]

Ideological nonchalance was evident even toward the most basic Marxist categories. The reform era saw disputes, for example, about the extent to which capitalism differed from socialism. The official, majority line was that these systems were basically contrasting. But some writers pointed out that capitalist governments (despite what Marx had predicted) passed laws to protect labor and to reduce monopoly capital.[60] Shanghai became the center of discussion about the Wenzhou model, which was a topic of much theoretical discussion aimed at proving the very dubious proposition that the wildly free markets of Wenzhou were, after all, fundamentally socialist.[61] Such basic questioning of Marxism did not, however, destroy all its credibility as a belief system. Religions do not cease to exist when they assimilate heterodox ideas or doubt.[62]

Some wits say that three "theories" (*lun*) guide China today. The "cat theory" relies on a dictum of Deng Xiaoping: "No matter whether it's a white cat or a black cat, if it catches rats, it's a good cat." Second is the "feel theory," from Zhao Ziyang: "Feeling the stones as you cross the river." Third was the "special characteristics theory," popular among conservative politicians, which referred to "Chinese" or "socialist" or other characteristics—all safely undefined.[63]

Ideological "confusion" was sometimes praised by Chinese theorists during re-forms.[64] Actually, the core ambiguity was whether individual and local norms might join the collective ones that had for so long been deemed the sum of all political ideas.

Traditionalist politicians periodically asserted the need for more intense and unified belief. To prepare for a National Day, Party chair Jiang Zemin addressed a "rally" held in the Great Hall of the People, and this was attended by old ralliers such as Yang Shangkun and Wan Li. Jiang announced there were two kinds of reform: a socialist kind that upholds Party dominance, and a bourgeois liberal kind that advocates "total Westernization." He said the second "actually constituted a transformation to capitalism and would bring China into the orbit of the capitalist system of the West."[65] He favored some foreign investment, but not "excessive decentralization" and certainly not structural reform in politics. Jiang Zemin, Deng Xiaoping, and many other high Beijing leaders were fair-weather reformers only. They supported change so long as it helped to legitimate, and did not threaten, their own stability at the top of the CCP. Toward any other kind of reform, they were willing (especially when foreign investors were out of the room) to express strong opposition.

Ambiguousness about the extent to which the government would support or repress change has been a prominent feature of other postrevolutionary periods, too. The English Restoration is often called the "years of doubt."[66] The state could still be somewhat arbitrary, but wide tolerance in ideological matters has also been a popular hope in periods after social violence. Restoration scientists such as Boyle wrote about religious topics from a "Latitudinarian" viewpoint, espousing moderation in dogma, emphasis on only a few essential points of theology, and the pursuit of science as an activity that supported the newly peaceful social order.[67]

The practicality of "unifying thought" (tongyi sixiang) to achieve "ideo-logical uniformity" (sixiang yizhi) was a subject of major debate during re-forms.[68] Few in China openly supported the Durkheimian notion that modernity required diverse, nonuniform mentalities and personalities. But uniformity became an ideal for the past and the future, not the present, and its realization became indefinitely delayed.[69]

What Are the Ostensible and Actual Audiences for Ideology?

Although most regime propaganda is in public, in fact not all kinds of people are supposed to receive it equally. The listenership comes in several types, and these are officially distinguished from each other. The broadest audience for PRC claims during reforms is by definition the huge national one: all Chinese. Official orthodoxy speaks of "building socialism with Chinese characteristics," when actually a market economy involving collectives is what is being built. The main "Chinese" characteristic is something untraditional: the leadership of the

Communist Party. According to a theory that stirred interest among many officials, China is said to be only in the "primary stage of socialism" (*shehui zhuyi chuji jieduan*); therefore, the CCP should rule for a long time. This is a political argument rather than a national trait. It justifies continued rule by an incumbent elite.

The end of the building process is officially not supposed to be capitalism, which like socialism has actually combined with the national characteristics of many different countries. What it will be, if China follows the pattern of other high-income countries, is a mixture of institutions that create market efficiency with government regulation. This could surely exist in a context that retains strong Chinese traditions (as it does in several modern Chinese environments outside the PRC). It does not take a linguistic philosopher to note that the term "Chinese characteristics" is almost always used in contexts that have less to do with China than with the incumbent elite.

This nationalist emphasis made public sense, however, because adulation of foreign things was occasionally carried very far in reform China. The national airline, CAAC, had its flight attendants' uniforms designed by Pierre Cardin.[70] This did not solve all its problems. Imports of foreign popular music, and of the norms many pop songs suggest to youth, caused conservative heads to shake. Against these trends, clear Chinese virtues of courtesy were propagated in official campaigns by the early 1980s. There was a general moralistic campaign, in true Confucian style, for "five emphases and four points of beauty."[71] In industry and transport, there was a campaign for "double renovation," both spiritual and productive. In rural areas, there were campaigns for "civilized villages." In banks, accountants were supposed to be "double good." In primary schools, students had to "study Lei Feng." Women's groups campaigned for "six goods," while youth organizations urged the "revival of China." Although these were all called "campaigns" (*yundong*), they lacked the violence of many previous movements in the 1950s and 1960s.

Campaigns for courteous obedience were officially combined with the 1979 campaign against dissidence at Democracy Wall, with the 1980–81 campaign against bourgeois liberalism and against "scar literature" and Bai Hua's films, with the 1983–84 campaign against spiritual pollution (*jingshen wuran*), with the repressions of student activism in 1986–87 and 1989, with the critique of "peaceful evolution" in 1991, and with many other campaigns that the central authorities have announced throughout these years. The effectiveness of such movements was fragmentary, but they held together as a continuing ideological reaction to reforms.

These were moral-political campaigns addressed to all Chinese. Other movements had more specific intended audiences. As early as September 1979, for example, the Shanghai Party Committee launched a campaign to reduce the number of leaders who had multiple jobs, to make meetings shorter, and to reduce the number of offices under the municipal administration. In early 1981, the Party raised the need for its own cadres to undergo criticisms and self-criticisms. These remained rituals within the CCP, although they disappeared from other organizations.[72] Such intensive propaganda would have been ineffective during reforms in public formats.

Shanghai's *Liberation Daily* at this time was publishing general retrospective articles, urging readers to recall "the glorious history of the Party" and to realize the CCP could guide everyone.[73] The early 1980s saw propaganda about "three principles" proposed by a Party secretary. The first rule was innocuous enough: that leaders should make friends among the masses. The second was Maoist: that cadres should restore the system by which they engaged in regular physical labor. The third was orderly: that they should be taught to hold themselves by the same rules that applied to ordinary citizens.[74] These bits of advice would be relevant to people who already had Party posts. Movements were mainly for cadres in the state network or in its wide periphery, not for large numbers of other people. These local leaders were the boundary of the state, but in the reform context it was unclear to what extent campaigns would discipline them to become effective agents of the central government, rather than of their local friends.

Official ideological education was still actively sponsored throughout the reform era, but the addressees were captive audiences less frequently than in Mao's time. Sometimes on Shanghai TV, and far more often on the central stations in the city, large amounts of time were used for didactic speeches on social or political topics, generally presented by a male lecturer. When important politicians used this format, the surveyed audience was larger than most Westerners would expect—especially if the Party sermonizer had an interesting topic. Lesser functionaries also held forth, seated before the camera for long programs that did not garner large audiences. Their subjects were many, such as the proper role of modern journalism, the contemporary meaning of "independence," and other broadly political subjects. Viewers were fewer for these speeches, but the central stations broadcast them nonetheless.[75]

Intellectuals were more subject than less-educated people to intensive ideological address by the regime. Shanghai universities had required courses in politics ever since October 1949.[76] In the same month, it had been decreed that textbooks would be produced by the state only. But thirty years later, such controls at universities were haltingly loosened. At Fudan University, "Friday political study" was sharply reformed.[77] In the mid-1980s, students were divided by departments and classes into relatively small groups, each of which was presided over by a faculty member. These sessions were fairly formal, and everyone had to attend. Newspaper editorials, sometimes supplemented with sermons by the instructor on how the class was doing, formed the main agenda of these meetings.

By 1988, this structure became less formal. Various students could organize the lectures, usually on political or social topics but perhaps on literature or other subjects. The school authorities at Fudan still arranged some lectures, including a weekly "information briefing" (*xinxi fabu*), but young people took responsibility for most of them. Student associations with particular disciplinary interests might invite professors or visitors to talk. Speakers came from many units, and some were from abroad. The university's Propaganda Department, under the Party committee, also organized talks. Generally there were three or four such offerings each Friday afternoon, and maybe one or two more in the evening.

Because Fudan students had a choice of which lecture to visit, attendance was not taken—and some students skipped them all (although the university's role in the job assignment system was still powerful enough that playing hookey on political lectures was informally kept secret). Some sessions were far more popular than others. According to one estimate by a student in 1988, about half of the humanities and social science students normally went to one of these lectures, and the percentage was probably somewhat less among natural scientists.

Political education sometimes works, but it takes resources—especially resources of legitimacy to mobilize the political educators and students. Before the Cultural Revolution, the government had enough cachet for an extensive program. Political education supplemented by many kinds of organizational control was powerful in influencing actions then, even if it did not always result in behavior that all central leaders foresaw.[78] After the peak of violence in the late 1960s, the CCP's resources of legitimacy were scarcer. Even during reforms, however, the Party attempted political education among some groups that it deemed important, especially university students. Some evidence suggests this was effective.

At East China Normal University, two students got into a long argument about whether a tourist to Shanghai should go first to see the Jade Buddha Temple or the Yuyuan Garden. A third student, bored by this debate and wanting to change the subject, suggested that, instead, the first visit should be paid to the house in Shanghai where the Chinese Communist Party was founded, a place that is not very scenic but politically more correct. The other two students immediately agreed. None of the participants in this conversation was reportedly fond of the political education class each of them was required to attend. Many surveys have shown that most students at this time were willing to speak anonymously against the value of such classes. Yet the witness to this small debate believes all three were sincere in their consensus. This outside observer said he could speak quite easily about the general merits or defects of China's political leadership with workers and ordinary Shanghai citizens—but not with students, whom the government had designated as a group to be watched closely and propagandized intensely.[79] For limiting topics of discussion, if perhaps less for stirring enthusiasm, propaganda at this time sometimes worked.

Curricular reforms in some places aimed at making courses in politics more interesting. A university teacher of politics, who was aggravated that so many students were obviously bored in them, wrote a spirited brief for making political economy an optional rather than mandatory subject. Then the students who enrolled might actually be interested in the topic. He did not want to teach students who did not want to learn, so he put the case in personalist terms that would have brought sure criticism during the Cultural Revolution but by 1987 were acceptable: "Individuals' enthusiasms, interests, and original backgrounds are different."[80]

This Fudan professor also argued strenuously against "taking one or two Marxist classics" as core texts and said that real students of political economy not only should read the most serious and complex books by Marx (including *Capital*) but also should study bourgeois Western theories—not just to criticize them, but to find what is of value in them. He said universities too often covered such subjects apologetically, in courses whose titles included the word "history" (*shi*) or emphasized the content as foreign (*wai*)—for example, in offerings with names like "The History of Foreign Economic Theories." But he said these subjects were relevant to China here and now, not distant and dead, and they should be taught critically.

He advocated that students really interested in social science should learn not only a wide variety of theories, but also foreign languages, econometrics, statistics, and how to teach. They should get out of classrooms and do practical survey research on real social problems (as apparently his own students had done in Shanghai). This reformist professor of political economy at Fudan was no doubt Marxist. But he had a far more eclectic, exploratory, and nonpropagandistic view of the social role of political economy than would ever have been tolerated in Mao's time. A professional in his subject, he wanted to teach it to modern specialists, not to others who lacked a need to know it.

When ideology becomes an intellectual specialty, rather than an uncritical gloss for power, its audience becomes narrower and its content becomes more complex. Highly placed CCP theorists disagreed in the early 1980s about the extent to which Marxism itself could be subject to scientific disproof. A critical approach to it could conceivably lead in that direction. The director of the CASS Institute of Philosophy, Xing Bensi, sounded like Heraclitus:

> Marxism, whose nature is revolutionary and critical, does not recognize any absolutes except that all things in the world are in absolute motion. This Marxist spirit is, of course, completely applicable to Marxism itself. The history of Marxism is a history of continuously substituting new conclusions for old ones.[81]

But a conservative retired Politburo member, Hu Qiaomu, sounded like Parmenides:

> In building socialism with distinctively Chinese characteristics, of course, it is impossible to find the answers from the works of Marx and Lenin. However, we must always bear in mind the fundamental principles of Marxism-Leninism and study new situations and solve new problems in light of Marxism-Leninism's stand, viewpoints, and methods.[82]

This was a debate between criticism and nationalism. Hu Qiaomu and many other conservatives so regularly associated the term "Chinese characteristics" with the idea that there is some absolute truth in Marxism, which happens to be an import, that the inconsistency became unrecognized because of the repetition.

A similar irony lies in the fact that the most articulate ideologists for Party conservatism, ostensibly for the dictatorship of the proletariat, were personally from capitalist backgrounds. This is an international phenomenon. Raymond Aron claimed that "the ideologists of the proletariat are bourgeois intellectuals."[83] But in his context, that meant intellectual ideologists of a kind whose ideas were for changing rather than preserving rule. Bourgeois intellectuals are also the ideologists of every other modern group, radical and establishmentarian alike, because these are the people who most often articulate belief systems and create ideological innovations.

Especially in reactionary periods such as the early 1990s, conservative propaganda stressed simple, unphilosophical topics. It urged the emulation of heroes, especially soldier Lei Feng, cadre Jiao Yulu, and child-hero Lai Ning. Lai, for example, was a Young Pioneer from Sichuan, who in 1988 (at age 14) died fighting a forest fire. He had protected state property. According to Chen Yun, Beijing's top elder statesman in the economic field, the "spirit and mental state" of Lai Ning were a model of "what our Party hopes to find in the next generation."[84] Chen was old enough to know he would presently die (as he did, a few years later), and old revolutionaries like him looked rather desperately for reliable successors. They found few, and many of those were also aging.

For the Qingming Festival in 1991, top police specialist Qiao Shi went to the grave of Jiao Yulu, traditionally to clean it but also to give a speech on "promoting the Jiao Yulu spirit." Jiao had died of exhaustion because of his work for the masses and his self-discipline. "He wore socks that were mended time and again; he sat on the same old rattan chair all his life; he did not have the cash to buy a movie ticket."[85] This was sentimentalism, perhaps fit for a wide audience but best believed by old Party cadres.

Many awards, based on pure ideological incentives, were designed mainly for CCP members. This group and intellectuals were the main groups of interest to the state in propaganda efforts. So the reform period did not bring the abolition of nonmaterial labor incentives, such as medals. In mid-1988, Shanghai newspapers praised the highly selected "May 1 Labor Medal" winners, of whom 97 percent were CCP members.[86] The Women's Federation also gave awards to fifty female entrepreneurs, of whom practically all were Communists. Among a group of highly selected scientists who won awards, however, less than two-thirds were in the Party. Among teachers chosen for such high awards, four-fifths were Communists. So were 93 percent of those who took high military awards.

Other suasion campaigns were aimed at wider audiences, but usually in local areas. The localist pride of China's reforms was published in books about the particular glories of regional history. A ten-volume series on Shanghai and its people appeared. So did *A Shanghai Dictionary, An Encyclopedia of Shanghai, A Shanghai Lexicon, Studies in the Cultural History of Shanghai, A Chronicle of Modern Shanghai, Modern Architecture in Shanghai,* and *A Dictionary of Famous People, Events, and Things in Shanghai.*[87] Below the municipal level, too, both governmental and nonstate agencies ballyhooed local virtues.

In each of Shanghai's urban districts and rural counties, detailed gazetteers and local memorabilia were published. The thick volume on Luwan district, for example, contains loving descriptions of the origins of each street name, the histories of local factories, several kinds of maps showing all buildings, hydrographic maps with the locations of creeks (long since paved over), the histories of schools, and expensively produced cartography of each street area within the district.[88] Songjiang county, in Shanghai's suburbs, became a place for special research, and some survey reports on Songjiang were so detailed they remained classified.[89] But many places produced materials, and by no means were all of them for academic or administrative use only. Guidebooks, gazetteers, compendia, and various popular and formal histories appeared from practically every locality in the Shanghai delta.

Public sponsorship of local pride became evident in other contexts, also. Lanes and courtyards (*lilong*) in central Shanghai were extremely crowded, and many were in dilapidated buildings. Local committees were in charge of sprucing up these neighborhoods. Above each entrance to a lane, the place name was generally carved. Most lanes gilded or recarved these signs. In some, the names had been changed during the Cultural Revolution—but now they reverted to their previous titles, adding new signs if the old ones could not be found. This trend was not exactly a movement. Certainly its audience was not national, but it strengthened local loyalties. Not all communal ideas are in very large groups.

Alternative Ideologies from the Intellectual Elite

Localisms of this kind, especially in rural areas, seemed not to challenge the state elite—and perhaps for that reason, they together somewhat eroded the state's power during reforms. The mechanism by which this occurred was indirect; localisms certainly did not challenge official ideology, but they legitimated behavior that ended up hurting the state. Ideological challenges that were more direct had less immediate influence, because they could be repressed as more obviously dissident.

Intellectuals are the people who could replace the regime leaders. Especially when the intellectuals in question were not young students and were old enough to threaten such replacement, Party conservatives did everything possible to prevent the spread of their ideas. Many of these challenges originated very close to the center of the Party-state. As early as August 1980, *People's Daily* deputy editor Wang Ruoshui argued that the CCP in power had created some political alienation (*yihua*).[90] Many writers of the time also stressed the need to implement a Marxist variety of "humanism" (*rendao zhuyi*). This was a period in which some old cadres, who had been hard-liners among writers and artists, made self-criticisms. When Zhou Yang, who under Mao had been China's foremost bureaucrat for literature,[91] made a self-criticism in 1983, he called for a "rectification of the Party, which we will soon undertake, for the aim of overcoming economic and political alienation."[92] Deng Liqun, head of the Central Propaganda Department and often the most prominent opponent of "bourgeois liberalization," in early 1983 also called for more public debate about alienation and the link between Marxism and humanism, saying public discourse on this subject was "an excellent thing."

Reform in Beijing is often less consistent than elsewhere. By the autumn of 1983, Deng Liqun, Deng Xiaoping, and others veered to an opposite ideological line and attacked "spiritual pollution." Their spokesman specified the danger clearly, in terms of people who thought that "the roots of alienation are to be found in the socialist system itself."[93] Even in this mood, though, they insisted the fight against spiritual pollution was no "movement" (*yundong*) but merely "an ordinary item of work in building socialist civilization."[94] The conservatives' sporadic effort to hold movements that were not campaigns was already a major reform.

Other intellectuals such as Wei Jingsheng or Fang Lizhi, farther from the center of the state, could publicize their ideals of more radical change to large audiences in the context of mass demonstrations that were temporary. The Democracy Wall movement of 1978–79, the student demonstrations of late 1986 and the spring of 1989 are well known in the West, as are the articulate spokespeople who emerged at those times. Because this topic is more thoroughly covered in English than any other important aspect of recent Chinese ideology, only a few examples and background need to be offered here.[95]

In November 1986, Fang Lizhi spoke with extraordinary bluntness at Shanghai's Tongji University:

> Socialism is at a low ebb. There is no getting around the fact that no socialist state in the post–World War II era has been successful, and neither has our own thirty-odd-year-long socialist experiment.... I am here to tell you that the socialist movement, from Marx and Lenin to Stalin and Mao Zedong, has been a failure.... I think that complete Westernization is the only way to modernize.[96]

At Jiaotong University, also in Shanghai, Fang urged the youths to take action: "Students are a progressive force for democratization.... Chinese intellectuals should demonstrate their own strength. In fact, they already have this strength, but they are not conscious of it or have not dared to demonstrate it. If only they dare to stir up trouble, the impact will be very great."[97]

This stress on international science and the supposed power of intellectuals had a major tradition, but it also had major weaknesses. Science does not capture the most popular political platform in China, which is nationalist. Also, scientists are a tiny minority. The ideology of scientism can be resented by nonintellectual leaders as just another claim by political entrepreneurs who want power. Science is inherently international. As Fang Lizhi said, there is no distinctively Chinese science. The findings work for all countries, or for none. But an emphasis on the scientific nature of Marxism has arisen in Chinese politics in two senses that are opposite to each other. Some intellectuals stressing science do so partly to show how China, to be strong, must become more cosmopolitan and international. But conservative intellectuals who stress that Marxism is scientific, thus providing a means to truth that can withstand tests, have exactly the contrary political intent: They mean that Marxism (really, the Party) cannot be abandoned if China is to be strong. Reformers use "science" as an argument against too much Party control, but conservatives use "science" as an argument for more Party control.

Scientism remains oddly crucial for both as a claim to legitimacy. The conservatives resist the notion that science is international, with no country's "specific characteristics," but they use it as a universalist ideology. The reformers, who are mostly technocrats, also have a problem: Science is very useful as an ideology for getting them posts when they have technical educations, but only if they can show its result is national strength. Reform technocrats are at some political disadvantage in their conflicts with conservative technocrats. Even though their position is more consistent, it can sound less patriotic.

China's intellectual reformers all strongly recall the May 4th Movement at the end of World War I. When the early socialist Chen Duxiu introduced "Mr. Democracy" and "Mr. Science" about this time, he conjoined the two and declared, "We are now quite sure that only these two gentlemen can save China and get rid of all political, moral, academic, and ideological darkness."[98] Chen called for a "new ideology." Its elements, as he first expressed them, were "science" and "human rights" (although the political part of his prescription was later changed to "democracy" rather than "human rights"). Chen argued that "after the rise of science, its role will not be less than that of the theory of human rights," and he posited that the two would be "a chariot with two tires." But democracy, as his waffling about it suggests, was even more difficult for him to define than science.

Chen did not admit the extent to which traditional China had developed science.[99] He urged Chinese scholars in effect to adopt Western methods and to discard theories of *yin* and *yang* and the five elements.[100] He thought peasants needed science to choose good seeds and fight insects; workers needed science to avoid wasting materials so that China would no longer have to depend on foreign war matériel; and businessmen needed it so they would not seek short-term interests and could calculate better for the future.[101] The aim of such science, however, was not truth but national strength.

"The enlightened awake the others," according to Mencius. Intellectuals form a natural elite, in this view; and in China, they have very self-consciously followed the traditions of moral protest inherited from their predecessors in the movement praising Mr. Science (*Cai xiansheng*) and Mr. Democracy (*De xiansheng*). Enlightenment has long been seen as the main basis of politics led by scholars in China, and the antidemocratic aspects of this belief have been ignored. Student banners at Tiananmen in 1989 lamented, "Seventy years already!" and "We have waited too long for Mr. Science and Mr. Democracy!"[102]

By stressing the novelty of Mr. Science, rather than deconstructing the interests of a modern knowledge elite, Chen and other intellectuals obscured the most obvious connection between imperial norms and their own movement. By criticizing Confucian traditions in a wholesale way, they likewise neglected the democratic potential in Mencius's doctrine of a "natural mandate" (*tianming*). As Roger Des Forges has written:

> Of course, Mencius was an aristocrat who accepted a social division of labor ("those who work with their minds/hearts rule, those who work with their hands are ruled") and emphasized patriarchal virtues such as filial piety and the subordination of women. Yet his radical belief in the goodness of human nature and in the "right of rebellion" inspired popular uprisings and frightened aristocrats from his day forward.[103]

The stress on the proper limits of leaders in a hierarchy depends entirely on self-restraint by the leaders. China is "civilized," and all that discipline is supposed to be individual and normative. Mr. Democracy was called *De xiansheng,* where the *De* was formally just a sound—but it was written with the character meaning "morality." This connotation may have been ex-Confucian, an attempt to modernize an ethical tradition, but as such it was wrong: Democracy arises when people are not cocksure what is moral.

Chen Duxiu said there could be no contradiction between science and democracy, because both were based in human rationality. If individuals understood external scientific things, this would raise their internal sense of freedom. The truth would make each individual free.[104] This argument was proposed as a means to save Chinese collectively, not just individuals. It hardly justifies the personal sureness evident in many Chinese intellectuals, as fostered especially in the country's most prestigious universities. As Schattschneider put it, "Democracy is a political system for people who are not sure that they are right." Not just in China, sages seldom stress how wrong they can be. They are publicly expected to preach comprehensive truths. But this self-image discourages candidness in admitting that "nobody knows enough to run the government."[105]

Divergent Ideologies from Nonstate Functional Leaders

Functional and generational leaders, especially among youth, also may conceive counterclaims to official ideology. Localisms, such as are treated above, are more important than these; they involve no such counterclaims because they are mostly tacit. Past treatments of rural ideologies have mainly stressed mass political culture, e.g. among "the weak." James Scott admits what he is doing: "By definition, we have made the public transcript of domination ontologically prior to the hidden, off-stage transcript .... Our analysis here privileges the social experience of indignities, control, submission, humiliation, forced deference, and punishment."[106] But actually, the ontologically prior experience may instead be that of freedom. There is no need to assert the priority of any particular type of experience. The strong and the weak will be seen in what they do, not by whether they are often thought so. Situations and norms interact, the full normative transcript includes both public and hidden texts in many sizes of groups, and there is no reason either to resent or to respect priority for the public one when the other is politically more effective. There are some conditions (as contemporary China makes clear) when the supposedly strong are really weak and the cultural nexus of power becomes localized.

The effectiveness of official controls determines many reactions to nonstate ideas. "The disparity between public action and off-stage discourse depends heavily," as Scott says, "on the severity of the domination." Yet measuring absolute degrees of rule is harder than finding changes in it. Scott continues: "Other things being equal, the more involuntary, demeaning, onerous, and extractive it is, the more it will foster a counterdiscourse starkly at odds with its official claims."[107] This relationship might be seen not just in separated unofficial groups, but also in many of them acting together—and sometimes proving strong vis-à-vis the state. Such "counterdiscourse" is not a type of symbol, but something that is most likely to become powerful at specific historical moments, for example, after a revolution's height of repression (in China, after the 1960s), when resource arrays also support it. It is a way of thinking that coexists with and provides alternative options to more-statist norms in the "cultural nexus of power."

This last notion, developed by Prasenjit Duara to describe early traditional domination in China, puts the regime's efforts in a context of local leaders who have broad, multifunctional powers. China is not the first country in which governments have spread ideologies trying to centralize revenue collection and police control. Nor is it the first in which local communities have resisted that intrusion.[108] The reform era is not the first time this has happened in China. Duara points out how "the overtly consensual character of ... values [has] masked how they were produced and used in society." The state is not the only actor in this drama:

> This subtle and complex process continually involves competition, accommodation, and adjustment of perceptions and interests among different social groups, including the state.... Unlike material resources, symbolic ones are plastic, capable of being molded and manipulated even for opposing goals, while still retaining their connotative power—the power to motivate, inspire

and impel. . . . The competition over the symbols of legitimate authority took place not only among contenders within local society, but also with outsiders such as the imperial state. . . . This state did not always find it easy to direct the normative materials in the nexus [of power] toward its own interests and often had to struggle to inscribe its own hegemony on popular symbols.[109]

This formulation has several strengths, because it suggests interaction between material and symbolic resources and it suggests that popular symbols are a field of struggle between the regime and local patriarchs who are not always weak. That story could be expanded to account for situations in which the leaders of functionally diverse local groups, not claiming to replace the state, nonetheless erode it ideologically and materially. The variety of cultural symbols in rich urban areas, such as those surrounding Shanghai, is larger than in poor areas. In cities, and in families that produce local leaders, this diversity is even greater.

Urban China shows many examples of semistrong groups, such as university students or unionized workers, who for generational or functional reasons do not challenge the regime with an ability to replace it, but who have ideas about how it should be run. No less an authority than Deng Xiaoping put this in substantive terms in 1980: "Some people, especially young people, [are] skeptical about the socialist system, alleging that socialism is not as good as capitalism."[110]

It is difficult to know what an individual at a single time is thinking. The content of an idea, its scope, the intensity with which it is believed, and the total audience among whom it echoes can all vary enormously. The individuals in large groups of bright people, such as students, of course do not all think alike. A few polls have been worded to take account of this fact, for example among Shanghai youths. Stanley Rosen, summarizing several questions from the best available 1988 poll of Shanghai university students, concludes: "Honesty has become situational. Some students report that, 'If exam questions are easy and I can answer them, or I'm not concerned with high grades, then I won't cheat; otherwise I will.' "[111] During the reforms, Shanghai young people might be believed when they claimed they had scant moral sense. Only 25 percent of Shanghai university students in 1988 disagreed with the statement "It is very difficult today to say clearly what is correct and what is wrong."[112]

This was hardly an ideological claim to rule. The main result of apathy among nonstate leaders and potential leaders is skepticism about the regime elite who do claim that right. Communist enthusiasm, in all good and bad respects, withered severely during China's reforms. Shanghai university students in the late 1980s are quoted as saying, "The trouble is, no one wants to be thought of as a Lei Feng." "Everyone is sick to death of government slogans and models like Lei Feng. If you gave your seat to someone [on a bus], people would think you were trying to get yourself praised for being like him."[113]

A late 1980s ditty about China's three liveliest cities was "*Beijing aiguo,*

Shanghai waiguo, Guangzhou maiguo" (Beijing is patriotic, Shanghai goes abroad, and Guangzhou sells out the country). But the tone of the joke suggests some sense in what both sets of southerners are doing. This does not attack patriotism, of course, but puts it in practical perspective. It recalls a sardonic early-1970s joke about the youth who was asked where he was going to vacation. He replied, "*Xin Xilan,*" which is Chinese for "New Zealand." But he meant *Xin*jiang, *Xi'*an, and *Lanzhou*—all in western parts of China that received many reluctantly rusticated youths. Individuals' interests do not end just because a state says they should. The tension can be a rich source of humor, but it is also a source of recreation and renovation for more collective ideologies. Fun that challenges official values, if only as a joke and as from individuals, is a hallmark of the productive and ambiguous times evident in China after its great violence in the 1960s. This has happened in other countries after their revolutions too, and the later modern results are not bad.

Notes

1. This is the very beginning of the famous classic by Lao Zi and perhaps the least translatable passage in all literature.

2. Lucian W. Pye, *The Mandarin and the Cadre: China's Political Cultures* (Ann Arbor: Center for Chinese Studies, University of Michigan, 1988), p. 81.

3. See Harry Eckstein, "The Idea of Political Development: From Dignity to Efficiency," in *Political System and Change,* Ikuō Kabashima and Lynn T. White III, eds. (Princeton: Princeton University Press, 1986), pp. 311–46, and Clifford Geertz, *Negara: The Theatre State in Nineteenth-Century Bali* (Princeton: Princeton University Press, 1980).

4. Clifford Geertz, "Deep Play: Notes on the Balinese Cockfight," in *The Interpretation of Cultures* (New York: Basic Books, 1973), p. 443.

5. Suzanne Langer, *Philosophy in a New Key: A Study in the Symbolism of Reason, Rite, and Art* (New York: Penguin, 1942) and *Feeling and Form* (New York: Scribner's, 1943). Although culturalists in social science sometimes cite Langer, they shy away from her finding of functions for symbolic forms.

6. An attempted application, raising this problem earlier, is the present author's book about fury in the Cultural Revolution, *Policies of Chaos* (Princeton: Princeton University Press, 1989).

7. James C. Scott, *Domination and the Arts of Resistance: Hidden Transcripts* (New Haven: Yale University Press, 1990), p. 220.

8. Neglecting that literature has structure, Darnton also says such an approach "has a rigor of its own, even if it may look suspiciously like literature to a hard-boiled social scientist." Robert Darnton, *The Great Cat Massacre and Other Episodes in French Cultural History* (New York: Basic Books, 1984), pp. 5–6.

9. This last is an interpretation of Lakoff to which he might not subscribe. But what else should one do with a book from Berkeley that encourages such free associations? The word "radial" is Lakoff's. This linguist, following a tradition that Wittgenstein's "clouds of meaning" began and referring to empirical work by cognitive psychologists, can be read to suggest that sets (categories) come in two main logical kinds. First, classic sets are defined such that each member has a full list of specific traits. Second, human minds in practice frequently define sets "radially" from an especially "good example" (e.g.,

Geertz's cockfight) whose traits can generate the set by various different metaphorical or metonymic operations; so some members may lack any specific traits in common (except an association with the central member). See George Lakoff, *Women, Fire, and Dangerous Things: What Categories Reveal About the Mind* (Chicago: University of Chicago Press, 1988), passim, especially chap. 6, and p. xii.

10. Prasenjit Duara, *Culture, Power, and the State: Rural North China, 1900–1942* (Stanford: Stanford University Press, 1988), p. 39.

11. Ibid., p. 41.

12. For the complexities, which are many, see Rudolf G. Wagner, *The Contemporary Chinese Historical Drama: Four Studies* (Berkeley: University of California Press, 1990), pp. 219–35.

13. This change was about individuals, so it is considered here; it was in collective norms, so it is also considered in the next part of the book. Lynn White, "Changing Concepts of Corruption in Communist China," in *Changes and Continuities in Chinese Communism: The Economy, Society, and Technology,* Yu-ming Shaw, ed. (Boulder: Westview, 1988), pp. 316–53.

14. Wang Anyun and Po Xiangyuan, *Shanghai Dashijie* (Shanghai's Great World) (Wuhan: Changjiang Wenyi Chuban She, 1988), p. 3 and passim.

15. The mirrors are *"haha jing."* See the nostalgic treatment (whose publication is also evidence of Shanghai's change) in ibid., pp. 82, 85, and passim.

16. "Making a name for oneself" loosely translates as *chengming chengjia,* which was once deemed a form of *geren zhuyi.* The article specifically mentions 1957, when the Antirightist Campaign set a pattern of broad social violence in China that lasted for more than a dozen years. *WHB,* October 18, 1980.

17. Victor Nee, "Peasant Entrepreneurship and the Politics of Regulation in China," in *Remaking the Economic Institutions of China and Eastern Europe,* V. Nee and D. Stark, eds. (Stanford: Stanford University Press, 1991), p. 182.

18. See Clifford Geertz, "Deep Play," especially p. 452, or most other works of recent anthropology.

19. *SJJJDB,* August 15, 1988.

20. Perry Link, "China's 'Core' Problem," *Daedalus* 122:2 (Spring 1993), pp. 203–4.

21. Fredric Jameson, *The Political Unconscious: Narrative as a Socially Symbolic Act* (Ithaca: Cornell University Press, 1981), p. 20. This work, from a literary critic, may please a student of politics. But the premise in the quotation could as easily lead to a more circumspect conclusion, that "everything" is related to the political, not that it can be reduced to the political.

22. The functional definition of ideology proposed here depends on Karl Marx and Friedrich Engels, "The German Ideology," in *The Marx-Engels Reader,* ed. Robert Tucker (New York: Norton, 1978); Max Weber, *The Protestant Ethic and the Spirit of Capitalism* (New York: Scribner's, 1958); and Karl Mannheim, *Ideology and Utopia* (London: Routledge, 1936). The interpretation of Mannheim is related to ideas about "pure ideology" that helps system stability or "practical ideology" that helps change systems, in Franz Schurmann, *Ideology and Organization in Communist China* (Berkeley: University of California Press, 1966).

23. Gaetano Mosca, *The Ruling Class* (New York: McGraw-Hill, 1939).

24. Although the phrase "both red and expert" (*you hong you zhuan*) in Chinese does contain "both," the Cultural Revolution clearly put a premium on redness. See a summary of this history from an interesting date, January 13, 1977, in *RMRB.*

25. The Nanjing paper is *Xinhua ribao;* the first report of this sort came in the *Shanxi ribao* of April 9, 1977. *Zhongguo xueshu jie dashi ji, 1919–1985* (Chronicle of Chinese

Academic Circles, 1919–1985), Wang Yafu and Zhang Hengzhong, eds. (Shanghai: Shanghai Shehui Kexue Yuan Chuban She, 1988), p. 267.

26. "*Ni yao shehui zhuyi de cao, buyao ziben zhuyi de miao.*"

27. *WHB,* October 24, 1979.

28. Also present, in addition to Mao, Dong, Chen, and He, were Chen Gongbo, Zhou Fohai, Liu Renjing, Li Da, Wang Jinmei, Deng Enming, Chen Duxiu—and almost surely the host, Li Hanjun, whose house in present-day Luwan district is a museum. *WHB,* October 24, 1979.

29. *Shanghai shi wenxue jiang huojiang zuopin ji (1982–1984 nian lilun pinglun)* (Collection of Prizewinning Works in Shanghai Literature [Theory and Criticism, 1982–1984]) (Shanghai: Shanghai Shehui Kexue Yuan Chuban She, 1986), p. 12.

30. Karl Mannheim, *Ideology and Utopia.*

31. The cults of Mao and Deng were revived less consensually in the 1990s. This was supported by some conservatives, but apparently not by all officials.

32. Fu Zhengyuan, "The Sociology of Political Science in the PRC," in *The Development of Political Science: A Comparative Study,* D. Easton, J. Gunnell, and L. Graziano, eds. (London: Routledge, 1991), p. 239.

33. Adapted from *FEER,* December 11, 1985, p. 51.

34. Marlowe Hood interview with Wang Ruoshui in *Post,* May 13, 1989.

35. *FBIS,* January 2, 1991, p. 29, in Troy Shortell, "The Party-Building Campaign in China" (senior thesis, Princeton University, 1991). This author agrees with analyses that distinguish different kinds of Chinese conservatives, although a stress on them is more apt for discussing politics in Beijing than for the issues in this book. The contrast between "reformers" and "conservatives" in the USSR is similar to usages in Stephen F. Cohen, *Rethinking the Soviet Experience: Politics and History Since 1917* (New York: Oxford University Press, 1985).

36. *FBIS,* January 4, 1991, pp. 29–30, source found by Troy Shortell.

37. Barrett L. McCormick, *Political Reform in Post-Mao China: Democracy and Bureaucracy in a Leninist State* (Berkeley: University of California Press, 1990), p. 4.

38. Ibid., p. 3.

39. Stevan Sangren, "Traditional Chinese Corporations: Beyond Kinship," *Journal of Asian Studies* 43:3 (May 1994), pp. 391–415.

40. *Shehui xue tongxun* (Sociology Bulletin), Shanghai, 1983, p. 72.

41. Andrew J. Nathan, *China's Crisis: Dilemmas of Reform and Prospects for Democracy* (New York: Columbia University Press, 1990), p. 6.

42. Stanley Rosen, "The Effect of Post–June 4 Re-education Campaigns on Chinese Students," paper for the annual meeting of the American Association of China Studies, 1992, p. 22.

43. See Stanley Rosen, "Political Education and Student Response," in *Education in Mainland China,* Lin Bih-jaw and Fan Li-min, eds. (Taipei: Institute of International Relations, 1990), p. 368.

44. Stanley Rosen, "Students and the State in China," in *State and Society in China: The Consequences of Reform,* Arthur Lewis Rosenbaum, ed. (Boulder: Westview, 1992), p. 173.

45. *Shijian shi jianyan zhenli de weiyi biaozhun.*

46. For a circumspect treatment of the origins of Mao's ideas, see Frederic Wakeman Jr., *History and Will: Philosophical Perspectives of Mao Tse-tung's Thought* (Berkeley: University of California Press, 1973).

47. Richard P. Suttmeier, "Party Views of Science: The Record from the First Decade," *China Quarterly* 44 (October–December 1970), p. 154.

48. Jürgen Habermas, *Toward a Rational Society: Student Protest, Science, and Politics* (Boston: Beacon Books, 1970), pp. 85 and 107, quoted in Li Cheng, "The Rise of Technocracy: Elite Transformation and Ideological Change in Post-Mao China" (Ph.D. dissertation, Princeton University, 1991).

49. Daniel W. Y. Kwok, *Scientism in Chinese Thought, 1900–1950* (New Haven: Yale University Press, 1965).

50. *Zhonghua renmin gonghe guo xianfa* (Constitution of the People's Republic of China) (Beijing: Falü Chuban She, 1986), p. 55.

51. The information in this analysis comes from correspondence with Lyman Miller.

52. It is good to know that the stars take such interest in all this. The material comes from Lyman Miller as well as from James Williams of the University of California, who is writing about Fang Lizhi.

53. Old traditions link natural events with mandates to rule. These are not unique to China, and many Chinese urban people speak of them mainly as light suggestions (e.g., the near coincidence in 1976 of the Tangshan earthquake and Mao Zedong's death). The idea that major natural-science theories should somehow mesh with political legitimacy, however, continues to come up in print.

54. This was suggested to the author by Lyman Miller, who has sources on it from *Red Flag*.

55. See this author's "Bourgeois Radicalism in the 'New Class' of Shanghai," in *Class and Social Stratification in Post-Revolution China,* James L. Watson, ed. (Cambridge: Cambridge University Press, 1984), pp. 142–74.

56. Clifford Geertz, *The Interpretation of Cultures.*

57. The Chinese expression was *"yi jieji douzheng wei gang."* Jiang Zemin et al., *Shanghai dangzheng jigou yange* (The Transformation of Shanghai's Party and Administration) (Shanghai: Shanghai Renmin Chuban She, 1988), p. 143.

58. Richard D. Baum, *Burying Mao: Chinese Politics in the Age of Deng Xiaoping* (Princeton: Princeton University Press, 1994), chap. 9, refers to Hong Kong *Wenhui bao,* December 24, 1987, and *China News Analysis* 1351 (January 1, 1988).

59. *Mo shitou guo he.* See also *FBIS,* December 21, 1987, p. 21, reporting radio of December 18.

60. "Reunderstand Capitalism and Socialism," in *Liaowang* (Outlook) (overseas edition), July 19, 1988, and John P. Burns, "Strengthening Central CCP Control of Leadership Selection," *China Quarterly* 138 (June 1994), pp. 458–91.

61. See Part 1, volume 1, for further discussion of Shanghai reformers' reasons for having initiated propaganda about the Wenzhou model. Also, *Wenzhou moshi de lilun tansuo* (Theoretical Exploration of the Wenzhou Model), Lin Bai et al., eds. (Nanning: Guangxi Renmin Chuban She, 1987).

62. In Christianity, some theologians have explored the sacredness of doubt. See also Clifford Geertz, *Islam Observed* (New Haven: Yale University Press, 1968).

63. The "cat theory" (*mao lun*) caught Deng in a playful mood: *"Buguan baimao heimao, zhuazhu laoshu jiu shi haomao."* The "feel theory" (*mo lun*) relies on Zhao's advice, romanized above. The "special characteristics theory" (*tese lun*) is as imprecise as the foregoing two.

64. See the article "How to Look at Some of the Current Phenomena of Confusion" in *GMRB,* September 1, 1988, cited in John Burns, "China's Governance: Political Reform in a Turbulent Environment," *China Quarterly* 119 (September 1989), p. 497.

65. *CD,* September 30, 1989.

66. "Years of Doubt" is the title of a central chapter in Ronald Hutton, *The Restoration: A Political and Religious History of England and Wales, 1658–1667* (Oxford: Clarendon Press, 1985), pp. 185–219.

67. Michael Hunter in *The Restored Monarchy, 1660–1668,* J.R. Jones, ed. (London: Macmillan, 1979), pp. 185–86.

68. Stuart R. Schram, *Ideology and Policy in China Since the Third Plenum, 1978–1984* (London: Contemporary China Institute, School of Oriental and African Studies, 1984), pp. 78–79.

69. Tolerant "balancism" has been described as a norm that helps contain consensus in bureaucratic policy making at such times. Susan L. Shirk, *The Political Logic of Economic Reform in China* (Berkeley: University of California Press, 1993), p. 277, writes: "As an ideology, 'balancism' shapes the thinking of even those groups who are penalized by it."

70. *Post,* July 4, 1988.

71. *Wujiang simei* stressed decorum, manners, hygiene, discipline, and morals, as well as the beauties of mind, language, behavior, and environment. The other items listed below were respectively called the movements for *shuangxin, wenming cun, shuangjia, xuexi Lei Feng, liuhao,* and *zhenxing Zhongguo.* See *Shanghai shehui xiankuang he qushi, 1980–1983* (Situations and Trends in Shanghai Society, 1980–1983), Zheng Gongliang et al., eds. (Shanghai: Huadong Shifan Daxue Chuban She, 1988), p. 233.

72. *JFRB,* March 28, 1981.

73. *JFRB,* August 23, 1981.

74. These principles of CCP secretary Wang Chonglun are publicized in *JFRB,* August 17, 1981.

75. Chinese interest in lecturing of this kind is not restricted to the mainland; somewhat similar programs were occasionally seen by the author in Taiwan also during the summer of 1993. They are fewer there, and some are evangelical (including sermons on Buddhist teachings, presented by both monks and nuns). On Hong Kong television, they are very few.

76. Required courses are *bixiu ke. Zhongguo xueshu,* pp. 125–26.

77. This study was *xingqi wu zhengzhi xuexi. Fudan Daxue de gaige yu tansuo* (Reforms and Explorations at Fudan University), Fudan Daxue Gaodeng Jiaoyu Yanjiu Suo, ed. (Shanghai: Fudan Daxue Chuban She, 1987), p. 163.

78. On the effectiveness of political education, see Anita Chan, *Children of Mao: Personality Development and Political Activism in the Red Guard Generation* (Seattle: University of Washington Press, 1985). On the ways in which pre-1966 political education was powerful but in ways not intended by the leadership, see Susan Shirk, *Competitive Comrades: Career Incentives and Student Strategies in China* (Berkeley: University of California Press, 1985). On the point that such education, while powerful in cities where few had starved during the post-Leap famine, lacked a basis in rural areas where Party cadres lost resources of legitimacy because of the famine, see Yang Dali, "Making Reform: The Great Leap Famine and Rural Change in China" (Ph.D dissertation, Politics Department, Princeton University, December 1992).

79. Based on a conversation with a former teacher at Shanghai Normal University, July 14, 1992.

80. "Dui zhengzhi jingji xue zhuanye gaige de jidian jianyi" (Some Suggestions for Professional Reform in Political Economy), in *Fudan Daxue de gaige,* p. 219.

81. *RMRB,* October 10, 1980.

82. *NCNA,* September 24, 1984. This and the previous source were suggested by Prof. H. Lyman Miller.

83. Raymond Aron, "The End of the Ideological Age?" in *The End of Ideology Debate,* Chaim Waxman, ed. (New York: Funk and Wagnalls, 1968).

84. *BR,* April 16–22, 1990, and *FBIS,* May 30, 1990, p. 21, cited in Troy Shortell, "The Party-Building Campaign."

85. *FBIS,* January 25, 1991, pp. 18–22, and also *FBIS,* May 10, 1990, pp. 22–23.

86. *JFRB,* June 28, 1988. There were 4,304 winners of this *wuyi laodong jiangzhang.*

87. This list appears in editor Li Cheng's introduction to an English translation of Yang Dongping, *Chengshi jifeng: Beijing he Shanghai de wenhua jingshen* (City Monsoon: The Cultural Spirit of Beijing and Shanghai) (Beijing: Dongfang Chuban She, 1994), in *Chinese Sociology and Anthropology* 29:2 (Winter 1996–97).

88 See *Shanghai shi Luwan qu diming zhi* (Gazetteer of Shanghai City's Luwan District) (Shanghai: Shanghai Shehui Kexue Yuan Chuban She, 1990). Another example is *Shanghai shi Xuhui qu diming zhi* (Gazetteer of Shanghai City's Xuhui District) (Shanghai: Shanghai Shehui Kexue Yuan Chuban She, 1990). The bibliography contains references to many county publications, cited elsewhere in this book; but by no means were all the local publications for academic or administrative use.

89. Interview with an official of the Shanghai Municipal Committee Party School, June 1991. But UCLA historian Philip C. C. Huang has obtained access to some material for his book *The Peasant Family and Rural Development in the Yangzi Delta, 1350–1988* (Stanford: Stanford University Press, 1990). See also *Songjiang nianjian, 1987* [1988] (Songjiang Yearbook, 1987 [and 1988]) (Shanghai: Shanghai Shehui Kexue Yuan Chuban She, 1987 [and 1988]); and *Songjiang zhenzhi* (Gazetteer of Songjiang Town), Che Chi et al., eds. (Shanghai: Shanghai Renmin Chuban She, 1988).

90. This article by Wang appeared in the journal for journalists, *Xinwen zhanxian* (News Front), August 1980; see also Stuart R. Schram, *Ideology and Policy,* p. 43.

91. See Merle Goldman, *Literary Dissent in Communist China* (Cambridge: Harvard University Press, 1967).

92. Stuart R. Schram, *Ideology and Policy,* p. 45.

93. Ibid., p. 46.

94. *RMRB,* November 16, 1983, in Schram, *Ideology and Policy,* p. 47.

95. The sources are far too many to cite, but among many interpretations and many anthologies are: Merle Goldman, *Sowing the Seeds of Democracy in China: Political Reform in the Deng Xiaoping Era* (Cambridge: Harvard University Press, 1994); and Han Minzhu (pseud.), ed., *Cries for Democracy* (Princeton: Princeton University Press, 1990).

96. Benedict Stavis, *China's Political Reforms: An Interim Report* (New York: Praeger, 1988), p. 94, from *China Spring Digest,* March–April 1987, pp. 12–13.

97. Benedict Stavis, *China's Political Reforms,* citing *BR,* February 23, 1987.

98. Chen Duxiu, "Xin qingnian zuian dabian" (Defense of the New Youth Case), *Xin qingnian* (New Youth) 6:2, in *Chen Duxiu wenzhang xuanbian* (Selected Works of Chen Duxiu) (Beijing: Sanlian Shudian, 1984).

99. Joseph Needham, *Science and Civilization in China* (Cambridge: Cambridge University Press, 1954 et seq.).

100. In Chinese tradition, *yang* was a generalized principle of male active brightness, while coexistent *yin* represented the opposites. The five elements (*wuxing*) of traditional chemistry are metal, wood, water, fire, and earth. See Liu Guisheng, ed., *Shidai de zuowei yu lilun de xuanze: Xifang jindai sichao yu Zhongguo qimeng sixiang* (The Achievements of the Time and Theoretical Choices: Modern Western Thoughts and Chinese Enlightenment Thought) (Beijing: Qinghua Daxue Chuban She, 1989), p. 170.

101. *Xin qingnian* (New Youth), September 15, 1915.

102. Vera Schwarcz, "Memory, Commemoration, and the Plight of China's Intellectuals," *Wilson Quarterly* (Autumn 1989), p. 121.

103. Roger V. Des Forges, "Democracy in Chinese History," in *China: The Crisis of*

1989, Roger V. Des Forges, Luo Ning, and Wu Yen-bo, eds. (Buffalo: State University of New York Press, 1990), pp. 29–30.

104. Liu Guisheng, ed., *Shidai de zuowei,* pp. 169–70.

105. E.E. Schattschneider, *The Semi-Sovereign People: A Realist's View of Democracy in America* (Hinsdale, IL: Dreyden Press, 1960), intro. David Adamany, pp. 54 and 133.

106. James C. Scott, *Domination and the Arts,* p. 111, cites Michel Foucault, making the same point. Scott elaborates in a footnote, with a more realistic view: "We ought not to assume that the real subjects of our analysis have absolutely nothing else to talk about except domination and resistance."

107. Ibid., p. 134.

108. See Charles Tilly, ed., *The Formation of National States in Western Europe* (Princeton: Princeton University Press, 1975).

109. Prasenjit Duara, *Culture, Power,* pp. 24–25.

110. Deng Xiaoping, *Selected Works of Deng Xiaoping, 1975–82* (Beijing: Foreign Languages Press, 1984), p. 235.

111. Stanley Rosen, "Political Education," p. 371.

112. Although the current book generally avoids attitude surveys, this was a careful poll and is reported by the best Western critic of the genre in ibid., p. 369.

113. Joan Grant, *Worm-eaten Hinges: Tensions and Turmoil in Shanghai, 1988–89, Events Leading Up to Tiananmen Square* (Melbourne: Hyland House, 1991), p. 27.

Chapter 2.2

Reform of Religion

*The gods? Worship them by all means. . . . Now you want to have
your rent reduced. Let me ask you how will you go about it? Will
you believe in the gods or in the peasant association?*

—Mao Zedong, 1927[1]

The religious impulse veers away from secular contexts or the collective state; it
is about individuals trying to face ultimate reality. A social scientist can approach religions in terms of the activities they support. To say vaguely that
people have "spiritual needs" can underspecify their condition. People become
sick and eventually die; they would like to know why. They become married and
have children; they want for themselves and their offspring a kind of recognition
that religious congregations provide. When bad things happen to good people,
they want to live despite injustice.

What good is the state in solving such problems? It can help with some of
them, but its special forte is coercion, which is marginally helpful at best. Taxes
can support a health system that delays death, but evidently nothing prevents it.
Mutual faithfulness in a marriage may need protection, but the army is not what
makes fidelity. The state's courts sometimes rectify injustices, but they have also
been known to perpetrate them. China has lately seen much revolutionary coercion, many officially mandated separations of families, and more rural and urban
deaths in the early and late 1960s than have been yet fully recorded in the
national politics. So it is hardly surprising to find that many individuals and
small groups there turn to nonstate religious ideals.

Urban Shanghai during reforms has seen less religious enthusiasm than many
rural parts of East China. But in fast-developing hilly areas, and to a lesser extent

in rich parts of the flat delta, religious organizations have flourished—sometimes with the support of local Communists despite the antireligious views of the central CCP. As a 1984 Zhejiang source reported, "Communist Party members, even some basic-level cadres, have become religious believers. They read 'the Bible,' offer prayers, solicit donations, build shrines and temples, and worship Buddha [*qiu shen bai Fo*]."[2]

A journalist has asserted that China during reforms has "no greater set of moral values than the pursuit of profit." This does not bother economists. Normative ambiguity in the reform era can be easily interpreted as a "spiritual vacuum." But if so, different people have different concerns about it. A Chinese sociologist claims that "religion, Confucius, and much of our traditional culture have been repudiated in the last forty years. Without them, it is impossible to guide society."[3] It indeed became impossible for official intellectuals to have the degree of influence to which they had traditionally become accustomed. By the same token, the ethics of different kinds of Chinese became more varied; and by any reasonable definition, there has been a quick increase of corruption. But it would be shortsighted to neglect the nonmaterial covenants even with the god of wealth (*cai shen*).

Prosperity in families is not praised in China merely because it means more material things, but because it means more in general, cosmically. It means more to offer the hungry ghosts of the ancestors on altars as proof that the communities they started still do well. It means more candles or joss sticks, more oranges on a New Year tree, more prayers to betters who understand compassion, more from the cornucopia of life. In the traditional cosmology it also meant more sons, but the one-child policy and more careers for women now somewhat discourage that interpretation among urban Chinese. This is not a spiritual vacuum. The pursuit of wealth, especially in South China, is popularly conceived in very cosmological terms. Northern thinkers and officials, who get less now from this faith than do others in their area, may well rue it. Chinese are not all alike. Neither are their beliefs, but the justification of new wealth is something that their various religions do during reforms.

The Pervasive Chinese Religion: "Confucian" Hierarchy

Despite the variations in this large country, there is arguably a single Chinese religion. Formally, many aspects of diverse Chinese creeds cohere. This religion is not usually monotheistic but is generally fatalist and very syncretic. It is not terribly concerned with any difference between the habits of close groups and the purposes of individuals; faith comes as often from status or birth as from conscious, intentional declarations. To develop a social science that can discuss this Chinese religion in terms of its effects, separate analyses are needed for Confucianism, Daoism, Buddhism, Islam, and the Christian sects (and some of these are of course doctrinally monotheistic and demand restricted, personal declarations of

commitment). But very many Chinese in practice combine creeds. Most Westerners implicitly define a religious belief so that it cannot be syncretic; for most
Chinese faithful, however, this exclusivist preference holds no interest at all.

Common ideals of Chinese families and other local networks have been well
described by many anthropologists, and here is a convenient summary:

> Harmony will bring wealth, prosperity, and happiness, while disharmony will
> bring poverty and disaster. In pursuit of harmony, an entity such as the cosmos
> or the society is conceived and treated as a system of interrelating parts. . . . If
> divination or just plain common sense indicates that a system is in disharmony,
> then people can take measures to put it right again.[4]

Some scholars argue that the Daoist *yin-yang,* five-elements cosmology is
"the basis of Chinese religion," a set of symbols that tends to frame the way folk
Confucian and Buddhist elements are understood. A Daoist adept traditionally
should preside at major rites of individual passage, as well as at the most important communal rite of village renewal (which is often called the *jiao* ritual,
although in the PRC such village services cannot easily be held). Buddhist rituals
on such occasions "do not differ appreciably from similar rituals offered in a
local temple, under the direction of a Taoist."[5]

Worship of Chinese deities in a Daoist or Buddhist temple, on one hand, and
reverence for ancestors in a "Confucian" lineage hall, on the other, are now seen
by many anthropologists as just two ends of a continuum.[6] Anthropologist Joseph Bosco has shown the continuing pervasiveness of folk religion in China,
along with the close formal parallelism between societies such as the Yiguan
Dao and state-approved structures.[7] The similarity is so great, local people often
do not consider such organizations heterodox, even if the state deems them so. In
a number of similar avatars—secret societies, Protestant congregations, *qigong*
and martial arts groups, or others—such organizations filled the spiritual vacuum
the Party left in many rural areas after the Cultural Revolution. Most of their
leaders want to remain scrupulously apolitical in public, if only to attract converts and waylay the attentions of the state. But ideologically, most are millenarian. They are inherently political, whether or not they advertise this fact, because
despite minor differences they all propagate the Chinese tradition of obedience
to moral leaders.

Worship of organizational hierarchy is one of the clearest facts about Chinese
political life. The religion of China is generally more fatalist than theist, and both
state and local organizations (as well as imagined organizations) can affect fate.
The powers that be are not assumed to be perfect. Folk Buddhism and Daoism
have some fallible gods; even Confucians warmly respect their forebears, teachers, and heroes. These are all humans or very much like humans. When they are
ghosts, they should be placated, but they are often deemed to be remarkably
unintelligent, more stupid than omniscient. Ordinary people can try to guide

them. The intentions of ghosts (like those of recent state leaders) are normally fuzzy, but ghosts too are hungry. Specifically, ghosts are fed at a late summer festival in which food is set out for them on altars before being consumed by a very living family. If they are evil, they may be fooled, for example by a baffle wall, to stay out of a house. At the birth of a son, the traditional midwife can shout "It's just a girl!" so that any malicious spirit will not think the infant worth bothering. Spirits are dangerous, but they can be led. The greatest such power is only a bit more clearly secular, and it is the state. Governments and local cadres alike promote these kinds of reverence, and they have been doing so for millennia. Reverence for official organizations in China is like the worship of these foolish gods.

Theme and Variation: The Creed of the Chinese Religion

It is easier to sense the unity of China's most general creed than to specify its doctrines. Themes are easy to suggest, but all the evidence comes in the form of enigma variations. Perhaps it is sensible to rely on a quasi-official Chinese source to begin a discussion of orthodox themes before attempting to explain the many partial heterodoxies. A Shanghai Marxist author, trying in 1985 to explain religious belief to people who read books, argued that there must be five "special features" of a properly Chinese faith:

1. Since the traditional ancestors of the Hans (figures such as Pan Gu, Nuhuo, and Fu Xi Si) were humans rather than gods, a national Chinese religion would tend not to be theist.

2. Since Chinese "have worshipped Buddhism's Amitofo and Guanyin, Daoism's God of Wealth, the stove god, and the three gods of prosperity, longevity, and good fortune," Han religious beliefs are "nonexclusive." As this Shanghai author points out, "the proportion of Han [exclusivist] religious believers in China's total population has been quite small for over two thousand years."

3. Nonetheless, "gods and ghosts," "souls and spirits," have been endemic in Chinese peasant religion. The implication was that an urban intellectual reader of a secular book, such as this one, could never take mere peasant beliefs seriously.

4. "The ruling class throughout China's history has never legally forced one religion, a so-called state religion, on all the people." (Actually, creeds such as Buddhism under the Sui, Confucianism under the Ming, or leftist radicalism under Mao Zedong received state support. But the periods of nonexclusivity predominate.)

5. This secular book claimed that "the ruling thought system, Confucianism . . . imposed restraints on the development of organized religion. The principal concept of Confucianism, the concept of the 'will of heaven,' and the general principles of feudalism were in conflict with the teachings of Buddhism and the other great religions. . . . This 'heaven-determined fate' way of thinking led many of

the people away from reliance on religion to reliance on themselves to 'change' their own destinies." (Max Weber denies this progressivist reading of Confucianism and calls it a religion. But the Shanghai book, following official categories, likes Confucian intellectual statism and so calls it a "thought system" lest anybody confuse it with religious superstitions.)[8]

For Chinese, the appropriate belief would thus be a humanistic, nonexclusive, nonpeasant, nonestablished, and nontheist philosophy. The amalgam would be, in this Communist exegesis, much like a modernized and socially responsible form of Confucianism.

The 1985 Shanghai book was by no means the first attempt to create a "national religion" for modern China.[9] It was a circumspect retreat from the cocksure and violent antireligious line of the 1960s. Its five characteristics for a patriotic credo—offered during reforms when many said they sought belief—were based on justifiable readings of past Chinese practice. But its upshot was obviously designed for intellectuals and the state, not for most people and other power networks.

A more complete description of popular doctrine would modify the list somewhat. Certainly humanism, syncretism, and nonmonotheistic animism are common ideas in China. Peasants and ex-peasants also entertain a practical interest in multiplicity, not just of spirits but also of more sons, more dollars, more oranges on the ceremonial trees, more years in long lives. These are all happily honored, so long as the things counted are standardized and at least potentially useful. Multiple beliefs in different religions joins this potpourri with no problem.

The many forms of little-tradition "Confucianism," which stresses familial and face-to-face links particularly, makes government control more difficult than state officials stress, because it undergirds small patriarchies, not just the large one. Confucianism (like Buddhism) is not theistic in its formal doctrines, even though it is unmodern. Atheistic modern Marxists did not fully know how to approach it. The main form of Confucian organization is the social unit that creates the strongest political bonds of all: the family. This gave Chinese Communists pause, since very few of them have been radical enough to advocate abolishing families.

CCP faith in organization has strongly echoed the Confucian premise that people of one blood, organized with discipline to work together and led by a patron, can do anything. Although there are explicit associations of Confucianists centered on the Sage's old family home at Qufu, Shandong, this formal quasi-religious organization (although it has prospered during reforms) is politically trivial in comparison to the endemic family relations that powerfully inform local politics throughout China. The pervasive appreciation of kin and kinlike relations, whether seen as specifically Confucian or generically Chinese, was scarcely dented by the Cultural Revolution. Family members sometimes criticized each other then, but coercion gave these terrifying events unusual meanings to the participants as family members. Often the people attacked (usually parents) saw that violence against them was necessary so as to save their own kin, who were forced to be aggressive. The structure of factions in 1966–68, even of radical groups, showed strong Chinese biases for familylike organizations, much as commercial structures in the later reforms have done. The recent rise of rural collectives, household contracts, and better-educated cadres, while certainly not just a matter of Confucianism, freely draws on Chinese traditions that Confucius articulated.

Open praise of the Sage became legitimate during the reforms, because his name had been used by radicals in the campaigns to criticize Confucius. The most famous Chinese philosopher had been damned along with the ancient Duke of Zhou, a stand-in for Zhou Enlai. But this movement, like many other radical campaigns, had unintended local effects: Many Chinese greatly enjoy reading the ancient masterpieces about themes that range from love to morals to folly. These are as different from each other as the ancient peasant *Songs,* the *Analects,* and the Daoist mystical writings. Many also like to learn the old literary languages (*wenyan*) in which these classics were written. Some interviewees report that the campaigns to "criticize" Confucius, Lin Biao, and the Duke of Zhou in the early 1970s gave them a state-legitimated opportunity to study works they secretly relished. How could they incisively criticize Confucius or other "feudal" writers, after all, without reading them? So they attended the political meetings, said whatever negative things they had to say about China's most famous teachers—and enjoyed the chance to learn the old forms of their own language and the extremely diverse contents of these timeless texts.

Confucianism involves temples and services, but the Chinese government has flinched from damning it as a "religion." The reasons for this are at least triple. The first and most obvious, during the reform period, is that the Cultural Revolution threatened the unity of so many urban families—while actually strengthening their internal bonds because of this external violence—that the legitimacy of the Party-state had been put in conflict with the extremely strong local legitimacy of the Chinese family. All but a few very radical Party members, during most of the reforms, have steered clear even of faint critiques against Confucius, lest they be thought to want another Cultural Revolution. The Sage's home temples and grave site at Qufu, Shandong, have been restored, partly at government expense. The 1982 Central Committee policy statement on China's religions, which is a long document, did not mention Confucianism at all.

A second and more important reason for the official reformed attitude of generally suspending judgment on the doctrines of the Sage lies in the civil-social emphasis in his beliefs. Confucianism is nontheist rather than quite atheist; doctrinally, it is agnostic about gods. Nonetheless it involves rituals, practical worship of the power of organization in the abstract, and clearly nonrevolutionary commitments against hasty change and unnatural sacrifices. Leninist discipline could easily conflict with Confucian respect for one's body and its role in the sequence of generations. This sect also has a spiritual headquarters, the major establishment for respectful pilgrimages at Qufu. The ambiguity of the Party's stance toward Confucianism is striking, not just because of the CR attacks, but also because most Communists have usually idealized a more thorough totalism about beliefs than the recent tolerance of Confucianism would imply.

The Marxist ideal still applies (even if it can no longer be implemented) to other religions: to "foreign" Christianity, to indelibly theist Islam, and to "super-stitious" Buddhism and Daoism.[10] But Confucianism is treated differently, per-haps because its formal doctrines link legitimate power to educated elites. This stress on education went down well in a Party geared toward reforms, as tech-nocrats claimed power on a current political platform of modernization for na-tional strength. Also, Confucianism is humanistic and thoroughly Chinese. It is localist, not just statist. It was ostracized in the Cultural Revolution. These are all good qualifications for a belief system in reform China.

Confucius was an intellectual who advised princes on how to be legitimate. Elder Communist princes by the 1980s not only had reason to feel legitimacy was a problem. They also needed confirmation that the union of knowledge and hierarchy would be effective. No belief system affirms the rightness of educated rule more thoroughly than Confucianism. Also, few others have such tolerance for long-winded public moralizing, a perquisite that many Communist cadres had come to enjoy. After the CCP's botching of the Great Leap Forward and the Cultural Revolution, any doctrine (especially a native Chinese one) that could convince individuals of the inherent virtues of stable order was music to Com-munist ears. Such useful faith could not be deemed "religion."

No "rites controversy" has been waged by the Communist hierarchy in the reform period against the respect for ancestors. Respect for beliefs runs in lin-eages. Other religions in China have evinced this pattern strongly, and it applies to Marxism too. "Ancestor worship" means that members of young generations tend to uphold whatever beliefs were bequeathed to them, as part of their basic identity. Confucian rites, nontheist and based in local communities, strengthen over the long term *any* other system of values that accommodates them. They stabilize and legitimate whatever previous beliefs a lineage had.

Local and State Support for Obedient Orthodoxy

Sectarian interests come after this stress on the family. Chinese people during the reforms acquired or revived many kinds of these—whether Buddhist, Daoist, Islamic, Catholic, or Protestant—if they knew their ancestors had committed to the same sect. Empirical evidence suggests this is the main, though not exclu-sive, explanation of why Chinese people become formally "religious," when they do so. Some never see a need to go so far. Many, especially in urban and rich rural areas, apparently considered that reverence for family and affection for local friends made sufficient faith.

Lineages that had lost records in the Cultural Revolution pooled local sources to reconstruct their genealogies. Such activity challenged high-level CCP interests, and a few bureaucrats expostulated against it. But that did not stop it. Like all other religious activities, genealogy writing went underground if repressed. Lineage rituals have returned endemically during China's reforms. In one place, more than five hundred members of the Wu family gathered to clean their ancestral graves at the sweeping rite in 1990. One reporter claimed that "the clans begin to have an administrative, judicial, and commercial power that is on a par with, or even excludes that of, the properly constituted authorities."[11]

Official cadres on religious affairs, apparently realizing that any hope of expunging Chinese people's interests in their families would be utterly vain, deftly identified family rituals with "Confucianism"—which was declared not to be a faith so much as organization. Most intellectual CCP reformers' attitudes toward religion relate to the somewhat tolerant views of one of the Party's earliest intellectuals, Chen Duxiu. Chen argued, "Religion, law, and morality are all from [scientific] truth. Religion bases itself on human beliefs, and law is operated by power. Morality manages human affairs, which are beyond the control of belief and power."[12] Chen saw what he took to be a historical progress in Western religions, from dogmatic Catholicism to Protestantism to Unitarianism and ethical societies. He wanted to use religion as a spiritual buttress of the movement toward China's new culture. In the long run, he thought, ethics and aesthetics would replace theisms, but he would be patient. There was plenty of time to wait. This mélange of patience and futurism was also the official mindset toward religions during the reforms.

Later, Chen became more materialist, less tolerant of theism, and more insistent that truth be found by inductive rather than deductive methods.[13] Science became for him something individuals needed, not just in their material lives, but also in their spiritual lives. Many urban intellectuals, whose need to make careers may affect their views of religion, believed this faith in irreligious science. Many leaders of collectives, and local cadres in rich parts of the Shanghai delta, had similar views.

When a group of Sunan rural people was asked in 1989 whether they believed in Buddhism, Daoism, Islam, Catholicism, or Protestantism, only 5 percent identified specifically with any of these religions. As one of the careful surveyors reported, the vast majority of them believed more generally in "fate" (ming), not in any more elaborate or exclusive doctrine.[14] Their conviction was probably not weaker than in many other parts of the world. Religion is not something that comes only with the Boolean values of 1 or 0, such that a person clearly has it or lacks it.[15] In southern Jiangsu, many people were aware of religious doctrines as something of possible future interest; a small minority was converted during the reforms to enthusiastic forms of Protestantism. Older people reportedly said they would like to hold more Daoist-Buddhist rites if their local leaders would allow that. But only a few areas of Sunan showed anything like the gaudy ebullience of folk religions that became evident during the reform period elsewhere, for example in Fujian. Folk Confucianism was of interest to Sunan lineages whose genealogies had been destroyed and could be reconstructed. This was presentable as research into local history. Small household altars to assorted deities were also common in the Sunan countryside, as was generalized respect for ancestors; and at the Spring Festival, candles and joss sticks were lit. But most local Sunan leaders, even in the early 1990s, were more interested in secular pursuits.

The difference between Sunan and some other booming parts of China (including Taiwan) seems to have been sharp in this respect. Part of the discrepancy may be explained because the fabric of temples and shrines in the Yangzi delta had largely disappeared. The Cultural Revolution and earlier movements had reused or destroyed rural Sunan's temples more thoroughly than in most parts of China. Major historical shrines were available for worship in Hangzhou, Suzhou, Shanghai, and other cities, but the minor ones had mostly been converted for use as offices or schools.

Postviolence Theodicy and Official Distancing from Religions

Revolution tended to make more Chinese religions officially heterodox. The Cultural Revolution strengthened the sects it most virulently attacked. No matter what the intentions of the radical participants may have been, the result was to turn major religions against the state. An official CCP report lays this on the line:

> the anti-revolutionary gang . . . radically did away with the work the Party had done on the religious question. They forcibly forbade legitimate religious activity of the mass of religious believers. They treated patriotic religious personages, as well as the ordinary mass of religious believers, as "targets for dictatorship," and fabricated a host of wrongs and injustices, pinning these on religious personages. They even misinterpreted some customs and practices of the ethnic minorities as religious superstitions. . . . They used violent measures against religion, with the result that this enabled religions to go underground and owing to the disorganized state of affairs to make some headway. . . . Any action which forces a non-believer to believe in religion, just as any action which forces a believer not to believe in religion, are both infringements on others' freedom of religious belief and, as such, are both grave errors and not to be tolerated at all.[16]

Why do good people suffer bad things, if there is some omnipotence that has compassion? This is hardly a new question.[17] The Cultural Revolution increased the faith of many Chinese in whatever religion they believed, rather than weakening it.

Religious freedom is formally guaranteed in the PRC constitution, but local laws to implement these provisions have been slow to come. The constitutional guarantee for freedom of belief is administered to cover only the organized forms of five specific religions: Daoism, Buddhism, Islam, Catholicism, and

Protestantism.[18] "Shamans and sorcerers," along with fundamentalist adepts in any of these religions outside state-monitored organizations, have in Party documents been termed "absurd and ridiculous." They are not protected. The Party's own factotum evil spirits, Lin Biao and the Gang of Four, have been officially blamed for the fact that such unorganized enthusiasms "have been increasing in villages where the disaster [the Cultural Revolution] was serious.... They must be suppressed."

Piety revived in response, and the widespread rural prosperity helped it. It emerged not just in state-authorized and unauthorized congregations of all five recognized religions, but also in quasi-Daoist shamans and other folk forms, as well as invocations of lineage ancestors.[19] The constitution does not protect fundamentalisms, and the government of intellectuals actively tries to suppress them. Many people believe in them anyway.

Some sects that are officially marginal or heterodox nonetheless served state goals during reforms. Most could maintain stable discipline among their members, and some have shown great success in the economy. Max Weber's ideas about a correlation between transcendental asceticism and practical work throw some light on East China during the 1980s. In a county of Zhejiang that had relatively many Protestants, that group was publicly admitted to be "not at all backward." They were very forward in entrepreneurial terms. The productivity of Christians in the metropolis was also praised in "award meetings for patriotic-religious advanced elements," where in the mid-1980s many Shanghai doctors, engineers, teachers, workers, salespeople, and Christians in other professions were praised as "labor models."[20]

Scattered Buddhist communities, and especially rural lineages in towns that contained their family names, also participated in economic reforms by becoming prosperous. Religious leaders sometimes criticized "self-seeking materialism." As the state-recognized Catholic bishop of Shanghai Jin Luxian thundered in 1988: "People are only concerned for money. The religion of worshipping money and materialism has taken root in many people's hearts.... Most young people pursue material enjoyment and neglect the spirit."[21] But his own organization became subject to the same critique, as a rent collector on lands that had been returned to it after the Cultural Revolution. Many of his flock used their religious ties in business.

Sectarian communities of any religion grew in their particular economic circumstances and were strongly local. In 1986, for example, Wuxi had thirty-five Catholic villages, served by three chapels and the head church, St. Joseph's. The nearby hamlet of Guangyi had forty-three households, of which forty were Catholic; and just as important, it had two large and prosperous Catholic fish farms on the shores of Lake Tai. As a Chinese-Canadian visitor explained about these Catholics, "People seemed to take pleasure in speaking of 'wan yuan hu' (literally, '10,000–yuan households').... It is easy to understand how praising the rich who enjoy the fruit of their labor becomes an expression of freedom." The

two priests, assisted by catechists, spend much time visiting dispersed parishio-
ners, "claiming churches back for worship, supervising repairs in those churches,
[and] making sure ... that units occupying church properties pay rent at appointed times."[22]

The economic proceeds from "superstition" are not minor, and the reform
economy absorbs them. In Shanghai's Chuansha county, a sandy agricultural
area part of which is now known as Pudong, "six sorceresses and fortune tellers
have used the money they swindled to rebuild their houses." But sometimes
peasant religion leads to modern losses, as a particularly sublime example from
Chuansha shows:

> Early this year [1982], rumor in the villages had it that paper ingots made of
> toilet paper were worth a lot of money in the netherworld. Consequently, many
> peasants rushed to purchase toilet paper [rather than gold or silver paper] to
> use as a substitute for paying condolences to the netherworld, to be burned for
> deceased relatives. One peasant bought forty rolls of toilet paper at once; so
> more than 10 *yuan* turned into ashes in an instant. Not only was money wasted,
> but it exhausted the toilet paper stock of some stores.[23]

Ritual spending soared as the economy prospered and the state tended to
withdraw from matters of religion. In one rich area of East China by 1989, the
average price of marriages had risen above 9,000 yuan.[24] The cost of weddings
by this time could reach 30,000 yuan or more. Officials were supposed to disapprove, but in practice they often participated.

To show that extremely unofficial folk Daoist religious practices exist and are
widespread even in such a perimodern suburb as Chuansha, it is most effective to
quote at length from a 1982 article by Gong Jianlong, who published in the
important PRC academic journal *Shehui* (Society). The material is so sensational, commentary would only obscure it. The Marxist writer found

> more than twenty people's communes and towns in Chuansha County where
> superstitious activities are widespread. The activities mentioned here refer to
> the specific seeking out of professionals [engaged] in superstition (*mixin
> zhiyezhe*), in "fortune telling," "divining by the Eight Diagrams" (*bagua*),
> "catching ghosts to cure sickness," etc. As for those who generally believe in
> ghosts and deities, in holding memorial ceremonies on New Year's Day or
> other festivals, they are even more common. Devout believers in ghosts and
> deities are not only limited to old folks and women; a sizeable number consists
> of young people. For instance, among a total of 461 members of the Qingsan
> Brigade in Cailu Commune, over 95 percent are believers, but less than 5
> percent are non-believers. There is an old sorceress, Zhang so-and-so, in
> Jiangzhen Commune, self-proclaimed as being able "to call immortal celestial
> beings," "to capture demons," "to cure the terminally ill," who set up in her
> home our incense tables; every day a continuous flow of people go to her for
> "fortune telling" and healing, making her front door and courtyard like a
> marketplace. At Lianqin Brigade in Cailu Commune, fortune teller Mr. Xu

so-and-so at first charged two *jiao* [0.20 *yuan*] for fortune telling each time; later seeing that people wanting their fortunes told came in droves, and having more business than he could attend to, he raised the service fee to 1 *yuan* and still "the business is brisk." At one brigade in Huanglou Commune, where also in vogue was "arranging ghost marriages" (*pan guiqin*), eight couples were so arranged, of which surprisingly the parents of three couples were Party cadres. The so-called ghost-marriage arrangement consists of making a match, with the sorceress as the go-between, for a marriage in the netherworld, joining the deceased son of the Zhang family with the deceased daughter of the Li family. However, the occasion of their wedding is not inferior to that of the living, with the bride price and dowry from both sides [technically illegal], and relatives and friends invited for wine; the only difference is that the bride and groom have only memorial tablets instead. A cadre of Shiwan Commune made a computation about a peasant believer in superstitions; the latter's household was busy with superstitious activities the whole year round, with the new year welcoming the God of Wealth [Cai Shen—who is especially popular during the reforms], making sacrifices to ancestors at Spring Festival, by the Seventh Lunar Month worshiping "Dizangwang" [a Buddha who saves souls], by year's end sending the Kitchen God [on his way to report to powers above the doings of the year], and, in between, deaths bringing monks to chant Buddhist scriptures for the deceased every seventh day for seven times, on the one-hundredth day, the anniversary, etc. Some other commune members climb over mountains and wade through rivers distant from their hometowns to burn incense and worship buddhas at the Lingyin Temple in Hangzhou and Putuo Mountain near Ningbo; these practices are on the increase.[25]

Other reports refer to the troubled ghosts of the dead who suffered violence in the 1960s. Sorceress Diao Qiujiu of Chengzhen, Chuansha, claimed to be possessed by Mencius. She undertook to cure a boy of typhoid by exorcising from him the unquiet spirit of a person who had been "executed by shooting near the Wang home, the ghost of one who has suffered a wrong that has not been righted." Another sorceress, in Sanwang brigade, charged 1,000 yuan for trying to exorcise a fox-spirit causing sickness in a young woman—whose family went so far as to sell their house to pay the expense, which they deemed necessary.[26] The center of Shanghai may be reached from any Chuansha town in an hour or two. Certainly these "superstitious practices" were very unmodern. However that may be, the government had lost its credibility in efforts to end them. Peasant culture has its attractions, and after the Cultural Revolution these impressed some who now ignored the official faiths.

Ideal and Concrete Conditions for "Heterodox" Religions

The central state was mostly disserved, despite some benefits, by trends in Chinese religion during reforms. Official repression of religions had increased the enthusiasm of believers, as official publications freely admitted. Even if believers had not themselves been severely persecuted, as one analysis put it, they tended toward secret activities and religions if their futures were unclear. PRC books recorded that the Cultural Revolution had encouraged conspiratorial movements and secret activities, including secret belief in religions.[27]

Religious feelings among many young Chinese in Shanghai rose because of the previous violence. As a local nonreligious publication put it, these youths had grown up "under the red flag" and at first had high social ideals. But they became dispirited because of corruption and memories of the Cultural Revolution. They "could not correctly analyze the roots of these phenomena and actively treat them; so they accepted the supernatural ideas of religion." As this report pointed out, many older people—including some cadres—had similarly been disgusted by the willingness of official "living Buddhas" to accept bribes and gifts.[28] They came to the conclusion that religious ideas could provide a better moral order. This same analysis repeated the classic idea that "some contents of religious morality can guide believers to give up bad things and take up good ones, thus benefiting unified social stability." Buddhist and Christian organizations supported charities and many other good works, and accordingly they came in for public appreciation.[29]

Good works as defined by state intellectuals could be different, however, from those seen by religious believers. The sects and the state had different ideas about public health, for example. During the spring of 1986, in Xinmong, Jinshan county, Shanghai, the *Xinmin Evening News* reported that more than a thousand worshipers "lit joss sticks and candles and prostrated themselves before an ancient gingko tree." This tree stood next to a primary school built on the site of a former Buddhist temple. "Local people believed the Goddess of Mercy [Guanyin] in the former temple could cure all illness, [so they] lit firecrackers and made offerings before the hallowed tree."[30]

Traditional local hierarchies, including religious-coercive organizations, could be separate from the central state yet closely linked to local cadres. As *Youth News (Qingnian bao)* reported on the notable date June 2, 1989:

> Recently, secret societies have developed quickly, especially in rural areas. Five or six years ago, a portion of the peasants got rich because of the development of the commercial economy. They established various kinds of guard organizations [and these] attracted many peasants. But these organizations now are evolving in a traditional way. . . . Some peasants ask secret societies to help them resolve conflicts, but they do not ask the local public security or judicial organizations to help them. If peasants are not satisfied with a given secret society's decision, they ask another secret society to help them. In such situations, serious conflicts occur between two secret societies. Moreover, some township governments also often ask secret societies to deal with difficult problems that local governments cannot resolve. Reportedly, a secret society can resolve problems more quickly than government. But some secret societies also dare in public to oppose governmental or legal organizations.[31]

Religions solidify kin and villages. These local ties during reforms became more autonomous from official direction than in the past; some were like small coercive states. In poor rural areas of East China, traditional chiliastic kinds of religion flourished. A peasant leader of a secret Great East Asia Buddhist Society, Li Lianting, was sentenced to death for having attracted 130 members "in the name of curing diseases and explaining scriptures. . . . He conducted reactionary propaganda, advocated dynastic changes, viciously attacked the leadership of the Party and the socialist system, and slandered and abused Party and state leaders."[32]

Antistate heterodoxy built on local traditions that often recalled White Lotus Buddhism, but these normative factors combined with specifiable kinds of concrete situations to produce radical nonstate hierarchies at some times. It is possible at least to hypothesize that throughout South China, there are two kinds of villages that might be differentiated initially on the basis of soil types. At least one kind of tentative thesis is as follows:

Hamlets on poor or sandy soils, especially in broad regions that now have medium or high levels of income, apparently saw extensive urban emigration in the eighteenth and nineteenth centuries. They also saw the development of secret societies based in nonagricultural occupations such as transport, construction, and trading. In Guangdong and Fujian, such areas are called "overseas Chinese districts," where most of the people have relatives abroad.[33] In East China, most of the migrants went to places such as Shanghai. Perhaps the ground beneath these villages tends to be relatively light in color, and rice does not grow well, especially with traditional agricultural technologies, although there is sometimes cotton. Especially in certain periods, e.g. from the mid-1920s to the late 1930s or the mid-1970s to the present, investment money and entrepreneurial spirit related to earlier emigrations overseas have made these places boom industrially. Local leaderships there have foreign reasons to foster the revival of traditional religious rites and genealogical researches; temple building and tomb restoration have recently proceeded apace. Some villages are even able to sponsor large village rituals. A visitor to such places today sees multistory buildings of concrete, hotels, gas stations, restaurants, light-colored dust, and pipelines being laid; these villages currently resemble nothing so much as construction projects. Reform has come quickly to such places.

By contrast, around villages where the soil is darker, perhaps containing relatively more carbon and less silicon, crops have been reliably better and there was less need for migrants to leave. Local leadership was traditionally less often exercised through secret societies than in the previously medium-poor places described above. Hiring networks for nonagricultural activities were less important. These areas (and probably other very poor locales, whence emigration also never took place) still lack overseas Chinese connections or perhaps quite as many urban connections, relatives who could now come back to invest in ancestral places. The local leaderships tend to have either less interest or less outside reason, presentable within the CCP, to nurture religious revivals. So new temples and tombs tend to be built less conspicuously than in the other places. Research on lineage genealogies has a low priority in public, even if some of it goes on privately. There may often be new rural industry—after all, most of these areas are traditionally rich and can generate capital locally—and it tends to be organized by somewhat high-level local administrations (*xiang* rather than *zhen*, *zhen* rather than *cun*). Reform certainly comes to these areas, especially in the form of enterprising collectives that are closely linked to the local government. But many of their religious and local-political aspects change less quickly than their economic aspect. Organization in such places tends to be at somewhat higher levels of local administration.

The Shanghai delta is mostly in this second category. Old sediment soil in Sunan and northern Zhejiang is extremely rich, occasionally renewed by flood silt (not just in premodern times), and covered with self-refertilizing paddies. Recent reforms of rural industry there have been largely generated from local capital. Although some families have overseas relatives through parts of their lineages in urban areas, especially Shanghai, the percentage of families in this category is much lower than in many Guangdong, Hainan, or Fujian districts. Middle levels of the administrative hierarchy have been extremely important in most of the Shanghai delta, creating new factories and stores in the reform era—at the expense both of small networks and of the high state.

Exceptions test rules, and the delta contains some exceptions. The most conspicuous recent evidence of major religious revivals and secret societies in the Shanghai delta comes from relatively marginal groups in transport and fishing. Very close to the sea, e.g. in Shanghai's Chuansha (literally, "river sand") county, are areas that fall clearly in the sandy-soil category, as most of Sunan does not.[34] All the expected correlates can be evidenced in Chuansha: rural emigration has occurred, especially to the very large city nearby; traditionally more cotton than rice has been grown; recently there have been sharp decreases in agricultural production; there are clear signs of relatively high secret-society activity; recent shamanism has been reported; there have been religious revivals in established Buddhist and Christian sects; and the local history shows periods of particular local florescence (in the 1920s and 1930s, as well as in China's current decades of reform).[35] Du Yuesheng, Shanghai's most famous secret-society leader from the 1920s through the 1940s, was a native of Chuansha. That county also has a high proportion of Roman Catholics, who have been heterodox because of Rome. Chuansha is now called Pudong.

Empirical tests of the correlations suggested above might be attempted on different parts of the China coast. Some of them might prove valid. They could involve data ranging from soil composition, the frequency of new tombs, the percentages of employment and output in rural factories that are formally licensed by different administrative levels, and many other indices. The Shanghai delta is not the ideal place for such tests, because so much of Sunan is in the rich-soil category. Regions of China that are on almost wholly laterized ground might also not provide enough contrast to show such differences clearly. There seem specifically to be relations between outside investment and religious activities that deserve particular study. Religious festivals have certainly attracted overseas investors in Guangdong.[36]

These hypotheses are in some tension with many comparative theories of migration, but there is enough evidence from a variety of China coast places to put them tentatively.[37] Different kinds of Chinese heterodoxy may have grown in different kinds of marshy or sandy locations, and these concrete factors might be used together with norms about family prosperity to explain aspects of both religion and emigration in East and South China, as well as to show some differences between these two regions.

Local Support for Heterodox Enthusiasms

Official tolerance for some religious beliefs during the reforms sprang partly from Communist cadres' understanding that earlier coercive repression had not weakened shamanist and theist beliefs. Religions were better tolerated in the 1980s than before, and the official reason was that believers could be patriots and could contribute to China's modernization. As a thoroughly Communist, basically antireligious Shanghai analyst pointed out in 1986, "a latitudinarian policy must be adopted. To launch debates on issues between theism and atheism is harmful."[38]

Some of the doctrines that were tolerated, however, meshed badly with Chinese Communism. An obvious example is Islam, although that religion was politically far more important in western China than near the coast. Islam was heterodox, yet it had to be legitimated both for PRC foreign policy and because of its legally recognized minority status. Islam in Shanghai and other parts of China retained its organizational integrity even during the Cultural Revolution more effectively than any other religion. The Hui (Chinese-assimilated Muslims) of Shanghai form a tiny portion of the city's population, but they are the city's most numerous officially recognized minority, and some are concentrated in a few districts. Because this community lives in a major urban center of communications, any violence or discrimination against the Islamic minority would be quickly reported to the many Muslim countries with which China tries to maintain good relations. During the Cultural Revolution, however, when this kind of diplomacy became difficult anyway, most mosques were closed, and some Muslims were forced to raise pigs. But Muslim Red Guards organized to fight such insults, on communal rather than religious grounds. The Muslim Middle School formed its own youth gang, the Baozi Hao, to protect themselves.[39] Even in 1969, one mosque was still open in Shanghai—when all other public temples and churches were closed. The Chinese Islamic Association was reestablished as early as 1970.[40]

The rise of Islamic fundamentalism coincided with a decrease of state legitimacy in China during the 1980s, and both urban and rural Muslims were affected. Even though Shanghai Muslims posed no political threat, the local government treated them very gingerly because of communications with Muslims elsewhere.[41] As Islamic teacher Ma Liancheng said in 1990, "More people are attending prayers, more are going to the mosques to study the Koran, and more are going on pilgrimages to Mecca."[42] When a book entitled *Sexual Customs* was published in Beijing in 1989, its references to Muslim practices were considered insulting by Muslims, who marched in protest against it.[43] A fundamentalist sect called Ishan was tightly organized under a clannish hierarchy whose leadership posts were hereditary, and the government tried to ban it.[44] What the state could effectively do, however, was less than before.

Buddhism-Daoism, Shamanism, and Qigong

Buddhism-Daoism is China's main folk religion. This system of beliefs refers to names and concepts that derive from the "high culture" philosophic versions of either Buddhism or Daoism. For most people, though, the two are blended into a single religion whose temples hold sanctuaries for deities from both traditions. Piety is shown by waving lighted incense sticks, placing them in an urn, and praying for fortune in human affairs. Aside from folk Confucianism, this is by far the most widespread religion in China. It is difficult to discuss well, because the state Buddhist and Daoist associations that publish information are different from each other, and both are somewhat separated from the yeasty amalgam of their beliefs in popular culture.

Daoist monasteries, which had loose links with anti-Communist secret societies, were closed by the late 1950s. Also, Daoism (unlike Islam, Buddhism, Protestantism, or Roman Catholicism) lacks adherents abroad who are important to PRC foreign policy. Another handicap for the folk version of this religion is that intellectuals and Communists have identified Daoism more than any other belief with "superstition," and they deemed it a hindrance to Chinese economic progress and national strength. This was the least rationalist of the major Chinese cults, and the Communists found nothing in it to serve their state. The "high" form of Daoism represented by the classics of Lao Zi and Zhuang Zi is not subject to such charges, but the kind of Daoism-Buddhism that peasants revived enthusiastically in the 1970s and 1980s had been straightforwardly repressed in earlier years. The resurgence of popular Chinese religious devotions since the end of the Cultural Revolution represents a mass return to "superstitions" that most Chinese intellectuals have rejected.[45] But intellectuals are a tiny minority, even though they seldom seem so.

"Wind and water" geomancy, for the siting of new houses, became important with the rise of rural prosperity. Peasants in some localities also restored shrines, dedicated to local deities that had been destroyed during the Cultural Revolution.

For certain groups, such as boat people, these temples revindicated their identity as communities, even if their occupations and living arrangements had changed. Shamans' influence apparently remained low in rich areas of China such as the Shanghai delta, because of the spread of standard Chinese and Western medical systems. But the reform pattern was stronger in rich areas than poor ones, where a different picture was sporadically reported.

In the early 1970s, a young rural boy was seen with his hair in a topknot, to look like a girl so that evil spirits would be less likely to harm him. Fortune tellers did business in cities, not just in the country. According to a 1979 report,

> in a village near Shanghai, a witch and her assistant sought to heal a woman by exorcising a ghost. In the process, the witch attacked and killed two six-year-old boys in the watching crowd. The witch poured boiling water on them, then strangled one and set fire to the other. The witch accused one of the boys of being "possessed by the spirit of a drowned man." According to the *New China Daily* account . . . "the witch told the anguished parents that if they wanted to conceive 'noble babies' to replace their dead sons, they would have to bow down before 'the Buddha,' meaning herself, and burn incense in her honor.". . . The newspaper made no mention of any effort by the villagers to save the boys.[46]

This kind of thing does not happen every day near Shanghai. The police, unsurprisingly, have opinions about such events and try to stop them. But the Chinese state itself in the Cultural Revolution legitimated spectacles of violence, so the police have a difficult job.

Qigong is, after Confucianism, perhaps the most important officially unrecognized faith in China. As a popular 1990s saying had it, "East, west, south, north, center, everybody's practicing *qigong*."[47] Nominally, *qigong* is an old Chinese medical practice, involving exercises to channel the flow of energy through the body. *Qigong* was based on the Daoist notion that people learning to discipline their breath could also control the cosmic ether (*qi*), the force that composes everything. These ideas certainly have Chinese characteristics, and they loosely relate not only to traditional medicine, but also to sword wielding, to supernatural abilities seen in popular films, to the happy antistate warrior heroes of the classic novel *Water Margin,* and to the popular exercise routines of *taijiquan.*[48] Literally, *qigong* is the "ability to control ether." It was named as late as 1955 by a CCP cadre named Liu Guizhen, but it is a very old tradition and has long had some state support. Recent Chinese gerontocrats such as Chen Yun, Ye Jianying, Bo Yibo, and perhaps Deng Xiaoping were reportedly interested in *qigong*—which was not surprising in view of its medical claims for prolonging longevity. For many residents of crowded cities such as Shanghai, *qigong* was a way to provide "breathing spaces." Nancy N. Chen reports estimates of the number of *qigong* practitioners in the 1990s from sixty million to two hundred million.[49]

About twenty million belonged to popular *qigong* organizations. Many high

Communists, especially in the military, are *qigong* adepts. The 1988 *Shanghai Public Security Yearbook* includes, prominently near its title page, a picture of policemen splitting bricks with their bare fists. The caption is simply *"qigong."*[50] A *qigong* master taps the force of a "higher realm" (*gaoji jingjie*), thus acquiring supernatural powers to tell the future, to see through objects, to levitate, and so forth. Such heroes were the topic of a best-selling book in 1990.[51] Most of them were nationalist to the point of xenophobia—as are the *qigong* masters who hold fundamentalist rallies at which people absorb the cosmic force. *Qigong* is highly idealist and basically anti-Communist despite some of its famous followers. Even when it takes the form of a millenarian sect, the government cannot or does not stop it.

Qigong and martial arts movements receive enthusiastic support from many kinds of local leaders, especially those involved in militia or police work. It would be inaccurate to say that the diverse traditions of folk Daoism had ended, partly because *qigong* is one of them. A few PRC books have been recently published on *qigong* as a medical therapy, but apparently none cover the movement's very important religious or political sides.[52] *Qigong* enjoyed a particularly sharp renaissance in a millenarian and organized form during August and September of 1988, when rampant inflation and elite conflicts, combined with the recently unprecedented influx of foreign culture, provided a salubrious climate for *qigong* revival meetings. This phenomenon was more apparent in North China than in the Shanghai delta, but data from there are relevant because the movement shows an aspect of Chinese nationalism that might spread further and has at least some following throughout the country.

The tenor of this faith is captured in a news report that a foreign correspondent filed from Beijing about his attendance at an auditorium full of 1,500 people in August 1988:

> I was dumbstruck by the silence. Never had I seen a Chinese audience so utterly rapt. . . . On the stage, a young man in his mid-30s gave instructions in a measured, reassuring voice on the best way to sit and breathe in order to receive his *qi*. . . . Master Zhang's announcement that we were about to hear his recorded voice struck me as a bit cheap: At 10 *yuan* a head—three days' wages for most of those present—I expected a live performance. Before I could register my indignation, however, the gates to bedlam suddenly swung open. . . . The auditorium reverberated with loud animal-like noises. . . . The young woman directly in front of me began to shake so violently that her wooden seat came unhinged and slammed into my knees. A People's Liberation Army soldier in uniform to my right shot out of his chair, stretched his arms toward the ceiling and sobbed hysterically, pausing only to gulp for air. . . . When the tape ended about 40 minutes later, Master Zhang, who had been patrolling the aisles examining his handiwork, resumed the stage. The mayhem slowly subsided. . . . For the next part of the program, half-a-dozen invalids were wheeled on stage. . . . Master Zhang's disciples, including two women, set to work projecting *qi* through their outstretched palms like so many faith

healers laying on hands. Some of the ostensibly paralyzed limbs recovered; others remained motionless.[53]

Nativist millenarian movements have been known in many countries at times of economic dislocation. They are often antiforeign, and China's 1988–89 *qigong* movement falls into this pattern. In a later interview with master Zhang Hongbao, he reportedly said, "I face three obstacles in my work. The first is Western-trained Chinese intellectuals, who are suspicious of *qigong*. The second is the media, which must be won over. The third is the Communist Party itself."[54]

A novel called *The Great Qigong Masters* was published from the pen of Ke Yunlu in 1989. The protagonist was based on a real-life model, Yan Xin, an adept in his late thirties. Marlowe Hood writes:

> As early as 1987, stories of [Yan Xin's] ability to cure the incurable, see through walls and project both his *qi* and himself over huge distances were eagerly exchanged throughout the land. But when two prominent national newspapers and China Central Television reported in mid-1988 that Yan's powers had been scientifically verified under supposedly rigorous laboratory conditions at Qinghua University (China's MIT), Yan's fame—and, according to many who know him, his ambitions—soared to new heights. With the blessing of state-sponsored *qigong* associations, he traveled the land like a living Buddha, received by rhapsodic crowds wherever he set foot. . . . When Yan Xin packed the 15,000–seat Beijing Worker's Stadium three nights running in September, 1988, flaunting his popularity right under the leadership's collective nose, a crackdown soon followed.[55]

Yan had to leave China in 1990—a postponement, at least, of his imperial ambitions.

"Local emperors" (*tu huangdi*) have appeared frequently in reform China. In Hunan during 1981, a would-be "emperor," Li Laiyong, started a movement that lasted many months as a "counterrepresentation" of the PRC state.[56] Shandong has also nurtured at least two recent "emperors" (probably more, if reporting were complete). Li Lianting created "a reactionary secret society, advocated dynastic changes, and viciously attacked the leaders of the Party" before he was shot. Lin Yishi was first a peasant, then an entrepreneur—but he became so wealthy locally during reforms, he claimed the mandate of heaven in an area near Yimeng Mountain, Shandong, with ten thousand "subjects." His sect grew until a policeman member of it was killed (while making love to one of the imperial concubines). Lin Yishi escaped the public security's dragnet and was apparently never caught.

In 1984, an adept named Zhang Xiangyu had a vision in which Buddhist and Daoist gods dubbed her a daughter of the Jade Emperor and taught her "the language of the universe." Originally from Qinghai, in 1987 she moved to the Beijing Academy of Qigong Science and Research, and by the end of the next year had reportedly garnered many million yuan and half a million followers. After her 1990 prediction of an earthquake caused so much panic that officials went on television to deny its accuracy, she was put in jail.[57]

Qigong sects, shamans, and protoemperors are most unlikely to replace the CCP. They are not in a position to garner enough kinds of talent for China's modern administration. Historically, Red Eyebrow Daoists did not replace the Han, nor did White Lotus Buddhists or Taiping Christians replace the Qing (nor were many other such movements successful between these two dynasties). Millenarian movements are common in many countries.[58] Periods of widespread collective and personal concern can bring popular bouts of "soul-stealing" or "cat massacres."[59] These cults show that a political system can change; they do not show exactly how it will change.

The state reacted to new religious trends negatively, but it could do nothing effective to stop them. A Party proselytizer said, "Religion is preaching that the real world is illusory, insignificant, and that human life is 'the life of a mayfly,' brief and ephemeral, without meaning. Religion induces people to give up interest in the present life and to cease all efforts to find happiness and prosperity in this world."[60] This official critique of religion was socially serious and ethical, distorting only some popular beliefs. But it could not gainsay the fact that many Chinese during the reforms were turning to chiliasms different from the Communist one. People find meaning, even about society's future, in many places. The CCP had unintentionally taught them to seek it outside the official antireligion.

Organization and Funding of Reform Religions

Theist religions were more acceptable to state intellectuals than were shamanism or *qigong*. Both the Party and organized sects gathered information about the changing demography of belief, and these statistics during the reform era showed quick expansions of all institutionalized sects. Buddhism, like Confucianism and Daoism, is so widespread in China—and the intensity of belief in each of these denominations is so variable—that no estimate of the number of adherents could mean much. Suffice it to say that the numbers for Buddhism and Daoism (and for Confucianism were it considered a religion) would be extremely high, and any attempt to count believers in these three as exclusive of the others would be misinformed. As a Central Committee document has said, "Buddhism, including Lamaism, has almost the entire population among the ethnic minorities of Tibet, Mongolia, and Liaoning. . . . Among the Han race, Buddhism and Daoism still have a considerable influence at present." Official estimates of the number of believers in various congregations were confidentially published in 1982, as Table 2.2–1 shows. The numbers became much higher later, although it is very difficult to know to what extent the many disparate reports on this subject are comparable.

Table 2.2–1

Religious Believers, Clergy, and Temples (in China and three provinces: Shanghai, Jiangsu, and Zhejiang)

	China, 1949 adherents	China, 1982 adherents	3 Provinces, 1990 adherents	3 Provinces, 1994 adherents
Muslims	8 million	10 million		
Catholics	2.7 million	3.8 million		
Protestants	0.7 million	3.0 million	c. 1.6 million	c. 2.2 million
Buddhists	Many Hans are Buddhist; so are almost all Tibetans and most Mongols			
Daoists	Very many Hans have at least some interest in Daoism			
Confucians	Practically all Hans revere lineages, at least; so c. 1 billion			

Clergy and Temples (officially registered; China and Shanghai, various years)

	China 1982	Shanghai 1949	Shanghai 1965	Shanghai 1990	Shanghai 1994
Muslim clergy	20,000	60	50	19	
mosques		*19*	*3*	*6*	
Catholic	3,400	780	287	48	
churches		*392*	*39*	*43*	
Protestant	5,900	553	171	115	n.a.
churches		*280*	*38*	*23*	*32*
Buddhist	27,000	3,299	971	198	
temples		*1,950*	*339*	*19*	
Daoist	2,600	3,716	1,235	58	
shrines		*236*	*28*	*6*	
Confucian	Confucianism is unrecognized as a religion; no registered clergy				
temples	*Many Confucian sites are officially just "historical places"*				

Notes and sources: "Clergy" in some cases probably include religious associations' employees who do not lead services. The most precise available figures (specified by even more local disaggregations) were on a small but interesting minority, the Christians. Of the c. 2.2 million Protesants in the "three provinces" by 1994, nearly six-tenths were in Zhejiang, about four-tenths in Jiangsu (increasing very rapidly in the early 1990s, by official reports of the Jiangsu Provincial Religious Affairs Bureau), and about 3 percent in Shanghai. The number of believers in various religions is notoriously difficult to estimate, because for some creeds many are unregistered; in any case, strength of faith cannot easily be counted. It is uncertain that the criteria used by various sources (including official reporters) are kept standard. But see Document 19 of the CCP Central Committee, 1982, in Beatrice Leung, *Sino-Vatican Relations: Problems in Conflicting Authority, 1976–1986* (Cambridge: Cambridge University Press, 1992), pp. 118 and 355. The 1990 estimates of Protestants in the three provinces come through the courtesy of Dr. Philip L. Wickeri; two-thirds were in Zhejiang, with estimates as follows: Zhejiang (0.9–1 million), Jiangsu (0.4–0.6 million), and Shanghai (50,000+). The total number of Protestants in China as of 1990 was estimated between 5.0 and 7.4 million. Most Shanghai data come from *Dangdai zongjiao yanjiu* (Contemporary Religious Research) 1991:1 (a publication of the Shanghai Academy of Social Sciences), p. 8. By the mid-1990s, the numbers of adherents to the two Christian religions were between two and three times their numbers in the early 1980s. Intensity of devotion among Muslims was increased. Confucian and Buddhist rites affected larger numbers of people.

The government could do little to stop the expansion of religious sects throughout China, so it found retreat the better part of valor. This official withdrawal, partial though it was, depoliticized many believers except among groups such as Roman Catholics that had suffered severely during earlier decades. In the 1989 democracy movement, because most Chinese intellectual dissidents had doubts about all religions and because many believers eschewed all political views, theists were scarcely to be heard at Tiananmen. A draft law to specify some rights of religious sects was approved in August 1989.[61]

Forty religious colleges had been established with official blessing before this time, teaching sixty thousand Buddhist monks and nuns, Taoist priests, Christian clergy and sisters, and Islamic imams.[62] In East China, many large Buddhist monasteries acquired monks as well as paint jobs during the reforms, although smaller establishments did not receive so much attention. For Protestants, the Nanjing Union Seminary was revived as a major institution. So was the seminary at Sheshan Basilica in Qingpu county, Shanghai, for the Catholic Patriotic Association. Although more information is easily available about the organization and funding of the minority Christian sects than about the more diffuse and larger institutions of Buddhism and especially Daoism, the relative prosperity of all these churches during reforms reveals much about the interests of millions of ordinary people, as the revolution wound down.

Restoring the Fabric of Destroyed Religious Buildings

After the Cultural Revolution, many CCP leaders saw no great problem in offering restitution for damages caused by radicals. Restored religious sites, into which the state put some money after the Cultural Revolution, included many in the greater Shanghai delta: the Jade Buddha and Longhua temples as well as St. Ignatius Cathedral and Sheshan Basilica in Shanghai proper, the North Pagoda in Suzhou, the Putuo Mountain temples in Zhejiang, Daming Temple in Yangzhou, Guoqing Temple on Zhejiang's Tiantai Mountain, and the rich Buddhist and Daoist shrines of the Southern Song's old capital at Hangzhou such as the Lingyin Temple. The government could easily justify restoring these as national monuments. This suggested some regret for pillage in the Cultural Revolution. But many ordinary Chinese took these places to be not just patriotic landmarks, but destinations for live religious pilgrimage.[63]

The Cultural Revolution wreaked destruction of religious establishments throughout the Shanghai delta, even at some distance from major cities. At Qingcun, Fengxian county (in Shanghai, but rural), 475 lineage shrines, 16 Buddhist temples, 186 Buddhist statues, and assorted other Daoist and Buddhist places were destroyed in the months following mid-1966. These facilities had served about twenty thousand people in dispersed farming settlements then. Although some of these might be restorable, little evidence has been found that massive repairs have been undertaken on such establishments in the Shanghai delta generally during reforms.[64] Intellectuals could not see them as museums. Certainly there has, through the mid-1990s, been far more such restoration in coastal areas farther south.

Buddhist temple restoration by the 1980s became a major movement, although more on the coast south of Shanghai than in the Shanghai delta. Shrine construction could be justified by local cadres, because the high state was at the same time atoning for its own guilt in allowing the Cultural Revolution; it authorized repairs of famous monuments that 1960s violence had damaged. As one localist cadre put it, "The state has built large temples, and so the peasants have built small ones. Why should we bother about this?"

Temples for Guanyin, for Tianmu, for Mazu, for Erlang, for the Earth God, for the God of the Southern Hemisphere, for Guan'gong, and for other more local spirits sprang up widely in rural areas. This could not have happened, and did not happen, without the connivance of local cadres. As a critical Zhejiang report had it, "Apart from building temples, some people even use cement to build tombs for themselves. A few young people have gone so far as to build high-quality tombs for themselves, although they are only in their twenties."[65] This account went on to explain, in rational modern terms, that good cement should be used to build schoolhouses instead. But a zealous state had unwittingly put such official modernity out of fashion for many. Ex-peasants replaced it with their own tastes. Development has always meant *nouveaux riches*. On the mainland, as even more spectacularly in Taiwan, rural growth finances a resurgence of popular piety. Intellectuals in the government may disdain all this, but they simply do not have the resources to stop it.

Buddhist-Daoist Institutions

Folk Daoism has scant organization, except locally. It also has scant doctrinal unity, since adepts are supposed to find their truth and strength within themselves. Few of its believers reject other religions, except for the state-appointed professional Daoist masters. These traits make Daoism difficult to analyze—and easy to downplay. The Daoist religion might be dismissed as unimportant by now, except that most of the population actively participates in non-Buddhist, non-Confucian, broadly Daoist rites both in homes and in rural villages. Also, a few urban intellectuals are very taken with philosophical high Daoism as a native and sophisticated doctrine. This religion merges with ancient animisms for most people, with traditional cosmology for specialists, and also with very respectable, modern, nontheistic science for a very few scholars. Like its major scripture, the *Dao de jing,* which has been translated hundreds of times into modern languages (e.g., modern Chinese), the social organization of Daoism also opens itself to many interpretations.

Since Confucianism is not considered a faith by the government, Daoists can claim their belief is China's only indigenous religion. Shanghai by mid-1987 had two active Daoist monasteries. The main activities at the larger, the White Cloud Temple, were to reprint thirty-six volumes of Daoist scriptures (such as those that Red Guards had destroyed there), to record Daoist rituals and music, and to train new priests. The secretary-general of the Shanghai Daoist Association, Chen Liansheng, was old by the late 1980s, but most Daoist novices were in their twenties. According to "a 23–year-old student from a traditional Daoist family in Jiangsu . . . the Daoists of the 1980s are different from what they used to be, because they have talents and intellect." Some express an interest in applying Daoist methods to modern topics such as the conservation of energy or the conservation of ecological resources. As with all other faiths, it is clear that the revival of formal Daoism in East China has been financed and staffed by young members of families traditionally enthusiastic about this creed. It is especially clear of Daoism (but also true of all four major imported creeds)[66] that the religion comes in two forms, one popular and one intellectual—and that the revival of Daoist piety after the Cultural Revolution is in tension with the state.

Prereform Communist treatment of Buddhism, as of the Daoism and Confucianism in which most Buddhists participated, was schizoid. On one hand, the abbots of monasteries were often classed as "landlords" because their foundations often collected rents. The Cultural Revolution saw extensive closure of temples and smashing of old pagoda-stupas. As with other religions, Buddhism was legitimated in the late 1970s because it had been so egregiously attacked earlier.

On the other hand, Buddhism as a part of the culture of peasants, who were the popular backbone of the early revolution, could never be suppressed by the CCP. Many ideas and organizational techniques of the Chinese Communist movement itself—from small-group criticism sessions to the particular emphasis on self-cultivation and boddhisatvalike socialist heroes—probably owe more to Buddhist precedents than to later imports from the West. These elements—and the cult of Chairman Mao, who inherited his god-king role lineally from Buddhist Turkic rulers under their sacred umbrellas since the Sui and earlier—were obvious in the millenarian Cultural Revolution. Though that movement aimed to attack all religions, the Cultural Revolution faithful drew so much from Buddhism that the Red Guards did not realize the extent of their piety. These symbols were natural to them. Because of the past assault and new prosperity, reforms saw a massive revival of Buddhism.

As late as 1980, the apparently weak underground organization of Buddhists made the resurgence somewhat slower than in other sects. In that year, for example, it was reported that the Jade Buddha Temple in Shanghai was open just one day each month, whereas St. Ignatius Cathedral already celebrated mass every day. Islamic and Christian scriptures were reapproved for publication before 1980, whereas Buddhist scriptures were delayed.[67] But the much larger size of the potential congregation with family memories of Buddhism in China, along with the government's interest in Japan and Thailand and its inclination by the early 1980s to ignore any kind of piety that was politically innocuous, soon led to a sharp and spontaneous rise in Buddhist observances. Abbots and lamas could claim this religion is nontheist and more Chinese than the later imports.

Christian Organization and Funding

The relation of the Chinese state to more recently imported religions, especially to Catholicism (because of the Pope's claims to authority over bishops collectively), is a good measure of the state's changing tolerance of diversity. Although Christians are a minority in Shanghai, they are disproportionately important in the economy, and they present the question of state tolerance in a clear way. They will be accorded some space here, despite their minority status, because they are a litmus test of reform diversity. The conclusion, of course, will be typical reform ambiguity.

Protestant Christians in Shanghai were slightly less subject to official doubts than Roman Catholics, because their foreign connections now claimed no authority over them. The original idea for the Three-Self Movement in the 1950s was that it should encourage Chinese believers to rely on themselves: self-governing, self-financing, and self-nurturing in all practical ways. During that decade and into the Cultural Revolution, most Three-Self Protestants clearly wanted to keep their loyalty to China—but nonetheless suffered for their beliefs. This experience delegitimated the government's previous stress on patriotism as, in effect, an essential aspect of religion. Even that kind of belief was attacked; so the economic "opening" to the West was soon followed by religious openings and some quasi-dissident autonomy in fundamentalist groups outside the authorized Protestant church. There was no longer any convincing way for officialdom to insist on very strict control of contacts with foreigners. More important, the state's credibility as a defender of loyal religionists had been shattered earlier.

The Three-Self Movement incorporates Anglican-Episcopal, Baptist, Methodist, and Presbyterian groups, as well as some of the more fundamentalist sects. It is in many ways postdenominational.[68] Coastal East China, especially hilly regions and small cities in Zhejiang, is an extremely important area for this Protestant movement. Shanghai was the site of the National Standing Committee meeting of the Three-Self Movement in early 1980, whose "Open Letter" was not in the cocksure administrative language still heard from the state. It was a widely circulated and graceful song to divinity:

> We cannot but thank God for being able to address you once again openly in this manner. . . . Although many of our clergy and leaders of Three-Self organizations had to suffer all sorts of persecution . . . it heartens us to learn that large numbers of Christians all over China have persisted in their faith, that their service, prayer, and waiting before God has not ceased.[69]

After the Cultural Revolution, some of the waiting was over. The previous official organization had clearly abandoned loyal Chinese Protestants earlier, so the pastors at this assembly declared their hope of founding a "new national structure" alongside the Three-Self organization, whose relationship to the latter "is going to be like that between the two hands of a body. There will be no question of one giving and the other accepting any leadership."[70] The Cultural Revolution had destroyed the credibility of some cadres in the previous organization. The state's Religious Affairs Bureau was no longer in a position to supervise people who had remained more faithful than it had during the Cultural Revolution. So a new institution was needed to serve the Protestants—or even to serve the government as an effective liaison to them. East China Protestants, in particular, protested with sufficient cogency to obtain some autonomy. To the extent they needed organization above the congregational level, it was provided by a set of institutions centered at the Nanjing Seminary.

Zongjiao (Religion), published since 1979 in Nanjing and widely available as a semiannual since 1986, is the main academic journal on this subject in post-Mao China. Its style is analytic, the language is often Marxist, and the articles concern all major religions. The calligraphy on the journal's cover is that of Zhao Puchu, head of the Chinese Buddhist Association. But the most active writers are Christians. The editor is Bishop Ding Guangxun, the most prominent Chinese Protestant, whose background is Anglican and who now leads the government-recognized Protestant church in China while in that capacity also trying to keep track of unofficial house churches.

Zongjiao has been an East China project. As the main foreign student of these developments has written, many of its writers live in Shanghai, often working at the Institute for Religious Research of the Shanghai Academy of Social Sciences. "Also significant is the fact that the writings of prominent religious theorists such as Ren Jiyu, Jiang Ping, Huang Zhu, and Lei Zhenchang—all from Beijing—do *not* appear in the journal."[71] The East China approach to religions was different and less statist or conservative than the line sponsored by institutions closer to the center of the state.

Protestant tradition includes millenarian phases, which are difficult to monitor and which cause representatives of the state great concern. But this tradition also includes phases of skepticism about the potential of all human organizations, including churches. The Communist government, during reforms at least, has been able to accommodate such modesty. Chinese Protestants have been authorized to recruit foreign help, on the condition that their own agencies remained in charge. The authorized groups were Chinese, with the allegiance to their state that implies, even though they also were faithful to an imported religion.[72] Some of the "house churches," however, simply ignored the state and kept their organizations smaller.

Social services remained an important part of the religious commitment for the authorized Protestant church, as also for Buddhists and Catholics. All these religions became active as public organizations. Medical work was particularly important. Amity Foundation, a Protestant group with a major office in Hong Kong, organized donations from Chinese Christians of large sums for handicapped children and for the Jiangsu Artificial Limb Factory. Classes in English and German were taught under Christian auspices by expert foreign teachers. Various Buddhist and Christian groups organized disaster relief on several occasions when it was needed. Communist leaders, whatever their aversion to religion may have been, did not turn down such help.

Social services were also a specialty of organizations informally connected to religious sects. The Shanghai YWCA resumed its activities at the end of 1987 (after a suspension since 1966). The YWCA's all-China general secretary, Cora Deng, had held her post since 1950; she was the third incumbent since the association's founding in Shanghai during 1923, and Shanghai had the largest branch in the nation. Deng in 1987 held a press conference to announce the YWCA's resumption of "social services based on Christian principles."[73] The association ran nurseries, kindergartens, medical classes, and (together with the YMCA) youth choruses, painting classes, calligraphy groups, English classes, academic lectures, and cultural performances, along with concerts of Christian music. This revived YWCA was financed by public donations and small government grants.

Shanghai by October 1985 had twenty-two officially recognized Protestant churches with active congregations, but many prayer groups also met in individuals' apartments. Zhejiang province reported eight hundred thousand Christians and "more than 1000 church buildings—many newly built in the countryside—with more going up all the time."[74] Jiangsu had at least four major Protestant churches in Nanjing, with others in Suzhou, Wuxi, Zhenjiang, Yangzhou, and elsewhere.

"Home churches" that sprang up in many parts of China, notably in the Shanghai delta, were embarrassing not only to the government but also to religious organizations trying to do legalized work. Yet Anglican bishop Ding Guangxun, president of the Three-Self Movement and a member of the Chinese People's Political Consultative Conference, pointed out in 1982 that the Party was not providing enough alternative places for worship. "Few churches have been reopened, and most Christians hold their prayer meetings in private homes. . . . I, as one of the leaders of the Three Self Patriotic Association, should not like to say these home meetings are illegal."[75] Bishop Ding also protested that home churches met the Three-Self criteria: "Those meeting in homes are self-governing, self-supporting, and self-nurturing, too. Thus they are very much a part of our Three-Self movement, just as much as the big crowds worshipping in churches now being reopened. Many go to both. They will be furious to be named 'the underground church.' "[76]

The Party's policy on religious services by 1982 had become murky. A decree stated that "all places for religious services are under the administrative control of the Bureau of Religious Affairs, but the religious organizations and the professional clergy themselves are responsible for their management." It was also ordained that "with the approval of the responsible government departments, Buddhist and Daoist churches can sell a certain quantity of religious reading matter, religious articles, and religious works of art"; but auditing the "certain quantity" was easier to plan than to accomplish.

Many religious activities took place in the homes of believers, from Buddhist chanting to Muslim fasting to Christian services and last rites. It was hard to make a clear distinction between activities permissible in homes and those against the law there. A good symbol for the obscurity of this policy is the provision that "as for Protestants meeting to hold religious services in their homes, this in principle should not be allowed. Yet this prohibition should not be too rigidly enforced."[77] Reform ambiguity thus made Protestant "house meetings" technically illegal but very frequent. As a certain Pastor Chen put it in the mid-1980s, "Small family meetings are all right. The government won't interfere. But when several families with many people get together, as many as 100 or even 200 persons, that is illegal. The government used to try to force them to quit, but now they only cajole. Thus far, they don't dare to use force. They are very polite, just urging them to attend [the official] church instead."[78]

A 1994 estimate counted twenty-seven Three-Self churches in Shanghai—and two thousand homes where Protestants gathered for worship with official permission. Gatherings without state approval reportedly occurred in at least another thousand homes, many of which held multiple services per week and organized Sunday schools.[79]

Roman Catholic Organization and Funding

China's state-guided Catholic Church, not recognizing the authority of the foreign Pope, first ordained bishops in the enthusiasm of the Great Leap Forward of 1958. This denomination has had a particularly hard row to hoe, because the Chinese government has been unable to abide by Rome's administrative claims that many Chinese Catholic leaders have honored—all the more vehemently because of extensive violence against them in the 1950s, 1960s, and later.

The first Catholic Patriotic Association (CPA) suffragan bishops were not chosen until late 1984, when the bishop of Shanghai, 92–year-old Aloysius Zhang Jiasu, nominated Stephen Li Side and Louis Jin Luxian for these posts.[80] Jin Luxian became CPA bishop of Shanghai in 1988.[81] Shanghai has other Catholic leaders whose stock has been very much higher in Rome.[82] But describing this conflict as if it were entirely between two centralized authorities can neglect the role of much larger numbers of people in it.

Papal claims to believers' allegiance are based on criteria of apostolic succession that the CPA also arguably met, depending on variant interpretations of canon law. The ordination of new bishops remains one of the reforms' many ironies—because state involvement apparently reduces the legitimacy of CPA appointments in the eyes of many local Catholics, no matter what views on legal procedure either Rome or Beijing may hold. From the state's viewpoint, this is important because it makes the CPA less effective in its officially conceived role.

In the 1950s, Catholics in Shanghai suffered traumatic tensions between their Chinese and Catholic identities. The state attacked them as traitors, in effect. Shanghai Catholics felt strains between their patriotism and their religion that were more severe than Western church propaganda, which stressed only their Catholicism, has suggested. Cultural Revolution violence largely solved this dilemma, very much in Rome's favor, for the faithful who remained. At least some Shanghai Catholics in the 1970s and 1980s honored priests inversely to the extent they were seen as agents of the Communist state. But because even the state needed new prelates who would be widely perceived as legitimate to run the CPA by then, it served government interests that some of the new CPA bishops were thought by local Catholics to be secretly loyal to Rome, so long as they did not flaunt this loyalty too much in public. The equivocal tenor of all of China's reforms were never in fuller voice.

In this clouded context, May 1980 saw the first national Synod of the Patriotic Catholic Church for many years, at which plans were made to reopen Sheshan Seminary in Qingpu county and to publish a journal.[83] Shanghai was at once the most important center and most difficult place for Chinese Catholics. As Beatrice Leung reports, "Shanghai. . . has been relatively tough on religion. . . . It is less under pressure to tolerate religious practices than more 'backward' places."[84] Many CPA Catholic churches, such as those in Beijing and Guangzhou, reopened in 1979, but the resumption of many official Catholic activities except masses was delayed in Shanghai until 1982.

One reason for special problems at Shanghai was that the city's bishop recognized by Rome, Ignatius Gong Pinmei, had been consistently faithful to the Vatican. Bishop Gong was released after decades of imprisonment in 1979, simultaneously with the pardon of rightists.[85] He never recanted any of the actions for which he had been jailed. Bishop Gong became a cardinal on June 30, 1979, when the Pope said, in Latin at a consistory to confer red hats, that he had determined one other cardinal secretly "in the breast."[86] The Chinese state could not object, only because the identity of the new cardinal was not public.

Lack of a formal agreement on how to choose bishops has remained the core practical issue between Rome and Beijing. Bishops in the early church had been "chosen in the view of all" not just by the bishop of Rome, as a 254 A.D. Council of Carthage decision put it and as CPA documents point out—making a nice point that is historically true but hardly germane to the post–Cultural Revolution ideas of many Chinese Catholics. Treaties between the Vatican and many nations, ranging from Spain to Australia, have created procedures by which governments propose episcopal candidates for the Pope's selection. A new bishop under many of these treaties must specifically vow fealty to the state.[87] From the

Vatican's viewpoint, the problem with the CPA has been the lack of an accord to normalize this process. From the PRC's viewpoint, the problem is that the Vatican then claims other legal authority over its appointees. Also, the Pope has not been Chinese.

China is not the first country to hive off a separate national church from Rome's authority, and the Vatican probably has enough experience by now to be wary of such situations.[88] So the Pope has concurrently recognized many Chinese prelates in the CPA, when their allegiance to him has been arguably probable in religious matters. For other purposes, these prelates can be understood as Chinese. But a 1989 document suggests that the PRC government's policy was exactly identical to Rome's—from the opposite viewpoint, of course, but equally ambiguous. As the CPA put it:

> We designate the underground as consisting of those bishops secretly conse-crated by the Vatican, those priests these bishops have in turn ordained, as well as key leaders they control. . . . As for underground bishops and priests, we treat each case individually, winning them over or isolating them if not. . . . Those whose political attitude is not so clear, or who lack sufficient theologi-cal knowledge, can take part in training courses or be sent to seminaries.[89]

Rome and Beijing have taken the very same political approach, which leaves room for an ambiguity that is typical of reforms in general. Each side has tried to test the loyalty of candidates for ordination, granting titles whenever an individual's case seemed plausible. The difference between the reform period and the era before the Cultural Revolution, however, was the government's greater handicap because of Communist violence against Catholics.

The CPA bishop of Shanghai, Jin Luxian, reports himself a Jesuit. Before 1949, he was inducted into that order, which once had the main responsibility for Catholic administration in Shanghai. When a Hong Kong correspondent asked him in 1985 about his relationship with the Vatican, he replied, "We want communion—as brothers, not as subjects. . . . *Ubi caritas et amor, Deus ibi est.*"[90] Rome does not regard Bishop Jin in the same communion, but because of the ambiguity of so many similar situations in China, neither he nor the Vatican normally publicizes this circumstance.[91]

The loyalties of Shanghai's bishop are documentably complex. When Jin Luxian was ordained as the CPA's auxiliary bishop of Shanghai, he asked to use the Latin rite (a seeming protest, no doubt popular with the cadres, against the 1963 Vatican Council) rather than a Chinese text. But the Chinese service in-cludes a section in which the candidate swears independence from Rome; the Latin version omits this. Bishop Jin has sometimes criticized the Pope, but he has also visited Hong Kong and Germany, with many opportunities to express him-self in private to coreligionists there.[92] A person in this position may not need to find full closure on the matters that divide Beijing and Rome, because he may be most useful to each side by vacillating between them. Here is a hinge leader on an international scale though not a quiet one.

Various kinds of PRC Catholics respond to this two-pole situation variously, and both of the central authorities defining the two sides of the debate have had to accommodate the positions of believers whose interests on local grounds are more complex than simply declaring for one side or the other. Sister Beatrice Leung describes this exquisite murkiness:

> Because of the [reform] relaxation there are some who until very recently were in the underground, but who now publicly participate in liturgical services offered in the open churches sponsored by the CPA. There are some bishops and priests who have never been members of the CPA, but who are now allowed to exercise their pastoral ministry publicly. A few years back, this was not possible. . . . It is reported that a number of bishops of the CPA deep down in their hearts are deeply pained by the separation from Rome. The authorities have told them that whatever their personal feelings may be, they must openly refuse allegiance to the Holy See; yet there are some bishops in the CPA who never speak against Rome and are known in China for their pro-Rome attitude.[93]

Jaime Cardinal Sin of Manila, an ethnic Chinese with major political skills who has engaged in tentative diplomacy between Rome and Beijing, stressed the practical value of accommodation to the PRC state: "We must not ignore that a number of nonofficial, semi-underground Catholic communities, now flourishing in many regions, are able to operate more freely because of the silent approval and benevolent regard of the so-called 'official' [CPA] Catholic authorities."[94] He advised against the "grave injustice if we give the impression that all the bishops ordained in China" without Rome's mandate were excommunicated. Cardinal Sin's pragmatism had, according to informal reports by the 1990s, created serious tensions with a rather less flexible Pope.

None of this wrangling prevents social services, which run smoothly because they are local. The CPA, like the Three-Self Movement and Buddhist monasteries, raises considerable money in the reform economy for social work and for its own activities. Although since the Cultural Revolution the government has claimed to help finance religions, all sects' money during reforms has come overwhelmingly from private donations. Most of it is donated by newly wealthy social groups—whose independence of attitude may have helped them prosper during the mixed reforms. Interviews with Buddhist and Daoist monks strongly indicate unofficial sources of funding as major. When Shanghai Catholic bishop Jin was asked in 1985 how his diocese would pay for its new seminary at Sheshan, he replied, "Our new seminary will cost about 2,000,000 *yuan* [then about U.S. $705,000], just for the buildings. Furnishings will be extra. . . . The Shanghai Diocese will pay half; the other dioceses contribute some. The money of Shanghai Diocese comes from two sources: we collect rent from church-owned property, the rest comes from the gifts and offerings of Christians. There are more than 100,000 [Catholic] Christians in Shanghai, and they are very generous."[95] By the end of 1988, the Shanghai diocese was China's largest, with a clinic, a mortuary, a foreign-languages school, a Catholic Intellectuals' Association, the Guangqi Press, and thirty reopened churches.[96]

Underground Churches

These activities do not necessarily command all the faithful, because of the CPA's connection with a government that many Catholics still see as problematic. In a late 1988 talk, Bishop Jin Luxian admitted with some asperity that

> Catholics who belong to the "underground" church are more than those who follow us. . . . [At an unspecified time] there were 120,000 Catholics in Shanghai. The 20,000 Catholics in Chongming [Island] were also incorporated in the Shanghai Diocese. So there should be 140,000 Catholics in Shanghai, but this number did not go to church at Christmas. Before, there were 10,000 in Xujiahui [Xuhui urban district], but how many go to church now? Some Catholics go to pray at the three holy shrines of Sheshan, but they do not want to go into the [CPA-run] church. Some people are working actively at Jinshan, Suzhou, etc., and make Catholics who begin to go to church not go anymore. One or two people [in the underground] can do so much. What about ourselves, who are so many? Are we, who form the "visible Church" not so energetic as those of the "underground"?[97]

The CPA was frustrated by its inability to control underground Catholics, but so on occasion was Rome. When the Vatican authorized simplified procedures for the consecration of bishops in some parts of China, the underground church responded with enthusiasm and ordained far more than Rome had expected.[98] After the Tiananmen massacre of June 4, in November 1989 at the village of Zhangerce in Sanyuan district north of Xi'an, twenty-one underground Catholic bishops from all over the country convened their own secret conference. After the meeting ended, all participants were arrested. But what is most interesting about this meeting is that the Vatican did not instigate it—on the contrary, it was untimely for Rome's diplomacy then—but also could not disavow it. Before the session, the Vatican had reportedly sent specific instructions not to convene it. Underground Chinese Catholics did this on their own. The Pope's position was like that of the Chinese government. Both were intensely interested, but neither could control what was happening.[99] These Chinese Catholics had their own agenda, and they followed it despite contrary wills in both Beijing and Rome.

The Three-Self Movement ran into parallel problems because of the power of local networks. Because fundamentalist Protestant millenarianism was common on the China coast before 1949, and because old evangelist families in the 1980s produced proselytizing members, there has been quick expansion of these sects during reforms. Certain groups, such as the Children of God and the "Yellers" (*Huhan pai*), are periodically banned by officials, though no government action has effectively made them disappear.[100] Officials have more trouble monitoring millenarians than they do keeping track of more established Protestants. Fundamentalists in house churches by the mid-1990s were multiplying at a rate roughly double that of the officially recognized Christian churches. Leaders of the latter sometimes feared that the illegality of house churches would turn CCP conservatives against Protestantism in general, and they avowed even more concern that new do-it-yourself preachers had little training. A glory of the Protestant tradition is arguably that dogma has not been its most prominent problem. In China after the revolution, however, orthodoxy became an issue.[101]

Religious Recruitment: Villages and Lineages

Enrollment in any Shanghai denomination was not mainly a result of organizational efforts. Although Buddhism and Protestantism made some converts from new families and in new areas, piety grew fastest during reforms in rural localities and in urban lineages. The main determinant of interest in any religious sect was whether the new believer had a personal connection, local or inherited, with others who believed.

Buddhist belief was important in the histories of many of the city's families. So the Shanghai People's Press sold its 1988 paperback *Chinese Buddhism and Traditional China,* and the East China Normal University could sell its *Concise History of Modern Buddhism in Shanghai.*[102] Factual information about religions was available in Shanghai in the 1980s and later. Religious creeds were still frowned upon by many who believed in scientific socialism, but fervent beliefs could be discussed under the guises of international studies, minority studies, or social science. Anyone interested, for example, could buy a concise paperback entitled *Ten Great Religions of the World,* which offered descriptions of the origins and doctrines of Buddhism, Christianity, Islam, Judaism, Shintô, old Brahmanism, modern Hinduism, Jainism, Zoroastrianism, Manichaeanism, and the ancient religions of Babylon and Egypt.[103] Information of this sort did not, by itself, create many converts; but such matters had not always been legitimate discourse in the PRC. A 1987 analysis from the Department of Research on Religions at the Shanghai Academy of Social Sciences concludes with this crucial point: "A very important reason that some of these young people came to believe in Buddhism is the influence of family members who are Buddhists."[104]

Daoist clergy claimed that many neophytes came to them independently, but if so, recruitment in this sect was different from all others, and the claim probably reflects a Daoist ideal. The few professionalized Daoists were aware of their own loose organization's relation to Buddhism, and a majority of lay people interested in either of these doctrines received exposure to the other also. A Daoist nun was proud that "this temple is not private property, it is not state-owned, nor is it a collective like a factory. . . . We depend on ourselves to find resources. . . . One can become a Buddhist by simply shaving one's head, but one must have both talent and virtue to become a Daoist monk or nun."[105]

The situation in the Christian sects has been better documented, and it also shows a correlation of family with piety. China as a whole had at least four times as many Protestants, and about half again as many Catholics, in the early 1980s as in 1949. Exact numbers are hard to know because of underground churches, but the pattern is clear. Protestant numbers continued to soar during the 1990s, largely because of proselytizing, irrespective of what the law prescribed.

Protestant believers had been numerous even before 1949 in a working-class neighborhood of Shanghai that was surveyed during reforms and included many women textile workers. Only one-twentieth of the people surveyed confessed religious faith to the pollsters, however. Of these, three-quarters were women. Half had come to their Christian beliefs before the Cultural Revolution, but half were post-1966 converts.[106] The reasons why Protestant churches gained members in a workers' residential district, according to this survey, included fears of disease and death among the elderly, past wounds from Communist political movements, family problems such as those that arise when husbands beat wives who are thought to be infertile (sending them into religious communities that console them), and the need of the elderly for companionship in their last years. The evangelistic "propaganda" of ardent believers was also publicly credited as a factor in attracting converts.[107]

This section of Shanghai had five or six Protestant churches and evangelical centers before the 1950s, and many followers among the proletarian population. The system of "joint services" (*lianhe libai*) was mandated in that decade, and in the Great Leap Forward the number of church-goers declined. A reform-period book admitted that "the left" had interfered with religious activities excessively after 1957.[108] Some residential areas of Shanghai that contain many professional and shopkeeping families also have relatively high concentrations of Catholics or Protestants, and observation of the people who attended churches there during the late 1980s showed a wide distribution of believers by both gender and age.[109]

Many pre-1949 Catholic lineages retained or revived their faith.[110] Many boat people in Shanghai are reportedly Catholics (although most Catholics are not boat people). That church also includes some farmers, as well as higher-income families long resident in the Xuhui district of urban Shanghai, named for the Xu family that long ago provided support and converts. The congregation is thus a diverse one, ranging from professionals to peasants, both currently and before 1949. New priests are mainly recruited from old Catholic families.[111]

Qingpu Visions as an Example of Local Piety

Fishing people in Qingpu county, a Shanghai suburb, have for generations been Catholic. The traditional livelihood of these people, who numbered about ten thousand in 1949, was to catch fish, shrimps, and crabs as their boats meandered along the many miles of canals in Qingpu. Their group was poorer than local non-Catholic peasants, and they did not intermarry with the people who farmed adjacent fields. Conflicts arose between fishers and peasants, especially when vegetables or livestock were found stolen. Partly because these Catholic families were aquatic nomads, a major CCP interest in them during the 1950s was apparently to prevent any transport of goods unauthorized by state plans. Some of the fisher families were moved onshore, and the Party made efforts to ensure that boat children would attend a newly nationalized rendering of the previously parochial Wangdao Primary School. The main church, at Zhujiajiao, was brought under the government's authorized Catholic organization. These families, despite being obviously proletarian and poor, were subject to increasing pressure from officials.

Fewer than a hundred attended Christmas mass in 1964 at the church in Zhujiajiao. As a Marxist writer says, "This did not mean that the Catholic fishermen had given up their faith; it showed that they were again doubtful about the religious policy, and that there was again a barrier between them and the Party and government."[112] During this time most of them also curtailed their annual May pilgrimage to Sheshan in Qingpu, where they would dock their boats and form a procession up the hill to pay respects at the basilica dedicated to St. Mary.

The Cultural Revolution was predictably a disaster for Qingpu Catholics—and then for radicals who misjudged them. As a Party writer says,

> When churches are destroyed and Christians are assaulted, the faith of devout believers is strengthened. Their firm faith gave the Catholic fishing people of Qingpu courage when they were wrongly attacked. Now they are all saying that they followed the example of "Jesus, who was nailed to the cross and died," and that their sufferings were their "gift to God," believing that God would compensate them. When they were not allowed to read the Bible, many resorted to silent reading in their hearts. Others, together with their whole families, and even groups of boat families, read aloud while sailing out of earshot of the shore. They used every means to hide the few "rosary beads" and "holy medals" which escaped detection. Thus it turned out that while the "ultra-leftists" attempted to stifle religion by administrative methods, the final results were exactly the opposite of what they had intended. This proves that banning religion by administrative decree will not work.[113]

Adherents did not give up their faith during the Cultural Revolution. In Qingpu, for example, the local Catholic church was closed and smashed during 1966, but the parish continued to celebrate masses in secret. In a local production brigade of boat people, a Catholic had his boat searched repeatedly and he was jailed for two years for his belief. There were many other examples of similar persecutions in the Shanghai area, among hard-to-monitor boat people and suburban peasants as well as among Christian and Buddhist professionals and workers in the city.[114] But in general, the more religionists were repressed, the more ardently they believed.

During the early 1970s, the family faith of Qingpu Catholics flourished in part *because* it remained secret. Bringing it into the open could have weakened it, by lessening the integration that comes from external opposition more than because of external threats the radicals could muster.[115] A visiting Roman cleric attended a mass in China during 1971, although he found no full-time priests. He reported that the clergy could "perform their pastoral ministry—that is, the administration of the sacraments, funerals, etc."[116] It is clear from many anecdotal reports that Catholic priests and nuns visiting China as tourists early in the reform period fostered illegal churches and connections with Rome. But little seemed to be happening, because the maintenance of faiths was overwhelmingly in local groups then.

The next major event in Qingpu Catholicism was also not organized by any hierarchy. A Shanghai Academy of Social Sciences report covers it well:

> In March, 1980, before any of the Shanghai district churches had reopened, Qingpu Catholics heard the rumor that the "Blessed Mother" would show her power and presence by appearing on Sheshan hill surrounded by a halo. For over ten years they had not gone to Sheshan to worship the "Blessed Mother," so when they heard the rumor passed around by some people, they quit working and went to Sheshan to see the "apparition and radiance of the Blessed Mother." When they arrived at Sheshan, the people who had spread the rumor, hiding themselves among the crowd, shouted reactionary slogans, breaking, smashing, and abusing the government.[117]

This was not at all what Communist reformers had in mind. Officials discovered very quickly that locals had more notions than anybody in the state apparatus had dreamed. It was clear that the government needed a new policy toward these people. One cadre claimed, "The decisive factor in regaining Qingpu fishing people's confidence in the religious policy was the return to them of the Zhujiajiao Catholic church, its repair and reopening, and the restoration of normal religious activities."[118] The reconsecration of the church, by a priest of the new Qingpu Catholic Patriotic Association who apparently was trusted among his flock and thus autonomous, occurred just a few months later on Christmas, 1980. No state plan had guided this timing.

The sharply rising incomes of families without land was just as important in Qingpu Catholic life. So was the continuing mobile lifestyle, which officials still found hard to monitor. Some rural industries were now established, however, by fishing people onshore. The Baihe Aquatic Brigade, composed of Catholics, went into nonaquatic activities such as founding a leather shoe factory and a box factory. "In recent years, the income of every household has increased. Many have bank deposits of more than 1,000 *yuan*. Bicycles and sewing machines are popular, and many have TV sets and tape players."[119] The Zhaoxian Aquatic

Brigade bought twenty TV sets wholesale, apparently for distribution to its members. This becomes religion, too.

During the three years from 1984 to 1987, fifteen hundred Catholics were baptized in Qingpu. The Zhujiajiao church choir was largely young. New religionists came mainly from the old families, not from others, but those lineages stubbornly stuck to their traditions—which were Catholic in this case, but might have been otherwise. The CCP surely did not like this development, but cadres did not have the capacities they once had imagined in their state. By the 1990s, most masses in CPA churches were surely said by priests whose ordinations were validated in the Vatican, although neither Rome nor Beijing advertised this example of postrevolutionary fuzziness.

Religion and Revolution

Political violence has affected each of the religions named above many times in the past, both in China and outside. The Cultural Revolution and the market have, however, made the practice of revived religions crucially new. Anthropologist Helen Siu shows that the religious revival is not entirely traditional, if only because believers think the atheist state has angered the gods:

> Observers of the resurgence of popular rituals in the Chinese villages today may conclude that tradition is being restored. On closer examination, the worship of gods, ghosts, and ancestors will be seen to have taken on a very different meaning for contemporary practitioners. Peasants in traditional China believed in a supernatural power structure that interacted with the material world to which they belonged. If a deity failed, the believer did not cease to believe in the authority the deity symbolized. Appeals to deities expressed faith in a culturally defined system of power. The "revival" of popular rituals today does not entail the same perceptions of power on the part of the faithful. If a deity fails, believers tend to blame the atheist state power. . . . Contemporary popular rituals express a lack of faith in both the supernatural and material power structures, and a pervasive sense of alienation among the practitioners. These cultural fragments paradoxically show the extent to which popular beliefs have been affected by the Marxist state.[120]

China is not the first country in which a revolution has altered religion. Beliefs have often been strengthened because of repression. They have often been partly secularized by the tumultuous effects of a revolution on people's lives. But especially in China, whenever members of the current generation know their ancestors were believers, religion does not die out.

Religious change was fast during the first part of this century, even in poor rural areas.[121] But the symbols of religion do not always mean the same things in different contexts or for different people, so general reform change was bound to affect beliefs. James Watson has shown how Tian Hou, the main goddess for southern Chinese fisherfolk and many others, whose worship in the past was often officially encouraged, has long meant different things to different believers.[122] Religion involves ongoing choices, and the reform context in China partly conditions which of these people use.

Religious organizations claim functions that are so intimate to people, they can never fully succeed in their apparent purposes—even when they use methods more subtle than the state's coercion. At times of quick change, such as China's reforms, individuals and families search their communal pasts for ways to solve their current problems. These personal religious searches can be very syncretic. A woman who had been left alone, because her husband had been posted out of Shanghai, reported in 1994 that a "fox fairy put awful dreams in my head." She wanted to sleep with men she met on the street, and even with her father-in-law, who rebuffed her advances. Then someone told her she could rid herself of the fox possession if she ate excrement, but "I still had these dreams." Other friends advised her to pray at Daoist and Buddhist temples, which she did; she also joined a Protestant home-prayer group.[123] Community support for this troubled woman eventually helped her, after a tour of most of the available creeds. Her quest for personal peace was an odd one, and official pressures tended to keep it apolitical. But with breakneck economic change following close on the heels of the Cultural Revolution, many in Shanghai sought contentment widely.

Notes

1. Mao was addressing Hunan peasants and is quoted in Donald MacInnis, *Religious Policy and Practice in Communist China* (New York: Macmillan, 1972), p. 10.

2. Donald E. MacInnis, comp., *Religion in China Today: Policy and Practice* (Maryknoll, NY: Orbis, 1989), p. 80. This book is an anthology.

3. For example, see *Newsweek,* Pacific edition, September 20, 1993, p. 29.

4. Stevan Harrell sees Taiwan religion, which he describes above, as "a variant of a similar set of beliefs and practices found outside the educated elite in all parts of China." See "Men, Women, and Ghosts in Taiwanese Folk Religion," in *Gender and Religion: On the Complexity of Symbols,* Caroline Bynum, Stevan Harrell, and Paula Richman, eds. (Boston: Beacon Press, 1986), p. 98.

5. This is the argument of Michael R. Saso, *Taoism and the Rite of Cosmic Renewal* (Pullman: Washington State University Press, 1989), p. 8.

6. See Robert P. Weller, *Unities and Diversities in Chinese Religion* (Seattle: University of Washington Press, 1987), concerning Taiwan, or David Faure, "The Lineage as a Cultural Invention: The Case of the Pearl River Delta," *Modern China* 15:1 (1989), pp. 4–36. The author extends thanks to Prof. Weller of Boston University and to Prof. Joseph Bosco at the Chinese University of Hong Kong for help with this anthropology.

7. Joseph Bosco, "*Yi Guan Dao:* 'Heterodoxy' and Popular Religion in Taiwan," unpublished manuscript shown to the author.

8. Another author, from a Suzhou elite but now Western background, has written: "Like most Chinese, I am basically a fatalist—too sophisticated for religion and too superstitious to deny the gods." This credo, a concise summary valid for many Chinese intellectuals, is in Bette Bao Lord, *Spring Moon* (New York: Harper and Row, 1981), pp. 256–57. For the PRC patriotic religion, see Donald MacInnis, *Religion,* pp. 96–97.

9. See Joseph Levenson, "The Draining of the Monarchical Mystique: The Hunghsien Emperor as a Comic Type," in *Confucian China and its Modern Fate: The Problem of Monarchical Decay,* vol. 2 (Berkeley: University of California Press, 1964), pp. 3–21.

10. There is also a new-class aspect to this Party favoritism for high Confucianism. Buddhism and Daoism are strongest among mere peasants (even though they also have many urban adherents, especially in poor classes). Even Catholicism has survived best in rural areas, notably in the Shanghai suburbs and among the previously despised "boat people," many of whom are Catholics. See Richard Madsen in *Unofficial China: Popular Culture and Thought in the People's Republic,* Perry Link, Richard Madsen, and Paul Pickowicz, eds. (Boulder: Westview, 1989), for a suggestion that icons of Mary at the basilica of Our Lady of Sheshan, in Songjiang county, Shanghai, strongly resemble images of the goddess Mazu. She is the traditional patroness of Chinese fisherfolk and the main focus of their piety in Daoist-Buddhist temples all along the China coast.

11. The festival is *qingming.* David Kelly, "Representative Culture: Official and Unofficial Values in Tension," in *China Review,* Kuan Hsin-chi and Maurice Brosseau, eds. (Hong Kong: Chinese University Press, 1991), p. 16.19.

12. *Daode zhi gainian ji qi xueshuo paibie* (Concepts of Morality and Currents in Moral Theory), orig. March 17, 1917, in *Chen Duxiu wenzhang xuanbian* (Selected Works of Chen Duxiu) (Beijing: Sanlian Shudian, 1984), vol. 1, p. 194.

13. Ibid. contains Chen's articles *"Yougui lun zhiyi"* (On Theism) of May 1918 and *"Kexue yu shenshen"* (Science and Dieties) of the following month.

14. This is based on an interview with one of the surveyors, Lu Feiyun, a doctoral student in the Sociology Department of the Chinese University of Hong Kong, whose family came originally from Suzhou. The surveyors were Chinese, careful, and speaking Wu dialect; it is doubtful that peasants in this situation would have much overstated weakness of their beliefs because they thought the Party expected them to do so. Lu and others see a considerable difference between the quality of religious belief in Sunan and, for example, in Fujian, where more research has been done partly because the religious revival there offers more to report.

15. A fine study of the varying qualities of religious experience, though without the references to algebra, is Clifford Geertz, *Islam Observed* (New Haven: Yale University Press, 1968).

16. Document 19 of CCP Central Committee, 1982, confidential but translated in Beatrice Leung, *Sino-Vatican Relations: Problems in Conflicting Authority, 1976–1986* (Cambridge: Cambridge University Press, 1992), pp. 353–55.

17. This is called by specialists the problem of theodicy, though a fancy word hardly solves it. The wording in the text is meant to suggest Buddhism, in which many Chinese believe; but most readers of this book will be mainly aware of the issue as raised by Job. Some Chinese in the Cultural Revolution developed an impatience with dogma similar to Job's. At the end of the Book of Job, that struggler rejects finite explanations about his agony that come from his three friends; and with a combination of pain and faith he simply says, "Now I see." This tale is artfully topped off with an absurd happy ending: Job regains his health and all else, to drive home the main point that life is never primarily covered by human rationality.

18. In Chinese, Protestantism (*jidu jiao*) and Catholicism (*tianzhu jiao*) have had different names since long before 1949. This convention has somewhat obscured their commonalties throughout the Chinese world.

19. Donald MacInnis, *Religion,* p. 4; for the next quotation, p. 34.

20. *Zhongguo shehui zhuyi shiqi de zongjiao wenti* (Problems of Religion in China's Socialist Period), Luo Zhufeng, ed. (Shanghai: Shanghai Shehui Kexue Yuan Chuban She, 1987), pp. 131–32, gives 1985 statistics showing that Shanghai's "advanced and

model people at various levels" included 650 Protestants and 350 Catholics (out of a total including non-Christians that was not published). This important book has been translated by Donald E. MacInnis and Zheng Xi'an as *Religion Under Socialism in China,* Luo Zhufeng, ed. (Armonk, NY: M.E. Sharpe, 1991).

21. *Sunday Examiner,* Hong Kong, March 10, 1989; James T. Myers, *Enemies Without Guns: The Catholic Church in the People's Republic of China* (New York: Paragon, 1991).

22. Donald MacInnis, *Religion,* pp. 269–70.

23. Ibid., p. 389.

24. *Jingji xinwen bao* (Economic News), January 26, 1989, cites a survey of marriages in Qingdao indicating that parents there paid on average 52 percent of the costs, while 36 percent came from the couple's savings, with another 8 percent from friends and relatives, and 5 percent from loans.

25. This quoted section is in Donald MacInnis, *Religion,* pp. 387–88, from the English translation in *Chinese Sociology and Anthropology* 16 (1983). Some of the bracketed material is added.

26. The quotation is from ibid., p. 389. Stevan Harrell interprets "evil fox-spirits that manifest themselves as beautiful women and seduce men to their ruin" as representing "the seductive female who threatens the patrilineal order." See "Men, Women, and Ghosts in Taiwanese Folk Religion," pp. 113 and 116.

27. Luo Zhufeng, *Zhongguo shehui zhuyi,* p. 104.

28. These "living Buddha" cadres were sarcastically called "*huo Pusa.*" Ibid., pp. 103–4.

29. Ibid.

30. Donald MacInnis, *Religion,* p. 393.

31. *QNB,* June 2, 1989.

32. This case was tried in a Shandong court. *Post,* August 14, 1989.

33. See Chan Ka Yan, "The Role of Migration in China's Regional Development: A Local Study of Southern China" (M.Phil. thesis, Department of Geography, University of Hong Kong, 1990), p. 40. This is a map showing that from some rural Guangdong counties (Chaoyang, Jieyang, and Puning, in the Teochiu area; Meixian, the Hakka capital; and Taishan, on the coast west of Macau) emigration has been major. But from adjacent areas (Jiexi or Luhe; Meizhou; Yangjiang), there was practically no emigration. Even within counties, there is sharp local variation; for example, most Taishan emigrants come from the northern, inland part of the county, not from the coastal part. Also, emigration was not just to one place; for example, ibid., p. 74, reports that although 38 percent of all Taishan emigrants by 1950 were in the United States, 42 percent were in Southeast Asia.

34. Another example that should clearly fall in this category, even though less recent evidence has been found, is Jiangsu's Qidong county, which provides both entrepreneurs and cotton for mills in Nantong and Shanghai. The argument here refers partly to standard maps of soil types, of which an interesting example is in Hsieh Chiao-min, *Atlas of China* (New York: McGraw-Hill, 1973), p. 131.

35. Please consult other references to Chuansha county in the index to the present book for specific data on these trends.

36. Helen F. Siu, "Recycling Rituals: Politics and Popular Culture in Contemporary Rural China," in *Unofficial China,* Perry Link, Richard Madsen and Paul Pickowicz, eds., pp. 121–37.

37. These ideas were inspired by a late 1993 bus journey from Shantou (Swatow) to Xiamen (Amoy). Especially in southern Fujian, different valleys showed the contrasts suggested above. Some had light-colored soil, and many new multistory concrete buildings,

especially hotels and gas stations. Other valleys had dark-colored soil, lush green crops, and more concentrated groupings of old, gray, onestory houses, with less new wealth. Further research in such areas would be required either to confirm the correlation suggested or to amend its elements. Although soil type is suggested in the text above as a major generating factor of such differences, another basic cause (effective concurrently with soil type) might well be proximity to cities with modern transport facilities. If these two variables were treated together, there might be no need to restrict the analysis to the China coast. The ideas set forth here are not necessarily in conflict with theories of migrants' motives that stress hopes of economic betterment, as in Michael P. Todaro, "A Model of Labor Migration and Urban Unemployment in Less Developed Countries," *American Economic Review* 59 (1969), pp. 138–48.

38. Xiao Zhitian, "A Tentative Enquiry into the Problem of the Compatibility Between Religion and Socialist Society in China," in Zhang Zhongli et al., *SASS Papers* (Shanghai: Shanghai Academy of Social Sciences, 1986), p. 373.

39. See Lynn White, *Policies of Chaos: The Organizational Causes of Violence in China's Cultural Revolution* (Princeton: Princeton University Press, 1989), p. 283, and *WHB*, March 3, 1967.

40. Robert G. Orr, *Religion in China* (New York: Friendship Press, 1980), p. 124.

41. On April 5 and 6, 1990, separatists in Akto county in the Kizilsu Khirgiz Autonomous Prefecture near Kashgar proclaimed an Islamic republic and announced a *jihad* against the heathen in Xinjiang, who are Han Chinese. The immediate issues concerned Party restrictions on Islamic studies and on building schools, but the longer-term problem was Han immigration to Turkic areas. See *FEER*, May 3, 1990.

42. *New York Times*, July 3, 1990. Cheng Wen-Ting, a student at Princeton, deserves thanks for offering this reference.

43. Sheryl WuDunn, "Muslim Students March in Beijing," *New York Times*, May 13, 1989.

44. Lynn Pan, *The New Revolution in China*, rev. ed. (London: Penguin, 1987), p. 284.

45. Julian Pas, ed., *The Turning of the Tide* (Hong Kong: Oxford University Press, 1989).

46. Apparently the whole "watching crowd" was cowed by the witch—and that says as much as the fact of her craziness. Robert G. Orr, *Religion in China*, p. 108.

47. *Dong, xi, nan, bei, zhong, dou zai lian qigong.* David Kelly, "Representative Culture," pp. 16.16–18. This essay and Marlowe Hood have supplied most of the material concerning *qigong* here.

48. *Shuihu zhuan*, translated as *All Men Are Brothers.*

49. Nancy N. Chen, "Urban Spaces and Experiences of Qigong," in *Urban Spaces in Contemporary China*, Deborah S. Davis et al., eds. (New York: Cambridge University Press, 1995), p. 347.

50. *Shanghai gongan nianjian, 1988* (Shanghai Public Security Yearbook, 1988) (*neibu*), *Shanghai gongan nianjian* Editorial Department, ed. (Shanghai: Shanghai Shehui Kexue Chuban She, 1988), n.p., opposite the list of editors. Another of the eight pictures is a cheerful photo of Shanghai's current police chief, Li Xiaohang, standing with four of his predecessors—including Yang Fan, the oldest, who was purged in the mid-1950s with Rao Shushi but by the late 1980s was living in Shanghai in honored retirement.

51. *Zhongguo de qigong shi* (The History of China's *Qigong*) (Beijing: Renmin Wenxue Chuban She, 1990), mentioned in David Kelly, "Representative Culture."

52. For example, Zhang Mingwu et al., *Chinese Qigong Therapy* (Jinan: Shandong Science and Technology Press, 1985).

53. Marlowe Hood, "Mystics, Ghosts, and Faith Healers," *Los Angeles Times Magazine*, April 19, 1992, p. 22. Much of what follows is based on Hood's article; another report suggests credit for some of this information may be due also to Prof. Nancy Chen,

writing a book about *qigong*. Neither of these is responsible for any interpretations here, however.

54. Ibid., p. 35. The Rev. Jerry Falwell, talking about the East Coast intellectual establishment, the media, and the mainstream parties, could have been no more concise than *qigong* master Zhang.

55. Ibid., p. 23.

56. Ann S. Anagnost, "The Beginning and End of an Emperor: A Counterrepresentation of the State," *Modern China* 11:2 (April 1985), pp. 147–76.

57. Marlowe Hood, "Mystics, Ghosts," p. 33.

58. Vittorio Lanternari, *Religions of the Oppressed: Studies of Modern Messianic Cults* (New York: Knopf, 1963); Eric J. Hobsbawm, *Primitive Rebels* (Manchester: University of Manchester Press, 1959). See also Chalmers Johnson's comparative work relating millenarian threats to other threats against the state, in *Revolutionary Change* (Boston: Little Brown, 1966).

59. See Philip Kuhn, *Soulstealers: The Chinese Sorcery Scare of 1768* (Cambridge: Harvard University Press, 1990); Robert Darnton, *The Great Cat Massacre and Other Episodes in French Cultural History* (New York: Basic Books, 1984).

60. Donald MacInnis, *Religion,* p. 82.

61. *WHB,* August 15 1989.

62. *DGB,* Hong Kong, June 2, 1988.

63. An obvious project for Chinese anthropologists, on which some may already have embarked, is to relate Victor Turner's theories about pilgrimages to the revival of ritual travel in reform China. For Taiwan, Robert Weller of Boston University has studied pilgrims' tourism.

64. In addition, over three hundred houses were ransacked by Red Guards, many of whom were local. Qingcun was chosen by a Japanese researcher mainly to study rural economic progress, and he records information about the Cultural Revolution there mainly because he could obtain it easily in the course of other work. Qingcun seems as credibly "typical" of the Shanghai delta as any place can be. See Ishida Hiroshi, *Chūgoku nōson keizai no kiso kōzō: Shanhai kinkō nōson no kōgyōka to kindaika no ayumi* (Rural China in Transition: Experiences of Rural Shanghai toward Industrialization and Modernization) (Kyōtō: Kōyō Shobō, 1991), p. 91.

65. Donald MacInnis, *Religion,* pp. 88–90.

66. The four major imported creeds are officially listed as Buddhism, Islam, Catholicism, and Protestantism. For the quotation, see Donald MacInnis, *Religion,* pp. 210–12.

67. Robert G. Orr, *Religion in China,* p. 112.

68 This ecumenism appealed strongly to some foreigners. One American, Philip L. Wickeri, was ordained together along with five Jiangsu candidates at a 1991 ceremony in Nanjing. See his book *Seeking the Common Ground* (New York: Orbis, 1988; a 1984 Ph.D. dissertation at Princeton Theological Seminary). On the ordination, see *China Talk* (United Methodist Church China Program newsletter), Hong Kong, July 1991.

69. Robert G. Orr, *Religion in China,* p. 60.

70. Ibid., p. 62.

71. Philip L. Wickeri, in *Christianity in China: Foundations for Dialogue,* Beatrice Leung, ed. (Hong Kong: Centre of Asian Studies, University of Hong Kong, 1994),   pp. 135–39; quotation p. 137, emphasis in original.

72. The most sensitive treatment of this subject, which draws implications for Christian belief in general, is Philip L. Wickeri, *Seeking the Common Ground.*

73. *FBIS,* December 7, 1987, p. 37, reporting radio of December 3.

74. Britt Towery, *The Churches of China* (Hong Kong: Amazing Grace Books, 1986), pp. 159, 178, 197.

75. Beatrice Leung, *Sino-Vatican Relations,* p. 129.

76. Robert G. Orr, *Religion in China,* p. 64.

77. All quotations are from the CCP's confidential Document 19 of 1982, in Beatrice Leung, *Sino-Vatican Relations,* p. 358.

78. Donald MacInnis, *Religion,* p. 322.

79. *Eastern Express,* March 8, 1994.

80. A suffragan bishop is auxiliary to the main bishop of a diocese, usually a younger helper. *FBIS,* December 12, 1984, p. 5, reporting radio of December 11.

81. Jin Luxian is from Chuansha county (cf. note 35, above), born there in 1916 to a Catholic family. He went to religious schools and then into the church, which sponsored his theological studies in Europe during the late 1940s and early 1950s, after which he returned to China. By 1982, he was head of Sheshan Monastery in Shanghai's suburb of Songjiang—an institution that reported jointly to the Catholic organizations in all East China provinces. The Administrative Committee of the Shanghai Catholic Church in early 1988 elected him as full bishop of Shanghai. See *FBIS,* March 1, 1988, p. 30.

82. One of these may be Jesuit father Vincent Zhu Hongsheng, who was released from more than two decades of prison in 1979 but was re-arrested in 1981 because of contacts with visiting foreign priests, diplomats, and journalists.

83. Robert G. Orr, *Religion in China,* p. 80.

84. Beatrice Leung, *Sino-Vatican Relations,* p. 113.

85. Robert G. Orr, *Religion in China,* p. 80.

86. *In pectore* describes a secret ordination of this kind; the primate of Lithuania had the same secret status in Soviet times. Eleven years later, in exile at Rome, Cardinal Gong could in public be given his red hat—an event that the Shanghai Public Security Bureau celebrated in a different way, by arresting several Catholics. Beatrice Leung, *Sino-Vatican Relations,* p. 209, and Robert G. Orr, *Religion in China,* p. 80.

87. Also, in most Orthodox-rite churches that recognize the primacy of the Pope, bishops are selected by the Eastern Patriarch. This tradition is interpreted in Rome to represent a standing papal consent for a traditional practice that Beijing does not enjoy; the need for such consent is challenged by the CPA (and, incidentally, by Protestants everywhere). For more on the facts, see Beatrice Leung, *Sino-Vatican Relations,* pp. 370–71.

88. The English case, under Henry VIII, is best known. The Swedish case was even clearer: A whole national hierarchy, from the cardinal primate in Uppsala on down, asserted autonomy from Rome, with only scattered resistance. The status of the Swedish bishops in apostolic succession could not easily be questioned. The Chinese case is more complex, because xenophobic/patriotic PRC repression of Catholics has encouraged trust in the administrative aspects of a Roman church. Also a Protestant tradition already exists in China, and Catholics there have not deemed it their own.

89. Beatrice Leung, *Sino-Vatican Relations,* Appendix V.

90. "Where care and love are, there is God." The Pope accepts this old motto but reads it differently. Donald MacInnis, *Religion,* pp. 291–92.

91. This 1994 information came from a reliable Hong Kong source, who pointed out that the Vatican already had a bishop of Shanghai: Cardinal Gong, then in very old age half a century after his episcopal ordination, and in exile.

92. Beatrice Leung, *Sino-Vatican Relations,* p. 179.

93. Ibid., p. 178.

94. Ibid., p. 332.

95. Donald MacInnis, *Religion,* p. 294.

96. *Sunday Examiner,* Hong Kong, March 10, 1989; James Myers, *Enemies Without Guns: The Catholic Church in the People's Republic of China* (New York: Paragon, 1991).

97. *Sunday Examiner* and James Myers, *Enemies Without Guns.*

98. Hong Kong interview, 1994.

99. Beatrice Leung, *Sino-Vatican Relations,* pp. 131–32.

100. Donald MacInnis, *Religion,* p. 323.

101. Based on conversations with a young person who had worked with PRC Protestants.

102. Fang Litian *Zhongguo Fojiao yu chuantong wenhua* (Chinese Buddhism and Traditional Culture) (Shanghai: Renmin Chuban She, 1988); and Yu Youwei, *Shanghai jindai Fojiao jianshi* (Concise History of Modern Buddhism in Shanghai) (Shanghai: Huadong Shifan Daxue Chuban She, 1988).

103. See *Shijie shida zongjiao* (Ten Great Religions of the World), Huang Xinchuan, ed. (Beijing: Dongfang Chuban She, 1988).

104. Donald MacInnis, *Religion,* p. 156.

105. This nun was not from Shanghai. Donald MacInnis, *Religion,* p. 209.

106. A knowledgeable Shanghai informant guessed the surveyed street area was in Yangpu district (although the published source did not divulge any location). The area included 5,179 people, including 800 who were retired. It can be calculated that the portion of Party members in this workers' area was only 2 percent (98 persons)—notably lower than the city's average ratio. See Luo Zhufeng, *Zhongguo shehui zhuyi,* p. 214.

107. Ibid., pp. 215–17.

108. Ibid., p. 220.

109. Author's observations in Shanghai during late 1988.

110. Richard Madsen, in *Unofficial China,* Link, Madsen, and Pickowicz, eds.

111. Among four Sheshan seminarians interviewed in 1988, all came from multi-generation Catholic families (two were fifth-generation; another said, "My whole family is Catholic"; the fourth averred that his family had been so "for over three hundred years"). Most knew of previous priests in their lineages, as well as unmarried aunts who had acted informally as catechist nuns during the 1960s. The interviewees' home villages were widely separated—but in each, practically all the households were Catholic. See Donald MacInnis, *Religion,* pp. 304–9.

112. Ibid., p. 277, from a 1987 report of the Shanghai Academy of Social Sciences. Shanghai Catholics already by late 1964 were a target of radicals under Yao Wenyuan and Zhang Chunqiao, running Shanghai's cultural bureaus in a Cultural Revolution–like manner before their movement fully began. This book questions the standard periodization of the end of the Cultural Revolution, setting it instead at the end of the 1960s. But there is also much evidence to show that the militarization and radicalization of politics before the 1966–69 violence was established in some spheres at Shanghai by mid-1964. A similar argument by Barry Naughton, albeit on a very different topic (investment), periodized the Cultural Revolution from 1964 to the early 1970s on the basis of time series; cf. his "Industrial Policy during the Cultural Revolution," in *New Perspectives on the Cultural Revolution,* W. Joseph et al., eds. (Cambridge: Harvard University Press, 1991), pp. 153–81.

113. Donald MacInnis, *Religion,* p. 278.

114. Luo Zhufeng, *Zhongguo shehui zhuyi,* pp. 238–39, refers particularly to "fishermen believers" (*yumin jiaotu*).

115. See Lewis Coser, *The Functions of Social Conflict* (New York: Free Press, 1956).

116. The priest, Father Leon Triviere, was apparently visiting China incognito. The present author, on trips to China in 1979, 1991, and other years, has been aware of other travelers using the same transportation who were Roman Catholic clergy sent for such missions. See Robert G. Orr, *Religion in China,* p. 79.

117. Donald MacInnis, *Religion,* p. 278.

118. Ibid., p. 280.

119. Ibid., p. 281.

120. Helen F. Siu, *Agents and Victims in South China: Accomplices in Rural Revolution* (New Haven: Yale University Press, 1989), p. 300.

121. Prasenjit Duara, *Culture, Power, and the State: Rural North China, 1900–1942* (Stanford: Stanford University Press, 1988), chap. 5.

122. James L. Watson, "Standardizing the Gods: The Promotion of T'ien Hou along the South China Coast, 960–1960," in *Popular Culture in Late Imperial China,* David Johnson, Andrew Nathan, and Evelyn Rawski, eds. (Berkeley: University of California Press, 1985). Clifford Geertz shows, for example, how many aspects of Islam differ between Morocco and Indonesia, even though formal Islamic doctrines are unified. See Geertz, *Islam Observed.*

123. *Eastern Express,* March 8, 1994.

Chapter 2.3

Reform of Media

*With public sentiment, nothing can fail; without it, nothing can
succeed. Consequently he who moulds public sentiment goes
deeper than he who enacts statutes or pronounces decisions.*

—Abraham Lincoln[1]

East China's broadcast and print media during the past twenty years have diversified in many ways: in their organization to address different audiences, in their sources of revenue, in the ways they recruit staff, and in the criteria for choosing their content. These environmental and intentional changes of media loosely correlate with other changes in Chinese society, and they can be analyzed in the same categories. Over the long and bumpy run, government policies affect the media only in a complex context of changing technologies and mixed, increasingly international messages. It is difficult for a regime to govern everything that people think.

This does not mean that the Chinese Communist Party (CCP), whose top leadership often views media as tools aiding Leninist discipline throughout the nation, has tamely forsworn hopes of controlling the press. On the contrary, in 1989 the editors of many major CCP newspapers were relieved of their duties.[2] Even CCP top politicos suggested that the number of Communists who opposed this round of purges was "not a small handful." It was a very important group of the Party's own membership.[3]

The year 1989 was surely the most difficult, during reforms, for the state's efforts to justify itself normatively with individuals. This was not, in the larger scope of PRC history, the first time for such difficulties. Greater coercion had been used to remove dissidents from the media in 1957, 1966, and other years.

The PRC government's policy toward intellectuals has taken the form of a sine wave: sporadic periods of state repression have been followed by eras of qualified state apology and partial "reversals of verdicts" when the Party found it needed critical intellectuals, not just statist ones.[4] Freedom of the press, which actually comes in many degrees and kinds, varied not just with the attitudes of top leaders toward dissent, but also with the contexts in which ideas could be communicated to individuals.

During reforms, most observers downplayed what one of them was premature to call "signs of a shift from an 'obligation-directed' to a 'rights-directed' society."[5] "Reform" in the journalistic field, as in others, is nonetheless basically stable because it did not originate as a policy gift from Beijing. It is grounded in the broadening opportunities and interests of large, widely scattered Chinese constituencies.[6] Reform is less a policy than a social reaction (unintended by Beijing) to previous policies and to profitable divisions of labor.

This analysis will run the risk of being lowbrow, paying special attention to truly mass media—not just to prestigious media for sophisticated audiences. The popular press (especially evening newspapers and television) creates effects that are slow and indirect, but pervasive.[7] Industrialization in rich rural places, combined with new technologies for broadcasting, is quickly changing the ways Chinese gather information and the reasons they have to gather it. This chapter will look at four aspects of media in sequence: the ways they have been organized, the ways they have acquired resources during the reform era, the ways they have recruited reporters, and the ways they decide what to publish. Media in recent decades have given residents of the Shanghai delta more sources of information than they earlier had. Editors who comply with Beijing policies have also needed to make their articles and programs credible in this new and more diverse context.

Establishing the Many Media

The Foundings and Functions of Newspapers

About 1950, only 800 million copies of Chinese newspapers were issued per year. Distribution grew quickly thereafter, even though the variety of content in the press sharply decreased. By 1956–57, the annual number of newspaper copies was about 2.5 billion. It doubled by 1960 as part of the Great Leap Forward—and then receded to its mid-1950s level in 1962. In 1970 (after the closure of many short-lived Cultural Revolution radical broadsheets), distribution was still below its peak a decade earlier. But in 1971—before the reforms began in official high policies, yet after China's most intense social violence—total circulation soared to 8.4 billion copies. This was an increase of by more than four-fifths in the single year 1971. By 1972, the number was up to 10 billion. (The next large annual jump, in 1976, was only 13 percent.)[8]

Chinese newspapers can be categorized into several types according to their readerships. First are the "organ papers" (*jiguan bao*), in Shanghai notably the *Liberation Daily,* which is the bulletin of the province-level CCP committee. A second type is called (by the former chief editor of the *Wenhui News,* the oldest Shanghai example) "influential papers."[9] These cover all major social and political topics, and they are usually produced for intellectuals. In the late 1980s, Chinese journalists widely debated whether these unofficial papers could be "run by the people" (*minban*), as certain kinds of schools and enterprises were. Their partial independence from the Party was sometimes recognized to be a source of their influence. The *World Economic Herald,* a Shanghai weekly that conservative politicians opposed from the mid-1980s—and effectively shut down in June 1989—claimed to be "unofficial" (*feiguan*), part of a loyal opposition to the bureaucracy. The *Herald* had become China's premier reformist paper, and it was by no means just local in Shanghai. It did not have a mass circulation, but it was read by intellectuals throughout the country and internationally.[10] A third major category of newspapers includes evening papers and other media that carry community and entertainment news. The most obvious example of this species in Shanghai is the *Xinmin Evening News,* which is truly a mass medium and the largest-circulation newspaper in all China.[11]

By the mid-1980s, among all the newspapers published in China, about one-fifth (including many dailies) were formal Party organs.[12] Another fifth were issued by large enterprises. Another tenth were technical. Some were for specific readerships, such as managers, workers, peasants, or other particular categories. The papers with the largest circulations were "comprehensive," for the common reader. When these were dailies, they were usually published in the evening.

An editor of the *Liberation Daily* frankly said all of the city's journals were "Party papers," and the *Liberation Daily* might most accurately be called the Shanghai Party's "institutional journal."[13] All papers have an explicit mandate to support current state policies through propaganda (*xuanchuan*). All periodicals, including Party organs, at the same time are supposed to maintain their credibility and interest among readers by reporting news fully enough to seem "transparent" (*touming*). The *Liberation Daily* carries more articles on Party affairs than do other journals that have different readerships—but this is ideally just a difference in the list of subscribers, not a difference of orthodoxy.[14] When policy disputes have been obvious in public, the *Liberation Daily* has occasionally taken clear implicit or explicit stands on them, as other papers have also sometimes been able to do.[15] *All* important editors receive their appointments only after Party approval. In periods such as mid-1989, when one policy group within the CCP could exclude those with other views, orthodoxy becomes more important than "transparency." The press is effective only when credible, however; so transparency and loyalty are in tension.

On a nationwide basis, the first half of the 1980s was a banner period for the creation of new journals. More than half the newspapers existing in China at the beginning of 1986 were less than five years old. Somewhere in the country, a new paper started in each two-day period during this half decade.[16] Such rapid creation of new newspapers did not mean that they all equaled the more established press in circulation or importance. Nor were they free of many direct and indirect official controls on content. But at least there were more of them.

Printing

Each newspaper by the mid-1980s could decide in what factory to publish its copies. The number of Shanghai publications coming out of the main *Liberation Daily* plant decreased from more than sixty in the mid-1980s to about forty in late 1988, partly because of the paper shortage. The *Wenhui News* set up its own plant—which also put out forty other kinds of weeklies and other publications. The *Liberation Daily* printing facility in the mid-1980s was used by two of the three major dailies (that paper and *Xinmin Evening News*), by all locally reproduced national newspapers, and by about fifty periodicals. That plant put out not only the Party paper, but also (in fewer copies) six national dailies: air editions of the *People's Daily, China Youth News, Economic Daily, Guangming Daily, Sports Daily, Workers' Daily,* as well as *Labor News* and the limited-circulation summary of foreign reports entitled *Reference Information*. The only non-Beijing newspaper from any outside province that printed issues in Shanghai during the late 1980s was Guangzhou's *Yangcheng Evening News*.[17]

The *Liberation Daily* plant could print nearly four million folios each day in mid-1988.[18] The centralization of printing for so many journals in this factory reflects the concentration of authority over the Chinese press. If ever the Party wishes to stop a journal quickly, it can do so at the factory. But this has not prevented some diversification of journals.

The Role of the Evening Press in Popular Culture

Evening papers deserve special attention because of their importance to the urban populace at large. Scholars (like officials) have paid scant attention to them. They seem to lack political importance, because their influence emerges over long periods, over broad groups, and indirectly through cultural channels, not just overtly political ones. Over one-quarter of the urban readers did not, in the early 1980s, get to their newspapers until evening.[19] Evening papers are especially important among youth.[20] These rival the national papers in the total number of copies issued, even though they receive less state support.[21] As one of the *Xinmin Evening News* editors wrote in 1982, "If you meet [the interests of] cadres, you can lose the masses; but if you meet [the interests of] the broad masses, the cadres will want to read that too."[22]

All of Shanghai's major newspapers in the late 1980s wrote their own histories. This was evidence of local pride, and for Shanghai the crucial example was the *Xinmin Evening News*. A brief review of that history tells the main story of Shanghai journalism generally. As soon as the city came under army management in 1949, newspaper work became "united front work," and Party spokesmen such as Xia Yan placed particular emphasis on evening papers. "These are read after tea and food; the contents must be relaxed."[23] Already by 1951, as the Party sought to build a mass constituency of support among workers, popular papers such as the *Xinmin News (Evening Edition)* were asked to write in Shanghai dialect and to emphasize the need for pride among workers. In 1953–54, after this paper formally became a joint enterprise and fell completely under the Municipal Party Committee Propaganda Department, it was instructed to study the experience of the *Moscow Evening News* in producing a "paper for the streets."[24] But during the Hundred Flowers Movement of 1957, the head of the *Xinmin Evening News,* Zhao Chaogou, put forward slogans for journalistic reform that were somewhat similar to those of the later reforms.[25] Oddly, he was not declared a rightist.

By 1964, most of this newspaper's educated cadres had been sent out to "live, eat, and work" with peasants during the Four Cleans Campaign. From June 1966, in the Cultural Revolution, the *Xinmin Evening News* was attacked as a "revisionist black paper." In August, it changed its name to the *Shanghai Evening News,* and by December the paper was run by radicals. New people took over the editing, many previous reporters were sent to a May 7 cadre school (not far away on the coast, in Shanghai's Fengxian county). Some journalists were murdered or committed suicide.[26] Other Chinese newspaper staffs had similar experiences, and of course these memories affected their later political views strongly.

The *Xinmin Evening News* was reconstituted only in 1982, sixteen years after it had ceased under that title.[27] Old staff were recalled to publish the paper again. They soon ran into major difficulties. More than one-quarter of the staff had died during the years of stoppage. The previous offices of the paper had been occupied by a succession of "rebels," and then by squatters. Efforts to move these residents elsewhere proved unsuccessful. Also, as the paper's historian delicately put it, "the accumulated internal problems [within the staff] were extraordinarily many."[28] The newspaper found temporary quarters. Finally the Municipal Party Propaganda Department arranged a "provisional" abode until a new two-tower skyscraper was built, the News Building (Xinwen daxia, to be shared with the two morning dailies, *Liberation Daily* and *Wenhui News*). Despite these problems with facilities, the *Xinmin Evening News* increased its circulation from over 800,000 copies per day in 1982 to nearly 1,500,000 by 1986.[29] This increase was faster than that of any other major paper in China. It was even faster than the increase for Guangzhou's flourishing evening paper, and much faster than for Beijing's. When the chief editor of the *Xinmin Evening News* was asked why the *Liberation Daily* and *Beijing Evening News* did not have as much success in circulation as his own newspaper, he waxed poetic. Judiciously answering only about the Beijing paper, he replied that his paper was "like a swallow," light and fast. By August 1988, the *Xinmin Evening News* had the largest circulation in China, with 1.8 million subscriptions.[30]

Nine-tenths of the *Xinmin Evening News* copies (and of evening papers in other cities) are ordered by households. In contrast, about nine-tenths of subscriptions to morning papers are paid by work units, not individuals. About 1,000,000 copies of the *Xinmin Evening News* in the mid-1980s were distributed in Shanghai. Less than 500,000 copies went to the suburbs, and many of these were delivered to nonpeasant households. About 200,000 copies are sold on the streets. (The non-subscription sales of other Shanghai dailies are much less.) The paper was by 1986 also published in identical "air editions" at "separate printing points" in Beijing and Chengdu.[31] Approximately 800,000 copies were soon distributed in other provinces, at least half of these going to people who originally lived in Shanghai. This was "horizontal liaison" of a wholly voluntary kind.

Like the *Wenhui News,* the *Liberation Daily,* as the organ of the Shanghai Party Committee, is a somewhat more official, staid, prestigious publication. In August 1988, it had a total circulation of 900,000, seven-eighths subscribed by offices and only one-eighth by individuals. During the reform period, official papers have not much been subscribed by individuals. Partly to counteract this trend, their young staffs have periodically launched interesting series of articles about local problems—as the *Liberation Daily* has occasionally done about environmental problems near the Baoshan Steel Mill, for example, or very gingerly about the high rate of central budget extraction from Shanghai. In other words, some popularization of the press's cultural styles by evening papers (and especially by television) created a context that sometimes strengthened the positions of reforming journalists even in official papers.

The Foundings and Functions of Broadcasters

Radio and television have been more important than morning newspapers in reaching mass audiences. Their political effects are indirect and broad, like those of the evening papers. In 1949, the metropolis had forty radio stations, which were mostly private. These broadcasters underwent "socialist transformation" earlier than most firms. By September 1953, they had all been nationalized, becoming part of a unified Shanghai People's Station. In later years, the independence of programmers varied inversely with the severity of China's political campaigns. Broadcasting, like many other sectors, for more than two decades followed the principle "First the center, then the localities."[32] In the 1953–57 Five-Year Plan, the expenditures of central stations during this Soviet-influenced period were 84 percent of the whole broadcasting budget; only 16 percent went to local stations.[33] The Central Television Station was simply the Beijing station.[34] But a Shanghai Television Station was established in 1958. In the beginning it broadcast only a single frequency, twice a day, for just two or three hours at a time—and only four hundred sets in this huge city could receive the signal. The 1958–62 Five-Year Plan explicitly called for more centralization of stations.[35] Many local radio and some television stations were abolished during a national campaign to "unify broadcasting" in 1962. Then in the Cultural Revolution, from 1968 to May 1972, the Shanghai station transmitted only two programs. As a later local report said, these were simplistic and didactic.[36]

By 1971, more local programming became possible in almost all of China's province-level units, including Shanghai.[37] Because of greatly accelerated sales of TV sets in the 1970s, and because of a diversification of programs that attracted more viewers, television's impact on the population rose. In 1971, the TV station moved to larger new premises on Nanjing Road, and it began broadcasting from a new 210–meter tower that became the tallest landmark in the flat city. (This spire was displaced in that symbolic landmark role during later reforms by the Pudong tower.) By 1973, it was airing programs on eight frequencies, and it began experimental programs in color—largely red, of course, but not exclusively so.[38] The local network was reorganized, and it started transmitting on four channels coordinated by two separately organized stations in 1973.[39]

The Shanghai First Television Station even through midreforms was relatively staid, spending some hours of prime time on speeches concerning political and social topics. The Second Television Station has aired more sports and music. Both rebroadcast Western, Japanese, and Russian programs dubbed in Chinese. Both generate their own variety shows, crooners, and stars. The Shanghai Television Station, through each of these channels that were separated for most programming, reached over 90 percent of the households in the city and its suburbs by the mid-1980s.[40]

The Shanghai station made five major surveys of its audience from 1953 to 1983.[41] According to one report, however, sampling was almost continuous, and quasi-Nielsen ratings were published secretly and frequently. Each day in the late 1980s and 1990s, an independent organization of the city government, the Shanghai Urban and Rural Survey Team, polled 1,000 households (apparently chosen at random, and at various times on different days) to complete a questionnaire that included queries about media use and many other subjects of interest to the authorities. This survey, whose results were limited-circulation, reportedly showed that by 1988 the typical Shanghai TV set was turned on for two hours each day, mostly in the evening. Housewives, retired workers, and nonstudent youths were the most intensive viewers.[42] Statistics from such surveys were reportedly often biased in favor of the organizations running them, which claimed greater effectiveness and coverage for media than they actually had. But they nonetheless showed some trends.

These polls showed that the two Shanghai stations were viewed far more intensively than the two central government channels broadcasting in the city. Programs on Shanghai's central channels came largely from Beijing. Their content was similar to that of the centrally sponsored station in each provincial capital (although Shanghai viewers did not necessarily have the same interests as viewers, for example, in Qinghai). These channels were organizationally distinct from the city-run ones. But they attracted fewer viewers. Insipid state broadcasting is not an exclusively Chinese characteristic. In India too, the central Doordarshan network has long presented programs that "ranged from dull to extremely dull."[43] But by the 1990s, the arrival of dish antennae gave Indians other options, including CNN, MTV, and the BBC. This caused the state network to create parallel news services, in an attempt to garner larger and more diverse audiences. In China, this role has largely been filled by regional networks.

If Shanghai audiences are like those in Beijing, from which more comprehensive surveys have been published, certain media are especially important to certain groups. In an analysis by gender, newspapers were said to be more influential than radio, TV, or other sources for 45 percent of men, but only for 31 percent of women. Radio was said to be most significant for 38 percent of women and one-third of men, largely in rural suburbs. Television was by 1982 already especially important for youth.[44] Shanghai surveys suggest that a household's average time with the radio turned on during the 1980s was half as much as with TV, just one hour, generally in the morning. An average of only ten minutes was spent reading newspapers, mostly in the evening.[45]

When the 1982 media audience was divided by occupation, newspapers were claimed to be the main source of information for 74 percent of cadres, 70 percent of technicians, 51 percent of teachers, and 42 percent of workers. But radio was still the most prominent medium among peasants—reportedly most important for 48 percent of them. The reasons seem to be several: Literacy is not required of radio listeners, reception of radio is often better than that of TV in rural areas, and peasants can listen through headsets while tending their fields.[46] By the mid-1980s, rural industrialization gave many families in the countryside the funds to purchase television sets.

The Shanghai People's Broadcasting Station found in July 1986 that as many as 82 percent of the city's employed people received most of their news from the broadcast media rather than newspapers. The continuing importance of radio and growing importance of television is a notable fact in many countries, including China. Television schedules now seriously compete with evening papers in terms of numbers of readers. In Shanghai, the *Weekly TV Log* (*Meizhou guangbo dianshi*) is reportedly referred to more often than any newspaper.[47]

Reports from elsewhere on the Shanghai delta were like those in the metropolis. A Zhejiang survey in 1983 determined that three-quarters of the population "often watched television."[48] A Jiangsu poll of the same year showed that considerable numbers of peasants watched television, even when they lacked enough money to buy a set. Among a group of individuals who made less than 20 yuan per month but nonetheless told the surveyors they were regular TV watchers, only 7 percent owned sets. The same survey showed that, for respondents who said they were regular viewers and who came from households making over 50 yuan per person each month, 43 percent by 1983 had bought their own monitors—and this number rose to become a majority in the mid-1980s.[49]

To meet the demand implicit in this technological and market change, the number of broadcasting stations in the PRC doubled between 1980 and 1985, from 106 to 213. The number of television stations more than quadrupled, from 38 to 202. In these same years, China's total number of newspaper issues went up 42 percent, and the number of books printed rose 45 percent.[50] Yet not all important media were new. Word of mouth is probably the most credible means of conveying information. One way to suggest the multiplicity of means that Chinese people use for communication is to mention a medium that is nearly distinctive to the PRC.

Wired Broadcasting: A Local Medium That Is Neither Print nor Radio

Nonradio broadcasting networks remained surprisingly important in many areas of China until midreforms, although little scholarly attention has been devoted to them. Shanghai's suburban county governments began investing in wired networks as early as 1956. By the early 1970s (when, as we have seen above, some innovation was also occurring in the television medium) these suburban authorities joined together and established a wired "county radio" station.[51] Wired networks provided local leaders with means to contact each other, even when dispersed in different villages, by hooking their offices together for virtual conferences. This system was based on China's telephone grid, so that branch lines were financed from the budgets of low-level jurisdictions, including townships and collectives. Households had to pay for connecting and maintaining their own loudspeakers.[52]

The wired broadcasting network was not abandoned just because wireless media (especially television) expanded quickly during reforms. Rural leaders remained very fond of their wired broadcast systems. When dealing with sensitive questions such as tax collections or deliveries to state factories, the wired medium allowed cadres to express themselves in local telephone conferences and to keep in contact. This was the early rural equivalent of the later urban fad for networking by cellular phones, which swept the metropolis of Shanghai in the 1990s. It was financed with central encouragement, but local leaders had their own passion and uses for it. In 1983, the Central Committee sent down Document No. 37, which instructed county governments and Party committees to expand the wired network. The excuse was military and centralist; the actual use was far more diverse. The continued importance of this system can be illustrated by the fact that in 1984 China had 86 million loudspeakers, directly or indirectly reaching 43 percent of all rural households in the whole country.[53]

By 1984, there were more than a million horns in Shanghai's suburbs, reaching directly into 74 percent of the rural homes. Wired broadcasting networks also reached 72 percent of the rural households in neighboring Jiangsu province by the middle of the 1980s—and even more in Zhejiang, which had an exceptionally high rate apparently because the provincial cadres put special funds into the wired network. (At the same time, in 1984, television in Jiangsu reached 59 percent of the homes; in Zhejiang, it reached only 46 percent.)[54]

The density of wired speakers was particularly high in Nantong county near Shanghai, or in Zhejiang's Sushan county, for example, where these horns were established in more than 70 percent of the individual rural homes. Their density in Shanghai's immediate suburbs was similar, although the speakers there may have been less often used.[55] The tolerance of urban people for frequent wired broadcasts during the reform period has generally been restricted to schools and factories. Although the loudspeakers of urban residence committees were often noisy in earlier years, these horns were not as often heard within the city during the 1980s.

The wires were originally installed to strengthen communitarian rural leadership and defense, but they might well be further adapted (with new switching equipment) for individual telephone use. Their evolution in the 1980s showed in miniature a sort of localization that also affected more widespread regional networks, as the next subsection shows. The wired broadcast stations run by suburban counties prided themselves on programs that were in easily understandable Wu dialects (unlike most radio and TV programs, which were largely in Mandarin). They carried fresh news from places that their listeners knew well. They were under Party leaders, to be sure—but local ones, in charge of industrializing rural areas.

Regionalism in East China Media

Professor Wang Zhong of the Journalism Department at Shanghai's Fudan University as early as 1956 advocated that some media be published not by single administrative jurisdictions, but jointly by more than one. "Economic regional papers" of this sort, he thought, would spur practical cooperation between cities.[56] Wang was dubbed a rightist for wanting a change in the way the Party then ran newspapers. But what happened in the East China media by the mid-1980s, despite the interests of the central Party, was essentially what he had espoused.

Regionalization was more obvious in television than in newspapers. The *Liberation Daily* is sold almost entirely within the city. Less than one-half of 1 percent of its copies are sold on the streets, and only 5 percent are sold outside Shanghai (mostly in other cities of East China).[57] The *Wenhui News* offers a different picture: Only about one-fifth or one-sixth of its circulation is in Shanghai, and another two-fifths go to other East China cities.[58] The proportion of *Wenhui News* subscribers in nearby cities has increased during the reform period.[59] By late 1988, the *Wenhui News* was distributing 1,310,000 copies each day, nearly 300,000 of them in the metropolis—whereas the total circulation of the *People's Daily* was only 50,000 in Shanghai. The *Wenhui News* was also the main Shanghai paper with a national following.[60]

To reach its subscribers, the *Wenhui News* had to depend on the vagaries of postal delivery to reach its scattered constituency. No more certain recipe for bureaucratic conflict has ever been conceived than between Chinese newspapers (which have some capacity to voice complaint) and the Chinese post office (which is a big bureaucracy with a difficult job).[61] In Tianjin and Guangzhou, most dailies by the 1980s had abandoned the post office and bought fleets of trucks to distribute their own copies. Shanghai's *Liberation Daily* and *Xinmin Evening News* in the late 1980s were about to do the same thing. The *Wenhui News,* with two fifths of its circulation going to East China cities outside Shanghai and an equal portion going even further, had no choice but to stick with the post office—though staff at the paper did not withhold their opinion that postal service to outlying subscribers was "too slow."

Interviewees report that, despite the postal delays, Shanghai newspapers sold widely, not just on the delta but also in major cities of northern Zhejiang and southern Jiangsu. In the major Jiangsu city of Wuxi, for example, Shanghai papers such as the *Xinmin Evening News* were reportedly read by larger numbers of people than any journals from Wuxi or from the provincial capital of Nanjing. When Shanghai editors were asked what Jiangsu Party and province officials thought of this, they said only that before the 1980s Shanghai papers were so similar to those in other provinces, they could not compete. Press regionalization has been less important in the printed media, however, than in television.

The Rise of Regional and International Broadcasting

Shanghai's television audience now extends throughout East China. That city's broadcasting network had more radio frequencies, more television channels, more programs, and more varieties of them than any other place in the country by the mid-1980s.[62] Programs are transmitted from the metropolis to the city-run stations of all large settlements in the region. So the regular audience for the Shanghai city-run TV channels, in particular, is one hundred million people (about one-tenth of China's whole population).

This situation emerged quickly. By 1984, the two city-run TV channels aired thirty hours of broadcasts daily. Just one year later, this rose to thirty-five hours. Shanghai programs were sent by microwave to stations covering Jiangsu and Zhejiang, as well as much of Anhui and Jiangxi.[63] Shanghai's own transmitters covered most of this area for radio, and the most densely populated part of it for television. With the leverage of microwave transmission and amplification through the broadcasting antennae of about thirty East China cities, these programs could be heard and seen widely.

Just as in print journalism there are official and less official newspapers—and the less official ones make stronger links between Shanghai and other East China cities—a similar pattern has emerged in television. The Shanghai TV Station has become one of China's three main centers for the production of programs. The features it generates (like similar ones produced in Guangzhou) have more audience throughout the country, especially in coastal provinces, than the usually more staid presentations from Beijing. Nanjing and Hangzhou, the capitals of the two rich provinces adjacent to Shanghai, both receive central programs from Beijing without cost, as Shanghai's central station also does. These are broadcast regularly, and some of them are of high quality, but reportedly the surveys show they garner less audience than do programs created within the region.

Provincial governments originally invested in the microwave equipment, at central behest, to connect all major cities in East China for distributing the central programs. But according to Shanghai officials, they now regret having done so, because the same equipment sends the livelier output of the Shanghai TV Station to broadcasters in Nanjing, Changzhou, Nantong, Qidong, Wuxi, Yangzhou, and Zhenjiang in Jiangsu, as well as to Hangzhou, Jiaxing, Ningbo, Shaoxing, Wenzhou and other Zhejiang centers, and farther afield. Local stations in these places, administered by the cities, can normally choose to broadcast what they wish. All of them have very close relations with the Shanghai city-run station, which in practice provides most of their programs.

In particular, Shanghai provides news items for many other East China municipal stations. When a lively story about police breaking a criminal case arose in Zhenjiang, Jiangsu, the local authorities telephoned the Shanghai TV Station directly, asking it to send its closest crew for the scoop. (This was despite Zhenjiang's proximity to Nanjing's provincial newscasters; Shanghai is about four times farther away.) When Shanghai TV officials were asked whether incidents of this kind made cadres at the Jiangsu provincial station angry, the sheepish but proud answer was that they certainly did. There was nothing, however, that Jiangsu authorities could readily do at that time to gain more control over broadcasting in their own province. Even in the city of Nanjing, the surveyed audience for Shanghai TV newscasts (broadcast over the city-run station there) was greater than that for the provincial station. So the cadres in Zhenjiang, who wanted their story to get out, knew what they were doing.[64]

In August 1988, this extensive informal cooperation between Shanghai and other places in East China was formalized for the purpose of sharing news stories. Thirty-one TV stations, all run by cities outside the central system, joined to form the Shanghai News Center (*Shanghai Xinwen Zhongxin*) which covered the Shanghai Economic Zone. In effect, Shanghai's local station was competing for audience, with great success, against Beijing's network of provincial stations. Officials of the Shanghai station said they were only providing "what people want." Of course they provided these data with pride and interest, but they had many data to offer.

This relationship in popular culture between Shanghai and other delta cities is like the "horizontal relations" (*hengxiang lianxi*) in trade. It is not directed by any state plan. It parallels old family ties, which link individual Shanghainese with other places in southern Jiangsu and northern Zhejiang, whence the ancestors of most of them came. These bonds, which involve markets, consulting, technical help, and retirement plans, are now reforging relationships that were prominent before 1949—but were suspended in the 1950s by central mandates.

Economic reporting, in particular, was by the mid-1980s not split between East China provinces. The Zhejiang provincial station, for example, produced a program called *Economic News* that summarized highlights from about eight journals (not limited to those published in Zhejiang). The Shanghai station similarly had a *Selections from Publications* program that collected stories from any of 90 newspapers or 120 magazines, to disseminate largely economic information, but also news about politics, culture, and new techniques.[65]

One of the reasons why the central broadcasting stations in Jiangsu and Zhejiang had difficulties attracting audience in the reform period was that they had traditionally taken rural peasants as their main constituency. As ex-peasants became richer, tastes changed faster than the ideals of Party programmers changed. With quick rural industrialization in places such as southern Jiangsu, ex-peasants watched a good deal of Shanghai TV. Local broadcasters in cities and counties also initiated their own newscasts that were popular in townships and villages.[66]

The Shanghai city-run TV station's link with the Guangdong provincial station was particularly strong, and the Shanghai city station exchanged tapes with many other places. Similar, sometimes competing, news services were established by other regions in China at about the same time—notably one centered in Xuzhou, in northern Jiangsu, called the Jiangsu-Shandong-Jiangxi-Anhui Adjacent Districts News Cooperative.[67] The salience of the Beijing national media was reduced during the 1980s, both by the rise of regional networks and by the popularity of programs that were aired in China from videotapes from Taiwan, Hong Kong, Japan, and farther abroad.

Foreign broadcasters such as the Voice of America, Taiwan stations, and the BBC had some impact in China, because of their services in Mandarin. During major political upheavals, notably the student demonstrations of December 1986 and May–June 1989 (when the whole world's reporters were in Beijing to cover Gorbachev's visit), the importance of these media was immense. They became, for a while, the most accessible source of reliable information for important groups of Chinese people. What is less appreciated outside China is that both the central and city-run television stations had during the previous decade accustomed Chinese viewers to seeing stories from foreign sources. Daily coverage of international news by these stations had for many years relied on American, British, French, Japanese, and other foreign sources, which came to China instantly by satellite. When controversial PRC stories broke, in late 1986 or mid-1989, these were by no means the first stories from foreigners that ordinary urban Chinese had experienced. The likes of CBS or NBC had long shown

Israeli or South African tanks in action; so when by mid-1989 the tanks were in Beijing, the audience knew this kind of thing can happen in the world, and that foreigners report it.

The PRC, for its own part, also broadcast outward—notably to Taiwan. Shanghai TV programs, including a weekly concert jointly produced with a station in Fuzhou, were transmitted to the island over a channel called the Voice of the Straits.[68] Shanghai radio at the end of 1987 established a special station, broadcasting in both Shanghainese and Mandarin to Taiwan, called the Voice of the Huangpu River. Its aim was to "spread news about Shanghai among natives of the city living in Taiwan, so as to promote patriotism and help unify China."[69]

Nonbroadcast electronic media proliferated too during these years throughout the world. Videotapes were also a medium of increasing importance, shown at venues that ranged from restaurants to street committees' "culture palaces" (*wenhua guan*). The pirating of tapes, especially from TV, became common by the late 1980s. The Shanghai Broadcasting Station bought programs from many sources, including some from abroad, under agreements prohibiting piracy. Under the terms of these contracts, the network's officials could often let inland units use such tapes—and the renters reportedly "signed away their lives" with promises they would not copy the tapes. More than a hundred television stations from all over the country concluded such agreements with the Shanghai network. But the antipiracy provisions were completely unenforceable. New media, such as facsimile machines, satellite dishes, and then the Internet, stupefied official efforts to control the content of public information in China.

Finding Funds for Media

Costs of Paper and Diversification in the Reform Press

China's Leninist system, which placed all newspapers as well as broadcasters under official finance and control, worked acceptably well as long as the government faced no major budget crunch. During reforms, state revenues dropped sharply as a portion of national income; yet officials still claimed rights to tell media what to do. With its budget in the red, however, the government had no spare money to provide incentives. High cadres still got most of what they wanted from the press, because of appointment controls. The reasons lay in old rules and procedures, especially for approving jobs, not in any concrete or new incentives.

Budgets tell more than editorials about when the reforms began. A telling example of early 1970s reform comes from journalistic finance. Advertising revenues to newspapers had been nil at the height of the Cultural Revolution, because many radicals considered all advertising to be bourgeois. At the *Liberation Daily,* for example, the intake of advertising funds as late as 1973 was only 40,000 yuan. But then this source of revenue became very important very quickly: In that and the next four years to 1978, advertising revenues rose on average by 94 percent *each year*. In the next five years, to 1983, the rate of increase was understandably more modest (15 percent annually), but in the following half decade to 1988, it accelerated again, and the annual increases were about half the breakneck speed of 1974–78. By the first half of 1988, the *Liberation Daily* generated advertising revenues at an annual rate of 15.5 million yuan (after it paid the 4 percent advertising tax).[70]

This situation might have affected the state's control of newspaper budgets—except that the government clamped price controls on the advertising rates media could charge. At the same time, the collapse of price-and-delivery controls made costs soar. Inflation has been the bane of journalistic finance in China. The total cost of producing an issue of the *Liberation Daily* in August 1988 was 15 fen, up from 13 fen at the beginning of that year. Because the price of the paper was 10 fen, the publisher lost 5 fen on each issue sold. Circulation decreased—which was marvelous news to the financial departments, but a horror to the editors. For the loss on eight million subscribed issues, this Party organ in Shanghai required an annual subsidy of 4,000,000 yuan. Greatly increased advertising revenues by 1988 could cover only a bit more than 10 percent of this loss, because the government restricted advertising rates that newspapers could charge.[71]

Subscriptions to the *Xinmin Evening News* covered paper costs (as well as postage) as late as 1986, but they did not always do so afterward. The price of paper was raised on several occasions in the next two years. Although national economic plans mandated that state-run paper companies were supposed to supply specific amounts for each news organization, the chief editor of the *Xinmin Evening News* said emphatically "They do not guarantee the quality." They also did not deliver at the legally planned rate, and late performance was less performance.

Newspapers (like housing, transport, and staple foods) have for years been priced uneconomically low by state fiat. As part of the general reform program, the *Liberation Daily* planned to raise its price by 250 percent, to 25 fen, beginning in 1989. The *Wenhui News* was scheduled to go up by 300 percent, to 15 fen, and the *Xinmin Evening News* by 75 percent, from 8 to 14 fen. But especially for *Xinmin,* which relies heavily on individual subscribers, price increases during earlier stages of the reform proved that Shanghai readers have a demand curve after all: The 1987 increase from 5 to 8 fen resulted in an average of 300,000 fewer copies of *Xinmin* bought each day.[72]

In search of more and better paper, the *Xinmin Evening News* by the late 1980s sent buyers to many provinces (Guangdong, Fujian, Jiangxi, and the Northeast). Because most physical aspects of the journal's production were handled in the centralized printing plant, this effort on the part of the editorial staff was remarkable. *Xinmin,* because of its popularity, used almost half the plant's daily paper supply. So its staff had to take a lead in the search for newsprint.

Xinmin tried to solve its problem by assembling a "supply consortium" (*baogan jituan*) that would provide funds for direct investment in a Northeast

China paper factory, to meet the needs of various Shanghai papers. The *Xinmin Evening News,* the *Liberation Daily,* and the *Wenhui News* together made a large 1988 investment in a Northeast China paper mill. But there were many difficulties. Paper making is China's most devastating source of environmental pollution. One-sixth of all the waste water in China and one-quarter of the most noisome organic pollutants come from paper making.[73] The Environmental Protection Committee of the State Council in early 1989 issued regulations under which paper factories were supposed to meet standards for the cleanliness of waste water—but only by 1995.

A three-year wait for construction was expected before the *Xinmin-Wenhui-Liberation Daily* paper factory would be in production, by 1991; prospects for the interim were bleak. This kind of horizontal contract—whose aim was to create surer supplies in a time of market chaos by integrating the production process vertically—may seem a throwback to the Maoist era. Vertical integration isolates companies from markets. But the organization in this case involved interlocal agreements that were not under a state plan. The agreement depended on the reliability of local leaders.

If the *Xinmin* price rose too much, readers could find alternatives subsidized by work unit subscriptions. They could read the more staid amd statist morning dailies instead. Ironically, it was unclear when *Xinmin* could become economically viable—even though its editors and correspondents arguably had the best record in all China for producing a newspaper that large numbers of people really wanted to read. The price of their paper was controlled effectively. The price of their newsprint was not. So they soon lost money on each issue. The more popular they were editorially, the more indebted they were financially. This sort of irony was common during midreforms, when remnant constraints from old-style planning interacted in almost random patterns with new market trends. As paper prices soared, the very success of the *Xinmin Evening News* threatened to undo it.

The subscription structure of the *Wenhui News* was between that of the *Xinmin Evening News* and the *Liberation Daily.* As late as 1987, when the *Wenhui* price was only 5 fen, 40 percent of the issues were bought by individuals. Because it is a morning paper, many of these were apparently read on buses as office workers rode to their jobs. By late 1988, however, the total number of subscriptions was falling—and only 20 percent were paid by individuals. In 1989, when the price rose to 15 fen, the *Wenhui News* staff feared that individual subscriptions might drop to 5 percent of the total (with the other 95 percent bought by units); but the journal had to raise its charges to pay for the paper on which it was printed.

The *Liberation Daily* was expected to hold on to most of its subscribers, which were work units. Even though the number of daily issues would decrease because of the price rise, the content of the Party organ would not be allowed to change merely for market reasons. The *Wenhui News,* however, braced for big

Table 2.3–1

Wenhui News Finances (revenues net of profits, in millions of yuan)

	1986	1988
Newspaper sales after costs	1	-15
Advertising revenues	8	9
Management, subsidiaries	3	-3
Other Profits and Losses	1	-3
Totals (rounded)	12	-12

Note: Interview with *Wenhui News* staff, November 1988, which gave rough figures on the basis of which this table was constructed. Rising blank paper prices are the main cause of the change.

change: It planned to run more feature articles and international news, but less domestic news from outside Shanghai; and it planned to raise its printing quality, as well as the number of weekly supplements and accompanying publications. Even with these up-market changes, the *Wenhui News* expected a 40 percent decrease in circulation. The *Xinmin Evening News* expected even more drastic cuts, because it depended heavily on individuals' money.

Costs rose so fast, a typical office that spent 100 yuan each month in 1987 for subscriptions to ten newspapers might, by 1989, be able to afford only two or three. The three Shanghai dailies could survive this onslaught because of their popular or political importance—but with difficulty. Less prominent publications were under more pressure (especially if Party leaders disliked them). Even the *Wenhui News* in late 1988 predicted a decrease from 120,000 issues daily to just 80,000 a year later; the *Xinmin Evening News* was also expected to fall below 100,000 copies per day. Ironically, only the *People's Daily* stood to sell more than 200,000 copies in the whole country until prices stabilized—not because its editorial policies attracted more readers than those of other newspapers, but because as the national Party organ, it would continue to be subscribed widely by units. Secondary papers, including media in many other cities that competed locally with Shanghai publications, faced the possibility of having to close.

Advertising could have supplied more funds. For print media (though not for television), the demand curve for advertising was elastic with respect to price. Many big enterprises did not in any case have a great deal of money for publicity by the late 1980s. For this reason, newspapers' revenues from advertising were limited. Table 2.3–1, concerning the *Wenhui News,* shows a pattern of change in the late 1980s that could apply to many though not all print media: Higher paper prices overwhelmed other facts in the economics of journalism then.

At *Xinmin,* however, advertising was more important; this change was wrought by reforms. The costs of all writing, editing, printing, and some of the paper during reforms have been fully borne by advertisements. During most of the 1960s, this source of revenue did not exist, because all ads were politically suspect. By late 1988, the paper made 10 million yuan per year (more than twice the total of its subscription revenues) from selling advertisements. Half of this money went for printing. Some paid for additional paper, although the staff received more glory than money from selling these copies. The rest was for writers and editors. Especially because "cultural units" (*wenhua danwei*) in China, including newspapers, generally need not pay much tax or remit much profit to the state, this new revenue from advertising was crucial for *Xinmin.*

The main reason why taxes were a minor problem for Shanghai newspapers was that they had scant profits to tax. The government in the late 1980s gave them a three-year holiday from the enterprise tax, the real estate tax, the resources use tax, the transport tax, and other levies that would otherwise have been applicable. Before this holiday, the *Liberation Daily* paid as much as 10 million yuan just for the taxes that were suspended, and 17 million yuan in total remittances. In 1988, the paper paid only 3 million yuan total, including a small tax on advertising revenues. With journalistic companies, as with other firms in Shanghai, the government could not collect money that was not there.

Wenhui needed government subsidies to stay afloat: 7 million yuan for fiscal 1987 and more than 10 million for 1988. Its total bank indebtedness in late 1988 topped 64 million yuan, but the loans had been negotiated on favorable terms. Interest was a low 6 percent, and the repayment periods were generally ten years or more. The economy was inflationary, and *Wenhui* editors knew such a long-term financial burden was safe.

The post office distributed all newspapers in Shanghai, and its charges (paid by the newspapers) were tied to nonmarket negotiations between offices, as were the related subscription fees. Partly because the postal service raised its rates several times during reforms, including a big increase in 1989, the editors of Shanghai papers had to negotiate with each other and with many other agencies about any increased subscription rates. No single paper could decide its price alone. Each was still tied to a structure in which planning was supposed to prevail.

Major capital improvements for Shanghai papers depended on the city government. When *Xinmin,* for example, could not reclaim its old quarters on Yuanmingyuan Road, the government provided temporary space. It also provided funds for the new two-tower skyscraper, containing computerized equipment, into which all three of Shanghai's dailies moved at the turn of the decade. The News Building cost 80 million yuan, supplied by a loan from the People's Bank. For financial reasons, reforms in some ways made newspapers more, rather than less, dependent on government concessions. Yet to interest their readers, they increasingly had to report facts, rather than just policies.

Commercials and Costs in Broadcasting

The amount of money spent on broadcasting in China has risen sharply as the receivers and audience have expanded. Station costs totaled 22 million yuan in 1950, 50 million in 1957, 119 million in 1967, 391 million in 1977, and 1.3 billion in 1984.[74] The 1967–77 annual rate of increase in broadcasting expenditures was thus 13 percent, while from 1977 to 1984 it rose only somewhat, to 19 percent. In the latter period, costs increased sharply for television programming, although in the early 1970s most new money was spent on equipment.[75] The main infrastructure for TV reform was built in the early 1970s.

The main television tower on Nanjing Road was not used to capacity until 1989, when the new antenna (twice as high) rose in Pudong. These towers were, like the News Building in print journalism, financed outside the media. But in broadcasting, the need for these capital funds was one of the few financial contributions from the state. If the government had not fixed advertising prices low, the broadcasters—as they freely said in the late 1980s—would have needed no official money.

The very first advertising on PRC television was broadcast by the Shanghai station in January 1979.[76] "Advertising programs" (*guanggao jiemu*) positively littered Shanghai's airwaves by the mid-1980s. Cooperation between provincial stations was largely justified by efforts to advertise products. In 1984, for example, Shanghai joined with a number of other provinces, including Jiangsu, to produce an "advertising program," called *Wishing You Health,* "to introduce pharmaceuticals to the audience."[77] The prices of commercials in this medium (as in print) were state-controlled, but the demand for TV advertising time was very high.

As station officials were quick to point out, companies "line up" to advertise in Shanghai's electronic media, and there was not enough airtime to accommodate all of them. Managers of the city's station were sure they could become a self-financing enterprise—while also using much less airtime for commercials— if only the government would let them raise their advertising prices. But because state-owned companies would pay, such a proposal was controversial. The station thus long remained a public enterprise (*shiye danwei*), paying taxes but also offering its services at nonmarket low prices. It is likely that side payments, in addition to the published revenues, came to TV stations that would carry particular ads. More money from this source for broadcasters—combined with the fact that air media use no costly bulk resource like paper—lessen the indirect control from government. The relative youth of television staffs also affected this situation. Careful censorship of TV became, from the conservative point of view, important for these reasons.

The budget of the Shanghai city broadcasting station in 1988 was about 30 million yuan, one-third coming from the municipal government and two-thirds from commercial activities, especially advertising. Other businesses run by the station also contributed. The network owned the Qichong Tian (Seventh Heaven) Hotel as well, prominently located on central Nanjing Road in a tall building from which the station had transmitted before 1973. It also operated another hotel and a company for selling and renting videotapes. Like any Chinese unit flush with funds, it diversified its business. Most of the 20 million yuan that came commercially in 1988, however, was from advertising. By that time, station executives thought the reform era preference for changing units into self-supporting enterprises (*qiye hua*) should apply to their whole company. To the extent that occurred, these broadcasters would in practice be more independent of the state.

Recruiting Personnel for Media

Choosing Shanghai Media Reporters

At the *Liberation Daily,* an interviewee frankly reported that the Party deals with all "big matters," especially personnel questions. But even in conservative eras, staffs are not completely replaced—and during most of the 1980s, appointments were made on broader grounds, prominently including educational qualifications. The propaganda departments that try to run PRC journalism are Party, not government, units. All important editorships are on the *nomenklatura* list, so that all incumbents must be approved by relevant CCP branches. These are usually local. Before 1989, and then after a relapse gradually in the 1990s, the most cogent links between newspapers and propaganda departments were reduced to two fields: (1) designation of some sensitive topic areas for stories that were to be managed directly through the New China News Agency, which is centralized more directly than local media; and (2) approval of new employment to journals' top positions.

Head editors of important newspapers nonetheless often had so much personal prestige that in normal times and as regards most subjects, they could effectively run their own shops. Editors in Shanghai (which because of the importance of its daily media is unlike most Chinese cities in this respect) compete for news, staff, official subsidies, and especially political prestige in top CCP circles.[78] Nothing less than death itself is likely to cut the influence of some of these editors radically, even after their formal retirements.

The staffs of different newspapers have not fared identically in the broad tides of Chinese politics. For example, the *Wenhui News* had a higher percentage of "rightists" in its ranks than any other newspaper in the whole country—about forty rightists in the Maoist period. During 1979–80, all of them were invited back to the paper—and most were still quite lively. The retirement programs of the early 1980s soon took many of these cadres out of their work units. An editor freely admitted, however, that tensions between rivals in the Cultural Revolution nonetheless persisted well into the 1980s. They were periodically revived by events such as those of mid-1989. For actuarial reasons, some of these conflicts within units will last for a long time.

Newspapers' Personnel and Compensation in the Reform Era

The portion of Party members on late 1988 Shanghai newspaper staffs varied considerably, but less at the top of each journal's hierarchy than at the bottom. Employees at the *Liberation Daily* altogether numbered nearly a thousand people, of whom 43 percent were cadres and 40 percent were members of the CCP. Among the reporters and editors, 68 percent were Party members.[79] Another 13 percent were in the Communist Youth League. These ratios were higher than for most newspapers, but understandably so, because the *Liberation Daily* is Shanghai's Party organ. At the *Wenhui News,* whose constituency is different, only a fifth of the writers were members of the Party by late 1988. One-third of the editorial department were CCP members, however (as was the chief editor, whose prestige clearly made him the main leader in this unit). Only a few reporters were members of the Youth League. Not only did the *Liberation Daily* have a higher ratio of Party members, but also its personnel, especially at the top, received higher salaries than at other Shanghai papers.[80]

The chief editor of the *Wenhui News,* when asked for the criteria he used in hiring reporters, specified three major factors: First, their "cultural level" and quality of education—especially in writing—had to be high. Second, a potential recruit should be effective with other people. Third, the "thinking" of the candidate had to be sound. The editor opined, apparently protesting too much, that such a criterion was less a political problem than an ethical or social requisite. Employment decisions were supposed to be made on the basis of personnel files, which this editor described as containing more information about work ability (*gongzuo nengli*) and professionalism (*yewu nengli*) than about political attitudes. But in practice, it seems clear that the criteria for recruitment included both technical expertise and acceptable politics.

By the late 1980s, at the *Wenhui News* and many other papers, effectively all staff recruitment not from universities came among "stringer" correspondents. Few reporters had joined from other units during the reforms. At least by 1988, the army had supplied far fewer than it had during the prereform era. By that year, only 5 percent of the newspaper's total staff had any full-time military experience, and most of these were in the *Wenhui* administrative rather than editorial departments. This trend away from ex-soldiers may be important in many civilian posts during the 1990s.

The 1988 staff of the *Xinmin Evening News* included about 150 reporters and editors. Although the Cultural Revolution closure of this paper (as of other media) created more staff turnover during the first part of the decade than was usual in economic organizations, two-fifths of this journal's people by 1982 were retained from the previous era. Because this paper's policies encouraged both retirements (*tuixiu*) and special-benefit retirements (*lixiu*), the pre-CR staff was by 1988 down to one-tenth of the total.[81] Nine-tenths, but not at the top of the hierarchy, had graduated from universities during the 1970s or 1980s. A majority come from Fudan University, which is Shanghai's premier institution in the humanities. Many majored not in journalism, but in history or literature. The *Xinmin Evening News* chief editor said that although his paper could interview prospective employees before hiring them, and both the paper and graduating students could express their preferences, the "state distribution" (*guojia fenpei*) of graduates to jobs was in late 1988 still handled within universities. This system gave the schools' personnel departments, which are important branches of the Party there, some influence over a part of Shanghai's population that was most liable to make political dissent. As economic growth provided more career alternatives for students, this influence declined.

Not many at *Xinmin*, reportedly, were members of the Party when they joined; some were not even in the Youth League. Few had served in the army. But the ratio of Party members in Shanghai newspaper staffs generally suggests that some new hires were soon recruited or co-opted into the CCP. In any case, the portion of Party members on the senior staffs of all papers was high. Not all these CCP editors, however, necessarily shared identical policy views.

The educational backgrounds of news staffs clearly improved during the 1980s. By the end of August 1988, the *Liberation Daily* had 406 cadres, of whom slightly more than half were reporters. Five-eighths of all the personnel were university graduates. Among these, 78 percent had completed various kinds of colleges during the 1980s. A small 5 percent (the "lost generation") got their degrees during the 1970s; 13 percent did so in the 1960s; 4 percent in the 1950s; and just 1 percent before 1949.[82] One-quarter of the graduates had majored in journalism.

Some old cadres had been hired at this Party organ in several prereform eras from other units. Some, especially among administrative personnel, were ex-soldiers. In 1988, 7 percent of this staff were still on active duty with the army reserves. One-tenth of all the cadres (forty of the youngest members) had been hired on the basis of tests given by the *Liberation Daily* itself. This was one way in which the journal could vet its large staff of stringers, as well as other youths of interest to the editors, for possible full-time employment. The paper actively sifted the dossiers of potential recruits from universities (just as the Shanghai Television Station did, and the *Xinmin Evening News* reportedly could not). The *Liberation Daily* did not rely just on the advice of school personnel cadres.[83]

In the *Wenhui News,* which addresses an educated readership and was particularly hard hit by both the Antirightist Campaign and the Cultural Revolution, only one-fifth of the 1977 editorial department had been to college—but ten years later, two-thirds of the editors had university degrees. Half came from Fudan University, many from its Journalism Department; and the other half came from diverse universities (including some from far less prestigious TV colleges or vocational schools). Most of the remaining editorial staff, without degrees, was close to retirement by the late 1980s.[84]

The editor of the *Wenhui News* complained that the professional competence of most university graduates after the Cultural Revolution, except for the famous classes of '81 and '82 discussed in chapter 3.2, was lower than that of graduates before 1966. He was particularly concerned by the graduates' declining ability to write the Chinese language well. The main reasons, he said, lay not in universities, but in the damage that years of neglect had done to high schools. Some of these academies had, before the mid-1960s, been truly elite institutions, with competitive academic standards and discipline. But as promotion rates to schools rose, and as Maoist disruptions and then quasi-capitalist reforms undermined the previous norm that hard work should lead to good livelihoods, "universities can now do little."[85]

Among the publishing directors of Shanghai's most important newspapers, four-fifths had university educations by the mid-1980s. This distinguished group was on average older, at 56 years, than in any other Chinese city. They had averaged longer (at fifteen and one-half years) in journalistic work. Among the sixty-five top editors, 82 percent had college educations; their average age was 50, and the average number of years in their newspapers was thirteen (somewhat less than in most other provinces).[86]

The Jiangsu Press Corps

Although no comprehensive survey of all Shanghai's journalists has been found, a large 1986 poll of all media employees in the neighboring province of Jiangsu has been published.[87] Among these journalists, men outnumbered women by a ratio of 3:1 in total staff, and more than 6:1 in writing and editing. Many women were kept in secretarial and janitorial jobs. The whole Jiangsu press corps was not generally old—partly because writing demands some education. Over two-fifths of all editors and reporters were less than 35 years old. But more than half of the "leading cadres" were over 46, and a quarter were over 56, presumably old revolutionaries then nearing retirement. Newspaper staffs were older than broadcast staffs, with nearly three-fifths over 46 and more than one-third over 56. Seventy percent of all these journalists were in the Party or League; among leading cadres, a majority were in the CCP. A big majority of broadcast writers, editors, and announcers were Party members. Hints from other evidence suggest that, in this whole-sample census of the Jiangsu press, many broadcasters had at least some experience in the army. There were more highly educated people on newspaper staffs (55 percent overall) than on broadcast staffs (36 percent).[88] Party membership may have helped journalists obtain their jobs, but in reforms it was also probable that the Party wanted to co-opt them because of their important political functions.

A surprisingly high portion of these newspeople (39 percent) had begun their careers during the years 1966 to 1976—usually in the early 1970s—but very

Table 2.3–2

Cohorts Entering Jiangsu Journalism (percentages of 1986 staff)

	Year entered journalistic work			
	Prior to 1957	1958–65	1966–76	After 1977
Leading cadres	16	13	26	42
Midlevel cadres	14	18	22	44
Editors and reporters	5	6	12	76
Announcers and directors	1	3	24	71
Others	6	11	14	65

Source: Zhongguo xinwen nianjian, 1987 (China News Yearbook, 1987), He Guangguang et al., eds. (Beijing: Zhongguo Shehui Kexue Chuban She, 1987), p. 194.

often in careers other than journalism. Another 29 percent had begun before that era, and 30 percent after it. Over two-thirds had not entered the journalistic profession (as distinct from other jobs) until after 1976. Table 2.3–2 shows the distribution, by level and date of vocation, of people entering the Jiangsu press corps. About half of those who had joined since the beginning of the reform period had college educations; and this portion almost surely rose in later years.

There may be some tension, usually latent, between people who joined journalism from the army and the increasing portions at all levels who joined later and after college. Among leading cadres, as the table shows, 42 percent had begun their press careers after 1977. But in urban units, only one-third of the leaders had begun in journalism during the reforms. Two-fifths of the leading cadres directed rural media, largely at the county level. So the most important *urban* media in Jiangsu were more often led by *non*–college-graduates, at least in 1986, than were more local county newspapers or more specialized urban publications. Party notables or old revolutionary soldiers, if they had specialized in journalism, could get work and residence in big cities, apparently, whereas younger and better-educated cadres got leading jobs mainly in smaller towns. The most competent of them would not necessarily stay there forever.

Just one-eighth of all these journalists had attended Party schools at one time or another, and over 80 percent had begun their careers doing work other than journalism.[89] Young educated editors were not always as well placed as their titles implied. They were nonetheless many, by the later reforms. Relatively few young conservatives had much experience producing newspapers.

Broadcasters in Reform

Radio broadcasters in the 1950s and 1960s were sometimes expelled from their jobs after accusations of being rightists, having "complicated social relations," or coming from "bad family origins."[90] But the newer electronic media, especially television, were less affected by this kind of problem than were most other politically sensitive organizations in China, because they had not yet begun in 1957; their organizations mostly did not exist then. Large increases of new broadcasting units' employment occurred in the 1970s, for technological reasons.

At the end of 1966, the total number of employees in all of China's stations was 43,873. Because of political disruptions, few more could be hired for the next three or four years. But by the end of 1976, all broadcasters in the nation had 160,448 staff. These data imply that for some years in the early 1970s, there was a quick expansion of employment in broadcasting stations, between one-fifth and one-quarter annually. Many of the early 1970s hires lacked complete educations, and presumably some had been replaced by the end of 1984 (when the total number of workers in the broadcasting industry had risen to 271,218). Even allowing for some expulsions, however, the rate of new hiring in the post-1978 broadcast industry was almost surely lower than in the 1971–74 era.[91] In China as a whole, province-level "leadership groups" in broadcasting were relatively younger and better-educated than in most fields. By 1984, for example, 72 percent of this cohort had university degrees; the average age of these high cadres in broadcasting was only 51.[92] Technological opportunities, not just politics, drove the timing of these changes.

Some reforms in media staffs (as in rural industrialization, state budgets, and many other fields) apparently began about 1971. Broadcast media in the 1970s were largely staffed by ex-military personnel; college graduates seldom went there. In 1980 and 1983, however, the Shanghai station held "open recruitments."[93] The bureau was choosy and did not hire many people on these occasions. Already by the start of the decade, recruitment to the Shanghai TV station involved an exam that the station administered.[94] The criteria for hiring included school records, past performing or directing experience, assessments of personal character, and the results of a professional test.

Staff were then sought from universities including Fudan's Journalism Department, which offers courses in broadcasting. Personnel officials at such schools could try to "distribute" graduates to jobs in the usual manner. But the TV station would not hire them unless they also did well on the test.[95] The station was thus a state-run analogue to collective and private enterprises, and to some newspapers, in not automatically accepting all new recruits whom the CCP personnel departments of schools recommend for employment.[96] This procedure undoubtedly made the universities' personnel departments choose more carefully for the TV station than for other companies (e.g., the *Xinmin Evening News,* whose less active hiring policies are noted above). This policy gave units seeking workers every incentive to set up exams of their own, lest they end up with less good staff members.

The television station also hired employees among "intellectual youths" in the countryside, government organizations, and the army. The average age was low.

By the mid-1980s, some people on station staffs had been allowed to go abroad for study.[97] Broadcasting wages were typical for journalists.[98] The Shanghai Television Station expanded so quickly during the reform, it has inherited less elderly staff than any other institution in the city with such a high public profile.

Local authority in hiring was increased as the reforms moved into the mid-1980s. In 1983, new regulations affecting broadcasters specified that personnel decisions would be approved by the whole Party committees of the relevant bureaus, rather than by the smaller and more office-bound CCP "groups."[99] In the same year, power over all appointments below the section (*ke*) level was decentralized, and in the next year, this happened also in larger divisions (*chu*). Most important, the stations themselves took over appointments to all lower levels, without a need for higher-level approvals.

Outreach programs allowed the Shanghai Broadcasting Station to establish useful liaisons with many other local entities. In September 1985, the station joined the Shanghai Journalists' Association and the Jing'an District Education Bureau to set up the Shanghai News Radio and TV Employees' School.[100] It graduated 120 students in the first year, who studied all aspects of the station but seem to have been mainly stringer reporters. In particular, they studied the commercial side of the enterprise—which was fast becoming more important for television than for newspapers. State politics was, for better or for worse, no longer the sole topic of concern among journalists.

Deciding the Contents of Media

Censorship with Chinese Characteristics

The main Maoist method to make sure that journalism followed high politicians' ideas was to have Party notables themselves do much of the writing. This practice made censorship redundant. Top Chinese leaders used to publish important editorials in official newspapers. Mao himself did this regularly for the CCP's organ at Yan'an (the *Liberation Daily* in its earlier form). Liu Shaoqi, Zhou Enlai, Chen Yun, Bo Yibo, Hu Qiaomu, and other leaders in the 1950s and early 1960s wrote often for the *People's Daily*. By the 1980s, however, this practice had generally stopped. Hu Qiaomu in 1983 wrote a few small commentaries under a pseudonym, but this was a pale and nostalgic reference to a bygone era of directly authoritative journalism. Leaders' speeches were still excerpted in newspapers, when they were not too long-winded. Journalists in prestigious newspapers remained politically well connected; many were professional writers for specific politicians. The practical identity of leadership and journalism, however, ended during reforms.[101] This was a vocational specialization.

Contemporary Chinese censorship (like other aspects of the PRC) has been uneven over time, place, and type of unit. This topic is complex for China, because most censorship there is indirect or secret; news of it is censored. The severity of criteria for imprimaturs has varied sharply in different eras of reform. Also, serial media are often censored less than books. Shanghai newspapers have published many kinds of information that seldom appear in books available for open sale. As sources of social information, the evening papers are often as telling as limited-circulation books. Shanghai newspapers reported Zhejiang silk growers' failure to supply local mills with the planned amounts of raw silk in the mid-1980s, for example, but few books printed such material. When news involves conflicts between units, dailies and weeklies sometimes may report it. Newspapers also carry stories about problems that involve human interest as well as politics. When five thousand families had to be resettled because of a project to expand the Shanghai railroad station, anybody who bought a local paper could read all about it.[102] But many books steer clear of practical issues, unless they are published in times of particular political thaw, by organizations that have reform-minded patrons, and in limited or small circulations.[103]

The basic criteria for censorship have remained ambiguous in the reform era, because the government's desire for popular credibility has strained against its desire for political loyalty. Some Chinese editors try to distinguish news that is "informational" from news that is "propaganda."[104] Sometimes this is expressed as a difference between "reporting" and "advocacy."[105] All countries have some limits on journalistic freedom, and frank Chinese reporters admit that the PRC limits are stricter than most others. Inspectors, however, are reportedly not assigned to Chinese newspapers—in part because, before 1949, the Kuomintang made extensive use of censors (*shencha yuan,* who came with a law to govern their work), and the CCP had criticized the practice then.

Official institutions for mediating between "reporting" and "advocacy" were inherited in the 1950s from Soviet precedents, but they became less authoritative by the 1980s. For example, *News Front (Xinwen zhanxian)* was created in December 1957, at the height of the Antirightist Campaign. Its mandate was to tell journalists what kinds of stories to write, and it was secret for internal use only. With a change of name in 1960, it continued publication until 1966. As one newspaperman said of Mao's time, "Little papers copied big papers, and big papers copied radicals."[106] Local and evening media then carried more lively information than did national and official papers, but controls over content were severe.[107] Especially after the closure of many transient Red Guard newspapers in 1967–68, the number of local journals throughout China decreased sharply.

From 1971 to 1975, newspapers printed more economic news. In some media, the kinds of propaganda were reduced. The circulation of *Reference Information (Cankao xiaoxi),* an internal-use daily with extensive news translated from international wire services, sharply increased—and this change was backed by Zhou Enlai (and then by the de facto premier in 1974, Deng Xiaoping). *Reference Information* was also a pet project of Mao Zedong himself.[108] Reform was slower in news content than in many fields, but quick technological change in TV was matched by limited-circulation news stories of considerable variety, and often translated from foreign sources, in the early 1970s. Despite its legally secret status, *Reference Information* soon became the largest-circulation newspaper in China.[109]

Protoreformers could raise questions about matters that had been previously forbidden—and they reportedly began to do so within the *Liberation Daily* staff in 1971, and especially in March and April of 1972.[110] At this time, Shanghai journalism was still deeply influenced by the Gang of Four. But the tenets of that group were not so inflexible as to preclude debate about the extent to which newspapers should support production, not just revolution. The *Liberation Daily* in particular had been a center of leftism ever since it moved to Shanghai in April 1949, with the purpose of transferring guerrilla traditions from its Yan'an predecessor to China's capitalist metropolis.[111] By 1973, for example, politics was partly consumed with a campaign to "criticize Confucius" (the Zhou philosopher implied Zhou Enlai on this occasion). Jiang Qing was reported to believe that "Confucianists [support] production, but Legalists [support] rebellion."[112]

Ex-bureaucrats were also returning, during the 1971–73 era, from political exile in great numbers. By 1974, Deng Xiaoping and the economic politician Wan Li were already influential. Despite the continuing importance of more radical politicians in Shanghai, newspapers could carry somewhat more articles emphasizing the importance of production than had been possible during the violent Cultural Revolution. Then in the transitional period of 1976–78, according to a cadre of the *Liberation Daily,* there was not much liberalization of policies on journals' content. In this, as in many other areas, the 1973–75 protoreform (milder though it was in journalism as compared to other fields) was not furthered in the year of Mao's death or under Hua Guofeng. The greatest lapse in the modern history of all news reporting—the neglect of the Tangshan earthquake, a case that had nothing to do with advocacy—occurred in China during late July 1976.[113]

Critiques of leftism could be printed after the April–May 1978 plenum of the Central Committee. As late as that year, however, newspapers such as the *Wenhui News* still carried no serialized fiction, and there was scant coverage of arts. By 1979 and in the early 1980s, many new topics could appear in newspapers—including the Party organ in Shanghai—that had previously been communicated mainly by informal word of mouth. Reporting became much broader politically, because of pro-democracy demonstrations, the return from rural areas of young intellectuals who had been exiled there, and the removal of most labels from "rightists."

The *Wenhui News* launched an early discussion of "practice as the sole criterion of truth." There was a sharp temporary increase of economic reporting during 1979, presumably because there was some good news to tell, especially in agriculture.[114] But 1980 saw an increase in cultural reporting and nonpolitical articles—and at this time, it was possible to criticize Mao gently. The beginning of the 1980s also began occasional news about sports and family matters, both in the relatively staid morning papers and (to a greater extent) in evening papers. By the mid- and late 1980s, feature articles (*zawen*) became main attractions in papers such as the *Wenhui News,* as did articles on arts and household life and on economic topics as novel as stock prices.

Official calls for urban reform throughout the early 1980s, culminating in the middle of that decade, further broadened the content of Shanghai newspapers. Articles on science and technology became more frequent. The norm of "transparency" (*touming*) justified many news articles that would previously have been unprintable on the grounds that they lacked sufficient interpretive "standpoint" (*lichang*). A new norm took news as primary (*xinwen wei zhu*), and more articles about social affairs were published.

Local leaders increasingly became their own censors. When *News Front* reemerged with its original title, it no longer controlled journalism effectively. It was still published by the *People's Daily,* the national organ of the Communist Party, but by 1980 it was just a monthly. It was no longer limited in circulation.[115] Its change of function—from being a political guide for journalists to being a professional publication—reflects a reduction in the central state's hopes of controlling the press absolutely. No other national guide for journalists took over the early directing functions of *News Front.* All limited-circulation Chinese serial publications on journalism by 1982 were apparently published at the province level or lower, and none were in Shanghai.[116] Informants inside China, when asked about this by the late 1980s, said this kind of Party guidance had ceased. Less constrained interviewees, outside the PRC, reported the existence of a *Propaganda Bulletin* (*Xuanchuan tongxun*), published by CCP propaganda authorities at various levels, that still carried directives to editors and reporters. For example, the Central Propaganda Department once warned media not to print stories about a Chinese student group visiting Taiwan.[117] Workers' strikes and certain other categories of news have also been unreportable.

The chief of the New China News Agency urged simply contradictory principles on journalists, saying they should "bring to light falsehoods and shameful events so that people can judge and criticize"—but in the same speech, he warned them that they were politically responsible for actions their words might cause:

> In filing critical press reports, we should analyze whether our exposition and criticism of problems can produce educative results. . . . There is no need to file press reports on shameful events that do not have educational or press value. In addition, in filing press reports we should consider the image of the Party, the government, and the people's army. Individual, occasional events harmful to the image of the Party, the state, and the people's army, should not be given publicity.[118]

What, then, were reporters supposed to do? Plainly two-sided directives were efforts by high editors to safeguard themselves against any political wind that later might blow. To say that either rights-conscious or duty-conscious attitudes prevailed among Chinese journalists during the reforms—or that either choice could be separated from the external situations they faced—would distort too much good data for the opposite argument. Dissonance, not unison, was the order of the day.

"Transparency"—a demand for rights to factual information—became a pervasive slogan in the spring of 1989. Some Western intellectuals claim that public articulation, civil expression, and true or false consciousness are central to politics. But in this case, bureaucratic secrecy was more noisome for local power networks than nonofficial expression would have been. A true Chinese liberal at this time noted that free expression about state politics, even if it could be completely achieved, would not by itself assure the free flow of argument that was actually more important to most people in localities:

> The media ask to have transparency; but also, people in many units ask for transparency because they want to know something about their own welfare. People want the state particularly to be transparent about major state affairs; but they also want the police to be transparent about household registration management cases. Asking for transparency is asking for democratization. If people are unclear about facts, how can democracy be carried out, how can the people be the country's masters, and how can they exercise supervision over government? . . . People have stressed the transparency of high-level leadership before. Certainly, this was important. But we cannot overlook local-level transparency, such as household registration processes. . . . It is important to ask whether [police] carry out policies correctly or whether they establish local policies (*tu zhengce*). . . . In a word, they are asking for more transparency about officials.[119]

In early 1989, a period of relative thaw in China, Shanghai's most popular newspaper, the *Xinmin Evening News,* published a column bemoaning the difficulties faced by editors and writers who were supposed to follow instructions from "leading departments" and at the same time were supposed to meet the interests of their "broad readership." The result in many articles was an "emptiness," because many readers neither believed the propaganda nor much cared about the distant statist categories in which it was written. These were mainly matters for intellectuals who wanted government jobs, not for most people who wanted wealth and local prestige. As the paper put it, the social effects of such articles were at once "pitiable and laughable."[120]

Self-censorship by PRC media has nonetheless been extensive, though less so in periods of political thaw than in conservative times. A particularly striking example of criticism against such censorship was issued by Shanghai's Wenhui Publishing House. A reformist writer pointed out that pre-Liberation papers were able to report anything, even trivial matters; but some important issues were hard to publish during China's reforms.[121] Conservatives argued that some subjects were inherently unpublishable—and they made the point by stressing the case of pornography.

"Yellow" (*huangse*) materials were periodically banned during reforms, although they were often obvious on Shanghai's streets. Pornography was subject to occasional campaigns, for example, in late 1987. As one official admitted, "These materials are not easy to trace." Police confiscated "hundreds of thousands" of "obscene" items that year. "In some cases pornographic books were burned at public rallies. In Shanghai in August, a man was sentenced to death for organizing pornographic video shows and encouraging audience participation in sex acts."[122] Not all of the seized materials were salacious, in fact. Many publications taken by police were merely printed by firms lacking government licenses. In Shanghai alone, officials reportedly seized many millions of copies of illegal publications each year in the late 1980s.

In the 1990s, these campaigns continued, though with decreasing results. A State Press and Publication Administration official claimed in 1994 that his unit would "continue to ban illegal publications, including those that are pornographic or tasteless." But, he said, "this does not mean censorship." Although "SPPA officials do read and check publications," this was only to ensure a "healthy development of China's press and publishing industries for the good of all people." Another official averred, "Unless the problems in a certain publication are exceptionally serious, we do not take measures against them." Of 2,039 newspapers and 8,000 other serials in 1993, just "four or five" were reportedly shut down for "grave problems."[123] But the definitions of phrases such as "tasteless," "healthy," "grave," or "the good of all people" were left totally vague.

Broadcast Contents

Similarly changing restrictions applied to the airwaves. During the Cultural Revolution, and in this field continuing into the early 1970s, the reigning radicals in Shanghai had a great deal of newspaper experience. (Half of the Gang of Four, Zhang Chunqiao and Yao Wenyuan, were print journalists.) They trusted only a few of their fellow editors—apparently not enough to distribute to broadcast media. So radio and TV programs at this time tended largely to be spiritual readings from the printed press. At the beginning of 1967, all of China's broadcasting stations formally came under military control. They stopped producing "independent programs."[124] Shanghai radio broadcast a limited repertory of shows, repeating them day after day on a continuous basis.[125] The most important sources of such programs were editorials in the then-radical *People's Daily*, although two other Beijing publications (*Red Flag* and the *Liberation Army News*) also had their leftist editorials broadcast. Arts programs of the Central Broadcasting Station were limited to eight model operas, eight songs, and three movies.[126] Journalistic freedom was suppressed in the Cultural Revolution, but China's correspondents had also been fettered in some earlier periods such as the Great Leap Forward, before the Gang of Four had great power.[127]

As most open violence of the Cultural Revolution ended, broadcasting stations slowly resumed more autonomy in creating their own productions. This hesitant reform was temporarily reversed in the mid-1970s. By June 1974, Mao's wife, Jiang Qing, was fighting back in several ways, one of which involved a TV program called *Caring for the Masses*.[128] Radicals occasionally still tried to smash old recorded disks and to destroy tapes of arts broadcasts that did not meet their fancy. But some stations, including that in Shanghai, managed to preserve many recordings.

By 1979, the Shanghai Broadcasting Station began airing its own "autonomous commentaries."[129] In the middle of the 1980s, radio news was broadcast forty-two times a day in Shanghai. Two years later, there was a nominal policy that "each [commentator] walks his own road." This kind of maxim was not uniformly honored, but it showed the continuing tension between norms of orthodoxy and credibility.

Propaganda vs. "Transparency" in Print

By the 1980s, prominent editors could frankly castigate the journalism of earlier periods as being "false, boastful, and empty" (*jia, da, kong*). The aims of the "reform of journalism's content" were varied at different times, because some politicians called for more news that was coordinated with official policies, whereas others called for diversification. In the first category, a major aim was to stress the reporting of economic models. An East China broadcasting station in 1981, for example, publicized eight hundred "advanced persons," and the next year, this number was raised by half. A contrasting kind of emphasis, at this same time, was on "critical reporting."[130]

Faddism that misdirects the power of the Fourth Estate was sporadically recognized as a problem in China. A much-publicized East China case was the press treatment of Bu Xinsheng, who directed Zhejiang's Haiyan Shirt Factory, and who was at first lionized as a daring reformer but then fired—pilloried in the press—when his factory ran into the red. As the *China Daily* said, "The media did not mention any of Bu's weaknesses while he was extremely popular." It quoted the comment of a worker to a journalist: "Bu was not so good nor so bad as you pictured him." The problem is that

> in China, when an authority such as a senior official or a leading newspaper like the *People's Daily* takes a stand or gives an opinion, it is common for the media to chime in. The chorus of one-sided views often makes such a deep and dominant impression on the public that it seems impossible for anyone to raise a different voice.[131]

"The press needs reform," a journalist in Zhejiang said. "The dated mentality that makes journalists consider someone or something either entirely good or bad should be changed."

The varied content of Shanghai media in the long term arose not just from official intentions, but also from interaction with audiences. As readerships expanded, and as special interests became more recognized for their contributions to the economy, newspapers could occasionally follow suit. Specialized journals began for many groups, ranging from lawyers to dressmakers. Specialized supplementary publications were added to newspapers or published by the same staffs. The *Liberation Daily* founded a *Digest of Periodicals* in 1979, and this summary has become one of the city's main journals. The same paper in 1980 took charge of *Branch Life,* a limited-circulation periodical for Party members that has 600,000 subscriptions. In 1983, the daily paper also began a literary supplement called *Novel Extracts;* 1984 saw the inauguration of the *Liberation Daily Rural Edition,* as well as of the *Shanghai Economic Information News* (both of which later had to cease publication, mostly because of paper shortages). By 1985, this same paper even began the *Student's English Daily.*[132] The *Liberation Daily* also runs a branch that publishes books.

Many other Shanghai newspapers, notably the *Wenhui News,* have likewise offered extensive supplements and magazines in the 1980s, as well as more varied books. Their diversity stands in contrast to the prereform era, when supplementary publications did not exist. The number of Shanghai titles, both of serials and books, increased most sharply after 1978; but the acceleration of this increase was highest, especially for books, in the early 1970s. There was a decrease or stagnation in 1975–77.

The daily circulation of newspapers per person within Shanghai trebled from 1978 to 1986.[133] Subscriptions to all serials multiplied almost six times. In absolute terms, the rates of circulation were low (by 1986, the average Shanghai reader still got about half a newspaper per day, and about two magazines per month). But the increase reflected greater prosperity, an increasingly literate population, and some perception among officials that more specialized interests should be addressed. Although no sudden or perfect one-to-one relationship exists between new constituencies and the sources that emerge to inform them, publications ultimately need readers. So if the audience becomes more varied, the media do too. This is not the place to present data proving 1980s Chinese social diversification, especially among literate people.[134] But over a span of years, changing constituencies affect media policies.

In comparison with the Maoist era, fewer important journals during the reforms were classified. The most significant internal serial in Shanghai during the 1980s has been *Branch Life,* the Municipal CCP Committee's journal for Party members. By the end of 1982, it came out in 390,000 copies (roughly an issue per member), but just fortnightly. It was a journal of essays on the current Party line, Marxist theory, and Shanghai Party members' experiences.[135] For most of the 1980s, *Branch Life* was apparently not a major source of new information even for its recipients. Its publication paralleled similar magazines put out by each provincial CCP committee in China. Reforms, when they were

Table 2.3–3

Diversifying Publication in Shanghai from the Early 1970s

	Books		Magazines		Newspapers
	Titles (number)	Copies (millions)	Titles (number)	Copies (millions)	Copies (millions)
1965	3,238	296	58	72	303
1966	1,786	365	51	70	346
1967	319	459			424
1968	273	185			511
1969	16	47			482
1970	180	204			469
1971	392	279			494
1972	829	281	1	10	588
1973	1,239	346	1	10	439
1974	1,475	373	12	30	614
1975	1,638	347	23	34	617
1976	1,485	304	32	40	625
1977	1,332	327	33	27	587
1978	1,666	392	42	47	641
1979	2,040	458	90	73	732
1980	2,338	562	126	122	855
1981	2,808	601	266	203	1,028
1982	3,395	607	308	231	1,493
1983	3,653	465	349	251	1,813
1984	3,848	537	402	310	1,963
1985	4,176	495	491	345	1,954
1986	4,531	365	541	303	1,994
1987	5,103	426	546	313	2,245
1988	5,538	433	535	266	2,138
1989	6,765	328	527	186	1,585
1990	7,767	298	522	173	1,676
1991	8,141	311	504	175	1,916
1992	8,095	275	527	179	2,476

Source: Unlike some other information here, the numbers of Shanghai newspaper titles were not available in *Shanghai tongji nianjian, 1986* (Shanghai Statistical Yearbook, 1986), Li Mouhuan et al., eds. (Shanghai: Shanghai Shi Tongji Ju, 1986), pp. 380–82, and *Shanghai tongji nianjian, 1988* (Shanghai Statistical Yearbook, 1988), Li Mouhuan et al., eds. (Shanghai: Shanghai Shi Tongji Ju, 1988), pp. 350–52. Data for the last five years are in the 1990 edition, p. 536 for 1988–89 data, the 1991 edition, p. 380; the 1992 edition, p. 415; and the 1993 edition, p. 359.

followed, brought more formal similarity in the journalistic services offered to Party members and other specialized constituencies.

The Party's influence even within news staffs varied considerably over time. Some editors in the 1980s expressed an opinion that the content of newspapers, even when largely political, should be deemed a technical matter within their jurisdiction. In this reformist view, the Party organization in news staffs should confine itself to personnel questions, choosing journalists but then letting them write. But unintended circumstances, not just principles and policies, usually determined the actual outcomes of any conflict between Party and reporting cadres. In the face of some news stories, such as the December 1986 student demonstrations in Anhui and then Shanghai, propaganda and transparency were hard to mix. When such a story broke, who decided how to report it?

A *Liberation Daily* editor said his paper wanted to report the December 1986 events squarely—since the public was hearing a great deal about them through media such as the Voice of America and the "grass telegraph" (*xiaodao xiaoxi*) anyway. But higher municipal officials, apparently those appointed from Beijing, said the reporting of such a sensitive issue should be done by Xinhua, the central New China News Agency, which apparently has rights to take over in periods of crisis for the government. The chief editor of another major Shanghai newspaper, two years after the December 1986 student demonstrations, said the job of reporting them had been handled "badly." The *Liberation Daily* editor implied that Shanghai journalists should be allowed the same degree of trust as central ones, since the locals were also concerned to avoid possible destabilizing effects of their news. The prevailing institution varied over time: In ordinary periods and for ordinary issues, local papers could do their own reporting. For sensitive topics and eras, they ran Xinhua text.

Shanghai's hepatitis epidemic in early 1988 seemed to be a different kind of case, because propaganda about the problem helped solve it. Many aspects of the matter were sensitive, including the decline of Shanghai production, the serious cases and deaths, the lack of adequate hospitals or ambulances for such a large epidemic, and the obvious need for better public inspection of food. Shanghai media could offer tips about how individuals might avoid the disease, what the symptoms were, what kinds of home care were useful, and what steps kitchens and other institutions should take to stop the infection. Local newspapers and broadcast media reported extensively on these aspects of the epidemic, and their information surely hastened its end. High CCP politicians seldom think that other social problems (e.g., cadre nepotism, workers' strikes, or plan failures) can be similarly relieved through public information and debate, as the epidemic was. So reporting on these tended to be centralized, especially in Xinhua. Both procedures remained available for media to use, however, and the choice depended largely on the topic.

Some media are taken as more serious than others, and these are more constrained.[136] Although a paper such as the *Xinmin Evening News* is supposed to convey the Party line subtly, its mandates for "transparency" and for "serving the interests of the masses" tend to overwhelm its political mandate. This puts it in a somewhat different position, for example, from that of the *Liberation Daily* or *Wenhui News,* which are for official-intellectual readerships. Aside from relatively straightforward domestic and international news, published without editorial comment on the first and fourth pages of *Xinmin,* each day's issue in midreforms had a page of feature articles entitled "The Night Light Cup" (*ye guang bei*), as well as a page on sports and cultural attractions. At least on a weekly basis, other pages concerning "The Pleasure of Reading," "Home Life," "Recreation," "Science Hall," and similar apolitical topics also appear. None of these subjects directly bears on questions of authority. But if a proper Leninist newspaper is supposed to convey the Party line, either *Xinmin* is relatively free of such constraints or the content of orthodoxy has mellowed during reforms, despite conservatives' frequent efforts to harden it. Orthodoxy—for some units, some times, some places, some generations, and some issues—has been fairly easy to neglect.

Newspapers had to make frequent decisions on whether material should be printed on an "open" (*gongkai*) or "internal" (*neibu*) basis. Openness was supposed to be an important general preference of the reform era, but of course the bureaucratic preference was for secrecy. In newspapers and publishing houses alike, editors determined for each article whether open publication was allowable. Except for security matters, the guidelines were vague—and were applied very inconsistently by different editors and at different times. A frequently cited criterion for secrecy was the notion that controversial issues should not be published while they were still under "theoretical discussion" (*lilun tantao*). With ever fewer people interested in Marxist theory, this rule was hard to use.

A prominent Shanghai editor in the late 1980s said it was standard journalistic practice that when an article was based on official sources, the bureaucrats who supplied the data would ordinarily be sent a copy before publication. But he was also eager that papers should have some freedom to criticize official mismanagement. Most articles were subject to scrutiny only within the paper's staff before they were run. This influential editor described two broad criteria on which he might decide not to print stories: First, if the report would harm China's international policy, it would be omitted. Second, if it would harm political or economic stability within the country, it would also be censored. In particular, this editor confirmed his paper did not run 1988 stories in Shanghai about student demonstrations against the Japanese consulate (because of Japan's controversial work visa policy) and about industrial strikes, as well as many items about inflation. But he claimed he did not want to censor just complaints against bureaucrats. "Criticisms of higher levels" were in principle fit to print whenever their contents were true, and stories about unofficial social movements such as the nativist martial arts and *qigong* fads had also been published.

In 1988, the chief editor of the *Xinmin Evening News* was asked whether directives such as the old *News Front* still guided journalists. He replied in general that newspapers should help the movement for reform. He said there was no kind of news that should not be printed, except news that would destabilize the reforms. His colleagues at the interview raised questions about whether Chinese reporting of events such as the December 1986 student demonstrations in Shanghai had been handled well, implying they had not. The ideal was to be "transparent" enough so that many facts could be reported without taking an official position on them.[137] But one prominent Shanghai editor in a different newspaper said frankly that the "transparency" of Chinese media is low.[138]

The prestige that is assigned officially to leaders in almost all Chinese workplaces militated against a formal system of official censors. A distinguished editor would generally have been able to overrule a censor anyway. The editor is the "responsible person" (*fuze ren*), who is fully authorized to take credit or blame for everything that appears from that unit. The chief editor at *Xinmin* claimed he alone decided the content of each issue. When asked whether the Party took any role in deciding what stories would be run, he said it did not—but this reply should be put in perspective of the fact that he and most others at the editorial meeting (which has several members, although he chairs it) are Party members. He said his paper has no censor. When asked why, the chief editor pointed his finger at his own nose.

If Shanghai editors are asked how they can be both "transparent" and propagandistic at the same time, they freely admit the "contradiction"—and unapologetically welsh on it. They say they have to support both of these opposite goals. The tension gives them options, a language for debate, which may be more useful than any straightforward formula could be for their situation. Expression is not totally free in the ideals of any country.[139] Editors can try to come to terms with both their journalistic vocations and their Party loyalties by maintaining this contradiction rather than by resolving it. The issue always arises untheoretically in any specific case; it requires decisions about particular manuscript articles.

Newspaper Logistics and Deadlines as Constraints on Censorship

At the *Liberation Daily,* the ratio of the number of available stories to the number needed to fill the eight-page, quarto-format paper varies considerably from day to day. About one-tenth of the articles come over the transom from stringers or others outside the paper (who occasionally send the same item to several journals simultaneously). Some reports come from neighborhood committees or the police. Letters to the editor (*duzhe lai xin*) arrive at the rate of about six hundred each day. The paper's Mass Work Department sorts these, flagging any that might warrant sending a reporter to investigate—either for the sake of a story, or to solve a problem that the letter raises.

The content of the *Liberation Daily* is decided at a meeting of about twenty editors each day at 6:00 P.M. Because this is a long (eight-page) paper, the session often must break to eat dinner before completing its work. Details do not come before the plenary editorial meeting. The chief editor stresses questions about the content of the next issue's first page, as well as critiques of the previous issue, published just that morning. Any editor who has come across ideas for news stories may also present them. The editors in charge of each department report very briefly about their pages for the next day. If further news breaks in the evening, the paper ordinarily can "go to bed" as late as 1:30 A.M. In extraordinary cases, it can even take a story after that.

At the *Wenhui News,* by the late 1980s, four-fifths of the articles were not features but arose directly from news of the previous day. Most drafts came in by 6:00 P.M. on that day, and by 10:00 or 11:00 at night, all the local stories had gone to bed. By 1:00 A.M., the last three pages of this four-sheet paper were fully prepared. By 2:00 A.M., the last Xinhua story could be accepted over the wire; an hour later, the first page was final. Printing began at 3:30 A.M., and by 5:30, the post office trucks arrived for distribution. By 7:00, this morning paper was commonly available, and by 9:00 the last subscriber within Shanghai had a copy.

An editor's main task, according to the chief at *Wenhui,* is not to change the content of drafts submitted by correspondents, but to put it in lively Chinese prose. He claimed meetings were ordinarily not called to discuss articles in progress. Many stories go through three or four revisions—still by hand in the late 1980s, not on computers—mainly to improve the language.[140] At that time, only final versions were sent to electronic machines for typesetting. In fact, editors sometimes did considerably more than advise on style. Reporters were supposed to know what was expected. If they turned in marginally heterodox material, there was not a great deal of time each day to censor it.

The content of the *Xinmin Evening News* was basically decided at an 8:00 meeting each morning, under the editor's chairmanship. By 11:30, the last story was edited; and during the noon hour, typesetters in the late 1980s plucked characters by hand from boxes, set them in frames, and proofread the galleys. These frames were sent to the *Liberation Daily* printing plant, where the first copy of *Xinmin Evening News* came off the presses about 1:00 P.M. The post office still did the distribution in Shanghai, and it got the evening paper to most subscribers' homes in the city at about 4:00 or 5:00.

House traditions within a particular paper can influence the stories it runs. *Wenhui News* staff are proud of having carried articles of pathbreaking importance in some past national politics. This tradition may give them some independence. The most famous example (of which the reformed paper's staff is ashamed) was Yao Wenyuan's 1965 review of a drama, *Hai Rui Is Dismissed from Office,* which was an opening salvo of the Cultural Revolution. But by 1980, *Wenhui* also pioneered the rehabilitation of Liu Shaoqi's memory, publishing an extensive interview with his widow, Wang Guangmei. In 1985, this newspaper was the first to publish articles reversing the 1955 purge of writer Hu Feng (whose attackers had later gone on to give China the Antirightist Campaign and the Cultural Revolution). *Wenhui* often fostered seminar discussions of arts and social theory that were much publicized. In the mid-1980s, it was the first to broach the Liu Zaifu case, and it was prominent among media discussing a controversial television documentary, the *River Elegy* (*He Shang,* on which more follows in this chapter and especially the next).

Most topics for *Wenhui* articles reportedly come from its own correspondents. The head editors also make suggestions for stories, based on their sense of current state issues. This mode of originating news stories (to the extent it is really dominant) is different from the one that was used in China before reforms. As long ago as the Yan'an guerrilla period, secret directives for journalists were supposed to be crucial in deciding which stories to print. This pattern continued into the 1960s and beyond, but official mandates to journalists became far less prominent later.[141] By the late 1980s, *Wenhui* had eight foreign correspondents, but most of its international stories nonetheless came from Xinhua.[142] Half of the *Wenhui* domestic articles from outside Shanghai also came from Xinhua, although the other half originated in an extensive network of forty stringers in other Chinese cities and the paper's own three "reporter's stations" (*jizhe zhan*) at Beijing, Guangzhou, and Tianjin. All *Wenhui News* articles about Shanghai were written by its own reporters.

The *Liberation Daily* used more stringer correspondents (*tongxun yuan*) than other Shanghai papers—three thousand of them by 1988—partly because it could fairly easily co-opt any CCP members with writing ability. Half its stories were found, cowritten, or completely written by these outside correspondents. On some pages, such as those for "social news," more than four-fifths of the articles came from stringers. Party policies helped to determine which of these to run, but such rules depended on circumstances far beyond official intentions.

Press reform, like all other aspects of change in China's slowly ending revolution, rose and subsided like a wave, even though the long-term pattern was toward more diverse media content. During campaigns against "bourgeois liberalization," journalistic reform efforts cooled. At other times, the "wind of press reform rose again."[143] Reporters at a Beijing meeting in mid-August of the relatively liberal year 1987 discovered that "press reports have been filled with so much of the same old stuff that the readers just do not go for it." Hu Jiwei published an article in the *People's Daily* arguing, "All [journalistic] work of the state should be placed under the supervision of the masses." At the Thirteenth CCP Congress, for the first time in two decades, correspondents could come to the meetings and report them directly (although this practice was reversed at the Fourteenth Congress, which postdated the crackdown of mid-1989). Press reform was not consistent; it was a bumpy trend.

What Was Broadcast During Reforms

Before reforms, newspapers provided radio and TV announcers with much of their material. During reforms, this relationship was partly reversed. Broadcast media, both national and international, supplied much of the news that increasingly kept print media concerned about their public credibility. Newspapers used wire services, of course, but their content over time was increasingly driven by topics that reader-viewers had seen on TV. This effect was partly dependent on technical changes in signal transmission, reductions in the real prices of receivers, and the rising ability of Shanghai people to see and hear broadcast programs. Such factors, which are not mainly political although they influenced politics, became more important in the 1970s and later.

Since 1971, the Shanghai Television Station has formally been able to make its own decisions on programming, although these are of course influenced by current Party lines. In the 1971–74 era, the content of programs haltingly changed from "great criticism" (*da pipan*) to news about politics and model examples of factory production—although these still did not attract much audience. As a programmer put it, "Ordinary people did not welcome that." By 1973, when the TV tower was built and the station first broadcast in color, the number of sets within range of its transmitter was about ten thousand. Most were still owned by work units rather than families. After 1976, programming acquired somewhat more variety. Public debate was still not seen on the screen, but factory news was spiced by dramas. The number of sets increased sharply after 1978. A decade later, by 1988, the count of TV receivers in the urban area was 98 percent of the number of households.[144]

A survey outside Shanghai showed that in July 1977, about half (54 percent) of all local news broadcast reports still came from "newspaper copy," whereas a year later this was down to 22 percent.[145] "Station editorials," which were aired but not published, also increased at this time. Throughout the country, broadcasters were now supposed to go out and develop their own stories. In 1980, the State Council sent out Document No. 107, declaring that broadcasters fell mainly under the leadership of their local governments, which in Shanghai was represented by a municipal bureau. In 1983, an all-China "working conference" of broadcasters passed resolutions that called strongly for more local management.[146] The stations were supposed to follow the functional agency for broadcasting at the next higher level.[147] For province-level Shanghai, that office was far away in Beijing, and the institutional changes gave broadcasters more opportunities to explore local news.

During the 1980s, the variety of entertainment programs also increased, especially in popular music. The Shanghai Television Station received letters from conservative viewers, including some in the army, disapproving of this trend. But it also received many appreciative letters, especially from youths.[148] The TV officials thus could often act as they wished. They continued to show new programs. Later in the decade, even the military took up these new styles and sponsored the production of conservative programs that aimed to attract young audiences. Crooners in PLA uniforms, often chanting patriotic songs but also showing considerable artistic technique in quasi-Western styles, appeared on Shanghai TV singing *tongsu* music (as described in chapter 2.4). Chinese folk tunes were also converted into a form of national popular music that the station proudly broadcast—and could justify continuing to transmit on the basis of frequent audience surveys.

After 1981, the amount of international news carried by Shanghai television rose, as did programs on general family topics (often with broad titles such as *Friend of Life*) and sports. By the middle of the decade, the station initiated more investigative and social programs, including a conservative one called *Law and Morals,* and a program of features called *News Perspectives.*[149]

In February 1984, as part of a general journalism reform, the Shanghai TV station established a "news center" that separated, more distinctly than before, the four steps in creating daily stories: choosing the topics, editing, recording, and broadcasting.[150] By the middle of the decade, TV news broadcasts had increased to five each day, and there was a strengthened emphasis on news that came from other East China places. Video footage from city stations elsewhere in the Shanghai delta, as well as from international news networks, was by this time perfectly normal on Shanghai TV. Video technology provided a kind of "transparency" for the TV medium that is difficult to match in print.

By 1986, there was a move to enliven the "social education" programs, which often in previous years had been "sit and talk" lectures, failing to attract much audience. Most of these lectures on political topics had involved one man, sitting at a desk and talking toward the camera, often reading from notes. Such programs in 1986 were thus reformed from a "closed" style to an "open" one. News features, for example, carried investigative reports often interesting for their scandals, not just their morals. Programs called *Conversations on the Marriage Law* and *Officials Can Intervene in Family Affairs* contained a good deal of human interest.[151] In 1986, Shanghai's regular television news broadcast hours were also more than a third longer than in the previous year.[152]

Broadcast entertainment programs were allowed more hours during the reforms, from 41 percent of Shanghai airtime in 1976 to 64 percent in 1985.[153] The Shanghai Television Station in the seven years ending at mid-decade created almost a hundred new productions, and it received national prizes for more than twenty.[154] Plans at that time called for more "comprehensive arts programs."[155] This slogan justified shows such as *The Great World,* named after Shanghai's main amusement park, or *The Great Dance Stage,* which attracted a wide audience. Whether or not this should be considered progress, puritans in the Party clearly disapproved of it. Much of the surveyed Shanghai audience spent time looking at it.

Stand-up dialogues between two comedians (*xiangsheng* in Mandarin, or *huaji* in Shanghainese) have been shown often on TV during the reforms. These "cross-talk" dialogues were very popular—and inexpensive for the television station to produce. The next chapter describes them and their political importance in more detail. As late as 1981–82, the Shanghai Television Station made only five or six feature programs annually, but this pattern changed sharply by the middle of the decade. In 1988, Shanghai TV produced about eighty features—which meant about that many hours of prime-time broadcasting. Somewhat over a hundred hours more were imported from foreign countries, with the rest coming from other parts of China. In 1970, the Chinese Central TV station in Beijing imported only 6 percent of its programs, but Shanghai TV already imported 13 percent. The 1990 portion of foreign programs was up to 17 percent for the central station, but for Shanghai it rose to 43 percent.

Chinese programs arrived in Shanghai from elsewhere partly through the Central Broadcasting Station in Beijing—which by government mandate obtains features from all over the country, much as emperors in bygone days once got tribute grain over the Grand Canal. Although the Central Station made some programs, Shanghai and Guangdong directors were by the late 1980s making a larger number of features. Shanghai regularly bartered its own feature programs with those from producers elsewhere, and it could usually obtain these more quickly this way than through Beijing. Shanghai's station acted, in effect, as the representative of city-run stations throughout East China. Important documentaries for intellectuals were made in Beijing, but for general audiences the capital became more important as a redistribution center than as a producer.

The most important television feature of the late 1980s came from the North: the interpretive documentary *River Elegy*. This six-part series, running in June 1988, showed the import of broadcast media for politics in China—as one year later, televised broadcasts of meetings with students and foreign radio on the Tiananmen killings also did. These programs were more significant for national politics than anything that happened in print media during those years. The purpose of Su Xiaokang's *River Elegy,* according to one article praising it, was to explain China's backwardness, dictatorship, inertia, and conservatism.[156] In this sense, it was seen as "a manifestation of patriotism." But the content was a radical critique of Chinese civilization as a basis for modern development.

The medium was new for this kind of message. A great deal could be said—and in all major Chinese media *was* said—about how such problems ought to be analyzed. A TV documentary was used to present unprecedentedly controversial ideas about the link between China's culture and modernization. Many political conservatives found these themes difficult to accept, almost traitorous, just as soon as they were aired.[157] The creators of the documentary were thus purged in mid-1989. Such ideas are bound to emerge again, for criticism and praise as well as clarification, in later debates about China's future. *River Elegy* will be analyzed in more detail, as a product of China's reform culture, in the discussion of China's new ideas.

Far less attention has been paid to *River Elegy*'s less sophisticated predecessors, especially the political soap opera entitled *New Star* (*Xin xing*). This series, beginning in 1986 but rebroadcast later, depicted conflict between an old cadre and a young reform leader. The twelve-part series was produced by Taiyuan

Television, the regional station in Shanxi. It was shown by several other local networks before its obvious popularity caused the central television network to run it. Tension between the two generations of leadership, along with the corrupt connections of old cadres in this story, made the subject politically tender—and interesting to audiences for that reason. Both the characters and the plot were complex: The protagonist, a young reformer, took an extremely activist attitude toward change, but the plot involved a love triangle, with the "new star" leader at its apex. The pasts and ambitions of his female interests were both rather murky. The story ends in uncertainty about the success of local reforms, though not about their great popularity.[158]

This electronic novel would almost surely have run afoul of high-placed politicians, and would not have been shown, if any one of a host of conditions had applied: if it had been produced by the central network as a high-profile presentation initially, if it had been easy for censors to review together in its many episodes (which emerged one by one), if the personality of the reformer had been more realistic, if the end of the plot had resulted in a straightforward reformist victory, or if the love subplots had become arguably salacious. The moral ambiguity of the story—a good cadre who fails to end a corrupt structure—caught the spirit of the times well, and the show became popular. *New Star* created much less stir among intellectuals than newspaper reportage by Liu Binyan on cadre corruption or than *River Elegy*. But this and less forward soap operas inspired as many people, including many less educated ones. Modern technologies—especially movies and television—brought the political concerns of literati to unprecedentedly wide audiences.

By the late 1980s, Shanghai broadcasters were producing and acquiring a greater variety of programs for listeners and viewers than anyplace else in the PRC.[159] The formal autonomy of stations to create their own programs in the short term rose and fell inversely with the government's demands for national uniformity.[160] In the long term, this autonomy was rising. Chinese broadcasters increasingly gave their audience more chances and reasons to learn new things.

Conclusion on Politicians, Journalists, and the Truth

Journalism tells its listeners or readers what they do not know, rather than what was implicit already in the structure of things they did know. This role, like any other intellectual function, tests for alternatives, for the unexpected, for "news" in the most comprehensive sense. Journalists are inherently in the business of distinguishing between choices of reality and unreality, fact and falsehood, but state authorities in China traditionally like to think they are the proper ones to make such choices.

Many modern alternatives arise from occupational groups. It is difficult for governments to benefit from the specialized efficiency of such groups without also putting up with their viewpoints. The Shanghai weekly press in the late

1980s diversified to address them. New journals were printed in many fields. Papers were published in business areas particularly, and magazines appeared with titles such as *Shanghai Mechanization News* or *Shanghai Industry and Economy News.* The late 1980s also saw a revival of *News Report,* a paper for businesspeople carrying stories about the international and domestic trading of Shanghai firms.[161] *Social Sciences Weekly,* published by the city's academy, raised theoretical questions in a less popular vein than those of the *World Economic Herald,* edited on the same premises. New publications also emerged in fast-expanding service fields, including the *Shanghai Legal System News* and a bimonthly journal called *Lawyers and the Legal System.*[162] A few of these closed in the 1990s, but others were established to serve functional groups.

Precisely because Chinese bureaucrats had long treated journals as legitimate tools of the state, specialized interests could take press diversification by the 1980s as official concessions of status. Journals have long played direct governmental roles in China, for example in the way they have handled letters "to the editor"—often in fact written and read as complaints to the government. Although newspapers are not legally organs of the state in the PRC, old Chinese customs of petition to authority have continued in letters to newspapers.

The fully governmental nature of this role is underlined by the fact that government offices also receive many such letters.[163] Often petitioners send the same missive to state offices and to newspapers, in the hope that someone who can help may respond. At least one citizen said, "We have a lot of things to tell the leaders, but we wonder whether the leaders hear and see them." Another said the leadership's frequent critiques of corruption would not mean much until cadres who were found guilty had their names printed in the papers—because publicity was the best solvent of official corruption.[164]

China's media are inherently powerful, as unavoidably the Fourth Estate is in any country. As journalists become more professionalized in the future and address more specialized audiences, they may emerge further from their subordinate relationship to government. It would be naïve to expect this change to be fast or smooth, but evidence suggests that the infrastructure for it is stronger now than before the reforms began. The uncertain trend of change in Chinese journalism over the reform years correlates with some very hesitant specialization of the role of the state. Politics is not quite so all-consuming a business in late revolutionary China as it once was—for example, during the late 1950s or 1960s. Old leaders try to restore the previous atmosphere, in which they developed their own personal abilities. But many Chinese, having experienced that the state's coercive force is often used in ways that violate their common ethics, have tentatively and implicitly begun to doubt the ancient tradition that governments have a role in morals.

When the chief editor of the *Wenhui News* was asked why the circulation of his paper had risen more slowly than that of the *Xinmin Evening News,* he cited two broad and revealing reasons: Politics, he explained, had become a decreasing focus of popular interest during the reforms. Also, there was an increase (by more than one million) in the number of Shanghai retired people. The editor said they were less concerned with public issues because their careers had ended. Their lives had not been easy. They now had a great deal of free time to read newspapers, but their interest in serious public material was less than he thought it should be.

Satellite dishes may well further this trend in the future. In late 1993, Minister of Radio, Film, and Television Wang Feng justified rules against satellite dishes, saying, "Such control is beneficial to the cultivation of patriotism among our citizens, safeguarding the superior traditions of the Chinese race, promoting socialist civilization, and maintaining social stability."[165] By 1996, the PRC government required licenses for these satellite antennae in urban areas, but not in rural areas. The main means of control was commercial threat against satellite programmers, such as Rupert Murdoch's company, which had other interests in China. Most satellite programs in Chinese were designed for Taiwan and Hong Kong markets; they had PRC viewers but were politically self-censored. This policy was, from a conservative PRC viewpoint, successful in the mid-1990s; it made no hermetic seal against uncensored information, however. Any striking political news about China, e.g. in case of future urban demonstrations, would come into the country through many channels.

New media, especially regional and international television, only complement the oldest medium: word of mouth. Surveys near Shanghai have showed that some decrease in reliance on radio among peasants was balanced by increases in newspaper reading—but especially by greater reliance on face-to-face talking.[166] There is now an increased variety of public information, and more about which to talk. People over most of the past dozen years found they could speak more freely as the reforms progressed. So the "grass telegraph" apparently became even more important than previously as a source of credible news. New electronic media almost surely spurred the increase of its influence by providing more news about which to gossip.

The press corps, both in and around China, may further the Fourth Estate's inevitable role in limiting politicians when they abuse authority. State leaders may oppose the press in this function. But long-term diversification of the media, such as is now occurring, would correlate with real political development more closely than would the temporary rise of better politicians—or editors—unless they furthered this trend toward more structural independence.

Notes

1. Quoted in John Street, "Popular Culture = Political Culture? Some Thoughts on Postmodernism's Relevance to Politics," *Politics* 11:2 (1991), p. 22.

2. See Jiang Shan, "The Complex Purge of the CCP in Journalism Circles," *Zhonggong yanjiu* (Chinese Communist Research) 23:8 (August 15, 1989), pp. 46–52.

3. See Jonathan Mirsky, "China Braces Itself for the Great Purge," *Observer,* August 27, 1989.

4. This dynamic equilibrium of thaws and freezes is classically detailed in the books of Merle Goldman, *Literary Dissent in Communist China* (Cambridge: Harvard University Press, 1967) and *China's Intellectuals: Advise and Dissent* (Cambridge: Harvard University Press, 1981), where the overall logic shows a balance only somewhat less stable than is commonly assumed in the field of her spouse, who is an economist.

5. Godwin Chu of the Institute of Culture and Communication at the East-West Center in Honolulu provides evidence from attitude surveys (as this present research does from technological and economic data) to suggest that this shift "is definitely beginning to take place." See his article in *Centerviews,* July–August 1989, p. 7.

6. A parallel argument, that the Cultural Revolution was an unintended rather than a direct or well-controlled result of anyone's thought, may be found in Lynn White, *Policies of Chaos: The Organizational Causes of Violence in China's Cultural Revolution* (Princeton: Princeton University Press, 1989). Another description of recent hotchpotch policy, serving no coherent interest at all, involves economic arguments; see the same author's *Shanghai Shanghaied? Uneven Taxes in Reform China* (Hong Kong: Centre of Asian Studies working paper, University of Hong Kong, 1989). That research also contains notions about the effect of rural industrialization on the profits of state enterprises, and thus on government revenues—and the desperation of high officials now that old sources of money are no longer available. Unintended decentralization, uncontrolled markets, and new technologies also affect media and their audiences.

7. Jacques Delors, president of the European Commission, has put this in a stark and narrow fashion, saying that "the lightning flash of freedom through the communist countries," was partly caused by "rock music and American movies." See *World Press Review,* September 1989, p. 28.

8. *Zhongguo xinwen nianjian, 1983 ban* (1983 China News Yearbook), An Gang et al., eds. (Beijing: Zhongguo Shehui Kexue Chuban She, 1983), p. 16. Information about the earlier history of Shanghai newspapers can be found in Mary Backus Rankin, *Early Chinese Revolutionaries: Radical Intellectuals in Shanghai and Chekiang, 1902–1911* (Cambridge: Harvard University Press, 1971).

9. He used the term "*you yingxiang de bao*" and included major Party organs—of which the *Wenhui News* is not one—in the category. He unabashedly said the third category of media mentioned below, including all evening papers, was "uninfluential" (*mei yingxiang*).

10. This book devotes less attention to the *Herald* than to other Shanghai papers, both because its reach extended far beyond Shanghai and because more specialized research on this has been done by Hsiao Ching-chang, Yang Meirong, and others. See also Li Cheng and Lynn White, "China's Technocratic Movement and the *World Economic Herald*," *Modern China* 17:3 (July 1991), pp. 342–88.

11. Evening papers are often mentioned generically as *wanbao*. The second-largest circulation newspaper in the nation, after *Xinmin wanbao,* was or is Guangzhou's *Yangcheng Evening News (Yangcheng wanbao).* This chapter takes evening papers more seriously than state discourse in China does.

12. The figure 21 percent (367 papers) was given in *Xinwen yuekan* (News Monthly) (Beijing) 1986:1, p. 4.

13. He used the expression "*dang de baozhi*," and "institutional paper" translates as "*jigou bao.*" Most information not otherwise referenced in this book comes from interviews.

14. A 1986 "random sample" of nearly two thousand *Liberation Daily* (*JFRB*) readers showed that 66 percent were male, with 34 percent female. By occupation, 25 percent were cadres, another 24 percent were workers, 20 percent were cultural workers (mostly

teachers), 19 percent were managers, 9 percent were students, 2 percent were retired, and 2 percent were others. By age, in 1988, nearly half—47 percent—of the readers of this Party organ were "young," and another 44 percent were "middle-aged," i.e., between 35 and 55. Only 9 percent were older. Unsurprisingly, more than half (53 percent) of the *Liberation Daily* readers were in state-owned enterprises, whose Party cells presumably encouraged these firms' subscriptions to this particular paper; and another 35 percent worked in CCP or government offices. Only 10 percent worked for collectives. Two percent of the copies went to other people, and less than one-half of 1 percent went to private workers.

15. An example for which *Liberation Daily* took the lead in doing this was during the intense October-December 1979 local Shanghai questioning of the economic and environmental advisability of the Baoshan Iron and Steel Factory, heavily advocated by central ministries but openly and scathingly criticized on the pages of the Shanghai Party organ. See almost any issue of the paper in those months.

16. An additional 6 percent of all 1986 papers were pre-Liberation, 4 percent were from the 1960s, and 9 percent were from the 1970s. *Xinwen yuekan* 1986:1, p. 4.

17. For three months in 1986, another provincial paper was also printed in Shanghai until this proved uneconomical—and the most interesting aspect of this experiment is that the journal was the *Guangzhou Daily,* also Cantonese.

18. The amount of paper consumed in 1987, according to one interviewee, was 34,600 metric tons.

19. This was based not on Shanghai figures, unfortunately, but on a 1982 Beijing survey. The time of reading for 39 percent of the sample, however, was "uncertain." *Zhongguo xinwen nianjian, 1983,* p. 277.

20. Ibid., p. 294.

21. A survey of Beijing readers of *China Youth News* (*Zhongguo qingnian bao*), asking what else they also read, showed that more than three-quarters also looked at the *Beijing Evening News* (*Beijing wanbao*)—whereas the runner-up, *People's Daily* (*RMRB*), interested less than half. This was based on a 1982 survey in Beijing and throughout China published in *Zhongguo xinwen nianjian, 1983,* p. 527. The other kinds of papers mentioned, in declining order of total issues, were "local comprehensive newspapers," "national papers," "evening papers," "scientific and technical papers," and "specialized enterprise papers."

22. *Zhongguo xinwen nianjian, 1983,* p. 80.

23. Zhang Linlan, "Women de tansuo—jiefang hou de Shanghai 'Xinmin bao' " (Our Exploration—Shanghai's *Xinmin News* After Liberation), in Chen Mingde et al., *"Xinmin bao" chunqiu* (The Spring and Autumn of the *Xinmin News*) (Chongqing: Chongqing Chuban She, 1987), p. 408.

24. A *lilong bao* could also be "specialized" for that purpose, thus a *zhuanye bao* too. The movements for such papers are discussed in Zhang Linlan, "Women de tansuo," pp. 410–11.

25. Zhao said news should be "short, shorter, then even shorter; broad, broader, then even broader; soft, softer, then even softer." (*Duan xie, duan xie, zai duan xie; guang xie, guang xie, zai guang xie; ruan xie, ruan xie, zai ruan xie*). Although he was not dubbed a rightist in the turmoil that followed, two members of his editorial board and several reporters were sent to places such as Qinghai province for labor reform. Mao Zedong personally met with Zhao at this time (and later, also in 1958 and 1961), and Zhao turned over the chief editorship to the head of the new CCP group in the paper, Shu Renqiu.

26. Zhang Linlan, "Women de tansuo," p. 421.

27. The evening papers in Guangzhou (*Yangcheng Evening News*) and Beijing (*Beijing*

Evening News) were allowed to resume publication in 1980. The *Xinmin* chief editor, when asked about the delay of his paper in an interview, gave no reason for it, although a general lack of central budgeters to give Shanghai money for any purpose may be relevant.

28. *"Baoshe neibu jilei de wenti ye feichang zhi duo."* Zhang Linlan, "Women de tansuo," p. 422.

29. Calculated from *Zhongguo xinwen nianjian, 1983,* p. 539, and *Zhongguo xinwen nianjian, 1987 ban* (1987 China News Yearbook), He Guangguang et al., eds. (Beijing: Zhongguo Shehui Kexue Chuban She, 1987), p. 410.

30. Guangzhou's *Yangcheng Evening News* by mid-1988 had a slightly smaller total circulation (at 1.7 million the second-largest paper in China)—including some among Shanghai residents, especially those whose families were originally Cantonese.

31. These *hangkong ban* and *fenyin dian* were mentioned in Zhang Linlan, "Women de tansuo," p. 429, and in several interviews.

32. *"Xian zhongyang, hou difang."* Dangdai Zhongguo de guangbo dianshi, shang* (Radio and Television in China Today, volume 1), Li Hua et al., eds. (Beijing: Zhongguo Shehui Kexue Chuban She, 1987), p. 174.

33. *Dangdai Zhongguo, xia* (volume 2), p. 80.

34. *Dangdai Zhongguo, shang,* p. 38.

35. Ibid., p. 51.

36. *Shanghai wenhua nianjian, 1987* (Shanghai Culture Yearbook, 1987), Liu Zhenyuan et al., eds. (Shanghai: Zhongguo Da Baike Chuban She, 1987), p. 133.

37. The only two exceptions are an interesting and odd pair: Beijing and Tibet. *Dangdai Zhongguo, shang,* pp. 40–42.

38. By mid-1975, five of the frequencies were normally in color. *Shanghai wenhua nianjian, 1987,* p. 133.

39. Not just in the research on media, but also in many economic fields, there was more important change in the early 1970s than most periodizations suggest; these 1973 events are only examples. See *Shanghai wenhua . . . 1987,* pp. 451–52.

40. The year on this technical survey concerning signal reception was 1984, and the claim was 97 percent coverage; *Dangdai Zhongguo, xia,* p. 406. A very knowledgeable informant who had left Shanghai, however, put this lower in that top decile—and suggested that many media inflate the results of surveys to claim greater influence.

41. The conclusions of these surveys have not been published. On this and many other PRC subjects, the amount of secret information available in government files is immense. See *Dangdai Zhongguo, shang,* p. 317, however, and the work on Beijing audiences by Brantly Womack.

42. *Shanghai shi chengxiang diaocha dui,* whose results were reported (proudly) at an interview in the Shanghai Television Station.

43. See the summary of work by Sevanti Ninan in *Wilson Quarterly* (Winter 1996), p. 138.

44. *Zhongguo xinwen nianjian, 1983,* p. 258.

45. Interview at the Shanghai Television Station, August 1988.

46. Television was the most important for 28 percent of peasants, in next place after radio. *Zhongguo xinwen nianjian, 1983,* p. 259.

47. The city's *Publications Digest (Baokan wenzhai)* and *Shanghai Translations (Shanghai yibao)* are collected from both domestic and foreign presses. Information about the popularity of Beijing's digest *Wenzhai bao,* whose readership compares only to the TV guide and *Beijing Evening News* in that city, is in *Zhongguo xinwen nianjian, 1983,* p. 277.

48. *Dangdai Zhongguo, xia,* p. 154, also reports that the portion in Beijing was over 90 percent, although it is unclear whether the city/province difference, rather than differences in the questioning procedure, accounts for this difference.

49. Shi Tianchuan, *Guangbo dianshi gailun* (General Outline on Broadcasting and Television) (Shanghai: Fudan Daxue Chuban She, 1987), p. 52.

50. The number of magazine issues soared by 129 percent. *Zhongguo shehui tongji ziliao, 1987* (Chinese Social Statistics, 1987), Social Statistics Office, State Statistical Bureau, ed. (Beijing: Zhongguo Tongji Chuban She, 1987), p. 5. Figures for the intervening years, and for earlier ones, are provided in *Zhongguo chuban nianjian, 1985* (China Publishing Yearbook, 1985), China Publishers' Association, ed. (Beijing: Shangwu Yinshu Guan, 1985), pp. 2–3.

51. *"Xian guangbo zhan." Shanghai wenhua . . . 1987,* p. 133.

52. *Dangdai Zhongguo, shang,* p. 399.

53. Ibid., pp. 365 and 375.

54. The reports from Zhejiang are too high to be credibly compared with those from other places, but the strategic location of that province (and fears of invasion that date from the 1950s) may explain part of this. See *Dangdai Zhongguo, xia,* pp. 407–9.

55. *Dangdai Zhongguo, xia,* p. 405.

56. Wang called these *jingji diqu bao. Xinwen ziyou lunji* (Collection of Essays on Journalistic Freedom) (Shanghai: Wenhui Chuban She, 1988), p. 89.

57. These figures come from a survey taken by the *Liberation Daily* concerning its own distribution on August 31, 1988. A passion for exact numbers that typifies many recent Chinese efforts in the statistical field meant the figures were reported to the last issue.

58. Very few copies of this paper find their way into rural areas, though a few are ordered by county schools. The chief editor of the *Wenhui News* also confirmed the heavily urban distribution not only of other papers for intellectuals such as the *Guangming Daily,* but also of the *Xinmin Evening News.*

59. Interview with a journalist who is very familiar with *Wenhui News.*

60. *Wenhui News* was the only newspaper not published in Beijing to appear significantly in a 1982 survey of that city's readers. At the time, it was the tenth most widely perused publication in the capital—where many people spend much time reading newspapers. One-third of the *Wenhui* readers were state cadres, and only a quarter were workers. *Zhongguo xinwen nianjian, 1983,* pp. 273–74.

61. For more on this, see Lynn White, "Local Newspapers and Community Change," in *Moving a Mountain: Cultural Change in China,* Godwin C. Chu and Francis L.K. Hsu, eds. (Honolulu: University Press of Hawaii, 1979), pp. 76–112.

62. This Shanghai boast comes from a national, not a local, source: *Dangdai Zhongguo, xia,* p. 405.

63. *Shanghai wenhua . . . 1987,* p. 134.

64. This information comes from interviews with Shanghai television officials, but also from watching the news coverage of local stories from all parts of East China on Shanghai stations in 1988.

65. The Zhejiang program was *Jingji xinxi* and the Shanghai one *Baokan wenxuan. Dangdai Zhongguo, shang,* p. 104.

66. Ibid., p. 86.

67. Su-Lu-Gan-Wan Jierang Diqu Xinwen Gongzuo Xiezuo Hui; see *Jingji xinwen bao* (Economic News), January 26, 1989.

68. The name of this *Haixia zhi sheng* station may have been inspired by that of the Voice of America, *Meiguo zhi yin.* See *Shanghai wenhua . . . 1987,* p. 135.

69. On January 1, 1988, this station broadcast a feature about Zhao Zukang, the

KMT's acting mayor of Shanghai, who remained in the city and later became a deputy mayor under the Communists. *FBIS,* December 27, 1987, p. 50, reporting radio of the same day.

70. Interview at the *Liberation Daily.* The figures reported were 9,040,000 yuan for the period January through July 1988; 2,190,000 for all of 1983; 1,100,000 for 1978; and 40,000 for 1973.

71. This is based on calculations from figures offered in Shanghai interviews with journalists.

72. Interview at the *Liberation Daily.*

73. The State Council declared that no new paper mills could be constructed in tourist regions, near hot springs, or in other nature protection areas. *Jiangsu fazhi bao* (Jiangsu Legal System News), January 24, 1989.

74. *Dangdai Zhongguo, shang,* p. 26.

75. From statistics in ibid., it can be calculated that the 1967, 1977, and 1984 portions of total broadcasting budgets that went for buildings and equipment ("basic construction costs," *jiben jianshe fei,* as distinct from operating costs, *shiye fei*) declined respectively from 38 to 28 to 22 percent. These figures should probably be treated with caution, because they may understate the extent of spending by localities for microwave relays and city-run stations.

76. *Shanghai wenhua . . . 1987,* p. 133.

77. This *guanggao jiemu* was called *Zhu nin jiankang* and is documented in *Dangdai Zhongguo, shang,* p. 104.

78. This emphasis comes from an ex-reporter in Shanghai, now living in the United States, to whom the author is grateful.

79. The exact number of employees in early October 1988 was 949. This included 141 CCP members on the writing/editing staff of 207. Calculation from the figures implies that only 32 percent of the paper's nonwriting staff were Party members.

80. The average basic wage at the *Liberation Daily* in August 1988 was 101 yuan per month, with reporters receiving a slightly higher average of 109 yuan. The thirteen top cadres on the whole staff got an average of 180 yuan. The total value of average compensation was about double this basic amount—a pattern that was very common in the late 1980s also at other units in the state sector, no matter whether they were government offices or economic firms, and when they were large urban businesses, no matter whether they were state-owned or cooperative. About half of the increment above the basic wage, i.e. an average of 47 yuan at this newspaper, comprised subsidies (*butie*) for haircuts, commuting, newspapers, and other items—plus a basic wage supplement (*jintie*) that was mainly a means for firms to compensate their employees, when they could get authorization to keep the money, at rates higher than the standard wage rates, which were low because of nationally mandated rules. The other half of the total increment over the basic wage was the bonus (*jiangjin*). This was highly variable, depending mainly on each supervisor's assessment of the employee's productivity. In the newspaper, it was also based—as presumably the basic salary was—on the political sensitivity of the employee's work. The number and quality of articles that had been written or edited was a major factor for determining bonuses of the writing staff. The person with the highest salary at the *Liberation Daily* earned about 400 yuan per month in the late 1980s because of a high bonus, over 200 yuan. For most employees, the average bonus was about 50 or 60 yuan. Bonuses were less important in the wages of the *Wenhui News.* The chief editor, with the highest salary, got only 280 yuan per month and 20 more yuan in bonus. Other leading cadres received 160 yuan, with bonuses of about 40 yuan; good editors received salaries of about 140 yuan, with similar bonuses. Regular reporters got about 100 yuan in salary, but with larger bonuses of about 60 yuan. The portion of bonus in total pay thus rose as

the basic salary decreased. Nonbonus supplements to compensation, however, presumably correlated directly with seniority, responsibility, and salary. (*Jintie* wage increases may have begun in hardship posts, where they are still used. Miners in dangerous jobs, for example, receive "post subsidies" [*gangwei jintie*]; and staff sent to work in difficult places may get "area subsidies" [*diqu jintie*]. But the *Liberation Daily* and other Shanghai employers had few hardship posts, and these *jintie* seem to have evolved as a means of raising compensation without violating rules against higher wages [*gongzi*].) Based on interviews in Shanghai and Hong Kong.

81. In the autumn of 1988, forty-five cadres had left the *Liberation Daily* on a *lixiu* basis, in most cases still coming to work there on most days; and seventy had retired with *tuixiu* status.

82. In exact terms, there were 207 reporters and 253 university graduates, according to an editor at *Liberation Daily*. Of the reporters, 77 percent graduated in the 1980s, 5 percent in the 1970s, 13 percent in the 1960s, and 4 percent in the 1950s.

83. This pattern at *Liberation Daily* contrasts with the procedures at *Xinmin Evening News*, although the latter paper hired fewer new reporters in the late 1980s.

84. Interview with an editor at the *Wenhui News*, November 1988.

85. Ibid. Statistics on actual promotion rates in Chinese schools could be used to paint a picture of this situation that would show more differences in various years of Mao's time. But this editor's views are more interesting without such refinements. His main points, about the long-term harmful educational effects of the Cultural Revolution and of some economic reforms, reflect the views held by many Chinese intellectuals, including some young ones.

86. *Xinwen yuekan* 1986:1, p. 13.

87. *Zhongguo xinwen nianjian, 1987*, pp. 193–94.

88 The total portion of all these personnel with college educations was 45 percent: 49 percent among reporters, 51 percent among leading cadres, and 56 percent among mid-level cadres. Of the college graduates, only 15 percent had specialized in journalism; over two-thirds had majored in other humanistic subjects. Ibid.

89. A portion, 29 percent, had begun in teaching, and some of these surely had been sent-down youths; 17 percent had been in industrial labor; 13 percent in the army; and 11 percent in Party or mass work. Over 30 percent had begun as stringers, often reporting from these earlier careers, not as professional journalists. The Jiangsu press corps was not highly paid, then averaging 70 yuan per month, not counting bonuses, which may have doubled that. Ibid.

90. *Dangdai Zhongguo, xia,* p. 278.

91. The raw data are in ibid., pp. 278–79.

92. Ibid., p. 284.

93. These were "*gongkai zhaoping*." Ibid., p. 298.

94. Interview with a professional director at the station, who was in charge of the testing procedures, August 1988.

95. In addition to Fudan, there is also a Beijing Broadcasting College (Beijing Guangbo Xueyuan). "Distribution" (*fenpei*) is the common word, even during the middle reform period, for the way people get jobs.

96. There was, however, a difference: Because TV jobs were popular, the wages were lower (though more stable) than in the few private or collective sector jobs that similar youths might sometimes obtain.

97. *Dangdai Zhongguo, xia,* p. 391.

98. Average wages in television were about 100 yuan per month only. Bonuses (*jiangjin*) totaled a similar amount, but these were divided into two approximately equal parts. For this television station and most other work units in Shanghai by the late 1980s,

roughly half (50 yuan) of the bonus did not depend on work performance but was the sum of small compensations—often in kind rather than money—for transport, for books and newspapers, for cold drinks in summer, for food (especially in the station canteen), for coming to work on any summer day when the temperature reached 35 degrees Centigrade, and for other small amenities. The rest of the bonus, averaging about 50 yuan in the TV station and many other units but varying considerably among workers, was based on supervisors' estimates of the employee's productivity. Some typical names for these allowances were the *jiaotong fei* for transport, the *shubao fei* for books and newspapers, the *lengyin fei* for drinks in summer, and the *tianre fei* for extra money on hot days—but this is not an exhaustive list. The categories of such fees differ from unit to unit and from time to time, but the habit of having them is general in the PRC (and to some extent, in other Chinese places such as Hong Kong or Taiwan). Chinese broadcasting stations, like many other institutions, use more people than are on their books as "permanent employees." At the end of 1984, throughout the country, "employees outside the plan" comprised 15 percent of the total in broadcasting. "Temporary workers" were another 8 percent, and "contract system employees" were 1 percent. The Chinese terms, respectively, are *guding zhigong, jihua wai yonggong, linshi gong,* and *hetong zhi zhigong,* out of a total of 271,218 *zhigong. Dangdai Zhongguo, xia,* p. 280.

99. Ibid., pp. 294 and 296, does not entirely clarify the significance of this change. If other writers are able to help here, they are asked to do so.

100. *Shanghai wenhua . . . 1987,* p. 136.

101. Prof. Wu Guoguang supplied this information while he was a graduate student at Princeton.

102. Interviews reported that these resettlements were arranged not by the Railroad Bureau directly, but by the work units of affected residents. The extent to which the Railroad Bureau had to bear these costs of its project is unknown but may be small.

103. Some books, not labeled for internal use (*neibu*), contain information that is restricted only because they are also not labeled with any price. They are merely "distributed" (*faxing*), not sold—a status that makes nearly as much economic sense as is implicit for most books, which are actually sold but at prices set far below cost. Friends of the author in Shanghai could loan him some such books legally, because these were not formally limited in circulation—but the data in them would otherwise have been hard to obtain, since they are not available in libraries or bookstores.

104. *Xinxi xing* vs. *xuanchuan xing.*

105. This formulation was used in 1996 by Lu Ping, the Party's spokesperson for Hong Kong, when he was asked what freedom of speech would be available there after mid-1997 for any journalist who might advocate independence for Taiwan. Lu's distinction between "reporting" and "advocacy" was better PRC politics than general epistemology. Authority (here the state) alone knows which is which, in any particular case.

106. Interview with Shu Renqiu. The term "radicals" in this paraphrase translates as *liang xiao,* the "two schools" of radicals at Beijing and Qinghua universities important during the early 1970s, but used in this saying with a more general meaning.

107. See Lynn White, "Local Newspapers," pp. 76–112.

108. Interview with the chief editor of Shanghai's most prominent national newspaper for intellectuals. This distinguished cadre had been in a position to know about Mao's role in the rise of *Reference Information.*

109. For more, see Henry G. Schwartz's early work "The *Ts'an-k'ao Hsiao-hsi:* How Well Informed Are Chinese Officials About the Outside World," *China Quarterly* 27 (July 1966), pp. 54–83; and the more recent monograph of Jörg-Meinhard Rudolph, *Cankao-Xiaoxi: Foreign News in the Propaganda System of the People's Republic of China* (Baltimore: University of Maryland School of Law, 1984).

110. Interview with an editor at *Liberation Daily*.

111. The *Liberation Daily* history during the Antirightist Campaign and Great Leap Forward, then during the periods of criticism by and against Peng Dehuai, and then in the era when radicals led by Zhang Chunqiao and Yao Wenyuan of the Gang of Four controlled Shanghai journalism, are all large stories beyond the scope of this book. Staffers of the newspaper in late reforms were writing this history.

112. *Rujia shengchan, Fajia zaofan. Zhonghua Renmin Gonghe Guo jingji dashi ji, 1949–1980* (Chronicle of Economic Events in the PRC, 1949–1980), Fang Weizhong et al., eds. (Beijing: Zhongguo Shehui Kexue Chuban She, 1984), p. 528.

113. An all-time world record for careful failure to report the news was set after the Tangshan earthquake of July 27, 1976, in which some 250,000 people died. This was, in terms of the number of lives lost, the worst urban earthquake in history. Two Xinhua reporters, Zhang Guangyou and Luan Zhongxin, rushed to Tangshan overland, saw people frantically trying to dig out seventy thousand who had been trapped in building cave-ins, and interviewed responsible managers who said that ten thousand coal miners had also been buried alive. Using a military telephone to Beijing, the two reporters were able to file this story. But it was never published. Radical editors thought it might distract people's attention from the really vital news of mid-1976 (the grand successes of the class struggle against Deng Xiaoping). In 1990s terminology, they deemed it not "reporting" but "advocacy" because it might take minds off more important facts. Public newspapers later reported the earthquake only in terms of the official rescue efforts, after these had begun. See Jing Jun, "The Working Press in China," unpublished paper sent to the author, 1985, p. 21.

114. In the first half of 1979, economic reports took up 56 percent of the airtime on Liaoning radio, for example; but this was up to 73 percent in the next six months. A national survey on the second half of the year showed that 61 percent of the airtime was dedicated to economic topics then. *Dangdai Zhongguo, shang*, p. 99.

115. *Zhongguo xinwen nianjian, 1983*, p. 489. *News Front* (*Xinwen zhanxian*) changed its name in 1960, just for a while apparently, to *News Profession* (*Xinwen yewu*).

116. *Zhongguo xinwen nianjian, 1983*, p. 491ff. cite *neibu* serial guideline publications for Heilongjiang, Jiangsu, Anhui, and Beijing broadcasters only.

117. The author is deeply indebted to an informant for this and other information.

118. Allison Liu Jernow, "An Attempt at Amicable Divorce: Legislating for a Free Press," *Human Rights Tribune* 3:2 (Summer 1992), p. 16.

119. *XMWB*, March 19, 1989.

120. This was a case of *"kebei, kexiao"* results of conflict between *lingdao bumen* and *guangda duzhe. XMWB*, February 28, 1989.

121. *Xinwen ziyou lunji*, p. 83.

122. The First Emperor (Qin Shi Huang) is famous for burning the books of scholars. On the Shanghai events, see *Post*, December 29, 1987.

123. *CD*, March 5, 1994.

124. This *junshi guanli* prevented the production of *ziban jiemu. Dangdai Zhongguo, shang*, p. 96.

125. Ibid., p. 122.

126. Ibid., p. 65, lists the names of these model productions.

127. This was pointed out by the famous editor Hu Jiwei in *Xinwen ziyou lunji*, p. 5 of the introduction. The same point is made by another writer on p. 3 of the main text.

128. *"Guanxin qunzhong"* was refused broadcast time by the Tianjin TV station. *Dangdai Zhongguo, shang*, p. 97.

129. *"Ziban pinglun."* The "road walking" in the next sentence was under the slogan *"ziji zoulu." Shanghai wenhua . . . 1987*, p. 133.

REFORM OF MEDIA 139

130. These advanced folk were "*xianjin renwu*," but the critical reporting was "*piping xing baodao.*" The examples are from Zhejiang, within tuning distance from Shanghai. *Dangdai Zhongguo, shang,* p. 125.

131. *CD,* February 9, 1988.

132. The Chinese titles of these supplements, in the order the text mentions them, are: *Baokan wenzhai, Zhibu shenghuo lianzhai xiaoshuo, Jiefang ribao nongcun ban, Shanghai jingji xinxi bao,* and *Xuesheng Yingwen bao.*

133. *Shanghai jingji 1987* (Shanghai's Economy, 1987), Xu Zhihe, Ling Yan, Gu Renzhang et al., eds. (at the Shanghai Academy of Social Sciences) (Shanghai: Shanghai Renmin Chuban She, 1987), p. 12, indicates that each reader received only 0.16 of a daily newspaper on average in 1978, but by 1986 the number rose to 0.45. The average annual increase in magazine issues was sharp: from 4.31 to 24.78.

134. See Lynn White and Li Cheng, "The Diversification of China's Intellectuals," *Issues and Studies* 24:9 (1988), pp. 50–77.

135. *Zhongguo xinwen nianjian, 1983,* p. 501. At least seven of the parallel secret journals for members, published by other provincial CCP committees, are also entitled *Zhibu shenghuo.* This source remarks that although the Cultural Revolution period staff of Shanghai's *Zhibu shenghuo* was controlled by supporters of Jiang Qing, the publication ceased (oddly) in April 1971. Why this occurred more than five years before the ouster of the Gang of Four is unclear, but it may be further evidence of 1971 being a watershed toward reform (despite the emphasis on 1976 and 1978 in both CCP and Western periodizations, which tend to pay almost exclusive attention to events in Beijing, as if the rest of China did not really exist).

136. This parallels an argument by Lucian Pye that dissent in some (young) generations is more acceptable in China than dissent in other (older) ones. See Pye's important book on *The Dynamics of Chinese Politics* (Cambridge, MA: Oelgeschlager, Gunn, and Hain, 1981).

137. At this time, for example, a Japanese tourist had been murdered in Shanghai— and newspapers were prominently carrying the story, even though the police work was not finished, the culprit had not been apprehended, and the motives were unclear. In this case, a suspect was later indicted, and officials claimed the motive was robbery. It is important that, in the reform period, journalists can sometimes print the information they have, even before a case is officially or finally evaluated.

138. This editor was speaking openly to a foreigner. In mid-1989, he took an apparently conservative stance; but a wide variety of people at that time were more disturbed by the killings in Beijing than they admitted in public.

139. U.S. law, for example, frames some limits on free expression, in cases of immediate danger. Efforts to restrict political expressions, such as flag burning, have been obvious even in countries whose elites idealize freedom more than China's do.

140. The *Wenhui News* editor was not optimistic, when interviewed shortly before 1989, that good software would soon be available to computerize news drafting; the slowness of learning and using the current systems had been discouraging. He was willing to be proven wrong (presumably by faster chips to access larger random access memories, which could contain dictionaries accounting for the disyallabic and tonal traits of Chinese). But he wanted to be shown first, before making any big investment. His newspaper at that time used computers only for typesetting and accounting.

141. Interviews with editors in Shanghai's three largest-circulation newspapers all included questions about *Xinwen zhanxian.* Their responses about *News Front* were uniform and seemed not especially designed for foreign consumption.

142. Interview with the chief editor of the *Wenhui News.* The foreign offices were in New York, Washington, Paris, Tokyo, Mexico City, Manila, and (assigned but not yet

accorded a visa) New Delhi. In late 1988, the only other Chinese papers with correspondents abroad were believed to be the *People's Daily, Guangming Daily,* and *Economic Daily.* There was also an office in Hong Kong, associated with the *Wenhui News* there, which is a different newspaper—as became obvious when it castigated the army's violence against students in mid-1989, and when the CCP (apparently referring to a secret *nomenklatura* covering some Hong Kong corporations) urged the sacking of the chief editor.

143. *FBIS,* December 7, 1987, p. 25, reporting radio of December 6.

144. Interview at the Shanghai Television Station, August 1988.

145. This decrease of broadcasted *baozhi gao* in Liaoning is described in *Dangdai Zhongguo, shang,* p. 101. The "station editorials" are *bentai pinglun.*

146. Ibid., p. 52.

147. Ibid., p. 397.

148. This comes from interviews at the Shanghai Broadcasting Station. Contemporary Chinese music, either serious or popular, is a topic that musicologists have largely ignored. The most informative study, dealing with the fate of classical music and musicians in the PRC during recent decades, is by a political scientist: Richard Kraus, *Pianos and Politics* (New York: Oxford University Press, 1989).

149. *Falü yu daode* and *Xinwen toushi;* and above, *Shenghuo zhi you.* Based on Shanghai television viewing and interviews at the station.

150. The four stages were abbreviated: *cai, bian, lü, bo.* See *Shanghai wenhua . . . 1987,* p. 133.

151. The "social education" genre was called *she jiao,* very often just "sit and talk" lectures. The titles of the other programs mentioned (some of which the author has seen while in Shanghai) are respectively *Hunyin fa duihua* and *Qingguan neng duan jiawu shi.* See *Shanghai wenhua . . . 1987,* p. 134.

152. The number of such hours was 1,110 in 1986; the increase from 1985 was 34 percent. Ibid., p. 134.

153. Ibid., p. 133.

154. Ibid., p. 134.

155. *Zonghe xing wenyi jiemu.* Ibid.

156. *ZGQNB,* July 5, 1988.

157. *Jiefang jun bao* (Liberation Army News), August 14, 1988.

158. A summary of the episodes is in James Lull, *China Turned On: Television, Reform, and Resistance* (London: Routledge, 1991), pp. 103–16.

159. *Shanghai wenhua . . . 1987,* p. 134.

160. A somewhat nuanced history of this, discussing the Lushan Plenum era and the mid-1960s, is *Dangdai Zhongguo, shang,* pp. 91–94.

161. Issues of *Shanghai jixie bao, Shanghai gongye jingji bao, Shehui kexue bao,* and *Xinwen bao* have all been seen for February 2, 1989.

162. *Shanghai fazhi bao* has been seen for January 30, 1989, and *Lüshi yu fazhi* in the January-February 1989 edition.

163. When Mayor Zhu Rongji took that post at the end of April 1988, his office was receiving three or four thousand letters per month; by September, the rate had not declined much. Many concerned inflation. *JFRB,* October 17, 1988.

164. Ibid.

165. *Post,* October 16, 1993. Wang's dictum is broad-minded, drawing strengths equally from both Honecker and Hitler. Liberals may hope it will end as they did.

166. This is based on two surveys by the Jiangsu Journalists' Association in 1983 and 1985, reported in Shi Tianchuan, *Guangbo dianshi,* p. 97.

Chapter 2.4

Reform of the Arts

This process of coming to see other human beings as "one of us" rather than as "them" is a matter of detailed description of what unfamiliar people are like and of redescription of what we ourselves are like . . . . The novel, the movie, and the TV program have, gradually but steadily, replaced the sermon and the treatise as the principal vehicles of moral courage.

—Richard Rorty[1]

When I hear the word culture, I reach for my gun.

—Hermann Goebbels

What has sparked the lightning flash of freedom through the communist countries, if not rock music and American movies? You can like or dislike them, but you have to take notice of them.

—Jacques Delors[2]

Chinese leaders have long been avid users of arts, notably calligraphy, to further their own legitimacy.[3] By tradition, artistic brushwork has been valued as an aspect of leadership to present written orders. Arts were thought seemly in governors, and many Chinese recall past regimes such as the Southern Song under Huizong, who was an elegant calligrapher (albeit a weak emperor). Ideals of social unity, in both the Confucian and Marxist philosophies, brought aesthetics closer to morals.[4] Revolutionary impulses by the twentieth century challenged many Chinese artists to address wide national audiences and to develop new styles. The Communist Party supplied institutions for this, of which many were Soviet imports.

The Stalinist ideal for organizing art was that a revolutionary state should recreate culture, not just politics, by destroying all earlier forms of creativity that did not serve its own ends. This required new and more centralized institutions. Stalin fostered new corps of Soviet ballerinas, painters, musicians, and film directors, restricting the style and content of their work in exchange for state support. Beginning in the 1930s, these groups replaced previous artists who had been less subject to official controls through the mid-1920s. Mao's government inherited this Stalinist vision of how to organize art, but for many reasons implemented it less thoroughly. So in the reform period, change was quick.

Were merely cultural movements integral to reforms of politics? Timid thinkers in political science, who are now a majority in that field, have been professionally trained to doubt that cultural change can relate to politics in any important way. What difference in political outcomes can evidence of free styles prove, they ask, as distinct from evidence about external constraints on actors? That is a good question, like any other calling for closer links between data and conclusions. Evidence that rulers and rebels all say cultural ideals are crucial to legitimacy does not deter this line of skepticism. Neither rulers nor rebels, in general, are properly trained in social science. The methodological fad now is only to look at the contexts of action, not at the intentions behind it.

The trouble with this view is less that it is wrong than that it needlessly discards useful information. It takes the coherence of a profession to be more important than understanding. The counterpart of the "so what?" inquiry about culture is the "so what does it mean?" inquiry about context. That cultural question asks that conclusions be linked more closely with data from informants. The standard objection to it is that the logical categories obtained from mere actors may not match those understood by real scientists. But analysts have no ground to privilege their need to apprehend their own theories over the need that their notions should be tied with the data they gather. The search for more evidence often leads to multicausal explanations, and real politics is not simple. Habitual intentions are just like situational constraints at the point of each action; they may be different sorts of factors, but the logic of their effect on results is the same. Because they are human, like the people they study, scientists of human affairs can gather a kind of evidence unavailable in natural science. Serious researchers do not throw out information that may throw light on what happens. This book will explore cultural change in China since 1970, to see what those trends show about politics then.

Art reform was national, because symbols travel well throughout China. The material on arts to be presented below will emphasize the Shanghai region, as all parts of this book do, but it must also discuss styles elsewhere that found major audiences in Shanghai. Salient trends throughout PRC art during the reforms can be summarized as "declining political supervision, a growing cultural market-place, increased artistic professionalism, and new access to outside culture."[5] There were changes both in ideal content and in the concrete organizational support for artistic activity. Because the formal characteristics of the main kinds of art differ somewhat, and these differences affect their links to politics, each major field of art needs to be treated chronologically to avoid overgeneralization. Some patterns that typify most of the arts can nonetheless be listed.

Tentative artistic reforms began early, even though two of the antireform Gang of Four had strong personal interests in the arts. Jiang Qing, a movie actress before she became Mao's wife, fancied herself an expert on drama and music; Yao Wenyuan was a writer and literary critic. Their tastes were narrow, so public presentations of Western-style music and theater remained mostly monotone in the early and mid-1970s. But at home, artists who managed to stay in Shanghai could paint. Some musicians could practice away from the hearing of busybodies on neighborhood committees. Gross invasions of privacy were fewer after 1971 than they had been in 1967–69. So reforms of cultural life came more slowly than in other fields such as rural industry. But beginning in secret, and in time, they did come.

Public expression has been bumpy, alternating between periods of reform and reaction, even though actual artistic production has been more steady. Another parallel with many other fields is that artists' dependence on the state plummeted along with official budgets to support them. A great deal of reform art has been in obvious reaction against violence remembered from the Cultural Revolution. Yet especially in conservative years, these political meanings were kept obscure or tacit. Artistic content and style have diversified greatly since the early 1970s, sometimes along local lines, as China's political centralization waned in the twilight of the revolution. Cultural topics are seen by many social scientists as radically separate from other subjects, especially in economic and political areas. One of the purposes of addressing art in this book is to show that cultural change has many specific resemblances to change in other social fields during China's reforms.

Painting and Visual Arts

In Mao's time, especially in Beijing and Hangzhou, the state appointed master artists to lead academies. They received salaries, which were low for them (as for other teachers) but which linked them to the Party. Many of the best works were not sold, but instead were given by artists as gifts "in an elaborate exchange system that helped to smooth the path in making various arrangements."[6] Art, like newspapers or book publishing, was another form of expression to be subsi-dized by the state, either because ideologists assumed such activities had to be controlled, or because they were deemed socially worthy and thus unfit for commercialization.

Shanghai's pattern was atypical—very different from that in Beijing or Hangzhou. As China's metropolis, Shanghai had been by far the most important center of pre-1949 Chinese painting. Chinese painters who had been influenced by impressionism, cubism, and abstractionism drifted to cosmopolitan Shanghai, but no art academy was established there during the 1950s.[7] Many Shanghai painters violated the precepts of socialist realism, which was the official standard before the Antirightist Campaign. Even before the decentralization of art academies and some diversification of styles in the Great Leap Forward, Shanghai was unique in China because teaching there was dominated by individual artists' studios. They generally received no state support. Some, such as Catholic sculptor Zhang Chongren, maintained themselves by charging high tuitions—which students paid because they admired the quality of his art. Then by the 1960s, Shanghai-based illustrators produced "works of superb aesthetic quality," especially for graphic novels (*lianhuan hua*).[8]

The aesthetic independence of some Shanghai artists until about 1963 tells a story that is different from patterns in nonartistic fields, or even in other cultural fields that require collective work. Shanghai landscapist Wu Hufan, for example, remained largely untouched by socialist aesthetics during the first fifteen years of the PRC. Some of Wu's paintings even after that, such as a shocking 1965 scroll of China's recent mushroom cloud, are on politically acceptable subjects but may well have been meant ironically. When this artist was asked for a painting that was "both red and expert" (*you hong you zhuan*), he reportedly offered a picture of a red brick (*hongzhuan*).[9] Most of Wu's painting was totally nonpolitical.

Much of the painting that could be publicized in the early 1970s was folk art. Shanghai's suburbs nurtured a local school of peasant painting (*nongmin hua*). Suburban Jinshan became China's most famous source of these colorful primitives. They were salable on foreign art markets during the reforms. This genre could flourish early in the reforms because some of these pictures were interesting, and at least some of the artists were impeccably proletarian. In 1972, for example, the Nanhui County Culture Palace in suburban Shanghai organized an "arts core group" to foster such paintings, whose style was heralded as a combination of socialist realism and peasant traditions. Communes, brigades, and teams set up painters' groups. The organization was presentably bureaucratic, but officials did not much constrain these painters.[10] An exhibition of two hundred such Shanghai pictures was held in January 1976.[11] More than three hundred Jinshan county artists gave an exhibition in late 1979—by which time the local pictures were in somewhat more varied styles.[12] Shanghai peasant paintings continued to be shown throughout the reforms.

Socialist realism was still the radicals' official style for public production in the early 1970s, despite actual work that was done in other styles. A political compromise was to mount photographic exhibitions that offered scenery, still lifes, and other apolitical subjects. An exhibit of New Year pictures (*nianhua*) could be shown, with images of peasant boys holding fishes (*yu*, a traditional pun on the prosperous "surplus" desired for the coming year).[13] Although these pictures were publicized as "new accomplishments at a new level," presumably because the artists were peasants, the contents were arguably feudal. Not all the art at this time was realistic, and not all the realism was socialist.

Early Reform Art: Content and Support

With the PRC's thaw of international relations during the early 1970s, the Foreign Ministry and Premier Zhou became concerned that China did not have adequate hotels to house visiting traders. Planning was in vogue, so the Foreign Ministry estimated that ten thousand pictures would be needed to decorate the necessary accommodations. As Ellen Laing reports:

> Efforts to remold traditional-style painters were carried out in 1972 in Zhejiang, Canton, Shanghai, and presumably elsewhere. . . . Jiang Qing's supposedly monolithic hold over the arts, however, had its cracks. With all this effort expended in rectifying traditional-style artists [and with her presumption that Chinese always bow to the state], she was understandably appalled at events that surfaced in 1974 and that crystallized in the so-called Hotel School.[14]

Premier Zhou suggested that traditional-style artists be brought back from cadre schools (sometimes from confinement in "ox sheds") to paint these pictures. The hotels, where the artists were temporarily bedded and boarded, provided better living conditions than their previous abodes. The painters were told to be creative, because foreigners like traditional Chinese paintings. "Zhou declared that the subjects of the pictures should be birds-and-flowers and landscapes. There did not need to be pictures of peasants, workers, or soldiers with guns."[15]

Toward the end of 1973, when Zhou was hospitalized for cancer, Jiang Qing began castigating this "unapproved" art as "revisionist . . . wild, strange, black, reckless." Some painters went through struggle meetings, but the very criticisms suggested the artists' boldness: A painting of the burial of fading flowers was taken to represent the fate of the Cultural Revolution. Many of the pictures used black ink, which the radicals did not like. A scroll showing a bird over eight lotus flowers was interpreted as Jiang Qing swooping above her eight model operas. Ellen Laing has publicized (in the title and on the dust jacket of her own book) a particularly fine Hotel School piece, Huang Yongyu's *Winking Owl,* the first version of which was probably painted in 1972. Owls do wink, but this bird had a particular secret: Chinese folklore makes the owl a devil in disguise, a symbol of death (perhaps Jiang Qing herself). This nocturnal bird of prey begins its reign when the sun (Mao) starts to drop.[16]

The Hotel School represented no single style, but the early 1970s showed that some artists were willing at least privately to challenge political radicals. After the Cultural Revolution's high point in 1969, many artists of course also wanted to be politically careful. An example is the painter Wu Guanzhong, who was originally from Yixing in the Shanghai delta, just west of Lake Tai. In 1972, he returned to his studio after serving as a peasant: "I started to paint again at home. I did not have to worry about things but could travel freely and produce new works. However, that good time did not last long. There was a movement to denounce so-called 'black paintings.' I had to wrap up my paintings and hide them in the homes of friends who were not in the art world."[17] Wu's pieces are not full abstracts, but many are explorations of periodic patterns such as fractal mathematicians of "chaos" and "complexity" have recently made famous. In most cases, the colors are light or white, and the canvases are fully used. There is little political content. The paintings were expertly done, and the government could also approve them. PRC arts officials often help to publish books of reproductions that do not reflect the full diversity of Chinese art.[18]

In the early 1970s, as Julia Andrews says, "stimulated by the thaw, *guohua* [national painting] artists such as Shi Lu and Li Keran painted some of the most beautiful landscapes of their careers."[19] But nonrepresentational painting could also be done in China before Mao's death, so long as the artists were reasonably discreet. Impressionist and postimpressionist styles could occasionally be seen without official sponsorship in public places during the mid-1970s.[20] Exhibitions of such works could not be held, and official honors were not accorded unless the artist or style was arguably proletarian. But some painted in these ways anyway. The first non-archaeological fine arts journal to be revived after the Cultural Revolution was the irreproachably realist *Chinese Photography,* in September 1974. Because of the particular interest of radicals in arts and publishing, public reforms were slower in these areas than in others.[21] That fact did not entirely prevent private painting.

In art and other fields involving intellectuals, 1974–75 was a period of temporarily reversed reforms. Urban houses had not frequently been raided for several years, in part because Red Guard groups had largely been disbanded or sent to rural places. But in a 1974 campaign, the works of some artists were seized for exhibits of "black paintings," including many of the informal Hotel School. Yao Wenyuan himself, at a Municipal Party Committee meeting on January 2, 1974, attacked art from a catalogue that had been published by the Shanghai Foreign Trade Administration.[22] The *Liberation Daily* and *Wenhui News* soon castigated a wide variety of old and young painters, especially those who painted *guohua* or who could already sell works in Hong Kong. Shanghai artists had a trying year in 1975—mostly because they had been able to paint privately with some freedom in 1971–74.

This mid-1970s movement was more repressive than the socialist morality crusade in 1981 or the 1983–84 drive against spiritual pollution. But like these, and like the sporadic pressures for conformity after June 4, 1989, the 1974–75 movement against artists was clearly not sponsored by the whole government. By that time (as distinct from 1966–68), there was no sustained mass participation in the movement for political purism. Also, just as some intellectuals enjoyed reading Chinese classics at this time ostensibly to criticize the Duke of Zhou (a symbol for the reformist Zhou Enlai), they enjoyed attending exhibitions of "black paintings" to see how cleverly the radicals had been rebuked.

Soon after the fall of the Gang of Four, artistic creativity in public was on a less short political leash. Cartoons had long been a major means of artistic-political expression in Shanghai, and the events of 1976 did not change that pattern. Soon after the Gang of Four's arrest, Shanghai staged an exhibition of political pictures to lampoon the Gang members' quirks.[23] Another exhibit of 250 cartoons criticizing the Gang of Four opened in Shanghai during February 1977. The artists came from factories, villages, and schools all over the city. This movement showed some obvious continuities with Cultural Revolution styles. On one hand, the public insistence that satire against the Gang come from all places and walks of life in Shanghai echoed the form of criticisms in 1966–67. At that time, each victim was "dragged out" not just by one type of citizen, but by model representatives of all types. On the other hand, the new cartoons were characterized by a great variety of creative styles. The satirical aspects of this movement were no longer combined with vituperative struggle meetings against the victims or their associates. Humor used against the Gang was harsh, but at least it lacked the dead seriousness of the Red Guards. Punishment was now the business of courts.[24] Some in Shanghai expected that modern change would become endemic, creating a politics that could dispense with campaigns.

Grass became a particular symbol of protest, not just because it grows on graves. Death images were common in the experiences of many Chinese intellectuals during the Cultural Revolution, even though they seem emotive to people without that experience. Grass, the least presumptuous of plants, became a symbol for the weakness of intellectuals. But grass is also persistent, the first green to return after a red fire. As a symbol, grass has ambiguous formal traits: both inextinguishable and bending, but in single blades everywhere.[25]

Rice, wheat, cane, and bamboo are all botanically grasses. They can all spread by sending out side shoots, and often these are underground. Chinese artists who used grass as an emblem meant it to stand for something like the pervasive resilience of people, in contrast to the seemingly strong but ultimately ineffective coercion of the state. Grass is flimsy but also is a symbol of inevitable renewal, the first sign of life after a blaze (such as the Cultural Revolution had been). As a broadly suggestive simile for the situation in which many intellectuals found themselves, the traits of grass were accurate for purposes of dissent by the weak, whose weapons included symbols.

The most important reform-era group of Shanghai artists called themselves "Grass Grass."[26] After a February 1980 exhibit at the Luwan District Culture Palace, the group dissolved because no cadre would take responsibility to approve further exhibitions of abstracts. This official disapproval—without overt struggle meetings, as would have been customary before the revolution reversed course—did not prevent members of the group, such as Qiu Deshu and Chen Jialing, from continuing their careers in other ways.

The appropriateness of nude figure studies became a center of debate among formal painters. This was an old controversy, partly because Mao had once condoned nude drawing. He had said that the painting of nudes was not a bourgeois corruption but a necessary step for painters to master their art. But as soon as this issue was raised again during reforms, it became for conservatives a litmus test. "The deeply ingrained puritanism which has always existed in China side by side with a great erotic tradition," as Stuart Schram says, "has been carefully cultivated by the authorities since 1949 and now represents a major non-political force for conservatism."[27] Culture is controversial, in China as in other countries, and political entrepreneurs against change make the most of it. As reforms became a public slogan in 1978, Shanghai artists knew that foreign traditions could again be studied openly. This meant nudes could not just be painted but could be shown. Because conservatives were so offended by such works, artists wanted to exhibit them.

At the behest of an unidentified "leading comrade," a letter by Mao confirming his view was included in a collection of Mao's epistles published in the early 1980s.[28] *Jin ping mei,* China's most famous erotic novel, also became available in Shanghai in versions less expurgated than had been usual during earlier years.[29] Shanghai commentators defended the right of artists to exhibit nudes. When a show of such paintings was mounted later, about eight thousand viewers came daily. The deputy head of the Shanghai Art Gallery gave these risqué oils a good critical review. He denied they were painted just for the masses; they were for the leadership too.[30] His statement was ambiguous at the least, since some leaders reportedly did not appreciate them at all.

Whether or not this debate about the propriety of painting nudes is very important for art, it became so for politics. The most public national example of the genre, a mural entitled *Water Festival, Song of Life,* depicted bare-breasted minority women and was painted by Yuan Yunsheng, who came from Nantong near Shanghai. Yuan (one of the few painters who can be covered in this summary) is worth some attention here, because his work brings out several different aspects of Chinese avant-garde painting during reforms. Yuan Yunfu and his brother Yuan Yunsheng have expressed their autonomy in different ways. Yunfu, who is older, graduated from the Hangzhou Academy of Fine Arts in the 1950s and avoided major political trouble (although as an intellectual, he was sent during the Cultural Revolution to learn from peasants). As Joan Cohen explains, "By 1972, his third year in the countryside, political tensions had become so relaxed that when Yuan and his colleague Wu Guanzhong went off on their daily task of collecting dung, they managed to include paintbrushes in the bottoms of their buckets. Their artist friends teased them as the Dung Bucket School of Painting."[31]

Street Scene in Hubei Village (plate 1), a 1972 gouache on paper, is not an abstract—but the pattern of light-colored rectangles (white and yellow walls, light brown roofs, even pink wall posters) is what holds the painting together. In 1980, Yuan Yunfu painted *Flags* (plate 2), which is an abstract somewhat influenced by Mondrian. If questioned, the artist could explain it as just a picture of flags. The rectangles here are all in bright single colors, hanging from absolutely straight horizontal black cords. The representational explanation would be a patent excuse, but apparently it was enough to put the canvas in the Oil Painting Research Association Exhibition of 1980.

Yuan Yunsheng, on the other hand, got into political trouble early. He criticized Stalin during the Hundred Flowers Movement in private chats with his fellow art students, so by 1957 he was dubbed a "rightist" and sent to a labor camp. Returning to art school in 1962, he tried to put Tang period historical styles from Dunhuang to modern use. His graduation painting of peasants at New Year was severely chastised for its elongated rather than realistic-photographic figures, and Yuan Yunsheng spent the whole 1963–79 period exiled near Changchun in the Northeast.

Almost immediately upon his return in 1979, he joined a group of artists (including his brother Yunfu) painting murals at the Beijing Airport. His contribution was *Water Festival, Song of Life,* depicting a ritual of the Dai people in Yunnan. Because national minorities have some legal immunities in China, and because their ways of life and thinking provide a principle that variety is legitimate in the PRC, they have long been sources of special interest and envy to Han reformers. *Water Festival* used a Sinified art-deco style to show lithe Dai beauties bathing nude.

The Beijing Airport is a very public place. But national leaders did not by 1979 have a unified idea what to do about this kind of scene. Their would-be puritanical predecessors ten, twenty, or thirty years earlier would surely not have taken so long on this question. Party hard-liners were upset. But Deng Xiaoping, perusing the mural, remained vague: "Is that what they [the conservative critics] are afraid others will see?" Hua Guofeng, still in top posts but obviously in decline, was given the dubious honor of passing judgment. He carefully passed the buck: "The Dai people themselves must decide."

A Dai delegation was duly flown to Beijing, and they approved the picture. Dai women did indeed bathe nude, they reported. The delegates were apparently both amused and honored that Han grandees would put a mural of Dais in such a prominent place. But the matter did not end there, because conservatives raised a larger question. Should such a diversity of "Chinese" customs be approved, even by means of a mural? (Another part of the picture showed two Dai boys chasing a girl, as reportedly happens at the real Water Festival; but some asked whether such a practice should be shown to Hans too.) The principle of modern diversity would suggest it is moral for people to think and behave in different ways. The minorities, if respected as such, are traditional but also a standing threat to unified Chinese communitarianism.

Criticisms came in the only presentable guise: letters from Yunnan suggesting the mural was, after all, an insult to Dais. So a curtain was installed over the wall, closed during political reactions but open during thaws. This was a neat symbol for the schizophrenia of the whole reform period. Even when the curtain was closed, however, airport visitors could look under it to peek at part of the mural. By the spring of 1981, with the movement for socialist morality in full swing, a layer of wallboard was added on top of the mural. Presumably it could be removed in the future.

Later paintings by Yuan Yunsheng refer boldly to Cultural Revolution persecutions of himself and other artists. *Black Figure,* an ink on paper from 1981, is a picture of torture. The figure is contorted, tied, confined, kneeling but with hands high in the air behind the back in a painful pose vaguely reminiscent of the "airplane position" into which many intellectuals were forced during 1966–68 struggle sessions.[32] Such paintings could not, of course, be exhibited—as the happier *Water Festival, Song of Life* could be, at times when the curtains were open.

Later Reform Art: Protest Content, Political Carefulness

Some critics see no change in PRC art until after 1979, but this is true only of works that were extensively publicized at that time—e.g., the hundreds of thousands of satirical cartoons that lampooned the Gang of Four, or the much-advertised China Art Museum exhibition in 1977 whose aim was "enthusiastically to congratulate Comrade Hua Guofeng on becoming CCP Chair, Chair of the Central Military Commission, etc."[33] Many artists were already painting, in a diversity of styles, subjects that were less politicized. Privately, a few had been doing so for most of the 1970s.

Beijing is sometimes thought to be the center of the Chinese world, but a 1982 compilation of major active Chinese painters listed 322, almost half of whom had their studios in Shanghai. Of the dozen chosen in that book to have biographical write-ups and painting reproductions, at least three-quarters hailed from Shanghai or the two adjoining provinces.[34]

Jiangnan prominence in Chinese painting was not restricted to artists listed as professionals. At Fudan University, the student-run "salon" in part of the early 1980s had wall paintings of a reclining nude, as well as of obviously depressed people presented in shades of gray.[35] Much art remained traditional, full of plum blossoms and karst formations rather than politics. But protest against Cultural Revolution injustice, and for the liberation of individuals, was evident not just in the work of professionals, but also in many amateur and student pictures.

Such trends were national. By the 1980s, all forms of Chinese art had diversified. Traditional Chinese painting (*guohua*) sometimes adapted aspects of international styles ranging from French impressionism to abstraction.[36] Oils (*youhua*) had already gone far beyond the bounds of socialist realism. Although

New Year paintings (*nianhua*) were still primarily used by peasants, these now reflected fewer political themes and more emphasis on the pursuits of wealth and happiness. Block prints (*banhua*) and watercolors (*shuicai hua*) were still often used to tell stories, but with more diverse themes in the reform era than before.[37]

Abstraction became less reprehensible politically. Much traditional Chinese art, for example calligraphy, is extremely abstract. Chinese painters using many traditional styles could be safely national while producing abstracts that bore no resemblance to socialist realism. Wu Guanzhong said he tried "to appreciate different types of human beauty, even the distorted beauty in Western modern art." He could be openly dubious, though in a nonconfrontational way, about the imported socialist dislike of abstraction, which had come from the USSR. He pointed out that Chinese characters, house and roof decorations, and the arrangements and shapes of stones in traditional gardens were all abstract.[38] The abstract zigzags of old Jiangnan designs, for example in Suzhou gardens, is also likely to have a fruitful future in modern Chinese buildings, as emigré Shanghai architect I.M. Pei has already begun to show. Certainly in China, and probably everywhere, there is nothing modern about abstract art.

Partly for this reason, some top PRC leaders also became interested in the creation of new art. Deng Lin, the eldest of Deng Xiaoping's five children, began painting traditional Chinese plum blossoms in the 1950s, but then the Cultural Revolution became "the major influence in my life."[39] She was put to work making soy sauce and paper, and her artistic career stopped. As she says, "During the Cultural Revolution, people were only allowed to paint Mao images and political slogans. Individual creativity was suppressed." During a 1985 visit to New York, the museums there converted Deng to abstract impressionism. In 1993 she mounted a one-woman show entitled "Distant Echoes" at the posh Hanart Gallery in Hong Kong. Eleven large silk tapestries, all abstracts in black, white, and gray, were based on designs taken from a source so old it was really prenational: neolithic pottery patterns from the Yellow River valley. These could be had at prices ranging from U.S. $23,000 to $46,000.

Either traditionalist or dissident art could be sold abroad for high prices. Politically safe Shanghai artists (including Chen Jialing whose modernistic plum blossoms disturb no censors) excoriated dissident and radical painters, calling for a calmer reconciliation of old with new. Chen fumed, "Some artists neither have a profound understanding of traditional Chinese painting, nor have they the patience and the will to explore. They blindly follow the Western mode and think it is generating something new." Chen claimed they were "unable to break away from the contemporary mode, 'ingesting modern art without assimilating it,'" but he also reviled those who were "ingesting the old without assimilating it." He called for "transformation" (*huajing*, apparently a code that might be translated as "modern art with Chinese characteristics"), "to reconcile complex relationships of old legacies and current needs."[40] The result, from Chen Jialing's own brush at least, is a kind of semiabstract impressionism, usually ink on paper and clearly based on Chinese subjects. Such work would be far easier to criticize for social effeteness than for lack of beauty.

While stressing the conservatism of many state artists in Shanghai city proper, Joan Cohen chooses pictures by three different Shanghai delta painters for the most prominent places in her pathbreaking book about reform art: a semitraditional piece by Chen Jialing, of Shanghai University, for the cover; an abstract collage by Qiu Deshu, of the Luwan District Culture Palace, for the frontispiece; and an ex-realist oil by Chen Yifei, of the Shanghai Painting Academy, for the back. City-limit analysis does not, of course, tell the whole story. Conservatism in Shanghai's state sector of art is nonetheless congruent with the pattern shown elsewhere in this book about Shanghai conservatism in management, tax compliance, and many other fields. But the culture of this city certainly breeds individualism, too. Two of the three artists mentioned above were originally from delta locations in Jiangsu and Zhejiang.

Qiu Deshu, whose images are painted more for intellectuals than workers, became in the mid-1980s a major pictorial commentator on the Cultural Revolution. This artist "may well be the outstanding painter and theoretician of his generation."[41] A Shanghainese born in 1948, Qiu's works differ sharply from the traditionalist paintings that emerge from most of the city's state-sector artists. Qiu often uses ink and paper, and at first his abstracts seem devoid of political content. In some of his pictures, the general shapes come from calligraphy used on Shang oracle bones, so this art is certifiably Chinese. Heat applied in ancient times to inscribed bones or shells made patterns that fortune-tellers read, but the cracks provide Qiu with a means of comment on current China. He paints paper but then tears it, pasting the pieces into collages. Because of the abstractness of Qiu's style, he temporarily had to stop painting during the 1983 movement against spiritual pollution. Nothing in his creations is overtly political, but Qiu, who had a factory job during the Cultural Revolution, uses the torn-paper method to "represent my own pain and suffering" and that of other artists. Collages such as *Cracks* (plate 3) take a formal approach to the theme of alienation.

Qiu Deshu's paintings during some periods could not be shown in Shanghai for political reasons, and many were soon sold abroad. But galleries in the city during liberal periods could exhibit new works. Shanghai held the PRC's first oil painting exhibition, according to the organizers, in late 1987. Jiang Zemin himself came to the opening.[42] Paintings selected during the reforms for exhibition and popular publication were unlike any in the PRC receiving such publicity before. For sale at a nominal price were two portfolios of reproduced oils, designed for people to hang on their walls at home. These were chosen from a major 1988 show at the Shanghai Exhibition Hall, then published that year for widespread distribution. They were still available at the largest bookstore on Nanjing Road well into the 1990s.[43]

These paintings came in a great diversity of styles. Although there were no pure abstracts in the set, most showed strong interest in repetitions of stylized shapes. Nonrepresentational elements in many cases covered more than half of the canvas. The painting *Woman Shepherds* (plate 4), by Jier Gebang (who as a minority person may have more freedom than Han artists), is one of the more eccentric in the portfolio. It is mostly covered with simplistic designs, looking like commercial tiles. These make an abstract wall. Four women stand before it, dressed in their best minority clothes, which may not be the best choice for herding but show they have political security.[44] Two figures look away from the viewer, and the faces on the other two are clearly glum. The geometric decorative designs behind them seem irrelevant—and no more inspiring than the herders are inspired. This picture is arguably so bad from an aesthetic viewpoint that the artist may be trying for that effect. This style could be used to express discontent at the modernized, safe, controlled status into which minorities have been pigeonholed. Three of the women carry cameras, perhaps suggesting their obeisance to the official preference for photographic art. Alienation is apparently a theme of this strange picture, which can easily be interpreted as an expression of the artist's cynicism. But the painter could deny this political interpretation, and may have done so in order to have the work shown. Despite such ambiguity, or conceivably because the selectors agreed with the message, *Woman Shepherds* was chosen for reproduction and posting in Shanghai.

A more interesting piece of art in the same collection is *Facial Designs and Girl* (plate 5), by Guan Xiaobin. Six different Chinese opera masks, representing stern generals or judges, are juxtaposed to a girl, whose face is realistic but like the masks. This picture is an example of the "rationalist" school, borrowing somewhat from surrealism.[45] The painted masks are mostly of warriors, except for the white one. The picture leaves open many questions of interpretation. Is it castigating the girl's ability to don various guises that do not represent her real self, as many feared they did not represent themselves during the Cultural Revolution? Or on the contrary, is it contrasting her straightforwardness or innocence with that of the traditional masks, which are not alive? Like the reform era's "murky poetry," to which a PRC interviewee likened this painting, this painting asks the viewer to make choices. Passive receipt of the visual information is not enough to specify a meaning.

The girl might don these guises (although the artist could deny such a suggestion, because the masks are of different sizes). If so, this could be a critique of people who assume odd and fierce personalities, as did many in the Cultural Revolution and in the 1980s movement against spiritual pollution. Other interpretations are possible—indeed, they may have been necessary so that the picture could be displayed—but the visual evidence allows this strongly political one.

Xu Mangyao's *My Dream* (plate 6) is a startling selection to have been published in such a popular format. It shows a young man, perhaps the artist in a self-portrait, breaking out of a red wall into which his whole midriff has been bricked and plastered. To his right is a light switch, apparently still turned off.

Below is some greenery that was also encased in the wall. On the left are two white gloves, painted full but without hands, reaching for a door handle connected to no door and apparently trying to open it. A surgical suture in the wall extends below the handle. Further to the left is a bust, resembling Karl Marx almost as much as a Greek philosopher, toppling to the ground.

A student from Jiaotong University mentioned he had seen *My Dream* and controversy about it published in Shanghai when it was first exhibited. But many elements of the painting—the light switch, the gloves, the handle, the suture, and the falling bust—are all subject to divergent explanations, some of which are apolitical. That was the normal prerequisite for public exhibition.

Other pictures chosen for this mass-produced portfolio in Shanghai flouted literalism more abstractly. Wang Hongjian's *Soundless Song* showed the central figure, a poor minority woman on a totally barren desert, kowtowing to the viewer—with her young boy imitating her motion. Several other pictures in the series had the central figures with their backs to the viewer (this arrangement fails to fulfill Jiang Qing's critical criteria of "three prominences"). Wang Zhenghua's *Evening Years* depicted decrepit old people whose lives had obviously been hard. Another contribution was titled as a harrowing remembrance of Picasso's *Guernica*.[46] Paintings with this much protest, perhaps especially because of the foreign reference, could be published.

Pessimism does not always sell well, however, and in later reforms Shanghai painting changed partly in response to foreign tastes. Qiu Deshu's designs were still full of cracks, but by the late 1980s and 1990s they were often done in bright colors. Socialist realism was adapted by Shanghai painter-filmmaker Chen Yifei to nostalgic and very unsocialist purposes. Chen had once painted the PLA *Taking the Presidential Palace* in Nanjing.[47] But in later reforms, he offered nearly photographic oils of Chinese imperial palace beauties, Western women playing string instruments, and slightly fuzzier depictions of canals at Suzhou—and at Venice.[48] Chen spent time in New York, Hong Kong, and Taipei as well as Shanghai. Over the reform years, he painted less and less, earning more and more per canvas sold abroad.

Then Chen became yet more photographic as a movie director, making *Shanghai jiumeng* (*Reverie on Old Shanghai,* 1993). Without dialogue, this movie is a series of visual vignettes on pre-1949 Shanghai: architecture, street hawking, vintage cars, red lanterns, opium smoking, and Western businessmen pictured while eating meat—all loosely held together because the images are centered on a comely woman who usually wears a slit dress. The film's main audience was overseas, eliciting nostalgia for Shanghai in the 1920s and 1930s. This trend of art, stressing symbols about the inevitability of greed, clearly diverged from an interest in anything collective. After so much idealistic politics in Chinese art, it is not surprising that some artists had such a detached reaction. Others took a more confrontational tack.

When a more avant-garde art exhibition, which had found no sponsor in

Shanghai, opened in the capital during 1989, it was dominated by dramatic "action" exhibits. In one of these, an artist fired bullets into her own masterpiece (a concoction based on telephone booths). Another artist used his allotted space for a perfectly ordinary stall selling shrimps. He said he wanted to show that "the concept of business had penetrated every aspect of Chinese life, including the exhibition itself."[49] "Installation works," often requiring the artist personally at the center of the art, became notorious by the late 1980s.

Condoms and money were thrown on the gallery floor. An artist wearing no shirt sat in the middle of his own work, atop a pile of hay. He was "hatching eggs," according to the title. He wore a vest printed with the words "No reasoning during incubation, so as not to disturb the next generation."[50] The reference to tutelage theories of politics was clear enough. News of such art spread fast, albeit not on a mass basis. The police closed this show—but they soon allowed it to reopen on the condition that the "action art" (xingwei yishu) was excluded.[51] A Shanghai fashion designer still came to the gallery in baggy clothes covered with African designs and plaited cotton in his hair. He declared he was not part of the show, but plainclothes police asked him to leave. The logo of this art show was a road sign prohibiting a U-turn to the left. An East China example of "action art" was entitled Violence, Shanghai Street Cloth Sculpture. The artists swaddled themselves tightly, head to foot in sheets, and sat in public restaurants to suggest how constrained they were.[52]

Liu Dahong, whom a foreign critic calls "artist laureate of China's reform," did not need action exhibits to convey messages that were similarly skeptical of state authority. Liu graduated from the Zhejiang Art Academy in the early 1980s and then moved to Shanghai. "Many of Liu's most extraordinary works exude the atmosphere of this city, yesteryear's adventurers' paradise and one of China's most intriguing carpetbagger enclaves today." On the other hand, despite his artistic quality "his reputation is mostly limited to Shanghai—the Peking art scene is jealous of outsiders who do not take up residence."[53]

Liu Dahong's canvases, too complex to reproduce effectively here, are full of figures; they are something like a cross between Hieronymus Bosch and Chinese Spring Festival paintings. The dominant colors are usually browns or reds. These large pictures are episodic, containing many subscenes in which different figures are performing different acts, usually risqué or greedy. Liu depicts famous personages from different historical periods together and he paints geographically separated buildings as if they were together, so the viewer is forced to think about logical connections. The relevance of such art to the ambiguous mix of old memories and current lusts in China's reforms is captured in critic Lu Jie's comment on one painting, Old Theater, which gives a good sense of Liu's other works too:

> The figures in the picture are both actors . . . and audience (witnesses). The
> mischievous boy, traditional mandarins, waiter, ancient generals, and Red

Guards from the Cultural Revolution appear together in the same scene. . . . The painting maliciously incorporates several extremes: the alienated technique used to depict the figures on the one hand, and its conventional application on the other; the contrast between the accuracy of the depiction and the allegorical significance of the figures; and, most importantly, the clash between the simplicity of Liu's artistic language and the complexity of the painting's contents.[54]

Liu's *Shanghai Bund* (1987) shows the Great World amusement center, which is actually located inland on Tibet Road, as if it were among the financial and administrative centers along the Huangpu shore. A Chinese emperor in yellow dances on the Bund to disco music with his empress in red. American GIs chase a Chinese woman down an alley lined with bars and brothels. Cultural Revolution hero Ouyang Hai saves a Japanese bullet train (rather than the Chinese train he was supposed to save) while the main thoroughfare of the Bund hosts a parade of marchers. To one side is a dissection: a direct quote from Rembrandt's *The Anatomy Lesson*.[55] Liu asks his viewers to be similarly analytical and detached.

The political reaction of 1989–90, like similar roars of the conservative lions earlier in the reforms, affected the ability of artists to exhibit politically controversial works. But they continued to paint or sculpt in their own various styles, selling some of their best work abroad. Even after the *Goddess of Liberty* had been toppled, memories of Tiananmen inspired some Chinese artists to make new works. These could not soon be shown in public, although a visiting foreign scholar privately saw "a fair number" in January 1990. By the beginning of 1991, the journal *Artist* (*Huajia*) published several works that could only refer to the massacre.[56]

A sympathetic Western critic found that artists living together near the Summer Palace in Beijing "are not particularly distinguished. They imitate each other, unimaginatively combining Cynical Realism and Political Pop. In fact, when you look closely at the paintings, you feel that most of these artists are only a half step away from jade carvers or other practitioners of local handicraft for foreign consumption." He stressed the effects of Western money on these artists. One of them was quoted as claiming that "before '89, there was hope, political hope, economic hope, all very exciting." Another added, "Now there is no hope, we've become artists to keep busy." The critic found this "a flattened cynicism, more the stuff of student cool than of despair."[57] But these artists were northern intellectuals. In other, less controlled and more entrepreneurial contexts, especially those far from the capital, there was more evidence of hope. Southerners and nonintellectuals, including many with tastes for the gaudy, affect Chinese art more than an examination of the Beijing scene alone would imply.

Foreign Money, Foreign Tastes

It is still somewhat controversial among critics to discuss PRC art. Many specialists express strong, broad doubts about its aesthetic quality, and with this they usually stop. As Julia Andrews writes, "We are so accustomed to the twentieth-century idea of 'art for art's sake' that it is extremely difficult to contemplate artists working in a society that has rejected this concept."[58] A linked problem is that art patrons are wealthy and China remains Communist, but that does not answer the question about aesthetics. Details of prereform ideas about the social role of Chinese art, as well as Maoist pressures on artists, make a sad history.[59] This has inspired skeptical views, such as those put bluntly and immodestly by Hugh Moss:

> State patronage, political upheaval, and methods of marketing have left artists divorced from a critical audience as we know it in the West. . . . Artists are encouraged to produce repetitions of their own standard works. . . . Students seldom stray from the styles of their masters. Without unfettered critical feedback, the whole process has become somewhat incestuous and painting standards are lowered so subtly and pervasively that the artists themselves hardly notice it happening. There are exceptions, but recently they seem disappointingly few. . . . It is my view that posterity will select many of the great Chinese artists of the present time from outside the People's Republic of China.[60]

Another well-published, nonacademic art critic in 1990s Hong Kong has suggested unattributably that most current mainland painting would make dubious "wallpaper."[61]

The strength of such views might be enough to daunt anyone less gauche than a social scientist. Since aesthetic consciousness, like any other kind, comes from traditions involving many people, not just individuals, it may be wise to delay judgment for a long time. Art can have meanings, including aesthetic ones, in many spheres, and its political context is one of these. It can be interesting from many angles, and the best approach is not to begin with a sense that a single aesthetic criterion should be evident. A search for more aspects of art in reform China not only shows some of the passions in Chinese elite politics, it also explores new ways to find meaning in the art. Although some Western critics claim that recent PRC art is derivative, a Chinese painter retorts, "Chinese art is no more Western than Picasso's art is African or the impressionists' pictures are Japanese."[62]

Shanghai painters found they made better livings in the 1980s and 1990s reforms by selling abroad. Many of them had their own briefs against socialism, though in fact they adapted various styles that had been developed in Mao's years. No matter whether they were relatively traditionalist or relatively iconoclastic, their market during the reforms was increasingly foreign. When artists of the less radical type were as presentable as Chen Jialing, they could easily mount exhibitions and sell paintings at venues ranging from Smith College to Hong Kong. In this respect, they did not differ from the socially critical painters, who could enjoy similar financial success abroad—with the advantage that overseas associations may have provided some degree of political safety, even aside from the money.

International commercialization became a major trend in Chinese fine arts during reforms. Salaries to serious artists from the state had always been paltry, even for those who qualified through their membership in official associations. By the 1980s, many of the best new scrolls or paintings were sold—for convertible currencies—to foreigners or overseas Chinese. Both buyers and artists made extensive efforts to avoid the heavy state price markups, so that the official artists' associations became outdated. After the confinements of the Cultural Revolution, many artists thought they should receive any money purchasers were willing to pay. Galleries abroad, such as Peach Blossom or Hanart II in Hong Kong, organized shows for good PRC artists. Even if only a small fraction of the works on offer actually sold, and even after such a gallery took its commission, the revenue to the artist from one such show could be many times greater than a year's salary from the state.[63]

What happened in the art trade, therefore, closely paralleled the evolution in many other reforming fields such as rural industry. Resources (in this case, the best new art works) were increasingly removed from the state system. After Mao's years, state officials lacked sufficient social legitimacy to monitor those resource flows. The most desirable or scarce goods tended to sell for foreign currency, especially before the devaluation of the yuan in the early 1990s. Above all, state imposts on foreign sales have been extensively evaded.

The effect of this pattern on art is difficult to determine. Andrews and Gao judge the issue sensibly, in comparison to earlier years: "A new commercial standard has replaced previous political demands on the themes and styles of official art. . . . The art world is now dominated by a concern for commercial success to the point that most other critical criteria have been discarded."[64] Dissident artists have moved abroad, making money partly because of their dissent. At least in the early 1990s, most who remained in China painted official works or found other jobs. Good art and music often grow like asparagus, in bunches. Inside the PRC, the 1990s have seen less of them than earlier periods of reform.

Analytic efforts to find sociological bases for any major aspect of high culture have in the past foundered on the problem that artists have a choice: They can either react against social constraints or reflect them (or do both in different ways at the same time). If there are causal actions and reactions in this field—as there almost surely are—they flow in both directions, mirroring both social and individual interests.[65] Models to capture this complexity will be multicausal, notes of partial correlations that suggest patterns.

The post-Tiananmen era saw a temporary reduction in the frequency of major PRC art exhibits abroad. But by 1993, in conjunction with the Hong Kong Arts Festival—and with the interested support of up-market Hong Kong dealers—a show was mounted of "China's New Art, Post-1989." Shanghai artists figured very prominently. A 1991 painting by Li Shan, *The Rouge Series, No. 21* (plate 7), became the most frequently reproduced work in the show. This acrylic is dominated by the face of a man covered with Chinese opera makeup in white and red, with a flower of the same colors growing from his mouth. The face might well be that of an ex-cadre sophisticate; the skin is smooth, the eyes Buddha-like, and the hair part severe, central, and proper. Clearly he has pleasant-sounding things to say, but the viewer is not asked to believe him. The Bund is the background, mostly obscured by our dubious hero, but showing masses of people in dark clothes making their way toward a shiny limousine.[66]

"Political pop" artists in Shanghai included Li Shan, Yu Youhan, and the latter's student Wang Ziwei, who were all shown at a 1993 exhibition, "Mao Goes Pop," at the Sydney Museum of Contemporary Art. Stylized depictions of the Great Helmsman, using the same poses and gazes as in the most frequent posters of him during the Cultural Revolution, dominated this revival of the Mao cult, whose clear purpose was to ridicule it. A Hong Kong Chinese critic praised this art for its "light side that glamorizes the mundane, teases the dogmatic, and pokes fun at high station." Conservatives seldom appreciate restoration humor, however. This art was the saucy protest of a small intellectual elite. It was banned from public view—although the artists seemed perfectly free to work privately, in their studios. Most Shanghainese would probably not have much liked it if they had seen it: "After I gave a painting to an old uncle of mine," Yu Youhan admitted, "he didn't get back in touch for a year."[67] Many of Shanghai's best artists protested all the way to the bank, where they could deposit their foreign exchange.

Conclusion: Elite Art and Popular Culture

Some Chinese artists in the late 1980s were children of former intellectuals who had been dubbed "rightists" in 1957. Their iconoclasm had often prevented their admission to art academies. One critic claims, "Perhaps the most significant social contribution was made by artists who had been turned away from art schools. . . . They tenaciously held out at the periphery. . . . In the 1980s, artists began to achieve an individualism that was anathema to the cultural establishment."[68] The work of these artists is full of irony about the unintended bad results of high-flown ideals. Many of the major reform schools by the 1990s, variously dubbed "Political Pop," "Cynical Realism," or "Endgame Art," used symbolic clichés to convey ironic meanings radically different from their original significations. Purposes go awry, as PRC history richly showed. Painters could often express this fact, while writers of sentences and lines of words could not so naturally do this, because most state censors expect proper criticism to be discursive, taking one predicate at a time, rather than planar and simultaneous. The gist of much of the 1990s reform art could even be put in the far less lively language of social science: Situations affect norms.

Artistic reforms responded to their contexts, with some differences from other social changes to which they were loosely correlated. Painting and sculpture reforms began in the early 1970s, but top radicals then cared so intensely about symbolic subjects, cultural fields changed more slowly and secretly. They were not in lockstep with other kinds of reform. Public articulation was a consuming passion for the high radical intellectuals; expressive politics in art was dangerous. The Hotel School flourished then, because very few understood the paintings' political critique. So did crypto-abstracts (art whose ostensible subject was representational but whose real interest was abstract, such as Yuan Yunfu's *Street Scene*). This resurgence of diverse art was not obviously greater than in the late 1970s, when reforms officially began, or than during the "new current in art" (*yishu xinliu*) that started about 1985.

Even in later years, artistic reforms remained somewhat out of synch with other kinds of reform. Editorials and conferences against decadent modern art have been sporadic throughout the reforms, but repression of modern artistic work has not always come at the same time. So in this field especially, it is easy to overperiodize or to insist that central and local politics follow the same schedule. More obvious than the to's and fro's of the official line in culture is the constancy of tension between artistic conservatives and reformers, because each is based in specific networks of prestige and power.

There was a particular run of new exhibitions in early 1989, but the Tiananmen massacre did not become a "main move against 'bourgeois liberalization.'"[69] The new conservative campaign against artists did not strike until May 1990 and later months, and then it was based on much earlier preparations for similar hard-line campaigns that had quickly fizzled in 1986 and May 1987. Even in 1990, this campaign to purify art politically was ineffective. Many of the best artists moved abroad. In fields where individuals face norms, such as art or faith, government policies seldom brought their intended results as the revolution receded. The content of artistic reform was clearly related to broad political changes, but the timing of reform in art was only loosely linked to the timing of changes in fields that deal with resource situations. An intellectual interviewee claimed in 1994 that while painting nudes might still be attacked by reactionaries, the practice was "commonplace. . . people became more tolerant, or indifferent." It is not necessary to accept the primacy of social constraints on imagination in order to see a link between art and politics.[70]

Literature, Theater, and Film

Jiang Qing's radical aesthetic, before reforms, called for characters in any literary work to evince "three prominences": positive personalities should stand out; among these, the art should emphasize heroes; and again among these, there should always be one main protagonist. The aim was to make artistic messages clear—and political. The only legitimate kind of hero was a Communist leader. The result was sometimes inspiring but devotedly one-dimensional.

The early 1970s showed signs of literary revival, whose chief exemplar was the politically radical writer Hao Ran. His 1972 book *Bright Golden Way* depicted stubborn but compassionate revolutionary heroes who were, as the title of one of his best stories puts it, "Firm and Impartial."[71] The themes in Hao's works were limited; the writing was spare and realistic. The characterizations already showed a hint of the ambivalence that flourished in post-Mao literature. For example, the heroine of "Firm and Impartial" is first described as somewhat bossy and distant. Her deeds are shown as unambiguously virtuous, but much of the interest of the story comes from a tension between her pushy style and the substantive compassion of what she does. There is no character change, but the story reveals her personality to the reader in progressive stages.

The technical quality of Hao Ran would be difficult to impeach, no matter what a critic might think about the limits politics placed on his work. This point applies to most of the presentable artistic products of the early 1970s. It is easier to criticize the radical repertoire because of its official monopoly and its thematic narrowness than because of its technical quality. The proficiency of narrative in Hao Ran's stories was high, whatever else might be said about the content. The dancing of the prima ballerina in the film *The Red Detachment of Women* would have pleased audiences in St. Petersburg, no matter about the plot. The issue with *The Yellow River Concerto* was not that the pianist could not play his instrument; the difficulty lay instead in the grandiose quality of the music, composed by a committee that tried to imitate Rachmaninoff in his least circumspect mood.[72] In each case, the Chinese writer, dancer, or pianist did a good job. The problem was in context and content, not performance. In Hao Ran's case, the work was so clever that it could also point to interests in character ambivalence and development of which later reform years would see much more.

Early Reform Literature

Writing is easier to do in secret than is music performance, which can be heard through walls. Even the visual arts require studio space. So some of the best writing of the early 1970s went into drawers, for publication later. Little was available in bookstores. By the end of the 1970s, however, many of these works as well as new ones became available, and many genres—poems, short stories, novellas, plays, and reportage—flourished in public then largely because of quiet work writers had done earlier.[73] Many authors could write in the early 1970s, but few could publish then. A writer named Yang Mo, for example, resumed writing in 1972. Although she was slowed by criticisms, she finished ten chapters of a novel—which was finally published in 1979. Wu Qiang, who had authored a novel called *Red Sun* (*Hong ri*), lived in Shanghai and wrote part of his next work, *Fortress* (*Baolei*), in the early 1970s. Some of his manuscripts had been taken by Red Guards in one of their house searches, but that did not bring his efforts to a complete halt.[74] The novelist Ke Ling, although he could not publish in the early 1970s, was "gathering materials and preparing work" then. The famous Shanghai novelist Ba Jin, whose wife died because of the Cultural Revolution, returned in the late 1970s to translating the memoirs of a Russian, writing his book *Random Thoughts* (*Sui xiang lu*), and collecting his previous essays for publication together.

By 1975, there was public criticism of the literary uniformity. The *Wenhui News* in that year praised the elegant style of speech in the feudal novel *The Dream of the Red Chamber*, to exemplify how well ideas can be expressed. "A thousand pieces all in the same style" (*qianbu yiqiang*) were seen as too dull. Characters in contemporary stories were deemed generally too monotone. Articles called on literature to "reflect class struggle . . . . But the problem is how to reflect it." Literature was deemed by the mid-1970s to have become pedestrian, and even radicals called for a greater variety of voices.[75] In July 1975, Mao Zedong on two occasions said, "One hundred flowers are not blooming anymore . . . . Party policy should be readjusted a bit, to expand the spectrum of arts in one, two, or three years. There is a lack of poems, essays, and art reviews."[76] The literary supplement magazine of the main national newspaper for intellectuals, *Bright Daily,* was restarted in August 1975, even though this change could hardly be described as a rebirth of literary freedom. Style, content, and choice of literary topic were still severely constrained, for any writer who wished to publish.

This current book presents data to show that, in many fields, reforms began during the early 1970s. It does not claim that officially recognized art *in public* was one of these. Even in fields such as rural industry, where reform during the early 1970s was as fast or faster than in most later periods, some of that early development was secret and/or illegal. Writers were sufficiently few, expressive, dissident-tending, urban, and identifiable to be closely monitored by the state. Writing as a genre is often more difficult to keep safely ambiguous than, for example, music. So reforms of literature were repressed and slow in comparison with other fields.

Some variation of popular literary output was nonetheless needed in the early 1970s, because reducing China's national literature to a few plots created boredom. Although Jiang Qing and her friends in arts circles approved only eight "model operas," the variety of Chinese folk genres was so great, they had no way to prevent experimentation in all of them. In February 1976, Shanghai held "mass art performances" of many kinds, and the best local artists offered their concerts in the city center. Shanghai light opera (*Huju shuochang,* which involves speaking as well as singing), musical imitations of various kinds of personalities (*biaoyan chang*), revolutionary stories (*geming gushi*), Wuxi short operas (*Xiju xiaoxi*), Pudong musicals (*Pudong shuoshu*), "mountain" songs (*shange biaoyan chang*), fishers' calls (*puyu haozi*), hauling chants ("yo-heave-ho" songs, *dahang haozi*), story plays (*gushi ju*), and accompanied singing (*zuochang*)—all these genres were publicly available in Shanghai by the mid-1970s, before the Gang of Four fell.[77] The performers were supposed to observe political decencies, as in some respects they have done throughout reforms. They could be in deep trouble if they criticized reigning leaders directly. Also, they remembered the severe restrictions on local artistic presentations that began in 1964 (before 1966) and intensified during the next eight years especially. Most of the genres were folk, even though many of the artists were professional. The content of these shows by the mid-1970s was less tightly regulated than before, and the genres were mostly "feudal," in fact.

After the radicals were purged in 1976, most of the works they had pilloried became available for presentation. A play about the Long March, entitled *Ten Thousand Rivers and a Thousand Mountains,* was presented largely because it had been forbidden during the reign of the Gang of Four.[78] This drama had been produced as early as September 1976, despite the radicals' disapproval. Between the October 1976 arrests of the radicals and the Spring Festival of 1977, there was not much time to write new plays and songs. But material had been composed during the early 1970s, and this could now be performed. At the same time, popular works from the Cultural Revolution were still onstage. The model revolutionary opera "The White-Haired Girl" still attracted audiences in 1977.[79] The range of artistic options diversified at this time.

In early 1977, the *Wenhui News* criticized the way in which radicals had celebrated previous New Years. Now, it claimed, "the Spring Festival is really coming."[80] Old Chinese art forms were revived for this occasion, including barely ex-"feudal" styles in theater, dance, and the formal recitation of poems. The messages in this new art did not change overnight. Chairman Hua Guofeng's picture was hung beside (or instead of) Chairman Mao's in the middle of theater stages across the country. The cult of persons was not ended just because Hua had less personality. Also, public adulation of Mao was maintained after the old chairman's death, because Hua's friends used it to boost his own pallid legitimacy.

As soon as the Gang of Four was deposed, Shanghai troupes adapted Shaoxing and Yangzhou operas to praise the wisdom of Chairman Hua. A 1977 poem entitled "Shaking Hands with Chairman Hua" had a prominent place in the 1977 Spring Festival ceremonies. Those who attended Shanghai's 1977 festival also could hear "Ode to Struggle at the [Daqing] Oil Field." A piano sonata for the festival, entitled *Fighting the Typhoon,* suggested that some officials still had a preference for fortissimo over quietism. The army's bravery provided a theme for other presentations. The *Great Wall of the South Seas* praised the efforts of Fujian's local militia against the danger of invasion from Taiwan.[81] The invasion was indeed soon coming, not militarily but musically.

Political language in 1977 remained as fervent as in the late 1960s, even though actual violence had sharply decreased. An allegorical fable, written for presentation at this Spring Festival, promised to strike the Gang of Four with "merciless whips" (*wuqing bianda*). Moderation was phrased, in this odd art, with radical stridency.[82] But by 1977, vehemence was already giving way as the main artistic style.

Poetry of the 1970s

A dissident literature emerged most clearly in poetry first, perhaps because poetry can be the least discursive written genre. Novelists and story writers could not reach readers easily. The best-known prose writer during the early 1970s was Chen Ruoxi, who was able to publish only abroad, in Hong Kong and Taiwan, whence a few copies of her work filtered illicitly back into China. But poems, unlike short stories or novels, can be memorized and copied with relative ease. Their conciseness and openness to interpretation makes poems more difficult for officials to control.

Poetry posted at Tiananmen, during the 1976 unauthorized demonstration in memory of Zhou Enlai, became the most important example of dissident literature during the mid-1970s.

> I sorrow, I hear ghosts howl,
> I cry, the wolves laugh.
> I shed tears mourning the hero,
> My eyebrows raised, I draw my sword.[83]

Poetry was particularly hard for radicals to domineer, for two specific reasons inherent to their own movement. First, their sometime protector Mao Zedong was himself a poet. He had strong and authoritative opinions about technical aspects of this field. Three standard issues for the analysis of Chinese poetry concern the extent to which old or new language is employed, whether poems should be short and evocative or long and narrative, and which stanza forms are best.[84]

Along none of these three dimensions was there a clear Cultural Revolution position. On the first point the radical theorist Yao Wenyuan, for example, was constantly torn between the value of classic allusions (which he used frequently in his polemic works) and the need for nonallusive writing that every common worker could understand. Second, on the matter of long or short forms, the radicals might logically have been expected to prefer long heroic epics containing so much explicit narrative that nobody could misread any meanings. But Chairman Mao's own poems—and preferences—took precisely the opposite form. Third, as regards stanzas, the Chinese tradition provides so many varieties that public debates about the most appropriate types remained hard to resolve. So on these three formal aspects of poetic style, the radicals never reached definitive conclusions. Many poets, like all other kinds of intellectuals, suffered in this period unconscionably. Most could nonetheless avoid publishing in the worst periods. Even in the best of times, what they do is rated not at all by its volume but by its quality.

Criticisms of the Cultural Revolution, beginning with the 1976 poetry in honor of Zhou and continuing with public recitations by poets, were direct and emotional. Lei Shuyan's fervent "A Tiny Blade of Grass Is Singing" was read at an open meeting:

> The wind says
> Forget her
> I have buried the crime with dust!
> The rain says
> Forget her
> I have cleansed the humiliation with tears! . . .
> Only a tiny blade of grass is still seen
> So mournfully on starless nights. . . .
> She
> Was shot to death. . . .
> I am ashamed that I,
> A Communist Party member,
> Am no better than a tiny blade of grass. . . .
> Let me keep awake!
> Living in the doldrums is more lamentable than death;
> Living in ignorance is worse than a pig's life![85]

The audience "shuddered, then broke into a hurricane of applause that went on and on." In another country, Yevtushenko had once led such scenes.

In the wake of the Cultural Revolution, writers produced "murky poetry" (*menglong shi*). These poems asserted the worth of individuals by refusing the need to be clearly intelligible. The national capital, rather than Shanghai, was clearly the main center for reform poetry; in this respect poetry was different from painting, although the audience of intellectuals was nationwide. Alienation is a fact of life in an untitled, formal poem from Bei Dao:

> To the world
>> I will always be a stranger.
>> I do not know its language,
>> It does not know my silence.
>> We exchange
>> Only a touch of nonchalance,
>> As if we meet in a mirror.
> To myself
>> I will always be a stranger.
>> I fear darkness.
>> But I let the body block
>> The single light.
>> My shadow is my lover.
>> The heart is the enemy.[86]

Choice of literary topics had been subject to intense debate during the Cultural Revolution. The social and political grounds on which writers chose subjects had been matters for conflict and violence. Radicals had pressed for the propagation of writings about model heroes. Now the poet him- or herself became the hero, and the "three prominences" were replaced by a formal interest in their opposite, murkiness.

Prose in Memory of Violence

There was a "thaw" from 1976 to 1978 in Shanghai literary circles. Authors started to break taboos. Short-story writer Liu Xinwu introduced new themes just after Mao's death. "The Class Teacher" appeared in November 1977, and the summer of the next year saw "The Scar." As McDougall says, these stories "introduced elements into literature that had been absent for a decade or more: intellectual protagonists, questioning of the philosophic basis of populist and antirightist movements, problematic or unresolved endings, and the insinuation that tragedy could be an appropriate mode in a socialist society."[87]

After the publication in Shanghai of works by Zhong Fuxian, and especially of Lu Xinhua's "Scar," the *Wenhui News, Liberation Daily,* and other journals printed essays about "scar literature" (*shanghen wenxue*). These debates mooted the relationship of literature to life, the need to find truth in practice, whether writing could cover typical characters, "the socialist tragedy," and other topics that generally suggested a political demand: that the state should give less advice to writers. In 1979, the *Wenhui News* criticized the conservative idea that "praising virtue" was the main business of authors. *Shanghai Literature* castigated the notion that writing is merely an instrument of class struggle.

Zhong Fuxian's play *Where the Silence Is* resembles the poems in praise of Zhou Enlai. A careful critic noted "the re-emergence of the writer's subjective ego. . . . [These writers] are scornful of being the trumpet of their age and of writing about heroic events outside their own world of feeling. In their poems, one can hear individual voices of regret and sorrow, of hope and despair, in sharp contrast to the uniform utterance of encomium for the Party and the regime."[88] Not just in poems and plays, but also in novels such as *Man, Ah Man,* by Dai Houying, the new writers made clear that their art aimed at more than just copying an objective and verifiable reality. It also imitated the subjective feelings of individuals.[89] Realism of most kinds, and certainly narrowly political socialist realism, does not do this, so writers after the CR used methods that can.

Alienation was the topic of a September 25, 1980, essay by Wang Ruoshui in the *Wenhui News.* "From then on, *Shanghai Literature, Academic Monthly, Studies in Literary Theory, Wenhui News, Liberation Daily,* and other journals published many essays discussing the relationship between Marxism and humanism, between the natural and social character of human beings."[90] These were real debates, because opposite views were aired in print. The *Wenhui News* in 1981 published an essay by writer Ai Qing criticizing "obscure poetry," but then another by Li Li praising the genre. *Shanghai Literature* sponsored a similarly controversial forum on the "modern literature" school. The issue was whether writing had to be modernized while society developed. These questions did not much concern most people in the city, but Shanghai media participated very fully in this debate about the legitimate range of content in literature.

Freedom for PRC writers was relatively great in the late 1970s, through 1980, so this period is sometimes called the "Second Hundred Flowers."[91] In the critiques of liberalization at this time, the explicit target was bad art, not bad artists. As the head of the Party's Literature and Art Bureau put it, "criticizing the intellectual tendency towards liberalization is not equivalent to censuring a certain individual, but is the purification of . . . mistaken thinking. There must be absolutely no personal attacks."[92] Published damnations of liberal art were to mention the titles of dubious books and articles without mentioning the names of authors—even though everyone with an interest in literature knew quite well who the writers were.

A Shanghai literary critic by the early 1980s could win a prize for an essay showing how discussions of evil figures, even when not contrasted to good models, might be socially useful. Most intellectuals still held the premise that public teaching is a major aim of literature. A piece of fiction, for example, might describe how street urchins get into fights; this could, it was argued, reflect the extent of Cultural Revolution damage to society. Another example arose in a film called *Reaching Middle Age,* in which a moralizing, leftist old woman cadre refuses to let a young woman doctor perform a cataract operation for an honored leader, simply on grounds the medic is too young. This movie held up a bad example—and used it to teach the need for more tolerant social attitudes.[93]

Since 1957, published critiques of artists had ordinarily meant they had to stop working openly, and often they had been physically abused. But after 1979, direct violence against artists had certainly stopped. The reason was apparently not that state leaders felt more sure of their institution's legitimacy, so that the silencing of literary dissent would have been needless. Quite the opposite: Reactionaries during reforms tried some coercion to further their visions of goodness and beauty, but they discovered this technique no longer worked efficiently to those ends.

Scientific Fiction and Detective Stories

Science is one of the most important bases on which modern Chinese elites have claimed legitimacy in politics. So science fiction stories are inherently dangerous, in a country long ruled by intellectuals, because they can poke fun at a realm the government likes to think crucial. Usually official censors are able to ignore this problem and enjoy the tall tales of science fiction along with everybody else.

But in sporadic puritanical moods, when top politicians became nostalgic for the disciplined Leninist order of the 1950s, science fiction came in for political criticism. During the drive against spiritual pollution in 1983, official reviewers castigated pseudo-scientific and "superstitious" elements in science fiction (as if anybody ever expected the genre to be otherwise). Thrill-seeking and macabre scenes were usual in this literature, and these have been tolerated as nonpolitical fun in some periods of reform.[94] But during others, authors have been rebuked for taking a lighthearted approach to science, the Marxist key to the universe, to which state leaders suggest their rule must have some cosmic connection. *Lèse-majesté* toward science has been interpreted by some Chinese conservatives as the same attitude toward government.

While the revolution was still centralizing, popular frivolity about science was officially tolerated only to the extent it was useful. As science fiction critic Wu Dingbo explains:

> Due to Soviet influence, science fiction was regarded as a subcategory of the popularization of science. Therefore, all the stories [of 1950–65] fall into two modes: (1) intriguing accidents plus scientific explanations; and (2) an interesting visit to the future or another planet. They are short, simple, and written in children's language; they are crude and incidental in nature, while meager in plot and characterization; and they contain too much reasoning squeezed into action-oriented linear narratives. These stories are not comparable in literary or artistic quality with the stories of the 1980s.[95]

The first Chinese science fiction after the Cultural Revolution was published in Shanghai during 1976.[96] By 1978, China's top award for all short stories went to a science fiction piece by Tong Enzheng, "Death Ray on a Coral Island."[97] A laser specialist working on PLA ray guns is confronted by a foreign consortium, which tries to steal his invention. But he is a patriot, and before he is killed, he gives his secret to a younger Chinese scientist. This story later became a film and a Shanghai opera. The plot is exciting for teaching nationalism rather than science.

Yan Jiaqi in 1979 published a novella entitled *Flight Spanning the Ages,* showing how practice determines truth in the past, present, and future. This was published in Shanghai and was soon translated into French and Japanese.[98] Yan's early fame was as a science fiction writer. After 1983, many science fantasy writers switched to more established kinds of fiction. But *Scientific Literature and Art* (renamed in 1989 *The Fantastic*) continued to turn out six issues annually.[99] In 1986, it founded the Chinese Nebula Awards for the best science fiction stories. This genre revived slowly, because it had variable prestige among intellectuals. Its popularity tells much about the culture surrounding politics during reforms.

Perhaps an even better index of the new relaxation can be found in detective stories. A private eye such as Holmes or Poirot is famously smarter than the government's public security officers. Forensic plots often poke fun at the police.

Such stories treat crimes as intellectual puzzles, not overwhelming moral problems. They are deeply reformist, rather than conservative, in a Chinese setting; and they were so in other countries before reaching China. This genre first flourished in England during a period of quick economic change that challenged some traditional values. In China, detective stories are barely beginning (except for imported Holmes on television), but Ye Yonglie published a series of such stories in twelve booklets called *The Scientific Sherlock Holmes,* of which the Popular Science Press by 1982 distributed eight million copies.[100] And for every Chinese who came across the image of an incompetent policeman in a detective story, many more saw the same image in a movie or broadcast from Hong Kong.

Literature Becomes Theater and Film

Cinema, especially if televised, is the means by which literature reaches most people during the late twentieth century. Whether or not this is desirable, it is what happens. Shanghai cinema was once, in the 1930s and 1940s, among the liveliest in the world and was overwhelmingly dominant in China.[101] It has not regained this position, despite the rise during reforms of a new generation of Chinese film directors who are world-class. They will be discussed below, because their films have much effect in Shanghai even when not made there.

Radical influences on film production, which is a relatively costly and very popular medium, remained strong in the early 1970s. Jiang Qing's personal feuds with film artists who knew her from the 1930s led, by one estimate, to more than thirty deaths in Shanghai during the 1960s. When nonopera films began to reappear, for example *The Fiery Years* in 1974, they usually retained the radicals' prescription for a single central character. That protagonist was joined by friends, then by masses to be won over; finally the enemy loses, at the end of the story. A director in 1974 explained his preference for this ascetic aesthetic: "Like good poetry or painting, the film must reject all tedious and ineffective frills."[102]

In China's cinematic world there was nonetheless evidence of diverse views during the early 1970s. More than half the workers at Shanghai's Haiyan and Tianma studios were sent away from their work to labor reform and cadre schools during at least part of this time. But the radicals had few personnel who could fill their shoes. Even within the government, some leaders expressed an awareness of a need for more films—and by implication, for the directors and actors and photographers who could make them well. Zhou Enlai echoed widespread opinions in 1973 when he urged that the lack of new non–model-opera movies "is a big shortcoming of ours. . . . Fill in this blank. . . . The masses' needs are urgent."[103] As in many other fields of reform, 1975–76 was a period in which the radicals counterattacked—in this case, by ordering studios to make films about "capitalist roaders in the Party." Sixty such films were planned for 1976. Although the early reform movement in Chinese cinema did not have any signal output, neither did these plans for a revival of radicalism.

As Paul Clark says, "A careful reading of accounts of studio activities before October 1976 tends to cast doubt on the presumption that that month was a sudden turning-point. As in other fields of literature and the arts, changes in the film world had started before 1976 and have continued to be slow and cumulative." He also writes of a "continuity of personnel in the Chinese film world in the 1970s— even if few movies were produced initially . . . . The personnel remained, apparently, largely the same after October 1976 as they had been in the first half of the 1970s."[104] A similar periodization applies in many other fields too.

Political control of movie makers in the early 1970s did not stop all their work. Because resources were partly controlled by radicals, the main obstacles to completing and showing new films were logistical. There was little point in making a movie if theaters could not show it. But "by 1973 some members of the older generation of film makers were back at work." In 1974, a children's film called *Sparkling Red Star* (*Shanshan de hongxing*) was released. This was hardly a work of political dissent, but it required enough humor to appeal to young audiences. In 1975, a controversial feature called *Haixia* was produced by Xie Tieli, who was sharply criticized by radicals but nonetheless made his movie. When his production group complained to the Ministry of Culture against bureaucratic pressure that had been applied to them, Premier Zhou Enlai saw the film. Chairman Mao Zedong himself had their antiradical letter of complaint distributed to the whole Politburo. It would be inaccurate to say that the Gang of Four, which clearly wanted *Haixia* suppressed, had its way in all cultural matters before 1976.

The radicals' film techniques evinced a "staginess," a set-piece quality, which merely reproduced what could be done on a live stage.[105] "Filmism," using methods peculiar to that medium, took hold in the late 1970s and 1980s. To jump in time for the sake of contrast, a good example of reform cinema is *Ju Dou,* shot largely through colored and misty filters in a family dyeing factory. The abstract beauty of long sheets of colored cloth hanging from poles, or the images of bubbling vats of dye, contrast starkly with the light-or-dark crispness of Cultural Revolution cinema. The radicals' artistic tenets prevented them from using the most distinctive aspects of this medium.

Characters in the plots of these two eras show a parallel contrast. In Jiang Qing's operas, the persons do not basically change; they are good or bad depending on their class consciousness. But the 1975 film *Haixia* shows its title character as an early orphan and then an adult militia woman. These are two very different stages of life, and the person evolved. This way of depicting character development strained at the limits of constancy on which the radicals insisted. Such boundaries were broken with far more abandon by the increasingly nuanced, often ambivalent personalities in later films.

Because it takes at least two years, and sometimes four, to convert a plot idea into celluloid, political changes at high levels never mean instant films. The 1976 change meant that nonradical scripts, mostly written during the early 1970s, could be produced and shown. As Clark says, "Many of the over sixty feature

Plate 1. *Street Scene in Hubei Village* by Yuan Yunfu. 1972. Gouache on paper.

Plate 2. *Flags* by Yuan Yunfu. 1980. Oil on canvas.

Plate 3. *Cracks* by Qiu Deshu. 1984. Collage of ink and color on paper.

Plate 4. *Woman Shepherds* by Jier Gebang. 1988. Oil on canvas.

Plate 5. *Facial Designs and Girl* by Guan Xiaobin. 1988. Oil on canvas.

Plate 6. *My Dream* by Xu Mangyao. 1988. Oil on canvas.

Plate 7. *The Rouge Series, No. 21* by Li Shan. 1991. Acrylic on canvas.

films produced after October 1976 were shot from scripts written a few years earlier." *The Battle of Leopard Valley* was released within six months, on the basis of a 1964 plot and a script from 1973. *The Great River Rushes On* was first shown in early 1979, although its screenplay dated from 1975.[106] This movie, which was mostly produced before Deng's resurrection in 1978, had "certain directorial embellishments" that "reflected a new awareness of audiences."[107]

By the turn of the decade, it was possible to screen films about Cultural Revolution sufferings. Depictions of human failings, constancy or inconstancy in love, and a suspension of certainty whether a plot will end happily or tragically—these elements all reentered the cinema. *Bitter Laughter* (1979, Shanghai) shows a reporter who is frustrated by having to write only prescribed kinds of good news rather than writing about the corruption he sees. He finds a way out of his dilemma by nearly random chance, rather than because of any particular heroism or ideology. *The Legend of Tianyun Mountain* (1980, Shanghai) explores the strength and fragility of love during a Cultural Revolution that tried to smash such links between people. *Rain on the River* (1980, Shanghai) concerns an early 1970s Yangzi boat voyage of a poet condemned for his opinions; most of the passengers slowly come to realize he should not have been criticized, and he is finally liberated. *The Alley* (1981, Shanghai) does not let viewers know the conclusion of the plot until the plot actually ends, and that much alone directly violates the prereform principles of narrative. *Longing for Home* (1981, Shanghai) concludes without any clarity at all on how the plot ends.[108]

Seeing a movie can be like having a dream; the image can be misty and complex, recalling the past with great or little specificity. The new films expressed in public new ways of thinking and feeling about the Cultural Revolution experience. After a showing of *The Legend of Tianyun Mountain,* apparently in Shanghai, Xie Jin reports that "the audience was moved to tears. When the film ended, a lot of spectators didn't rise. They just sat there and wept."[109] Such situations have been seen in the West, too, with films such as *Schindler's List* or *The Sorrow and the Pity.*

The cinema may at first seem to have a bias toward realism. It seems to be a medium of direct representation. An art historian of China quotes a prime theorist of cinema, André Bazin, that film is "the apogee of the drive towards realism that has dominated the Western arts since the discovery of perspective, reproducing reality in both space and time. The Chinese arts have no such drive. There is no adherence to realism, and no tradition of perspective in painting."[110] Movies ordinarily have to be explicit. They fill the whole screen, and with photography. Traditional Chinese poetry and painting studiously avoid such clarity, so as to involve the imagination of the individual.

Despite these appearances, however, the experience of watching a film is dreamlike and Daoist. The cinematographer can use lens filters, sudden shifts between different scenes, and many other techniques to obviate the inherent realism of the photographic medium. In many ways, film can acquire "Chinese characteristics," and during reforms PRC directors took full advantage of these possibilities to portray the widespread cloudiness they saw about them.

Cinema theorists for several years engaged in public debate about how closely films should adhere to the aims and methods of the theater or of literature. Bai Jingyi in early 1979 said, "There's no denying that film art has indeed derived much from drama. . . . But now that film has become an independent art, will it walk with the support of the walking stick forever? . . . It's high time that we threw away this crutch!" If live theater received a pink slip from most of the film theorists, literature certainly did not. The malleability and ambiguity of words and long stories were qualities they thought they could reproduce on the screen—and they wanted to try, because the radicals had insisted on so much stark clarity in both plots and characters. As Qiu Mingzheng said, "The more developed and mature a film is, the stronger its literary qualities and the more important a role they have."[111]

Changes of technology, not just changes of ideals, made movies more independent of control by the centralized state. The ability of the new generation of directors to make films more freely was not just a result of temporary reformist thaws. It also depended, indirectly, on a new generation of cameras. When nonbulky Japanese video equipment arrived in China, the potential costs of cinematography plummeted. Video cameras did not require a large budget to buy. They were easy to transport and required no developing lab. They were relatively unobtrusive, convenient to hide. So film production became potentially more difficult to monitor. In fact, the aesthetic of the best of the new film makers, Zhang Yimou, required bulkier equipment for wide angles and especially vivid colors. But as regards political control of the explicit content of movies, the small video cameras let the cat out of the bag. New alternative equipment gave the censors less reason to attempt tight control of the heavier cameras, more complex color processes, and even the art budgets. This technological change, like many others in different fields, gave reformers more freedom, allowing them to work with just local authorizations.

A measure of the widespread influence of films in the early 1980s was that *Popular Cinema* became the largest-circulation magazine in China.[112] This partly explains the sharpness of the conservative political reaction to Bai Hua's *Unrequited Love* (1981, Changchun). If such a production had appeared merely in writing, it would not have been such political dynamite.

Unrequited Love suggested that the collective state has obligations to individuals. The script included several lines to which severe criticism brought worldwide attention. A young girl proposing to emigrate asks, "Dad, you love your country. Through bitter frustrations, you go on loving her. . . . But Father, does this country love you?" In another scene, a Buddhist monk advises more circumspection about social acts than any simple ideology uses: "You will find, my child, that in this world the actual result is often the exact opposite of the good intention."[113]

Bai Hua therefore became the focus of a major attack against "bourgeois liberalization" in a newspaper article on April 20, 1981. Many Chinese intellectuals after the Cultural Revolution were determined they would prevent the return of any such critique. "Never again" was their resolve, and Bai Hua among them was especially outspoken. Bai made a speech at the Fourth Congress of Chinese Writers and Artists, ridiculing authors who did not write but instead spent their time currying official favor:

> I often receive letters from well-meaning comrades and readers cautioning: "You are in a dangerous position!" . . . Quite a few nonworking hypocrites rely on intimidating others to gain reputation, profit, and official rank. Of course they are people who upset the boat and fall into the water like Yao Wenyuan [the polemic writer who was one of the Gang of Four], but when all is said and done these are in the minority.
>
> I call for democracy! The China Federation of Literary and Art Circles and the Chinese Writers Association are organizations of writers themselves. They are popular associations under the leadership of the Party. I hope they are not disguised bureaus or offices of a certain ministry.[114]

Conservatives in high places declared cultural war, because they understood Bai to be attacking a resource of their legitimacy. Many of China's best-known writers decided that enough was enough, and they marched very publicly in the opposite direction. Because such a clear majority were absent without leave, the hard-liners could do little. In May, the Chinese Writers' Association defiantly awarded Bai its top poetry prize. That same month, its highest nonfiction award went to Liu Binyan, who had angered powerful hard-liners by publishing factual reports about corruption in the Party.[115]

The message of Bai's film received far more attention than it would have, if the *Liberation Army Daily* had not published the April 1981 attack. Leaders of the Party-state themselves were divided, because as individuals many of them had also suffered at collective hands. They could not bring themselves to levy coherent sanctions against this writer or his defenders. By December, Bai Hua still managed to retain his Party membership. CCP general secretary Hu Yaobang, himself an ex-rightist, said that Bai Hua's partial recantations should be accepted. The issue stopped there, without violence. The contrast with the Cultural Revolution, when intellectuals suffered far more for protesting far less, was evident to all. The Chinese revolution was winding down. The rampage against Bai Hua did not silence him. On the contrary, he soon wrote another play, *The King of Wu's Golden Spear and the King of Yue's Sword,* which was staged in May 1983—and received a good review in the *People's Daily.*[116]

Directors could thereafter more freely stage plays and make films. *Yellow Earth* (1984), has a story that makes it a propaganda film. It shows poor peasants being served by Yan'an Communists in 1939. All aspects of this movie that can be described uninterpretively and incontrovertibly allow it to be defended as rock-solid Communist. But the aesthetic is 180 degrees from that of the Cultural Revolution. The plot could be interpreted as a love story—a totally unspoken one, the peasant characters say so little. Haunting folk melodies occupy much of the soundtrack, but they are all bitter songs. Above all, cameraman Zhang Yimou offers long, slow, hard looks at barren Shaanxi hillsides—through the same deliberate eye that he later used as director of his own reformist and then international films.[117] *Yellow Earth,* directed by Chen Kaige, is bleak and introspective, and the characters are complex individuals despite the fact they say practically nothing in words.

By the mid-1980s, China was producing about 150 feature films per year, roughly the same number as in the United States.[118] Some of the mid-1980s productions (especially *Under the Bridge* [1983, Shanghai]) show the revival of a "Shanghai sensibility" bequeathed to that city's movie industry by its strong cinematic traditions of the 1930s.[119] The relatively small budgets available for such productions did not preclude making movies of high artistic quality, even though many less good films were also made.[120]

In the 1980s, at least three politically controversial Chinese films, *Hibiscus Town, Red Sorghum,* and *Old Well,* won international awards. All of these, after delays and disputes, later also won Hundred Flowers awards inside the PRC.[121] Belated honors in their own country also came during the 1990s to Chen Kaige's *Farewell to My Concubine (Bawang bieji)* and Zhang Yimou's *Raise High the Red Lantern (Dahong denglong gaogao gua).* In the early 1990s after Tiananmen, however, the Chinese films that garnered most international awards could not easily be shown in China, and they could be produced there only with the support of local networks. Zhang Yimou had created *Red Lantern* with the help of officials in Shanxi, who gave access to a feudal mansion where most of the film is set. Financial support came from a Taiwan tycoon, and production support from Hong Kong. The elegant, bare-brick pavilion in which most of *Red Lantern* takes place correlates with the precise but inhuman rules of the lineage that owns it. Together they represent Chinese culture, and perhaps also a decadent CCP.

Zhang's previous two films were both set in workplaces (a winery and a dye factory), but *Red Lantern* totally neglects the economic basis of the family's power. The heroine, who unintentionally causes two deaths, becomes a flawed personality. The clan head is seldom on-screen (never at the center of it) and is marginal to the coldly mechanical tradition that drives the tragedy. For all its stark beauty, this kind of production, in which the educated heroine (played by Gong Li) goes mad, can be seen as overstating its case for a China that has a growing stratum of middle-income people. For better or worse, they already affect its culture more than intellectuals or high politicians like to admit.

Most of the films that implicitly raise questions about CCP authority, such as *Red Lantern,* do so only by implication. A post–June 4 film, *Bloody Morning,* set a Gabriel García Márquez novel in the Chinese countryside. While nothing in this film is directly political, the story is very violent and the images show rural China in unremitting squalor. A young schoolteacher deflowers a rural woman and is axed to death by her brothers, all in a bleak and backward setting.[122] With a plot and scene like this, the government could be totally absent from the film and still emerge as totally incompetent to protect people against local tyrants.

A review of films by "Fifth Generation" directors Zhang Yimou, Chen Kaige, and Tian Zhuangzhuang generalizes about their reticent and suggestive style:

> Nothing, it appeared, could be more challenging in the wake of the Cultural Revolution than sharply defined pictures devoid of any obvious didactic purpose, surrounded by silence and open to multiple interpretations . . . a style at once lush and laconic, guarded in its statements while insistent on the right to linger over compositions as gorgeous as they are elusive in meaning. . . . Purposely empty images and gestures clearly have a liberating significance, when they follow such oppressively legible productions as *The Detachment of Red Women* and *Flowers of Friendship Blossom in the Table Tennis Tournament.*[123]

This indirect style was also needed because political statements could be public only if muted. As director Tian Zhuangzhuang said candidly in an interview, "If I had to depend on explanation, I couldn't have made films." By the 1990s, Tian was still able to make *The Blue Kite* (*Lan fengzheng*). This lambaste of CCP campaigning against ordinary people in the 1950s and 1960s is relentlessly steady but all implicit. The style remained fully Chinese, and in this case, support was foreign only by default. The government banned *The Blue Kite* from being shown in China, claiming it had been made "without permission" from the proper high authorities.[124]

Suggestive messages could be powerful in a context of some continuing political control. Most films containing them could be publicly shown and financially supported in China, especially in local networks, as openly articulated political demands could seldom be. Formal aspects of the film medium allow it to convey such messages well, and new Chinese directors during reforms took this opportunity with verve. Poetry has the same capacity to make suggestions that can be explained away even if attacked politically. Ghosts often appeared in the parts of 1989–90 Shanghai dramas that might prove politically sensitive, because the authors (if later questioned) could claim these were obviously just dream sequences, not intended to represent any reality.[125]

Later some directors, like musicians and painters, chose for financial reasons to do more work for foreign audiences (and the booming eminence of the Chinese film industry was enhanced by Lee Ang, a director from Taiwan working with both Chinese and Western materials). Painter Chen Yifei's nostalgic film *Reverie on Old Shanghai* was followed by Zhang Yimou's *Shanghai Triad,* which is not nostalgic but is also set in the bad old Shanghai of the Republican era. Despite differences between these films, their audiences, technologies, and finances were largely foreign. They were products of late reforms, and they were not about the PRC. The midreform films, by contrast, because of shifts between thaws and freezes that typified those years, arguably made a more important artistic contribution.

By no means, however, were most Chinese movies in the reform period "fine art cinema." The best directors have worked with state subsidies and then with overseas revenues. Light "entertainment films" (*yule pian*) have made higher profits inside China.[126] Like "decent" *tongsu* popular music rather than rock, and like popular art rather than dissident painting or abstracts, "entertainment films" could be supported by state conservatives.

Theater, Pingtan, *and Brecht*

Theater also diversified. In Shanghai, the summer of 1979 saw a restaging of several dramas from the odd period after 1937 when the International Settlement was an "orphan island" (*gudao*). The city was at that time surrounded by Japanese-occupied territory, but it was able to support a lively Chinese theater. *Shanghai Night,* a 1939 drama by Yu Ling, and *The Night Inn,* by Shi Tuo and Ke Ling, returned to the local stage four decades later.[127]

More public in the late 1970s were street artists, who sang songs, offered Shanghai operas, told stories, or otherwise indulged their hobbies in places such as Fuxing Park at the center of the old French residential quarter. Sometimes they made money, but the government regarded the content of their art as unhealthy or of low quality. These "freedom performances" (*ziyou yanchang*) were officially disapproved, and some were deemed illegal, but they occurred frequently.[128] They are a good introduction to a distinctive element of East China's theater during the early reforms: the use of an old Suzhou presentational style, combined with ideas from Germany, to stage the message that political conservatives most wanted to suppress.

Alienation, usually in humanist rather than Marxist guise, was the main literary idea that China's reform directors conveyed. Tragedy because of injustice was their most common theme. The Shanghai delta happens to be the center of a traditional Chinese genre whose formal traits allow it to express a kind of sharp, detached consciousness—a nearly ideal medium for wry remarks about injustice.

Pingtan (literally, "comment and pluck") is a mixed medium involving long critical narratives, accompanied by raucous plucking on a guitarlike *pipa*. Suzhou, near Shanghai, is the most important old cultural source for the metropolis, and *pingtan* are commonly performed throughout this area. They are a form of ballad singing, in local dialect, that both engages audiences and distances them. The director of the Shanghai Youth Theater explained this "comment and pluck" genre as follows:

> The performer is at once actor, storyteller, singer, and instrumentalist. He/she narrates the text, often breaks into singing, plays all the characters during

extensive dialogue sections, while assuming an appropriate facial "mask" for each character . . . and accompanies the text by the occasional plucking of a long-necked string instrument, or the banging of a small hand drum, while other sound is created with the human voice or a wooden gavel slapped on the top of a small table, behind which the performer is sitting. The audience is always directly addressed . . . and frequently encouraged to form opinions or draw conclusions from the story. . . . It is presented as a serial . . . somewhat like a "Brechtian" soap opera. . . . The dialects and the delight of *pingtan* create a V-Effect [alienation effect][129] which Brecht could not have improved upon.[130]

Bertolt Brecht himself had heard China's premier opera singer, Mei Lanfang, at a Moscow performance in 1935 and had written a highly laudatory critique: "The audience can no longer have the illusion of being the unseen spectator. . . . The performer's self-observation, an artful and artistic act of self-alienation, stops the spectator from losing himself in the character completely. . . . The Chinese performer is in no trance. . . . He does not mind if the setting is changed around him as he plays."[131] Brecht opined that Western dramatists could learn from Chinese traditions how to get audiences thinking about their alienated condition.

By the 1980s, East China intellectuals greatly appreciated the best current performer of *pingtan,* Jiang Yunxian. What Brecht did with Kurt Weill's music, storyteller Jiang did with the *pipa.* Sharp irony, quick shifts of plot, violence, and banging—and social content with a wink—were all standard fare in these epic Suzhou ballads. Here were strong means to tell the story of the 1960s.

It was only grist for the Brecht mill that Shanghai Gang of Four polemicist Yao Wenyuan had in 1963 specifically attacked "the dangerous tendency of capitalist artists acclaiming the bourgeois dramatist Brecht."[132] Yao's unintended effect was to legitimate productions of Brecht's plays after the radicals fell. The reform reasoning was politically airtight: If Yao disliked it, then it had to be good. Brecht's plays advocate kinds of thinking that mock patrimonial hierarchies and seek concrete freedoms. Very explicit stamps of disapproval from Yao Wenyuan (and also Zhang Chunqiao) were the factors that put them firmly on the PRC's reform stage.

Brecht was not entirely new to the PRC theater. Producer Huang Zuolin, originally from Shanghai, had staged *Mother Courage* in 1959, but this bleak play about the Thirty Years' War was by the producer's own account "a flop" in the 1950s. Twenty years later (half of which Huang spent in solitary confinement and at hard labor) in 1979, Huang and Chen Yong produced Brecht's *Life of Galileo.* The play ran for more than eighty performances, "full house all the way through."[133] The Cultural Revolution had given Shanghai audiences more taste for complex tragedies.

Galileo was particularly easy to stage, since it had come in for especially vituperative attack from radicals. The protagonist is a scientist who recants. For astronomers the sun is an object of investigation, but for Maoists it is a sacred metaphor of the Chairman himself. According to a summary of the radicals' pious critique, "Brecht dared to let Galileo point the telescope towards the sun, as if it were a cannon. . . . Moreover, Brecht was propagating an anti-hero [because of Galileo's forced vacillations]."[134] The great success for *Galileo* was followed by a *Threepenny Opera* in Nanjing and three other Brecht plays, including *The Good Person of Sichuan*. There were Shanghai productions of *The Respectable Wedding* and scenes from both *Mr. Puntila and His Servant Matti* and *Fear and Misery in the Third Reich*.

Party conservatives fumed. But with Yao's radical critiques to justify them, the Brecht directors marched even further. The Shanghai Comedy Troupe "made a satire out of Brecht's noted saying that 'if you digest beforehand what you are going to offer the audience, then you would be serving them shit.'" This was a sufficiently clear critique of the political meetings held before the staging of any play. The satire "ironically switched the dialogue to another inflexible rule that 'the proof of the pudding is in the eating.'"[135] Such thoughts were new to China's stage. But they showed the distance between free-thinking theater professionals and a historically embarrassed Communist Party by the late 1970s.

An interest in theatrical distancing also influenced Chinese playwrights such as Liu Shugang, whose *Visit of a Dead Man to the Living* was staged at Beijing's Central Experimental Theater in 1985. The aim of the plot is to pique ethical sensitivities in the audience: A young man on a bus encounters two pickpockets. Showing public spirit, he challenges them, but in a quick fight he is killed. Returning from the dead to a patently unreal stage, he asks each of the other passengers (workers, cadres, and peasants, including some who know martial arts) why they did not intervene on his side, since he was trying to help them. He forgives each in turn. As a Chinese critic writes:

> A drummer was placed at an outstanding place on the stage, and the drum beats would control the rhythm of the performance. . . . Xiao Xiao forgave all the passengers, but whether the audience forgives them or not is the choice of real people. . . . after he died, he was posthumously admitted as a member of the Communist Party. According to the necessity of social propaganda, he was propagated as a "hero." Society not only distorted the living beings but also distorted the dead. There was a funeral and a memorial meeting in the drama, but the hero always wanted to laugh, so he was always destroying the solemn and respectful atmosphere of the meeting. The elegiac couplet of the meeting wasn't in praise of the dead. The first line of the couplet was "How could the story on the stage not exist in the world?" The second line of the couplet was "The character in the drama is often among the audience."[136]

It would be difficult to conceive a sharper moral challenge to an urban Chinese audience after the Cultural Revolution. Many of them knew they had done nothing while good people were being killed.

This enthusiasm for the beat of the wake-up drum or the pluck of the *pingtan* string was mainly among intellectuals. But large groups of people on the Shanghai delta liked this genre, which has great potential for detached commentary. As James Scott notes, "oral culture is irretrievably decentralized."[137] A performance of *pingtan* is sufficiently long, and its discursive tradition is sufficiently unofficial, that the presenter can voice broad political views with great freedom. This is a tradition to vie with hierarchy.

Shanghai's local theater was less constrained than Beijing's, especially at the peak of freedom in late spring 1989, just before the Tiananmen crackdown. An example was *Sacrifice to the Mountain,* a drama of barely concealed political satire that a diplomat in the audience judged "could not have been performed in Beijing" even at that time. The protagonist was "The Old Man Who Moved the Mountain," made famous in Mao Zedong's essay about that persevering hero— but it clearly referred to the gerontocracy governing in Beijing. When the old man in the drama was asked why he tore down one mountain, only to make another from the pile of rubble, he replied, "If I did not continue to do this, I could no longer be emperor. And as emperor, whatever I say is law." The diplomat who saw the drama on June 3, 1989, reported that "the audience that evening loved the play, laughing hilariously at the innuendo and the constant and pertinent cracks about the leadership in Beijing. . . . If the play could have been shown in Beijing on any night in the preceding fortnight, I doubt that many people would have laughed, though, for in Beijing the immediacy of the threat from The Old Men was very real—whereas in Shanghai, the acrobatics of the bureaucrats and politicians in the capital seemed rather irrelevant, if not comic."[138]

Popular Xiangsheng: *Politics Can Be Funny*

Other traditional genres also had formal traits that made them politically potent. The audience for "face and voice" (*xiangsheng,* alias "cross-talk") performance is probably the largest for any traditional art form in China. These colloquies are always lighthearted, full of puns, jokes, impersonations, miming, and satires. Usually they involve two comedians, but sometimes just one or more than two.[139] These stand-up dialogues, called *huaji* in Shanghainese, are an old tradition in East China. They have been very common on Shanghai TV, as well as in stage performances, during the reforms.

These dialogues always include odd logical sequences—often obliquely commenting on politics. Much audience enjoyment of Chinese cross-talk in recent years has clearly come from satire aimed at authority figures. As soon as the Gang of Four was purged, its members provided rich material for impersonation. Cross-talk artists could ridicule deposed radicals safely, but in ways that also portrayed *whatever* arrogant bureaucrat the audience wished to imagine.

These comedy dialogues are extremely popular not only among intellectuals but also in blue-collar audiences. They are often included in variety programs that also involve singing and dance segments as well, but some programs are devoted to humorous dialogues alone. Television stations broadcast as many good ones as can be organized or found on tape. Competitions between pairs of comedy interlocutors are sometimes held, and these generate long stretches of stand-up punning that can be broadcast together—and always attract big viewerships. Face-and-voice dialogues are easy to produce quickly, at minimal expense. The flexible, funny logics that hold the routines together capture the waggish, practical mentality that has appeared also in other societies during periods of tentative toleration and decompression. In English, the most renowned examples are comedies of the Stuart Restoration, when the mix of purist and reformed styles also became a fertile ground for farce.

In one of the cross-talks of the master comedian Ma Ji, an intrepid group of young women are depicted as they venture out "to catch fish for the State." This short example is political only because of their official mission, and because the twist of expectation in it became a popular logic after the Cultural Revolution.

A: When they got on board they were full of talk and laughter.
B: Sure! They were happy!
A: And in a moment were shouting and singing.
B: Happy!
A: Everyone together skipping and jumping!
B: Happy!
A: And in the end vomiting and groaning!
B: Happy! (suddenly realizing) Huh? Vomiting?[140]

The surprise at the end is funny, following an ancient comic tradition of establishing a firm rhythm of thought and speech, then giving the audience a big laugh because of a semantic jolt or pun. This is standard procedure in cross-talks, as in many other forms of comedy. It is tricky to show specific social meaning in this example or most others.[141] The logic of cross-talk may nonetheless be inherently subversive, because it shows how easily people deceive themselves. The few lines above were not intended as a summary of the Cultural Revolution, nor are they a heavy discourse on how policies at any time can go awry. But their form could cover all that in any case. They encourage forms of thought that are ironic, subversive, and nonhierarchic.

Comedians were in trouble from Maoists in the late 1960s (when for this reason cross-talks were seldom performed). But by 1976 and later, the state at least got out of the business of censuring comic logics unless they were openly political. That policy missed a point: This traditional style of thinking, even if it is taken as purely formal rather than more substantively social, offers challenges to any fixed notion of power. It is in tension with charismatic authority because it encourages finding alternative bases of belief, with patrimonial authority because it makes fun of pompous patrons, and with legal rationality because bureaucrats are so dully predictable. No ruler is safe from these jesters, even if they say nothing directly about ostensible politics.

Real-life cross-talk, with a less fixed script, sometimes occurs between CCP politicians and non-Party intellectuals. When Jiang Zemin attended a "discussion meeting on literary and art creation," for example, he had

> cheerful and humorous conversations with Shanghai writers and artists. . . . After hearing speeches by [prominent local musicians and artists], he said: "If we do not know something, we must say so truthfully. I am not an expert on literature and art, so I am here to have a heart-to-heart talk with you only as an enthusiast of literature and art." Carefree conversations began, amid laughter.[142]

Nervous humor is a response to tense situations not just in China, and intellectuals recall that their interactions with high CCP politicians have not always been carefree. Uncertainty about humor, which is typical of restoration periods after violence, was paralleled by the uncertain norms on the extent to which the state should claim a role in thinking. A book on the linguistics of humor was published by 1987 in Shanghai, detailing Chinese and Western views on what was funny (back to Aristophanes on the Western side, though only to the early Qing in China). Policy studies were all the rage during reforms, and this book gave advice on how to tell jokes.[143] Everyone by 1987 could agree that state power had been obviously misused against artists during the Cultural Revolution. Nobody seemed clear whether that meant the politicians had no further legitimate role to play in matters of human sensibility, or whether they were still as important in this realm as they had once pretended to be. This ambiguity, typical of the times, allowed a great deal of circumspect fun.

Alienation on TV: River Elegy and New Star

The most widely appreciated example of impressionism by the late 1980s was not a story but a television documentary: Su Xiaokang's *River Elegy*. This broadcast feature emphasized China's insularity. The Yellow River was taken as the center and cradle of the country, surrounded by the Great Wall on the north, deserts and high plains on the west, water to the south and east. This made for an inward-looking civilization, in which people had strong attachments to a land they could not leave.[144] According to this line of thinking, the wall that the First Emperor completed in the third century B.C. has affected Chinese people ever since. It kept them in, although it did not always keep aliens out. The makers of *River Elegy* note that foreigners came across both land and oceans to influence China, and they ask why more Chinese have not likewise gone to foreign places. The Great Wall is taken as a symbol of China's closed tradition—and inability to protect itself. The authors of *River Elegy* wonder why China is so proud of this wall, which has proven useless. The conclusion of the film report, however, is that Chinese culture has changed. Now, according to this view, China has been forced open, even at the expense of the integrity of her own culture.

Patriotic sinocentrism and foreign searching are inextricably mixed in this emotional documentary. The conclusion of *River Elegy* is that China must face the world, and the TV serial is clearly consistent with national goals of modernization. The program was made for Chinese—and some nationalistic intellectuals explicitly liked the idea that its vagueness would prevent it from being universally communicable, in particular to foreigners. One praiseful reviewer wrote, "Even if a hundred foreign experts come, they would not be able to understand a tenth of its deep meaning."[145] The same reviewer thought it would be useful to Chinese for many generations.

What the film said was much less than what it suggested. Broad metaphors, Proustian flashbacks, shifts in style from exhortation to seminar, quick breaks from themes that are later reprised, repetitions for effect, chants and drums, and especially colors—all these together produced a powerful impressionistic effect that contributed at least as much to the documentary's influence as did the discursive looseness of its argument. *River Elegy* relied above all on colors. Yellow was the tint of China and of the river's water. Red was the color of blood, reminiscent of sacrifices in wars and oppressions that were largely in vain because of feudal leadership. Finally, deep azure blue (*weilan se,* the title of the documentary's last episode) was the foreign ocean and space, where the river ended, the color of hope. For its art, this presentation depended specifically on color television. The whole concept of this documentary, impressionistic and popular as it was, would not have worked in black and white.

River Elegy was designed to "cure the root" (*zhi ben*) that brought forth tragedies like the Great Leap Forward and Cultural Revolution, so that they could not occur again. Chinese culture was taken to be the cause of the problem, insofar as national tradition came from an "agricultural civilization," not a modern one, and it had been formalized in Confucian terms. The "four little dragons" of Singapore, Hong Kong, Taiwan, and South Korea also have Confucian roots, however, as a Shanghai reviewer pointed out. Yet these places have not run into the same problems.[146] The reviewer doubted that causal, "one-way" (*danxian*) logics relating factors to consequences would easily explain the extent of China's tragedies. He said *River Elegy* brought out the shape of the problem nicely, and he thought the documentary provided as much "historical resolution" as was likely to be had on this subject.[147] Above all, it challenged people to take a "thorough," intellectualized approach to the nation's problems. The vision that China was in some sense dying brought out the problem of how to make it live. What clearly wasn't dying, though neither the movie producer nor the intellectual critic mentioned it, was the claim of neomandarins that a single normative key to truth must exist. So the intellectuals who found it should be in charge.

One review emphasized the documentary itself less than the broader "*River*

Elegy phenomenon." The TV series did not, according to this assessment, have any special artistic merit; its virtue was that it starkly discussed "theoretical questions." Its main ideas were not original, and the malaise that *River Elegy* expressed was already evident in the "culture fad" (*wenhua re*) of the previous few years.[148] The popular TV medium communicated, to a wide group of Chinese people, notions that had been common among Chinese intellectuals ever since the Cultural Revolution. It created a "consensus" efficiently. Some admiring reviewers said this message, in this medium, would allow China to reach a new stage of "planning" for the future.[149] The steady presumption was that the educated elite is the group that can plan.

The ideas in *River Elegy* were not new. Liang Qichao at the beginning of the century bewailed the fatalist passivity of Chinese culture and argued in Darwinian fashion that China must either change or die.[150] Chen Duxiu warned that China's hoariness did not guarantee her survival: "The Babylonians are no more; what good does their civilization do them today?"[151] These thinkers called for "new people," for an "awakening"; they still suggested, very traditionally, that mere willpower and intellectual understanding might be enough to accomplish such a feat. Norms were everything, for them and for other intellectuals. Sun Yat-sen also claimed, "Knowledge is difficult; action is easy" (*zhinan xingyi*).[152] This motto, if deconstructed, would justify rule by a few thinkers, not by many people. *River Elegy* typified reforms in its impressionism and its ambiguities, but this film was oddly nostalgic, trying to look back to an age of wise mandarins, not just forward to an age of democracy.

The Cultural Revolution, the Expanding Economy, and Art Reforms

Reform literature and drama, as well as *River Elegy,* mainly carried the political recommendation that intellectuals should have more power. But this message was not synchronized with the actual course of reforms, in which influence increasingly went to less articulate power networks. Some artistic reforms dwelt on the past and on intellectuals' interests. Others, especially in most television programs and in most music, were more oriented to the future and to more popular interests.

The Cultural Revolution understandably remained on the minds of dissident literary intellectuals as the principal event in their lives. A Shanghai writer in February 1989 was bold enough to suggest the establishment of a Cultural Revolution museum.[153] This idea received domestic and overseas support, because such a museum would teach young people what that disaster was. Although objections to such an exhibit had been raised on grounds it would undermine people's confidence, a columnist in early 1989 could argue that the opposite was true. The famous writer Ba Jin was praised at this time for publicly advocating more discussion of the Cultural Revolution. The Communist writer Wang Li was criticized in print for having falsified some of this history.[154]

If a Shanghai Cultural Revolution museum were too difficult to establish, according to one proposal, at least people could remember this tragedy by reading books by its victims. *Life and Death in Shanghai* by Cheng Nien (Zheng Nian) became available in the 1980s from the Zhejiang Arts Press in one translation, and from a Shanghai publisher in another.[155] By this time, many books about the Cultural Revolution were appearing—mostly on a limited-circulation basis, because this was still officially a "forbidden area." An author named Feng Qicai published serialized articles that traced the lives of many people through the Cultural Revolution.[156]

As time passed, however, many younger Chinese who could not easily remember the Cultural Revolution developed other interests. These were often intimately personal, and many were materialistic. Money had a democratizing influence on culture, even if it also affected the content of art. Literature changed as the means of its communication became more popular and electronic. Current interests made old hurts fade into memory. Artistic content diversified, as the kinds of people art addressed also became more varied.

Music

The most abstract of the major arts is difficult to relate in a formal way to social themes. "So easy to love, so hard to grasp" was Carl Schorske's complaint of music, in a research whose scope was almost as broad as this one.[157] One of the problems is that contemporary musicology is practically schizoid. "Masterpiece culture" still dominates most of this field, while a rejection of this culture dominates the rest. Virgil Thompson, a distinguished critic as well as a composer, grumbled in 1961, "What music needs right now is the sociological treatment, a documented study of its place in business, in policy, and in culture." Theodor Adorno, who is more famous for his Marxist socialism than for his musical scores, joined many others in trying to make connections between music and politics—but by the 1980s, musicologist Joseph Kerman grieved that such trends had "produced relatively little of intellectual interest."[158]

Yet music readily attracts great popular interest. Even in reform China, popular musicians could make money, while classical musicians, no matter whether their scores were Western or traditionalist, generally found themselves playing for love rather than money—and to small audiences. Minimalist pop music conveyed a kind of frankness, often more or less explicitly sexual, that many Shanghai youths found refreshing in contrast to the puritanical Marxist morals that were still their official fare. The abstraction of music, and the technical ease of its diffusion in tapes and broadcasts, gave pop musicians and audiences a powerful way of making quasi-political statements that the government could usually conserve its own resources by ignoring.

Formal changes in small-audience music during the reform era are harder to link with social trends at that time than are, for example, the more obviously political changes in small-audience visual arts. Dutch musicologist Frank Kouwenhoven warns against seeing "the interaction between political and cultural history" as "a one-dimensional, linear process."[159] The "new tide" of Chinese music, serious and popular alike, nonetheless contained a "threat and inspiration pluralism" that came not just from politics but also from a diversity of Chinese and Western traditions. Cultural elites in the reform era heard more polyphonic writing in Chinese classical music. Old instruments such as the *erhu* and *zheng* were sometimes tuned to "depart from the traditional to accommodate the use of incidentals, while the character of traditional performance techniques is retained."[160] Regional styles received great emphasis, as they had in previous eras also. Several of these genres, including some from East China, enjoyed new adaptations during the reform era. Influences from Western music, ranging at least from Rachmaninoff to Gershwin and rock, were evident during reforms.[161]

This mixture at least offered more choices than had been available before reform. The Gang of Four had labeled practically all Western music of which they were aware as "bourgeois romantic." So by 1977, Shanghai's radio stations were broadcasting many hours of Beethoven, Schubert, Chopin, and Tchaikovsky. In this first stage, composers as early as Bach or as late as Stravinsky received scant attention. The classical and romantic periods stirred interest among urban Chinese audiences first, as they have also done elsewhere in East Asia. Even Monteverdi or Milhaud, not to mention Machaut or Messiaen, took a very long time to gain even very small elite audiences. Works by these figures and by contemporary Chinese composers predominated for a few years, when lighter music ranging from the *Blue Danube* to violin fantasias such as *Liang Shanbo and Zhu Yingtai* began to displace them.

By the 1980s, official Chinese versions of Western popular styles (other than rock music, which bureaucrats disapproved) took up much airtime. Chinese rock musicians in the PRC, Hong Kong, and Taiwan became heroes among students—with political commentary at or very near the surface content of their presentations. This later stage of China's quick musical evolution during reforms, which has received more attention in the West, can be put in terms of a preceding period in which the germs of change in serious and popular music were closer to each other than the growing diversity of music would make obvious later.

Early Reform Music: Beethoven to Light Pop

In the early 1970s, some young musicians could be taught—but only in private, and only if they made little sound. Chen Zuohuang, a young prodigy from an intellectual Shanghai family (the parents were both professors), was accepted in 1972 as a student conductor by orchestra director Zhang Xiaoying. She gave him private lessons for two years. As Chen later told a reporter, "At that time, it was politically risky to learn Western and classical music. . . . I tried my best to get hold of some scores and copy them down. We dared not play the piano or any other instruments." Since any conductor's most important work before rehearsals is a matter of quiet thinking about scores, this imposed silence was not a decisive disadvantage. Chen said of himself and Zhang, "We were lucky, because we both were quite familiar with the scores. My teacher could help me, whenever I made mistakes." At first this may seem a parody of education: Chen waving silently in the air, with Zhang sometimes interrupting to make comments. But the result was a fine conductor.[162]

Classics Revived

Late 1972 publications, including the *People's Daily,* praised the value of some Chinese traditional and Western artistic styles. In 1973, the London Philharmonic and the Philadelphia Orchestra both came to China, playing Western composers from Haydn to Elgar, who were all essentially identical "bourgeois romantics" in the view of radicals. The Shanghai Symphony made a tour as far as Europe and New Zealand as early as 1975, playing both Western and Chinese music.[163]

Foreign music had a big following just as soon as the Gang of Four fell. In 1979, when the Shanghai Translation Press printed fifty thousand copies of a songbook with lyrics from the United States, Australia, Britain, and Canada, they were sold out on the first day.[164] Many of these could be justified as folk melodies, which are the explicit basis for many classics. But this period was also a high tide for serious Western music, especially for orchestras and pianos but even for chamber groups. These were all broadcast after 1976 with a verve that only the reverse imprimatur of the Gang of Four could have inspired, and their beauties easily attracted some listeners in cosmopolitan Shanghai.

Music education remained a very low priority of the Chinese government during reforms, but some urban families devoted immense amounts of time and energy to musical practice. By early 1980, the Shanghai Conservatory had five hundred students and three hundred teachers. Much of the best musical equipment had been destroyed in the Cultural Revolution, so the conservatory ran its own factory for making wind, percussion, and string instruments—everything except pianos, which are more complex. Multiple scores had been lost, and photocopying was still expensive, so new scores were hand-copied by students.[165]

As memories of the Cultural Revolution faded, however, classical music again came to be a more elite activity. More popular Western styles displaced it. One ex-member of the Shanghai Philharmonic, who had left to join Shanghai's opera company, complained of a brain drain from classical ensembles: "With pop music and dancing parties catching on, cafés, hotels, and guesthouses are competing to form bands. They advertise for players, promising big pay. For financial reasons, some of our best players have already left to join the bands." The end of socialist leisure also meant people had to work harder at their regular jobs. "Players nowadays simply have no time for rehearsals."[166]

The Shanghai Music Conservatory in mid-1985 organized a month-long Mozart festival, including symphonies, chamber music, concertos, and the opera *Cosi fan tutte*. This ended with a performance of the *Requiem* at the Majestic Theater.[167] Pianos became very scarce about this time, when the newly wealthy could afford them. "Buyers have to order at the factory and pay the money a year before the instrument is delivered. . . . In Shanghai, people formed a long queue six days before a new piano shop opened" in 1986. "Some families think a piano at home is a symbol of wealth and education." The price of pianos skyrocketed, when they were available at all. The state tried to control this inflation, even though the product is very difficult to standardize, and makers justified the price hikes because of rising raw materials costs.[168]

The instruments of the Shanghai Symphony still "appalled" visiting members of the Hongkong Philharmonic Orchestra in the late 1980s. "The Hongkong musicians had been astounded that the Chinese tuba player could get a sound out of his instrument, it was so full of holes."[169] An overseas critic in 1987 called most Chinese orchestral concerts "ill-tuned," mostly because of the instruments. The strings factory at the Shanghai Conservatory was crucial, he said, because "the breaking of violin and piano strings is commonplace, even in mid-concert." The supply of auditoriums was no better: "Shanghai has just one symphonic facility—the run-down, spitoon-equipped, 1,500 person Concert Hall—to serve a city of 12.5 million."[170]

Yet among an ardent constituency of cosmopolitan families, classical music was still valued very highly. In the mid-1980s, the Shanghai Conservatory was receiving ten serious applications for each opening.[171] Some of the best PRC musicians, like some of the best painters, left for foreign countries. Zhang Xiaoying, conductor of the Central Opera House, reported that fully one-third of her orchestra had absconded abroad. She bluntly opined that musicians should be paid higher wages in China, and she pointed out that gifted young people dropped out of school early so that they could go abroad without facing the restrictions imposed on those who matriculate at Chinese universities.[172]

The main difference for music between the Cultural Revolution and reform eras needs to be specified. It was not that the state supported only certain styles of music in the radical period but many types during reforms; all official support for music was constrained as government deficits rose. Instead, the main difference was that the state came to recognize the popularity in local networks of a greater variety of music, including many that it could not prevent but sporadically discouraged. In this sense, the reform of music was like the reform of rural industry. It was a change from the earlier usual unanimity among different kinds of local and central leaders about what they desired.

National flavor, in music "with Chinese characteristics," was generally one of the desiderata. But all music is somewhat abstract. Its reform nicely exemplifies the difficulties of guiding change in a way that distinguishes nationally desired from internationally imported elements. This field's reform, more clearly than the reforms of other fields in which the same problems exist but are obscured because of overdetermined symbolism, shows that what Chinese people wanted and what came from abroad are not identical but are intertwined.

Shanghai composers—writing light music in a variety of styles for both Chinese and Western instruments—have used Han and minority folk melodies in a mixture of styles that is very eclectic. Most of the pieces on one such Shanghai recording originated well before the reforms, mingling Chinese and Western styles freely. Zhejiang opera fashions are evident in a violin concerto depicting the folk tale about cowherd Liang Shanbo and weaving maiden Zhu Yingtai. Another violin piece, adapted from an earlier composition for the two-stringed *erhu,* presents Chinese folk tunes but in a manner apparently indebted to Max Bruch.[173] Other composers have adapted to old Chinese peasants' songs the same style that Bartók used to good effect with Hungarian folk melodies. Although a few of the finest young Shanghai musicians, such as cellist Wang Jian, have been able to seek their fortunes abroad, the reform period has made far less contribution to the repertoire they actually play than have either Western or pre–Cultural Revolution Chinese composers.

It can be very hard to distinguish imported modernism from Chinese traditionalism in PRC serious music. Some of the freedoms of tonality and structure that twentieth-century Western composers have found are very compatible with old Chinese music. The tuning may be less standard, not necessarily adhering to absolute pitches. Pentatonic intervals (in more than one kind of five-tone scale, actually) "sound Chinese" but may also be found in twelve-tone music. Dutch musicologist Frank Kouwenhoven cites a 1979 song by Luo Zhongrong (who studied in Shanghai before 1949), calling it "the first strict twelve-tone melody ever written in China . . . an attractive but entirely Western type of art-song on a pentatonic basis."[174]

Serialism, not just atonalism, could also be linked to Chinese traditions, especially to the rhythms of percussive ritual music. An old style, for example, used a series of equal-time lines, all containing the same number of beats (e.g., two quarter notes along with six eighth notes each) but with the placement of the two longer sounds varied in each line. This creates a tight serialist "pulse of quavers with rapidly shifting long accents." Especially when the pitches were based on Chinese folk songs, this could sound very national in the PRC—but also like Bartók. Except for these Chinese traditions (and perhaps despite them), Bartók could be identified as the greatest foreign influence on modern Chinese music. As composer Qu Xiaosong (b. 1952) said of his 1981 string quartet that uses Chinese folk melodies: "I began writing it before I had heard any Bartók. So you can imagine how surprised I was when, shortly afterwards, I discovered Bartók and found striking similarities to my own music."[175]

Another resonance between contemporary Western music and a Han musical tradition is the extensive use of percussion. Rhythm is, of course, a crucial element of most music. But Ge Ganru, writing *Lost Style* (*Yi feng*), a solo for amplified cello at the Shanghai Conservatory in 1983, created "a truly astonishing piece, in which Ge employs the cello mainly as a percussion instrument. . . . It may well be termed the first genuine avant-garde piece in mainland China."[176] Like many other talented composers, Ge soon moved to America, where he spent part of his time earning money at ordinary jobs and his leisure composing string quartets, works for prepared piano, and a Buddhist requiem for choir and orchestra. A surprising number of China's artists were attracted to the West, and the musicians went especially to New York.

Back in China, the atmosphere was especially restrictive after mid-1989. Kouwenhoven notes that the output included "full-scale Stravinskian ballets, as well as works of well-nigh Elgarian pomposity for all sorts of official occasions. . . . At present, the absolute limit of 'modernity' seems to be drawn at twelve-tone music."[177] In serious music as in rock music, however, some artists simply refused to wear official straitjackets. They traded government support for creative freedom—and even after 1989, the cultural bureaucrats fumed about them but seldom could stop them.

Just as valid aesthetic questions can be asked about late-reform commercialized paintings and "entertainment films," many traditionalist players of "national music" (*guoyue*) were highly critical by the mid-1990s that reforms were destroying competence in their art. *Pipa* player Tang Liangxing, for example, wrote an essay skeptical of modernist influences on Chinese music. After a nostalgic reminiscence about growing up in Shanghai to the dulcet sounds of the many varieties of "Jiangnan silk and bamboo" (*sizhu*) music, he complained:

> The opening up of Chinese society has triggered a decline of Chinese music. Most performers have turned to hotels, night clubs, and dance halls to earn a living. With a cut in government subsidized salaries, orchestras are encouraged to seek alternate sources of income. The Shanghai Traditional Orchestra has begun leasing long-term space to pop music groups and its practice rooms to outside businesses for office use. . . . If not for an occasional major concert, recording and touring engagements, the orchestra might have been dissolved.[178]

Chinese abroad became crucial for the financial preservation of Chinese music. "The Shanghai Traditional Orchestra is [in 1993] assiduously planning and rehearsing in preparation for its upcoming concert tour to Taiwan. In recent years, most of the leading Shanghai and Beijing musicians have accepted invitations from Taiwan, Hong Kong and Singapore to lecture, perform, record and teach. While continuing to work, they have improved personal circumstances as well."

For most young musicians in Shanghai, however, major overseas support was not available. On any day after 5:00 P.M. at conservatories, sounds of practice were seldom heard, because the best students and teachers were working in more lucrative styles at hotels. Practice is essential to preserving quality in music, so critic Tang also complained, "I've viewed the annual televised Chinese New

Year's Eve cultural show, but I've never seen good quality programming of Chinese instrumental music or *Kunqu* [Kunshan opera]." An irony typical of reforms is that this severe critic himself emigrated to the United States. In the 1980s, he plucked his *pipa* on Broadway in *M. Butterfly* and performed *pipa* concertos with the symphony orchestras of Denver, Sacramento, and Long Beach.

Back in Shanghai, both commercialism and a reaction against it were evident in music as in many other fields of reform. A humorous example of the cash nexus comes from efforts to use music in medicine. "Music therapy," which is relatively inexpensive to administer but for which charges can easily be made to patients or their insurers, has been much touted by Shanghai psychiatrists for treating residual schizophrenia. The Shanghai Mental Health Center built a room with "a pleasant and comfortable environment" and "an advanced sound system with multiple sets of earphones" for its patients. In a one-month experiment, a group of patients was treated to light music, ranging from "Deep Affection" to "Rain on the Bananas," victory marches, and popular songs such as "Picking Betel Nuts" (which is "a community inspiration song"). The listeners were then tested for their degree of schizophrenia—as was a control group, in this truly modern mixture of science with art—and the treated group did better on these tests at the end of the month. Whether the good effects would be permanent, after the end of such soothing treatment, was unclear.[179] But it was evident that the Shanghai Mental Health Center had found a new and profitable activity.

A very few other contributions to 1990s music in Shanghai were more critical, less commercial, and much less soothing. On December 27, 1991, Yu Qiang, a student at the Shanghai Conservatory, organized a musical "action art" at the garage of a metropolitan garbage disposal station—after he had been strictly forbidden to perform it on the conservatory campus. Kouwenhoven mentions that Yu could explain the details of his music ritual in terms of Buddhist and Daoist precepts:

> The center of the garage was cleared and Yu decorated this space with music scores hanging from ropes: fragments of Beethoven, bits of traditional *guqin* music, scraps of Haubenstock-Ramati, of He Xuntian, even some pages of Yu's own compositions. Tape recordings of all this music were simultaneously heard through loudspeakers. The garage floor was strewn with tiny clay and wooden musical instruments.... The audience—a handful of students and some factory workers—observed it all in bemused silence, and some even joined in spontaneously. While the opening bars of Beethoven's Fifth Symphony pounded through the loudspeakers, the music sheets were plucked from the ropes and quietly torn to pieces. These were collected in a big pot and boiled in water. Ginger, soya bean oil, pepper and other ingredients were added to transform the wet paper mash into a spicy Sichuanese soup—a symbol for the "soup of life." When the soup was ready, it was eaten with spoons.... One might say that in Yu's experiment, the spirit of John Cage has found its way to China. Or is it rather a spirit which happens to be akin to Cage, but which has always been native to China?[180]

Toward the end of his concert, Yu smashed the clay models on the floor, rearranging the debris first to depict the Chinese character for person (*ren*), and then the shape of a musical note.

The Hobbesian and Stalinist idea that art should support politics was certainly not dead among conservatives in the government—or among many people older than youths. But repressive means of guiding art had proved ineffective and controversial. State leaders still wanted to govern music, but during reforms they lost confidence that they knew how to do this kind of job effectively. Western classicism was in any case far less obviously threatening to them than was pop. Old revolutionaries reacted to mass tastes based in nonstate communities—often young ones—that were both beyond their control and beyond their understanding.

Pop Music

Vocal music for youths offers the clearest examples. After the Cultural Revolution, as a Chinese music critic said, PRC composers "put their true feelings back into their songs, and their melodies broke away from the rigid pattern of high-pitched, harsh sounds of the years of turmoil. The range of subjects has widened. . . . The songs, full of poetic sentiments, have strong individual feelings and are characterized by a sense of intimacy with the audience."[181] The advent of pop to the PRC came from the West, but indirectly, through Taiwan and especially Hong Kong. Conservative northerners might have reacted against this music more quickly if they had been able to understand the early lyrics, which were certainly "bourgeois romantic" but largely (safely) in Cantonese.

The most influential musical imports to the PRC in the era after 1978 were cassettes by Taiwan torch singer Teresa Deng Lijun—and not just because she sang in Mandarin. Some of her songs explicitly reworked Shanghai pentatonic tunes from the 1930s that CCP cultural czars had castigated as pornographic or "yellow music" (*huangse yinyue*).[182] Mid-1980 saw a major debate in the *Wenhui News* about "decadent" music. This paper had published an article claiming that music should never be banned on grounds it could harm youths. A conservative reply to the editor, however, said such tunes kept the young from work and study, caused them to violate the law so as to get tapes and recorders, and encouraged them to hold dances at home "until the wee hours of the morning." Yet another letter asked how music could be called "pollution" if people liked it. Yet a third letter to the editor took a middle position, saying that many of the new songs had words that were dubious, but they also had good, catchy tunes.[183]

Chinese conservatives fully realized the political importance of pop music (even if some American political scientists may have more difficulty with this). The hard-liners wanted to define what they opposed; so a conservative press in late 1982 published a book called *How to Distinguish Decadent Music*. The problem with yellow music lay in its effects: "After listening to bad music, one must be very careful to avoid harm." Even a march by John Philip Sousa was criticized: "It slyly avoids the beat that people expect and forces them to accept the unexpected, the abnormal beat. . . . Dancing to this kind of beat is like having nervous spasms."[184] Formally, this was in some ways like cross-talk; conservatives saw danger in the unplanned spontaneity of such music. But unlike crosstalk, such music did not have the cover of being Chinese. A jazz club was closed in Shanghai during 1982; and this book gave reasons: "The rhythm of jazz is against the normal psychological needs of people. It leads people into an abnormal, demented state." In general, decadent music could be distinguished by "how the song is sung, the timing, the quivery rhythm, extra notes, and unclear, loose, drunken pronunciation."

Even an ability to recognize such evil is no guarantee against its deleterious effects, because such music is like a vortex for people's imaginations, according to this view. The book's straightforward advice was simply to stay away from it.

> Because of the massive use of soft, turbulent, and alluring rhythms, one may find one's body movement will coordinate with the beat against one's will. . . . No matter how excellent your ability to distinguish pop content and feelings, there is no escape, and you are bound to be attracted and influenced as long as you listen.[185]

This critique suggested, but avoided stating, the novel feature of most popular music during reforms: Its topic was the naturalness of naked truth, especially sex. Explicit sexual content in these presentations attracted urban youth, and it was inseparable from an appeal for more frankness in politics. Youths found this exciting and liberating in a stuffy society. The older generation had to admit how badly it had managed in recent decades, but elders were divided on how fast to bring in new managers who could act more effectively and express themselves more frankly. The individual and political aspect of China's new music raised modes of free thinking that endangered conservatives at least as much as it endangered youths.

Old politicians avoided public discussion of the sexuality in new music, and singers were only sometimes less careful.[186] Shanghai's young people nonetheless became more self-conscious as a group during reforms—even though they mostly remained unorganized (except in the Youth League under Party direction). This age cohort does not ordinarily articulate interests politically in China, as in most countries. But much evidence shows that youths became increasingly conscious of lifestyles. In the summer of 1988, the most frequently seen T-shirt slogan on Shanghai streets was "*Xinyidai*" ("a new generation"), printed in romanization without characters and clearly identifying its wearers.[187] Attire became far more varied than in earlier years, and Shanghai youths clearly came to care about it as much as do youths in other modern cities. New popular music was the main, though not the only, media for symbols that held together a generation who, by midreforms and in 1989, went into politics on a larger stage.

The suggestive minimalism of popular music—both the notes and the lyrics—clearly appealed to many Shanghai youths. It was seldom directly about politics. But it hindered the possibility of youth mobilization in support of older elites, such as Mao had used effectively during parts of the PRC's first two decades. Music provided the clearest symbols for a generation whose politics was usually inarticulate and was basically changed.

Later Reform Music: Minimal State Funding or Control

The government found itself unable to displace the particular kind of youth culture that emerged, partly because it could not find good alternative players and singers. The Chinese Musicians' Association, the clearinghouse for official efforts to guide music education, ran six magazines by 1986. But lack of funds was described as "a major stumbling block" for new music even of the government-approved kinds.[188] The Shanghai Philharmonic was specifically praised by the association for its efforts to persuade government officials to fund classical music—a problem very well known to orchestras in other countries also—but the audience even in this most cosmopolitan of China's cities was increasingly limited. Pop music was the growing kind, and for that too, state support was limited.

The prosperity of newly rich entrepreneurs, often without education, correlated with an invasion of Western culture that many Chinese intellectuals considered low-class: too much Madonna, not enough Mozart, and both of these were foreigners. The government had financial problems, while suburban entrepreneurs lavishly financed imports to their taste. Westernized intellectuals and conservative politicians thus had some common interests. A 1986 article by a vice president of the Chinese Musicians' Association in effect pleaded with conservatives to help "right-thinking" musicians more: "With China opening to the world, 'unhealthy' foreign pop music has become prevalent. . . . Such a phenomenon is a result of the neglect of aesthetic education . . . . Music teaching in middle and primary schools is still poor, and musical entertainment is thin."[189] This gap was filled by music from Chinese pop artists abroad.

Pop Politics Becomes Rock Politics

Music, especially when televised, was the main medium for conveying overseas Chinese culture to many in Shanghai. Taiwan songs were reprinted there in bulk, often as "folk music." When it could be claimed that the lyrics were from Taiwan's aboriginal (*gaoshan*) minorities, this added not just anthropological but also political correctness. Cassettes from Taiwan and Hong Kong were often copied for resale.[190] Thirteen million tapes of pop songs were sold in Shanghai during the first half of 1986. Some classical items also sold well, and official reports emphasized these, but pop music from Hong Kong and Taiwan was the overwhelming bulk of the new market.[191]

Conservatives were wary these songs would propagate ideas to weaken their own cause, and they objected. Many elderly people, whom they presumed socially more important than youths, agreed with them—which made conservative criticism of the youths' new music seem solid politics. The head of the Chinese Musicians' Association in mid-1985 roundly condemned the imports: "Most Hongkong and Taiwan pop songs are the products of capitalist societies and meet the needs of customers in their bars. . . . We do not give them our support, and we should boycott them." He said PRC composers should write songs to "stir patriotic hearts."[192]

Popular songs in the 1980s were increasingly "pornographic," according to conservatives. A *Wenhui News* journalist was dismayed by the popularity of a song from the Japanese occupation period, which he found booming from cassettes in several Shanghai parks. He called it "bitter, demoralized, and pessimistic." He thought reform music should instead be "happy tunes, especially marches."[193] But that had been the Cultural Revolution style, which was one reason why composers did not adopt it readily later.

Conservatives tried to sponsor alternative music that might appeal to youths. The words of a state-supported song transformed the obviously sexual allure of other pop songs into terms that were more acceptable to those who wanted stability rather than excitement: "I hope for the day, / I hope for the day of no tears and hatred, / No more bloodshed and chaos; / Let us share a world of beauty. / Oh, year upon year we welcome our tomorrows, / Oh, let this world be overflowing with love."[194] This was not class struggle, but it was not like the more risqué Hong Kong croonings, either. Many youths, for better or for worse, preferred the latter. Young people could be detained by police for attending parties at which they "danced in a vulgar way under dim lights to the accompaniment of unhealthy music on a tape recorder."[195]

Approved popular music (called *tongsu yinyue*) became publicly distinguished from rock music (*yaogun yinyue*), but not on the basis of formal style. The official genre, as Andrew Jones shows, is particularly multifarious as to form. The basis for the distinction was politics: Approved popular music was explicitly supported as propaganda, while the rock style became a separate genre because of the CCP Propaganda Department's explicit rejection of it. The main reform in mass-audience music was that rock nonetheless became available in China. The cultural commissars lacked the resources effectively to prohibit it.

Rock music did not take off in China until the crucial mid-1980s crisis of reforms, as noted in the economic and fiscal chapters in Volume One. Cui Jian, the most creative and prominent rock musician, did not compose his own songs before 1984. He began as a trumpeter in the Beijing Philharmonic. He founded his first band in 1985, along with six classically trained colleagues from that orchestra. The link between classical Western music and rock is a clear one, although Cui's musicians soon moved beyond Mozart and Mendelssohn. They had no official financial support, of course, and they lacked money to buy new instruments or to stage large performances. So they were largely unknown until May 1986, when Cui performed "I Have Nothing" (*Yiwu suoyou*) at a large variety concert involving many more approved groups. Cassettes of his music spread like wildfire in this relatively liberal year—which ended with the campaign against bourgeois liberalization. Cui's performances were then banned, and he was fired from the Philharmonic. A Party official asked, "How could a young person in new socialist China have nothing?"[196]

Rock lyrics sometimes suggested the remorse of ex–"educated youths" who were recently returned to cities early in that decade and were reassimilated as part of the urban scene. Other rock lyrics appealed to students, who were supposed to be a young elite but whose job prospects early in the 1980s were somewhat hindered by the influx of superb candidates from the cohorts who would, if there had been no Cultural Revolution, have graduated from tertiary institutions before then. By the mid-1980s, official popular music could be broadcast on TV; rock could not. Rock music was played only on cassettes, at semisecret concerts (often held under "extraterritorial" protection at foreign joint venture restaurants that police were loath to enter), and occasionally by hunger strikers at Tiananmen.[197]

The main origins of Chinese rock music are clearly foreign imports. Formally, the rock style is often percussive but otherwise very dissimilar to anything in Han tradition. Many styles of PRC government are traditional—as the rock musicians explicitly mean to suggest by contrast. Standard rhythm, 4/4 time, is overwhelmingly usual in rock. Rhythmic variations, if any, practically never follow the mathematical patterns common in some elite Chinese music, either ancient or contemporary. Pentatonic tunes are very rare in rock, although they are common in traditional Han music. The rock lyrics are seldom pastoral; on the contrary, they often refer to an individual's resentment of oppression, and the individual is represented by the singer, who croons sentences in which the grammatical subject is often the pronoun "I." The vocal tone is usually rough rather than pure. Melodic lines tend to be short rather than long or involved.

The essential attraction of rock was political defiance. As a Communist songwriter put it:

> Rock is essentially a kind of emotional release, something that's out of step with society, a way to let off steam about oppression and depression. It's like a public toilet where people can express things they otherwise couldn't express. . . . Rock is anti-tradition, anti-morality, anti-logic. You can hear that in the lyrics. This is reasonable, but it isn't suitable under present conditions in China.[198]

A 1986 performance of the British pop duo Wham! left an especially bitter taste in the mouths of Chinese authorities. So then the Shanghai Bureau of Culture identified an all-woman Los Angeles group called SheRock that it considered more acceptable. After trips to America by cadres in the bureau and the local broadcasting station, the women of this group gave a "pop rock miscellany" concert, with an emphasis on "good clean fun," in Shanghai's Jing'an Hall.[199] All the musicians had classical training. Their trip in China was supported by officials as a healthy foreign influence. The lead singer told a Hong Kong journalist, "We had to modify our dress and some of the lyrics.... For example, we had to change the word 'freedom' to 'friendship,' as freedom has rebellious connotations. But that didn't worry us. We were representing America, and we were prepared to make a few adjustments to our act."[200]

The December 1986 student demonstrations in Shanghai began because of a rock concert. An American group was performing in the Jiaotong University gymnasium, and a graduate student responded to the rock band leader's invitation and started dancing—although the police had apparently thought of this event as a concert without a dance. After the student returned to his seat, "two plain-clothes policemen took him to a room backstage and allegedly punched him. The authorities were notified of the incident and the dancer was brought back to campus by representatives of the Students' Association. The next day, big character posters calling for democracy appeared on the walls of Jiaotong University.... The incident was the immediate cause of the student unrest at Jiaotong, the first university in Shanghai to use campus posters and hold demonstrations [in 1986]."[201]

Pop music does not by itself cause riots, but it can become a summary symbol for groups that espouse new politics at least latently. It was seen by both sides as such in Shanghai during the 1980s. Some authorities attempted to respond by preempting this symbol, to use it as a flag for their own cause. For example, national CCP congresses have long been occasions for documentary specials on Chinese state television and for patriotic music. Before 1987, these were normally introduced with "rousing Communist anthems," but in that year "millions of Chinese waiting to see their leaders on screen were regaled with a medley of [American] pop, followed by a spirited rendering of Josef Haydn's *Surprise* symphony." The main surprise was the news, officially resolved by the Party Congress, that China was still merely in a "primitive stage of socialism."[202] Such surprises may have provided more relief than Communist anthems could, for a while at least, in the middle of the uncertain 1980s. The Party had a difficult job recruiting either Haydn or pop, but a sign of the times was that some of its cadres tried.

The state-run Chinese Musicians' Association in 1987 officially hoped to promote certain "successful pop songs" and to discourage others. As its deputy head said, "The problem is that we haven't composed enough good songs to meet the demands of the masses."[203] Pop tunes with lyrics that were deemed more suitable than the Taiwan and Hong Kong imports were honored with awards in state-run competitions. Their authors received jobs in artistic organizations of the sort that Stalin pioneered. The clear aim was to demonstrate official support for specified kinds of culture, and to encourage cultural workers to reciprocate by supporting the state.

The trouble was, during reforms nonstate arts also flourished. The extent to which unauthorized networks penetrated official organizations of the late 1980s was evident in an agreement between the PRC national broadcasting network and a U.S.-based company called Chinamerica. They contracted to air a "soft, easy listening" pop music program, "which will reach China's estimated 500 million radios."[204] The opening show began with Ronald Reagan addressing listeners with "*Ni hao*" (how are you?), followed by introductions of songs by a well-known woman announcer from the state network. Almost five hundred songs were suggested by the American side for broadcasting. The Chinese station rejected only thirteen, on minor but interesting grounds.[205] The basic reason for the state radio network's enthusiasm was clear: The American network could buy the station's time and seek foreign advertisers at high rates in hard currencies.

Pop music was one of the few arts that could find good financial support within China. The people who benefited most, however, were not the artists but the heads of firms selling music. Pop singers made far less money from their successes than did recording companies. For example, torch singer Zhang Qiang was occasionally criticized for offending socialist morality because of her tight clothes, frizzy hair, and liking for fox-fur shawls. But she received less than 1 yuan for each 2,000 yuan the recording company grossed from her tapes.[206] Her mother, who was also an ex-crooner (with a local hit in the 1960s called "Thinking of Chairman Mao") defended the daughter: "Her songs are all healthy; and anyway, love songs have nothing to do with politics. They belong to the world." However this may be, the proceeds went to the company. Pop music was fully part of the reform economy, exploitative even at this level.

The most popular PRC musician by 1988 was Cui Jian, the singer trained on classical trumpet whose "baggy grey trousers, sloppy sweatshirts, and heavy army-style boots are unlike the glittering, sequined singers in tight trousers who grace most Chinese stages." Cui's lyrics were full of allusions to politics, but in concert he "jokingly dismissed calls to perform some of his most popular—and controversial—songs." Cui's styles were diverse. Some songs, such as "I Have Nothing," had lyrics that were nearly nihilistic. His rendition of a 1930s revolutionary tune called "Nanniwan," using words from a 1960s Maoist musical, shocked conservative politicians partly because the old themes they liked were now sung in rock style. An antiwar song, "The Last Bullet," was officially attacked as pacifist propaganda. But Cui retained his popularity with youth, at least through the 1989 rallies at Tiananmen, in which he participated. After the crackdown, Cui Jian apparently avoided prison because he was careful and because the state leaders were conscious of his continuing renown among many young people. Cui remained a public figure even after the Tiananmen tragedy, offering the proceeds of some concerts to support the Asian Games of 1990.[207]

The new decade saw conservative efforts to revive Shanghai's own pre-1949 popular music, which was politically less laden than the rock music attracting youths. A cassette tape sold as "typical Shanghai music" in the 1990s contained songs in Mandarin, practically all with fast Latin beats supported by light percussion in common 4/4 time, as if from south of the Rio Grande. The texts concerned love, Shangri-la, and other themes that Jiang Qing had not countenanced in public.[208] Many of the songs, such as "Shanghai at Night" (*Ye Shanghai*), were taken directly from the most famous period of the city's popular music before 1949.[209] A few made slight allusions to chord sequences from Chinese folk music, but these were overwhelmed by Western styles and instrumentation—coming not just through Hong Kong and Taiwan, but also through Shanghai's own pre-1949 music.

To connect with an audience infatuated with rock and not much drawn to these old styles, the conservative government ended constraints against rock singers who were careful to eschew politics. There was positive publicity, even in mid-1991, for PRC rock stars such as Wang Weihua. She had resigned from a TV broadcasting job shortly after the Tiananmen massacre to set up her own band, in which she was the lead singer. Her purple lipstick, gyrations on stage, "cowboy pants," and general delight in raucousness and sexual innuendos were much like Western prototypes—and helped this singer prosper in the 1990s. Such an artist was not openly political, but impartiality was not her object: "Basically our songs are about human hope. It is our inner feelings. We focus on ourselves and analyze ourselves."[210] To keep open her chances of giving concerts, Wang Weihua (like many other pop artists) conspicuously and publicly refused to talk about politics. Many Chinese, especially political conservatives, considered rock performances such as Wang's to be lewd. But the government no longer attempted to control as much as it once did. It was now content with the lack of public challenge to its particular institutions. No one could tell—and the pop singers did not need to decide—whether this was political articulation.

Conclusion: Individual Taste and Collective Steering

The PRC offers much evidence that artistic taste does not correlate with any particular kind of politics. Richard Kraus points out that the social organization of the arts can proceed in any of three ways: radical mobilization, bureaucratic planning, or market constraints.[211] These use respectively charismatic, traditional, or rational authority. The kinds of art that are guided by these three types are different in several respects—none of which either precludes or ensures aesthetic quality, even though the political matrix in which artists work certainly can affect styles and content.

Charismatic art, for example, as it emerged among radicals in the Cultural Revolution, was designed to inspire the masses rather than to reflect their tastes. A small group of vanguard artists produced works legitimated by a practical ideology. Jiang Qing, ordering her prickly pianists and prima-donna ballerinas, was an ideologist representing a small group that wanted to change the unwashed "masses." These were in fact not collectivists; they were most proud of their prowess in conflict with others. They claimed to assert a truth fully revealed only to a few. Lenin, Mannheim, and Selznick have described the type.[212] What their art does is to attack normative incoherences, trying to change others while knowing the road to success in such a task is long and tortuous. An individualist painter or performer who had less political ambition could easily adopt a similar stance on an art-for-art's-sake basis, still justifying the artistic product in terms of norms fully understood by one or few people who had special insights on truth. Cultural Revolution radicals, in ways they did not intend, set the stage for the reforms' self-consciously individualist "murky poetry."

Traditional patronage networks may alternatively be used to support and plan art, and most classic works in the West and East have emerged with such aid. Other intellectual activity in China, e.g. in universities, is generally organized in this manner. The harmonious, "pure ideology" art that comes from this means of arranging artists is supposed to further the establishmentarian goals of a stable state. Plum blossoms on scrolls for the elite will do as nicely, in this genre, as pictures of happy children for peasants. So would an impressionist piece, especially if it pleases a Frenchman and might promote trade; but nothing conflictual is planned this way. A majority of Chinese professional artists earn their livelihoods directly from the state. Historically, on a worldwide basis, state patronage has long been a crucial support even for the artists who became famous because of their social and aesthetic independence.

Markets have now become important for Chinese artists who either have exceptional talent or have an ability to please wealthy tastes, e.g. in Hong Kong. This principle of organization produces art that sells at high prices. It has more influence in arts for which individual creators can produce physical objects (scrolls, sculptures, cassettes, copyrighted novels or scores) than in arts for which collective troupes produce more ephemeral experiences (dramas, ballets, Chinese operas, or novels or scores whose copyrights are held by official collectives). Markets abroad have recently lured many of the PRC's best artists out of the country.

Each mode of organization implies a different kind of education for artists in training, a different means of compensation, and a different view of connoisseurship. But none, apparently, requires different aesthetic standards. China's greatest modern novelist, Lu Xun, had the sharp will of a charismatic prophet to find the truth and speak individually. The anonymous state employees in many large orchestras work in a traditional environment of collectivist planning. Some of China's finest modern contemporary painters, such as Liu Dahong, now sell on the open market and care what prices they receive. All three kinds of authority, claimed by either individuals or collectives, can result in either good or bad art.

Aesthetic standards are subject to quick change in reforming societies. Historically, the most famous example is Restoration England, which produced both witty comic plays and (as a holdover from Cromwell's Revolution) the greatest work of popular Puritan literature, *Pilgrim's Progress* by Bunyan. In China, the early reform period saw a flourishing of safe, classic art forms: ink-on-paper bamboo paintings, and much foreign art that will be familiar to readers here. Beethoven had a new political message then, because the Gang of Four had opposed him as a bourgeois romantic. Michelangelo was in fresh vogue. Manet, with his nudes, took a few years longer, for those interested in painting. Popular Western dance styles, and the music and lyrics to go with them, entered more surely. Pornography and the "Hong Kong breeze" (*Gang feng*) were seen as ever-present dangers by conservatives, who kept questions of taste on the public agenda as long as they could.

Some of the most interesting recent Shanghai art does not attract big viewerships or audiences. The abstracts of Yuan Yunfu were not seen by peasants, even rich suburban ones. Most rural entrepreneurs, who did more in the short run to change China than any painter could, might well disapprove of nudes and disregard abstracts. Serious art programs were shown each night on Shanghai television in part of the 1980s, covering all periods of Chinese art except the most recent and all Western eras from the Renaissance through the nineteenth century. The soundtracks offered appropriate music by Chinese composers of various eras and by Western ones from Bach to Brahms. Also on these TV programs, an announcer with an overwhelmingly cultured baritone voice read Tang and Song poems.[213] The extent of the audience among nonintellectual workers, peasants, or new entrepreneurs may not have been large. But as a sign of the greater cosmopolitanism and freedom in Chinese art, the contrast with earlier stages of the revolution was very sharp.

Pop songs and pin-up art were more popular. The main challenge of these new forms to the conservative political order was in a single field: their portrayal of sex. This was important in ways that are hard to prove.

Cross-talks and films, which were also very popular, for that reason attracted the censors' attention. These were not much easier to regulate, however, and like *pingtan* presentations they flourished well during reforms. Their basis of support was increasingly local or overseas, rather than from the national state. Form in art ceased to interest the politicians much, even after they still hoped to control content. Political evaluations of artistic works in the 1970s and 1980s were conducted on fewer criteria than in the 1950s and 1960s, when the revolution was rising. Some intellectuals still revered the state so much, their memories of this became oddly short. In Mao's time, literature and art could be politically criticized for having inappropriate forms, as movie director Teng Wenji reminisced; but in the mid-1980s

> they don't care about form, they always talk about content. The meaning of a film like *At the Beach* lies in the form, in the cinematography, the structure. The same story told another way wouldn't be this film. But in China, if you want to issue a film, a book, an article, and they want to determine how good it is, they'll spend 90 percent on the content. They don't care about form. They should.[214]

Formal principles to guide the state in artistic matters became defunct; there was no semblance of agreement among high leaders about what such principles might be. Official decisions on art now mattered much less than they once had, as new foreign and local markets became the main source of livelihood for all kinds of painters and performers alike. State budgets supported art rarely, and then on the basis of audience and content, not quality or form.

Art was regularly censored during the reforms' conservative stages, but there were no laws to rationalize such controls. During the relatively liberal autumn of 1988, this legal lacuna became subject to public debate. A PRC publication put the situation frankly: "Arts censorship, although not specified in law, is actually carried out in China. Some art works such as films and plays must be approved by the authorities . . . . The process of censorship is a mystery to the public and the artists themselves."[215] The problem was that artists did not know what they could create and show while remaining within their rights. Journalists, who for their own reasons wanted a press law to clarify the definition of libel, were very sympathetic to this problem and publicized it widely. A *Guangming Daily* commentator had a modest proposal:

> Lawful and authoritative censorship organizations must be set up, with their power and responsibilities stated in detail. Only personnel in these organizations should have the right to censor art works. Censors must be elected democratically, so they represent the feelings of the public. They must be honest, determined, and knowledgeable about national arts. Artists should have the right to appeal against a censor's judgement.[216]

Less Official Support, Less Official Art

The state did not get the art for which it did not pay. Performing and visual media alike require some public infrastructure. In Shanghai, neglect of this for many decades created practical problems. The number of theaters in Shanghai before Liberation was over a hundred; but by 1983, it was down to thirty. Shanghai was still China's most productive province in 1983, but it was below the national average among provinces in the number of theater seats per capita.[217] The reason was not a relative lack of interest in culture among Shanghai people, but a relative discrimination against them among central budget makers.

Cultural institutions in general received low budget priority. Investment in museums, academies, theaters, and other facilities for cultural activities (even including schools) in the mid-1980s was only 0.4 percent of Shanghai's total construction budget. A discontented professor of Chinese literature at East China Normal University wrote that the lack of cultural facilities in Shanghai had become "intolerable." He suggested, possibly with tongue in cheek, that the central government should declare Shanghai to be a "Special Cultural Zone," on the analogy of Guangdong's special economic zones.[218]

Overseas support became important in both elite and popular arts during reforms, but the Ministry of Culture still attempted to keep tight oversight of

Shanghai artistic exchanges with foreign countries. The bureaucrats in Beijing were reportedly concerned with "equality between various places in the country," but they were also said not to know enough about the cultural resources of various cities. A professor in Shanghai complained that they made many faulty decisions. Art exchanges were, according to this professor, too centralized.[219]

State representatives ruefully admitted the general lack of support for arts and the consequent lack of official control over their contents. Even the minister of culture, by early 1988, was quoted as supporting the view that

> evidently the way to bring about prosperity in literature and art is to tap both state and social resources and to encourage the simultaneous development of government- and civilian-run literature and art. . . . This is quite similar to what is being done in many countries in the rest of the world: Ordinary cultural undertakings are run by civilians, whereas important cultural undertakings that are more widely representative, including philharmonic orchestras and operas, are run [with] state financial support. . . . In opposing unhealthy culture, oversimplified methods should not be used.[220]

Artists readily concluded that if the state's moralizers stopped support, then creators could rightfully go their own ways. Tang Dacheng, secretary of the Chinese Writers' Association, said in 1988 that "the association is a voluntary mass group. . . . Although literature cannot be separated entirely from politics, the Association is not a political organization but a 'home' for authors. We have no model to follow; we cannot follow the Soviet Union's experience." He went on to specify the political implications of this new loyalty: "The Writers' Association must . . . protect authors' legal rights against any violations, free authors from any illegal or unreasonable attacks, provide welfare for authors, create conditions which are favorable for literary exchange, and carry out legal business activities and increase authors' income, which will let authors devote time to their creations."[221] The new norm was clear, and it could be openly articulated in an organization even though hard-liners did not agree with it.

When the Shanghai Literature and Art Association met in early 1989, many participants argued that artists must not depend on state appropriations alone. "The association itself now has the capability to collect financial resources to support its own activity. But existing policies look upon the association as a kind of Party or government organ; they impose too many constraints on the association's ability to collect money from society. They do not allow the association to engage in profitable businesses. . . . The association can reform itself through its own forces and can provide a model for the government to use in reforming other groups."[222]

Reform Ambiguity About the Autonomy of Art

Salons have long posed indirect threats to old regimes. Especially from early 1989 into the next decade, when intellectuals with common interests could establish clubs, they did so in Shanghai. Readers concerned with the city's novelistic traditions, for example, set up a Shanghai Popular Literature Research Center—and apparently no state or Party organizations were involved.[223] Many of the authors, professors, and reporters who founded this organization noted that official literary societies did not have time to work on really popular literature. These salons did not remain merely civil; they involved mutual exchanges of prestige, separate from state control, so that they acquired some importance as local political networks. China is not the first country in which literary salons have served this role, even though the intellectuals forming them have been few and thus somewhat more subject to state control than the larger numbers whom they influence.

As elderly writer Wei Wei remarked in a May 1991 edition of the Propaganda Department's journal, "Frankly speaking, the task of opposing bourgeois liberalization is formidable." Hard-liners could not control artists, and for specialized types of art they lost interest in doing so. Even General Secretary Jiang Zemin apparently realized the government needed a broad approach in its attempt to mobilize support for post–June 4 cultural policies. Many writers had remained silent, fearing either criticism from the conservatives or complicity with them. On March 1, 1991, Jiang called a meeting of thirty eminent writers—without consulting the conservative minister of culture He Jingzhi.[224]

This gala session was held in the Cherish Benevolence Hall of the CCP leadership compound, Zhongnanhai, in the old imperial palace. The writers had sweet dumplings with their tea, but the warm official welcome scarcely mollified them. Novelist Shen Rong rose to opine that authors would be willing to follow Party policy if the CCP leaders themselves could agree on it. Another writer got up to ask whether the Politburo was really of one mind about fighting bourgeois liberalization "to the death." He noted that campaigns in the recent past had begun with great fanfare but had not lasted long.

Secretary Jiang's speech in reply was platitudinous, repeating shibboleths about writers becoming workers. They were supposed to "make socialist literature prosper." The Politburo member overseeing propaganda, Li Ruihuan, said more plainly that after Tiananmen political education would work "only if people are willing to listen to it and accept it. . . . If people run away upon seeing you, what work can you do?"[225]

The mice often won this kind of cat-and-mouse game. In early 1991, the Shanghai People's Art Theater produced a play entitled *Old Forest*.[226] One part of the plot concerned a master who had trained his dog to chase wolves. This was a political statement, critical of the gerontocrats behind polemicists who still threatened to hound artists. Long political meetings were held at the theater to discuss this matter, but the author consistently said his play was just a story, with no political intent. The People's Art Theater put on the drama, albeit to an invited rather than public audience, without further damage to any of the participants. As a connoisseur of paintings said, "So long as art can assert its own danger, it succeeds."[227] This is as true for pop songs as for intellectuals' works.

Notes

1. From Richard Rorty, *Contingency, Irony, and Solidarity* (Cambridge: Cambridge University Press, 1989), quoted in John Street, "Popular Culture = Political Culture? Some Thoughts on Postmodernism's Relevance to Politics," *Politics* 11:2 (1991), p. 24.

2. Jacques Delors, president of the European Community, is quoted in *World Press Review,* September 1989, p. 28.

3. See Richard Kraus, *Brushes with Power: Modern Politics and the Chinese Art of Calligraphy* (Berkeley: University of California Press, 1991).

4. There is no space here to cover this evolution before 1949 or even 1970, but Mao's discourses at Yan'an and other relevant topics have been analyzed well by several authors.

5. Richard Kraus argues that these trends re-create an "aesthetic realm," in "Four Trends in the Politics of Chinese Culture," *Forces for Change in Contemporary China,* Lin Bih-jaw and James T. Myers, eds. (Taipei: Institute for International Relations, 1992), p. 223.

6. Joan Lebold Cohen, *The New Chinese Painting, 1949–1986* (New York: H. N. Abrams, 1987), p. 12. This book, which is richly illustrated, pioneered the presentation of reform painting and remains a valuable compendium.

7. For the very complex details, see the best available book on the political fates of Chinese artists: Julia F. Andrews, *Painters and Politics in the People's Republic of China, 1949–1979* (Berkeley: University of California Press, 1994), pp. 46–49 and passim.

8. See ibid., p. 246, passim, and especially the stunning figures 79–80 (pp. 250–51) by Shanghai illustrator He Youzhi. Anyone who thinks of *lianhuan hua* as mere comic strips will change that idea after viewing these.

9. Ibid., pp. 303–5, especially p. 304 for the mushroom cloud scroll.

10. *WHB,* December 20, 1975.

11. *WHB,* February 1, 1976.

12. *WHB,* December 25, 1979.

13. *WHB,* September 30, 1975.

14. There are too many reform painters for this book to cover, and there are even too many whose origins are in the Shanghai delta. Fortunately, several art historians, including Joan Cohen, Julia Andrews, and Ellen Laing, have done the critical groundwork that makes this job easier. On points in the text above, see Ellen Laing, *The Winking Owl: Art in the People's Republic of China* (Berkeley: University of California Press, 1988), pp. 84–85.

15. Ibid., p. 85.

16. Ibid., p. 86.

17. Wu Guanzhong, *Painting from the Heart: Selected Works of Wu Guanzhong* (Chengdu: Sichuan Art Publishing House, 1990), p. 14.

18. UNESCO, *Chinese Paintings: Catalogue of the Thirteenth UNESCO Travelling Exhibition* (Paris: UNESCO, 1979).

19. This claim can be illustrated by Shi's *Mount Hua* (1972) and Li's *Landscape of the Pure River Li* (1975); see Julia Andrews, *Painters and Politics,* pp. 368–71.

20. This author, on a February 1976 trip to China (before the Cultural Revolution was officially over) took a stroll in a park at Jinan, Shandong, that was not on the organized tour to that city. An artist sat there, doing an oil painting of a pond that the aesthetes of the Gang of Four (then still apparently in power) would have abominated. The style was French-influenced, not at all realist. The painter was bothering no one, and no one was bothering him.

21. The Shanghai magazine *Wenyi luncong* (Arts Compendium), for example, was not

republished in Shanghai until September 1977. See *Zhongguo xueshu jie dashi ji, 1919–1985* (Chronicle of Chinese Academic Circles, 1919–1985), Wang Yafu and Zhang Hengzhong, eds. (Shanghai: Shanghai Shehui Kexue Yuan Chuban She, 1988), p. 269.

22. Julia Andrews, *Painters and Politics,* p. 373.

23. *WHB,* December 9, 1976.

24. *WHB,* January 22, 1977.

25. The foreign notion that "all flesh is grass" makes a comparison, but grass could be an original Chinese symbol. From early prophets to Luther, Brahms, or Whitman, grass has often found metaphoric uses in the West too.

26. *Cao cao* is a pun on the name of a very famous ancient general. See Joan Lebold Cohen, *The New Chinese Painting,* p. 67.

27. Stuart R. Schram, *Ideology and Policy in China Since the Third Plenum, 1978–1984* (London: Contemporary China Institute, School of Oriental and African Studies, 1984), p. 74.

28. See *Mao Zedong shuxin xuanji* (Selected Letters of Mao Zedong) (Beijing: Renmin Chuban She, 1983), p. 605, cited in Stuart Schram, *Ideology and Policy,* p. 73.

29. Conversations with John Balcom, a doctoral candidate in literature at the Shanghai Academy of Social Sciences.

30. *LDB,* February 18, 1989.

31. Joan Lebold Cohen, *The New Chinese Painting,* pp. 34–35; and for the paintings described below, p. 36.

32. Based on ibid., pp. 40–44.

33. Xiao Zhenmei, "Dalu huatan sishi nian" (Mainland Painting for Forty Years), *Zhongguo dalu yanjiu* (Studies of Mainland China) 35:11 (November 1992), pp. 95–96.

34. The portion of studio locations in Shanghai was 44 percent. Computed from material in Victor Wu, *Contemporary Chinese Painters* (Hong Kong: Hai Feng Publishing Co., 1982), which mostly deals with traditional-style painters.

35. Benedict Stavis, *China's Political Reforms: An Interim Report* (New York: Praeger, 1988), p. 29.

36. The current author attended an exhibition in Hangzhou during late 1988 and saw traditionally mounted scrolls, including one in Chinese black, gray, and white ink whose style clearly referred both to old Chinese landscapes and to French impressionists. Another was a misty abstract, almost an expanded detail of clouds in an old Chinese scroll in an area with no other representation. The author has photographs of these, and other relevant works have been published widely.

37. Xiao Zhenmei, "Zhongguo dalu de xiandai hua" (Contemporary Painting on the Chinese Mainland), *Zhongguo dalu yanjiu* 36:4 (April 1993), pp. 75–86. The last words of the article's title, *xiandai hua,* are a pun; with a different *hua,* this means "modernization," not "painting."

38. Joan Lebold Cohen, *The New Chinese Painting,* p. 122.

39. The Cultural Revolution also harmed Deng's four other children, especially his elder son, Deng Pufang, who was thrown (or jumped) from a window, still cannot walk, and heads the China Welfare Fund for the Handicapped. He also participates in several businesses, in which he has been accused of corruption. See *Time,* International Edition, May 17, 1993, p. 43.

40. Chen Jialing, *Huajing* (Transformation) (Hong Kong: Plum Blossoms, 1990), p. 6 for the quotations and *passim* for photographs of the results from Chen's Shanghai studio: plum blossoms, karst formations in fog, lotuses, and similarly traditional subjects.

41. Joan Lebold Cohen, *The New Chinese Painting,* pp. 67–69.

42. *FBIS,* December 29, 1987, p. 50, reporting radio of December 21.

43. The author bought several portfolios at the New China Bookstore, Nanjing Road,

in 1991. Sample pictures were spread prominently in a glass display case. The paragraphs in the text refer to Shao Chuangu, ed., *Zhongguo youhua zhan xuanji* (Selections from an Exhibition of Chinese Oil Paintings), portfolios 1 and 2 (Shanghai: Shanghai Renmin Meishu Chuban She, 1988). The number of reproductions was twenty-six, not bound and easy to post. The overall aesthetic quality of these paintings, while not giving the likes of Velázquez any major cause for concern about reputation, was presentable.

44. A possible interpretation of the painting—and one the artist could use if he were accused of expressing cynicism—is that the wall suggests a modern city, and the well-dressed women are tourists with their cameras. If so, some of them nonetheless look unhappy on tour. A PRC informant suggested that, from left to right, the minorities may represent a Miao or Yi, possibly a Manchu, a Tibetan, and a Mongolian (apparently like the artist).

45. Julia F. Andrews and Gao Minglu, "The Avant-Garde's Challenge to Official Art," in *Urban Spaces in Contemporary China*, Deborah S. Davis et al., eds. (New York: Cambridge University Press, 1995), pp. 221–78.

46. *Zhongguo youhua zhan*, n.p. The paintings' names in Chinese are respectively *Muyang nü*, by Jier Gebang, *Lianpu yu nühai*, by Guan Xiaobin, *Wode meng*, by Xu Mangyao, *Wusheng ge*, by Wang Hongjian, and *Wannian*, by Wang Zhenghua.

47. See Julia Andrews, *Painters and Politics*, plate 11.

48. For reproductions, see Chen Yifei, *Chen Yifei huigu zhan* (Chen Yifei: A Retrospective) (Hong Kong: Plum Blossoms, Ltd., 1992).

49. Joan Grant, *Worm-eaten Hinges: Tensions and Turmoil in Shanghai, 1988–89, Events Leading up to Tiananmen Square* (Melbourne: Hyland House, 1991).

50. This exhibition was in Beijing, although Shanghai artists knew a great deal about it and several participated in it. See ibid., p. 86.

51. *Post,* February 11, 1989.

52. A photograph of this October 1986 performance is in Julia Andrews and Gao Minglu, "The Avant-Garde's Challenge," p. 256.

53. Geremie Barmé, "Liu Dahong: Artist Laureate of China's Reform," *FEER,* March 4, 1993, p. 60. Liu was born the son of a "rightist" in Qingdao (whose beaches he sometimes paints, full of bathers). He then studied in Hangzhou, and now his studio is in Shanghai. He has not been a Beijing man. An anthropological fact that needs to be explained about intellectual communities is why they perpetuate the notion that the best thinking naturally occurs in just some locations: Beijing, Tokyo, Oxford or Cambridge, Paris, sometimes Shanghai.

54. See Lu Jie, in Liu Dahong, *Paintings, 1986–1992* (Hong Kong: Schoeni Fine Arts Gallery, 1992), p. 187.

55. *Shanghai tan,* like most of Liu Dahong's canvases, is too complex to be reproduced effectively on pages as small as the ones in this book. Only details of particular scenes could be presented here, but Liu's point is that his visual vignettes must be taken together. A physically larger book, containing photographs (even then too small) of the whole picture and of some subscenes, is ibid., pp. 42–47.

56. One of these is illustrated in John Clark, "Official Reactions to Modern Art in China Since the Beijing Massacre," *Pacific Affairs* 65:3 (Fall 1992), p. 349; cf. also p. 347.

57. Andrew Solomon, "The Fine Art of Protest," *Post Magazine* (January 23, 1994), pp. 10–11.

58. Julia Andrews, *Painters and Politics,* p. 9.

59. One of the first books in this field was Arnold Chang, *Painting in the People's Republic of China: The Politics of Style* (Boulder: Westview, 1980).

60. Hugh Moss, *Some Recent Developments in Twentieth Century Chinese Painting: A Personal View* (Hong Kong: Umbrella, 1982), pp. 15–16.

61. This oral source remains anonymous. But readers are also referred to Edmund Capon, "A Sense of Unreality: Painting in the People's Republic of China," an atypical chapter in *Twentieth-Century Chinese Painting,* Kao Mayching, ed. (Oxford: Oxford University Press, 1988).

62. Quoted in Andrew Solomon, "The Fine Art," p. 10.

63. Interview with a member of the Department of Fine Arts at the University of Hong Kong who is familiar with the situation of PRC painters.

64. Julia Andrews and Gao Minglu, "The Avant-Garde's Challenge," pp. 232 and 278.

65. The Maoist period saw much stress on the link between art and "substructure," although artists were often treated then as if their influence on history was greater than they thought. Concerning the expressive possibilities of art, as analyzed by a formal symbolic logician, see Suzanne K. Langer's classics *Philosophy in a New Key: A Study in the Symbolism of Reason, Rite, and Art* (New York: Penguin, 1942), which mainly concerns music, and *Feeling and Form* (New York: Scribner, 1943), which mainly concerns visual arts.

66. A review of that exhibition is Nicholas Jose, "Next Wave Art," *Art and Asia Pacific Quarterly* 1 (1993), pp. 25–30; Li Shan's painting is reproduced on p. 28.

67. The quotations are in *Newsweek,* Pacific Edition, August 8, 1994, pp. 16–17.

68. Karen Smith, "In With the New: China's New Art, Post-1989," *Asian Art News* 3:1 (January-February 1993), p. 36.

69. John Clark, "Official Reactions," pp. 335–36.

70. A brilliant but involuted approach to interpretation, which is ultra-intellectual and would make no sense at all to workers despite its avowedly Marxist argument, is Fredric Jameson, *The Political Unconscious: Narrative as a Socially Symbolic Act* (Ithaca: Cornell University Press, 1981).

71. This story is in Helen F. Siu, ed., *Furrows: Peasants, Intellectuals, and the State* (Stanford: Stanford University Press, 1990), pp. 147–55. Hao's book's title is *Jin'guang dadao.*

72. *Hongse niangzi jun* and *Gangqin xiezou qu "Huang he."*

73. See Yu Shiao-ling Shen, "The Cultural Revolution in Post-Mao Literature" (Ph.D. dissertation, University of Wisconsin–Madison, 1983).

74. The fearsome "house searches" (*chaojia*) were a phenomenon of the late 1960s, and nothing in the interpretation above should be read to imply they were not serious hindrances to all literary and scholarly work. By the 1970s, however, they had mostly stopped. *WHB,* May 23, 1979.

75. *WHB,* September 4, 1975.

76. *Zhongguo xueshu,* pp. 263–64.

77. *WHB,* February 4, 1976.

78. The title, *Wanshui qianshan,* is taken from a poem by Mao Zedong. *WHB,* December 12, 1976.

79. *WHB,* January 1, 1977.

80. *WHB,* January 2, 1977.

81. *WHB,* January 1, 1977.

82. *WHB,* January 2, 1977.

83. *Yu bei, wen gui jiao, Wo ku, cai lang xiao. Sa lei, ji xiong jie, Yan mei, jian chu xiao.* Hsu Kai-yu, "Contemporary Chinese Poetry and its Search for an Ideal Form," in *Popular Chinese Literature and Performing Arts in the People's Republic of China, 1949–1979,* Bonnie S. MacDougall, ed. (Berkeley: University of California Press, 1984), p. 260.

84. The text above does not consider whether Mao was a good poet, because that

question has become unnecessarily knotted with political controversy. Ibid., pp. 248–49. Hsu categorizes the kinds of Chinese stanzas into these types: modern free verse (as in Mayakovsky), "long songs" (*fangge*), folk songs, the "new *ci-fu* style," traditional *shi, ci,* and *sanqu,* as well as "sets of poems" (*zushi*), pp. 250–61.

85. This recitation was in Beijing, not Shanghai, where such events were less frequent because of a lower density of intellectuals, their fewer connections with high cadres, and local pride in a habit of avoiding public confrontation with the state. But Shanghai intellectuals knew, of course, about such events and contributed to them. Quoted from an essay by Ke Yan, "A Few Words in Defense of New Poetry and the Literature and Art Contingent," in *Chinese Literature for the 1980s: The Fourth Congress of Writers and Artists,* Howard Goldblatt, ed. (Armonk, NY: M.E. Sharpe, 1982), p. 80.

86. Helen F. Siu, tr., "Introduction," in *Furrows,* p. 1.

87. "Ban zhuren" and "Shanghen" are the stories' titles. Bonnie S. MacDougall, "Writers and Performers, Their Works, and Their Audiences in the First Three Decades," in Bonnie S. MacDougall, ed., *Popular Chinese Literature,* p. 302.

88. *Yu wusheng chu.* See Yu Shiao-ling Shen, "The Cultural Revolution," p. 275.

89. *Ren, ah ren* by Dai Houying has been translated as *Stones of the Wall* (London: Sceptre, 1987). A symbolic logician's parsing of the formal means by which various arts can echo subjective situations is Suzanne K. Langer, *Philosophy in a New Key,* largely about music (which is discursive), and *Feeling and Form,* largely about fine arts (which are mostly nondiscursive).

90. The Chinese names of these journals, in order, are: *Shanghai wenxue, Xueshu yuekan, Wenyi lilun yanjiu, Wenhui bao,* and *Jiefang ribao. Shanghai shehui kexue* (Social Science in Shanghai), Institute of Information Studies of the Shanghai Social Science Academy, ed. (Shanghai: Shanghai Shehui Kexue Chuban She, 1988), pp. 76–78.

91. This term has also been used for the 1961–62 era in which the Party tried to neutralize intellectuals' dissent about economic failures by having them discuss other topics in public. See Lynn White, *Policies of Chaos* (Princeton: Princeton University Press, 1989), p. 174. But on reform writers, who by 1977 faced a declining revolution rather than the rising one of 1957, see Michael Duke, *Blooming and Contending: Chinese Literature of the Post-Mao Era* (Bloomington: Indiana University Press, 1985), chap. 1.

92. John Clark, "Official Reactions," p. 337; see also p. 341.

93. *Shanghai shi wenxue jiang huojiang zuopin ji (1982–1984 nian lilun pinglun)* (Collection of Prizewinning Works in Shanghai Literature [Theory and Criticism, 1982–1984]) (Shanghai: Shanghai Shehui Kexue Yuan Chuban She, 1986), pp. 4–5, discusses the film *Ren dao zhongnian.* For much more on allied topics, see ibid.; see also Wu Liang and Cheng Depei, eds., *Xin xiaoshuo zai 1985* (New Novellas in 1985) (Shanghai: Shanghai Shehui Kexue Yuan Chuban She, 1986) and *Xinwen xiaoshuo zai '86* (News Novellas, '86) (Shanghai: Shanghai Shehui Kexue Yuan Chuban She, 1988). The reform of Shanghai literature, as it reflects general trends of reform in the metropolis, is only a small part of the present book—partly because literary writers can speak for themselves without the need for mediation by a social scientist, and partly because fine scholars are already thinking about the topic. A young member of this group is John Balcom, once of the Shanghai Academy of Social Sciences.

94. Wu Dingbo and Patrick D. Murphy, eds., *Science Fiction from China* (New York: Praeger, 1989), p. xxxii.

95. Ibid., p. xx.

96. Ibid., p. 168, refers to Ye Yonglie's *Shiyou danbai* (Strange Cakes) in Shanghai's *Shaonian kexue* (Juvenile Science), no. 5, 1976.

97. *Shanhu dao shang de siguang* in *Renmin wenxue* (People's Literature), August 1978; see Wu Dingbo and Patrick Murphy, eds., *Science Fiction.*

98. Yan Jiaqi, *Kuayue shidai de feixing* (Shanghai: Shanghai Renmin Chuban She, 1979); Wu Dingbo and Patrick D. Murphy, eds., *Science Fiction*, p. xxiii.

99. *Kexue wenyi* and *Qitan*.

100. Wu Dingbo and Patrick D. Murphy, eds., *Science Fiction*, p. xxiv.

101. Fu Poshek of Colgate University is currently writing a book about films in "orphan island" and Japanese-occupied Shanghai. Most of the directors from this golden era of Shanghai cinema later came to Hong Kong, where they created the main Chinese film industry after the early 1950s.

102. Paul Clark, *Chinese Cinema: Culture and Politics Since 1949* (Cambridge: Cambridge University Press, 1987), pp. 133–36.

103. Ibid., p. 138.

104. Paul Clark, "The Film Industry in the 1970s," in Bonnie S. MacDougall, ed., *Popular Chinese Literature*, pp. 178–81.

105. Ibid., pp. 183–86.

106. These films are *Baoziwan zhandou* and *Dahe benliu;* ibid., p. 182.

107. Paul Clark, *Chinese Cinema*, p. 147.

108. *Ku'nao ren de xiao, Tianyun shan chuanqi, Bashan yeyu, Xiaojie, Xiangqing.* This relies heavily on Paul Clark, *Chinese Cinema*, pp. 162–65.

109. Quoted in "Interviews," in *Chinese Film: The State of the Art in the People's Republic*, George S. Semsel, ed. (New York: Praeger, 1987), p. 110.

110. Catherine Yi-yu Cho Woo, "The Chinese Montage: From Poetry and Painting to the Silver Screen," in *Perspectives on Chinese Cinema*, Chris Berry, ed. (Ithaca: Cornell China-Japan Program, 1985), p. 21.

111. Quoted in Xia Hong, "Film Theory in the People's Republic of China: The New Era," in George S. Semsel, ed., *Chinese Film*, p. 44.

112. *Dazhong dianying*. Paul Clark, "The Film Industry," p. 188.

113. *Kulian*. This relies on Paul Clark, *Chinese Cinema*, pp. 169–70.

114. In Howard Goldblatt, ed., *Chinese Literature*, pp. 61 and 66.

115. Merle Goldman, *Sowing the Seeds of Democracy in China: Political Reform in the Deng Xiaoping Era* (Cambridge: Harvard University Press, 1994). There is not space in this book to do justice to Liu Binyan, the author's fellow Princetonian and friend, or more generally to the rise of "reportage" (*baogao wenxue*) on CCP corruption. Most of Liu's work concerned North China, although Shanghai and places farther south certainly suffered corruption too. Link, Goldman, and many others—including Liu—have already published extensively in English about this.

116. *Wuwang jinge Yuewang jian*. Yu Shiao-ling Shen, "The Cultural Revolution," p. 279.

117. After shooting *Huang tudi* (*Yellow Earth*), Zhang's first effort as a director was the extremely successful *Hong gaoliang* (*Red Sorghum*), which was also a major vehicle for the Chinese cinema's foremost actress, Gong Li. *Red Sorghum*, even though set during the Japanese occupation in a very poor area, is not so introspective as *Yellow Earth*—but is just as personal, because of the sexual links between the main two characters.

118. George S. Semsel, "Film in China," in *Chinese Film*, p. 1.

119. *Daqiao xiamian*. Paul Clark, *Chinese Cinema*, pp. 176–78.

120. An example of the latter sort is *Daihao Meizhou diao* (Code Name Cougar), a film about terrorists-without-a-cause hijacking an airplane from Taiwan to the mainland. This movie for a popular audience includes gunfights mixed with slow, merely quasi-political suspense. Zhang Yimou codirected, and Gong Li was the main actress; but surely nobody thinks this was their best work.

121. *Post*, September 29, 1988.

122. *South China Morning Post Spectrum*, June 2, 1991.

123. Geoffrey O'Brien, "Cinema: Blazing Passions," *Yale-China Review* 1:1 (Spring 1993), p. 20.

124. *The Blue Kite* was released in video by Chuo Eyetos and Co. in 1993. Zhang Yimou, Chen Kaige, Tian Zhuangzhuang, and Lee Ang (for his films involving Taiwanese, not just because he directed *Sense and Sensibility* superbly) made clear to an international audience, by the 1990s, that Chinese film directors could make a very major contribution.

125. Interview with a Westerner who follows cultural life in Shanghai.

126. See Paul G. Pickowicz, "Velvet Prisons and the Political Economy of Chinese Filmmaking," in Deborah S. Davis et al., eds., *Urban Spaces,* pp. 193–220.

127. *Ye Shanghai* and *Ye dian.* Productions continued underground in Shanghai even after the "orphan" area was seized by the occupying army, though with more ambiguous contents than French Resistance's *Les enfants du paradis.* See Edward Gunn, "Shanghai's 'Orphan Island' and the Development of Modern Drama," in Bonnie S. MacDougall, ed., *Popular Chinese Literature,* p. 36. Also, Fu Poshek, *Passivity, Resistance, and Collaboration: Intellectual Choices in Occupied Shanghai, 1937–1945* (Stanford: Stanford University Press, 1993), and Fu's future book about film.

128. *WHB,* May 21, 1979.

129. Form meets function here, because the German sounds frightful: *Verfremdungseffekt.*

130. The director's remarks are summarized by Carl Weber, "Brecht is at Home in Asia," in *Brecht in Asia and Africa: The Brecht Yearbook XIV; Brecht in Asien und Afrika, Brecht-Jahrbuch XIV* (in English and German), John Fuegi, Antony Tatlow et al., eds. (Hong Kong: University of Hong Kong, Department of Comparative Literature, 1989), p. 36.

131. Brecht, tr. Willett, "Alienation Effects in Chinese Drama," quoted in Ding Yangzhong, "Brecht's Theater and Chinese Drama," in *Brecht and East Asian Theatre,* Antony Tatlow and Tak-Wai Wong, eds. (Hong Kong: Hong Kong University Press, 1982), pp. 35–40.

132. Li Jianming, "Brecht and the Chinese Theater in the 1980s," in John Fuegi et al., eds., *Brecht in Asia and Africa,* p. 61.

133. Huang Zuolin, "A Brief Account of Brechtian Reception in China," in John Fuegi et al., eds., *Brecht in Asia and Africa,* pp. 1–2.

134. Adrian Hsia, "Reception of Brecht in China," in Antony Tatlow and Tak-Wai Wong, eds., *Brecht and East Asian Theatre,* p. 55.

135. Ibid.

136. Xue Dianjie, "Brecht's Drama and the Modern Chinese Stage," in John Fuegi et al., eds., *Brecht in Asia and Africa,* p. 55.

137. James C. Scott, *Domination and the Arts of Resistance: Hidden Transcripts* (New Haven: Yale University Press, 1990), p. 161.

138. Shelley Warner, "Shanghai's Response to the Deluge," in *The Pro-Democracy Protests in China: Reports from the Provinces,* Jonathan Unger, ed. (Armonk, NY: M.E. Sharpe, 1991), pp. 216–17.

139. See Perry Link, "The Genie and the Lamp: Revolutionary *Xiangsheng,*" in Bonnie S. MacDougall, ed., *Popular Chinese Literature,* p. 83.

140. See ibid., p. 104.

141. Later in this particular cross-talk, *"Haiyan"* (Stormy Petrel), there are clues to further intent. See ibid., p. 106.

A: She's spirited! Stormy Petrel dares to think and dares to act! She's like a boy—exceptionally strong!

B: Oh!

A: She'll grab a hundred-pound load in her arms and take it away!

B: Wow!

A: . . . toss a two-hundred-pound load on her shoulder and take it away!

B: Fantastic!

A: Raise up a one-ton load of steel and take it away!

B: Huh? Raise a one-ton load and take it away?

A: She runs the crane!

B: Hah! I thought so!

No one in the audience would fail to think of Jiang Qing. The piece also betrays some general antifeminism, as Link suggests.

142. *FBIS,* December 31, 1987, p. 25, reporting *JFRB* of December 26.

143. Jailed Shanghai journalist (and Gang of Four member) Yao Wenyuan would not have thought well of Hu Fanzhu, *Youmo yuyan xue* (The Linguistics of Jokes) (Shanghai: Shanghai Shehui Kexue Yuan Chuban She, 1987).

144. This is the interpretation of *WHB,* June 28, 1988. A literal but long translation of the documentary's title would be *Premature Death of the Yellow River.*

145. *ZGQNB,* July 5, 1988.

146. These dragons are the *si xiao long.* The *River Elegy* documentary and many other analyses of these problems by Chinese intellectuals (including by Chen Kuide in *WHB,* December 6, 1988) emphasize Confucian traditions in their popular rather than formal versions; they do not stress that China has non-Confucian traditions too.

147. Chen Kuide likened the methods of *Heshang* to those used by Hegel and Toynbee.

148. *Heshang xianxiang;* see *WHB,* December 6, 1988.

149. This "consensus" *(gongshi)* is mentioned in *WHB,* December 6, 1988.

150. See John Fitzgerald, *Awakening China: Politics, Culture, and Class in the Na-tionalist Revolution* (Stanford: Stanford University Press, 1996), as well as Andrew J. Nathan, *China's Crisis: Dilemmas of Reform and Prospects for Democracy* (New York: Columbia University Press, 1990), p. 124.

151. Quoted in Lucien Bianco, *The Origins of the Chinese Revolution, 1919–1949* (Stanford: Stanford University Press, 1967), p. 42.

152. This exactly reversed the motto of Ming philosopher Wang Yangming, who claimed that action was hard but knowledge easy. Both neglect that norms and situations are linked. The separation between these is purely analytical; the whole show lies in interactions between particular norms and situations.

153. *Wenge bowu guan. XMWB,* February 7, 1989.

154. *XMWB,* March 11, 1989.

155. The Zhejiang translation, by Cheng Naishan, was called *Shanghai shengsi jie,* whereas the Shanghai translation (in which bibliographical data are not supplied) was entitled *Shengsi zai Shanghai.*

156. These books were apparently not published openly, but Feng's articles appeared in a serial called *Dangdai (The Present Age). XMWB,* March 11, 1989.

157. Carl E. Schorske, *Fin-de-Siècle Vienna: Politics and Culture* (New York: Vintage, 1981), p. xiv.

158. See the *New York Times,* November 26, 1995, sec. 4, p. 5.

159. Frank Kouwenhoven, "Developments in Mainland China's New Music," part 1, *China Information* 7:1 (Summer 1992), p. 18; see also part 2, *China Information* 7:2 (Autumn 1992), pp. 30–46.

160. This describes a 1990s work by Wang Ming with the patriotic name *Guofeng* (National Wind), a trio for *dadi, erhu,* and *gu zheng,* in *Changfeng yuexin/Music from China Newsletter* (bilingual) 2:3 (Autumn 1992), p. 1. The *erhu* is a two-string violin,

held vertically, with the bow hair running between the strings. A *zheng* is a horizontal set of strings with individual bridges over a resonating box (plucked, much like its descendant, the Japanese *koto,* which is better known in the West). The ensemble of traditional Chinese instruments is much wider, including a great variety of horizontal and vertical flutes, guitars and zithers, tuned metal and stone bells, and other instruments including drums and gongs.

161. The author in February 1975 attended a Nanjing concert, including an accompanied violin piece presenting a Shaanxi folk dance in a style that was much like Bartók.

162. Chen directed two major orchestras by 1977, when he went back into music study first in Beijing—and then, following many other Chinese artists abroad, to the United States. *Post,* July 29, 1986.

163. *Post,* October 7, 1986. As *CD,* December 19, 1986, reports, the Shanghai Symphony is China's oldest. It began in 1879 as the Shanghai Municipal Public Band, headed by a German named Rudolf Buck with six other European wind players. By 1907, it was a full-fledged orchestra.

164. *Post,* December 12, 1979.

165. *Post,* January 6, 1980, based on reports of an American musician's visit to the conservatory.

166. *CD,* April 13, 1985.

167. The choice of *Così fan tutte,* which has an especially complex and elegant plot including much about power relations (especially between the sexes), must have been made without conservative CCP advice. The Majestic Theater, an old Shanghai name, was the Meiqi Da Xiyuan. Some intellectuals, when speaking English, still use the old names. *CD,* May 23, 1987, and interviews.

168. *CD,* September 6, 1986.

169. *Post,* October 7, 1986.

170. Paul Hertelendi, in *Post,* August 1, 1987.

171. *Post,* August 1, 1987.

172. *CD,* November 23, 1987.

173. These may be heard on the cassette tape *Yu Lina xiaoti qin duzou jingxuan* (Selection of Violin Solos by Yu Lina), with the Shanghai Philharmonic Orchestra (Shanghai: Zhongguo Changpian Zong Gongsi, 1987).

174. Frank Kouwenhoven, "Developments," part 1, p. 20.

175. Ibid., pp. 22–25; see also p. 29.

176. Ibid., p. 36.

177. Frank Kouwenhoven, "Developments . . . ," part 2, p. 40.

178. *Changfeng yuexun* Music from China Newsletter (bilingual) 3:1 (Spring/Summer 1993), p. 4. The following two quotations are from the same place.

179. Wenzhong Tang, Xinwei Yao, and Zhanpei Zheng (tr. Michael R. Phillips), "Rehabilitation Effect of Music Therapy for Residual Schizophrenia: A One-Month Randomised Controlled Trial in Shanghai," in *Psychiatric Rehabilitation in China: Models for Change in a Changing Society,* Michael R. Phillips, Veronica Pearson, and Ruiwen Wang, eds., Supplement 24 to the *British Journal of Psychiatry,* vol. 165 (August 1994), pp. 38–44.

180. Frank Kouwenhoven, "Developments . . . ," part 2, pp. 43–44.

181. Quoted in the *Post,* June 8, 1987.

182. Andrew F. Jones, *Like a Knife: Ideology and Genre in Contemporary Chinese Popular Music* (Ithaca: Cornell East Asia Series, 1992), pp. 11 and 16.

183. *Post,* June 3, 1980.

184. *Post,* December 8, 1982.

185. Ibid. A Chinese air force pilot, who liked the "sweet, vampy renditions of old

love ballads" by Deng Lijun, very popular in the mainland by 1982, flew his airplane to Taiwan and defected. The Taiwan authorities obligingly introduced him to his favorite crooner, and they sang a duet. When this particular Deng passed away, at an early age in the 1990s, many mainlanders mourned.

186. Two girlfriends of Shanghai male singer Zhang Xing had nine abortions between them; so the police finally arrested Zhang. *Post,* February 26, 1986.

187. The second most frequent T-shirt motto in this odd time when the author lived in Shanghai was enigmatic and offered in English only: "Evolution: Somehow It's." Other slogans were equally suggestive, often also in English, such as one calling simply for "Dialogue." Colophons on T-shirts are not so stately, or ultimately so important, as clauses of the constitution. But they are more frequently read.

188. *CD,* March 16, 1986.

189. *CD,* July 14, 1986.

190. *Post,* May 8, 1980.

191. Hong Kong *Standard,* October 13, 1986, also reports that when tapes and records of the Berlin Philharmonic's rendition of Beethoven's *Ninth Symphony,* conducted by Karajan, appeared in Shanghai, they were (despite a high price) sold out on the first day.

192. *Post,* July 24 and 25, 1985.

193. *Post,* February 9, 1980.

194. *Post,* June 9, 1987.

195. *Post,* April 16, 1982.

196. Andrew F. Jones, *Like a Knife,* pp. 93–94.

197. Ibid., p. 20 and passim.

198. Ibid., pp. 87–88.

199. *Post,* August 16, 1986.

200. *Post,* September 6, 1986.

201. *Post,* December 28, 1986. See also Benedict Stavis, *China's Political Reforms,* p. 92.

202. *Post,* October 26, 1987. The "primitive stage of socialism" is *shehui zhuyi chuji jieduan;* perhaps it was surprising to see the Congress (not just a few theoreticians) admit this. Less surprising, because it had been mooted for some time, were the formal retirements from government posts of Deng Xiaoping, Chen Yun, and other old revolutionaries at this meeting, and their replacement by colleagues of Zhao Ziyang.

203. *Post,* June 8, 1987. In a 1985 Guangzhou light music contest, the competitors were forbidden to present songs written outside the PRC, even though a Hong Kong tobacco company paid for the concerts. See *Post,* October 16, 1985.

204. *Post,* April 20, 1988.

205. "Roll Over, Beethoven" was omitted, apparently because the station did not want, after the Cultural Revolution, to offend classicists. "Everyone Wants to Rule the World" and "The Gambler" were rejected because of their titles. But "The Gambler" was later approved after the announcer promised instead to call it "The Rambler." With principles like these, the revolution had truly ended. *Post,* April 20, 1988.

206. Calculated from figures in *Post,* February 26, 1986.

207. "Nanniwan" is titled after a town in Shaanxi where Communist guerrillas had heroically resisted Japanese and Nationalist attacks in the early 1940s. Interviewees stress the importance of figures such as Cui Jian. Also, *Post,* February 20, 1988.

208. Hear the tape *Meng Shanghai* (Dreaming of Shanghai), Yin Pinzhang et al., singers (Shanghai: Shanghai Shengxiang Chuban She, n.d., probably 1993).

209. A revival of this music occurred in Hong Kong during the early 1990s, with the issue of compact disks taken from old records and film soundtracks from pre-Communist

Shanghai. Obvious even to the casual Hong Kong visitor was a similar influence in architecture. Few new Hong Kong skyscrapers were then considered complete unless topped with a pyramid referring directly to the Sassoon House/Peace Hotel. In Shanghai, some of the more distinguished Western buildings away from the Bund were in danger of destruction; but Shanghai art deco strongly affected Hong Kong, which had more money for expensive construction.

210. *Sunday Morning Post Magazine,* Hong Kong, July 28, 1991.

211. A more cumbersome analytic way of describing these three is to say they are steering mechanisms for art based on interests in normative-individual, normative-collective, or situational-individual issues. The original typology is in Richard Kraus, "China's 'Liberalization' and Conflict over the Social Organization of the Arts," *Modern China* 9:2 (April 1983), pp. 212–27.

212. See Karl Mannheim, *Ideology and Utopia: An Introduction to the Sociology of Knowledge* (London: Routledge, 1936); Philip Selznick, *The Organizational Weapon: A Study of Bolshevik Strategy and Tactics* (New York: McGraw-Hill, 1952).

213. The author enjoyed such programs on many evenings in Shanghai during the second half of 1988, though perhaps even some Chinese viewers did not follow every word of the poems.

214. Quoted in "Interviews," in George S. Semsel, ed., *Chinese Film,* p. 123.

215. *CD,* September 28, 1988.

216. Ibid.

217. The city then had thirteen theater seats per thousand population, as compared to a national average of fifteen. *Shanghai shehui xiankuang he qushi, 1980–1983* (Situations and Trends in Shanghai Society, 1980–1983), Zheng Gongliang et al., eds. (Shanghai: Huadong Shifan Daxue Chuban She, 1988), p. 186.

218. *"Wenhua tequ."* See Prof. Wang Yuanhua in Hong Ze et al., *Shanghai yanjiu luncong: Di yi ji* (Papers on Studies of Shanghai: First Set) (Shanghai: Shanghai Shehui Kexue Yuan Chuban She, 1988), p. 13.

219. Ibid., p. 15.

220. *FBIS,* February 9, 1988, p. 19, reporting the Hong Kong *DGB,* February 8.

221. Tang Dacheng in *LW* 45 (November 1988), p. 16.

222. *Shehui kexue bao* (Social Science News), March 9, 1989.

223. *Shanghai wenhua yishu bao* (Shanghai Culture and Arts News), February 24, 1989, reports this *minban* literary club, the Shanghai Tongsu Wenxue Yanjiusuo, which may be distinguished from its official (*guanban*) counterparts.

224. *South China Morning Post Spectrum,* June 2, 1991.

225. Ibid.

226. *Lao lin.* Interview with a Westerner who follows cultural life in Shanghai.

227. Andrew Solomon, "The Fine Art," p. 11.

Chapter 2.5

Reforms of Entitlement Support

*The unity, the ubiquity, the omnipotence of the supreme power, and
the uniformity of its rules, constitute the principal characteristics of
all the political systems which have been put forward in our age . . . .
Our contemporaries are therefore much less divided than is commonly supposed; they are constantly disputing the hands in which
supremacy is to be vested, but they readily agree upon the duties
and the rights of that supremacy. The notion they all form of
government is that of a sole, simple, providential, and creative power.*

—Alexis de Tocqueville[1]

The problems of obtaining basic welfare and shelter for people, arranging transport for them, supplying medicine, building schools, and providing other kinds
of common public support are often treated merely as issues of efficient production. Of course, allocating resources for these is supposed to be a role especially
of socialist governments. But these commodities are not optional for people.
They relate to human environment, time, or identity more closely than do most
goods that come on markets.[2] Consumption of these things is widely expected to
be adequate for each person or family, as a matter of decency. The politics of
dispersing such goods is shaped by habitual values more than by unintended
situations.

Housing and Residents

The norm that each household head provides shelter, along with the severe
scarcity of nonstate housing, has made residential space allocation the

Table 2.5–1

Shanghai Employment by Ownership Sector (millions of regular staff and workers, and percentages)

	1957	1965	1970	1976
Total number (m.)	2.31	2.76	3.08	3.99
State-owned (%)	75	77	79	78
Collective (%)	16	22	20	22
Other (%)	8.5	1.8	(0)	0.3

	1982	1985	1990	1992
Total number (m.)	4.77	4.93	5.08	5.11
State-owned (%)	78	78	78	78
Collective (%)	22	21	20	19
Other (%)	0.5	0.6	1.8	3.2

Note and source: The state firms are *guoying*, the collectives are those legitimated by reasonably large jurisdictions (*zhen* and bigger), and the "other" category includes private firms but mostly comprises joint enterprises of various sorts and especially in early years is almost trivial. Calculations for 1970 and later years (except the ''other'' calculation for 1976 and 1982) are from data in *Shanghai tongji nianjian, 1993* (Shanghai Statistical Yearbook, 1993), Shanghai Statistical Bureau, ed. (Beijing: Zhongguo Tongji Chuban She, 1993), p. 77. Figures on the early years, and slightly different figures for other years, are in *Shanghai jingji, neibu ben: 1949–1982* (Shanghai Economy, Internal Volume: 1949–1982), Shanghai Academy of Social Sciences, ed. (Shanghai: Shanghai Shehui Kexue Yuan Chuban She, 1984), p. 963.

government's main continuing hold on ordinary Shanghai people during reforms. So through the mid-1990s at least, reforms did not mean a flight of workers from state-sector jobs. Everyone wanted a job in a nationalized work unit, because everyone needs a place to live. As Table 2.5–1 makes clear, people did not formally give up their jobs in state agencies, unless relatives took the jobs so that cheap housing would stay in the family. Shanghai people's productive energy devoted to state firms fell during reforms, but even into the 1990s the state portion of Shanghai employees was reported as amazingly constant (near 78 percent). Also, the table shows that collectives remained far more important than private enterprises, at least as means for official registration of jobs, since collectives often had access to housing allocations if they were "dependent" on state firms. As long as the government was giving away essentially free urban apartments, few workers were so rash as to turn down such beneficence.

Low rents were the main buttress of this last bastion of state power over families. But reforms to raise rents, making them closer to scarcity prices, were for political reasons, extremely difficult to engineer. Amounts of rent in Shanghai are determined, per square meter, on the basis of categories of areas within the city and on the basis of the quality of construction materials.[3] Rents have been lower for residential than for industrial and commercial space. Housing became a political entitlement of the CCP's worker constituency in Shanghai. This situation became subject to reform because market pressures raised land prices, not just because the earlier vision of land as a nearly free good has led to dilapidation.

Available Amounts of Residential Space

The long-term deterioration of Shanghai's housing began because of Japanese invasion and civil war. Much of the best living space in Shanghai during the early 1990s was built before 1937.[4] Unmet depreciation continued after 1949, when the new municipal government set up its Housing Management Section (later a bureau) to take over property and control rents. But little new money was spent for housing. From 1952 to 1954, the standard rent rate for residential space was only 32 fen (Chinese cents) per square meter, and it remained low thereafter.[5] No agency would invest for financial reasons at such low rents. New construction was sparse relative to population, although state units built some flats for their own employees.

The main means by which the people's government for years dealt with the Shanghai housing problem was to use campaign pressures that forced families into more equal (often smaller) amounts of space. This development occurred over a number of years, and some periods such as the mid-1950s Transition to Socialism were particularly important in it. Because these sporadic forced migrations into less space were part of a recurring, persistent campaign rather than the main publicized aim of any single period of struggle, and because the Party did not advertise them abroad, they have received insufficient attention in scholarly literature.[6]

From 1949 to 1982, two million people (only 21 percent of Shanghai's average population in those years) moved into newly built housing, but this space constituted 57 percent of Shanghai's total space at the end of that period. Older residential buildings housed the great majority of the people. New residences were practically all distributed to the families of regular, permanent, unionized employees of state firms. Throughout the whole province-level municipality, including its rural areas, there was a 21 percent increase in the average living space per person in this long era (from 3.9 square meters to 4.7 square meters). But much of the rise came in the suburbs during the last three years of the period. Many urban families, even in professional classes, had decreased amounts of space in which to live.[7]

In other words, the early 1970s saw some building, as did the Great Leap Forward and other periods. In 1976, Shanghai had 4.3 square meters of residential space per person; and by 1978, this was up to 4.5 square meters. But in 1979, the average declined again to 4.3 square meters, because of the return of "educated youths" from the countryside. By 1981, the average living space rose again, to 4.5 square meters.[8] By 1986, the figure was up to 6.0 square meters.[9] Even this meant very tight crowding, but it represented some improvement.

In the early 1980s, Shanghai's government could not, after excoriating the Gang of Four, reestablish its legitimacy among Shanghai's many ex-capitalist families without returning some residential space that Red Guards had (to use the plain word) stolen from them. Publicity about a big reallocation of space might have offended the state's main urban constituency of workers, so the press seldom reported these restorations of property.[10] At the same time, Shanghai state enterprises could not build much new housing after 1982, because massive remittances to Beijing still continued then.

China's "national bourgeoisie" comprised capitalists who had adequately cooperated with the regime in its early years. Yet during the Cultural Revolution, their bank savings, public bonds, gold, silver, and much other property were confiscated. A January 1979 decree of the CCP maintained, "All these properties are legal private assets, protected by the Constitution. . . . All confiscated property should be returned to the original owners."[11] This was followed by a provision that national capitalists' salary losses, which had begun during the Cultural Revolution, were to be reimbursed. "Occupied private houses should be returned to their former owners." Also, "The capitalists' positions should be readjusted, and experts among them should be given formal titles." All these rules about returning property were much easier to announce than to accomplish, and often they remained paper apologies only.[12]

Such regulations were most apt to be enforced when previous predations against a family had been egregious. One "national capitalist" family, which had been pushed into one-seventh of its former dwelling, also suffered the murder by Red Guards of their eldest son; so in the 1980s, the whole house was restored. Far more common were cases of partial restoration to familes from whom space had been taken but had suffered only ordinary injustices during the late 1960s. (The government does not publish information about this or any other topic that might further stoke the outrage of many Shanghai families about their treatment during the Cultural Revolution.) During the first four years of the decade, 12 percent of the city's households reportedly received better space.[13] This was, for Shanghai's government, largely a political necessity during reforms because of the continuing local power and capacities of families that had been wronged. When families that might have moved out had cadre or army status, the reallocation of housing was far more difficult.

The situation was worse for new families. The housing crunch was probably as effective as the late-marriage policy in depressing Shanghai's birthrate. In July 1982, 129,000 nuclear families had legal registrations in Shanghai but without any rooms. Most were newly married couples. It was estimated that

408,000 people could not be normally married, because of lack of housing—even though all the grooms were above the recommended marriage age of 27, and all the brides were over the officially ideal minimum of 25.[14] In the eyes of the law, these couples were married; they had certificates. But apparently they had not yet held the celebratory party that gives informal, social recognition of marriage, because they had no housing and could not live together. Another 99,600 households contained more than one couple living in space that had been allocated to just one family. At this time, 60,000 households had less than 2 square meters per person. The total of Shanghai households affected by these various difficulties in 1982 was about 591,000, or about one-third of those in the urban districts.

Housing was so short by mid-1982 that 23 percent of all families in urban Shanghai were officially listed as having insufficient housing space. For 15 percent, the amount of space per head was less than 3.5 square meters. For 8 percent of households, no space was allotted at all. "They lived in kitchens, passageways, public sidewalks outside houses, attics, and so forth."[15] Another 38 percent of all families were officially declared to suffer from "inconvenient" accommodations (as defined by any of several criteria: a single room sleeping parents along with children over age twelve, adult sisters having to share a bedroom with adult brothers, three generations in one room, or two married couples having to share one room).[16] Local opinions about the housing crunch were very strong, though unorganized. A 1982 poll showed that 70 percent of Shanghai residents thought their "most serious difficulties" in the city came from the housing shortage.

One-quarter (26 percent) of all Shanghai's households in 1983 were living in residences with less than 4 square meters per person. "Inconvenienced households," with only a bit more space, were an additional 22 percent of the families. Another 4 percent of the city's households had no place of their own to live.[17] A survey at the end of 1983 showed that more than half of all Shanghai families were classified as "households in difficulty" because they lacked enough space.[18] Within this disadvantaged half of all Shanghai families, half (51 percent) had less than four square meters of space, another two-fifths (41 percent) of this group were "inconvenienced," and 8 percent had no space at all.

Residential facilities other than space were also scarce. One-fifth of all Shanghai's people during the early 1980s lived in buildings with no running water; three-tenths had no separate kitchens; and two-thirds used public toilets. The three particularly crowded urban districts of Zhabei, Huangpu, and Nanshi had about one toilet for each five households.[19] This situation became politically sensitive because it was not typical elsewhere in the PRC. Other Chinese cities during the early 1980s began to see much more investment in residential space. But Shanghai's major move toward more building was delayed at least half a decade by the high extractions for central budgets. Housing construction expenditure per person in 1981 was 39 yuan for Shanghai—but 135 yuan in Beijing.[20] Even by 1985, Shanghai people on average had only 4.4 square meters of housing space, 0.47 square meters of recreational space, and 1.6 square meters of road area—"figures that are among the lowest in the world."[21]

In all of China's cities together, in the early 1980s, 4 percent of GNP was spent on urban housing. But in Shanghai, residential construction investment in 1979 was less than 1 percent; in 1980, 1 percent; in 1981, 1.6 percent; and in 1982, still only 2 percent.[22] Other administrative cities with light industries (including many provincial capitals, but not Beijing) were, like Shanghai at this time, short of money to spend for housing. Guangzhou residences remained on average much worse than in other large Guangdong cities. That provincial capital by 1985 had 5.6 square meters per person (up from 3.8 square meters in 1980); but Foshan nearby had 12 square meters.[23] Shanghai was, in fiscal terms, the most monitored place in China, so its residential infrastructure received the least attention. Total living area rose, from 1950 to 1985 in Shanghai urban districts, by only 35 percent even while the total residential space available in all Chinese cities rose about 400 percent.[24] The main reason is not hard to find: Very little money was spent to build new Shanghai housing.

The government's preferred solution was to move people out of the city into satellite cities, which were often envisaged as company towns associated with major state corporations. A classic example of this genre was Minhang, south of Shanghai and dubbed an urban district after it was financed in the 1950s by electrical machine companies. But satellite cities such as Minhang had limited success, despite the money poured into building roads and amenities. Many urban people did not want to move, and household registrations were not supposed to be given to rural people. By the mid-1980s, only 40 percent of the value of infrastructure laid down for Minhang was in use.[25] Shanghai's twelve largest satellite towns together had a population density of only 8,000 per square kilometer—reportedly just one-fifth the density of the contiguously built-up city. People did not leave the central city in droves, despite official plans for state workers to do so.

Shanghai people clearly did not want to live so far from the cultural and commercial attractions of the metropolis. A mid-1996 report claimed dubiously that residents were leaving Shanghai for the suburbs so fast that "the population density in urban areas went down to 4,650 persons per square kilometers in 1995, from 27,230 persons per square kilometers in 1982."[26] This kind of change might apply to quite limited areas that were officially slated for conversion from residential to business use. It might have counted expected departures of residents who had not yet been effectively forced to move elsewhere. Without more incentives, however, the number and size of satellite suburbs that had been state-planned for Shanghai were greater than residents would support by moving there. Bureaucrats did not revise these plans, on which their jobs depended, even years after it was evident that residents were not responding easily. If fewer satellites had been financed, each of them might have been more successful.

Because the PRC state by the 1970s had less capacity to stop the growth of rural industries in the Shanghai delta than to monitor the high tax structure in the metropolis—in other words, because particularist reforms could be implemented earlier than standardized reforms—industrial labor became more dispersed from the 1970s to the 1990s. But this development was no result of the long-term bureaucratic fad for satellite cities; it was not guided by any state plan. Many people stayed in rural areas because the state could less effectively tax the rural factories that therefore could provide them jobs.

Residential Construction Lags Behind Local Politics

By 1987, the Party's paper in Shanghai claimed that residential "problems left over from the Cultural Revolution" were "basically solved." Over 98 percent of the 500,000 square meters of private housing that had been illegally occupied had, by this report, been returned. The newspaper claimed that 96 percent of the 57,800 households from which art objects had been stolen had been compensated.[27] At the same time, the "Seek truth from facts" slogan was said to be useful in dealing with a number of pre–Cultural Revolution "old historical cases" that had (as 1980s officials admitted) wrongly maligned non-Communist local leaders in Shanghai. The extent of fair compensation remained controversial. The state had to say it was making amends—and the fact that it did so told something about its officials' informal view of their own popularity—but everyone knew it was impossible fully to compensate for such a disaster. In any case, this rectification did begin to solve the housing crunch in Shanghai, which had been caused by decades of underinvestment.

Almost half (47 percent) of the new residential space built in Shanghai from 1949 to 1983 was constructed in 1979–83 only.[28] This building campaign continued, although the neglect of residential infrastructure for the previous forty years meant that the amount of available total space remained below many Shanghai people's hopes. In 1987, the average residential floor space per dweller in Shanghai's urban districts was only 6.15 square meters. But the average for other East China places, e.g. for all urban districts in Zhejiang cities, was at 8.00 square meters, about one-third higher.[29] Suburban peasants had very much more space in which to live.

Part of the problem was that Shanghai had scant land per person. The 1987 residential population density in Jing'an district was 64,000 people per square kilometer, the highest in the PRC.[30] In commercial areas, especially those around Nanjing and Huaihai Roads, the ratio rose to at least 170,000 per km^2.[31] These places compare, per unit of ground space, with the most densely populated areas of the world. The extreme case is apparently Mongkok, Kowloon, Hong Kong, a high-rise area in a richer city. But for lack of *floor space* per person in an urban region, the tracts surrounding Nanjing and Huaihai Roads, Shanghai, almost surely set the global record.[32]

This metropolis had much the highest population density among Chinese cities. There are various ways of measuring this phenomenon, the most usual of which counts residents in all urban districts.[33] In these, by 1987, Shanghai's density averaged 19,200 persons per square kilometer, as compared with only 1,300 in Tianjin, 1,500 in Beijing, and 2,400 in Guangzhou (respectively, just 7, 8, and 12 percent as dense). Shanghai was and is egregiously crowded, even in comparison with other large PRC cities. Because urban districts are defined by administrative fiats, rather than more directly by the functional uses of land, it would be most accurate to consider population within the contiguous built-up area. If the density is figured by dividing nonagricultural population into this area, Shanghai has almost 36,000 people per square kilometer, as compared to Beijing's 13,000, Tianjin's 17,700, or Guangzhou's 15,100. On this basis, Hangzhou's density is 8,900, and Wuxi's is 17,200. Even by this calculation, Shanghai is more than twice as packed as the second most crowded city, Tianjin.[34] Accounting for the unregistered population would change the densities more than the intercity ratios. "Cities" differ from each other far more than most people realize.

Shanghai citizens tended to be somewhat disaffected from government because of this extreme crowding. State leaders, lacking concrete resources to satisfy all their constituencies, did little but express sympathies. At one of Mayor Jiang's meetings with local residents in February 1987, however, he heard complaints that ten thousand urban Shanghainese had an average floor space of 2 square meters only. A later newscast averred, "As a result of this session, more than 60 percent of the individuals in this predicament had been moved to bigger housing by the end of October."[35] The most severely underhoused families, if they were legally registered, could be given attention in a campaign whose political benefits exceeded the economic costs. By National Day, late in 1988, all registered Shanghai households with "special difficulties" (tekun hu)—that is, ones with 2 square meters or less per person—were reportedly moved into larger quarters.[36] The General Federation of Trade Unions was involved in this change, as well as the Housing Management Bureau, but less than 1 percent of the urban residents were affected.

Residential crowding in Shanghai strengthens Chinese kinship traditions because it forces members of more than two generations to live together. Parents and adult offspring cannot get enough floor space to live apart. Nuclear households in separate residences remained the ideal of most, as a survey in Shanghai showed, but the housing crunch made them impracticable. "Strong obligations to newly married children and to frail elderly parents repeatedly overrode the desire to have each married couple maintain its own home."[37] Filial duties, combined with the state's long-term unwillingness to maintain the buildings it said it owned, created many two- and three-generation households. Among a sample of Shanghai households, nuclear-family residence was even less common in 1990 than in 1987. Shanghai young people were quoted as saying, "Here it is harder to find an apartment than to find a spouse."[38]

Motives for Housing Reforms and Conservative Reactions

Socialist cadres, suburban peasants, urban female workers, male entrepreneurs, and many other specifiable groups had distinctive and different attitudes toward housing reform. The slowness of this actual reform cannot be understood separate from the motives of unorganized groups of individuals that received personal disadvantages or benefits from the prereform structure of housing. Cadres had the clearest interests in holding on to their relatively generous space at low rents. They could present socialist reasons against reform in this area.

Housing was, in thoroughgoing Communist thought, supposed to be like hospitals, fire stations, sewers, or schools—a commodity so infrastructural that it was taken to be social, an early candidate for free supply. Marxist ideals for urban housing reform prescribed that it should not only liberate workers from exploitative rent, but it should also sever them from urban residential "private plots." Here is one of Engels's eloquent flights in his book *The Housing Question:*

> It is precisely modern large-scale industry which has turned the worker, formerly chained to the land, into a completely propertyless proletarian, liberated from all traditional fetters and *free as a bird;* it is precisely this economic revolution which has created the sole condition under which the exploitation of the working class in its final form, in the capitalist mode of production, can be overthrown.[39]

The Communist answer was thus collective- or state-owned housing, at rents that were purely nominal. Bauhaus architects, followed by Soviets (N.A. Miliutin and others), designed hundreds of housing projects that aimed to fulfill this ideal. Chinese urban planners of the 1950s followed such precedents.

The problem was that construction is expensive and the workers are numerous. Especially in China, all possible methods were used to save costs. The Shanghai government's first main approach to residential housing reform, beginning in the 1950s, was to use all existing floor space by dividing old buildings among many families. Only the flimsiest shacks were torn down. The center of Shanghai was left intact. Socialist pricing assumed that the value of all land, and of already-built floor space too, should be roughly equal (and near zero). Thus the face of central Shanghai, at least until the late 1980s, was basically unchanged from 1937. Residential buildings were more crowded, since more denizens had moved in. When new rooms were needed, plasterboard was installed to divide old ones. The Shanghai Real Estate Management Bureau, which obtained ownership or administrative rights over most houses, built few new structures and did not maintain old ones.[40]

A second means to save money, when housing was urgently needed for state workers, was to standardize construction materials and techniques. The lack of remaining large Chinese forests and the expense of foreign wood meant that the most important building materials were bricks and prefabricated panels of reinforced concrete. "New towns" (*xincun*) grew around Shanghai—not inside the city, lest old structures be torn down and state budgets be expected to finance new ones. Apartment houses in new towns overwhelmingly took the form of rectangular blocks, laid out either like library stacks or in quadrangles.[41] These apartments forced a kind of collective spirit, because they too were often crowded, usually having communal kitchens and bathrooms.

The same sort of involuntary community had been created by subdividing houses in more central parts of Shanghai, because families there generally had to share cooking space and toilets. Both the new apartments and the subdivided houses inspired a thirst for family privacy. For most Shanghai families, quenching it would have to wait for reforms more extensive than had been fiscally possible even by the late 1990s.

Individuals' interests for or against such reform were affected by wealth, cadre or noncadre status, urban or suburban residence, and location in or out of an area slated for redevelopment. The housing shortage hurt women more than men. Male employees in practice received some preference in the state allocations. Forty percent of the mostly female staff of all Shanghai's textile mills in 1979 had less than 2 square meters of living space.[42] Seven percent of single women over the legal minimum marriage age, according to one 1980s estimate, would have had no access to more residential housing if they got married, either through their spouses or on their own account. Peasants in Shanghai's rural suburbs met some of the need by leasing space to newly married couples—at rents that doubled in two years of the mid-1980s alone.[43]

Shanghai's housing allocation system depressed regular workers' job mobility. If an employee shifted jobs but an apartment had been "distributed" from the limited pool of residences the old employer had, either the job shifter had to move between residences or the previous employer wanted compensation for the loss of a flat. The Housing Management Bureau or the business enterprises, if they could cooperate, might solve this problem; but with residences in great shortage, job transfers often posed real difficulties.[44] Sometimes the job leaver or the new employer paid a handsome sum to the previous unit in order to keep the housing. Sometimes the employee was able to retain good rapport with the previous unit's head, or the two agencies wanted to maintain amicable relations so that the problem could be solved. Sometimes the transfer involved just one of two spouses working for the same unit, so that the home could be retained in the name of the other. But especially for young employees wishing to make transfers, the link between jobs and housing could create great problems. Often a person changing jobs either had to leave home or had to pay a substantial sum to the previous employer.[45] This created a form of indenture.

When some areas were slated for redevelopment, as occurred increasingly in the 1990s, new housing was owed to evicted families. The State Council paid for renovating the Shanghai railroad station, because this was a "national key project."

So the local Railroad Bureau was able to pay the work units of people whose houses had to be removed to make space for the new terminus. The bureau did not deal with mere residence committees for such an important project, but with the geographically scattered employers of the residents instead.

When slums were torn down and people were moved into better-quality housing, the amount of new space they received was specified according to the amount of shack space they had to relinquish. They received less, but in sturdier buildings.[46] Relocations of this sort had been important during the 1950s, but they often violated the official ideal that residential space should be connected to jobs. In any case, the weakening of controls over unregistered migrants by the late 1980s, combined with the state budget crunch, meant that squatter areas in Shanghai grew rather than contracted. New construction was hard work, and the recent immigrants who did most of it also increased the extent of Shanghai's slums.

Rents in the suburbs were not controlled, and the demand for housing there rose. So the portion of incomes spent on housing, among all people living in Shanghai rural areas, increased sharply, from 20 percent in 1980 to 30 percent in 1983 and higher thereafter.[47] Suburban peasants charged rent to migrants who often lived in sheds that had once held the pigs they no longer bred for organic fertilizer. Former hog pens were spruced up for human habitation. Rural housing reform was much quicker than urban. In cities, the cost of residential construction remained high, and rents remained subsidized. Even by the mid-1990s, no real takeoff for Shanghai urban housing had started.

Sales of Urban Space

Housing reform depended on selling residential space, but for political reasons far more places were advertised than sold. Many reformers in the central government wanted the state to sell apartments to their occupants, creating a real estate market, derogating maintenance costs away from the state, and raising vast amounts of money for official coffers. But this plan was effectively subverted by local interests.

The reformers' ideal had precedents in the PRC. Peasants owned their houses. Overseas Chinese had long been allowed to buy, at high prices, a few plots even in cities. But with real estate reform, as with the slow emergence of the stock market, propagandistic hoopla exceeded substantial action. Conservative leaders insisted that, for the insult to socialism, land purchase prices must be kept high.

The Shanghai government nonetheless sold some housing to private buyers in the reforms of 1982. This policy soaked up money that otherwise would have added to inflation. Since the proceeds went directly into the local government's budget, it also helped staunch the city's fiscal deficit. A small portion of Shanghai's housing was scheduled to be renovated or built each year—and although two-thirds of this space was still earmarked for "distribution" by state agencies, one-third was to be sold. Units such as Jiaotong University would pay a substantial part of the cost, on a grant or loan basis, for valued employees (in lieu of finding them housing to rent). Because the value of the few privately owned houses in Shanghai shot up during the reform period, those who bought these properties in the early 1980s were generally satisfied with their purchases as the end of the decade approached.[48]

Little, however, was sold, and the buyers were mainly speculators. Eighty-one percent of Shanghai's residential urban housing in the mid-1980s was still directly under the Real Estate Management Bureau.[49] Less than one-fifth was under collectives or state factories that oversaw housing separate from this municipal bureau. A trivial amount was under private ownership. By the end of 1986, Shanghai residents were again encouraged to purchase their own apartments from the bureau.[50] But the procedures for setting prices remained unclear, and the alternative of paying low rents was usually more attractive.

The first serious step in Shanghai's housing reform began very modestly in 1988 with yet another survey of the problem. A 1 percent sample was selected from among the 1.8 million households (which included 4 million employees and 1 million retirees from about 100,000 work units). The survey probed popular expectations of the housing reform; unsurprisingly, it found that many Shanghai residents feared the purchase subsidies would be insufficient.[51] This survey accompanied an auction of state-owned apartments in Shanghai, beginning in March 1988, when two buildings were sold. The high bidders were both from the part of Shanghai that had the most funds, i.e., the suburbs. A deputy manager of a rural enterprise group and a director of a collective factory offered the winning bids. A newspaper report admitted that "the prices were regarded as a bit high by the public." But the manager of the newly founded Shanghai Housing Auction Company claimed, "The prices are not too expensive, presuming buyers can conduct good business in the city." Both the suburban entrepreneurs said they intended to use lower floors for commercial display windows.

The director of the Shanghai Housing Management Bureau said, "The city intends to sell most newly constructed housing as commodities, instead of allocating it to Shanghai citizens at low rents." Vacant state-owned buildings were also slated for sale, but the director admitted, "No breakthroughs have been made in how to sell housing now occupied by people."[52] The problem was partly psychological: Taking away benefits already enjoyed by people lowers their satisfaction by a greater amount than it would be raised by any plan to give them additional benefits in an equal amount.[53] So long as rents remained pleasantly low, people could be induced to switch to a new system only by high purchase subsidies. These were politically impossible. So the new real estate market was, in effect, restricted to newly built quarters. Official low rents for old housing stock made the new buildings seem very expensive; so the state sold few and had to forgo considerable revenues. By late 1988, almost 1.2 billion square meters of residential housing were authorized to be sold in all Chinese cities, and the average price was 200 yuan per square meter. If this could all be sold, revenues to the state would have been 240 billion yuan, but the market lagged partly because the average price for ordinary buyers who were not employees of state enterprises was twice the price available to state workers.

When Shanghai authorities offered twelve thousand apartments for sale in 1988, fewer than 7 percent of the flats were actually sold. Most were bought by work units and businesses, rather than individuals. As a PRC paper explained, "The price of homes has rocketed out of the reach of ordinary wage earners. . . . In Shanghai, it has gone up to 1,000 yuan per square meter, from about 300 yuan in 1982." Also, "a variety of government departments levy fees on these sales," which were "apparently irrational" but were "the main cause of the increasing burden," accounting for about two-thirds of the rise in the price of housing.[54]

A "housing fair" was held in Shanghai for two days in January 1989, offering 570,000 square meters for sale; but of all this space, buyers again only took 7 percent. The government wanted too much money.[55] Cartoons ridiculed the cost of housing that was put on sale. At 1,500 to 2,000 yuan per square meter, this space seemed out of reach to workers who continued to receive low wages. And they had no need to buy.[56]

Residents had become accustomed to cheap rents, and they had plenty of experience seeing the PRC government change its general politics from quasi-capitalist to quasi-socialist and back. As an interviewee put it, these "psychological uncertainties" made them wary of purchasing better space for their families. Such hesitations even affected those with large savings accounts (of whom there were many), for whom the high price alone was not a crucial factor.

For young families, work units still had a formal responsibility to find and "distribute" rented housing to employees. The delays in this process were ordinarily counted in years. The quality of such homes, when they were finally available, was often unsatisfactory. The locations were often inconvenient. But at least the rents were cheap, state-owned apartments would not be confiscated in any future political movement, and they had generally became too small for families to face requests that they further subdivide the space. Past memories reduced demand on Shanghai's new housing market, no matter how reasonable the prices seemed to state officials.[57]

Other cities sold more space. Yantai in Shandong, Bengbu in Anhui, and Tangshan in Hebei held early experiments in housing reform. The basic idea was that as rents went up, urban employers would issue certificates that could be used only to pay for housing. The value of these chits was based on employees' wage levels. Because rents had been very low for decades, and great amounts of money would have been needed to bring them near scarcity values, a step-by-step introduction of the reform was generally advocated—especially by budget cadres, who needed this gradualism because they could scarcely afford the reform at all. In Tangshan, for example, housing reform was planned in three slow stages, each involving a rent increase and a subsidy for allocated space that was over a threshold cost.[58] In Yantai, prices were slashed 50 percent, "limited property rights" were offered to the purchasers, and a special bank was established to provide low-interest loans for urban house purchases.[59] But the experiment cities were all much smaller than Shanghai, and many of their buildings were newer.

In most cases, the experiments did not work. Changzhou, on the Shanghai delta, was one of six Chinese cities chosen nationally to test ways of creating a market for houses. Workers there stopped paying ordinary rents and instead purchased their homes in installments. The monthly amounts were very much higher than the rents to which they were accustomed, and "this program was not popular."[60]

The government's main interest was clearly to make more sales, so as to finance the ballooning public debt. But rent increases, which could raise buyers' incentives, were politically sensitive among local cadres and workers who were crucial supporters of the state. So essentially nothing happened. Because practically all real estate in Shanghai was owned by the city government, rent revenues might have been important for the municipal budget—as was the case in Hong Kong, where most housing was also managed officially. But the rents were set so low since the early 1950s, this money was insignificant. Shanghai economists reported that 37 percent of Hong Kong's government budget came from land sales and rents.[61] But the control of scarce housing space was increasingly important to Shanghai managers as other resources they could offer to their workers decreased. Central impositions on Shanghai budgets continued to give low priority to construction of new residences. For basically political reasons, mostly at the local level, rents and land sales were forgone as a source of public revenue until the 1990s.[62]

Urban rents in China as a whole were still estimated in 1994 to be "less than a sixth" as much as they would have been under free market conditions. In Shanghai, rents were very much less than a sixth of the value to which they entitled renters. Even officials sometimes admitted the political aspects of this problem: "Some people have abused their power to get large homes. The public is extremely angry about this. Reforming the system will improve relations between the Party and the people."[63]

Cadres' Resistance to Housing Reform

In Mao's China, urban neighborhoods had been ideally, though not in fact, self-sufficient. A trend toward more functional specialization among neighborhoods can be shown during reforms.[64] In Shanghai, new "foreign enclaves" have appeared near Hongqiao Airport and in Jing'an district. The government, which by the 1990s was in need of funds because of the financial collapse of state industries, apparently became uninterested in housing reform for old residents of central Shanghai. It was more profitable to move them elsewhere and rent the space at higher prices to more specialized and wealthier clienteles.

Although there was a great deal of propaganda in newspapers and in the media about the need for housing reforms, this was "much thunder with no rain."[65] One major specific obstacle to reform could not be published: Corrupt leaders could often give unoccupied housing illegally to their own children. Cadres' apartments are low-rent, and as one source put it, "The more housing space, the better, because the renter can get more subsidy from the state. A family which has 8 square meters per head each month gets 30 more yuan of subsidy from the state, in effect, than does a family which has only 4 square meters per head. This is one reason it is so hard to reform the housing system."[66] Cadres had bigger flats, so they had personal stakes in seeing the old system continue.

In their role as managers, cadres also had other reasons to resist reforms. Ninety-five million workers by 1988 in all of China received urban housing from state-owned firms. The annual subsidy cost the government 2.5 billion yuan annually. The national budget for construction in that year, at 3 billion yuan, was scarcely more. Rent revenue supplies more money than housing expenditures use, and much of the rent collected goes to pay not for maintenance but for production.[67] Factories consider residential rent income as production funds proper, and a housing reform would put this money to new uses, thus straining managers' budgets.

The incentives are complex because a rent increase would have to precede wide sales of houses to workers. In some cities, such as Yantai, Bengbu, and Tangshan, rents were actually increased. The compensation to workers came from managers' budgets. Some cadres feared this change would bring complaints, but widespread grievances did not arise. The cabinet minister responsible for housing opined that reform could be carried out if propaganda calmed public attitudes toward the reform and clarified the need for it. In fact, resistance to housing reform may come more from cadres than from the public.

The high state was defeated by its local officials in this reform. Since high-level budgets had scant money for Shanghai housing, and since local leaders would not allow extensive sales of old space, national leaders sought an alternative policy. The state's deficit stoked official enthusiasm for housing cooperatives that could finance themselves. The Gonglian Housing Co-op, the first of its kind in China, was founded in 1987 at Shanghai; by mid-1990, it had built three large apartment buildings. Half of the 4 million yuan that members contributed came from four hundred households, and the other half came from the enterprises where they worked. Most of the construction money, 10 million yuan, came in bank loans. Using similar procedures, many other housing co-ops began in Shanghai—but conservatives in the government pressed to keep the prices high. The loans carried interest, because these local residents' collectives were outside the network of officialdom.

Orthodox statists wanted to make sure the government would be amply compensated for this lapse of socialism. Reformers, on the other hand, raised their goals for the improvement of Shanghai housing. They had a plan for the year 2000, when the average residential area per citizen was supposed to reach 8 square meters. These visionaries aimed far, since one-fifth of Shanghai residents in 1990 still had an average living space of less than 4 square meters. In 1990, "about three-quarters of urban houses lack self-contained facilities such as water, electricity, gas, and toilets." Yet fiscal imperatives ruled all: "According to housing officials, the current reform has yielded various ways of collecting funds for housing construction, shifting the heavy financial burden from the government alone."[68] Housing reform was not just about housing; it was also about production budgets, cadres' client networks, and the daunting accumulated costs of decades of neglected maintenance. There were no cheap ways to change the prereform system of assigning shelter.

A survey of Shanghai residents showed that many thought urban housing allocation was a festering corruption. Families with insufficient space and old Red Army soldiers were cited for special treatment, but many ordinary citizens worried that most of the subsidies in any reform would go to the families of cadres. If this happened, it was predicted that the housing reform would "lose meaning" for most residents. The main public opinion, which this survey found, was that cadres should receive the same treatment as other residents. The interviewees also expected far more money would be needed than the government ordinarily appropriated for Shanghai's social problems. As a respondent said, "If housing reform is going to make an entrance, the leaders must take the stage."[69]

As another source put it, "There are two kinds of empty apartments. First, cadres or officials 'occupy' such flats to prepare for their children's marriages, or even for their grandchildren. Second, some apartments cannot be allocated in a timely way after they are built . . . . In Shanghai, there are already 10,000 empty flats. But 51,000 square meters have been occupied by illegal residents, mostly cadres."[70] An ideal underlay this corruption: that land was naturally a common good and unmarketable, so it should be subject only to political or moral allocation. Local leaders could count on high CCP fears of workers' reaction to any large increase of rents. So housing reform was mostly stymied.

Transport Infrastructure and Commuters

As a distinguished Chinese scholar of urban development put it, "There are considerable economic and social advantages in living in metropolitan areas; and the larger the city, the greater the advantages."[71] Crowded urban life can also offer disadvantages if housing and transport infrastructure are not maintained. Although this kind of question is often treated as if it were purely economic, the political and social threat it presents reflects not just a failure of adaptation, but also the habits and ideals of urban people. The danger is that individuals and families become apathetic, because the life patterns they have to maintain involve too much standing on crowded buses, too often waiting in traffic, and too long commuting to work. Liu Xinwu's 1990 short story "Bus Aria" describes the resigned anger of urban people who find daily that they cannot get on board.[72]

"Changing consumption cities to production cities" became the rationale for a studied neglect of all expensive infrastructure. Socialist governments might well make it their special job to build up infrastructure for long-term growth. This was an ideal in China, but the demands of central ministries for immediate funds made the state overwhelmingly interested only in the production of fiscal revenues. Capital was put largely into state-owned heavy industries. Urban transportation, housing, sewers, nonindustrial water and electricity supplies, tertiary education, and many other kinds of infrastructure in Shanghai received little money for a quarter century.[73] Socialist policies for Shanghai's development in Mao's time built infrastructure for factories that benefited the state, but these policies left out many ordinary people.

Reforms were slow to start, in this area. Public infrastructure investment was three times higher in the period from 1977 to 1982 than between 1966 and 1976, although this partly reflects its low level during the earlier period.[74] The period of radical rule in Shanghai poured money into military and heavy industrial plants, but not into infrastructure. The most obvious aspect of Table 2.5–2, on Shanghai's infrastructure for living, is the generally low level. The trends are more presentable than the performance (which was not comparably reported after 1987). Residential housing, water supply, and urban transport are problematic in many Third World cities, including other cities of China, but Shanghai's fiscal burden made them special problems there. So were many other aspects of infrastructure, including household telephones, electricity, sewers, residential streets, and sidewalks. The level of supply in Shanghai was low through the mid-1980s, and it rose more slowly than the city's production. Such problems were especially evident in the 1978–80 period, when the particular dependence of central bureaucracies on Shanghai money (as other reforming provinces cut their central remittances) created a situation in which the city had even less money than usual to spare on residential infrastructure. After 1987, the problems persisted but became less egregious as Shanghai's fiscal reforms took hold.[75]

Over the long term, e.g. between 1952 and 1987, the per-person measures of square meters of residential housing, kilometers of water pipes, and number of buses in Shanghai's urban districts did not decline in absolute terms. On the contrary, the stocks of infrastructural capital in each of these fields increased (despite spells of decline in the per-capita housing stock during the 1970s, in the water mains at the end of that decade, and sporadically in buses during the early sixties and most of the years from 1978 to 1985).[76] Shanghai's infrastructure in all these areas nonetheless aged badly, even though some new facilities were added. This metropolis also fell notably behind other large Chinese cities in providing such facilities to its residents.

Table 2.5–2

Indices of Infrastructure for Living in Shanghai: Housing, Water-pipe Length, and Buses per Urban Person (in urban districts)

	Residential housing (m²/pop.)	Water main pipes (km/pop.)⁻⁵	Buses (vehicles/pop.)⁻⁵
1952	3.4	.189	.040
1957	3.1	.205	.054
1962	3.8	.217	*.095*
1965	3.9	.241	*.093*
1970	*4.4*	.298	.094
1975	*4.2*	.345	.108
1978	*4.5*	*.386*	*.123*
1979	*4.3*	*.377*	*.116*
1980	4.4	.386	*.114*
1981	4.5	.392	.115
1982	4.7	.398	.130
1983	4.9	.409	*.131*
1984	5.0	*.398*	*.126*
1985	5.4	*.396*	*.126*
1986	6.0	*.396*	.130
1987	6.15	.424	.133

Notes and sources: Italics denote runs of declining years. The indices are calculated from *Shanghai tongji nianjian, 1988* (Shanghai Statistical Yearbook, 1988), Li Mouhuan et al., eds. (Shanghai: Shanghai Shi Tongji Ju, 1988), p. 77 on population, p. 381 on housing, p. 389 on water pipes, and p. 391 on buses. The vehicles counted are trolley buses (*wuguei dianche*), which at least since the 1950s have been the main basis of mass transport in Shanghai. The population figures, from public security records, are incomplete but probably more consistent as time series than from other sources; see p. 76 of the source for an alternative set of population data, the use of which would not alter conclusions of the kinds drawn here.

Transport as the Main Scarcity Linked to Housing

Decentralized housing construction during the socialist period might have led to a quick growth of civilian transport. But for political and institutional reasons—housing was linked to productive factories, while public transport was not—residential and transport development were separated. Much new housing was far away from workplaces in the city. Factories might provide buses for their own workers, but these were inefficient users of road space because other commuters could not embark. The average number of times people boarded buses daily in Shanghai more than doubled between 1978 and 1986.[77] The number of buses rose; but not only were there more people, they also traveled more often.

The shape of built-up Shanghai as late as the 1980s can be broadly described as a crescent facing southeast. The unoccupied sector, needed to complete the circle that would be spatially more efficient, was across the Huangpu River in Pudong, where some housing had been built during the 1970s. This space was difficult to use because the ferries were slow. In October 1970, a tunnel under the Huangpu had been built by the army; and after it opened in 1971, it was for years the only way to cross that river without a boat.[78] But this first tunnel was exclusively for the military. and more than two decades later, civilians still could not ride through it. Not until after the mid-1980s did Shanghai retain some money to fund links across the Huangpu.

Before the bridges were built, new apartments in Pudong, east of the Huangpu River and not easily accessible to most of the city, were sometimes taken as allocated housing by workers—but then locked up and left uninhabited. Rents were nominal, so Shanghai employees had scant reason not to take these apartments if their work units made the offer. But in practice, these workers also tried to avoid the crowded transport from Shanghai's outskirts to most of the locations of good jobs.[79]

In central Shanghai, traffic became slower. Although the average speed of all Shanghai traffic in the 1950s was clocked at 25 kilometers per hour, by the mid-1980s this had already decreased to 15 kilometers per hour.[80] For reasons evident to commuters, this index was published less frequently in later years. Another report clocked it at only 10 kilometers per hour.[81] Traffic jams became the norm of the 1990s.

The reasons concern consumption, not just production. After the Cultural Revolution, people demanded more. This was a matter of values, not just efficiency. City dwellers wanted to live on time patterns that differed from rural norms more than earlier socialist institutions in Shanghai had been designed to support. For this, they traveled more. The number of trips within Shanghai that people took each day rose dramatically during reforms—up 64 percent between 1978 and 1983. The difficulty of getting on buses was so great that by the mid-1980s at peak rush hours in Shanghai, there were more than ten people per square meter of bus space.[82]

The early 1980s census had shown that already one-quarter of Shanghai workers took more than an hour and a half to commute each way. A report a few years later suggested that this situation had become worse, partly because large numbers of new laborers could find housing only on the city's outskirts. Many commuters had to spend more than two hours going to work.[83]

The number of Shanghai's vehicles grew rapidly. By 1983, Shanghai had more than 80,000 motorcycles and 2.75 million bicycles, so traffic congestion was intense. More than twenty major traffic accidents occurred daily.[84] In later years, as rural prosperity throughout the country made the number of China's imported and domestic vehicles soar, city planners' main reaction was to scurry for ways to keep these cars and trucks out of Shanghai. Some construction was

financed, but not enough. By the 1990s, the six-lane Nanpu Bridge linked southern Shanghai with industrial areas across the river, and the similar Yangpu
Bridge did so on the east. To connect Pudong to the center of the city, a subway
tunnel linked Yan'an Road (just south of the city hall, on the Bund) to Lujiazui
on the eastern side of the Huangpu.[85] But socialist budget planners resisted
spending very large amounts for civilian transport infrastructure. They hoped
foreign investors would take up these slow-return projects.

Satiric articles appeared about the difficulty of getting onto Shanghai buses.
The efforts of crowds to jam through bus doors each day were said to make the
vehicles fatter and older. The insistent clicking of the bus conductor's ticket
punch was taken, in one story, to be a symbol of a tense scene.[86] Bus society in
Shanghai became a rich subject for humor, because anybody who has tried to
board a trolley in Shanghai's rush hour remembers the experience.[87] This was a
twice-daily trauma for most of the city's population. It was never a directly
political experience, since bus crowds are not highly organized, but Shanghai
people developed a mordant discontent about the inconvenience.[88] The state ran
the buses, and in Shanghai they were obviously underfinanced.

Lampoons of the government's failure to offer enough urban transport came
readily from reporters, sometimes as tongue-in-cheek science. A journalist obtained the number and size of all available Shanghai buses, and then he figured
the total floor area of all these vehicles together. He also obtained data on the
total number of passengers at the middle of rush hour each weekday. To discover
how many people could possibly stand in this available total bus space, he went
to shoe stores—and found that twenty-four pairs of average-size shoes could, if
pressed together, fit into one square meter. A calculation showed that all
Shanghai's buses together did not have enough standing room for all the people,
wearing two shoes each, who were actually traveling in rush hour. The answer to
this ingenious paradox was unclear until the reporter boarded a rush-hour bus
and made a further observation: Many commuted for hours while standing on
one foot, like a crane.[89]

The Bangkok/Jakarta Syndrome and Shanghai's Future

Governments can lose control of such situations. Shanghai's inherited conditions
for transport are particularly unfavorable. This city has a planar rather than
stringy spatial structure (like Los Angeles, for example, but unlike Hong Kong).
This means that concentrated development of a few fast-transit routes in Shanghai still will not move a large portion of the traffic. The extremely scarce road
space per person (unlike, for example, Beijing, whose imperial walls became
wide avenues) also hinders effective development.[90] Shanghai's land for transport in the mid-1980s was only 8.3 percent of the entire built-up area, much
lower than in other Chinese cities.[91] Shanghai had less road surface—only 1.58
square meters per resident in 1983, as compared to 2.42 square meters in Tianjin,

or 4.52 square meters in Liaoning's large industrial city of Dalian.[92] By the middle of 1988, Shanghai had raised this figure to only 1.9 square meters of road space per person; but there were 6 square meters in Beijing, and nearly 10 square meters in Tokyo.[93] The national average road space per person for all cities in China was twice Shanghai's. A city official confessed that the infrastructure for road transport in this metropolis was "appalling."[94]

Buses were the main medium-term solution, even though new investment in them was not fast. Every square meter in a bus holds nine people on average, and twelve to sixteen in rush hour. Buses are far more space-efficient than bicycles, and buses are used in Shanghai by a higher portion of commuters than in other Chinese cities. Only 33 percent of Beijing workers ride to work by bus, while 51 percent ride bikes. In Tianjin, fully 81 percent use bicycles. "One bus can carry a hundred people, but twelve bikes take one bus's road space. In other words, *one* bike takes *eight* bus riders' space," noted one analyst. "In Chinese cities, the growth rate of motorized vehicles is higher than that of road length, but the growth rate of bikes is even quicker. This necessarily leads to terrible traffic." This source blamed the state directly: "The government for a long time has subsidized bicycles. . . . In addition, bike riders do not return money by buying bus tickets and do not need to pay road taxes. Government policy itself has discouraged the development of the bus system."[95] By the 1990s, it was compounding the problem by encouraging an even less road-space-efficient kind of vehicle, the automobile.

High officials' preferred option was not to spend money for either new buses or new roads, but instead to pass traffic rules. The costs of these regulations were not borne by high-state budgets. A campaign to stagger the opening and closing times of offices was launched in 1979, to reduce pressure on transport. In that year, on an average day Shanghai people boarded buses 8.6 million times, so the government wanted to spread these events as evenly as possible over time. The new office hours were set not just according season, but also by the municipal bureaus under which various factories and stores operated.[96] This use of bus space was the equivalent of the government's response on housing: intensify use of old stock rather than invest any real money.

A similar strategy was to illegalize the use of certain vehicles at specified times. Before the busy Chinese New Year of 1989, in order to lessen Shanghai traffic jams between 2:30 and 6:00, nonbusiness cars with odd-numbered license plates could travel only on Mondays, Wednesdays, and Fridays. On Tuesdays and Thursdays at these rush times, cars required even-numbered plates.[97] Rich units and suburban entrepreneurs, however, were not to be stopped by whims of the calendar. Some bought two fleets of vehicles, with even and odd plates for use on different days. This wasted capital, but (unlike other methods to solve the dilemma) it was legal—and perpetuated the traffic jams.

Yet another possibility was to encourage major outside funding sources for a rail transport infrastructure. By the late 1980s, Shanghai planners were drawing maps with great enthusiasm. A subway system of 7 lines and 137 stations was projected, along with 7 tunnels under the Huangpu River. Underground malls were projected along the shopping streets of Nanjing and Huaihai Roads, as well as at the railway station, Jing'an Temple, and three other locations. A futurist professor at the Underground Areas Center of Tongji University pointed out that Tokyo doubled 3.4 percent of its land area by adding facilities belowground, while the figure in Shanghai was 1.2 percent. Digging was recommended. One of the Tongji specialists claimed, "The twentieth century was one of high-rise buildings, but the twenty-first will probably be the century when people go underground."[98] Mao's old advice on excavation for civil defense was reformed to make subterranean malls.

Foreign investment was found by the late 1980s to aid construction of infrastructure: a thirteen-station Shanghai metro system, a new bridge and two tunnels across the Huangpu, a new sewer system, and an extension of Hongqiao International Airport.[99] Perhaps more important, the possibility of foreign funding had spurred support from official budgets that previously did not spend so much for transport. The rate of progress nonetheless remained slow. The Shanghai metro's first line was to run from Xinlonghua in the suburbs to the main railway depot. In the late 1980s, work began at three of the planned subway stations: at People's Square, Xujiahui, and Shanghai Stadium. About half of the funding came from abroad.[100] But Shanghai's subway in 1994 still served as a suburban and tourist line only, from Xujiahui toward Meilong township to the southwest. This initial line would later follow Hengshan, Huaihai, and Tibet Roads to the railroad station, but construction plans were very slow, considering Shanghai's population and renewed prosperity. In earlier years, the city's money had largely gone to the national capital, which built its subways in the 1960s. In the 1990s, less fully public infrastructure projects with quicker economic payoffs had higher priority.

The construction of major road arteries, which could be used by many kinds of vehicles, showed one large success in the 1990s. A ring highway around central Shanghai followed the route of 1950s Zhongshan Road in its south, west, and north sections. But in the east, it crossed the Huangpu on two new suspension bridges, circling far into still-rural parts of Pudong that were slated for development. These reform-era bridges helped expand the city, although traffic in the center remained slow. It was not clear whether plans being pursued in the mid-1990s would be sufficient to prevent further slowdowns of a kind that had become politically important in other Asian cities, notably Bangkok and Jakarta. Perhaps the greater ability to retain funds in Shanghai during the 1990s, together with the regime's care for its urban constituencies, would be enough to prevent a transport disaster in Shanghai. But traffic was going to get worse before it got better, and the change in fiscal policies for Shanghai had come slowly.

The patchwork of urban asphalts revealed fast change throughout the metropolis. This transformation was not just economic; it reflected politics too, because it showed the extent to which individuals had new opportunities. Municipal transport for civilians was a government function that the Shanghai government conceived as supporting the economy; but for residents, the availability of rides was a matter of their lifestyles and political temper, too. It was still unclear, by the mid-1990s, whether the regime would ever be brought to task for its dilatory funding of Shanghai transport and residences. But only the most saccharine officials claimed that the socialist government had made most Shanghai families content with their commuting and housing.

Relief and Pensioners

The Chinese government has been enjoined to aid distressed people since the time of Mencius at least. But total relief aid funds plummeted almost every year after the mid-1980s. Rural people were most affected. In 1985, relief funds for the aged and for uninsured disabled went to 38 million rural people; but by 1992, only 8 million benefited from them.[101] In urban areas also, official spending for welfare dropped— though less sharply, because city families are more important in politics.

Low Retirement Ages and an Increasingly Old Population

The elderly portion of Shanghai's urban population was important, about twice that of China as a whole: 14 percent of Shanghainese were above 60 years of age in 1987, and 2 percent were above age 80.[102] The aging of this urban population was relatively fast. Old people were not distributed as evenly in the city as might be expected; the concentration was highest in Nanshi district (economically the city's poorest).[103] Shanghai had about one million residents age 60 or older by 1992, a minority of whom were not covered by social insurance.

Families in Shanghai urban districts supported ever fewer non–wage-earning retirees or children as the city modernized. This trend continued during the reforms, although at a slower rate than in the PRC's first decade. The average number of unemployed dependents that each Shanghai urban laborer supported at home in 1982 was only 0.56 of a person (not including him- or herself)— much less than the 1.97 dependents per worker in 1952.[104] Many households in the city were either individual employed persons or else working couples with-out children or parents in the same flat. Most of the change, during reforms, was in post–working-age cohorts, not among children. The ratio of retired to actual workers rose sharply during reforms. For each hundred current laborers in 1978 Shanghai, there were only eleven retirees. But by 1992, the number of retirees per hundred workers had soared to thirty-two.[105]

This pattern was very costly to the state. Retirement pensions were generally 60 to 70 percent of final monthly pay, depending on the length of continuous service. For any laborer who had "participated in revolutionary work" before 1949, the pension was higher: 80 to 90 percent of final pay.[106] In China as a whole during the 1980s, the number of retired state workers increased at an average rate of 1.8 million a year. The number of pensioners rose sixfold in this decade. The government in 1988 spent 37.3 billion yuan in welfare benefits. There were still 6.4 active workers for each retired worker in the state system, but the campaigns for retirement since 1979 had brought this ratio down—and the greater income that retirees could make on the side, once they left the state sector, gave them incentives to abandon state jobs as soon as they could.[107]

The socialist government could not cope financially with the effects of this demographic transition, which made the number of elderly people soar. The family was in fact still Shanghai's main social security system. One-third (33 percent) of the household heads over age 60 in a 1985 survey lived with their married sons. Another 14 percent lived with their married daughters. Interestingly, 5 percent of these households whose heads were over age 60 contained multiple generations that were not consecutive, i.e., households of grandparents living with grandchildren. The missing middle generation in these families had usually been assigned to work elsewhere in China, though it had been able to send the youngest generation back to Shanghai for schooling and residence.[108]

The sociologists who made this survey apparently asked their informants, all over 60 years old, what the family situation had been half a century earlier.[109] Although fifty years earlier, in the mid-1930s, half of the old people in these families had lived with their sons, the portion by 1985 had declined to almost exactly one-third. Correspondingly, only 6 percent had lived with their daughters half a century earlier, but the portion by 1985 was up to 14 percent. So there had been some changes, but the traditional Chinese care procedures for old people remained very strong.

Among very elderly people in Shanghai (over age 80), 57 percent lived in three-generation families during the mid-1980s.[110] An additional 19 percent lived in four-generation families, with 14 percent living in two-generation households. The portion of persons over 80 who lived just with their spouses was 7 percent, and 8 percent resided alone. About 8 percent lived with another couple, in a "joint family."[111] A plurality (35 percent) of the elderly over age 80 in 1985 were in families of five to six people.[112] The Chinese family system was the most important basis of social security, even in this most modern of PRC cities.

These bonds were important to people's lives not just because the socialist government limited most welfare entitlements to its own markets, but also because it pensioned people early. Official retirement ages in China have long been lower than in many other countries: among most cadres, retirement comes at age 60 for men and at 55 for women; and among ordinary workers, the age was 55 for men and just 50 for women. The number of retirees in Shanghai in 1984 was 26 percent of the size of the listed workforce, 4.9 million. These older people were a very large labor reserve, including many who still drew salaries in nonstate sectors while continuing to collect state pensions. But the pensions were often low: less than 40 yuan a month for 31 percent of retired ordinary workers,

Table 2.5–3

Second-Job *Reported* Earnings of Shanghai Retirees (end of 1986)

Portion of the 1.4 million retirees (percentage)	Annual rate (yuan)	Monthly rate (yuan)
39	860 or less	72 or less
37	861 to 1,200	72 to 100
13	1,201 to 2,400	100 to 200
6	2,401 to 3,600	200 to 300
5	3,601 or more	300 or more

Source: This table includes both ordinary (*tuixiu*) and favored (*lixiu*) retirees, and it counts those working in Shanghai, in the suburbs, and elsewhere. In addition to the amounts shown above, all these retirees also drew pensions—in many cases ranging between 50 and 100 yuan per month. *Tansuo yu zhengming* (Investigation and Debate), March 1988, p. 51.

and below 50 yuan even for one-third of retired cadres.[113] Many elderly ex-workers got less, and inflation during reforms was quick. Among Shanghai's urban retired people over 80 years old in 1985, a majority (58 percent) had no pensions at all. Among the remaining 42 percent, who apparently included many ex-soldiers who had become cadres, the average pension was 90 yuan per month.[114] Retirement funds, according to the socialist ideal, are collected in a fixed ratio to wages.[115] But by the late 1980s, inflation caused fixed pensions to lose value fast. So 80 percent of retirees depended for at least some money on their children.

Somewhat younger retirees, ages 60 to 80, often had good enough health to take second jobs while collecting pensions. A local survey in a relatively poor district showed that the portion of people age 60 or older who were actually working in 1985 was 76 percent.[116] Practically all the remaining 24 percent were women. More than a quarter of the elderly who had no employment (28 percent) said they would have preferred to keep working. Nonpension state welfare was practically unknown, even in the proletarian part of Nanshi district where the survey was conducted. The portion of persons over 60 who received nonpension welfare there in 1985 was one-half of 1 percent. This area was somewhat atypical, and it almost surely contained many contract workers.

In 1986, Shanghai contained 1.4 million retired people overall, of whom 23 percent reported having second jobs.[117] Their compensation was considerable, as Table 2.5–3 shows. Nearly six-tenths of all retirees reported monthly 1986 earnings over 100 yuan, and they were in fields such that the reporting was surely incomplete.

Many young retirees thus paid their way in their families and were not just dependents. When a sample of Shanghai people over 60 was asked whether they liked to live with their children, about three-fifths said they did. These were about equally divided on the benefits that came from such living, between those who mainly needed the younger generation's help and those who mainly liked to help their kin. Among the two-fifths who preferred to live separately (whether they were actually doing so or not), a plurality said they wanted "peace" in their last years, and nearly half admitted they had conflicts in joint-generation living.[118]

In crowded multigeneration households, 16 percent of the old respondents declared that they had major trouble getting along with the younger generation—and almost half of these difficulties were of the most classic type, i.e., complaints by mothers of sons against their daughters-in-law. A major specific occasion for conflict was competition for housing space; 16 percent of the surveyed old people had to live in kitchens, corridors, lofts, or without any fixed bed at all. Some elders also opined that the "morals" of Shanghai youth were unbearable by the mid-1980s.[119]

Insurance for Temporary Workers

As reforms raised the number and variety of nonpermanent workers in Shanghai and the surrounding delta, the portion of all laborers with social insurance fell. The vast majority of the three million "peasants" working in Shanghai's industrial and service sectors by 1987, as well as several hundred thousand contract workers then, had no social security at all. "Few of these people are entitled to old age pensions from employers after retirement."[120] The salaries of nonunion new workers could be garnished with official imposts, however, if they were registered. So three million in 1988 were put under life insurance policies, with premiums of 66 million yuan, as charged with a high administrative overhead by the city government's Life Insurance Company. Mandatory deductions from salaries were the standard method of paying premiums.

Many workers were simply not covered. In plants licensed at low levels, most employees were unregistered. The newly penurious state's ideal was that they should form social security cooperatives, for which they would pay. In the early 1980s, "social insurance" schemes were already being tested in Shanghai cooperatives. Collectives were expected to pay, for example, 3 yuan monthly for each worker into a medical insurance scheme. Drugs were available on a copayment basis, with the patients paying 30 percent. Collectives were also supposed to pay between 5 and 10 yuan monthly into a old-age pension fund.[121]

Employees of state firms and large collectives were covered for many benefits in the early 1980s, when about 4.2 million Shanghai workers enjoyed labor insurance. Of these, 77 percent were in state units and 23 percent were in collectives.[122] An additional set of workers, adding about one-fifth to the total of regular unionized employees, received smaller benefit packages because of their work in small collectives or service units including neighborhood committees. Retired workers in the city by 1982 numbered 1.16 million (more than a quarter the number of active employees). Of the retirees, 72 percent came from the state system, with only 28 percent from collectives. Total labor insurance expenditures in 1982, of which the bulk went for retirement pensions, were 29 percent of the costs of direct wages.[123]

So Shanghai had a social security system, but the ability of the state sector to fund it fell during reforms. The number of urban people enrolled on either a temporary or permanent basis declined from 1980 to 1983. A few employees were put on "simplified retirement" schemes, but this number also declined in the same period.[124] Throughout the country, the number of urban Chinese on state insurance programs in mid-1991, including pensions, unemployment benefits, and medical programs for workers and spouses, totaled 150 million. Because most of the beneficiaries were state employees, the government had to subsidize these programs, and the bill for 1990 was more than 10 billion yuan. In a "reform" to lower this drain on the government budget, selected coastal cities including Shanghai approved insurance deductions at a higher rate from workers' salaries.[125] Like the bond-purchase deductions, these were in many cases offset by higher bonuses—so the nominal amount that workers took home was not greatly affected. Inflation, however, meant a major real deduction in worker incomes. The state's rearrangement of the salary and welfare components of its urban wage bills during the early 1990s was one of the more interesting shell games in town. So long as the cuts in real income were offset by rising bonuses, top officials clearly hoped worker unrest could be calmed.

Health and Environment for Citizens

Biological and chemical processes operate separately from human intentions, but when they affect the health or surroundings of individuals, people often hold the government responsible for them. Shanghai's environmental pollution in the mid-1980s stage of reforms was described as "very serious." The death rate from cancer was China's highest. Food pollution was also "the most serious in the country." About 500 tons of waste water flowed into the Huangpu River every day.[126] Conservation and health require infrastructural investment of kinds that Shanghai's government largely postponed until late stages of reform.

The political aspects of this problem emerged from widespread popular desires to extend the public health institutions of the 1950s and 1960s to larger groups of people. Chinese medical insurance came in three kinds: Workers' insurance (*laobao*) was the traditional socialist sort, covering permanent unionized industrial employees and including full coverage for the employee, with dependents paying half fare. Public paid (*gongfei*) coverage was for office workers, especially in the government and often female, who were also fully covered although their dependents were excluded. Cooperative medicine (*hezuo yiliao*) was for peasants and co-op workers who were legally registered in their locality, but it covered only minor ailments and drug prescriptions; major illnesses were excluded.[127] Many in China during reforms were without medical insurance of any kind.

Communication Against Contagions, Specialization Against Chronic Diseases

Communalist approaches had proved highly effective, especially during the 1950s, against many contagious diseases that vaccinations can prevent. Yellow fever, polio, rubella, cholera, measles, mumps, and smallpox all decreased sharply in Mao's time. Although mobilizational policy proved especially effective against viral and bacterial contagions, such normative campaigns based on "human organization" principles are less useful in preventing—and are not useful in curing—chronic individual maladies, such as cancer, schistosomiasis, stroke, and heart disease. Specialist, "technical organization" measures are needed actually to cure these, in individuals who already have them. Normative education is also useful in preventing, but not much in curing, diseases such as dysentery, malaria, leprosy, or AIDS, to which the body generates few effective antibodies.[128] Reforms, while they have helped Chinese medics control "modern" ailments such as cancer and heart disease that are hard to cure, have lessened the previous emphasis on normative medical campaigns that proved very successful against communicable diseases during the high tide of revolutionary organization after 1949.

By the early 1970s, China's production brigades each had an average of two "barefoot doctors" with minimal medical training. Collectively financed medical systems had been established in about 70 percent of the brigades by that time. This was a tremendous accomplishment, even though the Cultural Revolution created an estimated shortfall of 130,000 graduates from medical schools.[129] Doctors and medical researchers suffered along with all other intellectuals in that movement. When the medical education system was restored, its adherents served (as Mao predicted they would) rural and poor patients less, and urban and rich patients more. The new medics were far more adept at their science, but in effect they prescribed benign neglect for China's rural people. Fortunately, clinics to maintain the vaccination and basic medical education campaigns remained largely in place.

As Sheila Hillier writes:

> Many parts of China, particularly the cities, are experiencing the "epidemiological transition"—the causes of sickness and death begin to resemble those of a developed country. Instead of parasitic and infectious diseases and high rates of infant death, the longer-living population increasingly suffers from chronic complaints like heart disease, cancer, and hypertension.[130]

As better medicine lets people live longer, there are more geriatric cases. Community doctors may have fewer epidemics to face, but they need more time for work with individuals and for efforts to give people healthier living habits. Many of the increasingly relevant diseases are incurable. The old socialist enthusiasm for mobilization is relevant to some new medical problems such as AIDS, but it is really effective with a decreasing number of the diseases that are most common, especially in a city such as Shanghai.

The campaign method was not entirely dropped during the reforms. In May 1978, for example, the Shanghai Revolutionary Committee launched a "patriotic public health campaign."[131] Although tuberculosis decreased in Shanghai during the early 1980s, high blood pressure, digestive disorders, and various cancers all increased.[132] The most important diseases among Shanghai's elderly, according to a 1985 survey, were coronary problems, arthritis and rheumatism, and bronchial ailments. Three-quarters (74 percent) of surveyed persons over 60 were eligible for public medicine, and another 22 percent needed to pay just half of their doctor's bills, while only 4 percent had to pay entirely by themselves. But the quality of care left much to be desired. The main support of a Shanghai old person during a time of illness was certainly within the family.[133]

Some easily communicable diseases, notably hepatitis, rose. Hepatitis A became widespread in Shanghai during the spring of 1988, originally because of a large batch of contaminated clams. Once the contagion started, human contact of many kinds could convey it. Shanghai reported 700,000 to 800,000 cases of hepatitis by early 1988—more than one-tenth of the urban population (and a survey suggested that another 300,000 individuals falsely claimed to have that disease, in order to take three months of paid leave).[134] The State Council held a special meeting to seek ways of combating this threat to Shanghai's production and China's revenues. Hepatitis A clearly affected Shanghai's production; the city's output was 17 percent less in February 1988 than in January.[135] In the first month of that year, the epidemic was blamed for 30,000 deaths.

The hepatitis epidemic did not harm youngsters or elderly people as much as those of working age. Ninety percent of the reported cases were contracted by people 20 to 40 years old.[136] The reasons for this high working-age portion are epidemiological: Children and teenagers with hepatitis often have light subclinical cases, which go unreported. Among old-age cohorts, the chances of previous exposure and thus immunity are relatively great. The childhood years of people who were elderly in 1988 predated the Maoist campaigns against contagious diseases, so many who survived had built immunities against hepatitis early in life. For these reasons, middle-aged workers were hit more severely than any other group. They will, in later life, be vulnerable to liver cancers.[137]

The production loss in Shanghai because of hepatitis was estimated at 2 billion yuan during the first half of 1988. The epidemic made local state managers' problems even more intractable, but it also brought some relief from government remittances. In fact, it surely speeded structural change for Shanghai's economy. In later months, because of a very normative campaign that would have made Mao proud, Shanghai's restaurants and food handlers cleaned up their act impressively. Memories of mobilizational medicine had not been entirely lost, and there was a real need to revive them against this epidemic.

Health vs. Revenues: The Cigarette Problem

New health problems in Shanghai mostly came from less communicable diseases. Furthermore, the reform state's urgent need for revenue exacerbated chronic diseases for a specific reason: official coffers got so much of their money from tobacco. Cigarette addiction had become a major financial interest of the state. Health officials were interested in propaganda against cigarettes, and the medical costs of smoking were well known. The state's cigarette monopoly nonetheless created profits and taxes directly providing about 8 percent of funds at all levels of government in early reform years, and perhaps one-tenth of official budgets as other state industries foundered.[138] Tobacco revenue, as a portion of all state income, was high, fairly stable, and calculable as follows: in 1982, 8.68 percent of all official revenues came from tobacco; 1983, 8.20 percent; 1984, 7.12 percent; 1985, 6.43; 1986, 6.42; 1987, back up to 7.18; 1988, 7.99; 1989, 9.16; 1990, 8.45 percent. Addicting the public to nicotine became an official need, because of the state's addiction to money.

China has well over 330 million smokers.[139] The public health costs of cigarette addiction on this scale would be difficult to calculate—and it is unclear who will pay, to the extent the loss is merely financial. The monetary and unmonetized medical costs of this tobacco use are mostly delayed, so they can be easily neglected; but they are immense. A more immediate concern of financial officials, however, was that in the reform environment local entrepreneurs could illegally break the government monopoly of this high-profit industry.

The reform boom created not just smokestack industries, but also smoking people. Before 1978, the annual per-capita consumption of cigarettes was less than 1,000; but by 1987, Chinese smoked 1,750 cigarettes on average.[140] Since tobacco accounts for 30 percent of all cancer deaths (and almost 90 percent of lung cancer deaths), as well as four-fifths of deaths from chronic lung diseases and one-fifth of deaths from heart disease, this reform in smoking was not good news. A 1993 survey at Minhang in the Shanghai suburbs found that 67 percent of men regularly used cigarettes, and the portion of smoking women was low but quickly rising. Practically none of the respondents had ever tried to quit, and 86 percent of smokers did not even say they wished to quit. Most were quite aware of health risks, but they considered smoking a "social asset" that helped them do business and make friends. Most surprisingly, expenditure for cigarettes was "an average of 60 percent of personal income and 17 percent of household income" among smokers. The amount spent by poor smokers was equal to that spent by rich ones.[141] Nicotine addiction during reforms resulted in very large profits and taxes for the government, on an income-regressive basis.

Rural companies that manufacture bootleg cigarettes abound, despite their illegality. Smuggling of foreign cigarettes into China is also massive. Profit margins in this industry are so high that state efforts to control this reliable source of funds have been stymied by local power networks protecting illegal plants and trade routes. Despite competition—and partly because of police campaigns in 1989 and during the 1990s against illegal tobacco companies—the Shanghai Cigarette Factory topped all of the city's firms for its deliveries to the state of profits and taxes.[142] Much more research is needed to trace tobacco politics in China and in other countries. Postrevolutionary reforms, not just in China, show great competition for market share between official, illegal, and international suppliers of cigarettes. The fiscal and medical implications are great, although there is no space for most of them here.

Healthy Environment

Any effective national health system must be related to resource flows in the economy.[143] As China has decentralized and collectivized, the national government has lowered its commitment to medical care, intending that families and individuals will handle these tasks better. As Minister of Health Cui Yueli said plainly in 1984, "for a long time, our principle of [government] monopoly has affected the development of public health services. . . . It is necessary to discard this principle and fully arouse people's enthusiasm for building hospitals."[144] This reformed approach to medicine will deal with chronic diseases among individuals better than with contagions among groups. If past experiences are a reliable guide to the future, it will lead to less egalitarian medical delivery. Most of the highly communicable diseases have already been defeated by clinics that were established during the years of revolutionary organization, and the health hazards that remain are largely environmental.

"Pollution first, management later" was a policy decried by many in Shanghai during the late 1980s. "Economic development should provide welfare for people, not dangers for people." Shanghai ecologists, hoping that breakneck economic growth would not spell environmental disaster, noted the "current in foreign countries for ecological or green parties" and claimed "it is right that we should learn from other countries."[145] But such policies cost money. Powerful forces were arrayed against paying much capital for mere cleanliness, when it might be invested instead to produce marketable goods. These forces were strong both in the central state and in localities. Conservationism tends to be seen by some Chinese political conservatives as a Western imported concept. Indeed, many modern ecological ideas can be traced to particular kinds of religious thought in the West.[146] Aspects of Buddhism or Daoism can also be read as conservationist. Most important, China's crowded land demands care in the use of water, air, soil, and the biosphere. People suffer specific and identifiable harms when these are degraded. Environmentalism is a cultural option in many places, but it enters the political agenda when there are messes to be cleared.[147]

Ecological laws came slowly to China. The urgency of pollution problems by 1990 encouraged the State Council to decree two sets of regulations for the protection of ocean coasts.[148] Resistance to environmental laws apparently came from state-owned enterprises that would have to pay the costs if they were enforced. Articles 9 and 26 of the PRC constitution of 1982 concern ecology, although they are phrased in broad terms. Tension between economic bureaucracies and environmental care is a frequent theme on the Shanghai delta, where dense population makes the need for such care politically important. Newspapers could raise environmental problems freely, but they were not automatically solved without more public funding than the state used for this purpose. One report suggested that 80 percent of Shanghai's domestic sewage was still dumped directly into rivers (mainly the Huangpu) without treatment during the mid-1990s.[149]

Nuclear pollution is potentially the worst environmental catastrophe that could strike the delta. The Qinshan Atomic Power Plant, in Zhejiang near the Shanghai border, was built during the late 1980s to generate 300,000 kilowatts for the East China power grid. This was China's first nuclear electric station. To plan more such installations, the Shanghai Nuclear Engineering Institute had been founded in 1984.[150] The Qinshan equipment was designed by this institute and largely produced at the Shanghai Turbine Works. It was completed by April 1989—and was said to have been inspected by "the state."[151] Many, but not all, were reassured after this.

Ecological debate about the Qinshan project was not published openly. The Chernobyl catastrophe and Hong Kong's political turmoil about the PRC's Daya Bay nuclear plant, which largely used French designs, nonetheless stirred a great deal of private concern in the Shanghai delta. Qinshan is near the middle of a large, very densely populated region where about one hundred million people live. A nuclear disaster there would do more than make the news.

Other nuclear hazards existed, although news of them was also suppressed. When the Chinese navy commissioned a new missile frigate, which Shanghai's Hudong Shipyard equipped with automatic guns, antisubmarine weapons, and a panoply of systems for electronic warfare, the navy also gave public assurances that the ship "measures up to international standards for preventing pollution."[152] The missiles were not counted as pollutants, although some may well have been nuclear.

Most environmental problems at Shanghai were far less dramatic but very evident. More of Shanghai's land surface is used for industry than in other cities. According to one Shanghai economist, a "world standard" for industrial land in a city is 15 percent—but by the 1980s, industry took 37 percent of Shanghai land.[153] This pattern made it difficult for new enterprises to find space, and it also mixed industrial with residential land closely. Pollution of living space was, in these circumstances, hard to avoid.

Campaigns to "green" (lühua) both urban and rural areas have been pressed in the 1980s nationally, partly because roots hold soil and river silting limits navigation. Shanghai's green area per person was only half a square meter in 1983, as compared with three times as much in Tianjin, or nearly a dozen times as much in Guangzhou.[154] The green space per person in Shanghai increased to 0.90 square meters in 1986.[155] This would have represented a doubling of green space by midreforms—if the expansion of the urban districts by administrative whim did not account for much of it.

Air, water, and noise pollution were the most obvious concomitants of reforms. "Severe contradictions between factories and masses" by 1979 affected over three hundred plants, and there was "conflict" at eighty-one of these. Almost fifty Shanghai factories had to stop work for some days in that year because of pollution. The frequency of conflicts and days lost decreased by 1982, but "the problem still was not fundamentally solved."[156] In fact, it worsened as the whole Chinese economy boomed without any effective kind of regulation. A report in 1989 confessed, "Air pollution is a serious problem. In Shanghai, there are 7,000 stovepipes, 8,000 boilers and 800,000 briquet stoves. Nobody knows how much air pollution they cause every day . . . . Statistics show the rate of death from [lung] cancer is three times that in nonindustrial cities. Beijing, Tianjin, Shanghai, and some cities in northeast China are most seriously air polluted."[157]

Haze and fog induced by particulates became common in the 1990s over wide parts of Shanghai and the surrounding region. In previous years, when Shanghai's 800,000 coal-ball stoves were major contributors to the bad air, localized air pollution had sometimes been severe. But during the reforms, smog often spread more widely, over the whole delta. It came not just from more industries and vehicles in urban districts, but also from suburban factories. Planes landing at Shanghai's Hongqiao Airport on early morning schedules had, more often than in previous years, to fly in circles until the sun burned away enough of the mist. An impressive new TV tower was completed in 1994 at Lujiazui, in Pudong opposite the Bund; but its top was often barely visible.[158]

Water pollution was also serious. One Shanghai source estimated a 1983 discharge of 4.9 million metric tons of untreated waste liquids into the city's public waterways. Shanghai's traditional source for urban water was the Yangzi River, since flow tides push fresh water up the Huangpu, and this supply requires somewhat less purification than water coming down the Huangpu at ebb tide. Intake pipes have for some years also been run far into the estuary of the Yangzi, and during the 1980s, pipes were built to take more water from large Dingshan Lake in Qingpu county, on Shanghai's border with Jiangsu.

Suzhou Creek was reported to stink continuously during the warm half of each year.[159] The Huangpu River, which is geologically a tidal slough, was declared "smelly" by a standardized criterion for 41 percent of the days in 1983.[160] In light of records kept over eight decades concerning the Huangpu, which showed that water quality was on average unacceptable 41 percent of the time, the 1983 finding was bad but normal. As reforms accelerated in urban Shanghai, water pollution became worse. A 1986 estimate, using the same measure, put the Huangpu as unacceptably smelly 53 percent of the time. Then just two years later, in 1988, a government office certified the Huangpu "black and smelly" 63 percent of the time.[161]

These water pollution problems increased so rapidly, some response to lessen them was forthcoming in the 1990s. Newspapers could report this issue. "There is serious environmental pollution in the Yangzi delta," a local journalist complained. "The Grand Canal connecting North and South China has become the biggest sewer channel in this area. Many factories along the canal continue to discharge [untreated] waste water. The Huangpu River in Shanghai is black and smelly for half the year. . . . Once polluted water flows on the land, soil and crops also become polluted."[162] Stringent controls on the Huangpu and Suzhou Creek had somewhat ameliorated the problem in central Shanghai by 1994, but really clean water was difficult to arrange in such a quick-developing place.[163]

Noise pollution was also serious in areas that contained both factories and residences. In some of these, the decibel level was measured at ten to twenty times the safe maximum.[164] Such problems were handled by the people who suffered most from them, those who lived in the area. Local residence committees approached local noise-polluting firms in such cases, and state organizations seldom played any role.

The best-researched environment in the Shanghai delta is in northern Zhejiang. At Xiang Lake, between Hangzhou and Shaoxing on the prosperous north Zhejiang plain, a historian records a period of new "local rule" during reforms. County-level posts had been "almost completely monopolized from 1949 to 1980 by men from Shandong province," but thereafter they were filled by local people.[165] This change had consequences for policy, too. Rural prosperity in this region during the 1970s and 1980s led to so much house construction, the local clay quarries supplying the raw material for bricks from areas that had once been lakebed were threatened with exhaustion. Rather than leave them as pits in the ground, the new town leadership filled them with water for fish farming and better scenery. Xiang Lake, once very large, had been reduced gradually over centuries, and an early-PRC decision taken by cadres from Shandong (who presumably arrived in the area with Gen. Chen Yi's Third Field Army) would have filled all the remaining water area with land. But local control by the 1980s boded to give part of the lake a rebirth. In general, people who live in an ecology care for it better than corporate or government officials do. Environmental health is a natural field for local networks.

Birth Planning and Parents

The Chinese government, backed by most intellectuals but with less support from other groups, during reforms has stressed a national economic need to have fewer people. The highlight of this campaign lay in high leaders' proclamations since 1979 that each married couple should have just one child. In this connection, it is notable that China's total fertility rate (TFR) had its sharpest decline *prior to* the state's stress on a one-child policy. The TFR is the average number of children that a woman has during her life. Technical demographers tend to use it as the best index of fertility. In China, this statistic plummeted from 5.7 in 1970 to 2.3 in 1980—mostly before the one-child propaganda. Then it dropped very gradually to 1.9 in 1992 (about the same level as in the United States or United Kingdom at that time).[166] If fertility reduction is taken as the hallmark of China's reforms in population policy, then behavioral data show these reforms occurred mostly before 1978.

Demographic control was still officially prominent as the first-listed priority for social development in Shanghai's 1981–85 state plan.[167] Birth control policies have been hortatory in style; the national constitution itself obligates citizens to follow birth plans. Individualism has not been an ideal of China's formal law, even in this field that is very intimate to families. The PRC state cites the naturally communal origins of people to arrogate to itself a right of regulating how many children a couple will have. The official propagation of this state right, however, does not automatically prove that it is the effective cause of most behavior in this field. The situations and ideals of individual women and small families have changed since the early 1970s, in ways that suggest at least some unofficial origins of the fertility reduction.

Procedures for Birth Planning

One child was the official norm for urban families during most of the reform period. Families with one child who promised to have no more could obtain a "one-child certificate." Officials might ask to see this, and it was supposed to confer various advantages, but the extent to which it affected families varied greatly by time and place. Parents could nonetheless apply for permission to have a second baby. The procedures for arranging this were complex.

For an urban family, letters of approval from both the husband's and wife's work units had to be brought to the local street committee (of the wife's residence, if work or housing forced them to live apart). These documents were supposed to be forwarded to the district or county birth planning committee, which could issue a certificate allowing two children (upon return of the one-child certificate that the family had previously received), under any of the following conditions: if the first offspring was disabled, if the couple had adopted a foster child and five or more years after marriage the wife became pregnant, or if both the husband and wife were themselves single children.[168] Otherwise, in general, the pregnancy was supposed to be aborted.

Peasant couples, even in Shanghai's suburbs, could be legally authorized to have a second child under the three conditions listed above for urban-district residence—or under any of *eleven* other conditions.[169] Applications always had to be made through a work unit, urban or rural, which sent its "opinion" to higher levels for approval. The authority to issue birth permissions was one of the more important powers retained by officials during reforms, but these cadres were at least as beholden to local networks as to the state bureaucracy.

In practice, the complex rules gave local cadres some discretion, although in theory their role was only to interpret the facts of each case and issue certificates accordingly. A change during the reforms was that a manual specifying these criteria and procedures was on sale in Shanghai. It could be used by anyone interested in making an application to the bureaucracy on this or any of the other subjects it covered. The reforms made people more lawyerly.

Birth Campaigns and Modernization: Effort and Results

Shanghai has long been the place in China with the highest per-capita expenditure on birth control. Together with other modern factors, this contraception effort has brought results: In 1954, of all China's twenty-nine provinces, Shanghai had both the highest rate of natural increase and the highest birthrate; but by 1981, Shanghai had the lowest rates both for natural increase and for births.[170] A sharp decrease in the local birthrate was wholly responsible for this reversal of Shanghai's rank among the provinces. By 1981 most other provinces reported lower mortality than Shanghai, apparently because relatively strict household registration in Shanghai had discouraged young immigrants and made for many old people there. Shanghai had enjoyed the lowest death rate among China's provinces in 1954. Several factors lowered Shanghai's birthrate, and not all depended on the main intended results of policies. Some came from the long and bumpy growth of institutions to send youths out of Shanghai, which had reduced fertility there.[171] Together, the campaigns and other modern factors proved to be effective from an antinatalist point of view.

The official effort to control Shanghai's birthrate, while always strenuous, relaxed somewhat in the mid-1970s, during the temporary conservative period after the first spurt of reforms in the early 1970s. The rate of per-capita expenditure on birth control in 1974–76 Shanghai was 15 percent lower than 1971–73 spending.[172] The reform process, in this and many other fields, suffered an interruption in 1975–76.

The death rate had already dropped by the early 1970s, largely because of the success of Maoist communitarian campaigns against contagious "crowd" diseases that produce antibodies. Socialist campaigns had been less effective against chronic "individual" diseases which community education campaigns can help to prevent but not eradicate.[173] China's death rate had already stabilized far below its premodern norm by the early 1970s. Irrespective of anything the state might do, this modern mortality rate was not about to go down much further.

So reducing births became the only available means of demographic planning for those who wanted such a plan. *And China's population growth was more than halved between 1970 and 1977* (from 26 to 12 per thousand annually). This was the essence of reform in population policy. Only later was there a major rise in female infant mortality, at least between 1979 and 1984—a tragic topic that will be discussed more fully below.[174] The overall results of demographic reform were more evident in the early 1970s than after 1978.

In Shanghai during the early 1970s, fertility reached an unprecedented low. From 1971 to 1977, the local birthrate averaged 10 per 1,000 people—as compared with an average of at least 13 per 1,000 from 1978 to 1992.[175] The early 1970s, while the pro-natalist Mao was still alive, give evidence that could arguably show the greatest effectiveness of the birth control policy that is usually attributed to enlightened reforms. The figures below show how Shanghai's rate of births per thousand people fell in the early 1970s. Then it rose irregularly—especially because of natality in built-up areas, not in the suburbs—until the late 1980s, when registration rates and birth rates both fell.

1952	39	1973	10	1980	12	1987	15
1957	46	1974	9	1981	17	1988	13
1962	26	1975	9	1982	19	1989	13
1965	17	1976	10	1983	15	1990	10
1970	14	1977	11	1984	14	1991	8
1971	12	1978	11	1985	13	1992	7
1972	11	1979	11	1986	15		

The overall picture after 1970 is of a rate that was low for many reasons. Government policy was important in the result, but not exclusively so.

In China as a whole, the pattern is somewhat similar. The main reform in birth planning was to reduce the rate. Because of internal migration, this matter may best be analyzed on a nationwide basis. The early 1970s saw a very sharp decline in comparison with births during the decade after 1978, when the rate fluctuated about a flat low level.[176] In 1969 and 1970, births were 34 and 33 per thousand people, respectively; but by 1976 and 1977, they had fallen to 20 and 19 respectively—a drop of 14 points in about seven years. After 1978, the figure varied only slightly: it was up to 21 in 1982 and 1987, then down to 17.5 per thousand in 1984. Any post-1978 decreases were temporary, unlike those of the early 1970s. Since lowering the birthrate and keeping it down is the main reform, the early 1970s qualify as reform years at least as well as do the years after 1978. In the first period, natality dropped; in the second, it was held fairly low.

More education and career opportunities have, in some reform years, become available for young women. Birthrates fluctuated upward and then downward, but they never approached the premodern high levels. When they later come down in effect to equal death rates, China's "demographic lag" will end—as has happened in the permanently registered population of Shanghai already. The country's eventual population will depend heavily on the fast decrease of birth-rates during early reforms. The 1970–77 birthrate reduction was arguably the most important of all reforms because of its permanent effect in determining China's population size.[177]

State policy was a factor reducing birthrates in urban Shanghai, but this policy was not the only cause of the lower fertility. A careful study tested the relative contributions of two broad causes: general socioeconomic development and state birth planning. Did Chinese women have fewer children because they had more education, for example, so that their own local motives may explain more of the result? Or did they have lower fertility because of state birth control policies, as mandated by the central government? The conclusion of a complex correlation exercise, involving seventeen general development variables and eleven specific family planning variables, was that although the quick fertility transition in China has been partly induced by policy, the contribution to low fertility of very fast socioeconomic development is also great.[178]

The proportional contributions of state policy and economic growth are strictly impossible to measure, because some growth results from state policy. Some acceleration and deceleration of growth also come from unintended effects of government measures. Policies for birth control almost surely did not cause all the fertility decline that China has seen, and individual contexts have surely impelled some of that change. But rational-actionists still have to explain why China's fertility has fallen faster and earlier than in other densely populated countries with similar per-capita incomes. And statists might allow the possibility that the government does not administer all social norms; it does not even implement all the ideas that people have about their large collective. State propaganda for birth control has been effective in part because many Chinese people, on the basis of their own thinking, concluded they were too crowded. The results of a 1990 attitude survey would tend to support this hypothesis.[179]

In central Shanghai, household size fell faster than the birthrate. Average urban household size, surveyed there in 1980 and again in 1992, plummeted from 4.06 to 3.11 people.[180] A continuous birth control campaign, based on explicit collective and habitual coercion, was a factor contributing to this result. So were other correlates of economic growth.

In the suburbs, prosperity encouraged marriages, but industrialization and policy discouraged the bearing of children.[181] Birth control apparently achieved its aims in suburban Shanghai by the end of the 1970s. Registered population size was almost totally stable from 1976 to 1988 in the best-studied village there—even though from 1976 to 1980 alone, the number of households in-creased by almost one-fifth. Even a few years later, the rise of the registered population in this suburban place was not great, although the number of house-holds continued to grow quickly.[182]

Rural wealth correlated strongly with family size. A major reason was an ironic and unintended result of the equalization of rural land plots in the early 1950s under Mao. When plots for cultivation were assigned in the 1970s to many households on responsibility contracts, the amounts of contracted land were at first roughly equal; Maoist precepts were followed at least to that extent. These plots were closer to each other in size, for example, than had been typical of household holdings before land reform in the early 1950s. So in the 1970s stage of agricultural contracting, the amount of labor each contract plot demanded of its peasant family was also roughly equal. The amount of *extra* labor any household could devote to industrial work was thus dependent on how much labor remained, i.e., on family size—and industrial work paid better.

As late as 1984, these figures on Shanghai rural families showed how incomes were a function of the number of members a family could send into factory work:[183]

Rural families with:	Household size	No. of industrial workers	Household income (yuan)
All agriculturalists	3.57	0	876
1 industrial worker	3.86	1	1,065
2 industrial workers	4.35	2	1,170
3+ industrial workers	4.83	3.1	1,223

State birth policies encouraged young working couples to bear an approximately equal number of children (ideally, just one) who then went to school. Early retirement policies dismissed from their jobs many who still lived with their families. So the number of modern sector workers per household varied far more sharply than family size. The amount of income families made showed a similar variation. These policies—especially the early land reform that meant post-1978 redistributions to families had to be fairly even—had been largely designed to equalize household prosperity. Not only did they have unintended effects completely irrelevant to the leaders' apparent intentions and explicit ideology, but they also produced precisely the opposite effects: Measures for equalization could lead to inequality. Birth controls designed to raise per-capita prosperity could disadvantage peasant families that followed them. In these families, no surplus members contributed nonagricultural income.

Birth control, and departures of family members to even higher-paying jobs in the urban area of Shanghai, combined to make average suburban household size drop from 4.26 to 4.09 persons between 1980 and 1984.[184] The average number of industrial workers per rural household nevertheless rose by 40 percent. More labor for all purposes was mobilized per family (from 1.02 workers at the beginning of this short period up to 1.43 at the end). The portion of rural laborers working in industry rose very sharply in these five years, from 36 to 52 percent.

Some relaxation of state control in the 1980s led to family decisions about the use of women's time for labor, for unpaid work, or for other activities that affected birthrates. During reforms, more people got married. Shanghai's marriage rate topped those in all Chinese provinces in 1985, at 3.0 percent of the population annually (compared to the next highest, that of Beijing at 2.7 percent, and Tianjin's 2.4 percent).[185] At the same time, Shanghai was the only province in China where more than half of all married women of reproductive age had one-child certificates. Shanghai was also the sole province in which that portion was over 60 percent among women living in urban districts. Inland provinces showed strikingly different patterns in all these respects.[186]

Yet it was difficult for Shanghai neighborhood committee cadres not to take the avuncular and welcoming attitude toward new babies that is natural in all societies, including China. A late 1980s Shanghai regulation, which codified local practices common before then, provided that "for babies born in violation of birth control policies, the Household Registration Office should approve and register them. But their parents should be given education about birth control policy."[187] Enforcement by that time in Shanghai did not punish children along with their parents, after unauthorized births took place. Every kind of measure was attempted to reduce births in advance. After parents actually had their children, that policy had failed. When local officials faced a *fait accompli,* then state policy had been displaced and they could acquiesce.

What, over the years, was the effect of these varied pressures on Shanghai's birthrate? Demography is a field in which long views are needed, because a population is like a large ship; it does not change course quickly. Reforms have depressed the birthrate in cities because of stringent antinatal campaigns and because some women have more diverse career possibilities, and especially more education, than in the past. A counterforce to these factors is the broader prosperity, which allows parents to support children more easily. Official demographic projections in 1985 "aimed at" a Shanghai population by 2000 of 13 million— but 14 million had already been reached in 1990.[188]

Urban Fertility in Perspective of Nationwide Migration

The influx of cheap labor during reforms debilitated demographic planning. Birth control was practically impossible to enforce among migrant workers, especially suburban farm workers:

> Recently [1989], many people from Jiangsu, Anhui, and Shandong have come to Shanghai seeking jobs because they were impoverished back home. After they got a female baby, they still wanted a male baby. Many had two children or more.... Some couples came to farm, so as to avoid the local urban government's birth control. Almost all these workers had one or more "black" children [unauthorized by the state]. Because the workers migrated, it was difficult for leaders on suburban farms to carry out the birth control policy among them. Some cadres were aware of this problem and wanted to adopt

effective methods; but if so, the workers just floated to other places. Workers would move repeatedly until they had a male baby.[189]

Women who immigrated to Shanghai, especially those who came illegally, easily eluded birth control cadres. They "generally had little education; 13 percent were illiterate, although 47 percent had been to middle schools.... 40 percent had lived in the city for more than five months. They actually had become Shanghai 'residents.' About half of these women engaged in economic activity. Many women thought that if they could make money and could pay their over-quota birth fines, they could have more children."[190]

Monetary penalties for extra births unintentionally made new wealth—and thus work outside of the high-tax state sector—the key to success for parents who wanted a traditionally large Chinese family. Illegal immigrants to Shanghai often made better money than state employees in the late 1980s and early 1990s. "The local [district and street] governments where they lived could not manage, because they were in Shanghai but the offices had no information about them.... As a matter of fact, they were free to have more children."[191]

Especially in rural areas, cadres put themselves in danger if they tried to enforce the one-child policy without concern for the interests of local networks. A survey of the causes of peasant attacks on local cadres during the late 1980s in twelve towns of Suining county, Jiangsu, showed that almost one-third (32 percent) were directly caused by contraception and abortion policies. Resentment about birth control was even more important than taxes and other imposts as a reason for physical reprisals against officials.[192] Reports of such violence come from rural areas, not cities, but they are sufficiently frequent to show that insensitive birth planning could threaten the very lives of the officials who tried to implement it. In some cases, cadres or their families (especially their sons) were murdered by peasants who were enraged by this policy.[193]

A more usual local response to unpopular birth control in both rural and urban areas was evasion. "Extra-birth guerrilla bands" (chaosheng youji dui), comprising both pregnant mothers and illegal midwives, often could "move to another town for births" (yixiang shengyu). State cadres stood no chance of catching up with this underground railway.[194] The availability to women of jobs in collective and private firms reduced the state's influence over them—while also reducing their motives to have children quickly. Many nonetheless resisted abortions, on their own or their husbands' wishes. As one official put it, "Few rural women agree to have abortions, and many who do first put up a strong fight." The reasons are often traditional or practical—invasive medical procedures are unpleasant and can be dangerous—but very seldom religious in any other sense. A birth control cadre reported, "If women know we are coming, they frequently run away. Usually they come back at night. As a result, a lot of my visits take place after hours. Even then, they sometimes run away." Mothers-in-law tended to be strongly pro-natalist, telling officials to "mind their own business."[195]

Female Infanticide and the Uncivil Side of Society

Infant girls surely suffered most, as government pressures and traditional prejudices combined to kill them. Largely for this reason, total life expectancy actually declined in China from 1979 to 1984.[196] Infant mortality rose sharply in this
period, from 3.7 to 5.0 percent annually. The change included a clear sex bias
against girls. Although almost identical infant mortalities were reported for boys
and girls in 1978, the death rate for infant girls in 1984 was double that for boys.
In 1978, the mortality of Chinese boy babies was 3.68 percent, and that of girls,
3.77 percent, was not radically different. But just half a decade later by 1984, the
male figure was 3.39 percent, and for female infants, a reported (perhaps underreported) 6.72 percent.[197]

The discussion that must follow is not about abortions; it is about the deaths
of unwanted babies, most often girls, after they were born. This was a reform—a
local one—and it shows a sharply uncivil, unsocial, inarticulate, and barely
speakable aspect of the reform process. The central government wanted "birth
planning," but it unleashed local administrators who in practice did that job by
acquiescing to ancient prejudices against women. The result was powerful: Girl
babies were found abandoned in increasing numbers during the most coercive
periods of urban birth control.[198]

Orphanages were supposed to take care of deserted babies, and in Shanghai
they probably did so at least as well as in poorer parts of China. But this city
provided gruesome reports about maltreatment of unwanted orphans, mainly
girls. A Shanghai medic, Dr. Zhang Shuyun, left China with considerable concrete evidence of these problems, after failing to ameliorate them through petitions to the offices that run Shanghai orphanages. She gave her evidence to
Human Rights Watch, which issued a scathing report:

> The brutal treatment of orphans in Shanghai, which included deliberate starva-
> tion, torture, and sexual assault, continued over a period of many years and led
> to the unnatural deaths of well over 1,000 children between 1986 and 1992
> alone. . . . This campaign of elimination could be kept secret through the com-
> plicity of both higher- and lower-level staff, and because the city's Bureau of
> Civil Affairs, responsible for the orphanage, also runs the crematoria, where
> starved children's corpses were disposed of with minimum oversight, even
> before a death certificate had been filled out by the attending physician.[199]

The State Council in Beijing soon issued a statement retorting "The so-called
accusations of 'torture and abuse of disabled children' by the Shanghai Welfare
Institute are completely groundless." But Dr. Zhang and others brought documentary evidence of their charges, as well as photographs that would have been
difficult to fake, showing children near death. While still in China, she had in
1992 enlisted a member of the Shanghai People's Congress, an economist and
Party member named Hong Dalin, to protest these abuses with the orphanage

authorities. The bureaucrats were unresponsive, apparently because they saw no overwhelming problem in the deaths of abandoned babies, most of whom were girls. The birth control campaign also had other costs in terms of family structure, but the heaviest resulted from the callousness of educated officials who acquiesced to female infanticide.

Pensions for Birth Control, Less Money Against Mortality

On a national basis, from 1982 to 1987, the average size of households in China declined from 3.4 persons to 3.2.[200] Because a traditional reason for having more children was their expected support when parents became elderly, urban pension schemes were altered to reinforce birth planning: Upon retirement, both members of a working married couple that had just one child or no children would receive a 5 to 10 percent increment to their normal pensions, in compensation for the fact that they could receive less or nothing from their offspring.[201]

The reform government did less, however, to finance medicine. The decline of "barefoot doctors" from 1.8 million in 1977 to 1.3 million in 1984 matched a decline in funds for rural health services particularly. The drop in China's mortality stopped (although considering China's low average income, mortality had already reached very respectable international levels earlier, and there were inherent difficulties in making further major progress after the traditional contagions had been tamed). The reforms brought back traditional male biases in nutrition and health care. The previous achievements of communitarian policies under Mao were mostly retained, even as reform-era individualism swept the country. But they were not furthered, and in some important areas (including primary education and public health) they partially receded. This was the context in which the antinatalist campaign was conducted in China. The state effort at population planning showed the considerable extent of what a late-revolutionary regime can do, and also the greater extent of its public claims. Propaganda for birth control was partly an excuse for bad economic management; but especially in crowded areas like the Shanghai delta, it was also a response to extreme crowding over limited resources.[202]

Birth Control, "Little Emperors," and
Modern Career Politics

Birth planning created many one-child families. Since both urban parents often had jobs, their child would be left in a nursery or kindergarten, or with a grandmother or an amah (usually a peasant woman with far less education than the parents, often in the city for long periods but with no formal household registration). Child neglect was a possibility under these circumstances. A much greater danger, given the strength of Chinese families, was that these only children would be overindulged, treated like "little emperors" (*xiao huangdi*) or princesses.

Chinese writers on this subject express a keen sense that today's children become the adults who will decide the community's future. Not just lineages, but also the nation as a whole, depend on the quality of upbringing that children have. Parents and officials alike, in both public and private, have during the reform years shown great concern that the "little emperor" phenomenon and the low moral tone set by the Cultural Revolution together pose dangers to the future of China and of Chinese families.

This concern was itself a lifestyle reform. It made increasing numbers of middle-income urban parents demand a great deal of their children (at least after babyhood, when by tradition Chinese children are coddled unrelentingly). Grades in school became, in some families, the overwhelming micropolitical issue. "Piano mania" (*gangqin re*) was a fever for parents and a fear for children. Delia Davin reports a Chinese conversation:

> One woman told me how unrealistic such parents are, recalling a newspaper story of a boy who had chopped up his piano with an axe because he was so fed up with practicing. Yet she had forced her own seven-year-old girl to practice for three hours a day until friends advised her to reduce it to two hours. When I asked how the little girl felt about this, she admitted her daughter had said that the best place in the world must be one without a piano. I asked her if she was not repeating the mistake of the parents whose son had chopped up the piano. "Oh no," she said. "It's different. My daughter has real talent."[203]

Street committees run "schools for household heads" (*jiazhang xuexiao*), which parents and grandparents may attend to learn more about raising children and to discuss perennially difficult issues such as corporal punishment. The state in the reform era officially opposes corporal punishment (though some, not all, of its public actions, such as at Tiananmen suggest that it teaches an opposite lesson too). Rules forbid teachers to hit their pupils. In big city schools, especially after the Cultural Revolution whose beatings some people recall, this standard seems to be observed. Urban parents, however, sometimes think they have to hit children, especially those who receive low grades at school.[204]

Pressures to succeed in densely populated, individually competitive Chinese environments, where resources are sparse relative to the number of claimants, cause most of China's politics and much of its political violence. None of these problems is unique; nations as different as Japan and the United States continue to face many of the same issues. But the single-child policy has been a major contributor to the "moral panic" that Davin describes in Chinese urban society during reforms: "China's obsessive search for the right way to educate her children reflects the much more general uncertainty with which she now faces the future."[205] This search is China's only in the sense that many families and local networks share it at the same time, after a revolution disrupted the careers of their members.

Table 2.5–4

Portions of Women Among Employees in Chinese Provinces, 1985
(percentages)

Shanghai	*41.8*	Heilongjiang	37.6	Ningxia	34.2
Tianjin	41.8	NAT'L AVG.	36.4	Guizhou	33.9
Liaoning	40.9	Fujian	36.0	Yunnan	32.9
Beijing	40.7	Hunan	35.7	Shaanxi	32.7
Xinjiang	39.7	Sichuan	35.6	Shandong	32.4
Jilin	39.1	Inner Mong.	35.5	Henan	32.3
Zhejiang	*38.8*	Jiangxi	35.1	Qinghai	32.1
Hubei	38.2	Tibet	34.7	Hebei	32.0
Guangdong	37.8	Guangxi	34.6	Gansu	31.1
Jiangsu	*37.7*	Anhui	34.3	Shanxi	30.4

Note and source: "Employees" (*zhigong*) refer mostly to staff and workers of enterprises; peasants and shepherds are not included. The index on this table correlates with many other indices of modernization, including urbanization and per-capita wealth. Put in order from data in *Zhongguo tongji nianjian, 1986* (China Statistical Yearbook, 1986), State Statistical Bureau, ed. (Beijing: Zhongguo Tongji Chuban She, 1986), p. 135. The three East China provinces of major interest in this book are italicized. Note that an ideal feminist rate, for this index, would be near 50 percent; but only the four most urbanized provinces registered over 40 percent on it.

Opportunities and Women

Shanghai contained a higher portion of women in 1987 (49.68 percent) than any other Chinese province.[206] Women in Shanghai also comprised a greater portion of workers, as Table 2.5–4 indicates. Women were 42 percent of the city's total labor force in 1985. Many of their jobs, e.g. in textile mills, were menial; but female participation in paid work correlates by province very highly with per-capita wealth.[207] Shanghai, northern Zhejiang, and southern Jiangsu made up the most populous large region in China with high rates of working women.

Modernization or Mobilization Approaches to Women's Progress

Most literature about women's opportunities in China, to the extent it explores the causes of change in them, can be classified in two categories. One of these explains action in terms of the situational context where it occurs; the other treats what people do in terms of their intended meanings. Sociologists who study modernization tend to treat greater equality for women as just one aspect of a very large correlation of changes (including the rise of per-capita incomes, urbanization, and a more complex division of labor). This view of the situation can organize most of the empirical data.[208] In no country has the process gone far enough to equalize men's and women's salaries or educational opportunities, but such differences are lower in measurably modern countries than in others. Marxist official approaches to the problem of women's liberation have been compatible with the view of many non-Marxist sociologists that overall progress for women does not occur as an isolated phenomenon, but instead as one part of a large historical process that may variously be described as modernization or revolution.

Avowedly feminist authors tend to think that such an approach, even if useful for making static comparisons, misses the political potential for dynamic change. They advocate community education to mobilize women for their own better-ment. Early revolutionaries in China, especially before 1949, included many for whom ending the patriarchal oppression of women was the main aim.[209] After the PRC's establishment in 1949, the centerpiece of national policy for women was a Marriage Law that allowed women to divorce spouses who harmed them. Enforcement of this law was slow, and the context created many ambiguities in its meaning.[210] The Women's Federation became an arm of the government, supporting all its policies. Women's liberation was officially subsumed as just one aspect of revolutionary modernization, having particular interest to half the population but having no inherent priority over the production of more tractors, the collection of more taxes, or any other government cause.

Women workers were crucial for socialist capital accumulation, because they tended to have jobs at low wages in light-industrial and retail firms that could generate huge amounts of revenue for Beijing's coffers. Although surprisingly little capital was put into such firms, these plants expanded on the basis of cheap urban female labor and mandated sales, to the state, of the low-priced agricul-tural inputs that many of them processed.

By the late 1980s, almost fifty times as many women worked in PRC state industries as in 1949. Even after the Transition to Socialism of the mid-fifties, the number of women in state factories rose eleven times by the late 1980s.[211] But the wages of these female employees went up very slowly. Women workers had, on average, more schooling than male employees by the late 1980s. During 1986 in China as a whole, 81 percent of female staff had at least a middle-school education, while only 73 percent of male employees did.[212] Retirement ages account for part of this difference (women retire earlier than men, leaving their younger, better-educated sisters to raise the average for women's education). But the main story to be told is the contribution—and exploitation—of women work-ers in light-industrial state factories.

State-Led Modernization and Problems for Women

The development of socialist light industries, to support central budgets, ex-panded employment opportunities for women. It did not ensure that they would have good jobs. Their organizational connections with the bureaucracies that ran their careers were generally weaker than in the case of male employees. After the Cultural Revolution, the Shanghai Women's Federation was officially revived in 1973; it was one of the last mass organizations to be resurrected.[213] But it continued to do little by way of representing women workers to the state agencies that employed them. In the textile-weaving center of Nantong, for example, women comprised nearly two-fifths of the workers. But few could easily move to high-paying jobs, reportedly because state companies were pressed during reforms to make bigger profits.

"Women employees found they are likely the first to be fired when a unit is overstaffed and the last to be hired when employees are needed. . . . The reason women are not welcome is that they are likely to ask for more leave, such as paid maternity leaves."[214] A 1980s solution for Nantong was to require each company in the city to contribute 20 yuan a year per woman employee to a public fund, administered by the Women's Affairs Department of the All-China Federation of Trade Unions, as partial protection against layoffs for these women. But this fund did not solve the problem. Rather, it could justify state managers in getting rid of female workers.

When the state sector slowed down, women were often the first to be laid off payrolls. "These women have to return from society to family, although they are reluctant to do so." Many were well qualified to work. A 1989 survey in downtown Huangpu found that most without jobs were young and had educations: 87 percent of unemployed women there were age 40 or younger, and 91 percent had at least attended middle school. "They came home because there was not enough work to do in the factories. . . . Ms. Zhong was employed in a processing factory before she had a baby. Because she gave birth, she had to leave the plant temporarily and she received 80 percent of her wage. But after March [1989], she will only receive 60 percent." Short-term absences could turn into long-term unemployment. "The baby is growing up, and she wants to return to work. But she is not fortunate enough to go back, or even to get a temporary job. The living standard of this new generation of housewives is clearly decreasing."[215]

Even if excess workers remained on a payroll at a percentage of their previous low wages, the main means by which factories compensated active workers in this era of quick inflation was to give bonuses. These often equaled or exceeded wages. Laid-off workers were, of course, not eligible for performance bonuses. So many women

> had to do other businesses without official registration. . . . Some sold everyday commodities in streets. Most such women have a strong desire to go back to work. But their old enterprises have no capacity to absorb them, for reasons such as insufficient tasks, financial losses, and a surplus of labor. How should we deal with these unemployed women? Do they want to be housewives forever?[216]

Most of them did not, and the loss of income to their families was a cause of dissatisfaction among Shanghai's workers even before the 1990s, when this problem became worse.

The state's stress on financing itself in consumer goods markets did not always work against the practical interests of women. Housework was still far more often considered the responsibility of wives than of husbands, and new consumer appliances eased this burden somewhat. The 1980s demand for washing machines, refrigerators, and similar appliances is understandable, because housework took considerable time for Shanghai residents. A 1982 survey of state employees showed they averaged 2.4 hours of housework per day in Shanghai, with female employees averaging more than 3 hours.[217]

As more textile manufacturing moved inland, a major question for the maintenance of women's jobs was the extent to which Shanghai and surrounding cities could develop electronic industries. The mixed record, showing that such development was slow, has already been discussed above. Although electronic firms have not developed as quickly as the metropolitan planners would have liked, these industries—as well as pharmaceuticals and new service industries such as hotels and consultancies—have hired many women. The degree of freedom or exploitation they encountered in such jobs varied between industries, and female workers in new factories under high administrative levels tended to do better than those in enterprises linked to villages.

Some women's rights that had been normalized in state plants during the 1950s nonetheless came into doubt because of state deficits in the 1980s. Pregnancy leave was controversial among Chinese managers, because state enterprises paid the costs. In 1981, under Shanghai's birth control regulations, Shanghai's pregnancy leave was just 15 days, and the new mothers' salaries were reduced 20 percent during this period.[218] Sometimes arguments for pregnancy leave were explained by the idea that men and women have a social "division of labor."[219] The growth of state budget deficits tended, however, to trump the virtues or faults of any theories during reforms.

For good jobs, which required educated women, the state-sector decline combined with ancient male biases in hiring. The portion of women among Shanghai's scientific workers decreased during reforms, from 36 percent in 1978 to 34 percent in 1983. This falloff may not seem great, but the number of people involved (a total of 320,000 specialists in the city by 1983) was considerable, and there was increasing competition for such posts. The trend was especially surprising in light of high job turnover among these professionals during the same years. Ten percent of all Shanghai scientists at the end of 1981 were newly promoted to their posts in that year; the figure was 8 percent in 1982. The portion of women varied by specialty: more than two-thirds of medical officers in these years were female, but only about one-fifth of engineers were.

Shanghai's employment structure in 1982 showed many working women, as Table 2.5–5 indicates, but most had low-level jobs. This pattern of discrimination

Table 2.5–5

Shanghai Employed People by Occupation and Gender (percentages in 1982)

Percentage of work-force in each occupation	Occupation	Men	Women	Number
3	Gov't/Party (of which:)	83	17	235,715
	State agencies	(90)	(10)	11,718
	Party and mass orgs.	(76)	(24)	58,962
	Street and rural orgs.	(56)	(44)	7,959
	Enterprises	(86)	(14)	157,076
3	Work in offices	65	35	229,145
4	Commerce (of which:)	55	45	299,074
	Wholesaling	(85)	(15)	77,680
7	Service work	46	54	556,423
11	Professional	54	46	792,770
24	Agriculture/fishing	41	59	1,769,976
	Farm work	(37)	(63)	1,584,858
48	Industry/Transport	57	43	3,543,989
	Textiles	(24)	(76)	398,694
0	Other	—	—	9,715
100	Municipal total	53	47	7,436,267

Source: Shanghai shi di san renkou pucha ziliao huibian (Compendium of Materials on Shanghai Municipality's Third Census), Shanghai Census Office, ed. (Shanghai: Shanghai Shi Renkou Pucha Bangong Shi, 1984), pp. 331–41. Percentages may not sum to 100 because of rounding. See a related table in this book, on changes in educational level from 1982 to 1987, for more data classified by occupations.

was particularly obvious in the high official sector, comprising the 3 percent of registered workers in Party and government jobs. Only 10 percent of the employees in government jobs were women, whereas in street and rural organizations the rate was 44 percent. Females comprised just 14 percent of enterprise cadres. Among wholesalers in commerce, only 15 percent were women, but the portion behind ordinary retail counters was surely much higher. One-quarter of all Shanghai registered workers were agricultural, and 63 percent of these farmers were women. In textiles, women were 76 percent of workers. This pattern in China's largest city is typical of many countries, and it shows more sex equality than do figures from other parts of China. But the distribution of jobs by gender nonetheless remained very unequal. A striking aspect of Table 2.5–5 is the conclusion that, even in Shanghai, nine-tenths of the state was male.

When the government ran into financial difficulties, local leaders (mostly men) made sure they kept their own jobs. Women had more trouble finding or holding work. An Australian teacher reported clear job discrimination against women in 1989:

> The general belief [at East China Normal University] was that a bright woman had less of a chance of being employed in a good job than a duller man, and that the university authorities connived with employers to assign women graduates to lower status and lower paid jobs. When I raised this with university authorities, their response was to warn students to stop talking to foreign staff about the job assignment system.[220]

A comparison of census findings in 1982 and 1987 shows that the portion of working women declined—just the opposite trend from what might be expected in a period of quick modernization.[221] Chinese statisticians explained that more young women were in school and more were doing housework. But in rural areas, many did agricultural work, freeing male relatives for labor at higher wages in rural factories.

The state sponsored a Stalinist vision of womanhood even in late 1980s Shanghai, when production and reproduction were equally honored in state rhetoric. Some Shanghai women who distinguished themselves in both professional and household work could receive the title "Red Flag Holder." "Five-Good" families were also dubbed as models if they were internally harmonious and socially productive. In these officially lauded households, 44 percent of the family heads were Party members, and 32 percent were cadres.[222] Most of the household heads, of course, were men.

Patriarchy is a strong local political tradition in most of China, and the reform period eroded it very slowly, even in modern Shanghai. More overseas Chinese businessmen came to the city in this time of international opening, and some took Shanghai "wives" in addition to their spouses in places such as Taiwan. Punning on the phrase "one country, two systems" (*yiguo liangzhi*), some wags pronounced this "one country, two wives" (*yiguo liangqi*). But this joke has limited humor for feminists. Sex and power are so related, their connection even extends to law. Women are subject, as a sinologue sociologist has argued, to particular legal controls: "The frequent use in China of administrative detention of females for 'sexual transgressions' [*xing zuicuo*] must be seen in light of protection of moral boundaries in general. As such, female sexual crime is probably the prime example in China of what can be called 'constructed crime.' What is 'criminal' for females is not necessarily so for males."[223]

A few intellectuals sharply criticized all this patronizing. Zhang Jie's 1982 story "The Ark" has been called "the first genuinely feminist literature published in the People's Republic." Its protagonists are

> three single women, two divorced and one separated, who live together. They have consciously broken the rules for proper female behavior: They don't care

about their looks. Their skin has become like "air-dried sausage." They smoke and swear, never wash up, and live in permanent disorder. They have meaningful jobs but constantly have to fight against male chauvinism, gossip, and humiliations because of their sex.[224]

Zhang Jie's feminism is not unique among well-known women writers of the reform period. Dai Houying, Yu Luojin, Zhang Xinxin, and others write extensively about women's problems. This kind of literature was absent during the Cultural Revolution and scarce before that. It did not affect a large part of the population during reforms, but it proclaimed some women intellectuals' sharp frustration at the continuing pervasive sex bias against them.

The official approach to women's liberation in the 1950s and 1960s brought only limited improvements, but it was less communitarian than were policies in many other fields. During reforms, for reasons presented in many sections of this book, market modernization also made a very mixed record in this field. Community propaganda and situational change are the main alternative strategies for improving the status of women. Neither has brought very quick results yet, in China or other countries; but these are both just analytic ways to talk about the issues. There is no reason always to prefer communitarianism over modernization, or vice versa, if each of these approaches can bring at least some good results for people.

Near the conclusion of her book on the changing identities of Chinese women, Elisabeth Croll describes "ambiguous women" of the reform era, "hovering within a plurality of expectations . . . so that the identification of 'proper' or 'appropriate' female behavior and priorities seems difficult in the absence of a single rhetoric defining proper female needs and interests appropriate to a modern women."[225] Mixed cues from the economy, the outside world, the commercialized environment, lineage traditions, and the state created many tentative opportunities for Chinese women during reforms. Different age cohorts and individuals did not react to these identically. The communitarian and market policy approaches to approving women's situations were also ambiguous, because neither of them solved all problems. That did not mean a bleak future, however, if women could choose whatever identities and policies boded to serve them best at each time.

School Finance and Students

Rule by the educated was a strong ideal of intellectuals during China's reforms, but state support for education dropped. Shanghai's exceptional tax burden had for many years meant downward pressure on educational budgets in the city. During the 1978–88 decade, the allocation for schools in Shanghai's local budget was 16 percent. Central controllers earmarked a lower portion of Shanghai revenues for education than was the case for twenty-one other Chinese provinces in

1988, although only Beijing has a larger number of university students. In Shanghai that year, the ratio of per-pupil education expenditures to per-capita GNP for primary, secondary, and tertiary education was respectively 7, 13, and 69 percent. This was much lower than the respective averages for all developing countries (10, 19, and 88 percent), even though Shanghai is a modern city.[226]

Niggardly financing could discourage the growth of schools even in a Confucian culture. The central state had long considered universities, which train future elites, to be within its purview, so the tertiary sector especially suffered when the state ran out of money. University enrollments increased in Shanghai during early reforms, but then they decreased: 117,644 university students in 1986, up to 122,500 in 1987 and 128,200 in 1988, then down to 126,100 in 1989, 121,300 in 1990, and 116,900 in 1991, before a rise to 119,500 in 1992.[227] Public support per Shanghai college student was notably lower than in the two comparable province-level cities, Beijing and Tianjin.[228] Shanghai's universities did not share in reform prosperity during the 1980s, because the central state continued to take heavier remittances from this place than from anywhere else. Education—especially university education after 1989—was far below the top of official priorities. The schools that relied on central finances ran into increasing trouble, while those able to call on local money could still afford to teach.

When local and central budgets are added together, the portion for education in *all* Chinese budgets rose in the early 1970s (except for slight declines in 1978 and 1982), as these figures show:[229]

1970	4.24%	1975	5.88%	1980	7.77%	1985	9.98%
1971	4.51	1976	6.26	1981	9.19	1986	n.a.
1972	5.03	1977	6.29	1982	10.03	1987	11.31
1973	5.20	1978	5.90	1983	9.89	1988	11.95
1974	5.81	1979	6.05	1984	9.98	1989	13.19

Reform decrees from Beijing abjured most national-level responsibility for supporting China's schools. As a 1980 State Council and Central Committee manifesto on education put it, "In a large country such as ours, which is heavily populated and economically underdeveloped, the task of universalizing primary education cannot be shouldered by the government alone." Education builds human infrastructure, and this pays off handsomely—but slowly. Central budgeters, needing quick money to finance state deficits, clearly bet that local Chinese families would discount the future less heavily. They promised only that "the government may provide some subsidies as it sees fit." The same decree nonetheless intoned that "no school should have a dilapidated building, each class should have a classroom, and each student should have a bench and a desk."[230] Beijing did not volunteer to pay, but it ruled this goal should be achieved "in two or three years or a little longer." Schooling was on the state's reform agenda, but far down the list.

Chinese schools had long been divided into several types, which determined their budgetary arrangements. Top universities (including Shanghai's Fudan, Jiaotong, Tongji, East China Normal, East China Chemical Engineering, Shanghai International Studies University, and thirty others elsewhere in the 1980s) were under the State Education Commission and received part of their money from central funds.[231] Another group of universities, more than four hundred, were subject to various ministries and other agencies of the central government, including many military academies. More than six hundred additional tertiary institutions were run by province-level administrations. In general, high schools were managed by rural counties or urban districts. Primary schools were mostly under townships or street offices, although their budgets came traditionally from the next higher level of government. [232] Under reforms, the main change was that school managers were plainly told, either by the administrative hierarchy or the keypoint prestige hierarchy, that they would have to round up more of their own money.

Different educational managers varied in their ability to support their local institutions. For some purposes, such as the maintenance of school buildings, money had been scarce for decades. When top secretaries of the municipal CCP committee inspected a primary school in Xuhui district, the teachers complained roundly about run-down classrooms. These politicos did little but "asked the district leaders concerned to help primary schools solve the problem of inadequate school buildings."[233] They did not contribute funds to solve the problem.

The educational portion of all Shanghai city expenditures from 1981 to 1983 was about 12 percent. By 1984–85, this figure dropped to less than 10 percent. Lack of school funds caused problems that are familiar in many countries: "Because of lack of investment, the cost of relocation ... and the difficulty of procuring space, we can only move at a snail's pace when repairing the dilapidated buildings and revamping alley primary schools."[234] This pattern was evident also at the secondary and tertiary levels. To a surprising extent, it is possible to speak of a single reform policy for all levels of Shanghai schooling: reduce the drain from public budgets by making students and local institutions pay.

This lessening of official support was not just for schools, but also for many allied activities. Shanghai's 1983 spending for all civilian services—culture, education, and social welfare all together—was only 3.9 percent of the amount invested for construction. China's other 265 officially designated "cities" in 1983 averaged much more (10.2 percent). Shanghai had the very lowest portion of budget allocated for culture and education among all large cities.[235]

Learning is, however, far more than a national pastime in China. When high and province-level state politicians declined to appropriate money for education, local institutions often sustained it. This change occurred with particular speed from 1982 to 1984. Suburban Shanghai county and its lower administrative levels (above the village) had paid just 1 percent of the local school budget in 1979 and just 3 percent in 1982—but by 1984, the portion was 17 percent.[236]

Educational institutions were expected, during reforms, to become more like businesses. They were supposed to finance themselves insofar as possible. "Schools run by the people" (*minban xuexiao*) charge tuition and have existed in China since the 1950s. Legally, these are cooperatives. Beginning in 1979, and expanding in the early 1980s, many small "private schools" (*sili xuexiao*) also appeared, mostly to teach foreign languages or vocational topics such as typing and sewing. They were supposed to have government licenses, but officials lacked any resources to control them. More regulation was publicly mooted in 1981–82, when local and central conservatives averred that the private schools were expensive or did not provide high-quality training.[237] Since these leaders declined to finance any alternatives, their objections were not a policy.

Local schools raised their tuitions sharply. Average annual student fees in suburban Shanghai county rose, between 1978 and 1984, from 63 to 157 yuan—up 2.5 times, while the county's local education budget also rose 2.1 times (partly to cover inflation).[238] This pattern was typical of reform in many fields: The central state decreased its funding and influence in a field from which it did not garner money. So nonstate networks and local state leaders took up the slack, using resources the state no longer had. Public norms of hierarchy remained strong, but local leaders, who now paid the piper, could call the tune.

Nonstate sources of new school budgets became important very quickly. Extrabudgetary income was 34 percent of total income for all Chinese education in 1986, and this portion rose to 38 percent just one year later. Of these extra funds, which were absolutely crucial for schools in strapped financial straits, almost two-fifths in 1986 came from "community collections and donations, and contributions from enterprises, mines, and factories."[239] A Shaoxing township collected "several hundred thousand yuan from local people" and built a new three-story primary school with well-lit classrooms and a separate office for each teacher.[240] The state, even when it had been better organized, very seldom spent such money on rural primary schools. The new order apparently limited enrollment to locals; but total funding, in places where the leaders cared about education, rose sharply.

Sunan schools in particular benefited from the rush of local prosperity, because town governments began demanding "education surcharges" from rural industries: "Fuqiao Township of Taicang County is a place where rural enterprises are doing well. In 1985, it collected 450,000 *yuan* in education surcharges, a truly sizeable revenue for a township. In Taicang County, however, Fuqiao is the only township that is capable of collecting this much. For other townships, such as Xinhu Township, the education surcharge only amounted to 83,000 *yuan*." Some local leaderships valued education; others conspicuously did not. "For example, Xiashu, a township that is economically better off than others, had, in 1985, 143,000 *yuan* at its own disposal. Out of this, only 9,300 *yuan*, that is 6.5 percent of the total amount, was spent on education." One-third was reinvested in industries, another third went to pay off earlier business loans, and more than one-fifth was "dispersed as administrative expenses including salaries for the township cadres."[241] Shanghai delta prosperity brought help to education when—but only when—local leaders wished to use the new money for schools.

Extrabudgetary expenditures for education by subprovincial cities and towns throughout Sunan rose between 1985 and 1989 by fully 220 percent, while the rise in budgetary expenditures was much less, 79 percent.[242] Local appropriations became crucial, as the center mostly withdrew from education and provincial budgets barely kept up with inflation. Especially at the preprimary level, practically all new schooling was nonstate, and much was private. By the mid-1980s, Shanghai parents had founded many collective and private nurseries for infants. Before the reforms, practically all registered nurseries in the city had been state-run, usually to help mothers who worked in factories or stores. More than two-fifths of Shanghai children between the ages of one month and four years were in nurseries by 1988. Of these, the largest portion (39 percent) were in quasi-private collectives. Another 22 percent were under the auspices of townships or villages, 25 percent were in state nurseries, and 14 percent were in household and street committee nurseries. State-run institutions had ceased to do much of this job.

Kindergartens were better supported by higher-level budgets. The Shanghai Education Bureau, with its local agencies, still ran institutions for 59 percent of the children ages 4 to 6. Of the others, 27 percent were under collectives, 11 percent under factories, and 3 percent under village and township auspices.[243] Going up the educational ladder from these low levels, parallel statistics show that the state's financial contribution rose. But even the most prestigious key-point universities in Shanghai were all, by the late 1980s, accepting "self-pay" (*zifei*) students, sometimes in regular curricula and sometimes in special ones. In a later section of this book, on controlling student politics, such broad generalizations about nurseries and universities will be abandoned; but in school finance, the similarity across age groups was strong.

"Thatcherism" is the closest recent Western analogy to what happened to Chinese education during reforms. High leaders avidly supported these changes. Obeisance to high officials allowed structural reforms that boded later to change that custom. Deng Xiaoping, along with Politburo member Wang Zhen, visited Jiaotong University in February 1984. They declared their "satisfaction" with the reforms on that campus, and especially with Jiaotong's political head, Ding Xuchu. This put pressure on other top Shanghai municipal cadres to pay a formal call on Jiaotong two months later. The Shanghai CCP Committee declared, "The basic experience of management reform at Jiaotong has a general significance, and it is suggestive for all fronts."[244]

Jiaotong made its own experiments in organization during the 1980s. The content of these reforms was to emphasize the potential of economic incentives to spur better school performance. Economic profit centers were established throughout Jiaotong University. Engineering consultancies and scientific experiments could often bring in considerable money. From 1978 to 1983, the university's revenues from such projects were over 12 million yuan. About 15 percent of total staff time was used by the mid-1980s for economic projects.[245] Engineering universities such as Jiaotong benefited most from the marketization of academics. But even a largely humanistic university such as Fudan boasted about fifty economic contracts by 1982, and three times that number two years later.[246] Tongji University by 1984 generated one-third of its entire budget from outside contracts.[247]

Almost any activity was legitimate if it made money. In the summer of 1988, the Shanghai Academy of Social Sciences rented space for a "beer festival." This brought together executives from breweries throughout East China to "exchange experiences" and see how they might cooperate with the aim of increasing their total sales of beer.[248] This may have been unacademic, but it was hardly unprecedented. Financing Chinese academic institutions compares in oddity with the same process abroad.

Famous academic institutions could make considerable money by having their scientists develop patents, by establishing factories making computers and other high-tech products, and by founding subsidiary schools where faculty could teach for high tuitions. The new industrial and commercial sources of money for institutions such as Fudan and Jiaotong (as for Beijing and Qinghua Universities in the north) were quite lucrative, so institutions of this sort could raise professorial salaries handily by the middle of the decade. Most educational institutions, however, were not so talented or lucky. So the gradient of differences between intellectuals' salaries in different units became sharply steeper in the mid-1990s.

Shanghai schools acted in the same manner. Many had a history of running factories during the Cultural Revolution. At that time, the reasons were ostensibly moral and educational. In any case, these factories were continued during reforms "to improve teachers' material benefits and facilities." The plants also taught "professional skills after class."[249] Fuxing Middle School started a radio factory and three clothing shops, whose profits consolidated its position as one of Shanghai's best schools. Taxes on these economic activities were minimal, because educational institutions receive exemptions. From 1989 to 1992, Fuxing could renovate its cafeteria, basketball and volleyball courts, jogging track, and table-tennis; it computerized its library and provided sixty study terminals; and it raised the bonuses for teachers. Some instructors worried that the school's quality should not depend so much on mercantile prowess. A history teacher said, "It took a while for me to get adjusted, because traditionally Confucius does not think highly of commerce. Most teachers don't want to go into business. It's not easy to do, and you have to have the gall to chase after money." The principal admitted, "This issue was debated for a long time, with people asking: Wouldn't this influence the school? But now, everyone is running businesses. And our school is in great demand. Lots of students want to come here, but we can't take them because we have no space."[250]

Local governments in poorer parts of China by 1992 sometimes ran out of money to pay their schoolteachers. Instructors in an unidentified place were compensated only through July of that year, although most of them kept working. Deductions from the traditional Spring Festival bonus were so great that each teacher ended up receiving only 20 yuan. Local authorities in Jiangsu were said to be "extremely concerned" about delays in paying teachers' salaries.[251] This problem was greatest in areas less prosperous than Shanghai, but publicity about it shocked intellectuals nationwide. In the 1990s, the State Education Commission placed pressure directly on provincial governors, through telephone conferences and by other methods, threatening to publicize provinces that did not pay teachers' salaries. The effects of this central state attempt at moral suasion are unclear.

To some extent, the reform era's greater variety of schools, combined with more local control of them, may head off in China problems that have arisen in other educational systems, e.g., that of the United States. The spread of learning to larger portions of the population has correlated, over the course of the century, with a clear decline in the quality of typical classroom work. It has also correlated with a growing isolation of teachers from other professionals. China is not exactly like any other country, of course; and some of these problems may be acceptable to Chinese because a longer-educated population may obtain more cultural and technical skills. Evidence from Hong Kong or Singapore can buttress an argument that Confucian culture in households lends effectiveness to modern education. However this may be, the PRC central state is investing much less in education than it once did. The quality of schooling will depend, more than in the past, on decisions made in local power networks.

Ethnic Respect and Minorities

Discrimination against minorities might at first seem an unlikely problem to emerge in Shanghai, since the people there can present themselves as overwhelmingly the same: almost all Han Chinese. The city government keeps careful track of such matters, and the members of all twenty-nine resident non-Han minorities (excluding foreign citizens) have been regularly and punctiliously counted. Muslims are a clear majority among Shanghai minorities, but the city also has a few Mongols, Manchus, Tibetans, and Koreans. Their formalistic representation in the Shanghai Political Consultative Conference increased between 1979 and 1982.[252] In that latter year, however, the Muslims numbered only 44,300.[253] Other minorities in the city totaled scarcely over 5,000. Non-Hans comprise just one-twenty-fifth of 1 percent of all Shanghai people. They are more conspicuous than this tiny portion suggests, because their separate ethnicity carries special rights.[254] Since the local Muslims were helped by a reduction of antireligious persecution after the Cultural Revolution, when they organized special Red Guard groups that effectively defended their secular rights, prejudice against minorities would not seem to be a big topic for Shanghai. But it would be a mistake to understate the talents of solid communities anywhere in finding "others" to help define themselves.

Han people discriminate against other Han people on "subethnic" regional lines. A majority in Shanghai are Jiangnan, speaking the Wu language to which the city has given its name, Shanghainese. But a very considerable minority—roughly one-quarter of Shanghai's population—are Subei people, originally from northern Jiangsu. They speak distinctive dialects of Mandarin, and many have distinguishing characteristics that feed a lively Jiangnan prejudice against them.

"Subei," like "Jiangnan," is a term with varying uses. The best scholar of this subject defines "areas that are uncontestably part of Subei" as the tract from Yangzhou to Yancheng, Funing, and Huai'an in the north.[255] Other less professional accounts take even Nantong, which is north of the Yangzi but closely connected with Shanghai in many cultural and economic ways, as part of Subei. Nanjing, Jiangsu's capital, is sometimes considered neither Subei nor Sunan.

The Subei subethnic group is difficult to specify, partly because northern Jiangsu areas are different from each other, and mostly because people from these places are deemed Subei only when they reside in Jiangnan. Ethnic stereotypes are cultural constructions, determinable only as people determine them. The city of Yangzhou is as famed for cuisine and culture as most Jiangnan places (and such traits are central to the Jiangnan self-conception), but Yangzhou is usually considered Subei. Further north, the rail center of Xuzhou has sent few immigrants to Shanghai, and other areas of northern Jiangsu are distinctive, so that the notion "Subei" does not arise there. The label is applied in Shanghai, not in the areas from which these people come.

Language determines these subethnicities, according to some in Jiangnan. Nanjing and cities further north, such as Yangzhou and Yancheng, speak dialects of Mandarin. So does Zhenjiang, on the southern bank of the river, despite that city's very close ties with quintessential Jiangnan places such as Changzhou, Wuxi, Suzhou, and Kunshan, near Shanghai. In Nantong, north of the Yangzi but not far from the metropolis by boat, the tongue is a strong dialect of the Shanghainese language.[256] Jokers use a pun to complain they cannot understand it; the name Nantong is homophonous with the Chinese words for "hard to communicate."[257] Other Wu dialects are spoken in Zhejiang, including inland Jinhua and southern Wenzhou, which were outside the early compact version of the Shanghai Economic Zone, as well as along the Hangzhou–Ningbo corridor that is discussed here as fully part of the Shanghai delta. The most frequent subethnic tension is between people from economically poor but politically powerful northern Jiangsu groups and economically richer Jiangnan groups.

Discrimination against Subei people in Jiangnan is old, and Shanghai people confess it volubly. It predates the rise of Shanghai, although in modern times it has been most obvious in that city.[258] Northern Jiangsu has been perennially impoverished for centuries because of recurrent floods and droughts. Sporadic natural disasters have kept Subei poor (as violent typhoons and volcanoes do in much of the Philippines, or cyclones and inundations on the geological flood plain where Bangladesh is located). Huaibei, an overlapping or adjacent area to the west, is similar.[259] People from Subei have long served as "defining others" for residents of richer Chinese areas.[260]

Subei denizens of Shanghai are in many cases evident on the streets. Some are garbage pickers, equipped with steel tongs about the length of an arm to salvage metals and other useful items from trash. Many of these are permanent workers, employed by neighborhood committees. Subei people coming to Shanghai have taken jobs as hairdressers, cooks, bath attendants, and cart pullers.[261] During reforms, many more have come as construction workers, in which jobs they are joined by migrants from many inland provinces. Jiangnan people often speak with remarkable candor about their willingness to see their Subei compatriots remain in such jobs.

Another Subei part of Shanghai's population, however, consists of high Party cadres who were recruited in northern Jiangsu anti-Japanese guerrilla bases by Gen. Chen Yi's Third Field Army, which liberated Shanghai in 1949. Many of these cadres later took high positions in the municipal government. A Yangzhou native, Mayor Jiang Zemin, certainly did not play down his Subei connections. On the contrary, within two weeks of assuming the mayoralty, he promoted a cleanliness campaign—and for a brief time he joined a contingent of garbage collectors.[262] This was comely in a mayor, but the style was not at all Jiangnan.

A disadvantage of Subei people, in this context, is the continuing poverty of the area whence they come, as compared with other parts of China where most Shanghai people maintain connections. Relative to Subei, the high levels of education, industrialization, and wealth in Jiangnan remain a stark contrast. A census of Jiangsu, for example, provided figures from which it can be calculated that in the four large Sunan cities of Wuxi, Nanjing, Changzhou, and Suzhou, the ratio of university graduates to secondary-school graduates was 2.2 percent—but in the four large Subei cities of Xuzhou, Lianyungang, Huaiyin, and Yancheng, that ratio was only 0.8 percent. Economic contrasts between these two sets of cities were just as sharp. The portion of working people engaged in agriculture in the four Sunan places (including their extensive suburban counties) averaged 30 percent, but in the Subei places, this nonindustrial and nonservice part of the working population in 1987 still averaged 75 percent.[263] The four Sunan cities and their subordinate counties that year had a per-capita income 2.5 times that in the four Subei cities. The Sunan cities' fiscal contributions to central coffers were 8.1 times that of the Subei cities on a per-capita basis (and 5.2 times on an absolute basis). Although the Sunan cities' educational expenditures were only 35 percent greater per capita (and in absolute terms were 16 percent less, because the southern part of the province subsidizes budgets in the north), the two areas remained sharply and obviously different.[264] Shanghai and Jiangsu top politicians, who hailed largely from Subei, knew very well about such contrasts. Their will to aid Jiangnan, and Shanghai, was surely lessened by that knowledge, although they had scant interest in advertising this.

The geographical distribution within Shanghai of families from other East China places is fairly even among the ten districts, except that natives of counties close to the city are somewhat concentrated in parts of Nanshi district. In Changning, Huangpu, Jing'an, Luwan, and Xuhui, a great majority of families are Jiangnan.[265] In streets and smaller neighborhoods, concentrations of families from particular regions are often higher. Much of southern Nanshi (with an adjacent part of Luwan) as well as sections of Yangpu district and the Xingguo Housing Project provide many homes for Subei people.[266] A residents' committee area in the circular "old city" was entirely Subei, although most families surrounding that area were not.

The concentration of subethnic groups in certain services and light industries has also been traditional. Yangzhou people are still often barbers and managers of bathhouses. Nantong immigrants once had a near monopoly on street sales of hot water for tea. "Shanghai" textiles are actually produced all over the Jiangnan region, and the managers come disproportionately from Hangzhou, Suzhou, and Wuxi. Menial tasks in Shanghai's transport, construction, and other industries have long been held by Subei people, although the heads and staff of many construction companies come from Nantong and especially its nearby city of Qidong.

Ningbo, along with areas farther south along the coast all the way down to Guangdong, provides many of Shanghai's most entrepreneurial families. According to one informal estimate, Ningbo people constitute about 30 percent of Shanghai's population—somewhat more than the portion identified with Subei.[267] Immigration to Shanghai from Ningbo and nearby areas began extensively during the Ming, and Ningbo people were already very prominent in Shanghai by the beginning of the Qing. Before Liberation, people from seven counties between Ningbo and Shaoxing along the north Zhejiang coast ran the Siming Public Office (Siming Gongsuo), which the French sometimes called the "Ningbo Temple." This was like other common-place associations (*tongxiang hui*), bringing together residents in Shanghai from particular areas elsewhere. In pre-1949 Shanghai, especially in parts of the "French Concession," Ningbo people dominated much business.[268] Some led important secret societies. They were the most obvious single provincial group, but many other Shanghai people also have strong family ties with specific parts of Jiangsu, Guangdong, and inland provinces.

Jiangnan people's continuing discrimination against outsiders has been heightened by immigration during the reforms, and it was articulated in a 1988 article by two writers from Shanghai's Party School.

> When the outside laborers inhabit a region, it is very likely to be a dirty place. They lack a concept of public morality. . . . There are some who come to

Shanghai with the thought of getting rich by foul means. . . . Behavior that harms prevailing social customs occurs time and time again. . . . The city residents are dissatisfied, because [transients] disturb normal life and livelihood.[269]

Subethnic discrimination in Shanghai may continue to increase because the economic boom has brought migrants. "More and more outside people come to Shanghai to seek jobs. . . . This has two results: On one hand, Shanghai unemployment becomes worse. On the other, some enterprises employ too many outside workers."[270] Unionized employees see themselves without work to do, because state-sector firms cannot obtain inputs, so they ask why Shanghai needs immigrants. Humans create communities from their situations, and subethnic differences could become more important in the future of Chinese politics if rival leaderships emerge to vie for popular support on any basis they can muster.

Conclusion

What was the effect of individual-normative factors on China's reforms? Since this postrevolutionary change is a new syndrome in Chinese politics, and since actors can always select old cultural options in any particular situation, causation is hard to prove from data about ideal meanings. But it is possible to observe—after research, rather than before it—that some activities in pursuit of new truths and lifestyles became far more widespread and controversial than others. These reforms were generally organized in terms of social groups.

The renaissance of all kinds of religions affected large numbers of people even in the most blasé part of China, the Shanghai delta. A thread running through all the legitimative institutions, from newspapers to churches to art studios to orchestras to writers' associations, was a clear decline of state financial support. This was accompanied by great ambiguity among local leaders, in all these fields, about their dependence on the state. The government no longer paid them, so what they legitimated in practice tended to be structures different from the government.

The appointment of important leaders in cultural fields (except some performers) was still formally regulated by the state's *nomenklatura* control system. But high-state leaders were more divided than they had been in earlier days about the criteria to be used for such appointments. Religious prelates were more effective if the unwashed faithful believed they were not atheists. Singers got bigger audiences by aping Hong Kong and American models. For some groups, there was nothing much the government could do after the Cultural Revolution to persuade them that high officials would benefit them.

Rational-actionists would argue that external material constraints on popular and elite legitimating activities sufficiently explain their changes. No doubt those factors were important. But the available information also suggests that personal or family identification was crucial as well: identity as believers in one or another religion, as journalists who should generally report the truth, as artists or performers who show people experiences they had not known before, as scientists explaining the natural world in its own terms rather than in terms of anybody powerful, or as ideologists trying to find a more comfortable relation between the state and other groups in China. It is possible to assert, but impossible to prove, that those identities all came ultimately from unintended external facts. It is much easier to show that, for the actors who exercised them, they represented intended values.

No such assertion, one way or the other, is convincing if it is abstracted from a circumspect look at evidence about what these people did. Method follows research, not just the other way around. Failed experiments to find situational causes and blind alleys in search of cultural causes are as important as the searches that succeed. Before looking at the foreign and elite interests of many late-reform leaders of cultural groups, it would not be possible to see their roles in reform. Only the contrast of relative successes and relative failures in lines of specific research can give a circumspect view. Meanings as well as facts, and individuals as well as nations, must be in that view—and perhaps dimensions other than these two. Presuming that human consciousness has evolved with the species, not even a full list of the dimensions to search can be surely given. Any philosophy of method is merely metascience. Science is knowledge, including the tools that have *already* found it.

Notes

1. *Alexis de Tocqueville on Democracy, Revolution, and Society,* John Stone and Stephen Mennell, eds. (Chicago: University of Chicago Press, 1980), p. 87.

2. The classic source on this is Karl Polanyi, *The Great Transformation: The Social and Economic Origins of our Time* (New York: Rinehart, 1944).

3. *Shanghai shimin banshi zhinan* (Citizen's Practical Guide to Shanghai), Shanghai Municipal Government Office, ed. (Shanghai: Shanghai Renmin Chuban She, 1989), p. 12, gives a table of nonresidential monthly rents charged per square meter (as measured on a "constructed area" basis), ranging from 7 yuan for downtown space in good buildings to 1.5 yuan for fourth-rate space. Page 13 has a table for residential space, whose price per square meter ranged from 2 yuan down to 0.4 yuan—very cheap.

4. Some of these places were photographed for Tess Johnston and Deke Erh, *A Last Look: Western Architecture in Old Shanghai* (Hong Kong: Old China Hand Press, 1993).

5. *Shanghai jingji, neibu ben: 1949–1982* (Shanghai Economy, Internal [classified] Volume: 1949–1982), Shanghai Academy of Social Sciences, ed. (Shanghai: Shanghai Shehui Kexue Yuan Chuban She, 1984), p. 791.

6. There are some exceptions, often linking the economic and police aspects of the question. Michael Dutton of Adelaide, Australia, is contributing important new work on incentives to households in China; see his "Policing the Chinese Household: A Comparison of Modern and Ancient Forms," *Economy and Society* 17:2 (May 1988), pp. 195–224, and his forthcoming translation of Zhang Qingwu's book *Basic Facts on the Household Registration System,* Also, important research about housing policy in Shanghai is currently

being undertaken by Guilhem Fabre of Paris; on the broader scene, see his "Le réveil de Shanghaï: Stratégies économiques 1949–2000" (The Reawakening of Shanghai: Economic Strategies, 1949–2000), *Le Courrier des pays de l'est* 325 (January 1988), pp. 3–40.

7. *Shanghai jingji,* p. 791. The 21 percent is calculated from this source and from averaging populations of the city, 1949–82, offered in *Zhongguo renkou: Shanghai fence* (China's Population: Shanghai Volume), Hu Huanyong et al., eds. (Beijing: Zhongguo Caizheng Jingji Chuban She, 1987), p. 77.

8. *Shanghai shehui xiankuang he qushi, 1980–1983* (Situations and Trends in Shanghai Society, 1980–1983), Zheng Gongliang et al., eds. (Shanghai: Huadong Shifan Daxue Chuban She, 1988), p. 21.

9. *Shanghai jingji 1987* (Shanghai's Economy 1987), Xu Zhihe, Ling Yan, Gu Renzhang et al., eds. (Shanghai Academy of Social Sciences) (Shanghai: Shanghai Renmin Chuban She, 1987), p. 12.

10. There was similar silence in the press about the 1950s movements to subdivide houses and apartments. See Lynn White, *Policies of Chaos* (Princeton: Princeton University Press, 1989), pp. 99–100, 132, and 292.

11. *Tongyi gongzuo shouce* (Handbook of Unification Work), Office of Unification Studies and Voice of Jinling Broadcasting Station, eds. (Nanjing: Nanjing Daxue Chuban She, 1986), pp. 124–26.

12. Some housing was returned in full, albeit in dilapidated condition. The author knows families in Shanghai that had been forced out of practically all their residential space, but then received it again in the 1980s.

13. *Shanghai shehui xiankuang,* p. 125.

14. *Shijie xin jishu geming yu Shanghai de duice* (The Global Revolution in New Technology and Shanghai's Policies in Response), Shanghai Economic Research Center and Shanghai Science and Technology Committee, eds. (Shanghai: Shanghai Shehui Kexue Yuan Chuban She, 1986), p. 362. Although engagements (*dinghun*) are not officially registered in China, these people had apparently asked for marriage certificates and were legally entitled to them.

15. Zhe Xiaoye, *Chengshi zai zhuanzhe dianshang* (Cities at a Turning Point) (Beijing: Zhongguo Funü Chuban She, 1989), pp. 54–59, and many other published Shanghai sources.

16. The one-child and late-marriage policies in Shanghai were largely advertised in terms of the severe residential space crunch (which had been caused in turn by the unadvertised official distaste for investment in housing). Under the official criteria, a family not classified as short of housing would not become so, at least for twelve years after the birth of a single child (living in the parents' bedroom). Also, with one child there would be no question of a brother and sister over age eighteen having to share a room. With delayed marriage, the actuarial chances of having three-generation families might slightly decrease (although the need for child care by grandparents, especially when late-wed mothers had begun careers of their own, created a countervailing effect that was reinforced by traditional Chinese family ideals). The official criteria were framed in terms of sleeping accommodations, but sleeping rooms were of course also ordinarily used for dining, conversation, listening to radio or television, homework, and all other family purposes (in many but not all cases, cooking too).

17. The "inconvenienced" families (*bu fangbian hu,* which might equally be translated by a bureaucrat as "inconvenient") apparently had a precise definition, which this particular source does not give. *Shanghai shehui xiankuang,* p. 58.

18. Specifically, 52 percent of all Shanghai households were *kunnan hu.* Ibid., p. 121.

19. Jing'an and Luwan were not surveyed, apparently, although lack of facilities there was probably more severe; see ibid., p. 121.

20. *FEER*, December 12, 1985, p. 28.

21. This article at another place reports 2 square meters of road per person, but that is apparently a rounding from 1.6. Ibid., p. 29.

22. The basis for these Shanghai percentages is the locally generated national income. There is some difference between national income (*guomin shouru*) and GNP (*guomin shengchan zhi*), because the latter includes depreciation; but this difference does not obviate the obvious pattern of the figures, which have been rounded to standard percentages in the text in any case. The original figures were: 1979, 0.78 percent; 1980, 1.03 percent; 1981, 1.6 percent; and 1982, 1.95 percent. See *Shanghai shehui xiankuang*, p. 122.

23. Ezra Vogel, *One Step Ahead: Guangdong Under Reform* (Cambridge: Harvard University Press, 1989), chap. 6.

24. This "four times" approximates a calculation that indicated a 402 percent increase—but this estimate involves several complexities. An unknown portion of the rise may come from additional "urban" housing as more towns were officially designated "cities," though this factor could not account for all of the difference between 35 and 402. Residential "constructed area" (*zhumian*) differs from residential "living space" (*zhumian*, but with an exactly homophonous *zhu* that means "live" rather than "construct"). The estimates here all refer to usable living space inside residential buildings, which is always about three-fifths of the constructed area of ground that the houses cover. Shanghai had 161 million square meters of such space in 1950, and 378 million square meters in 1985, implying that 217 million square meters had been built (a rise of 35 percent). China as a whole had 355 million square meters of space in 1950, and the yearbooks reported 6.7 square meters for each of the 213 urban people on average, implying 1,427 million square meters (a rise of 402 percent). See *SHTJNJ86*, pp. 52 and 412; Kang Chao, "Industrialization and Urban Housing in Communist China," *Journal of Asian Studies* 25:3 (May 1966), p. 382; *ZGTJNJ86*, p. 686; and *China: Urban Statistics, 1986*, State Statistical Bureau, PRC, compiler (Hong Kong: Longman, 1987), p. 207.

25. *FEER*, December 12, 1985, p. 30.

26. This is a brief and unsourced report in *Post,* June 17, 1996.

27. The calculation comparing this figure with *SHTJNJ86*, p. 412, indicates that 2 percent of the city's total residential floor space in 1967 was illegally occupied—or at least, this portion needed to be returned to previous occupants who were still alive two decades later. The families affected were, however, far more important to the city's social and economic structure than this low figure might suggest. The "old historical cases" mentioned in the next sentence were called *lishi lao an*.

28. *Shanghai shehui xiankuang*, p. 21.

29. Calculated from *Zhongguo chengshi tongji nianjian, 1988* (Statistical Yearbook of Chinese Cities, 1988), State Statistical Bureau, ed. (Beijing: Zhongguo Tongji Chuban She and Zhongguo Tongji Xinxi Zixun Fuwu Zhongxin, 1988), p. 304.

30. In Luwan District, there were 59,000 people per square kilometer. *SHTJNJ88*, p. 82.

31. *FEER*, December 12, 1985, p. 28.

32. Hong Kong, a rich city without much land but with enough capital for many high-rise residential and commercial buildings, probably has a world record in the sweepstakes for densities per unit of ground in an extensive place. Sham Shui Po, in Kowloon, achieved 165,000 residents per square kilometer of land in 1985, according to *Hong Kong 1986* (Hong Kong: Hong Kong Government Printing Department, 1986), p. 186; the economy there attracts even more in daytime hours. But on a per-unit-of-floor-space basis,

an area with less capital and fewer skyscrapers is required. Long-term official hindrances against building in Shanghai also exacerbate this per-person lack of space in which to live. Counting both residents and economic transients, the world's first and second most dense areas of that scale are almost surely corridors on either side of Nanjing and Huaihai roads, in Jing'an and Luwan districts, Shanghai.

33. These districts (*qu*) and the suburban counties (*xian*) are the main submunicipal administrative jurisdictions in the city, and together they cover its whole area. But in fact, parts of the counties are built up and now very industrial, and relatively small parts of the urban districts are green. The data that follow, rounded to the nearest hundred, are from *Zhongguo chengshi tongji nianjian, 1988*, pp. 41–47.

34. These 1982 figures are from *Zhongguo shehui zhuyi chengshi jingji xue* (Chinese Socialist Urban Economics), Zhu Linxing, ed. (Shanghai: Shanghai Shehui Kexue Chuban She, 1986), pp. 162–64.

35. *FBIS*, December 7, 1987, p. 39, reporting radio of December 5.

36. *XMWB*, October 4, 1988.

37. Deborah Davis did interviews in Shanghai during separate years of the 1980s, reported in "Housing and Family Life in Shanghai," *China Update* 11:3 (Fall 1991), p. 9.

38. *JJRB*, January 20, 1988.

39. Friedrich Engels, *The Housing Question* (New York: International Publishers, 1935), p. 24, quoted in Danielle S. Pensley, "The Socialist City?" [about Neubaugebeit Berlin-Hellersdorf] (senior thesis, Woodrow Wilson School, Princeton University, 1993), p. 11.

40. The history of stages in which the Real Estate Management Bureau acquired its vast holdings was more gradual than many other important events in Mao's China—although the campaigns of 1956–57 were important. For a bit more, see Lynn White, *Careers in Shanghai* (Berkeley: University of California Press, 1979).

41. A gap, however, was always left in any quadrangle design. After a large crane raised the concrete panels to create the inner walls of the courtyard, a space had to be left in the design so that the crane could exit.

42. Most of these workers were women, and many lived in very old dormitories. *WHB*, August 10, 1980.

43. *Shanghai shehui xiankuang*, p. 125.

44. Based on an interview in Hong Kong with an economist who had some knowledge of these matters in China.

45. Zhang Jian deserves credit here for his useful information on this topic.

46. *Shanghai shimin*, p. 16, has a table showing these conversions.

47. *Shanghai shehui tongji ziliao, 1980–1983* (Statistical Materials on Shanghai Society, 1980–1983), Group on the Shanghai Social Situation and Trends, ed. (Shanghai: Huadong Shifan Daxue Chuban She, 1988), p. 35.

48. Interview with a professor of economics at Jiaotong University, who had bought a house in Shanghai and was pleased not only with the advantages of private ownership in economic theory, but also with the paper profit he had made. But few made such decisions when he did, in the 1980s—and in the 1990s, the government became even more interested in garnering increases in land values, so that urban real estate property rights were sometimes precarious.

49. This agency was the Fangdi Chan Guanli Ju. *Shanghai jingji 1987*, p. 790.

50. Harry Harding, *China's Second Revolution* (Washington, DC: Brookings, 1987), p. 124.

51. *RMRB*, August 15, 1988.

52. *CD*, March 9, 1988.

53. Experimental psychologists have studied this problem in many ways, and they have apparently found that measurable increments to pleasure change a person's sense of

well-being less (by about half) than measurably equal increments of pain. By the same token, when people have something good, it is about twice as painful to have some of it removed than it is pleasurable to have an equal amount added. This rough 2:1 ratio is surprisingly robust over a very wide variety of experimental situations. It seems to apply in real life too; and it might be of some use in explaining the institutional rigidities that hamper reforms in countries emerging from socialist eras. The author owes thanks to the experimental psychologist Daniel Kahneman, who nonetheless bears no responsibility for this interpretive rendition.

54. *CD*, November 23, 1988.

55. *CD*, January 31, 1989.

56. Hong Kong per-square-meter costs were ten times as much for residential space. Of course, there was a big difference in wages and some difference in land scarcity; but the main contrast was the popular thinking that four decades of nominal rents had engendered. *XMWB*, February 17, 1989.

57. Based on several interviews of Shanghai people, in that city and in Hong Kong.

58. *JJRB*, January 25, 1988.

59. These *youxian chanquan* rights and other provisions are mentioned in *Zhongguo jingji tizhi gaige* (Chinese Economic System Reform), 1987, p. 21.

60. Benedict Stavis, *China's Political Reforms: An Interim Report* (New York: Praeger, 1988), p. 79.

61. This percentage applied in 1981. Shanghai Duiwai Kaifang de "Kaifang Du" Yanjiu Keti Zu (Research Group on Shanghai's "Degree of Openness" to the Outside), *Shanghai duiwai kaifang de "kaifang du" yanjiu* (Study of the Degree of Shanghai's Openness to the Outside) (Shanghai: Shanghai Shehui Kexue Yuan, 1988), part 2, chap. 3, p. 1.

62. The main exception to this rule was foreigners, i.e., their companies, which pay rents at literally hundreds of times the rates for resident PRC citizens. Interviewees reported plans to raise Shanghai rents about ten times for local people—and to raise their wages so they could pay. The local politics of this was much chancier, however, than the economics, so it occurred haltingly, by slow institutional replacements more than by quick or sweeping economic policies.

63. *Eastern Express,* April 6, 1994.

64. Piper Rae Gaubatz, "Urban Transformation in Post-Mao China," in *Urban Spaces in Contemporary China,* Deborah S. Davis et al., eds. (New York: Cambridge University Press, 1995), pp. 28–60.

65. "*Gan da lei, bu xia yu.*" *JJRB*, January 20, 1988.

66. Zhe Xiaoye, *Chengshi zai zhuanzhe dianshang,* pp. 61–63.

67. If one assumes, on the basis of these figures in ibid., that the average urban rent was 5 yuan per month and that the number of residents paying it was 95 million, then the state's total rent income would be 5.7 billion yuan a year. This is larger than the new construction and maintenance expenditure. (Many of the households contained two or more employees.) See *JJRB*, January 20, 1988.

68. *SF,* July 2, 1990.

69. "*Fanggai yao chu tai, lingdao yao shang tai.*" The soldiers were called "*lao hong jun.*" *RMRB,* August 15, 1988.

70. Zhe Xiaoye, *Chengshi zai zhuanzhe dianshang,* pp. 54–59.

71. Reginald Yin-wang Kwok, "Metropolitan Development in China: A Struggle Between Contradictions," *Habitat International* 12:4 (1988), p. 204.

72. Nancy N. Chen, "Urban Spaces and Experiences of Qigong," in Deborah S. Davis et al., eds., *Urban Spaces,* pp. 349–50.

73. For more, see Zhe Xiaoye, *Chengshi zai zhuanzhe dianshang,* pp. 43–45, and many other sources.

74. *Shanghai jingji 1987,* p. 798.

75. An attempt to compute statistics for later years on the table might be made, but the figures are hard to find or to compare. The 1993 Shanghai statistical yearbook, for example, on p. 408 conspicuously omits the per-person residential space in urban areas—although the parallel table on p. 414 offers such information for farmers living out in the suburbs where there is more room. Shanghai infrastructural resources rose in the early 1990s, but less for personal-use resources such as these than for projects with a quicker return, and much less for such items on a per-capita basis because of new migrants in the population.

76. Calculated from *SHTJNJ88,* p. 77 on population, p. 381 on housing, p. 389 on water pipes, and p. 391 on buses.

77. Ibid. shows that each day the average number was 686 per 10,000 people in 1978, but by 1986 it had risen to 1,419.

78. *Shanghai jingji 1987,* p. 783.

79. This is based on interviews and observations in Shanghai.

80. *Shanghai qiye* (Shanghai Enterprise), August 1985, p. 2.

81. *Shanghai shehui xiankuang,* p. 22.

82. The *meiri keliu liang* rose to eleven million people-trips daily in 1983; and its rate of growth slightly accelerated from 10 percent annually in those six years to 11 percent in 1984. For more on the *shengche nan,* see *Shanghai shehui xiankuang,* p. 58.

83. Ibid., pp. 22 and 58.

84. Ibid., p. 22.

85. Zheng Zu'an, "The Historical Development of Pudong," in Zhang Zhongli et al., *SASS Papers* (Shanghai: Shanghai Academy of Social Sciences, 1986), p. 540.

86. *XMWB,* January 12, 1989.

87. This author's memories of the Number 26 trolley bus are strong—and nostalgically positive, except for thoughts about the somewhat easier job of boarding a bus in Beijing in the same era.

88. Parallels in Soviet society were recorded by the Russian humorist Ivan Ivanov.

89. *SJJJDB,* October 21, 1985.

90. This is a contrast also with Vienna, whose Ringstrasse replaced old imperial moats and walls and is beautifully described in Carl E. Schorske, *Fin-de-Siècle Vienna: Politics and Culture* (New York: Vintage, 1981).

91. From 1949 to 1984, Shanghai's industrial output increased 30 times, but the length of the city's roads and transport space rose only 1.4 and 1.8 times respectively. Yao Shihuang, *Jin sanjiao de tansuo* (Search for the Golden Delta) (Chongqing: Chongqing Chuban She, 1988), pp. 105–32.

92. These are 1983 figures. *Zhongguo shehui zhuyi,* p. 209.

93. *SHJJ,* June 1988, p. 6.

94. *FEER,* December 12, 1985, p. 28.

95. Zhe Xiaoye, *Chengshi zai zhuanzhe dianshang,* pp. 76–91; emphasis added.

96. *WHB,* December 11, 1979.

97. *XMWB,* January 24, 1989.

98. The groundwater level in Shanghai, however, is shallow. It is unclear how these plans squared with others in the Yangzi watershed for flood prevention. *CD,* September 19, 1988.

99. Charles F. James in *The China Traveller,* December 1987, p. 3.

100. *SF,* May 29, 1989.

101. Because of massive flooding, 1991 saw an increase in such funding—large amounts coming from Hong Kong and Taiwan charities. Also, *ZGTJNJ93*, p. 808.

102. The comparable portions in China as a whole were less. Those over 60 were only 7 or 8 percent (as compared with 14 percent in Shanghai); the difference mainly arises because old people in Shanghai long ago established legal residency, which youths could less readily obtain. Those over 80 in China as a whole were only one-half of 1 percent (but 2 percent in Shanghai). To obtain the all-China figures, partial data were summed from *Zhongguo renkou tongji nianjian, 1988* (China Population Statistics Yearbook, 1988), State Statistical Bureau, comp. (Beijing: Zhongguo Zhanwang Chuban She, 1988), pp. 479–80; and for the Shanghai figures, *Shehui xue yanjiu* (Sociological Research), March 1987, p. 75.

103. *Shehui xue yanjiu* (Sociological Research), April 1986, p. 86.

104. By 1956, the comparable figure was already down to 0.71, according to one report. *Shanghai jingji 1987,* p. 85.

105. *SHTJNJ93,* p. 91, unfortunately does not provide pre-1978 data. The quickest increases in this ratio came in 1989 and especially 1979.

106. There was, also, a minimum pension of 27 yuan monthly. *Shanghai jingji 1987,* p. 974.

107. *CD,* April 29, 1989.

108. The area of the city where this survey was conducted, though relatively poor, was also old and probably rather stable in its population makeup. See *Shehui xue yanjiu* (Sociological Research), April 1986, p. 87, which gives a table—taken to tenths of percents even for the half-century-old estimates from memory!—that provides the basis for the next few sentences of the text above.

109. *Shehui xue yanjiu* (Sociological Research), April 1986, p. 87, indicates that none of the surveyed old people could recall missing generations in any local family half a century earlier. This phenomenon clearly results from PRC job assignment policies.

110. *Shehui xue yanjiu* (Sociological Research), March 1987, p. 76.

111. Ibid. This *lianhe jiating* sounded like a reform-approved kind of "joint enterprise." *Shehui xue yanjiu* (Sociological Research), April 1986, p. 86, reports that another 1985 survey of Shanghai people over 60 showed that 7 percent in that group lived in "joint families."

112. *Shehui xue yanjiu* (Sociological Research), March 1987, p. 76.

113. *Shanghai zhigong tiaojian ziliao shouce* (Handbook on the Conditions of Shanghai Employees), Shanghai Statistics Bureau, ed. (Shanghai: Shanghai Tongji Chuban She, 1985), pp. 8–10.

114. More precisely, the figure was 90.33 yuan, with a standard deviation of 35.14 yuan. *Shehui xue yanjiu* (Sociological Research), March 1987, p. 76.

115. Peter Nan-shong Lee, "Reforming the Social Security System in China," in *Public Policy in China,* Stewart Nagel and Miriam Mills, eds. (Westport: Greenwood Press, 1993), p. 34.

116. *Shehui xue yanjiu* (Sociological Research), April 1986, pp. 86 and 95.

117. The number in absolute terms was 1,388,000 *tuixiu* and *lixiu* retirees.

118. *Shehui xue yanjiu* (Sociological Research), April 1986, p. 90.

119. Ibid., p. 91.

120. *FBIS,* December 21, 1987, p. 42, reporting radio of December 18.

121. On these tests of *shehui baoxian* and *yanglao jin,* see *Shanghai jingji 1987,* p. 100.

122. An additional 0.45 million had the medical benefits that went with normal labor insurance, because of their work in public service units, especially neighborhood committees. These public service (or "cause") units are *shiye danwei.* Also, 0.36 million members

of "small collectives" received some but not all the benefits of normal labor insurance. *Shanghai jingji 1987*, p. 975. All percentages are calculated from raw figures in the source.

123. The total costs of Shanghai's labor insurance that year was 1.8 billion yuan, so it can be computed that the city's total wage bill was about 4.14 billion yuan. The retirement fund is called the *tuixiu fei*. *Shanghai jingji 1987*, p. 975.

124. *Shanghai shehui tongji*, p. 108, gives numbers of recipients and dollar costs for "fixed term relief" (*dingqi jiuji*), "temporary relief" (*linshi jiuji*), and "simplified retirement" (*jingjian tuizhi*). The numbers of people in the first and third of these categories, however, were small, and the money spent in the middle category was small on a per-capita basis.

125. *CD*, May 21, 1991.

126. In the thirty-five years after 1949, while Shanghai's output value rose 30 times, the city's capacity to process waste water only increased 3.2 times. Yao Shihuang, *Jin sanjiao*, pp. 105–32.

127. This information comes from the author's friend, Prof. Li Cheng. The evident discrimination against women in the *laobao/gongfei* difference inherited from revolutionary times is a subject that needs more study. Socialist practice in urban housing allocation almost surely strengthened patriarchalism within families.

128. The other side of this coin is that individualist policies (e.g., in medical research) found the techniques of prevention that Mao's communitarian state applied with such great success against diseases that produce antibodies. Individualist medical policies remain important along with communitarian ones in dealing with the chronic diseases that now cause most deaths in developed countries and in China. The purely analytic nature of this norm-situation divide is brought out clearly in the medical case: Everybody wants to avoid becoming sick—and, when sick, wants to become well. There is no sensible way to make a general choice between these two types of medical policy, because each is useful in preventing or curing specific diseases. Also, there are some diseases (e.g., the common cold) against which none of these approaches makes much progress.

129. Sheila Hillier, "Health and Medicine in the 1980s," in *Reforming the Revolution: China in Transition*, Robert Benewick and Paul Wingrove, eds. (Basingstoke: Macmillan, 1988), p. 150.

130. Ibid., p. 152.

131. Jiang Zemin et al., *Shanghai dangzheng jigou yange* (The Transformation of Shanghai's Party and Administration) (Shanghai: Shanghai Renmin Chuban She, 1988), p. 143.

132. Precise 1981–83 Shanghai frequencies of these diseases are offered in *Shanghai shehui xiankuang*, p. 65.

133. Only 27 percent of people over 60 in the 1985 Shanghai survey were widowed. Of these, just one-twentieth were men; only 1 percent of the whole sample had never married. *Shehui xue yanjiu* (Sociological Research), April 1986, p. 86, also mentions that about 1 percent of the whole sample were divorced.

134. Marlowe Hood in *Post*, March 3, 1988. The same source on March 5 quoted a Public Health Ministry spokesman as having declared the newspaper's earlier estimate as being "impossible," while also declining to offer an alternative figure.

135. *FBIS*, March 7, 1988, p. 76, reporting radio of March 4.

136. *ZGQNB*, July 1, 1988.

137. Liver cancer is often a long-term aftereffect of hepatitis. Therefore an increased incidence of liver cancer, because of the 1988 disaster, is a danger that Shanghai surely faces as the middle-aged group which suffered most of the hepatitis cases becomes older. The author's friend Prof. Anthony Hedley, who heads Hong Kong University's Department of Community Medicine, inspired some of these interpretations, although he bears no responsibility for the rendition of them here.

138. The numerator series on tobacco is found in *Zhongguo qinggong ye nianjian 1992* (China Light Industry Yearbook, 1992), Light Industry Research Center, ed. (Beijing: Zhongguo Qinggong Ye Nianjian Chuban She, 1992), p. 254, and later editions. The denominator, fiscal revenue, is easy to find in any recent *ZGTJNJ.* On related topics, see also Sheila Hillier, "Health and Medicine," p. 158.

139. This is a mid-1980s estimate, from an interview, that apparently includes only users of machine-made cigarettes. By the 1990s, cigarette use had increased.

140. Yu Jing Jie et al., "A Comparison of Smoking Patterns in the People's Republic of China and the United States: An Impending Health Catastrophe for the Middle Kingdom," *Journal of the American Medical Association* 264: 12 (1990), p. 1576.

141. You Long Gong et al., "Cigarette Smoking in China," *Journal of the American Medical Association* 274:15 (October 18, 1995), pp. 1232–34.

142. *SF,* June 25, 1990.

143. See Robert Blendon, "Can China's Health Care be Transplanted Without China's Economic Policies? [Answer: No.]," *New England Journal of Medicine* 300 (1984), pp. 1453–58.

144. Quoted in Sheila Hillier, "Health and Medicine," p. 153.

145. *Chengshi shengtai jingji lilun yu shixian* (The Theory and Practice of Urban Environmental Economics), Chen Yuqun, ed. (Shanghai: Shanghai Shehui Kexue Chuban She, 1988), pp. 43–44.

146. The author is indebted to his father for this idea.

147. London Kirkendall, a student of the author, is writing about the politics of ecological management in China.

148. *RMRBHWB,* August 2, 1990.

149. A friend reported this, on the basis of a book published by Tian Fan and Zhang Dongliang that the author has not seen.

150. Yao Shihuang, *Jin sanjiao,* pp. 35–68.

151. *SF,* October 2, 1989; also June 5, 1989, not a propitious day.

152. See *FBIS,* December 29, 1987, p. 39, reporting radio of the same day.

153. *Zhongguo shehui zhuyi,* p. 108.

154. But Ningbo had only 0.3 square meters per person, even less than Shanghai's 0.5 square meters. See ibid., p. 209.

155. *Shanghai jingji 1987,* p. 12.

156. *Shanghai shehui xiankuang,* p. 23, refers to "conflicts" (*chongtu*) without further specification.

157. Zhe Xiaoye, *Chengshi zai zhuanzhe dianshang,* pp. 98–102.

158. Smog might be taken as an apt symbol for the haziness of norms in China's quick development during these years. Increased nonlocal air pollution was a noticeable aspect of reforms not just in the Shanghai delta, but also in other parts of China, including Hong Kong and Shenzhen. Such conditions in other countries have not, however, been permanent. London "pea-soup fog" and Los Angeles's smog are now under considerable control, because public resources have been spent to reduce them. A later revival of Chinese state capacity to enforce pollution laws can eventually clean the air there, too.

159. Yan Tingchang, Cai Beihua, Xu Zhihe et al., *Shanghai lüyou ye de jintian he mingtian* (Shanghai Tourism Today and Tomorrow) (Shanghai: Shanghai Shehui Kexue Yuan Chuban She, 1987), p. 2.

160. *Shanghai shehui xiankuang,* p. 60.

161. *Heichou.* Shanghai's 1988 drinking water was declared to be only at the "second-level standard of the state"—though further data were not offered to allow much interpretation of this. *XMWB,* February 13, 1989. For much more, see Vaclav Smil, *The Bad Earth: Environmental Degradation in China* (Armonk, NY: M.E. Sharpe, 1984), pp. 102–4.

162. Yao Shihuang, *Jin sanjiao,* pp. 10–12.

163. Based on discussions in Shanghai during 1994. "Suzhou Creek" is more formally named Wusong Jiang.

164. *Shanghai shehui xiankuang,* p. 60.

165. Keith R. Schoppa, *Xiang Lake: Nine Centuries of Chinese Life* (New Haven: Yale University Press, 1989), p. 237.

166. Erica Strecker, "The One-Child Campaign in Rural China: Limits on its Implementation and Success" (Thesis for the Program in East Asian Studies, Georgetown University, 1994), p. 1, based on Peng Xizhe in *China Report* 26:4 (December 1990), pp. 385–405, and Nicholas Kristof, *New York Times,* April 25, 1993.

167. *Shanghai jingji 1987,* p. 14.

168. *Shanghai shimin,* p. 57.

169. The de facto main condition for peasant couples to have an authorized second child was that they got along well with the very local power network. Formally, the additional criteria are worth describing because they exemplify the elaborations that are necessary so that the state can mobilize resources and save costs. Thus, in addition to the three standard criteria, peasants may also have a second child: (1) if the wife or husband is disabled (legally, or perhaps arguably); (2) if the couple lives with elderly parents who have no other child and need support; (3) if, among more than two sisters or brothers, any one has no possibility to be fertile and each of the others has no more than one child; (4) if the family has had its income from fishing for more than five years [this was certainly not presented as a state concession to Catholic religious belief, but it applies to many Catholic families in Shanghai's Qingpu and Chuansha suburbs and may lessen resentment among them about the PRC's strongly pro-abortion policies]; (5) if either spouse is an oceangoing sailor; (6) if either has been a miner in the pit for five years; (7) if either has overseas Chinese status; (8) if either belongs to a national minority (some reports suggest these last two criteria informally apply in urban areas too); (9) if either's parent was designated a martyr for the PRC; (10) if either is a disabled soldier of the official grades A or B; (11) if either married a second time and they together had fewer than two children before the second marriage. See *Shanghai shimin,* pp. 56–57.

170. Other factors—some growth of jobs for women in Shanghai's consumer product industries, for example—also contributed to this result. But it would take the usual argument of this book, against the full effectiveness of policies, too far to claim that "birth planning" had no link to these data on births. For the statistics, see Peng Xizhe, *Demographic Transition in China: Fertility Trends Since the 1950s* (Oxford: Oxford University Press, 1991), Tables 1.1 and 2.1. The 1954 figures for Shanghai crude births, deaths, and natural increase per thousand are respectively 52.74, 7.12, and 45.62. By 1981, these had declined to 16.14, 6.44, and 9.70. Similar figures are offered in the source for the other provinces.

171. See Lynn White, "The Road to Urumchi: Approved Institutions in Search of Attainable Goals," *China Quarterly* 79 (October 1979), pp. 481–510; and White, "A Political Demography of Shanghai After 1949," *Proceedings of the Fifth Sino-American Conference on Mainland China* (Taipei: Guoji guanxi yanjiu suo, 1976), reprinted over several weeks in *Ming bao* (Bright News), Hong Kong, in November 1976.

172. Peng Xizhe, *Demographic Transition,* Table 2.2.

173. This summary does not cover some further aspects that must at least be mentioned. Although communitarian policy proved effective against viral and bacterial contagions, education campaigns based on communitarian principles are also of some use in preventing the "individual" diseases listed. They are also useful against diseases with mixed biological traits, such as dysentery, malaria, or AIDS. By the same token, individualist policies (e.g. in medical research) must be credited for finding the cures that the

socialist-communitarian state applied so successfully, and individualist medical policies remain important along with communitarian ones in dealing with the second list of diseases—which are now the causes of most deaths in developed countries and in China.

174. *ZGTJNJ93*, p. 82. But also see J. Dreze and A. Sen, *Hunger and Public Action* (Oxford: Clarendon Press, 1989), Table 11.2, based on work by Judith Banister.

175. Such comparisons even over fairly long periods are subject to many factors other than the intended effects of birth policy. *SHTJNJ93*, p. 67. Partly estimated from a chart at the bottom of this page. The next page shows the acceleration during the early 1980s in Shanghai's urban districts.

176. Ming Juzheng in *Zhonggong zhengquan sishi nian de huigu yu zhanwang* (Recollections and Prospects on the Forty Years of CCP Power), Wu An-chia, ed. (Taipei: Guoji guanxi yanjiu zhongxin, 1991), p. 358.

177. Empirical testing of the pattern presented here has been extensive, and the theory seems to apply well in a variety of cultural settings. Readers unfamiliar with demographic literature might imagine a graph, with rates on the vertical and time on the horizontal. Birth and death rates begin at the same high level at an early time, then death rates fall while birth rates do so more slowly, until the two lines flatten and converge again at a low level after the end of the demographic lag. The eventual population of a country is its traditional size plus the difference of the integrals that represent the areas under the two curves. The speed at which the birthrate falls thus has a strong effect on the eventual stable, replacement-rate size and on the year when it is reached. For China, this stabilization may occur at somewhat less than two billion people in approximately 2020. See World Bank, *World Development Report, 1993* (New York: Oxford University Press, 1993).

178. Path analysis, which is a kind of multiple regression, was used in this important study. It is difficult to assign a specific portion of the lowering of fertility to either family planning behavior or to general socioeconomic development, partly because these factors themselves are interrelated. But this massive number-crunching exercise, in which twenty-eight provinces were considered although the published article presented no geographically specific data below the national level, deftly corrects the usual public assumption that the only reason for China's low fertility is state policy. See Dudley L. Poston Jr. and Saochang Gu, "Socioeconomic Development, Family Planning, and Fertility in China," *Demography* 24:4 (November 1987), pp. 531–49.

179. One-quarter (24.7 percent) of Chinese (not just of urban or educated people, but of a large and carefully stratified sample for the PRC) in 1990 opined that the government was paying "not enough attention" to population control. Half (50.4 percent, although decimals mean nothing in attitude surveys) thought the amount of official attention to birth planning was "just right," and the other quarter in this high-response-rate survey was equally divided between the "too much attention" and "no interest" categories. Individuals, even in China, do have views about collective norms. See Andrew J. Nathan and Shi Tianjian, "Left and Right with Chinese Characteristics," *World Politics* 48:4 (July 1996).

180. *SHTJNJ93*, p. 408. Ibid., p. 414, shows that from 1980 to 1992 the average size of rural households in Shanghai's suburbs also decreased almost as sharply, from 4.28 to 3.43 people.

181. To what extent did rural industrialization, rather than birth planning policies, account for the low natality on the Shanghai delta (even while the number of households and marriages rose)? To answer such a question, it would be useful to compare two kinds of rural places, with relatively high and low industrialization rates but with similar amounts of local birth planning effort. How well or badly would industrialization correlate with low natality? How much of the result of China's birth planning can actually be attributed to occupational changes?

182. These data come from Tangjiacun, Fengxian county, a credibly typical place in suburban Shanghai. See Ishida Hiroshi, *Chōgoku nōson keizai no kiso kōzō: Shanhai kinkō nōson no kōgyōka to kindaika no ayumi* (Rural China in Transition: Experiences of Rural Shanghai toward Industrialization and Modernization) (Kyōto: Kōyō Shobō, 1991), pp. 94–95.

183. *Shanghai shehui xiankuang,* p. 113.

184. Ibid., p. 114.

185. The lowest marriage rate, 0.5 percent of the population, was in Tibet; and the other low province was Guizhou. Shanghai's divorce rate, involving 0.11 percent of the population, was eighth among the provinces, far below divorce-prone Xinjiang (0.83), which was followed in order by Qinghai (only 0.15), Heilongjiang, Jilin, Shanxi, Beijing, and Liaoning. The reasons for Xinjiang's high divorce rate deserve research, partly because the Han population there is largely Shanghainese. *Zhongguo shehui tongji ziliao, 1987* (Chinese Social Statistics, 1987), Social Statistics Office, State Statistical Bureau, ed. (Beijing: Zhongguo Tongji Chuban She, 1987), p. 28.

186. Fully 56 percent of fertile-age women in Shanghai had one-child certificates. By contrast, the much poorer provinces of Guangxi, Guizhou, and Jiangxi all reported this statistic at just 4 or 5 percent; such things were not taken so seriously there. See Peng Xizhe, *Demographic Transition,* Tables 2.6 and 2.7.

187. *Shanghai shimin,* p. 1.

188. Gilles Antier, "New Planning Trends in Shanghai" (Paris: Institut d'Aménagement d'Urbanisme de la Région d'Ile-de-France, 1993), p. 2.

189. *XMWB,* April 7, 1989.

190. Zhang Tanming in *Shanghai liudong renkou* (Shanghai's Floating Population), Shanghai Statistics Bureau, ed. (Shanghai: Zhongguo Tongji Chuban She, 1989), pp. 162–64.

191. Ibid.

192. In addition, about one-eighth of the peasant reprisals can be traced to each of these three factors: cadres' insistence on cremations rather than burials, disputes over housing sites, and "other" causes. The percentages add to 100 and are reported in Yang Dali, "Making Reform: The Great Leap Famine and Rural Change in China" (Ph.D. dissertation, Politics Department, Princeton University, December 1992), Table 7, quoting *Nongmin ribao* (Farmers' Daily), September 26, 1988.

193. See *FBIS,* October 7, 1988, p. 13, and Kate Xiao Zhou, *How the Farmers Changed China* (Boulder: Westview, 1996, and Ph.D. dissertation, Politics Department, Princeton University, 1994), chap. 8 of thesis, p. 14.

194. Ibid., all of chap. 8.

195. *Asian Wall Street Journal,* July 23, 1988.

196. Judith Banister calculates that life expectancy at birth was 65.1 years in 1979, but down to 64.6 in 1984. See J. Dreze and A. Sen, *Hunger and Public Action,* Table 11.2.

197. Ibid., Table 11.3. The infant female disadvantage in 1978 was only .09 percent; but by 1984, it was 3.33 percent.

198. The best study is centered on a Wuhan orphanage. See Kay Johnson, "Chinese Orphanages: Saving China's Abandoned Girls," *Australian Journal of Chinese Affairs* 30 (July 1993), pp. 61–87.

199. *New York Times,* January 6, 1996. By this time, the particular orphanage in Shanghai where Dr. Zhang had worked was presentable enough to host foreign journalists. The Chinese government at this time was receiving about U.S. $3,000 for each baby adopted abroad. Periodic reports of policies to neglect orphan infants nonetheless appeared from other parts of China, e.g. from Guangxi in Hong Kong media. This lack of care may be traceable to official-intellectual traditions or to very old biases against women, not just to revolutionary hubris.

200. *RMRBHWB*, November 12, 1987.

201. There was also a minimum pension of 27 yuan monthly. *Shanghai jingji 1987*, p. 975.

202. This is a field in which intellectuals' perceptions of China's best interests were probably not far wrong. But there is a major international controversy about such issues. A testy summary is Nick Eberstadt, "Population and Economic Growth," *Wilson Quarterly* 10:5 (1986), pp. 95–127.

203. Delia Davin, "The Early Childhood Education of the Only-Child Generation in Urban Areas of Mainland China," in *Education in Mainland China*, Lin Bih-jaw and Fan Li-min, eds. (Taipei: Institute of International Relations, 1990), p. 324. This essay has many insights on a crucial topic that has been neglected in the social science of China for too long. Works cited in its footnotes, e.g., by Kessen and by Liljeström, should become a field that even political scientists begin to read.

204. Ibid., p. 323.

205. Ibid., p. 326.

206. *Zhongguo funü tongji ziliao, 1949–1989* (Statistical Materials on Chinese Women, 1949–1989), Research Institute of the All-China Women's Federation and Research Office of Shaanxi Provincial Women's Federation, eds. (Beijing: Zhongguo Tongji Chuban She, 1991), p. 25, shows Shanghai moving from one of China's least female populations to the highest (with the possible exception of Tibet, for which the relevant table apparently includes a misprint).

207. The lowest provinces on this index include a populous and contiguous group in China proper: Henan, Hebei, Shandong, Shaanxi, and Shanxi (north-central bedrock conservative territory for the most part). The overall index for Jiangsu is sharply lowered by rates in Subei. According to *Zhongguo 1987 nian 1% renkou chouxiang pucha ziliao: Jiangsu sheng fence* (Chinese 1987 1% Sample Survey: Jiangsu Province Volume), Jiangsu Province Statistical Bureau and Jiangsu Province Census Office, eds. (Nanjing: Zhongguo Tongji Chuban She, 1988), p. 165, women comprise much higher portions of the southern Jiangsu industrial workforce (in Suzhou, 69 percent; or Wuxi, 64 percent) than they do in Subei (Xuzhou, 36 percent; or Lianyungang, 25 percent).

208. The best treatment of Chinese cities in this vein, with many international comparisons, is Martin K. Whyte and William Parish, *Urban Life in Contemporary China* (Chicago: University of Chicago Press, 1984), esp. pp. 1–6, 195–227, 390–98.

209. A striking reportorial account is Jack Belden, *China Shakes the World* (New York: Monthly Review Press, 1970), pp. 275–307. There is no space here to detail the deeds of China's revolutionary heroine-martyrs, such as Qiu Jin of Shaoxing near Shanghai, whose main interest was feminist; but their memory provides a strong basis for future feminism. A notable literature in English has emerged on the situations of Chinese women, and readers are referred to works by authors including Phyllis Andors, Claudie Broyelle, Elisabeth Croll, Delia Davin, Kay Ann Johnson, Stacey Peck, Judith Stacey, and the anthropologist Margery Wolf (who gets beyond a sharp distinction between the modernization and mobilization approaches, sensibly seeking good results from either of them). It is too odd that most recent writers on this topic, unlike Belden, are themselves women. Further publication about the Women's Federation during reforms will be forthcoming from Irene L. K. Tong.

210. Recent interviews about the Marriage Law suggest that one of its effects was to facilitate divorces by Communist male ex-soldiers, newly urbanized and empowered during the early 1950s, from their previous rural wives. They often found more interesting women in cities than in guerrilla bases.

211. Calculated from *Zhongguo funü tongji ziliao, 1949–1989*, pp. 241–42.

212. *JFRB*, March 5, 1987.

213. Interview with Irene L. K. Tong, whose research partly refers to Shanghai and to Jinhua, Zhejiang.

214. *CD*, February 13, 1989.

215. *XMWB*, May 16, 1989.

216. Ibid.

217. This *jiawu laodong* time is discussed in *Shanghai shehui xiankuang*, p. 59.

218. *Shanghai jingji 1987*, p. 975.

219. *XMWB*, November 22, 1988.

220. Roy Forward, "Letter from Shanghai," in *The Pro-Democracy Protests in China: Reports from the Provinces*, Jonathan Unger, ed. (Armonk, NY: M.E. Sharpe, 1991), p. 188, n. 1.

221. The percentage of working women, in age cohorts from 15 to 50, dropped only a bit, from 70 to 69 percent. The direction of this change (in a sample of such huge size as virtually to eliminate statistical error) is the point of interest; the amount of change was minor. *RMRBHWB*, July 29, 1988.

222. *JFRB*, March 1, 1987.

223. Borge Bakken, "Crime, Juvenile Delinquency, and Deterrence Policy in China," *Australian Journal of Chinese Affairs* 30 (July 1993), pp. 49–50.

224. Anne Wedell-Wedellsborg, "Literature in the Post-Mao Years," in *Reforming the Revolution: China in Transition*, Robert Benewick and Paul Wingrove, eds., p. 199.

225. Elisabeth Croll, *Changing Identities of Chinese Women: Rhetoric, Experience, and Self-Perception in Twentieth-century China* (Hong Kong: Hong Kong University Press, 1995), p. 171.

226. *Shanghai jiaoyu fazhan zhanlüe yanjiu baogao* (Research Report on the Strategy of Shanghai's Educational Development), Kang Yonghua, Liang Chenglin, and Tan Songhua, eds. (Shanghai: Huadong Shifan Daxue Chuban She, 1989), pp. 7–9.

227. The best source is *SHTJNJ93*, p. 344; and it is mainly confirmed (with more detail) in *Shanghai jingji nianjian, 1989* (Shanghai Economic Yearbook, 1989), Xiao Jun et al., eds. (Shanghai: Shanghai Jingji Nianjian Chuban She, 1989), p. 569, and by *Zhongguo chengshi jingji shehui nianjian, 1987* (Economic and Social Yearbook of China's Cities, 1987), Zhongguo Chengshi Jingji Shehui Nianjian Lishi Hui, ed. (Beijing: Zhongguo Chengshi Jingji Shehui Chuban She, 1987), p. 86.

228. The 1987 expenditures per university student in Shanghai were only 2,521 yuan; but in Tianjin it was 2,904 yuan, and in Beijing 3,007 yuan. Aside from heavily subsidized Tibet, Shandong topped the list at 3,139 yuan. Confucius would have been pleased with his native province. *Shanghai jiaoyu fazhan zhanlüe yanjiu baogao*, p. 1.

229. Most figures come from *Zhongguo jiaoyu chengjiu: Tongji ziliao, 1949–1983* (Achievement of Education in China: Statistics, 1949–1983), Department of Planning, PRC Ministry of Education, ed. (Beijing: Zhongguo Jiaoyu Chuban She, 1984), p. 371; and *Zhongguo jiaoyu chengjiu: Tongji ziliao, 1980–1985* (Achievement of Education in China: Statistics, 1980–1985), same editor and publisher, p. 104; those after 1986 are from *Zhongguo jiaoyu tongji nianjian* (China Education Statistics Yearbook), State Education Commission, ed. (Beijing: Zhongguo Jiaoyu Chuban She, 1991 and 1992), p. 112 of 1990 edition, and p. 126 of 1991–92 edition.

230. This motto was "*yiwu liangyou*" (one without, two with). Cheng Kai Ming, "Reform in the Financing of Education in Mainland China," *Chinese Education: A Journal of Translations* 25:2 (Summer 1992), pp. 11–12.

231. The State Education Commission also claimed charge of two universities in Jiangsu (comprehensive and humanistic Nanjing University, as well as the newer

Dongnan [Southeast] University), and one in Zhejiang (Zhejiang University, which is famous in technology and sciences). These and the Shanghai ones mentioned above are all keypoint universities. Complete descriptions are in *Zhongguo zhuming daxue gailan* (A Brief Overview of China's Famous Universities), Huang Zhanpeng, ed. (Jinan: Shandong Renmin Chuban She, 1990) and new work by Suzanne Pepper.

232. Different provinces' degrees of financial support for education vary somewhat; Shandong, for instance, has a reputation for generosity to schools. Based on an interview with a professor at Beijing Normal University.

233. *FBIS,* December 3, 1984, p. 2, reporting radio of November 29.

234. Cheng Kai Ming, "Reform in the Financing of Education," pp. 18–19.

235. *Shanghai shehui xiankuang,* pp. 186–87.

236. Calculated from *Xian de jingji yu jiaoyu de diaocha* (Survey of County Economies and Education), Task Force for Research on China's Rural Education, ed. (Beijing: Jiaoyu Kexue Chuban She, 1989), p. 134.

237. Private schools were mainly evident in PRC newspapers because of the advertisements they placed, rather than because of adequate reporting about them. Interview, and *Post,* December 4, 1981.

238. Calculated from *Xian de jingji yu jiaoyu,* p. 130.

239. Calculated from data that Cheng Kai Ming reported in a March 1990 "Issues and Studies" article from *Jiaoyu jingfei yu jiaoshi gongzi* (Educational Funds and Teachers' Salaries), State Education Commission, Educational Funds Research Unit, ed. (Beijing: Jiaoyu Kexue Chuban She, 1988), pp. 101, 107.

240. Schools in areas from which rich overseas Chinese families originated often gained from their generosity, but this Zhejiang report is interesting because it specifies that the new money was local. Yao Shihuang, *Jin sanjiao,* pp. 35–68.

241. Cheng Kai Ming, "Reform in the Financing of Education," pp. 33–35.

242. Some of these increases countervailed inflation. Calculated from raw data in *Sunan fada diqu jiaoyu fazhan zhanlüe huanjing yanjiu baogao* (Research Report on the Environment for Educational Development Strategy in the Developed Region of Southern Jiangsu), Task Force on the Environment for Educational Development Strategy in the Developed Region of Southern Jiangsu, ed. and pub. Mimeographed "discussion draft" (*taolun gao*), n.p., 1991, p. 70. Prof. Gerard Postiglione kindly lent this book.

243. *Shanghai jiaoyu fazhan zhanlüe yanjiu baogao,* p. 228.

244. *Shanghai Jiaotong Daxue guanli gaige chutan* (Preliminary Research on Management Reform at Shanghai's Jiaotong University), Shanghai Jiaotong University, Communist Party Committee Office, ed. (Shanghai: Jiaotong Daxue Chuban She, 1983), introduction, pp. 6 and 9 for the quotations; also passim.

245. Ibid., p. 14.

246. Tony Saich, *China's Science Policy in the 80s* (Atlantic Highlands, NJ: Humanities Press, 1989), p. 75.

247. The remaining two-thirds were almost equally divided between the Ministry of Education and money from other state agencies, including the municipality. Ibid., p. 96.

248. Interviews with East China brewers attending the August 1988 "beer festival" at the academy. Although most of the visiting cadres were from cities in the Shanghai Economic Zone, a few were from Fuzhou, as well as from breweries in Guangdong and Haerbin. Certain American academic institutions also sponsor beer festivals (the rental charges are taken mainly in the form of contributions from alumni). A comparative anthropologist should study this.

249. *FBIS,* December 4, 1987, p. 24, reporting radio of December 3.

250. Sheryl WuDunn in the *New York Times,* December 27, 1992.

251. *LW* 13 (March 19, 1993), pp. 18–19.

252. *XMWB,* January 5, 1982.

253. This was half again as many as in 1953—but the number of Shanghai Hans over the same years had nearly doubled. Fewer birth restrictions applied for minority groups, but intermarriage is a powerful reducer of the number of small minorities; apparently many children of Han-Hui (Han–Chinese Muslim) Shanghai marriages opted simply to be Han. The numbers are based on police registrations—and surely underreport Uighur and Kazakh traders or illegal residents whom this author has seen in the city—as calculated from *Zhonghua Renmin Gonghe Guo renkou tongji ziliao huibian, 1949–1985* (Compendium of PRC Materials on Population Statistics, 1949–1985) (*neibu*), Population Office of the State Statistical Bureau and Third Bureau of the Ministry of Public Security, eds. (Beijing: Zhongguo Caizheng Jingji Chuban She, 1988), p. 932.

254. Muslim beef restaurants prosper in Han areas throughout China. One establishment on Yan'an Road in central Shanghai, at which the author ate in the 1980s when it was unprepossessing, became rich during reforms because the chef was good. By 1994, it sported an impressive Taj Mahal–like onion dome, brightly floodlit at night in properly Muslim green.

255. Emily Honig, "Migrant Culture in Shanghai: In Search of a Subei Identity," in *Shanghai Sojourners,* Frederic Wakeman Jr. and Wen-hsin Yeh, eds. (Berkeley: University of California Institute of Asian Studies, 1992), p. 240.

256. See *Nantong jingu* (Nantong's Today and Yesterday), issues 3, 4, and 6 (1989) and 2 (1991), for articles praising Nantong dialect as culturally distinctive—which it certainly is. Here is another example of reform localism. Prof. Qin Shao of Trenton State College kindly sent the author copies of these articles.

257. The pun uses a different *nan* and the same *tong.* This very important city, like booming Wuxi across the river, is in a strip of dialectical no-man's land between the northern (Mandarin) and Wu (Shanghainese) systems, although the languages of both places are basically Wu. Nantong and Wuxi speakers, especially if elderly, can present listeners from elsewhere with formidable challenges; they may think they are speaking the emperor's Chinese when they are not. A scholar friend of the author, originally from Nantong but now living in Taiwan, identifies as Subei for the sake of argument, since his city is on the river's northern shore; but his view is unusual. Qidong, another prosperous city near the northern mouth of the Yangzi close to Chongming Island in Shanghai, speaks a Wu dialect like Nantong's. Another border case is Zhenjiang, which is usually considered here a Shanghai delta city because of its many connections to the metropolis—but it is geographically much closer to Nanjing and speaks a dialect of Mandarin.

258. See Emily Honig, *Creating Chinese Ethnicity: Subei People in Shanghai, 1850–1980* (New Haven: Yale University Press, 1992).

259. For a sharp sense of the particularly harsh environment of politics in Huaibei, see Elizabeth J. Perry, *Rebels and Revolutionaries in North China, 1845–1945* (Stanford: Stanford University Press, 1980), especially chap. 2.

260. Antonia Finnane, "The Origins of Prejudice: The Malintegration of Subei in Late Imperial China," *Comparative Studies in Society and History* 35:2 (April 1993), pp. 211–38.

261. Hong Ze et al., *Shanghai yanjiu luncong: Di yi ji* (Papers on Studies of Shanghai: First Set) (Shanghai: Shanghai Shehui Kexue Yuan Chuban She, 1988), p. 283, contains a short essay on U.S. studies of modern Shanghai history, written by Chen Yang, a Shanghai academic whose family was originally from Subei, who was interviewed by Emily Honig and reports that experience.

262. *FEER,* December 12, 1985, p. 29.

263. Calculated from *Zhongguo 1987 nian 1% renkou chouxiang pucha ziliao: Jiangsu,* pp. 136–37 for the educational figures and pp. 156–57 for the data on agriculture, forestry, husbandry, fishing, and water conservancy.

264. All calculated from raw data for each of the cities separately in *Zhongguo chengshi tongji nianjian, 1988,* p. 25 for the eight urban populations, p. 619 for national incomes, p. 583 for revenues to the central government and for educational spending.

265. Interview with a Shanghai social scientist who had done much research in the city.

266. Conversations with a scholar at Fudan University.

267. Interview with a Ningbo person in Shanghai. This estimate counts not just families from Ningbo proper, but also from Zhoushan and neighboring areas of Zhejiang (but not so far west as Shaoxing); the area was captured in a common pre-1949 identification, memorable in the informal Pidgin as "Ningbo more far." This refers, however, to a proud, large, and prosperous group of Shanghai people.

268. Pre-Liberation Shanghai had two Ningbo Roads, on both of which there was some concentration of people from that city. One of them, which still retains the name, is just north of Nanjing Road, parallel to it and east of Tibet Road. The other, which became Huaihai East Road after 1949, was the residence of an even larger number of Ningbo people.

269. Dorothy Solinger, "China's Transients and the State: A Form of Civil Society?" *Politics and Society* 21:1 (March 1993), pp. 91–122.

270. This report concerns a shipyard, whose total staff size (or name) was not divulged in *Shanghai fayuan* (Shanghai Court), March 1989, pp. 20–21.

Part 3

Sanctions: Commanders Reform Political Tradition —Coercive Incentives by State and Nonstate Communities

We rely largely on men for our evidence about women, on conform-
ists for our evidence about deviants, and on élites for our evidence
about non-élites. . . . How, why, and in what ways did bias work?
Precisely how did it affect interpretation, and how can it be used
against itself? The study of group ideology, of mentalité, is not the
opposite of empirical revision, but its necessary partner.

—James Belich[1]

The ultra-centralism advocated by Lenin is not something born of
the positive creative spirit, but of the negative sterile spirit of the
watchman.

—Rosa Luxemburg, 1904[2]

Political integration is an ideal. Practically everybody, however, chafes at the state's use of coercion and positive sanctions based on communal norms to achieve it.[3] Mao Zedong was not reknowned for hesitations about organizing violence. But when asked in mid-1949, "Don't you want to abolish state power?" Mao replied in a politic tone: "Yes, we do, but not right now; we cannot do it yet. Why? Because imperialism still exists, because domestic reaction still exists, because classes still exist in our country. Our task is to strengthen the people's state apparatus—mainly the people's army, the people's police, and the people's courts—in order to consolidate national defense and protect the people's interests."[4] By the time of reforms, however, imperialism and classes had become more distant concerns, and domestic opposition was a worry for the ruling elite. The state by the end of the century was hardly withering, despite its problems. Much of its remaining power relied on collective habits of coordination.

One Chinese tradition holds that beating people is educative. A good father beats his son, in this view. Otherwise, if discipline is absent, the result might be Western-style children, whom many Chinese intellectuals consider unruly. The discomfiting of mere material bodies, some think, is a small price to pay for the instillation of right ideas—in societies, not just families. Yet other Chinese traditions, which are at least as hoary, take a diametrically opposite view of coercion. Violence is not something in which gentlemen engage. Nobody should get credit for being forced to do something good. Fearless censorship of any evil lord—and if necessary, willing martyrdom for a right cause at the hands of a power that is merely stronger—receives great praise. This view simply contrasts with the different notion that virtue can be beaten into people. There is no single relation between right and might in China. The culture provides diametric alternatives, and they both appear in recent politics.

It is always possible to ask, concerning any action, about either the internal motives or the external incentives that caused it. And it is always possible to ask whether the action should best be conceived as done by large collectives that nurture people or by individuals or family-like groups. Explanations in terms of collective norms have caused particular confusion, when officials offer them, because state leaders are everywhere interested in promoting the notion that they exhaustively represent the ideals and traditions of the people whom they try to govern. Leaders' usual activities largely concern a different area: practical and external situations. The links between that sector and the other three have been most famously described by Max Weber. In Weber's terms, "traditional" authority connects administrative politics to the establishment of regular group norms—largely through "coercive" incentives that can be either negative or positive. "Charismatic" authority links politics to ideal truths as believed by individuals or small groups, and this is the basis for legitimative politics and "normative" compliance. "Legal rational" authority coordinates the situations of individuals and small companies, so that they are efficient and act in complementary ways, gaining benefits of a "utilitarian" sort.[5]

Many other social thinkers, more idealist and less comprehensive than Weber, have suggested that collective traditions (e.g., national or Communist habits) explain most politics. But the issues have been obscured, because traditional authority—often conceived as a middle form, between the other two—has been linked to more specific ideas about time, about cycles, about positive or negative incentives, and about "hegemony." Weber saw his analytical types predominating in sequence; so the death of a community's founder would "routinize charisma," passing rights of legitimate judgment to more established courts. Other scholars can document a cycle of calls to compliance (normative, then coercive, then utilitarian, then normative . . .) with each type solving the particular problems of its predecessor.[6] Still others suggest that specifically Weberian "neotraditionalism" operates only through positive incentives, denying that it can also operate through negative or totalitarian sanctions.[7] Most authors, including these at some times, write as if collective ideas (rather than anything individual, or anything contextual) frame politics. Their main questions have been about the coherence of this mental hegemony. Or they have asked how the hegemony has been internalized within individuals.[8] Actually, politics are not just about collective norms. But these habits and ideals have been for many researchers a fruitful direction from which to approach politics, and they provide important ways to study China's reforms.

Sanctions and Communities in Reforms

Norms of political integration in China are often seen as so overweening that all power in that country can be comprehended in terms of them. This view oversimplifies the evidence, and during China's reforms it becomes decreasingly adequate. But it is easy to link with classic social thinkers who protested tight political integration, for example, in Europe; and the comparisons lend it credence. Antonio Gramsci distinguished a "dominant" state that controls society mainly through norms of coercion from a "hegemonic" state whose ideas about hierarchy infuse society so thoroughly that they are perceived as natural.[9] The Chinese polity, with its more or less continuous record of more than two millennia, is the longest-lived example of the hegemonic type. In recent years, increasing evidence from prospering parts of the country shows that, while the norms of hierarchy remain very strong at both state and local levels, they explain less than heretofore about behavior, about power, or about the full distribution of political resources. In reforms, the PRC's specific ideological hegemony has continued to inform the Communist Party to some extent; but more diffuse, pre-Leninist traditions of organization have combined with market and other interests to inform most local political networks.

This certainly does not mean that internalized deference to authority has disappeared or that norms justifying violence by powerholders are weak. The reform era has seen severely repressive crackdowns—but in response to opening political structures. During April 1976, popular memorials to Zhou Enlai were hindered on Tiananmen Square; but radical revolutionary rule ended (after its last fling in the summer) later that year. By March 1979, the "democracy wall" movement was similarly suppressed, and critics of the regime were jailed; but in the fall of 1980, competitive local elections were held in a few places, and trade unions became more independent. This led to yet more clampdowns and trials in 1982.[10] In later years such as 1986, political reform was on the agenda again, stirring major rallies in December of that year—followed by a conservative backlash the next month. The cycle of 1988–89 took the same form.[11] The lions and the foxes regularly clashed at the state level. Dissident intellectuals made clear, in their loud way, that even if the state had hegemony, the regime did not. Rural entrepreneurs also made this clear, in their more lasting but inarticulate ways.

Do norms supporting external negative coercion exclude internalized norms of positive compliance? Various kinds of writers, ranging from some "postmodernists" to others who argue against the concept of totalitarianism, have suggested this. But, as evidence from China shows, the positive and negative types of collective norms are mutually reinforcing. Laura Engelstein, assessing Michel Foucault's distinction between punishment and discipline, points out that Russia for a long period showed a "combined underdevelopment" of both forms of control.[12] She also criticizes Foucault's fixation on control by bourgeois professional disciplines (e.g., medical and police experts) because that perspective slights the continuing effects of very old traditions in arbitrary law. These critiques of European theorizing, made from the viewpoint of Russia, might as well have come from farther east.

It is nonetheless fruitful to use Foucault's insight that the norms and resources behind coherent power in any society are fine-grained. They run far beyond the boundaries of the state. Foucault saw power in many structures, even very parochial and inarticulate ones.[13] Other analysts such as James Scott have shown how norms can shape the local politics of the weak. Foucault also suggests how, by acting in parallel, they can shape politics on a big scale. This disciplines the state itself. It is unnecessary to adopt Foucault's radical doubts about science to see that such a view can show some things about collective habitual power in reform China.

Internalized or External, Local or State Power

Collective sanctions seem such a striking but dangerous topic, many analysts have preferred other ways of explaining politics. Samuel Popkin, writing about a traditional Vietnam that is not wholly different from rural China during reforms, starkly contrasts coercion and incentives in an effort to see how the collective state related to villages there:

> Emphasizing village autonomy and the *collective incentives* to withhold information and handle village affairs locally leads to undue emphasis on the concept of penetration by the state and the need for force to gain compliance. In fact, the national system in large part gained compliance and made its impact on the village through the use of *incentives* that *induced* villagers to seek connections with the larger system on their own behalf and on behalf of their village.[14]

It is unclear why these two emphases are incompatible. In any case, two separate contrasts are involved here: between incentives and force, and between nonstate local networks and the state. It is hard to see why either the state or the villages would avoid using either incentives or force, if these methods boded success in attempts to achieve their aims with the other. In empirical application, the data on this subject actually fall into all the boxes; so none of these kinds of evidence wholly invalidates its opposites. James Scott stressed collective incentives, especially normative ones and especially in villages; Popkin preferred more attention to situations and to other levels (individuals ideally; small groups in practice). Yet it would be surprising if any of these units ignored, in their real politics, any of the options open to them. States, villages, midlevel leaders, and individuals all try to use both incentives and sanctions. More elegant theories would be possible, were this not the case. That is insufficient reason to adopt them.

James Scott writes about "infrapolitics," unobtrusive and anonymous forms of political struggle. Antebellum American slaves told *Brer Rabbit* stories to each other, glorifying the weak but clever. Malay peasants went out at night to smash combine harvesters that deprived them of work, ridiculing the landlords (but not solving their employment problem) with this anonymous, inarticulate, nocturnal Luddism.[15] In southern Italy, in Andalusia, in parts of Ukraine, and in many other places these traditions of infrapolitics have been vividly documented for centuries.[16] Infrapolitics starts in the collective consciousness of people who are low in a power hierarchy; they have to be seen as weak, or they would not be "infra." But the same hierarchy might be explained in individualist and situational terms, albeit less colorfully.

There is no need to choose between James Scott's "moral economy" and Samuel Popkin's "rational action," in order to follow the multiple reasons why oppressed people eventually comply or resist being manipulated. There is no need on an a priori basis to exclude either material or normative factors, nor individual or collective factors, from accounts of action. The popularity of the debate between culturalists and rationalists may come from academic fads for using arbitrarily narrowed rather than circumspect analytic logics. The choice of one against the other is purely aesthetic. Scientifically, these two approaches are incomplete without each other. Each already implies the need to examine phenomena in the light of the other, because the categories each uses are merely opposite analytic options, not actual facts. Convincing conclusions require both methods. "Most of the political life of subordinate groups," as Scott indicates, "is to be found neither in overt collective defiance of powerholders nor in complete hegemonic compliance, but in the vast territory between these two polar opposites."[17]

Norms on Violence

Fear of coercion is an evident generator of much Chinese politics. A general climate of violence, such as China suffered during the Cultural Revolution, becomes a reason for complying with orders from the controllers of force. There was more coercion and torture even among state leaders in the late 1960s than has yet been fully recorded.[18] Well before the Cultural Revolution, the state channeled specific sanctions against landholders and some capitalists in the early 1950s, against intellectuals who were dubbed "rightists" after mid-1957, and often against others because violence has administrative uses.[19]

Memories of coercion are naturally strongest among those who suffered it, especially intellectuals. "It is the horror of the *laogai* ["education through labor" prison camps] that provides China with apparent stability," according to an ex-inmate.[20] Negative, not just positive, sanctions crucially buttress the PRC state. But the state in the process of reform has both fewer carrots and fewer sticks, relative to other networks, than in its first two decades.

Campaigns have slowly gone out of style as a standard operating procedure for administration. A study group of Party cadres at Fudan in 1979 discussed the general utility of these implicitly or explicitly coercive political movements—and concluded with a low assessment of their efficacy for any useful purpose. In the previous twenty years, this group noted with rue, only three or four years had been relatively free of campaigns.[21]

Local nonstate coercion, however, was on the increase during the reforms, as crime statistics below will show. Civility was not ensured, when the high state sporadically began to forswear campaigning. The frequency of local sanctions became a subject of open debate. In the early 1980s, there was public controversy on the appropriateness of children's corporal punishment (*tifa*). As a *Liberation Daily* editorial said, "Even capitalist education opposes uncivilized corporal punishment. . . . It could produce greater antagonism between students and teachers." The paper said that the Cultural Revolution had "left some teachers without training in educational methods, theory, and psychology; so they tended to try to solve problems with corporal punishment." It recommended that such people be shifted to other work.[22] But local tyrants of many sorts often could and did continue to employ violence to bolster their power.

Families and Their Imitators

The most frequent exercise of habitual, more or less legitimated, violence in China, as elsewhere, occurs not in the state but in households. These collectives are small, but here they are units to be taken as self-sufficient wholes. The effect of these and other quite hermetic local power networks is less different from the effect of the state than either politicians or political scientists generally avow. These power networks represent institutions that have hegemony for many purposes. They are not subordinate to the state, but they can compete with it at least tacitly—when the state is a unified entity. Dense, active, powerful local networks are possible in traditional or modern situations. States in China often explain their own legitimacy by reference to analogies about the care and power of parents over children. Confucian traditionalists understand the distant rule of an emperor largely on the basis of more primary ties between parents and their offspring. Families are far more important to more people; infants need parental protection more urgently than adults need rulers. Mencius suggests that emperors who cease to perform their proper roles may fall; but mothers and fathers, who gave life to their offspring, have a claim that is almost absolute. The Chinese state derives its authority from its leaders' hope for similar power, though they practically never achieve it. Nobody argues that family hierarchy derives authority from its likeness to the state.

The Chinese state, borrowing a Western practice, now nonetheless attempts to regulate the formation of families. To obtain a marriage license, both the bride and groom need proof of previous marital status (single, divorced, or widowed) from their work units or residence committees, as well as a medical exam certificate and a photo. Work units or residence committees during the reforms were still supposed to be consulted formally before a couple could marry, but their only legal function was to certify that the applicant was not making an illegal second marriage (*chonghun*).[23] Bureaucrats could not easily stop marriages—as they once claimed power to do—on other grounds.

Families are overwhelmingly important in China. This may seem a commonplace and dull observation, but it is nearly an understatement. The family is "still the most basic, universal, and versatile institution that the Chinese people inherited from history," as two PRC scholars have recently written. The family's "survivability and cohesion" remain "extremely strong."[24] A 1990s survey suggested that more than seven-tenths of inland villagers thought the protection of individuals by family forces was indispensable. A slight majority thought that cadres worked "for the interests of their lineage groups." Only 15 percent thought they worked "for the village."[25]

This does not mean any kind of quasi- or neo-family; it means the family as such, extended or not, bonded usually by blood. Anybody who has lived among Chinese people cannot but be struck by the extraordinarily tight—often warm, often tension-filled—links that hold their families together. Chinese organizations that are not families, including the state but not restricted to it, often take structures and use symbols like those in families. This kind of hypothesis cannot be greatly improved by complex interpretations of its terms. It may be asked, for example, whether patronist authority in China is a modern creation of Leninist organizational techniques or is part of the cultural legacy of Chinese (not abstracted Weberian) tradition. Current trends only clarify that it is the latter, and fully Chinese. Another effort might be to distinguish various uses of the word "family." Does this, for example, mean the nuclear family or lineage? The answer, which could be tested in comparisons with patterns in other cultures, would almost surely be: both of the above. "The subversive family," according to one author, is "the enduring permanent enemy of all [other] hierarchies, churches, and ideologies."[26]

What is a state, compared to a family, in the most crucial human affairs such as the creation of life or the mourning of death? Whatever faults Chinese may have (and overestimation of what government can do has been among these) in ordinary situations they have almost always understood that the state is not really omnipotent. In particular, for the overwhelming majority of Chinese, as for other people, the state means much less than do kin taken as a whole collective unit. Chinese leaders often liken their other institutions (states, parties, offices, shops, factories) to families, but this influence is not seen as particularly private rather than public. It is political; or at least, the purpose is to justify forceful coherence. If this influence is seen as an abstract authority type, rather than a specific communal tradition among people who think of themselves as filial because they are Chinese, it obscures the central importance in local politics of real families as created by births, child care, and a sense of continuity between ancestors and descendants.

In a typical Shanghai suburban settlement, the surname of a majority of the household heads is still included in the geographical name of the place. Such hamlets are groupings of houses. In Tang Family Village, i.e. Tangjiacun in Qingcun township, Fengxian county, the hamlet size ranged from about 25 to 60 households. In the largest, Tang Family Hamlet (Tangjiatang), in 1988 the most common surname was Tang. Parallel situations, with other surnames, existed in two Xu Family Hamlets and in the Gu Family Hamlet, to mention the most populous cases. So although most people in the larger Tang Family Village (as distinct from the smaller hamlet) did not have the Tang surname, nonetheless Tang Family Hamlet with a majority of Tangs is geographically at the center of the larger village, located where the main bridge crosses the largest canal.[27] Once such places became rich independently, as they did during the reforms, they were the main solidarities for their members.

In each of this locality's hamlets, at least three family surnames are represented; so this is not strictly a one-name village situation such as remains common in rural China coast settlements farther south. But just one (or sometimes two) lineages were numerically overwhelming in each hamlet of Tangjiacun. The data to show this come not from deep history but from 1988, in an ascertainably typical part of the Shanghai delta, checked as such by a foreign scholar. The third, fourth, and any less frequent family names were held by an average of one-seventh as many households as was the most frequent surname alone. And that main family was also designated as obviously important, in most cases, by the hamlet's very name on the map. Local leaders from that lineage, whenever they might agree with one other, could easily get a sense they owned the place.[28]

Identity Groups Define Corruption or Rent

If exchanges of many sorts become legitimate among members in any Chinese network, as such exchanges are in families, the networks become stronger. Their leaders gain more power over the members, although not in public. State collective norms and network collective norms can easily conflict under these conditions.

The kinds of interaction that are supposed to be based on normative or coercive compliance become hard for people to distinguish from the kinds to be based on utilitarian compliance, and moral ambiguity is endemic. China's partial market reforms give rise to corruption.[29] The problem is not that divergent authority and compliance types can be chosen—they are always available options. Instead, the problem is that people become uncertain which to choose in specific kinds of situations. Every modern country has a mixed socialist-capitalist system, in which governments encourage individuals and small groups on markets for the efficiency they bring, but also regulate markets against exploitation. Socialism is corrupt when it prevents efficiency and prosperity. Capitalism is corrupt when it fails to restrict markets against ills like child labor, pollution, or financial collapse. The mixed quality of a regulated *and* unregulated system is not what breeds corruption. The lack of clearly accepted norms, for example in quick transitions such as China's reforms, is what breeds it.

Certain kinds of corruption were rampant in Mao's state, but sometimes they were not seen as corrupt then because they were public. Vast amounts of money were wasted, especially from 1964 to 1971, on national inland projects that produced little.[30] Chinese accepted that these investments were in the collective interest of the whole nation—as surely they were intended, though objectively they were not. The referent group, all of China, was so large that the problem with these projects was not perceived as a form of corruption.

State planning, when it was effective, also meant very high rake-offs of profit for the government, whose funds are controlled by high leaders. Markets that replace planning also require extra costs of operation when norms are unclear. To conclude market contracts, kickbacks (*huikou*) often go to any agent who must approve documents. These "fees for worshiping the gods" (*bai shen fei*) are a normal expense of market development in reform China. The main difference from Mao's era is that the main recipients are local captains, not the coffers under state leaders.

Local spending for banquets and presents could be very lavish. Many reports of ordinary corruption are available from all periods of China's reform, including the early 1970s.[31] A large portion (often several tenths) of the budgets of many established families in poor areas of rural China reportedly still goes for ritual gifts, including those to officials.[32] As Jean-Louis Rocca has written, "Corruption in China is not merely the result of the desire of a leading class to remain in power or of the delegation of the state's power. Many cases have revealed clearly the policies adopted by the new class of entrepreneurs." In other countries during periods of breakneck economic development, local leaders have similarly taken money. Corruption in the reform era has become "an indispensable means of operation." It comes in two forms: " 'predatory' corruption when those in power make use of their position and thus preserve their monopoly, and 'creative' corruption—a means of renewing society and a vehicle of modernization."[33]

When is a gift a bribe? A rent to one person may seem a kickback to another. The groups with which people identify can determine whether an act is corrupt or merely kind. It tends to be corrupt when the obligation of service that it establishes fails to create something like the general bond that exists in a family. The need for highly reliable ties of mutual help arises especially among people who want to protect themselves against a power such as the state, which may be a potentially great threat because it tries to garner resources widely. Mayfair Yang writes about the "symbolic violence of the gift economy" that "is also an 'art of the weak' . . . which assumes an oppositional role to state power." She finds that gifts in unofficial networks are a means of local social control that favors producers. But "the official economy favors redistributors."[34] Gifts in reform China usually support hierarchies not under effective state control.

In rich areas such as Sunan, new dependencies are greatest when local entrepreneurs exploit nonlocal workers, giving them low wages—in exchange for which, they often become general clients. This relationship is sometimes called a form of "symbolic violence," but actually it is neither very symbolic nor usually violent. It strengthens local captains by giving them financial resources to use in both the upper and lower constituencies they previously faced with less independence. It is an art of the leaders of the weak—which makes them really stronger than either state leaders or their followers, with all of whom they are interdependent.

Links above and below hinge leaders can become tenuous because the span of administrative control is wide, because state extractions are heavy, or because specialization increasingly gives these leaders and their groups particular interests. Administratively higher or lower authorities are likely to think these middle leaders corrupt, if links to them are infirm. Corruption is also associated with patronist politics, because clients' networks divide on general grounds, discouraging complementary interactions between them and encouraging separate communities that can see each other as corrupt.[35]

The relationship between patrimonialism and corruption is not linear; it is curved. When the patrimonial state works well and covers many levels of networks (for example, when state plans deliver goods, and police enforce them as intended), then local leaders do not frequently go outside legal channels to serve themselves and their constituents. If, at the other extreme, markets are free and patrimonially organized plans are minimal, then there is also little corruption because "right" prices clear the markets, making goods available, but allowing scant surplus that can be given away free to clients. At middle levels of patrimonialism, corruption is greatest. When the Leninist state declines in effectiveness, as at present in China, public definitions of corruption become more lax and corruption by any set definition rises.[36] Social norms often treat corruption as less corrupt, when there is more of it.

Corruption is not the sole or main evidence for patrimonialism. Patrimonial pollution is not the only type anyway; malfeasance comes in charismatic and legal-rational forms too. Corruption is always in the eye of the beholder. No specific form of political behavior can be shown, probably, to be viewed as corrupt everywhere. Corruption inherently involves consciousness and group networks. That is one reason why rational-action theorists (who like to test the limits of explaining such phenomena by external incentives and individuals) find it a challenging topic.[37] Evidence of corruption is a claim from one group's viewpoint that an action benefiting another group or individual is dirty.[38] The same action is not demonstrably corrupt in the absence of such a claim. Shanghai wisdom on corruption is summarized in a local proverb: "A big embezzler gives a lecture against corruption; a medium-sized embezzler listens to the lecture; only a small embezzler goes to jail."[39]

Suppose there is a failure of substantive justice. Patron-client networks, whose most usual authority is traditional, will see it as corrupt—while networks that are addicted to legal-rational authority could see the selfsame event as a victory for formal rather than arbitrary justice. Either traditionalist hard-liners or modernizing reformers in China often consider activities inspired by charismatic authority as reminiscent of the Red Guards, disturbing to public order, while a Maoist enthusiast can see both the CCP traditionalist and the proto-capitalist as corrupt in different ways.

Many Chinese and foreigners currently think the PRC is becoming more corrupt, and they generally blame this on remnants of patrimonialism. This analysis is accurate only insofar as it means that patron–client traditionalist behaviors are now being challenged more often by different senses of propriety based in different networks, held together by other authority types. The coexistence of alternatives as increasingly live options, not the dominance of any one of them, is what makes the corruption.

These choices involve linkages between groups that have structures. The leaders attempt what Weber called "social closure." This is the process of excluding other groups from access to opportunities that are monopolized by the elite.[40] Even non-elites sometimes attempt to exclude others by social closure, but political leaderships and their families—not necessarily in the state—most usually do so. Invitations to eat together are, not just in China, prime symbols of who is in a group and who is not. Banquets were a symbol of a "bureaucracy that developed out of an eating culture" and was "extremely greedy."[41] They caused a "demonstration effect," so that the cost of getting married or doing business "skyrocketed to a ridiculous degree." When exchanges are perceived as a cost of integration in a group that the perceiver approves, they can hardly be thought corrupt. But to someone cut out of that group, or in another that is not necessarily integrated by the same principle, the exchange is corrupt.

State regulation of such rituals would have extended state power, had it been successful. The Shanghai Meat Import and Export Corporation held an early 1989 campaign to have "more honest administration." It was decreed that business banquets should cease (except for "necessary" wining and dining of foreign businesspeople). Commercial discussions were supposed to occur in offices only.

Gifts of food, if accepted, were either to be sent to public canteens or else announced in a public notice. No two family members were supposed to be hired in the same company. When a banquet with foreigners was held, only the relevant officials were to be invited, not their relatives. This corporation estimated that if its top manager were to attend all the functions which the subordinate firms ordinarily held, he would use sixty days of work a year for this purpose alone.[42] But the decrees against such practices did not, interviewees say, deeply affect actual business practices.

Corrupt cadres find ways to absorb newly produced wealth; and high cadres tend to charge more than low ones, if their blessings are needed for an enterprise. So top–down reform distresses many Chinese local leaders more than bottom–up reform, because they have to pay more for it. As one manager complained, "If only we didn't have to sully ourselves by paying cadres under the table to stay in business! The sand in the rice of every entrepreneur is corruption."[43]

As the multitier price system continued to breed corruption, the main government response was to set up centers at which citizens could hope for anonymity in reporting officials' economic crimes. By October 1988, about 2,000 procuracies throughout the country had established reporting centers, and in the previous three months they heard 50,000 cases of "graft, bribery, tax evasion, misappropriation of public funds, speculation, and profiteering." Only 27 percent of the accused were government cadres, and just 11 percent were Party members. A small 2 percent had positions as high as bureau (*ju*) directors.[44] Either Party norms had not completely disappeared, or citzens reported malfeasance among private or collective entrepreneurs more readily than among officials, who had more access to agencies of coercion.

From 1983 through 1987, only 1.6 percent of the 40 million CCP members throughout China were punished for various mistakes. Only 0.4 percent were expelled—and comparison of this with other statistics suggests that political or "cultural" failings were more frequent among these cases than punishments for economic corruption. In 1987 nationally, just 109,000 CCP members were dismissed—a trivial portion of the Party membership.[45] The top called a campaign, but for the most part bureaucrats managed to avoid its effects.

The "cadre-crooks" have been called "nomenkleptocrats."[46] By early 1989, there were 48 million Party members, but only 23,000 (0.05 percent, or one-two-thousandth of the total) had been expelled in 1988 for various breaches of discipline. Another 51,000 received punishments for various infringements such as "bribery, corruption, embezzlement, dereliction of duty, or other misdeeds"— but these had avoided the "most severe" sanction, which was expulsion.[47] It was a scandal among local non-Party leaders that CCP members very seldom had to face courts for their misdeeds.

The "circles of compensation" that form the communal and political basis of state agencies in China did not disappear with reform modernizations, but the market made them larger. Marketization makes the cadres who head these networks interact more than they otherwise would. The central meaning of reforms after elite violence in China (and in other countries) has been an accommodation between such groups and between their leaders.[48]

Corruption flourished because it lubricated business and showed the symbolic utility of wealth; so external sanctions were unlikely to reduce it. Corrupt leaders mostly thought they were being communal. Most of their ill-gotten lucre was usually spent on their whole groups, not on themselves. (The accounts are not available, but testimony from many strongly suggests this.) Hinge cadres' responsibility to the state could easily be lost in corruption, because the state was not their only network. If less hierarchal and more specialized relations between people became more common in the course of change, the current epidemic of corruption might be assuaged. Symbols, not just sanctions, were crucial for local leaders. A letter to Mayor Zhu Rongji in 1988 opined that the city fathers' frequent diatribes against corruption would not mean much until cadres who were found guilty had their names printed in newspapers, because publicity was what they feared most.[49]

Protest against corruption was an issue that galvanized everyone. China is so large, with so many sizes of collectivity between leaders in local places and those at the top of the state, that almost everyone there has both detested corruption and participated in it. This is usually conceived by its perpetrators as rent-seeking for the solidarity of a legitimate group. Corruption was sufficiently egregious by the 1990s that wide political support could be mustered for attacking it. But disagreements persisted among Party leaders about the extent to which newspapers should report malfeasance, since CCP members were often involved. Wan Li, then the elderly chair of the National People's Congress, received "most enthusiastic applause" at a 1990 propaganda work conference when he said, "If you do not talk about what really exists, and do not allow [corruption reports] to be carried in newspapers, the people still know how things stand, because they have either seen or heard many of them."[50]

Patronism and Leninism

Not all networks among people are hierarchal. Even when they are, they can impede state capacity just as often as they increase it. A recent researcher on the Chinese "art of social relationships" (*guanxi xue*) writes about nonstate and antistate potentials in the Chinese popular emphasis on networking:

> Seldom is the art of *guanxi* [social relations] spoken of in public as the only way for people to get anything done, to penetrate an impersonal bureaucracy. That is to say, the discourse on *guanxi* generally draws attention away from the possibility that the art of *guanxi* is produced by certain systemic conditions and that it serves to loosen state control over all aspects of society.[51]

People speak of their hierarchies as strengthening the state, even when they are in fact weakening it.

The Variety of Political Networks and the Power of Smallness

The Turkish political scientist Ergun Özbudun has summarized the situation concisely. "All definitions of patron-client ties stress at least three core elements: inequality, reciprocity, and proximity."[52] Only the first element, inequality, is easy to maintain in large organizations. Networks differ most crucially according to their size: large, small, or many gradations in between. Face-to-face small networks, in the extreme case dyads of two persons but usually families or coteries of friends, create strong bonds between people. Larger groups such as the state attempt to create imitations of the family form. In small networks, which enjoy greater mutual dependence, debts can be postponed. Gifts can be exchanged with the reasonable expectation that, when at a later date some recompense is needed by the giver from the receiver, it will be forthcoming.

But in large networks, *regular* and *planned* contributions from each side to the other (such as taxes, continuing wages for continuing work, or reserved residences in a context where these are allocated politically) remain the strongest glue of the relationship. Social obligations develop, but the degree of personalism becomes more attenuated as face-to-face experiences decrease in large organizations. "Gifts" are the mode of exchange in small networks. But "bribes" (current payments for current benefits) become more common between distant nodes in a large network.[53] They are simply payments for one-time assistance, rather than symbolic gifts cementing a relationship.

Network size, more than the educational diversity of members, often sets the extent to which a Chinese group can become like a family, able to create strong ties of solidarity. The difference between peasants and brain surgeons may not, in this respect, be as important as the number of people in the group to be organized. Even informal groups of Chinese intellectuals tend toward hierarchy. They often seek a single guru—not just a top artist or astrophysicist or anthropologist, but a top intellectual who is generally deemed wise on many subjects. Sometimes they seek a small group of sages (as with the Daoist eight immortals, a *number* is regularly cited) whom they may all follow. The state does not have to organize this process on a current basis. In fact, such a group might oppose the incumbent governors—whom their hierarchal organization might allow them to replace. Yet the long precommunist tradition of Chinese states relying on intellectuals has slowed the fading of this habit in academic circles. Elsewhere in Chinese society, for example in the economy, the pattern of having self-identifying intellectuals in power is becoming somewhat less salient.

The hierarchical habit of intellectuals is in an ironic tension with what intellectuals do best: propose independent ideas. A critic of 1990s artists "understood that what was radical in this work was its originality, that anyone who cleaved to a vision of his [or her] own and chose to articulate that vision was at the cutting edge of Chinese society."[54] Not just in China, intellectuals want *both* to imitate the best *and* to say something new. The first task may imply hierarchy; the second implies separate initiative. This second, creative role is the goad that maddens China's conservative lions, who guard the collectiveness of Chinese norms even more fiercely than they guard the content of any particular value. Past attacks from stately lions, for example in 1957 or 1966–69 but also in many earlier centuries, also generate data to show the coercive reasons why Chinese intellectuals accept hierarchy more readily than do those in Europe, for example. Educated people in China are, in any case, a small and urban part of the population; the state elite manages them with more ease than either group pretends. More dangerous to the state are groups beyond the pale of control, in general many southerners and in particular rural entrepreneurs.

Constancy of communication between group members becomes a sign of the generality of commitment that binds them. The most widespread high-tech symbols of popular Chinese interest in personal networks are beepers and cellular telephones. In May 1990, the Shanghai Communications Development Corporation established a new radio paging system that doubled to 60,000 the number of potential subscribers in the metropolis. Ordinary and conference modes were both available, as well as message checks and automated statistics collection— all wireless, so that no member within Shanghai would ever have to be away from a network. The cellular phone company had begun in the city as early as 1983, and by the end of the decade it was broadcasting from three transmitter-receivers. In the PRC, only Guangzhou had more subscribers.[55] If Hong Kong or Taipei is a guide, Shanghai will need more paging capacity very soon. Networking is a strong collective tradition in China, which never required state promotion.

Beepers and portable phones help unofficial collectivities as well as governments. Modern electronics allows members of tight-knit groups to be physically separate yet spiritually together. These facilities affect the watershed from which their network can absorb resources. The density of communications in a political system has long been deemed an indication of its development, and reforms in China have meant more frequent communications.[56] The number of PRC long-distance telephone calls, for example, never increased less than 11 percent annually between 1982 and 1986. The number had grown only 7 percent yearly in 1975–80, and just 3 percent from 1980 to 1981—but 15 percent annually during the early reforms from 1970 to 1975.

Letters mailed grew in number more than twice as fast from 1970 to 1975 as from 1975 to 1980, and clearly faster from 1970 to 1975 than in later reform years on average. An analyst notes that, "press reports leave one in little doubt that the chief users of postal and telecommunications facilities are the newly established small or medium-sized collectively owned firms."[57]

Networks woven in these ways can be hierarchical or horizontal. They can also vary along many other dimensions. Patron–client relations are just a subset of the great variety of links that people establish among themselves, and they should be put in perspective of the other kinds. They are a hierarchical type of the species, but other relations (as between heads of equal lineages or equal companies) are not hierarchical. Patronist links are a type involving transfers of power and protection, but other types (e.g., between regular customers and sellers on a free market) involve transfers of economic goods rather than power. Still others (as at a meeting of intellectuals) often exchange symbolic vouchers of social prestige, rather than either goods or power.

Furthermore, the patron–client model has been developed theoretically to describe dyadic situations. The motives of people in power relations are, in this logic, shown to be rational for them as individuals. But in practice, patronist networks almost always involve more than two people. The actual structure of such units is like that of a traditional family, with several members doing different things on a regular basis, not just one father with one son. Networks are important in China, and it is usually better to talk about structured groups than about inchoate ones. But much more needs to be said: First, they transfer economic and social goods, not just political goods. Second, they are often nonhierarchical, as in markets. Third, they recruit many people, not just two. Fourth, they are really traditional in China, not just a neotraditional form of authority for modern uses. Fifth, they weaken the state at least as much as they strengthen it.

The Weakening of State Patronage

Kenneth Jowitt argues that Soviet-style states are "neotraditional" because their sporadic attempts to attain more efficiency through legal-rational reforms have been periodically defeated by patrimonial Leninist organization.[58] This syndrome stifled efforts to diversify the monolith that Stalin bequeathed to Khrushchev, and then to later reformers. But it should be clear by now from Russian data that the Jowitt thesis is incomplete. Social diversification can defeat clientelist organization, as Russianists such as M. Lewin, S. Bialer, and S. F. Cohen have long argued.[59] Jowitt was right to say that modern prebendal organizations are in frequent conflict as Leninist systems decline, but he was wrong to suggest that the traditional forms usually win in politics or that reform efforts by the government were all in vain. For one thing, Leninism was not the only factor in their behavior; and for another, traditionalism in small networks could be a powerful destroyer of neotraditionalism in large ones. In China, where Mao never accomplished nearly as much centralization as Stalin did in the Soviet Union, strong Chinese habits of patrimonial rule eroded at the state level more quickly than in smaller groups. The effect of Leninism was probably never as great as the available documents to footnote it suggested. The organizations that published these never admitted the extent to which they were disorganized.

A Definition or a Finding? Neotraditionalism and Chinese Politics

Several scholars, following Jowitt, argue that Communist-Leninist regimes should be conceived as essentially clientelist. This is a definitional proposition about the close ideal relationship between this kind of communism and patrimonialism. As Jean Oi says in her study of village politics, "My point is not that clientelism as a model is useful, but that at the village level a communist system *is* clientelist."[60] This assertion is of course accompanied by rich empirical material. It does not exclude that other (e.g., nonstate) systems in Chinese villages might also be clientelist, or perhaps even that nonclientelist systems might be there. It would be different from saying that *all* aspects of Chinese village politics are communist/traditional (as distinct from totalist/charismatic or pluralist/rational)—though similar statements have certainly opened themselves to such misreadings.[61] But this approach is by intention an explicit tautology. It does not depend on data. To the extent that it is accurate about communism, its relevance decreases as the communist aspect of politics decreases.

Such assertions are often combined with sharp denials of the usefulness in Chinese studies of thinking about the other two Weberian authority types (charismatic/"totalitarian" and legal-rational/"pluralist"). These suggestions, that only the traditional type applies, may provide a zesty emphasis on the importance of patron–client relations; but they also imply that traditional authority is something other than an ideal type.[62] A Weberian authority type is not concrete; it does not exclude its alternatives, which are the other two types. The logical equation of Communism with traditionalism shows some interesting things about Leninist organizational ideals. But no mere definitional equation can cover a situation as complicated and transitional as the recent reforms of China's politics—or even the organizational behavior (as distinct from the state policies) of the Maoist era.[63]

Chinese Tradition's Continuing Power, Especially in Rural Areas

This does not deny the possibility of showing an overlap between Leninism and patrimonial or patron–client relations. That point is valid, as a means to explore how initiatives of the Party, which is largely though not exclusively integrated in a patrimonial way, foster patronistic structures throughout society. But the Chinese evidence for the importance of patron–client relations was always strong by itself. To show that, it is unnecessary to rely on specifically Communist neotraditionalism; the argument is stronger when it rests on specifically Chinese legacies. Its main buttresses are not matters of communicated consciousness, but are also the resources and protection that families and family-like networks provide their members. In practice, Chinese people obtain resources and protection in that way, but also increasingly through structures organized by other sorts of authority—including the charismatic/totalist and legal-rational/pluralist types. When they use traditions of family-like solidarity, what they are doing is mainly Chinese and old, rather than imported and new.

The literature to the contrary equates Leninism and patrimonial authority. The data in these categories were seen as so overwhelmingly correlated that they were the same thing. That net catches fewer fish, as time goes on. The broad restructuring of political situations and norms in China during the 1970s and 1980s amounts, whether top officials say so or not, to a basic political change. Evidence is more compelling than definitions, and the state is not as able to co-opt local Chinese political structures to its ends as it could during the high tide of the revolution. Large groups of local leaders, using all the kinds of authority they can muster—prominently including patronist authority, but also other kinds—are changing flows of money, typical symbols, patterns of sanctions, and views of how current opportunities can be related to current needs in China.

In the face of this quiet onslaught, the state's campaigns to preserve its powers often split the government, because their unintended long-term effect is often to strengthen the autonomy of low-level forces that get more resources temporarily by supporting high authorities. Academic literature has described this process insofar as it strengthens low-level patrimonial units.[64] It may also strengthen the local politics of interests among different groups. It certainly strengthens claims by local leaders to particular effectiveness, whenever the campaign is mounted through functional groups or captains who are not fully integrated with the state network. In other words, state campaigns can have the unintended consequence of strengthening all three kinds of authority in nonstate leaders. As Jean Oi writes,

> cadre power has changed. It is now much less complete, much less direct, and much more dependent on the cadre's own entrepreneurial skills than on his office. . . . Now it seems more the case that the cadres work to frustrate the aims of both the state and the peasants, manipulate policies more to their own personal advantage, and deprive peasants of the benefit of the new state policies.[65]

Good patrons, in other words, are now harder to find. Whatever the previous Chinese village polity was like (and it contained a few charismatic and legal-rational elements, not just patrimonial ones), it is now slowly changing. Local politicians have no reason to forgo any options they have for gaining compliance.

Neotraditionalism may also be seen as a mixture of Weber's modern and traditional authority types. It is not a new secret of organization; forms very like it have long been used in other polities (e.g., for some purposes, in the Catholic Church). Leninism includes clearly legal-rational elements of procedure—rights inherent to positions such as general secretaryships or Party membership, and appointment rules—although it also includes clearly traditional elements. It is not a logically new authority type.

In most contemporary social science, simple words like tradition or heritage have acquired undeservedly bad names. When anybody mentions culture, too many social scientists (inspired especially by the habits of mainstream economists) reach for their guns. The main objections are that "the continuity of culture itself must be explained by its relation to institutional structures that serve to perpetuate it, [and] we cannot safely assume there is a 'tradition' with which contemporary social institutions exhibit continuity."[66] But cultural traditions are themselves institutions. They are inseparable from regularly predictable patterns of behavior. Many empirical data suggest their importance without the need for brave assumptions. Works by historians on capitalist institutions such as banks in the Republican period, for example, show that very non-Communist institutions in China could produce patterns of incentive and provision that are very like those in units recently called "neotraditionalist."[67] Of course, the elements of any culture have accreted over long periods of time and reflect many different past experiences among the people who hold them. So they are not necessarily consistent with each other. They nonetheless constrain each other partially. A culture shows patterns, as in a "chaotic" complex, a system that can bring some predictable and some unpredictable results. There is no need for so much wariness as most modern analysts show, when talking about plain tradition.

Collective Authority Habits Change, as Reforms Set New Goals

The neotraditional idea was striking when applied to urban factories during Mao's time. But during reforms, as organizational goals changed, typical authority types also altered somewhat. The main analyst of neotraditionalism suggested an involution that would become more static:

> Leninist forms evolve, by their own logic, into a form of clientelist rule. The particularism remains embedded in "decayed" Leninist institutions. . . . These conditions—the freeing of labor from social and legal encumbrances to land or social institutions . . . the universalization of labor and commodity markets and their associated money ethic . . . and the universalization of the profit motive that embeds formally rational means-end calculation more deeply—are instead conspicuous by their absence. On the contrary, in China labor is tied to the enterprise, labor and commodity markets are weakly developed, and the enterprise is a budgetary arm of the state whose existence and prosperity are linked weakly to capital and labor efficiency. China's revolution has succeeded in creating a type of modern civilization that is profoundly anticapitalist.[68]

Well before the fall of the Leninist state, however, extensive data suggested trends toward many of these aspects of "capitalism." The neotraditional perspective could be somewhat modified to become a "local state corporatist" view—but then the link to Communist centralism was lost. Local corporatism is in evidence throughout reform China. Whether this should be called "local *state* corporatism," simply because the government tries to co-opt local leaders by giving them official titles, is a knottier question.[69] China's many actual local corporatists have been dubious representatives of a top-to-bottom Leninist structure. They were far more "local" than "state."

A better view, suggested for example by Karl Polanyi, is that communitarian-patrimonial and capitalist-individualist types of change coexist or alternate dialectically, even if one or the other is usually more evident during a particular period.[70] Each is a political approach to problems that the other cannot solve. It would be a mistake to write off either the capitalist or the socialist tradition too quickly in China.

Alternation along these lines can be found in local power networks, not just in the state. For example, during the late 1980s, a Shanghai chemical company, faced with intense international competition, had failed to export its products. So after 1987, it restructured its organization to make better use of technicians switching from a "direct line responsibility system" to a "direct line matrix responsibility system."[71] Under the first regime, each of the company's projects or production lines had its own corps of specialists. This organizational form meant that each person reported upward to a single overseer; it was like the traditional family structure, in which a father rules. Under the second and more efficient system, groups of specialized technicians cooperated to form offices within the company, offering specialized help to any of its production lines. With such a structure, each specialist became responsible for performing a function well and could have several monitors, not just one patron. Also, the company established a new department for product development. This reorganization fostered "horizontal relations" within the company. It was spurred by the need for more efficiency, and it moved the organization away from neotraditionalism.

Some cadres lost their "iron chairs" (tie jiaoyi). Better trained officials reportedly assumed their posts. To raise labor incentives, the company set bonuses according to the principle "more work, more earnings" (duolao duode). As a result of the changes, the company garnered 62 percent more foreign exchange from its exports than in the previous year. International competition—and official desires for hard currency—brought a management restructuring that the domestic environment within the PRC alone had not engendered.

The organization creating a firm has usually also controlled it: "whoever establishes, manages" (shei jian, shei guan).[72] Some reformers aimed at changing this pattern. In the hotel business, for example, early 1985 saw the establishment of a Shanghai Hostelry Association to train personnel and coordinate economic information among hotels that had already been established. But a more basic reform was that new, less-official institutions were created by new people.

Rural industrialization weakened state patronage through many mechanisms, while creating local clienteles. New rural factories, for example, attracted peasants away from growing grain; some became factory workers, and the remaining farmers tended to grow more profitable nongrain crops, so that the main product the patronist state had extracted became scarcer. The state had to pay more to buy grain. This food had previously been bought at low prices and sent to cities, where workers got it by presenting grain ration coupons (liangpiao) that were disbursed by offices under state work-unit patrons. But during reforms, as the state and free prices for grain converged, people living in cities less often needed the coupons. Supplies of food had risen, and the patron–client networks that had distributed coupons lost a source of their previous power.[73] Also, when some urban people made more money during reforms, they no longer so urgently needed household registrations or links to the patrons who could induce police to register them. They could obtain rice to eat in Shanghai more easily than before, even if they lacked good relations with official networks.

This is not to say that rational standardization has overwhelmed particularism in China. To the contrary, the strengthening of local leaders has left the country with widespread authorities that are anything but meritocratic, utilitarian, or fully legalized. There has as yet been no incurable epidemic of rationality in China or elsewhere, but it has infected higher reaches of the state more than other parts. The relations of Chinese leaders to their followers, whether coercive or incentive, can be relatively particularistic or relatively standardized. Particularist loyalty, despite the nostalgia of some old Party leaders to restore it nationwide, is now overwhelmingly local.

Chapter 3.1

Sanctioning Agencies

Any violence which does not spring from a firm spiritual base
will be wavering and uncertain. It lacks the stability which can
only rest in a fanatical outlook.

—Adolf Hitler[74]

State security depends largely on collective coercion. This is obviously a sensitive topic; so the first noteworthy reform relating to it is some increase of public information. Not just the army and police, but also courts of law, have by tradition been deemed inherently secretive in China. The coercive agencies would have to be covered more thoroughly in a more adequate treatment of Chinese politics—as the police, army, and intelligence networks of some Latin American countries have actually been treated on the basis of kinds of data for which no PRC counterparts are available.[75] For China, this comprehensiveness is currently not possible.[76] Most questions of high and medium-level reform politics involving official coercive agencies—like many other interesting questions about top leaders—remain difficult to answer with good evidence because those leaders hide information to stay where they are. The main matters that can be addressed are the security concerns of large numbers of people.

Police

"Georgianization," the growth of mafia-like groups, is common after the high tide of revolution, when local networks regain ground previously lost to the state.[77] These groups penetrate the state, just as the state during its revolutionary rise penetrated other power networks. Implementing norms for the whole collective, insofar as the state can represent it, becomes largely a matter of police work. But police coercion is often used for nonpublic or partisan purposes too.

Conservatives and reformers alike have been aware in the 1980s and 1990s that public knowledge of official corruption became a very major cause of antagonism toward the government.[78] So the police were enjoined to publicize any efforts against corruption. "Economic crime reporting centers" were planned for Shanghai in mid-1988.[79] Similar institutions had already been set up on an experimental basis by public prosecutors' offices in Shenzhen (where the opportunities for official economic malfeasance were many), in Beijing (specifically in its Western district, which contains government offices), and later in Guangzhou and Shantou. The main aim of the reporting centers was to gather information about particular bribery and corruption cases among state cadres.[80] Telephone reports were entertained, as well as letters and visits. The prosecutors promised to keep the identities of accusers secret, to avoid retribution from the sometimes-powerful officials who were thus investigated.

These "telephone report centers" encouraged callers, who might remain anonymous, to report corruption. In 1988, such centers numbered 550 nationally; but 3,706 more were added from July 1989 to January 1990. Corruption reporting centers at the beginning of the new decade were attached to nine-tenths of China's county- or district-level procuracies. Of the evidence these prosecutors obtained from all sources, the portion from telephone reporting was 80 percent.

Procuracies received "twice as many reports from the masses" in the first ten months of 1989 as in the same period of 1988. But in the country as a whole, their offices were insufficiently staffed—and were sufficiently resisted by powerful corrupt cadres—that only one-quarter of the reported cases were "chosen for processing."[81] The three-quarters of reported corruption cases not chosen for processing by procurators were apparently omitted. Either the accused cadres were too powerful, or else the factual evidence was not so clear as to admit a quick decision. Lawyers, few in number and swamped with work, were mandated to cover as many cases as they could. Almost a thousand Party members in 1988 were inspected by CCP authorities because of legal violations, although only 21 percent were expelled from the Party.[82] The ratio of Party expulsions to corruption cases was usually about one-fifth, although interviewees report a very strong public consensus that it should have been much higher: 19 percent in 1988, down to 17 percent in 1989, then up to 21 percent in 1990. The number of prosecuted corruption cases nationwide soared in late 1989. They were at about the 200,000 level both for that year and for 1990—up sharply from about 80,000 in 1988. But only a small portion of expelled cadres nationally were at or above the county/district level: 8 percent in 1989, and 7 percent in 1990. There were some prosecutions for corruption, but there were also many bitter jokes in Shanghai—uttered very freely by 1995—that the police efforts against corruption were a ritual. High cadres were thought exempt from corruption charges, practically all midlevel leaders were also exempt, and the anticorruption bureaucracy only caught small fish.[83]

Punishment against corrupt cadres was rare and slight because of their own political networks. They garnered local legitimacy for economic successes that corruption enabled. Young members of leading families, at both the national level and locally, constructed nonpublic economic networks that could support followers more surely than the socialist state's more diffuse efforts to do the same thing. The posts held by these "princelings" (*taizi*) in the 1980s were impressive. Yang Shangkun's younger half-brother headed the army's General Political Department. His son was president of a company in Shenzhen and Hainan. Liao Chengzhi's son directed the Overseas Chinese Affairs Office. Li Weihan's son (Li Tieying) was a member of the Politburo. Deng Xiaoping's daughter directed the State Science and Technology Commission. Zhou Enlai's adopted son became premier of China.

This pattern, obvious in public at the top of the PRC structure, normalized a similar model locally. "Princes' factions" (*taizi dang*) included many relatives of high Shanghai cadres. When they were actually caught in egregious violence, they were not always immune from punishment. The son of Hu Lijiao, head of the Standing Committee of the Shanghai People's Congress, was executed by firing squad in February 1986 for membership in a gang that reportedly had raped or molested fifty-one women over four years. Other members of this gang included the son of former first secretary of the Shanghai Party Committee Chen Guodong, as well as the sons of other senior officials in the city government.[84] But when the corruptions were more economic than violent, or when they were coercive but less egregious, many relatives of high cadres reportedly were able to use their positions profitably. Such notables made the CCP look indistinguishable from a triad society. But some leaders were surely more horrified by this similarity than others; the triads, among conservatives, at least had the virtue of not disregarding all authority.

Shanghai Party head Wu Bangguo in late 1993 publicized that proper CCP members should observe the "five don'ts," against profits, bribes, drunkenness, gambling, and prostitution. But there is extensive evidence from many sources that all five were sharply on the rise at that time. Nightclubs and karaoke bars catered not just to rich foreign and overseas Chinese businessmen, but very extensively to midlevel PRC cadres, military and police officers, and "princeling" sons of government and Party cadres. Especially when these discos offered hostesses and discreet bedrooms, the prices were reportedly high: U.S.$1,000 just for the cover charge at some such establishments. Shanghai has laws against prostitution. The journalist providing the most detailed report on these new brothels writes that would-be patrons sometimes had to know passwords before they were admitted.[85] Coercive offices of the state were needed as active sponsors of such businesses, not just because of their illegality. They earned a great deal, and these resources required protection.

Many kinds of entrepreneurs could try to set up sex establishments. But as in Shanghai during the 1920s and 1930s, the profits were so great that any such place needed shielding by a forceful organization, in order to maintain itself. Coercive cover could be had from any of three sources: the army, the Public Security Bureau, or underworld gangs. As one report had it, "If the PLA is a partner in your brothel, or the PSB shares the girls from your karaoke bar, who's going to crack down on you?"[86]

The People's Liberation Army, with experienced and professional cooperation from Hong Kong's Sun Yee On (in pinyin, *Xin Yi An*) triad, which provided very effective unofficial operatives, in 1994 reportedly ran the "Top 10" club and other bars in an area north of central Nanjing Road. This partnership was also said to manage other discos ("Casablanca" and "Galaxy") near the intersection of Yan'an and Zhongshan roads. As in other cities, particular coercive organizations dominated particular districts. It is possible to draw a map of Shanghai, indicating regions of such influence by the PSB, the PLA, and various overseas mafias.[87]

Taiwan's Bamboo Gang, perhaps because of favoritism to an island of particular official interest, seems to have needed no PRC institutional partner in its karaoke and massage enterprises along Siping Road.[88] The manager of the "Dedo Club" on Nanjing Road claimed that he did not arrange assignations for men who came to his disco—but he also did not restrain independent female entrepreneurs who might come: "Well, doing P.R. work for herself is okay, but she should not overly harass my customers. Public Security wants this to look like a cultural place, not a red-light zone." He felt that official sponsorship was essential: "You need a good partner to run a club in China, and the Public Security is a good partner."[89]

Other forms of vice also grew in Shanghai during the 1980s and 1990s. What most changed, however, was the state's inability or unwillingness to prevent "its" cadres from running these activities. Compared with the situation in Shanghai during the first half of this century, much of the public's sensitivity against these forms of corruption apparently remained high. But as long as such an activity recruited willing participants and followed its own collective "rules of the game," the government could no longer prevent it. An official campaign against gambling dens in Nanshi district in early 1989, for example, netted a large number of poker den owners, who were sentenced to several years of prison each—not because they had run the dens (which were many and illegal) but, reportedly, because they had cheated at cards.[90]

In many rural parts of China, all coercive forces of a quotidian sort were fully under local leaders' control. The central state, following an ancient pattern, farmed out the administration of justice to hinge leaders. In an extreme case, the head of a very rich township outside Tianjin reportedly set up his own prison, into which he threw his local rivals without a need for any regular legal procedure. When an inspection team from higher-level police and judicial departments arrived to check on this situation, the local autocrat's followers physically block-aded all the roads into town (reportedly parking their new domestic and imported automobiles across every entrance). So the inspectors could not get into town by any route. Only after several weeks of negotiations, and after regular PLA rein-forcements were brought up, did the township leader have to back down.[91]

Prosperity did not necessarily breed liberalism, at least in the short run and in most localities. As China's economy grew apace during reforms, the rents col-lectable from coercion rose. Even when the police were centralized, they were just one such agency in a context of many. Most crimes were not committed by private actors, but by representatives of reasonably large communities. State and collective enterprises, rather than private ones, were responsible for over nine-tenths of a group of "serious cases of fraud" investigated by the State Industrial and Commercial Administration nationally in 1987. More than 90 percent of these cases also involved raw materials shortages and the overpricing of goods, especially steel, nonferrous metals, cigarettes, cars, chemical fertilizers, timber, and diesel oil. Another 8 percent involved false trademarks.[92] Most civil and criminal violations were perpetrated by collective agencies that had at least some status in the bureaucratic structure—and were much like the agencies supposed to control them.

When laws were violated, it was often unclear which agency had the responsi-bility for enforcing them. Police were expected to stop crime, but so were agen-cies of the Party. "Actually, discipline inspection commissions are regarded as suborgans of the Party. . . . They have no legal rights. Commissions for inspect-ing discipline have great difficulty in examining Party committees or members at the same level."[93] For CCP members suspected of wrongdoing, the partisan inspection committees often replaced the procuracies and courts that dealt with most crimes or torts.

Ordinary people, not just in China, make fewer sharp distinctions between state and nonstate coercion than the government does. A TV drama called "Shanghai Bund," made in Hong Kong, was a series of hour-long programs about the world of secret societies, full of godfathers and conspiracies. When broadcast in Shanghai, it attracted 82 percent of its audience from people who had only junior high and technical school levels of education.[94] Most Chinese acquiesced in the norm that the state could be coercive. Most—but least often intellectuals—were acquiescent to the facts that the state has many different parts, and that it is not the sole coercive agency.

Reported Crime Rates

Periods of postrevolutionary decompression are, in comparative perspective, eras of rising crime. Reform in the Soviet Union began when Gorbachev came to power in 1985, a record year for Soviet crime. The anti-alcoholism campaign, and perhaps temporarily greater social hope in a time of "openness" (*glasnost*),

Table 3.1–1

Serious Crimes in Shanghai, 1980–1983
(major crimes as a percentage of all Shanghai crimes)

	1980	1981	1982	1983
Murder (and attempted)	3.2	2.6	2.9	3.8
Armed robbery	2.4	2.3	1.5	2.0
Hooliganism	1.4	1.5	1.9	1.8
Rape	0.1	1.2	2.3	5.0
Larceny/embezzlement	85.7	87.7	86.9	80.7
Other (approx.)	7.0	5.0	4.0	7.0

Source: Shanghai shehui xiankuang he qushi, 1980–1983 (Situations and Trends in Shanghai Society, 1980–1983), Zheng Gongliang et al., eds. (Shanghai: Huadong Shifan Daxue Chuban She, 1988), p. 245. The last row is a residual.

caused the crime rate to drop in the following two years by more than one-quarter. But this initial effect against crime was reversed in 1988, and by 1989 the USSR reached another all-time high crime rate.[95] The emergence of nonpublic coercive agencies throughout the ex-Communist world has become a major phenomenon. Most of them are classified as criminal by the state, but of course they take a more favorable view of themselves.

Crime statistics are ordinarily difficult to find for China, and then they are difficult to interpret because they may correlate with government policy, not just with social trends. According to one report, however, there was a slight decrease in the number of Shanghai criminal cases during the first two years of the 1980s, followed by a sharp (34 percent) decrease by 1982 below 1981, and a further 21 percent decrease by 1983.[96]

The police solved a generally increasing portion of these cases during the first four years of the decade (respectively, 57, 54, 58, and then 62 percent). And among "serious criminal cases," the police solved a much larger proportion: in 1981, 86 percent; 1982, 92 percent; 1983, 93 percent. They reportedly broke even higher proportions of the "especially severe cases," including all of the murders in 1983 and 98 percent of the rapes. Nonetheless, the number of these serious cases increased during the reforms—and the decrease of less serious cases may have been caused in part by the rise of police time and attention that the increase of major crimes demanded. Also, the reported rates of police success in solving crimes are so high, the published figures may be illusory.[97] Reforms meant more violent crimes, however; and these were usually reported only after the police claimed to have caught the culprits.

The number of serious cases increased during the reforms, as Table 3.1–1 shows, and the decrease of less serious cases may have been aided in part by the rise of police time that the rise of major crimes demanded. Although there was some decrease in reported embezzlements between the last two years of this short period on which figures are available, increases in serious crimes (especially rape and "hooliganism," *liumang zui*) were sharp. Violent crimes were up, even though ordinary ones were down. Burglaries were down, but corruption cases rose: from 11 percent of ordinary criminal cases in 1982 to 15 percent the next year.[98] Bribery cases similarly rose, from 8 to 10 percent, and fraud cases from 3 to 5 percent of the total. There was a rise of economic cases among all crimes deemed "especially severe." Increases were also registered for crime rates among state employees, retired people, and youths, even though there were decreases among cadres, peasants, and students.

In rural areas and cities alike, open violence by local groups has been higher during reforms than in the recent past.[99] The Shanghai suburbs accounted for a rising portion of the municipality's criminal investigations, up from 9 percent in 1981 to 13 percent in 1983.[100] Because suburban residents comprised 46 percent of Shanghai's population at this time, however, they were either more law-abiding or more adept at hiding their crimes from the police, or perhaps both.

Nationally, an epidemic of major crimes, such as murders and armed robberies, began in the mid-1980s and accelerated into the 1990s. Major crimes had increased slowly through 1984; but in 1985, their rate rose by 31 percent; then by another 17 percent in 1986, by 25 percent in 1987, and by 66 percent in 1988. So there were more than three times as many major crimes in 1988 as during any of the first few years of the decade. This crime wave accelerated into the 1990s, and it was probably linked in many ways to the economic boom.

If the much larger number of minor crimes are added to the accounts, however, this acceleration disappears until the 1990s. The best available summary of PRC crime rates shows surprisingly little variation (always 40 to 60 cases yearly per 100,000 people) from the early 1970s to 1978. The 1979–82 rates exceeded that range, up to a high of 89 criminal cases in 1981. The total reported crime rate in 1982 was higher than in any of the next five years, and in 1988 there was a jump of only one-tenth; the 1983–87 rates were again all between 40 and 60. Then criminality soared, exceeding 200 cases per 100,000 people by the early 1990s. The perpetrators were increasingly young; 1985 was the first year in which more than 70 percent of arrested criminals were less than twenty-five years old. The portion before 1980 had always been lower than 50 percent.[101] It is possible that post-1989 state conservatives' interests in showing reports of police solving crimes—but not getting themselves or their kin caught—may affect this picture of an overall flat rate through 1988, and then a rise in the 1990s.

Why were there many more large crimes after the mid-1980s, while public criminality as a whole rose far more slowly? The answer is not entirely clear, but it may well relate to the opportunities that economic decentralization and growth caused for major embezzlements. Neither the state nor local networks that depress criminality countervailed the rising power of local communities.

Strengthening the Police

China's civilian public security apparatus became somewhat more separate from the army in relatively liberal periods of the reforms, and Shanghai had an interesting role in this change nationally. When Wang Daohan became mayor in 1980, his foremost deputy mayor was Ruan Chongwu, a civilian bureaucrat. Ruan's background had not been in police work or in the army, but later in 1983, he was appointed minister of public security—the first civilian to hold that highly sensitive job. He left the post as China's top police officer in 1987 after the student demonstrations, but the fact that a person of his background had this job at all was a sign of change.[102]

Reformist politicians at the top of the state fully supported the strengthening of coercive institutions to police ordinary citizens. As Zhao Ziyang told those attending the first session of the Sixth National People's Congress on June 6, 1983,

> Over the next five years, it is necessary to speed drastically the setting-up of a strong contingent of lawyers and public security agents [Zhao, the reformer, lumped together these two types of detectives] . . . and to improve, on every level, the political and professional training of cadres and all personnel. We must also improve their social standing, renew their technical equipment, and strengthen their fighting spirit, so that the public security contingent really becomes a well-trained force, liked by the people and fulfilling the function of a pillar of public security.[103]

Accordingly, the police were modernized. From Swiss firms, they bought electronic scramblers to maintain the confidentiality of their telephone conversations, as well as hi-fi equipment to listen discreetly to suspects.

"People's armed police forces" (renmin wuzhuang jingcha budui) were established in April 1983 by joint directives from the top of the CCP and government—and the Party's Military Commission. These forces were organized as if they were an army, although their obvious and explicit mission was domestic rather than international.[104] More mobile armed police forces were funded in many large Chinese cities during 1988.[105] After June 4, 1989, when these units had shown themselves to be ill-armed for nonlethal attacks on demonstrators, these specialized police units reportedly received much larger budgets. The government clearly expected these riot squads would be required to repress urban dissent in the future.

The actual use of sharp sanctions for political rather than integrative purposes was an issue that often separated the lions from the foxes. Both these state elites depended for confidence on much larger groups of local leaders, to whom the use or nonuse of police violence sent important signals. At each major crisis in reform China (as in the developing polity of Thailand, for example), local urban reformists sporadically or hesitantly condoned public demonstrations that pressed for change, clearly hoping their favorite foxes in the state leadership could defeat the lions there.[106] During 1976, 1979, 1986, and 1989, this uncoordinated strategy of local leaders mostly failed in the short term, although it would probably prove somewhat influential in the long term. In China as a whole, it worked far less well than in cities. Conservatives at the top of the state agreed with Emile Durkheim that deviance provides "occasions for the affirmation of common norms and beliefs among the conforming, and thereby promotes solidarity."[107]

Reformist and conservative intellectuals alike, not just when they were in government, clearly thought that retribution against criminals was a valid means of reaffirming the political solidarity of China. Faced with rising dissent in the early 1980s, the hard-liners pressed for law and order in 1983. They refused to distinguish crime from dissent. The police announced a campaign in support of "severe blows" (*yanda*) against all violations of law. Toward intellectual dissidents, the conservatives tried a simultaneous "campaign against spiritual pollution." The results of these two campaigns tell much about reforms: The movement to discipline intellectuals slowly fizzled, and the movement against criminals was important only in some locales.

Although the national crime rate had actually fallen in 1982, the number of public executions after quick trials rose mainly *pour décourager les autres*. Such spectacles were often scheduled just before public festivals like National Day or Chinese New Year, for reasons that derived more obviously from hard-liners' ideas about collective norms than from the timing of offenses. Most reports of sentencing in stadia, before large crowds (which, according to one reporter, "could not help but clap and cheer") come not from places like Shanghai, but from inland provincial capitals such as Kunming, Lanzhou, or Chengdu.[108] Shanghai traditionalists seem to think the coercive buttresses of solidarity are more effective if they are more subtle.

Top leaders apparently disagreed on how to administer the police. The Ministry of Public Security was legally part of the government, not the Party. In practice, however, it had always fallen under the CCP, whose general secretary until 1987 was Hu Yaobang—a relative liberal. In an irony that is only apparent, this was a case in which reformers were helped (as in Andropov's USSR) by a fusion of state and Party. The Ministry of Public Security retained many old cadres who deeply distrusted the effects of the reforms espoused by new Party leaders—but the latter largely controlled the police.[109]

Public spectacles of state coercion were often approved by reformers, who were more intellectual-elitist than liberal. In early 1989, more than thirty thousand people came to a public execution of seventeen people, arranged by the police in Guangzhou, one of China's most cosmopolitan cities. These victims were criminals rather than political dissidents, but reports indicate that attendance at their killing by the state was enthusiastic. Young Chinese intellectuals are nearly unanimous on the need for capital punishment.[110] They have seldom opposed harsh sanctions as such; they have mainly opposed its use against educated people.

In mid-1989, these tenets were partially challenged by events at Tiananmen. But the greatest number of casualties in that repression were nonintellectuals, killed elsewhere in Beijing. Student demonstrators were allowed a route by which to leave Tiananmen Square, before the tanks rolled in. Shanghai weathered this storm with fewer deaths because police were ordered off the streets on June 4. News of the 1989 violence in Beijing nonetheless caused in Shanghai major political effects that will be discussed later in this book. Shanghai's conservatives insisted primarily on the maintenance of public order, but in later months all types of causes were cited to relegitimate state coercion.

Violence from local and very unofficial power networks, especially resurgent groups in rural areas, was clearly on the rise at this time. During early 1990 in Tiantai county, Zhejiang, 5,000 people from 43 villages were involved in an armed battle between coalitions involving eight lineages—and the local leaders of each group were Party members and state cadres, not just clan heads. The "Li Committee" in Wugang, Zhejiang, took charge of mediating disputes between Li family members, and many state cadres in clan posts were quite frank about implementing only those state policies that would benefit their clans. In Tiantai, lineages fielded their own candidates in the 1989 township elections, and they made sure that all kin voted within the family.[111] More broadly in the 1990s, the number of gunfights in China between police and criminals or mafia-like groups exceeded 3,000 per year.[112]

One way for the lions in the 1990s to legitimate the role of police was to publicize that the constabulary should expel illegal residents. This met with strong approval among most long-term residents. Local conservatives also called press conferences to stress the need to clamp down on the drug trade. They warned that traffickers would be punished by death.[113] China's "Strike Hard" campaign of the mid-1990s was a classic state exercise in attempted solidarity. During this period, the PRC was executing more people per year than the rest of the world combined. Politicians who liked this leonine style found nothing better to confirm communal solidarity than an occasional execution. Reform foxes, for shorter-term political purposes, usually concurred in public.

Comparisons with other countries after revolutionary centralizations suggest nothing unusual about China's slowness in changing collective norms that justify extensive state violence. High politicians in many Far Eastern countries propound this as a special Asian tradition. In Singapore and its two larger neighbors, all the top leaders (apparently to distract from potential conflicts between them) stress the glory of harsh punishments. In the West, late Stuart legal sentences after Cromwell's centralization also tended to be extremely severe, especially in criminal cases. In civil cases, such as those involving equity, land, and trusts, procedural reforms made application of the law more uniform. This did not end retributive criminal law. There were real reforms then (hearsay evidence became inadmissible, and writs of habeas corpus were more often demanded). But convictions still led to severe penalties.[114] Recent research by Michael Schoenhals has documented that in China, especially among high politicians, the "Central Case Examination Group" before reforms organized sharp coercive violence against "cadres managed by the center" (*zhongyang guanli de ganbu*).[115] Occasional violence to posit political unity may eventually provide a basis for civil experiments in fairness, but only after memories of revolutionary injustice make many in the elite want less arbitrary use of sanctions.

Army

Police officers at or above the county or district level in China have long been concurrently officers of the People's Liberation Army. They are at once subject, for different purposes, to the Ministry of Public Security and the Ministry of Defense. Among the passing generation of China's high politicians, there has also been a wealth of army experience, so the distinction between military and civilian people has been a relatively fuzzy one in China.[116] The presence of military officers in high Party and state posts has varied over time but has always symbolized the coercive agencies' political role. At the time of Liberation, the field armies established governments in all the areas they liberated.[117] Less well known is that Beijing ministries also tended to be staffed, at least originally, by one or the other of the field armies.

Reform Demobilization:
From Government and from Officerships

Military people have, until recently, been the usual appointees to civilian jobs that the Party held most crucial for its own security. Just after Liberation, the main mandate of the CCP was to establish regional governments. This task fell naturally to the field armies that had liberated specific areas; in Shanghai, this was Chen Yi's Third Field Army. Political security was the major aim of the early 1950s' Suppression of Counterrevolutionaries campaign. Because of such experiences, soldiers moved naturally into police work.[118] The 1956 Transition to Socialism absorbed many officers demobilized from the Korean War as "public" representatives in new joint state-private enterprises. The economic incompetence of most such cadres, which was criticized roundly during the 1957 Hundred Flowers Movement, sent many in the 1958 Great Leap Forward to less-urban centers, where they became involved in rural work. During the economic upturn after the early 1960s, more soldiers than before were given positions of importance in universities and technological research institutions—whether or not they had expertise in these fields. During the Cultural Revolution, after local Party officials were embarrassed by mutual and outside criticism designed to root out "people in authority taking the capitalist road," the army became the main administrative structure remaining in China; it staffed most of the local revolutionary committees.

By 1972–73, Premier Zhou Enlai was able, after the demise of Lin Biao, to establish more civilian control of his government by rotating army officers to posts in new areas, where they had fewer personal connections. So the army became somewhat more professionalized at that time.

Military participation in central bodies of the Party (the Politburo and Central Committee) dropped sharply after 1971. But as Table 3.1–2 shows, the portion of military members later rose again, between 1973 and 1977, dropping again until the mid-1980s. At local levels, the importance of the early 1970s watershed was more obvious—and the decline of soldiers in provincial Party politics (as evidenced by the number of officers who served as CCP first provincial secretaries, or even as members on the small "leadership groups" of Party provincial committees) was in steady decline after a peak reached in 1971.

By 1988, only 3 percent of the top 115 Party and government leaders had army backgrounds. This tiny portion rose slightly again later, and it does not measure all political power. But it represents a drastic long-term decline from the zenith of military influence in 1969–70.[119]

Even at much lower administrative levels, where past careers in the military were once sure tickets to good civilian jobs, such guarantees ended—especially for jobs that involved culture and norms. By the late 1980s at *Wenhui News*, for instance, effectively all staff recruitment that was not from universities came from among civilian "stringer" correspondents. Only a small part of the staff had joined the paper from other workplaces during the reforms.[120] Many fewer than in the pre-reform era came from the army. By the late 1980s, only 5 percent of the newspaper's total staff had any full-time military experience. Most of these were in administrative and security rather than editorial departments.

This change was paralleled by changes within the army itself—which many soldiers had to leave, either through retirements or discharges. Army demobilization occurred in two main waves: in 1982, and in 1985–86. The first campaign failed to retire many officers; they simply declined to resign. So reformers offered more incentives in the second wave. The 1985–86 cutback also involved reorganizations of China's military regions, reducing their number from 11 to 7 and installing new commanders. This change did not occur by consensus. Marshal Ye Jianying reportedly refused to retire and opposed the whole policy. Earlier in the decade, demobilized veterans had staged uprisings in Wuchuan county, Guangdong, and also on Hainan Island. Pressure to send demobilized soldiers to frontier areas such as Xinjiang was also effectively resisted in the early 1980s. Massive noncompliance with the 1982 demobilization drive taught the government that soldiers, like civilians, would often defy orders. The second spate of reduction, in 1985–86, had more success particularly among officers who were five years older by then, and among those who could move to entrepreneurial positions in the newly expanded low-tax sector of the economy.[121]

Military retirement has been, along with periodic reshuffles of commanders between army districts, a major pillar of central reform policy. Reformers in the

Table 3.1–2

Army Officers in the Politburo, Central Committee, and Provincial Party Commitees, 1956–1987 (percentages)

	CCP first secretaries, provinces	Leadership groups, provinces	Central Committee	Politburo
1956	21		35	30
1965		11		
1966	25			
1969			45	40
1971	72	62		
1973		49	24	24
1975	38			
1977			30	31
1978	31	12		
1982		3	22	21
1983	5			
1985	0	0	15	18
1987		0	17	11
1992			24	9
1997			22	13

Notes and sources: In years when data are missing, elections may not have taken place; but when the number of attritions in a continuing group for a later year are known, these affect the figures. Peaks are italicized. These figures are partly tabulated from a graph in *Yearbook on PLA Affairs, 1987*, Richard H. Yang, ed. (Kaohsiung: Sun Yat-sen Center for Policy Studies, 1987), p. 36, compiled by Yü Lin-yü from Hao Mengbi and Duan Haoran, *Zhongguo gongchan dang liushi nian* (Sixty Years of the CCP) (Beijing: Jiefang Jun Chuban She, 1984), *Feiqing nian bao, 1967* (Yearbook of Chinese Communism, 1967) (Taipei: Intelligence Bureau, Ministry of National Defense, 1967), and Hong Kong *WHB*, November 2, 4, and 5, 1987. On 1992, see Li Cheng and Lynn White, "The Army in the Succession to Deng Xiaoping," *Asian Survey* 33:8 (August 1993), pp. 757–86. On 1997, see Li Cheng and Lynn White, "The Fifteenth Central Committee of the Chinese Communist Party: Full-Fledged Technocratic Leadership with Partial Control by Jiang Zemin," *Asian Survey* 38:3 (March 1998), Chart 1 and Table 14.

state would almost surely have been under more effective pressure from conservatives, if fairly high midlevel officers (of the sort who make coups in countries other than China) had not been pleased with the fact that they could now assume commands vacated by retiring older soldiers. These promoted officers knew by the mid-1980s that their PLA was under unprecedented competition from other Chinese institutions for both money and talent. Some of them surely resented pressure from old revolutionary officers whom they viewed as antediluvian, not to boost the professionalism of their army. Especially after the "lesson" by Vietnam in 1979, they were determined to improve the PLA's war-making capacity. But funds from the general treasury were scarce, and young officers had much about which to complain. In their personal careers, many could advance to higher commands in 1985–86; and that was a silver lining on the clouds they saw. Marketization opened up opportunities for army units to make money using scarce goods such as gasoline, to which the military had privileged access. Such local and short-term career considerations almost surely helped neutralize military doubts about the national and long-term policies of reformers.

To replace the retirees, the army was supposed to recruit "intellectuals with both ability and political integrity."[122] The Nanjing Military District, accordingly, promoted more than 300 intellectuals to higher officerships. These commanders' relatively high level of education reduced the role of the commissars. Political officers in army units, as originally envisioned by Trotsky, had been supposed to assure the dominance of the Party within the military. This was an ideal structure, which nonetheless may not have worked as intended even in the land of its birth. In China, the army's political commissars did much less to promote civilian rule than to bolster the political power of the military.[123] These political advisers have not been watchdogs over the commanders; they were for many years the army's political arm. Now, during reforms, commanders can contribute more to that cause.

When new cadre recruitment policies were established on a nationwide basis in the military, the reform had several aspects. The first was a program to train leaders; so from 1980 to 1986, the PLA trained 438,000 new officers. Second, when a command post became vacant, it might be filled not just from subordinate units (as had been traditional) and it did not even have to be filled from the same branch of the armed forces. A more general pool of all qualified soldiers was established. A third project was to pension off superannuated officers; and in the five years after 1982, 20,000 elderly cadres retired.[124] Fourth, there was a program to limit the number of personnel, restrict military payroll budgets, and rationalize the organization chart to accord more exactly with functions. Fifth, a goal was established that at least one-third of specialized technical cadres in the army should be placed under a separate personnel management system.

After the interlude of guerrilla commanders and intellectual commissars, China's military–civilian relations became more comparable to those of other countries. The establishment in 1980 of the National Defense University, amalgamating three earlier military academies, allowed future officers to certify their qualifications on the basis of technical training and an old school tie. This has been seen in the armies of many nations. Professionalization of the army was also furthered when it withdrew from certain civilian activities. In 1984, the PLA Railway Engineering Corps was abolished, and its units came under the Railway Ministry. The army's Capital Construction and Engineering Corps was ended, with its personnel farmed out to various government ministries.[125]

A late 1980s' survey of more than 200 top PRC military officers showed that three-quarters had received higher educations. Admittedly, more than half were at military academies. These schools were nominally at the university level, but it is easy to doubt that the education they offered was liberal in all senses.[126] Most top officers had received their tertiary schooling during the 1950s or early 1960s. Almost all who were included in the 1988 survey, which was not a sample but covered all top-ranked 224 military officers, had risen to their high posts between 1985 and 1988.[127]

Confucianism may still discourage praetorianism. Intellectuals' traditional disdain of soldiering in China, along with soldiers' recent education there, may create differences from Latin America, for example, where area specialists acknowledge that Iberian traditions nurture military *golpes*.[128] Educated Chinese commanders may continue to avoid taking direct administrative control of agencies and enterprises outside the sector of the economy that the PLA already owns. Generals may be political "kingmakers" at the state level, and they may tend to support lionlike conservatives more than foxlike reformers. But to do that, they need not govern directly.

Army Budgets

Military budgets plummeted in 1971. Defense spending is difficult to measure in any country; but in China, one aspect of their political content may be best captured by expressing defense costs as a percentage of the state budget. Despite the problems of obtaining accurate data, it is safe to say that immediately after the 1971 downfall of Lin Biao, Chinese military procurement plunged.[129] Bureaucratic secrecy and peculiar accounting shroud many details, but the general trend in Table 3.1–3 is clear enough: After the early 1970s, the army's fractions of either the PRC state budget or of gross national product dropped very sharply. By the mid-1970s, as China's economy continued to expand, the PLA portion of GNP generally continued to fall, though at a more moderate rate, even while its absolute value and portion of the state budget increased.

Some reduction of militarism may be natural after periods of centralizing violence. In Restoration England, for example, Parliament granted the king money to expand his army only in times of war. Then the Commons would appropriate money only for demobilization, to have regiments disbanded, requiring the king to pay for permanent troops from his own revenues. A specialist on this subject puts this case strongly: "Charles's restoration indirectly resulted from Parliament's deep-seated hatred of the rule of a standing army, so that opposition to any form of regular land force after 1660 was perfectly natural."[130]

In reform China, during a later century when practically all states thought they needed standing armies, the military did not disappear. Shanghai and other regions along the southern coast had more military construction than ever, because of PRC interests in the South China Sea islands including Taiwan. China's

Table 3.1–3

Estimates of Military Spending in the PRC State Budget, State Spending, and GNP (percentages)

	In GNP (RY)	In GNP (JF)	In spending (LN)	In budget (RY)	In budget (JF)	Total % change (JF)
1975	13					
1976	14					
1977	13		18	15		
1978	12	5	15	17	15	
1979	13	6	17	22	17	33
1980	10	4	16	19	16	−13
1981	10	4	15	17	15	−13
1982	9	3	15	18	15	5
1983	8	3	14	18	14	0
1984	8	3	12	18	12	2
1985	7	2	10	19	10	6
1986		2	9	20	9	5
1987		2	9	20	9	4
1988	5	2	8	8	8	4
1989		2	8		8	15
1990		2	9	9	9	15
1991		2			10	12
1992	8	2			10	14

Notes and sources: Numbers are rounded from the sources—which in Richard Yang's (RY) estimates are less directly from the PRC than in John Frankenstein's (JF) (although neither claims total coverage of all military spending, and both would emphasize the extent to which such spending is hidden). The last column, calculated by Frankenstein, is the nominal percentage change of defense spending in yuan over the previous year—not counting inflation. The last figure in the first "RY" column is not Yang's; and in each author's works the most recent numbers come from different sources than the earlier ones. There is no certainty that the accounting procedures are invariant over different years; these estimations are extremely difficult to perform, and the differences between these particular authors result not from different viewpoints but from estimation problems that have more than one reasonable solution. The profits of army-run factories making civilian products became particularly important in military budgets after 1984. The "LN" columns are from Lee Ngok, "The People's Liberation Army," in *China Review,* Kuan Hsin-chi and Maurice Brosseau, eds. (Hong Kong: Chinese University Press, 1991), p. 5.15, who reports military spending in state spending. The RY columns are rounded from *Yearbook on PLA Affairs, 1987,* Richard H. Yang, ed. (Kaohsiung: Sun Yat-sen Center, 1987), p. 45 [material by Harry G. Gelber] and p. 171; for 1988 (and confirming 1978), *The Military Balance, 1988–1989* (London: International Institute for Strategic Studies, 1988), p. 147; and for 1992, *U.S. and Asia Statistical Handbook, 1993 Edition,* Richard D. Fisher and Jason Bruzdzinski, eds. (Washington: Heritage Foundation, 1993), p. 29. The JF columns are rounded from John Frankenstein, "The People's Republic of China: Arms Production, Industrial Strategy, and Problems of History," in *Arms Industry Limited,* Herbert Wulf, ed. (Oxford: Oxford University Press, 1993), p. 310.

security environment after 1971, with the slow American withdrawal from Vietnam and the slower collapse of the USSR, also changed in ways that justified
savings, a peace bonus. As the central state's reform budgets became smaller,
spending on the army from central coffers continued to drop.

Reform Bureaucratization of the PLA vs.
Military Budget Shortfalls

The state was not the military's only source of funds. The army came to rely, for
increasing amounts of money, on its own local factories and commercial activities. Since centralized socialism was becoming defunct, some officers moved
quickly into business. Before 1972, macroeconomic planners in China had a
sharp bias in favor of industries that might help the military—but after Lin
Biao's fall, this principle became somewhat less important. The State Planning
Commission developed a bad case of bureaucratic arthritis; it became an agency
to balance the demands of provincial magnates and high Beijing politicians.
When powerfully directed planning for specific sectors became vital for the
future development of the military (as electronics investment clearly was by the
1980s), the Planning Commission published exhortations on the need to move
forward in these areas; but the center alone did not control that advance. The
Seventh Five-Year Plan (1986–90), for example, tended to spread money for
electronics all over the country—some to Gansu, some to Shanghai—because it
was a dependent document, mainly summing the separate provinces' plans. Regional interests set the plan, although the army as a national institution might
have expected more real coordination.[131]

Local control over defense industries was strengthened, even in the early
1970s, when the military economy was already becoming regionalized after its
relative centralization in the 1960s. In 1972, a Shanghai office was established at
the behest of Beijing to deal especially with national defense industries. In 1973,
this was merged into the more generic bureaucracy of the city's Industry and
Transport Group under the Revolutionary Committee. By 1974, three more offices were put under the governmental system. In the next year, the army Recruitment Office was added to the same order (xulie).

The quickest increase of the PLA's economic activity is easiest to document
after the mid-1980s' watershed, when the government's budget crisis became
much worse. Military-run civilian industries began largely under local auspices,
and nonmilitary production in army enterprises boomed during the 1980s. Because Chinese spending for defense dropped, while the inertia against disbanding
military factories persisted, 51 percent of the value produced by "ordnance enterprises" were "civilian products" by the end of 1985—up from 24 percent in
1980. More than 400 military production lines had been converted in the early
1980s to make nonmilitary items.[132]

The Nanjing Military Region held a weeklong "forum on basic level construction" in late 1984, urging the army to take "modernization as its central task."[133] Even the Good Eighth Company of Nanjing Road, which in Mao's years had been a symbolic bastion for military radicalism, "introduced their experience" in reforms. Part of the 1984 industrial reform required "all major units" of the Nanjing district to work out "assistance plans" to support key construction projects that were designated by local authorities.[134] Officers were supposed "humbly to solicit the opinions of the local governments," and they were particularly supposed to help with civilian police functions, even maintaining order at railway and bus stations at peak times.

Industrial reforms thus pressed the army into civilian service. Many facilities had been built for exclusive use by soldiers in previous years, and by the mid-1980s they proved to be profitable assets only if civilians were also allowed to benefit from them. Seventy military rail lines, throughout East China but under the PLA office within the Shanghai Railway Bureau, were opened in December 1984 to civilian traffic. They were described as "well equipped" but had been "unable to operate at full capacity because of limited transport volume, while rapidly growing local [civilian] transport had been in urgent need of more rail lines and loading sites."[135]

The PLA's section of the economy has long been organized into state corporations, like the civilian section.[136] The General Logistics Department of the army runs the Xinxing Corporation which produces clothes, food, vehicles, fuels, and construction materials—far from all of which are supplied to military units. This is just one example in the long list of the agencies in China's military-industrial-commercial complex of the 1990s.[137] By 1986, the PLA's Xinxing Corporation was already producing 5000 kinds of products at 400 factories and farms, organized in 21 large branches throughout China. It was authorized to retain all its foreign exchange earnings, which were considerable.

PLA firms competed handily with civilian companies for some inputs of production, and also for many outputs that found their way onto regular markets. Army units could often wheedle special rules that made the commercial side of their enterprises more profitable—this gave them business advantages over civilian firms. Quarrels between local politicians and officers often arose over the army's use of increasingly high-value urban land for military businesses that often competed with those under local civilian bureaus. Newspapers in the 1990s were ordered not to report any conflicts between PLA units and other jurisdictions, especially civilian governments; but news of them occasionally emerged anyway. The taboo against publishing such cases was justified on grounds that any report smacking of military business—especially if corruption were involved—could weaken China's international image of strength.[138]

Various units of the army came to rely on their industries as a major source of funding. The available data do not permit a precise estimate of the extent of this reliance, because some officers wanted to present it internationally as low. But figures from sources that have no political axes to grind suggest that the portion of military funds from civilian businesses was substantial, and in some units very large. By 1990 PLA spending rose to 29 billion yuan—a 15 percent increase over the year before and much higher than the general increase in government spending. This formerly revolutionary army, in whose service many had died, seemed in one of its aspects increasingly to resemble a business federation. It was certainly still dedicated to defending China, but it also had many other fish to fry. The decline of central state capacity to raise funds, more than any other factor, brought about this change to PLA commercialism, which some soldiers deeply resented.

A report by two naval officers, looking at the long-term decrease of governmental funding for the military during reforms, had three complaints: "First, the modernization of China's national defense has been held up. Second, the livelihood of officers and soldiers . . . has become difficult. Third, the program for production, extensively launched in the army for maintaining the original scale of military expenditure [i.e., using profits from army-run factories to supplement the low regular military budget] will inevitably result in lax discipline and a decrease in the army's combat effectiveness."[139] Even if such opinions do not cause coups because of China's civilian traditions, they will surely affect policy successions. As Deng Xiaoping grew older and less able to take an active role at the top of the state, the government in fact used greater portions of its budget for the army. It would have been difficult for any high civilian politician to oppose such allocations, and Jiang Zemin in particular was not prepared to win an antimilitary reputation.

In 1992, almost surely because politicians in Beijing were entering a period of top leadership succession, the PLA received 30 billion yuan from the government (and approximately as much from its businesses). By 1993, the military budget again rose, by more than one-fifth in nominal terms.[140] The army, like the police and other coercive organizations in China, was benefiting immensely from the economic boom. Some high PLA officers vehemently decried or denied their fiscal reliance on doing ordinary civilian business, but this element of reform was changing their political roles.[141]

Courts and Lawyers

Chinese law has mostly been punctiliously formal, even though it has not traditionally guaranteed individuals any sure rights. Some legal scholars of China emphasize that the government sometimes interferes in particular cases at will, whereas others stress that Chinese law has mostly been systematic, procedural, and rationally organized. This difference reflects a much broader debate in comparative law. Some writers stress the legal role of the regime. Others note that the state often forbears to meddle with established procedures or lacks the resources to interfere regularly.[142]

"Law" is a general word, obscuring its many kinds. During Mao's time, the

Chairman often made broad pronouncements that had the force of law; but these were expressions of value, usually without details about implementation. They affected state actions without always defining them. For Mao, the flame of revolution could not be fossilized in a law or a constitution—and documents of these latter sorts were unimportant to him except as political tools and because they were important to others. They were frequently honored in the breach, and the Party constitution in particular often changed. Article 1 of the 1954 state constitution of the People's Republic of China provided that the PRC was "led by the working class," whose representative was the Communist Party. So it suggested, in effect, that the Party constitution was the supreme law of the land. Seldom in Mao's time did a National Party Congress meet without drafting a new CCP constitution.[143]

Reform began very slowly in some functional areas during the early 1970s, and one of these is law. Legal regulations from the 1950s had not generally been repealed, so some proto-reformers in the early 1970s urged their codification. Leftists reportedly prevented the formal adoption of legal codes, and law schools at many universities were the last departments to reopen in the 1970s. But the call for codification at that early time suggests that the legal field was not completely defunct then though it was almost so.[144]

The formulation of consistent policies was necessary for government work—and a different set of leaders, below Mao, took charge of that. Zhou Enlai preached less than Mao, but he administered more.[145] The State Council during the reform period has inherited a tradition from Zhou, during his long period as premier, of relying not so much on laws as "regulations" (*guiding*). These acknowledge the need for revolutionary change in the sense that they can be enacted quickly—by the cabinet without a need for a National People's Congress. This also means they can be changed quickly, and therein lies their weakness as laws. After reforms began, the State Council was specifically empowered to issue economic regulations. It decreed them in such great numbers that they interfered with each other. When cadres in any locality or department did not like the effects of a regulation, they often were able to ignore it, refer to other rules, or plead special circumstances. Because there was seldom an effective way to reverse selective biases against regulations that parts of the bureaucracy did not like—and because all agencies engaged in rule avoidance at one time or another—it became normal that regulations were impermanent. They could sometimes be neglected in localities. Usually they would be honored, at least in propaganda, for a few months after they were issued. Then, if they were inconvenient, they might be forgotten.

Norms are inherently flexible, not just according to Chinese but also according to cognitive sociologists: "People enter into conversation with an attitude of trust and a willingness to overlook a great deal, doing 'accommodative work' to 'normalize' interactions that appear to be going awry. Rules and norms possess large penumbral areas; an 'et cetera clause' implicit in every rule leaves room for negotiation and innovation. Actors 'ad hoc' when they encounter unexpected circumstances and employ legitimating 'accounts' to define behavior as sensible."[146] As part of a theory of action, this view organizes many verifiable data. As part of a legal system, it serves the interests of any actor or institution that can, because of coercive capabilities, delay or welsh on a commitment longer than others can. Realism and dependability are a tradeoff in the legal field.

Early Reform Law: Accumulating Disputes

Formal law is one of the areas in which the early 1970s provide practically no evidence of reforms. For many other functions described in this book, it has been possible to show some greater or lesser (sometimes very great) surge of reform that began in 1971–72. That claim is not made here for certain other fields, including formal law as administered by courts. Jurisprudence at that time remained a small, very stately, rather unimportant but tightly monitored part of Chinese life.

Courts in the PRC, like the military, have been deemed instruments of state security. When a visiting group of lawyers from the Philippines asked to visit PRC courts in the early 1970s, they were simply informed: "The legal organs are not for sightseeing." When the American scholar-lawyer Jerome Cohen made a similar request in mid-1972, the response was somewhat more revealing; he was told that many legal officials were at "May 7" cadre schools.[147] Practically all of China got along without any visible activity in formal courts at that time, largely because there were few legal experts with sufficient political status to staff them.

Yet there had to be some dispute settlements in this period. Local street committee mediation was the judicial process that could be put on public show at this time. Tocqueville wrote that, "The institution of the jury ... imbues all classes with a respect for the thing judged, and with the notion of right ... teaches men to practice equity [and] invests each citizen with a kind of magistracy."[148] If so, street mediation (which had begun earlier in China, but was spread during the early 1970s) might be considered real reform. But it was not an extension of the consistent, reasoned, systematic sort of law that typifies most of China's legal past and is important for future development, especially in the economy. Early 1970s mediation committees may have educated more Chinese people in simple law, and they may have combined the legitimation brought by lay assessors with the expertise of a judge.[149] But the element of technical consistency was largely missing in early 1970s China, even though some popular education in legal norms occurred then.[150]

The standard taxonomy of dispute settlement procedures is tripartite: *Mediation* involves a third party who tries to arrange a completely voluntary agreement between the disputants. These parties may reject either the process or the agreement at any point (although in actual Chinese "mediations," there is much evidence that the mediator is often more authoritative and the decision far more binding than strict use of this method would imply).[151] *Arbitration* normally involves a prior commitment by the disputants to accept the arbitrator's decision as binding. In Chinese law, there is no appeal from a mediated or arbitrated judgment. *Adjudication* is the formal route, in which both the process and the verdict are binding. By one estimate, five to ten times as many decisions emerge from the mediation (*tiaojie*) process as from full-fledged courts.

The problem with emphasizing these three institutional forms is that they do not distinguish the main aspect of any dispute settlement: whether the verdict is meaningful in the sense that it is actually enforced. All legal personnel, including judges in courts and "judicial assistants" that supervise People's Mediation Committees, are hired and promoted by local governments (and approved by local Party leaders). There is no "separation of powers" because of conservative objections about that idea as an import. Judges are thus in practice, though not in law, dependent on local executive organs; the judiciary is administratively dependent, not autonomous.

The lack of formality caused specific problems. "Sincerity" was still officially seen as a potential substitute for law. Jerome Cohen was told by the top lawyer in China's national trade council that, "no contract could anticipate all possible disputes . . . yet as long as both sides resorted to friendly negotiations, disputes could usually be settled to mutual satisfaction."[152] Despite such optimism, this official nonetheless wanted to gather as much technical information as possible about trade contracts elsewhere. The formal legal profession in the early 1970s was small and reticent, but it looked forward to more business.

A 1974 criminal procedure, on which a report is available, illustrates at least some of the style of Chinese justice at this time. A worker who had stolen factory materials was brought to trial, because the prosecutor said the case was too serious for a local mediation committee. But the trial was held at the plant, before an audience of 200 co-workers of the accused. This procedure provided character witnesses—positive ones in a case that local leaders probably had agreed to punish but not very severely. A trade union leader said, "The defendant was honest and confessed to the theft . . . it was the defendant's first crime." Many spoke to the judge and lay assessors, who decided on a light sentence, two years of supervised labor. There was also a "postverdict discussion," at which participants claimed that the trial "had added to their education regarding law and regulations." There was also much said about class struggle and the malevolent influence of the Liu Shaoqi line on this worker, who had previously been "honest."[153] Mass involvement in deciding a legal case, or perhaps in legitimizing a decision that might have been a compromise between prosecutors and factory officials, was probably educative whether or not it was crucial to the result.

Summaries of PRC civil disputes indicate that some cases, especially those involving divorce, were heard in the early 1970s by formal courts.[154] Procuracies (*jiancha yuan*) in China, which perform functions like those of public prosecutors in liberal countries, had been temporarily abolished in 1969. Apparently

after intense discussion during the proto-reformist surge of 1973–74, their abolition was reconfirmed in 1975, but then they were re-established in 1978.[155]
Reported court activity during the early 1970s, though low, was greater than
during the years of violence in the late 1960s. It may not differ much from the
relative juridical inactivity of some years in the early 1960s, too. Most civil cases
that are now summarized as interesting precedents in surveys were decided in the
1980s—or before 1957. A report on a divorce case, for example, mentioned that
a county-level people's court worked actively on that case in the few years after
it was revived (*huifu*) in 1973.[156] No decision was reached until mid-
1976. Ephemeral laws made for verdicts that could be revisited.

An assessment of this early reform period in law involves many problems of
evidence and interpretation. Mediation committees largely replaced formal tribunals. The courts were hamstrung because many top legal experts were still called
"rightists" and worked in pigsties as often as at law. A few avoided this fate and
gathered information about international law, because of expanding PRC trade
and diplomatic relations. Memories in the early 1970s of earlier repressions still
kept the legal system—to the extent that it functioned—under tight wraps of
state secrecy. Many of the cases adjudicated were divorces, but this is also
ambiguous in its meaning for reform. Many of the cases separated couples so
that the political sins of one spouse would not so badly infect the other or their
children.

When procedure was rationalized, causes could still remain politically biased.
The ambiguity of law in mediation committees—for which the early 1970s was
the period of greatest florescence—came from their amateurism. Class struggle
was invoked frequently in these processes; but also, actual problems of justice
were placed before public audiences and solved jointly by jurylike lay assessors
and professional judges (who were, despite Maoist apologies, actually supposed
to know some law). This was a mixed system, speaking with many voices. The
road to reform was even bumpier in the state-oriented field of law than in other
fields.

The Backlog of Cases

Many substantive problems that need adjudication arise in local networks rather
evenly over time, without respect for periodizations that may make sense in
studies of high politics. Numerous civil disputes, for example, are reported in
compendia as having begun in the early 1970s or as involving evidence from that
half-decade. But in state courts, few such cases seem to have been finally resolved until later (sometimes in 1975, or in 1976 before Mao's death, or in the
1980s). An old backlog of difficult civil processes—such as had at last to go into
formal processes because street mediation could not satisfy both parties—piled
up relentlessly after the legal system was incapacitated in 1957 and temporarily
destroyed in 1966. Even the tentative, weak revival of the early 1970s,

though indicating a need that was solved better in later stages of legal reform, could not make much of a dent in this dammed-up flood of local disputes.

Some married couples fell out with each other (wanting divorces) for reasons that were unconnected to national politics. Some people had the *lèse-majesté* to die (generating inheritance disputes) in years different from the times top leaders selected. Crimes and civil contract or plan violations fluctuated only somewhat with Beijing high politics, even though reporting on their solutions was more sensitive to the state. Local power networks in a country as big as China show a nearly limitless capacity to hatch disputes on their own. The government essentially ignored this accumulation for nearly two decades after 1957. It defaulted entirely from 1966 to 1970, and it largely defaulted in the early 1960s and early 1970s. Mediation committees came to fill the breach, especially in the early 1970s; but their origin as a state policy granted from on high is dubious. Localities needed them, because the state was paralyzed and could not perform one of its basic functions: dispute settlement.[157]

Cultural Revolution Crimes and Legal Rehabilitations

In all of China, a total of 1,200,000 criminal cases were decided during the official ten years of the Cultural Revolution. By June 1980, practically all of these (1,130,000) had at least begun a review process. More than a fifth had their verdicts changed. About 30 percent of the altered verdicts were "real" criminal cases, with the other 70 percent classified as political.[158] Because 64 percent of the political cases that had already been retried were deemed to have involved wrong sentences, it can be inferred that the total number of political cases was at least 273,000. In addition to these cases, another freshly raised 290,000 disputes were also investigated in the last two years of the 1970s. Many of these were apparently ancient cases of perceived or real injustice, revisiting old issues from the Antirightist Campaign of 1957 and the Four Cleans Campaign of the mid-1960s. More than a third of the "political" verdicts from the Cultural Revolution were reviewed, but were not yet reversed, as late as mid-1980. The stakes for many important local cadres were very high. In some geographic areas, the proportion of verdicts in political cases that were reversed was as high as 80 percent. Liu Shaoqi was reported to figure personally in cases involving 280,000 people. Although Liu scarcely could have known these quarter of a million henchmen well, allegations of links with him were raised in about one-tenth of all the political cases.

Jiang Hua, chief judge of the Supreme People's Court, admitted that the revisions of previous verdicts stirred opposition among some people, who thought that the movement to remove rightists' labels was dangerously "right-leaning" (*youqing*). Some bureaucrats refused to reinstate and compensate victims of unjust past persecutions, even after the courts told them to do so. On the other hand, Judge Jiang said the work of exoneration should be done more quickly—and he favored court procedures that would accelerate it. The execution of judicial decisions in these cases had been too slow, according to this judge; but he said the courts' work on such cases was mostly completed by the end of the 1970s. This specialist in rehabilitation stressed that all future legal proceedings in China should go forward on the basis of evidence, that forced confessions (of which he had seen many) were wrong, and that factual information should be weighed more heavily than personal expressions in deciding guilt or innocence. Law alone, he said, must form the criteria for judicial decisions: "Outside interference," for example from bureaucrats, must not be allowed in court.[159]

China's legal system reached a watershed in mid-1979, when the National People's Congress passed a new code of procedure to be used in criminal cases. It also approved a clearer definition of criminality, as well as new civil laws for joint ventures and an election law. This 1979 change had many local precedents. Soon after the Gang of Four was overthrown in 1976, the Shanghai CCP and Revolutionary Committee leadership established a "small group" to gather materials about "the Gang's" previous activities.[160] Many of the accused malfeasants had scant direct connection with any member of the Gang of Four; but by 1979, courts at many levels had to declare open season for the airing of grievances, as the central state leaders put on trial the radicals they had overthrown.

The Shanghai Public Prosecutor's Office received during 1979 a flood of about 25,000 letters. It handled just 7 percent of these, apparently, when legal action for political reasons seemed imperative.[161] Letters to editors also deluged the "mass work departments" of newspapers, which were publicly known to be official agencies for vetting complaints. Courts also received many grievances directly. By 1979, the Shanghai Superior People's Court had opened almost 200,000 letters about "judicial mistakes" made during the Cultural Revolution. As regards many of these, cadres of the court said that the letter writers' demands were "unreasonable" or that for various reasons the time was inappropriate to solve their complaints. They called for patience, propaganda, and "education by persuasion" (*shuofu jiaoyu*), not immediate litigation.[162]

The Public Prosecutor's Office by the end of 1979, in addition to its immense backlog of criminal cases, looked into civil disputes that arose because of production breakdowns. Reported violations of commodity-testing procedures and environmental laws also soared, and officials could not handle them all. The procuracy was a general investigative agency, which could bring charges in courts for certain problems and could hand others to various administrative agencies. It could also seek "model cases" in any of these areas to be publicized in media.[163]

The most important rehabilitations were handled in the Higher People's Court. By March 1979, this tribunal in Shanghai had reviewed more than 3,400 of the most important "cases of grievances, falsifications, and mistakes."[164] These had been originally tried under the Gang of Four. Many of the victims had died, but rehabilitation of their reputations was nonetheless very important for their surviving family members. In addition to reversal of these actions against important citizens in the superior court, 1,500 "rightist" labels were legally removed in the same proceedings. Some cadres who had manipulated information resulting in unjust imprisonments also came to light in 1979, although very few of these were jailed.

These rehabilitations of prominent citizens were only, however, the tip of an iceberg. According to an estimate in late 1979, there had been during the 1966–76 period more than 220,000 Shanghai cases that called for reversals of grievances, of falsifications, and of mistakes (*pingfan yuan, jia, cuo an*).[165] By the end of the decade, more than 90 percent of these had been retried and corrected. Only then was the removal of "rightist" caps in Shanghai said to have been completed. All Shanghai landlords and rich peasants who had earlier been sent to labor camps because of those labels were released. Most—though not all—of the cadres, intellectuals, and businessprople who had received wrongful treatment also had these injustices reversed, at least on paper, by the end of the 1970s. Some, though not all, of the former cadres were restored to their previous posts.

After the Gang of Four trial, more local radicals who had been especially destructive in Shanghai were also put into the dock. A two-year suspended death penalty, for example, was given to Hu Yongnian, who had led the Sports Movement Committee under the city's Cultural Revolution government. He had set up a Red Guard group of ruffian athletes, who had "struggled against" and injured large numbers of people—some of whom died while in captivity. Hu had personally whipped some women workers with electrical cords, and he was held responsible for the death of a doctor, an actor, and a telephone operator.[166]

Shanghai local leaders' extreme resentment of criminals, including officials who had abused them during the Cultural Revolution, can be contrasted with the somewhat more blasé amnesties to cadres in the national capital. In Beijing by 1979, a surprisingly small number of wrong verdicts had been listed for review (55,000, as compared with 220,000 in Shanghai). More than 99 percent of these had been reviewed by October—apparently with great speed for these cadres in the capital, lest they worry—as compared with about 90 percent in Shanghai.[167] One-fifth of all cadres in Beijing were nonetheless subject to these investigations.[168] The Shanghai CCP Committee's Office to Reveal and Criticize the Activities of the Gang of Four was abolished in September 1979 because its work was deemed "complete."[169] A vast majority of dubious officials were exonerated after cursory investigations, apparently because the government could not do without their services.

Various units convened "correction conferences" (*pingfan dahui*), and the resurrected cadres included secretaries on the municipal Party committee, as well as many other luminaries. Of the 579 "high" Beijing cadres in these cases, referring to those from leadership groups at the county level or above, 98 percent were exonerated. This process involved the "correction of files" for no fewer than 210,000 officials—and the paperwork was enormous. Some rejected documents were thrown away, but most contained other information that the Party did not want to lose. Thus the offending sections of many reports were blotted out and replaced with new wording. "Untrue libels" against each of these 210,000 cadres had to be corrected. In the second quarter of 1979, an assessment survey of one-third of all cadres at these levels in Beijing concluded that their morale had been raised. This, as much as delivering justice, was inevitably a goal of the post–Cultural Revolution legal system.

Civil Law and the End of Socialism in the 1980s

Disputes between unofficial parties, in which the state's main interest is peace that comes from fairness, has seldom been of major interest to revolutionaries. A higher profile for civil law has correlated with more equality among agents who had a hierarchical relationship before reforms. As contracts increasingly replaced state plans, civil courts became responsible for enforcing bargains that in Mao's time had been state orders. Laws were revamped, as plans ended.

During the fully socialist period of the PRC, "factory-to-factory transactions were generally based on 'gentlemen's agreements' with no legal support." The early 1980s, however, saw an official passion for contracts. The Shanghai Materials Bureau made contracts with more than a hundred companies to buy, supply, or transport coal. These agreements were supposed to guarantee the timing, quality, and amount of deliveries. If the agreements were violated, the responsible companies were supposed to "bear the economic responsibility." The amount of coal products that were supplied to Shanghai by contracting companies, rather than by plan allocations, rose twenty-eight times from 1979 to 1982.[170] This meant less high-level control of prices and plans. It meant that economic problems landed in courts more often. The Materials Bureau signed contracts directly, because it had a fairly high bureaucratic rank and was in a good position to insist on deliveries at least within the municipality. The bureau's or any Shanghai court's powers of enforcement in other jurisdictions were more tenuous.

About 1981, some Shanghai firms began engaging lawyers to monitor trade. In the next five years, attorneys dealt with 27,000 disputes. When a Jiangsu factory failed to deliver 30,000 yuan that it owed to the Shanghai Three-Star Meter Plant, which had shipped goods there, lawyers helped to secure the payment without a court fight. PRC attorneys also often do general economic research on behalf of their clients. When the Shanghai Lead and Tin Materials Plant wanted a million tons of aluminum, for example, it contracted for them with a company outside the city. Prepayment of 100,000 yuan was requested. "But legal advisers discovered it was an 'empty promise company' and was unable to honor the agreement."[171] The number of lawyers available for such jobs throughout the city was grossly inadequate for the task. So during reforms, increasing amounts of unpaid debts accumulated. The lack of legal enforcement of contracts gradually became a major danger to the Chinese economy.

Shanghai still had only about a thousand lawyers, many part-time, in twenty-six law offices by mid-1986. Two-thirds were over 50, while there were a few newly graduated lawyers. The ratio of legal professionals to population in Shanghai at this time was about 1 to 10,000. Perhaps because attorneys in the city dealt with issues that before reforms were under hierarchies rather than laws, lawyers were unpopular with conservative cadres: "Many law graduates would like to become lawyers, but somehow only a few are assigned to law offices." Their pay was "relatively lower than that of public security personnel, procurators, and judges." Reformers on the *Liberation Daily* suggested salary increases for them, more assignments of law graduates to law offices, and "more freedom in management."[172] But socialist cadres were not accustomed to what lawyers do.

More Contracts, More Lawyers

Contracts are not supposed to be broken; but in planned economies, if a breach occurs, this is often regarded merely as a delay. The offender might be liable for a penalty, but was still morally and legally obligated to perform the terms of the socialist contract that was part of a much larger national plan, notionally a law. The other party was also not released from contracts that might prove hard to fulfill because of earlier contract defaults elsewhere. In practice, direct settlement of disputes (involving neither lawyers nor courts) was strongly encouraged. Such issues were seen as essentially administrative, not legal.

During China's reforms, these standards had to change. The Technology Contracts Law of late 1987, for example, allowed parties whose contracts had been broken to repudiate their other agreements and not do their part. It also encouraged disputing parties to agree on binding arbitration or to sign a settlement agreement (thus not bothering the severely overburdened courts). Firms' new powers to choose arbiters and accept their terms—whether higher administrative levels liked the result or not—showed their greater independence.[173]

Only 441 enterprises hired lawyers as advisers in 1982 throughout all of China. By 1986, forty thousand companies did so—an increase of about a hundred times over four years.[174] The earlier and continuing paucity of lawyers may be easily decried. But Japan's economy, for example, has not over many years been devastated by that country's paucity of lawyers. Japan has many law graduates, not fully qualified as lawyers, who nonetheless do legal work in offices. The Chinese pattern is likely to be similar. Shanghai as late as 1985 had 434 people serving as full-time lawyers plus another 904 with full legal credentials but also doing other work. By 1989, the number of full-time lawyers had only gone up to 635. Apparently these jobs did not attract many people, although the number of lawyers in other jobs was 1,917.[175] By New York standards, this was a risibly small staff for a large urban economy. It is small even by current Tokyo standards (though not by Tokyo standards when Japan's domestic economy was growing faster). The economic value of lawyers is a topic that deserves more comparative research. After the mid-1980 watershed, Shanghai apparently needed more of them.

Many gradually became counsel-managers. By late 1987, half of Shanghai's largest ten thousand enterprises, practically all state-owned, had "legal advisers on the staff." In the two years 1985–87, the number of Shanghai firms with legal counsel on their payroll increased ten times. As the director of a rubber factory put it, "The enterprises cannot do without legal advisors, since they have become our important think tanks." The vice president of the Shanghai Lawyer's Association claimed, "Legal advisors no longer simply act as agents and arbiters. They serve more as directors, who provide guidance."[176]

Staff lawyers in the Baoshan Steel Plant once helped recoup a 140–million-yuan debt. The Legal Consultancy Office in the No. 5 Iron and Steel Plant settled nearly a hundred disputes by the end of 1987, recovering several million yuan in losses. A commercial businessman, with the help of his staff lawyers, won a suit about the quality of clothes he had received from a Jiangsu manufacturer. As the head of Shanghai's Wusong district put it, "With the development of a socialist commodity economy and the expansion of inter-regional cooperation, legal means rather than administrative measures will play a dominant role in government management."[177]

Other places on the Shanghai delta also hired more counsels to aid reform. Jiangsu's export drive led to a rise of lawyers there. By 1988, Jiangsu's two hundred joint ventures were generating cases at the rate of four thousand annually, a rate of litigiousness that was extraordinary by Chinese standards. Local towns not registered as cities in Jiangsu already had 1,600 "legal offices," probably most of them attached to large collectives, even though the number of qualified lawyers and notaries was small.[178] The need for lawyers, and for the bureaucratic rationality that they monitor, was caused by the state's inability after 1984 to supply enough raw materials or enforce marketing contracts. Socialist neotraditional organization did not deliver the goods. So business cadres looked elsewhere, even to the law.

"Unresolvable" Disputes in Clogged Courts

Economic quarrels became more numerous, as lawyers did. Civil courts in China during 1980 tried 6,000 cases; but by 1987, they had to try 333,000—an increase of more than fiftyfold in just a few years.[179] The courts were not staffed with enough professionals to handle this load. Judges knew they could not enforce decisions on most disputes, which they therefore had to refuse to hear. Contracts replaced plans; but neither of these forms of mandate meant anything if they hurt the interests of local networks that had scarce goods. Courts lacked the capacity to countermand local politicians in enforcing solutions to contract breaches. Raw materials shortages made inoperable many guarantees and agreements.

Of all economic litigations filed in Shanghai courts during October 1988, more than half were classed "unresolvable" as soon as three months later. One-quarter of the resolvable cases, before courts during those months, had still not reached conclusions.[180] The main immediate reasons for the unresolvable cases reportedly lay in enterprises that had closed, or managers who had absconded ("*xialuo buming*"), or political pressures on judges and prosecutors in favor of manager-defendants who had friends in high places. Legal cadres pointed to a need for some concept of limited liability (*youxian zeren*) that would make the criteria of managers' responsibility clearer, and thus give the overburdened courts a chance of dealing more systematically with this deluge of contract breaches.

Most of the economic cases naturally involved money. A common difficulty was the extent to which companies (not just banks) lent each other money, for example, for paying state profits and taxes. The "collateral" in such cases was often no more than mutual need and trust among socialist managers. But if a debtor firm had its assets frozen for any legal reason in this situation, then its creditor companies would also be unable to repay their own loans—and this syndrome could spread quickly throughout the economy. For example, the local office in Shanghai of a Shanxi company received a loan from a chemical company in Jiangsu, which then had its assets frozen. So none of its downstream debtors could pay their loans either. This syndrome of "triangular debt" (*sanjiao zhai*) could stop production. Courts, tax collectors, banks, and other institutions of economic control could therefore seldom freeze any company's assets, no matter how bad its legal violations and no matter how bad a risk it had become.[181]

The inflation motivating many of these disputes was outpaced only by their number. In 1987, as compared with 1986, the number of civil cases tried in China rose more than one-fifth.[182] The number soared over the next five years, as Table 3.1–4 suggests.

After mid-1989, and continuing into 1990 because of the implicitly anti-reformist *Zeitgeist* then, fewer cases were brought and more of these received penalties—and harsh ones for a while, although a time-series to show that change has not been found. The portion of decisions appealed was constant and low, between 6 and 7 percent. It has been usual in China for plaintiffs to avoid the state's courts whenever they have any other way of righting injustices they perceive. These statistics suggest that the tradition was somewhat reversed in relatively reformist years of the recent era.

In Shanghai, the rise in the number of civil cases was fast, and the pattern remained bumpy. Different kinds of court cases and other legal activities showed surprisingly varied rates of change. The total number of cases remained tiny, in relation to the size of the economy (more cases had been tried before the elimination of independent firms in the 1950s). But the involvement of judges and lawyers was on the rise, even when the total remained relatively low. The cases for available years are offered in Table 3.1–5.

Table 3.1–4

Chinese Civil Cases, 1986–90: Tried, Sentenced, Appealed, Appeals Judged

	Cases tried	% change from previous year	Tried, but not sentenced	% of sentences appealed	% appealed, but not judged
1986	989,409		c. 10,000	7	4
1987	1,213,291	+23	c. 19,000	7	3
1988	1,455,130	+20	c. 36,000	6	3
1989	1,815,385	+25	c. 7,000	n.a.	n.a.
1990	1,851,897	+2	c. 2,000	6	2

Notes and sources: The numbers of cases filed but not tried were unavailable. Differences are rounded from exact figures in the sources because some cases were carried from one year to the next. Second appeals are disallowed under Chinese law. For raw data, see *Zhongguo baike nianjian 1990* (Encyclopedic Yearbook of China, 1990), Luo Luo, ed. (Shanghai: Zhongguo Da Baike Quanshu Chuban She, 1990), p. 430 for 1990; and especially *Zhongguo falü nianjian* (China Law Yearbook), various years' editions (Chengdu: Zhongguo Falü Nianjian Chuban She, published in the following year): for 1986, p. 883; for 1987, p. 816; for 1988, pp. 1081–82; for 1990, pp. 933 and 936.

Percentage changes in economic contract cases may be a sensitive measure of the extent to which reforms are seen to have effective official support. The number of civil cases brought to courts rose nationwide in 1986 and 1987. Perhaps because the decisions in so many could not be enforced, the rate of growth declined thereafter. Partly because the courts could not handle their load, a further purpose of law firms was to settle cases without the state. Outside courts, China's lawyers accepted 55,000 cases in 1987; this was eleven times the number in 1981.[183] A service was clearly being performed by courts at this time, and more especially by lawyers.

Enforcement Campaigns

Police procedures are much of the law in practice, and they had to be reviewed intensively during the reforms' quick changes. The Ministry of Public Security established new, confidential rules to "raise the level of implementing the law" in September 1988.[184] The most obvious method to reduce the load was to have fewer laws that would need enforcing. So Shanghai abolished fifty economic "statutes, rules, and regulations ... not suitable to the current reform" in the mid-1980s.[185] Many new kinds of specialized rules were added during reforms, however. "Simplification" went the way of "legal briefs." It was an ideal, not a behavior. Some of the abolished norms were locally still enforced, and many

Table 3.1–5

Legal Cases in Shanghai, 1985–1989 (thousands and percentage changes)

	1985	1986	1987	1988	1989
Civil cases	5.7	8.6	14.2	15.3	19.0
% change		51	66	8	24	
Economic contracts	4.3	5.5	8.1	16.0	14.5
% change		27	47	99	-10	
Legal papers	5.5	8.1	10.2	11.1	30.2
% change		48	26	9	71	
Legal advice	48.0	51.6	57.8	55.2	56.0
% change		7	12	-6	1	
Mediations	52.4	48.1	64.3	72.4	75.5
% change		-8	34	13	4	
Criminal cases	4.5	5.0	4.1	4.1	5.3
% change		10	-17	-2	32	

Notes and sources: The sharp increase of criminal cases, by almost one-third, in 1989 over 1988 suggests that the adjudication of criminality depended partly on political campaigns. The term "legal papers" refers to documents written on behalf of clients, at their request, by Shanghai lawyers. The term "legal advice" refers to the number of cases (almost surely civil in the great majority of cases) in which clients came to lawyers' offices for advisory services. Few of these issues ever reached courts. "Mediations" refers to civil disputes handled by "people's mediation committees" (*renmin tiaojie weiyuan hui*), which as the figures suggest do a great deal of Shanghai's legal work and in the 1980s often had professional legal assistants. The line on economic contracts reports the number that were legally notarized. Computed and rounded from *Shanghai tongji nianjian, 1990* (Shanghai Statistical Yearbook, 1990), Li Mouhuan et al., eds. (Shanghai: Shanghai Shi Tongji Ju, 1990), p. 380.

new laws had no quick effect. Legislation differed, in both cases, from what people were actually doing.

The *People's Daily* in 1988 reported a survey of the implementation of forty-four national laws in Shanghai, claiming that only 34 percent of them were "fairly enforced," 59 percent were "not strictly enforced," and the rest were "completely ignored." Yet Shanghai was apparently the most obedient of the jurisdictions surveyed. In Heilongjiang, noncompliance with laws was "even worse." In Guangdong, "only half of the cases in which officials were involved were decided by the local courts; the rest were exempted from prosecution or punishment because of interference by leading officials of the local governments." One of the reasons for lax enforcement was that

> Forty-eight percent of the country's courts do not have the facilities to hold trials. The strict and fair enforcement of law is also affected by the poor quality of some judicial personnel.... Education in China's public security sector should be improved.... Police officers who have not received any professional training still make up a fairly large proportion of the total.[186]

The lack of legal facilities was later rectified, especially in the 1990s, so that in many Chinese areas where the economy is booming, the courthouse, procuracy, and police department have some of the most modern buildings in town. An extreme example is Shenzhen, where a very large and handsome new building was constructed for the court. On its top sat a huge sign in fluorescent paint, with the characters for "court" (fayuan). The procuracy, not to be outadvertised, put a similar sign atop its adjacent quarters, which in the 1990s were also new. Presumably the state is allocating money for such facilities, but they must be costly.

At the same time that the state tried by all means to raise the prestige of courts, it ran into many hindrances to the ideal of legal uniformity. Enforcement of regulations, for example concerning birth plans, was especially lax in rural areas. Although China's average marriage age for women rose from less than nineteen in 1950 to more than twenty-three in 1979, the average in 1980 and again in 1981 fell—despite a 1980 law raising the *minimum legal* marriage age for women from fifteen to twenty. Farmers often could simply ignore new laws they did not wish to follow.[187]

Some kinds of commerce were illegal or semilegal, but were nonetheless praised in public if they reduced market bottlenecks. Shandong traders in early 1989 were importing large quantities of peanuts and sunflower seeds to Shanghai illegally, according to the particular plans for these products. When they needed licenses to conduct such trade, forged certificates might be bought for only 80 yuan. A newspaper article about this trade complained more about the traffic and rubbish it generated in local markets than about its technical violation of law. Despite such problems, the journal reported that this kind of trade enlivened Shanghai's urban economy.[188]

The most serious legal problems came from the effects of the nonstate industrial boom on factor prices. Raw materials prices continued to rise in the early 1990s, and the authorized prices for finished goods from state enterprises remained low partly because the government, fearing urban unrest, issued fiats to control retail inflation. Shanghai product quality by this time was often lower than that of competing merchandise from inland collectives. Contracts to deliver raw materials were still broken at a high rate.[189] Three townships in Shanghai's Jiading county, which borders Jiangsu, had to report armed robberies, apparently of goods that were being exported illegally from Shanghai to fetch higher prices in the adjacent province. "Boat people," whose families lived on their craft, were identified as ringleaders in gangs that regularly patrolled anchorages to rob illegal traders.[190]

Resurgence of the Legal Profession

Mao Zedong liked the old tradition of Qin and Han dynasty Legalist philosophers, who taught that the purpose of law was to further the aims of the ruler.[191] Stalin, without benefit of such an ancient tradition, nonetheless became the best-known impresario of show trials that followed legal procedures. He was, ironically, the great Soviet law-giver, the father of the 1936 constitution (which lasted nearly until *perestroika*).[192] China in the early 1950s, like the Soviet Union before Stalin, had lawyers. The PRC had eight hundred legal offices in 1957. But in that year, "Many lawyers were regarded as rightists; so China had no lawyer system for twenty two years." By 1986, the national bar association was resurrected, and many cities followed suit with their own local bar associations. By 1988 throughout the PRC, 3,300 law offices and 27,000 lawyers were back in business.[193] The figure soon became higher.

An ancient Legalist habit, which persists in the PRC, is the nonpublication of laws. Counsels face difficulties if they do not know what the legal norms are. Although many detailed local regulations remained secret in the reforms, there was more effort in Shanghai than in most PRC jurisdictions to publish important rules. These came out in a legal compendium, widely distributed every year after the mid-1980s, in paperback at a nominal price, covering the most important municipal laws and regulations applicable then, no matter in what year they were passed since 1949. These rules were conveniently organized in sections on agriculture and industry, communications, construction, management, finance, market pricing, foreign trade, culture, labor, security, and other topics.[194] Even more publications describing Shanghai's laws could be bought in local bookstores by 1988.[195] Presumably people could cite them, if authorities tried to prevent actions that they showed to be within the law.

Legal education was popularized during reforms, no matter whether it was education to follow state dictates or education to learn about rights. Even the middle school curriculum was said to include a smattering of law by mid-1981, though this was largely advice to respect the police. A basic knowledge of law was included on the entrance exams for high schools and vocational schools.[196] Broadcast sermons about law became common on television. A thirty-four–part Shanghai television series on *The Effect of the Law* was published in book form.[197] This series for adults was not just civics moralizing; it offered detailed information on many kinds of legal procedures, and it tried to inform people of their rights. Popularization of this message required professionals; and they proliferated in Shanghai during the 1980s.

The number of Shanghai law firms by the end of 1987 was forty-four, including thirteen hundred lawyers.[198] All were still formally employees of the state, but their work required considerable autonomy. As was frequent during reforms, norms lagged behind behavior; so many lawyers were, at least in quasi-liberal eras, more independent of the state than many state cadres were. In May 1988, the "Li Guoji Law Office" was founded in Shanghai, the first to register under the personal name of a lawyer. Li was sixty-three years old, a graduate of the law department that Fudan University still had in 1952, and by 1957 already a right-ist. He could not practice law for twenty-two years and had become a factory worker. But in 1979, Li resumed his legal career. With the reforms of 1984, he could represent enterprises. His office by 1988 included eight lawyers, doing advocacy for more than ten big corporations and 118 small firms in Shanghai and the Yangzi River delta. This agency financed itself entirely, unlike prere-form legal offices that were inside the state bureaucracy. There was far more work than the lawyers could handle. "Several thousands" of potential cases had gotten as far as interviews, but the legal staff in this office had actually taken on fewer than one in twenty.[199]

A vice president of the China Lawyers' Association called in 1988 for more private law firms. Technically, all law offices were still state agencies, even though lawyers often disserved the interests of state cadres. Private or even collective ownership in the legal field was prohibited. But the association's advocate said this socialized system "lacks competition and adversely affects lawyers' initiative and creativeness." It also advocated more functional differen-tiation among lawyers: "We will gradually set up various specialized commit-tees, which will consist of some members of the Association and lawyers involved in various types of legal practice."[200]

By the summer of 1988, the minister of justice in Beijing was belatedly mooting the possibility that lawyers might form cooperative or collective legal firms that could represent clients in court.[201] Pressure for legal reform at this time came from southern provinces, whose economies needed it. The director of the Guangdong Judicial Department called for reform of "the old system in which the government controlled all legal offices." His counterpart in Fujian said that "legal offices of different forms should coexist," and a deputy director of the Shenzhen Judicial Bureau wanted "the opening of private legal offices."[202]

Five legal cadres, who quit their state jobs in late 1988 to form a Shanghai Cooperative Economic Law Office, were soon joined by seven others. This new lawyers' cooperative set up a hotline to provide twenty-four–hour responses on inquiries about its legal services. The group promised to handle urgent cases within one day—very much faster than the usual pace of the bureaucracy.[203]

In 1989, a directory of Chinese lawyers and offices summarized in sixty pages the special competences of Shanghai lawyers, with law office addresses and phone numbers. Jiangsu lawyers were covered in 37 pages—but the list for Zhejiang took 110 pages, including many in China's most reformed city, Wenzhou.[204] The number of lawyers remained tiny, in relation to the need for civil law in China's booming economy and for criminal law in its decentralizing coercive structure. A mid-1990s estimate noted that in America, 230 million people had 750,000 lawyers (one for every 300 people). In China, 1.2 billion people had 70,000 lawyers (i.e., one professional advocate for every 170,000 people).[205]

Lion Law vs. Fox Law

Party conservatives did not generally like lawyers. A CCP secretary was reported to opine at a public meeting, "There are several people in the law advisory office, and they always tend to support bad people. They stand opposed to the Party Committee. Can you in judicial and procuratorial organs get together to cope with them? Let us make a careful investigation of their behavior."[206] In the more reactionary periods of reform, young people who knew this stayed away from legal careers. Those admitted to law schools throughout China in 1990 fell from the previous year's 14,191 to 11,119, a 22 percent drop of new law students in one year.[207] During eras when more liberal foxes became prominent, however, legal professionals became more numerous and asserted their rights. Lawyers convened a national meeting in late 1990 to press for rules that would protect them against political persecution for doing their work—even when their advocacy on behalf of clients was disliked by high cadres.[208]

The Zhejiang procuracy, in the first quarter of 1989, sued in 27 percent more cases than during the same period of the previous year—including one trial of two high-ranking Party officials that was called "the most serious bribery ever to occur in the province since the founding of New China."[209] A city in Jiangsu established an "honest government mailbox" (*lianzheng xinxiang*) to receive public accusations against corrupt cadres.[210] The PRC auditor general in mid-August 1989 assessed fines of 51 million yuan against five state firms, including the China International Trust and Investment Corporation (CITIC) and the Chinese Rural Trust and Investment Corporation. The auditor admitted that these companies "have played positive roles in foreign trade, use of foreign investment, importing techniques and equipment, and economic development. . . . But activities violating administrative regulations exist in their management." They were found to have been "evading tax and buying and selling foreign currency without permission." The Rural Trust and Investment Corporation was said to have illegally drawn on massive savings deposits made by government and military units.[211] Criminality and corruption involved not just small actors in China, but also the largest state corporations trying to develop foreign and domestic trade, despite the will of conservatives to plan and tax everything. Serious reformers sometimes used courts successfully to bring large and famous state agencies within the bounds of law.

Use of the law against state entities or even peristatals was nonetheless very rare, and it had some success only when its politics were moot, situational, or monetary, rather than high-profile, normative, or symbolic. The most famous such case in Shanghai followed the firing of *World Economic Herald* editor Qin Benli by Jiang Zemin, then the top Party secretary in Shanghai (who was not Qin's boss, because the *Herald* was under the local Academy of Social Sciences). But Qin's independence threatened symbols of state control. When he was dismissed, a prominent group of intellectuals abroad wrote to Jiang, "By taking this step, you have trampled on freedom of speech and freedom of the press. You have contravened the Constitution."[212]

The *World Economic Herald* filed a civil suit against Jiang for "harming the reputation" of the newspaper because of his remark that its April 25, 1989, issue would "exacerbate certain factors for social disorder."[213] The staff issued an open letter entitled "The Truth of the Matter: Our Attitude and Demands," which called the sacking of Qin Benli "illegal." The letter said the Shanghai CCP had "acted in a simplistic and violent way" and had "hurt the image of the Party and government." Jiang tried to explain his action by contacting liberals in both Shanghai and Beijing, claiming that his goal was to preserve the *Herald* as a voice for reform. Many intellectuals publicly doubted his good faith. Jiang was not convicted; he was promoted to head the CCP.

Libel suits could be used by conservative bureaucrats, not just reformers, to discourage publicity for events that they wished to keep secret. For example, when a young woman gave birth to a girl (her husband wanted a son) her work supervisors supported the husband's action in evicting her from her home, sending her back to her natal family. A newspaper ran the story for its feminist content. Then the husband's mother threatened to sue the paper, unless it printed a retraction on the front page; and even bureaucrats in the young mother's work unit supported this litigation. The young mother, who by that time feared more serious reprisals from her relatives, denied having complained earlier to reporters about her treatment. The first such case that journalists won took nearly two years to prosecute.[214]

Courts in Postrevolutionary Social Diversifications

It is usual, during ebbs from revolutions, to have more business in courts that become relatively autonomous from the central state. The rise of common law courts, as distinct from prerogative courts, after Cromwell's revolution increased judicial independence. During the time of Charles I, the Court of Star Chamber, the Privy Council, and other courts would summon judges to hear royal policy before they went throughout the country on assize circuits. Local magistrates were subject to discipline by the Star Chamber or Council. But after the revolution, although common law courts did not neglect the power of the Crown, the demise of prerogative courts reduced the extent to which Charles II could change the law's application in local cases.[215] Judges were still supposed to be instruments of the Crown; but when the king conflicted with a group of them over an issue in 1672, he could not dismiss them quickly. When he finally succeeded in removing some judges, he was nonetheless constrained. It was "difficult too for the Crown to find adequate replacements to fill so many high judicial offices."[216] He needed them, as postrevolutionary PRC leaders did, because of their effect on the economy.

Conservatives and reformers could agree that law was a tool of economic development. As President Ren Jianxin of the Supreme People's Court said in late 1989, "At present, the people's courts center their work on serving economic construction and the reform program."[217] But about law as a tool for political change, there was disagreement. Reformers proposed many kinds of new laws, for example, for elections (which were passed) and for the press (on which no consensus could be reached). New economic laws had political results that often went beyond what conservatives wished.

Defining rights for managers and for property holders meant better-secured local powers. As an analyst of Chinese law put it:

> Legal institutions have in some respects reached such a level of sophistication that they can function as an ideology which masks the political functions of Party and state in administration, and serve to legitimate the political and economic orders.... New procedural law, which allows individuals to sue government, went into effect in 1990, and cases have skyrocketed. Yet in other respects, Party rule cannot be obscured.[218]

Statist norms persisted side by side with reformist changes. In 1988, the constitution was finally amended to recognize private property "within the framework of a socialist economy." Actually, some private property had existed earlier, and much collective property was de facto private.

Similarly, the constitution (like Stalin's of 1936) guaranteed freedom of speech. Yet this right is nowhere absolute, and the audience was deemed especially prone to panic in China's theaters, were someone to shout, "Fire!" Conservatives perceived the dangers as clearer and more immediate than reformers did. A Shanghai student, who returned to the city from the United States in 1985 but had joined the dissident Chinese Alliance for Democracy while abroad, was arrested during street demonstrations of January 1987. He was sentenced to two years' imprisonment on account of his "demagogic propaganda for counter-revolutionary ends," after a trial open to some Chinese only. This student's articles for the alliance's journal, *China Spring*, were the explicit cause of his incarceration. That organization's charter challenged the "four cardinal principles" (upholding the socialist road, the people's democratic dictatorship, Party leadership, and "Marxism-Leninism-Mao Zedong thought"—in short, CCP rule). A Shanghai Public Security Bureau cadre specified at a press conference that it was a crime to oppose socialism, a belief that the first article of the PRC constitution attempts to mandate for all Chinese.[219]

The Stalinist practice of committing political dissidents to asylums does not appear, at least in the many Chinese case files that a Western analyst has read.[220] Because the Ministry of Public Security administers some mental hospitals, there may well be exceptions. Although the Ministry of Public Health's mental hospitals contain many patients whose insanity can be linked to political campaigns, the government has reportedly seldom used psychiatric services as quasi-prisons for sane dissidents. Chinese practice on the commitment of people to psychiatric care nonetheless violates many norms of individual rights. Although patients' families are regularly consulted on whether insane members could be treated at home, the patients themselves are generally thought unfit to have any say in this. The CCP has followed so many Stalinist precedents in its coercive system, the apparent reticence to use psychiatric wards as prisons may at first seem surprising—until notice is made of the size of its "labor education" archipelago.

Rectitude and rights were conflicting themes during China's reforms. Sometimes lawyers stressed the need for law and order. At other times, they stressed the need for fairness. The legal presumption of innocence, as a rule befitting reform, became a cause for one writer in the *China Youth News:* "The principle has strong moral sense, because the protection of citizens' personal rights and respect for people's characters and reputations are interdependent.... In addition, the principle can push courts to seek justice."[221] This and other liberal ideals were common, albeit usually with less articulation, among Chinese intellectuals during reforms. Persuading the state to honor them was another matter.

A top Zhejiang lawyer, in an interview, said that prosecuting attorneys should not go all out to obtain convictions. Instead, they should consider the complexities of the cases with which they deal. When this prosecutor was assigned to pursue an assault case, for example, and the Public Security Bureau admitted that the balance of evidence was not against the accused, the attorney investigated the case herself. She found the evidence to be based on false information. So occasionally lawyers can change the minds of police about the people they have arrested.

A traffic case, in which a truck driver caused three deaths and thirty injuries, brought the man to court on very severe charges. A local leader, who had witnessed the accident, publicly demanded the maximum punishment. But local prosecutors, whose examination of the details of the case convinced them that the truck driver was not solely responsible for the extent of the tragedy, showed their independence by refusing to sue on the basis of the harsh original charges. A province-level lawyer was therefore brought in, at the behest of a prosecutorial committee (*jiancha weiyuan hui*). The court agreed with her opinion that charges should be brought for a lesser offense, and the driver was convicted on that ground.[222]

Quick economic change forced a need for whole new kinds of law. Environmental degradation, for example, became subject to more serious laws than before. Fake or mislabeled goods became subject to regulation, because the reform era brought a deluge of them. The protection of consumers' interests came up as a political topic. A national magazine propagated the need to educate consumers against accepting products that were unsafe, were of low quality, used counterfeit brands, or were sold at illegal prices or short-shipped. Laws were passed against goods that were never delivered after advance payments, that were based on deceitful mail-order ads, or that were tied to other sales.[223] False representations in a booming market raced ahead of the law in China as elsewhere, and the state was trying to catch up.

Progress against such abuses was slow, but at least some was publicized. When the wronged consumers were local collectives, they often had enough political clout to get their money back. When household appliances were imported to Shanghai from somewhere in Zhejiang, the Commerce Bureau in the metropolis would not let them be sold because they were found to be faulty. So the sales representative took them to Chuansha in the suburbs, thinking that would be a place "to avoid difficulties" (*bi nan suo*). He was wrong; the lemons were discovered and rejected there too.[224]

Consumer protection was supposed to be a concern of the legal system toward the turn of the decade. For example, the Luwan district court in early 1989 propagated rules on food cleanliness and on the quality of products sold in that area.[225] Luwan was an especially appropriate place for such rules, because shoddy shops selling fake goods on Daxing Street there had become notorious in Shanghai by the 1990s. "Daxing" became the standard Shanghainese phrase for commercial deceit.[226]

Statist Norms Without State Capacity

Nostalgic revolutionaries hoped to hide the extent of legal problems as much as to solve them. Litigation, especially when the state was directly involved, was serious—a symbolic challenge because of the *lèse-majesté* that would result if the government should lose in court. Conservatives expressed the view that public prosecutors, before coming to court, should remain totally secretive about cases. Periodic campaigns were launched to "plug leaks." In early 1991, it was announced that too much judicial information had been published. Officials "received specialized training in the art of guarding secrets."[227]

More open and adversarial procedures, however, emerged in reform Shanghai despite their tension with hierarchic norms. Private litigation in Shanghai soared during the late 1980s and early 1990s. Three types of civil disputes became particularly frequent: Divorce cases, especially, rose in number. Commercial disputes in Shanghai began to involve amounts of money unprecedented for the PRC, mostly for contract violations in deliveries or sales. The third largest number of cases was land-leasing disputes, both urban and suburban. The government published regulations in an attempt to clarify the ways of settling various kinds of conflicts between private or collective parties—but dispute resolution often followed irregular rules and involved implicit coercion, so many felt that legal decisions were often unjust. The main problem came after the verdicts: Especially after rulings in contract disputes, court mandates often became dead letters. Losing defendants simply did not obey them. A Hong Kong legal scholar informally estimated that the portion of contract violation decisions that were actually implemented was less than one-fifth.[228]

Like all other cadres in China, judges have bureaucratic grades. A decision from a court in another locality or functional system, especially if a higher-grade bureaucrat protects a defendant against whom a verdict is issued, becomes unenforceable. As a former president of the Supreme People's Court said in 1988, "the most outstanding problem in the administration of justice in the economic sphere" was the courts' inability to see that their decisions would mean something. As a county-level CCP secretary put it, "Tell me what matters more: official rank or the law? I can definitely tell you, rank matters more. Law is made by man; without man, how could there be law? Without man, how could law matter at all? That's why I say that rank matters more."[229]

This affects not just formal courts, but also the less stately forms of law. Donald Clarke has pointed out that no matter whether a settlement comes from mediation, arbitration, or adjudication, a much more important question concerns the bureaucratic relationship of the mediator-arbitrator or judge to the supervisors of the side that loses a case. Judgments mean much more, if both parties are under the same geographic or functional superior, so that the settlement is internal to an official system. If the decider is external, especially to the geographical or functional system of the loser, court rulings bring scant results. The court president often has a lower bureaucratic rank than the head of the jurisdiction over the party against whom a verdict is issued.

Despite such looseness in the legal system, statist legal norms remained strongly consensual among practically all Chinese. They did not necessarily follow these, but they verbally upheld them. Even reformist lawyers, if sympathetic to dissidents, could want to separate their specific legal work from their politics. Only on the legal work could they make progress. A lawyer defending artists in 1993 said, "I avoid speaking publicly of human rights and democracy. It's too dangerous. I work on individual cases in legal terms. The Chinese people have no idea of using the law to protect themselves. They imagine laws exist only to constrain them. We want to stand against that."[230]

The state was the litigator in criminal cases, but it was shown during the transitional reforms to be a decreasingly competent factor in civil cases. During later reforms, it was sometimes sued. New PRC regulations of August 1990 allowed foreign investors in China "to sue government officials for interference or other unfair treatment."[231] Chinese law could not in principle affirm foreigners' right to sue regime agents, while denying the same right to PRC citizens. Yet few such suits went far.

Shanghai's Huangpu district court twice turned down an appeal by long-time dissident Fu Shenqi against his sentence of re-education through labor in 1993, when conservatives nationally were concerned to show their toughness. He filed a civil suit against the government, alleging that it violated its own rules by not allowing him to present his case, and also by not allowing a public trial. Fu was detained for having argued with court officials.[232] Law was not, in this intellectualized view that was traditional in China, supposed to be a means for solving disputes so much as a place for the reassertion of stately truths. But reforms saw some suits against the government.

If disputing parties went to court, they lost control of the settlement. It was ordinarily better to coalesce locally, forge an agreement among the disputants, hide information from the state, and thus have matters settled.[233] Most political actors preferred to work without law, on a premise that they could pull together locally. The Chinese tradition, weakened only slowly during reforms, was to create ideal links with local officials—and to avoid conflicts. Modern law is normally a noisy field, but China's reforms changed the job of law more quickly than its style. In the long-term future, China's legal norms will almost surely reflect more of the diverse talents in its economy.

Notes

1. Anyone who wants a subtle read about a really fresh topic should look at James Belich, *Victorian Interpretation of Racial Conflict: The Maori, the British, and the New Zealand Wars* (Montreal: McGill-Queen's University Press, 1989 [orig. New Zealand, 1986]), here p. 335.
2. Quoted in Juan Linz, "Authoritarian and Totalitarian Regimes," in *Handbook of Political Science,* vol. 3, Fred Greenstein and Nelson Polsby, eds. (Reading, MA: Addison-Wesley, 1975), p. 206.
3. The word "sanctions" is used instead of "coercion" in the title of this chapter, even though "coercion" is more often cited by political scientists alongside "extraction," "legitimation," and "steering." Positive community-based incentives, not just negative coercion, are logically part of this subject.
4. Mao Zedong, *Selected Works of Mao Zedong* (Beijing: Foreign Languages Press, 1969), vol. 4, p. 418.
5. This way of relating Parsons's four functional types to Weber's three authority types has not been found elsewhere. See the source notes on the diagram in the introduction in Volume One. The terms for compliance types come from Amitai Etzioni, *A Comparative Analysis of Complex Organizations* (New York: Wiley, 1961).
6. The best application has been in the China field; see G. William Skinner and Edwin A. Winckler, "Compliance Succession in Rural Communist China: A Cyclical Theory," in *A Sociological Reader in Complex Organizations,* 2d. ed., Amitai Etzioni, ed. (New York: Holt, Rinehart & Winston, 1969), pp. 410–38.
7. See Andrew G. Walder, *Communist Neo-Traditionalism: Work and Authority in Chinese Industry* (Berkeley: University of California Press, 1986).
8. This sentence refers especially to Michel Foucault, *Discipline and Punish: The Birth of the Prison* (New York: Pantheon, 1977); and the previous sentence, to Gramsci (see note 9).
9. Antonio Gramsci, *Prison Notebooks* (New York: International Publishers, 1971), p. 229.
10. Benedict Stavis, *China's Political Reforms: An Interim Report* (New York: Praeger, 1988), pp. 3–4.
11. Richard Baum, in *Burying Mao: Chinese Politics in the Age of Deng Xiaoping*

(Princeton: Princeton University Press, 1994), traces eight such cycles, as suggested by Hu Qiaomu, from 1978 to 1993. Each involved a stage of loosening (*fang*) and then a period of tightening (*shou*).

12. This is, by origin, a difference between feudal French *ancien régime* macro-tyrannical law and modern bourgeois micro-tyrannical discipline. See Laura Engelstein (with reactions from Rudy Koshar and Jan Goldstein, and a reply by Engelstein), "*AHR* Forum; Combined Underdevelopment: Discipline and the Law in Imperial and Soviet Russia," *American Historical Review* (April 1993), pp. 338–81.

13. In addition to Engelstein's criticisms, there is also this problem of "false consciousness"—an evidentiary pothole to be avoided. But Foucault (like Marx and Gramsci and most of their critics) was an intellectual to a fault. Consciousness is not a Boolean variable—true or false, 1 or 0, wholly present or wholly absent—except for people who have to earn their keep by writing about it. It comes in many degrees of articulation. If these thinkers would speak of partial rather than false consciousness—often leading to unintended consequences and stupid mistakes—and if (as Scott says) they would not make the stately assumption that everyone else believes whatever the ruling intellectuals may deign to say, then they would be on much firmer ground.

14. All italics are in the original. Samuel L. Popkin, *The Rational Peasant: The Political Economy of Rural Society in Vietnam* (Berkeley: University of California Press, 1979), p. 109.

15. James C. Scott, *Domination and the Arts of Resistance: Hidden Transcripts* (New Haven: Yale University Press, 1990) and *Weapons of the Weak: Everyday Forms of Peasant Resistance* (New Haven: Yale University Press, 1985).

16. The most literary report is Carlo Levi, *Christ Stopped at Eboli* (New York: Farrar, Straus, 1947). One of the most comparative is Eric J. Hobsbawm, *Primitive Rebels* (Manchester: University of Manchester Press, 1959).

17. James C. Scott, *Domination and the Arts of Resistance*, p. 136.

18. The research of Michael Schoenhals, John Gerson, and others has lifted this veil to some extent, however. See Schoenhals, "The Organization and Operation of the Central Case Examination Group (1966–1979): Mao's Mode of Cruelty," *China Quarterly* 145 (March 1996), pp. 87–111.

19. An unintended effect, the Cultural Revolution, is explored in Lynn White, *Policies of Chaos* (Princeton: Princeton University Press, 1989).

20. Harry Hongda Wu spent nineteen years in the *laogai*, then lived in Berkeley, California before an ill-timed return to China and briefly to the PRC's gulag again. See *Post*, March 6, 1994.

21. This survey could have gone back a further ten years, to 1949, reaching much the same conclusion. But many still thought nostalgically of the early 1950s. *WHB*, October 12, 1979, reports a *Dangyuan ganbu dushu ban*.

22. *Hongkong Standard*, October 24, 1981.

23. *Shanghai shimin banshi zhinan* (Citizen's Practical Guide to Shanghai), Shanghai Municipal Government Office, ed. (Shanghai: Shanghai Renmin Chuban She, 1989), p. 49.

24. Zhang Renshou and Li Hong, quoted in Alan P. L. Liu, "The 'Wenzhou Model' of Development and China's Modernization," *Asian Survey* 22:8 (August 1992), p. 708.

25. Wang Xu, in a communication to the author, cited work by Chen Yongpin and Li Weisha in *Shehui yanjiu* (Sociological Studies) 5 (May 1991), pp. 31–36.

26. Ferdinand Mount, *The Subversive Family: An Alternative History of Love and Marriage* (New York: Free Press, 1992), quoted in *Wilson Quarterly* 17:1 (Winter 1993), p. 105.

27. The hamlets are sometimes called "natural villages," but this usage can become confusing. See Ishida Hiroshi, *Chūgoku nōson keizai no kiso kōzō: Shanhai kinkō nōson*

no kōgyōka to kindaika no ayumi (Rural China in Transition: Experiences of Rural Shanghai toward Industrialization and Modernization) (Kyôto: Kōyō Shobō, 1991), interpretation of a chart on p. 7.

28. Ibid. for the data only. None of this, of course, ensures that local leaders in a lineage always agree with one another. Compare the description of a Guangdong case in politically strenuous years, in Anita Chan, Richard Madsen, and Jonathan Unger, *Chen Village* (Berkeley: University of California Press, 1984). Compare especially Madsen's book on the same town, *Morality and Power in a Chinese Village* (Berkeley: University of California Press, 1984), which mentions that the most traditionalistic (for a while, Liuist) sublineage of Chens lived geographically in the center of the village.

29. For example, see Jean C. Oi, "Partial Market Reform and Corruption in Rural China," *Reform and Reaction in Post-Mao China: The Road to Tiananmen*, Richard Baum, ed. (London: Routledge, 1991), pp. 143–61.

30. See Barry Naughton, "Industrial Policy during the Cultural Revolution," in *New Perspectives on the Cultural Revolution*, William Joseph et al., eds. (Cambridge: Harvard University Press, 1991), pp. 153–81.

31. For example, see Lü Xiaobo, "Organizational Involution and Official Deviance: A Study of Cadre Corruption in China, 1949–93" (Ph.D. dissertation, Political Science Department, University of California at Berkeley, 1994), p. xiii.

32. On this topic in Heilongjiang, Northeast China, see Yan Yunxiang, *The Flow of Gifts: Reciprocity and Social Networks in a Chinese Village* (Stanford: Stanford University Press, 1995).

33. Jean-Louis Rocca, "Corruption and Its Shadow: An Anthropological View of Corruption in China," *China Quarterly* 130 (June 1992), pp. 413–14.

34. Mayfair Mei-hui Yang, "The Art of Social Relationships and Exchange in China" (Ph.D. dissertation, Anthropology Department, University of California at Berkeley, 1986), pp. 307–8. This dissertation has now been published as *Gifts, Favors, and Banquets: The Art of Social Relationships in China* (Ithaca: Cornell University Press, 1994).

35. A rational-action approach to corruption is discussed in Barrett McCormick, *Political Reform in Post-Mao China: Democracy and Bureaucracy in a Leninist State* (Berkeley: University of California Press, 1990), pp. 76–78.

36. See Lynn White, "Changing Concepts of Corruption in Communist China," in *Changes and Continuities in Chinese Communism: The Economy, Society, and Technology*, Yu-ming Shaw, ed. (Boulder: Westview, 1988), pp. 316–53.

37. Melanie Manion of the University of Rochester is studying corruption with a social choice approach.

38. See Lynn White, "Changing Concepts," pp. 316–53.

39. Thanks go to Li Cheng for reporting this to the author.

40. See Frank Parkin, "Strategies of Social Closure in Class Formation," in *The Social Analysis of Class Structure*, Frank Parkin, ed. (London: Tavistock Press, 1974), p. 3.

41. *CD*, February 9, 1988. Richard Solomon, *Mao's Revolution and the Chinese Political Culture* (Berkeley: University of California Press, 1971), describes an eating culture, although adoption of this Freudian interpretation seems optional. Frederic Wakeman Jr., *Strangers at the Gate: Social Disorder in South China, 1839–1861* (Berkeley: University of California Press, 1966), uses fewer assumptions to describe Cantonese views of the eating parasitism by Manchu bureaucrats in the middle of the last century

42. *LDB*, February 2, 1989.

43. See Bette Bao Lord, *Legacies: A Chinese Mosaic* (New York: Knopf, 1990), p. 151, where this is a recurring theme.

44. *CD*, October 20, 1988.

45. In China, "cultural" level refers merely to years of formal education, though this is

a revealing and dubious proxy for culture. The text above is based on calculations from *RMRB*, August 16, 1988.

46. See Richard Smith, "The Chinese Road to Capitalism," *New Left Review* 199 (May–June 1993), p. 98.

47. *CD*, March 16, 1989.

48. The term "circles of compensation" comes from Kent Calder, *Crisis and Compensation: Public Policy and Political Stability in Japan, 1949–1986* (Princeton: Princeton University Press, 1988).

49. *JFRB*, October 17, 1988.

50. *FBIS*, August 17, 1990, pp. 13–14, cited in Troy Shortell, "The Party-Building Campaign in China" (Senior thesis, Princeton University, Woodrow Wilson School, 1991), p. 50. Liu Binyan, China's most famous journalist reporting corruption, is discussed in other parts of this book.

51. Mayfair Mei-hui Yang, "The Art of Social Relationships," p. 184. See also Yan Yunxiang, *The Flow of Gifts*.

52. Ergun Özbudun, "Turkey: The Politics of Clientelism," in *Political Clientelism, Patronage, and Development,* S.N. Eisenstadt and René Marchand, eds. (Beverly Hills: Sage, 1981), p. 250.

53. This uses ideas from, but is not quite identical with, the stimulating interpretation in Mayfair Mei-hui Yang, "The Art of Social Relationships," pp. 295–96.

54. Andrew Solomon, "The Fine Art of Protest," *Post Magazine* (January 23, 1994), p. 8.

55. *SF*, May 14, 1990. Hong Kong almost surely has the world's highest per-capita expenditure on paging and wireless telephones. No one witnessing contemporary weekday *dim sum* there can fail to be impressed that the modular telephone on the table is now as standard as the pot of tea.

56. See Karl Deutsch, *The Nerves of Government: Models of Political Communication and Control* (Glencoe, IL: Free Press, 1963), and Deutsch's "Social Mobilization and Political Development," in *Comparative Politics: A Reader,* H. Eckstein and D. Apter, eds. (Glencoe, IL: Free Press, 1963), pp. 582–603.

57. Alan P. L. Liu, "Communications and Development in Post-Mao Mainland China," *Issues and Studies* 27:12 (December 1991), quotation from p. 79 and figures estimated from a graph on p. 80. This analysis, like many others, does not mention the early 1970s even though the figures it presents on them are clear.

58. Kenneth Jowitt, "Soviet Neo-Traditionalism: The Political Corruption of a Leninist Regime," *Soviet Studies* 35:3 (July 1983), pp. 275–97.

59. See Moshe Lewin, *The Gorbachev Phenomenon: A Historical Interpretation* (Berkeley: University of California Press, 1988), and Stephen F. Cohen, *Rethinking the Soviet Experience: Politics and History Since 1917* (New York: Oxford University Press, 1985).

60. Jean C. Oi, *State and Peasant in Contemporary China: The Political Economy of Village Government* (Berkeley: University of California Press, 1989); emphasis added.

61. For a clear statement on the difference between analytic and concrete categories, which is crucial to the case for classic functionalism, see Marion J. Levy Jr., "Structural-Functional Analysis," in *International Encyclopaedia of the Social Sciences,* David L. Sills, ed. (London: Macmillan, 1968), pp. 21–28.

62. Weber's three types of authority are ideal and analytical. They are adjectives that do not wholly exclude one another (rather than adjectives of the other kind, which do so). A leader may gain compliance from a follower for more than one reason simultaneously: because the leader is deemed to have some special insight into the charisma of truth, *and* to stand in a tradition of prophets, *and* to head an organization that provides utilitarian

benefits. These appeals can come all at the same time, even if one of the three potential reasons for compliance is most commonly cited. For a contrasting interpretation, which treats these types as mutually exclusive (and negative or positive sanctions from any of them also as mutually exclusive), see Andrew Walder, *Communist Neo-Traditionalism,* pp. 5–7 and passim.

63. In a book on *Policies of Chaos,* e.g., p. 319, the present author cites the links of clients to their official monitors, but also to the quasi-legal labels that helped create conflict groups and to the charismatic/totalitarian campaigns that served some individuals or frightened others, both before and during the Cultural Revolution. That book explicitly refers to all three of these categories of policy (campaigning, patronizing, and labeling) as Communist variants of efforts to gain compliance on grounds like those of Weber's authority types.

64. See Barrett L. McCormick, *Political Reform,* and Jean C. Oi, *State and Peasant.*

65. Jean C. Oi, *State and Peasant,* p. 226.

66. Andrew G. Walder, *Communist Neo-Traditionalism,* p. 10.

67. Recent work by Yeh Wen-hsin of the University of California at Berkeley is relevant here. Professor Yeh gave a seminar at Princeton in 1995, to which this author is indebted for such ideas.

68. These words are on the last two pages of the concluding chapter of Andrew G. Walder, *Communist Neo-Traditionalism,* pp. 252–53.

69. See Jean C. Oi, "Fiscal Reform and the Economic Foundations of Local State Corporatism in China," *World Politics* 45:1 (October 1992), pp. 99–126.

70. See Karl Polanyi, *The Great Transformation: The Social and Economic Origins of Our Time* (New York: Rinehart, 1944).

71. These were called the *zhixian zeren zhi* and the *zhixian juzhen zeren zhi.* The term "horizontal relations" (*hengxiang guanxi*) was used in this article with reference to links within offices of a company, although the more common use of this important reform phrase denotes market relations between different firms. *Shanghai jixie bao,* February 2, 1989.

72. *Hengxiang jingji lianhe de xin fazhan* (The New Development of Horizontal Economic Links), Shanghai Economics Association, ed. (Shanghai: Shanghai Shehui Kexue Yuan Chuban She, 1987), p. 179.

73. This change was predicted in Lynn White, *Careers in Shanghai* (Berkeley: University of California Press, 1978).

74. Quoted in Juan Linz, "Authoritarian and Totalitarian," p. 223.

75. See Alfred Stepan, *Rethinking Military Politics* (Princeton: Princeton University Press, 1988), which relies on direct interviews with very high military and intelligence officials (and ex-presidents), after their descents from power. Such a research context cannot yet be found in the PRC.

76. Two long-term projects are currently under way by scholarly members of the British Foreign Service: John Gerson is writing a political history of the current century as seen from behind the bars of Qincheng, China's most elite prison. David Chambers is writing about 1950s' United Front and police work in Shanghai by Pan Hannian and Yang Fan. See also Nicholas Eftimiades, *Chinese Intelligence Operations* (Hong Kong: Naval Institute Press, 1994). Other foreign and Chinese researchers are working on this—and some of them are secretive too, so few academics see their work.

77. Steven Sampson's term is quoted in Lü Xiaobo, "Organizational Involution," p. 352.

78. Corruption was the hottest topic among academics in the China field during the mid-1990s, as this current book was being edited. Among researchers on this subject at that time were: Michael Agelasto, Gao Xin, Ho Pin, Carol A.G. Jones, Julia Kwong, T. Wing Lo, Lü Xiaobo, Stephen K. Ma, Melanie Manion, James Mulverson, Gong Ting, Andrew Wedeman, Helen Xiaoyan Wu, and Kate Xiao Zhou.

79. *"Jingji zuian jubao zhongxin,"* or sometimes called *"jubao shi."* *JJRB*, July 7, 1988.

80. In Shenzhen, 54 percent of the crimes uncovered in the first stage of this program (apparently in 1987) were classified as "economic," including corruption, bribery, misuse of public funds, illegal income, and unlawful private transactions by officials. Although the intent of the program was to catch economic criminals, an almost equal number of charges (46 percent) arising from these investigations apparently did not involve money. A similar breakdown was not offered from the Shanghai program, which was just beginning; see ibid.

81. This "one-quarter," 27 percent, is calculated by the current author, assuming the rate at which procuracies received reports (presumably of cases) can be compared with the number of investigations begun. Nine-tenths of these (89.5 percent) were "handled" within the year 1989; but the process of choosing cases is very liable to involve local politics. This is a topic on which various scholars are now working. The current author has also computed the portions of expelled Party members (mentioned in the sentences after this footnote reference). See underlying numbers in *RMRB*, April 11, and *FBIS*, January 16, 1990, p. 17; also July 11, 1990, pp. 34–35; and *CD*, January 26, 1991. Some are cited in Troy Shortell, "The Party-Building Campaign," p. 17. *BR* (January 15–21, 1990), pp. 26–17, also deals with the telephone report centers.

82. A CCP secretary announced this at a regular bimonthly meeting (*shuangye zuotan hui*), which he held with "leaders of democratic parties and nonparty democratic persons" (*minzhu dangpai* and *wudangpai minzhu renshi*). *XMWB*, January 31, 1989.

83. A clear aspect of public feeling about corruption by the mid-1990s was that rumors about particular officials' malfeasance were almost always widely believed—with or without evidence. Mayor Huang Ju, who might have been more popular on the basis of his Ningbo background, had family members rumored to be involved in sharp businesses. The current author has no way to prove—or disprove—this and other rumored charges about high officials.

84. Many national leaders' children studied abroad, including the youngest son of Deng Xiaoping, who went to the University of Rochester in 1981; the daughter of Vice Premier Bo Yibo, who studied in Massachusetts; the daughters of Liu Shaoqi, who went to Boston University and to West Germany; a son of former foreign minister Chen Yi, who studied at the University of Texas; the son of Marshal Ye Jianying; who studied at Georgetown University; and the son of Huang Hua, who went to Harvard. But this is a very incomplete list. *FBIS*, November 5, 1986, p. K-4, reporting from *Hong Kong Standard*, November 3. A less common, more literary phrase for *taizi dang* is *yanei*.

85. This information comes from a Hong Kong Indian journalist for a business magazine. See Angelina Malhotra, "Shanghai's Dark Side: Army and Police Officers Are Once Again in League with Vice," *Asia, Inc.* 3:2 (February 1994), pp. 32–39; see also the comment from editor Sondhi Limthongkul, p. 4. The author's own discussions in Shanghai during the early 1990s confirmed the existence of vice rings involving not just family members of high officials but, reportedly, high officials themselves. He does not know which reports were true, but their commonalty was an obvious fact.

86. Angelina Malhotra, "Shanghai's Dark Side," p. 35.

87. The Malhotra article supplies such a map.

88. The most important was "a blue glass, neon-crowned tower called Shanghai Taiwan City." Ibid., p. 32.

89. This manager, whose club was jointly owned by the PSB and by "an anonymous Japanese group" that may have been like the underworld *yakuza* that made similar investments near Huaihai Road, had previously managed a nightclub at a hotel run by the army. See ibid., pp. 35–36.

90. One of these card sharks made 2,200 yuan in just fifteen rounds of poker. *Shanghai fazhi bao* (Shanghai Legal Paper), January 30, 1989.

91. This report comes from an oral source in Shanghai, January 1994, based on newspaper reports the author has not yet found.

92. *CD*, December 3, 1987.

93. *SHKXB*, March 23, 1989.

94. *Shehui* (Society), Shanghai, June 1985, p. 9.

95. Jennifer Roney, "Relaxing the Iron Hand: Crime under Perestroika" (Senior thesis, Politics Department, Princeton University, 1991), p. 2, quoting a Soviet statistical collection on crime. These published data were far more complete than their Chinese counterparts.

96. *Shanghai shehui xiankuang he qushi, 1980–1983* (Situations and Trends in Shanghai Society, 1980–1983), Zheng Gongliang et al., eds. (Shanghai: Huadong Shifan Daxue Chuban She, 1988), pp. 242–43, gives the percentages but not the absolute numbers. On the *zhongda xingshi* and *teda xingshi,* reported in the next paragraph, see ibid., p. 243.

97. Ibid., pp. 242–43, gives the percentages but not the absolute numbers.

98. These were the only two years on which specific figures were offered in ibid., p. 247.

99. The effective privatization of land led to disputes over "boundaries, water rights, and woodlands—the very stuff of which rural violence is traditionally made." See Elizabeth J. Perry, "Rural Collective Violence: The Fruits of Recent Reforms," in *The Political Economy of Reform in Post-Mao China,* Perry and Christine Wong, eds.(Cambridge: Harvard University Press, 1985), p. 179.

100. On this suburban crime statistic, which fluctuated a good deal but generally rose from a low base, see *Shanghai shehui xiankuang,* p. 250.

101. This report combines two sources: Borge Bakken, "Crime, Juvenile Delinquency, and Deterrence Policy in China," *Australian Journal of Chinese Affairs* 30 (July 1993), pp. 30 and 38, and reports of Zheng Yongnian from *Shehui xue yanjiu* (Sociological Research) 6 (June 1989).

102. Ruan Chongwu did not join the CCP until 1952, after which he studied automotive engineering in Moscow. The identification card system, which allowed people to travel within China more easily, was established during Ruan's term as minister.

103. Roger Faligot and Rémi Kauffer, *The Chinese Secret Service,* trans. Christine Donougher (London: Headline, 1989), p. 430.

104. An interviewee reports that these police were explicitly responsible for internal security, the patrol of internal (e.g., interprovincial) borders, some fire fighting, and the security of some high officials.

105. See Hong Kong *Wenhui bao,* August 28, 1988.

106. See Joseph J. Wright Jr., *The Balancing Act: A History of Modern Thailand* (Oakland, CA: Pacific Rim Press, 1991), whose Paretan analysis remained germane to Thai politics even after his book was published.

107. Summarized in the premier book on deviance under Communism, Walter D. Connor, *Deviance in Soviet Society: Crime, Delinquency, and Alcoholism* (New York: Columbia University Press, 1972), p. 14.

108. The clapping crowd was in Lanzhou, Spring Festival, 1991. Kunming's prominence in such reports relates to the ability of Yunnan (and adjacent Burma and Laos) to grow opium; Chengdu's may relate to its status as the capital of China's most populous province. See Borge Bakken, "Crime, Juvenile Delinquency," pp. 50–56; the quotation on p. 56.

109. This ministry is the *Gongan bu.* Roger Faligot and Rémi Kauffer, *The Chinese Secret Service,* p. 435.

110. *Post,* January 20, 1989, and separate interviews with two residents of Guangzhou, one of whom was a teacher who had long discussions with his students at a local university about their liking for capital punishment.

111. See Lü Xiaobo, "Organizational Involution," pp. 267–69.

112. Solomon M. Karmel, "The Neo-Authoritarian Contradiction: Trials of Developmentalist Dictatorships and the Retreat of the State in Mainland China" (Ph.D. dissertation, Politics Department, Princeton University, 1995), p. 418, quoting *FBIS,* October 12, 1993, p. 23.

113. *Kuai bao,* Hong Kong, October 26, 1990.

114. Jennifer Carter in *The Restored Monarchy, 1660–1668,* J.R. Jones, ed. (London: Macmillan, 1979), pp. 83–84, characterizes the harsh sentences given after the "Popish Plot" and the "Bloody Assizes," and she also gives a broad description of late Stuart civil law.

115. Michael Schoenhals, "The Organization . . . Mao's Mode of Cruelty," pp. 87–111, especially p. 88.

116. See Lynn White, "The Liberation Army and the Chinese People," *Armed Forces and Society* 1:3 (May 1975), pp. 364–83.

117. William W. Whitson (with Huang Chen-hsia), *The Chinese High Command: A History of Military Politics* (New York: Praeger, 1973).

118. The Suppression of Counterrevolutionaries was decreed in October 1950, and as a formal movement it was mostly completed within a year. But it set urban political precedents for more extensive coercion in 1957 and 1966–69, which began to ebb only in the 1970s.

119. These were the ministers of defense and public security, a deputy director in the Central Committee's office, and the Party secretary of a border province, Inner Mongolia. See Li Cheng, "The Rise of Technocracy: Elite Transformation and Ideological Change in Post-Mao China" (Ph.D. dissertation, Politics Department, Princeton University, 1991), p. 138.

120. The data from the interview with an editor were roughly confirmed by a later yearbook, which reported 882 *Wenhui bao* employees in the next year. *Zhongguo xinwen nianjian, 1990* (China Journalism Yearbook, 1990), Chinese Academy of Social Sciences Media Research Unit, ed. (Beijing: Zhongguo Shehui Kexue Yuan Chuban She, 1991), p. 341.

121. June Teufel Dreyer, "The Demobilization of PLA Servicemen and Their Reintegration into Civilian Life," in *China's Defense and Foreign Policy,* June Dreyer, ed. (New York: Paragon, 1988), especially pp. 320–21.

122. *FBIS,* December 11, 1984, p. 1, reporting radio of December 8.

123. The commissars, although they were not career military officers, had some battle command roles even though they reported to the Party. Trotsky's organizational model does not inform Chinese practice (just as the Communist totalitarian model as a whole fails to cover much evidence from Communist regimes). See Cheng Hsiao-shih, *Party–Military Relations in the PRC and Taiwan: Paradoxes of Control* (Boulder: Westview, 1990), p. 148.

124. *RMRBHWB,* November 10, 1987. Apparently these retirements were from units as high as company (*lian*) level.

125. Ellis Joffe, *The Chinese Army After Mao* (London: Weidenfeld and Nicolson, 1987).

126. The geographical origins of these officers—almost nine-tenths of whom had joined the army before Liberation—were striking: 27 percent from Shandong, and 21 percent from Hebei. See Li Cheng and Lynn White, "The Army in the Succession to Deng Xiaoping: Familiar Fealties and Technocratic Trends," *Asian Survey* 33:8 (August 1993), pp. 757–86.

127. Concerning the retirements that vacated these posts, see June Teufel Dreyer, "The Demobilization," pp. 297–326.

128. For China, this argument is suggested by Cheng Hsiao-shih, *Party–Military Relations*.

129. U.S. Congress, Joint Economic Committee, *China: A Reassessment of the Economy* (Washington: Government Printing Office, 1975), p. 462, has a graph by Sydney H. Jammes on this drop in China's military procurement (by approximately one-quarter) in 1972 below 1971.

130. John Childs, *The Army of Charles II* (London: Routledge and Kegan Paul, 1976), p. 218.

131. The paragraphs above—notably the critical tone in them—are based on interviews with Chinese economists.

132. The author attended an exhibit of army factories' civilian products, ranging from cosmetics to heavy machines, at the Beijing Museum of Military History in the summer of 1987. *CD*, February 1, 1988.

133. *FBIS*, December 12, 1984, p. 4, reporting radio of December 8.

134. *FBIS*, December 19, 1984, p. 3, reporting radio of December 17.

135. *FBIS*, December 7, 1984, p. 1, reporting radio of December 6.

136. Although civilian products are made in army plants, the China North Industries Corporation also makes land arms, the China Precision Machinery Import-Export Corporation makes missiles, the China Aviation Technology Import-Export Corporation produces planes, the China State Shipbuilding Corporation does what its title suggests, as does the China Electronics Import-Export Corporation; but the China Nuclear Energy Industry Corporation makes bombs too. Also, the PLA controls the Great Wall Corporation. Many of these titles contain the words "import-export," and all of them have foreign clients and are mandated to raise foreign exchange. Jane's Information Group, *China in Crisis: The Role of the Military* (Coulsdon, Surrey: Jane's Defense Data, 1989), p. 69.

137. John Frankenstein, "The People's Republic of China: Arms Production, Industrial Strategy, and Problems of History," in *Arms Industry Limited,* Herbert Wulf, ed. (Oxford: Oxford University Press, 1993), pp. 276–77 and 299, provides a more full presentation.

138. *Post,* December 29, 1993.

139. Quoted by Harlan Jencks in *Forces for Change in Contemporary China,* Lin Bih-jaw and James T. Myers, eds. (Taipei: Institute for International Relations, 1992), p. 106.

140. Oral information from analyst Cheung Tai Ming, at a spring 1994 talk in Hong Kong.

141. A distinguished Western sinologist gave an academic paper in mid-1994 at a conference in China, where he was roundly scolded by a senior PLA officer for asserting (with documentation) the extent of the army's involvement in civilian work. The scholar's data were good and germane, but the officer apparently thought foreigners would fear the Chinese army less, if information about its civilian involvements were published. He apparently thought nonmilitary work would weaken the army.

142. Roberto Unger is identified with the statist view, but his account has been criticized. Alison Conner of the University of Hong Kong stresses some systematic traits of Chinese law. For further references, see Philip C.C. Huang, "The Paradigmatic Crisis in Chinese Studies: Paradoxes in Social and Economic History," *Modern China* 17:3 (July 1991), pp. 322–23.

143. *Zhongguo gongchan dang dangyuan da cidian* (Dictionary for CCP Members), Cheng Min, ed. (Beijing: Zhongguo Guoji Guangbo Chuban She, 1991), in the appendices, pp. 701–26, gives documentation from the Eighth Party Congress of 1956, then also of 1969 (the 9th), 1973 (10th), 1977 (11th), 1982 (12th), and 1987 (13th).

144. James P. Brady, *Justice and Politics in People's China: Legal Order or Continuing Revolution?* (New York: Academic Press, 1982), p. 234, makes this one interesting point.

145. Revision of older views of Zhou's politics, showing his coerciveness, is furthered in Michael Schoenhals, "The Organization . . . Mao's Mode of Cruelty," pp. 87–111.

146. This description of Harold Garfinkel's views is written as general sociology, without any reference to Chinese or any other cultural tendencies, by Walter W. Powell and Paul J. DiMaggio, in their edited book, *The New Institutionalism in Organizational Analysis* (Chicago: University of Chicago Press, 1991), p. 20.

147. Jerome Alan Cohen, "Chinese Law: At the Crossroads," *China Quarterly* 53 (January–March 1973), p. 138. The law-as-a-state-secret position has been slow to change in China. In a 1992 article, Donald Clarke remarks offhandedly in a note, "It is still extremely difficult to obtain reliable information about the functioning of courts." That is a particularly concise statement of what many researchers have found. See Donald C. Clarke, "Dispute Resolution in China," *Journal of Chinese Law* 5:2 (Fall 1990), p. 245.

148. Tocqueville also says, "I do not know whether the jury is useful to those who are in litigation, but I am certain it is highly beneficial to those who decide the litigation," and he calls a jury "a free public school." See *Alexis de Tocqueville on Democracy, Revolution, and Society,* John Stone and Stephen Mennell, eds. (Chicago: University of Chicago Press, 1980), pp. 90–91.

149. See ibid. Tocqueville noted that judges are inherently undemocratic, while ordinary people are inconsistent at law. The strength of the judge-and-jury system is that each of these parts makes up for the weaknesses of the other.

150. Stanley Lubman has been a major contributor in this area, starting very early with "Mao and Mediation: Politics and Dispute Resolution in Communist China," *California Law Review* 55:5 (November 1967), pp. 1284–1359.

151. This paragraph relies almost totally on work by Donald C. Clarke, a former student of the author who is teaching at the University of Washington School of Law. See Clarke's lucid articles "Dispute Resolution" and "What's Law Got to Do with It? Legal Institutions and Economic Reform in China," *UCLA Pacific Basin Law Journal* 10:1 (Fall 1991), pp. 1–76.

152. Jerome Alan Cohen, "Chinese Law," p. 142.

153. Franklin P. Lamb, "An Interview with Chinese Legal Officials," *China Quarterly* 66 (June 1976), pp. 324–25.

154. Legal cases in two surveys this author has scanned suggest much activity by legal mediation committees in the early 1970s. The PRC compilers may have been reluctant to include cases in which mediation committees' decisions were later reversed by formal courts. A very few summaries on early 1970s court hearings are in *Dalu hunyin jicheng fa* (Mainland Marriage and Inheritance Law), Xu Penghua and Chang Feng, eds. (Taibei: Weili Falü Chuban She reprint of a PRC case book, 1989). See also *Dalu ruhe jiejue minshi jiufen* (How the Mainland Solves Civil Disputes), Chang Feng, Yang Jiandong, and Qiu Haiyang, eds. (Taibei: Weili Falü Chuban She reprint of a PRC case book, 1988), a scan of which suggests that other civil disputes seldom reached settlement in the 1970–74 era. But these books only offer heuristic, illustrative examples of precedents in categories of legal interest. They do not claim to be representative in any other sense, and so they are only suggestive rather than adequate for drawing firm conclusions about changing levels of formal court activity over time. Information on the exact year of final court adjudication is not available on all the civil cases (about 400 of them) in these two compendia together. A back page of the 1988 book advertises yet a third, compiled and published in the same way but not yet located by the current author and left for analysis by proper legal scholars: *Dalu ruhe jiejue shangwu jiufen* (How the Mainland Solves Commercial Disputes). Neil Diamant receives the author's best thanks for alerting him to the existence of these legal compendia, which will surely receive much further and more refined analysis by legal scholars.

155. Chen Benlin et al., *Gaige kaifang shenzhou jubian* (Great Change in the Sacred Land [China] During Reform and Opening) (Shanghai: Jiaotong Daxue Chuban She, 1984), p. 124.

156. The province and county are not divulged, perhaps because the purpose of the compendium is only to present precedents, but the 1973 revival of a court is clear. Formally, a 1966 court's denial of divorce in this case was not reversed until July 1976, although legal officials were working on the complexities by 1973. Further case research of this sort is being done by scholars in the legal field. See *Dalu hunyin*, p. 125.

157. This functional interpretation differs from totalitarian views of China's legal system, from views that might explain its changes by Chinese or neo-Communist organizational traditions, and also from the romantic view presented in Victor H. Li, "Law and Penology: Systems of Reform and Correction," in *China's Developmental Experience*, Michel Oksenberg, ed. (New York: Praeger, 1973), pp. 144–56.

158. The "more than a fifth" is 22 percent, or 251,000 cases. The "30 percent" are 76,000 cases, and the remainder are 175,000. Percentages have been calculated mostly from raw figures in *JFRB*, September 5, 1980. The figure in the next sentence can be checked because the article also says that 9 percent of the verdicts on ordinary criminal cases were changed, as compared with 64 percent for the political cases.

159. The quoted phrase was *"wailai de ganshe."* See *JFRB*, September 5, 1980.

160. Jiang Zemin et al., *Shanghai dangzheng jigou yange* (The Transformation of Shanghai's Party and Administration) (Shanghai: Shanghai Renmin Chuban She, 1988), p. 133.

161. *JFRB*, December 29, 1979.

162. For more on letters to the editor, see other sections of this book on the media and gathering views. *JFRB*, December 29, 1979.

163. *"Dianxing anjian." JFRB*, December 29, 1979.

164. *"Yuan, jia, cuo an."* Ibid.

165. *JFRB*, December 22, 1979.

166. *WHB*, October 5, 1980. An informant from China guessed that a suspended death penalty against a Cultural Revolution criminal, of this sort, in all probability would not have been carried out.

167. *JFRB*, October 7, 1979.

168. Ibid. The total number of Beijing cadres at this time was given as 328,000; and the total number of them subject to mistaken verdicts was 56,000.

169. Jiang Zemin et al., *Shanghai dangzheng*, p. 148.

170. The quoted phrase is *"ying chengdan jingji zeren."* The 1979 figure for contracted coal was 40,000 metric tons; 1981, 800,000; and 1982, 1.1 million. *Shanghai jingji, neibu ben: 1949–1982* (Shanghai Economy, Internal Volume: 1949–1982), Shanghai Academy of Social Sciences, ed. (Shanghai: Shanghai Shehui Kexue Yuan Chuban She, 1984), p. 683.

171. *CD*, June 6, 1986.

172. Ibid.

173. Edward J. Epstein, "China's Legal Reforms," in *China Review*, Kuan Hsin-chi and Maurice Brosseau, eds. (Hong Kong: Chinese University Press, 1991), pp. 9.15–16.

174. Liu Jinghuai et al., in *LW* 41 (November 1988), p. 14.

175. *SHTJNJ90*, p. 380.

176. *NCNA*, November 27, 1987.

177. *FBIS*, December 4, 1987, p. 25, reporting a journal of December 3.

178. Fifteen of the 210 joint ventures in which Jiangsu participated at mid-1988 were located in other provinces. *CD*, August 3, 1988, also cheerfully volunteered, "Work put in by prisoners has proved to be beneficial for them and for the [Jiangsu] economy. The

export production value of prison factories in the province totalled more than 57 million *yuan* last year." Prison-made exports became an international issue by 1989—but the issue, beyond standard protectionism, involved the reasons why some prisoners were jailed, not the matter of whether prisons can properly finance themselves.

179. Pitman B. Potter, "Riding the Tiger: Legitimacy and Legal Culture in Post-Mao China," *China Quarterly* 138 (June 1994), p. 351.

180. *Huadong xinxi bao,* January 28, 1989.

181. Ibid.

182. Barrett L. McCormick, *Political Reform,* p. 126.

183. Liu Jinghuai et al., in *LW* 41 (November 1988), p. 14.

184. *RMRBHWB,* September 29, 1988.

185. *FBIS,* December 21, 1984, p. 4, reporting radio of December 19.

186. These could be overestimates. *RMRB,* October 7, 1988, reported in *CD,* October 8.

187. Kate Xiao Zhou, *How the Farmers Changed China* (Boulder: Westview, 1996; and Ph.D. dissertation, Politics Department, Princeton University, 1994), chap. 8 of thesis, p. 12. See also Ansley J. Coale et al., "Recent Trends in Fertility and Nuptiality in China," *Science* 251 (1991), p. 390.

188. *XMWB,* January 30, 1980.

189. Interview with a knowledgeable foreign economist in Shanghai, June 1991.

190. *XMWB,* January 10, 1989, uses a somewhat old term when it refers to *chuanmin.* Gangs among this subethnic group, which was generally despised by Jiangnan business families, were common before 1949 and were often associated with conservative secret societies. Robbery of contraband is, of course, a lucrative practice among illegal gangs in many countries.

191. On the Legalists, see William T. de Bary, *Sources of Chinese Tradition,* vol. 1 (New York: Columbia University Press, 1960).

192. See Robert Sharlet, in *Stalinism,* Robert C. Tucker, ed. (New York: Norton, 1977).

193. Zhang Yijun in *LW* 41 (November 1988), pp. 14 and 16.

194. See, for example, *Shanghai shi fagui guizhang huibian, 1949–1985* (Compendium of Laws and Regulations of Shanghai City, 1949–1985) (Shanghai: Shanghai Renmin Chuban She, 1986).

195. *Shanghai shi fagui guizhang huibian, 1986–1987* (Compendium of Laws and Regulations of Shanghai Municipality, 1986–1987), Public Affairs Office and Legal System Office of the Shanghai People's Government, ed. (Shanghai: Shanghai Renmin Chuban She, 1988).

196. *Post,* August 9, 1981.

197. Each broadcast episode, or chapter in the book, is called a "talk session" (*jiangzuo*). See Xu Yiren and Cheng Pu, *Falü de shixiao wenti* (Issues of Legal Effectiveness) (Shanghai: Shanghai Shehui Kexue Yuan Chuban She, 1988).

198. *FBIS,* December 4, 1987, p. 25, reporting a journal of December 3.

199. Cheng Maodi in *LW* 41 (November 1988), p. 11.

200. *CD,* January 26, 1988.

201. Interview, August 1988, with a member of the Law Research Institute of the Shanghai Academy of Social Science.

202. *Beijing Review* 31:28 (July 11, 1988), p. 15.

203. *XMWB,* December 25, 1988.

204. *Zhongguo lüshi he lüshi gongzuo jigou* (Chinese Lawyers and Legal Work Units), Huang Min et al., eds. (n. p. [Beijing?]: Falü Chuban She, 1989).

205. Wang Hongying, "Transnational Networks and Foreign Direct Investment in China" (Ph.D. dissertation, Politics Department, Princeton University, 1996), chap. 2, p. 21.

206. Liu Jinghuai et al., in *LW* 41 (November 1988), p. 14.

207. *Zhongguo falü nianjian, 1990* (China Law Yearbook, 1990) (Chengdu: Zhongguo Falü Nianjian Chuban She, 1990), p. 378.

208. *CD*, October 23, 1990.

209. *CD*, April 15, 1989.

210. This was in Huaiyang city. See *Shanghai fazhi bao*, January 30, 1989.

211. *CD*, August 17, 1989.

212. *Post*, May 1, 1989.

213. *Post*, May 3, 1989.

214. *Post*, December 15, 1988. The Chinese paper involved was the *People's Daily*, which ran a photo of the mother in tears, holding her baby girl.

215. Jennifer Carter in *The Restored Monarchy, 1660–1668*, p. 86.

216. Ibid., p. 87.

217. *CD*, October 3, 1989.

218. Edward J. Epstein, "China's Legal Reforms," p. 9.3.

219. The case of Yang Wei is described in *FBIS*, December 21, 1987, pp. 15–16, reporting three articles.

220. See Veronica Pearson, "Law Rights, and Psychiatry in the People's Republic of China," *International Journal of Law and Psychiatry* 15 (1992), pp. 409–23.

221. *CD*, June 27, 1988.

222. The term "prosecutor" is used here because it is a valid translation of *jiancha yuan* and is understandable to most English readers, though "public prosecutor" or "procurator" would be more usual in legal texts. See *Lüshi yu fazhi* (Lawyers and the Legal System), Hangzhou (January–February 1989), p. 23.

223. *FBIS*, March 9, 1988, p. 42, reporting a journal of January 1988.

224. *Huadong xinxi bao*, January 28, 1989.

225. *Shanghai fazhi bao*, January 30, 1989.

226. The author thanks his friend Cheng Li for this report.

227. *Post*, March 16, 1991.

228. Conversation with an instructor of law in Hong Kong, who made a well-educated guess on the basis of many news reports.

229. "Contempt of court" was not a violation under Chinese law, at least into the 1990s, although various other provisions were substituted for it. See Donald C. Clarke, "Dispute Resolution," pp. 263 and 265. The text paragraphs here are indebted to this article by Clarke and, to a lesser extent also, to his "Regulation and its Discontents: Understanding Economic Law in China," *Stanford Journal of International Law* 28:2 (1992), pp. 283–322. Anyone with specialized interests in this subject should read these essays.

230. Quoted in Andrew Solomon, "The Fine Art," p. 11.

231. *Asian Wall Street Journal*, August 8, 1990.

232. *Post*, December 29, 1993.

233. A decision rule associated with reform China is fairly common in out-of-court settlements everywhere. See Susan L. Shirk, *The Political Logic of Economic Reform in China* (Berkeley: University of California Press, 1993), chap. 7.

Chapter 3.2

The Control of Social Groups

Often without noticing that they do so, the dominant groups project their own experience as representative of humanity as such.

—Iris Young[1]

The political control of groups such as workers, students, and intellectuals is a topic that liberal readers might think are most naturally considered from the viewpoints of individuals. Workers, academics, students, and job seekers do not generally conceive of themselves as elements to be welded together to serve a coherent political system. Yet their school admissions or rejections, employment or unemployment, and promotions or retirements are subject to powerful constraints, many of which are collective. People in workplaces, classrooms, or family contexts may often be most concerned with themselves or their immediate small groups, but decisions made by larger collective agencies set the parameters of their careers. It is possible to take their individual meanings and situations into account, while at the same time taking seriously the collective checks that affect them.

Workers

Employment and Promotion

Job allocations are the most obvious means by which central or local authorities try to guide employees. In Shanghai, as reforms began, a considerable proportion of the unemployed people had recently returned to the city from which they had been forced out in 1968–69, as "educated youths" sent to rural areas. It is clear that most wished to return for work in the metropolis, and a majority actually did

368

return to Shanghai by the mid-1980s. A 1979 rule specified that, "a former Shanghai intellectual youth who went elsewhere from January 1968 to October 1976 can apply to return to Shanghai, if he or she is currently working outside the city, is unmarried, has lost a husband or wife, or is a cadre."[2]

This rule did not mention employment for the return migrants, but their influx created a need for new jobs. Just as the central Party's policies for a green revolution had inadvertently created a later need for rural industries to absorb labor in the countryside, so also the Party's policy for "sending down" youths from city schools later created an unplanned need for urban jobs. Many of these youths returned to cities, and police had decreasing resources to keep them away. The state sector could not generate enough new jobs for them. Collectives in and around Shanghai during the reform boom relieved this problem by creating new jobs—and served the state by doing so because many returnees were politically restive, often angry at the officials who had sent them to the boondocks. The government had no option but to help many of these former "educated youths," no longer young, to find employment. From 1976 to 1982 in Shanghai, 1,563,000 people (one-seventh of the city's average population in those years) received work.[3]

By no means could the state system provide all these new jobs. After the Cultural Revolution, city officials approved having collectives hire returned youths. This trend kept many potential discontents busy. Immigrant returnees nonetheless obtained jobs only with great difficulty, especially in large cities such as Shanghai. As Chapter 1.5 on migrations shows, the first major reflux of youths came to smaller cities in the early 1970s. Returnees were politically active by 1976 in protests that called for quicker reforms then, and pressure from them eroded the coercive resources of police to keep them away. By October 1979, the whole country already had more than 8 million urban people "waiting for employment." Fully 57 percent of those officially listed then as needing jobs were educated youths who had come back to their native cities.[4]

The return of these potential dissidents was officially recognized and accelerated in the late 1970s; but it began long before then and forced the planning state to relinquish much of its control over urban jobs. In just two years, from 1977 to 1979, six hundred thousand people received work in Shanghai. This was as many as found employment there in the whole decade of the Third and Fourth Five-Year Plans together. The employment was largely outside state firms. Two-thirds of the new employees were hired in 1979, the same year that the labels of "rightists" were removed. More than seventy thousand went into light industrial jobs, and ten thousand into construction, food industries, transport, or public utilities. The jobs that many took did not require much education, although the program was publicly justified for "educated youths." The great majority went into collectives.

Replacement of Retirees as an Excuse for Local Hiring

One-third of the migrants to Shanghai urban districts from 1978 to 1986 were allowed to register permanently, because they were supposed to replace retiring workers.[5] In 1978 and the four following years, 550,000 sons and daughters of retired workers took their parents' jobs in Shanghai.[6] This number is higher than the total registered immigration to Shanghai during those years, and there is evidence that most returning "educated youths" got jobs in collectives and that most of their parents worked for state firms—and were not, in fact, required to retire immediately.[7] The substitution (*dingti*) rule could be used by managers to patronize workforces locally, not just for returning ex-rusticates. Many collectives were "attached firms" (*guahu*) of state enterprises, and the state's political need for urban job creation led to less central restraints on hiring than had been normal in previous years. High official permission for a parent to pass a job to an offspring in the state sector began in 1979, but this practice had sometimes occurred earlier. Time lags of retirements after "replacements," and diffuse links between state and collective firms, created a flexible situation in which local managers could act as they wished. The replacement rule was not officially abolished until 1986.[8] Even while it was in force, its main effect was not replacement but, rather, greater authority for local leaders to create jobs.

Many re-registrations of youths in Shanghai came on the official-ritual presumption of parental retirements that did not soon take place.[9] Especially after offspring had their urban residence rights restored, they could search for other jobs too. Local collusion between companies' public security offices and workers' families became impossible for central bureaucrats to prevent, even though it readmitted to cities large numbers of young people who had sharp grievances against earlier state policies. The practice of registering offspring in view of parents' prospective retirements had been known at Shanghai in the 1968–77 decade, when 9 percent of new registrations in the city were justified on this basis. (Earlier years averaged 1 or 2 percent.) By the 1980s, "searching for replacement work" (*zhaogong dingti*) was the most frequently recorded reason resulting in successful applications for new permanent registration in Shanghai. It accounted for twice as many legal immigrants as the next highest reason for registration, the "return of educated youth to the city," which is closely related but did not involve the promise of retirements.

Youths who "returned to the city to take work" were often associated, through relatives' employment, to factories that lacked the resources to hire them. Recent graduates and unemployed youths could benefit when a firm without state-approved vacancies might nonetheless declare such people in its "ranks of collective young workers." These "staff of a collective nature" (*jiti xingzhi de zhigong*) were not necessarily counted among those eligible for the centrally approved rosters of posts, but they could be employed by local managers.[10] Factory cadres often supported the careers of their regular workers' offspring. The lack of a central mandate to do this, and the sporadic state rules discouraging it, did not prevent new hires.

A survey of workers in the state-owned Shanghai steel industry indicated a sharp rise in the number of young returnees at the end of the 1970s. Only 10 percent of the steel workers were below age twenty-eight in 1966, but the portion rose to 26 percent in 1975, and then to 50 percent by 1981. Half of these young workers (49 percent) were on the "first line" of production, over four-fifths of whom were engaged in the hard jobs of "ordinary" steel making. One-fifth were in administrative work, mostly as technicians. Not all the laborers came into steel mills by replacing their parents; 14 percent of all staff by 1983 had done so, and they comprised 67 percent of the steel workers below age twenty-eight.[11] The replacement system shaped the employment practices of state firms strongly; but it did not achieve the state's aim of capping total wage budgets by balancing each new hire with a retirement. This official collective goal was tangential to the motives of Shanghai youths and their families. So the locals used it as a normative rationale, while largely ignoring it in their practical behavior.

Returnees came back to Shanghai not mainly for jobs like the ones their parents held, but for lives in the city that were better than the ones most of the older generation had endured. "Replacement" within the old system was not their sole purpose. Many knew that their hopes of promotion and prosperity would require more education than their parents had. In the first eight months of 1980 alone, thirty thousand Shanghai workers applied to spare-time universities; but their employing units prevented more than a third of them from attending. Cadres in many units refused to affix official chops to the enrollment documents, which therefore could not be filed. Factory personnel officials reportedly threatened that if workers took up study, deductions would be made from bonuses and wages. They would not promote employees who sought more education. Many firms would not subsidize education, on grounds that such learning would not serve their corporate aims. Cadres complained that "study influences production" negatively. In workshops, they said, there is "no place to put your writing desk."[12]

Such resistance often came from the selfsame officials who earlier had pressured parents to rusticate their sons and daughters. So many returnees and other workers signed up for more schooling anyway. The number of Shanghai adults in continuing education rose by 31 percent between 1980 and 1983.[13] By 1982, about one-quarter of all Shanghai employees were taking advantage of adult training courses.[14] The types of jobs that many Shanghai people were willing to take also changed. Their desires on this point were now recorded and published. Unemployed people often wanted to work in units such as hotels, not in textile mills, carpentry shops, or other places where the tasks were harder. But the official labor bureaus under street committees, which aimed to set everyone in employment, tended to offer them the kinds of jobs they disliked. People who had occupational training or good educations could get posts, but many of the unemployed lacked such qualifications.[15] Many went into urban services, day labor, or suburban factories.

Two Migrations: Returning Youths and Newly Urban Ex-Peasants

The migration of partly educated returnees back to their native cities in the 1970s and 1980s created a new proletariat of middle-aged workers, who had urban registrations but few affective connections to the state. The migrations of ex-peasants also expanded the contract proletariat, especially among collective sub-urban factory workers. They often lacked valid household registrations or extensive educations. The ex-peasants were willing to do hard jobs in construc-tion, stevedoring, and the like. They came to the central metropolis in Shanghai, but they were even more obvious in nearby suburban towns.

More than seven-tenths of all workers at collective factories in Shanghai towns (*zhen*) in the 1980s came from rural areas and lacked town registrations. For factories legitimated at lower administrative levels, this proportion was often more than 90 percent.[16] By the late 1980s, it included many immigrants who had come from poor provinces inland such as Jiangxi and Anhui. Because the regis-tration of this inland group has always been very incomplete, the exact meaning of published unemployment data is hard to know, but Table 3.2–1 collates re-ports that are available from Shanghai and the whole country. The available statistics do not include "hidden" unemployment. They almost surely understate the extent of regular urban unemployment because persons who seek work must sign up with offices that can check on the legality of urban household registra-tions. The trend in the figures is significant for what it suggests about policy. The data suggest government efforts to reduce Shanghai unemployment in 1981 and the next four years. By the late 1980s and 1990s, there was a rise of joblessness and a reduction of effective state striving to prevent it.

In 1985, the Shanghai government approved new regulations to "rationalize" the floating workforce. "This was the starting point of the Shanghai labor mar-ket," the city's Labor Bureau claimed. But the labor market had actually begun much earlier, and the official role in it varied over time and over specific cases. The government of the late 1980s revived "labor service stations" (*laodong fuwu zhan*) that have many predecessors in the 1950s and 1960s. "Shanghai worker exchange service offices" were established then at the city level and in districts and counties. The main task of these agencies was to "approve" job transfers, and they increasingly served as protective agencies that could resist objections from state firms workers wanted to quit. At other times, they tried to persuade the workers to stay. There was no coherent labor plan, but the state might exercise a role when local workers and managers disagreed with each other. The increase in job transfers struck at the heart of traditionalist power in many work units, because it gave disgruntled employees an option to leave posts under their previous bosses. "In 1987 alone, 107,000 workers re-arranged their positions, and more than 30,000 unemployed people found jobs."[17]

The Decline in Official Job Allocations

The collapse of planning in the mid-1980s watershed meant that the state also could no longer give managers effective caps on their staff sizes. Chinese work units had long used more people than were on their books as "permanent

Table 3.2–1

Reported PRC and Shanghai Urban Unemployment
(numbers and percentages)

	PRC number (000s)	PRC rate (*daiye lü*)	PRC portion who are "young" (age 16–25)	Shanghai number (000s)	Shanghai rate
1952	3,766	13.2	—	—	—
1957	2,004	5.9	—	—	—
1978	5,300	5.3	47	100	2.3
1979	—	—	—	52	1.2
1980	5,415	4.9	71	148	3.2
1981	4,395	3.8	78	35	0.7
1982	3,794	3.2	77	26	0.5
1983	2,714	2.3	82	10	0.2
1984	2,357	1.9	83	20	0.4
1985	2,385	1.8	83	12	0.2
1986	2,644	2.0	79	18	0.4
1987	2,766	2.0	85	29	0.6
1988	2,962	2.0	83	45	0.9
1989	3,779	2.6	82	70	1.3
1990	3,832	2.5	82	77	1.5
1991	3,522	2.3	82	76	1.4
1992	3,603	2.3	83	94	1.8
1993	4,201	2.6	79	130	2.5
1994	4,764	2.8	63	149	2.8

Notes and sources: Officially designated "young" people are those between the ages of 16 and 25, e.g. at work, in school, or in the army. Unemployment in China is called "waiting for a vocation" (*daiye*). *Zhongguo tongji nianjian, 1986* (China Statistical Yearbook, 1986), State Statistical Bureau, ed. (Beijing: Zhongguo Tongji Chuban She, 1986), p. 136. Later national figures are from the same yearbook, 1991, p. 116; 1993, pp. 119–20; 1994, p. 107; 1995, p. 106; and the Shanghai data before 1991 come from *Shanghai tongji nianjian, 1991* (Shanghai Statistical Yearbook, 1991), Shanghai Statistical Bureau, ed. (Beijing: Zhongguo Tongji Chuban She, 1991), p. 86. National data were not found for 1979, presumably because cadres did not want to register or report all the references from rural send-downs in that year. It is very likely that many of the 1990s reports are inaccurately low.

employees." At the end of 1984, throughout the country, "employees outside the plan," for example in the broadcasting industry, comprised 15 percent of the total staff. "Temporary workers" were another 8 percent, and "contract system employees" were 1 percent.[18] About a quarter of all Shanghai's state-owned firms, employing approximately the same portion of the whole city's workers, reformed their hiring practices in 1988. Employment contracts (*pingyong hetong*) were signed to define the responsibilities, powers, and compensation of each staff member. Under this reform, it was at least theoretically possible to fire people—and newspapers mooted what "surplus personnel" might do, after removal from their jobs. Economists suggested that labor service stations might arrange jobs for them, especially in new tertiary industries. They might go into training. Or they could work for street factories. Or they could go on unemployment rolls, expanding the reserve proletariat under "the system of waiting for work" (*daigong zhidu*).[19] Even these measures were not expected to find jobs for everyone. The government could not, in this new order, do everything. It no longer had the resources to hire all the urban workers that it could not keep at their present positions. Some economists foresaw a "marketization of employment" (*jiuye shichang hua*).

Markets fluctuate, however, and this can cost individuals their jobs. Officially, only forty-five thousand Shanghai unionized state workers who were clearly not at or near retirement age had been laid off by the end of 1988. For this small number, the state declared a responsibility to find new jobs. But among legally registered workers at other types of plants, apparently in large part because of the closures of firms, another ninety-six thousand had lost jobs in 1988. The *Liberation Daily* estimated that on a nationwide basis, state-owned enterprises had 20 million "surplus workers." Another 50 million were "expected to move from the countryside to the city in the early 1990s. . . . These unemployed and surplus laborers pose a serious threat to Shanghai."[20]

Slackness in Shanghai's labor market was much greater than the low registered numbers of various categories of unemployed would suggest. The agonies of state-sector factories, losing inputs and markets to rural collectives, gave many who remained on the payroll less to do. Women in light industries were disproportionately early among those who suffered layoffs. Over four-fifths of the female unemployment in Yangpu district, during late 1988, arose from a "lessening of duties" at their factories, apparently because of raw-materials shortages.[21] Another tenth was caused, or rationalized, by the retooling of plants that had to change their lines of production.

Unemployment is an even more unsettling prospect for Chinese laborers in full-time jobs at state factories than for workers in the West. Some were so disenchanted with state-sector jobs that they resigned, but a majority of unionized workers lived in flats linked to their jobs.[22] In Mao's PRC, medical care, urban housing, and many other benefits were generally perquisites connected to employment. If a worker in the West receives a pink slip, a generalized system of relief is usually available, at least for a while, to lessen the blow. But in China, where the Party has long fostered the dependence of employees on their bosses by linking social goods to work units, loss of a job could be a personal disaster. Firing workers was politically even more difficult at the local level in China than it is in countries with more open labor markets. As an economic reformer said in mid-1988, managers of large factories could not dismiss workers because of opposition from the police liaison offices. The supervising public security bureaus feared worker unrest.[23] In the reform period, when established unionized laborers saw their own factories idle because the planners could not deliver raw materials, these red-blooded proletarians could claim their rights under Communism. They could become angrier with the government for failing to finance those rights, precisely because it called itself socialist.

Unemployment was not just in the state sector. The revived nonstate sector stirred job transfers generally. A 1990 survey of Shanghai urban households showed that 55 percent of the "people laid off" had worked for state enterprises, and 45 percent had worked for collectives.[24] Since 78 percent of all Shanghai workers at this time were in the state sector, it was chancier from an employee's point of view to be in the nonstate sector. The principle of socialist pink slips, so to speak, came as a great shock. It was not very often applied, until the 1990s, especially to male workers in heavy industries.

The government knew it had to treat laid-off Shanghai workers well, lest they fear the collapse of their own state-sector factories and act up politically. By 1989, official regulations specified that those who had been "fired from bankrupt or near-bankrupt enterprises will be registered [for hiring priority elsewhere], if their status is certified and they hold household registrations." Similar promises also went to other groups that might form urban oppositions: "Students who do not obey the state's allocation but who discontinue their studies will be registered, after their former schools certify them and they show household registrations." Even "people who are out of 'labor education' or out of jail" as well as unemployed contract workers could claim state help, when seeking new jobs—if they were over sixteen, had Shanghai household documents, and held leave documents from their former units.[25]

Procedures for recruiting workers and signing labor contracts were published in Shanghai by the late 1980s and thus were usable by parties in disputes. A person without a job could go through a process to obtain a "waiting-for-work certificate" (*daiye zheng*) on the basis of which labor service offices in street committees would try to find employment. A law specified the criteria for unemployment insurance (*daiye baoxian*).[26] This was new, and it could become more important as the reforms allow inefficient firms to go bankrupt.

Unemployment in reform Shanghai resulted from frustration with state-sector work, not from slow business. Indeed, the economy was generally booming. One-third of all registered jobless people in Shanghai at the end of 1988 had not been laid off, but had resigned their previous posts.[27] People also left work units by unauthorized migration and by early retirement. A surprisingly large number of workers simply resigned. At least 15 percent of Shanghai's 1.5 million "retirees" at the end of 1988 were actually still earning incomes, at least from street or residence committees or as hawkers. Others found lucrative post-"retirement" jobs.

Another large group of people (variously reported from 1.65 million to 2.09 million) were migrants to Shanghai from other cities, whence they had left their previous work units—and bosses.[28] In Shanghai's private enterprises, more than half the employees were from outside the city. Train and bus stations in major Chinese cities become labor hiring stations. By the 1990s, especially in South China, posters near terminals were full of notices about jobs in construction, toy making, and other fields that do not require high skills. Each morning, labor contractors brought trucks to these stations and hired people for temporary day labor.[29] Such places became sites of tension between police and ex-peasants, since the former tried to regulate the job market, and the latter wanted to earn better livelihoods in the big city.

Wages and Inflation

Guidance of workers can be analyzed in terms of decisions to hire and be hired, but the same story was also written in terms of the amount of work that people did and the compensation they received for it. A famous criticism of the prereform pattern put the problem boldly: "Socialism is a system in which the workers pretend to work, and the state pretends to pay them." At the height of Maoism, compensation to employees was scanty and could be arbitrary. In 1968, a regulation came down that all new employees, regardless of their line of work, would receive 36 yuan monthly. In Shanghai, these Great Proletarian Cultural Revolution wages were even smaller than previously. During the incipient reforms of the early 1970s, total compensation seems to have risen slightly. In 1974, the "welfare fund" in state firms was fixed officially at 11 percent of the wage budget. But actual expenditures apparently strained at this limit, which local managers found ways to override.

"Distribution according to work" was a slogan of Deng Xiaoping already in 1975. Early reformers already reacted to state firms' loss of dynamism, which collective firms' buying of input factors was already beginning to cause. "Wages regardless of contribution" were castigated by Deng as unsocialist, because they "do not mobilize people's initiatives."[30] Radicals in the 1975 government did not approve of Deng's ideas then, and early in the next year they moved to repress him and all reforms temporarily. But neither they nor he controlled the local networks that made this issue important—and assured that it would soon reappear.

By 1976, another rule came down that gave many employees who had entered their jobs between 1968 and 1970 a raise to 41 yuan (and for a minority to 43 yuan). By 1977, the method of raising wages was to add bonuses, and complex provisions were introduced for "adjusting wages" (tiaozheng gongzi). These resulted in increases of about 5 yuan per month for 40 percent of Shanghai's total staff. Also, "subsidies" (jintie) were added for many purposes.[31] This complex structure of subsidies was not just communitarian quaintness; it was a way for local managers to circumnavigate central restrictions on their wage budgets.

So there was at least some change in the socialist wage system before reforms were announced in 1978. The agricultural contract system within just a few years created such widening disparities of income that urban workers took notice and demanded higher wages. The ratio of urban to rural incomes in Shanghai moved from 1980 to 1983 precipitously in favor of the countryside: In the earlier year, urban people made 36 percent more than rural people, but four years later, only 13 percent more.[32] The average total wage and bonus per Shanghai worker in 1982 was 883 yuan—and it had risen by 5 percent annually for the previous three years. In suburban villages, the 1982 average total "distributed income" was lower than in the city (at 512 yuan, 42 percent less). But these suburban incomes had risen faster, by 10 percent annually in the previous four years.[33] China's socialist state planners by the early 1980s espoused "pay according to work" (under the Marxist theory that free supplies could be granted according to needs only later, with the arrival of full Communism). So young Shanghai laborers joked that they would gladly "work according to pay"—which was still not much.[34]

The Shanghai Labor Bureau regularly makes estimates of work discipline, and data on this topic have been published for some time periods. According to 1981 research on thirty enterprises, only 20 percent of all workers and staff completely abide by labor rules (e.g., by always appearing for work at the stipulated hours). Another 70 percent "could" respect the rules, though they were sometime violators. Fully 10 percent were reported to break the rules "regularly," and 2 percent were found to make "serious mistakes" in this respect.[35] A 1981 campaign to raise compliance was said to do so by only 2 or 3 percentage points in the low categories. This describes real politics: the power of unionized workers to set Shanghai's production.

Wages

Shanghai salaries were higher than those in most other places, under a national scheme of "kinds" of wage places. Workers in that city had received some relatively minor wage increases during the early 1970s, as workers in other Chinese cities did not. Shanghai in the mid-1980s was of the "eighth kind" (*ba lei*).[36] Urban people had some wage raises in later years, although increases in their disposable incomes were small, especially before the 1990s and especially when compared with the galloping prosperity of peasants in rich, rural areas of the delta. In the short period between 1980 and 1983, for example, all Shanghai state employees' wages (not counting bonuses) rose 2.5 percent. Urban people in collective enterprises did far better; their wages rose 9.3 percent.

The increases of the early 1980s went to nonindustrial workers whose compensation had long been low. In Shanghai industrial firms, the rise was only 0.1 percent.[37] The productive efficiency of intellectuals is difficult to quantify; but apparently because of clear discrimination against brain-workers in Mao's time, the basic wages of scientific workers between 1980 and 1983 rose 12.7 percent, and that of teachers and public health workers rose 15.9 percent.[38] These catch-up trends of the early 1980s were reversed at the end of the decade, when the problems of state industries made the government apparently more concerned about unrest in the industrial proletariat, so blue-collar wages again rose faster.

Bonuses became very important for most workers. Examples from the media prove useful in examining white-collar wage trends in Shanghai. At the *Xinmin Evening News,* basic wages of the staff varied from 80 to 200 yuan per month. But nine-tenths of the staff were recent university graduates and received no more than 120 yuan as basic wages. Bonuses at this newspaper, and at many other enterprises, were of two kinds: a fixed amount (about 40 yuan) to each worker from a government-supplied fund, plus a variable amount (averaging about 40 yuan more) based on supervisors' estimates of the quality of work.

A "floating wage scheme" was sometimes used, generally allowing 30 percent of compensation to float above a fixed level of basic salary and benefits. But there were also cases in which all wages and bonuses floated. The basis for determining the variable amount differed from business to business, and it usually depended on both the individual's productive contribution and the whole company's profit.[39]

During reforms, basic salaries and bonuses both varied more between various workers than during earlier years. In state units, this stratification nonetheless seldom showed a wide spread. The average basic wage at the *Liberation Daily* in August 1988 was 101 yuan per month, with reporters receiving just a slightly higher average, 109 yuan. The thirteen top cadres on staff got an average of only 180 yuan. But the total value of average compensation was about double this basic amount—a pattern that was also common in the late 1980s at other units in the state sector, whether they were government offices or economic firms. State-owned and cooperative firms were similar in this respect, at least until the 1990s, if they were large and urban. About half the increment above the basic wage, that is, an average of 47 yuan at the *Liberation Daily,* comprised subsidies (*butie*) for haircuts, commuting, newspapers, and other minor items. Subsidies were tied to inflation for items deemed basic; so these supplements countervailed inflation in specific commodities such as meat, edible oil, and a host of other items.

Such practices varied among functional "systems" (*xitong*) as well as between specific employers and employees. The practices at *Liberation Daily* illustrate the kinds of compensations. The subsidies described above were additional to a wage supplement (*jintie*), which was mainly a means for firms to compensate their employees at rates higher than the standard, nationally mandated salary rates.[40] Such supplements were often added for night shifts, for assignments outside the main place of labor, for work under dangerous conditions—or for any other reason that allowed employers to give official accountants a rationale so that money could be issued.

The other half of the total increment over basic wages was generally a bonus (*jiangjin*). This varied greatly, depending on each supervisor's assessment of the employee's productivity. At the newspaper, it was also based—as presumably basic salary was—on the sensitivity of the employee's work. The number and quality of articles that had been written or edited was a major factor in determining bonuses for the writing staff. The person with the highest compensation at the *Liberation Daily* earned about 400 yuan per month in the late 1980s because of a bonus of more than 200 yuan. For most employees, the average bonus was about 50 or 60 yuan.

In this transitional period of the 1980s, when communitarian and incentive norms were both touted as valid by different kinds of local leaders, the pattern could differ even at similar institutions. Bonuses were less important in the wages of the *Wenhui News,* for example, than at *Liberation Daily.* The chief editor at *Wenhui* got the highest salary, only 280 yuan per month and 20 more yuan in bonus. Other leading cadres received 160 yuan, with bonuses of about 40 yuan; good sub-editors received salaries of about 140 yuan with similar bonuses. Regular reporters received about 100 yuan in salary, but with larger bonuses of about 60 yuan. The portion of bonus in total pay rose, in other words, as the basic salary decreased. Nonbonus prerequisites that supplemented wages, however, correlated directly with seniority, responsibility, and salary.

The Shanghai Television Station's average staff wages, about 100 yuan per month only, were typical for journalists despite the station's high prestige and profile. Bonuses (*jiangjin*) totaled a similar amount, but these were divided into two approximately equal parts: For this television station and most other work units in Shanghai by the late 1980s, roughly half (50 yuan) of the bonus did not depend on work performance but was the sum of small compensations—often in kind rather than money—for transport, for books and newspapers, for cold drinks in the summer, for food especially at the firm's canteen, for coming to work on any summer day when the temperature reached 35 degrees Centigrade, and for other small amenities.[41] The rest of the bonus, averaging about 50 yuan at the television station and many other units but varying considerably among workers, was based on supervisors' estimates of the employee's productivity.

Specific firms and industries differed increasingly, as Shanghai's wage structure diversified during the late 1980s and 1990s. The average basic annual wages of employees in Shanghai's centrally managed factories approached 2,100 yuan in 1987; whereas in locally managed firms, the rate was considerably lower, about 1,750 yuan.[42] The Shanghai Oil Machines Parts Company had a higher profitability in 1988 than most other firms in the city, reportedly because it used younger staff and gave bonuses on a strict piece-rate basis.[43]

Productivity, Piece Work, and the Partitioned Proletariat

Worker motivation was an endemic problem in Shanghai, because inflation kept state-sector wages low—and because the reforms made salary standards ambiguous. Although the problem was widespread throughout the state sector, it became particularly evident as more foreign companies came to Shanghai, wanting to hire and inspire their workers. Discussion of the issue can begin with the international sector, which was not wholly atypical as regards worker motivation except for the managers' unusual will to raise productivity. Joint-venture employees were technically seconded from the local branch of China's Foreign Enterprise Service Corporation (FESCO). Foreign companies paid FESCO much higher "salaries" than the employees actually received. But because foreign companies, unlike state ones, did not have their total wage budgets tied to a national plan, and because they wanted real effort from their workers, they paid bonuses directly. A problem arose because these amounts were substantial enough to put many employees over the relatively high minimum threshold for the personal income tax. Partly to discourage foreign firms' bonuses, which made other urban workers envious, the PRC tax authorities in 1991 asked the overseas companies to withhold part of the bonus remunerations, requiring them to act as tax collection agents for the government. This sent the foreigners' lawyers into a predictable dander: "How can I tell my Chinese employees, who already see 80 or 90 percent of their salaries go to FESCO, that I am now taking even more out? I'll have to make up the difference myself." Another complained, "They're turning us into tax collectors—and at the same time raising our taxes." An overseas attorney opined that the new law had "inconsistencies" and was "not well drafted." Expatriate employers easily became an interest group. "Leaders of the foreign business community hope the widespread opposition being expressed now could be translated into a unified, organized protest."⁴⁴ A classic bureaucratic error saved the day to prevent such unstateliness: The withholding forms were declared unavailable, and a delay in printing them was predicted. It was also unclear whether the new rules were enforceable. Foreigners could protest decrees sent down without consultation. PRC business cadres, when faced with similar arbitrariness, were less able to do this openly even if they were influenced by such foreign habits.

Market pressures to make firms more efficient were weaker than they would have been if bankruptcy had been a real threat, but the first socialist answer to the need for more labor efficiency was to hire temporary staff at piece-work wages. Payment for performance was more difficult to institute among workers who were guaranteed their jobs than among contract workers, who were paid for each product they made. Efficiency-based payment stratified the proletariat. It also produced a regimen of effective effort and predictable hours—a regularity in work—that promoted productivity.

The average real incomes of Shanghai's state employees rose slowly. Bonuses and salary supplements (*jiangjin* and *jintie*) created some increases after years of stagnant wages. The raises were larger in some trades than in others, especially in fields involved with building. Construction workers in Shanghai had the fastest raises; their average yearly total income by 1986 was more than 2,000 yuan—double the 1980 figure. Surveyors made about 2,300 yuan, a figure that had risen spectacularly in the 1980s. But many state employees by 1986 still made only about 1,500 yuan, up an average of 62 percent over their 1980 compensation. In 1990, the total nominal compensation of state employees was about three times that of 1980—but so were the prices for the living expenses that these people paid.

Among state employees, industrial workers generally fared better than commercial employees in the late 1980s and early 1990s, when both of these groups' salary raises outpaced those of civil servants and teachers. The government apparently became more concerned with industrial strikes than with anything storekeepers, office workers, or intellectuals could do. Even within industry, there was much variation. Electrical employees in Shanghai on average by 1986 earned more than 2,000 yuan per year, but workers under the Second Light Industrial Bureau (who are about 80 percent women) made only 1,550 yuan on average.

The effects of the new income differentials in state jobs—not to mention those in the private and collective sectors—demoralized many in Shanghai. Retailers became rich, while inflation made many other groups, including intellectuals, poor. "The maker of guided missiles can't be compared to the seller of tea eggs" (*gao daodan de buru mai chaye dan de*), according to a late 1980s joke that punned on the words for "egg" and "bomb." A "moralist" was quoted as moaning that, as regards income, "those who handle the scalpel are inferior to those who handle the razor" (*ba jiepodao de buru ba didao de*).[45]

Private enterprise attracted expert retired technicians and managers, but it also attracted many who had suffered "labor education" in Mao's time or had personal reasons for unsocial behavior. Party members, for their own reasons, stressed the moral impropriety of some private entrepreneurs. Conservative hardliners in Shanghai claimed that "mixed-up people are getting rich."[46] Intellectuals—even many who had historical reasons to distrust Party hacks casting aspersions on entrepreneurs—mostly agreed that the reform era's emphasis on making money had gotten out of hand.

From 1980 to 1989, annual average Shanghai wages rose from 873 to 2,512 yuan. The ratio of Shanghai to national average wages also increased during this decade, from 1.15 to 1.30. Labor productivity rose, reportedly from 6,136 to 14,867 yuan in terms of gross output, although during the 1980s the ratio of Shanghai to national productivity fell from 2.78 to 2.12.[47] These figures imply that the portion of Shanghai workers' productivity actually received in wages increased over the decade—although it was always low (by this measure, rising from roughly one-seventh to one-sixth).

Price Supports for Retail Products and Foods

The supplies of infrastructural amenities, such as housing and transport, were smaller in Shanghai than in many other Chinese cities. But the prices of consumer goods have been kept low there, and the supplies have been relatively adequate. On the whole, Shanghai has been a "price basin" (*wujia pendi*). Rates for both electricity and water remained reasonable during the 1980 reforms.[48] Utilities costs have been even lower to industry than to residents, and inexpensive for both. Retail food sales in Shanghai soared 48 percent between 1978 and 1982 (while the population rose 9 percent). But the microgeographic distribution of this change was very uneven and revealing: The rate of increase in suburban *rural* areas was sharp, though in large suburban towns (such as Songjiang or Jiading), the supply of retail foods reportedly decreased. For the central urban districts, there was only a "slight increase."[49] The newly rich and specialized farmers ate more; and more of their food came onto markets. Also, both they and the new immigrants to Shanghai's suburbs were increasingly in services and industry, not agriculture; so they had to go to markets to buy food.

Calorie intake per capita rose little from 1952 through the next two decades (except for quick recoveries from sharp downturns caused by agrarian disasters such as the Great Leap Forward). The 1952 level was 2,270 calories per person per day; by 1978, this had risen to only just over 2,300. Then came a sharp upturn: by 1983, this calorie consumption averaged nearly 2,900.[50] This pattern matches the official periodization of reforms, although it is unclear how much food during the early 1970s was grown and eaten in rural areas, without being reported to tax monitors then still trying to recover from the Cultural Revolution.

If the PRC eliminated urban food subsidies, the price of grain in cities would rise by at least half according to a mid-1980s estimate, and that of edible oils by four-fifths. If the same standard of urban consumption were maintained, this would require a state payroll budget increase of roughly one-quarter.[51] The government was eager to avoid this massive expenditure, whose main obvious value to the regime was as an insurance premium against urban discontent. Bonuses relieved some of the pressure, and subsidies relieved more of it. Neither was good news for the state budget.

The government did not get its full money's worth for these subsidies, since low-priced staples were often not sold to Shanghai consumers but "leaked" to other areas, where they fetched higher prices. Grain went at least as far as Hankou, three provinces away.[52] The loss of rice to elsewhere, from Putuo district alone monthly by late 1988, was estimated at 400,000 kilos.[53] The "rodents" and "insects" who were responsible for this hemorrhage were often the managers of Putuo's rice shops.

Shanghai prices were low, but this did not help citizens when the commodities became less available during some periods of the 1980s. Among 249 consumer products for daily use in mid-1986, about half were declared to be in shortage.[54] The situation was worst for items made of metals. A survey determined that 115 commodities were in insufficient supply, and only 13 were in surplus. But the city's tastes and the government's desire to keep wages stable in Shanghai combined to make the prices of some goods low. Non–export-quality beer, for example, was in the late 1980s about half as expensive in Shanghai as in other parts of China. Shanghai had the dubious distinction of leading China's provinces in the bibulation of liquor (except for nearby Zhejiang, famous for its Shaoxing rice wine).[55] This remained a high-consumption city. Cashmere wool was 10 yuan per kilo less in Shanghai than in the nearby provinces of Jiangsu and Zhejiang. The relatively high-wage, low-price system of Shanghai was inherited from Mao's time, and it served the purposes of maintaining a proletarian political constituency for the state. Reforms eroded this pattern slowly and unevenly.

Many items were removed from the rationing system in the mid-1980s. But increased Shanghai consumption and inland demand caused occasional reversals of this policy. Shanghai pork rations were brought back in late 1987, because of a shortage caused by more demand for meat and less production by farmers (who faced rising prices for pig fodder).[56] Although Shanghai's own production of hogs in 1987 rose 13 percent since 1986, three-quarters of the city's pork normally comes from other parts of China. A fast-rising taste for protein, combined with an exodus of peasants to industrial jobs, created a shortage to which the city government responded with rationing.[57]

The black market price of grain coupons rose in 1989, and early in that year the rise could be reported. These chits were needed by unregistered migrants to Shanghai who needed to buy food. They could be obtained in barter for consumer durables. *Xinmin Evening News* reported that an aluminum wok would bring enough coupons to purchase 50 catties of grain. A plastic wash basin brought coupons for just 20 catties. A fancy pottery wok was exchangeable for rations on 100 catties.[58] All these trades were illegal, of course; but the black market had become regularized because local people needed it. The largest-circulation newspaper in Shanghai had no compunction about publishing its current rates.

Eggs and other consumer goods were also exchanged for coupons, which became a "second currency," given along with wages to Shanghai workers.[59] Illegal "grain ticket peddlers" benefited indirectly from official money, since local grain prices in Shanghai were kept low by government subsidies. For rights to purchase 100 catties of rice, these traders could buy unused Shanghai ration coupons for 5 or 6 yuan. They could transport the rice over "120 Ho Chi Minh Trails and 270 underground railroads" (in practice, often by bicycles) to other provinces where the price was better. The profits on such transactions were worthwhile—about 50 yuan per 100 catties.[60] These crimes arose solely to absorb subsidies that the state wanted, for its own political reasons, to siphon through central budgets rather than leaving in the hands of unauthorized local leaders. Established institutions drove this policy, and it was easy to justify on grounds of high inflation and increasing inequality.

The distribution of per-capita family income became less equal in Shanghai quickly, during the first four years of the 1980s. Here are the percentages of households that earned various levels of income:[61]

	30 Yuan	30–40 Yuan	40–50 Yuan	50–60 Yuan	60–70 Yuan	>70 Yuan
1980 (percent)	6	20	37	36	0	0
1983 (percent)	1	11	30	29	18	11

This trend continued and accelerated in later years (although reliably compa-rable figures have not been found to show that in a single table). The reform continued to extend urban income gaps even during periods of conservative rule. A 1989 survey of household spending per capita showed that "high-income households" (apparently the top decile) averaged 268 yuan, up 51 percent over the previous year. But "low-income households" averaged 88 yuan, up by 19 percent.[62] Income gaps were widening within the city.

As compensations diverged, the state spent large amounts attempting to coun-teract the perceived unfairness of this trend in Shanghai. In 1992, for example, the registered households in built-up districts with annual living expenditures between two and three thousand yuan were almost half—45 percent. (These were paid about 200 yuan per month, for households averaging 3.1 persons.) The proportion of households with spending this high in 1980 had been less than half of 1 percent.[63] Inflation had been very high over the previous decade.

Consumer Price Rises

Inflation has long been a political topic in Shanghai. The KMT lost urban sup-port to the CCP in the late 1940s largely because of hyperinflation, which was not slowed until the early 1950s. In the minds of many, the main economic argument to keep socialist planners in power was that a free market earlier had made havoc of prices. Anti-inflation policies were enforced as thoroughly as possible for a quarter of a century in Shanghai, so any demand pressures were channeled to create shortages, not higher prices.

By the 1970s, however, rural industries were using more resources. Especially by the next decade, the effect of this pressure on prices had become obvious. China's overall record of inflation shows one watershed in the early 1970s and another in the mid-1980s. From 1973 to 1979, the inflation rate was positive, albeit mildly so; but it had generally been negative in the strict controlled-price regime of the mid- and late 1960s. A second watershed came after 1984. As even the official figures in Table 3.2–2 show, annual inflation was always in excess of 5 percent—except in the two immediate post-Tiananmen years. In 1988–89, the inflation rate was more than 15 percent; and in the early 1990s it was only somewhat lower and almost certainly underreported.

The extent to which published inflation figures are complete or accurate is debatable, but comparisons between published Shanghai price levels and those in other parts of China are particularly interesting. In China as a whole, retail price

Table 3.2–2

Retail Inflation in China

	Previous Year = 100	1950 = 100
1965	97.3	134.6
1966	99.7	134.2
1967	99.3	133.2
1968	100.1	133.3
1969	98.9	131.8
1970	99.8	131.5
1971	99.3	130.5
1972	99.8	130.2
1973	100.6	131.0
1974	100.5	131.7
1975	100.2	131.9
1976	100.3	132.3
1977	102.0	135.0
1978	100.3	135.9
1979	102.0	138.6
1980	106.0	146.9
1981	102.4	150.4
1982	101.9	153.3
1983	101.5	155.6
1984	102.8	160.0
1985	108.8	174.1
1986	106.0	184.5
1987	107.3	198.0
1988	118.5	234.6
1989	117.8	276.4
1990	102.1	282.2
1991	102.9	290.4
1992	105.4	306.1
1993	113.2	346.4
1994	121.7	421.6
1995	114.8	
1996	106.1	

Source: Zhongguo tongji nianjian, 1991 (China Statistical Yearbook, 1991), State Statistical Bureau, ed. (Beijing: Zhongguo Tongji Chuban She, 1992), pp. 229–30; 1993 edition, pp. 237–38; 1995 edition, p. 233; and 1997 edition, p. 267.

levels had nearly doubled (up 98 percent) by 1987 as compared to 1950. In Shanghai, they had risen only somewhat less (84 percent). Most, though not all, of this rise had come during the early reform period.

If only for purposes of accurate planning, more of the inflation had to be reported. Three particular spurts of retail price rises occurred nationwide in 1980, 1985, and 1988. The timing of these events is easier to determine than the annual rates of increase, which were officially published (and underestimated) respectively at 6.0, 8.8, and 18.5 percent.[64] A better measure would include unreported transactions, with an adjustment for some continuing shortages. Inflation, like politics, does not all occur in the state system.

Local leaders wanting more investment funds were less concerned in the short run about inflation than were conservatives and central politicians. In public, administrators spoke as if inflation was an even more crucial danger than continued stagnation. They often spoke as if, in reform development, inflation and growth were not different aspects of the same phenomenon.

A reduction of central control of Shanghai is shown in the city's catch-up inflation during the 1980s, when the "price basin" plan that had subsidized the price of labor for Shanghai's heavily taxed and monitored industries began to fail as a viable system. By 1987, national retail prices were 46 percent higher than in 1978, while in Shanghai they were 51 percent higher. Shanghai retail inflation in 1986 and 1987, according to the officially published figures which underestimate this statistic, was running respectively at 8 and 9 percent per year.[65]

In Jiangsu and Zhejiang, retail inflation was reported at 8 and 9 percent for those years; but over a longer period of reforms, inflation in Zhejiang was considerably higher. In that province, 1987 retail prices stood 58 percent above those of 1978. The parallel rise in Jiangsu was less than in Shanghai, at 45 percent.

The government also compiles an index of inflation in "employees' living expenses"—which is similar to another index for "social retail prices" but may be more important politically, because employees sometimes go on strike if price hikes are too fast.[66] In 1987 Shanghai, nominal inflation for employees since 1950 had been 77 percent. On the basis of 1978 prices, the rise had been 47 percent; and it averaged over 10 percent in 1986–87 even in the published figures. Zhejiang, again had a much higher rate on this index for 1987 employees' living expenses, a 68 percent rise since 1978—compared to 56 percent for the nation as a whole (or 81 percent for the most inflationary province, Guangdong). But Jiangsu's rate was lower, almost down to Shanghai's sharply controlled level, at 51 percent.

Retail price increases have been sharp at Shanghai during some years, as Table 3.2–3 shows on the basis of official reports or comparative underreports.[67] But this inflation was still lower than that in other developing countries, for example in South America or the Middle East, where the governments have not made so many direct guarantees for workers' salaries. The high 1988–89 rate was politically dangerous for the state, and one of the state's solutions in later years involved underreporting of the problem. Workers knew, however, how much they were getting for their yuan.

Table 3.2–3

Increase in Officially Reported Price Indices
(percentages over previous year)

	All-China retail	Shanghai consumer	Guangdong retail
1979	2.0	1.0	3.0
1980	6.0	6.5	8.5
1981	2.4	1.5	9.3
1982	1.9	0.3	2.3
1983	1.5	0.1	0.7
1984	2.8	2.2	1.2
1985	8.8	16.4	3.6
1986	6.0	6.7	4.8
1987	7.3	8.8	11.7
1988	18.5	21.3	30.2
1989	17.8	16.7	21.0
1990	2.1	4.8	−4.4
1991	2.9	7.9	0.6
1992	5.4	6.0	5.8
1993	13.2	21.9	18.2
1994	21.7	23.9	8.9
1995		18.7	

Notes and sources: Especially for politically conservative years, such as the early 1990s, these figures may be very considerable underestimates. Found or calculated from *Quanguo ge sheng zizhi qu zhixia shi lishi tongji ziliao huibian, 1949–1989* (Historical Statistical Collection on Provinces, Autonomous Regions, and Municipalities Throughout the Country, 1949–1989) (Beijing: Zhongguo Tongji Chuban She, 1990), p. 32 on China, 1965–89; p. 337 for Shanghai; p. 638 for Guangdong; also *Guangdong tongji nianjian, 1991* (Guangdong Statistical Yearbook, 1991), Guangdong Province Statistics Bureau, ed. (Beijing: Zhongguo Tongji Chubanshe, 1991), p. 283; 1992, p. 323; 1993, p. 331; 1994, p. 283; 1995, p. 333; *Shanghai tongji nianjian, 1991* (Shanghai Statistical Yearbook, 1991), Li Mouhuan et al., eds. (Shanghai: Shanghai Shi Tongji Ju, 1991), p. 318; and 1993 p. 294; and on 1994 and 1995, in 1996 yearbook, p. 80; *Zhongguo tongji nianjian, 1991* (China Statistical Yearbook, 1991), State Statistical Bureau, ed. (Beijing: Zhongguo Tongji Chuban She, 1991), p. 318; 1993, p. 239; 1995, p. 233; and for Guangdong figures until 1984 (that list's 1985 datum is lower by half), see Ezra F. Vogel, *One Step Ahead: Guangdong Under Reform* (Cambridge: Harvard University Press, 1989), chap. 3, based on *Guangdong jingji tizhi gaige yanjiu* (Studies of Guangdong Economic System Reforms) (Guangzhou: Zhongshan Daxue Chuban She, 1985), p. 126.

A popular Shanghai magazine commentator maintained that in 1987, 30 percent of the urban households suffered a loss of real income.[68] This represents a change from the previous relatively stable pattern (at least since 1963) of relatively small improvements but also small declines in urban livelihood. China's reported retail inflation between October 1987 and October 1988 was over 26 percent.[69] In Shanghai, the first half of 1988 saw a decline of living standards. During those few months alone, 13 percent of the city's households had less income. Another 24 percent had living expenses that rose faster than their wages—so a total of 37 percent suffered clear decreases of real income. The inflation annualized rate in this 1988 period was officially reported at 16 percent.[70]

Not only Shanghai residents but urban people all over China suffered major losses of real income during this period. In the first half of 1988, twenty-five of the country's thirty-two largest cities reported consumer price inflation of 20 percent in just six months. By August, consumers fearing more price hikes went on a spending spree larger than any seen since 1949. Shop shelves were cleared of low-quality goods that had remained unsold for years. Bank deposits dropped, and officials admitted, "The leadership was shocked by what happened last month. . . . It does not know what to do. . . . It has been holding endless, exhausting meetings."[71] The Central Committee met in September, and the pace of reforms was slowed.

Four 1988 "waves of overbuying" were reported in Shanghai. These caused stores to build up inventories, hoping that the high demand would continue. But 1989 markets were slack. In an April 29, 1989, speech, Mayor Zhu Rongji was reported to say frankly, "Because of inflation, some Shanghai residents' living standards went down last year. Some people and units made money by trading illegally, and they created economic disorder."[72]

The political events of June 1989 had an economic corollary. Shanghai retail sales in that month were 11 percent below those of May. By September, consumer goods inventories in Shanghai stood almost one-third higher than a year earlier. The inventory surplus proved to be temporary because a growth of wealth continued for many families, especially rural entrepreneurs who had been absent from either side at Tiananmen. The nominal incomes of Shanghai households and nonstate organizations in 1989 were 18 percent higher than the previous year, although reported output was only 7 percent higher.[73] An officially mandated credit crunch of 1988–89 greatly slowed inflation but did not stop it. A 1989 survey of Shanghai households found that nominal per-capita spending was up 9 percent from the previous year, but down at least 3 percent in real terms because of inflation.[74]

A longer perspective is most appropriate for analyzing the causes of these sporadic short-term inflations. By the early 1990s, the main structural change had already taken place. The state had lost control of prices, which became subject to market fluctuations. The big picture is that shortages were high and rising in the early 1970s and in the early 1980s, when they became evident in price levels. Free market and state prices, according to the published statistics summarized in Table 3.2–4 diverged after 1973. Later, after 1976, the state allowed more free markets to spur competition and lower prices for some commodities. Annual inflation (to the extent published national figures are complete)

Table 3.2–4

National Inflation and Excess of Free Over State Prices
(reported percentages)

	Consumer goods price rise over previous year	Market over state prices
1965	3	40
1966	1	41
1967	2	43
1968	0	43
1969	−1	42
1970	0	42
1971	*9*	*54*
1972	*8*	*67*
1973	*5*	75
1974	2	77
1975	4	84
1976	4	90
1977	−2	79
1978	−7	69
1979	−5	57
1980	2	48
1981	6	49
1982	3	48
1983	4	48
1984	0	43
1985	17	28
1986	8	17
1987	16	17
1988	30	17
1989	11	12
1990	−6	8

Notes and sources: The first column records year-by-year inflation for urban traded consumption goods (*jishi maoyi xiaofei pin*) throughout the country, rounded by one decimal from data in the source. The percentage excess column compares free market prices (*shijia*) with prices in state-run commerce (*guoying shangye*), presumably for the baskets of commodities bought in those years. Many items were removed from lists for which the state specified prices. See *Zhongguo wujia tongji nianjian, 1988* (Statistical Yearbook of Chinese Prices, 1988), Urban Society and Economy Survey Group, ed. (Beijing: Zhongguo Tongji Chuban She, 1988), p. 70. For the last three years, see *Zhongguo tongji nianjian, 1991* (China Statistical Yearbook, 1991), State Statistical Bureau, ed. (Beijing: Zhongguo Tongji Chuban She, 1991), p. 92. After this table was compiled, but just as it went to press, lower rates of consumer inflation were reported retrospectively for 1988–89, along with high national figures for the mid-1990s. Consumer inflation is so politically sensitive that different compendia give different numbers, although the trends of change are parallel. Rows from the early 1970s are italicized to stress that reform inflation began then.

was high and irregular only after 1984. But just as important, the excess of market over state prices plunged in the mid-1980s, from 43 percent in 1984 to just 17 percent two years later. Goods became more expensive, but the price structure became somewhat more rationally linked to scarcities, which varied over time.

By the mid-1990s, it was unclear whether quick inflation would remain an aspect of China's reforms—or instead, whether the traumatic experience with prices in the late 1980s was basically a temporary phenomenon in a period of decompression, when an ex-revolutionary state lost control of prices as of much other activity. Long-term inflation is guided partly by political factors, and few economists claim that models can predict it over long periods. So it is interesting to note that inflation has not been a necessary concomitant of other postcentralization eras that showed high rates of growth. This should be studied comparatively for the periods that followed Cromwell, Napoleon, Lincoln, Hitler, Tojo, Franco, and other political-economic centralizers. A rough survey suggests that relatively quick growth in the wake of all these centralization eras was in only a few cases accompanied by severe price rises.

Inflation has not been endemic after all major centralizations, even when it has been severe during short parts of these periods. Both inflationary and deflationary spells have punctuated these eras. In England after 1660, for example, there were price fluctuations in that basically preindustrial economy, showing a basically flat pattern over many decades despite the variations.[75] French wholesale prices generally fell from 1820 to 1850, and then (after two decades of somewhat higher prices) they fell again into the first decade of the twentieth century.[76] The patterns in comparable periods of other political economies are mixed, but they suggest that inflation is not a necessary correlate of postrevolutionary decompressions. The relatively quick growth of consumer goods in many such periods may be anti-inflationary.

Optimism based on comparative cases would be removed, however, from what many Shanghai people were experiencing during the late 1980s and 1990s. Published estimates of the costs of living in Shanghai urban districts—if they can be believed—kept slightly behind actual levels of consumption, according to data presented from various sources in Table 3.2–5.

Yet the main question is not whether the government was concerned with maintaining incomes, but whether Shanghai residents perceived this was being done successfully. This is a matter of subjective viewpoint, and the data do not provide any clear answer. It is likely that rising costs of living were underreported, but also that Shanghai consumers acted on their interest to encourage more politically based subsidies by complaining about their supposed impoverishment.

Employees' Reactions to Pressures on Income

Reforms worked havoc not just with the compensations that workers received, but also with what they expected from jobs. After decades of scant pay and scant

Table 3.2–5

The Cost of Living in Shanghai (yuan per person)

Year	Level of consumption (urbandistricts)	Estimated expense of living n Shanghai
1965	329	
1966	353	
1967	354	
1968	330	
1969	361	
1970	362	
1971	383	
1972	399	
1973	427	
1974	450	
1975	471	
1976	485	
1977	492	
1978	510	
1979	587	
1980	623	552
1981	643	584
1982	643	575
1983	667	615
1984	757	726
1985	1,024	991
1986	1,192	1,170
1987	1,286	1,282
1988	1,682	1,648
1989	1,976	1,811
1990		1,936
1991		2,167
1992		2,509

Sources: The living expense data for 1980–84 are from a survey of 500 worker families, and the 1985–90 data come from another survey of 500 resident families. See *Shanghai tongji nianjian, 1991* (Shanghai Statistical Yearbook, 1991), Shanghai Shi Tongji Ju, ed. (Beijing: Zhongguo Tongji Chuban She, 1991), pp. 272, 292, 419, and 431; the 1992 edition, pp. 455 and 468; and the 1993 edition, p. 408. The living expense data for early years come from ibid., 1986 edition, p. 441. See also *Quanguo ge sheng zizhi qu zhixia shi lishi tongji ziliao huibian, 1949–1989* (Historical Statistical Collection on Provinces, Autonomous Regions, and Municipalities Throughout the Country, 1949–1989) (Beijing: Zhongguo Tongji Chuban She, 1990), p. 338. Comparable data have not yet been found for the mid- 1990s, after the main patterns of reform inflation had been set. Rates for those years were high.

work, many urban laborers received more money (and saw in shops more to buy with it) during the early 1980s than previously. That experience, as expectations rose, made the late 1980s all the more disturbing. Real wages for state and collective urban employees nationwide rose roughly 50 percent between 1978 and 1988. But none of this increase took place in the last three years of that period, after 1985. Large provincial capitals such as Shanghai, which the state monitored closely because of their importance to revenues, saw less rise in real wages. Mao for two decades had attempted a policy of no change in either prices or wages, but this effort was eroded by reforms. According to the best data available from a large city (Tianjin), from 1976 to 1986 real wages rose only 7 percent.[77] Earnings adjusted for inflation almost surely declined among urban state workers during the next three years, 1987 to 1989.

There was, however, more for city people to buy in the mid-1980s than previously. Shops were full, and advertising was rampant, even though many state and some collective workers in large cities by the end of the decade had less constant-value money to spend than earlier. The boom in the urban economy was driven for consumption as well as production by nonstate sectors of many kinds, especially small unregulated collective firms.

This was a change in local situations, not in local norms. By the late 1980s, it led to some proletarian strikes, but not to extensive open unrest. Polls at this time showed that many Chinese wanted to be conservative and risk-averse, at least when they were questioned about their preferences at the most abstract level. A late 1980s' survey of more than 4,000 respondents, mostly urban, asked them to rank the "values" they most admired in individuals. They appraised the following options in declining order: diligence, frugality, pragmatism, conservatism, obedience, personal connections, face-saving, sociability, and (lastly) risk-taking. But their attitudes were also strongly affected by the spirit of the time: When the same respondents were asked whether they would prefer jobs with "high income and more opportunities ... but you have to work hard and also risk losing your job," or on the contrary, jobs from which "you can only get a low income but don't need to work hard and will not lose your job," more than 50 percent said they would take the high-income, high-risk option. A smaller portion, two-fifths, said they would take the easier, lower-paying jobs. Wealth, even with uncertainty, was preferred to the stable-but-poor life, especially by young age cohorts.[78] What the selfsame respondents said they valued abstractly contrasts with what they said they would actually do, if presented with more concrete choices.

Earlier surveys, although not strictly comparable to the one cited above, likewise suggest that attitude change may have been very quick in the late 1980s. In the tradeoff between a high income and a quiet life, money was becoming more popular. A 1985 poll had less than one-fifth of the respondents preferring "an unstable life but more risk and opportunity to increase income." But four-fifths in that survey preferred "a stable life, but less opportunity to increase income."[79] In just four years, Chinese urban people reported they had become far more covetous of wealth.

Shanghai workers acted on this desire for more money. Moonlighting became a "craze" in the late 1980s, and it "exerted a great influence on production." In Shanghai by early 1989, more than one million people (or one-eighth of the city's whole workforce) reportedly had second jobs.[80] "Because workers can get much more money from private businesses than from state-owned firms, they are willing to work for private managers. By contrast, some state enterprises cannot get the workers they need, e.g., textile workers. Obviously, the market mechanism is adjusting Shanghai's labor power distribution."[81] The market was in charge, but this particular report was unclear about whether to resist such impersonal power. The protest was that the "market mechanism" hurt state industries, but a much larger number of people were concerned that it endangered state workers' incomes.

Holding two jobs became widespread in Shanghai by 1990. A survey of almost ten thousand residents in various southern cities showed that 16 percent worked at secondary jobs that ranged from peddling to legal consulting. But in mid-1990, Shanghai state workers were still technically prohibited from taking such employment. Questionnaires showed that 66 percent of residents within the city said they would take second jobs if these were legal, and only 9 percent said they would not. Just 5 percent of Shanghai people favored continuing the prohibition against secondary jobs.[82] The socialist state could not long maintain its traditional surveillance over employment, unless its own firms became more profitable—as they did not.

Stalinist or Traditional Control of Workers

Because of the historical role of labor in Marxist theory, China's Communist government from its arrival in Shanghai tried to organize the proletariat as its main constituency there. The model for Chinese state factories and unions in the 1950s was specifically late Stalinist, not more broadly Leninist or Communist. It was partly communicated through Chinese translations of post-1945 Russian handbooks, but the vast majority of the Chinese organizers who established this model in PRC institutions had no experience in the USSR.[83] Stalin's industrial and military successes were the main claims for the legitimacy of the model; but its main role in a new, alien context was to legitimate the particular Chinese cadres the Party had placed in factories. The traditions of this paradigm, as applied, were at least as Chinese as they were Stalinist. The use of a new technique to control localities is common among political regimes that are just establishing power.

Administrative Organization vs. Proletarian Segments

Organizational tricks could not always restructure the proletariat, despite official hopes. Sharp divisions between young and old, locals and outsiders, supervisory and menial workers were the main causes of labor movement activism.[84] Throughout the PRC's first three decades, strikes and other worker protests were common, although generally unreported and regularly suppressed.[85] News of strikes was usually not published after 1956. Labor actions became fit-to-print news only after state-sanctioned settlements had already been reached.[86] Proletarian protests became intense in the late 1960s, and they continued into the 1970s.[87]

On February 1, 1974, workers in the Fifth Harbor District of Shanghai's port put up a big-character poster entitled "We want to be masters of the harbor, and we will not be slaves to tonnage [regulations]."[88] Dockworkers had been allowed to go home from their jobs early on any day after they fulfilled their tonnage quotas—and some had even been praised for doing this. The poster objected to such practices. The *People's Daily* came out in favor of the poster, which was pro-production. So there was serious conflict in 1974 between groups in Shanghai's local leadership that might be called proreform productionists and antireform protectionists.

On April 5, 1974, the Central Committee allowed the State Planning Commission to call a national conference for the sake of emphasizing production goals, despite the concurrent campaign to "Criticize Lin Biao and Confucius." The government at high levels was thus working at cross purposes to itself. The conference reflected cleavages among top politicians at that time along issues that just a few years later were to be defined in terms of economic reforms.[89] But the National Planning Conference did not meet in 1974, although it was normally held in April of each year, because of leftists and the movement to criticize Lin Biao and Confucius. On July 1, Jiang Qing's spokespeople noted, "Confucianists [support] production, but Legalists [support] rebellion."[90]

The Cultural Revolution enhanced and politicized the diversity of worker leaders in Shanghai. Mao Zedong maintained, "Strikes and boycotts are means of struggle against bureaucracy." A new labor law by 1977 nonetheless countered: "Rules and regulations ought never to be eliminated. Moreover, with the development of production and technology, rules and regulations must become stricter, and people must follow them more precisely. This is the law of nature." It became, at any rate, the law of Beijing. The 1978 state constitution mandated a duty of Chinese citizens "to maintain labor discipline."[91]

It would be misleading to suggest that in Chinese Communist factories every worker was accountable to just a single father figure. Work units took the form of outwardly cooperative hierarchies, with the operations of each level not fully known to others (either higher or lower).[92] Patrons often came in networks or committees, often with different functions between them. Laborers depended on their workshop foremen for coordinating production and recommending wages. But the foremen could, often with reason, blame state budget restraints for slack productivity when wages were kept low. For promotions, factory directors and CCP organization department cadres at a higher administrative level were very important. To provide materials and markets in the old planned economy, which were the bases of most workers' jobs, crucial roles were played by the leaders of bureaus outside the factory. Many state employees became aware of this to their chagrin as planning broke down. Reforms cut the state's ability to sponsor or benefit from traditional Chinese patron–client ties.[93]

The central state never publicized the diversity of local leaders. Both state and Party were always thin on the ground. They lacked very large numbers of local leaders on whom they could rely. As late as the mid-1990s, when the CCP somewhat relaxed its entrance criteria and expanded to 50 million members, it still comprised less than one-twentieth of the population. Central agents preferred that organizations be large, with single designated patrons who could be held responsible for remitting funds. This pressure from the state was decreasingly effective during reforms. In a 1983 survey of Shanghai factories, Party members comprised only 5.4 percent of the total workforce. Just 22 percent of work group leaders were in the CCP, and half the work groups contained no one in the Party (largely because workers with that much prestige could get out of shops that did hard jobs). Although only a tiny portion of Shanghai's workers were illiterate, 18 percent had been merely to primary schools (xiaoxue), 47 percent had been to middle schools (chuzhong, sometimes called lower middle schools), 30 percent had been to high schools (gaozhong, also called senior middle schools), and 4 percent had gone to tertiary institutions (called daxue of various kinds).[94] As a few official vanguards of Shanghai's proletariat got ahead in their personal careers, they left most of the city's industrial workers behind.

Labor organizations were always politically sensitive—and when the state could have its way, tightly monitored—because budgets depended on restraint of wages. Increasing evidence nonetheless shows that workers sometimes got their way. A description published in Shanghai about the internal politics of a joint venture elsewhere in East China implied that workers there had to be especially placated by the Party, in order to put forth the strenuous efforts that a Japanese investor demanded. The well-financed workers' club, kindergarten, canteen, and other benefits at this Hitachi factory had won awards for excellence. The union leader, who was the most important full-time Party cadre in the factory, headed a high-quality staff to do "propaganda work."[95] Material incentives, however, tended to replace exhortations.

To raise production, some factories urged workers to stay late. They were paid on a piece-rate basis for overtime but at hourly wages for their regular work. Financial cadres from the First Shanghai Wire Factory wrote to the Wenhui News, reporting the great successes of this piece-rate system. The factory had long realized that potential demand for its wire was far more than it could supply. When, to produce more wire, it offered junior employees just 1.2 yuan for each extra day of work, none of them bothered to stay overtime for such low pay. On an experimental basis, some workshops then introduced piece-rate compensation. This practice spread, and the factory was soon producing more than double its planned quota of wire. Although its finance office had to shell out some 40,000 yuan of extra wages, the added revenues were 90,000 yuan. Ordinary work still had to be paid on an hourly basis—unions, which influence the rules on this, deem piece-rate systems exploitative. Most real effort and profits in this factory were now after-hours.[96]

Shanghai people demonstrably work hard. A survey of the way they spend their time was made at the end of 1985, and the results were compared with data from city dwellers in twelve other countries. Shanghai residents spent notably longer hours on the job—about three-tenths of their time—while those in the international sample spent only two-tenths. Shanghai's six-day work week, its high portion of women employees, its few formal holidays, and the long time spent on travel to jobs that was counted as work hours in this survey may have affected the results, despite the untaxing production during job hours for some workers. The findings can be summarized in percentages of workers' time:[97]

	Shanghai sample	International
Work	31	21
Study	3	1
Housework	11	11
Sleep	36	34
Watching television	5	4
Socializing	3	4
Reading	3	1
Culture/sport	2	4
Other	6	20

The exactness of such comparisons is moot, but they suggest a self-report from Shanghai people who felt they were working hard. Wang Shaoguang shows that Chinese leisure time during reforms has become less political, more private, more diverse, more "Western," more commercialized, and more polarized between consumers who can afford high- or low-priced leisure activities.[98]

Factory team leaders, surveyed in the mid-1980s, were asked whether they liked their jobs. A majority said they did not. They complained of too much work. They were responsible for product quotas and quality in their teams, as well as for the safety of the workers; they were supposed to ensure "total quality control."[99] Their jobs were varied and vague: assuring "cultural construction," providing ration tickets for their team members, pouring cold drinks in hot weather, organizing lotteries and national savings bond campaigns among workers, campaigning for blood donations, family counseling, propagating the one-child policy, training workers in new techniques, raising public knowledge of law, and promoting several different kinds of study. The team leaders were not compensated much for all this work.

Media, whose mass work departments acquired news about grievances, increasingly published it. The newspaper *Shanghai Workers' Movement* was founded rather early during reforms.[100] The circulation was 125,000 weekly; the readership was "trade union cadres and activists." High officials clearly wanted any open political media for labor to dwell on the proletariat's historical glories, especially workers' past support for the Communist Party. Other stories, about labor problems, could nonetheless occasionally be printed in Shanghai's reform press. Not all of this news was good.

Shanghai's industrial safety record, for example, was rather bad. In 1979, fully 20 percent of all China's industrial deaths and major accidents occurred in Shanghai.[101] Concern about this scandal led to much propaganda about safety in the next few years, so that by 1982 the rate was down to 14 percent of China's very serious industrial accidents. But Shanghai's proportion of China's urban workforce was much smaller: only 4 percent.[102] So this city's laborers were more accident-prone, or less well-protected, than most in China.

Shanghai television and the *Workers' Daily* could cooperate on a series of reports about employee health. The fainting of a Shanghai woman labor model at a meeting spurred journalists to research stories about the effects of incentive pressures on workers' medical fitness. After several conferences, and with the involvement of a group from the national Federation of Trade Unions, a new regulation to protect employees' health was sent down.[103] Newspapers increasingly provided channels to air new kinds of information. But this incident reflected the reform's ambiguities because it articulated complaints about the fact that people were working harder.

The rise of new industries and informal unions in them increased protests about the conditions of labor. Reform journalists could report these problems. Pregnant women were found working at dangerous jobs handling poisons for ten or twelve hours a day. Their salaries were low (52 yuan per month, in a 1989 Shanghai county case). If they took maternity leaves, they received only 45 percent of their usual salaries. A local "Regulation to Protect Women Staff and Workers" was reportedly not enforced. Local leaders in workplaces ignored it. So did some husbands, whom journalists accused of illegal beatings and spousal abuse.[104]

A series of major industrial mishaps at the Shanghai First Steel Mill led to a "meeting to analyze the causes of accidents." A survey in the mill had found, for example, that 28 percent of the drivers had no schooling for their task and lacked licenses that they should have possessed. If accidents happened, cadres regularly claimed that workers themselves had violated regulations. Foremen also threatened to fire any employee who spoke in public about the causes of accidents.[105]

Official and Unofficial Workers' Movements in the 1980s

Shanghai's proletarians were increasingly able, during the more open subperiods of reform, to demand better conditions. Workers' real incomes generally rose in the early 1980s but then fell painfully because of rising inflation thereafter. The repertoire of conventional means for Chinese workers to protest bad conditions is wide: making suggestions, filing complaints with supervisory levels, holding meetings to air grievances, writing big-character posters, "going slow," striking, barricading managers in their offices, smashing company property, perhaps calling a general strike, or even attempting armed resistance. Each of these graduated techniques has actually been used by Shanghai workers at various times in the past, as Elizabeth Perry shows.[106] Local and national leaders know that these protests continue extensively, even when newspapers do not print reports of them.

Concern among officials about worker protest was probably the most important brake on management and ownership change in Shanghai. The state did not want to seem to abandon its proletarian constituency by closing or privatizing plants. Property right transfers are about people, not just laws and things. A great deal could be advocated, by the late 1980s, with the aim of shifting property rights *between* state-owned enterprises; but moving plants out of the state sector was chancier. The Party could somewhat rearrange workers, but it could not threaten their jobs without the danger of a major reaction. Dong Fureng, head of the Economic Institute of the Chinese Academy of Social Sciences, said explicitly, "Without a bankruptcy system, inefficient enterprises cannot be removed; and, in order to develop, efficient firms must take over others." This would strengthen the "profit-margin equalizing mechanism" and make capital more productive by turning more of it over to managers who made salable goods. But as this economist noted, it could also cost people their jobs: "The current practice of transferring the labor force together with enterprise property rights is not a long-term method. . . . This will involve the difficult problem of turning labor into a commodity."[107]

Unions in the late 1980s were officially mandated to persuade workers not to act against marketization of their time, while also encouraging more specialized production and maintaining their welfare. Unions were supposed to promote the "rationalization" of labor procedures and professional attitudes among workers. Employees were always supposed to follow factory managers. Shanghai unions reportedly called for more consultation about salaries, medical care, nurseries, and other topics on which workers had views.[108] Labor federations were instructed to pay special attention to small socialist factories and shops, which often were in straits for lack of facilities and space. Union cadres had an extremely difficult time, however, responding to these diverse demands from on high. They increasingly responded to interests in their more local constituencies, while seldom openly challenging central authorities. PRC unions for years had supported state capitalism. Now they spent more time helping their members.

The All-China Federation of Trade Unions (ACFTU) is theoretically not a state institution.[109] Within firms, unions run elections for workers' congresses. A mid-1986 poll by the ACFTU indicated that 70 percent of its members were "negative or doubtful about the role of workers' congresses in examining major matters and supervising cadres. There were demands that the power of the congresses be given legal status. . . . Moreover, the ACFTU demanded the right of democratically assessing cadres as well as electing and dismissing them."[110] Local leaders sometimes accommodated such demands, even though they did not establish a pattern the central government could afford to announce.

The state sector had scant money to solve these problems—or even to pay wages. Thirty thousand Shanghai workers were reportedly laid off in 1987. This was a small portion of the city's labor force, but was notable because it was reported.[111] The national Federation of Trade Unions admitted that Chinese urban workers staged at least 97 strikes in 1987 and 49 in the first half of 1988.[112] The actual number may have been considerably higher.

James Seymour recounts that,

> [T]he 1980s Trade Union Federation tended to take a neutral stance on the question of workers going on strike—neither encouraging nor forbidding the phenomenon. Furthermore, in the spring of 1989, the Federation, in a remarkable demonstration of independence, donated 100,000 *yuan* to the Tiananmen demonstrators (the only government agency to give them financial support). Then the Federation's executive committee reportedly voted to call a nationwide general strike. However, Federation head Zhu Houze hesitated, and then Li Peng declared martial law. The incident suggests the possibility of the union structure detaching itself from party control. . . . They started arresting workers before the June 4 crackdown, and after that, most of the arrests and all of the executions were of workers. The leader of the independent union in Shanghai, the most industrialized city, was shown on television being held at gunpoint, his face badly swollen from apparent beatings.[113]

A former Shanghai Party propaganda chief said, "The attacking of Mr. Hu Yaobang was very unpopular among workers in Shanghai."[114]

The Shanghai branch of the All-China Federation of Trade Unions—the Leninist "conveyor belt" to China's largest group of urban proletarians—was supposed mainly to convey the state's directives to workers. But for their own part, "Workers want a genuine democracy that would represent them in negotiations."[115] Communist parties since Marx and Lenin had long stressed the need to fight such "economism" in favor of another elite: the vanguard party of intellectuals (not workers) that could guide the proletariat.[116]

During the turmoil of 1989, the Shanghai ACFTU sometimes conveyed ideas from workers to the state. On May 10, Mayor Zhu Rongji and the relevant deputy mayor went to the local ACFTU office. (This was a reversal of the normal procedure that lower-ranked politicians call on higher-ranked ones.) The union chairman described "the situation of the workers" for them and opined that, "in some enterprises the workers' status has not reached that of the masters of the state . . . the level of workers' participation in management has not been satisfactory."[117] The mayor and the union head announced an eight-point agreement that was aimed to rectify this problem. This was corporatist government. Surely the state's propensity to make such agreements was heightened, at a time when it was trying to exterminate other Shanghai workers' organizations that it did not want to recognize.

State repression of independent workers' organizations was uncompromising in 1989. Dissident proletarians were killed by the state in far greater numbers than were dissident intellectuals. Many workers of the Shanghai Autonomous Federated Trade Union were harassed, and at least ninety-nine were arrested. These included contract workers, private entrepreneurs, and unemployed as well as state factory workers. The autonomous union's leader, Cai Chaojun, was accused of organizing demonstrations and making speeches as well as obstructing traffic and planning to establish a People's Party (*Renmin dang*) that would oppose the Communist Party.[118]

Other cities on the Shanghai delta also developed autonomous unions. The Hangzhou Public Security Bureau in early June arrested seven leaders of an illegal "Hangzhou Workers' Independent Union," which was based largely in a think tank for research on the garment market. They were accused of blocking traffic and creating disturbances "on behalf of democracy, freedom, and the struggle for human rights."[119]

These organizations did not last long, but they sprouted easily during reforms. The government's patronist unions were badly frayed. As Anita Chan has shown, official trade associations in China sometimes perform corporatist functions of interest aggregation, even if timidly.[120] They employ intellectuals, especially journalists for workers' newspapers. When official organizations linked to the workers' movement are abolished—as some were, in Shanghai during the late 1980s—their spokespeople and journalists associated with workers' newspapers protested. The Shanghai Worker Movement Materials Committee at its 1989 plenary meeting was instructed to dissolve itself. But member Sheng Yihang said, "Some leaders argued [wrongly, in his view] that trade unions have separated themselves from the Party and have become independent kingdoms. . . . We can end the committee but cannot end the study of the workers' movement." Sheng argued for more attention to both worker and student movements. "We should establish unofficial organizations to engage in this task."[121]

The most general problem was that the state could no longer support its establishment workers, as the employees of state-owned units quickly came to realize. By February 1990, "More than 800 [Shanghai] factories have halted production because of massive stockpiling. Meanwhile, many workers have been temporarily laid off and wait at home for work to resume, living on discounted salaries and temporary subsidies."[122] Of these firms, twenty-two were "entirely closed down," and many others were running "with token staff." Sluggish markets after the 1989 credit crunch were part of the problem, but an emphasis on this cause was clearly meant to forestall criticism of the state materials bureaus, which could no longer muster enough inputs for the socialist economy. Another explanation was "triangular debt," in which firms could not pay their workers because downstream companies defaulted on their own contracts. "Statistics show that such debts total 5 billion yuan" in 1989 Shanghai, "and the situation is getting worse."[123] State factories' debts were increasingly owed to rural industries in the nonstate sector, rather than to state banks or to each other.

The government had committed state factories to hiring more workers than they could afford. After-tax state sector profits plummeted during reforms: from 17 percent in 1978, to 13 percent in 1985, and only 3 percent by 1992. As a distinguished Chinese economist said, "If this pattern of decline continues, the entire Chinese public sector will become unprofitable within a few short years. . . . Moreover, the public sector employs a predominantly urban work force of some 45 million people, and together with their families these workers constitute about 45 percent of China's urban population."[124] Shanghai was particularly affected, since its state sector was large. The politics of this profit decline boiled down to potential and actual worker unrest.

State Workers Fear Layoffs in the 1990s

The conservatives in power wished to confirm their legitimacy after the Tiananmen massacre, and they did everything they could to make the economy *seem* stable to urban residents. The traditionally low portion of per-capita production value that compensated workers gave some buffer for generosity, and for political reasons more funds went to workers. But central budgeteers, who used to be spendthrifts, had scant money to spare. So top politicians ordered the managers of state plants to tighten their belts. Factory finances were hurt by "adjustments" on May 1, 1991. State workers received an across-the-board 2 percent increase of wages. But there was no compensation to factory budgets from the high offices that ordered this raise. Also on May 1, 1991, the state increased the retail sales prices of grain and edible oil in Shanghai. These rates were still subsidized, but they were generally doubled from their previous low levels.[125] Such changes rationalized the city's price structure. But a result was the extraction of even more money from Shanghai since the Beijing budget reduced its subsidies for local prices.

By mid-1991, the ACFTU leaders could do little more than plead with managements to help workers who felt threatened by layoffs. The ACFTU had 101 million members. Far more of them were concerned by state factories' declines than were actually let go. It was still a shibboleth that workers should become "the masters of their enterprises." Union officials had to acknowledge in public that, "the [workers'] democracy system . . . has come into conflict with the contract system and enterprise leader responsibility system brought in since 1984." They claimed, "It is wrong to excuse ignoring workers' rights for participation in management because of the director responsibility system."[126] Yet the original cause of socialism, protecting workers, had long since been subverted by exploitation. Communist planners and local entrepreneurs alike could justify their decisions against high wages in terms of market competition. The ACFTU was gigantic, semiofficial, and weak. Its local branches were still heavily influenced by management. It could not help workers very much.

Managers found novel ways to fire their employees, without admitting as much to higher administrative levels. The situations of many state-run factories were so dire that workers were happy enough to retain their housing and use their time that had been previously spent in state factories for more profitable pursuits. "There are serious shortages of energy, financial resources, and materials in Shanghai's enterprises. Workers thus get a lot of 'holidays.' Managers feel nervous and try to do their best to continue. But strangely, many workers (especially young workers) are indifferent. They are pleased not to do their work because they know that even if their enterprises cannot prosper, their wages and welfare will not be reduced at all." Practically all state firms were on contracts, "but there is no healthy contract *within* any given enterprise."[127]

The blame for this situation could be pinned on laborers, on managers, or on the state itself; and each of these actors naturally thought first of the others. Workers were chastised for having "no sense of crisis." "Although many companies already have no extra money, workers still insist on getting their annual bonuses and other benefits." The lack of incentives could also be laid on the heads of managers, who "do not inform workers about the real situation in enterprises when times are good; but when enterprises are in crisis, they ask workers to consider the company's future." This habit, bred in an earlier era when pressure to produce was administrative, was very ineffective under a market system. The state was the highest-profile target, and some Shanghai workers blamed reformers in Beijing for ceasing to subsidize their factories' input and output prices: "Many workers argue that the current crisis of enterprises results from the state's attempt to rectify the economic order, so their [individual] efforts are of no use."[128]

Some state factories in Shanghai during the 1990s could not afford to pay their workers, but they also could not use the labor for lack of raw materials. For political reasons, however, employees usually could not be laid off. So the factories bought consumer goods wholesale—which were given to "workers away from their posts" (*xiagang gongren*). These commodities were in lieu of wages, and the employees could try to retail them at whatever price the market would bear, keeping any proceeds.[129] State workers were thus asked to become hawkers.

State-sector workers became aware that their jobs might disappear completely. The previous special prestige of official employment evaporated in the 1990s because the government seemed to be impoverished. Employees in many units had little work to do. The reaction of some was to go on strike. A confidential PRC document, reported in Hong Kong, suggested that in 1993 China suffered six thousand illegal strikes and over two hundred worker "riots."[130]

Dependent workers were not always eager to break their ties of dependency so cleanly, however, because such action freed their bosses to try to punish them. Especially in nonindustrial units, or among educated dependents whose own identity was bound to the state, employees might simply withdraw quietly from work. Universities had been so severely handled in earlier decades that senior faculty members could easily save themselves a great deal of teaching work—legitimately making their late careers more comfortable than their earlier careers had been— by maintaining standards and admitting few students. State commercial enterprises lost business to private hawkers, to collectives, and to "workers away from their posts" who were selling the goods given to them in lieu of wages by state factories in financial straits. The previous panache of state employment, making many think they were officials, clearly waned.

Many employees nonetheless had to retain some tie to the state for housing, the urban commodity in shortest supply. Men in particular needed to do so. Since most women received housing because of their husbands' jobs, the incentives they faced were different. Most families in Shanghai had practically no reason to buy their own accommodation. At trivial rents, they could have minimally acceptable residential space. Land officials also proved unwilling to put much land on the market, lest they lose the special premium that foreigners, speculators, and overseas Chinese would pay. Space prices remained very high. Since housing was mainly the responsibility of the Real Estate Management Bureau, other state units such as factories or schools faced little difficulty in certifying their employees as legitimate residents, who should be given low-cost official housing. Both the workers and their units had short-run incentives not to change the socialist allocation of residences.

The previously ideal "organized dependency" of workers was quietly eroded. Strapped managers could approach state banks with sad tales about their changing environment, and they could get loans to give their workers "stability payments" (colloquially called *anding fei*). The basis for such loans was political, not economic. For the banks, they often became bad debts. But the amounts may have seemed to be reasonable insurance premiums against the horror of a free labor market in which some ex-state workers would be greatly discomfited if they did not find jobs.

Dependency often lasted longer than economic organization. Many state units did not need all their employees, and their workers needed their units only for housing. So some firms paid their staff but allowed them to be absent from work—and instead, to use time more lucratively in private or collective enterprises. For this permission, and especially for continued housing, some *workers paid their "employers"* back, in amounts that exceeded their continuing salaries.[131] The amounts of these kickbacks might be several times their low state salaries; and the units certainly needed the money. Such arrangements were acceptable to all of the actors involved.

Bureaucratic rigidities constrained state cadres far more than nonstate managers. Leaders of collectives could often cut payroll costs by retiring workers. State retirees' benefits were mandated at such high rates that their compensation was similar no matter whether they continued to work or not. Collectives generally paid less—in some cases, nothing—to ex-workers. The net incentives to local people largely determined what happened. In families where nonstate units employed the household head, the average number of retirees still at work in 1984 was 1.04. But for families of employees in state units, the average number of retirees still at work was much lower—only 0.56—because laws required state managers to pay them high fractions of their salaries even after they quit.[132] This official system reduced state employees' opportunities to make extra income. In some state firms, by the 1990s, half the payroll staff was retired.[133]

In 1992, for the first time in decades, the number of PRC registered employees declined, as did membership in labor unions.[134] By the mid-1990s, even though union rolls rose again, nonunionized workers in China outnumbered union members by a large margin. The All-China Federation of Trade Unions, according to a 1994 estimate, had 120 million members. But 180 million other workers lacked union protection in collective industries, various kinds of joint ventures, and private firms.[135] The dictatorship of the proletariat was paying little sustained attention to workers.

Academics

The Number and Size of Universities

Chinese universities, which had effectively closed for all academic purposes since 1966, began to reopen in about 1971. The campaign against intellectuals had nonetheless cowed so many intellectuals that little new research was started at that time. Teaching outside the applied natural sciences remained sporadic; but at least the doors of schools were again open. In safe subjects, a few new students were admitted.

Reforms proceeded far more slowly in famous, heavily monitored universities than, for example, among collectives or lower-level schools during the early 1970s. The revival of serious academic work, after extremely severe repression in the late 1960s, was hesitant to say the least—and in some areas, reversals in this pattern continued long after the height of radical control. This revival, because schools teach sensitive norms, was far from continuous. In 1971, the Shanghai Academy of Finance and Economics was sensibly closed, after having been incapacitated for several years, although it was later resurrected. In a few fields, notably Chinese archaeology or any science of use to the military, academic work was possible. By 1973, new research was being published on topics such as the ancient site of Turfan in Xinjiang, interpretations of Chinese philosophy, and analysis of a few foreign works including *Das Kapital*.[136] Much more was being written at this time than was put into print. The number of research papers completed annually at the Shanghai Iron and Steel Engineering School from 1972 to 1976 was nearly three times that of the previous half decade.[137]

Shanghai has a few excellent universities and many specialized tertiary institutions. Later during reforms, a book listed and described the considerable academic offerings of fifty-one such schools.[138] But the number of students per college remained very small, averaging only 2,500 in 1989 (compared with 6,000 in the USSR and 4,000 in Japan). This represented a reduction from prereform times, and the same pattern applied to secondary institutions as well. The student–teacher ratio of Shanghai's high schools in the early 1960s had been 21 : 1, but by 1989 it was only 11 : 1.[139] A major unintended effect of the Cultural Revolution was to reduce the work load of teachers later—apparently because that group had borne excruciating political burdens earlier.

For universities, the national government in Beijing by the 1980s sent down a regulation that the minimal number of students per lecturer was supposed to be 6.5.[140] But Shanghai by 1988 in fact had only 5.2 university students per instructor. This difference created several kinds of official pressure, for example to slow faculty hiring or to send current Shanghai instructors to inland universities (as had been done on a large scale in the 1950s). Such policies could be justified in terms of "streamlining structure" (jingjian jigou), a movement that had been revived in the 1980s after a similar campaign in the 1950s.

Another way to raise Shanghai's student–teacher ratio to the official Beijing's norm would have been to admit more students. This occurred somewhat, but the increase of faculty was even faster—and many of the new students were admitted to off-campus programs that used relatively little time or facilities of prestigious main campuses. China's major universities have a tradition of residential education; so their regular students generally live in dormitories and eat in cafeterias. During the 1980s, there was scant money to build more dorms. When more students came into tertiary institutions, they were on a day basis only (called "walk-and-read students," zoudu xuesheng). Universities set up branch campuses (fenxiao) for these pupils, often using the classrooms and lab facilities of good high schools. The entrance requirements at such campuses were not nearly as stiff as at main campuses. Students wishing to study at a famous university were divided according to their test scores into groups (fenshu duan), and those who did not make the grade for normal campuses might be admitted to the branches as day students.

The increase in the number of nonresidential students at Shanghai universities still did not raise Shanghai's student–faculty ratio to the level the central government had mandated. University instructors in many countries have a seldom-spoken interest in teaching only a few good pupils, in order to allow more time for other activities including research. The Cultural Revolution established in China a later tradition of low teaching loads. Even high school teachers (like other state employees) did not have a very heavy work load—often about twelve contact hours a week, less than in high-income countries. University instructors had fewer teaching hours. At the same time, faculty hiring accelerated. Shanghai's full-time university teaching staff increased during every year of the 1970s and 1980s for which data are available.

Shanghai university enrollments recovered from the Cultural Revolution in 1972–73. They then had slow growth in 1976–77, despite state dicta that teachers should accept more students. The ratio of pupils to professors remained very low by international standards. This tug-of-war between educational budgeteers and reluctant teachers remembering the 1960s' trauma continued for many years. As Table 3.2–6 shows, enrollment grew quickly in 1971–81, declined in 1981–82 as the most qualified members of the Cultural Revolution generation finally graduated, and then rose at a moderate pace—until 1989, when it fell for three years running. The effects of 1989–91 political fears are evident in these figures, but not all the causes were governmental. Good new teachers became hard for Shanghai universities to recruit because so many young academics went into business or abroad. The student–teacher ratio by 1992 had risen because of its decreasing denominator; the absolute number of students since 1989 had also dropped, but not so much as the number of teachers. Some interviewees ruefully suggest that old remaining professors, having been through so much hassle for decades, felt they should take fewer students and do less work.

As these figures show, the change in enrollments began before 1978. The data obscure, however, that enrollments *on main campuses* during the 1980s rose only somewhat faster than faculty hiring there. The Cultural Revolution, by demoralizing large numbers of educators and forcing later governments to treat them with care, brought them fully into the socialist norm of performing little work. Production pressure on them after that brought few results. Shanghai's overall student–teacher ratio for tertiary institutions remained well below the minimum specified by central state rules. The national regulations were practically ignored by local educators. Plans were loyally announced, but compliance did not follow.[141] In China as a whole, the number of universities has rocketed upward during the reform period—but not in Shanghai, apparently for lack of money. The number of Chinese tertiary institutions rose by 76 percent between 1978 and 1986.[142] In the first half of the new decade, from 1980 to 1985, the number of regular universities in China increased 51 percent.[143] But in Shanghai during this half decade, there was according to one report a decrease of such institutions by 10 percent.[144] In 1984, Shanghai had 37 universities and colleges and 79,000 undergraduates—somewhat less than Beijing's 53 universities and colleges (with 91,000 tertiary students in the capital). Jiangsu had 49 tertiary institutions with 79,000 undergraduates; and Zhejiang, 22 such universities with 39,000 students.[145]

The number of tertiary institutions in Shanghai began to rise after 1984, when Beijing budget makers' power to constrain it became weaker. By 1988, the city had 34 percent more universities than in 1984. But by 1991, Shanghai had one fewer university than in 1988. In Guangdong, for comparison, the number of universities during the first half of the 1980s rose 47 percent; and the number of tertiary students, 59 percent.[146] The number of tertiary institutions in Jiangsu also rose smartly: up 52 percent in the decade 1981–1991.[147] Shanghai has not received

Table 3.2–6

Teachers and Students in Shanghai Regular Tertiary Institutions, 1970–1995 (numbers, student-teacher ratios, enrollment rises)

Year	Full-time teachers	Student undergrads	S/T ratio	% enrollment rise over previous year
1970	10,957	3,755	0.34	
1971		3,510		−7
1972		7,946		126
1973		16,268		105
1974		24,617		51
1975	12,369	31,313	2.53	27
1976		31,862		2
1977		34,867		9
1978	16,309	50,584	3.10	45
1979	17,681	67,404	3.81	33
1980	18,624	76,731	4.12	14
1981	18,755	91,136	4.86	19
1982	20,510	83,918	4.09	−8
1983	21,874	78,696	3.60	−6
1984	22,169	89,879	4.05	14
1985	24,306	107,865	4.44	20
1986	25,664	117,664	4.58	9
1987	26,375	122,529	4.65	4
1988	26,603	128,163	4.82	5
1989	26,529	126,091	4.75	−2
1990	25,788	121,251	4.70	−4
1991	24,501	116,925	4.77	−4
1992	23,866	119,532	5.01	2
1993	22,841	131,034	5.74	10
1994	21,863	140,396	6.42	7
1995	21,522	144,082	6.69	3

Sources: The student–teacher ratio is calculated from figures in *Shanghai Statistical Yearbook, 1989 Concise Edition*, Municipal Statistical Bureau of Shanghai, ed. (Beijing: China Statistical Publishing House, 1989), p. 133, which has numbers of full-time teachers. Enrollment figures for some years in the 1970s come from *Shanghai jiaoyu, 1988* (Shanghai Education, 1988), Wang Shenghong, ed. (Shanghai: Tongji Daxue Chuban She, 1989), p. 212. The 1988–92 numbers are from *Shanghai tongji nianjian, 1993* (Shanghai Statistical Yearbook, 1993), State Statistical Bureau, ed. (Beijing: Zhongguo Tongji Chuban She, 1993), p. 346; and for 1993–95, see the same yearbook, 1996 edition, p. 337. Some data from the early 1970s are italicized to stress the rise of enrollments then.

as much state money as other places for building new universities, but the metropolis has founded them when it could.

The aims of higher education in Shanghai remained unstable because the state and the students had somewhat different ideas on what they should be. These goals had changed erratically during earlier periods. In 1956, for example, universities had been mandated to produce scientists. But by early 1957, they were urged to graduate more professional workers; and by 1958, more laborers. In the Cultural Revolution, official directives called for the graduation only of "revolutionary fighters against taking the capitalist road."[148] During reforms, the official mandates became broader and less restrictive in practice. Universities were supposed to train technical and scientific workers, but also some generalists, including many with scientific degrees, who could devote themselves to administrative vocations.

The Inbreeding of Academic Appointments and Research

Chinese university faculties reproduce with almost no new blood from outside. This can make academic standards slip, because personal relationships among senior and junior colleagues easily become cozy to the detriment of intellectual criticism. The fences between departmental fields become more rigid, as local professors in a discipline reach an implicit consensus to assign one another easier jobs by excluding a part of their field from their purview or by other means. This syndrome affects the intellectual life of many countries. In China, it became very important after the Cultural Revolution, as Party committees in universities unevenly withdrew from making administrative decisions for academics.[149] Most Western or liberal analysts assume any such depoliticization must lead to higher academic standards in universities. They presume the Leninist party in such a situation must be the sole source of stagnation among intellectuals. This premise is often useful because thinkers in the PRC have often lacked enough political power to protect their creativity. But this premise can also ignore some negative effects of local power within academe, especially organization that fosters intellectual timidity after an experience like the Cultural Revolution. Without any help from a Communist Party, professors can make their lives easier than the actual problems in their fields would imply.

This pattern continued strongly far into the reform period, perhaps because academic institutions had been subject to tight control in Mao's time. To the very limited extent reforms started in academe during the early 1970s, the change in this field was slower and less sure than in other areas (notably rural industry), whose spatial scatter and political quiescence meant that the Party's centralized controls were more fleeting, after the high tide of China's revolution.

Effects of Past Struggles on Research Work

Shanghai academic staffs by the mid-1970s had been through a great many griefs in campaigns since 1957. Many researchers were old. In 1977, the members of

Jiaotong University's "leadership group" averaged sixty-four years, and cadres who were "middle-aged or less" comprised only one-fifth. Only 60 percent had college educations. But by 1984, the leading group was 80 percent "young or middle-aged," and four-fifths had university educations. The average age had dropped ten years.[150]

Personnel reforms at Jiaotong University involved moving some staff members and promoting others. Previously, research groups had been set up under old professors, with "three generations in one hall," just "like relatives." But more circulation of personnel was a major aim of the Jiaotong reforms. "Past historical movements [the Antirightist Campaign and the Cultural Revolution] have left ineradicable schisms between people."[151] Old critics and their previous victims could not perform well together as colleagues. Reformers wanted to move them to different offices or labs, away from their local enemies of past years.

Three obstacles nonetheless prevented people from leaving Jiaotong.[152] The first was lower salaries in most alternative jobs. So it was declared that any person departing Jiaotong for an approved assignment elsewhere would receive at least as much pay in the new job—even if it was not in Shanghai—including any prospective salary increases that would later be normal in the metropolis. A second "obstacle" was residence; but if a job shift from Jiaotong were within Shanghai, the person changing employment could remain in a current home or in queue for housing. The third matter was rank; so the person shifting jobs would be considered for promotion at Jiaotong just before departure. Time at Jiaotong would count toward seniority for promotion in the new job. In the first four years of the 1980s, some five hundred people left Jiaotong under this plan. The total size of the staff before their departure was 4,600; so the portion that was encouraged to create vacancies was about 11 percent.

Academic Professional Associations

Think tanks, too, began to change after the trauma of the 1960s, even though reforms in academe came later than reforms of most other institutions. Academic work units had not generally been abolished. In the early 1970s, the Social Sciences Division of the Chinese Academy of Sciences still existed. Just seven months after Mao's death and eight months after the fall of the Gang of Four, as early as May 7, 1977, the philosophy and social sciences section of the Chinese Academy of Sciences was hived off to form a new establishment: the Chinese Academy of Social Sciences (CASS).[153] Most of its researchers had been viciously reviled during the Hundred Flowers movement of 1957, the Four Cleans Campaign of 1964, and/or the Cultural Revolution of 1966–69. In Shanghai at the start of 1978, the nucleus of the city's own Academy of Social Sciences also began.[154]

Previously repressed subjects received public recognition as valid topics of academic discourse—although intellectuals had thought about them unofficially earlier. Studies of mental health had not lapsed, and the pre-1978 period saw several, partly because some mentally disturbed patients remained in hospitals—very obviously needing treatment—so facile denials of a need to think about ways of helping them were untenable.[155] Child development became more researchable in China. A center to study human development received support from a group of nongovernment organizations (including several that were foreign).[156] By the next decade, it was possible for data to be published about sociological subjects that could never have been studied openly during the Cultural Revolution. A table could be presented in a book, for example, showing that illegitimacy among children was evidently the most prominent cause of social pathologies like petty thievery, loitering on streets at night, and youthful smoking and gambling.[157]

As new topics of research were admitted to academic legitimacy, further institutes were added to both the national and metropolitan social sciences academies. An Institute of Information Studies in the national unit traced its founding to 1975. Three years later, shortly after the academy's formal establishment, the Institute of World Politics and Institute of Journalism were added. An Institute of Sociology was created in 1979, as well as an Institute of Marxism–Leninism–Mao Zedong Thought that was headed by the famous quasi-liberal theoretical innovator Su Shaozhi. Five institutes to study various capitalist and developing regions were added in 1981. In 1984, Taiwan studies could come in from the cold, with the public establishment of a CASS institute for research on that island of capitalist China.[158]

An apparent purpose of the new structure was to make the rehabilitation of social scientists easier. The new Chinese Academy in Beijing had moved quickly to call five meetings in 1978–79 to discuss the professional revival even of the most difficult field: political science. December 1980 saw the founding of a Chinese Political Science Association.[159] By 1981, the Chinese Academy of Social Sciences established a preparatory version of an Institute of Political Science. Ten Shanghai scholars wrote to the CCP Central Committee, asking for the establishment of political science departments at Fudan and other major universities, and suggesting that each of these schools should admit fifty to one hundred new undergraduate students and some graduate students annually, to read course syllabi on political science, on the histories of Chinese and foreign politics and institutions, on the histories of Chinese and foreign political thought, on China's constitution and comparative constitutions, on Chinese politics, public administration, urban politics, and local government.[160] The first PRC undergraduate programs in politics were restarted in 1983, not in Beijing but at Shanghai's Fudan University.[161] By 1987, the Chinese Political Science Association was publishing two journals, *Political Science Studies* and *Foreign Political Science,* and it had a membership of 1,200 political scientists.

In Shanghai particularly, there was a renaissance of capitalist historiography. Several books recalled Chinese bourgeois entrepreneurs' patriotism in the 1920s and 1930s with thick nostalgia—and with a contemporary aim of restoring to political grace scholars who had grown up in capitalist families. The label "bourgeois" became less damning than it had been. The legal significance of the label was abolished in 1979—although informally, everyone in any workplace still knew which colleagues had been burdened with it. In a 1982 article, a historian confessed he had earlier written that Shanghai's late Qing and Republican capitalists were reactionary; they were "fearful that the revolution would cause them to suffer personal losses." But by 1982, this author avowedly changed his views (on the basis of further research, he claimed): The capitalists had actually been crucial to creating and extending the revolution, especially in its early stages, and their personal economic interests were not their sole concerns. According to this revisionist historiography, many Shanghai capitalists had been patriots.[162]

A group of historians did a careful survey of the role of Shanghai's bourgeoisie during the May Thirtieth movement of 1925, which involved a general strike against foreign-owned companies after a Chinese worker at a Japanese-owned factory had been killed by British-officered Indian police.[163] This new history stressed that the wealthiest Chinese "compradore capitalists," although they served foreign companies, often also set up their own businesses. This made them "national capitalists." Research on biographical statistics about leaders of the Shanghai General Chamber of Commerce, and also on an association of less wealthy shopkeepers, called the General Association of Businessmen of All Localities, showed that foreign-associated compradore capitalists were important in both. It claimed that most of these merchants were (on a part-time basis at least) mainly in business for themselves as national capitalists. Therefore,

> During the high tide of the May Thirtieth movement, they stood on the side of the Chinese people. Even if they were seriously frightened during the upsurge of the labor movement [which was the most impressive mobilization anywhere by the CCP during the 1920s], they donated large amounts of money to ameliorate the conditions of the striking workers, in spite of the serious economic losses suffered by the industrial and commercial enterprises during the period of the general strike.[164]

Revisionist historians thus claimed that, despite the capitalists' sometime "conciliatory attitude" toward foreigners, "To do them credit, . . . they strove to force the imperialists to make certain concessions through mediation and negotiation, and they were successful to a certain extent."[165] This view of the capitalists' role is sharply different from prereform official doctrines about them.

The Localization of Academic Employment

Mao had tried to follow Stalin by developing his own cadre of establishment intellectuals who could be hired by the central state. In the mid-1960s, more than half of Fudan University's graduates had become researchers or teachers working in units that were at least formally under management by the central state.

Table 3.2–7

Rise of Local Scientific Reseach Institutions in Shanghai
(total numbers, percentages local)

	% of units local-run	number of institutions	employees total	employees %local
1957	57	77	7,356	20
1965	41	88	30,235	33
1979	59	246	68,084	40
1984	67	803	125,107	44

Source: Percentages calculated from *Shanghai keji, 1949–1984* (Shanghai Science and Technology, 1949–1984), Wei Hu and Fang Kaibing, eds. (Shanghai: Kexue Jishu Wenxian Chuban She, 1985), pp. 1230–31. After the mid-1980s, the trend toward localization continued, and the published data were divided into more categories.

Among the students who graduated by 1981 and 1982, however, 21 percent were assigned to work for local governments' research units, and half worked for other local units.[166] There was a trend, in reforms, for fewer graduates of this "keypoint university" to work for the central government. Relatively more were hired by local jurisdictions. There was also a trend away from research and teaching, and toward work in practical management.

Central government support for research in science is important in China as elsewhere. Table 3.2–7 shows years for which information is available about the number of institutions and personnel in Shanghai's centrally and locally run scientific institutions. The reform period witnessed a sharp increase in the total number of research units, especially locally run think tanks, until by 1984 there were twice as many local as central ones. There was also a convergence in the numbers of investigators by level of administration, with local employees only somewhat less than half the total by 1984. According to available figures, the local portion rose most quickly between 1965 and 1979. The degree of Beijing control over nominally central think tanks in Shanghai had also decreased by the 1980s.

Economic think tanks were all the rage in reform Shanghai. The city's Academy of Social Sciences in 1978 established its Institute of Economics and soon also founded an Institute for Sectoral Economics and an Institute for International Economics. The city's Finance Bureau set up an Institute of Financial Research. Fudan University by 1979 had an Institute of Socialist Economics (the name may suggest that even intellectuals could be loyal). The municipal government in 1980 established its Center for Economic Studies. That same year, the local Social Sciences Academy founded a consultancy, selling advice on any aspect of Shanghai's economy, society, or law. In 1981, the Shanghai Water

Transport College set up a think tank; and the next year, the Shanghai College of Finance did the same. In 1983, the city government's Planning Commission founded its Institute of the Planned Economy, to provide better long-term analyses for its work. By 1984, the Commodity Prices Bureau finally set up a think tank. The local branch of the China Construction Bank created an Institute of Fixed Capital Investment Studies; the city's Accounting Bureau, its academic Institute of Accounting; and the Statistics Bureau, its Institute for the Application of Statistical Science. By the middle of the decade, Shanghai had thirty-one major economic think tanks, hiring eight hundred professional researchers.[167] The state also encouraged universities to make liaisons with the economy. In doing so, however, it weakened state control of academics.[168] The Party less easily controlled the professorate, after the professors found outside opportunities in business.

Administrative Reforms for Specialization and Money

Professors increasingly ran universities, during the less reactionary periods of the reform era. In the early 1970s, the situation had been confused because many academics were still under political stigmas. At Fudan, fully 90 percent of the professors and associate professors had been castigated during the Cultural Revolution.[169] Practically all university administrators, even in the Party, had lost prestige at the same time, and these dishonors were not forgotten quickly.

In 1977–79, new promotions to headships of Shanghai academic institutions were exceptionally numerous. Forty-two new directors or deputy heads of university-level schools were named from among faculty, as were ninety-three new chairs of departments. Forty-five new chiefs or deputies of hospitals were also appointed during these years.[170] At the same time, 332 professors and 6,339 lecturers were promoted. One aim of the reforms was "to begin to restore" the "system of dividing work and taking responsibility" (fengong fuze zhi) in Shanghai's academic institutions. This meant that more administrative positions went to specialists—although Party generalists did not all disappear.

In the 1980s, some professors were also admitted to the Party. No longer were all voices on university committees supposed to represent the same functional interest. Reforms at Jiaotong University, which received wide publicity, came in four categories that could apply to almost any institution. First, the "leadership structure" (lingdao tizhi) was supposed to be decentralized. Second, the "personnel system" (renshi zhidu) was said to be altered along meritocratic lines. Third, the "allocation system" (fenpei zhidu) was designed to make salaries proportionate with contributions. Fourth, the "work system" (gongzuo zhidu) was supposed to create incentives and raise academic productivity.

Deng Xuchu, the reform leader at Jiaotong, encouraged instructors to be creative. He claimed, "A cadre who parrots the Party Committee's resolutions with complete inflexibility is not good." People were no longer supposed to be promoted simply because they got along with their colleagues. An instructor whose curriculum vitae was like that of a businessman, because he made many trips to Hong Kong, aroused criticism from fellow teachers—but the university administration supported him for promotion. Another instructor, considered by his colleagues to have an immodest, grating, but bold personality, was made the head of his department because of his expertise. He promised he would not change his ways in his new administrative post.[171]

Jiaotong University extended the responsibility system to department chairs in particular. Each unit head was empowered to name a deputy who could act in his or her absence, as well as heads of subordinate offices and research groups. A chair was mandated to discuss these appointments with the department's general Party branch—but the CCP now was said to lack formal authority, on its own, to fill these posts.[172] Under similar rules, department heads obtained rights to make suggestions on the future employment of graduates. They could "hand over," for reassignment to other posts, department members who did not "meet the needs of work." They could recommend promotions to senior ranks and decide titles in junior ranks—and were supposed to be in charge of salaries, bonuses, and benefit decisions. They could determine leaves and vacations. The reforms increased the local powers, at least in some kinds of institutions, of midlevel cadres. Specifically Chinese patronism was still the rule, but central control of local patrons became weaker.

Deng Xuchu stressed the importance of having new personnel in Jiaotong's leading group, and in an interview he downplayed various worries that had been raised by other people about this change. These concerns explicitly included a fear of "disorder," apparently because some of the new leaders had not fared well under others in earlier campaigns. The idle worries also included a general fear of reform—Jiaotong's forwardness was said to put pressure on other universities—and "excessive" aversion to making money from scientific consultancies, even excessive concern about violating regulations sent from higher levels.[173]

In secondary institutions, administrative structures were reformed more sharply than in universities, perhaps because younger students are of great interest to China's most powerful political institutions (families). The government is mainly interested in older students. The traditional Maoist structure had each high school headed by a principal, who was paired with a Party secretary. They were usually assisted by about three vice principals.[174] Teachers, under an academic dean in the 1960s, were organized to serve classes of students graduating in the same year. With reforms, however, this structure was changed and was specialized less often by class, and more often by academic subject.[175] Especially by the 1990s, the fees charged in many of Shanghai's best secondary schools (as described above in the section on school finance) increasingly made school administrations resemble private companies. Patterns of change in Shanghai's secondary schools are summarized elsewhere in this book. Central control of teachers, at both the secondary and tertiary levels, gave way in part to more local and material concerns.

Students

Marianne Bastid describes two ideas that have dominated Chinese thinking about education for more than a century:

> One is the notion that influences coming from other civilizations constitute a risk of moral alienation and political subjugation. The other is that a distinction can and should be made among the elements which make up another culture, so that a selective assimilation is possible of those elements pre-judged as capable of enriching Chinese civilization. The two interlinked ideas were rooted in a vivid sense of the originality and coherence of Chinese culture and in the conviction that this culture was the very foundation of the existence and unity of the Chinese Empire.[176]

It may seem odd for members of the world's most populous nation to fear they might be educated out of an identity whose long history gives them obvious reasons for pride. This danger is prevented not just by norms, but also by China's situation. Because of its size, China is among the world's least likely countries to lose its national "characteristics" (except insofar as people there decide that they wish to lose some of these). Who exactly is spreading the exaggerated rumors of China's potential demise? Intellectuals, especially in government, are the public worriers about this, and they have their own interests to serve.[177]

Technical education in Western science and engineering did not seem to threaten continued rule by Chinese intellectuals. But other ideas from the West raised questions about whether people with knowledge have an inalienable right to run the government. Democratic ideas about the mere counting of noses, as if aggregated individuals could represent communities, threatened to suggest that intellectuals might not always deserve power. If they moralized in too haughty a manner, people might not vote for them. These ideas may or may not endanger China's "characteristics," but they suggest the most articulate people there might do more to get along with other kinds of their fellow citizens.

Students, especially those graduating from universities, inevitably had a career interest in seeing more turnover from official jobs into which they might be hired. Tertiary admissions during reforms certified potential leaders in government, but not in nonstate jobs. Since criteria for promotion in official posts were similar, the link between educational certification and state positions was strong—but the central state, at least, was not the most dynamic sector. Government leaders wanted to assure that Chinese education would not teach subversive errors. A practical procedure for this purpose was to use academic tests and loyalty reports to admit students in tertiary levels, and then to use the same criteria to promote graduates in jobs. These techniques are not new or unique to China. They have been used extensively in most eras of the PRC, however. During reforms, the main change was in their nonstate context.

As China's economy needed more educated workers and more diverse workers, a millennia-old connection between moral education and central power began to erode. This educational transition was partly a change from elite to mass attendance at universities. In China, the portion of the relevant age cohort that goes for higher education is still only about 3 percent—whereas in Japan or North America, it is over 50 percent. During past decades, China's educational change had been delayed by Maoist job allocations, which meant that each graduate was supposed to take a job as a state cadre. As that norm was broken, the state paid less to train talent for its own use. The political correlate was that many students were distanced from their previous direct dependence on officialdom, including the Party. The financial correlate was that the government could insist that their families, along with local governments and corporations, pay tuitions. Reforms made the state unable to give government-linked jobs to all the educated people the economy needed. The ancient legitimacy of learning as the royal road to government became weaker, and education licensed power networks other than the state. It made individuals more responsible for discovering their own careers.

Educational Admissions

Educational reform was slower in the early 1970s than were changes in other spheres, notably rural industrialization. During the periods of Mao's time in which university entrance was supposed to be based largely on political recommendations, admissions were often actually based on kinship. Political qualifications were hard to assess, but family relations were not. So it was administratively easy for evaluators to escape criticism by admitting the sons and daughters of high officials.

When Chinese universities reopened in the early 1970s, they admitted "worker-peasant-soldier students." Some of the new pupils who arrived were actually from those groups, but many others (no matter what their labels) were children of CCP leaders. When early 1970s' classes arrived at Qinghua University to start their studies, for instance, "Red Flag" limousines typical among top cadres reportedly left off many of the students. This kind of situation became so egregious that, in May 1972, the Central Committee decreed that "back door" university admissions should be stopped.[178]

No Chinese institutions had been more severely damaged by the Cultural Revolution than schools, and they did not recover quickly. Promotion rates from one level of schooling to another rose, as high schools and universities were allowed to reopen. But in 1973, academic test results were still unavailable to aid admission decisions. When new schools were established, or old ones renamed, they became "worker-peasant-soldier" colleges (*gongnongbing xueyuan*).[179] These tertiary institutions, attended by many who had earlier failed the entrance tests to regular colleges, included an array of television universities, employees' universities, and vocational universities (*dianshi daxue, zhigong daxue, zhuanye daxue*). Academic standards at these institutions were far below the standards of elite schools such as Fudan, Jiaotong, Zhejiang, or Nanjing Universities.

Even for research degrees, the educational system showed openings in the early 1970s. The first Chinese graduate students after the Cultural Revolution enrolled in Shanghai in 1973. Some research students had been formally at school but academically inactive during previous years. Between 1975 and 1977, the city's graduate enrollment declined somewhat, but the rate of growth from a low base was fastest from 1973 to 1975.[180] A specific result of the Cultural Revolution was that many "educated youths," whose educations had actually been interrupted by send-downs, could resume their studies as partial compensation for remaining at posts outside big cities. So correspondence courses by 1975 were widely available to Shanghai youth who had gone to work in the countryside.[181]

Another particular problem arose by 1979, when some of the last cohorts of students admitted under lax mid-1970s' standards at Shanghai universities came up for graduation. Many of these "worker-peasant-soldier students" were of relatively low academic quality, especially in comparison with the classes admitted by the 1977 exams. It was acceptable to wonder, in public by 1979, whether they should receive their diplomas. At the Shanghai Academy of Chinese Medicine, such students got their degrees, but they openly expressed fear that their educations would be deemed second-rate. Party committees launched efforts to console them.[182] Often they were assigned from Shanghai inland. But many declined such jobs. Instead, they came to protest at the offices that tried to move them out of the city, pestering the cadres and "exchanging experiences" (as during the Cultural Revolution). Bureaucrats reportedly "received them many times and patiently tried to persuade them" to go elsewhere in this reform-era rustication.[183]

University Admissions Criteria and Procedure

Pressure for university admissions had been very intense for several years. In 1977, age limits for university applicants were temporarily suspended. In that year and the next, people as old as thirty could take the entrance exams; but in the following year, the norm was reduced to students who were not much older than twenty.[184] By the middle of 1977, extra examinations were held out of season, to begin as quickly as possible the politically sensitive job of offering higher educations to the best students in the cohorts that had been denied education earlier for political reasons only. But these were the most dangerous potential rivals to noneducated cadres in leadership. This very high-powered group of students, who took the exams in 1977, entered universities in that winter (rather than in fall, as is usual), and they graduated in the middle of the 1981–82 academic year. The second group of students accepted on the basis of competitive exams (in 1978) also graduated in 1982. These two famous classes of '82 are, by all reports from Chinese professors, the most competent cohort of university students the nation had ever seen.

University admissions were still granted according to several different criteria, even though exams were most crucial. A 1979 Shanghai article claimed that three factors were important: health, morals (which could still be defined in terms of loyalty to the regime), and scholarly knowledge. The procedure nominally put health and politics as preliminary considerations, before academics.[185] The process was not changed much during later reform years, although its implementation has varied at different times. It started with assessments of each applicant's "inner and outer" aspects, as represented by health and politics. So when a student registered to take university entrance exams, the secondary school would file a report based on a political investigation (*zhengzhi shencha*) and another report on a health examination (*shenti jiancha*).

The political report was secret, based on the full dossier of previous annual assessments—though for a great majority of student applicants by the 1980s, this hurdle was relatively easy to clear. Every year, high school students were assigned to write a summary of their activities. This was presented to a "small group" for criticism. On this basis, the faculty director of the class wrote confidential comments, which went into the student's file. On graduation, either the guidance office of the school or else the local Party branch would write further comments. The student was not allowed to see any of these, but they were used as a partial basis for placement recommendations.[186]

The comments (*pingyu*) regularly contained three sections: on political behavior (*zhengzhi biaoxian*), consciousness (*sixiang juewu*), and moral quality (*daode pinzhi*). The reform period saw a huge increase of standardized, uninformative reports in all these categories—which made them all less important—but university admissions procedures still did not change structurally, in ways that would preclude arbitrariness in schools' guidance offices or CCP branches against particular students. The politics and health records, once they were written, were not ordinarily edited at any later stage.

On a university application form, the student would indicate a preference for either humanities or scientific education (respectively, *wenke* or *like*). Within one of these categories, the student would list preferences of school-and-department combinations. (For example, an applicant's first choice might be the Fudan University Journalism Department, the second choice might be the same university's English Department, and the third choice might be a department at the Shanghai University of Foreign Languages.) After 1978, each department announced in advance the number of students it expected to admit, and also a predicted number from each province or city. If the student wanted a major in the humanities, there were usually five exams: in politics, history, geography, Chinese, and a foreign language. For some specialities such as finance, there were also exams in mathematics. If a scientific specialization was chosen, there were seven tests: politics, Chinese, physics, chemistry, biology, mathematics, and a foreign language.

The grading procedures were complex, to make them fair, in ways that strongly echoed the nearly fail-safe processes used for civil service exams in China's imperial era. Specialist committees of Shanghai professors and middle-school teachers in various fields did the grading for specific tests. School instructors could only mark papers of applicants from outside their own urban districts. All papers were read "blind," identified by numbers rather than names. A uniform scale, from 1 to 100, was used for all tests. If this whole procedure contained any biases, they could scarcely have arisen from the scrupulous marking process.

Once the scores were known, the secretariat of an enrollment committee (*zhaosheng weiyuanhui*) at the municipal level summed them, with various weightings for various specialities, and then divided the students into score cohorts (*fenshu duan*) according to their marks as required by their first-choice departments. This committee's secretariat could also scan the politics and health reports, to see which folders should be presented first to a larger admissions meeting of university representatives—although from 1979 to 1988, relatively few folders were said to have been re-ranked at this stage of the process.

On a preliminary basis, each university tried to reserve many more than its previously announced quota of admits from each geographic jurisdiction to each department.[187] Representatives of "keypoint universities"—such as Shanghai's Tongji, Fudan, Jiaotong, or East China Normal University—attended the enrollment meeting (*zhaosheng huiyi*). They could reserve groups of students according to the preference lists, beginning with the top cohort. Officers of keypoint universities from other provinces (such as Qinghua or Beijing universities in the capital) were also present at this session in each major jurisdiction, for example, in Shanghai. All these proceedings had to be kept confidential; so they took place in a series of rooms, to which admission was restricted, where folders were presented according to specialities and were examined by representatives of the students' preferred universities in order.

Looking at the political and health reports, a university could later reject some of its reserved files, reducing the number of its actual admits to the level of its final quota. (If it was able to reserve too few, it might have to go further down the cohort list, to students not already claimed by other universities.) In some of the more reactionary years during the reform era, decisions on how to use the health and politics reports were handled in a relatively centralized manner. In more reformist years, the nonacademic reports were similar in so many cases, they seldom provided a basis for distinguishing between the applicants. In any case, the academic score cohorts were supposed to be dealt with together.

If a student in a cohort was not accepted by any university department on his or her preference list when that cohort came up for consideration, the file became part of the pool at the next lower cohort, for later processing. When any university's representatives filled their quotas, they left the meeting. After this procedure was complete, the enrollment committee secretariat posted the lists of admitted students.

Shanghai universities followed an explicit policy of not admitting students from remote parts of China, if they were deemed essential in their work at those places, and especially if they were working in "grass-roots" endeavors. They could also be prevented from coming to university in Shanghai if they were thought by their cadres to want a "gangplank" (*tiaoban*) to move their household registrations to the metropolis. But for exceptionally promising students, this policy was apparently bent.

Even for graduate work, political criteria remained a matter of some importance for admission. In 1983, a well-known Fudan professor named Tan Qixiang, head of the History Department, objected to the "leftist criterion" that was apparent in recommendation letters for some Fudan applicants. As chair of his department, he was authorized to select new doctoral students in history at Fudan. When two students received bad recommendations from their units—for example, one was said to be discontented with his job—Tan said bluntly that he felt such letters should be disregarded in entrance decisions.[188]

By no means were the mid-1980s a period in which all educational administrators agreed that politics should be unimportant for admissions. At a meeting in 1984 concerning the entrance of graduate students, for example, Vice Minister of Education Huang Xinbai said that some departments were lowering their political criteria to admit academically more advanced students. He disapproved of this trend, because of the difficulties these students created in "ideological work" after they reached college.[189]

Admissions Pressures

Because China's "educational transition" was just beginning, and because most élite officials believed that modern societies show no weakening of the traditional Confucian link between thinking and power, the state did not mandate high school places for most Chinese students. Also, very few could go to universities—only 3 or 4 percent of high school cohorts in the 1980s. Schools and teachers were deemed successful only to the extent that their students passed exams. But in 1977 and 1978, most of those who sat for the national tests had finished what schooling they could either before or during the Cultural Revolution. So very intense pressure on high school teachers did not start until the early 1980s. As educators then warned, "Chinese students are being hurt physically and mentally by the burden of competing for places in college." Teachers reportedly were fond of quoting an old Chinese saying about trying to pass a whole army (all the high school students) across a small wooden bridge (the tests). Premier Zhao Ziyang in 1981 opined that students were being overtaxed.[190]

In Shanghai, where relatively many youths receive good educations, there was evidence of strong pressure on high school students in the year before university entrance. The time they spent in school, during that sixth year of postprimary education, was notably longer each day than for first-year students.[191]

The extra homework they had to do, as assigned by their own parents eager to have them do well in university entrance tests, was also great. The total time they spent on Sunday homework almost tripled, to 3.8 hours on average, between the fifth and sixth years. The average amount of sleep they received each night went down, and the number of school tests they had to take in a ten-week period rose from six or seven in the first four years, to ten tests in the fifth year, to twenty-five in the last year.

Shanghai students by 1986 were working very hard, and some of them complained. One protested, "Homework intrudes on my time. Give me back a soccer ball!" Half of this student's twenty-day winter "vacation" was spent in study. Another said, "My book satchel is too heavy, about ten pounds." So students asked that the 1986 drafters of the Youth and Child Protection Law should stipulate how heavy their homework burden could be.[192] Nothing specific was done, however, on this score.

Promotion rates in China have been low, compared with the rates in more developed countries. But the chance of a young, ambitious Chinese student eventually going to university has varied since 1970 in ways that the official periodization of reforms does not capture. As Table 3.2–8 shows, promotion rates since the early 1970s varied irregularly, ending that decade with a low rate of university admission in 1979, followed by a sharply rising pattern especially after 1981 until the middle of the decade. Major reductions of the number of students effectively competing for China's limited number of university places are always made, however, before students reach the senior high school level.

The table shows some of the complexity in this situation, by combining promotion rates to senior high and tertiary institutions with a three-year lag. The rates into high schools, which have fluctuated considerably and were much higher in 1975 than in 1982 for example, must affect any social or political interpretation of the figures for university promotion. After the early culling, the promotion rates for regular university and college entrance among regular high school graduates during the reforms indicated troughs in 1971, 1974, and 1979, and then very sharp rises in the 1980s. This should be put in perspective of the low promotion rates to senior high in much of the early 1980s. The high but irregular pattern from 1989 into the 1990s reflects many factors, including widespread questions among prospective students about how much their lives would gain from education. Despite doubts, many young Chinese were able to spend more years in school.

Higher education during reforms remained a legitimate basis on which to hope for a government job, regardless of whether the schooling was certified by certificates from first- or second-rate universities. Diplomas (*wenpin*) were sought broadly by many, at least until the mid-1980s watershed of reforms.

Secondary Enrollments: Nonattendance at High Schools

Presenting the structure of Chinese enrollments is a complex job, not just because of incomplete comparable data but because of differences of schooling by

Table 3.2–8

Selection of Cohorts for Education: All-China Promotion Rates into Senior High Schools and (for many students three years later) into Universities
(years, percentages of graduates admitted from previous level)

Year	Promotion rate to senior high	Promotion rate to universities	Overall rate for university cohort
1970	37	6.2	
1971	39	4.2	
1972		6.2	
1973		4.3	1.6
1974		3.9	1.5
1975	60	4.3	
1976		4.2	
1977		4.7	
1978	41	5.9	3.5
1979	40	3.8	
1980	46	4.6	
1981	32	5.7	2.3
1982	32	10.1	4.0
1983	36	16.6	7.6
1984	38	25.0	8.0
1985	42	31.5	10.0
1986	41	25.3	9.1
1987	39	25.0	9.5
1988	38	26.7	11.2
1989	38	24.6	10.1
1990	41	26.1	10.2
1991	43	27.8	10.6
1992	43	33.4	12.7

Notes and sources: The last column is the product of rates for a single age cohort. The term "senior high" (*gaozhong*) refers to all senior secondary institutions; "universities" are all tertiary institutions. There are dangers in overinterpreting the righthand column; but they may balance other dangers of overinterpreting promotion rates to any particular level alone. When year data have to be omitted in some columns above, the reason is that none of these sources provide them: *Zhongguo jiaoyu chengjiu: Tongji ziliao, 1949–1983* (Achievement of Education in China: Statistics, 1949–1983), Department of Planning, PRC Ministry of Education, ed. (Beijing: Zhongguo Jiaoyu Chuban She, 1984), pp. 25–26, and *Zhongguo jiaoyu chengjiu: Tongji ziliao, 1980–1985* (Achievement of Education in China: Statistics, 1980–1985), Department of Planning, PRC State Education Commission, ed. (Beijing: Zhongguo Jiaoyu Chuban She, 1986), p. 7, for early statistics. For the years 1984 and 1985 only, this last source is lower on the university promotion rate than is *Zhongguo tongji nianjian, 1993* (China Statistical Yearbook, 1993), State Statistical Bureau, ed. (Beijing: Zhongguo Tongji Chuban She, 1993); p. 726 gives the high school promotions and a quotient of the second column, p. 718, over the third, p. 715, is calculated for the university promotion rate. For 1965, 1971, 1975, and 1973 see confirming data in *Zhongguo jiaoyu chengjiu: Tongji ziliao, 1949–1983* (Achievement of Education in China: Statistics, 1949–1983), Department of Planning, PRC Ministry of Education, ed. (Beijing: Zhongguo Jiaoyu Chuban She, 1984), p. 38.

location, by level, and over different years. In China as a whole—but not especially in Shanghai and mainly in recent years—rural industrialization seems to
have reduced primary enrollments. "More and more primary students have quit
their studies. According to 1988 statistics, 4.28 million primary school students
stopped their classes throughout the country—and this was 3 percent of all
primary students. Also, 2.87 million middle school students have left, and this
was 7 percent of all middle school students."[193] These youths went to work in
new sectors of the economy. As a vice minister of education pointed out, child
labor is illegal in China. But, he stopped short of saying, the laws against hiring
juveniles are not enforced.

In China's huge national population, the portion of primary graduates who
entered junior high schools dipped sharply during mid-reforms, as the following
percentages show:[194]

1975	91 percent	1980	76 percent	1983	67 percent
1978	88 percent	1981	68 percent	1984	66 percent
1979	83 percent	1982	66 percent	1985	68 percent
				1989	72 percent

Primary enrollment in Shanghai delta primary schools, however, was practically universal (between 99 and 100 percent of the relevant age cohorts). In
Jiangsu province, for the 1989–90 academic year, it was also nearly total. Primary enrollment at the start of the 1990s nationally was 97 percent. The falloffs
came gradually in secondary schooling, and they differed by locality.

Promotion rates to junior high after primary school were somewhat lower, but
Shanghai delta rates exceeded those of the nation: for the cities of rich Sunan,
between 92 and 94 percent in Suzhou, Wuxi, and Changzhou at this time; for all
of Jiangsu, 80 percent; but in China as a whole, only 72 percent. A strong
majority of Chinese students, and substantially all who have any ambition in rich
parts of the country, now graduate from lower middle schools.

A major winnowing—or a rash of family decisions against further education—nonetheless takes place after graduation from junior high. In the relevant
age cohorts, only about half the 1989–90 graduates went on to senior high in
Wuxi (51 percent), Suzhou (48 percent), and other Sunan cities. The rate in
Jiangsu as a whole was only 38 percent. Nationally, it was 35 percent.[195] People
with ambition go to senior high often for specialized career training; but even in
prosperous parts of China, most do not.

In Sunan at the start of the 1990s, the ratios of enrollment to relevant age
population were as follows: in universities, 2 percent; in high schools, 27 percent; in junior highs, 93 percent; and in primary schools, 108 percent (higher
than 100 because of adult education to teach illiterates). In all of Jiangsu, the
same proportions were lower, especially at the junior high and high school
levels: for universities, 2 percent; for high schools, 21 percent; for junior highs,

81 percent; but for primary education, 116 percent (because of much need for adult education in poor regions). For China as a whole, the proportions were lower yet, even for adult primary education: in universities, 2 percent; in high schools, only 16 percent; in junior highs, 61 percent; and at the primary level, 109 percent.[196]

The limited access to universities in China is widely known. Much less well-known, but evident in these figures, is the difficulty or disinterest in admission to high schools. Although a majority of Chinese students go through the junior high level, and a strong majority do that in rich parts of the country, nonetheless the proportions attending high school during reforms in Jiangsu (even in its richest part, Sunan) are much lower. Only about a quarter of youths in the relevant age cohort go to high school in this prosperous large part of China.

Shanghai–Jiangsu Educational Comparisons

Jiangsu is a large province, far more typical of China as a whole than Shanghai, with three-quarters of its population by the 1990s still in villages and towns.[197] About three-tenths of all people in the Jiangsu age cohort then in their early thirties, as Table 3.2–9 shows, had gone to high school. Less than a fifth had attended primary school only. In other words, young Jiangsu people had far more extensive education than their elders.

Shanghai differs both from all of China and from Sunan, as regards educational change. From 1970 to 1975, the number of Shanghai high school students increased 9 percent per year. This early surge of change (like many others in the same period) was not sustained in the mid-1970s. From 1976 to 1978, Shanghai high school students *decreased* 4 percent per year. In higher education, the trend was somewhat less bumpy; the number of university students increased sharply during both the early and late 1970s. In educational reforms as in many other fields, the early 1970s saw more change than did a short reaction against these reforms, centered on 1976.

Among Shanghai urban people aged twenty in 1976 and the next three years, 83 percent had high school (*gaozhong*) educations. This would be a fairly respectable rate anywhere; but it contrasts very sharply with the 14 percent for cohorts just ten years older (those who reached age sixteen in the period 1966–70). The "lost generation" is, as these figures show, at least as evident at the high school level as in universities.

A substantial increase began in the portion of high school age Shanghai youth who by the mid-1970s received high school educations. Universal attendance at this level had not yet been achieved, but the percentage was already approaching 100. It is hard to know what later consequences may follow from this most important early educational reform in the city, after practically all urban youths went at least to high school.

Nine-year compulsory education was announced for all Shanghai children in

Table 3.2–9

Jiangsu Adults, by Highest Level of Education (percentages in cohorts over age 19 in 1987)

Av. year age 18	Age	University			High school			Jr. high			Primary school		
		All	M	F	All	M	F	All	M	F	All	M	F
1983	20–24	2	3	1	19	23	15	53	56	49	19	16	25
1978	25–29	2	2	1	29	34	23	35	41	29	21	18	86
1973	30–34	1	1	1	13	17	8	31	40	21	32	33	151
1968	35–39	1	2	1	7	9	4	25	33	16	42	46	239
1963	40–44	2	3	1	7	9	4	27	33	17	37	41	192
1958	45–49	2	3	1	7	10	3	16	23	9	34	45	264
1953	50–54	2	2	1	4	6	2	10	15	4	30	45	374
1948	55–59	1	1	0	3	4	1	8	13	2	27	43	490
	60+	0		0	1	3	1	5	10	1	19	36	562

Source: Zhongguo 1987 nian 1% renkou chouyang diaocha ziliao—Jiangsu sheng fence (Survey Data from the 1% Population Sample in China—Jiangsu Volume), Jiangsu Statistics Bureau and Jiangsu Province Population Survey Office, eds. (Beijing: Zhongguo Tongji Chuban She, 1988), pp. 140–43.

Table 3.2–10

Adults by Highest Level of Education in Shanghai Urban Districts
(percentages in cohorts over age 19 in 1982)

Age groups	Av year when age 18	University	High school	Jr. high school	Primary school	Illiterate and half so
20–24	1978	5	83	12	1	0
25–29	1973	3	36	59	1	0
30–34	1968	5	14	75	5	1
35–39	1963	14	39	37	10	1
40–44	1958	20	27	30	20	4
45–49	1953	10	15	29	33	12
50–54	1948	7	11	26	37	19
55–59	1943	5	9	23	37	25
60 +		3	6	13	32	45

Notes and source: Percentages are figured from data in the source. The second column is calculated. In the third column, pupils still in universities have been added to tertiary graduates. Figures are available in the source for the whole municipality (not just the urban areas), but these have been omitted to make the table more readable; they diverge from the built-up area rates, which are shown, more sharply among older than younger age cohorts. When the census was taken in 1982, urban districts accounted for 54 percent of the whole municipality's population. Also, data on educational levels in Shanghai's prosperous suburbs did not differ as markedly from the urban statistics as from those of inland places. *Shanghai shi di san renkou pucha ziliao huibian* (Compendium of Materials on Shanghai Municipality's Third Census), Shanghai Census Office, ed. (Shanghai: Shanghai Shi Renkou Pucha Bangong Shi, 1984), pp. 56–57.

1978, although that goal had been mostly accomplished in previous years. A decade later, almost all of the relevant age cohort completed junior middle schools, and 98 percent of those graduates were entering high schools. The performance in Shanghai's suburbs was only slightly less good.[198]

From 1978 to 1987, the total number of students in Shanghai at all levels decreased by 14 percent, mostly because of the effect of birth control on school-age cohorts.[199] The corresponding figures for secondary schools showed a decrease in Shanghai of 37 percent (and 19 percent in the whole country), caused in part by the demographic factor but also by increasing doubts among families that secondary schooling by itself paved golden roads to success and prosperity. Intense family planning in Shanghai caused the number of primary school students to decrease in 1981–82.[200] Almost all children in primary school age groups had long entered schools in Shanghai, and this rate rose from 99.2 percent in 1980 to 99.6 percent in 1983.

The promotion rates from primary to junior high school were also nearly universal: over 98 percent in the early 1980s.[201] Of Shanghai's 1985 primary graduates, 99.4 percent went on to middle school—a very high rate that was 31 percent higher than the national average. The 1985 promotion rate from middle school to high school was also extremely high for a developing country: 98.9 percent throughout the municipality, including its rural areas. Even in the suburbs, where only nine years of education were mandatory (six in primary school and three in middle school), the proportion of the high school age cohort actually studying at that level was 82 percent.[202]

Because the city takes tertiary students from far outside its borders, because older age groups were not affected by the low birth rate, and especially because high-level diplomas were increasingly needed for good jobs, the intake at the tertiary level was considerable. During the 1978–87 period, the number of students in Shanghai's universities increased 142 percent (and 128 percent in the whole country). The real bottleneck in promotions nonetheless came at the time of entrance to universities.[203]

To summarize: While primary and secondary enrollments fell, the number of high school students in large and small cities since 1978 has generally risen. Urban senior high enrollments in China reached a peak of 3.5 million in 1977, as the "lost generation" found itself in classrooms. After this surge, the absolute number fell temporarily until 1982; but later, the increase at the high school level was steady at least in cities and large towns through the mid-1980s. In rural areas, however, the trend was downward, as many high school–age children clearly wanted to make money by working. Many county high schools closed their doors after the mid-1980s.[204]

No political conclusions would be easy to draw exactly from such data. Moshe Lewin, explaining change in Soviet Russia, cited educational expansion as a basis for later change, and his early predictions proved more accurate than those from most sovietologists.[205] China's university-educated intelligentsia remains very small, except in large cities. An unprecedented portion of all Chinese can now read and process information. As the grim reaper, who is the most powerful policy maker of all, culls old cohorts, this portion will continue to rise over the next three decades.[206] The political effects—if any—might arguably range from chaos to democracy to fascism; they are probably indeterminable. But the rise of education has at least compromised the status of China's people as a "sack of potatoes," a mass of ignorant bumpkins who could not possibly have any coherent notions of politics.

Generalized Politics vs. Specialized Educations

Chinese students who would later go to universities generally do not specialize in secondary school. In 1981, however, the Ministry of Education approved syllabi that allowed previously generalist high schools to focus on either the humanities (*wenke*) or the sciences (*like*). All major subjects were still taught in all high schools, but this reform encouraged more division of labor.[207]

High schools were increasingly of many kinds. In Sunan, slightly less than half of all high school students were in "regular" programs, while one-fifth each were in "specialized" and "vocational" schools, with the remaining tenth in "technical" schools.[208] Vocational, specialized, and technical students in upper-middle age cohorts outnumbered general students. They did so more in Sunan than in China as a whole, because the school system in this rich area was more diversified.

Specialized secondary education became very important. For every two Shanghai middle school graduates who entered regular high schools in 1985, three entered various kinds of technical or vocational high schools.[209] One of the reasons for the popularity of such schools is that their graduates had considerable leeway in finding their own jobs, which in some firms paid well.

Years of education did not, however, guarantee a good income. On the contrary, a 1984 survey of Shanghai's suburbs showed that households whose major financial contributor had graduated merely from local middle schools averaged 1,594 yuan, but if that person had any tertiary education, the average income was only 1,257 yuan—a fifth less![210] Educated people in low-tax rural and suburban areas tended to take state sector jobs, which paid badly. In urban areas, education and prosperity may have correlated positively; but their negative correlation outside the state-monitored cities is striking.

The Military Service Requirement for Fudan Applicants

The disadvantages of schooling were not just economic. In conservative periods, advanced graduates also tended to find themselves in political hot water. A symbol of this problem was that incoming students to Fudan University—Shanghai's main humanities school, like Beijing University in the north—were required after Tiananmen to train in the army for a year before they could begin their first-year courses. (Aspirants to scientific and engineering universities, such as Jiaotong and Tongji in Shanghai or Qinghua in the north, were not subject to this requirement.) This and other political purification campaigns after 1989 were designed to preclude a "peaceful evolution" of China away from socialism. Struggle was renewed as an ideal in Chinese politics, even though "class struggle" was often sublimated, in new propaganda, to become struggle against foreign styles, especially in politics. Educated Chinese were expected by state leaders naturally to be good mandarins and uphold norms of hierarchy.

Faculties at Fudan and Beijing Universities found that the military prerequisite sharply lowered the quality of their applicants. Many smart students from secondary schools clearly preferred the scientific universities in order to avoid the year of army service. Even before this, during the mid-1980s, the quality of students had declined because of the extraordinarily good classes recruited in the late 1970s from the large pool of applicants whose college careers had been delayed by the Cultural Revolution. So the additional condition, placed on Fudan and Beijing in 1989, added salt to a wound.

When it was announced that Fudan admits would have to spend a year in military training, some Shanghai parents urged their children not to apply there. China's best applicants were avoiding its two best humanities universities. A cadre of Beijing University reported that "the entrance examination score needed to enter the school had dropped sixty points . . . many of the best students are now applying elsewhere."[211]

In the admissions season of 1991, the conservative government budged, apparently because of pressure from Fudan and Beijing Universities. Applicants that year still had to do a year of army training before matriculation, but the procedure was changed: High school students in some previous years had been able to apply to just one keypoint university; but in 1991, they could apply to either Fudan or Beijing *and* to one other keypoint institution (for example, Jiaotong for science or engineering), as well as to nonkeypoint colleges as backups. Also, the preuniversity year in the army was now counted as an internship, of the sort that college graduates were previously supposed to fill during the first year of their normal postgraduation jobs. So students entering Fudan still had to join the military for a year; but their overall careers were not much slowed because upon graduation they could enter their regular work directly as full employees, not apprentices.[212]

Finally, an early admissions program was allowed for Fudan and Beijing universities by 1991, clearly as a response that the government was pressed to make after a decline in good applicants there. Fudan administrators that year claimed the exam grades needed for admission would be no lower than was traditional. But the psychological advantage for students, hoping to get into a good place early, made Fudan applications more attractive. For those who were rejected in the early round, "They got another opportunity to be admitted by a key institution, because they could later apply to other universities."[213] Two chances in one year was a big novelty for hard-pressed high school students in China.

Nonetheless, the minimum exam score needed to enter Fudan plummeted, because many of the best students in this rather reactionary period still opted to go elsewhere (to Qinghua University, if they could get in, because the old-school network of that university had long been especially prestigious in government circles).[214] So in 1992, the requirement for a year of army service before university entrance to these two universities was simply dropped. The early application program continued, and fine classes entered Fudan then and in later years.

Educations and Incomes

University educations became less attractive to some Shanghainese, who knew that graduates' salaries might later average less than those of ordinary workers.

After junior high, students and their families had to decide whether to continue in regular high schools or to attend instead the more popular vocational and technical schools. This was, for each Shanghai student, the most crucial decision of his or her educational career. Many junior high graduates were disinclined, by 1988, to continue in the regular system, opting instead for vocational training. A suburban county in Shanghai could then recruit only 10 percent of its graduating junior high students "to be willing to" take exams for entrance to regular high schools. But the keypoint vocational school, which had places for only twenty new students from that county, received hundreds of applicants.

In one junior high school's class of two hundred graduates, only three wanted to sit for the regular high school exams. Families calculated that the "seven-year burden," from high school entrance to university graduation, involved an opportunity cost of 10,000 yuan in forgone income.[215] For students, the work in school was fairly heavy and the rewards were minimal. Urban household registration was said to be more valuable than a university degree, and mere vocational school graduates in Shanghai could keep their registrations—and make good incomes.

The state's financial crunch, which reduced real budgets for education, caused universities to admit students who would pay their own way. If they had low scores on the entrance exams, this obstacle was not insuperable. The laxity began in 1985, the mid-reforms watershed, as an "experiment."

> By 1987, with the approval of the Education Ministry, twenty-one universities and colleges in Shanghai admitted 825 self-paying students. This figure was 7 percent of all new university admits.... Although self-paying students could enter universities more easily than normal students, they in other respects did not receive such good treatment. They could not, for example, get jobs in the state allocation plan; and they had no free medical care during their studies.[216]

Teachers were astonished to find that many self-paying students earned good grades. Mandarins had not expected the state exams to be bad predictors of academic performance. These pupils "often could feel pressure in their studies, because they had to pay and had to find jobs by themselves after graduation. These factors forced them to study hard." Although this surprise did not cause universities to rethink their still almost-exclusive reliance on the sacred entrance tests to judge academic potential among youths, it did improve conditions for the self-paying students. "As long as they perform well, they also could get fellowships or other kinds of rewards." In any case, "To admit self-paying students was a good way to reduce the state's financial pressure and to link education with society." Even intellectuals began to realize that their context was changing.

Self-paying students, who by the 1990s were present at many Chinese universities and good secondary schools, became more numerous but remained distinct from other students. Financial pressures on academe combined with avarice among intellectuals, who saw the incomes of other citizens racing ahead. The entrance exam requirements for students who could pay high tuitions were lowered on a permanent basis; this program was no longer an experiment. The proportion of self-paying students rose in regular classes. This pattern reduced the opportunities for good but penurious students to attend universities. At some schools, including the most prestigious institutions in China, special "classes of auditors" were taught, for students who later took no examinations but received certificates of attendance stamped with very impressive red seals. The state had reduced the inflation-adjusted value of public support to university staffs. Each separate department in many schools was asked by the 1990s to show a profit. Faculties made this money wherever they could.

Compensation for Teachers

Scholars in China are never ideally mercenary. The reform era's price inflation and rising anti-intellectualism nonetheless encouraged them to think about money. Teachers' salaries had long been low in Shanghai, but during the decade after 1978, payments to instructors increased on at least three occasions. These pay adjustments raised compensation from a level that was insulting to one that was merely dismal. The cumulative effect was approximately to double the nominal salary of most teachers in ten or twelve years (and to increase it in real terms despite inflation). So a Shanghai middle school instructor, who might have earned more than 50 yuan per month in 1978, could be earning more than 120 yuan a dozen years later. Teachers' salaries still compared poorly with the incomes of many workers, especially in the cooperative and private sectors.[217] The problem was that bright people could earn much more in other professions.

Teachers heading departmental offices (*jiaoyan shi*) received extra pay for that job. School instructors could also earn extra money by tutoring students who had failed university examinations but wanted to take the tests again. They could earn overtime by accepting more than their quota of contact hours in teaching. These extra sources of income were unavailable before the reforms.[218]

Teachers' compensation in Shanghai schools rose between 1985 and 1987, but it still did not equal the level of salaries even among other state employees. Counting basic wages as well as bonuses, supplements, and overtime, Shanghai primary teachers in 1987 averaged 1,649 yuan annually; but all state employees together made an average of 1,864 yuan, or 13 percent more. After 1985, the yearly incomes of all state employees rose 469 yuan, but primary school teachers' compensation had gone up only 386 yuan, or 18 percent less.[219] This was a raise: It was faster than in prereform years, but slower than for other workers.

Student–teacher ratios in secondary schools were low, in light of international comparisons, at about 11 : 1 in 1988 Shanghai high and middle schools.[220] The work load of teachers was lower than is normal in other countries—for example, about twelve hours a week for a high school teacher. A new holiday, Teacher's

Day, was first celebrated in Shanghai on September 9, 1984; it is unclear how impressed intellectuals were. Considering the low wages most teachers received, at any level from primary schools to universities, they may have enjoyed the traditional respect. Concrete emoluments would have kept more of them at their jobs.

Control of Curricula

What were students taught? Traditional, quasi-Confucian teaching methods remained fairly common even in high schools, and in cities as well as rural areas. Examinations were still conceived as tests of students' abilities to recite (*bei*) material that had been presented in lectures or texts. Even distinguished PRC experts in pedagogy, who advocated "flexible" (*linghuo de*) classroom teaching methods, nonetheless sometimes suggested that an emphasis on originality in exam responses could be subjective and unfair. They expressed fears that the criteria for judging tests would become more illusory if too much original thinking were expected in students' answers.[221] Political foxes might disagree, during reforms, but the lions' view of pedagogy remained widespread.

Curricular reform was already a high priority for schools and universities by 1978. In that year, Fudan University began experiments with the "elicitation method" (*qifa shi*) of teaching, in which students were asked to treat the texts they read more critically than before. They became subject to oral as well as written tests on the material. Questioners were supposed to probe whether students could think innovatively, rather than just parroting. These methods were tried even in courses that taught Confucian classics, whose pedagogy for centuries had emphasized exact recitation (*beisong*).[222]

Reform of teaching methods became a matter of broad public discussion in the 1980s; but the consensus was merely on vague aims, not on any specific educational techniques by which to implement them. The "overall development" of students was, as many analysts broadly argued, the main goal. "Book knowledge" was denigrated in speeches. Officially publicized ideals held that students should become adept not just in standard academic subjects, but also in a wide variety of fields ranging from music and chess to radio engineering and sports. The principal of the nationally known Yucai Middle School in Shanghai, Duan Lipei, wrote many articles to urge this kind of breadth in educating young people. But teachers and parents knew perfectly well that the structure of entrance exams was unchanged. The social emphasis on test scores still gave students very strong incentives to memorize books.[223] There was an official set of educational ideals during the reforms, but the exam and entrance procedures effectively squelched them.

Curricula were not sharply reformed, especially before the mid-1980s' watershed. Evidence about what actually happened, as distinct from what was mooted, suggests that state leaders still implicitly hoped that education to pass official tests for loyal jobs would remain the goal of families for children. In primary schools, all courses were taken in common; in high schools, practically all were similarly mandatory. Required offerings comprised about 70 percent of departmental curricula in universities (often more, in science and engineering departments). Less than three-tenths of tertiary courses were optional.

Experimental schools had existed for many decades; but after 1978, more educational experiments were tried. The Shiyan (Experimental) Primary School in Shanghai was well known nationally. By the early 1980s, as the texts first used in these schools proved successful elsewhere, the special designation for experimental schools was dropped. A teacher reported, however, that school budgets had not changed much, despite plans to increase them for the sake of more curricular improvements.[224]

Most primary and secondary curricula were still in principle unified. The same basic texts were used throughout the country, at least through the mid-1980s. This worked to the disadvantage of Shanghai and its delta, where existing levels of parental education were relatively high and more challenging textbooks might have been appropriate. In the 1980s, after reforms had begun, different texts were sometimes allowed, mainly when some schools could teach a subject more quickly and thus could move on to more advanced material. Texts slowly began to be issued for different "tracks" of students, labeled A or B (*jia* or *yi*). A senior high school might have both tracks, although the basic program of study (*dagang*) remained the same. One of the many mid-1980s' changes was that different schools were allowed to use different texts.[225]

Tracking students is unegalitarian; so this practice ran into conservative quasi-Maoist objections even during reforms. "Fast" and "slow" tracks were informally called by their frank names (*kuaiban* and *manban*). As the Beijing newspaper for intellectuals *Bright Daily* argued, schools should not be judged exclusively by the proportion of their graduates who went from fast tracks to universities. The paper applauded recent decisions in some Shanghai schools to eliminate the separate fast and slow tracks, but this was a matter of local debate.[226]

Tracking in high school was increasingly pronounced, but its main form involved differences among schools rather than within them. By 1988, of all Shanghai enrollments at that level, only 39 percent went to regular schools (*putong gaozhong*). Fully 26 percent were in specialized technical high schools (*zhongzhuan,* from which they emerged as technicians), 21 percent were in ordinary technical high schools (*jixiao,* from which they emerged only as "technical workers"), and 15 percent were in vocational high schools (*zhixiao*).[227] Education was increasingly stratified during reforms.

A different trend was that elective courses became more common in Chinese university curricula during the 1980s. Previously, the particular courses required for any degree were fixed; only students in their last year of study could usually take electives. In the reforms, this pattern was relaxed somewhat, and more laboratories and computers were available to increase students' "hands on" learning outside lecture halls. A few more humanities or social science courses were added to engineering and natural science students' curricula. Conservatives had doubts about introducing too much laxness into the curriculum, however. A change not set by state policy was that, in the required propaganda classes on Party history and civics, the student absentee rates often ranged up to 70 percent.[228]

Control of Extracurricula

Students learn a great deal from seeing the extracurricular attitudes of their teachers, as well as from one another. The CCP, at the height of the revolution, had tried to assure that any political aspects of informal education would benefit the state. In Mao's time, children from a young age had been differentiated into two contrasting groups: those who could join the Young Pioneers organization and wear red scarfs around their necks, and those who were not permitted to have this honor. The criteria for including some children and excluding others had usually been based on family class labels, not on behavior by the students.

Discrimination of this sort, which damaged the self-confidence of young Chinese at early ages, abated during the reforms. The Pioneers organization had its thirtieth anniversary in late 1979. Discussion of this event began early, and it was a sensitive subject then because young school children are highly impressionable and their political treatment in school during the Cultural Revolution was easy to criticize retrospectively. The standard cohort for membership in the Young Pioneers consisted of children aged seven to fourteen. As late as May 1979, only 53 percent of this age cohort in Shanghai had actually been admitted to the Pioneers.[229]

By October, the anniversary spurred public debate of the fact that more than two-fifths of all children in the cohort eligible for Pioneer membership had still not been allowed to join, although there had apparently been a campaign to increase membership during the previous six months.[230] Parents wrote to newspapers, demanding that their children should be admitted. They noted that the Gang of Four's policy on Pioneer membership, which was restrictive and based on families' class origins, should be halted. They said it should be changed not just in policy pronouncements from national leaders, but also in practice at local levels. A column in Shanghai's quasi-liberal *Wenhui News* implicitly criticized teachers who opposed the admittance of all eligible children to the Pioneers.

Conservatives argued that "Pioneers" should by definition be vanguards, and not all children were. The newspaper column, while accepting the premise of this argument, said that even children with faults should be admitted. Other hard-liners held that children of revolutionary families deserved their "feeling of glory" on entering this organization, but the newspaper writer countered that the effects of such pride were bad. A third argument for restriction was that nonautomatic membership became a good motivation for children. The *Wenhui* columnist retorted that it was mainly a motive for teachers, who had the power to exclude kids from this club. The paper concluded that all children who were not in the

Pioneers should be admitted forthwith. This became a reform ideal—though still not a reality—in Shanghai by mid-1981.[231]

Admission to the Young Pioneers slowly became almost universal for primary school students, but this did not happen automatically. Lapses in organizing Young Pioneer chapters may best explain why some children were kept out of this system. In 1980, the ratio of the number of Pioneers to the number of primary students in China was still only 58 percent. By 1985, it had risen to 92 percent. By the 1990s, it was generally assumed in Shanghai that any school child between the ages of seven and fourteen was (or could become) a Pioneer.

The ratio of the number of Communist Youth League members to the number of students in the relevant older age cohorts (ages fourteen to twenty-eight) also increased somewhat in the early 1980s.[232] Admission to the Youth League was supposed to be possible for many then, and League membership rose from 48 million in 1982 to 56 million in 1988, while the relevant age cohort did not rise so quickly. Most secondary students joined, and any could "retire" at age 25.[233] But interest in the League also changed, and "many tertiary students do not participate in Youth League life."[234] Their joining was a formality, a line on the c.v. This was a normal step, for an ambitious urban youth, before applying to join the CCP on a probationary basis.

Although the proportion of Party members among students at Shanghai universities was very low in 1983—generally less than 1 percent of the undergraduate student body[235]—this ratio was apparently higher in both earlier and later years. The classes that had entered universities in 1977 and 1978 were older and had more administrative experience; so they also contained many more Party members. The mid-1980s was a period of some propaganda on recruiting university students into the Party, so that by 1988 the portion had probably risen above 5 percent.[236] Party membership slowly became a perquisite, rather than a prerequisite, of successful careers.

Youths' Reformed Use of Vacations and Common Interest Groups

Activities were as important as membership in all these organizations. The early 1980s saw a revival of children's summer camps. These had been common in the mid-1960s, when the army and labor unions had organized summertime activities for youths in some parts of Shanghai. During the reforms, there were again many educational camps. The Ministry of Geology, for example, provided money for schools to send students on geological field trips. Private camps apparently were unavailable even in Shanghai by the 1980s; but school summer camps were increasing, and their types quickly diversified.[237] By the 1990s, there were specialized camps in subjects such as music. The children's summer camp—a hallmark of the middle class anywhere—has long been common in countries like France and the United States. In China, where a potent family system also shapes them, similar camps also began to make an appearance.[238]

School-year extracurricular activities also flourished throughout the reform era, as schools organized more events. They provided support for students and faculty who wished to found common interest associations. In the spring of 1979, Fudan students established the first autonomous special-interest association at a Shanghai university: the Calligraphy and Painting Club. Computer clubs, music groups, university theaters, airplane and ship model-building clubs, and sports teams became common. Before the Cultural Revolution, such groups had been less common. During that movement, in addition to Red Guard groups, applicants to the Party would spontaneously form "Party Charter study groups."

By the late 1970s, however, Fudan had many nonpolitical associations, such as the Spring Bamboo Shoots Literary Society, a History Fledglings Society, and a Students' Science Association. Departments also sponsored common interest groups for Fudan students who liked academic activities, for example, physics experiments.[239] By 1985, more than fifteen large student clubs had sprung up at Fudan, including the History Association (1979), the Chinese Literature Department's Writing Club (1979), a Fudan Poetry Club (1981), a Stamp Collecting Club (1981), a Chess Club (1981), and a Film Club (1982). In 1983, a temporary conservative interruption of these student club foundings ended, but then a "second stage of development" saw the start of the Northwest China Development Association (1984), the International Studies Club (1984), an Alliance of Young Theorists (1985), the Legal Science Club (1986), the Philosophy Club (1986), and the general Student Center (1986).

In the mid-1980s, students in Shanghai from different parts of China also organized regional groups. Fudan, for example, had its Northwest China Economic Development Association, mostly comprising students from that area.[240] Clubs of fellows from the same region, somewhat like the "native-place associations" that had been prominent before 1949, became common. Fudan had such unions for Guangdong, Zhejiang, and elsewhere. At the start of a vacation, they would often travel together back to their native areas.

By that time, the talented wave of post-1987 "lost generation" university applicants had subsided. Fewer students "came from society," that is, from worker or peasant families, and fewer were old enough to have experienced or perpetrated violence in the Cultural Revolution. Most applied directly from high schools. "They had no social experience and had narrow knowledge."

Realizing this, some students were interested in making connections with nonintellectuals—networks of just the sort to raise conservative Party suspicions, even though reform administrators were pleased to see pupils interested in making money. The third wave of student associations, after the watershed of 1984–85, saw many business-oriented clubs. Fudan's administration supported the founding of the Student Center for Consultancy and Exploration in Science and Technology, a Public Relations Association (1987), an Economic Management Club (1987), a Future Entrepreneurs' Club (1988), and a Journalism Association (1988). Such students "got both economic income and social learning opportunities . . . .

They set up a book store and a coffee bar. . . . Many association leaders won votes in the annual [student government] elections through a variety of club activities."[241]

Students also began to establish enterprises while they were still in school. Members of Fudan's Chinese Literature Department set up a tutoring service. Students of computer science set up a company with the user-friendly, humanistic name "Forest of Charts" (Tu Lin She) to offer classes in computer graphics. Electrical engineering students hired themselves out to factories, where they renovated equipment. Fudan's Communist Youth League passed a resolution to praise all these reform activities.

Fudan students on vacation in Henan carried out a "diagnosis of enterprises" (*qiye zhenduan*), reorganizing the financial management system of firms there. Other students set up shops in the Shanghai Cultural Palace, in the canteen aboard a ship on the Huangpu, in a garment factory, and in a neon light bulb factory. Others went to the Shenzhen Special Economic Zone during vacations to work. Some still complained that the university did not do enough to prepare them for the real world.

Although old Maoist policies had called for "managing study on an open-door basis," the reform's policies were not compulsory in this area. They "encouraged work to aid schooling."[242] Faculty were supposed to help students "aid" society by taking jobs, and these youths were seldom averse to making some money. Conservative ministers of education during the reform era repeatedly said that schools should teach more about Mao Zedong's ideas on serving the people and combining study with work.[243] A tenet of CCP educational doctrine was that university students should have experience in factories. But a 1990 survey involving fifty Shanghai universities found that "a lot of factories in fact refuse to accept students for work experience, regarding them as a great burden to their aim of achieving production targets. . . . Above all, most universities lack funds to support work placements."[244] In the 1990s, if schools wanted factories to help train students, the schools would have to pay them for this special instruction.

Education on Courtesy and Sexual Mores

The post-Confucian approach to education, although it would cost the state less money, put students in contact with a greater variety of networks beyond their families. Many of these were not effectively monitored by the state. A code on students' behavior was published in late 1981, recommending that they "love physical labor" and learn rules of better conduct. Etiquette and injunctions against spitting were included in this campaign.[245] This was part of a movement in 1981–83, to encourage more polite, obedient, quasi-Confucian habits. The result, these nostalgic old revolutionaries thought, would be a restoration of the kind of order they had controlled in years such as 1955 or 1963.

An analysis of rock music, as offered earlier in this book, goes at least as far as the resurgence of philosophical humanism toward explaining changes of habits during reforms. Authoritarians measured "spiritual pollution" especially by change in typical links between young men and women. Sexual relations, in China as elsewhere, are a topic that divides generations. Late 1980s' student papers, sent to a foreign teacher in Shanghai, reported that "pre-marital sex, which was regarded as immoral by our grandfathers, is more acceptable to our youngsters. . . . Hedonism has replaced asceticism." Other youths wrote, "Students are absorbed in dancing, dressing, and looking for lovers." "Old people take sex too seriously, while among the young it is quite common to have sexual activity before they get married."[246]

A 1981 conference called for more sex education. This was a reform. Most such teaching focused on China's population problem, although human sexual biology was also covered.[247] In China's largest school for juvenile delinquents, 40 percent of the girls had been incarcerated after "having sex." A smaller portion of the boys at that school were there for the same reason. Premarital sex among consenting minors was reportedly not illegal in China; but for girls especially, it could earn a year-long spell at a reformatory that had steel bars over the windows. In one case, a girl who became pregnant confessed to her parents and had an abortion—and despite repentance, she was sent to the reformatory. Her boyfriend was put "under observation" at his workplace.[248]

The best academic surveys of Chinese sexual behavior, which researchers at the Shanghai Sex Sociology Research Center were able to continue from 1988 into the 1990s despite furious criticism from political hard-liners, showed that Shanghai "students, male or female, were found to have their first lover at the mean age of about fifteen." In middle schools, as many as one-quarter of the youths were reported to have had lovers; and among high school students, "the figure rose to 40%."[249] Since average ages of marriage are much higher, and since doctors' prenuptial checks of urban brides show one-quarter had induced abortions before marriage, large Chinese cities evidently have considerable rates of premarital sex.[250]

This is apparently a change from prereform patterns. It results from many aspects of modern life, including a policy-induced and career-induced pattern of late marriages. Interviewees suggest that new sexual mores were normalized during the early 1970s by ex–Red Guards sent to rural areas after the Cultural Revolution. Rock music imported from the West, Hong Kong, and Taiwan has provided a means for youths to express their sexual interests. But this may be just an occasion for voicing an impulse that was, for better or for worse, traditionally repressed. Change in sexual habits shocks many and affects many. It becomes an issue around which political entrepreneurs (conservatives and reformers both) try to mobilize support.

Foreign influences may have encouraged this rash of promiscuity, as conservatives claimed. High on the list of domestic factors, however, was crowded housing.

In present-day [1989] China, sex crimes are common among youths. Many investigations have shown that this problem is related to housing conditions. Shanghai has a serious housing problem; a small flat often is shared by two couples, parents, and their children. Parents' [and presumably neighbors'] sexual life thus necessarily affects their children. Bad housing correlates also with the increasing rate of divorce. According to a 1987 Shanghai government investigation, 22 percent of divorces resulted from inadequate housing.[251]

Many Shanghai families clearly felt cooped up by the late 1980s. In this context, distinctions between the habits of parents and children were difficult to maintain.

Counseling and Control of Students

For students in schools, or especially in universities, the state assumed responsibility for moral education. The conservatives' favored means to this end had been developed in the 1950s, when Qinghua University began a system of selecting students to be prefects. The policy of selecting "political counselors" (*zhengzhi zhidao yuan*) spread to tertiary institutions in Shanghai, where Party groups did the choosing. These elite students in the 1950s and 1960s were supposed to be models for their peers, ideally both red and expert. Because their professional studies were somewhat slowed by leadership training courses, they might be given an extra year of university to make them proficient in their specialized fields. The best of them, on graduation, were offered prestigious posts as assistant instructors (*zhujiao*). That group of young teachers, along with elder Party administrators, ran many universities before the Cultural Revolution.[252]

In the 1980s, there was again a conservative effort to recruit student cadres to do ideological work. At Jiaotong, for example, young political instructors were hired. Some had been to the countryside or had other socialist experiences that qualified them as ideological workers. Conservatives hoped they could make closer connections with students than the cadres whom they replaced.[253] Reformists in the same period, however, could rely on another group of student leaders: the elected heads of new undergraduate organizations. At Fudan, the chair of the Student Union of the History Department, student officers of the Law Department's Consultancy and Propaganda Station, and the chair of the Student Union in the Economics Department became prominent on campus.[254] Elected young leaders had somewhat different interests from students who were political appointees.

Propaganda meetings also continued in universities, although the strength of belief they instilled is not confirmed by attitude surveys. In the mid-1980s, the Party secretary of the Fudan University Party Committee still organized a regular Friday afternoon political meeting. Attendance was required of all Fudan students. This leader opposed explicit suggestions that the meetings be canceled; instead, he said they should be strengthened to support the reforms.[255] The Fudan Party nonetheless decided to reform the Friday meetings instead, and also to support a consultancy center because students wanted opportunities to work. Undergraduates increasingly took the podium at the Friday meetings, and the topics gradually became less political and more professional. Subjects for discussion at the reformed meetings included "The Wind Blowing from the South" (i.e., from Guangdong), "A Nineteen-year-old Factory Head," and "New Viewpoints from a Tour to Shenzhen."[256]

For each entering class in each department, one faculty member traditionally took charge of overseeing all work that concerned students' livelihoods. This instructor was mandated to do ideological work in that class and to deal with any problems that might arise among students. Part of the reform at Jiaotong University was to require that all instructors in every department take this job on a rotating basis.[257] Since many were more interested in their fields than in propaganda work, moralist meetings became more professionalized.

The language of political control began to reflect amateur propagandists' interests in social sciences. Officials were concerned with the "unbalanced psychology" of students, for example, even before the December 1986 demonstrations. Survey research was a way to find how students led their lives—and the results were not reassuring. Polls showed that more than 40 percent of Fudan students received less than eight hours of sleep each night. The best students, in particular, were subject to psychological losses of self-respect if, after passing tough university entrance exams, their performance fell. The 1985 suicide of a senior at Fudan was interpreted along these lines.[258] Only sometimes did universities relinquish their role *in loco parentis* and relax rules. At Fudan in 1984, the traditional 11:00 P.M. lights-out was eliminated.[259]

Shanghai's universities were said to be controlled more tightly than Beijing's. By April and May 1989, when students throughout the country were mourning the death of reformer Hu Yaobang and planning to celebrate the seventieth anniversary of the May 4 Movement, Fudan officials pasted a prominent notice that unlawful demonstrations would not be tolerated. This billboard said, "the University has uncovered a small group of students who were plotting to incite strikes and protests."[260] When Hu Yaobang died, big-character posters appeared in many places on the Fudan campus, and some were pasted over the base of Chairman Mao's statue by the front gate. These were soon torn down.

As one paper said, "Unlike in Beijing, where foreign reporters have been allowed onto campuses, some Shanghai colleges have stopped all university visitors at the gate. Security guards have checked the bags of some people at East China Normal University. At Fudan University, police took down the name and car number of a taxi driver [helping a reporter]."[261] The events of the spring of 1989 are treated elsewhere in this book. Conservatives tried to control students more tightly then. Reformers within the state hoped for a gradual evolution, which the tanks at Tiananmen soon precluded. When students from the Shanghai International Studies University joined a rally on the Bund in 1989, political counselors were dispatched in an effort to persuade them to go home.[262]

Government editorials on April 26, 1989, accused people at the memorial meeting for Hu Yaobang of being "conspirators," trying to overthrow socialism. On April 29 in Shanghai (as in Beijing), the government sent relatively low-level representatives to a session with officially selected students that was televised throughout the city. Many youths' anger at the accusations in the editorials was intense, but the chosen delegates' statements to the assembled bureaucrats were carefully phrased; and the officials scarcely replied. Then, on camera, several youths criticized Shanghai's top leaders for not attending. Also, they said the new Shanghai Autonomous Union of Universities and Colleges should have been able to send its elected representatives, rather than having delegates from the government-influenced Shanghai Students' Federation only.[263] University pupils were quite capable of establishing their own organizations, and at some times they sought to make these unofficial.

Job Allocations and Careers

Individuals' desires to receive a good job through the "state distribution" (*guojia fenpei*) were until the 1990s a major hold that authorities had over students. Once they graduated and their careers began, the shortage of housing became the main hold that Shanghai work units had over subordinates. Threats of political ostracism, which had been in the 1950s and 1960s the main source of social and political control by the Party, became passé. Slowly, even the job and housing controls weakened too.

"Planned distribution" (*jihua fenpei*) of graduates was restrictive, but as late as the 1980s it also provided numerous jobs. At Jiaotong University, for example, the Student Section of the Personnel Bureau used to determine the careers of graduates. It wrote recommendation letters, performed deanly discipline functions, and could designate "three-good students."[264] This office also could approve merit scholarships on the basis of suggestions from departments. It also had other assorted jobs, for example, catering to the special needs of nonresident day students and keeping track of Jiaotong alumni. This office even had to approve any student's application for a marriage license or for travel abroad to study—even on a self-paying basis. Most important, this is the office that kept all students' files.

A long-standing problem, publicly debated by the early 1980s, was that graduates were often arbitrarily assigned by the Student Section to work for which they had not been trained—and which they disliked. An electrical engineer, cited in a 1980 article, had been required to do financial work in which he had no interest. For years, higher-level cadres had used a slogan, "if you do a job, you *should* like it," to staunch the protests of people who disfavored their assigned jobs.[265] As a Shanghai student wrote later in the decade, "We all know that a country has to pay a lot for cultivating a college student, and college graduates are part of the country's property . . . [but] they just distribute us like animals."[266]

Graduates whose families lacked personal connections, as well as many women and ex-rural students, liked the socialist tradition of having a state plan to allocate jobs. But a survey of Jiaotong alumni concluded that graduates of the early 1980s were talented; so they could find their own jobs. They could use computers, speak foreign languages, and fend better than alumni of earlier decades, according to this report. Because these graduates had originally been selected in academic exams, the previous bias in favor of poorer family backgrounds had been reduced. The Jiaotong survey also concluded they had a tendency to be "arrogant," and many did not want to leave their offices to do labor in workshops. Many of the students, at scientific universities in particular, were less good at writing and rhetoric than some of their predecessors during the Cultural Revolution years.[267] They were more independent, however—and the gist of this report was that the university did not need to find jobs for them.

As the allocation system for school graduates declined in effectiveness by the mid-1980s, because the state then had fewer jobs to fill and less money to pay salaries, conservative planners still fulminated that society would be harmed if youths could choose their own careers. This would, these non-theistic Puritans declared, lead to a "blindness" (mangmu xing) in the supplies of labor by vocation.[268] Official intellectuals set a number of new hotel workers, for example, that they thought Shanghai needed in mid-1986. When more than twice as many youths were allowed to sign up for hotel careers as their first choice in that hiring period, these planners could do little more than fume, because the state system could no longer provide jobs for everyone.

Shanghai's Jiaotong University was the first in all of China to experiment with a thorough reform of the job distribution (fenpei) system. From mid-1985 to 1988, half the graduates of Jiaotong were allowed to find their own jobs. In March 1988, Jiaotong was the first university to let all its graduates place themselves. The decision was made after a January meeting in Beijing that mooted many possible reforms of the employment system. The 1989 entering freshman classes at many universities (scheduled to graduate in 1993) were told, before matriculation, that their colleges would not be responsible to arrange their work after graduation. A great majority of Jiaotong graduates as early as the class of 1988 found their own work.[269]

Students from distant border regions (for example, Shanghai youth who had spent time in Xinjiang but were able to return to the metropolis for study) were not included in the plans to give graduates freedom on where to work. They were "in principle" expected to return to the border places whence they had come.[270] But this group was an exception to the reform.

Under the new system, students' experiences differed greatly. One Jiaotong graduate, whose father worked for a Beijing ministry and whose mother worked for a newspaper there, received offers from seven or eight units; his reaction was "long live parents!" (fumu wansui!). A girl graduate from a peasant family in Hubei, however, had parents who cultivated fields; and they wondered how they would "find the relationships" (*zhao guanxi*) to get her a job. So she hoped Jiaotong would help her. Under the new system it was easier for male graduates to find work than for female ones. Graduating students of "the second sex" (occasionally called such, "*di er xing,*" a translation of the Western phrase) spent a great deal of time outside enterprise gates, "fully savoring the hardships of seeking jobs."[271]

As soon as high school students heard that the government would no longer be responsible for finding university graduates' jobs by the early 1990s, they began to complain. Many worried they would not be able to find employment, and some wondered whether to take up factory work rather than attending college. Although most recognized that the removal of guarantees for future jobs was a useful reform to introduce competition into the labor market, they also feared that influential cadre parents would "use power to seek personal interests" (*yi quan mo si*) and would "enter through the back door" (*zou houmen*) on behalf of their children, which was unfair. Most students felt that to have a good father (*hao baba*) was more likely to give an unfair advantage under the new system than under the old one. Resistance to the find-your-own-jobs policies was especially strong among women students, who felt the reform would give them less incentive to study hard in universities, because good transcripts would later be of less use.[272]

For middle school and high school graduates, the Labor Bureau still "distributed" most regular jobs in Shanghai during the late 1980s, and most university graduates were brought under the new system very slowly. This bureau, cooperating with the CCP Personnel Department, sent rosters of vacancies, provided by units, to "student sections" in educational institutions, which recommended job assignments for specific graduates. The Labor Bureau's purview covered many kinds of occupations, however. It had a Labor Service Company that found menial jobs for people who had legal household registrations. The Labor Service Company was not well financed, but it had liaisons at the street level in many parts of Shanghai.[273] A Talent Exchange Department also arranged exchanges between some unionized and white-collar jobs. Because this source mainly provided job candidates who had rejected other posts, managers of state-owned units had a bias against hiring through it.[274] The Labor Service Company and Talent Exchange Department together organized less formal "talent exchange centers" (*rencai jiaoliu zhongxin*), which arranged interviews and provided rosters of information on lists of job candidates for a considerable variety of posts open to graduates. Companies sometimes ran advertisements in newspapers, offering jobs; but they were supposed to do this only after obtaining approvals from one of the semigovernmental units, the Labor Service Company or the Talent Exchange Bureau. Such rules were often decreed by the state, then honored in the breach.[275]

The partial demise of the job allocation system for university graduates arose from many interests, not just those of centralized agencies that lacked enough jobs for all new graduates. Employers had an interest in finding staff who really wanted to work with them. The *Xinmin Evening News* editor in 1988 said that his paper always interviewed prospective employees before hiring them; it did not rely solely on the employment distribution system, any more than job seekers did. Both the paper and prospective hires could express their preferences, so that the state distribution to jobs was still handled within bureaucratic offices, but with much more consultation than before. This system still gave personnel departments, which were in effect important branches of the Party, influence over the part of Shanghai's population most liable to political unruliness: students.

For students who graduated from Fudan in 1988, and from some other universities such as Jiaotong earlier, the state allocation of jobs was suspended, so that each person was to find his own way (*zizhao menlu*). The ideal distribution system by 1988 specified that, on jobs and hiring, "both sides decide."[276] At Fudan, for example, this meant that students might seek jobs on their own; but if they failed to find anything, the university's Personnel Department would still help them. A journal reported that university students who had worked hard and gotten high grades did not necessarily obtain good jobs, but those with mediocre grades might receive fine jobs if they had the right father or father-in-law.[277] The allocation of housing also depended on personal connections. To correct these abuses, it was planned in Fudan and some other universities (even before June 4) that, for the 1989 graduating class, the state allocation of jobs would be mostly restored. This change was temporary, however, mainly because the state was running out of good jobs to offer.

The new institutions for placement, combined with the new justification of doing anything for money, led in Shanghai to "negotiations which often took place between companies and universities that literally 'sold' desirable graduates to the highest bidder—another way of earning cash bonuses for the staff."[278] Especially by the spring of 1989, students were extremely concerned that suitable job placements would be unavailable for them under such a system. The conservatives in government did nothing to quell these fears, apparently in hopes of dampening their ardor for liberalism. In Shanghai,

> Students spilled over with stories of the bungling or indifference which assigned graduates in physics as secretaries in middle schools, English literature majors as translators of correspondence and instruction manuals in diesel factories, etc. ("Someone who studied agriculture was assigned to a foreign affairs office [*waiban*] to buy tickets for the foreign teachers. . . .") Everyone claimed to know at least one such misfit; would the next one be themselves?

As one student said in a paper, "The 'back door' class starts to seek help from their fathers, their relatives, their friends, or their leaders . . . some even go to the fortune teller. Funny? No, that is absolutely what has happened."[279]

A spring 1989 undergraduate senior asked:

Why did we want to go to college? First, we were idealists, and we wanted to realize our ideals through higher education. Second, we wanted to have a respectable social and economic status in the future. But now we are facing a serious problem: job allocation. Graduate job allocations (*biye fenpei*) are being carried out now; but universities can no longer manage the work and students are asked to find jobs for themselves. Except for those in some fields such as computers and English that society needs, most in other fields have not yet found work. We get a feeling that we are being abandoned. In the past, society regarded university students as people to be proud of; and we felt the same way, because so few go to college. But now what do we feel? Society cannot offer us a satisfying job.[280]

Widespread student participation in the 1989 protests, as well as much lower rates of articulated public protest among final-year students than among juniors, both relate to the state's decreasing ability to maintain its policy of finding decent jobs for graduates.

Graduates' Educational Exit Visas

Many Shanghai families hoped to educate their children internationally. When parents were asked, in an April 1989 survey about Shanghai tertiary students, what jobs they wanted for their children,

> More than a third wanted them to work in foreign trade and travel, 30 percent chose the job of taxi-driver (the glamour job that year because of its money-earning potential), and 9 percent chose shop assistants (with their access to scarce commodities), while scientists, journalists, engineers, and university professors were at the bottom of the list, followed at the very end by school teachers. These last, of course, are government not private enterprise jobs.[281]

"Fever to leave the country" (*chuguo re*) became rampant. By 1990, at least a third of the young teachers at Jiaotong University had already left for study abroad, and 80 percent of those remaining reportedly wished they could leave.[282] In April 1989, reporters castigated this situation: "Recently, we visited about ten universities in Shanghai and calculated that 60 percent [of graduate students] had withdrawn. Nine-tenths had gone abroad or were preparing to go abroad. . . . Many graduate students preferred to pay the education fee [charged, apparently, upon withdrawal without grades] rather than to finish their programs." They admitted that, "because of inflation, many graduate students indeed faced serious financial difficulties." But "many young people were attracted by such programs."[283]

Shanghai students, once overseas, usually stayed abroad even if they were on government scholarships. Before giving a passport to some, however, the regime required a contract naming a hostage financial guarantor in Shanghai, who would be responsible for the scholarship cost in case of defection. In early 1988, for example, a wife who had guaranteed the return of her husband from Japan was ordered by a Shanghai court to pay 40,000 yuan in lieu of his return—although her total property and savings were worth less than one-fifth of that.[284]

Just 285 Chinese students took the Test of English as a Foreign Language (TOEFL) in 1981, but 26,000 took it in 1987.[285] By 1991, about half of Shanghai high school students had taken the TOEFL exam, hoping for admission to undergraduate institutions abroad. At Fudan University, a "negative mood" (fu qingxu) about local education was rampant. Half the graduate students in biology and almost two-thirds in social sciences had left Fudan for study abroad or for more promising nonacademic local careers.[286]

Graduates' Choices in the 1990s

By the early 1990s, many universities in China practically forswore helping graduates to find jobs. The term "distribution of graduates" almost disappeared, and it was replaced by phrases describing "mutual choice" between job applicants and employers. Old school ties were apparently still important to job seekers, but university graduates of the 1990s tended to go into business, no matter what subject they had studied.[287]

The brain drain and local job distribution problems gave rise to many new plans for reform: for training students according to the actual economic needs of companies, strengthening relations between colleges and enterprises, trying to propagandize the attractions of rural work, and eliminating restrictions on the pay that firms in unpopular places offered graduates.[288] Before the reforms, some Shanghai students preferred not to attend national "keypoint" universities in other provinces because their careers after "distribution" might not be in Shanghai. But nationwide trends, which have made students responsible for finding their own jobs, have also made other cities newly attractive because of quick growth there. Some ambitious youth left Shanghai for cities in Sunan or Zhejiang, or for Shenzhen or Hainan. This pattern tended to reduce the avoidance of good universities outside Shanghai. The prereform PRC system of definite wage grades (gongzi dingji) was defunct by the 1990s, and Shanghai youths looked more widely for ways to make their careers. A joke from the city described four paths to success: the red path (power, the Party), the black path (corruption), the blue path (the ocean, going overseas), and the gold path (making money).[289] All of these were open.

Notes

1. Iris M. Young, *Justice and the Politics of Difference* (Princeton: Princeton University Press, 1990), p. 59.

2. "Cadre" (*ganbu*) in this context apparently refers to state or CCP employees. *Shanghai shimin banshi zhinan* (Guide for Shanghai Citizens), Shanghai Municipal Government Administrative Office, ed. (Shanghai: Shanghai Renmin Chuban She, 1989), p. 96.

3. Calculated from population figures and from *Shanghai jingji, neibu ben: 1949– 1982* (Shanghai Economy, Internal [i.e., classified] Volume: 1949–1982), Shanghai Acad-

emy of Social Sciences, ed. (Shanghai: Shanghai Shehui Kexue Yuan Chuban She, 1984), p. 85.

4. *Zhonghua renmin gonghe guo jingji dashi ji, 1949–1980* (Chronicle of Economic Events in the PRC, 1949–1980), Fang Weizhong et al., eds. (Beijing: Zhongguo Shehui Kexue Chuban She, 1984), p. 630.

5. The "one-third" was 32 percent, and *zhaogong dingti* was the most common entry; *zhiqing fancheng* (educated youths returning to the city) were 16 percent in 1978–86. The most frequent justification from the 1968–77 period was for returning demobilized soldiers; but in the later period, this reason dropped to fourth place. See *Zhongguo renkou qianyi yu chengshi hua yanjiu* (Studies on Chinese Migration and Urbanization), Editorial Group for Studies on Chinese Migration and Urbanization, ed. (Beijing: Zhongguo Shehui Kexue Yuan Renkou Yanjiu Suo, 1988), p. 277.

6. *Shanghai jingji, neibu ben,* p. 965.

7. See data in the section of the earlier volume that concerns migration, especially Table 1.5–1, which shows that the city's total immigration in those years was less than 500,000.

8. Whether some factories continued this practice of bequeathing state jobs after 1986, or began to reduce it earlier, is unknown. See Philip C.C. Huang, *The Peasant Family and Rural Development in the Yangzi Delta, 1350–1988* (Stanford: Stanford University Press, 1990), p. 292.

9. Absolute numbers of immigrants to urban districts alone have not been found for this period; but the 32 percent *zhaogong dingti,* reported above, and other data together suggest the conclusion that the text reaches.

10. New hires numbered 2,000 through the Shanghai First Steel Mill in 1983 alone, although the mill had to arrange temporary jobs for more than half of them in other enterprises. These *huicheng jiuye de zhishi qingnian* could be deemed in a factory's *jiti qinggong duiwu. Shehui xue tongxun* (Sociology Bulletin), Shanghai (1983), p. 71.

11. Ibid., p. 70.

12. *JFRB,* September 4, 1980.

13. *Shanghai shehui xiankuang he qushi, 1980–1983* (Situations and Trends in Shanghai Society, 1980–1983), Zheng Gongliang et al., eds. (Shanghai: Huadong Shifan Daxue Chuban She, 1988), p. 199.

14. *Shanghai jingji, neibu ben,* p. 979.

15. *LDB,* March 9, 1989.

16. *Zhongguo yanhai diqu xiao chengzhen fazhan yu renkou qianyi* (Migration and the Development of Small Cities and Towns on the China Coast), Liu Zheng et al., eds. (Beijing: Zhongguo Caizheng Jingji Chuban She, 1989), p. 188, suggests a rate slightly higher than that on p. 184.

17. *Shanghai fayuan* (Shanghai Court) (March 1989), pp. 20–21.

18. The Chinese terms, respectively, are *guding zhigong, jihua wai yonggong, linshi gong,* and *hetong zhi zhigong,* out of a total of 271,218 *zhigong. Dangdai Zhongguo de guangbo dianshi, shang ce* (Radio and Television in China Today, Vol. 2), Li Hua et al., eds. (Beijing: Zhongguo Shehui Kexue Chuban She, 1987), p. 280.

19. This list of suggestions for these "*duoyu renyuan*" comes from *JJRB,* August 6, 1988.

20. *CD,* May 15, 1989.

21. *XMWB,* December 20, 1988 describes this trend of *renwu shao.*

22. Some urban workers lived in housing linked to their spouses' jobs. State companies and offices found they could lay off women workers disproportionately, in part because some of them lived in residences connected with their husbands' posts.

23. Cheng Xiaonong is quoted in the *Post,* July 21, 1988.

24. Private firms were apparently not surveyed; see *SF,* April 2, 1990.

25. *Shanghai shimin,* pp. 81–82.

26. Ibid., pp. 81–82.

27. *LDB,* March 9, 1989, gives this figure as 33 percent.

28. *LDB,* March 9 and 19, 1989, offer these different reports on the number of non-Shanghai people in the city; but it is doubtful that any office had a very exact figure. The migrants were often called *yixiang ren.* The report on the later date said that more than half the immigrants had lived in Shanghai for more than six months.

29. An example is in "The Drifters," *Post Magazine,* December 12, 1993, p. 23.

30. *Xin Zhongguo gongye jingji shi* (A History of New China's Industrial Economy), Wang Haibo, ed. (Beijing: Jingji Guanli Chuban She, 1986), pp. 343–47.

31. *Shanghai jingji, neibu ben,* pp. 975–76 and 983.

32. *Shanghai shehui tongji ziliao, 1980–1983* (Statistical Materials on Shanghai Society, 1980–1983), Group on the Shanghai Social Situation and Trends, ed. (Shanghai: Huadong Shifan Daxue Chuban She, 1988), p. 34.

33. "Distributed income," *fenpei shouru,* includes compensation in kind. Calculated from *Shanghai jingji, neibu ben,* p. 85, which only gives the suburbs' 44 percent rise in total compensation to 1982 from one year (1978), and the urban areas' 15 percent rise from another (1979).

34. "*Anchou fulao.*" *Shehui xue tongxun,* (Sociology Bulletin), Shanghai (1983), p. 72.

35. *Shanghai jingji, neibu ben,* p. 967.

36. By 1994, a decade later, an interviewee suggested that the range of "kinds" of cities, based ideally on average wage levels, may have been broadened. This report placed many other important Shanghai delta cities (Hangzhou, Nanjing, Ningbo, Suzhou, and Wuxi) in the "sixth kind," but Guangzhou was a seemingly new "tenth kind," and Shenzhen perhaps higher. Cities such as Lhasa or Xining, to which the state sends some professionals with major salary inducements for political reasons, reportedly by the mid-1990s could even be a "twelfth kind."

37. Figures are calculated from a table in *Shanghai shehui tongji ziliao, 1980–1983,* p. 19.

38. Ibid. According to this source, the 1983 average basic wage of scientists was 89.7 yuan per month, whereas that of teachers and medics was 79.5 yuan.

39. *FBIS,* December 9, 1987, pp. 22–23, reporting radio of December 6.

40. *Jintie* wage increases may have begun in hardship posts, where they are still used. Miners in dangerous jobs, for example, receive "post subsidies" (*gangwei jintie*); and staff sent to work in difficult places may get "area subsidies" (*diqu jintie*). But *Liberation Daily* and other Shanghai employers had few hardship posts, and these *jintie* seem to have evolved as a means of raising compensation without violating rules against higher wages (*gongzi*). Based on interviews in Shanghai and Hong Kong.

41. Some typical names for these allowances were the *jiaotong fei* for transport, the *shubao fei* for books and newspapers, the *lengyin fei* for drinks in summer, and the *tianre fei* for extra money on hot days—but this is not an exhaustive list. The categories of such fees differ from unit to unit and from time to time, but the habit of having them is general in the PRC (and in other Chinese places such as Hong Kong or Taiwan).

42. *SHTJNJ88,* p. 406, gives figures on basic wages (which do not include bonuses).

43. The company also invested in better technology. *Shanghai jixie bao,* February 2, 1989.

44. *Post,* April 3, 1991.

45. Lei Ge, *Fansi gongping* (Reflections on Justice) (Beijing: Zhongguo Funü Chuban She, 1989), pp. 13–18; and *Tansuo yu zhengming* (Investigation and Debate) (March 1988), p. 52.

46. Ibid. "*Busan busi de fa da cai.*"

47. Miron Mushkat and Adrian Faure, *Shanghai—Promise and Performance: Economic and Stock Market Review* (Hong Kong: Baring Securities, 1991), p. 34.

48. *Shanghai shimin*, p. 37, offers a table of electricity charges in Shanghai for 1989.

49. *Shanghai jingji, neibu ben*, p. 553, and Tao Yongkuan et al., *Dali fazhan disan chanye* (Vigorously Develop Tertiary Industry) (Shanghai: Shanghai Shehui Kexue Yuan Chuban She, 1986), p. 72.

50. The 1983 calorie intake of China's urban dwellers was reportedly 3,183. Peter Nolan, "Petty Commodity Production in a Socialist Economy: Chinese Rural Development Post-Mao," in *Market Forces in China: Competition and Small Business, The Wenzhou Debate*, Peter Nolan and Dong Fureng, eds. (London: Zed Books, 1990), p. 25.

51. This is roughly stated from estimates in World Bank, *China: Long-Term Development Issues and Options* (Baltimore: Johns Hopkins University Press, 1985), p. 150.

52. *XMWB*, December 25, 1988.

53. *XMWB*, November 28, 1988.

54. This report, *SHGYJJB*, May 12, 1986, gave information on the number of kinds of products, not their value amount that was deemed in short supply.

55. Shanghai's consumption patterns reflected many of its people's interests. French cognac makers, aware that they earn far more per inhabitant from Hong Kong than from anywhere else on earth, were advertising very intensively in Shanghai by the mid-1990s. Shanghai was also first among the nation's provinces (not counting Hong Kong or Taiwan) in per-capita consumption of wristwatches, for example. After Beijing, it consumed the highest number of TV sets per person. After Xinjiang (where many Shanghai people were sent during campaigns of the Maoist years), the city also led China in per-capita consumption of silk. Tibetans imbibed more than twice as many liters of liquor per capita as the next highest province (Zhejiang) in 1985, and Shanghai was third on this list. Interpretations of such data could range from misery to happiness; but for the facts alone, already see *ZGTJNJ86*, pp. 680–83, and parallel pages in later editions. But through the 1993 tome at least, the surveyors were sensitive enough to avoid reporting the number of cellular telephones.

56. *FBIS*, December 1, 1987, p. 16, reporting radio of the same day.

57. Additional measures included planning an increase, by half, in the supply of fish, and also an increase of eggs. *FBIS*, December 10, 1987, p. 18, reporting radio of December 8.

58. *XMWB*, January 9, 1989.

59. *XMWB*, January 9, 1989, refers to *dier huobi*, traded by *liangpiao fanzi*. In the hypothetical example quoted here, the rice would have cost only 30 or 40 yuan.

60. Ibid. refers to *Hu Zhiming xiaodao* and *dixia hangxian*.

61. *Shanghai shehui xiankuang*, p. 48.

62. The percentages are calculated from yuan figures in the source. *SF*, April 2, 1990.

63. The portion of urban district households with lower incomes was 13 percent, while those with higher incomes was four-fifths, with 3 percent having 5,000 yuan or more annually (over 400 yuan per month). The data are in *SHTJNJ93*, p. 408. Ibid., p. 414, presents a 1992 income distribution for families in Shanghai's rural suburbs; but comparison is hindered because the cut-off points in the urban and rural surveys are different. The survey shows that 5 percent of registered suburban houses earned less than 1,000 yuan (83 yuan per month), and that suburban per-household living expenditures were lower than those in the city (for households averaging 3.43 people, rather than 3.11 people as in the urban districts). By 1992, however, over 35 percent of them had net incomes over 2,500 yuan (over 200 yuan per month). Reforms had made the rural suburban picture, especially for successful families, close to that in China's largest metropolis.

64. The main work on the politics of Chinese inflation control is by Professor Huang

Yasheng of Harvard Business School. These figures were reported to him from World Bank sources, relying on PRC statistics.

65. The urban and suburban 1978–87 increases in Shanghai were identical (to one-tenth of 1 percent), even though in the country as a whole, the urban increase was 58 percent and the rural increase only 38 percent. This is another, but here unwelcome, witness of the extent to which Shanghai's suburbs had become urbanized and industrialized by 1987. See *Zhongguo wujia tongji nianjian, 1988* (Statistical Yearbook of Chinese Prices, 1988), Urban Society and Economy Survey Group, ed. (Beijing: Zhongguo Tongji Chuban She, 1988), pp. 34–36.

66. The terms in Chinese are: *zhigong shenghuo feiyong jiage* and *quan shehui lingshou wujia.* For the figures that follow in the text, see *Zhongguo wujia tongji nianjian, 1988,* p. 84.

67. See also Nicholas R. Lardy, "Consumption and Living Standards in China, 1978–1983," *China Quarterly* 100 (1984), pp. 847–65.

68. *Shanghai tan* (Shanghai Shore) 7 (July 1988), p. 24.

69. Hong Kong *Dagong bao,* December 17, 1988.

70. *SHGYJJB,* July 25, 1988. A hepatitis epidemic made this period somewhat unusual, but its main effect was to dramatize longer-term trends from the early 1980s.

71. Reuters, *Post,* September 19, 1988.

72. *XMWB,* April 17, 1989.

73. *CNA* 1409 (May 1, 1990), p. 8.

74. The percentages are calculated from yuan figures in the source; the average 1989 expenditure was 151 yuan per month. *SF,* April 2, 1990.

75. D. C. Coleman, *The Economy of England, 1450–1750* (Oxford: Oxford University Press, 1977), p. 100, shows this with a useful graph.

76. B. R. Mitchell, *European Historical Statistics, 1750–1975,* 2d rev. ed. (London: Macmillan, 1980), pp. 772–74.

77. This 7 percent is a total, not annual, figure for the whole decade. See Andrew G. Walder, "Urban Industrial Workers," in *State and Society in China: The Consequences of Reform,* Arthur Lewis Rosenbaum, ed. (Boulder: Westview, 1992), pp. 106–7.

78. Shang Xiaoyuan, *Zhongguo ren de ziwo yizhi xing renge* (The Chinese Self-Restrained Personality) (Kunming: Yunnan Renmin Chuban She, 1989), pp. 30 and 222 was mentioned by a student and friend, Zheng Yongnian.

79. Institute for Research on the Reform of Chinese Economic Institutions, *Gaige: Women mianlin de tiaozhan yu xuanze* (Reform: Challenges and Choices Facing Us) (Beijing: Zhongguo Jingji Chuban She, 1986), p. 87, was also pointed out by Zheng Yongnian.

80. *CD,* February 17, 1989.

81. *Shanghai fayuan* (Shanghai Court) (March 1989), pp. 20–21.

82. *SF,* July 30, 1990.

83. Deborah Kaple, *Dream of a Red Factory: The Legacy of High Stalinism in China* (Oxford: Oxford University Press, 1994).

84. This is a major thesis in Elizabeth J. Perry, *Shanghai on Strike: The Politics of Chinese Labor* (Stanford: Stanford University Press, 1993). A sequel is Elizabeth J. Perry and Li Xun, *Proletarian Power: Shanghai in the Cultural Revolution* (Boulder: Westview, 1996), which uses new archival material and an essentially Weberian distinction between three kinds of proletarian protest—rebellion, conservatism, and economism—showing that each mode produced a specific kind of labor leader.

85. This book need make no effort to replicate the pathbreaking work by Elizabeth Perry, mentioned above, on Shanghai strikes during all decades of the twentieth century.

86. François Gipouloux, *Les cent fleurs à l'usine: Agitation ouvière et crise du*

model sovietique en Chine, 1956–1957 (Paris: Ecole des hautes études en sciences sociales, 1986), and ibid.

87. See Lynn White, "Workers' Politics in Shanghai," *Journal of Asian Studies* 26:1 (November 1976), pp. 99–116.

88. *"Yao dang matou de zhuren, bu zuo dunwei de nuli." Zhongguo renmin gongheguo,* p. 522.

89. Ibid., p. 525.

90. *"Rujia shengchan, Fajia zaofan."* Ibid., p. 528.

91. James P. Brady, *Justice and Politics in People's China: Legal Order or Continuing Revolution?* (New York: Academic Press, 1982), p. 241.

92. The reason lower levels kept information from higher levels is that such a practice increased the lower levels' power because of a usual decision rule described in Susan Shirk, *The Political Logic of Economic Reform in China* (Berkeley: University of California Press, 1993). Higher levels were secretive vis-à-vis lower ones, as in most hierarchies, to mystify their authority and to keep their operational options open when members there wanted to delay or avoid decisions.

93. These interpretations are based mainly on interviews by the author in Shanghai during late 1988.

94. *Shanghai jingji kexue* (Shanghai Economics), January 1984, p. 29.

95. See Lin Qibing and Chen Hua, *Fu–Ri de shengchan fangshi* (The Fujian–Japan Method of Production) (Shanghai: Shanghai Shehui Kexue Yuan Chuban She, 1987), pp. 104–6.

96. Piece-rates are *jijian zi,* and daily salaries are *rigong zi. WHB,* October 13, 1979.

97. The samples from other countries, from the 1960s, involve respondents in the United States, USSR, Yugoslavia, and other countries. See *JFRB,* February 21, 1987. The author's impressions from Taipei in 1993 indicate a similar sense among people there that they work a great deal.

98. Wang Shaoguang, "The Politics of Private Time," in *Urban Spaces in Contemporary China,* Deborah S. Davis et al., eds. (New York: Cambridge University Press, 1995), pp. 149–72.

99. This idea, romanized as "TQC" even in a Chinese language text, was borrowed from Japanese factory management. The complaints of the team leaders (*banzu zhang*) are in *JFRB,* January 6, 1987.

100. *Shanghai gongyun* is mentioned in *Zhongguo xinwen nianjian, 1982* (Yearbook of Chinese Journalism, 1982), News Studies Institute of the Chinese Social Science Academy, ed. (Beijing: Zhongguo Shehui Kexue Chuban She, 1982), p. 217.

101. Perhaps Shanghai reporting was more complete than that from other places. See *Shanghai jingji, neibu ben,* p. 972.

102. Ibid., p. 997, indicates that in 1982 Shanghai's registered workforce was 4.75 million, but China's was 112.81 million.

103. *Dangdai Zhongguo de guangbo dianshi, shang,* pp. 139–40.

104. *LDB,* March 9, 1989.

105. This was called a *shigu fenxi huiyi. JFRB,* September 7, 1980.

106. Raising suggestions is *ti yijian.* Petitioning higher bureaucrats is *gaozhuang.* Slowdowns are *daigong.* Strikes are *bagong.* Barricading managers is *baowei ganbu.* The Chinese phrase for Luddite machine smashing is *za jiqi.* The main book for this is Elizabeth Perry, *Shanghai on Strike.*

107. *FBIS,* March 8, 1988, p. 29, reporting a journal of February 10.

108. "Rationalization" is called *heli hua. JFRB,* February 9, 1987.

109. Several works make clear that the Federation of Trade Unions is not formally an organ of the state nor a collective, but by default—for lack of other officially conceivable

categories—it is listed as a political party. See *Tongzhan gongzuo shouce* (Handbook of United Front Work), Ma Fen et al., eds. (Shanghai: Shanghai Renmin Chuban She, 1989), and *Zhongguo minzhu dangpai: lishi, zhenggang, renwu* (China's Democratic Parties: Histories, Platforms, and Personages), Qin Guosheng and Hu Zhisheng, eds. (Jinan: Shandong Renmin Chuban She, 1990).

110. Robert Benewick, "Political Participation," in *Reforming the Revolution: China in Transition*, Benewick and Paul Wingrove, eds. (Basingstoke, UK: Macmillan, 1988), p. 55.

111. *GRRB*, September 29, 1988.

112. These strikes protested inflation and the obvious dangers of closure in companies that were not receiving raw materials. *Post*, September 3, 1988.

113. James D. Seymour, "China's Democracy Movement: What the Agenda has been Missing," paper presented at the conference on "Rights in China: What Happens Next?," London, June 28–29, 1991, p. 5.

114. *Post*, April 24, 1989.

115. Hong Kong Trade Union Education Centre, *A Moment of Truth: Workers' Participation in China's 1989 Democracy Movement and the Emergence of Independent Unions* (Hong Kong: Hong Kong Trade Union Education Centre, 1990), p. 62.

116. See Lenin, "What Is to Be Done," in *The Lenin Anthology*, Robert C. Tucker, ed. (New York: Norton, 1975), pp. 12–114.

117. Quoted in Anita Chan, "Revolution or Corporatism?" in *China's Quiet Revolution: New Interactions Between State and Society*, David S.G. Goodman and Beverley Hooper, eds. (New York: St. Martin's, 1994), p. 180.

118. The union was the Shanghai Zizhi Lianhe Zong Gonghui. *Xinbao* (Hong Kong Economic Journal), August 17, 1989.

119. *RMRBHWB*, June 13, 1989.

120. See Anita Chan, "Revolution or Corporatism?" pp. 162–90, which cites Philippe Schmitter on corporatism and extends the earlier work of Jeanne Wilson to offer a view of the potential of Chinese unions.

121. *SHKXB*, March 9, 1989.

122. *SF*, February 19, 1990.

123. Ibid.

124. Cheng Xiaonong, "The Chinese Public Sector: Heading Toward Zero Profit?" *China Focus* 1:2 (March 30, 1993), p. 1.

125. Ibid.

126. *CD*, June 14, 1991.

127. *QNB*, February 24, 1989. Emphasis added.

128. Ibid.

129. In January 1994, the author saw *xiagang gongren* picking up leather coats at a distribution point in central Shanghai, where these goods could be sold in particular to Chinese and other tourists. Such practices put state factories in direct competition with state stores, of course. But factory employment in the state sector was an even greater problem than commercial employment. Stores could more often accommodate reform changes more easily than production units could.

130. *Economist*, May 21, 1994, p. 38.

131. This information, and some of the argument in which it is used, comes from a conversation with Michael Agelasto, then a student of Chinese education at the University of Hong Kong and previously a teacher in China.

132. *Shanghai shehui xiankuang*, p. 106.

133. Bridget Williams, untitled manuscript, Hong Kong, July 1994, p. 6.

134. On this slight decline, see *ZGTJNJ93*, p. 806.

135. *Post Magazine*, March 13, 1994, p. 11.

136. Wang Ya'nan's book on *Das Kapital* was published by the Shanghai People's Press in 1973. *Zhongguo xueshu jie dashi ji, 1919–1985* (Chronicle of Chinese Academic Circles, 1919–1985), Wang Yafu and Zhang Hengzhong, eds. (Shanghai: Shanghai Shehui Kexue Yuan Chuban She, 1988), pp. 257–61.

137. This is calculated from data in *WHB*, November 2, 1977. There is no information about the quality of the research.

138. *Shanghai shi gaoxiao zhuanye jieshao* (Introduction to the Professions in Shanghai's University-level Academies), Fang Ren, ed. (Shanghai: Jiaotong Daxue Chuban She, 1988).

139. The student–teacher ratio in Shanghai primary schools, between these same times, had also plummeted, from 30 : 1 to 17 : 1; but clearly, the main cause in this case was the one-child policy that reduced primary age cohorts. *Shanghai jiaoyu fazhan zhanlüe yanjiu baogao* (Research Report on the Strategy of Shanghai's Educational Development), Kang Yonghua, Liang Chenglin, and Tan Songhua, eds. (Shanghai: Huadong Shifan Daxue Chuban She, 1989), p. 6.

140. Interview with an educational researcher, who was originally from the Shanghai delta but had worked for many years in Beijing.

141. *Shanghai jiaoyu fazhan zhanlüe yanjiu baogao*, p. 7.

142. Chen Benlin et al., *Gaige kaifang shenzhou jubian* (Great Change in the Sacred Land [China] During Reform and Opening) (Shanghai: Jiaotong Daxue Chuban She, 1984), calculated from pp. 95–96. The number of Chinese universities in 1978 was 598.

143. See *Zhongguo jiaoyu chengjiu: Tongji ziliao, 1980–1985* (Achievement of Education in China: Statistics, 1980–85), Department of Planning, PRC State Education Commission, ed. (Beijing: Zhongguo Jiaoyu Chuban She, 1986), p. 20, which reports 675 regular higher educational institutions in 1980 and 1,016 in 1985.

144. *SHTJNJ88*, p. 331, shows that the number of Shanghai institutions of higher learning in 1980 was 49, but by 1985, only 45. Local budgetary data would be available for comparison in education bureaus, and probably in the Beijing ministry, but they have not been published.

145. *Zhongguo jiaoyu chengjiu: Tongji ziliao, 1949–1983* (Achievement of Education in China: Statistics, 1949–1983), Department of Planning, PRC Ministry of Education, ed. (Beijing: Zhongguo Jiaoyu Chuban She, 1984), pp. 324–26.

146. Calculated from figures in *Guangdong sheng tongji nianjian, 1987* (Guangdong Province Statistical Yearbook, 1987), Guangdong Province Statistical Bureau, ed. (Beijing: Zhongguo Tongji Chuban She, 1987), p. 441.

147. Early figures are in *Zhongguo jiaoyu nianjian* (China Education Yearbook), Editorial Group of the China Education Yearbook, ed. (Changsha: Hunan Jiaoyu Chuban She), various years, esp. the 1986 edition, pp. 452 and 516; and also in *ZGTJNJ*, separately for each year.

148. *WHB*, October 12, 1979.

149. See coverage of the intellectual inbreeding and *concurrent* depoliticization of academe in Du Ruiqing, *Chinese Higher Education* (New York: St. Martin's, 1992).

150. The size of this group was reportedly about a dozen people; this is a set, not a sample. *Shanghai Jiaotong daxue guanli gaige chutan* (Preliminary Research on the Management Reform at Shanghai's Jiaotong University), Shanghai Jiaotong University, Communist Party Committee Office, ed. (Shanghai: Jiaotong Daxue Chuban She, 1983), introduction, p. 2.

151. "*Tou peng tou, jiao peng jiao.*" The generations, mentioned later in the text, were "*sandai tongtang.*" The statement on schisms in offices is worth romanizing fully: "*Lici zhengzhi yundong ye gei ren yu ren zhi jian liuxia yixie nanyu xiaochu de gehe.*" Ibid., introduction, p. 13.

152. These were called the "three noninfluences" (*san bu yingxiang*). See ibid., introduction, p. 3, and regular text, p. 14.

153. *GMRB,* September 22, 1977.

154. The Jiangsu Academy of Social Sciences opened in March 1978. *Zhongguo xueshu,* pp. 270–77.

155. See Veronica Pearson, *Mental Health Care in China* (London: Gaskell, 1995), pp. 18–27, on the Cultural Revolution period and passim for the whole subject.

156. *Hongkong Standard,* March 7, 1981.

157. *"Shanghai shi qingshao nian baohu tiaolie" lifa jishi* (Record on the Legislation of the "Rules for Protection of Youths and Infants in Shanghai"), Drafting Office for the "Rules for Protection of Youths and Infants in Shanghai," ed. (Shanghai: Shanghai Shehui Kexue Yuan Chuban She, 1987), p. 151.

158. This information was compiled by Lyman Miller.

159. Fu Zhengyuan, "The Sociology of Political Science in the PRC," in *The Development of Political Science: A Comparative Study,* D. Easton, J. Gunnell, and L. Graziano, eds. (London: Routledge, 1991), pp. 235–36.

160. *Shanghai shehui kexue* (Social Science in Shanghai), Institute of Information Studies of the Shanghai Social Science Academy, ed. (Shanghai: Shanghai Shehui Kexue Chuban She, 1988), pp. 125–26.

161. Beijing University began its political science major one year later than Fudan did. See Fu Zhengyuan, "The Sociology of Political Science," p. 241.

162. Ding Richu, "Xinhai geming qian Shanghai ziben jia de zhengzhi huodong" (The Political Activities of Shanghai Capitalists Before the Xinhai Revolution), in *Jindai Zhongguo zichan jieji yanjiu* (Studies on China's Capitalist Class in Recent Times), Fudan History Department, ed. (Shanghai: Fudan Daxue Chuban She, 1983), p. 523.

163. Most of these police were Sikhs in the employ of Shanghai's International Settlement. The history of Shanghai's Indians has never been written. But this author must mention two recent and relevant books (one by his wife): Barbara-Sue White, *Turbans and Traders: Hong Kong's Indian Communities* (Hong Kong: Oxford University Press, 1994), and Frederic Wakeman Jr., *Policing Shanghai* (Berkeley: University of California Press, 1994).

164. Xu Dingxin, Tang Chuansi, and Jiang Duo, "The May 30th Movement and the Shanghai Bourgeoisie," in *SASS Papers,* Zhang Zhongli et al., eds. (Shanghai: Shanghai Academy of Social Sciences, 1986), pp. 516–17.

165. Ibid., p. 516.

166. The portion working in universities was 29 percent. Fudan had about 37,000 graduates in the 1963–65 era, which this reports. See *Fudan daxue de gaige yu tansuo* (Reforms and Explorations at Fudan University), Fudan Daxue Gaodeng Jiaoyu Yanjiu Suo, ed. (Shanghai: Fudan Daxue Chuban She, 1987), p. 51.

167. *Shanghai shehui kexue,* pp. 28–31.

168. See Ruth Hayhoe, *China's Universities and the Open Door* (Armonk, NY: M.E. Sharpe, 1989).

169. *WHB,* October 12, 1979.

170. *JFRB,* December 3, 1979.

171. *Shanghai Jiaotong,* pp. 19–21.

172. This discussion was called *huishang,* and the CCP branch was the *dang zong zhi.* "Personnel not meeting the needs of work" were termed *bu heshi gongzuo yaoqiu de renyuan.* See ibid., p. 37.

173. Ibid., introduction, pp. 10–12.

174. One vice principal would head a business office (often still called, in military fashion, an office for "general logistics," *zongwu houqing*). Another would serve as the

academic dean of students. A third would head a group of teacher-administrators responsible for extracurricular activities, the student union, and the school's Communist Youth League.

175. Interview with a teacher.

176. Marianne Bastid in *China's Education and the Industrialized World,* Marianne Bastid and Ruth Hayhoe, eds. (Armonk, NY: M.E. Sharpe, 1987), p. 5.

177. A few intellectuals, notably Fang Lizhi, go to the opposite extreme by calling for "complete Westernization." Even if Westernism could be defined as coherent—which it clearly is not—this seems a surreal idea in a country of China's size and resources, both situational and normative. It may prove little more than Fang's sincerity when he says he lacks ambition in any field except astrophysics because as a political platform in China "complete Westernization" is certainly designed to provoke rather than to attract. For some of Fang's ideas, see his contribution in *The Broken Mirror: China After Tiananmen,* in George Hicks, ed. (London: Longman, 1990). It should also be noted that *most* imported Western ideas are suitably hierarchical from the government's viewpoint.

178. See Li Cheng, "The Rise of Technocracy: Elite Transformation and Ideological Change in Post-Mao China" (Ph.D. dissertation, Politics Department, Princeton University, 1991).

179. Interview with a professor at Beijing Normal University.

180. *Shanghai jiaoyu, 1988* (Shanghai Education, 1988), Wang Shenghong, ed. (Shanghai: Tongji Daxue Chuban She, 1989), p. 212.

181. *WHB,* September 22, 1975.

182. *WHB,* May 21, 1979.

183. *WHB,* October 22, 1979.

184. *WHB,* May 27, 1979.

185. Health criteria do affect university admissions in China (as athletic ones do, for example, in the United States)—and because the ratio of Chinese applicants to admits is so small, they can be important. Handicapped people have real difficulties in this process; the Chinese procedure clearly works against them, rather than for them. On the other hand, ethnic minority status was an advantage (in Shanghai, 0.4 percent of the population in 1987; but for the whole country, 7 percent). *WHB,* May 27, 1979. To calculate Shanghai's minority percentage, see *Zhongguo 1987 nian 1% renkou chouxiang pucha ziliao: Shanghai shi fence* (Chinese 1987 1% Sample Survey: Shanghai Municipality Volume), Shanghai City Statistical Bureau, ed. (Beijing: Zhongguo Tongji Chuban She, 1988), p. 8.

186. The summary is a *zongjie,* and the criticism is a *pingyi,* on which the *ban zhuren* writes *pingyu.* A school's guidance office is usually called its *jiaodao chu.* Interview in Hong Kong.

187. These paragraphs are based on interviews with educators and students. One administrator indicated that university representatives would try to reserve as many as three times their final quota of admits at this stage. The ratio of reserved names to final admits varies by year, place, and unit—and is in principle secret—but this would be a most important index of the degree to which academic criteria govern educational promotions in China, if more could be known about it.

188. *Fudan daxue,* p. 163.

189. Ibid., pp. 381–82.

190. Interview with a PRC educator, and *Post,* December 6, 1981.

191. The change was from 6.0 to 7.3 hours. See tables in "*Shanghai shi qingshao . . . ,*" pp. 166–68.

192. Ibid., p. 122.

193. *QNB,* March 24, 1989.

194. The 1989 figure comes from the source noted immediately below, and it may not be fully comparable with the others. *ZGTJNJ86*, p. 738.

195. *Sunan fada diqu jiaoyu fazhan zhanlüe huanjing yanjiu baogao* (Research Report on the Environment for Educational Development Strategy in the Developed Region of Southern Jiangsu), Task Force on the Environment for Educational Development Strategy in the Developed Region of Southern Jiangsu, ed. and pub., mimeographed "discussion draft" (*taolun gao*), n.p., 1991, pp. 55–56.

196. The primary school age cohort is 7–12 *sui* (c. years; Chinese reckon that they become one year older at each lunar New Year); and for junior high, 13–15 *sui;* senior high, 16–18 *sui;* university, 19–22 *sui.* Ibid., pp. 57 and 52.

197. Calculated at 74 percent in Jiangsu's *xiang* and *cun* (as distinct from *shi* or *zhen*) from *Huadong tongji nianjian, 1993* (Statistical Yearbook of East China, 1993), Statistical Information Network of the East China Region, ed. (Beijing: Zhongguo Tongji Chuban She, 1993), p. 33. A good aspect of age cohort data, as demographers have long known, is that they do not change much as the cohort advances through middle years; the text combines 1987 and 1992 sources on this premise.

198. *FBIS,* December 4, 1987, p. 24, reporting radio of December 3.

199. See *SHTJNJ88,* p. 327, and *Zhongguo tongji zhaiyao, 1988* (A Statistical Survey of China, 1988), State Statistical Bureau, ed. (Beijing: Zhongguo Tongji Chuban She, 1988), p. 105.

200. *Shanghai shehui xiankuang,* pp. 188–89.

201. Ibid., p. 192.

202. *Shanghai jiaoyu fazhan zhanlüe yanjiu baogao,* p. 2.

203. Interview with a PRC research specialist on education.

204. The data come from Stanley Rosen, reported by Leslie Nai-kwai Lo, "The Irony of Reform in Higher Education in Mainland China," in *Education in Mainland China,* Lin Bih-jaw and Fan Li-min, eds. (Taipei: Institute of International Relations, 1990), p. 40.

205. See Moshe Lewin, *The Gorbachev Phenomenon: A Historical Interpretation* (Berkeley: University of California Press, 1988).

206. The steepness of the rise depends partly on the extent to which the post-1985 decrease in popular enthusiasm for education, after the big increase from the mid-1970s to the mid-1980s, may continue or be reversed. The youngest reported Jiangsu cohort has lower levels of high school education, although it shows a high rate in junior highs. Some of these people were still in school part-time. Also, not all education is formal. Research by Alex Inkeles and others suggests that factory work, even in small rural plants, is a powerful source of modern education. (See Alex Inkeles and David Smith, *Becoming Modern: Individual Change in Six Developing Countries* [London: Heinemann, 1974].) The main message is in the text above: China as a whole is becoming better educated.

207. Interview with a PRC research specialist on education.

208. The percentages and romanizations are: *putong gaozhong* (49 percent in Sunan, 55 percent in Jiangsu, 58 percent nationally); *zhongzhuan xiao* (respectively 22, 18, and 18 percent); *zhiye gaozhong* (19, 20, 19); and *zhigong xiao* (10, 6, 5). *Sunan fada diqu jiaoyu,* p. 58.

209. *Shanghai jiaoyu fazhan zhanlüe yanjiu baogao,* p. 2.

210. This average wage for tertiary graduates was about the same as the 1,250 yuan received in households headed by graduates from regular high schools, and not much more than the 1,119 yuan for those from junior highs, or 1,088 yuan for those only from primary schools. If the household head was illiterate, however, the rate was only 742 yuan (and most of the people in that category were elderly peasants). *Shanghai shehui xiankuang,* p. 116.

211. Stanley Rosen, "The Effect of Post-June 4 Re-education Campaigns on Chinese

Students," paper presented at the annual meeting of the American Association of China Studies, 1992, p. 11.

212. Interview with a teacher at Fudan University.

213. *XMWB*, May 29, 1991.

214. For a pioneering treatment of these links, which have analogues among many Chinese leadership groups, see Li Cheng, "University Networks and the Rise of Qinghua Graduates in China," *Australian Journal of Chinese Affairs* 32 (July 1994), pp. 1–32.

215. *WHB*, June 27, 1988.

216. For this and the following quotations, see Ye Shitao and Liu Jun in *LW* 20 (April 1988), p. 20.

217. Interview with a teacher, and *Post*, November 23, 1981.

218. Interview with a teacher.

219. *Shanghai jiaoyu fazhan zhanlüe yanjiu baogao*, p. 12.

220. *Shanghai jiaoyu, 1988*, p. 220.

221. Interview with a professor of pedagogy, 1988.

222. Zhu Weizheng, "Qifa shi jiaoxue de yidian changshi: guanyu 'lianghan jingxue' taolun ban" (Trials of the Elicitation Method of Teaching: A Seminar on the Confucian Classics of the Two Han Dynasties), in *Fudan daxue*, pp. 244–45.

223. An interviewee emphasized the importance of students' "*quanmian fazhan*" and bewailed the actual stress on "*shuben zhishi.*"

224. Based on *Post*, December 21, 1981.

225. Interview with a professor at Beijing Normal University.

226. *Post*, October 16, 1981, and interview.

227. *Shanghai jiaoyu, 1988*, p. 225.

228. Leslie Nai-kwai Lo, "The Irony of Reform . . . ," pp. 55–57.

229. *WHB*, May 22, 1979.

230. Of 1.2 million children in those cohorts then, only 0.7 million were members of the Zhongguo Shaonian Xianfeng Dui. *WHB*, October 10, 1979.

231. *Post*, August 17, 1981.

232. It is difficult to make these calculations exact because not all Pioneers are in primary school, and not all Communist Youth League members are in high school or college. But data for these rough comparisons, which do confirm the trends, can be found in *Zhongguo shehui tongji ziliao, 1987* (Chinese Social Statistics, 1987), Social Statistics Office, State Statistical Bureau, ed. (Beijing: Zhongguo Tongji Chuban She, 1987), pp. 3 and 5.

233. See *Zhongguo gaige da cidian* (Dictionary of Chinese Reforms), Dictionary of Chinese Reforms Editorial Group, ed. (Haikou: Hainan Chuban She, 1992), *shang*, p. 330.

234. From an interviewee, April 1994.

235. Hong Yung Lee has found that the Party percentage at Fudan in 1983 was 0.56 percent, 0.35 at East China Normal University, and 0.3 at the Shanghai University of Science and Technology.

236. Interviews with students at Shanghai universities.

237. *Post*, July 28, 1981.

238. This would be an interesting subject for further study partly because middle-class *radicals* in 1964–65 were the second major patrons of summer camping from Shanghai (after expatriates to hill stations at Lushan and Kyushu much earlier). The radicals' aim was to prepare young students for later rustication farther afield, and they could use military camps in the mid-1960s. Comparisons with both Koreas and with Taiwan would also be apt. On the pre–CR youth camps near Shanghai, see Lynn White, *Policies of Chaos* (Princeton: Princeton University Press, 1989), e.g., p. 215.

239. The Party charter study groups were *Dangzhang Xuexi Xiaozu.* The literary society was the Chunsun Wenxue She; the history group, the Shiyu She; the science club, the Xuesheng Kexue Xuehui; for physics, the Wuli Shiyan Xingqu Xiaozu; for international trade, Guoji Maoyi Xingqu Xiaozu. See *Fudan daxue,* p. 45.

240. This was the Xibei Jingji Kaifa Xuehui.

241. Liao Mei, "Shinian lai Fudan daxue xuesheng shetuan de fazhan qi qushi" (The Development and Tendency of Student Associations in Fudan University over the Past Ten Years), a proposal for academic exchange among Fudan University, Taiwan National University, and Hongkong University students, January 1989. Also, interviews with people from Fudan University.

242. Managing schools on an open-door basis is *kaimen banxue;* and encouraging work to aid schooling is *qinggong juxue. Fudan daxue,* p. 149.

243. *Hongkong Standard,* August 25, 1981.

244. *SF,* March 19, 1990.

245. *XDRB* and *Post,* December 7, 1981.

246. Joan Grant, *Worm-Eaten Hinges: Tensions and Turmoil in Shanghai, 1988–89, Events Leading Up to Tiananmen Square* (Melbourne: Hyland House, 1991), p. 19.

247. *Hongkong Standard,* October 20, 1981.

248. *XDRB* and *Post,* both July 28, 1981.

249. Ng Man-lung, "Facing the Inevitable: Sex Among Youth," in *China Review, 1992,* Kuan Hsin-chi and Maurice Brosseau, eds. (Hong Kong: Chinese University Press, 1992), pp. 14.3–5, reporting *Zhongguo dangdai xing wenhua: Zhongguo liangwan li xing wenming diaocha baogao* (Sexual Behavior in Modern China: Report of the Nationwide "Sex Civilization Survey" of 20,000 Chinese) (Shanghai: Sanlian shudian, 1992), of which Dr. Ng, a psychiatrist at the University of Hong Kong, is one of the compilers. The authors of this pioneering survey do not pretend to fulfill their pre-1989 hope of attaining fair randomness in the national population. Like researchers in other areas, they report they had to rely disproportionately on data from Shanghai.

250. Ibid., p. 14.5, reports these results from a clinic in Beijing during 1990. It also reports that medical checks found that nearly three-quarters of new brides lacked proof of virginity—but such checks are dubious from several viewpoints, one of which is that they are not a sure test for previous sexual activity.

251. Zhe Xiaoye, *Chengshi zai zhuanzhe dianshang* (Cities at a Turning Point) (Beijing: Zhongguo Funü Chuban She, 1989), pp. 72–73.

252. This is based on Li Cheng, "The Rise of Technocracy."

253. *Shanghai Jiaotong,* p. 15.

254. *Fudan feng* (Fudan Breeze), Shanghai, 1 (March 27, 1988), pp. 5–7.

255. Ibid., p. 9.

256. Ibid., p. 10.

257. *Shanghai Jiaotong,* pp. 384–85.

258. Zhang Aizhu, "Dui bufen daxue sheng bu pingheng xinli de fenxi" (Analysis of the Unbalanced Psychology of Some University Students) in *Fudan daxue de gaige,* pp. 137–46.

259. Liao Mei, "Shinian lai Fudan daxue xuesheng."

260. *Post,* May 2, 1989.

261. *Post,* April 25, 1989.

262. Joan Grant, *Worm-Eaten Hinges,* p. 117.

263. Ibid., p. 109.

264. The "*sanhao xuesheng*" students were good at study, health, and work (*xuexi hao, shenti hao, gongzuo hao*). The section was the Renshi Chu, Xuesheng Ke. *Shanghai Jiaotong,* p. 146.

265. *Gan yi hang, ai yi hang. WHB,* October 23, 1980.

266. Joan Grant, *Worm-Eaten Hinges,* p. 94.

267. *Shanghai Jiaotong,* pp. 395–96.

268. Figures and fulminations alike may be found in *Shanghai jiaoyu fazhan zhanlüe yanjiu* (Research on a Strategy for Shanghai's Educational Development), Task Force on Shanghai Educational Development Strategy, ed. (Shanghai: Fudan Daxue Chuban She, 1988), pp. 459–61.

269. *JFRB,* May 4, 1988.

270. "In principle" is *yuanze shang;* there were ten such "distant provinces and [autonomous] regions" (*bianyuan shengqu*). Exceptions to this rule were apparently granted only if the distant regions sent certificates of approval, allowing the graduates not to return. See *JFRB,* May 4, 1988.

271. Ibid.

272. *JFRB,* May 31, 1988.

273. "Street" (*jiedao*) area offices may sound small because of their literal English translation, but in fact they are large. Only the district (*qu*) level is administratively higher within the city. Street areas vary, and in Shanghai at least one of them is worthy of special mention: The Yan'an Middle Road area, covering a broad region of old Western-style residences, probably once contained more "rightists" than any other street area of China. (The area around Beijing University is the only serious competitor for this record, but it is too seldom noticed that many rightists were educated nonacademics.) The following oral report would seem incredible except for other circumstantial information about Yan'an Middle Road: In 1980, that single street's public security officials approved more than half the exit permits—from all of China—for "self-paying" students going abroad to study. (Government-sponsored students are not included in this report; and in later years, families from other places began to send their offspring abroad in larger numbers.) Street neighborhoods would receive more attention, if more information were available about them, in part because they can differ sharply from one another.

274. Interview with Catherine Kwai Po Ip, lecturer at City Polytechnic of Hong Kong, who has done the best interview research on this topic in Shanghai. From the Talent Exchange Department's founding in 1984 to the time of her interviews in 1988, only 17 percent of the applicants to this organization had actually found jobs through its auspices. The Labor Bureau is the Laodong Ju, and the Personnel Department, the Renshi Bu. Student sections were usually called *xuesheng ke.* The service company was called the Laodong Fuwu Gongsi, and it may well have been based in part on secretaries and offices inherited from *laodong fuwu zhan* (stations), established especially during the depression of the early 1960s but then much attacked by disgruntled job-seekers during the Cultural Revolution. The Talent Exchange Department was the Rencai Jiaoliu Bu.

275. An interviewee from Guangdong reported that the legal rules requiring approvals for job advertisements, before they are run in newspapers, were often violated. Large newspapers, whose classified job pages are easily filled (and now important for income), follow the rules more readily; but "if the approvals take time and money, small papers will break this law."

276. *Shuangxiang xuanze.* Interview with a professor at Fudan University.

277. *Shanghai tan* (Shanghai Shore) 7 (July 1988), p. 24.

278. Joan Grant, *Worm-Eaten Hinges,* p. 92.

279. Ibid., p. 91.

280. *QNB,* March 10, 1989.

281. Joan Grant, *Worm-Eaten Hinges,* p. 36; the sample was apparently of parents of tertiary students only.

282. Chen Hao, cited in Stanley Rosen, "Students and the State in China," in *State*

and Society in China: The Consequences of Reform, Arthur Lewis Rosenbaum, ed., p. 177.

283. *XMWB,* April 9, 1989.

284. *Post,* March 15, 1988.

285. Leslie Nai-kwai Lo, "The Irony of Reform . . . ," p. 32.

286. Stanley Rosen, "The Effect of Post-June 4 Re-education Campaigns," p. 28.

287. Relatively few graduates were able to go abroad. The author thanks Michael Agelasto, who has published some of his own research about Chinese tertiary education, for insights in this area.

288. *JFRB,* May 13, 1988.

289. Joan Grant, *Worm-Eaten Hinges,* p. 103.

Part 4

Steering:
Statesmen Reform Political Structure—
Authoritarianism, Liberalism,
and Alternatives

Treason doth never prosper, what's the reason?
For if it prosper, none dare call it treason.

—Sir John Harington[1]

This book is about politics, which is neither an activity just of large collectives nor a matter just of deciding what to do about unintended situations. Power may be motivated by circumstances, but also by customs and meanings. It may be used in the name of a large group, but also by small groups and individuals. Nonetheless, the top of a state elite generally exercises power in situations as they arise, at least nominally for the nation as a whole. This is just one kind of power, and links between it and other types need to be studied. Many of the other sorts have been discussed in the three previous parts of this book on economic, cultural, and social reforms. So the remaining job is to cover what PRC insiders have sometimes have called "political policy": the aspects of politics that have to do with corporate steering, especially measures that the state elite takes to regulate mobility to its own ranks. This is sometimes distinguished from "public policy," meant to serve society.[2] State leaders naturally obscure any such distinction.

Reforms are often seen as decisions of the state, and leadership politics have of course shaped measures undertaken by the government. This is usually too exclusive a way to talk about reforms, but that does not invalidate it as a partial

461

explanation of events in China over recent decades. What needs to be added is that politics occurs in many smaller kinds of collectivity too. The state's efforts to create and enforce its overall political policy will be treated below in terms of the high elite's choices along several dimensions.

At the top of any system, the main political policy can be summarized by Machiavelli's or Pareto's old observation that leaders must *both* maintain order *and* permit change. In practice, these emphases alternate between conservative and reformist periods of politics, but neither of them completely disappears from any era. Political elites contain both lions and foxes, to keep enough harmonious integration of the networks that they lead, while also garnering new resources.[3] In an attempt to coordinate various functional "arenas" of politics, the state interacts with local leaders over space and time.[4] The presentation will show how reforms have affected three kinds of strictly political decisions: choosing leaders, deciding policies, and selecting the constitutional regime type.

Divisions by Flexibility:
The Combination of Lions and Foxes

"Conservatives" have dominated Chinese politics in many subperiods of "reform." Change has been a slow undercurrent, only a long-term drift of a trend line that is wobbly over short periods. The word "reform" may be confusing because it describes a long era in which reactionary leaders have often been potent. The conventional wording nonetheless makes sense. The overall tenor of the time, which names the period as a whole, comes largely from local changes. Making hinge leaders more independent than they were before is inherently a reformist program. That trend has been steadier than vacillating state efforts to accommodate or control the political power of local networks, as the revolution ends.

The broad tendency, by the 1970s toward some political diversification but before 1970 toward more revolutionary control, created the watershed between eras. During the late 1960s' violence, there was much propaganda about a "war between two lines"; and the radical line predominated in high politics. Especially after Lin Biao's fall, the two lines in Beijing became clearer; the ambiguity of Party conservatives toward reformers, and vice versa, began to stabilize. Zhou Enlai and other administrators (sometimes joined by Mao Zedong) espoused a revival of more civilian and more moderate rule. The Gang of Four, sporadically joined by new trade unionists, new Party members who had risen fast during the Cultural Revolution, and a scattering of naval and militia officers, kept to radical principles. Parallel patterns can be shown in the provinces, for example in East China. A detailed account of factional conflict in Zhejiang shows a "reestablishment of civilian rule" during the early 1970s at least until 1973. "Renewed radicalism" predominated in some Zhejiang places during 1973 and 1974, and a breakdown of authority was evident in Zhejiang by 1975.[5] This Zhejiang mid-1970s rerun of the Cultural Revolution was atypical but violent. Not nearly so many people participated as in the earlier chaos there. Conflict was largely within the provincial government, between groups led by cadres who were not originally from Zhejiang and were later replaced by native sons. In Beijing politics, as well as diplomacy, international trade, and local decisions about rural industries, fluctuation was also normal. The overall trend for most people on the Yangzi delta nonetheless turned toward somewhat more reform by the early 1970s.

As long as the Gang of Four was prominent, and sometimes powerful, this trend was obscured. Officials in the Deng era, later, were reluctant to take pride in the resistance, especially in rural areas, to radical dicta from Beijing and from the Shanghai city government at that time. This view neglected the roles of Zhou Enlai, Deng Xiaoping, and many lower officials in the early 1970s. A current motive for denying the seriousness of tensions between radical and proto-reform elements between 1971 and 1976 would be to deny the propriety of China's having any serious elite conflicts.[6] In any case, such divisions certainly existed.

Even for some periods after 1972 when Deng Xiaoping was in political seclusion (e.g., most of 1976), Deng remained a central actor in Chinese politics. He inherited the mantle of Zhou Enlai as leader of China's "Four Modernizations" policy. That reputation was useful to him in periods of forced withdrawal because it fostered his famous comebacks. Deng was temporarily exiled from his posts after the Qingming rally commemorating Zhou in the spring of 1976. Quarantine did not, however, end his fame as a good administrator or his identification with the Four Modernization reforms. This public reputation was almost surely one of Deng's main resources, in the obscure processes that gave him high posts or took them away.

Late 1974 and early 1975 saw intense conflict in Beijing. This fact has been hidden in later official historiography because of the continuing value to Party legitimacy of Mao Zedong's charisma. Because Mao so long remained the final arbiter of decisions at the state level, most Chinese scholars have neglected the liveliness of these 1974–75 politics. But the early and mid-1970s were not just a period of continued radical hegemony. It is now time to incorporate, into Chinese periodizations of their own political history, more facts about the reform roles played then by Zhou Enlai, Deng Xiaoping, and (to the extent he was everpresent) the senescent Mao Zedong.

The campaign to "criticize Confucius and Lin Biao" had, by late 1974, fizzled with almost as little result as its odd and incoherent title suggests. Ordinarily, earlier campaigns were supposed to bring major results; this one brought only some. Criticism meetings occurred under the rubric of the campaign's slogan, but they were not coordinated and they had diverse aims. This new kind of response to an official movement amounted to an important early reform. It was a precedent for many would-be campaigns after 1978 that met even more phlegmatic fates. People slowly realized that they did not have to react with great enthusiasm whenever a top politician ordered a campaign. A war might be called, but more of the soldiers might (if enough of them were apathetic) be absent without official leave.

On October 1, 1974, Deng Xiaoping made a speech downplaying the movement to "criticize Confucius and Lin Biao." A Central Committee document of October 11, 1974, quoted Mao Zedong "to the effect that the Cultural Revolution had already been going for eight years and that it was time for unity and stability in the Party and Army."[7] Actually, the national leadership was sharply disunited. The radical group sent Wang Hongwen to tell Mao on October 18 that Zhou and Deng were re-creating the kind of opposition Mao had faced at the Lushan Plenum of 1959. But in response, Mao "accepted Zhou Enlai's version of events by confirming his position as Premier [and] uttered critical remarks about Jiang Qing."[8]

On May 27 and June 3, 1975, Deng Xiaoping presided over a Politburo meeting to criticize the "mistakes" of the radicals. Deng's 1975 role at the top of the state was crucial, although this history has been obscured in later accounts. Jiang Qing, Zhang Chunqiao, Yao Wenyuan, and Wang Hongwen (later the "Gang of Four") all made self-criticisms in late June.[9] By early 1976, the Gang enjoyed a partial comeback against Deng, but his prowess against them in the early and mid-1970s has been officially deemed unimportant to publicize. It does not prominently enter the discourse even of many Western scholars who know about it. Presumably the CCP's reasons for downplaying the top leadership's disunity after 1971 were to maintain the pretense that China's leaders must always be sages thinking together. The Party had no incentive to advertise the extent to which actual events at that time sprang from local rather than high state networks. But in fact, the top chiefs were then divided among themselves. Their state agencies, weakened by Cultural Revolution attacks, were separated from many localities they pretended to control. Not just because the supremo Mao was senile, sick with amyotrophic lateral sclerosis (ALS, or Lou Gehrig's disease) and unable to guide any kind of consistent policy, but also because horizontal and vertical divisions sundered the Chinese political structure, the reforms had already begun.

Reforms did not end factionalism at high levels of Chinese politics—not in 1976, not in the early 1970s, and not later. The aftermath of the severe "cleansing class ranks" movement, mostly in the late 1960s, had included the "one strike, three antis" campaign that slowly wound down from 1970 to 1972. Shanghai radicals composed lists of previous high officials, purged in the Cultural Revolution, whose continued absence from power became the Revolutionary Committee members' main hope. The perceived need for such lists already showed a decline in radical power; the radicals were prescient enough not to assume that the politicians they had purged were out of action permanently. Efforts to regularize administration, by Zhou Enlai on some occasions and by less exalted bureaucrats more reliably, spurred the "Criticize Confucius and Lin Biao" radical campaign, which ended inconclusively. About a month after Mao's death, the Gang of Four was arrested in Beijing; but this news reached Shanghai slowly, through radio broadcasts from Taiwan. Senior Shanghai Revolutionary Committee bureaucrat Ma Tianshui and Garrison Commander Zhou Chunlin, and then worker leader Wang Xiuzhen and radical writer Xu Jingxian, were called to

Beijing after the arrests of radicals there in a palace coup. They returned to Shanghai and convinced their fellow radicals, whose first impulse had been that factory militias should resist the change of the state regime, to cooperate instead.[10]

For this service, most of Shanghai's top radicals were allowed to fade into political obscurity. A tradition of gradual retirement for the most important followers of those purged had earlier been followed in Shanghai for local leaders as diverse as non-Communist proletarian gang leaders in 1949 or followers of Rao Shushi in the mid-1950s. This tradition was again honored in 1976–78. It was politically ambiguous, and it was a cornerstone of reforms.

Academic periodizations of the reforms, and the Cultural Revolution, have been influenced by state policies against publicizing any real change from the early 1970s to 1976. Most factual sources that could be footnoted to the contrary are suppressed or are published for internal circulation only. Some appear in the local, popular, or evening presses that Chinese officials seem to think no self-respecting thinker would ever take seriously. This situation has influenced Western research, since those who publish lest they perish need footnotes and ordinarily use more established, statist sources. Censors and self-censors apparently think it most important to avoid any suggestion that the state fails to control everything. They might, instead, take pride in the extent to which local Chinese leaders undermined radical policies in the first half of the 1970s, thus in effect forwarding policies that were then being circumspectly advocated by recent "capitalist roaders" such as Deng Xiaoping.

With such disarray at the top of the political system, it was easier for lower-level officials to do what they wanted—so long as they hid their activities and avoided becoming "negative examples" for either the radical or reform factions. In Zhejiang, for example, "Throughout 1975, alongside articles exploring ways to restrict bourgeois rights and press on with the Maoist 'continuous revolution,' the Chinese media carried reports extolling production increases and industrial discipline and promoting economic policies designed to foster efficiency and profit. The propaganda publicizing the ideals of the four modernizations was of necessity dressed up in a Maoist garb, but nevertheless it was clear that two sets of voices were speaking in Beijing."[11]

Mao's thoughts about the "continuous revolution" were by that time already second thoughts. On May 3, 1975, Mao in a Politburo session criticized *both* the Gang of Four (which he had earlier chastised also in July 1974) and Deng Xiaoping. But Deng still pressed the Four Modernizations movement. This had to be presented as if it were a campaign, but obviously it was not going to be a short, usual, or wholly political movement. Deng was not stopped until early 1976, and then just temporarily. At that time, demonstrators in central Beijing clarified the strong mass popularity of "modern" accommodative political policies. This threatened high Party conservatives' illusions that they still controlled everything.

The main facts of top-level politics later that year were the death of Mao and the overthrow of the Gang of Four. These events of September and October 1976 have been so well recorded in English already that they need not take space here. The Third Plenum of the Central Committee in December 1978, the removal of Hua Guofeng's supporters in 1980, and Hua's demotions during the next two years were high-level continuations of these trends, in terms of the types of leaders, policies, and political structures they implied. But such stratospheric politics bear only a loose relationship to the main events for most people in a city like Shanghai. Top leaders wrote (and often still write) as if hierarchy ruled all; but a look at what they do, not just what they write, shows a more complex picture.

Dissension at the top of a political system usually increases the range of freedom for leaders of small collectivities. When one or another group of politicos wins temporarily in Beijing, the momentum growing over many years among millions of hinge leaders in their local political networks does not suddenly halt. The winning demagogues claim otherwise, of course, saying that everything important has completely changed. Right philosophy finally rules. The old order was bad, and the new one is said to have sprung from the wise and beneficent thoughts of the winning leaders. They claim all this to maximize the legitimacy of their power seizure at that level. But journalists, foreign officials, and scholars do not need to believe them. The extent to which this dynamic in high politics affects the information available for sourcing reports should be considered with care, because it threatens to make us describe politics in China (and elsewhere) inaccurately.[12] It distorts the picture by overemphasizing the effectiveness of policies, the coherence of leadership, and the causal efficacy of voluntarist and state factors. It discourages adequate treatment of the unintended effects of policies, the very frequent fuzziness of leaders' notions, and the importance of physical resource arrays.

Tentative and Unintended Reforms of Succession Politics

No constitutional reform had been evident in the succession of Hua Guofeng to Mao Zedong. Leadership changes at the very top are rare events in Leninist parties. In 1976, as in previous cases, these politics were unencumbered by legal procedures. Hua found support among the nearby armed police under Mao's ex-bodyguard, Wang Dongxing, and among a sufficient group of generals. The empress dowager Ci Xi with her military consort Rong Lu, along with their many predecessors in Chinese court intrigues, would have had no trouble understanding all important aspects of this late 1976 drama.

The succession of Deng to Hua, however, showed some signs that the memories of recent Cultural Revolution violence and growing social diversification had begun to affect even the top level of Chinese politics. Deng had important bureaucratic support, as well as support from groups that had previously been unimportant in short-term state decisions. Some leaders whose attitudes in the late 1970s were compatible with Deng's were promoted to high posts even before Hua's demise became evident. Toward the end of 1977, Hu Yaobang (an ex-"rightist" from 1957, and a veteran of the Long March in the 1930s though he had been young then) was chosen to head the CCP Organization Department and, under Mao's ex-bodyguard, to be effective head of the CCP General Office.

Militarists remained very important in this succession, but some of them expressed policy reasons for their opinions. There is evidence that as early as February 1977 Generals Xu Shiyou and Wei Guoqing supported Deng by declaring, "During his lifetime, Chairman Mao branded all comrades in the Party who dared to air opinions disagreeing with him as class enemies ... and this category includes the problems of Comrade Peng Dehuai and Comrade Deng Xiaoping."[13] Marshal Nie Rongzhen may also have supported Deng, perhaps because he thought Deng's politics were consistent with his interest in technological research.

Hua did not lose his position merely because he lacked sufficient patronage to retain it. There were also cogent critiques of his policies. His ten-year economic plan of 1977 stressed extractive and heavy industries; it resembled the Great Leap Forward, which had led to massive shortages. Hua's "flying leap" led to trade deficits that were not reduced even by oil exports, which were a main interest of one of his support groups, the so-called Petroleum Clique. These were rationalistic and modern arguments; they were made, and they may have had some effect on Hua's fate. Great emperors of the past, and Mao at his zenith of power, had occasionally been interested in public reasoning but had seldom been threatened by it. Hua was not so lucky.

The most striking novel aspect of the 1977–78 succession, however, was that Hua was not fully purged when his power declined. He remained nominally at the top of the Party for a while after his status had plummeted from its acme, which was Mao's old throne. Hua remained on the Central Committee even in the 1990s. He did not become the leader of an opposition party, of course; but he was alive, well, and living in Beijing for many years after his demotion from the top of China's political system. Under China's emperors, or Mao or Stalin, the fate of failed claimants to top power had been quite different.

The "Two-Track" System to Unify and Recruit Elites

The "two-track system" (shuanggui zhi) by 1979 described the concurrent use of reform and nonreform policies. These were the two tracks that Pareto discussed: recruiting new elites by restoring the legitimacy of many prestigious locals who had been excluded politically for more than two decades, but also retaining the vast majority of established CCP leaders—including some who were promoted during the Cultural Revolution. China's top leaders no longer wanted to have a recruitment policy that was narrow or inflexible, even if for the sake of legitimacy they always suggested that it was infallible. The first track recruited new political resources into the state leadership, while the latter upheld the pretense of integral unity in a regime undergoing fundamental change.

Karl Polanyi, E. E. Schattschneider, and many other theorists suggest that dual elites, in countries such as the United Kingdom or the United States, alternate in power. These writers, unlike Pareto, designate two kinds of substantive social policy that the two kinds of leadership serve. This specification applies in the case of reform China: Reformers serve aims of efficiency; and conservatives serve aims of support for regime loyalists whom the market weakens.[14] Since the networks that would benefit from these two kinds of aims never disappear—even though they may be temporarily disserved by the state—and since central politicians can seldom serve both goals at once, the alternation of elites does not cease.

Such interests are endemic in the modern era, whether or not they are articulated in avowedly different political structures. In China, because of the CCP, their separate articulation could seldom be proved at any given time, even though later disputes often brought out data about factional conflicts, about fast or slow elite recruitment policies, or about market or regulatory policies. China follows an old pattern among postrevolutionary regimes, where the creation of policy groups is much slower than the articulation of political parties. In Restoration England, for example, "Although parties came into existence, a two-party system did not."[15] The Whigs and Tories gradually became organized groups, but the institutional framework of Britain's political system remained fluid.

One reason for this pattern is that the top leaders in one-party systems usually benefit from keeping their policy options open as long as possible. This helps them keep their posts, because it lets them retain ties to different subordinates with alternative views. Proposals come to them for approval when policy makers of lower ranks cannot agree, but the top leaders usually maximize their own resources by delaying decision—and then after some gainful dithering, they may "lean to one side" sharply.[16] They can profit from the results of their arbitrations, and then sometimes from the solid constituency gained by making zesty or unexpectedly extreme choices. So the top leader in a monist system has a sharp disinterest in policy consistency. He (in the empress dowager's case, she) during many stages of policy making has an interest in expressing unclear preferences or in expressing one idea and then supporting its opposite. Mao Zedong showed this often (e.g., in 1956 and then 1957–58, or throughout the early 1970s). Deng Xiaoping, too, was alternately a lion or a fox, switching stances for Party stability or for market change.

Management shifts show this reform ambiguity well, and they show that it does not apply only to the top leader. Policy factions, united for one purpose, can sometimes reverse their ideas on how to attain it. Central government reformers provide many good examples. They have wanted each Chinese firm to prosper only insofar as it is efficient. So for years, reformers argued for more decentralization of managerial power to local levels. Factory heads, in this view, should make decisions on hiring and production; and local plants should retain more funds. But when "lower" hinge CCP cadres actually got control of locally retained funds, putting them to uses other than investment, the reformers' commitment to derogation of power became reversed—toward centralization—lest money be used inefficiently.[17] Foxes could sometimes become lions. This "cycle of reform," which has been evident in Eastern Europe as well as China, weakens the Party at both the central and the local levels in the long run. It strengthens other people who have local prestige, and its alternation is quintessential reform.

Experience with the unintended results of policy could also change lions into foxes; so the hard-line and reformist camps of politicians have by no means been hermetic. An important example occurred in the inflation of the early 1980s. These price rises, caused mainly by unplanned rural industries, were less steep than in later years (by the official reports, annually about 6 percent). But they deeply disturbed high PRC officials. The last major inflation, centered in Shanghai, was by all reports a major cause of Chiang Kai-shek's débâcle during the late 1940s. CCP leaders had apparently dreamed that unexpected price hikes could not occur in an economy that still defined itself as socialist. So they reacted very sharply, imposing credit restrictions especially in 1981. This measure, like many similar steps in later reform years, seemed to be centralizing. But in practice, its main result was that state managers could not obtain raw materials, since they were not supposed to pay higher-than-official prices.

The state's credit crunch placed more pressure on state bosses than on others, decreasing the ability of state managers to operate in the new price environment. This in turn gave the government's enterprise heads a real need for more autonomy from national ministries and municipal bureaus. Firm-level managers did not articulate a political demand for such autonomy (many had good reasons to avoid such responsibility), but knowledgeable cadres understood that more diverse, less uniform management was necessary to revive the state sector. So the original intention in Beijing, toward centralization to fight inflation, became the opposite of what happened. The command economy had to break step, going over this particular bridge of reform, because its commanders were among the first to realize they could no longer do their job in the old way.[18] The early 1980s' inflation changed central planners into decentralizing reformers by 1984. It made some lions into foxes.

Many high state leaders, saying they wanted quick reforms, appear from circumstantial evidence to have been honestly unsure how many changes were safe for their regime. To the extent that economic decentralization did not weaken state budgets immediately, they were supported because the consequent economic growth helped to legitimate the whole regime. But the climate of top elite uncertainty allowed much policy variation among leaders. Those who had suffered politically in earlier years tended to be more reformist. Ex-rightist Hu Yaobang's reformism was fairly consistent throughout the 1980s until his demise, and it infuriated Party hard-liners who had considerable power at the same time.[19]

Reformers sporadically proposed that "Party leading groups" in government offices should be abolished. Conservatives vehemently disagreed, since this change would have ended their policy roles. This conflict raged at high levels of the Chinese government, for example in late 1987. Zhao Ziyang was the newly appointed Party head, but there is no irony that this reformer was in favor of scrapping the CCP leading groups. The government head, Li Peng, stressed the Party's role and publicly took the opposite stance. As Zhao told a late 1987 CCP congress, "Party leading groups in government departments should be gradually abolished." The new Party constitution passed at the 1987 congress, in a classic display of reform ambiguity, made them optional. By March 1988, Li Peng said that whatever might happen to Party groups, the CCP committees in each firm should become "even more important. . . . Party work in state organs can only be strengthened and not be weakened in the slightest degree."[20] The politicians at the top simply wanted different things. No matter what they wanted, the Party in fact was losing prestige regardless of their debates.

High Chinese leaders admitted candidly by the late 1980s that reform and conservative policies divided them. In October 1988, CCP Organization Department director Song Ping said that "leading cadres" had "impaired the Party's authority and credibility and corroded the Party's organization." They were, in his view, "unqualified" to be members.[21] Song said that too many new Party members were joining just for the name. They wanted to be legitimated locally by their memberships, but they did not believe "the Party Center's ideology." This was hardly surprising, in view of CCP reformers' efforts to co-opt all dynamic managers into the Party, recruiting any new talent for the regime elite that could help run the economy.[22]

Changes among Chinese leaders at the top have been less sudden than journalistic accounts imply. The regime always obscures information about leadership tensions before they become public conflicts. The officials have a vested interest in advertising stability. Zhao Ziyang, for example, is sometimes described as having fallen from power in the spring of 1989, shortly before the crackdown at Tiananmen. This event could not be hidden, and Zhao then had to resign his post as Party head. But actually, he admitted more than half a year earlier, in the autumn of 1988, that his influence in the crucial area of economic policy had already ceased.[23] More than a decade before that, the shift of power from Hua Guofeng to Deng Xiaoping was similarly gradual and belatedly announced. Still earlier in the 1970s, Deng's emergence as Zhou Enlai's righthand man took place before it was publicly evident.

Losing leaders, before their demise is published, have a chance under this succession norm to retire quietly. At least one major police action at the top of the system (the arrest of the Gang of Four in October 1976) echoed older traditions in CCP and imperial Chinese politics.[24] After the purges of Cultural Revolution radicals, apparently for many years no very high Chinese political figures were killed or very harshly imprisoned, although this happened to many non-leaders. No one knows whether this conduct will last, but it suggests that China's lions and foxes see some roles for each other. As circumstantial events sometimes force them to switch their own policy positions, they may grow more tolerant of alternative positions.

A scholar has opined, "Neither repression nor reform is likely to solve the Party's difficulties."[25] This would be right about the Party, if reaction and reform could concretely exclude each other most of the time (as now they do not) and if the Party were fully disciplined with its members always in lock step (as now it is not). Pareto's view of politics tells more: A combination of repression by "lions" *together with* reform by "foxes" helps any elite solve its difficulties. If a leadership loses *either* its integrity *or* its flexibility, it will recede. The analytic difference between these two needs, in any elite, does not prevent the greater concrete need for their coexistence. The question is which of the two types of policy, at any particular time, recruits the most valuable intermediate hinge leaders to the service of the state, without swamping it. In a postrevolutionary decompression, neither policy works very well; so they very often alternate. But reformers and conservatives are always there, because the overall structure at some point uses them both. And they conflict in politics. This may on occasion strengthen their order, while slowly but fundamentally changing it.

Linkages to new leaders make state decisions more difficult; but if information flows improve in later years, it could also raise state resources. Alfred Stepan, writing about this issue in Perú, points out, "The phrase 'relative autonomy of the state' implies that the state elite is not *constrained.* . . . However, [government] autonomy may be a source of weakness because a state elite is not *sustained* by constituencies. . . . The other side of the coin of autonomy is thus isolation and fragility."[26] In China, the Communist government found by accident in the 1970s that quasi-private collective affluence created quick legitimacy for the state after the Cultural Revolution. The central state lost autonomy and thereby neutralized most groups that might have developed in open dissent. The price, in terms of resources, was high; but the top elite had no choice but to give this sequence its blessing. In the future, the slow thaw may allow a diversification of political networks that can emerge as stable. After these institutions that have local powers develop more permanent understandings with the state, the government's resources could in the future rise once again.

Divisions by Administrative Level:
The Community Consensus Rule

Both conservative and reform leaders exist at many sizes of collectivity, but this does not ensure that hinge leaders below the top will coalesce to form vertical networks for reform or reaction. Under some conditions, they do this. Under others, their behavior is more influenced by their local interests. One general condition already appears in many sections of this book. When symbols, rather than situations, are at stake, administrative hierarchy tends to prevail. When speaking as distinct from acting, hinge leaders practically always respond on normative issues to the constituency "above" them. But in practical matters, such as reporting taxable profits or actual numbers of workers hired, local leaders behave far more autonomously. This usual condition for the relative autonomy of hinge leaders is separate from the issues of whether they are reformers or reactionaries or are acting in the interests of large, medium, or small collectivities.

Another common condition determining whether hinge leaders act autonomously from state hierarchy has been summarized in a decision rule: "If the agents agree, let it be." If hinge leaders in a given place or meeting can settle a policy among themselves, then it is final. They implement it. Local agreement, on the whole, leads to automatic ratification by higher levels, when it is brought to the attention of formal superordinates at all. Only if agents differ must they either abandon the issue, taking no action, or refer it upward for decision.

When this rule applies, hierarchy is relevant only if some enfranchised agent exercises a veto. If that member cannot be convinced by local colleagues to go along with a consensus, then the decision becomes subject to uncertainties from above. Various authors have called this procedure "management by exception," "delegation by consensus," or "the veto rule."[27] This algorithm arises from the interests of administrative superiors in saving their own costs (especially when they have incomplete information or uncertain benefits) and from the interests of formal subordinates in maximizing their own net benefits. The rule is commonly used when local groups cohere tightly, and it often applies unless some local leader is dissatisfied and/or has greater incentives to blow the whistle on anti-central actions than to benefit from those actions.

This decision rule sounds "like China" (to paraphrase Geertz). The procedure it describes is a habit. The veto rule can be examined in terms of its typical results:

- The need for consensus is a guarantee of "sincerity" (the common Chinese compliment to any bargainer). Rule by consensus crucially respects each legitimated participant. This procedure extends both formal and substantive courtesy to all agents who have rights to be present for a settlement.
- Political status legitimation becomes all-important. If a leader who would veto a proposal can be excluded, the matter is perforce settled (to the benefit of the others). The ostracism of dissidents and the pretense of harmony for procedural reasons become customary, irrespective of any merits dissidents' policies may have. Harmony becomes the byword, regardless of any conflict among the real interests of legitimated leaders.
- This decision habit encourages each cadre to "horse-trade" among issue areas, abstaining rather than objecting on less significant issues so as to gain the acquiescence of colleagues on points of greater importance to the particular leader.
- Because unanimity is required, the sum of resources needed to adopt a policy is greater than with majority rule (requiring just over half) or one-person dictatorship (requiring less). All goods allocations under this rule tend to become politicized because if differences cannot be swept under rugs, the ensuing political battles are costly.

- The settled-unless-vetoed rule is inherently conservative. Since new decisions are expensive to achieve, many questions get postponed. The previous pattern, whatever it was, may continue. A really pressing substantive issue may "cycle" for years, deepening hostility between people. Delay can cause sudden violence, resolving questions by alternative procedures that are very different from consensus.
- The "let it be" norm also creates incentives to downplay conflicts within a network, even if major policy differences persist. Leaders often agree to disagree. Divergent measures easily emerge, for different places, times, or functions. Each network retains parochial authority, and the overall collective system is most calm when least uniform among its parts.
- From the viewpoint of high state politicians, the settled-unless-vetoed norm also has certain advantages. Making decisions by agents' consensus befits aged principals, who may no longer have the energy to intervene in specialized or local affairs very often. Gerontocracy would probably be infeasible without this decision habit.
- The ostensible prestige of high leaders soars. Potential vetoers in subordinate agencies must guess the likely success of demanding policy change, which depends wholly on higher politicos unless everyone around a local table acquiesces in any proposal. Offhand remarks by big chiefs in China are regularly taken as oracles on how they might decide, *if* an issue were to reach them. Extremely complex sets of policies are supposed to have been clarified, when a Deng takes a trip to Guangdong, or when a Mao divulges that "people's communes are good" or "it is right to rebel." Just a word from a sage is imagined to resolve all questions.
- Rule-by-consensus also helps the high state manage its scarce resources. It allows a pretense of unitary norms along with a fact of quasi-federalism. It lets local information undergird most decisions. But for all its rationality at the state level, this veto rule discourages complementary specialization between networks. It brings high costs of autarky.
- This decision culture is postrevolutionary because it decentralizes power. Reformist foxes in the central state could present their rival lions with local facts-on-the-ground that had really been put there by local leaders. High reformers apparently "played to the provinces."[28] But these foxes were much weaker than high conservatives. Throughout all three decades of reform, they sporadically seemed to have a power that was in fact mostly reflected. Central reformers' policy statements usually put them in tune with the interests of local leaders. No longer, however, was the central network penetrating local networks, as it had during the 1950s. Instead, local networks were by parallel, inarticulate, and secret decisions determining what happened in the central network. A consensus norm was the hinge leaders' trump: *omertà* in another setting, the political power of uncivil silence.

The consensus rule works much better for some issues, places, and political climates than for others. Consensus management is based in norms of low-conflict politics and low-level power brokerage. It is related to China's old traditional authority. It assumes that legitimated members of bureaucratic councils can easily agree on the basis of the leaders' backgrounds. In China under Mao, veteran revolutionaries were long assumed competent to judge all issue areas. As that generation dies and China diversifies, this habit is going out of style.

The consensus decision rule, like every other social phenomenon, has specific origins and limits. It seems not to have applied as widely in the 1950s or 1960s as later, partly because so many campaigns were launched by state leaders in those decades against it. It probably became more important during the postrevolutionary rise of local powers in the reform era. It certainly correlated with the slow victory of contracted management (including fiscal contracts) over any standard policy (e.g., uniform taxes or price reform).[29] Rational choice analyses often present decision rules as summarizing primary causes, rather than treating them as parts of larger correlations which have historical roots. But that academic habit need not lessen the usefulness of the collective choice approach, whose premises are no more than bland abstract possibilities until life is found for them in real cases.

Chinese leaders tend to stick together in face-to-face meetings, even when their interests are in tension, longer than their counterparts elsewhere would. That is the norm that makes the decision rule often apply. This habit also makes China look, to a national leader like Sun Yat-sen, like a "sheet of sand" that cannot hold together, even though each of its particles is hard. The revolutionaries wanted to consolidate all those grains into concrete. They began to do so, in the first years of the People's Republic, until the Cultural Revolution and more specialization eroded their work. The result, by the time of the late reforms, was a structure that mobilized a greater number of the sizes of collectivity in China: not just the center, regions or provinces, or counties and towns, but all of them separately.

Divisions by Space: Mid-level Rule from Cities

The integration of localities in China, such as reforms bring, does not mean their centralization under single rule. Integration coordinates the actions of individuals and sectors, making them complementary because of external incentives. Centralization would mobilize them by normative mandates. All wealthy countries have markets that are highly integrated but generally decentralized. The Chinese norm favoring consensus at *any* size of group is consistent with integration, but it impedes the information flows needed for state centralization. In China, where planning has decentralized so that separate managers must take actions that are often constrained by impersonal market forces, some integration has accompanied decentralization. But an analysis of centralization must face the question: At what relative sizes of collectivity, more differentiated than just local and national, is centralization or decentralization actually taking place? This question is essentially spatial. It allows the possibility (and in reform China, the actuality) that power can gravitate to the leaders of medium-sized groups, more than to either separate citizens or national leaders.

Different places in China interact heavily or less heavily with the state. No consensual procedures establish uniform links between the center and localities. When localities operate without reference to the central regime—neither openly opposing nor concretely supporting it—explicit bargains between sizes of jurisdiction are hindered. On a small scale within each jurisdiction, the distinction between state-owned and collective firms reflects this same kind of difference. Cities almost always contain more units that are supported and taxed by higher administrative levels than rural areas do. Otherwise comparable towns can nonetheless differ in this respect; for example in Guangdong, Jiangmen city has more state-affiliated institutions than nearby Xinhui, which has many independent agencies.[30] Larger cities such as Tianjin and Shanghai, and all the provincial capitals as a group, have been better connected with the central bureaucracy than other places. Whole provinces, such as Heilongjiang, enjoy particularly close links to specific bureaucracies (in that case, the defense and oil ministries). The "one country, two systems" notion that has been used for Hong Kong is a further extension of the norm that different places might relate differently to the Chinese central state.

Reformist Rule from City and District Offices

A 1984 national policy specified "three controls and three relaxations." This envisaged more control of large cities, of large and medium-sized state enterprises, and of places that are primary producers of any product. It foresaw relaxation of rules over medium-sized and small cities, over collective and private enterprises, and over merely secondary places where any product is made. But a statist critic said these measures caused "three difficulties," all involving price decontrols that lowered Shanghai revenues.[31] The government, by announcing this policy, in effect admitted it had to conserve its own resources by monitoring only some fields. That is the usual administrative reason for decentralization to a middle level.[32]

The emphasis on rule from cities was nothing new. Chinese under the emperors had often referred to rural areas by the name of the nearest large town. To this day, the name of most counties is identical to that of the county seat. The idea of tying each rural place comprehensively to a city was old; but its meaning became new after local power networks were collectively stronger than the state's. This was a matter of the central administration trying to license midlevel control, to cut losses as these jurisdictions were in a position to remit less to the high state.

The central government has often supposed that tinkering with administrative structures might solve major problems. By 1978, the national constitution was changed, making it more like the 1954 PRC constitution than the intervening 1975 edition. This early document had acknowledged and raised the relative powers of midlevel administrations. The rights of provinces, such as Shanghai, over rural counties and urban districts had been defined more clearly in 1954; and in 1958, three counties of Jiangsu were transferred to the Shanghai municipal administration.[33] The idea that cities should run counties (*shi guan xian*) was carried further in 1960, when 52 municipalities throughout the country were given charge of 243 counties (although within a year, many of these decisions were reversed). By 1966, only 25 counties nationwide were managed by cities. In the 1970s, the number began to expand again; and by 1985, fully one-third of all China's counties (666 of them) had been put under urban administrations. The same movement encouraged sizable villages (*xiang*) to upgrade their status to townships (*zhen*). They could extend the same principle, lower in the administrative hierarchy, by taking charge of smaller hamlets (*zhen guan cun*).

Each county in 1985 became subject to the largest city in its region. Rural administration was centralized around central market towns. Before this time, there had been four main levels of government: central, provincial, prefectural (*diqu*), and county. But the third, the prefectural offices that had been subject to bureaucrats in provincial capitals, rather than local cities, was eliminated in 1985. The overall change was expected to lessen restrictions on local trade, but by the same token, it could disadvantage rural factories. Now urban centers could try to monopolize their wares in their own hinterlands, and to keep out their competitors from other cities, even when more local town and county officials wished to stop them.[34] The extent to which they would actually be able to control these markets was less clear than that high government officials (and the laws, such as they are in rural areas) supported free trade. Top state leaders did not know how to harmonize the two conflicting goals of urban entrepreneurialism and rural free trade; so in practice, different kinds of local jurisdictions fought political battles to see what would happen.

Tensions between politicians in larger and smaller centers, and the hope in each leadership to produce more profitable products, led to conflicts especially because local nonmarket administrations remained important. The power of parochial authorities to contravene the interests even of national ministries became astounding during late reforms. Leaders at the county level sometimes openly resisted arrangements made by very high officials, and the locals in such cases were often more authoritarian than the state bureaucrats.[35] It is impossible to generalize, for any administrative level, about the degree of influence from above, because of great differences by place and by the personalities of the hinge leaders, more of whom assumed power than advertised it.

Zhao Ziyang was the politician most identified with the effort to put cities in charge of counties. Zhao expected that "in the future we won't . . . be able to rely on the old system of 'lines' and 'pieces' (*tiaotiao kuaikuai*), but instead should rely on central cities (*zhongxin chengshi*) and industrial bases." He hoped this new principle of large-scale management, using industrial cities to override both functional hierarchies and local-area cadres, would create "rational economic regions and networks."[36] The real trouble with the old lines was that they no longer caught revenue fish. And the problem with the old pieces was that borders between them were being washed away by new markets. Trying to strengthen administration in a manageable number of regional cities was a sensible approach. But the central government had not begun the decentralization, even though statists interpreted Zhao as if it had initiated this change.

China's prereform political system had been strung together precisely by balancing tensions between the functional "line" hierarchies and local "piece" leaderships—between subministerial bureaucrats and local Party cadres. So Zhao's idea of subordinating both to industrial managers in nearby cities was an innovation. Technocrats in market centers were to have the last word. All of rural China was to become a suburb. If this idea were carried to its logical conclusion, smaller cities would become hinterlands of larger ones.

Parallel changes occurred within urban areas, "sending down" more power to districts. These alterations were less consequential than in the countryside because urban communications are better and city governments leaders used them. The twelve districts (*qu*) in Shanghai municipality received greater authority during the mid-1980s. In 1984, this process involved an expansion of district-level functions in construction and finance, so that approvals of renovation projects could be speeded. By 1985, they could keep more of the revenue they raised, especially from district-managed firms. Their activity in other areas such as culture, public health, education, sports, and construction therefore expanded. In 1986, districts were especially ordered to help raise the rate of residential building in their areas, and they did more on enforcing birth control, encouraging enterprises to run nurseries, and boosting secondary education.[37] The relaxation of municipal control over districts was a "releasing of power" (*fang quan*), one of China's many new norms that had been led by practice.[38]

Unitary Ideals, Federal Situation

China is not legally a federation. Its constitution contains no lists of central, local, and concurrent powers, because all state authority is nominally central. A current issue is whether sovereignty, in the sense of real and effective influence, should be recognized as unitary or divided. Another issue is whether the present untidy arrays of power should be made constitutional—and that is a matter that an ardently behavioral scientist might too easily conceive as minor. Future constitutions might, conceivably, define the leeways of localities so as to put official ideals in line with actual patterns.

At present, negotiation occurs regularly between Chinese jurisdictions, local and central, without the support of any federal laws or publicly legitimated norms. There has been much good study of the ways that sovereignty is divided in other countries.[39] But China is unlikely soon to become normatively federal, despite PRC "one country, two systems" avowals to Hong Kong and Taiwan. What midlevel and high leaders actually do, therefore, remains in tension with the unrealistic ways in which they speak about the links among their jurisdictions.

It may be difficult for a Leninist party, whose officers are generally appointed from the top down, to promote institutions that decentralize power. When mobilization campaigns are used to get out the vote for an essentially one-party election, for example, the medium can become the message. Participation is far from autonomous; and democracy is not yet the result.[40] But would-be democrats in non-Leninist countries share the same problem. States run by Leninist parties have democratized, for example on Taiwan. The literature debunking any possibility that hierarchical elites with ex-utopian ideologies can sponsor liberalization makes many interesting logical points, but it also neglects the role of contexts and the vast extent of what states cannot accomplish. Admittedly, it is impossible for democracies, as also for Leninist states, to arise without elite support. But clientelist structures can become the bases for new political parties. Reasoning from ideological norms, even if they do shape some practice, is not sufficient to determine what will happen.

The unfettering of local powers from central control allows them to compete on free markets, and it also allows them to repress still smaller collectivities. Central reformers sponsor free trade, but local authorities can often prevent or tax it. County and township officials during reforms have sometimes imposed illegal fees on trucks running through their jurisdictions. Their noncentral power hinders the comparative advantage of large markets. But the same localities also set up new factories and new trading firms. They became Schumpeterian entrepreneurs, both in cases where that leads to more overall efficiency and in cases that lead to inefficiency. So the reform role of local officials, doing all these mixed things, is very ambiguous. In the long run, efficient markets bring prosperity and tend to prevail as resources and information proliferate. Before then, the search for advantage by local leaders is intense, and it leads to a wide variety of different results.

The dependence or independence of leaders is not a dichotomous variable because autonomy comes in many degrees.[41] But for the sake of analysis, two attitudes toward coordination may be distinguished. Vivienne Shue explores this autonomy/dependence difference where it counts most, at the intermediate level. Shue contrasts "the coordinative local state" in Shulu, Hebei, with "the competitive local state" in Guanhan, Sichuan. Neither of these places is closely monitored by the central state. Their internal politics are nonetheless very different. The Hebei county, a non-"keypoint" place in a conservative part of China, has regulatory cadres who are good socialists; at least when they were studied, they had not started their own enterprises. In the Sichuan county, cadres more quickly became venture capitalists; they were not content merely to sit back, reign, and tax economic activity. Instead, they were aggressive in making money for their offices, and for themselves, on newly opened markets.[42] In both cases, these different "local states" were strengthened. They both followed the reformist policies of decentralization. Whether these officials, in either of the two counties, were more statist or more local is a question that might be argued. But as the term "local state" suggests, China has more than one governmental network.

Leadership Localization, Despite Central Pressures

Before the reforms, many high leaders in Shanghai had helped Communist General Chen Yi's Third Field Army liberate the city. But at the municipal level, and to a greater extent in nearby areas outside Shanghai, new reform leaders often tended to be locals. Comparing the incumbents of the top Shanghai CCP and city posts, as defined by bureaucratic rank in the two periods 1976–82 and 1983–93, the proportion of local people rose.[43] Localization of the top municipal leadership posts was quick in Shanghai, as elsewhere, in the early 1980s. Counting as native to Shanghai all who were born there or in the two adjacent provinces, or who have spent large parts of their lives there, the proportion of natives among the top November 1977 municipal Party secretaries was 13 percent (just one secretary). But by 1983, the comparable proportion was 20 percent; and by 1991, it was 83 percent. The change toward native leaders among top Shanghai government officials, as distinct from CCP secretaries, was sharper.

In other parts of the delta, and nationally, the same change was occurring. Zhejiang gazetteers show that by the early 1980s county cadres were generally local-born, whereas in earlier years appointees at this level were to a surprising extent originally from Shandong province, far to the north. Shandong soldiers came to Zhejiang in great numbers with Chen Yi's Third Field Army in 1949, and they remained at their posts for three decades.[44] A major reform there was their retirement, and the appointment of local Zhejiang people to replace them.

By the late 1980s throughout China, half of all the top provincial leaders (governors, deputy governors, provincial Party secretaries, and their immediate deputies) were stationed in their native provinces. Among mayors, this figure was 58 percent.[45] After 1989, the central government tried to take steps against this pattern. Beijing during reforms was not firm enough to decree a "rule of avoidance" such as kept mandarins out of their own provinces under strong emperors of the past. But the state in 1989 transferred many cadres between local posts, explicitly attempting to smash local networks that sabotaged the implementation of central policies. Some localities refused to release their old cadres or to accept the new ones. This assertion of local power was not entirely new in China, but it increased during reforms.[46]

Divisions by Faith in Particular State Leaders

Much evidence above shows that China's reforms were not caused by just a few "great men." Carlisle's historiography could not explain what happened. But most Chinese people spoke as if it could, and not all PRC leaders were alike in popular opinion. In Shanghai and elsewhere, most citizens gave high leaders credit for directing everything, even if they guessed otherwise. They commonly reported popular preferences for some CCP politicians, as compared to others who had similar government posts.

This pattern is an old one; but even during the mid-1970s powerful politicians could sometimes be defied in public. When Gang of Four member Wang Hongwen told spinners at a Hangzhou silk mill, in August 1975, to make no demands for higher wages, someone in the audience rose to challenge him personally:

> Comrade [CCP] Vice-Chairman, aren't you presently on grade 2 [very high] of the central wage scale? Think back to what grade you were on at the No. 7 textile mill in Shanghai. Was it the 17th or 18th? You . . . rose to become party secretary of the municipality. In the last two years you've done even better and gone up to grade 2 at the center! But you ask us not to raise the question of wages and promotion in grades. What kind of work style is this?[47]

The next year, 1976, brought rich evidence of varying local evaluations of different state leaders. The Qingming Festival is a time each spring when Chinese pay respects at their ancestors' graves. Public demand for basic policy change was especially severe by April 1976 in the Shanghai delta, and it emerged on this holiday in the form of unauthorized demonstrations to commemorate the recently deceased Zhou Enlai. The 1976 Beijing demonstration at Tiananmen Square has been best reported; but on the Shanghai delta at Changzhou, Hangzhou, Jiaxing, Nanjing, Ningbo, Shaoxing, Taizhou, Wuxi, Yangzhou, Zhoushan, and other cities there were also memorial rallies. Shanghai itself was under thorough radical control at the municipal level in early 1976, but two workers unfurled a banner with Zhou Enlai's picture on Culture Square, before they were arrested. Zhou was honored by many graffiti of mourning on Shanghai walls at this time.[48]

Shanghai's highest administrators have always had later or earlier careers in the central government. Mayor Chen Yi in the 1950s had a base in his Third Field Army, not just in Shanghai; and he joined the top ranks of the State Council as foreign minister and one of its strongest members after he left the city. Mayor Ke Qingshi, Zhang Chunqiao, Yao Wenyuan, and Wang Hongwen all moved between Shanghai and radical politics on a national scale. Jiang Zemin and Zhu Rongji had similar career moves from Shanghai to very high positions in Beijing. None of these politicians was unknown in the capital before moving there, but it is easy to imagine that Shanghai's fiscal contribution to many other ministries and parts of China has played some role in the abilities of so many top Shanghai politicians to assume high-flying jobs in the capital later.

Because of this career pattern among top municipal leaders, local people were heard to complain that successive mayors and secretaries identified with the capital more than with the metropolis. They reportedly "spoke Beijing dialect, not Shanghainese" (though all of them actually could speak both languages). The city's fiscal role meant its political leaders were seldom perceived, in early reforms, as being pro-entrepreneur. Shanghai thus differed sharply from Guangdong, for example, in the early 1980s. Zhao Ziyang had served as Party secretary of that southern province before the Cultural Revolution, and he later became premier of China. The first Party secretary in Guangdong, Ren Zhongyi, was reportedly willing to stand up to important central politicians such as Chen Yun and Peng Zhen, to argue for more investment in Guangdong, which they opposed.[49] Also, Guangdong could rely on intervention with top-level Beijing officials by rich Hong Kong capitalists, when approvals for large new projects were needed.[50] Shanghai lacked this much strong backing, at least in the early 1980s, because its most prominent spokespeople were more clearly centrists. This slowed, but did not halt, Shanghai's growth and structural change in the era of reforms.

Examination of high Shanghai Party posts in 1980 gives a preliminary idea of the extent of this central careerism. Of the Shanghai officials high enough to be chosen for the CCP Central Committee in that year, just one (the youngest, Wang Mingzhang) was born in Jiangnan. Both Mayor Peng Chong and First Secretary Chen Guodong hailed from elsewhere in East China, having had army experience before going into civilian work.[51] Many other top Shanghai leaders in the early 1980s were from non-Jiangnan parts of East China or had pre-1949 experience in General Chen's Third Field Army.[52]

Political leaders acquired popular or unpopular reputations easily. Zhao Ziyang committed himself to policies allowing faster growth in coastal areas, whereas Li Peng, his successor as premier in 1987, committed himself to massive inland investment plans for the Three Gorges Hydroelectric Project in relatively poor areas of Sichuan and Hubei. It is unclear whether this difference between the reformist Party chair and the conventionalist premier related to Li's ties with the traditionally conservative leadership of Hubei.[53] Coastal critics raised severe questions about the economic and environmental wisdom of this huge, very expensive scheme to dam the Yangzi—which was clearly going to take great sums of Guangdong and Shanghai money. But bureaucratic backing for the project was strong in Beijing, and it appeared to include politicians in heavy industrial ministries and the army. Premier Li was educated as a hydraulic engineer in Stalin's Russia, and this huge dam was seen as his pet project.[54] A journalist has summarized the conflict:

> Analysts noted that the Three Gorges project, like the Economic Coastal Development scheme, the pet subject of Party chief Zhao Ziyang, could turn out

to be a major political issue. They use engineering statistics to camouflage a fight for control of the economy. The conservatives are in favour of slower consumer growth and stronger central economic control, placing emphasis on basic necessities such as laying a firm foundation for the nation's industry and energy resources. The reformists still believe that developing the coastal regions, thus bringing in faster economic returns, would help the interior and the whole country in a much shorter period.[55]

The 1985 appointment of Rui Xingwen to be the city's top CCP secretary showed—as did Mayor Jiang Zemin's promotion—a continuing central insistence that top officials in Shanghai should have strong ties to Beijing. Many more local Shanghai leaders, including high CCP cadres and members of the Municipal People's Congress whom this author interviewed in the 1980s, complained openly that such officials should not just be "sent down" from the capital, but should do more to represent Shanghai. Rui Xingwen, in his late fifties like Jiang, also had served in ministerial posts at Beijing, heading the Ministry of Urban and Rural Construction and Environmental Protection.[56] Although no important elections were held in Shanghai, a good deal of anecdotal evidence about these officials suggests that many people—and probably they themselves—knew their popularity had limits.

Jiang Zemin came to the mayoralty with a double disadvantage. Originally from Yangzhou, he identified as being from Subei and was subject to prejudice from Shanghai's Jiangnan majority. He also came to the mayor's office directly after serving in Beijing from 1983 to 1985 as minister of electronic industries, when Shanghai received scant central investment in computer technology—arguably the industry it most needed at that time. Jiaotong University received a visit from Mayor Jiang on December 18, 1986, during the national height of student demonstrations for democracy in Hefei, Beijing, and elsewhere. The Jiaotong students had put up posters, but university administrators ordered these removed. Taking posters from walls became a contentious issue. At a heated meeting in which Jiang insisted on the removals, one student asked him whether the citizens of Shanghai had "elected" him mayor. Rather than giving a substantive reply, Jiang asked for the student's name and department. Others leapt to their classmate's defense, denouncing the intimidation.[57]

After Jiang moved from the mayoralty into Party work, he again made himself the conspicuous focus of resentment against his firing of the *World Economic Herald* editor.[58] When Jiang was promoted to head the CCP, interviewees in Shanghai told journalists that "his handling of pro-democracy turmoil since mid-April showed his uncompromising style." Students were pleased he had said he did not want troops to occupy the city, but Jiang was said to be better known for adaptability than for principles.[59] Some in Shanghai say he was not liked.

Jiang's successor as mayor, Zhu Rongji, had worked largely in national economic planning. Zhu was originally from Hunan. His ascent to the mayoralty, in mid-1988, soon became widely popular; many prominent local leaders praised him sufficiently far beyond the standard requirements as to cast further doubts on his predecessor. As the head of a large Shanghai company said, "Zhu Rongji is the kind of leader that Shanghai needs desperately. . . . He talks big and takes quick action. I am confident that under his leadership the cumbersome government bureaucracy will see a much needed overhaul."[60]

Mayor Zhu Rongji took a startlingly low-profile position on the events at Tiananmen (which was not, after all, his current jurisdiction). He made a statement supporting martial law but then said practically nothing else in public. The *World Economic Herald* case involved Shanghai because this fully national newspaper for reformers was published there. But formally that newspaper was at first "suspended," not closed. Its readers and contributors were actually global, involving intellectuals but very few others in Shanghai.

The mayor himself met with a group of students who wanted to march in mourning for those who had died in Beijing. He gave them permission to do this, in exchange for a promise that it would be their last march. Not many participated because of fear for their careers. But on June 9, a small group of brave students, wearing black armbands, marched unobstructed along their usual route to People's Square, carrying flowers to lay there in memory of the dead.[61]

Workers had not made such promises. On that same day, several from one of the autonomous labor unions protested by laying down on railway tracks in the suburbs. An oncoming train from Beijing did not brake early enough to stop, and they were crushed to death. In the Shanghai station, enraged workers stormed railroad cars and set some ablaze. They were soon arrested. The next day, a small group of Fudan University students marched to the jail in support of the workers, who were executed. Zhu Rongji's previous record of finding ways to prevent open violence in Shanghai during the Tiananmen battles was of course broken at this time. But in view of the situation, he is credited by Shanghainese of several different viewpoints as having done creditably well.

China lacks meaningful elections to high posts, but this does not completely prevent expressions of opinion, especially by youths. When students marched in front of reform leaders in relatively happy times, such as the 1984 National Day anniversary celebrations, some carried cheerful signs inquiring "Deng Xiaoping, how are you (*ni hao*)!" But the impermanence of this esteem was clarified in 1989 Tiananmen signs, some of which read "Deng Xiaoping, how confused you are (*ni hao hu li*)!"[62] There is a great deal of evidence that many Chinese often see the top of their state as split among more than one high leader. They rate these politicos individually. They follow their favorites, not just if they have some imagined factional connection. And they change their views in accordance with what they see the leaders doing. Such "votes" are of course never counted; and they are meant as moments of local gossip, not of risky influence. But in modern parts of China, including the Shanghai delta, the opinions are clearly there.

Chapter 4.1

Leadership Selection

Power tends to corrupt, and absolute power corrupts absolutely.
Great men are almost always bad men, even when they exercise
influence and not authority. There is no worse heresy than that the
office sanctifies the holder of it.

—J.E.E. Dalberg (Lord Acton)[63]

The selection of leaders—national, intermediary, and local—is perhaps the most obvious political function. Change in the ways cadres were chosen, during subperiods of China's reforms, reflects the disparate views of the state's top elite in these transitional decades. It also reflects the increasing pool of educated talent that state reformers could try to recruit for service. The signals that the government sent to new and potential young cadres were mixed throughout the reforms, both because of pendular swings in national politics and because the availability of qualified candidates emerging from China's educational system was uneven over time. The main message, however, was that some people who had university training could be promoted rapidly. The most important governmental reform in China was the massive 1980s recruitment of young and educated people into high posts.

Cadre Appointments

Data to be offered below trace several aspects of cadre selection reform back to the early 1970s, but the greatest changes in personnel policy came at the end of that decade, and especially in 1983–86. Already by 1978, Deng Xiaoping and others at high levels in Beijing suggested that new graduates could help both themselves and their country by devoting themselves to the bureaucratic regime. In 1980, this "democracy movement" got out of hand, in the view of conservative

CCP leaders, partly because outspoken students at universities stood as candidates for election to local people's congresses and raised new questions about old leaders in public. So by 1981, together with a concurrent campaign against "bourgeois liberal" film director Bai Hua, fewer university graduates went into government offices, though about half of them had done so in earlier years. By 1982, however, when the highly talented classes from the 1977 and mid-1978 university entrance exams came to the job market, reformist leaders could easily make cases for hiring many of them in responsible posts. This occurred, and it began a process of massive change in China's bureaucracy.

The "third echelon" (*disan tidui*) of cadres was officially supposed to replace two kinds of predecessors. The "first echelon" comprised old revolutionaries from the 1920s and 1930s, for example, Deng Xiaoping and others in his age cohort who were supposed to become semiretired. The "second echelon" included leaders such as Zhao Ziyang and was a generation that had largely entered the Party during the civil war—and in the 1980s rose to China's top formal posts. Together, these two groups had governed China since midcentury. The most cogent instruction for choosing the new third echelon leaders was reduced to a slogan: that the country's elite should be made younger (*qingnian hua*), more intellectual (*zhishi hua*), more specialized (*zhuanye hua*), and somehow more revolutionized (*geming hua*). This slogan adequately describes, except for its fourth item, what in fact happened in cadre recruitment. It is also a convenient framework for an analysis of that process.

By 1983, systems were fully established to select the "third echelon," who were sent into specialized training programs even though more than half of them already had university educations. Middle-aged and young people, if ambitious, naturally wanted to obtain such favored status, which was nonetheless reserved for a select few.

Many who failed to achieve this proto-elite status became "students at five kinds of universities" (*wu da xuesheng*), and they went into spare-time, vocational, and TV curricula that gave degrees—but ones that received little honor. At this time, in offices connected with factories, many young cadres, not selected to be part of the third echelon there, were demoted to workshops.[64] The trend toward better-educated, more expert, and younger cadres was officially supported throughout the Chinese system, even down to the village level. What happened in practice was complex, as urban migration drained many talents from rural China. But one survey showed a sharp rise in the educational qualifications of brigade-level cadres from 1978 at least to 1984.[65] These changes will be illustrated below at the national level, in Shanghai's provincial offices, and also at more local levels.[66]

A Chinese "Chain of Being"

The politics of this massive succession were complex and halting. But the administrative mechanism that high-level reformers used to achieve such a quick change in middle-level leadership was ex-Soviet: the *nomenklatura* (*zhiwu mingcheng biao,* as this Russian and now English word is rendered in Chinese). This is a list of posts, including state offices, professorships, and the jobs of priests, factory managers, judges, "mass organization" cadres, candidates to be elected to legislatures or Party committees, CCP secretaries, and every other conceivable kind of notable.[67] China's top administrative levels are the premiership (*zongli ji*), vice premierships (*fu zongli ji*), ministries (*bu ji*), bureaus (*ju ji*), departments (*chu ji*), and sections (*ke ji*). State propaganda encouraged Chinese to think that the natural order of the cosmos was hierarchical; it took the same form as the arrangement of tablets at a lineage temple. China's government is not unique for having sown this fancy. The cosmic "chain of being" has been beautifully documented for early modern England, for example.[68] Such norms do not determine all behavior in China, but they are imagined widely. Chinese people converse in these terms, even when they do not act this way.

The system applies to *all* jobs that are visible in public. The official ranking system posits vertical relationships nationwide among all leaders, including major local cadres. It sometimes may discourage them from approaching their work on a more functional basis. Posts are commonly conceived to be more important than the work done in them—and the ordering of posts is a subject of constant comment. County-level leaders, for example, are all graded higher than professors. The *People's Daily* in 1988 reported that "Even a Buddhist monk, who according to Buddhist doctrine should take no interest in worldly affairs, has a level; otherwise, he would miss many favored treatments granted according to the system of ranks."

This was marginally an imported neotradition, but it echoed formally many old and specifically Chinese traditions. In the pervasive Han religion, a spiritual bureaucracy of gods parallels the human bureaucracy of mandarins, although members of neither are seen to be uniformly reliable.[69] In the PRC, all local leaders have been formally ranked, as if they were always loyal agents of the state that does the ranking. Everyone knows this habit of discourse does not automatically make them comply with laws. The system meant decreasingly little, even though it was still much discussed, as gaps between localities' wealth widened quickly. Ranking as a rule was in sharp tension with the equality of a seller and a buyer on a market.

By mid-1988, a *People's Daily* article could condemn the official classifications as feudal. The writer opined that during the wars of the 1930s and 1940s, "the Party had to commandeer all available facilities"; so a system of centralized hierarchal ranks reportedly made sense then. But "when the government started to promote a market economy, problems with regard to the grade system arose." People with high ranks have the impression they may meddle in matters about which they have no local or technical knowledge. "Administrative interference sacrifices efficiency. A project has to wait for years, before it is approved by superior departments. Profitable opportunities are thus missed."[70] In reformist 1988, even the Party's main newspaper could moot an end to ranks.

There is a standard method of leadership selection. It has been reformed variously for different posts at different times, but in the mid-1990s it still applied to all high positions. The Organization Department of the CCP committee at each administrative level has a *nomenklatura* roster of posts for which it is responsible. When an incumbency needs to be filled, it proposes an appointee. This had, before reforms, to be approved by the Organization Department at the next higher level; then the person took the post.

The "two rank down" appointment system, normal during Mao's time, meant that no *nomenklatura* cadre could be subject to a single boss. This system was clearly Leninist but not surely patronist. It did not define one clear patron for each appointee; in principle, at least two bosses were involved in each major appointment decision. This system was reformed in August 1984, to follow a simpler "one rank down" rule. At a stroke, all high levels had their spans of control reduced to just one lower level. The autonomy of each lower rank was expanded, since it needed to clear appointments only at the next higher rank.[71]

To control salary budgets, each manager in a state unit is also generally given a roster of the number and titles of nonleadership posts to be filled (the *bianzhi*). Both the *nomenklatura* of leadership posts and roster of ordinary jobs have become less important in reform China than they were previously. But constraints on the *nomenklatura* system came less from changes in its formal procedures than from an increase of diversity among the ideas of the people who ran it. There has been an increasing portion of *pro forma* approvals in the CCP organization departments at the higher level, and an increasing diversity in what appointed leaders are expected to know and do.

Toward Younger Leaders

The first of the main new criteria for cadre selection is the easiest to measure and is closely correlated with the others. This aspect of reforms did not really begin until the late 1970s; but the several years after October 1976 showed only somewhat less turnover in leadership than did later reforms. Old prestigious revolutionaries in many kinds of PRC institutions were often slow to retire. When they did, technocrats were appointed to replace them. Six-tenths of the top Shanghai government and CCP leaders, still holding posts in 1980, were formally retired by March 1983. Their replacements were much younger. It would be difficult to argue from data about the ages of high Shanghai municipal personnel that 1976 or 1978 was a more important watershed than, in particular, the year 1983.[72]

A Party-vs.-government comparison can be made of the approximately thirty-five top Shanghai CCP and city appointees, a set defined by their holding high bureaucratic rank in the two periods 1976–82 and 1983–93. The data show that, for top government leaders, their tenure in office increased from thirty-seven to fifty-two months on average between these two periods. For Party leaders, there was not yet a change: forty-two months for appointees in both periods (although many were still at their posts in 1993 when the survey was finished). The new group in the government had been specialized in office for longer.

The CCP and government leaders included many Shanghai people and many who had training in technical subjects, forming a relatively stable leadership for the city from the early 1980s for at least a decade thereafter. Their educational credentials were strong, as in general was the political support for them from both administratively higher (Beijing) and administratively lower (Jiangnan) constituencies. In other words, the increasingly successful early 1980s' campaigns to appoint young cadres also developed types of leaders defined not just by youth, but also by education, specialization, and apparently also geographic origin, that lasted in those positions for a long time.

When youth, intellectual qualifications, and professionalization became subject to administrative rules, they could be quantified. But these criteria were not easily accepted by everyone—especially the old, the self-schooled, and the generalists, some of whom still had very high political status. So the process became controversial. In Shanghai, a writer for the relatively liberal *Wenhui News* objected against rigidity in "drawing lines," especially to exclude old and experienced appointees from open posts.[73] The political effects of emphasizing "youth" as a qualification of new cadres were often different from those of emphasizing years in education or in professions. The specific problem with many "youths" was their previous violence in the Cultural Revolution.

Section-level cadres, for example, had been specified under interpretations of the new cadre-appointment rules as ideally not much older than thirty years of age. But practically all such people had been Red Guards after 1966. Some writers pointed out that they would not necessarily be better for the reforms than would more experienced cadres, for example, those aged over fifty.[74] Injunctions to recruit "young" cadres apparently did not discriminate against the appointments of ex-radicals in the early 1980s, and it is also not clear that the injunctions to recruit "intellectual" and "professional" cadres would have done so either.

This 1980 view, that the Cultural Revolution still tainted many potential cadres in their early-middle careers, came under fire from critics. A later edition of the *Wenhui News* carried letters from cadres at the Shanghai Chemical Fuels Factory and the Shanghai Oil and Coal Company, protesting that cadres over fifty lacked vitality. They claimed that an older age group, not the Red Guards, had basically been responsible for the Cultural Revolution. They denied that ex–Red Guards lacked an understanding of Party discipline. But another reader (who had been a Red Guard himself, but was apparently more in tune with the editors' views) wrote that people who had made their way into the CCP during the Cultural Revolution were inevitably influenced by the principles of the Gang of Four. He warned that the government should be "especially careful" before promoting cadres who were, at that time, in their thirties.

The debate does not clarify the actual policy stances of anyone. In fact, conservative and reform tendencies both existed in many age groups. But it suggests that the bases for argument between groups had changed by the 1980s. There was a full consensus that the Cultural Revolution had been a disaster. The question was how to be fair to local leaders, mostly young, who had been active in it but later rejected it.[75] The campaign to appoint youths favored them, especially when their Cultural Revolution experience had made them less radical politically rather than more so.

Actual appointments involved intense quiet politicking and compromises between different interpretations of the mandate that new cadres should be younger, better educated, and more professional. Many local leaders who had been attacked during the Cultural Revolution were younger than the top radicals of that violent time, and they assumed a great many high posts in Shanghai. The average age of the very top municipal officials (bureau heads or deputies and their Party counterparts) in 1979–80 was over sixty-three years. But the average age after a 1983 round of appointments at the same level was fifty-one—a dozen years younger. By 1985–88, the older cohort had almost completely left the scene; there was just one honorific retirement from such a high municipal post in those years.[76] The change in the city's leadership was momentous, and it occurred largely in the early and mid-1980s. This transformation took place not just at Shanghai's provincial level, but also locally and nationally.

Leadership became younger and better educated even at medium-low administrative levels. County heads and CCP secretaries nationwide had respective average ages of forty-nine and fifty in 1978; but by 1984, they averaged forty-four and forty-eight. This suggests that many old county heads retired, although fewer county Party secretaries relinquished their jobs. In 1978, just *1 percent* of county heads had university educations; but already by 1984, the figure soared to 69 percent. Some had dubious degrees from political colleges, but many had taken serious science curricula. In 1978, fully 83 percent of county heads had never attended middle school; but by 1984, this undereducated portion had dropped to 13 percent.[77] To call these changes sharp would be a major understatement.

In the national government, parallel shifts occurred not only in the bureaucracy but also in the state's most important political organizations, such as the CCP Central Committee.[78] The average age of CC members in 1977 was sixty-five; but it was down to sixty-two in 1982, and to fifty-five in 1987. For the next CC, in 1992, this average age rose to fifty-six, because the post-Tiananmen period was conservative. But the slight change did not gainsay the very sharp decline of the mid-1980s.

At the municipal level, too, the same pattern was strong—and data are available on the whole bureaucracy. By 1987, high Shanghai city cadres were mostly in their fifties. Older cadres comprised only about one-fifth of the top officials by that time. They were just 1 percent of the whole city bureaucracy. Seniority was still extremely important, because the correlation between age and rank remained very strong, as it does in many countries. But not far below the top of the system, as Table 4.1–1 shows, retirement at sixty became a norm.

Table 4.1–1

Shanghai Municipal Cadres' Age Structure, 1987 (percentages)

Age cohorts	All city cadres	Bureau-level cadres (*ju*, high)
<31 years	22	0
31–35	13	1
36–40	16	3
41–45	16	8
46–50	13	14
51–55	13	25
56–60	7	29
>60	1	21

Notes and sources: Shanghai shi ganbu tongji ziliao jianbian (Précis of Statistical Materials on Shanghai Municipal Cadres), Shanghai CCP Committee Organization Department and Shanghai Municipal Personnel Bureau, eds. (Shanghai: no press, February 1988), as conveyed to the author by a reliable Hong Kong source. This table covers all 836,880 Shanghai city officials at the section level and above, although cadres of the central government in Shanghai are excluded, as are other cadres not employed by the municipality. Percentages do not total 100 because of rounding. Bureau (*ju*)-level cadres include only the five or six top leaders of each of the most important functional offices, in all areas including state enterprises, under the municipal government. These bureau leaders are at the very top of the city's system, comprising about one-half of 1 percent of all cadres.

Toward Better-Educated Leaders

The severe late 1960s' attacks against intellectuals were also attacks against the prestige of learning as an activity. These were not fully reversed until a decade later, despite some surprising change in local recruitments during the mid-1970s. At high levels, members on the CCP Central Committee for example, the 1969 and 1977 CCs (and probably the 1973 one, on which less information is available) were only one-quarter college educated. By 1982, this portion had risen to an unprecedented high of 55 percent, then 73 percent in 1987, and 84 percent in 1992.[79] Change at high levels was sharp but delayed.

The local situation had presaged this. Proficiency exams for cadres had not yet emerged in 1975, but by May 8 of that year the central government was at least promoting the idea that newly recruited leaders should not be "soft, lazy, or undisciplined." Any workers and cadres who had been unjustly criticized in earlier years, or had justly engaged in criticism, were already in 1975 supposed to be given favorable treatment. "Leading cadres who were old or weak can become advisers."[80] These changes foreboded later major reforms based on the revival of university exams, though several years passed before the new students completed their courses of study.

Radicals in the press during the late 1970s sometimes still claimed that most cadres' abilities were adequate for the work they had to do, but the State Economic Commission propagated a contrary view. Reformers on this commission undertook a study to assess the skills of socialist managers and found many of them wanting. The commission specified that business cadres not only should understand socialism but also should be adept in science, technology, and management. They should have "creative" abilities. According to an early estimate, not more than one-third of Shanghai managers toward the end of the 1970s could pass serious tests according to these criteria. Initial surveys indicated that few factory cadres were up to snuff. Factory heads did not do much better.[81]

Angst about the quality of leadership at all levels in China derived from a mix of ingredients. Chinese traditionally assume that education is valuable. The actual level of schooling was low among cadres who had held their posts since army demobilizations in the mid-1950s. In the 1970s, many leaders had a widespread sense that educated people had been mistreated, that technical training helps modernization, and that school closures in the late 1960s hurt long-term economic prospects. Many kinds of Chinese elites, surveying in retrospect the gross mismanagement of talent in their society under Mao, were prepared at least in principle for personnel change. There was, however, a real shortage of seriously educated young people until the early 1980s.

The most severely affected part of the "lost generation" is called the "old three classes" (lao san jie), which are the classes that would have graduated from high schools in 1966, 1967, and 1968 but were prevented from doing so by the Cultural Revolution. Many of these had been highly active in the movement— and although they mostly lacked high school diplomas, they could sit for examinations in 1977 and later years. Only a few passed. Along with the graduating classes of later years, these helped comprise the academically most distinguished group of university students that China has ever seen, which graduated from four-year programs in 1982.

But most members of the 1966–68 middle school classes that did not graduate, and of the later less disadvantaged classes until 1976, did not survive the fierce competition for entrance to universities. Many had jobs as state cadres, and those who had Party membership were generally not cast out of the CCP simply because they had joined during the Cultural Revolution. The push to have better-educated cadres (like that to have younger cadres) was highly political, despite a consensus for it among many national and local leaders. It did, after all, involve people's jobs.

Because many state employees wanted more education by the late 1970s to meet the new criteria for promotion, their employers feared a brain drain from bureaucracies to universities. Work-study programs were the approved solution, since these enabled cadres to receive credentials, while their units did not lose them as employees.[82] Rules were strengthened against full-time university study by cadres unless their units approved. Also, rules were strengthened to prevent those who had no high school diplomas (which many had been unable to obtain during the Cultural Revolution) from applying to universities. The quality of education in work-study programs was often low. These curricula gave people credentials that may have been as useful for meeting new technocratic notions about promotion as for solving actual problems that arose in the course of work.

Beijing reformers then pushed a massive program to hire the 1982 graduating class into government offices; and it later pushed the same for lesser numbers in a few subsequent classes that also contained much talent. Tension was natural between these "best and brightest" recruits from the regular universities and cadres who had not been able to take that route, often because they had been unable to pass the exams in 1977. This latter group was of various ages, but some were in their thirties, like their more successful peers. To create more space in offices than the retirement program alone could provide, many young cadres from 1982 onward were sent to Party schools (*dang xiao*)—whence they by 1986 began to receive diplomas. Nominally, these were university-level certifications, and they appear as such in the publicly available statistics. But everyone knew that most of these diplomas in fact showed less talent than was usual from the certificates of regular universities in the early 1980s.

This schematized drama continued four years later. By 1986, when graduates from the Party schools began to return to their work units, they were often welcomed back by older cadres who had military backgrounds. Some of the Class of '82 thereupon began switching jobs. A few went into the booming private or collective economy; others went into state enterprises that valued their talents or into postgraduate work or research, consultancy, and many kinds of service jobs. By this time, state budgets did not support many new hires in offices; so the government's intake of new university graduates was sharply hindered by financial woes.[83] In other words, some of China's best talents left the regular government sector, often for collective or peristatal organizations, in the mid-1980s.

Cadres with jobs who lacked degrees continued to have strong incentives to raise their "cultural level" (*wenhua chengdu*, a standard index that was very sanguinely measured by the number of years of schooling). Adult education schools were swamped, as the "lost generation" tried to make up for the formal training it had missed. Spare-time universities in Shanghai had been restricted in the Cultural Revolution, but they came into their own again during reforms.[84] Ten of Shanghai's urban districts re-established spare-time universities as early as 1978, although these were not formally approved by the Ministry of Education until 1980.[85] In the same year, the city government approved thirty-nine new "staff universities" among municipal bureaus and companies.[86] With the return of many young, Shanghai educated people from rural assignments in 1979, the pressure among these youths to improve their skills was great. Sixty new colleges were founded in Shanghai during that period, and others were revived, so that in the next decade the municipal total rose to more than a hundred.

The appointment of educated cadres to high PRC posts during the 1980s has been extensively documented elsewhere.[87] Applied scientists in particular were recruited as leadership cadres, even in the Party. In Shanghai, the main objective was to promote technical research. The Party was to admit more scientists and business people to its own ranks, presumably to show more concern for them than in previous years. In the Biochemistry Institute of the Shanghai Branch of the Chinese Academy of Sciences, more than half the cadres on the Party Committee had technical backgrounds by late 1979. Among all fourteen institutes of the academy in Shanghai, during this end-of-decade promotion campaign, thirty new people were named institute directors or deputy directors, and nearly two hundred were promoted to similar headships in the constituent research offices.[88] Most of these new leaders were university graduates from the 1950s, and the directors and deputy directors averaged fifty-two years old, with the research office heads averaging forty-four years old. Less prestigious agencies had a far more difficult time finding leaders with many years of schooling. Urban and scientific institutions might find a few, especially for high posts. But the vast majority of older Chinese local leaders were able to deter the threat to their posts from educated people simply because such a small proportion of the population had degrees.

Only 8 percent of all new CCP members recruited in 1978 had some university-level education. This portion rose to 13 percent in 1979, and then to 19 percent in 1980. Among the recruits, in 1976 only 4 percent of the new educated members were classified as "high-level intellectuals," but this ratio went up to 33 percent at the end of 1980. From the 1978 Party Congress to the middle of 1980, about 2,200 intellectuals were admitted to the Shanghai Party. This was a tiny number, considering the period, the rehabilitation of "rightists," and the size of the modern metropolis. These intellectuals were officially supposed to be let in, if their "political behavior" was deemed good and if they made contributions to society. But local CCP leaders, who had to approve the decisions, could be reluctant to admit people whom they knew they had treated unjustly in the past.

The *Wenhui News* had a higher percentage of "rightists" on its staff than any other newspaper in the whole country—about forty rightists in 1957. During 1979–80, most were still alive; and these were all invited back from the border and rural areas to which they had been sent. The retirement programs of the early 1980s soon took many of these cadres, as well as their old attackers of 1957, out of work units. As the editor of a major newspaper freely admitted, however, tensions among rivals of the Cultural Revolution era nonetheless persisted into the 1980s. Because some of the contestants were not old, some of these discords within units would last until the turn of the century. Offers of Party membership were an inexpensive way of trying to reintegrate talents who had been excluded for many years from their vocations.

Much publicity attended the Party admissions of high intellectuals. A Fudan University mathematician was able to join the CCP, even though he had come from an "oppressive class" family background and had "complicated social relations."[89] The Party nationally, toward the end of 1981, had 39 million members, of whom just one-quarter had junior middle school or more education.[90] This was more than in the past, but it was not a large proportion. More important were the assignments of educated Party people to top-level jobs especially after 1983, and the rise of a consensus that leaders should be literate, as they had been in classical times.

The 1984 industrial reforms again included a campaign to "recruit Party members from among intellectuals." A new director of the Organization Department of the Shanghai CCP fulsomely urged that, "Party cadres should associate with intellectuals and become their bosom friends."[91] The proportion of Communists among Shanghai's officially designated "high-level" scientists and technicians was 38 percent in 1984. This density of CCP members was higher in some fields than in others: 45 percent among engineers, 43 percent among researchers, 30 percent among professors. Among "midlevel" experts of these sorts, the Party membership was less dense, averaging 30 percent; and among "basic-level" educated staff in the city, it was 17 percent.[92]

Education for cadres and potential cadres continued to boom in the 1980s. The reform history of such education can be divided into three stages: First came the period in the late 1970s, discussed above, when cadres attended short-term training courses of a kind that had also been usual in the 1950s and early 1960s. This was followed by an era when directives advised young and middle-aged cadres that their promotions would depend on degrees, even if implicitly some of these were from academically weak institutions. Many local leaders knew that scholastic degrees would aid career advancement, so they pursued these avidly as certifications. Party schools, cadre schools, regular universities, workers' universities, television universities, night universities, correspondence courses, and self-study programs (and their equivalents at the high school level) all proliferated in the 1980s. Shanghai by 1985 had 227 programs especially designed to attract cadres. After 1985, in a later stage of this history, these were supplemented by more on-the-job training.[93]

By 1986, four-fifths of all the city's cadres less than forty-five years old had obtained at least high school degrees. From their viewpoint, there was a difficulty: These curricula also attracted other students who knew education was now the golden road to stable jobs. Competition for places, among people who avoided the risks of the cooperative or private economies, became stronger even in second-rate schools. Each school was supposed to fall under one of four "systems" in the local bureaucracy: the Organization Department of the local CCP Committee, the Propaganda Department of that committee, the city government's Personnel Bureau, or its Scientific and Technical Bureau. Each of these ran an office to coordinate training for its own and associated staffs. Supervision over Party and cadres schools, however, was often concurrent or unclear among these agencies.

Most of the schools were set up to certify government and Party cadres under age forty-five, but ordinary workers and others in Shanghai wanted degrees too. In the class of 1984, because the entrance exams to the Television University were easy, many took the tests. A survey showed that 44 percent of the applicants were actually not government or Party cadres. Even an official might seek admission to study any subject, regardless of its relevance. A topic inappropriate to the jobs was acceptable, just so long as it led to a diploma.[94]

Local leaders' educational certifications thus rose quickly in the mid-1980s, but there was still a severe shortage of talented people who had studied the archetypical capitalist subject: business administration. According to 1986 Shanghai CCP Organization Department figures, 80 percent of bureau-level cadres below age fifty had tertiary degrees, and more than three-quarters (76 percent) had studied technical subjects. Only 7 percent had studied management. Three-fifths reportedly desired training in "leadership science" (*lingdao kexue,* a more acceptable monicker for the same topic). Half admitted they "urgently wanted to study" modern management. Not enough courses were available in these subjects.

Management was a field in which Shanghai really needed more manpower, as a survey of many large and medium-sized enterprises there showed. Accountants, economists, and management engineers were all in short supply. Only 42 percent of the companies in a tolerable survey had a chief engineer, only 6 percent had a chief accountant, and only 3 percent had a chief economist. The others needed experts in those areas. The people who did such work there did not have the education and experience to qualify as "chiefs."[95]

University degrees could, however, mean a great variety of things in China. One could obtain such certification from a television university or a tertiary Party school after only a few years of study, whereas a degree from a mainline university like Fudan generally took four years of serious study.[96] As in many societies, certification rather than learning was often used to justify careers formally. Enthusiasm for schooling depended on many factors, including individuals' calculations about whether taking classes was a more interesting current option than taking the jobs then available. In the early 1980s especially, possession of degrees nonetheless conferred a clear advantage in landing state jobs.

Posts in Shanghai's city government went to certified graduates in two phases: spring 1983 and summer 1985. This applied even to the topmost jobs in the city. Jiang Zemin, who became mayor of Shanghai on July 28, 1985, was an engineering graduate who had previously been the minister of electronic industries. His six deputy mayors were respectively specialists in metallurgy, architecture, physical sciences, finance, electronics, and medicine. Five had been appointed in April 1983, and the sixth (the first Shanghai deputy mayor who was a woman) came in 1985. All, including Jiang, were in their forties or fifties. All had college educations. Just as important, this pattern was a sharp trend throughout the municipal bureaucracy, not just among its six or seven top leaders. Shanghai had never before had such a technocratic top leadership.

Students who returned from graduate programs abroad sometimes had helicopter-like careers. Many went quickly to leadership posts. At Jiaotong University by 1984, for example, of the 63 ex-students back from foreign study, 25 were already heads or deputy heads of their departments, 22 others were on the faculty, and one was made vice president of the graduate school. Especially in technical fields, older returnees to China also received better positions during the reforms. By 1985 at the Shanghai branch of the Chinese Academy of Sciences, almost 90 percent of the "task groups" were headed by ex–foreign students.[97]

Old incumbent cadres at many levels could not assume, in this era, that their jobs were secure without educational credentials. In 1986, the national government ordered that all managers of large and medium-sized public firms should take a "state unified test," to check their competence. They were exempt from these tests only if they could offer good reasons for not participating. The full criteria for exemption were not published; but there must have been many valid excuses since only 45 percent of the managers in these Shanghai factories actually sat for the test.[98] Many frankly said their scores would be low. An important reason, which apparently excused many, was that "leadership groups change frequently."[99] Promises to retire fairly soon may have exempted some potential test-takers.

It was hard for Shanghai factories to keep their leaders, as the market environment became somewhat more competitive. The national unified test was in many cases deemed less vital than the need to avoid demoralizing local economic leaders further. Officials announced that managers who played hooky from the test, which was given in several rounds and supported by training classes, would be dismissed unless they had valid excuses. But there were no explicit sanctions for leaders who failed the exam. The ideal was clear, and it was largely implemented in areas such as Shanghai, where reformist rather than reactionary leaderships usually predominated, especially in economic bureaus just below the top of the city government.

In 1986, new regulations on cadre recruitment specified that workers could not be redesignated as cadres simply on the basis of receiving adult education certificates. This change dampened enthusiasm for schooling. Perhaps the change was practical: In new collective and private enterprises, the managers' priorities lay with profits, not worker training. So rather suddenly, after very quick expansion of extramural and regular schools in the early 1980s, there was a shortage of adult students. The Shanghai Office for Adult Self-Study found that in 1986–88, the number of pupils in self-teaching programs declined by half. Intellectuals predictably gnashed teeth at this untraditional norm, evident from context, that they were not the main kind of person China needed: "With the devaluation of knowledge, educated people cannot get better jobs than illiterates."[100] Later in the 1980s, "The high tide of adult education has passed, but these colleges still exist."[101]

The norm for appointing educated cadres was easiest to enforce for new hires in the state system—which at this time grew more slowly than booming nonstate firms, to which many adventurous intellectuals moved. This was untraditional, although the connections of many independent collectives with local government made the posts nominally more official. The Technical Cadres Bureau in Shanghai recognized this trend and reformed its policies in late 1987, proposing "a qualified personnel market" and a "contract system for newly hired professional, technical, and managerial personnel." This had two main aims: greater allowance for job-switching, and faster dismissals of incompetents from sinecures. These reforms ran into stiff opposition, but they were widely discussed. The *Wenhui News* called for relaxations of limits on part-time jobs, so that an expert could keep all the income made in moonlighting if he or she had found the job alone and could keep at least 70 percent if the firm had arranged the work. Professionals were reportedly entitled to leave without pay, and an "arbitration organization" was created to hear any complaints from technicians about their employment.

As regards changing posts, the *Wenhui News* proclaimed that:

> If an individual wants to resign, generally he should be allowed to do so. Professional technicians who lease and contract for the operation of village and town enterprises . . . should be allowed to resign. Those who request to go to three types of partially or wholly foreign-owned enterprises, or to key state and municipal construction projects, should be allowed to resign.[102]

Firing employees was also supposed to be part of the new hiring ethic, and the newspaper went on to describe two legitimate justifications for pink slips. Technicians could be dismissed if they "violated discipline." Also, incompetents could be fired if they "repeatedly failed examinations."

The proportion of government and Party cadres with university educations more than doubled in Shanghai between 1982 and 1987, as Table 4.1–2 shows. This proportion also doubled throughout the city's workforce. In commerce, the proportion of workers who had university educations remained very low. A majority of traders in 1987 had stopped their educations at the junior high level. Many in this field were women, for whom the educational admissions committees make entrance more difficult than for men. Many people with trading skills by the 1980s thought they could lead good lives without education.

Bureau and division cadres, near the top of Shanghai's government, were by 1987 much better educated than cadres in general, as Table 4.1–3 shows. The Tiananmen disaster, and the resurgence of reactionary conservatives at the top of the state, which had limited effects on the Shanghai delta, decelerated the trend toward more educated cadres—although that deceleration can be dated to 1988. After the appointment of so many better-educated incumbents during the mid-1980s, the rate of change slowed toward the end of that decade. Most important posts had already been filled with college graduates by 1987. June 4, 1989,

Table 4.1–2

1982-to-1987 Improvement in Educational Backgrounds of the Whole Shanghai Workforce, by Occupation
(1987 percentages/1982 percentages)

	University	High school	Jr. high school	Primary school	Illiterate/ half so
Shanghai total	6/3	25/27	42/37	19/21	9/11
Gov't/Party (of whom)	23/10	32/28	34/45	10/15	0/1
State agencies	—/19	—/38	—/39	—/5	—/0
Party and mass	—/6	—/31	—/51	—/12	—/0
Street and rural	—/1	—/16	—/48	—/32	—/2
Enterprises	—/13	—/27	—/43	—/17	—/1
Office work	11/5	40/36	37/47	10/10	1/1
Commerce	2/1	28/36	52/44	14/16	4/3
Professional	34/28	41/40	22/27	4/5	0/0
Service work	0/0	16/25	43/33	28/26	13/15
Agriculture/fishing	0/0	3/8	21/28	35/32	41/32
Industry/transport	1/0	25/33	52/42	18/19	4/5

Notes and sources: Shanghai shi di san renkou pucha ziliao huibian (Compendium of Materials on Shanghai Municipality's Third Census), Shanghai Census Office, ed. (Shanghai: Shanghai Shi Renkou Pucha Bangong Shi, 1984), pp. 357–61, and *Shanghai tongji nianjian, 1988* (Shanghai Statistical Yearbook, 1988), Li Mouhuan et al., eds. (Shanghai: Shanghai Shi Tongji Ju, 1988), p. 88. Percentages are calculated from raw data in the sources; but see a related table in this book, on gender and occupation in Shanghai, for absolute numbers of workers in each field. Because international lending authorities assisted the 1982 census, the PRC has released more data on that survey than on the 1987 one, as subheadings in the table suggest. Percentages may not total 100 because of rounding.

also sharply reduced the rate of overseas students returning to China; so the Shanghai municipal government issued a promissory statement on "Arranging Things for Students and Personnel Returning from Abroad."[103] It pledged to arrange jobs for them. Cadres from the Public Security Bureau routinely called on returned students, to debrief them and to diagnose how much antidote to the infectious foreign liberalism might be required in each case. The rate of new hiring, at least by the government, declined in the early 1990s.

The intense spate of educated cadre appointments was mainly a matter of 1983–86. The size of the change was gigantic. Accounting for the whole country, and considering the brief time period, this was the most massive peaceful bureaucratic transformation in human history. As with many other aspects of reform, this move toward better-educated cadres was highly political, not just administrative. By the 1990s, it had largely occurred, and no factor was liable to reverse it.

Table 4.1–3

Shanghai Municipal Cadres: Highest Diplomas, 1987
(numbers and percentages)

	University	Vocational/ professional	High school	Junior high school
Numbers	290,380	211,596	143,892	191,084
All city cadres (%)	35	25	17	23
Bureau (*ju*) level	71	3	21	6
Division (*chu*) level	53	8	24	15
Section (*ke*) level	38	13	25	25

Source: Shanghai shi ganbu tongji ziliao jianbian (Précis of Statistical Materials on Shanghai Municipal Cadres), Shanghai CCP Committee Organization Department and Shanghai Municipal Personnel Bureau, eds. (Shanghai: no press, February 1988), as conveyed to the author by a reliable Hong Kong source. Percentages may not total 100 because of rounding. Cadres of the central government in Shanghai are excluded, as are other cadres not employed by the municipality; but all 836,952 of the city's own cadres are included.

Toward More Specialized Leaders

A cadre might be young and educated, but still lack the experience to do much. The hiring criterion of "specialization," as measured by the number of years spent in a single profession, counterbalanced the emphasis on youth and schooling. People with many years of work were not young, and some might substitute technical experience for training. So the sloganized emphasis on specialization began with a distinct political thrust, which cut differently from those represented by the other parts of the slogan.

Other criteria for leadership hiring were also mooted in public at this time, and they also cut against favoritism for young post–Cultural Revolution graduates. In 1979, leftists remaining at the *People's Daily* led a movement to promote cadres on the basis of their "creativity." One editorial, for example, came out in favor of retaining competent cadres who had experience in the anti-Japanese and Liberation wars, but also for promoting people who had graduated from universities and vocational schools in the 1950s and 1960s.[104] The editorial said age should not be the only factor in promotions. Because there was a high correlation between youth and schooling, this stress on professionalism even cast doubt on degrees.

Increasingly, the reformist view prevailed over the "leftist"-conservative one.[105] By August 1979, in the Shanghai Metallurgical Bureau, there was a campaign to promote specialists to leading posts, rather than to promote people on other grounds such as family origins. During that year, a newspaper reported that in the bureau, "Some personnel cadres still retain the old leftist 'theory of origins only' (*wei chengfen lun*) or 'blood pedigree theory' (*xuetong lun*)."[106] But "fears of committing rightist mistakes" were not supposed to carry the day. The Metallurgical Bureau's Party Committee appointed, as CCP secretaries in some factories, several people whose pasts had been "complicated" (*fuza*). Some were promoted after they had been accused of being "politically unreliable." A woman whose Party membership had been approved by a local branch in the relatively liberal period of 1956, but shelved by higher authorities then, was finally admitted in 1979—and was promptly made the deputy factory head. Ex-rightists often could be specialized, too.

Applied science, as the reforms progressed, became the usual definition of professionalism. Other kinds of local leaders, ranging from political commissars to religious clerics, might be in nontechnical specialities for years but were not considered specialized. Engineering was more attractive, as a credential if not always as a career, to talented Shanghai people during the reform period. The proportion of engineers among all state experts increased from 46 percent in 1978 to 56 percent in 1984. Over the same period, however, the proportion of general researchers (including social scientists) actually decreased from 13 to 7 percent.[107] In China, as previously in the Soviet Union, a higher proportion of talented people with general abilities went into engineering than is usual in Western countries. Their educations were specialized, and they formed a very large group in the PRC bureaucracy, tending to trust each other more readily because of their common backgrounds.

Technocratic elites do not gain political jobs because of their technical expertise, but because of their ideology and their specific organizations. They are builders, and on the whole a proud lot. The ideology is: to each technician wanting power, a position should be assured among fellow technocrats. It explains to other groups why they claim power and gives them a rationale to organize politically to defeat other kinds of leaders—particularly fuzzy-minded humanist intellectuals. Qinghua University has been a "cradle of technocrats" from long before the reforms. That university's long-time president, Jiang Nanxiang, fostered young engineer-politicians by designating his university's best or most reliable students as political prefects (*zhengzhi daoyuan*) and giving them an extra year of training. A surprisingly large number of Qinghua graduates, such as Zhu Rongji, came to prominent national posts in the 1980s and 1990s. The political support group behind their concurrent rise began forming long before the Cultural Revolution, and it became arguably the single most powerful political network (after the army) in 1980s' China. Many, but by no means all, the members have at least some identification with Shanghai or its delta, where about a third of the Qinghua faculty were born.[108]

This group is a network of the "old boy" sort. But it is not mostly patrimonial, and not just hierarchical. It thus differs from most networks described in recent studies of China. The technocratic ideology behind this network is clearly legal-rational, while in other respects the group is patronist. Members of the Qinghua clique entered it while they were being trained as engineers. The network had an obvious patron in Jiang Nanxiang, but it consisted of horizontal relationships among people who joined as students on a fairly equal basis. Political networks are usually bolstered not just by one of the three Weberian authority types, but also by admixtures of the other two at the same time. Recent writings on the PRC do not stress this possibility, even though it is built into Weber's logic of analytic ideal types. There is a great deal of evidence that charismatic, traditional, and legal-rational authority types often combine in many actual Chinese networks.

The network of engineer-politicians at Qinghua created precedents for Shanghai's Jiaotong University and, to a lesser extent, for Fudan. All prestigious universities created "old school ties" between graduates, and these became a means by which various high Chinese elites tried to assure their continuity and coherence. The establishment of the National Defense University in 1985 was an important means to plan bonding between PLA officers in the future. In 1993, the National School of Administration was founded—not as a department of the Party School as some Communists had hoped, but under the government's State Council. This program taught advanced management, of course; but it also was a superb place for networking among civil servants.[109] Communions among graduates of the same university (*tongxue*) became increasingly important, as educated people took more leadership jobs. Most technocrats get support from patrons, but they also get political help from their ex-classmates and fellow alumni.

Legal-rational organization cannot be shown to succeed (when it does succeed) just because of any objective impulses toward modernization. Instead, it sometimes wins against other types of leadership because people who have faith in it fight political struggles against other kinds of leaders. The same is true of charismatic or traditional leadership. Change toward technocracy, such as intellectual reformists have partially made in China, requires them to call on all the kinds of authority and compliance that they can muster, in hopes of winning against conservatives. Successful authority is unlikely to be of just one type.

The overall shortage of people with technical training constrained early reformers' abilities to recruit them. In 1983, more than half (52 percent) of Shanghai's technicians were aged thirty-six to fifty.[110] Most of these professionals had been trained either from 1961 to 1965 (27 percent of the total) or else from 1981 to 1983 (25 percent). But in later years, the young cohort expanded very rapidly. The 1966–70 period contributed only 12 percent of the graduates in 1983, and 1971–75 contributed only 2 percent, with 1976–80 contributing 11 percent. So recent cohorts, graduated with several years of schooling after 1975, were an increasingly important part of the labor pool; but the early 1960s remained a very common time for 1980s cadres' graduations also.

Table 4.1–4

Effect of the Cultural Revolution on Shanghai Scientists and Technicians by Age (percentages in age cohorts)

	< 35 years	36–45	46–55	56–60	> 60 years
1980	28	46	23	3	1
1981	28	44	23	4	1
1982	30	41	25	4	1
1983	34	36	25	3	1
Year many in cohort were age 18	1970	1960	1950	Pre-Liberation	
Average %	30	42	24	4	1

Notes and source: Comparable data are available only for a limited span of years, but the main story in this table is on the horizontal of the bottom row. Calculations on the last two rows are very inexact, but they broadly show some effects of the Cultural Revolution in reducing Shanghai's educated staff. See *Shanghai keji, 1949–1984* (Shanghai Science and Technology, 1949–1984), Wei Hu and Fang Kaibing, eds. (Shanghai: Kexue Jishu Wenxian Chuban She, 1985), pp. 1240–42. For 1978, these pages also report similar percentages—but in differently defined cohort groups.

Shanghai's scientific and technical staff became much younger on average during the reforms, as Table 4.1–4 shows; and this trend accelerated in later years. The proportion of scientists and technicians in age groups whose educations had been adversely affected by the Cultural Revolution (and the post-1963 politicization of admissions and curricula) was low even in the early 1980s, when they might have been making their careers and contributions. Retirements of old technicians made room for new hires during the early reforms, for which these statistics are available.

Facing these labor-pool constraints, high-level reformers commissioned research about technical graduates who, once in the bureaucracy, they expected to recruit as political allies. The *Organization and Personnel Informer* (*Zuzhi renshi xinxi bao*) is a limited-circulation serial, begun in 1984, covering these issues in the Party and promoting the extent to which intellectuals should be hired as cadres. Shanghai's Party Organization Department in late 1988 edited a limited-circulation study on science and technology cadres.[111] Party administrators could also fare reasonably well in this political climate, if they could claim also to be professional specialists.

Appraisals for all Shanghai civil servants were planned in 1987, first on an experimental basis in Huangpu district and the First Commerce Bureau. Leadership groups and section heads came up to be assessed before their underlings. All civil servants were divided into two categories: those engaged in political affairs, and those who were professional managers. The second group had to take tests on political science, economics, law, and administration. The first round of these vettings, observed by officials from the organization departments of seventeen other provinces, involved only eighty-five leaders. The assessment results were officially supposed to become "important criteria for awards and promotions or penalties and demotions." For the sake of procedural fairness, "Authorities at higher levels made the final assessments known to [the civil servants]; they have the right of appeal to the assessment committees if they have any objections. Actually, none of the eighty-five expressed any objections."[112]

Party generalists were, until 1989, apparently urged to take lower profiles or timely retirement, rather than to sit for tests. Even in the army, more specialists were promoted to high posts. Among the top-ranked PLA officers in 1988, more than half of the youngest cohort had careers specialized in military command posts only—not political or other jobs—but among the oldest cohort, only one-fifth had specialized in command jobs only, and fully one-third had served just as political commissars.[113] New appointments of high-ranking military officers increasingly went to specialists. On the entire 1992 Party Central Committee, the most generalist members (whose careers had mainly been in mass organization work) comprised only 1 percent of the total. This contrasts with earlier Central Committees: in 1973, mass organization leaders had been 40 percent of the CC; in 1977, 29 percent; in 1982, 12 percent; and in 1987, 10 percent.[114]

By 1992, over half of the strong majority of CC members with college degrees were known to have majored in applied or natural sciences, while only 12 percent majored in arts or other nontechnical subjects.[115] Among all members of the 1992 Central Committee who had degrees from the top fourteen civilian colleges, more than one-third were graduates of Qinghua University. These included Zhu Rongji and Hu Jintao, who were also among the seven leaders of the Standing Committee. Shanghai's premier engineering university, Jiaotong, had an old-school-tie network that brought as many members to the 1992 CC as came from Beijing University (which is often said by some of China's hierarchically minded intellectuals to be the best in the country, although its graduates included more humanities majors than engineers).[116] Jiaotong was notably less active in the late 1980s' democracy movements than were humanities universities in the city, such as East China Normal, Tongji, and especially Fudan.[117] If democratic ideas are current in a country, as Robert Dahl suggests, this together with other factors can affect the likelihood of a democratic evolution there. Technocratic ideas, asserting the right of applied scientists to rule, are no different. They have been in great vogue during China's reforms, although they are not democratic.

The problem with technocracy as a leadership type became evident whenever specialists failed to deliver as expected. Practical difficulties arose, for example, if "technician heads of enterprises cannot get used to their positions as managers." A 1989 survey of Shanghai state firms showed that 73 percent of the top managers were engineers. Although 17 percent had studied economics, only 8 percent had studied management. Most universities had closed their business departments after 1957, and enterprise administration as a speciality conflicted with norms in both the Great Leap Forward and the Cultural Revolution. Business departments were widely restored only in 1979. Shanghai "enterprise leaderships were readjusted" in 1984, but "management people were not available; so engineers were appointed as managers." Too many of them lacked "a sense for markets, for competition," for gathering information, and for the legal aspects of management. "Engineering people are used to doing things by themselves. They are not good at getting things done through organizing and leading. . . . The focus of engineers is things, but managers' aims must involve people. Technicians are afraid of taking risks."[118]

Toward More "Revolutionized" Leaders

The fourth item in the official slogan on selecting leaders calls for them to be "revolutionized" (*geming hua*). The other three criteria are less unusual than this one, when the calls for youth, education, and specialization are put in their political context. Yet "revolutionization" remains an extremely odd phrase. In practice, it meant *no* kind of change (no *hua,* despite the name). In its reform usage, as applied to leadership selection, it has nothing to do with generic socialism or helping the poor. It also has no connection to the revolutionary overthrowing of anything. Quite the contrary, it only required that new cadres should have good connections with *old* revolutionaries. These last had become, by the 1980s and 1990s, mostly political conservatives.

Recruitment Reform in the 1970s

Good political standing could depend on diverse types of personal connections. Loyalty checks were supposed to be systematized by personnel files (*dang'an*) in Party organization departments. During the Cultural Revolution, attacks on personnel cadres and their offices made clear the depth of public resentment against files that might be used for secret manipulations. As early as 1970 in Shanghai, an organ of the Revolutionary Committee that had been called the Group to Purge Files (*qingdang zu*) was reorganized; it stopped destroying files and was told to perform a curatorial role, keeping libraries of them. Its name also became less rebellious, the Files Institute (*dang'an guan*).[119] The next year, the Revolutionary Committee also abolished its Considerations and Approvals Office (*shenpi bangong shi*), whose chop had apparently been needed on many documents. Less general and more functional chops, though still many, were now supposed to be required on submissions to personnel files.

Already by 1971, in January, the work by offices of the Party Committee was more clearly distinguished from that by offices of the Revolutionary Committee. Agencies that performed the most obviously political functions were put under the Party, and the Revolutionary Committee became a fancy name for the city government. The Party thus revived an Organization Group, an Office for Special Cases, and a Politics Group. By 1972, the city's Party Committee had consolidated its main functions into six major groups and offices.[120] At this time, there were fourteen main agencies under the Revolutionary Committee, including specialized ones for industry and transport, science and technology, finance, and other ordinary governmental portfolios.

It is typical, after periods of severe conflict between types of elites—none of which can easily manage without the other—that titles are bestowed on all. The nominal size of the elite expands. The late Bourbon kings, who recognized both pre-1789 and Napoleonic noble titles, offer the clearest historical example; but the same thing happened after the Cultural Revolution. Total CCP membership in 1973 was 40 percent higher than in 1966 (a 4.9 percent annual rise in that period). Many Party cadres who came under attack had never been expelled, even though the leftists, their attackers, had joined. This increase of the Party's size accelerated during the next four years, so that the August 1977 total of "more than 35 million" was one-quarter above the membership in the same month of 1973 (a 5.7 percent annual rise). The growth continued thereafter, because many younger and better-educated people were admitted:

1961 (middle)	17 million
1964	19
1966	20
1973 (August)	28
1977 (August)	35+
1982 (Sept.)	39
1984 (July)	40
1986 (end)	46
1989 (early)	48
1989 (August)	48
1996	54

Party growth was uneven, if these figures are correct.[121] Annual growth rates were only about 3 percent in 1961–66 and 4.9 percent in 1966–73, but then higher than 5.7 percent in 1973–77, down again to less than 1.9 percent in 1977–84, peaking at 7.2 percent for the 1984–86 influx of technocrats, then down again to 1.4 percent in 1986–89. The most obvious constancy of this recruitment roller-coaster was its fluctuation. Most still entered the Party in admissions campaigns, which now focused usually on people who were able to obtain degrees. Very few left, until they went to go see Marx. Although statistics for years such as 1970 and 1975 are still unavailable and would aid interpretation, the highest rates of increase (5.7 percent and 7.2 percent) are recorded for 1973–77 and 1984–86.[122]

In 1976, after the fall of the Gang of Four, various districts and counties set up "cadre examination offices," "checking offices," and "rechecking offices." Their purpose was to inquire which cadres should be purged for radicalism.[123] Beginning at the end of 1977, the Shanghai Party Committee resumed managing appointments to the full *nomenklatura* list of posts at the city level. The Personnel Office of the local CCP's Organization Department therefore again became crucial to the lives of many local cadres in the city.[124]

Recruitment of new cadres was well under way in local Shanghai units by 1978. This process did not wait for official proclamations of reforms in Beijing. It could be done on site, as it was in the Shanghai Textiles Bureau. During the last two years of the decade, about one-third of the 2,285 members of all "leadership groups" there—at the bureau, company, and factory levels—were young and middle-aged cadres. And almost all these new cadres (more than 700) had been recruited within the previous two years, 1976–77.[125]

The ex-supporters of Shanghai's previous leftist politicians were apparently able to retain their posts, if not their previous influence, at this time. It was proudly announced that by the end of 1979 only one-third of the Textile Bureau's leadership group cadres were "old," appointed before the CR. The new third was recruited from more diverse family backgrounds, and they were favored for their expertise, not just for politics. The remainder was apparently youngish ex-leftists. The new hiring of experts had already begun, but Cultural Revolution recruits were generally not dismissed at local levels.

Leadership groups simply expanded (by about one-third) in size to accommodate the new entrants. The pre-CR and CR cadres were joined by young experts. Old cadres remained powerful at the end of the 1970s. The average age of the Party secretaries in twelve of the Textile Bureau's companies was fifty-seven; and in a study of a very large number of its basic units, the average age of the Party secretaries was fifty-three. These figures were considered higher than ideal; but old cadres could retain their posts, especially if they could claim some expertise. In the basic leadership groups, 69 percent of the cadres were technicians; and in more than a hundred of the largest factories, technicians and engineers comprised 86 percent of the leadership groups.[126]

Efforts to create more serious, work-oriented managements were not limited to big firms in Shanghai. They were important nationally and in other parts of East China, where the supply of highly educated technical personnel was smaller. For example, the Changzhou Textiles Bureau declared a policy in July 1978 to get rid of the influence of "leftists" and of overly political managers. After that campaign, more than 70 percent of the leadership cadres were "experienced workers." This personnel reform involved a major round of promotions in late 1978 and most of the next year. Several distinct policies, which this Textiles

Bureau was praised for using, were clearly meant to be models for other East China industries, too.

A procedure for promotions was made public. First, more than forty "old cadres" were selected to begin forming a new "leadership group" for the bureau. Second, a few younger cadres "with outstanding scientific or business talents" were identified and added to this group; but the bureau chiefs could recruit only twenty-one of them—which suggests that the technical standards may have been serious. Third, a smaller cohort of eleven experienced midlevel cadres was added. All the leaders promoted in this way were Party members.

At the same time, the bureau "arranged appropriate work" (outside the leadership group) for other cadres, who were retired politically. Past promotions in the bureau had reportedly "stressed virtue rather than talent, politics rather than business, and status rather than performance."[127] The earlier policies had represented a "cage" that held the bureau away from progress, according to the reformers there in 1979. Only a third of the mid-1978 cadres were deemed able managers by the end of 1979, at which time purges-by-reassignment and promotions of new talents had raised the portion of the "able" from one-third to seven-tenths. (It is unclear what the other three-tenths did for their salaries.)

So the rate of personnel change in Shanghai by 1979 was fast. The local Party paper called this the "year of breezes" (feng nian), saying there were a "wind of human rights," a "wind for long hair and bell-bottom pants," a "pop music breeze," and a "breeze that everything old is bad."[128] The paper went on to speculate that people might think old cadres were bad, too. Sometimes people were promoted in 1979 precisely because they had been held back from fair advancements earlier. A man was nominated to be head of the School of the Shanghai Second Factory for Dying and Textile Machine Parts, for example; but his father, not from a working-class background, had past "political problems." After a thorough investigation, the factory's Party secretary decided to promote the man anyway.[129]

A man who had been declared a rightist in 1958 and a counterrevolutionary by 1969, in the Shanghai Second Tire Factory, had the skills to be a crucial buying agent for the factory's needs abroad. He was "an object made of two substances" (shuangliao huo), technically useful but politically dubious. A debate raged in the factory during late 1979 on whether it was proper to give this man an overseas task as the best qualified person. After much discussion, the Party secretary decided to trust him—and of course, he and his wife took this to be a burden off the family's back. He was allowed to become the company's chief purchasing agent, and for this purpose to go abroad.[130]

In March 1979, political changes affected Shanghai's administrative structure over cadres. The most important shift moved the powers of supervision from the Party's Organization Department into a new city office called the Personnel Bureau. The municipal government also restored its Files Bureau, to complement a Files Office that it took over from the Revolutionary Committee, and these became "one organization with two signboards."[131]

There was a campaign, by the end of 1979, to promote non-Party members to high cadre posts. Although some non-CCP people had been "democratically elected" to leadership groups, higher levels in the Party often had not approved them for those jobs.[132] Even when they were allowed into their units' nominal top-level leaderships, limits were placed on their activities: They could not attend meetings freely, nor read some limited-circulation documents, nor receive certain foreign guests, nor go abroad on the same basis as the CCP leaders who were supposed to be their peers in administrative work. Most important, their suggestions were often ignored. Also, Party members within a unit could effectively blackball the admission of non-CCP people to the leadership group.

This pattern was very slowly and partially defeated, against opposition, not only because many in higher levels of the regime wished to recruit more talent, but also because many respected local leaders in Shanghai were not Communists. Non-CCP experts were officially slated to be given more government posts, according to successive policies proclaimed from 1982 to 1986. So the Shanghai Party chose 244 non-Communists for "leadership groups" at the bureau level and above.[133] But this was still only about 6 percent of the four thousand or so cadres at those levels, a nearly trivial proportion. Pressure to change this situation was relatively ineffective, at least until the mid-1990s. It was more effective for lower administrative levels, which had increasingly specialized roles.

Many Party members in the early 1980s had to make self-criticisms about their behavior during the Cultural Revolution. Few were expelled, however. Those purged had all been involved in "big cases," usually having caused deaths or suicides. Many of those punished were CCP cadres who had been in charge of the "special case groups" (*zhuan an zu*) under local revolutionary committees, which kept confidential files on "bad elements."[134] Shanghai's *Liberation Daily* near the beginning of the decade carried an article asking people to "prevent the disruptive clique" (*zhenpai*) from "drilling into" the new leadership groups. This newspaper encouraged the advancement of young and energetic cadres, and it discouraged a reliance on seniority or number of years of experience in work as bases for promotion. In particular, it urged the removal of leftists who had "wormed their way into leaderships at various levels," especially if they were from any "shock faction," "wind faction," or "noise faction."[135] It also called for a purge (*suqing*) of cadres who were "feudal remnants."

Among local Party cadres in Shanghai, fifty thousand were required to undergo training in rotating groups during mid-1980. This program to combat "leftist" styles was for selected CCP cadres of the twenty-first bureaucratic grade or above, that is, about the section level or higher. Approximately 160,000 cadres in Shanghai then had such levels, and the three-tenths who were chosen for this program apparently received a message to tone down their "leftist" conservatism against the expanding elite. The cadre-training program emphasized the current need to assimilate more educated personnel into the bureaucracy. The cadres studied the "four don'ts" so that they would not be bureaucratic, "wear hats," "beat up" others, or hold others responsible for past errors.[136] It is very unclear how effectively this education created amnesia about the wounds inflicted and suffered after 1966.

Party recruitment of better-educated members became, by the mid-1980s, a high priority. Between January and May 1985, apparently in a campaign for this purpose, a large batch of new Shanghai CCP members was admitted. More than two-thirds had received at least technical secondary schooling, and one-third had "various professional skills."[137] But intellectuals remained a minority in the Party, and decreasing numbers of them wanted to join. Many felt they had to do so because the *nomenklatura* system was still operating. But the issue was not just whether people given formal leadership posts were already Party members. Increasingly, the question also became: Could the Party recruit and accept the people who were needed in those jobs?

An example of the increased complexity of leadership selection, especially at medium-low levels, comes in the early 1980s from Shanghai's Truck Transport Company. That firm had gone through three stages of "mobilizing, discussing, and recommending" new cadres.[138] The people who passed through this process were suggested for promotion to the Party's organization departments (*zuzhi bumen*). Approval from that quarter was also needed before any one could be promoted to leadership groups. This system had three alleged advantages: First, it encouraged leaders to hear and garner (*tingqu*) ideas from a greater variety of "the masses" than was otherwise apparently thought likely. Second, it was said to be an early step in a broader democratic reform that the cadre system needed, to make leaders connect with their subordinates. Third, it was a way to identify fresh talent from new sources. These arguments were all at least tacitly pluralist, and they implied a recognition that China's low-level elite should be more diverse.

The Transport Company Party Committee decided to solicit "recommendation letters" (*tuijian shu*) from ordinary workers. These were not free-form epistles, but they followed a specific official outline that asked, in addition to the name of the recommended candidate, his or her speciality, the particular leadership job that person could do, when the person might best be promoted (sooner or later), and other reasons for the nomination. Most important, the recommender did not have to sign the form. It only had to be dropped into a suggestion box.

The unit's leaders, clearly following orders from higher levels, laid down qualifications they expected the recommended cadres to have. These guidelines emphasized technical abilities rather than "redness," even in this very proletarian transport company. Educational prerequisites and other traits not usual among truckdrivers were apparently on this list; and at the start, "many cadres expressed that the criteria for the successors were high, so that it was difficult to find good people." Controversy arose among the truckers concerning the faculties that newly promoted leaders ought to have. Some thought that it was enough to foster

Table 4.1–5

Ways Factory Cades Were Promoted (percentages from a 1986 sample)

	Factory heads	Engineers/ technical	Production heads	CCP and government
Higher levels simply choose	48	46	55	66
Unit committee elects cadre	26	5	5	5
"Fermented" in mass organizations	22	2	8	9
Outside hire by higher level	0	14	20	10
Other methods/no information	4	33	12	10
[Number of cases]	[23]	[145]	[190]	[110]

Source: Laodong yu renshi (Labor and Personnel), May 1986, p. 12, reports on a survey of 500 cadres. Nonresponses and small-response categories are omitted, partly because they overlap in meaning with the headings shown above. The methodology warrants thinking of the percentages with broad margins of error.

young, healthy, and reasonably educated new cadres. But others, more in tune with ambitious reformers, insisted that new cadres should understand more technology and business than their predecessors, should have an "excellent cultural background," and should not be ex-supporters of the Gang of Four.[139] Political criteria remained crucial in promotions, but appointments at local levels tended to be made more consultatively than in the past.

By the mid-1980s, there were many methods of promoting cadres, as Table 4.1–5 shows. Factory heads were appointed by at least three methods in Shanghai then. A committee within the factory could promote submanagers who were already there. Alternatively, the supervising bureau or company could hold an open recruitment, soliciting outside candidates as well as internal ones. Or third, an exam could be held, and candidates' scores would provide a basis for decision.[140] Each of these three methods was seen to have its own faults and virtues. But the habit of appointment from within (which was still normal in most factories) was thought worse than open recruitments or exams in one crucial respect: Internal appointment lowered the number of candidates, and therefore the likelihood of finding a good manager.

Nearly half of factory managers and two-thirds of Party and government cadres were still chosen in the hierarchical manner, as Table 4.1–5 shows; but the other half were either elected locally or appointed after wide discussion. Although the forms of the *nomenklatura* system were usually followed, the need to have synaptic leaders who could control their subordinates led to a more participatory system of appointments. Bottom–up control, when it was local, was strengthened. Top–down control, especially if it came from a distance, was weakened.

Table 4.1–6

Shanghai Municipal Cadres: Party Membership and Gender, 1987 (numbers and percentages)

	CCP	Women
Totals (out of 836,880)	308,284	233,476
All Shanghai city cadres (%)	37	39
Bureau (*ju*) level percent	94	8
Division (*chu*) level percent	95	10
Section (*ke*) level percent	84	16

Source: Shanghai shi ganbu tongji ziliao jianbian (Précis of Statistical Materials on Shanghai Municipal Cadres), Shanghai CCP Committee Organization Department and Shanghai Municipal Personnel Bureau, eds. (Shanghai: no press, February 1988), n. p., conveyed to the author by a reliable Hong Kong source. Cadres of the central government in Shanghai are excluded, as are other cadres not employed by the municipality.

Localization did not mean democratization. Top leaders on the spot in any organization continued to have great powers, and the emergence of more consultative leadership selection methods did not change age-old traditions of familism overnight. The influence of distant superiors (e.g., in municipal offices far from the factories or stores that managers ruled) was nonetheless attenuated in these changes. When the chief editor of *Wenhui News* was asked for the criteria he used in hiring reporters, it became clear that he controlled those decisions totally. If ever his comrades in the personnel offices of the Shanghai CCP Propaganda Department did not realize this, he would tell them.

Localization affects the criteria of appointments because it makes paramount loyalty not to the state but to the immediate agency and to its head. The newspaper editor, for example, admitted three factors that he used in evaluating candidates for appointment: First, their "cultural level" and degree of education—especially in writing, and specifically not in science—had to be high. Second, a potential recruit should be effective with other people, and polite but not too shy. Third, the "thinking" of the candidate had to be sound; but the editor opined this was "more a moral than a political problem." Employment decisions are supposed to be made on the basis of personnel files, which now have more information about work ability (*gongzuo nengli*) and professionalism (*yewu nengli*) than about political thinking. In practice, the criteria for recruitment included both technical expertise and acceptable politics—in the unit, not just in the national context.

Being in the Party and being male remained usual prerequisites for high posts in Shanghai even well into the reforms. Information from 1987 on Table 4.1–6 shows not only that 94 percent of the very high bureau-level cadres were CCP members, but also that 84 percent of the section-level officials were in the Party.

The dominance of high posts by men, rather than women, was almost as frequent as the dominance of these offices by Communists. No criteria for more equal representation of the sexes was included in the slogan to favor young, educated, specialized, and "revolutionary" or well-connected leaders. Available statistics suggest that women were never particularly favored for appointment to offices, when men could fill them, except in fields that were thought related to women's concerns alone.[141] There is a relationship between CCP habits and male dominance in offices because at least nationally, more than 15 percent of the Party's membership has apparently never been female.

The point is not just that Party membership became an essential trait of high cadres. Equally important, high offices afforded their incumbents presumptive claims to Party status if they did not already have that. Two kinds of CCP members developed: Those who had close earlier affiliations with local or higher Party leaders, and those who had been recruited to the Communist cause because of their expertise and underwent a reformed sort of "revolutionization" (geming hua). The Party needed these people as much as they needed the Party. Before reforms, that relationship had been different.

These trends were opposed by Communist minidynasties, popularly called "princes' factions" (taizi dang). At the national level, the adoptive son of Zhou Enlai, Li Peng, became his successor as premier. A son of General Ye Jianying was governor of Guangdong. A son-in-law of General Ye was a conspicuous minister, Zou Jiahua. The son of the most prominent Mongol communist, Ulan-fu, became vice governor of Shangxi. A son of the former United Front Work Department head, Li Tieying, became a member of the Politburo. There are many further examples that could be mentioned here, and "princes' parties" were also present at local levels. Patronage of a straightforward familial sort, very traditional and new only because of its date, was an important basis for appointment decisions. Its beneficiaries often had good educations, but they could at some point find themselves in tension with cadres who had risen to office without such help.

Leaders' different previous work experiences, types of educational degrees, and other background traits were all important for appointments in reform China. Tensions between regular-university and Party-school graduates, many approaching the age of forty in the late 1980s, echoed the earlier conflicts between "white area" and "red area" CCP cadres after Liberation. But increasingly, the experience that legitimated recruitment was education in applied science. Although relatively unqualified cadres appointed during the period of leftist dominance were mostly not fired, and their presence in offices sometimes displaced others who were better qualified for their work, an essential criterion for leadership became more consensual in principle even though often ignored in practice. It was ability.

Recruitment of Leaders vs. Dangerous Dossiers and Low Salaries

This analysis would be too exclusively collective if the four-part official slogan about cadre recruitment framed all of it. Bringing talented individuals to leadership posts was difficult for the regime, at least during the 1970s, because prereform history made the dangers of incumbency obvious. Responding to these concerns, the Shanghai Party's Organization Department in 1980 began a process of reviewing the dossiers of all the city's cadres. The aim was to remove "erroneous documents" that had been filed there during the Cultural Revolution. Over the next seven years, more than seventeen thousand such papers were removed from dossiers, and apparently papers that "should never have been filed" were destroyed. In just twenty-three high-level Shanghai work units, as many as nineteen thousand papers were given to the people about whom they had been written. Despite this very high number of "erroneous documents" that were handed over to their victims, it is certain that some were simply too embarrassing to their writers and were destroyed. This suggests the nature of office work not just during the Cultural Revolution, but since the 1950s. The new policies may have assured past victims that charges against them had been officially dropped, but information from the files may also have moderated the ambitions of prospective office holders. The process of cleaning the files in Shanghai was deemed "almost complete" by early 1987.[142]

People still did not have access to most documents that remained in their personal dossiers. After the Cultural Revolution, in which many had suffered because of easily refutable misstatements of fact in their files, this continued to be a political issue. The dossiers were still classified as "state secrets" (*guojia jimi*), but high Party reformers knew that the incentives of local leaders to do their jobs actively were reduced by this secrecy. They faced the problem, but resistance from local conservatives stymied their hope of solving it completely.

Within the Shanghai CCP, there was thus debate—which conservatives in the Party tried to keep secret—about the appropriateness of the rule against persons having access to their own files. The reformist head of the *Wenhui News* CCP Organization Department, at an informal meeting of cadres in September 1986, said he thought this was a bad rule. He said some cadres were not careful enough with filed materials. But a high cadre from another Party organization department said, on the contrary, that dossiers were handled scrupulously; if anyone had questions, they could be raised with department officials. The journalist replied that statements in a file should be verified in face-to-face meetings with the person whom they concerned. His paper later printed news of this debate. By March 1987, the *Liberation Daily* averred that such a procedure would lead to "rumors" and was thus "incorrect" (as well as being at variance with central orders regarding files). This issue was a matter of far more concern to Shanghai local leaders than the tightly constrained public debate on it pretended.

Another kind of individual disincentive to assume leadership posts was the continuing low rate of salaries in many state positions. As the collective and private sectors boomed, and as the government became more fearful of the reaction of state workers if their managers' compensation rose more quickly than their own, state cadres' salaries remained low. Wages were controversial, as the reforms proceeded, because the state needed to promote more "activism" among both workers and managers. Now nationalized firms had to compete with collectives and private firms in many fields, and the state system's work ethic was laggard.

The prereform pattern of wages, if perks and intangibles are ignored, had been exceptionally egalitarian. A survey of 322 Shanghai factories from a wide variety of industries explored wage differences. The heads of these factories received an average compensation of 2,022 yuan (about 170 yuan per month) in 1986. Of this, 69 percent was base salary rather than bonus. By international standards, these managers did not receive much more than their employees—only 27 percent more than the average for all workers at the same factories. Members of these plants' deputy-level "leadership groups" received 1,917 yuan that year, almost as much as the top executives.[143]

There was some variation in this pattern. Managers at the Aviation Bureau had higher average wages than their employees by an average of 56 percent. This was the greatest differential among the many offices surveyed. Heads in the food industry averaged only 15 percent more than their minions. There were instances of directors who received two or three times the average compensation in their companies, but these were rare. A few ascetic managers had salaries and bonuses below the average in their units.

Differences in other cities, such as Guangzhou and Foshan, were considerably greater than in Shanghai. Historical data from Shanghai also showed that from 1952 to 1957, managers made an average of about double what their employees did; but by the late 1980s, this 200 percent was down to 150 percent. The main reason for the change was severe official restriction against raising Shanghai cadres' compensation. Salaries had been generally frozen since the 1950s. Especially since the depression after the Great Leap Forward, promotions had been dissociated from salary increases. New managers often "ascended to office but did not get rich."[144] Maximum wages for various jobs were decreed by regulation, and many managers could not obtain higher compensations because their salaries had long been at the top of their categories. Factory heads also could not receive higher bonuses than their employees, and for some time after the bonus system was introduced, they had been classified as government officials, ineligible for bonuses. Yet another constraint on managers' salaries in Shanghai was that when a chief was promoted, the new hand could receive a rise in bureaucratic rank of only two grades above the rank in the previous posting. This was a restriction that did not apply in other parts of China—yet another example of unusually tight control in Shanghai—and it may have contributed to making factory heads there less entrepreneurial than their counterparts elsewhere.

The low monetary premiums given to Shanghai managers might rationally be linked to the fact that, under the concept of the city as a center mainly for revenue rather than growth, they were only supposed to manage production, not markets. They bore low risks of failure, at least before reforms, because their factories were line items on government budgets. They were much like workers, so they were paid as such. But by the mid-1980s, only market-oriented managers could lead their firms to survive. Although the State Council at the end of 1986 published a mandate to increase salary differentials, this was "hard to administer" in Shanghai.[145] The low salaries that Shanghai managers had, in comparison to others in China as well as abroad, could be seen as a symptom rather than a cause of the city's decrease of entrepreneurialism from the 1950s to the 1980s.

The rigidities of China's personnel and wage systems clearly wasted talent. Practically anybody with a state job, even doing important or profit-generating work, could make a better salary in this inflationary time by switching to a collective or private firm. An experienced economist, for example, entered a three-year postgraduate course on the basis of which he might later change jobs—even though his articles had been translated into foreign languages and his professional reputation was already high. Without the new certification, he could not switch jobs. As the *People's Daily* reported, "this was an ironic event."[146]

When local talents could not switch jobs, they shortchanged their regular work. Moonlighting engaged at least 300,000 Shanghai state employees in 1988. Among technicians, 15 percent were known to moonlight, as did 6 percent of ordinary workers. Because their managers in regular jobs generally disapproved such activities, they often kept moonlighting secret. Statistics on this subject are therefore probably underestimates. A survey reported that technicians on average received about 600 yuan yearly in casual work. But a highly paid moonlighter could earn 5,000 yuan or much more.[147] This was a better salary than state jobs paid.

Local reformers realized that many talented cadres would be more productive if they moved elsewhere. The reasons often sprang from personal reasons, for example, humiliations in their work units dating from the Cultural Revolution. Many had attacked others so unjustly, or had been attacked so unjustly, that even after "rectifications of verdicts" it was often best to put space between them and their office colleagues. So a Shanghai Scientific and Technical Personnel Development Bank began in 1984 as a high-level employment agency. This office apparently did no "headhunting"; it was not supposed to recruit already-employed technicians, who were performing well, on behalf of other firms that might hire them.[148] It worked on behalf of the unemployed elite, especially serving specialists whose jobs had been eliminated in reform streamlining campaigns, or scientists or technicians who had resigned for "suitable reasons." The job-seekers had to pay a considerable fee for this placement service.

Most technicians who found jobs apparently did so on their own. An investigation showed that 20 percent of all Shanghai technicians were not employed in their specialities. Only about 2 percent of Shanghai's scientific cadres (estimated at 486,000 in 1984) had been transferred through official agencies. Of those who had applied for new jobs from the early 1980s to the middle of the decade, only 8 percent had actually been placed through the state-approved agencies.[149]

Although the incentives to switch jobs were great, the incentives *not* to switch were also strong. Often housing was associated with a job that a cadre wished to leave. This required an employee leaving a post to have the permission of the previous unit, or else lose the residence. So "new rules" governed a 1988 program of "open recruitment," held for 1,460 cadres in the Shanghai government law and tax departments' economic offices. Applicants did not need permission from their work units. This was a sharp change from previous practice, under which units had given leave mainly to inept members (and hiring units had gotten their best recruits straight out of schools). Apparently if applicants were successful, in the new scheme, they were supposed to get high-level official support to keep their apartments. Even current employees of state units could apply; previously, they were often ineligible to change jobs. A record number, 126,000 people, were registered in Shanghai for this opportunity to switch jobs, 8.7 times the number who could be employed. This was the beginning of a free labor market for professionals in the city, and reformers in the Shanghai Personnel Bureau were delighted—despite doubts from local conservatives, who realized this would weaken their client networks. An enthusiastic report confessed that, "what these applicants worried about is whether their former units would agree to let them leave."[150]

One solution, especially attractive to youths who had not acquired rights to housing, was simply to leave Shanghai, sometimes for other places in Sunan but often for points farther south. Beginning in 1988, the new province of Hainan was eager to recruit educated professionals from Shanghai (as well as from Beijing and other cities) to staff its many new investments. Some Shanghai youths had considerable interest in going. People could obtain application forms from Hainan and could submit extensive information about themselves, which was put into computer-readable records for later use in job placements. Middle-aged people with skills could also submit such applications, if they wanted to move out of their current units. The motives for going were mainly economic and micropolitical: to make better salaries and get better housing in an environment of fewer rules and fewer old cadres.[151]

When the Communist Youth League of Huangpu district wanted to recruit five new leaders for its own organization in 1988, it had trouble finding applicants. In the end, only five applied. Many youths were disinterested in politics at that time, and CYL cadres "after the reform of political structure" were no longer formally classified as state cadres.[152] Also, "after the reform of economic structure," talented youths sought more lucrative jobs than what the Youth League could provide. It was reported that people signing up to be League cadres would make 1,000 to 1,500 yuan less per year than they could elsewhere. So "the applicants were not strong, and the strong did not apply."[153] Among the five who did submit their papers, some admitted they hoped later to "jump the dragon gate" and get better positions, presumably in the Party. Others admitted they hoped to get out of their current jobs, and an offer from the League would allow them to accomplish that.

Official jobs attracted fewer applicants as the reforms progressed. In February 1989, when four technical jobs were open in the Changning district government, only seven people took the tests. The district CCP committees, people's congresses, and governments were all involved in this process, even though the number of officials tested was small. The whole group "passed," though apparently budget limitations prevented them from all being hired.[154] District government was not where most modern Shanghai youths wanted to work. The state had become like a church short of priests, because young people could get better jobs especially in the collective economy.

Reformers faced conservative resistance against admitting non-CCP leaders to the Party. And they also faced resistance against selecting non-Party cadres for high posts. The phrase "non-Party" (feidang) became controversial because lions in the CCP used it pejoratively. An early 1989 movement among journalists in Shanghai called for new terminology when referring to "non-CCP members" or "non-CCP cadres," calling them those names rather than simply "non-Party." "Other democratic parties also are political parties, and their members also are party members."[155] Even though the United Front Work Department called for this, it was a new form of politically correct speech and it went against the presumptions of old revolutionaries.

Ex–capitalist class status was a continuing basis for informal exclusions from appointments. This prejudice clearly went against high state norms by the 1980s, and in fact many ex-capitalists were appointed to leadership posts on the basis of their numbers and talents in Shanghai. Local conservatives in CCP personnel departments could still find other reasons to object to them. Household book forms had generally not been changed, even a decade after official policy denied the importance of "class status," "family origin," and similar dossier entries. Forms to register or apply for public services, such as schooling or housing, also sometimes included lines on family backgrounds. People paid little attention to this, partly because in any serious recurrence of "class struggle" they knew that the information was public or would come out anyway.[156] But the reaction of local CCP conservatives to policies favoring previously disfavored groups was to delay the effects of reforms.

By early 1989, there were some (by an official count, not enough) non-CCP members in high Shanghai government posts: one deputy mayor, ten deputy heads of districts, three deputy heads of counties, and "about thirty" deputy heads of government offices, industrial bureaus, universities, research centers, and important enterprises. The restriction to deputy positions was obvious. A reformer claimed "no reason to be satisfied" with the extent of leadership by non-Communists in Shanghai. It was lower than in the 1950s, and lower in 1989 than even in 1984. "There is a serious shortage of young non-CCP cadres. What causes this? First, a few years ago, the Central Committee of the CCP carried out a new policy toward intellectuals and tried to resolve the difficulty of intellectuals' joining the Party. Many intellectual cadres were recruited into the CCP. Second, the CCP has no complete system for employing non-Party cadres. Third, a united ideology exists in the CCP, and many Party members carry prejudices against non-Party cadres."[157] By June 4, 1989, just a few months later when the urban CCP found itself sharply divided, at least this problem of too much "unified ideology" had been solved.

Reformers and conservatives bickered more ardently about cadre appointments than the quasi-administrative slogans about youth, education, and specialization imply. The proper qualifications of new leaders remained a hot political debate through the mid-1990s, but the change of generations in China's leadership structure occurred because of that most influential politician, the Grim Reaper. The old revolutionaries were dying out, even if they refused to retire. Their passing created a situation in which consensus about leaders' abilities and aptness for jobs would become more possible.

Cadre Retirements

Many high-level cadres in Shanghai had held their jobs since the mid-1950s, often after soldiering to win the revolution. After the experience of the 1960s, many were in the next decade ready for retirement. The reasons have less to do with their chronological ages—some were still in their forties—than with their backgrounds. Most of those who had come with the liberating army were not Jiangnan people. The political bias that underlay their good jobs was obvious to all. Most important, during many years especially in the 1960s, they had led and been hurt by disasters. A writer for the Shanghai Party organ *Liberation Daily* argued in 1979 that these "old cadres," despite their sins, were not "bad enough to be hit once again." He pointed out that only three years had passed since the defeat of the Gang of Four. He urged other people, despite past repressions, to be patient. Moderation was needed, he said, so that the old system could change without being destroyed. Pareto could not have put his case more concisely.

This very authoritative CCP writer ended a major article with plaintive advice to the old revolutionary cadres themselves: They should correct their mistakes. Many people, as they well knew, wanted to find fault with these ex-soldier managers, scorned them, even thought they were "jokes" (*xiaohua*).[158] The political spirit of the reform era was well summed up in this tableau: A high CCP editorialist, clearly representing the state in its reformist phase at the end of the 1970s, had to remind his comrades that many other people had a tendency in secret to make fun of them.

Rules and Incentives for Cadre Retirement

Retirement from most state jobs, theoretically, was mandated for men at age sixty, and for women at fifty-five.[159] Exceptions and interpretations naturally abounded for such a rule. The incentives facing different cadres varied enormously. Some leaders had suffered so much in their work that they were glad to be rid of it. Others who had suffered wanted chances either to prove themselves or to get revenge by staying at their posts. Some retired merely to collect their pensions while doing postretirement work—often at salaries higher than the state had ever paid them. All conceivable kinds of motives to retire, or not to retire, were in evidence. The age rule could be evaded by many, until the mid-1980s at least. Shanghai issued its own slightly fuzzier regulation requiring male cadres to retire at age sixty, and female cadres at fifty-five, "unless there is some pressing reason for them to stay in office."[160]

"Retirement registration forms" were sent to men in Shanghai aged fifty-eight. Chinese reformers fully realized that retirements were a prime means to bring new blood into the official system. Until posts held by old revolutionaries became vacant, it would be difficult to circulate new elites into crucial roles. Accordingly, during the reformers' first temporarily unchallenged period of control at the top of the state, they announced big plans to encourage the superannuated to leave. By no means, however, did all cadres immediately comply with suggestions that they retire. The more important these old soldiers were, the less likely it was that they would just fade away.

For high-level Party members, exceptions could be arranged. For at least one important category of national leaders, an exception was formalized: The advised retirement age of the Party secretaries of provinces, as well as ministers and vice ministers of the State Council, was announced as sixty-five.[161] Even after retirement, the "political treatment" of Party members was unchanged from their status during active days; this means they could still attend meetings and read secret documents, as they did before. Often at local levels, as well as nationally, "advisory committees" of distinguished retirees were established. Membership on these bodies was offered as an incentive to powerful elders who relinquished their main jobs. But politically, the gerontocratic groups sometimes became as important as the leaderships of younger officials who were supposed to have replaced them.[162] There is, in any case, no retirement from the Chinese Communist Party.

Prestigious staff could often go into the "second line" (*er xian*) of leadership, which implies important "advisory" functions. Some showed up at their offices as usual, collected pensions often equal to their previous salaries, and issued orders as ever, even though younger people nominally had their old top jobs. When old revolutionaries attended the meetings of Party committees overseeing their previous work, they were all the more important. Of course, the Party was supposed in reforms to withdraw from management and to concentrate on inspirational and political functions only—but this did not always happen.

Lixiu *Benefits, and Ordinary* Tuixiu *Retirements*

A few favored cadres could retire on a *lixiu* (literally, active departure to rest) basis, which involved many kinds of special benefits over and above ordinary retirement (*tuixiu*) pensions. Even the regular pensions were, for ordinary cadres, generous by the standards of comparable developing countries. *Lixiu* status was so beneficial that it created exceptional inducements to depart. If cadres had been working in revolutionary areas or organizations before October 1949, and if they were currently at the division (*chu*) level or above, they were entitled to *lixiu*. People qualified for the two classes of treatment irrespective of the dates on which they retired. If their work was deemed "necessary," they could stay at their jobs. A few prominent national figures, such as Deng Xiaoping, did not hold very active administrative posts but also did not fully retire. This pattern was copied at many middle levels.

In order to encourage people to retire, the *lixiu* system, which had begun on a small scale in earlier years, was greatly extended in 1978.[163] Favored cadre retirees were of three kinds: Long March cadres (*changzheng ganbu*), who joined the Communist cause before 1937, Anti-Japanese resistance war cadres (*kangzhan ganbu*), who joined from 1937 to 1945, and Liberation war cadres (*jiefang zhan ganbu*), who joined from 1945 until the establishment of the PRC. Their treatment and retirement ages were not the same, and these also varied according to the units in which they worked. The reform policy was to encourage retirements in general, with a system of incentives that was graduated to move out the oldest revolutionaries first. Their local power was so great, however, that sometimes they would not go.

New kinds of Party members or management personnel—especially intellectuals—were periodically ordered to be hired in greater numbers by top reformers. Compliance by lower CCP levels, especially in personnel campaigns, was often lethargic or lacking at first. A section on the army, in Part 3 above, has already shown that early 1980s efforts to retire high officers met with very mixed success. A second campaign in the mid-1980s, during the next main spurt of reform, was needed to persuade the old soldiers to retreat to their verandahs. Civilian cadres were only somewhat less recalcitrant, but early mandates to retire were effective only if they matched local interests. When they did not, a second or third wave of a personnel campaign was more likely to succeed than the first directive.

These delays did not make the hiring of younger, better educated, and more specialized midlevel leaders a failed movement. On the contrary, China in the 1980s saw the largest bureaucratic staffing change in all its history. It was the most momentous aspect of the reforms within the state structure. Its timing at most bureaucratic levels postdated the 1979 efforts by some top leaders, including Deng, to establish an entente with intellectuals. During the early 1970s, there had been some antecedents of this personnel reform in the fields of international trade and diplomacy; but the 1980–85 changes involved far more people. The change, when it came, was massive and has been treated in other publications.[164] Aside from repeated exhortations in the 1980s from central leaders, some of whom (such as Hu Yaobang and Zhu Rongji) had themselves suffered as "rightists" after 1957, why did this reform go as far as it did?

Some local leaders resisted the change, but many favored it too. Cadres, embarrassed by attacks that they either launched or suffered during the Cultural Revolution, were often willing to retire in peace. This impulse was reinforced when everyone in a work unit, including the leader, knew perfectly well that someone else in the unit was better educated for the local top job. The generation of regional leaders who had come in with the field armies was aging. General Chen Yi's Third Field Army, recruited mostly in Shandong and northern Jiangsu, was the organization that founded the first revolutionary local governments throughout the Shanghai delta. An officer aged thirty in the early 1950s was sixty in the early 1980s. With the chagrins of 1957, 1959–61, and 1966–69 to live down, some of these cadres considered retirement a welcome option.

The change in civilian personnel throughout China was especially sharp during the twelve months beginning in December 1982. From that time until May 1983, two-thirds of the top 1,400 provincial officials retired or "retreated to the second line of leadership."[165] The number of posts at this level was reduced by about 30 percent, and the new appointees were younger and better educated. For the rest of 1983, a similar change transformed lower administrative levels.

In Shanghai, twelve of the twenty top government and CCP leaders, chosen or reaffirmed in their posts during 1979–80 elections, were given honorific "semi-retirement" by March 1983. They sat on advisory councils, but were no longer involved in day-to-day administration.[166]

At lower levels, especially in cultural institutions, the picture was similar. Newspaper staffs can provide examples. In the 1980s, forty-five cadres (about one-twentieth of the total staff) had left the *Liberation Daily* on a *lixiu* basis, in most cases still coming to work there on most days; and seventy had retired with *tuixiu* status. These are high proportions, but that paper is an important one. On the *Wenhui News* staff, the 1982–87 period saw seventy retirements of senior staff, although four-fifths of these were regular *tuixiu* retirements.

The gradations of the retirement scheme became a method, especially by the late 1980s, for the state to mollify some local notables whose careers it had previously harmed.[167] In principle, *lixiu* retirements were available mainly for cadres at the division level or higher who had been in Party or government work before Liberation. Some such cadres had joined the CCP after 1949, even though they had worked for it before then. July 1, the anniversary of the CCP's founding, is a date of induction ceremonies for new members. One hundred non-Party *lixiu* retired cadres in Shanghai were admitted to the CCP on that day in 1988.[168] One such cadre had previously been denied admission because of overseas connections. Another had been denied because of his family background. But the official propaganda about their admission had a dual meaning: They should be honored as retirees; they were not admitted because of their current posts. The CCP had not been fair to some of them. These old people were poignantly proud to retire into the Party that had manipulated their lives. Many young talents, at the same time, were not desperately interested in joining.

What Retirees Did

Retired workers, if they had talent, became more free to use their skills than they were when fully employed. Talented technicians and managers at fifty-five or sixty still had, in many cases, enough energy to work hard—and they could often raise their incomes upon retirement. In the 1980s, they could sometimes double or triple their monthly pay (from the range, then, of 100 yuan to 200 or 300) as follows: Their retirement pensions (*tuixiu gongzi*) might be 80 yuan, presuming they had previously held regular jobs in state-owned units. They could receive additional work supplements (*gongzuo jintie*) for continuing to help their original employer. In addition, they could spend time advising other factories, at high fees if they were experts.

Some of the most profitable retirements were by people who moved their skills from high-tax state factories in Shanghai to lower-tax factories elsewhere on the delta. At least one-third of the people whom census-takers found in 1988 to have "floated out" of Shanghai were retired people. Only 20 percent were workers, and 7 percent were nonretired technicians. "These people left Shanghai for other places to help local development. Most engaged in advisory work for local rural enterprises."[169]

Some Shanghai state factories tried to keep their best older workers from these temptations. In companies under the Electric Machines Bureau, many retired people could still work. Although 40 percent of the retirees were deemed too weak, at least 20 percent were said to have both good health and technical skills. The bureau therefore established a Retired Employees Management Service Committee.[170] This group was supposed to make sure that selected retirees, whom the company still wished to keep, would stay with the business. Their technical contributions in some cases saved a great deal of money.

The most striking aspect of the retirement system, by the late 1980s in Shanghai, is that the sixty-for-men and fifty-five-for-women rules were at last generally being followed. Available data show a very strong correlation between rank and seniority. About half of the city's cadres (the women) actually leave their work at age fifty-five. Practically all of the remainder retire at sixty—unless they are bureau-level cadres or higher. In the municipal government, the same pattern is strong especially if the whole bureaucracy of more than 800,000 staff is considered. By 1987, high-level Shanghai city cadres were mostly in their fifties. Older cadres comprised just one-fifth of the top bureaucrats at that time. Seniority was still extremely important, and the correlation between age and rank remained strong, as it does in other countries. But not far below the top of the system, as Table 4.1–1 earlier in this chapter shows, retirement at sixty became a norm. The group above that age comprised only about one-fifth of the leaders, even at very high levels.

Most high-level leaders did retire, but not seriously. As Fu Zhengyuan of the Chinese Political Science Association said of an October 1987 "informal compromise" among top leaders to retire: "There is always a limit within which academic discussion is allowed. Party members may retire, but the millennium of Party leadership should never be challenged, as stipulated by the Four Basic Principles written into the Constitution of 1982."[171] Even when high-level cadres formally retired, they could usually retain much influence. Deng Xiaoping gave up his last official post (the chair of the Central Military Commission) in November 1989. In his resignation letter he announced, "Our task of reform and opening has only taken the first few steps." The old man remained around for more than seven years to hope that it might take more steps.[172]

Local Elections

Appointments and retirements have thus certainly been the most important means for the circulation of China's elite during reforms. Yet these events are undramatic. Competitive elections are "liminal periods" of politics.[173] Elections solve a "collective action problem" of a kind that reformers generally want solved, and about which conservatives have doubts. Ordinarily, people with common interests have few incentives to organize, especially if a totalist government threatens disincentives for doing so. Competitive elections, however, provide a legitimate occasion for this. The net benefits of participating, if citizens have any chance to win the election or to have their views count in a representative process, are more likely to be positive than the net benefits of not participating.

Elections, if held, could replace the less-structured conflicts that still determine most major policy transitions in the Chinese state. But elections are not the only ceremonies that could perform this role, nor is competition in them (whatever its other attractions) an inherent requirement of the liminal passage rite as such. Elections are a modern alternative for renovating leadership. But because democracy (like any other political structure) performs more than one role, and because not all functions are always fully met, it is difficult to be sure that China will move in a liberal direction. This could happen soon, or later, or much later after passing through authoritarian and corporatist state forms. For most people, various kinds of regimes passably serve many modern needs. Much of the Chinese elite probably now sees elections, without too much competition at first, as a modern valid way of choosing leaders and as politically better than appointments. Doubts now center less on the method than on its appropriateness to China, in a period that is perceived as transitional and developmental.

Local Competition and Its Skeptics

Radicals, including Mao Zedong, had shown a far more confident contempt of elections.[174] Local elections are nonetheless held frequently in China, albeit under many controls. Direct elections to local people's congresses were held in each of China's nearly three thousand counties and urban districts in 1980, 1984, 1987, and 1992. There were supposed on each ballot to be more candidates than posts to be filled. Not all nominations were made by the Party. Just as important, local congresses were empowered to create standing committees, which could become political bodies not fully under Party control.

Most county deputies, after these elections, were nonetheless Party members who had been incumbents in these posts. Pressure for new election procedures came from central leaders and were presumably acceptable to voters, but they were predictably opposed by county-level bureaucrats who might be voted out.

Andrew Nathan reports cases in Beijing and Changsha, where real electoral competition took place among candidates in universities.[175] These were atypical because of the intellectual communities in which they happened, but they were certainly contested elections. Barrett McCormick has given a detailed description of the June 1980 election in two districts of Nanjing, showing that the process was mostly a matter of mobilization from above. Most stages of this election were like old-fashioned, undemocratic inspirational campaigns.[176] But in the Drum Tower district of central Nanjing, only half the elected deputies were Party members. Kevin O'Brien, Bruce Jacobs, Wang Xu, and others are also writing about local elections. Repeated practice of elections in the reform period, at the local level despite much organization from above, was new in the PRC. The main problems were a lack of serious competition in most races and a lack of transparency in candidate selections above the county level. Central policies often did not work well precisely because they were central, even when they were reformist.

Organizations that were not formally part of the state, especially if they were proletarian, often held elections. Some Shanghai trade unions obtained more democratic structures in the early 1980s. In the first year of that decade, 22 percent of basic-level union organizations set up "employee representative congresses."[177] By 1981, the proportion was up to 38 percent; and by 1982, 42 percent. In 1982, thirty-seven Shanghai factories even chose their factory managers by election.

These elections were important, even though the process was supposed to be monitored by the Party at higher levels. During reforms, local CCP leaders had to get along with the people who won these polls. Preparing for elections was as important as holding them, even though many cultural norms militated against serious competition in them. These events were very different from Tocqueville's town meetings, because they were less free-for-all, and their lessons in democracy were muted. The main datum did not lie in anything that unorganized individuals learned in this process, but in what local leaders learned: The unorganized opinions of many people can be worth attention.

In the 1982 Shanghai elections for district and county people's congresses, just one-eighth of the 7,791 seats were uncontested. As was traditional, the Party nominated candidates and the voters' role was to approve them, in this election for seven-eighths of the offices. More than one candidate, however, was on the ballot for the 13 percent of the places that were contested (977 of them, in a system that gave some constituencies more than one seat, elected from among 1,217 candidates).[178] Even for these seats, there was just one "over-quota" candidate for each four places to be filled.

More than 99 percent of the eligible voters, a group comprising all but 0.4 percent of Shanghai registered residents aged eighteen or older, participated in elections in 1982. Despite a lack of innovation in the electoral procedures that had been inherited from prereform times (and from Stalin), the results were slightly new because the CCP chose a modern set of candidates. In comparison with the previous people's congresses in Shanghai districts and counties, the proportion of elected members who had high school educations rose from 60 to 85 percent. Among the new Shanghai heads and deputy heads of districts and counties, the average age was forty-nine, and half had university-level educations (one-third more than after the previous election). In later local elections over the next decade, held as is traditional before the springtime National People's Congresses in 1988 and 1993, this slow-reform pattern did not much change.

Many reformers in 1980s' China were skeptical of having legislatures representing important nonintellectual groups, for example, rural entrepreneurs, private businessmen, factory managers, or other creators of new local politics. Reformers might disagree with conservatives on many issues, but they often hesitated before abandoning the conservatives' inherent elitism.[179] Yet in relatively open periods, younger reformers such as university students had more confidence in competitive elections—and nothing to lose from them. Nine-tenths of a group of students favored a "multiparty system" for China in a somewhat atypical early 1989 sample at East China Normal University.[180]

Elections of officials became more legitimate, especially at high tides of the reform. It was nonetheless easy for conservatives to limit the franchise. In late 1987, for example, the Jiangsu CCP Committee held a meeting of high department and bureau directors, "to evaluate the performance of the governor and deputy governors, and to nominate candidates for leading posts in the next provincial people's congress, the provincial government, and the provincial Chinese People's Political Consultative Conference committee."[181] This followed a "working conference" at which four hundred "leading comrades of provincial, municipal, county, and district organs" filled out "evaluation and nomination forms" on candidates of their choice. This was in effect an advisory election, but the circulation of elites was limited because it was so indirect.

The Party sometimes reversed itself on its own candidates, even after they won elections. Local CCP leaders who had already been duly elected to district committees could be reassigned by higher-level Party organization departments because they were thought "unqualified" for such posts. In January 1987, for example, four members of standing committees of suburban Shanghai CCP county committees were removed. In the previous three years, fifty-six leaders at the section level or above in Shanghai district and county governments had been similarly "reassigned." The reasons Party organization departments ordered these removals reportedly included the incumbents' lack of educational qualifications or a need for work to "raise their level of thought."[182] Circulation of cadres was also advocated among different kinds of posts—between urban and rural jobs, between developed and undeveloped areas, between leading and basic organs, and between economic and political work. But there was more exhortation than practice in all this, since cadres generally preferred urban jobs in leading political organs. Among the top leaders of Shanghai districts and counties, circulation had reportedly affected one-third of the CCP cadres. Different cadres spent very different lengths of time on such rotation.

These rules could be used to justify the promotion of expert cadres. And they sometimes allowed the still-powerful CCP organization departments to reward or punish local leaders whom Party leaders liked or disliked. In either case, the procedural checks on such work remained unpublicized.

Formally contested "elections with a different number" (of candidates and seats, *cha'e xuanju*) did not begin until 1988 for province-level officials. The previous pattern had been that a local Party Committee would nominate a number of candidates equal to the number of offices. But a 1988 rule allowed ten people's deputies to nominate additional candidates. Full and deputy headships of province-level governments, people's congresses, people's political consultative conferences, high courts, and high procuracies were subject to such elections for twenty provinces in January 1988, and in nine more during April. For these headships in governments and congresses in the first election, there were supposed to be at least two (and reportedly were sometimes as many as four) candidates for each post. In five provinces, there was more than one candidate for the top job as governor or mayor.

Nationally, in the provinces that had the first round of the 1988 elections, 190 candidates were nominated by petition. The success rate of these hopefuls was low; out of fifty-four unofficially nominated in two units (Beijing and Zhejiang), only eight were actually elected. For the provinces in this round, 341 out of the 349 Party-nominated candidates won—a rate of 98 percent.[183]

Ten candidates competed, at least in a formal sense, for deputy mayorships of Shanghai in April 1988. This was the first occasion when the Shanghai People's Congress faced more nominations than it had positions, but it is very unclear whether the ultimate result was less preordained than in previous elections. Of the candidates, one was a woman, nine were Party members (a larger proportion than had been usual among deputy mayors in some previous periods, especially the 1950s). The age range was from forty-nine to fifty-seven only, narrower than a less-guided process would probably have produced. The least-educated candidate had graduated from a vocational school, and the most-educated one had done postgraduate work. Eight of the candidates had been nominated by the congress's group of chairmen (*zhuxi tuan*), and two were nominated by petitions signed by ten members.[184] This was hardly an open process, and the vote was within the congress, rather than popular. But deputy mayors are important because of their connections. In early "elections with a different number," the important fact is not that some candidates win, but that others lose. These signals provided much political theater.

Nationally, the most important result from such an election occurred near Shanghai, in Zhejiang. Even during the conservatism after Tiananmen, in 1993, the Zhejiang Provincial People's Congress (like its counterpart in Guizhou) exercised its legal rights by electing its own candidate, rather than the person appointed by Beijing, as provincial governor.[185] The head of such a prosperous province is a very important official. Zhejiang is home to more than 40 million people. Seldom had a hinge leader at such a high level in China been so publicly beholden to a local constituency rather than to the central state. The formal structure of the regime was still unitary. But the locally chosen governor's assumption of office might have caused more stir than it did if everyone had not known for years that the top of the Chinese state is not its whole.

What does this mean for the future? Clues to answer this question can come from several sources, of which perhaps the closest is Taiwan. Electoral development on that island has been slow, beginning in the 1950s and the next two decades in very local "political space" where outcomes did not directly threaten the ruling party, the Kuomintang (KMT). By the mid-1980s, this was the world's first Leninist party to allow a legitimate opposition at the national level. Before then, the KMT was at least as separate from grass-roots politics among rural lineages as was the CCP on most of the mainland. In Taiwan, as local elections became more competitive, the KMT would often back the likely lineage-coalition winner in situations where two such coalitions were rather evenly divided, so as to gain prestige from the electoral victory. But where two local faction groups were unequal, the KMT would often back the weaker—with the aim of dividing local elites more evenly and thus creating a structure in which they could be more easily controlled.[186] By the mid-1990s, when all important offices became elective, policy issues and candidates' reputations explained somewhat more of the actual choices of Taiwan voters.[187]

Preferred Varieties of Elections

The litmus test for a democracy is often thought to require a positive answer to one question: *Does the state fill its important posts by periodic elections in which competition is legitimate?* The PRC is, by this definition, no democracy. Additional factors nonetheless affect the practical meaning of democracy for ordinary people. A list of questions can summarize these factors and suggest their importance for the future evolution of China's state form.

Do local networks outside the central state have much effective power? In China, clusters of influential leaders who are unconstrained by the top of the state have gained influence recently. So even if someone were to wave a wand and convert the *top* leaders of the PRC to believe in competitive elections, not all power there would be wielded democratically. No country is wholly democratic. In companies, schools, and many other institutions, alternative means of choosing leaders remain dominant. American political history, for example, can be divided into periods when business dominated government and other eras when officials regulated nonstate power centers, especially in the economy. The political history of democratic Britain may be treated similarly.[188] Competitive elections become less important if nonofficials make crucial decisions affecting most people's lives.

Are elections used to select low-level officials? Do voters have a chance to choose their local leaders separately from the high politicos of the state? Few democracies at their foundings had direct elections for top leaders, and some at present still do not. In China, competition has recently occurred in localities; but the highest officials affected, especially before the 1990s, have been at the county level. In Taiwan, which is on cultural grounds the best comparative case for the PRC, legitimate competition has developed—although county leaders were for many years the highest directly elected chiefs. Hinge leaders who do well in clientelist and brokerage forms of politics often favor the following mixture: indirect generation of high politicos, but direct election of themselves in their localities. This procedure has ended very slowly in developed democracies such as the United States, and in most parliamentary systems it is currently used. Change came either through constitutional amendments (as for choosing U.S. presidents or senators) or because voters became used to understanding that ballots for local candidates were mere cyphers for selecting top national leaders (as in the United Kingdom). In China, it is likely that neo-Communists and any future legitimate oppositionists at the state level will continue to prefer indirect elections for a long time. But in local communities, throughout China and in Taiwan earlier, "becoming an official" (*zuo guan*) has a very high traditional value. Many parts of China provide evidence that infringements of local election laws have sparked quick protests, because these laws concern means for local leaders to advance themselves. Competitive elections, a newfangled method of achieving cadre status, has proved extremely intriguing to local notables.

Within the state, which powers are wielded at its different levels? This spectrum can range from the Swiss confederacy, in which local cantons have wide authority, to Stalin's USSR, where the central regime was overwhelmingly important despite a formal, multilayered federal constitution. In China, the official ideal that all wisdom flows from Beijing has been mitigated in practice, even during Mao's time, by regional variations. China has a unitary system, not a federal one; but local corporatism is so widespread that legalities do not capture the picture.[189] Local state leaders actually wield many powers, and the state itself has become a lanky and ill-coordinated structure.

What method is used to count votes, if elections are held? This is a question that scarcely arises for the PRC, since electoral competition is scant there. But it can throw much light on options that are likely to become available there in the future—and are already controversial in both Taiwan and Hong Kong. First-past-the-post systems, counting single nontransferable votes (as in the United States or Britain), encourage the emergence of two parties.[190] Proportional representation methods favor the rise of multiple parties.[191] Also, in several Asian countries a single district may elect many incumbents. In Japan, the Liberal Democratic Party long used its organizational ability in large, multiseat districts to retain control of the government. For Hong Kong elections after that territory's return to China, PRC representatives insisted on multiseat jurisdictions, so that even if democrats receive the most votes in any district, some "pro-Beijing" and minoritarian business candidates are elected.[192] In Taiwan, multi-incumbent districts have sometimes given the KMT "bonus seats," amounting on average in large localities to more than one-third more than they would have won under a proportional system.[193] On the mainland, as in Hong Kong, election districting has already been a topic of some dispute. The CCP, if ever it submits to serious electoral competition as fellow ex-Leninists in Taiwan's KMT have done, will surely advocate multiseat constituencies. This system would give them an advantage in the results, if they have more capacity to organize votes than their diverse oppositions.

What is the extent of the franchise? The historical extension of voting rights has been better studied for old democracies than any of the other questions raised above. But now, in current systems, practically all adults may vote. This rule applies in China even before most elections are competitive. This issue is important to mention not because of any doubt that nearly universal adult franchise rule will remain legitimate in China, but instead because of the slow and conflict-ridden evolution of the franchise in each of the older democracies. This history shows how profoundly electoral systems can change. It is easy, even reasonable, to say that China's current voting is of no political importance. But the institutions exist, even if they are not now meaningfully used; and the dimensions along which their evolution could begin to affect politics are evident from past experiences elsewhere.

China's current trends are evident along each of the ranges suggested in the previous paragraphs: Nonstate economic growth and official budgets, such as are obvious in the PRC, now allow people to obtain an increasing proportion of their resources outside the state system. Democracy at the national level, even if it were instituted in China, would still not cover many important decisions affecting people under the current localized structure. The weight of the government, relative to other political institutions there, has shrunk lately.

Whether high state leaders are elected directly or indirectly may seem a trivial matter when the elections evince so little competition—but even *if* candidates were more varied, the issue would be of decreasing importance recently because local leaders' powers have grown. Indirect elections are likely to remain the norm for a long time, even if they become more competitive; and they would mesh well with national corporatist structures that could simultaneously develop. There are many stopping places between full authoritarianism and direct democracy, and China is likely to visit them all.

Recent developments also cast a new light on the question of which powers are wielded at different formal levels of the state. The central government nominally has total authority over its parts. But the quickly increasing tensions between this normative law and diverse actual practice could cause some official reformulations of a quasi-federalist (though not ideally federalist) sort. Administrators may need such rules to deal with each other in an orderly way when solving modern problems. The "one country, two systems" formula is an effort to create some kind of quasi-federalism, albeit still defined in the vaguest possible terms within a unitary state. It seems obvious that constitutional thinkers in the world's most populous country, claiming places as different as Tibet and Taiwan, are groping for a way to make the treatment of some areas actually federal and of others actually unitary. Unless they simply adopt a principle of unevenness, which invites political challenges from any areas that are disadvantaged by the structure, they have some major conceptual work yet to do.

As for the fine points of district sizes and vote-counting methods (first-past-the-post or proportional, transferable or nontransferable, single- or multiseat jurisdictions), only politicians are likely to care enough about the implications of these choices to advocate any of them strongly. The dominant party, if reformers in it ever seek the legitimacy that competitive elections can confer, will probably make sure that multiseat districts with nontransferable and nonproportional counting become the norm. Of course, nobody knows when any such choices may become meaningful in China. But the various authoritarian and tutelage ideologies that have predominated there throughout the twentieth century have always assumed that—after the country becomes richer and stronger—more democracy should be on the long-term agenda. As the time for it seems closer (and during reforms, some intellectual leaders have claimed it is near), these fine points become options with consequences.

Even if tutelage ideologies are not explicitly temporary, or are not followed, modern change affects the actual modes of solving problems in China. As more decisions require functional expertise, generalist patrons and power brokers have less to do. To the extent that the government can standardize social security and access to employment, the chance of arbitrary personal domination by bosses will decline. If the law can begin to control corruption, local power brokers will have less clout. As more people live in cities, they will acquire more choices of what to produce and what to consume. Many such changes are occurring in

China quickly—and they are not just social but specifically political on a local basis. It is difficult to guess the timing and sequence of their effects on state structure, but they will have such results. They may first create corporatist structures there, and then democratic ones at some more distant, later time.

Notes

1. Quoted in Lacey Baldwin Smith, *Treason in Tudor England: Politics and Paranoia* (Princeton: Princeton University Press, 1986), p. 1.

2. See Charles E. Lindblom, *The Policy-Making Process,* 2d ed. (Englewood Cliffs, NJ: Prentice-Hall, 1980).

3. Karl Polanyi, E. E. Schattschneider, Samuel Huntington, and Robert Putnam (and, for the analysis of ideology, Karl Mannheim) have in their ways adopted basically similar distinctions. This book does not claim, however, that all these theorists are exactly alike— or specifically, that Pareto would have distinguished the individual or collective bases of action quite as this book does. As a way to read these classic contributors together, however, the scheme here seems economical. See these authors' books noted in the bibliography.

4. The word "arena" is used in a somewhat similar way by Michel Oksenberg, "Chinese Policy Process and the Public Health Issue: An Arena Approach," *Comparative Studies of Communism* (Winter 1974), pp. 375–412.

5. Keith Forster, *Rebellion and Factionalism in a Chinese Province: Zhejiang 1966– 76* (Armonk, NY: M. E. Sharpe, 1990), chaps. 6–8.

6. See also Anita Chan, "Dispelling Misconceptions about the Red Guard Movement: The Necessity to Re-Examine Cultural Revolution Factionalism and Periodization," *Journal of Contemporary China* 1:1 (1992), pp. 61–85.

7. Keith Forster, *Rebellion and Factionalism,* p. 177. Even though Forster's focus is Zhejiang, his descriptions of national politics are extremely useful for this period.

8. Ibid., p. 178.

9. Yan Jiaqi and Gao Gao, *Wenhua da geming shinian shi* (The Ten-Year History of the Great Cultural Revolution) (Tianjin: Tianjin Renmin Chuban She, 1986), pp. 543–44; and Hao Mengbi and Duan Haoran, *Zhongguo gongchan dang liushi nian* (Sixty Years of the CCP) (Beijing: Jiefang Jun Chuban She, 1984), pp. 645–46.

10. See Elizabeth Perry and Li Xun, *Proletarian Power: Shanghai in the Cultural Revolution* (Boulder: Westview, 1996), chap. 6).

11. Keith Forster, *Rebellion and Factionalism,* pp. 179–82.

12. Foreign policy, however, is generally a function of the central government, at least over any short term after the resource constraints on it are taken as premises. Part of the problem described above is that some scholarly analysts transfer the processes that they know determine foreign policy (on which they have to report especially) to other fields. The obverse of this coin is that the actual and potential views of top leaders concerning specific foreign relations are difficult to know with certainty. See Allen S. Whiting, *The Chinese Calculus of Deterrence* (Ann Arbor: University of Michigan Press, 1975), on this last point in particular.

13. Richard D. Baum, *Burying Mao: Chinese Politics in the Age of Deng Xiaoping* (Princeton: Princeton University Press, 1994), chap. 2.

14. In Japan, these "policy tribes" are also in evidence and are called *zoku* (in Chinese, *zu*).

15. J. R. Jones, in *The Restored Monarchy, 1660–1668,* Jones, ed. (London: Macmillan, 1979), p. 48. The "fluidity" of the late Stuart political structure is the main theme of Jones's essay.

16. This refers in part to Susan L. Shirk, *The Political Logic of Economic Reform in China* (Berkeley: University of California Press, 1993), chap. 7.

17. This is based on chapters by Barry Naughton, Christine Wong, and Susan Shirk in *The Political Economy of Reform in Post-Mao China,* Elizabeth Perry and Christine Wong, eds. (Cambridge: Harvard University Press, 1985), which is also summarized in a review article by Daniel Kelliher, "The Political Consequences of China's Reforms," *Comparative Politics* (July 1986), pp. 480–81.

18. Barry Naughton, "False Starts and the Second Wind: Financial Reforms in China's Industrial System," in Elizabeth Perry and Christine Wong, eds., *The Political Economy of Reform,* pp. 223–52.

19. Hu's liberalism extended to ethnic minorities, as the Dalai Lama reports. Hu was aware of the massive subsidization of Han migration to Tibet (as suggested in this book's Table 1.2–4, "State Extraction by Province" in the first volume), and he once angrily inquired of his comrades whether all this money had been "thrown in the [Brahmaputra] river." The Dalai Lama claims that General Secretary Hu "went on to promise the withdrawal of eighty-five percent of the Chinese cadres stationed in occupied Tibet." If this report is substantially true, it shows a very different mentality from that espoused by the CCP's Paretan lions, the hard-liners. See Tenzin Gyatso, *Freedom in Exile: The Autobiography of the Dalai Lama* (New York: HarperCollins, 1990), p. 231.

20. Susan Shirk, *The Political Logic,* chap. 2; see also Zhao Ziyang in *FBIS*, October 26, 1987, pp. 10–34, and Li Peng in FBIS, March 23, 1988, pp. 15–16.

21. Cited from *FBIS,* December 8, 1988, pp. 24–33, in Troy Shortell, "The Party-Building Campaign in China" (Senior thesis, Princeton University, Woodrow Wilson School, 1991), p. 4.

22. See John F. Burns and Stanley Rosen, eds., *Policy Conflicts in Post-Mao China* (Armonk, NY: M. E. Sharpe, 1986).

23. Harry Harding, *A Fragile Relationship: The United States and China Since 1972* (Washington: Brookings, 1992), p. 220, cites a Xinhua source from Zhao himself.

24. A concise briefing on this pattern in the CCP is Mao's own proud account of "ten big struggles," each of which he won, in the "Summary of Chairman Mao's Talks with Responsible Cadres at Various Places During his Provincial Tour," in *Chairman Mao Talks to the People,* Stuart Schram, ed. (New York: Pantheon, 1974), pp. 290–93. The last such struggle purged Lin Biao.

25. Barrett L. McCormick, *Political Reform in Post-Mao China: Democracy and Bureaucracy in a Leninist State* (Berkeley: University of California Press, 1990), p. xii.

26. Alfred Stepan, *The State and Society: Peru in Comparative Perspective* (Princeton: Princeton University Press, 1978), pp. 301–2. See also Daniel Kelliher, *Peasant Power: The Era of Rural Reform, 1979–1989* (New Haven: Yale University Press, 1993), pp. 38–39.

27. See Susan Shirk, *The Political Logic,* chap. 7.

28. See ibid., and Vivienne Shue's incisive review essay, "Grasping Reform: Economic Logic, Political Logic, and the State-Society Spiral," *China Quarterly* 144 (December 1995), pp. 1174–85.

29. A related discussion, which posits the victory of contracts over price and tax reform as a result of consensus decision making, is Susan Shirk, *The Political Logic,* especially chap. 13.

30. Interview with an urban specialist in Hong Kong.

31. *Sanguan, sanfang;* but these led to *sannan. SHJJYJ* (January 1988), p. 3.

32. The classic discussion concerns the Great Leap and is in Franz Schurmann, *Ideology and Organization in Communist China* (Berkeley: University of California Press, 1966).

33. The three counties were Baoshan, Shanghai, and Jiading. On this and material

below, see Bao Ligui, *Jinxian dai difang zhengfu bijiao* (Comparative Modern Local Government) (Beijing: Guangming Ribao Chuban She, 1988), pp. 199–204. The reference to 1966, below the footnote in the text, quotes this source, which may refer only to cities below the provincial level.

34. Zhao Ziyang was the main politician in Beijing who pressed for this change, and his ideas on the subject may have arisen from his experiences in Sichuan.

35. A striking minor example occurred in 1993, when the U.S. State Department's chief official on human rights visited China and (because of the danger of revocation of so-called most favored nation trading status) was duly received by the Chinese Ministry of Foreign Affairs. This delegation, as is normal, was scheduled to visit the Great Wall. But a county-level Chinese leader, livid at the ministry's connivance with foreigners on such a mission, effectively prevented use of the usual road to the Great Wall. The delegation had to take another. (This ministry's explanation of the irregularity might be dubious, but American embassy officials who often arrange such trips believed it because of details in the event. The report comes from a friend of the author in Hong Kong.) Before the reforms county leaders did not, apparently, tell the Ministry of Foreign Affairs how to do its business.

36. *Shanghai jingji qu fazhan zhanlüe chutan* (Preliminary Research on the Development Strategy of the Shanghai Economic Zone), *World Economic Herald* and Shanghai Economic Zone Research Society, eds. (Shanghai: Wuxi Branch of Shanghai Eighth People's Printers, 1986), p. 23.

37. *Shanghai jingji nianjian, 1988* (Shanghai Economic Yearbook, 1988), Xiao Jun et al., eds. (Shanghai: Shanghai Renmin Chuban She, 1988), pp. 100–102, where phrases and slogans relevant to these reforms are presented profusely.

38. *RMRBHWB,* July 20, 1988.

39. For comparisons, see William H. Riker, *Federalism: Origin, Operation, Significance* (Boston: Little, Brown, 1964), for an analysis of such bargaining. See also Herman Bakvis and William M. Chandler, eds., *Federalism and the Role of the State* (Toronto: University of Toronto Press, 1987). Many specific works concern the United States, using logics developed first by James Madison. Recent contributions are: Thomas Dye, *American Federalism: Competition Among Governments* (Lexington, MA: Heath, 1990); and Daphen A. Kenyon and John Kincaid, eds., *Competition Among States: Efficiency and Equity in American Federalism* (Washington: Urban Institute, 1992).

40. Barrett L. McCormick, *Political Reform in Post-Mao China.*

41. M. Bonnin and Y. Chevrier, "Autonomy during the Post-Mao Era," *China Quarterly* 127 (September 1991), p. 147.

42. Vivienne Shue, "Emerging State-Society Relations in Rural China," in *Remaking Peasant China: Problems of Rural Development and Institutions at the Start of the 1990s,* Jorgen Delman et al., eds. (Aarhus: Aarhus University Press, 1990), pp. 60–80, especially p. 76.

43. This rise can be shown for almost any definition of Shanghai origin or of administrative levels covered. The sample sizes are not large, but the gradients of change are so dramatic that the qualitative points stand nonetheless. See "Towards Dominance of Technocrats and Leadership Stability: The Shanghai Leadership Change, 1976–1993" (Anonymous manuscript).

44. Keith Forster suggested this in a talk at the Centre of Asian Studies, University of Hong Kong, on August 6, 1991.

45. This "half" was 48 percent by 1987–88. See Li Cheng and David Bachman, "Localism, Elitism, and Immobilism: Elite Transformation and Social Change in Post-Mao China." *World Politics* 42 (October 1989), pp. 64–94.

46. Liu Binyan speaks of phenomena like this before the Cultural Revolution in

"People or Monsters," in *People or Monsters,* Perry Link, ed. (Bloomington: Indiana University Press, 1983), e.g., pp. 13 or 28–29.

47. Keith Forster, *Rebellion and Factionalism,* p. 220.

48. The author's first trip to China was in early 1976, just after Zhou's death; and he saw sad messages daubed in paint on walls at several places in the central city then. Cf. also Barrett L. McCormick, *Political Reform in Post-Mao China,* p. 44.

49. Ezra Vogel, *One Step Ahead* (Cambridge: Harvard University Press, 1989), chap. 11.

50. For example, the Princeton-educated civil engineer Gordon Wu of Hong Kong approached Zhao Ziyang directly for consent to a plan that divided tolls from a proposed Hong Kong–Guangzhou–Macau highway between foreign banks, the province, and county governments. This consent was obtained.

51. Wolfgang Bartke, ed., *Who's Who in the People's Republic of China,* (Armonk, NY: M. E. Sharpe, 1981), pp. 707–8 and alphabetical entries on each of the leaders listed there.

52. These included Deputy Mayors Chen Zonglie and Han Zheyi, Shanghai People's Congress Chair Yan Youmin and Deputy Chair Di Jingxiang, Municipal CCP Secretaries Xia Zhengnong and Wang Yiping, and many commanders of the Nanjing Military District whose regular work was in Shanghai. Ibid.

53. The chief politicians of Hubei province seem to be among the most conservative in modernizing parts of China. Many works by Dorothy Solinger, who has best written in English about that PRC province, suggest this; see especially her collected essays, *China's Transition to Socialism: Statist Legacies and Market Reforms, 1980–1990* (Armonk, NY: M.E. Sharpe, 1993). A mainlander on Taiwan reported a proverb, based on one of the many provincial stereotypes that Chinese hold of one another. He described Hubei people as stubborn and odd: "Heaven has the nine-headed bird, and earth has folks from Hubei" (*tianshang jiutou niao, dishang Hubei lao*). Comparative provincial studies are needed to explain this central place's somewhat separate ways.

54. Li studied from 1948 to 1954 in the Department of Hydraulic Power at the Moscow Institute of Power Engineering, according to *Zhongguo gongchan dang renming da cidian, 1921–1991* (Who's Who of the CCP, 1921–1991), Sheng Ping, ed. (Beijing: Zhongguo Guoji Guangbo Chuban She, 1991), p. 284.

55. *Post,* December 14, 1988.

56. *FEER,* December 12, 1985, p. 29.

57. See *Post,* December 24, 1986.

58. Jiang was a 1947 graduate of Jiaotong University, with a degree in electrical engineering. He trained for six years at the Stalin Automobile Plant in Moscow, and he then was a deputy manager at Shanghai's Yimin No. 1 Food Factory, at the Shanghai Soap Factory, and in the electrical machines section of the Shanghai No. 2 Designing Division of the First Ministry of Machine Building.

59. *Post,* June 25, 1989.

60. *Post,* June 27, 1988.

61. Joan Grant, *Worm-Eaten Hinges: Tensions and Turmoil in Shanghai, 1988–89, Events Leading Up to Tiananmen Square* (Melbourne: Hyland House, 1991), p. 147.

62. The author's friend and former student Solomon M. Karmel suggested this.

63. Quoted in John Walden, *Excellency, Your Gap Is Growing! Six Talks on a Chinese Takeaway* (Hong Kong: All Noble Co., 1987), p. i. See also Lord Acton, *Historical Essays and Studies* (London: Macmillan, 1907).

64. Based on interviews in Shanghai.

65. Victor Nee, "Peasant Entrepreneurship and the Politics of Regulation in China," in *Remaking the Economic Institutions of China and Eastern Europe,* V. Nee and D. Stark, eds. (Stanford: Stanford University Press, 1991), pp. 194–95.

66. The most thorough work on this topic in localities nationally is Li Cheng and David Bachman, "Localism, Elitism," pp. 64–94.

67. The classic is John P. Burns, "China's *Nomenklatura* System," *Problems of Communism* (September–October 1987), pp. 30–41.

68. See E. M. W. Tillyard, *The Elizabethan World Picture: A Study of the Idea of Order in the Age of Shakespeare, Donne and Milton* (New York: Vintage Books, n.d.).

69. The Confucian family altar is taken as a symbol of Chinese culture in Martin J. Gannon et al., *Understanding Global Cultures: Metaphorical Journeys Through Seventeen Countries* (Thousand Oaks, CA: Sage, 1994).

70. Quoted in *CD,* August 13, 1988.

71. Kenneth Lieberthal, *Governing China* (New York: Norton, 1995), pp. 210–11.

72. The top echelon comprises the mayors and deputy mayors and CCP secretaries. See "Towards Dominance of Technocrats."

73. "Drawing lines" is *hua ganggang. WHB,* October 14, 1980.

74. "Middle-aged" cadres are generally defined in China as those between thirty-five and fifty years old. A few cadres, notably top bureaucrats in the Central Committee or People's Congress, are however not termed "old" until they reach sixty. At these exalted levels, leaders are sometimes called "young" until the age of fifty. This is just one of many ways in which top politicos in China tend to overstate themselves.

75. *WHB,* October 23, 1980.

76. See "Towards Dominance of Technocrats," table 3.

77. The educational qualifications of the county CCP secretaries were not published, presumably because the improvement was not so striking. This is all based on a survey of more than three hundred secretaries and three hundred county heads in these years, published in *Zouxiang weilai* (Towards the Future) 2:2 (February 1988).

78. For the Central Committees from 1956 to 1987, see Li Cheng and Lynn White, "The Thirteenth Central Committee of the Chinese Communist Party: From Mobilizers to Managers," *Asian Survey* 28:4 (April 1988), p. 376; and for the 1992 CC, see Zang Xiaowei, "The Fourteenth Central Committee of the Chinese Communist Party," *Asian Survey* 33:8 (August 1993), p. 794. For the bureaucracy, such changes have been extensively documented in Hong Yung Lee, *From Revolutionary Cadres to Party Technocrats in Socialist China* (Berkeley: University of California Press, 1991), and Melanie Manion, *Retirement of Revolutionaries in China: Public Policies, Social Norms, Private Interests* (Princeton: Princeton University Press, 1993).

79. Li Cheng and Lynn White, "The Thirteenth," p. 379, also has figures on the Politburo (even for 1973), which are similar. The 1992 figure is from Zang Xiaowei, "The Fourteenth," p. 796. The decile rise (73 to 84 percent, 1987 to 1992) is of interest partly because of a contrasting trend on the age index; the later committee in this case was slightly older. The prestige of educational credentials apparently induced some elder cadres to take courses for rather easy degrees.

80. *Zhonghua renmin gonghe guo jingji dashi ji, 1949–1980* (Chronicle of Economic Events in the PRC, 1949–1980), Fang Weizhong et al., eds. (Beijing: Zhongguo Shehui Kexue Chuban She, 1984), p. 547.

81. *WHB,* October 24, 1979.

82. *WHB,* May 27, 1979.

83. This is based partly on an interview with a Chinese researcher, who indicated that the statistics to separate regular-university from Party-school graduates in offices by 1986 would be revealing but were not public.

84. Spare-time universities had also been very important in the early 1960s, which remained the half decade in which the most degrees had been given to incumbent bureaucrats, both civilian and military, even twenty years later. On these universities, see Lynn

White, *Policies of Chaos* (Princeton: Princeton University Press, 1989), pp. 162 and 193; and on the military, Li Cheng and Lynn White, "The Army in the Succession to Deng Xiaoping: Familiar Fealties and Technocratic Trends," *Asian Survey* 33:8 (August 1993), p. 781.

85. *WHB,* June 4, 1980.

86. *Zhigong daxue. WHB,* June 13, 1980.

87. See especially the works of Li Cheng: "Localism, Elitism," pp. 64–94 (with David Bachman); "The Thirteenth Central Committee," pp. 371–99 (with Lynn White); and "Elite Transformation and Modern Change in Mainland China and Taiwan," *China Quarterly* 121 (March 1990), pp. 1–35 (with Lynn White). Also, Hong Yung Lee, *From Revolutionary Cadres to Party Technocrats.*

88. *JFRB,* November 26, 1979.

89. *WHB,* June 8, 1980, cites "incomplete statistics" on this.

90. *Post,* December 11, 1981.

91. *FBIS,* December 13, 1984, p. 4, reporting radio of December 11.

92. *Shanghai shehui xiankuang he qushi, 1980–1983* (Situations and Trends in Shanghai Society, 1980–1983), Zheng Gongliang et al., eds. (Shanghai: Huadong Shifan Daxue Chuban She, 1988), p. 220, gives tables on the density of Communists in many professions.

93. On-the-job training is called *gangwei peixun.* Two-thirds (in the source, 66 percent) of Shanghai cadres were then younger than age 45, and 80 percent of these had qualified for these degrees (*wenping*). *Shanghai jiaoyu fazhan zhanlüe yanjiu baogao* (Research Report on the Strategy of Shanghai's Educational Development), Kang Yonghua, Liang Chenglin, and Tan Songhua, eds. (Shanghai: Huadong Shifan Daxue Chuban She, 1989), p. 260.

94. Ibid., p. 260.

95. These three "*qiye sanzhong shi*" were the *zong gongcheng shi, zong jingji shi,* and *zong kuaiji shi.* Ibid., p. 241.

96. An informant in Hong Kong supplied this information.

97. Tony Saich, *China's Science Policy in the 80s* (Atlantic Highlands, NJ: Humanities Press, 1989), p. 121.

98. This test was the *guojia tongyi kaoshi. SHGYJJB,* April 17, 1986.

99. *Lingdao banzi biandong pinfan.* Ibid.

100. *XMWB,* April 4, 1989.

101. *LDB,* April 8, 1989.

102. *FBIS,* December 30, 1987, p. 36, reporting *WHB* of December 24.

103. *WHB,* Hong Kong, February 13, 1991.

104. *RMRB* editorial, reprinted in *JFRB,* November 30, 1979.

105. This book normally uses "reform" rather than "rightist," and "conservative" rather than "leftist." The directional terms, still common in China, can confuse readers from Western contexts. The Cultural Revolution establishment was "leftist," as are conservatives who oppose reforms. Pareto offers the crucial distinction: between conservatives who wanted to restrict new elite recruitment and reformers who are willing to allow recruitment.

106. *JFRB,* October 11, 1979.

107. *Shanghai shehui xiankuang,* p. 222.

108. This "Qinghua clique," researched from the *1989 Who's Who in China* covering the country's c. 500 top leaders, had more than double the number of the second-best-represented university. See Li Cheng, "The Rise of Technocracy: Elite Transformation and Ideological Change in Post-Mao China" (Ph.D. dissertation, Princeton University, Politics Department, 1991).

109. Professor John Burns, University of Hong Kong, is the main Western academic expert on China's civil service.

110. These people are collectively called "specialized talent" (*zhuanmen rencai*). They are the graduates of universities, three-year vocational colleges, and vocational middle schools. The age group from 36 to 40 contributed 17 percent of the total; the 41–45 cohort, 19 percent; and the 46–50 cohort, 15 percent. See *Shijie xin jishu geming yu Shanghai de duice* (The Global Revolution in New Technology and Shanghai's Policies in Response), Shanghai Economic Research Center and Shanghai Science and Technology Committee, eds. (Shanghai: Shanghai Shehui Kexue Yuan Chuban She, 1986), pp. 452–53. These figures indicate that the vocational middle schools (*zhongzhuan*, for short), did not revive in the early 1970s or at least did not produce many graduates then. Graduates of the Cultural Revolution's "technical schools" (*jixiao*, for short) were apparently not included in these figures, although prerequisites for entrance to them generally included senior middle school education, and some of their graduates were competent. The exclusion of these students could affect interpretation of some of the figures.

111. The CCP Organization Department was aided in this by the Municipal Personnel Bureau and a group from the Shanghai Academy of Social Sciences. A tentative title of the *neibu* book, which the author has not seen, was reportedly *Keji ganbu zhiwei fenlei guanli yanjiu* (Studies in Science and Technology Cadre Management), Shanghai Party Organization Department, Municipal Personnel Bureau, and Shanghai Academy of Social Sciences, eds. (Shanghai: Shanghai Dangwei Zuzhi Bu, Shanghai Shi Renshi Ju, Shanghai Shehui Kexue Yuan, 1989).

112. *FBIS,* December 11, 1987, p. 33, and December 18, 1987, p. 26, reporting radio of December 11 and 18.

113. These PLA officers in 1988 totaled 224, the youngest cohort (not very young at such high levels, aged 45–57) numbered 59, and the oldest cohort (aged 64–75) numbered 53. See Li Cheng and Lynn White, "The Army," p. 776.

114. All figures except the latest are from Li Cheng and Lynn White, "The Thirteenth," p. 385; the 1992 statistic is from Zang Xiaowei, "The Fourteenth," p. 800.

115. This counts military science as an engineering subject; calculated from figures in Zang Xiaowei, "The Fourteenth," p. 797. About one-third of the major subjects of study were unknown, but many of these were probably also in applied sciences.

116. See Li Cheng and Lynn White, "The Army," p. 783.

117. The Shanghai International Studies University (still usually called by its old name, the Shanghai Foreign Languages Institute, or *Shangwai* for short) is smaller, and its graduates expect to need state jobs or permissions to go abroad; so it was also conservative. Joan Grant, *Worm-Eaten Hinges,* pp. 112–13.

118. The sample size of this survey of medium-sized and large Shanghai state firms was 2,000. See *JFRB,* May 5, 1989.

119. Jiang Zemin et al., *Shanghai dangzheng jigou yange* (The Transformation of Shanghai's Party and Administration) (Shanghai: Shanghai Renmin Chuban She, 1988), p. 132.

120. One of these had the odd name "Fourth Office," although some previously existing First, Second, and Third Offices had apparently been abolished. The Fourth Office's functions are suggested by the fact that its name in 1973 was changed to the Investigation Group, Diaocha Zu. The Organization Group was the Zuzhi Zu; the Office for Special Cases (whose functions are murky), the Zhuan'an Bangong Shi; and the Politics Group, the Zhengzhi Zu. Ibid.

121. This table updates figures in the chapter "Political Structure" by Frederick W. Mote and Lynn White, in *The Modernization of China,* Gilbert Rozman, ed. (New York: Free Press, 1981), p. 275; see also *Cambridge Handbook of Contemporary China,* Colin

Mackerras and Amanda Yorke, eds. (Cambridge: Cambridge University Press, 1991), p. 63. The latest figure is courtesy of John Burns. It is interesting that by the 1993 edition *ZGTJNJ* offered very few statistics on politics (e.g., the number of National People's Congress deputies and the proportion who were CCP members, p. 805)—but it did not trace the Party's membership.

122. The mid-1970s' recruitment needs more study. This was a period in which the state at its top levels was sharply divided, and it is not clear the extent to which Gang of Four radicals or Zhou/Deng moderates at that time had support among new members then. China is so large that it is possible that some recruitment was of local notables, co-opted rather than wholly controlled by any top faction.

123. These were called *ganbu kaocha bangong shi, qingcha bangong shi,* and *fucha bangong shi.* Jiang Zemin et al., *Shanghai dangzheng,* p. 134.

124. This unit was the Zuzhi Bu, Renshi Chu. An office of the Revolutionary Committee had previously done this task; but the Party resumed it long before the committee was abolished. See Ibid., p. 140.

125. *JFRB,* December 5, 1979. The calculations in this and the next paragraph rest on the fact that "leadership group" (*lingdao banzi*) defines a specific set of bureaucrats and on the fact that the age cohorts of cadres are also defined exactly.

126. *JFRB,* December 5, 1979. The number of basic-level units in the bureau was 467.

127. The arrangement of new jobs for expelled cadres was described as "*lingxing anpai shidang gongzuo.*" The items stressed, and those made light of, were put in these terms: "*zhong de, qing cai; zhong zhengzhi, qing yewu; zhong chengfen, qing biaoxian.*" The word "cage" (*kuangkuang*) used in this article was a favorite of Yao Wenyuan's; see Lynn White, "Leadership in Shanghai, 1955–69," in *Elites in the People's Republic of China,* Robert A. Scalapino, ed. (Seattle: University of Washington Press, 1972), pp. 302–77; also *JFRB,* November 5, 1979.

128. *JFRB,* October 18, 1979; these were called the *renquan feng, changfa laba feng, liuxing geju feng,* and *fan lao jie huai feng.*

129. *JFRB,* October 5, 1979.

130. *JFRB,* September 27, 1980.

131. "Yige jigou, liangkuai paizi" has been a very common situation in PRC bureaucracies. Jiang Zemin et al., *Shanghai dangzheng,* p. 145.

132. The procedure of these democratic elections was not specified in *JFRB,* November 30, 1979.

133. *JFRB,* February 24, 1987.

134. Interview with an intellectual who had experienced the Cultural Revolution.

135. *Zhengpai, fengpai,* and *naopai* were the terms for these factions. See *JFRB,* September 18, 1980.

136. *Budai maozi, buda gunzi, buzhua bianzi. JFRB,* September 20, 1980.

137. Tony Saich, *China's Science Policy,* p. 155.

138. The stages were "*dongyuan, taolun, tuijian*"; see *JFRB,* June 19, 1980.

139. *JFRB,* June 19, 1980.

140. This logic comes from an interview with an economist in Shanghai.

141. National data, not just those from Shanghai, confirm this conclusion. Although the Tenth CCP Central Committee in 1973 had a female membership of 10.2 percent, the Eleventh through Fourteenth Central Committees respectively included women in the following low proportions: 1977, 6.9 percent; 1982, 5.2; 1987, 5.7; 1992, 7.5. See Li Cheng and Lynn White, "The Thirteenth," p. 375; and Zang Xiaowei, "The Fourteenth," p. 794.

142. On these "*cuowu cailiao,*" see *JFRB,* March 22, 1987.

143. These groups comprised the factory head, deputy heads, and the "three chiefs" (*san shi*), namely the chief engineer, chief economist, and chief accountant (*zong gongcheng shi, zong jingji shi,* and *zong kuaiji shi*). See *SHJJYJ* (March 1988), p. 9.

144. The phrase is "*shengguan bu facai.*" Ibid., p. 10.

145. Ibid., p. 12.

146. *FBIS,* December 22, 1987, p. 14, reporting a Hong Kong journal of December 18.

147. *Tansuo yu zhengming* (Investigation and Debate) (March 1988), p. 51.

148. "Headhunting" is a common way to search for managers in capitalist places, including Hong Kong and Taiwan. The usual strategy is to reconnoiter a rival firm, find an especially competent specialist there at a wage level just below that of the vacant post, and then offer the promotion and higher salary to induce the switch.

149. Tony Saich, *China's Science Policy,* p. 134.

150. *XWB,* January 3, 1989.

151. This is based on an interview in Shanghai.

152. They were not part of the "*Guojia gongwu yuan de hanglie.*" *ZGQNB,* July 14, 1988.

153. "*Laizhe bu qiang, qiangzhe bu lai.*" "Jumping the dragon gate," into a metaphorical palace, is *tiao longmen.* Ibid.

154. *XMWB,* February 26, 1989.

155. In English (e.g., in this book and others about China), the word "Party" is capitalized to refer to the CCP but otherwise left in lower case. But Chinese, despite its glories, does not have an upper case. The CCP is a *dang,* like other parties. On the change in media language, see Huang Ping in *Renmin zhengxie bao* (People's Political Consultative News), April 4, 1989.

156. Two separate ex-PRC interviewees, one in the United States and one in Hong Kong, said people recorded their class and family statuses on applications by the 1980s without much concern. They separately volunteered the opinion that compliance of this sort was attributable to Chinese culture.

157. Huang Ping in *Shanghai shangbao* (Shanghai Business News), January 13, 1989.

158. *JFRB,* October 18, 1979.

159. The main Western source on this subject is Melanie Manion, *Retirement of Revolutionaries.*

160. Benedict Stavis, *China's Political Reforms: An Interim Report* (New York: Praeger, 1988), p. 47.

161. Laszlo Ladany, *The Communist Party of China and Marxism, 1929–1985: A Self-Portrait* (London: C. Hurst, 1988), p. 516.

162. The most famous example of this phenomenon was national, at Tiananmen in 1989, when a group of elders took command of the army. Their most important younger aide, Premier Li Peng, was by most credible reports not the crucial decision maker at this time, even though he reaped benefits and bore costs of taking some responsibility for the government's use of violence then.

163. *Zhonghua renmin gonghe guo,* p. 602.

164. See Li Cheng and Lynn White, "Elite Transformation," pp. 1–35; Li Cheng and Lynn White, "The Thirteenth," pp. 371–99; Li Cheng and David Bachman, "Localism, Elitism," pp. 64–94; also Cheng Li, *Rediscovering China: Dynamics and Dilemmas of Reform* (Lanham, MD: Rowman and Littlefield, 1997); Hong Yung Lee, *From Revolutionary Cadres to Party Technocrats;* and Melanie Manion, *Retirement of Revolutionaries.*

165. Christopher M. Clarke, "Changing the Context for Policy Implementation: Organizational and Personnel Reform in Post-Mao China," in *Policy Implementation in Post-Mao China,* David M. Lampton, ed. (Berkeley: University of California Press, 1987), p. 45.

166. See "Towards Dominance of Technocrats," table 3.

167. Other methods of similar restitution for loyal cadres, especially those who had been attacked during the Cultural Revolution, involved state permissions for trips abroad, payments of back salary, and restoration of living space that had been taken away earlier.

168. *JFRB*, July 1, 1988.

169. Zhang Kaiming in *Shanghai liudong renkou* (Shanghai's Floating Population), Shanghai Statistics Bureau, ed. (Shanghai: Zhongguo Tongji Chuban She, 1989), pp. 39–46.

170. On this *tuixiu zhigong guanli fuwu weiyuanhui*, see *Shanghai jixie bao*, February 2, 1989.

171. Fu Zhengyuan, "The Sociology of Political Science in the PRC," in *The Development of Political Science: A Comparative Study*, D. Easton, J. Gunnell, and L. Graziano, eds. (London: Routledge, 1991), pp. 237–38.

172. *Post*, March 20, 1990.

173. The quoted term is from Victor Turner, *The Forest of Symbols: Aspects of Ndembu Ritual* (Ithaca: Cornell University Press, 1967), p. 110, whose description of the Swazi *rite de passage* before a king comes to power tells much about a basic political function. The king goes into hiding and is submerged in the earth, and "in this fruitful darkness, king and people are closely identified. . . . Only in that Trappist sabbath of transition may the Swazi regenerate the social tissues torn by conflicts arising from distinctions of status and discrepant structural norms."

174. Stuart Schram, ed., *Chairman Mao Talks to the People.*

175. See Andrew Nathan, *China's Democracy* (Berkeley: University of California Press, 1985).

176. Barrett L. McCormick, *Political Reform in Post-Mao China*, pp. 138–45.

177. *Gongzhi daibiao dahui. Shanghai shehui xiankuang*, p. 233.

178. Ibid., p. 232.

179. See Li Cheng and Lynn White, "China's Technocratic Movement and the *World Economic Herald*," *Modern China* 17:3 (July 1991), pp. 342–88.

180. This was an informal but apparently large survey. The surveyor was a foreigner (an Australian), the students were interested in English, and the time was early spring in 1989; so the polling conditions were very far from typical in all of Shanghai at most times. The high nine-tenths proportion surprised even the surveyor and is the only reason the result can be reported, at least qualitatively and very roughly. See Roy Forward, "Letter from Shanghai," in *The Pro-Democracy Protests in China: Reports from the Provinces*, Jonathan Unger, ed. (Armonk, NY: Sharpe, 1991), p. 188.

181. *FBIS*, December 9, 1987, pp. 25–26, reporting radio of December 5.

182. "*Tigao tamen de sixiang*." *JFRB*, February 1, 1987.

183. *JFRB*, February 12, 1988.

184. *JFRB*, April 28, 1988.

185. *Shijie ribao* (World Journal), New York, February 1, 1993.

186. See Joseph Bosco, "Taiwan Factions: *Guanxi*, Patronage, and the State in Local Politics," *Ethnology* 31:2 (April 1992), pp. 157–83; and Bosco, "Faction versus Ideology: Mobilization Strategies in Taiwan's Elections," *China Quarterly* 137 (March 1994), p. 38. Selina Tay, a Singaporean student at Princeton, also deserves thanks for her ideas about Taiwan.

187. This is indebted to ongoing work by Shelley Rigger, a former student of the present author.

188. E. E. Schattschneider, *The Semi-Sovereign People: A Realist's View of American Democracy*, intro. by David Adamany (Hinsdale, IL: Dreyden Press, 1975); and the classic treatment of Britain in Karl Polanyi, *The Great Transformation: The Social and*

Economic Origins of Our Time (New York: Rinehart, 1944). Lay readers may be interested that many professional students of politics regard these two books as among the very best ever written in the field. The basic likeness of their arguments has seldom attracted attention, however.

189. See Jean C. Oi, "Fiscal Reform and the Economic Foundations of Local State Corporatism in China," *World Politics* 45 (October 1992).

190. See Maurice Duverger, *Political Parties: Their Organization and Activity in the Modern State,* trans. B. and R. North (New York: Wiley, 1954).

191. The effects of transferable vote rules deserve study in countries with extensive local clientelism and brokerage. Politicians who flourish in that environment would probably oppose transferable vote methods because they tend to succeed relatively more often against other kinds of politicians by organizing vote quotas themselves.

192. A first-past-the-post system was, however, strongly supported by a majority of Hong Kong Legislative Council (Legco) members—especially by the democrats among them—with some support from other Legco members who were appointed or chosen by functional constituencies. Because of extensive local fears of too much Beijing control in local affairs, this counting rule was adopted for the early 1990s.

193. The figure 36 percent for large multiseat jurisdictions is calculated in a manuscript by Gary W. Cox and Emerson M. S. Niou, quoted in Shelley Rigger, "Electoral Strategies and Political Institutions in the Republic of China on Taiwan," *Fairbank Center Working Papers,* No. 1 (Cambridge: Harvard University Fairbank Center, 1993), p. 19, which is the most lucid overview of these issues in Taiwan. On factions' attempts to coordinate votes for a very local multiseat election in Pingdong county, southern Taiwan, see also the anthropologist's view in Joseph Bosco, "Taiwan Factions," pp. 157–83.

Chapter 4.2

Policy Selection

I will not cut my conscience to fit this year's fashion.

—Lillian Hellman

The structure for selecting policies is a topic that may be divided into three main parts: the process of legislating or otherwise decreeing policies, the official channels through which the state tried to garner information from people without endangering itself in elections, and the unofficial custom of public demonstrations to express views. This is a steering function about which it is possible to generalize over many different substantive fields together. A good deal of fine research on policy making within the Chinese state has already been done. This allows a brief treatment of formal policy making here, so as to leave space for the policies of nonstate actors too.

Legislating

Formal policy making was practically nil during the Cultural Revolution. This is one respect in which the early 1970s resemble the late 1960s. No new ordinary laws (as distinguished from constitutions or other decrees) appeared in China for many years after April 1966. The National People's Congress (NPC) passed one enactment in January 1975. Further formal statutes had to wait until after Mao's death.[1] This index of legislative activity, however, is not comprehensive because China has at least three formal levels of rules: the constitution, laws, and orders (*xianfa, falü,* and *mingling*).

Local Uses of the Levels of Legislation

The cabinet, called the State Council, as well as local governments authorize the "order" genre of rule-making, which is by far the most frequent. The cabinet has issued so many different rules on related topics that local authorities can to some extent pick and choose among aspects of the national decrees that they like. These orders came in several forms—regulations, provisions, or measures (*tiaoli, guiding,* or *banfa*)—all of which had legal effect.

Major laws (*falü*), which need National People's Congress approval, are seen as more permanent. By the same token, these take much longer to pass. To streamline this process, the 1982 constitution gave the Standing Committee of the National People's Congress, acting for the whole legislature, authority to pass "basic laws" (*jiben fa*). But law is taken with great sententious seriousness in reform China, and any category of law that requires less consensus becomes devalued. Each lesser kind of law is supposed to be consistent with higher levels, and of course ultimately with the constitution. But the Chinese state during reforms has issued so many legal decrees that conflicts of laws are rampant—and very useful in localities.

The profusion of verbiage in the lower species of law has created an extremely complex body of regulations that various officials tend to interpret ad lib. Codification and uniformity therefore became a central task of legislation during reforms. Codification went through many stages in reform China.[2] Several summary codes, such as the Criminal Code and the Civil Code, were finalized in the late 1970s and mid-1980s. This was seen as a great accomplishment. But politically, three aspects of this fulsome regard for legal formality need to be mentioned: First, courts and police could not enforce many of the laws. Second, the decade-long delays in formal legislation for some fields (a press law, for example) showed deep political divisions on what the laws should say. Third, the relationship between local and central laws remained indistinct.

The 1982 Chinese Constitution is vague on the extent to which localities can pass their own laws. It makes clear that China is a unitary, not federal, state. It also mandates local governments to use regulations that maximize the "enthusiasm" of local people. People's congresses throughout China can and do pass laws. National rules are supposed to trump regional ones if there is a conflict, but this ordering has often been honored in the breach. During the reform era, it has been violated in principle for new and prospective parts of the PRC under the "one country, two systems" formula, which aims to persuade Hong Kong and Taiwan people that they will/would retain some independence. Another formalism is that minority peoples are supposed to be "autonomous" in their designated areas. But the State Council in 1990 sponsored a legal conference at Yinchuan, the capital of the Ningxia Muslim autonomous province, to encourage a review of laws passed over the years in minority regions and to "clear out" those no longer deemed appropriate.[3] Why this should be done on an all-PRC basis was unclear. The matter was particularly sensitive among Chinese Muslims, whose leaders declare that the Koran is for them the summa of all valid law. In Han areas, such as the Shanghai delta, conservatives also hoped for homogenization of the legal regime. But local diversity is so great throughout China that enforcement even of agreed rules is spotty. Clear consensus on permanent laws is hard to obtain even under authoritarian conditions, so the actual legal regime remains far from unitary.

Regional people's congresses also pass laws of their own. The Constitution of 1982 certified their right to do so, without any explicit restriction as to the topics of local laws. China's system is not federal, so there are apparently no published or exhaustive lists of topics under national, provincial, local, or concurrent jurisdictions. No crucial kinds of power were constitutionally denied to localities.

When and if national regulations on the subject of local laws are later approved, the local laws are supposed to become moot. But in fact, they often remain in effect where they were passed. Shanghai has been particularly active in generating "regulations" and "provisions" on a wide variety of subjects (housing, the treatment of juveniles, and other social topics in particular, and even a tentative press law) for which national resources or consensus were insufficient to pass a law.

Some important and controversial matters have been left to local regulation. The "one-child policy," for example, has never been a matter of national law. The issue is too intimate, and China is too diverse, to encourage national legislation of a unified code—despite the continuing official ideal of a unitary state. So Shanghai's government passed local provisions to implement the vague one-child norm. There have been national statements of intent on this subject, and some of them have legal standing. None of these include the implementing provisions that would make a serious law. Chen Yun in 1979 declared the one-child idea to be a "basic state policy."[4] The 1982 Constitution enjoined "both husband and wife" to plan their fertility, but the NPC has not legislated how they should make such family decisions throughout such a big country. That may indicate disagreement among the top politicos on exactly what sanctions such a law would lay down. The lack of a full-fledged law on this major demographic passion of the incumbent elite suggests not just that the state is not so powerful as it often pretends to be, but also that its leaders know as much.

Categorizing Codes

China's first national conference on legal theory, sponsored locally by the East China College of Law, was held at Shanghai in 1983. An aim of the conference was to discuss how to classify the kinds of law that require major codes. Most of the lawyers there favored a five-part division: civil law, criminal law, administrative law, law of the state, and law on litigation.[5] Others argued that the constitution was already the law of the state. Yet others advocated separate divisions for various kinds of social laws: on marriage and the family, labor, welfare, the economy, national resources and conservation, science and education and arts, military affairs, nationalities, and so forth.[6] It would have taken a great deal of time to reach consensus on all these areas. The meeting did not even try to do that much.

The most important achievements of reform legislation are evidently the 1979 Criminal Law (*xingfa*) and the 1986 Civil Code (*minfa tongze*).[7] Reformers in the mid-1980s were extremely active in lobbying for new laws in all functional areas. By early 1988, the national government was expecting to act on 37 draft laws and 176 sets of administrative regulations, about topics ranging from standardized weights to city planning. It also expected to moot "at least seventy-two sets of regulations" on a responsibility system for state-sector industries, on leasing, stock markets, private firms' income taxes, land transfers, and the management of foundations.[8] Not all of these were passed, of course. The need for consensus is always seen as great, and the substance of these matters often divides conservatives from reformers.

Consultative procedures involving experts were used to vet these codes. The best Western students of the National People's Congress show that these reforms were events of the mid-1980s, not of 1978 or any earlier stage: "It was 1983—not 1979—which turned out to be the real turning point in the NPC's effort to develop a serious subcommittee system," with the establishment of special committees (*zhuanmen weiyuanhui*) with functional mandates similar to those in many older legislatures.[9] "Drafts to gather opinions" (*zhengqiu yijian gao*) were circulated, and sometimes localities would enact these as temporary regulations, to try them out before more general legislation was proposed. Think tanks and specialists beyond the Party were regularly brought into these consultations, as well as organizations with interests in the final drafts. Reformers liked the expertise used in this process, while conservatives liked its snail-like slowness.

The Legal Work Committee that wrote China's Civil Code in the mid-1980s was divided between reformers and conservatives in a way that illustrates the politics of many drafting processes. Socialist-minded members thought that courts had a duty to preserve state-owned entities' property as "sacred," so that all government enterprises would have sovereign immunity in suits that others might bring against them. The code nonetheless put parties in civil cases on an equal footing—at least in theory. Any other decision would have only furthered the actual trend of nonstate entities distrusting official organs and contracting largely among themselves.[10] The wording of the code was a flexible compromise, which has been interpreted differently in relatively liberal or stabilizing periods of reform.

The business of establishing legislation to protect Shanghai youths and children in 1986 shows several common procedures for legislative reform. In the first place, the jurisdiction was local, not yet national. The drafting committee was chaired by a deputy secretary of the unit with jurisdiction (in this case, the Communist Youth League). The main deputy chairs included an expert (in this case, from the East China College of Politics and Law) and a member of the local people's congress.[11] This combination of government and expert leaders, chaired by a CCP official from the supposed "supervising agency" (*zhuguan bumen*), was typical. Before the draft was finalized, a delegation "went to the capital to report" (*pujing huibao*). In Beijing they met representatives of the national Communist Youth League, the Chinese People's Political Consultative Conference, the National People's Congress, the national Public Prosecutor's Office, and others—although Shanghai municipality had standing rights to finalize this law by itself. Whenever possible, central authority was honored; but in periods like 1986, the state leaders were largely reformist and accommodated local wishes. Surely not all the interests of all the consulted parties could be fully articulated or financed under this procedure. But there is evidence that the consultation for formal legislation, as distinct from political orders, was notably wide.

Careful Norms on Economic Interests

Economic laws in particular were subject to slow debate. The need for them was as obvious as the political interests against market regulation. The bankruptcy law was extremely hard to finalize. Without a bankruptcy law, foreign and Chinese economists regarded reforms in the state sector as laughable. Many cadres and workers took a much less theoretical view, since their jobs were on the line. As a reporter put it, "All workers, but especially those in state-owned enterprises, promised lifetime tenure, would be caught mentally unprepared. They would find it hard to accept that what they had been told since school days about socialist job security no longer held true."

An economic cadre admitted, "As bankruptcy is such a sensitive issue in a socialist economy—it had often been pointed out as a symbol of capitalist decay—few firms would really go broke. Rather, [the concept of] bankruptcy will be used more as a warning to debt-ridden enterprises." For this symbolic reason, the same cadre described his CCP's worst nightmare. He was,

> very worried about the possible backlash of protests from workers who lose their jobs, particularly in the case of mass layoffs. What if the workers who have been fired throng around government buildings, raising signs and chanting, "I want to work. I am hungry. I want to eat." . . . This is a far more serious problem than a bankrupt factory in debt to the tune of three or five million *yuan*.[12]

A bankruptcy law was passed in March 1988, but for many months thereafter no state firms were allowed to go under.[13] The draft of a new enterprise law (*qiye fa*) was well under way in late 1988, and it adumbrated many breakthroughs. It specified that basic-level state enterprises were to be "independent management units," whereas in the past they had been just "relatively independent"—that is, under the thumbs of their supervisory corporations. Also, the new draft distinguished ownership from management. "The whole people" (*quanmin*) owned a state enterprise, but the director was to become their nearly omnipotent trustee. The draft enterprise law loosened the national rules for compensating employees; it extended to state units norms for generous bonuses that were already usual in cooperatives. The draft guaranteed that a firm could use part of any foreign exchange earnings. It legalized enterprise rights to determine the internal administrative structure and roster of posts. Firms could buy the shares of other companies. Their managers were put in "the central position" for all decisions and responsibility. The draft also specified that, while managers might be punished by supervising firms for abandonment of duty, they would take responsibility within their units for any straightforward mistakes. This draft even provided that the police might be summoned to support a manager's rights, presumably against workers, in professional administration of the firm.[14] But this law was just a draft, and events in 1989 delayed its finalization in the 1990s as a statement of principles. Actual bankruptcies of state-owned enterprises remained a political anathema to conservatives.

Intellectual property laws also involved political conflicts, but of an easier kind since one of the usual types of parties was foreign and fairly easy to hoodwink. On April 1, 1985, the first Chinese patent law took effect. It was hailed in typical reform style: "From early morning, inventors formed a line in front of the Shanghai branch of the Chinese Patent Bureau, waiting to register their inventions. A lecturer at Shanghai's Second Industrial University began the queue at 4:15 A.M. and was the first to file." Xinhua News Agency declared, "From now on, the history in which intellectual property is used without compensation has ended in China."[15] This was a reformist hope, though not a communitarian one. Foreign countries pressed China to pass a copyright law, which it did in September 1990.[16] Even before that, a local law protected Shanghai inventors. Not until after 1994, because of American threats to cut trade, did the PRC more seriously enforce intellectual property laws. Legislation became serious only when political pressure, domestic or foreign, caused that to happen.

Regulatory laws to dampen market speculation had been long seen by conservatives as a pressing political need because inflation threatened the Party. Premier Li Peng in 1990 reported that his government "shall gradually explore ways to establish a system of macroeconomic regulation and control, based on the state plan."[17] But of course, this idea was not new. A "planning law" (*jihua fa*) had been mooted for the whole previous decade, in most years of which the need for better macroeconomic control was very obvious to everybody. The problem was that nobody, not even at the top, knew exactly what that law should say, to make it work in light of decreased state power. This weakness showed badly in the majestic 1990 assertion that there was, after all, a plan to have a planning law.

The need for a market-regulating securities law was evident by 1994. In the previous year, 43 percent of stock investors lost money, 32 percent approximately broke even, and profits were made by only 24 percent, even as the market generally rose. Insider trading and other abuses were rampant. A securities law "was to have been approved by the Standing Committee of the NPC in April," but ideological doubts by conservatives, who liked state company shares to be traded only under many restrictions (and who apparently represented a minority making money in this particular market), scuttled approval of the law. One of China's most prominent economists argued that "state shares should be traded, otherwise they are dead."[18] But such arguments did not carry the day politically, and passage of the securities law was put on hold for many years.

The Saga of the Press Law

No better example of reform legislating can be found than in a narrative of efforts to pass a press law. Reporters and editors needed to know what they had a right to publish, without being arrested for libel or sedition. Many cadres were very content with the prereform standard that nothing at all should be published if it might embarrass state officials. China's press law (*xinwen fa*) was a subject of intensive discussion during 1988, and three conflicting drafts of it were prepared—one by the relatively liberal ex-director of the *People's Daily* Hu Jiwei, one by a State Press and Publication Administration in the central government, and one by a group of Shanghai journalists. The main issues concerned "the supervision function of the press and the rights and obligations of reporters." Hu Jiwei's draft "stipulates the freedom of individuals to run privately owned newspapers," and the Shanghai version was explicitly allowed so that it could be enforced "as a local regulation on a trial basis if the central government failed to achieve a national law."[19]

The PRC has a public security law, some aspects of which are secret, but a press law seemed unattainable in the late 1980s. The number of libel suits against newspapers had, as a Shanghai editor said, skyrocketed during that decade; so the need for a clear code was very evident. He opined in late 1988, however, that disagreements about the content of this law were so extensive that there would be no conceivable way to finalize it soon. This reformist editor set forth his own criteria for a plaintiff's success in suits: that statements not be considered libelous unless based on falsified evidence, that the legal rights of the victim should have been violated, and (a political proviso) that the story should not have substituted the "public opinion of reporters" for that of the people.

The conservatives' criteria were tougher, but hard to specify because of their reluctance to lose Party prerogatives by setting these out in public. It was impossible to reach agreement on a law to protect reporters who uncovered scandals involving powerful cadres. The reasons go directly to Pareto's protofunctionalist needs of elites: To survive, leaderships must maintain both their integrity and their flexibility. Neither the conservative nor the reformist position was going to disappear in debates about rules like a press law. So a consensus needed for passage would take careful wording and a long time to achieve.

Aside from the issue of criteria for reporters' freedoms, many other matters were also confounded by continuing ambiguity between norms of public rights and norms of Party loyalty: whether private newspapers should be allowed in

China, whether licensing of newspapers was fully necessary if criteria for journalists' behavior were specified, and whether newspapers could report cases in which government policies differ from provisions of the constitution.[20] Such issues can only have been exacerbated by the state attack against intellectuals (including journalists) in mid-1989. The criteria for press content over the long run depended not just on more consistency in official policies, but also on the slowly evolving social interests of writers and readers.

According to a newspaper in early 1989, after about a decade of debate about this public libel rule, "The formal draft of China's Press Law will be submitted to the Standing Committee of the National People's Congress for examination toward the end of this year." Partly because of June 4, no such thing happened. Drafts of the law generally guaranteed citizens' rights to express opinions and obtain information in media, while not harming "the interests of the state, society, or collectives," and without interfering with the legal rights of other citizens.[21] Work on the press law continued into the 1990s at a slow rate.[22] But none of the three drafts of the press law had been published in the PRC, even by the mid-1990s. The ex–chief editor of the *People's Daily,* Hu Jiwei, formally retained his Party membership despite conservatives' resentment of his plea that, "there will be no genuine stability without press freedom."[23]

It was decided by the spring of 1994 that a "publication law" might be passed prior to a press law—which, however, was only "expected to be completed in two or three years."[24] This was apparently an agreement between reformers and conservatives to continue disagreeing, with all sides then presuming they could prevail in any succession dispute after Deng Xiaoping's death.

Reform Moderation in Formal Legislation

One sign of the depth of the reform process, as it affects the central Chinese state, is that even when conservatives replaced reformers in 1989, they generally held off from trying to impose major laws to their liking on most subjects (not including public demonstrations). They almost surely could have forced passage of wordings that matched their views on all topics—to do that much, they needed to control only a legislature, not the whole of China. But they apparently recognized that if the state did not conduct its business with some regard for the power of other networks, laws would soon become dead letters. That would be a *lèse-majesté;* so in this case, statist norms fooled the situation rather than vice versa.

A reformist commentator in the *Legal Daily* proposed three new ways of thinking about juridical reforms: First, "law depends on conditions of material life," so that law "cannot be replaced by class struggle"—and naturally, his main example of class struggle was the Cultural Revolution. Putting the matter this way rejected the standard Marxist argument that law is a historical result of class conflict. Second, denying a Marxist corollary that law is the tool of the ruling class, he argued, "The theory of law as the reflection of the will of the rulers actually abandons rule by law." Third, he related civil law to functional power networks, in effect, arguing, "In modern society, the legal system has an influence on various fields such as the economy, politics, culture, and science. It no longer serves political [state] struggle only." He referred to the need for better laws on ecology, population control, energy, and arbitration across jurisdictions—several of which are spheres beyond the control of a single government.[25]

Laws against sedition or counterrevolution were the focus of debates about whether all law should always be conceived as immediately political. "Counterrevolution" had been illegal in the PRC since the early 1950s. By 1991, two years after June 4, although counterrevolution was still on the books, doubts could be aired about the wisdom of keeping it a crime. Sedition, the *Legal Daily* averred, was an internationally recognized crime that would cover all the appropriate cases, so that "counterrevolution" was redundant. As the newspaper noted, "We cannot deny that the crime of counterrevolution has a political color." It said that "even learned experts" could not easily define the scope of this particular malfeasance, which made it legally "unstable," changing "according to historical conditions." The paper suggested dropping "counterrevolution" from the law codes, with its place taken by "sedition" or "endangering state security." This finally happened in 1997, but in 1991, this suggestion was necessarily conjoined with assurances that such a change would not lead to any perilous political relaxation. The essay cited a need to combat all plots that undermine the socialist system.[26] Debate continued into the 1990s, and would probably continue into the new century, on all aspects of PRC formal law in which equal fairness to citizens might discomfit the high elite.

Executive-Led Legislation

Passing laws did not ensure they would be applied, especially if they threatened the interests of hinge leaders. Exactly two months before June 4, 1989, the Administrative Litigation Law was passed, specifying the procedures by which Chinese citizens could proceed in court against bureaucrats. It was supposed to implement Article 41 of the constitution, which vows: "Citizens who have suffered losses through infringement of their civic rights by any state organ or functionary have the right to compensation."[27] But especially in conservative eras, for example. in the months after Tiananmen, PRC judges could severely limit the effect of this statue. They could, for example, classify cases into legally exempt areas (such as national security). Or else they could use narrow interpretations of the categories of abuse the Administrative Litigation Law specified, after its implementation in October 1990, and refuse to hear cases on grounds that the complaint did not fall within any relevant cause of action. Whenever they did this, of course, bureaucrats accused of abuses did not have to appear in court.

Communitarian approaches to law, emphasizing that the legal system should prevent infringements before they happen, rather than just curing them after breaches, can be espoused as a Chinese norm.[28] A conservative central government, not wanting to be pestered with litigation, naturally paints China as solidary. The actual evidence on whether law during reforms has been communitarian or individualist, centered on interdependence or on rights, is mixed. The vast majority of Chinese spoke in communitarian terms. On the other hand, a "legal reform constituency"—a "loose association of judges, legal officials, lawyers, legal scholars, and others who employ specialized legal knowledge"—wrote most of the major statutes before 1989. This group was rights-oriented.[29] PRC legal culture during reforms was based on commingled principles, both communitarian and individualist, to match the variety of political resources, norms, and elites that are obvious in the country.

Many cadres thought procedural law would be fine for saving resources on administering the masses, while special rules should apply to themselves. For some crimes, Party law applied to Party members while public law applied to everyone else. As a non-Party official openly complained in 1989, "CCP members must give up the privilege of not being punished by laws. Every human being is equal before the law. This is a common principle. But now most Party members or leaders who commit corruption are punished under the Party constitution, not under laws. . . . The CCP constitution predisposes its members to commit corruption. . . . China has laws, but the government does not emphasize them. Certain leaders' words may be more important than laws."[30]

The conservative government by 1990 explicitly tried to subordinate the rule of law to Party policies. As the president of the Supreme People's Court said in January 1990, "In the course of last year's counterrevolutionary rebellion, some people hoisted the flag of 'judicial independence.' In actual fact, these people were advocating the concept of 'the tripartite division of power' of the bourgeois class. They were opposed to the principle of the CCP's leadership of judicial work."[31] Judicial authority rested with the Political and Legal Committee of the NPC, headed by Qiao Shi, who also was chief of the secret police and of the Party's Central Discipline Inspection Commission.

Many legal codes remained incoherent or incomplete because consistency in them would have represented state promises to other people. The state's authority was declining, but this point could not be codified. So nonstate parties continued to suffer legal discrimination, as compared even to nominal state parties; and they simply avoided the law when they could. For a land law in 1990, for example, the Shanghai People's Congress passed two sets of regulations: one concerning public lands, and one on land dispute settlements.[32] But so many cadres had made so many administrative decisions about land on particularistic bases, creating precedents others could use as they chose, that the formal courts became swamped with more land business than they could handle. They made more land decisions than they could enforce. Reform norms were in practice ambiguous: In conservative periods, they used legislation wholly as a tool of the Party-state executives. At other times, they called for more fairness.

Independent-Minded Legislators

In relatively liberal periods of the reforms, some PRC legislators expressed themselves in defense of local interests more openly than at any time since 1957. As early as a mid-1980 session of the National People's Congress, Shanghai representatives spoke for the city's interests. They demanded fewer rules and less "overbearing control" of revenues by the central government. They advocated, along with Jiangsu delegates, more money for urban construction rather than capital construction. The Baoshan Iron and Steel complex was so unpopular that 150 Shanghai delegates grilled the minister of metallurgy intensively about its cost overruns, pollution, and expense for Shanghai.[33]

This pattern was repeated periodically in the liberal sub-eras of reform. A 1980 fire on an oil rig platform in China's Bohai Gulf led National People's Congress legislators to interpellate the petroleum minister and a vice premier. The former had to leave his post, and the latter was demoted. This was a famous instance nationally; but in all high-state reformist periods, legislators could be outspoken.

When Shanghai's representatives returned from a meeting of the National People's Congress on April 4, 1989, they were hailed for having put on a "great performance." "They appealed for democratization . . . asked questions about legal regulations and about the Shenzhen special economic area [which pays lower taxes and is less regulated than Shanghai]." The delegation had received notables such as Li Peng and Qiao Shi, who came "to answer the delegates' questions," so that procedures of interpellation were somewhat available even though the spirit was still statist. State Council Secretary General Luo Gan opined that this process was "very favorable" for raising the quality of decisions.[34] Perhaps some information was passed on to the central state. Ministers in China's future may come to regret that such precedents were ever set, even though they did not mean a great deal in 1989.

Modern political consultation may take this interpellative form, but a crucial part of its role is conscious institution-building. The main fact about people's congresses in China is that they are exploring what they can do. They are widely recognized as legitimate. As parts of the state, they have great prestige. But they are authorities without much real authority. Kevin O'Brien, the foremost student of legislative development in China, has concluded on the basis of extensive interviews and official sources: "Individuals on the front line of legislative work did not see themselves to be agents of pluralization, but agents of an organization scrambling for jurisdiction."[35] This describes the situation of most PRC elected officials, outside people's congresses as well as inside them.

The actual history of legislative development in many countries has occurred in two different stages. At times when kings or militarists could hold states together in an absolutist fashion, legislatures performed a relatively minor, rubber-stamping or information-gathering role. This remained the usual situation in the

PRC at least into the 1990s; and under it, legislatures could extend their jurisdiction so long as they did not contravene the will of the ruling Party, which at high levels and at most times presented an image of unity. This kind of institutional development could continue only so long as the assemblies preserved their institutional integrity—by eschewing real politics, in particular any politics between the state and nonstate oppositions.

When dissidents had a realistic hope of affecting the regime's decisions, however, a very different kind of institutional development began. Legislatures then became more pluralistic forums, in which groups vied for support. In this second stage, such assemblies became sites for coalition-building. Their seizure by any one faction could be important in deciding which social forces would win. This happened in England during the late 1640s, in the United States during the 1770s and again after the 1860s, and in France variously during the 1790s and at other times. It would ignore too much history to claim that legislatures cannot evolve in either of these stages: in the first period, when they serve the executive's agenda by becoming embedded in official politics; and in the second, when they embed the state itself in larger political structures.

Taiwan provides some Chinese comparisons on this process. For many Chinese, even in the modern world, the pinnacle of any career is to become an official (*zuo guan*). In Taiwan by the 1990s, many talented people who had already made very prosperous careers for themselves in business, arts, or journalism remained unsatisfied. None of these accomplishments were stately enough. Competing in elections to assume state offices became, by the 1990s, a real possibility for them. Many local social leaders thus dropped everything else to run for the Legislative Yuan.[36] Campaigning for votes became the modern form of the old exams because it could give much-coveted official status. On the mainland of China, reaction to a revolution at least temporarily produced more privatism. But the state was still widely respected, feared, and loved. More hinge leaders in the PRC may later run for legislatures, and help develop them as institutions, when the Chinese top leaders admit that their state can benefit from such talents.

At a late reform meeting of the Shanghai People's Congress in a relatively open era, a representative from Huangpu district complained that the delegates included no private entrepreneurs. A representative from Yangpu district pointed out, "Most of the time at this People's Congress has been spent at reports and elections, and I wish we could increase the chances for the delegates to express themselves."[37] They could do so only in their "small group" meetings; the congress itself provided time mainly for leaders' speeches.

Some legislators bluntly protested the Party's monopoly of the state. "The Communist Party's expenses should come from Party members' contributions," said Qi Wansheng, an elected non-CCP representative to the April 1989 meeting of the Shanghai People's Political Consultative Conference. He was willing, in that atypically open season, to come forth with antiregime opinions expressed in operational terms. "The conference members are still too many; the smallest committee has twenty-nine people and the biggest has forty-eight people. If every delegate is allowed to speak for fifteen minutes, some could not make second speeches, [but] administrative leaders often make two-hour speeches. So conference members lack enough time to ask the officials questions."[38]

An index of the slow change toward more important representative institutions in Shanghai was the failure of some elected delegates to show up for meetings. A 1989 report on the Third Plenary Session of the Shanghai People's Congress bewailed this apparent laziness, as do formalist democrats in the West: "Among the 890 representatives, 98 failed to show up with no [apparent] reason; and 77 more had asked for leaves of absence. During the first session, 715 delegates came half an hour after the meeting began; and by that time, 82 were taking naps. Participation then decreased further. Although 788 representatives took part in the first meeting and 762 attended the second, only 715 came to the third." Perhaps these were seriously important people, with other work to do, like members of the U.S. Congress who often miss plenary debates and committee hearings. A journalist quoted a citizen's letter castigating the delegates' performance: "He expressed his view that . . . people had a right to supervise their representatives."[39] This was not competitive democracy, and apparently some of the legislators did not fully know why they were there. But it was quite different from the fully attended meetings that had listened to Mao.

Dissent in PRC legislatures can be equated with nonsupport of official motions. Even in the National People's Congress, 40 percent of the representatives did not support an April 1989 government motion to delegate special legislative authority to Shenzhen. Only 10 percent actually voted against, but 30 percent abstained (and in this case, none were present but not voting). The dissenting portion to approve the Three Gorges Dam project in April 1992 was 33 percent. In March 1993, 19 percent dissented from a plan to streamline the government. A year later, 28 percent dissented from approval of the work report containing the state budget. A year after that, in March 1995, a new education law was not supported by 26 percent of the NPC representatives. At the same meeting, 20 percent refrained from voting to approve the work report of the Supreme People's Procurator, and 17 percent dissented from the work report of the Supreme People's Court.[40] In no case was this a majority; but in each case, it was certainly a message.

Gathering Opinions

Serious electoral contest or legislative interpellation threatened the autonomy of the state elite. But leaders during reforms increasingly felt they should know the views of the masses as a partial basis for their own decisions. So they tried to gauge these opinions by all the means, not threatening to the CCP elite, that were available. Polls, especially secret ones, were the favored method for this work.

But sampled groups of individuals do not always test the strength of feeling about issues in structured networks, and many kinds of institutions—notably newspapers—were used to gather policy information.

Government by Petition: Newspapers' Mass Work Departments

The government adapted an old Chinese tradition: humble petitions. Their new form was "letters to the editor" (commonly "letters from readers," *duzhe lai xin*) that were really to the government. The *Liberation Daily,* which receives more such letters than any other paper in Shanghai because it is the Party organ, at the height of political reforms in the early 1980s had a staff of more than forty people, whose full-time job was to handle the problems these letters raised. Its Mass Work Department (*qunzhong gongzuo bu*) was a major means for the Shanghai government to assess the severity and extent of its problems. This was a highly political job, not really a journalistic one.

Most letters to the editor that came to the *Liberation Daily* in 1979, the main year for reviewing Cultural Revolution cases, were not published. But a feature writer who had access to them expressed amazement at their variety and at the intensity of feeling in them. Expressions like "this is enough to make anybody angry!" or "resolutely struggle against this!" occurred in many such letters.[41] The exact content of most letters remained secret, but clearly their writers were many and frustrated.

Letters would not be printed if the problems they raised were "too personal, too insoluble, or too complex."[42] In such cases, they would be sent to the relevant organizations (*youguan bumen*) and to limited-circulation journals for officials. The number of letters reached a peak in 1980. Many "rightist" labels had been removed shortly before then, and many youths had just returned to Shanghai needing revival of their urban household registrations; so *Liberation Daily* was flooded with 180,000 letters that year. The Shanghai People's Congress and its subordinate courts, prosecutors, and other organizations from 1980 to 1982 also received 15,329 letters and 7,650 personal visits.[43]

Gradually, as reforms continued, fewer people wrote letters about personal grievances, either because these had been solved or because victims had given up hope of a solution. This work rose and fell with the cycles of reform. By 1986, only 51,000 letters came to the *Liberation Daily* editor; and by 1987, the mails brought only 40,300. This still meant an average daily intake of such letters, at this one newspaper, of well over a hundred per day.

The Mass Work Department divided all petitions into three categories: "supervisory" (i.e., complaints from citizens against particular cadres or official agencies), "participatory" (i.e., policy suggestions), and "informational" (i.e., new facts that were brought to the attention of these journalists).[44] One quarter of all the contacts were "supervisory," mostly concerning accusations against officials who were deemed arrogant or badly behaved. There was a slight decline in the frequency of "supervisory" complaints during the second half of 1986 over the first half, probably because people were warier of bringing such complaints then as political tensions rose. On the other hand, the letters or visits that involved political participation greatly increased as larger numbers of people came forward to advocate particular policies. Shanghai's "construction plans" were often the topic of these advances, which was unsurprising, in light of the backlog of projects that had been unfunded for decades. The "informational" approaches also rose in 1986, especially concerning news on commodity shortages.

The staff then handled each missive in one of four ways: First, a few were published in the weekly column of letters to the editor. Second, some were published alongside other articles dealing with allied topics, and occasionally the letter was the original basis for reporting the subject. But these two methods covered only a tiny fraction of the cases that the letters brought to light. One-fifth of the mails received by editors were handled in the third possible manner, by being printed in limited-circulation "internal publications" (*neibu kanwu*), which exist for just this purpose on both a daily and a weekly basis locally in Shanghai and nationally. The fourth category of letters (about 65 percent of the total received) were sent to other organizations, usually the Party office that supervises the work unit of the sender. These agencies were supposed to solve the problems—not a very effective procedure, since they were usually headed by the leaders who had caused those problems.

Polls and Meetings

Opinion surveys are a special fad of authoritarian regimes. They promise political information without politics. Pollsters seemed useful, perhaps as a means less dangerous than democracy for gathering public opinion. Wu Xin, a Chinese statistician who was dubbed "China's George Gallup" (and favored "tweed sports jackets and modish shirts") said, "Since the reforms, the economic system has been changed a lot. The government wants to know if the mass of people will go along with it." This pollster tried to develop "methods to surmount the hurdles of inhibition" among PRC survey respondents, such as assuring their anonymity.[45]

Surveys became a veritable movement in China. From 1984 to 1987, the State Statistical Bureau developed "opinion sampling groups" with ten thousand investigators nationwide. Between May and June 1987, these groups conducted the first big survey on how reforms affected ordinary citizens' daily lives. In July, another survey concerning political reform was performed in eight large cities, including Shanghai.[46] These polls need not be discussed at length here because they are used to treat their subjects in many other sections of this book. But their currency was a governmental reform. They supplemented more classic means of gathering information.

Meetings between CCP leaders and groups of citizens often occurred, both to suggest the officials' sensitivity and to gather information. Mayor Jiang Zemin made highly publicized efforts to consult ordinary Shanghai residents. In 1987, for example, he held six roundtable discussions with workers, students, teachers, scientists, peasant leaders, and "public figures." This public relations campaign was explicitly designed to make contact with local leaders, in a population that had grievances. Jiang Zemin suggested his consciousness of the main problem: "Holding these discussions is not paying lip service, but is aimed at really helping to solve difficulties so that we can win their confidence."[47]

State leaders could not always control the agendas of such sessions. When Mayor Jiang in late 1987 called a meeting of the city's branch of the Chinese People's Political Consultative Conference—to talk about another subject—he nonetheless got questions from the floor about Shanghai's egregious traffic congestion (a topic reported to be "of much interest to Shanghai people") and about the housing shortage.[48]

The mayor of Shanghai also receives letters. When Zhu Rongji took that post at the end of April 1988, his office was receiving three to four thousand letters per month. At least one citizen said, "We have a lot of things to tell the leaders, but we wonder whether the leaders hear and see them." A university student in the field of politics and law wrote a letter responding to a speech by the mayor, who had said taxi drivers charging too much would be punished. The student asked how serious such infractions would have to become actually to receive the attention of the police. He also asked whether a temporary, campaign-like emphasis from the mayor's office (as distinct from more permanent rules in the specialized unit, the taxi company) should be the basis for punishing people.[49] Resentment at the arrogance of cadres was a major theme in many letters.

Discussion Within the Party and Administration

The difficulty of individual petitions and group meetings with leaders was the medium, not the message. These means of gathering information all implied that the Party-state was the only effective structure for political communication in China. When ordinary citizens or groups of leaders met with CCP potentates, or when an individual sent a letter to the state via a newspaper, the main content was often not the petition, but the hierarchy.

Probably the most effective information gathering during China's reforms occurred in Party meetings that were not public. With more intellectuals in the Party, more free-ranging discussions occurred in many reform era CCP meetings. Since such conclaves are secret, the evidence for this is mainly circumstantial—from traits and changes of policies or from interviews that cannot easily be cross-checked. But there is much evidence of these kinds. The Party organization in the Shanghai Economic Planning Commission, in relatively open subperiods of reform, for example, made efforts to establish a "system of democratic life." This followed a national regulation to encourage such change, and it involved rules that mandated more regular meetings among all CCP members in subordinate units.

New regulations also required that top Party secretaries come to these meetings, which they often had not done in some earlier periods. They were supposed to be patient when hearing new ideas and criticisms. The topics at such sessions were various. At the Shanghai Plastics Factory, for example, seven "democratic life meetings" convened in 1980.[50] Participants criticized the continuing influence of leftists in the company's Party apparatus. Complaints were aired about the need to improve equipment in basic-level factories, to raise standards for the company's housing for workers, and to alleviate excessive pressures to work overtime (presumably at the ends of plan quota periods).[51] Managers were urged to "seek truth from facts" at these "democratic life meetings."

After such sessions, the Party Committee of the Inland Rivers Docking Company changed its leaders in 1981. The aim was to promote leaders whose views were consonant with norms before and after the Cultural Revolution, rather than during that period.[52] Some leaders were accused of corruption at public assemblies that had been billed as normal meetings. For example, when three cadres did not go through the proper procedures to expand their apartment sizes, questions arose at a "democratic life meeting." They had to submit self-criticisms and give up rooms to other families that had amounts of living space below average. Such meetings might also unearth evidence that helped the tops of hierarchies, rather than hinge cadres. For example, when a factory's leaders failed to report above-quota production and illegally converted it directly into bonuses for workers, this fact emerged at a meeting and led to a local change. The meetings sometimes could resolve conflicts between factory managers and Party secretaries. When a manager disagreed with his CCP secretary on the question of which workers should receive bonuses, a "democratic life meeting" was called to decide the matter.

Regular, rather than ad-hoc campaign-style, consultations between Communist and other leaders in economic affairs were encouraged during some periods of reform. Shanghai's Golden Triangle Club by 1987 was holding activities at least twice a month. It organized many "salons" for lawyers, economists, business consultants, and Party secretaries.[53] More than four hundred entrepreneurs were regularly involved, and every month they contributed to a limited-circulation journal called the *Information Insider*.[54] The club also organized conferences, including a "consultancy meeting on horizontal economic liaisons."

"Building more intimate links between the government and the masses" was the stated purpose of the 1991 administrative reforms. Officials certainly did not advocate liberal democracy, but they felt there was a need to "perfect the decision-making mechanism and ensure that policies are decided in a scientific way." The "external relations" of state agencies were said to require improvement. Many agency bureaucrats' reply to the rise of local power structures in their areas was to resent the loss of their influence, serve applicants even less well than before, pull in their heads, and collect their salaries.[55] But this pattern separated the state from local evidence that would have been required for effective administration.

"Democratic" Parties and Intellectuals' Timidity in Politics

Chinese intellectuals can hardly be blamed for reticence, after the Party's preda-tions against them for expressing their views. In 1978, Deng Xiaoping claimed at a National Science Conference that intellectuals were members of the working class. By the next year, many of their leaders had their pejorative "rightist" labels removed. They nonetheless remained politically weak, as their return to politics in tame "democratic" parties attests.

These "satellite parties" in Shanghai revived their activities in late 1979. Many had not met at all since before the Cultural Revolution. Democratic political parties had branches in districts and in major universities, as well as in some financial institutions. Because most of them were created to attract intellec-tuals, they had only a few members in the industrial economy.[56] New entrepre-neurs, especially in rural areas, were not represented in these groups, most of whose members joined in the 1950s and by midreforms were fairly old.

A full list of the democratic parties registered in the 1980s, with membership totals and types for some of them in 1984, in rough order by size, is as follows:[57]

- The Democratic League (*Minzhu tongmeng,* or *Min meng* for short; first established in Shanghai, 1953), 50,000 members, stresses members in cultural and educational work, especially universities.
- The Revolutionary Committee of the KMT (*Guomindang geming weiyuanhui,* or *Min ge* for short; established in 1949), 20,000 members, specializes in ex-members of Chiang Kai-shek's party who became loyal to the PRC, but who are now mostly old like their copartisan mainlanders on Taiwan, with whom the PRC state enjoins them to make connections.
- The Association for Promoting Democracy (*Minzhu zujin hui,* 1949), 15,000 members, contains mainly school teachers.
- The September Third Study Association (*Jiusan xueshe,* 1946), 12,000 members, a party composed largely of scholars and scientists.
- The Democratic National Development Party (*Minzhu jianguo dang,* 1956), 12,000 members, recruits teachers in primary, middle, and high schools, normal universities, cultural fields, and the press.
- The Farmers' and Workers' Democratic Party (*Nonggong minzhu dang,* 1949), despite its name, contains many medical and health-care workers.
- The Justice Party (*Zhigong dang,* a United Front effort during the reforms, established at Shanghai in 1980, its name might also loosely be translated "Extend the Public Party") is mainly for returned overseas Chinese, many of whom had difficult years during the Cultural Revolution.
- The Taiwan Democratic Autonomous League (*Taiwan minzhu zizhi tongmeng,* or *Tai meng,* 1949) is for Taiwanese who live on the mainland, some of whom—like some members of each of the groups listed above— are concurrently members of the Communist Party.

To use a single word, "party," to describe these groupings and the CCP together is to strain the very concept of definition. To call them "democratic" refers to the conscious values of many members in some of them, rather than to any function they perform in a larger context. Very few Chinese, even in the population of a city like Shanghai, were members. The membership of the Communist Party in China was several hundred times that of all the "democratic parties" combined. Some prominent intellectuals nonetheless participated, and (as with national minority groups) it was a norm of the United Front that leaders from non-CCP parties should hold some seats in political assemblies.

Many of these in particular were concurrently CCP members. About one-tenth of the 1988 Chinese People's Political Consultative Conference members were at once in the CCP and a democratic party. Their ability to represent the "democratic" parties, as distinct from their other Party, must be questioned. But the main criterion for leadership during reforms was in any case educational. Four-fifths of this assembly's members had university degrees, and more than one-half were in academic or cultural work.[58] These were certainly not China's main politicians, although they had a good deal of social prestige. In some years, especially during relatively liberal times in the 1980s, CCP reformers solicited their help, which often came timidly.

The *People's Daily*, at least in early 1988, encouraged intellectuals to complain more. An engineer who had been sent to the loess plateau in poverty-stricken Shanxi had been "dogged with misfortunes," even though after graduating from university he had volunteered for hard work, had "transformed pieces of barren, uncultivated land into fine, fertile land," and had "persisted in his ideals." Apparently he came from a dubious family background, but the *People's Daily* itself said he deserved the high title of "iron man." At the same time, this Party organ criticized him for his willingness "to be wronged, to be oppressed, and to be falsely accused in social and political life." Cadres in his unit had brought charges in 1984 that he was involved in economic corruption and "had committed millions of crimes." The *People's Daily* said that an intellectual should "not have been unaware that he could employ a lawyer to protect his legal rights." He had not resisted accusations that later proved to be groundless. The newspaper said this meekness was "a common characteristic of many Chinese intellectuals. . . . Confronted with a violent oppressive force, they will show their weak points—they dare not wage determined struggle against a situation in which power is abused."

The CCP paper rightly blamed this fault on "the harm done to intellectuals by previous political movements." It said, "Over a long period, many comrades praised intellectuals without analyzing them. . . . The practice of suffering a wrong in the general interest and enduring humiliation in order to carry out important missions are considered as sublime moral traits; the practice of leading a non-practical life and neglecting family in order to fulfill tasks are considered as unselfish contributions."[59] But the intellectuals had reasons—built into the polity for which the *People's Daily* was trying to mobilize their talents—for doubts about this new world, in which political conflict was said to be allowable.

Demonstrating

Mainstream Chinese tradition is supposed to give expressive people, who generally have advanced educations, a special burden in government. During Mao's time, for just this reason, the lowest of low statuses in politics had been nationally reserved for intellectuals. As the revolution was centralizing after 1949, the traditional formal offices of censors, whose main duty was to urge morality on emperors, had long since been abolished as a bother to the state. Traditionally, upright officials might, for cause, "curse the emperor" or even metaphorically "hit the emperor."[60]

Modern intellectuals sometimes assumed this old job, even though they seldom enjoyed any official mandate to do so in the PRC. The habit was sharply curbed after the Antirightist witch hunt in 1956–57, which can be seen as the most important watershed in PRC political history before the early 1970s. The number of "rightist" critics of the CCP at that time may have been half a million.[61] This was not a large part of China's population, but the rightists were overwhelmingly intellectuals, and their number was large enough to cover most of China's independent minds then. Their critical tradition was very strong, but that by itself did not give them legal opportunities to guide the state by censoring it.

Constitutional Expression and Movement Democracy

The Cultural Revolution gave political expression a dubious name, but some concepts of political rights survived even this attack. As early as January 1975, Article 13 of a new state constitution spelled out the "four big freedoms" (so called because the Chinese phrase for each includes the word *da,* "big"):

> Speaking out frankly, airing views fully, holding great debates, and writing big character posters are new forms of carrying on socialist revolution created by the masses of the people. The state shall ensure . . . the right to use these forms to create a political situation in which there are both centralism and democracy, both discipline and freedom . . . and so consolidate the leadership of the CCP over the state and consolidate the dictatorship of the proletariat.[62]

This wording already contained tensions between the ideals of freedom and discipline, such as pervaded the reforms. Leftist support for freedom of expression made it an easy target, later, for reform conservatives. The wording of the 1982 state Constitution was less broad for this right, which nonetheless remains a vital plank for liberals.

Public demonstrations were a right enshrined in Article 35 of the 1982 Constitution, but that edition deleted references to the "four big freedoms." Not all public demonstrations were authorized. When, as in rallies expressing resentment against Japan, for example, the demonstrators did not challenge PRC state interests, they could march with state acquiescence and without repression. But when Shanghai students demonstrated for political reform in 1986, for example, the more conservative Articles 51 and 53 of the constitution were said to limit Article 35.[63] These illiberal provisions made any exercise of rights contingent on service to the interests of the state.

Political rallies occurred in several Chinese cities during the mid-1980s, but until December 1986 they were mostly outside Shanghai. These usually reflected broad frustrations among urban youths, rather than any more specific political platform. In May 1985, for instance, the defeat of China's soccer team by Hong Kong's led to a riot in Beijing that involved thousands of people and damaged two dozen vehicles. A few months later, several cities saw student demonstrations against Japan's "economic invasion" of China; but many observers said that students were also expressing vexation with their own lot. In June 1986, Tianjin fishing people demonstrated at their city hall for higher wages. In Shanghai, rusticated youths demonstrated to get their household registrations restored; and suburban farmers demonstrated against incursions by state companies on their lands. In July, a soccer riot involving several thousand youths erupted in Xi'an. In early September 1986, Nanjing was the site of yet another rampage after a soccer match; but the game seems to have been less important than many of the fans' discontent at being unemployed. More than two thousand people jammed traffic in downtown Nanjing for more than two hours, singing a theme song from a television series, in which a militant Buddhist monk chants, "My hat is tattered, my shoes are full of holes, my clothes are shabby, and you laugh at me. But wherever there is injustice, you will find me."[64]

During the December 1986 demonstrations, Shanghai students marched to each other's universities, to the city hall on the Bund, and to the municipal Congress on People's Square demanding democracy, freedom, human rights, and an end to police beatings.[65] Jiaotong and Fudan universities were especially active in these 1986 rallies, which began in Shanghai before they spread to Beijing.[66] The rallies in many cities nationwide, especially in the context of Soviet *perestroika,* gave conservatives an opportunity to sack the reformist Party head Hu Yaobang. But the central government was still split between and lions and foxes. Their conflict was already muted by a sense that, even if either group could defeat the other, neither could greatly affect the rate of China's change in many places.

June 4 in Shanghai

The famous sequel to Hu Yaobang's death, in the spring of 1989, needs no full retelling here. Shanghai's students and populace, following their peers in the capital at this time, exercised their freedoms of expression far beyond what either the high-level state reformers or conservatives had expected. A *People's Daily* editorial of April 26, 1989, became infamous for claiming that the student movement was "a planned conspiracy . . . a disorder fabricated by a small minority of people." Perhaps because of many intellectuals' interest in "neoauthoritarianism" at this time, the students wanted to make sure that they were at least potentially in authority. They rallied to protest their elders' corruption and mismanagement, and thus to assume Chinese intellectuals' ancient duty of moral censorship in public.

At an East China Normal University meeting, Shanghai students raised one major political demand—freedom of speech—with a set of related specific requests: an end to censorship of the student newspaper, time on the university radio station, enactment of an earlier promise to raise student stipends, and no punishments for demonstrators. Six thousand students marched from Fudan and East China Normal Universities to People's Square on May 2, carrying banners that read "Give us Democracy and Freedom," "Oppose Privileges," and "The Media Must Tell the Truth."[67] They had asked no official permission for the rally. The whole event was peaceful, and this encouraged further demonstrations. By May 8, even a government source reported that the number of people at the rally was "over ten thousand."[68]

On May 16, several Shanghai students began a hunger strike. That same day, a crowd of 4,000 sat down for this purpose on the Bund. The main issues were freedom of speech, corruption, and dialogue about these topics with high government officials. Banners designated the schools from which the demonstrators came, but not all in the crowd were young. One sign, over an elderly group, bore the simple title "Citizens of Shanghai."

Ba Jin, one of China's most famous novelists and an honored senior citizen of Shanghai, was now often in the geriatric ward of Huadong Hospital; but on May 18, Ba Jin went on Shanghai television. He compared the May 4, 1919, movement for democracy with the 1989 one: "Not enough has changed in the last seventy years. Everyone should support the students one hundred percent."[69]

Media broadcasts, such as had been less open in previous years, made the rallies important. The arrival of Gorbachev in Beijing, and the concentration of newspeople there, meant that most listeners in Shanghai could follow events in the capital as easily as those in their own city. Most Shanghai people were extremely reluctant to confront the government. But the students were obviously pressing the regime to be less corrupt, and that cause was popular. Many ordinary citizens could "have their cake and eat it too," watching from the sidelines, respecting the old language of obeisance, naively hoping the intellectuals in government and in dissent were smart enough to know what they were doing. The structure of official institutions was no more democratic than before, and many urban people felt the students were pressing for good goals with jejune tactics. But the vague goals of the movement had much support among nonintellectuals in

Shanghai. This was a case of informal, partial, unsolicited representation by the students, without stable laws to make anything like it permanent.

Four hundred students held a hunger strike in front of the Party's headquarters on the Bund. By the time Li Peng in Beijing called on "the whole Party, the whole army, and the whole nation to make concerted efforts and to act immediately at all posts to stop the turmoil and stabilize the situation . . . and play the role of the core leadership and fighting fortress," the core of demonstrators in Shanghai was accompanied by twenty thousand other students and workers. Some waved banners, saying "Li Peng does not represent us." Others erected on the Bund a ten-foot polystyrene replica of Beijing's Goddess of Democracy.[70]

The challenge to the Party extended quickly among many citizens not just because of recent inflation and corruption, but also because of long-term grievances from the Cultural Revolution and earlier movements. The Shanghai Symphony, on May 21 and 26, held a concert to raise money for the students, playing Beethoven's Sixth Symphony, the Chinese national anthem, and the "Internationale." Because city officials disallowed ticket sales, money was collected directly inside the music hall. Funds for the students came not just from intellectuals, but also from many others. In a street market, students passing a basket between stalls collected money for their movement—and some donors put large bills in the basket, even though this was a relatively poor part of the city.[71]

The next few days were nervous, as many in Shanghai thought the government might move troops into the center of town. May 28, 1989, was the fortieth anniversary of Shanghai's liberation by the PLA; a festive commemoration had long been planned at People's Square. Students joined in, but for a different purpose.[72] June 4 brought shocking news from the north, which traveled throughout Shanghai by both electronic means and grass telegraph immediately. The municipal government was careful: The rallies continued. Police disappeared from the streets, and no tanks came.

Shanghai was in a general strike as students set up roadblocks on all major streets (which are narrower in Shanghai than in Beijing). They easily commandeered buses, parked them across roads, and deflated the tires. This blockade was effective from June 5, when the Shanghai media reported 123 intersections impassable, until late June 8 (although some barricades were temporarily removed by worker militia on June 6 to allow food deliveries).[73] The city government sent a message by doing nothing.

Mayor Zhu Rongji's June 8 television speech was—like previous statements from the local regime—less strident against the Tiananmen demonstrators than the vitriolic statements then emanating from Beijing and most other provinces. According to one report, hard-liners in Beijing had sent Zhu a speech to read; but "when the show went on the air, he reached into his breast pocket, seemingly for his eyeglasses, and conspicuously patted his clothes in search of them; he then laid aside the text and delivered his own ad-lib speech."[74] Not once did Mayor

Zhu refer to "counterrevolutionary elements," although he mentioned "unlawful elements." He said he had never considered ordering troops into Shanghai, although he would have to enforce the law and would send workers to remove the street blockades.

Broaching thoughts that had obviously occurred to the demonstrators—while perhaps separating his own views from what his job required—Zhu warned, "Do not misjudge the situation. Don't dream of a change in dynasty." He promised to hold discussion meetings with students (and the next day, a group of them marched peacefully for a vigil at People's Square, Shanghai, in memory of the people who had been killed in Beijing). Zhu's ambiguous but sensitive politics in this speech was capped by his reference to the "rumors" of killings in the capital. "I am not going to discuss these rumors with you. All I want to say is: Things that occurred in Beijing are history. No one can conceal history. The truth will eventually come to light. Why do you have to believe those things? Why do you have to listen to one-sided rumors?"[75] But Zhu did not say the reports were false. Indeed, most people in Shanghai knew they were true.

This subtle politics, which was well adjusted to the ambiguity of reforms and to the tenor of this city, prevented extensive violence in Shanghai. The only serious incident that occurred was on the night of June 6, when a train outside the Shanghai train station ran over workers trying to block it. A leftist Hong Kong newspaper reported that eight people were killed and thirty were hurt.[76] In Shanghai, as in the capital, most casualties in 1989 were workers, not students; but the number in Shanghai was relatively small. Many could see that the city government had not instigated the disaster near the train station, although it executed those who caused it. Shanghai's Party administrators at this time certainly included both lions and foxes. The mayor was able, even at this tense time, to present a surprisingly balanced regime in public.

Less publicly, and to reassure conservatives, the regime took the chance to move against local networks that were allegedly seditious. Shanghai police arrested leaders of the China Youth Democratic Party (Zhongguo Qingnian Minzhu Dang) and the Freedom Society (Ziyou She) on June 10. Police reported that since 1986 the general secretary of the former group, Wang Zhengming, had called for the Communist Party to "step down." They claimed that since 1989 Wang had formed branches of the China Youth Party at Fudan, Tongji, and other Shanghai universities. The head of the Freedom Society, Li Zhiguo, had since March 1989 reportedly recruited students for the establishment of a "kingdom of great freedom," allegedly asking them to learn gunnery and establish guerrilla base areas. His society was said to use formal red seal chops and to have designated its new flag, official flower, and currency.[77]

Autonomous trade unions were similarly repressed, but these were reported even less fully or reliably, because labor dissidence is extremely sensitive in a would-be proletarian state. On June 15, 1989, three workers who had protested the Tiananmen crackdown by burning a train at the Shanghai Railway Station were sentenced to death. Treatment of intellectuals was less severe, even though some journalists at the *World Economic Herald* were imprisoned and questioned.

June 4 and Afterward, Elsewhere on the Shanghai Delta

The 1989 unrest affected other cities of East China at least as much as Shanghai. Discontent with inflation and corruption was high in many cities. Intellectuals even after the June 4 repression were willing to say they supported the movement for democracy. A survey taken shortly after June 4 among students at the Hangzhou Electronics Industrial Institute revealed surprisingly high percentages who were willing to trust the interviewers (or imperil their own careers). Only 2 percent of seniors or juniors at that school said they had "opposed, looked down on, or resisted" the June 4 movement. Another 2 percent of the juniors—but 10 percent of the seniors, then seeking job placements—said they were "unconcerned and did not participate." Of the overwhelming remainder, about one-third "did not support but sympathized and observed," and about two-thirds said they "supported and participated in" the democracy movement.

Almost as striking were these students' reactions to the government's propaganda after the repression. One-quarter said the official publicity "had no result; turned a deaf ear to it." About half said it had only "some result, but only grudging." Only the remaining quarter (who were practically all seniors needing career recommendations) said they accepted the official line.[78] Propaganda was, among these students, not very effective at least in the short run. The state elites, receiving this kind of poll information regularly, were quite aware of their unpopularity among students. In Mao's time, PRC police had been more active against the leaders of dissent. But by the reforms, people who held antiregime opinions were not in great danger so long as they did not express these openly. This pattern was usual in the most tense periods of basic decompressions after political centralizations. Dissent had become tolerable, so long as it was not public. A British law of 1661 forbade the submission of public petitions to the king or Parliament by more than ten persons.[79]

Temporary Halts of Most Reforms, but Repression of Parades

The Tiananmen massacre put conservatives in power at Beijing for a while, and it slowed reforms for a while. But the state leadership could not, even if it wished, reverse most structural changes from the mid-1980s. Even in legislation, reforms merely stalled; they were not rolled back. The press law and the planning law had each been mooted for a dozen years by the early 1990s; but after Tiananmen as before it, there was so much disagreement about what they should say, they were still very difficult to finalize.[80] A "Law on Administrative Litigation" (*xingzheng susong fa*) had been passed exactly two months before June 4,

1989. It was not repealed, although its provisions restricting bureaucrats were not much enforced yet.[81] The law went into effect in October 1990.

The "Law on Assemblies, Parades, and Demonstrations" (*jihui youxing shiwei fa*), which came into force on October 31, 1989, very clearly reflected the determination of conservatives never again to allow an event such as had stung them so badly at Tiananmen.[82] Although the accompanying propaganda assured the public that the law on demonstrations had been under preparation for more than a decade, its harsh provisions—if followed—would give the state complete control over any public expression on the streets. This was an exception to the more persistent principle that very formal legislation should represent a consensus between lions and foxes, and the conservatives clearly meant it as a symbol of their anger.

The provisions of this ukase outlawed collective political expression against the regime. Prior demonstration permits were required in all cases, except for memorial meetings run by units on their private premises. The applicants had to be state-recognized organizations, whose leaders took personal responsibility for any violation of laws or conditions that later occurred. The application had to declare an assembly's "aims, forms, slogans, posters, participants' names, vehicle license numbers, kind of sound equipment, the time period, place, route of march, and the responsible people's names, occupations, and addresses." It was explained that outside or later participants could not be admitted because "other people's joining of the demonstration will increase the difficulty of maintaining order and may lead to unexpected results." All such expressions were to be held within spatial "cordons" that the state or any of its organizations might decree, and between the hours of 6:00 A.M. and 10:00 P.M. only (thus on no more than one day running). No bones were made in the warning that "if participants refuse to dismiss themselves, police have the right to dismiss them through necessary forceful methods."[83] These were procedures, as formal and legal as anybody could wish, but with the clear aim of slowing reforms. They would succeed only if people followed them.

Notes

1. Xu Guangtai in *Zhonggong zhengquan sishi nian de huigu yu zhanwang* (Recollections and Prospects on the Forty Years of CCP Power), Wu An-chia, ed. (Taipei: Guoji Guanxi Yanjiu Zhongxin, 1991), pp. 310–11.

2. Frances Hoar Foster, "Codification in Post-Mao China," *American Journal of Comparative Law* 30 (Summer 1982), pp. 398–410, details the difference between seven such stages from August 1977 to November 1981 alone.

3. "Clear out" is *qingli,* a word with a revolutionary history. The world press did not come to Yinchuan for this meeting. The growth of local laws in earlier years is, however, the main news. *RMRBHWB,* September 12, 1990.

4. *Jiben guoce.* See Wong Siu-lun, "Consequences of China's New Population Policy," *China Quarterly* 98 (June 1984), pp. 220–40; and Tyrene White, "Postrevolutionary Mobilization in China: The One-Child Policy Reconsidered," *World Politics* 43 (October

1990), pp. 53–76. Cf. also Kate Zhou Xiao, *How the Farmers Changed China* (Boulder: Westview, 1995).

5. These types are *minfa, xingfa, xingzheng fa, guojia fa,* and *susong fa.* See Xu Guangtai in *Zhonggong zhengquan,* p. 312.

6. These were respectively called *hunyin jiating fa, laodong fa, shehui fuli fa, jingji fa, ziran ziyuan he huanjing baohu fa, ke jiao wen fa, junshi fa,* and *minzu fa.*

7. Xu Guangtai in *Zhonggong zhengquan,* p. 310.

8. *CD,* March 24, 1988.

9. Murray Scot Tanner, "The Politics of Lawmaking in Post-Mao China: Institutions, Processes, and Democratic Prospects," (book manuscript), pp. 4–20. See also Kevin J. O'Brien, *Reform Without Liberalization: China's National People's Congress* (New York: Cambirdge University Press, 1990), pp. 150–51 and 158–64.

10. Alex B. Clavel, "Law and Authoritarianism in China, 1978–1995" (Senior thesis, Princeton University, East Asian Studies, 1995), p. 50.

11. *"Shanghai shi qingshao nian baohu tiaolie" lifa jishi* (Record on the Legislation of the 'Rules for Protection of Youths and Infants in Shanghai'), Drafting Office for the "Rules for Protection of Youths and Infants in Shanghai," ed. (Shanghai: Shanghai Shehui Kexue Yuan Chuban She, 1987), pp. 402 and 406.

12. This official was in Beijing. *CD,* October 31, 1988.

13. *Post,* July 21, 1988.

14. *LW* 41 (November 1988), p. 6.

15. Yao Shihuang, *Jin sanjiao de tansuo* (Search for the Golden Delta) (Chongqing: Chongqing Chuban She, 1988), pp. 35–68.

16. The Chinese text of this law is in *WHB,* Hong Kong, September 9, 1990.

17. Quoted in Margaret Y. K. Woo, "Legal Reforms in the Aftermath of Tiananmen Square," *Review of Socialist Law,* 1991, p. 55.

18. The economist was Professor Li Yining. See *Eastern Express,* March 8, 1994.

19. *CD,* November 25, 1988.

20. *SHJJDB,* August 29, 1988.

21. *CD,* February 13, 1989.

22. *WHB,* Hong Kong, June 22, 1990.

23. This is the title of a column that Hu Jiwei wrote in one of the last issues of the *World Economic Herald.* See Allison Liu Jernow, "An Attempt at Amicable Divorce: Legislating for a Free Press," *Human Rights Tribune* 3:2 (Summer 1992), p. 15.

24. These words are from a spokesman of the State Press and Publication Administration. *CD,* March 5, 1994.

25. Zhang Zonghou, reported in *CD,* September 21, 1988.

26. *Fazhi ribao* (Legal Daily), quoted in *Post,* March 15, 1991.

27. On the *xingzheng susong fa,* see Richard Dicker, "A Law for Change—With Loopholes," *Human Rights Tribune* 3:2 (Summer 1992), pp. 7–9.

28. This approach was once advocated by Victor H. Li, when he was a professor at Stanford Law School but had also experienced legal justice in inner-city Detroit; see "Law and Penology: Systems of Reform and Correction," in *China's Developmental Experience,* Michel C. Oksenberg, ed. (New York: Praeger Publishers, 1973), pp. 144–56.

29. Richard Dicker, "A Law for Change"; also Pitman B. Potter, "The Administrative Litigation Law of the PRC: Judicial Review and Bureaucratic Reform," in *Domestic Law Reform in Post-Mao China,* Pitman B. Potter, ed. (Armonk, NY: M.E. Sharpe, 1993).

30. *Renmin zhengxie bao* (People's Political Consultative News), April 4, 1989.

31. *Post,* January 5, 1990.

32. *WHB,* Hong Kong, September 1, 1990.

33. Dorothy J. Solinger, *China's Transition from Socialism: Statist Legacies and*

Market Reforms, 1980–1990 (Armonk, NY: Sharpe, 1993), pp. 46–47, and Kevin J. O'Brien, *Reform Without Liberalization,* pp. 101–3.

34. *XMWB,* April 5, 1989.

35. Kevin O'Brien, "Chinese People's Congresses and Legislative Imbeddedness: Understanding Early Institutional Development," draft of paper for *Comparative Political Studies,* p. 9.

36. This is based on many conversations in Taiwan during the summer of 1993.

37. *JFRB,* April 20, 1988.

38. Ling Fang and Wu Xiaobo in *Lianhe shibao* (United Daily), April 28, 1989.

39. *XMWB,* April 24, 1989, covers both the quotations in this paragraph. E. E. Schattschneider, *The Semi-Sovereign People: A Realist's View of American Democracy* (Hinsdale, IL: Dreyden Press, 1975), contains eloquent sections that question hand-wringing about low voter participation. This is a problem for some intellectuals' democratic theories, but not for democracy. Most people may actually know what they are doing.

40. Vote totals are offered in Murray Scot Tanner, "The Politics of Lawmaking," table 2. During the Shanghai vote, Kevin O'Brien was in the gallery. He reports that the counting took fifteen minutes, after one thousand hands went up. "It was quite a sight." Personal communication to the author.

41. *JFRB,* October 18, 1979. This article postdates any major influence by Hua Guofeng in national politics; but interestingly, it praises his role in smashing the Gang of Four. It advocates change, but not too fast.

42. From a 1988 interview with an editor in Shanghai.

43. *Shanghai shehui xiankuang he qushi, 1980–1983* (Situations and Trends in Shanghai Society, 1980–1983), Zheng Gongliang et al., eds. (Shanghai: Huadong Shifan Daxue Chuban She, 1988), pp. 231–32.

44. The letters and visits are classed as *"jiandu lei," "canzheng lei,"* or *"xinxi lei." JFRB,* January 26, 1987.

45. On Wu Xin, read *Hongkong Standard,* November 1, 1987. On Chinese surveys, see Stanley Rosen, "Value Change Among Post-Mao Youth: The Evidence from Survey Data," in *Unofficial China,* Perry Link et al., eds. (Boulder: Westview, 1990), pp. 193–216.

46. *FBIS,* December 17, 1987, p. 17, reporting radio of the same day.

47. Mayor Jiang's political form, in these meetings, was remarkably similar to that adopted by the mainlander leader on Taiwan, Chiang Ching-kuo (Chiang Kai-shek's son), who also sought to win the hearts of a population that could air its own problems. See *FBIS,* December 7, 1987, p. 39, reporting radio of December 5.

48. *FBIS,* December 15, 1987, p. 27, reporting *JFRB* of December 6.

49. *JFRB,* October 17, 1988.

50. *Minzhu shenghuo hui. JFRB,* March 26, 1981.

51. Workers were compensated for "adding of shifts" (*jiabian jiadian*) toward the end of quota periods with extra pay, according to interviewees; but they were under pressure to produce at such times.

52. Inland river wharfs had been major centers of Triad and other activity that the CCP had difficulty controlling since the early 1950s. Workers from northern Jiangsu were common in trades there, as was a variety of other subethnic groups. The article in *JFRB,* March 26, 1981, does not delve into all aspects of the topic it suggests.

53. These meetings were called, from the French, *shalong*—and the CCP secretaries' *"dangwei shuji shalong"* had a particularly euphonious, reformist ring to its name. *JFRB,* February 2, 1987.

54. *Xinxi neikan.*

55. *Post,* January 21, 1991.

56. *WHB,* May 16, 1979.

57. Some official lists of local *minzhu dangpai* also include the Shanghai Federation of Industry and Commerce (*Shanghai shi gongshang ye lianhe hui*)—which would be less odd if the others acted more like political parties. *Tongzhan gongzuo shouce* (Handbook of United Front Work), Ma Fen et al., eds. (Shanghai: Shanghai Renmin Chuban She, 1989), a Shanghai source, refers to all of these but the Association for Promoting Democracy. The main source in English is James D. Seymour, *China's Satellite Parties* (Armonk, NY: M.E. Sharpe, 1987), cf. p. viii. A comprehensive book is *Zhongguo minzhu dangpai: lishi, zhenggang, renwu* (China's Democratic Parties: Histories, Platforms, and Personages), Qin Guosheng and Hu Zhisheng, eds. (Jinan: Shandong Renmin Chuban She, 1990).

58. These are approximate estimates, based on calculations from CPPCC respondents to a survey about journalism. Hou Jun, *Piruan de yulun jiandu* (The Worn-Out Guidance of Public Opinion) (Beijing: Zhongguo Funü Chuban She, 1989), pp. 92–95.

59. See *FBIS,* February 9, 1988, pp. 16–17, reporting *RMRB,* January 21.

60. *Ma huang* or even *da huang.* It might be argued that discipline commissions in the early 1950s performed this role, except that their mandate was to assure compliance with "lines" established at the top, rather than with broad principles such as those Confucian censors were supposed to advocate. See Rudolf G. Wagner, *The Contemporary Chinese Historical Drama: Four Studies* (Berkeley: University of California Press, 1990), pp. xi and xiii.

61. The estimate 400,000 to 700,000 is offered by Merle Goldman in the *Cambridge History of China,* vol. 14, part 1 (Cambridge: Cambridge University Press, 1987), p. 257.

62. *Zhonghua renmin gongheguo jingji dashi ji, 1949–1980* (Chronicle of Economic Events in the PRC, 1949–1980), Fang Weizhong et al., eds. (Beijing: Zhongguo Shehui Kexue Chuban She, 1984), p. 539. The freedoms were *da ming, da fang, da bianlun, da zibao.* Also James P. Brady, *Justice and Politics in People's China: Legal Order or Continuing Revolution?* (New York: Academic Press, 1982), p. 243.

63. Robert Benewick, "Political Participation," in *Reforming the Revolution: China in Transition,* Robert Benewick and Paul Wingrove, eds. (Basingstoke, UK: Macmillan, 1988), pp. 51 and 57.

64. *FBIS,* November 5, 1986, pp. 1–2, reporting Hong Kong, Agence France-Presse of November 4, supplemented by observations by this author in Shanghai.

65. Benedict Stavis, *China's Political Reforms: An Interim Report* (New York: Praeger, 1988), pp. 98–99.

66. Fang Lizhi had shortly before given speeches at these universities, and the spread of the rallies corresponds to his previous itinerary. See Richard Baum, "The Road to Tiananmen," in *The Politics of China, 1949–1989,* Roderick MacFarquhar, ed. (New York: Cambridge University Press, 1994), pp. 340–471.

67. *Post,* May 3, 1989.

68. Joan Grant, *Worm-Eaten Hinges: Tensions and Turmoil in Shanghai, 1988–89, Events Leading Up to Tiananmen Square* (Melbourne: Hyland House, 1991), pp. 104–5 and 112.

69. Ibid., p. 130, and, for what follows, pp. 122–23.

70. *Post,* May 21, 1989.

71. Joan Grant, *Worm-Eaten Hinges,* pp. 132–33, describes the market scene.

72. Ibid., p. 135.

73. Shelley Warner, "Shanghai's Response to the Deluge," in *The Pro-Democracy Protests in China; Reports from the Provinces,* Jonathan Unger, ed. (Armonk, NY: M.E. Sharpe, 1991), pp. 222–28.

74. *Time* (Asian edition), August 16, 1993, p. 19.

75. Shelley Warner, "Shanghai's Response," p. 227.

76. Ibid., p. 226, reporting *WHB,* Hong Kong, June 7, 1989.

77. *RMRBHWB,* June 13, 1989.

78. Rounded and further interpreted from Stanley Rosen, "The Effect of Post-June 4 Re-education Campaigns on Chinese Students," paper presented at the annual meeting of the American Association of China Studies, 1992, tables 1 and 2. Rosen is thanked for allowing the use of this fascinating material.

79. Jennifer Carter in *The Restored Monarchy, 1660–1668,* J. R. Jones, ed. (London: Macmillan, 1979), p. 82.

80. An analysis that appeared after this was drafted is Judith Polumbaum, "To Protect or Restrict: Points of Contention in China's Draft Press Law," in *Domestic Law Reforms in Post-Mao China,* Pitman B. Potter, ed.

81. *Zhonghua renmin gonghe guo xingzheng susong fa jianghua* (Talks about the PRC's Administrative Litigation Law), Propaganda Office of the Judicial Department of the People's Republic of China, ed. (Beijing: Falü Chuban She, 1990).

82. *Jihui youxing shiwei fa jianghua* (Talks about the Law on Assemblies, Parades, and Demonstrations), Propaganda Office of the Judicial Department of the People's Republic of China, ed. (Beijing: Falü Chuban She, 1990).

83. Ibid., pp. 51–64.

Chapter 4.3

Selection of Political Structure

The location of the United States is in the Far West. It is the most un-
civilized and remote of all countries . . . an isolated place outside
the pale, solitary and ignorant. Not only are the people entirely un-
versed in the forms of edicts and laws, but if the meaning be rather
deep, they would probably not even be able to comprehend.

—Qiyang (Manchu official, 1842)[1]

A fool who thinks he is a fool is for that very reason wise.
A fool who thinks that he is wise is called a fool indeed.

—Gautama Buddha, *Dhammapada* 63

Constitutions are prescriptive documents. The best way to analyze them is nonetheless behavioral. They define the formal structure of government, along with
the rights of people and groups—and sometimes they influence what happens
after that. Even when constitutions are not followed, the inconsistency between
what constitution-makers say, on one hand, and what leaders do, on the other,
reveals much about state power.

Constitutions in the PRC have seldom restrained the government, and their
exalted legal status must be examined in the context of their references to the
Communist Party (which has its own separate constitution) as the leading element in politics. The date of Mao's main constitution for the government was
1954; not until 1975 was it replaced. The 1978 and 1982 state constitutions
contained wordings that could be interpreted to their benefit by either reformers
or conservatives. These were documents for both foxes and lions, designed to be

such. Both kinds of leaders found them useful for the functions, places, and times they could dominate. Replacement of China's constitution has sometimes occurred when the topmost state leader changes or when the incumbent of that position is trying to leave a legacy or trying to assert himself vis-à-vis rivals.

Constitutional Rights and Duties

The 1982 Constitution has lasted longer than most of its predecessors; but its meaning can be found in the ways it has been implemented, as well as in the proposals that Chinese people have made to amend it. State constitutions in many countries express ideals that are not yet realized. The U.S. Constitution at first created a system that let states grant votes, for example, only to white males who owned real property—and this restricted group directly elected just half of one-third of the government (the House of Representatives, but not the Senate, the chief executive, or the Supreme Court). Yet the document that proposed all this began with the words "We the people . . ." After many later experiences—a civil war, suffrage and populist movements, a great depression, and world wars—politics in that country gradually involved more of the people. As Schattschneider writes, "Somewhere along the line, the owners of the government decided to read the Constitution as if it were a democratic document."[2] This process, which in practical terms has not been finished, continues currently. Similar evolutions can also be seen in the constitutions of quite different countries.

The 1936 "Stalin Constitution" in the USSR contained many inoperative joke-clauses: all the political rights anybody could wish, even the right of the republics to secede. These were long honored in the breach; but as later events showed, they were not all meaningless. State documents and local leaders, not just unorganized people, help build popular government—and they sometimes do so even when state elites disdain such change.[3]

In China, it is easy to ridicule the rights clauses of the PRC Constitution that the government regularly violates. Even if they do not represent some twinge of conscience among CCP elites that future politics should embrace more people, at least Chinese liberals in practice will continue to demand that these provisions mean something—until eventually, perhaps they will. The 1982 state constitution formally enshrined many rights, including the "negative freedoms" from state interference that are near the center of individualist theory.

Article 35 guarantees "freedom of speech, of the press, of assembly, of association, of procession, and of demonstration." Article 36 posits "freedom of religious belief," prohibiting state and public organizations from trying to "compel citizens to believe in, or not to believe in, any religion, nor may they discriminate against citizens who believe in, or do not believe in, any religion" (except that "religious affairs are not subject to any foreign domination"). Article 37 claims, "No citizen may be arrested except with the approval or by decision of a people's procurate or by decision of a people's court . . . and unlawful search of the persons of citizens is prohibited." Article 39 declares, "The home of citizens of the People's Republic of China is inviolable. Unlawful search of, or intrusion into, a citizen's home is prohibited." Article 40 speaks of the "freedom and privacy of correspondence." Article 41 asserts that "citizens have the right to criticize and make suggestions to any state organ or functionary." The scolded unit (rather than a court) is supposed to take care of an accusation against itself; but constitutionally it may not "suppress such complaints, charges, and exposures, or retaliate against the citizens making them."[4] The constitution suggests much hope that sweet reason can prevail over politics—as if words, rather than structured conflict, could ever create a constitutional framework.

What do the liberal clauses mean? Many other provisions of the 1982 constitution, beginning with Article 1, insist that citizens must "support socialism"— which is interpreted to mean rule by the CCP. Several sections, such as Article 24, warn that "the state . . . combats capitalist, feudal, and other decadent ideas."[5] Article 51 makes all the other provisions moot, because it requires that "the exercise by citizens of the People's Republic of China of their freedoms and rights may not infringe upon the interests of the state, of society, and of the collective."[6] These interests are defined by the government, and the thrust of Articles 51 through 54 is simply opposite to the meaning of the clauses about rights. So this constitution can be complaisantly read by either a reformer or a conservative. Different people can see different things in it.

Time and politics determine what it means. According to a *Beijing Daily* headline of May 21, 1981, "Socialist Law Does Not Give Counterrevolutionaries Freedom of Speech." China's Penal Code, Article 90, refers broadly to "counterrevolutionary crimes." PRC courts in the trials of Wei Jingsheng and others have interpreted this as criminalizing "counterrevolutionary speech."[7] These vague terms are legally defined only by the Party, the arbiter of revolution, not by any court or legislature. Counterrevolution has long remained a crime.

The liberal words of Articles 35 through 47 may nonetheless eventually come to have a more comprehensive effect. Some leaders who wrote this document were at least partly aware of the surrealism of many of their words. The clear conflict of norms within the Chinese constitution is not different—at least formally—from similar tensions among laws of any other country. Every freedom of speech, a norm that comes very close to the center of liberalism, must be conditioned by laws against libel or slander and by rules on "clear and present danger." Each liberal norm is under some conditions subject to other factors, including collective claims. The fact that the PRC Constitution explicitly conditions individual rights on state interests goes beyond the verbiage, though not the practice, of basic laws in some other countries. It presupposes that relations between state and people could become tense, and it skews the laws to serve the state. It may also suggest a premise among intellectuals (who are a minority in any society) that the state cannot very effectively be constituted by all the people.

The clauses enshrining liberal rights have scarcely been honored in China, but they could prove to be more effective in the future. They avoid some of the broadest liberal ideas, which are found in some other constitutions but have been difficult thus far to implement anywhere.[8] The Chinese government has often ignored guarantees in its own constitution, especially in the field of criminal procedure. The most egregious of these involves arrests, not just of "political criminals" but of ordinary miscreants. Article 37, for example, prohibits arrests without the approval of procuracies or courts, and it bans unlawful detentions. China's implementing code on criminal procedure allows only a ten-day period after a suspect is detained, in which police must either obtain a judge's or procurator's arrest warrant or else release the person. This law is, to the extent that it is public, crystal clear—yet what it ordains is often not what happens. On the contrary, police have a frequent custom of placing people under long-term "shelter for investigation" (*shourong shencha*), a habit that may be legitimated by unpublished (*neibu*) regulations that end up having more practical effect than the formal laws or constitution.[9]

A similar difficulty arises because China has a particularly rich diversity of judicial decision-making forums: Courts handle major cases. Administrative tribunals adjudicate many minor ones. Various mediation committees hear complaints with which the relevant higher officials do not want to deal. But the police (including Party branches within public security offices) are in charge of determining which of these benches will hear any particular case. Procedural guarantees vary considerably between these different kinds of judiciaries; but the punishments they can mete out are not so graded, especially in civil cases. Administrative tribunals, not just courts, can issue very severe sentences.

So the arm of the law that most directly has instruments of coercion (police in their various forms) determines procedures too. Public security departments are far more important in determining the effects of law than are the ideally more thoughtful arms (regular lawyers and courts). No country's record of living up to its own constitutional ideals is or perhaps should be unimpeachable, because in that case the ideals would be too modest. But much evidence from China is grossly out of line with many provisions of the document that is supposed to be its supreme law. The state's coercive arms are often so arrogant, that their practice in effect repeals large parts of the constitution. These medium-level power networks have in some periods been more conservative than the top of the state, and in other periods they have been more liberal. In either case, local police have often pre-empted the central state.

In places where human rights have become respected in the past, that change has happened for identifiable historical reasons, not because of uncaused changes of values. They have become respected because of conflicts that cannot be finally resolved but are too expensive for the combatants to continue. When no faction or party can win, each may tend to tolerate new, more liberal institutions that maximize its benefits minus its costs under circumstances that are from its viewpoint less than perfect. This habit of respecting rights may later be retained as an institution, even after the conditions that gave rise to it change. For example in the West, human rights expanded after bloody but fundamentally inconclusive religious wars. The crucial argument for liberalism is not a matter of philosophy; it is a memory of conflict. Its crucial opponents are not always utopians but are people whose status depends on suggestions that there is some unified large-group identity that should affect all politics. Intellectuals are the people most prone to make such a suggestion, just as they are also the people most able to show its inadequacy.

Proposals for Changing Political Structure

Radicals, especially during the Cultural Revolution, expressed skepticism about permanent law as such. Chinese politics was personalized at every level then, so proposals for constitutional change were few. Shanghai's Revolutionary Committee on November 13, 1977, changed at least the names of most of its subordinate units.[10] By the end of 1978, the Revolutionary Committee ran sixty-six offices. Its title was not changed to that of a municipal government until the decade finished, in 1979. Structural change was tardy, at this august level. The symbolic "revolutionary" name was quietly dropped, long after most actual activities of the government had become reformist. Reform China inherited, however, as anticonstitutional a polity as has existed in recent times.

To analyze structural change in state form, a whole-country perspective including local politics is needed. Brave proposals for change were set forth in 1978 by dissident Wei Jingsheng, who demanded the "fifth modernization," that is, democracy.[11] From that time on, whenever the reformist foxes ran China in years of relative relaxation (*fang*), intellectuals came forward with similar or further proposals for more democracy. Whenever the lions roared, in alternating years of tightness (*shou*), these proposals were attacked.[12]

The early 1980s saw new constitutions for both the Party and the state. Deng Xiaoping opined that "unconditional power is the source of all unhealthy tendencies."[13] Deng embraced political reform, at least hesitantly and sporadically. In an August 1980 speech to the Politburo, he called on his Party comrades "to develop in full measure people's democracy and to ensure that the people as a whole truly enjoy the power to supervise (*guanli*) the state ... especially to supervise political power at the basic level, as well as all enterprises and undertakings."[14] Deng rejected, at least indirectly, much of the Soviet inheritance from the 1950s. He admitted that Stalin had "gravely disrupted the socialist legal system." Deng could give a convincing list of reasons why China's political structure by the 1980s was faulty:

> Bureaucracy remains a major and widespread problem in the political life of our Party and state. Its harmful manifestations include the following: standing

high above the masses, abusing power, divorcing oneself from reality and the masses, spreading a lot of time and effort to put up an impressive front, indulging in empty talk, sticking to a rigid way of thinking, being hidebound by convention, overstaffing administrative organs, being dilatory, inefficient and irresponsible, failing to keep one's word, circulating documents endlessly without solving problems, shifting responsibility to others, . . . vindictively attacking others, suppressing democracy, deceiving superiors and subordinates, being arbitrary and despotic, practicing favoritism, offering bribes, participating in corrupt practices in violation of the law, and so on. Such things have reached intolerable dimensions.[15]

About the same time, CCP ideologist Liao Gailong, in a speech at the Central Party School, went even further, criticizing not only Stalin but also Lenin, whose name is normally sacred in Communist countries: "Lenin's political theories emphasized the aspect of violent suppression of the dictatorship of the proletariat, and neglected the democratic aspect. He even did so to such a degree that he said the proletarian dictatorship was an iron dictatorship not bound by any laws."[16] Liao called for more "freedom."

This could all be said because democracy had an odd panache even among hard-liners. Conservatives talked about democracy because they knew it was attractive to many, but they were eager for public opinion not to associate it only with capitalism. This climate encouraged proposals that central power might become more limited, so the middle of 1986 saw a high tide of discussion about structural reforms of politics.

A researcher at the Shanghai Academy of Social Sciences Legal Research Institute could justify radically new views by citing the founder of Bolshevism:

Lenin once pointed out that "Socialism cannot win its victory unless it carries out full democracy." To carry on a full democracy, we cannot just completely deny bourgeois democracy, which is still effective in today's world. We should actively absorb its rational parts. For example, the principle of "the separation of three powers" is an important element in capitalist republics. It has been proven by history to be an important measure toward preventing the restoration of feudal dictatorships.[17]

Proposals for separating powers took many forms: dividing Party from government roles more clearly, dividing central, provincial, county, and township powers, sometimes even dividing the sovereignty of the state from that of individuals. Yan Jiaqi, the most famous Chinese political scientist, argues that the PRC would become more democratic, and individual rights would be better respected, under a federal system (*lianbang zhi*).[18] A structural change of this sort might have some effect toward decreasing the tendency of Chinese leaders to fold coercion into their administrative policies. But either of two other changes might have a greater effect: the rise of intellectual politicians who claimed electoral popularity rather than moral rhetoric as their right to rule or the rise of politicians from other strata who could defeat them nonviolently, for example, in elections. A stress on federalism or other forms of administrative tinkering as a bridge to democracy could well lead to that promised land more slowly than a more direct stress on the most crucial aspect of democracy, which is legitimate diversity. That, and de facto federalism too, actually bloomed in China during the reforms, no matter what the government did.

In mid-1986, Deng Xiaoping called for more basic political change, but he said it would take "at least a decade," and China should wait "twenty to thirty years before national [direct] elections."[19] Sometimes he and other Chinese Communist leaders have predicted longer waits. But democracy of some vague, undefined kind remained the consensual ideal among practically all Chinese intellectuals, both in government and in dissent. They said it, yet they avoided doing it. It was the goal; everything before the democratic millennium was transitional, not yet quite legitimate, requiring explanations. Theories of a need for tutelage still remained most convincing to incumbents. Ideologically, this position was unstable.

Wang Ruowang of Shanghai wrote about the possibility of multiparty systems in China. For this suggestion against the Four Cardinal Principles, which were still sacrosanct for the nonce, he was criticized and purged from the CCP in January 1987. Many educated people in Shanghai still recalled his ideas during later years, but the media were apparently asked to publish nothing about him. Wang's and others' proposals for political reform by 1987 emphasized new procedures for making government decisions, an independent judiciary, the hiring of better-qualified bureaucrats, stronger elected congresses, and above all the separation of the Party and the government.[20] "Checks and balances" (*zhiheng*) within the Party, though not between it and other groups, were much discussed among intellectuals from 1981 through 1986. A "division of powers" (*fenquan*) was mooted in the mid-1980s.[21] The endemic vagueness of these ideas may be one reason why, at least in the short run, they came to naught.

The main motive for these proposals is probably not that so many Chinese intellectuals had suffered so much during the revolution, or even that they have such a strong tradition of moralizing what other people should do. These were prerequisites—and healthy ones because the nation needed ideas for new structures. The main cause of public interest in these liberal proposals was different and concrete: the quick economic change, which brought many practical problems of management. From a modern elite perspective, the main problem with dictatorship was not its arbitrariness, but its slow inefficiency. The modern market required timely decisions, and the old Party structure was not rendering them.

Xu Xuejun, vice president of Shanghai Industrial and Business College, in a lecture on the "Entrepreneurial Spirit of Modern Shanghai's National Capitalist Class," argued forcefully in 1989 for a restoration of the city's administrative creativity. "Existing enterprises have no strong driving force to be competitive, to initiate new programs, and to accumulate capital. High centralization and too many levels of administration deprive enterprise managers of sufficient autonomous rights to run firms, killing entrepreneurial spirit. Economic and political institutions must be reformed if an enterprising spirit and a rich economy are to develop."[22]

Nonstate companies in the 1980s were very forward in proposing new political forms. China's largest private electronics consortium, the Stone Group, set up a research institute headed by Cao Siyuan, who called himself a "lobbyist" to study constitutional revisions.[23] Cao was prominent in debates about China's bankruptcy law and its basic law. Other large companies also had formal or informal think tanks. In the spring of 1989, high Chinese intellectuals stressed the need for structural reform. A May 4 petition drafted by a former senior official at the CCP Propaganda Department called for "comprehensive reform," saying, "The Party must be separated from government. There must be free popular elections, and the judiciary must be independent.... We cannot pit democracy against [fears of] instability. Only with democracy can all the factors for instability be eliminated."[24]

A reply was to charge that such notions were unpatriotic. According to one commentator in the *River Elegy* documentary, Chinese people cannot change their laws and methods easily, because political reforms raise questions about their identity as Chinese. For years, as a Shanghai intellectual wrote, Confucianists espoused a "treasure of method," a morality that had some uses but lacked any spirit of progress or "mechanism for cultural renovation."[25] This commentator alleged that in Europe's "religious revolutions," people never doubted their identities as French or Italians or the like—so they could remain what they were, while making big social changes.[26] Only in China, this writer said, is identity such a huge problem. In fact, just a small group of urban Chinese intellectuals raised such worries. Most people in China have no doubt about being Chinese and know they can remain so as their country develops. Agonizing about symbolic identity, when something concrete needs to be done, is not most people's style even though statist intellectuals enjoy it.

Political structure, rather than the personal characters or values of wise leaders, is the mainstay of democracy. But during the Tiananmen period, few intellectuals did anything specific to propose new political structures. There is an odd bit of negative evidence to the contrary: The students supported Zhao Ziyang because of his relative openness to procedural changes—even though they knew that his policies had led to inflation and that his family was as corrupt as any in the land. What they liked about Zhao, as about Hu Yaobang earlier, was that he favored structural reforms. These two advocated reducing the managerial role of the Party. With the winds of economic change behind them, they had somewhat more success in actually changing the old situation of Party dominance at local levels than in persuading their elite colleagues of the reasons for that change.

Intellectuals are, of course, needed for writing constitutions. "Founding fathers" and tennis court debaters have been crucial in the development of democratic rules. But intellectuals have been effective in this way only while less philosophical types manned battle lines to protect them. Chinese intellectuals ask themselves why they have generally failed as constitution makers, even at Tiananmen while the populace of Beijing was in fact shielding them.[27] A search for democratic documents from the 1989 chaos unearths stirring but extremely vague speeches, street banners demanding freedom of expression, a memorable statue, mock-humble petitions, and philosophical editorials—but surprisingly few proposals for specific governmental rules, or for new institutions to enforce them. Why?

In the early 1980s, political scientists such as Liao Gailong and Yan Jiaqi—writing as individuals—actually came forth with such proposals for procedures. Particular intellectuals suggested reducing the size of the National People's Congress, making it bicameral, lengthening the sessions, and having direct elections of deputies.[28] But comprehensive and collective efforts of this sort, especially when conjoined with mass protests that the holders of official power could not ignore, have been conspicuously absent. When students and citizens were at Tiananmen, some older intellectuals held meetings at the Chinese Academy of Social Sciences; but no famous new structural proposals for politics emerged.

Chinese intellectuals may think their reticence on such occasions is caused by conservative incumbents' powers. Or possibly it arises from traditions that make political collaboration between young and old dissidents difficult. A greater likelihood is that democratic procedures would give more power to commercial businessmen, workers, even peasants—and less to scholars—than the latter think seemly. Developments in South China (not just Hong Kong and Taiwan) may slowly be changing the pattern of political engineers' near-monopoly of civilian politics. But few northern intellectuals have welcomed such change. The main issue is whether legitimate rule in China should be restricted to educated people whom the Party elite chooses or instead should be based on the opinions of very large numbers of people.

Antidemocratic Scientism

Intellectuals are generally thought to be democrats. Since many urban educated Chinese suffered badly during the Cultural Revolution under a highly illiberal structure, they have reasons to favor tolerant democracy. Many of them talk about it often, and previous publications have covered this subject.[29] In the future, bright writers will be crucial for conceiving new political forms in China. But knowledge has also been connected in China with some right to rule. Perhaps the main obstacle to Chinese democracy lies in the idea that academic achievement among leaders would assure just government. The main hindrance to Chinese democracy may not lie in the factors usually said to cause it (hierarchical traditions, economic poverty, extensive illiteracy, or population size), but instead in hesitations among the Chinese intellectual elite to aid the rise of norms of social toleration.

The Enmity of "Mr. Science" for "Mr. Democracy"

Chinese educated people—governmentalists and dissidents alike—often continue to stress that, in order for China to be strong, the nation should be run by a knowledge elite (*zhishi jingying*). This notion discourages competitive elections that might empower entrepreneur, labor, and agricultural leaderships. It encourages "movement democracy," whose sporadic outbursts have scant lasting effect on decision-making procedures. The cultural, economic, educational, and demographic conditions in China might, at some future time, sustain more liberal structures. But they are unlikely to do so until the classic scenario of a liberal transformation begins: An urban populace, supported by some military and police, shields a group of relatively open-minded intellectuals who begin to operate a constitutional framework providing competitive elections. The result would be some elected officials who are not intellectuals. This has not happened yet. "Mr. Science" has been a false friend to "Mr. Democracy."

Much evidence shows the currency of antidemocratic scientism in China, even during the most liberal periods. Philosopher Li Zehou argued, at two spring 1989 conferences commemorating the seventieth anniversary of the May 4 Movement, that "democracy must be more scientific."[30] The famous astrophysicist-dissident Fang Lizhi once said, "Because science and technology have become more and more important in the world in which we are living, there are a great many problems that only people with some background in science or culture may be able to grasp clearly."[31] This is true, but it could be antidemocratic. It does not stress the questions: Who finally decides? In whose interest are problems that require specialized techniques going to be solved? The main question about technocracy or any other claim to rule is an old one: *Cui bono?*

Intellectual Elitism

Intellectual elites, both governmentalist and dissident before Tiananmen, published together in journals such as the *World Economic Herald* to plump for rule by intellectuals.[32] On May 1, 1989, the *Herald* carried a full page on "China's Modernization and the Ideological Trend of Populism," arguing squarely against the populist trend. Rather than uniting with ordinary citizens who protected intellectuals at Tiananmen, the *Herald* said the Cultural Revolution had been caused by populism. It straightforwardly favored "elitism" (*jingying jingshen*).

Earlier, from 1987 to 1989, the period after Zhao Ziyang replaced Hu Yaobang at the head of the CCP as quasi-liberals thrived, many would-be reformers praised "neoauthoritarianism" (*xin quanwei zhuyi*). Scholars at the Chinese Economic System Reform Institute argued against any structural reform of politics.

They criticized the notion that checks and balances, multiple parties, or direct elections could help China. These reformers explicitly called for "elite politics" (*jingying zhengzhi*), and they opposed "democratic politics" (*minzhu zhengzhi*). They only wanted to bring "knowledge elites" into the "power elite" (*quanli jingying*).[33]

Rocket scientist Qian Xuesen proposed that the way to assure an expert elite in China was to require high academic degrees of incumbents at high government posts. He wrote in 1983 that, by the year 2000, all cadres should be college graduates, all leaders at the county/bureau level should have M.A. degrees, and all ministers, deputy ministers, and governors should hold academic doctorates.[34] Anyone who has worked in a university, where Ph.D.'s actually govern, must be extremely skeptical of Dr. Qian's hopes.

"Neoauthoritarianism" received crucial support from abroad. Its foreign side, like many other aspects of reform, is treated elsewhere in this book, ranging from art to credit. The Chinese political scientist Fu Zhengyuan uses very careful wording to say, "Paradoxical as it may seem, the discussion of neo-authoritarianism was allegedly stimulated by the publication of the Chinese translation of Samuel Huntington's *Political Order in Changing Societies* in late 1987. A few of the propounders were young scholars who had just returned after studying in the U.S. This is a typical case where a foreign idea may be transfigured."[35] The extent to which migration to China distorted Huntington's ideas is a question. There can be no doubt, however, that a structured critique of political participation from a distinguished foreign scholar greatly heartened the new Chinese literati who wanted state offices.

Huntington's book, *American Politics: The Promise of Disharmony,* is as important as *Political Order* because it proposes a gap between democratic ideals and institutions. Huntington defines these ideals as egalitarian, individualistic, open, antihierarchal, and suspicious of government. He claims that "Americans find it congenial" to assert "principles that cannot be practiced." He admits that other countries have similar tensions in their political cultures; for example, France has strong traditions of both elitism and revolution. But to make an argument, Huntington points out that Americans are "hypocritical" when they strongly espouse democratic ideals yet order each other about.[36] What he might also note is that elitists, especially in the modern diversified world, make excessive claims for governments. Many states fail to deliver what they promise.

Chinese, following his line, raised practical objections to democracy. Reflecting the opinions of both reform and conservative intellectuals, political scientist Yang Baikui wrote that,

> the majority are actually unable to participate in decision making themselves, much less make right and informed decisions. Taking into account the reality in China today, popular participation in decision making is not as important as the quality of the minority who make decisions.[37]

The problem of getting a structure of government that serves people, without requiring from them more than they can or want to give, has also confounded Western liberals. Thinkers as good as Tocqueville or Schattschneider tried to solve it in various ways. Yang is traditionally Chinese in his certitude that "the quality of the minority" is crucial, but increasingly, other Chinese may develop in their situations reasons to disagree.

Neoauthoritarianism was, at least until mid-1989, clearly the dominant trend of Chinese reformist thought. These protodemocrats wrote that individual freedom was desirable; and it would emerge historically—but gradually, by tutelage in stages whose duration was unspecified but long. During a lengthy transition to modern nirvana, according to this view, only intellectuals could be trusted with power. They thought they could keep the democratic millennium in their heads as a goal, despite the seductive distractions of office. Theorist Wu Jiaxiang, writing in the *World Economic Herald* in early 1989, said that stages of real totalitarianism and then milder authoritarianism (the transitional phase) would have to precede democracy in China.[38]

There is nothing new about "neoauthoritarianism" except the view that the authorities should have modern educations. Chinese reformers before June 4, oddly calling themselves democrats, in general supported this plainly undemocratic idea. After Tiananmen, conservatives in power attacked this phrase, perhaps to confuse their reformist opponents. Old bossiness was enough for them. Neoauthoritarianism was roundly condemned by actual authoritarians because most articulate dissidents had supported it. The would-be neoauthorities were too exclusively intellectual for their own political good.

Conservative Chen Xitong on June 30, 1989, saw the origins of the "evil pro-democracy movement" in a meeting of Zhao Ziyang with Nobel laureate Milton Friedman. Here was a certified sage, advising Chinese leaders how to run their country while admitting they knew much more about the place.[39] Chen said meeting with the Nobel laureate raised Zhao's prestige, so Zhao could be a "new dictator," pressing ahead with "bourgeois liberalization." Chen also excoriated student leader Wang Dan for his love affair with authoritarianism.[40] These critiques have a ridiculous side since "authoritarian" Zhao was under house arrest and "authoritarian" Wang was about to be jailed. Chen Xitong was far more authoritarian (and corrupt) than either. Yet such an effort at debate also shows the unanimity of China's elite on the supposed need for firm central rule. This position of practically all national leaders, both governmentalist and dissident, made them hesitate to campaign seriously for support among mass constituencies. More local leaders, who increasingly ran the country, also favored strong domination over their own constituents—but in practice, they powerfully undermined authority in the state.

Public protests became an instrument that students could use against the government, both because of their own intellectual and protoelite status and because the official elite had no tradition of taking appeals in public seriously. Even reformers at the national level were very wary of mass demonstrations, thinking them a flaky approach to politics. The boundaries around leadership groups were assumed to be more important for political success than the quality of decisions they took. The only use of rallies, in this view, was to send signals between types of elites. Sometimes the language even of the top reformer suggested that his listeners must think of democracy separate from struggle: On May 3, 1989, Zhao Ziyang said, "If we allow these disturbances again, a China with a future will become a China with no future at all. . . . Stability, progress, order, law: these are the needs of reform and of science and democracy."[41]

Critique of the Argument That a Culture Can Exclude a Regime Type

Foreign factors, including advice from Singapore and legislative riots in Taiwan, tended strongly to confirm PRC elite doubts about the chances of channeling political struggle usefully.[42] Actually, government authority can bring confusion too, even though disorder is what authoritarianism is supposed to prevent. In nations like China, which have recently seen much revolutionary violence and where memories of coercion are fresh, authority acquires a reputation not much better than that of chaos. Although some Chinese traditions incline people toward order and justice, much of China's actual state practice has been based on other, harsher traditions that overwhelm civilized customs.

Elite reformers point out that Chinese dynasties have been overthrown only every two or three hundred years.[43] They complain that when Liu Shaoqi was imprisoned during the Cultural Revolution, the laws of the PRC could not even protect the head of state—or ordinary citizens. But they seek more hopeful traditions in Chinese culture too: Near Liu's jail was a temple dedicated to the hero Bao Gong, a sage with a black face, famed for integrity and fairness toward all people.[44] Intellectual elitists tend to identify tolerance with educated people, and intolerance with peasants. Constructions of culture vary, depending on the interests and situation of the constructor. Intellectuals tend to forget that peasants are a structured network, not a "sack of potatoes" mass; and their leaders are broadly able to seek rural people's interests.

Deng Xiaoping reportedly told George Bush that "China is in the process of economic development. If we seek formal democracy, we not only cannot implement it but also cannot have development. This would only lead to disorder in the country and in people's spirits." He referred to the Cultural Revolution and said, "China must persist in its open door and reform policies . . . but we need stable politics. China has a huge population, and different people have different opinions; so if today some people hold demonstrations and tomorrow others do, we will have protests 365 days a year and cannot engage in economic construction."[45]

Many young Chinese intellectuals believe that the obedient attitudes of all Chinese (except themselves) have been continuous for thousands of years, "since Confucius."[46] They see no real prospect for change in China, and they describe all the obvious changes of the Deng era as mere surface impressions. China's traditions, they say, overwhelm any serious chance for "democracy," which they posit as the only change that would make a real difference. Reformers who are this pessimistic have difficulty proposing structural reforms. Their inactivity aids the interests of state leaders.

Practically all Chinese political elites, not just those in government, have in effect tried to persuade ordinary Chinese people that they cannot trust themselves with power. Elites accuse most of their compatriots of being immature—too poor, too illiterate, too many. If this logic were surely true, then India could not have maintained competitive elections (such as it has, at least) for half a century. Smaller countries like Costa Rica would also not have had much chance at democracy, even allowing wide formal variance for their national characteristics. Nor would many countries of Western Europe or North America in the nineteenth century have done so, since most people then were poor.

Types of Liberty

This view neglects that ideals of freedom in the past have very often come bound with ideals of order. This is possible to show by looking at a variety of traditions in a single country. Historian David Fischer discusses different immigrant waves to America of Massachusetts Puritans, Virginia planters, Pennsylvania Quakers, and Appalachian Scots–Irish borderers. Each of these migrations, in a specific time period, carried from specific parts of Britain to specific parts of America four different kinds of liberalism. The example that has most resonance for China is that of the Virginia gentleman, who:

> was required to lead others of lower rank, and they were expected to follow his high example. The moral authority of a gentleman derived from his material independence . . . but others in that society lived in various degrees of unfreedom and many had no freedom at all. Their bondage supported a gentleman's freedom and independence, which thus became a hegemonic idea, very different from libertarian thinking in New England [or] Pennsylvania.[47]

Mencius, mandarins, or many modern Chinese intellectuals would share an interest in this particular concept of liberty.

Most Chinese elites' views are close to this case—and much further from the moral individualism of Quakers, the quasi-anarchistic "natural freedom" of backcountry Scots, or perhaps even the more collectivist "publick liberty" of Massachusetts congregations. The point is that even in countries like the United States, where liberty is often supposed to find some behavioral definition, notions of freedom actually exist in a much richer diversity than high politicians of the united state have wanted to publicize.

Individualism or collectivism (like also materialism and idealism) are not just categories that academics can use. Political entrepreneurs often claim these as typical of the groups they are trying to mobilize or regulate. They imply their special understanding of their people's characteristics gives them a right to lead. An incumbent state elite often suggests that some specific version of individualism or collectivism should typify all proper action in its polity, and no other action ever natively happens. Even social scientists have been taken in by such efforts. What most people do, however, shows no merely analytic constraints; it comes in all the types.

State Leaders' and Citizens' Presumptions About Effective Legitimacy

Elites who disdain the selection of leaders by masses, no matter whether they are authoritarians of the left or right, tend to underestimate the legitimating power of free elections. They think that elections are a joke. Marcos, on the right in the Philippines, thought that he could safely call a poll and then rig it; but Aquino won, and Marcos never recovered. Kim Dae Jung and Kim Young Sam, on the left in South Korea, were at first more interested in the internal cohesiveness of their separate client groups than in allying for electoral victory; so Roh Tae Woo received a fair plurality and became president constitutionally. The Kims won later. Daniel Ortega Saavedra in Nicaragua thought he was safe from the risk of an election, because he ran the most patriotic and populist party; yet even in a nation then fighting a civil war, after the voters spoke, Ortega knew what he had to do. Much of Eastern Europe is now littered with ex-Communist elites who held elections, content that the invincibility of their clever Leninist organizational forms would surely sustain them. They discovered otherwise, at least until they developed newer forms of organization later.[48]

Hierarchical norms in culture are historically no more a trait of China than of the West. PRC intellectuals have sometimes suggested that Westerners are enterprising individualists, or have always been so, and that Western institutions (markets, explorations for trade, and democracies) have grown mainly on the basis of individualist norms. Communitarianism has indeed been strong, especially within Chinese families; but there are alternative individualist traditions in China too.[49] And the West is not so monotonously individualist as some of its cowboy-style leaders claim.

All countries develop structures that pay attention to both order and divisions. Traditions of stability ensure that few institutions in any country are democratic. A glance at the way American or European businesses, universities, or bureaucracies are organized will quickly show they are overwhelmingly hierarchical. Information sometimes flows upward in these organizations, but directives, resource allocations, and appointments are all top–down affairs. Even in elected assemblies, the legislators represent their constituents. They are beholden to common voters only at the next election. Of course, democratic norms affect hierarchical organizations in liberal societies, and they sometimes mitigate abuses by local autocrats. But popular sovereignty is an occasional and very partial thing, even in the most democratic countries and even at the turn of the twenty-first century.

Historically, norms of hierarchy have been just as strong in the West as in China. Most Americans have forgotten how sharply norms of social rank have changed in the lifetime of one generation. The predominance of the Anglo-Saxon ethnic group (not Catholics, not Asians, not Jews, certainly not blacks) was taken as a certainty just one generation ago. In Britain, which is a credible democracy, there is still a nobility. Below this, every old schoolboy wants to have a "Sir" in front of his name before retirement; and his wife wants to be called "Lady" if "Dame" is unavailable. If a somewhat longer historical view is allowed, English culture provides elaborate philosophical accounts of the supposed naturalness of hierarchy. Elizabethans widely believed in a "chain of being," a full cosmos of hierarchy that included everything. This justified absolute monarchy and much else.[50] Mencius was a rebel in comparison.

Political culture in China has offered ambiguous empirical results concerning the relative strength of authoritarian or participatory cultures. When an old survey on attitudes about "civic culture," once conducted decades ago in other countries, was repeated in China shortly after Tiananmen, citizens expressed little confidence about their own political effectiveness. Many Chinese felt separate from government. They did not (theories about totalitarianism to the contrary notwithstanding) report that their daily lives were greatly affected by Beijing politics. Analysts of this survey saw this as a hindrance to any structural change in politics. If government really does not matter much, then there is no point in arguing who should head it. Such findings led to the analysts' conclusion that, "if a political crisis between the regime and the intellectuals occurs again [as in 1989], the majority of the population may once again not offer much backing for the demands for democratic change. But . . . the attitudinal gap between the educated and the uneducated that now helps to stabilize the regime may moderate the violence of a regime transition and provide a reserve of deference to help an infant democracy survive. Nothing in our data supports the theory that Chinese political culture is an absolute bar to democracy."[51] But most Chinese still speak of "politics" as if it were in another sphere far above them.

It is possible to show in surveys that Chinese intellectuals as a group, not just published writers among them, still tend to hold undemocratic attitudes.[52] About two-thirds of a large group of them, polled in early 1989, said that it was inconsistent or unfeasible simultaneously to disagree with a view and to support the right of others to express it in public. Only three-tenths of the surveyed intellectuals found any practical sense in the liberal position that disagreeable viewpoints might be advocated.[53]

The Chinese state for centuries has supported knowledge elites, justifying their power with claims to specially defined moral virtues. Under such a stable regime, intellectual tolerance has often been a repressed citizen. If the structure for obtaining office changed from knowledge certification to electoral victory—even if this change were brief or temporary—it is difficult to be sure how the new structure would affect attitudes. Procedures affect notions of what is feasible, not just the other way around. Ideas can change quickly; they are less stable than pollsters or intellectuals have an interest in admitting.

Democracy and authoritarianism are popularly contrasted, but modern politics can be constructed in syndicalist or corporatist ways, too. China's strong patriarchal traditions at the local level may eventually foster a more consultative political structure among the patriarchal units. These traditions can support corporatist or authoritarian regime types immediately. In at least two ways, China's mixed legacies and situation would also support democracy:

First, the association of wealth with liberalism is not just a modernization theory; it is a public claim that leaders use, as they seek to defeat their rivals who also try to associate the growth of wealth with authoritarianism. The world's richest large countries are all democratic; so for whatever reason, leaders who become liberal may have a long-term advantage in such contests.

Second, Chinese traditions legitimize local—not just national—hierarchies. Authoritarians in Beijing understandably do not stress this point, but they have no monopoly on Chinese characteristics. Local patriarchal units are the bricks that make political coalitions in that country. They may well, in the near future, coalesce into larger corporate units, and perhaps eventually articulate interest groups. At first, the grounds for such association will almost surely remain personalistic; but factions could evolve into recognized corporate groups, and then policy groups.

Democracy, Its Alternatives, and Leaders' Choices

Many treatments of conditions for liberal transitions stress positive or negative effects of modernization on political structure. By the early 1960s, when a form of functionalism dominated social science, writers such as Lipset, Cutright, and Almond stressed the high correlation between democracy and per-capita income. Later forms of functionalism complicated this story, as postindependence dictators became more obvious in the Third World. So Samuel Huntington theorized about the problems that economic growth created for polities. Both the optimistic and pessimistic versions of functionalism, however, relied on logics that link local political networks throughout a society with the structure of the state.

In later decades, various social scientists such as Rustow, O'Donnell, Schmitter, Bermeo, and Di Palma complicated this story further by stressing the importance of state elite choices. The ideas and resources of elites were "brought back in" to the discussion about regime types, after a period in which broader social causes of state structure had been sought. This "new institutionalist" approach to political explanation is compatible with its functionalist predecessors, however, if the difference between the broad and elite approaches is conceived as merely a difference between state and nonstate *political* institutions.

Dankwart Rustow and Adam Przeworski, in particular, both treat democracy as a bargained equilibrium. Rustow emphasizes its preconditions, including national unity and a prolonged struggle in which diverse elites habituate themselves to democratic processes. He underplays the socioeconomic bases of stable elites. Przeworski doubts that elites, when they conflict, often seek benefits within democratic procedures as their first preference. He implies they would usually rather opt for authoritarianism, even though he sees democracy as the least unacceptable option for large groups trying to further their interests. Both Przeworski and Rustow suggest that the emergence of democracy depends on structures of power distribution, not on modernization.[54]

Yet there is a link between modernization and power distribution (including resource distribution), as the Chinese reforms show. An emphasis on leadership choice makes good sense, if the types of leaders are seen as many and the time frame for effective change is seen as not necessarily short. On that basis, it becomes possible to ask not just what might create democracy, but also what might make for other regime types that leaders could prefer: authoritarianism, corporatism, or other forms of interest aggregation. Democracy's emergence or nonemergence depends on political factors, not just economic factors, as Rustow and Przeworski stress. But they are oddly uncurious about why these factors arise, and they can frame the discussion not just in terms of authoritarianism or democracy, as if these were the only options. Intermediate and transitional ways of relating diverse modern interests to state power—especially corporatist and syndicalist ways of doing this—are as important as either authoritarianism or pluralism.

Critique of the Argument That Crowded Poverty Precludes a Regime Type

The most usual argument for neoauthoritarianism is functional: that strong rule will bring about a healthy economy. As a corollary, it is asserted that rule in China must be especially firm because of the gigantic national population size. Chinese intellectual leaders, official and dissident alike, treat this positive relationship between authoritarianism and economic demography as if it were a sure fact.

The past performance of East Asian "tigers" or "dragons" has been seen as the conclusive proof—even though Taiwan, Hong Kong, South Korea, and Singapore are all much smaller than China, internationally more open, militarily less secure, and in fact far more liberal. Most Chinese intellectuals think their country will become rich if it follows policies like those used in the "four dragons." They describe these policies as a combination of "markets" with "government intervention." Such concepts may provide a framework for discussion, but they do not specify why markets have arisen anywhere.[55] Also, such ideas do not specify what kinds of government intervention bring growth and what kinds hinder it.

Finally, the majority of Chinese intellectuals who share this way of thinking have not looked at another factor that applies in each of the four dragons to a much greater extent than in the PRC: The political elite in each of these small countries had, especially at the time its economy was growing fastest, a major problem of security and legitimacy as against potential rivals.[56]

There is a common problem with each of the blinkers that prevents vision in this discourse: They are all based on the premise that some unified idea, rather than struggle between networks contending over resources and norms, is what brings prosperity. Treating markets as natural neglects the historical contest in each current market polity between groups that benefit from the situational efficiency that markets bring and groups that want to protect labor and its surroundings from becoming priced commodities. Treating government intervention as uniformly wise neglects the many historical cases (e.g., China's "Great Third Front" 1964–71 investment program) in which it has been disastrous. Treating the "four dragons" as comparable to the PRC neglects not only their smaller size. More important, it neglects the fears and vulnerabilities of their governments in each case, which made those regimes more sensitive to the results of their actions than the PRC elite was. The usual discourse on this topic is easy to "deconstruct" as a gloss justifying continued rule by establishment intellectuals and soldiers. In China today, the politicians who are actually bringing prosperity tend to be rural, outside the effective reach of the state, not unified in any sense, and often without much education. When intellectuals have tried to run everything, they have done less well.

China's own experience of strong rule in periods like 1958–61, a time of major depression, also suggests a nonauthoritarian lesson about the link between state form and economic results. Growth clearly has not accompanied strong dictatorial rule in many other countries, ranging from Cuba to Haiti to Ethiopia to North Korea to Burma to Vietnam. Long periods in each of these countries have seen strong and internally disciplined governments presiding over economic basket cases. PRC elitists, especially intellectuals, tend simply to ignore the many countries that fail to confirm the economic value of dictatorship. The policies of leaders do not always work.

Does strong rule bring wealth? Does China need an authoritarian government, in order to have good economic performance? Lee Kwan Yew of Singapore says so, and other Chinese intellectuals have written myriad articles in agreement. The substantive question is empirical and comparative, and it has several parts. Both firm government and economic performance may be defined variously. Conclusive evidence for an answer is complex, because the query can be put in several different ways.[57]

Empirical Data on the Economic Effects of Regime Types

It is clear that high per-capita income correlates with democracy. Stephan Haggard used World Bank figures to create lists of countries in income groups (e.g., greater than $6,000 for a high group, and less than $500 for a low group). These he compared with the same countries' Freedom House ratings on two measures related to democracy. He found that four-fifths (79 percent) of the high-income countries were classed as having "the most extensive" political rights, among the seven categories along that scale. But two-thirds (67 percent) of the low-income countries were in either the sixth or seventh low ranges for political rights. Poverty correlates with authoritarianism.

The linkage between income and civil liberties was very strong as well. Fully 83 percent of the high-income countries were in the two "most extensive" civil liberties categories, and 93 percent of the low-income countries were in the three "least extensive" ratings.[58]

Atul Kohli examined groups of selected "more democratic" and "more authoritarian" countries. He found that although average annual GDP growth rates were slightly higher in relatively authoritarian countries, this correlation was not strong. Crucial nongrowth economic indices showed better performance: Democracies did better than illiberal regimes at reducing income inequality. They also were much better at lowering the portion of export earnings that went for external debt service.[59]

Although some authoritarian states in recent decades have shown high growth rates (e.g., Taiwan or South Korea), many others have been economic disaster areas. Average growth under illiberal regimes is fairly low. Although most of the states that bring down the average economic performance of authoritarian regimes are geographically far from China, some such as North Korea and Burma (and, at some stages, Vietnam) are very near China. Also, as "democratic transitions" in many East European and Latin American countries have shown, liberal regimes often inherit economies where authoritarian regimes had previously created massive inefficiency. Generals who lead *juntas* sometimes discover that they are inept economists; this can lead them to hand power (and economic messes) back to civilian politicians.[60] What happened in China at the fall of Lin Biao may not be totally different from this pattern (even though Lin's demise was involuntary). The high tide of wasteful PRC investment, especially in factories of the inland Great Third Front that depressed China's growth, dropped sharply after 1971.[61] Liberal regimes have no monopoly on bad economic policy.

Strong regimes are not all of a single kind. Authoritarianism may come in two distinct sorts, which have very different effects on economic growth. First, there are regimes like those of Stalin, Mao, "Papa Doc" Duvalier of Haiti, or Mengistu of Ethiopia—governments that try to be heavily extractive. When these leaders are fortunate to rule countries such as the USSR or the PRC, which have abundant primary industrial resources, whose mining the authoritarian state can monopolize, they can create quick but inefficient growth. Output rises, while total factor productivity declines. New sectors are created, and the state sets their product prices high, while keeping the costs of inputs and labor low. The government in this way can gather new capital from profits in the state industries from which these manufactures are sold. Initially, in the short run, the economic statistics from extractive authoritarianisms look superb. Later, when the wastefulness of the mobilization effort becomes more obvious and gross production rises more slowly, consumers want a greater variety of goods, and the statistics begin to look worse. Less well-endowed authoritarian regimes sometimes attempt this growth strategy without much ability to mobilize resources (perhaps because the ground they rule contains few minerals); so they turn in disastrous economic performances.

A second, less extractive kind of authoritarianism—as in Taiwan, South Korea, and for some periods in countries as different as Spain and Zimbabwe—is based (whatever its pretensions) on a shakier political constituency. For that reason, its leaders may choose to be less illiberal in both politics and economics than the extractive authoritarians mentioned above. Governments in these less-extractive states are greatly constrained by a need to assure that economic growth provides them legitimacy. Each such case involves large groups that are potentially antigovernment oppositions. Ethnic Taiwanese, for example, comprise 86 percent of the island's people. Since 1947, the KMT's industrial and land policies have been designed to neutralize their potential opposition to the slowly declining control of the state by mainlanders.[62] In South Korea, since the civil war of the late 1940s populist southerners have remained a major and very demonstrative threat to governments filled with ex-generals.[63] In Zimbabwe, Ndebeles and whites have been a continuing concern for the Shona leadership.[64] In Spain, Franco won his civil war, but not everyone (especially in high-growth provinces) was an ardent Franquista. Authoritarian regimes that have obvious ethnic or class-based latent oppositions are more likely to develop economic policies that lead to efficient growth than are authoritarian regimes with less need to use economic policy to neutralize such threats.[65]

China, considering its size, is relatively homogeneous in ethnic and social terms. For this reason, it is unclear whether authoritarians in the PRC have enough political incentive to use efficiently the economic resources that they extract. In any case, democracy is not merely a factor of production. Like authoritarianism, it has too many other effects to be treated so narrowly. Democracy is not just an investment good. Most Westerners, and even most political scientists, think that democratization comes mostly as a loose correlate of economic growth. Democrats in China, or least the urban clerks and intellectuals who most often claim to be democrats, have lost both income and prestige because of modern markets. Some Chinese dissidents therefore have conceived of democracy not so much as the concomitant of economic modernization but instead as a means to restore their traditionally high status, which economic reforms have eroded. Urban intellectuals have liked political modernization because it justifies complaint against a government that is unable to make the new economic modernization serve old elites.

The fast growth of prosperity in the world's largest nation must, at first face, be seen as a benefit to humanity as a whole. Surprisingly, it has not been widely welcomed by non-Chinese, who tend to fear China's future strength. The present author, taking a more optimistic view, sees China's boom in the long run as a nearly unalloyed good thing. This Chinese strength is a correlate of decentralization and undeclared practical democracy. More governmental control would, for the most part, impede it. Although there is surely a danger of xenophobic leaders in central politics, they emerge from the same intellectual strata as do their rival reformers who are more likely to succeed in postrevolutionary politics. A stronger China, presuming its internal violence is over, will for some time mean what it has already meant for the past quarter century, that is, a relatively weaker Beijing.

Demography and Regime Types

China's huge population size is often blamed by intellectuals for creating a need for authoritarianism. This defines the problem both too vaguely and too narrowly. Japan, Taiwan, and the Netherlands have very dense populations and sparse natural resources. Yet few would argue that these countries need more authoritarian population control. They have diversified and efficient economies, which provide many goods per person. Can a dictatorial planner do a better job for China's apparent surfeit of people than they themselves are doing? Authoritarian planning, which lowered total factor productivity during Mao's period, is much of the problem. In agriculture, which still employs most people for at least some of their time, total factor productivity (including labor productivity) declined 6 percent between 1952 and 1957, and then again 8 percent between 1957 and 1965.[66] Only after central authoritarianism in agriculture was reduced, in the 1970s and 1980s, did people produce more crops per farmer—so in that important sense, the population problem became less severe. Perhaps illiberal rule can solve some aspects of the population problem, but such rule also helped create it. The present PRC elite nonetheless stresses population size as a justification for police powers, control of the press, and centralized rule. A more direct effect of these policies is to suppress the government's critics. People are not the problem. Educated planners are, when they justify their status by claiming more than they can deliver.

Economic Interests and Reform Interests Among Citizens

Reforms, if there were truth in advertising, should always be sold with the proviso "results will vary." The State Institute to Study System Reform surveyed three groups—intellectuals, cadres, and randomly chosen individuals—to assess their expectations and satisfaction with the reforms. The findings (not published openly in exact statistics) showed that, in 1984, the gap between expectations about reforms and satisfaction with them was small. But by 1988, this gap had widened.[67]

Urban young people in the 1980s, who had not experienced the Cultural Revolution directly, were often less enthusiastic about democratic slogans than were either more-educated people in the same age cohorts or older groups who recalled the post-1966 disaster. The *China Youth News* surveyed Chinese citizens' interest in democracy during 1987. According to this poll, a slightly lower percentage of ordinary urban youths below age twenty-five felt that democratic freedoms were an essential condition of modernization than of respondents in the 26–35 age bracket (although in both groups, the proportion was only about one-fifth).[68] This survey was of course attitudinal. By the 1980s, the government was constraining young people less severely than it earlier had done. Articulate expressions of opinion about political structure may vary to match the contexts.

The public venting of opinions, especially by experts, begins to get at a particular strength of modern rule.[69] The expertise of a democracy is to choose the experts who will serve more basic values. One need not know how to make a machine before making an intelligent decision on which brand of machine to buy. The same is true for decisions about which politicians and structures to empower.[70] Now China has elections at least at low levels, some experts in legislative committees who interrogate cadres closely, some independent editorials, and some other checks on bureaucrats. China is probably not about to become a democracy soon, despite these changes. Its sporadic changes in that direction have occurred, not just because these make intellectuals feel safer, but also because they serve other kinds of people. Intellectuals may be China's best hope, as is often claimed.[71] But an alternative view is that some of the professional thinkers now provide some hope to nonintellectual and nonstate actors.

Regime Types: Modern Options in Theory

Standard elite arguments about the difficulties of democracy in China all presume the main causes of action are ideal and normative, rather than situational and concrete. If so, political will could maintain order, culture would determine state form, and disciplined plans would bring growth. Also, order, culture, and plans would all be conceived only as collective on a national scale, never as local. Yet in practice, local situations frame most of Chinese politics. If the PRC is to grow under the stability of rule by one party, this elite will need more institutional mechanisms to become responsive to local leaders.

Corporatism has been shown at local levels in China, but it could also emerge at the state level. Philippe Schmitter defined corporatism as:

> a system of interest representation in which the constituent units are organized into a limited number of singular, compulsory, noncompetitive, hierarchically ordered and functionally differentiated categories, *recognized or licensed (if not created) by the state* and granted a deliberate representational monopoly within their respective categories in exchange for observing certain controls.[72]

Local corporatism, if it is not licensed by the state, falls outside this definition. In reform China, some local power networks are officially recognized, many are effectively known only to local hinge leaders who are often decisive on their own but nominally in the "state," while others are illegal. Most leaders of corporate bodies have an interest in speaking as if they were fully loyal, inside the pale. Whether or not this claim is true, it can help them do whatever they wish. Central state license is, for most Chinese local corporations during the reform period, inessential to their power; but they want official approval to the extent that it does not put a crimp in their practical business. When the state derecognizes local entities, as it has often done in conservative periods, many go underground and wait for a more realistic or tax-hungry regime to relicense them. Geography, time, and functions all define the corporate entities in China, with which the leaders of the state are slowly finding they must come to terms.

Corporatism has usually been studied not in localities, but in whole countries. A corporatist system at the national level may be conceived as a modern form of government that, while undemocratic and probably transitional, allows diversified political work to be done. Leaders of the corporate groups articulate their interests to top policy makers (though not always in public). Such a system relates power networks to one another, and it may be described alongside pluralist democracy and totalitarian monism, which historically have been longer-lasting kinds of regimes.

Two Keys Generate Four Regime Types

Schmitter suggests that state systems come in four basic types, which he calls corporatist, syndicalist, pluralist, and monist. He does not suggest these four may also be ordered by the dimensions on the big diagram in the introduction in Volume One of this book, but they can be (as can some of his later formulations).[73] Schmitter's list is about politics and making decisions that represent interests, so it concerns "steering." But the diagram's two dimensions also apply either within that sector or to political aspects of the three other sectors.[74]

Schmitter is primarily interested in corporatism, which he presents as one of the decision-making types that is collectivist. A corporatist state grants recognized monopolies of influence to a limited number of noncompetitive groups, in which membership is compulsory to represent "their respective categories in exchange for observing certain controls on their [the corporate group's] selection of leaders and articulation of demands and supports." Although corporatism at the state level in China has not been high profile, the annual conferences in Beijing to decide tax rates closely resemble this structure (even though the corporations involved are mostly regional, not functional, and their effective power often fails to reach local polities). Corporatism is also a frequent political structure in entirely local Chinese power networks. It is certainly a regime type that, in some partly regionalist variation, could well emerge as obvious in the national structure during future reforms.

Schmitter specifies that corporatists (like pluralists) particularly recognize "the burgeoning role of permanent administrative staffs, of specialized information, of technical expertise. . . . Corporatists of whatever stripe express confidence that an 'enlightened statesman' (or an 'enlightened state') can co-opt, control, or coordinate [what Madison called] 'the most common and durable source of faction . . . the various and unequal distribution of property'."[75] Corporatism is a system for making *collective* decisions about the arrangement of *external situations* and resources, under the premise of regime unity. It can be considered a fairly modern regime type.

Monism, a.k.a. totalitarianism, is in some respects similar to corporatism, as Schmitter says. A monist state similarly licenses monopolies to noncompetitive compulsory groups. But the difference is that a corporatist state deals rationally with situations the system did not create, while all parts of a monist system are "ideologically selective," following *normative* values that the state specifies.[76] Monist systems are *collectivist* and coercive. They are, even ideally, willful and dictatorial. Mao's first-preference regime type was clearly of this kind, although in practice it never quite fit the model as well as the international classic cases of the 1930s, Stalin's and Hitler's. This is the state form against which various kinds of political reform in China are most often directed. Specifying the three different alternatives to it is one way of showing how diverse reforms can be.

Pluralist states have one specific similarity to corporatist regimes. They both face modern problems of trying to deal efficiently with *external* situations. The difference between them is normative: Pluralist states do not intend to license interest groups or control their leaderships. The pluralist assumption about *individual and small group* interests is that they are naturally incoherent; they are separate data; they will naturally conflict. (Both corporatist and monist regimes are based on exactly the opposite premise.) Pluralist group memberships are not compulsory; individuals make their own choices. Pluralist groups are like corporatist ones because they deal with situational goals, not ultimate values. They assume "the persistence and expansion of functionally differentiated and potentially conflicting interests," as Schmitter says.[77] When most liberal states concoct their foreign policies toward the PRC, they are sometimes explicit about designing their actions to encourage the evolution of a pluralist regime in China. But there are at least two nonpluralist structures that could replace China's monism, that is, the corporatist or syndicalist forms.

Syndicalist political systems use *normative* means of reaching decisions, but they (like pluralist systems) assume that *individuals and small groups* will differ. Syndicalist groups consist of "an unlimited number of singular, voluntary . . . categories, . . . resolving their conflicts and authoritatively allocating their values autonomously." The state does not license any monopoly of representation for them. But like monist groups (which are instruments of the state), syndicalist groups are ideologically selective, often "radical and utopian" in their values.[78] In sum, a comprehensive categorization of political systems can be made along the same dimensions that sociologists explicitly (and anthropologists implicitly) have used to structure their approaches to societies and communities.

Chinese Choices Among the Four Options

In these terms, what kind of regime does China currently have? There are different answers to this question, depending on the way it is asked. The first, most analytical answer must be all four, in varying degrees, since these are basically kinds of activities that any political system may perform. But the surest way to parse a polity is, first, to look at the interests the leaders propagate as most important (either individualist or collectivist, either normative or situational); and then second, to make a critical analysis by testing alternative sets of interests and noting how they are being served. Most PRC leaders are conservatives and *say* they are oriented to a large Chinese community of patriots and to social ideals (i.e., moving toward the monist direction). Indeed, until the reforms they did less well by individuals and by criteria of external efficiency than by the whole nation and by the expression of clear values. But during the reforms, even the top of the Chinese state is paying more attention to the opposite tasks. So it is changing—often in a more corporatist direction. All real polities mix these types.

A second answer is that different parts of a whole regime ordinarily serve these four different functions. These concrete institutions are often in tension with one another because they are good for different things. Conflicts in the Chinese state between economic and cultural politicians have been very common—not just in the 1960s, for which these tensions became best known.[79] The styles needed for the "technical organization" and "human organization" roles of government are essentially different. Attention to situations and to norms often call for opposite styles of leadership, and these can become bases for factions. Another difference arises between the styles needed for "pure ideology" politics aimed at harmonious stability and those for "practical ideology" politics aimed at change.[80] Some leaders are better at articulating consensus values, while others are better at inspiring vanguard small groups to lead transformations.

Yet a third answer is that not all these roles need to be performed. Even if in some sense they "should" be served, they are often simply neglected. In general, the Chinese system, at least in most of its units larger than families, still seems to do an especially inept job of being sensitive to interests that individuals express. The PRC has, even during reforms, done much better at integrating or disciplining its parts reliably as regards norms than at coordinating them for efficiency. Actual political systems "satisfice," and they never perform with anything remotely resembling perfection. The most common regime type is a partial failure.

The use of such categories is to gauge, probe, and compare directions of change, not to specify the immutable characteristics of any system. If reform norms give more allowance to small groups and individuals, this should become evident in purposes that can reasonably be attributed to people's observable conduct. When behavior and statements alike evince more efficiency in dealing with external factors, then local and state leaders' interests are becoming less strictly normative and more situational. Both of these trends in the PRC since the early 1970s have been uneven but can be documented. They are the substance of reforms. They come from many kinds of power networks, and the evidence for them comes from many fields that are usually studied separately. But they show how the Chinese political system, despite all its continuing variety, slowly changes between regime types.

What is needed, for the Chinese political structure to become more responsive to larger numbers of people, is a greater sense on the part of top Communist leaders that their fate depends on local leaders, who are watching them. No change has not been proposed by high intellectuals in China, but a pattern of state responsiveness is the trend. If the resources and views of hinge captains affect state leaders' own success against their rivals, then national corporatism, and perhaps later a more open system, could emerge in China.

Actual Reforms of Structure: Party or Management

The changes that have occurred in China, at least as much as those that have been proposed by the country's few legal writers, head in the directions suggested above. In Xiaoshan, Zhejiang, for example, there is a Private Enterprises Association, which all nonstate and noncooperative firms are supposed to join. Of the twenty-five members of the association's administrative committee in 1991, fifteen were private businessmen. The other ten were officials from municipal bureaus. Some of these came from offices with claims on the firms (such as the Tax Bureau and the police). Others came from offices that entrepreneurs often had to contact (the Land Administration Bureau, the Electricity Bureau, the Township and Village Industry Management Bureau, and the Industrial and Commercial Management Bureau).[81] The association represented Xiaoshan's private entrepreneurs locally, in a fully corporatist fashion.

In many work units before the reforms, a single person controlled everything. Economic diversification made this pattern obsolete. Multimember "leadership groups" (lingdao banzi) formally predated reforms, but they slowly became somewhat more prominent at many administrative levels after 1971. The prereform stress on having a single "responsible person" in each unit was reduced as a requirement imposed by the state. Many local groups still had clear chiefs, who did not always have the nominal top jobs as defined administratively. But Chinese traditions, not just state dictates, supported "one-man management" where this form arose. It was no longer, in reforms, the requisite form everywhere.

Before the 1980s, most Chinese organizations possessed "unified leaderships," with the same person acting as the Party and administrative head. In the 1980s, administrative jobs became separate and more important than Party jobs. Managers, rather than CCP generalists, were supported by high reformers in claiming all vital functions in organizations, except that most appointments also went through a Party approval process.

Many companies and schools held two meetings each week: one led by the management to talk about professional and technical matters, and the other held by the Party to talk about loyalty and mobilization. The "political" meetings contrasted, however, with sessions the Party used to organize before the reforms. They became less formal, not always based on prescribed readings such as editorials or Beijing directives.

These structural changes would have been difficult without personnel changes. New kinds of leadership often required new leaders. So both nationally and locally, sporadic campaigns purged "leftists," who had benefited from the Cultural Revolution in any of the last three years of the 1960s. These leaders were castigated as "three [bad] kinds of people" (sanzhong ren). In 1983, the CCP established a Central Discipline Inspection Commission, which soon launched a drive to expel many young leftists—a putative quota of 3 million, according to one report—who had joined the Party during the Cultural Revolution.[82]

Well into the reforms, China nonetheless still had two kinds of cadres: Party generalists and professional managers. Even in 1985, throughout China, a vast majority of demobilized soldiers who had gone on to cadre posts as heads of units (either Party or state) made their later careers in the Party stream, not the state one. Slightly more than half of the country's top local cadres of this sort who had previous experience in administration (xingzheng) also stayed with Party careers. But most cadres with technical, professional, or grass-roots leadership experience went into managerial jobs. This bears a strong resemblance to the pattern Seweryn Bialer reported in the late 1970s' USSR, as he studied changes in the Leninist party of that country. Data on the Chinese case are shown in Table 4.3–1.

The aftermath of the Cultural Revolution was generally a demotion for the soldiers and a promotion for the managers. Yet Party cadres, no matter how strong their love of discipline or how much they wished to follow national leaders, did not all surrender their previous powers readily. Deng Xiaoping said in early 1986, "All comrades should consider the problem of reform of the political structure." Deng announced that the Party should be "subject to restrictions" and that without such changes, economic reform would be forever stymied. "What good is it to decentralize power [to enterprise managers] if it is always being taken back again [by Party committees]?"[83]

The main reason for such high-level concern about retirements was economic. Many Party members had scant education, and 8 percent of them nationally were illiterate.[84] As Fudan University professor Wang Huning wrote in 1986, "Reform of the economic system is breaking up the old government." He noted a wide range of linkages that had to be altered for economic efficiency: "Political power in the central government, horizontal power relations in the central government,

Table 4.3–1

Party or Managerial Careers of 1985 PRC Unit Heads, by Background
(percentages)

	Secretaries in 1985, or deputy secretaries	Managers in 1985, or deputy managers	
% of the two groups above, by previous backgrounds:			
Demobilized soldiers	36	9	
Administrators (incl. CCP)	27	15	
Grass-roots leaders	15	23	
Professionals	14	24	
Technical backgrounds	8	28	
Totals	c. 100	c. 100	
% of the cadres below by whether they were 1985 secretaries or managers			Totals
Demobilized soldiers	72	28	100
Administrators (incl. CCP)	54	46	100
Grass-roots leaders	29	71	100
Professionals	28	72	100
Technical backgrounds	15	85	100

Source: From nontabulated data in Wang Yu et al., *Da juanbian shiqi* (The Era of Great Transformation) (Shijiazhuang: Hebei Renmin Chuban She, 1987), pp. 48–49. These figures are rounded from the source. The percentages in the upper panel are calculated on the premise that these five categories exhausted the sources of such 1985 cadres, as apparently the classified survey had intended them to do.

vertical relations between central and local governments, horizontal power links among the local governments, and the relations between government and enterprises must all be adjusted. Otherwise the ossified model in the economic system will never be wiped out."[85]

The industrial reforms of the mid-1980s stressed the importance of giving more authority to the heads of stores and factories. Managers' rights were further expanded in another set of regulations in September 1986. This trend gained momentum, despite resistance from "mother-in-law" planners and Party conservatives. Later, a regulation decreed that the "director responsibility system" should apply in all state firms. As reformers could rightly conclude:

At the high-point of China's economic reform in the summer of 1988, the Party's role and influence within state enterprises had contracted to the extent that its secretary and committee experienced considerable difficulties even in fulfilling their basic formal obligation to "guarantee and supervise" the implementation of Party and governmental policies.[86]

Factory directors, under the reforms, were supposed to take responsibility for practically everything, and in some plants, they actually exercised this right. The "one-man management" system during reformist periods aimed to reduce the Party's "guaranteeing and supervising" (*baozheng he jiandu*) nearly to extinction. In conservative periods, and in most local units, this change was stymied.

Enterprise heads were still supposed to submit important issues to their units' management committees, which included the Party secretary, department heads, and up to one-third of the delegates representing the enterprise workers' congress. But the manager theoretically had authority to exercise his judgment, rather than the decision of the management committee.[87] To hire or fire a deputy director or department head, the manager was supposed to have the approval of the personnel department in the supervising corporation. The enterprise Party committee could also offer its "opinion." These restrictions on personnel decisions were important, but heads of firms nonetheless increased their authority in the 1980s. In reformist years and modern offices, even a manager who did not himself run the local Party needed to consult CCP colleagues less than in Mao's time. In conservative years and most units, a manager had to consult local Party leaders more than in reformist years.

The "two-track system" still gave local Party committees charge of political work. Mayor Jiang at the end of 1987 called for a "one-track system." The CCP in units were supposed to be reduced to merely "supervisory" roles and had to "support the director or manager in assuming full responsibility for the enterprise."[88] This reform at Shanghai began in Minhang district, whose factory CCP committees in the main local bureau (for electrical machines) were put firmly under the jurisdiction of the district Party committee. Their decisions were supposed to override any made by functional Party committees at the municipal level, that is, by the supervising corporation. But there is no doubt that, even in this much-publicized local instance, some Party cadres resisted the diminution of their authority. As Mayor Jiang put it plainly, "To achieve this historic change, cadres of Party committees at all levels should voluntarily, actively, and happily take part in this reform."[89] He suggests they did not all give up their power joyfully.

State managers and Party cadres could be put into fairly serious conflict, especially in local units where their previous relations had been uneasy, when the state told managers to take charge. A law of early 1988 gave factory directors "full power over management." This was supposed to include personnel decisions, which had earlier been mostly a Party matter; and companies' CCP committees were again enjoined to "support the factory director in fully exercising power according to law."[90] These exhortations were repeated many times. If the reformist state at this time had been effective over local conservatives who directly opposed its policy, once would have been enough.

Party heads were supposed to confine themselves to propaganda and assorted community roles, for example, guiding trade unions, the militia, security guards, the women's federation, and the youth league.[91] A Party secretary at a Nantong industrial plant protested, "To guarantee and supervise are only hollow words. There are no criteria attached to them. There is no practical and proper way of implementing them. The central purpose of the director responsibility system is to reduce the Party's leadership in enterprises." In another Nantong plant, a Party secretary was more powerful and was consulted by his manager frequently, mostly because this secretary had previously held the directorship himself. Even then, when the chief accountant (not a CCP member) drew up the factory's profit-and-loss sheets for mid-1988 in a manner that the Party secretary did not like, the latter was unable to have the accounts written in the way he wished.[92]

In government offices, not just factories, this change was officially supposed to reduce the power of Party generalists in the late 1980s. The municipal Party committees of many Chinese cities during 1988 created "reform plans" that shifted specific management functions to government offices. Beijing and apparently Shanghai abolished Party groups (*dangzu*) in most government departments. In their stead, the CCP established "leading small groups" over large functional areas. The same top leaders tended to remain in charge at high levels, but there was a partial change of formal structure: They increasingly did so wearing their government hats rather than their Party hats. The number of "administrative personnel" (*guanli renyuan*) in state-owned units rose during the reform period, but the number of "engineering technicians" rose much faster.[93]

Many cultural units kept unified managements because propaganda departments are Party, not government, units. But the main relationship between newspapers and propaganda departments seemed, by the late 1980s, to have been reduced to Party approval of new appointments to journals' top management positions. CCP advisers outside the media might urge coverage of some issues, topics, or persons. But heads of particular media remained crucial. Chief editors—who were always important Party leaders in their own right—often had so much personal prestige that they could run their shops autonomously most of the time. If problems arose, conflicts would arise directly and secretly between these chief editors and CCP propaganda department cadres, who were no more than their peers. The Party's residual powers to disapprove promotions might have become important, at least temporarily, as the old generation of prestigious editors with pre-1949 revolutionary credentials retired or passed away. Their influence on their staffs often remained so great that nothing less than death itself was likely to attenuate their power.

In journalistic staffs, it is difficult to separate technical from political functions. Some editors in the 1980s expressed a view that the content of newspapers, which is obviously political, should be deemed a "technical" matter within their jurisdiction—and that the Party in news staffs should confine itself to personnel questions only, not journalism. At *Wenhui News,* only a fifth of the writers were members of the Party in 1988, although one-third of all members of the Editorial Department were CCP members, as was the chief editor, who was the main political as well as technical leader in this unit. Only a few further reporters were members of the youth league. The *Liberation Daily,* as the Shanghai CCP organ, predictably had a higher ratio of Party members on its staff.

Managers in the late 1980s reported that they spent a great deal of time resolving conflicts between their department heads—a major task, previously, of Party secretaries. Also, managers in interviews agreed that CCP meetings were held less frequently than in previous years and were taken less seriously.[94] Activists were seldom created in political campaigns by the late 1980s. But people with worker backgrounds could still extract special benefits from the personnel system, especially when they joined the CCP themselves.

Party organizations in factories could initiate their own investigations of management, but they were not supposed to usurp the authority of experts. They could encourage "suggestions" to factory directors. The CCP was mainly supposed to deal, during reformist periods, with propaganda and morale rather than technical matters. Actually, Party cadres had many informal roles, and their continued oversight of hiring and promotion decisions gave them great local power. Workers who were CCP members felt relatively free to express their opinions to managers. This helped flows of information from the shop level to executives. In one factory where informal consultations of this sort became usual, workers with ideas or ambitions were said to want to join the Party; in a workshop of five hundred people, one-tenth of the staff in early 1988 submitted applications for Party membership. Everyone was supposed, still, to "respect and depend on" Party organization.[95] Some pathos, in this call for respect, was consistent with continued special pride among proletarian members of the Party, even after the reforms had been under way for many years.

Structural reforms of politics in China during the 1970s and 1980s have taken place outside the institutions of Party and government, not just inside them. As an ideal, reform of official institutions has been on the agenda of some reformist PRC leaders; but they find it harder to accomplish than to promise. They downplay the extent to which local leaders have been making de facto political reforms already in units that are supposed to liaise with local or functional groups but are often mostly autonomous. Power institutions from families to economic collectives are restricting the structural options available to state leaders. The major change in this regime is that nonstate forces are "bringing themselves back in" to Chinese politics. Local networks are now busy penetrating the state.

Notes

1. Earl Swisher, trans., *China's Management of the American Barbarians* (New Haven: Yale University Press, 1951), p. 48.

2. E. E. Schattschneider, *The Semi-Sovereign People: A Realist's View of American Democracy* (Hinsdale, IL: Dreyden Press, 1975), pp. 114–15.

3. A classic analysis of the crucial role of state organization is Reinhard Bendix, *Nation-Building and Citizenship* (New York: Wiley, 1964).

4. *Zhonghua renmin gonghe guo xianfa* (Constitution of the People's Republic of China) (Beijing: Falü Chuban She, 1986), pp. 58–59.

5. Ibid., p. 55.

6. Article 52 concerns a "duty . . . to safeguard the unity of the country and the unity of all its nationalities." Article 53 requires citizens to "keep state secrets, protect public property, and observe labor discipline and public order and respect social ethics." Article 54 enjoins them to "safeguard the security, honor, and interests of the motherland." Ibid., p. 62.

7. Frances Hoar Foster, "Codification in Post-Mao China," *American Journal of Comparative Law* 30 (Summer 1982), p. 419.

8. American courts have seldom used Articles 9 and 10 of the Bill of Rights because these are subject to conflicting interpretations—some of which are radical and futuristic. Article 9 can be read simply as an astonishing attempt to split sovereignty because of the powerful understatement of its verbs and its last noun: "The enumeration in the Constitution, of certain rights, shall not be construed to deny or disparage others retained by the people." Political fury has seldom been so channeled. The judges have to read all this; it glares at them; but, for once speechless at the implications, they still largely think that they have to ignore it. Also, the institution of the common law jury, which has implicit quasi-legislative powers, carries the same meaning.

9. See, on this and some material in the next paragraph, Timothy A. Gelatt, "Book Review," *China Law Reporter* 7:3–4 (1993), pp. 237–38.

10. Jiang Zemin et al., *Shanghai dangzheng jigou yange* (The Transformation of Shanghai's Party and Administration) (Shanghai: Shanghai Renmin Chuban She, 1988), p. 140.

11. The official four modernizations—none of them political—had been of agriculture, industry, science and technology, and defense. See Wei Jingsheng, "The Fifth Modernization," in *China's Fifth Modernization: The Human Rights Movement, 1978–1979,* James D. Seymour, ed. (Standfordville, NY: Human Rights Publishing Group, 1980), pp. 47–69; and David Goodman, ed., *Beijing Street Voices: The Poetry and Politics of China's Democracy Movement* (London: Marion Boyars, 1981).

12. For more on *fang* and *shou,* and a diverting mnemonic that they tended to alternate in even and odd numbered years respectively, see Richard Baum, *Burying Mao: Chinese Politics in the Age of Deng Xiaoping* (Princeton: Princeton University Press, 1994).

13. Quoted in Tony Saich, "Reforming the Political Structure," in *Reforming the Revolution: China in Transition,* Robert Benewick and Paul Wingrove, eds. (Basingstoke, UK: Macmillan, 1988), p. 32.

14. Stuart R. Schram, *Ideology and Policy in China Since the Third Plenum, 1978–1984* (London: Contemporary China Institute, School of Oriental and African Studies, 1984), p. 20.

15. From *Selected Works of Deng Xiaoping (1975–1982)* (Beijing: Foreign Languages Press, 1984), p. 310.

16. Stuart R. Schram, *Ideology and Policy,* p. 21. A February 1989 Shanghai journal also criticized Lenin for allegedly having a mistress, "a Russified French beauty," who died

in 1921. According to this report, he was so aggrieved that his ability to handle Party affairs was hindered. The report is sketchy at best; but see the Hong Kong liberal magazine *Zhengming* (Dispute) (April 1989), p. 17.

17. Wei Haibo in *Reform of China's Political System* [vol 20, no. 1 of *Chinese Law and Government*], Benedict Stavis, ed. (Armonk, NY: M.E. Sharpe, 1987), p. 76.

18. Yan's proposals are sensibly directed toward difficulties that the PRC faces in capitalist China, especially Hong Kong, Macau, and Taiwan. He makes the proposal of federalism for Chinese provinces, too, and he seems to neglect the possibility that cultural-political entrepreneurs in Tibet or parts of Xinjiang would not call for China's division (a result that Yan might not like). In fact, a kind of federalization is taking place in China without the benefit of law. See Yan Jiaqi, *Lianbang Zhongguo gouxiang* (Plan for a Federal China) (Hong Kong: Ming Bao Chuban She, 1992).

19. Robin Munro, "Reform, Students, and Conservative Backlash," in Robert Benewick and Paul Wingrove, eds., *Reforming the Revolution,* p. 70. As things turned out, the decade was not to be a smooth one; and Deng knew that he would not be the one pronouncing on national elections in that time frame.

20. See Benedict Stavis, *China's Political Reforms: An Interim Report* (New York: Praeger, 1988); also Andrew J. Nathan, *China's Crisis: Dilemmas of Reform and Prospects for Democracy* (New York: Columbia University Press, 1990), p. 179.

21. Benedict Stavis, *China's Political Reforms,* p. 52.

22. *SHKXB,* January 19, 1989.

23. *Post,* May 13, 1989.

24. Li Honglin was the official, but other signatories included political scientist Yan Jiaqi, legal scholar Yu Haocheng, journalist Dai Qing, and social scientists Xu Liangying and Zhang Xianyang. See Willy Wo-lap Lam in *Post,* May 6, 1989.

25. *"Wenhua de gengxin jizhi."* The "treasure" was called a *fa bao. ZGQNB,* June 30, 1988.

26. This view, in ibid., is interesting as a statement from contemporary China. It is extremely dubious in light of much historical research about the West. See, for example, Eugen Weber, *Peasants into Frenchmen* (Berkeley: University of California Press, 1977).

27. An heroic general once sent a concise victory report: "We have met the enemy, and he is ours." But the malapropists, as usual, made a subtler version that is more applicable here: "We have met the enemy, and he is us."

28. Some of this information comes from a personal communication by Kevin J. O'Brien. For more, see Liao Gailong, "The '1980 Reform' Program in China," published in Hong Kong during 1981 and translated in *Policy Conflicts in Post-Mao China,* John P. Burns and Stanley Rosen, eds. (Armonk, NY: M.E. Sharpe, 1986), pp. 87–101, and parts of *Yan Jiaqi and China's Struggle for Democracy,* David Bachman and Dali L. Yang, eds. and trans. (Armonk, NY: M.E. Sharpe, 1991).

29. See Merle Goldman, *Sowing the Seeds of Democracy in China: Political Reform in the Era of Deng Xiaoping* (Cambridge: Harvard University Press, 1994). A particularly sensitive account is Perry Link, *Evening Chats in Beijing: Probing China's Predicament* (New York: Norton, 1992).

30. *"Minzhu yao kexue hua."* Vera Schwarcz, "Memory, Commemoration, and the Plight of China's Intellectuals," *Wilson Quarterly* (Autumn 1989), p. 124.

31. Christopher Buckley, "Science as Politics and Politics as Science: Fang Lizhi and Chinese Intellectuals' Uncertain Road to Dissent," *Australian Journal of Chinese Affairs* 25 (January 1991), p. 16, from Fang's *Selected Works,* published in Singapore in 1983. Li Cheng gave me this reference.

32. See Li Cheng and Lynn White, "China's Technocratic Movement and the *World Economic Herald,*" *Modern China* 17:3 (July 1991), pp. 342–88.

33. *SHJJDB,* January 30, 1989, p. 10.

34. *SHJJDB,* October 10, 1983, p. 2.

35. Fu Zhengyuan, "The Sociology of Political Science in the PRC," in *The Development of Political Science: A Comparative Study,* D. Easton, J. Gunnell, and L. Graziano, eds. (London: Routledge, 1991), p. 245.

36. Samuel P. Huntington, *American Politics: The Promise of Disharmony* (Cambridge: Harvard University Press, 1981), passim, e.g., pp. 35, 50, and 66.

37. *CD,* February 3, 1988.

38. *SHJJDB,* January 16, 1989.

39. Nobel prizes are more generally respected in China than in other countries because most are for intellectual accomplishments, especially in science. When overseas Chinese scientists win Nobel prizes, and then return on trips to the motherland, they have audiences with the most prestigious leaders of the state. Friedman receives similar treatment, even though Friedman is not well known for his commitment to socialism. Mother Teresa, who also visited the PRC, received more international fame for her work in Calcutta slums than for her Peace prize; but in China, the Nobel was her best visa. When the Dalai Lama won this prize in 1989, the rebuke to PRC policies of oppression was strongly felt in China because of the immense prestige of such awards there. When the first PRC intellectual wins a Nobel, the effect on the Chinese elite will be even more impressive than has been achieved at the Olympics.

40. Wu Guoguang has referred me to Chen's article in *RMRB,* July 7, 1989, p. 2, and a related piece by Chen Yeping in *Qiushi* (Seeking Truth) 20 (1991).

41. *Post,* May 4, 1989.

42. Singapore may require more self-discipline than China, in the medium term, because of 200 million Indonesians nearby. Riots in Taiwan's Legislative Yuan, whose violence PRC television shows out of journalistic instinct and presumably at the behest of Beijing hard-liners, have given competitive democracy a bad name in some PRC intellectual circles. This violence in Taiwan may have developed from an unusual history there: The opposition Democratic Progressive Party legislators sat for years in a parliament along with old members from mainland China elected in the 1940s (and with KMT members recently elected on Taiwan). The tradition of legislative violence grew from resentment that their votes were counterbalanced by mainland assemblymen whose electoral mandates were egregiously stale. This pattern will not be replicated in the PRC, if that state allows a legislative opposition. Violence is not inevitable in competitive Chinese assemblies—even on Taiwan, local people have became surprisingly blasé about it. Elections are profoundly disturbing to people whose careers are in parties that can lose. Coups sometimes overthrow electoral results, but there is scant evidence to show that fights among legislators delegitimize them.

43. The avowedly reformist *River Elegy* documentary claims that the Chinese people fear disorder and avoid talking about it. It likens this to the regular flooding of the Yellow River—and mentions that even a dauntless leader like Mao Zedong, who wrote poems about many rivers, did not much refer to the Yellow River. *ZGQNB,* June 30, 1988.

44. Bao Gong (990–1062) was chief mandarin of Kaifeng under the Northern Song, famous for never taking bribes or yielding to unjust pressures from his own family—or even from the imperial family—and renowned among the populace for his fairness. Bao Gong projects a severe, fair, straight-arrow image, much like that of George Washington in America, with whom he is compared in the *Zhongwai lishi renwu cidian* (Who's Who of Historical World Figures), Wang Banghe et al., eds. (Changsha: Hunan Renmin Chuban She, 1987), p. 81.

45. *Jihui youxing shiwei fa jianghua* (Talks about the Law on Assemblies, Parades, and Demonstrations), Propaganda Office of the Judicial Department of the People's Republic of China, ed. (Beijing: Falü Chuban She, 1990), pp. 9–15.

46. Based on an interview with three young intellectuals from Shanghai. They did not represent the whole city, as the text above suggests.

47. David Hackett Fischer, *Albion's Seed: Four British Folkways in America* (New York: Oxford University Press, 1989), p. 413.

48. There are exceptions, e.g., in Burma or Algeria; but history is not finished in those countries.

49. See William Theodore de Bary, *The Liberal Tradition in China* (New York: Columbia University Press, 1983).

50. The standard source is E. M. W. Tillyard, *The Elizabethan World Picture: A Study of the Idea of Order in the Age of Shakespeare, Donne and Milton* (New York: Vintage Books, n.d. but c. 1942).

51. Andrew Nathan and Shi Tianjian, "Cultural Requisites for Democracy in China: Findings from a Survey," *Daedalus* 122:2 (Spring 1993), p. 116. This research used the famous survey questionnaire that underlay the classic in this field, Gabriel A. Almond and Sidney Verba, *The Civic Culture* (Princeton: Princeton University Press, 1963).

52. Li Cheng, "The Rise of Technocracy: Elite Transformation and Ideological Change in Post-Mao China" (Ph.D. dissertation, Politics Department, Princeton University, 1991), p. 310, from a study by Wang Fuchun and Wu Xiaojian in *Zhengzhi xue yanjiu* (Political Science Research) 1 (1989).

53. Ibid., p. 311, from Min Qi, *Zhongguo zhengzhi wenhua* (Chinese Political Culture) (Kunming: Yunnan Renmin Chuban She, 1989), p. 123.

54. Dankwart Rustow, "Transitions to Democracy," *Comparative Politics* 2:3 (September 1970), pp. 337–63; and Adam Przeworski, *Democracy and the Market: Political and Economic Reforms in Eastern Europe and Latin America* (New York: Cambridge University Press, 1991).

55. Most Chinese intellectuals regard markets as a natural phenomenon with no political history, as if people's time, environment, and proper earnings are completely unproblematic as market commodities. Like most Western economists, they avoid reading any books describing the history of political struggle surrounding markets, e.g., Karl Polanyi, *The Great Transformation* (New York: Rinehart, 1944)—or they avoid understanding such books in terms that might threaten the notion that intellectual planners have a natural right to decide everything alone. The terms quoted in the previous sentence are from a Chinese economist, interviewed during 1994.

56. In Taiwan, this problem during the island's period of quickest economic growth came mainly from the fact that the government was run by mainlanders but 85 percent of the population was Taiwanese. In Hong Kong, it arose because the government was essentially British, with 98 percent of the people Chinese. In Singapore more than in any of the other three (although they all have security problems), tight but prosperous government can easily be justified by the existence of about 200 million Muslim Indonesians nearby, whose economy is controlled by a small Chinese economic elite; this situation puts Singapore in some long-term great danger that its leaders would not reduce by mentioning, so that they talk about the "Asian way" of hierarchy instead. In South Korea, the instability came mainly from an old and rather xenophobic opposition to the military–business regime coalition; this opposition is represented most in places like Kwangju and universities; its importance in Korean politics goes back to the mid-1940s at least. See Bruce Cumings, *The Origins of the Korean War* (Princeton: Princeton University Press, 1990).

57. See the review article by Robert Wade, "East Asia's Economic Success: Conflicting Perspectives, Partial Insights, Shaky Evidence," *World Politics* 44 (January 1992), pp. 270–320.

58. Stephan Haggard's paper for the Agency for International Development, June 15, 1990, used 1987 figures from the World Bank's *World Development Report* and from

Raymond Gastil, *Freedom in the World: Political Rights and Civil Liberties, 1986–87* (New York: Greenwood, 1987).

59. Atul Kohli, "Democracy and Development," in *Development Strategies Reconsidered,* John P. Lewis and V. Kallab, eds. (New Brunswick, NJ: Transaction Press, 1986), p. 157.

60. John Londregan has mentioned data suggesting that, although democracies do not have a much better or worse economic record than authoritarian regimes, shifts from illiberal to constitutional rule often produce one-time increases of GNP. This statistical finding may be linked to the interpretation offered above.

61. See Barry Naughton, "Industrial Policy During the Cultural Revolution," in *New Perspectives on the Cultural Revolution,* W. Joseph et al., eds. (Cambridge: Harvard University Press, 1991), pp. 153–81.

62. See Lynn White, "The Political Effects of Resource Allocations in Taiwan and Mainland China," *Journal of the Developing Areas* 15 (October 1980), pp. 43–66.

63. Most people still think that the civil war in Korea began in 1950, but they have not seen Bruce Cumings, *The Origins of the Korean War.* Cumings proves definitively that the Korean War was internal, not just external, and that it began before and (in effect) continued after the 1950s. In the early 1980s, for example, the Kwangju uprising showed the resilience of political divisions that go back for decades. In other specific places, e.g., Cheju Island, the situation is similar.

64. This case is perhaps more complex because Shonas comprise four-fifths of the population. But the Ndebele 17 percent is relatively consolidated (in territory and in ZAPU) and decisively led. And the whites have economic influence far greater than their numbers would imply. Robert Mugabe and ZANU have to consider these factors constantly. See Jeffrey Herbst, *State Politics in Zimbabwe* (Berkeley: University of California Press, 1990), pp. 28–29, 169–72. Perhaps more important for the argument above, Zimbabwe's economic growth has not been high; but again, the situation is complex. If the partial withdrawal of whites' capital and entrepreneurial expertise after independence is considered, and certainly if a comparison is made to the economic performances of most other African states, Zimbabwe's recent growth stands up rather well.

65. The city-states of Singapore and Hong Kong have been omitted from this discussion only because of their size and the decisive effects of the international economy on their growth over time (even though these effects are also important in much larger areas such as Taiwan or South Korea). But in Hong Kong, the British government had almost no ethnic constituency, and uncertainties from over the border provide arguments for unified rule. In Singapore, ethnic and subethnic strife among Malays, Indians, and various sorts of Chinese are quite conceivable; and Sukarno did much to bolster Lee Kuan Yew's authoritarianism by showing Singapore as a rich Chinese island in a relatively poor Malay sea. Hong Kong and Singapore have authoritarian regimes that are minimally extractive because of the strong latent internal and external oppositions they face. These governments are certainly not authoritarian in the sense that the intellectuals who run them can do anything they want.

66. See Ramon Myers and Lynn White, "Economic Structure and Growth," in *The Modernization of China,* Gilbert Rozman, ed. (New York: Free Press, 1981), p. 342.

67. *SHJJDB,* August 29, 1988.

68. *FDXB* (June 1988), p. 63, and *ZGQNB,* December 12, 1987.

69. Lenin understood this less than his contemporary, Weber. See the discussion in Barrett L. McCormick, *Political Reform in Post-Mao China: Democracy and Bureaucracy in a Leninist State* (Berkeley: University of California Press, 1990), pp. 23–24, referring to A. J. Polan.

70. E. E. Schattschneider, *The Semi-Sovereign People,* has this and much else.

71. Many of them have shown no modesty in claiming this very publicly. China's

future dependence on intellectuals (not just past mistreatment of them) is a major theme in many of their own productions, for example, the famous documentary *River Elegy*.

72. Philippe C. Schmitter, "Still the Century of Corporatism?," in *The New Corporatism,* F. Pike and T. Stritch, eds. (South Bend: Notre Dame University Press, 1974), p. 85; italics added.

73. Although Schmitter makes no exact specification of the field these four exhaust, he suggests that his list of them "seems to round out in logical terms the combinatorial possibilities." Indeed they do, and an especially careful aspect of Schmitter's analysis is the single dimension that it omits in a studied and explicit way: whether the state or other (local or functional) units were most crucial in founding the regime type. See Philippe C. Schmitter, "Still the Century," p. 98. Later, writing with Wolfgang Streeck, Schmitter has suggested that there are four main kinds of social institutions—markets, states, communities, and associations—which are defined similarly by lists of traits that capture the concrete "aspects" (to use Parsons's word, though the sociologist did not separate the analytic and concrete axes that can generate these) of the AGIL categories, clearly in that order. (More is in the appendix to the introduction of the first volume of this book.) See Wolfgang Streeck and Philippe Schmitter, "Community, Market, State—and Associations? The Prospective Contribution of Interest Governance to Social Order," in *Private Interest Government: Beyond Market and State,* Streeck and Schmitter, eds. (Newbury Park, CA: Sage, 1985).

74. The spatial representation is much more useful for referring to directions, which compare the relative differences between the four types, than for implying any absolute positions. The latter task would require so many definitions and measurement tools that an attempt to describe them would make even this book look short. The shortcut, here and in most treatments, is to write about institutions in which functions are "embedded," without an overweening concern about the danger they become "reified." Of course, that makes for some arbitrariness in organizing material—but it also allows work on specific people, times, and countries.

75. See Schmitter,"Still the Century," pp. 94 and 96–97.

76. This agrees with Juan Linz, who says a totalitarian system has a "more or less intellectually elaborate ideology" that excludes the more varied norms allowable in a flexible "mentality" such as a merely authoritarian system has. See Linz, "Authoritarian and Totalitarian Regimes," in *Handbook of Political Science,* vol. 3, Fred Greenstein and Nelson Polsby, eds. (Reading, MA: Addison-Wesley, 1975).

77. Schmitter, "Still the Century," p. 96.

78. Ibid., p. 98, does not mention Karl Mannheim; but *Ideology and Utopia* suggests some basic ideas in the work of both Schmitter and Linz.

79. This is well known in the Beijing government, but such divisions ran through the system. In Shanghai during the early 1960s, for examples, Mayor Ke Qingshi, Zhang Chunqiao, and Yao Wenyuan were interested mostly in symbolic and normative matters; and for nearly a half decade, they avoided fundamental conflict with other politicians such as Cao Diqiu, Chen Pixian, and others, who were readily given charge of the economy. See Lynn White, *Policies of Chaos* (Princeton: Princeton University Press, 1989).

80. The terms in quotation marks are from Franz Schurmann, *Ideology and Organization in Communist China* (Berkeley: University of California Press, 1966), who explicitly equates his concept of "pure ideology" with Mannheim's "utopia"; and "practical ideology" with Mannheim's "ideology." Schurmann structures his analysis of China during the 1950s (and at other times, both later and historical) entirely by using this distinction or else by using Durkheim's—which he recognizes as different—between policies based on normative/human organization/"mechanical" solidarity and those based on situational/technical organization/"organic" solidarity.

81. Gordon White, "Prospects for Civil Society: A Case Study of Xiaoshan City," in *China's Quiet Revolution: New Interactions Between State and Society,* David S. G. Goodman and Beverley Hooper, eds. (New York: St. Martin's, 1994), pp. 207–8.

82. Richard D. Baum, *Burying Mao,* chap. 6, refers to *Asiaweek* 43 (October 28, 1983).

83. Ibid., chap. 8, refers to *Beijing Review* 30:20 (May 18, 1987), and other sources.

84. Troy Shortell, "The Party-Building Campaign in China" (Senior thesis, Princeton University, Woodrow Wilson School, 1991), p. 64, quoting a *China News Analysis* tabulation from *Nanfang ribao* (Southern Daily), Guangzhou, June 3, 1989, and *Nongmin ribao* (Peasant Daily), September 27, 1989.

85. Wang Huning in Benedict Stavis, ed., *Reform in China's Political System,* p. 53.

86. John Child and Xu Xinzhong, "The Communist Party's Role in Enterprise Leadership at the High Water of China's Economic Reform" (Beijing: China-EC Management Institute Working Paper, September 1989), pp. 1–2.

87. Ibid., p. 9.

88. *FBIS,* December 15, 1987, p. 27, reporting *JFRB* of December 6.

89. *FBIS,* December 18, 1987, p. 27, reporting *JFRB* of December 12.

90. *CD,* January 12, 1988.

91. For organization charts that lay out this structure clearly in a university, see *Shanghai Jiaotong Daxue guanli gaige chutan* (Preliminary Research on the Management Reform at Shanghai's Jiaotong University), Shanghai Jiaotong University, Communist Party Committee Office, ed. (Shanghai: Jiaotong Daxue Chuban She, 1983), pp. 28–29.

92. John Child and Xu Xinzhong, "The Communist Party's Role," pp. 32–36.

93. The percentages of *guanli renyuan* among the employees rose from 8.4 to 9.5 percent from 1976 to 1983, but the number of *gongcheng jishu renyuan* soared from 3.6 to 5.1 percent. *Shanghai shehui xiankuang he qushi, 1980–1983* (Situations and Trends in Shanghai Society, 1980–1983), Zheng Gongliang et al., eds. (Shanghai: Huadong Shifan Daxue Chuban She, 1988), p. 38.

94. John Child and Xu Xinzhong, "The Communist Party's Role," pp. 23–24.

95. *Cunzhong he yikao dang zuzhi. SHGYJJB,* February 2, 1989.

Conclusion

China Changes

One can only describe here and say: this is what human life is like.

—Ludwig Wittgenstein[1]

If you take consent seriously, you have to take seriously the capacities of the person who is supposed to consent. . . . All choice is opaque—we always choose with a limited understanding of what we are doing.

—Onora O'Neill[2]

The most general laws, because they are most devoid of content, are also the least valuable. The more comprehensive the validity— or scope—of a term, the more it leads away from the richness of reality, since in order to include the common elements of the largest number of phenomena, it must necessarily be as abstract as possible and hence devoid of content.

—Max Weber[3]

What damn good is this country? You can't compare it to anything.

—plaint of an area specialist
(a political scientist who happens to study Thailand)[4]

Questions asked partly determine the answers found. If Chinese policy making is deemed solely a function of the central government, whose result as an index of power is publicized policy documents, then research about the personalities and knowledge of top leaders should be enough to explain it. In particular, the charismatic authority of the top leader and the traditional or bureaucratic authority of agents below him should give the whole answer, especially if the question asked is with regard to the short run. But if long-term policy making, even by Beijing leaders alone, is the object of research, then it is also necessary to consider influences on them that are beyond their control. Most of these factors, which are needed to explain a historical syndrome as large as China's reforms, involve both the situations and ideals of small power networks.

Local leaders make policies (widely called "counterpolicies," or *duice,* to distinguish them from state policies, *zhengce*). Their power is thoroughly political, not just social, and it is often uncivil. It affects both central Beijing decisions and regional decisions. Distortions of implementation by nonstate actors force— and amount to—new policies. This is not just a matter of "social forces"; it is a matter of local power. Noncentral elites are real elites, when their effects overwhelm results from other actors. Geographic space makes a serious political difference, because it reduces the ability of central leaders to monitor what is happening locally. The time periods of basic-level politics often do not synchronize with the time periods of central politics, especially when localities respond to technological changes or to unintended secondary effects of central policies. Functional and regional "tendencies of articulation," which are usually inarticulate, make their own policies and play on divisions between high state leaders.[5] The overall hierarchical-"bandwagoning" or anarchical-"bargaining" structure of politics affects political results.[6] The policy process in China is fragmented and incremental, and the main reason is local power.

Long-Term Rationality

As Lieberthal and Oksenberg have argued, "the fragmented, segmented, and stratified structure of the state promotes a system of negotiations, bargaining, and the seeking of consensus among affected bureaucracies." But "in the case of China, scholars to date have tended to neglect the complex structure of the state itself as a significant determinant of the political process and policy outcomes."[7] The solution is to stress "structural dimensions of the Chinese bureaucracy." This present book aims to complement such views by looking at the structure of politics also in local power networks. Many of these include leaders with low bureaucratic ranks nominally inside the state, but that factor is often minor in determining their behavior if not their speech. The combined force of many such networks, acting together, has constrained what the Chinese state can do. Not only is the state becoming less solid internally, it is also becoming more porous to nonstate influences. To treat this topic requires making more links than have been usual, in either Chinese studies or political science, between the ways people speak and the ways they act, and between the sizes of the networks in which they do both.

"Great Men" vs. Policy: Behavior as Inherently Federal

High-level policy has been the explanandum of most studies in Chinese politics. "Rationality models" that trace policies to national needs or "power models" that trace measures to the personal interests of high leaders have thrown different lights on Beijing decisions.[8] But this book takes political behavior, which is all applied policy, rather than merely state policy as the thing to be explained. It stresses that leaders at many levels of the Chinese system have policies, as soon as that word is freed from its usual governmentalist connotation. Their collective rationality and personal networks are increasingly powerful.

People do not ordinarily conceive of policy in this way, and psychology suggests one of the reasons. Experimental psychologists have documented what they call the "fundamental attribution error," a tendency to understand the behavior of actors solely in terms of premises about personalities, rather than in terms of the contexts in which they operate. Controlled tests have shown how stubbornly people hold to assumptions about innate traits of actors, once these have been taught to the observers. They do so with higher frequency when others about them are doing the same. Even after total and full information is divulged about a context (as is possible at the end of a psychological experiment), people often cling to their earlier views even in the face of facts to the contrary, which show these premises about actors' attributes to have been wrong. Many Chinese, when talking about their political structures, do not report how much their postrevolutionary quick-growth context affects them. They speak of the state as powerful because it once was more so. They do new things, explaining and perceiving these in old languages.

Many social scientists, faced with a China that has ancient stately traditions, do the same thing. They suggest that China, especially its political structure, can never really change. Evidence of unprecedented reforms cover the landscape, but these are often explained solely as old habits in new guises, lest Western readers mistake China for their own countries. Of course, the extent and permanence of changes can be overstated. But during the high tide of revolution, coercive and fiscal centralizations changed the structure of Chinese politics fundamentally. The country is now unevenly emerging from a period in which the force of the central state was influential in establishing some institutions that are still kept and others that are now dismantled. This pattern of political compression and decompression has been seen before in other countries, during and after their own spates of centralized violence.[9]

Stately language is an important interest that the state nurtures. Chinese top leaders, autonomous leaders, dissident leaders, and many Western scholars alike speak as Stalin did: "Cadres decide everything." The prestige accorded to politicians has widely obscured the constraints under which they operate. At all levels, they are reverently addressed as "leader" (*lingdao*), not just by the titles of their posts. Lü Xiaobo has complained:

The Chinese love to look up to the famous, thereby saving themselves the trouble of thinking; that is why the Chinese rush into things en masse. . . . Why do the Chinese constantly re-enact the same tragedy, one starting with Qu Yuan's drowning in the Miluo River? Why do the Chinese mourn, as tragic heroes, people like Zhou Enlai, Peng Dehuai, and Hu Yaobang, while they forget such tragic [anti-state] figures as Wei Jingsheng?[10]

Thomas Carlisle's "great man" method of writing history has survived better in studies of Chinese politics than in any other field of social science—except perhaps in studies of diplomacy, where it may apply better. A researcher need not use *Annales* or Frankfurt methods exclusively, to see that such extensive attention to so few leaders in such a big country as China is likely to leave gaps. One need not become a Marxist concerned solely with concrete substructure to see that context influences action. Evidence available to foreign scholars of China is deeply tainted by hierarchical preoccupations that come from the Chinese state, from Western leaders who are equally interested in claiming efficacy for rule, and from journalists who like to quote officials.

Intellectual dissidents, who often oppose specific PRC hierarchs, use hierarchal symbols for this purpose and want to uphold the principle that educated people should rule others. Students on the steps of the Great Hall of the People at Tiananmen Square in 1989 conveyed intellectuals' power eloquently by miming total subordination. They kowtowed toward officials in the hall, knocking their heads on the pavement in an effort to shame corrupt governors into rectitude. This was an "art of resistance." Expressing subordination in an ostentatious but ironic manner, as the Beijing students did, raises the logical issue of who defines hierarchy.

James Scott criticizes "social science . . . focussed resolutely on the official or formal relations between the powerful and the weak." He notes that "it hardly exhausts what we might wish to know about power. Eventually we will want to know how the *hidden* transcripts of various actors are formed, the conditions under which they do or do not find public expression, and what relation they bear to the public transcript."[11] This view may overrate publicity, but it is one basis for knowledge about nonofficials' influence. Scott claims that "the hidden transcript can tell us something about moments that carry the portent of political breakthroughs."[12] The larger point is that politics can be found by seeking what people do, not just what they express (whether hidden or open). Even revolutions are less complete changes than the revolutionaries claim. Local politics always constrains state elites, and top leaders do not publish this fact.

"The weak" acting together because of parallel interests can be very strong—whether or not these interests are articulated in any kind of transcript. They make political breakthroughs using resources, not just symbols. Their transcripts in China are at least as hierarchical as those propagated by the state, but that does not require them always to obey government decrees. As Daniel Kelliher writes,

"When reform came, it was not the tame follower of anyone's vision. It was not fully subject to the new-found initiative of the peasantry or to the dictates of the central state."[13] The people who mainly decided on reform in China were the hinge leaders of local networks, using all the types of authority that they could muster.

Why should political science pay attention to "the weak," if they always and surely were so? If its focus were on the ways in which actual power is used or abused, then would it not stress only the influential instead?[14] One legitimate and moral answer is that the weak deserve attention because they are oppressed. Another answer, to be emphasized here, is that they deserve attention because in some circumstances they are strong—and those conditions can be studied. For every person, as well as every group, weakness and strength can only be tentative predicates. There is no need to be interested exclusively in the meanings of the oppressed, rather than in the causes of their actions that actually prove effective. The weak are not so impotent, or at least not eternally so, as mainly normative approaches to them might suggest. Their collective reactions, often against the stately strong, determine in large part what the latter can or cannot do. The reason for seeking their meanings is to improve the reliability of causal predictions, by using maximum evidence from habits that both they and their researchers can comprehend. An occasional effect is that they find ways to use their resources to gain influence.

Every finding of power is a causal statement (a leader's wish sufficiently causes a follower's behavior), and power involves both norms and situations. Both the leader's and the follower's wishes are ideal, and the follower's behavior is in principle unintended. It can nonetheless be difficult to apply this definition of power in specific instances, even though none of its elements can well be avoided. A common way of talking about power is to assume that it is easy to get a full sense of what leaders want. But this premise is dubious; leaders' and followers' wishes alike are often understood and communicated implicitly or indistinctly. Another common way of talking about power is in terms of the top–down organization chart of the state. But when the leaders of small collectivities constrain what the leaders of the state can do, then the "lower" leaders are powerful and the "higher" leaders are weaker.

The definition of state power depends partly on the clarity of the state's intention. It is often easier to tell what an apparent follower does than to tell what an apparent leader really wants.

1. Policy wishes are not restricted to the public results that leaders announce. They also want policies to raise their own individual resources, and they require administrative implementing policies that are not always as subsidiary as public statements suggest. Leaders need to find local agents, to categorize groups that will be served or taxed, and to estimate how much coercion can be used to achieve any substantive goal. In China, the manipulative aspects of state policy have often overwhelmed other goals that they ostensibly aimed to achieve. Policies

are practically always impelled by diverse motives, which may conflict with one another. In any practical situation, a leader wants more than one thing.

2. Policy intentions are inconsistent over time. Followers can often choose which of many instructions-from-above they will obey. PRC policies for secondary education, for example, have been sufficiently various over time that local school authorities could pick from a large inventory of past measures.[15] "Latest directives" receive special publicity from the central government, but that does not mean these are always the directives followed.

3. The state includes many sizes of jurisdictions, and preferences of cadres at each of them often differ. This book is full of Chinese instances when various kinds of notables formally within the government acted on different interests. The state, when playing the leader, has many guises.

4. Wishes at any level are choices among options, but leaders often do not need to foreclose each such choice. They may suggest one alternative, but may be able also to leave others open for later decision (or for avoiding choice), after the results become clearer. An emphasis on one aspect of a policy—the main thing the leader wants—does not require final action on other choices, including inconsistent options. Mao Zedong, for example, often made cogent arguments for one policy line, but then in practice supported another.[16] Powerful actors *usually* see advantages in remaining ambiguous about some aspects of the policies that they espouse in public.

5. State leaders' announced intentions, as declared for example in editorials, may conflict with what those same leaders fully want—because publicity for a policy, rather than its formal content, is sometimes its main substance. Shanghai's state factories during reforms, for example, benefited from cheap immigrant labor to cities, and police benefited from the popular legitimacy in gestures against "vagabonds"—so official editorials railed against "blind immigration" more than official actions stopped it.[17] To infer the desires of the state only from its public documents would, in such cases, miss half the story.

We cannot do without some definition of power in political studies. Dahl's concept, discussed earlier and involving those algebraic folk A and B, is clearer than any other. But the five reasons offered above suggest five ways in which it is necessary to take care. Researchers must keep an eye out for implementing and personal-political intentions, for choices based on past rather than current policies, for local leaders who are not consistently part of the state even when they want their clients to think they are, for ambiguity and changes in high leaders' positions, and for rational decisions by leaders not to articulate some of their own wishes. This might seem to make research on power impossible, but it only makes the project more interesting.

These issues of ambiguous and scattered power have entered Chinese studies before, but they have often been sidetracked because of unrealistic definitions. For example, these problems have arisen particularly in discussions of policy implementation. "Success" in policy implementation can be measured in either of two ways. The "congruence method" evaluates implementation by looking for parallels between policy intentions and outcomes. The "procedural approach," an alternative, asks whether implementation was "consistent with the procedures called for in the policy document, [and] if procedures were followed, [implementation] was successful by definition."[18] Many political scientists of China, including the one who developed these types, prefer the procedural method. It has a major advantage: Intentions can be very difficult to ascertain, whereas evidence about procedures is more available. But this approach sets an easy test for the officials; it tends to regard implementation in a governmental, short-term way. Procedures are often left vague in published policy documents. Public mandates stress broad goals instead; so the legalistic, procedural method of determining implementation success is often no more practical than the hope of finding the extent to which official intentions prevailed. Also, since the best definition of power implies one actor following the intention of another, the procedural view of implementation divorces it from politics. Intentions as influence may be judged over time, on the presumption that actors wish to flourish, through evidence about whether or not they actually prosper.

A less bureaucratic, longer-term, spatially broader outlook is needed, in order to curb the common bias toward concluding that the top of the PRC government effectively runs everything in China that it claims to run. The "congruence method" mentioned above can be used, especially if the time period for seeing the results of policy is longer than a few years. All an analyst needs is a single safe assumption: that the regime wants to strengthen itself. The government tries to do this in many ways that are measurable, for example, by expanding its fiscal resources or the number of its firm followers. If its policies, which may be deemed to have these intentions whether or not they are explicit, fail to achieve the result of strengthening the political elite and its institutions, then the congruence method shows unsuccessful implementation. China lately has seen a great deal of this.

Reforms were, as Dorothy Solinger has written,

> designed as an instrument to fine-tune a decrepit machine. But since the wielders assigned to manipulate this tool grasped it with untrained hands, they were bound to use it crudely, to resort to practices familiar to them, and to rely on associates with whom they had worked before. And each time the tool faltered, those who had bestowed it saw fit to take it back again, as they sought other modes of temporarily tinkering with their machine. But through it all, they never meant to trade the new tool for their own machine.[19]

What they meant, in all this bumbling, was not what they got. Local leaders almost always speak deferentially of designated high leaders, but they often act autonomously when resources are involved.

Under what conditions did the boom of China's local industries, to cite the main factor, erode the state? In the short term, it clearly weakened the budgets and planning capabilities of many offices in the central state. But the main argument of this book too easily could be misread to contradict a valid long-run point that has emerged from the researches of Vivienne Shue, Helen Siu, and others: Reforms do not just restore the same kinds of local patterns that predated the revolution. Market expansion tends, sporadically over time, to induce standardization in contracts, in regulatory rules, and in authority relations. This takes time. For the nonce, the state is weakened—though neither central nor local leaders publicize its infirmity. Later, it may be stronger.

As Zhou Xueguang argues, "the institutional structure of state socialism reduces the barriers to collective action, by producing 'large numbers' of individuals with similar behavioral patterns and demands that cut across the boundaries of organizations and social groups."[20] The state tries to prevent autonomous organization, but it cannot prevent interests. The state unintentionally strengthens nonstate power networks by trying to use Leninist precepts to strengthen just its own state networks. Traditional and local institutions increasingly reap the rewards of modern resources that the centralist revolution generated. Chinese politics is not all contained within the structure of the state, and it is not all guided by the formal hierarchy.

"Chaos" vs. Policy:
Behavior as Alternating Between Poles

When reform is viewed as a rational policy, its pattern is generally assumed to be smooth: a logically planned, usually moderate upward trajectory of output, specialization, trade, education, cosmopolitan opening, and then perhaps democracy or some other version of political nirvana. It is unsurprising that the PRC's socialist leaders should propagate this smooth notion of reform. In doing so, they serve their interests in trying to persuade everybody that they do and should control such changes for the public benefit. It is scarcely less surprising that foreign potentates, either because they share with China's state leaders a presumption that governments are effective or else because they are also heirs to the Enlightenment belief that it is easy to use coercion rationally, also tend to think of reform as a smooth process, which can be planned. Journalists, who must file stories daily, can obtain quotations about planned successes more easily than about other results. But academics at least try to take, as one of their jobs, the task of interpreting behavioral patterns separately from the interests of officials, journalists, businesspeople, or others who have more immediate interests.

If reform is viewed as a pattern of action, without the premise that it must be conceived as a rational policy, it looks like a random walk. Reform turns out to be a halting and bumpy process, not at all smooth, inseparably mixed with reaction. Unintended consequences of policies that were rational for immediate ends at one time often turn out to overwhelm similar policies later. Although the pattern shows broad trends over long periods (more growth, specialization, trade, education, and cosmopolitan opening), it also shows "two steps forward, one step back" irregularities that are for many purposes as important as the overall trends. Reforms of different types march to different drummers, of which the high state is just one.

China's leaders before reforms trumpeted communitarian policies based on "human organization" and aimed at the "support-led security" of a socialist safety net. The real-world problems of welfare, which these policy options address, do not disappear simply because most coalitions of reform-era leaders ignore them. Reformers, for their part, have trumpeted more individualist "technical organization" aimed at "growth-mediated security" and market efficiency.[21] Both before and after the reforms began, the kind of policy opposing the mainstream (either communitarian or individualist) remained available. What changed was the state elite's preference for thinking in one set of terms, rather than the other. Human-organization and technical-organization political coalitions have alternated over time, and they have also subsisted in particular bureaucratic or geographic units. They are means of publicizing easy-to-follow—but inherently temporary—policy lines.[22]

Institutions evolve not evenly but in spurts. This insight has been stressed in many diverse fields: by Arthur Stinchcombe in organization theory, by Stephen Jay Gould in evolutionary biology, and by Daniel Kahneman and others in explaining "endowment effects, loss aversions, and status quo biases" in the psychology of economics.[23] But recent formal thinking about complexity mainly concerns not-yet-wholly-disintegrated systems. Less purist approaches to realism are even more necessary to begin accounts of greater chaos. Scientists are discovering that they are most unlikely, ever, to understand everything. After the Enlightenment, too many think this is very bad news.

Many social scientists still prefer to find a single cause for each event. It is a nostalgic but odd idea that, ideally, there should be just one predicate to each subject. Modern people actually encounter an onslaught of complexity every day in diverse fields ranging from controversial judgments of fault or no-fault in law, to multiple regressions in econometrics that can become inconclusive, to difficulties that emerge from attempts at simultaneous coprocessing in computer science.[24] This onslaught of causes understandably discomfits them, because it suggests that they should try to keep in their heads many kinds of factors at the same time. Jugglers show that many balls can be kept in the air simultaneously, but this kind of feat is not always easy.

In social science, the two main considerations that have to be juggled together are normative and situational predicates. These are opposite types, but they can modify a subject simultaneously; they are not mutually exclusive. This creates difficulties. It would decrease the work load of social scientists, by decreasing the number of topics that they have to scan, if either normative or situational predicates could simply be outlawed. If either could be classed beyond the pale of the knowable, then scientific method would involve fewer steps, and the efforts of research could be economized. A common strategy is to suggest that in *my* discipline (economics, anthropology, politics, history), we need to think only about situations or about norms; other work is for the oddballs in other departments. From an intellectual viewpoint, this is unpresentable; nonetheless it flourishes in institutions. The most common tack, in this effort to simplify the complex, has been to argue either in a rational actionist vein that only situational predicates can be causal, or else in a hermeneutic vein that only noncausal predicates are interesting. But these viewpoints are made no more valid by their frequent repetition, nor by the fact that the lives of both humanists and naturalists would be easier if they were true. The trouble is, either norms or situations can cause effects. Academic life might be more elegant if this were not the case, but it is the case.

This problem is sufficiently troublesome that some have tried to get around it by changing its terms. A recent effort has stressed another knotty but basically different question: whether a factor can be considered causal if it is just partially present. This is a particular issue in any study that concentrates on a "case," such as the present book does with respect to China's reforms as an example of a larger set of postrevolutionary political changes. Charles Ragin advocates an "algebra of logic" in his attempt to resolve "the gulf between case-oriented and variable-oriented research."[25] Actually, mathematical variables and relations are not always clearer than verbal ones.[26] But the approach in this book is consistent with Ragin's insistence that concept formation and data analysis cannot be completely separated. Ragin's Boolean algebra "simplifies complexity through experiment-like contrasts."[27] It shows that steps in formalizing causal links can be inductive. But its use is limited because it depends on forced choices about whether each possible cause or result is wholly present or wholly absent.

If that approach were taken here, this book would have to ignore too much of the best available information on China that offers proportions, very often shown as percentages on the pages above. Straight up-or-down truth values of 100 percent or 0 percent are unavailable for most of the predicates on which we have data from the real world. While the Boolean attempt at inductive primness may inspire formalists, it is about math, not about society. Comparative politics, as applied to any real event and place, cannot sensibly throw out data about partial conditions and results. Science is knowledge, not just etymologically. If knowledge is what we want, this method restricted to experiment-like contrasts would discard a great deal of information prior to research. It cannot stand alone as sufficient for understanding any real politics.

The present study is not designed to provide a formal test of any wholly general principle in political science. The author has never heard of any study that is widely held to accomplish such a task, despite having heard a great deal of rumor about the possibility. Harry Eckstein has provided the most careful categorization of types of case studies in politics, ranging from "ideographic" to "crucial" case studies.[28] The current book is, in his terms, mainly a "plausibility probe" of the hypothesis that, despite statist language suggesting otherwise, local power networks tending to act in parallel ways can seriously constrain political behavior in a large-scale national network.

Although this idea certainly does not qualify as a law, China is a "crucial" place to look at it. If power in small networks can be proved real in that avowedly authoritarian environment, then their power elsewhere might a fortiori be likely. This might even be true in countries with states that less often suggest they are omnipotent. A much costlier study would be necessary to extend the argument that far, but the purpose of a "plausibility probe" is exactly to put such a conjecture on the intellectual agenda. Not all China scholars will agree that the thesis here is correct or important, but at least they can face the evidence in the book. The best thing about case studies is not that they show the usefulness of many kinds of ideas at once, but that they require notions to be compared with facts.

Causal Circumspection: Reasoning in Multiple Dimensions

It is oddly difficult to persuade social scientists that causal explanations of really major events might be the best aim of their theories. Wonder about such events (including many even larger than China's reforms) is, however, at the origin of every big idea they have had. The historical rise of commodity markets bred the general equilibrium model at the heart of mainstream economics. The quandary about how society could hold together, as the division of labor threatened traditional beliefs and elites in modern development, was the spur to Durkheim, Pareto, Mannheim, Weber, and the others who founded sociology. The actual practice of competitive elections and legislative voting was the impetus for choice theory and its paradoxes, which many political scientists regard as the only important part of their profession. Intellectual historians could show how the most general and sweeping theoretical claims of economics, sociology, and political science have emerged from efforts to figure out how specific time-bound events could have occurred.

In contemporary China studies, too, the big notions have come out of identifiable events. Without the Liberation of 1949, scholars would not have begun arguing so fiercely about the relative importance of Chinese nationalism or Communist socialism in explaining what happens there. Without the Great Leap Forward of 1958, they would not have become so interested in applying a closely linked set of ideas from organization theories: "decentralization to the middle level," cellular or national taxation, the efficiency of natural or imposed rural markets (and cultural) systems, and the issue of how much a charismatic leader, as compared to a bureaucracy, can guide state policy. Without the Cultural Revolution of 1966–69, scholars who assert the constant importance of clientelist-traditional patterns of bondage would not have conflicted theoretically with those who stress that Weber's three types are all ideal and that nascent pluralist and fading totalitarian authority also explain some facts.

China's reforms after 1970 are yet another event to be explained. They have already spurred conversations between those who favor an account of power in local institutions, structured under hinge leaders who effectively "kick the state back out," and those who instead adduce data to show the importance of central state reform policies. No matter how any of these debates turns out (and the truth is probably mixed in each of them), positions are usually offered as forever-and-always keys to sociopolitical Reason. When and if the intellectual historians of the future bother with contemporary scholarship on the PRC, they will record that, despite theoretical pretensions, writers were mainly trying to figure out what happened.

To find factors that change the long-term institutional structure of politics, it is necessary to look for causes. The contrast to this method—the alternative forgone here—comes in various forms of reductionism. This book aims to complement others of two types: those concerning short-term fluctuations of state leadership in Beijing and those explaining Chinese politics mainly in terms of traditions (e.g., Chinese or Communist). The first of these approaches largely concerns the alternation of conservative "lions" and reformist "foxes." Institutionalism, if focused on state decisions rather than on nonstate institutions, examines top leaders' resources and is good at explaining changes of interest among some well-known people. But the PRC state elite's relationship to functional and local leaders has changed over a long period, and the number of relevant political institutions has become large. This book does not pretend to provide a way of predicting the immediate fluctuations between reformers and conservatives. Fine work is already available about the cycles of reform.[29] The topic here is the longer trend in which local authoritarians are now conflicting with national ones. This may lead to further structural changes to diversify, and perhaps pluralize, the centralized system that the revolution bequeathed to China.

Many writers of the second, more cultural kind imply that almost everything one needs to know about Chinese politics can be summed up in the need to understand the styles of relationships among individuals there. These links have, as they emphasize, been modal in Chinese culture for generations. If we want to know the effects on recent structural changes in Chinese politics, however, the most interesting aspects are inconsistencies, unstable or ambiguous aspects that need to be resolved in a modern context, rather than age-old coherences showing cultural constancy. That is the main reason for using plural words like "values" or "norms" to describe culture. Old ideals subsist in the heads of people who are in specific situations; so the problem is always how norms (both old and new) interact with situations. The zest of reductionist explanations is lost if all these are considered; but that toll is worth paying to gain greater confidence in explanation that comes from the effort to be circumspect.

An adequate account of any social phenomenon is likely to use both norms and situations as causal factors. It is also likely to examine both collective and individual actors. Daniel Little, who has looked at modes of explanation both in Chinese studies and in general, summarizes the view of a "methodological individualist":

> A social event, occurrence, or condition is best explained as the aggregate consequence, intended or unintended, of many individuals acting on the basis of specific motives within a particular environment of action. . . . Social structures, institutions, practices, and the like have causal powers only insofar as they influence the behavior of individuals.[30]

This is unobjectionable (and the present book takes a rational-action approach), so long as it is understood that habitual "structures, institutions, practices, and the like" socialize and create individuals. Separate from them, people are not even born. So they inherently "influence the behavior of individuals." At least, the chance that they do so is as high as the chance that the rest of an actor's environmental context does, unless specific research shows otherwise. Any good causal explanation must thus be translatable into institutional, habitual, cultural, collective terms, *as well as* into individualist terms. This constraint on a good explanation, arising from the fact that groups make individuals, is not a whit less severe than the constraint arising from the fact that individuals make up groups.

Really good causal accounts would undertake both viewpoints and could be expressed in either. These would be, however, more difficult to produce than either the rational-actionists or the culturalists promise. Both these professions are no more than ways of structuring essays. An American national self-image has made the rational-action trend mainstream (and this has been aided by the prominence in academic administrations of economists, who tend to be missionaries for natural individualism). So maybe it is most useful here to speak for the culturalists, even though their viewpoint is equally flawed and narrow. Collectively learned habits beget most of the options among which rational actors choose. Preferences do not come out of thin air. To say that such categories are useful "only insofar as they influence the behavior of individuals" is not to say a lot when much evidence suggests they influence it a great deal. Little asks that study be limited to tastes that may be universal: "Balinese peasants are as likely as anyone else to do their marketing in the market town that is easiest to get to. . . ."[31] But a rational actionist could also use symbolist methods to lay out the options that people consider when making less universal kinds of choices. There is nothing incompatible about these approaches for the kinds of topics to which they apply.[32]

Norms and groups are part of the environment of action. Daniel Little is ambiguous on whether to admit this much. The rational actionist wants to malign "normative, religious, magical influences on action" as "extrarational"; but he confesses limits to his purism and admits that "religious or familial behavior *may* reflect motives which are quite uncalculating and independent of material interests." He even suggests that other approaches may be better to comprehend processes in historical time.[33] In other words, collective and normative factors may be taken as effective causes for major events. An explanation that has not sought them is incomplete, unable fully to test its causal hypotheses against other categories that may cover more of the empirical data.

The search in this book for multiple causes of China's reforms incorporates a rational-action approach, which is a subset of a neo-functionalist one even if its exponents do not realize that. But the options among which actors choose can be normative (not just external), can be generated collectively (not just individually), and can be subject to evolution over time (not just as set preferences). Each of these three facts affects the meaning of rationality: First, environments include stable, hard-to-change normative habits of thinking, which provide evidence as reliable as any from material situations. Ideas can serve as either underlying or spark causes of events, just as concrete conditions can. Second, there is a continuum of many sizes of collectivity—from individual through family, village, local area, province, nation, and world. Causes of behavior in any of them may appear in any of the others. For a country as vast as China, it is near-sighted to speak of individuals alone, even though it is also inadequate to speak about any other level of collectivity as if it were not composed of people. This dimension often appears as spatial because different networks are often strong in different places. Third, causation occurs in the dimension of time. Additive rationality theorists oddly shy away from looking at the calendar when trying to compute from structures of preferences. But this is unnecessary, and it weakens their case that rational action approaches are especially useful for explaining the causes of events. Time is at least as clear an analytic variable as any other.

Since Aristotle, "cause" is a word with many meanings. Cultural patterns can be causative.[34] Correlation is not the only linkage that occurs among variables in a model; identity, difference, and combination are diverse types of ties—and models often tell good stories about culture.[35] The point that the naturalists make, when they claim a monopoly on explaining causation, is that *no* humanist proposition (causal or other) can be validated by evidence totally separate from its subject. Since the humanists want to use data direct from the people they study, this critique of them is true but not damning. It applies, in any case, equally to noncausal and other propositions, although naturalists cite it as if it gave them sole title to talking about the reasons for events.

The humanist and naturalist approaches to social topics differ in their sources of data. The issue is whether ideas start with subjects or with scientists. Both approaches can actually make causal arguments and can offer noncausal insights. The two approaches are necessary logical complements to each other, despite all the adrenalin spilled and all the academic careers made in fights between them. Interpreters despite their efforts are not identical to their subjects, and modelers do not create all their premises without reference to their subjects.

Choices Within Tradition, and Causes of Events

Chinese culture has so many aspects that have proved useful to many people for so long that it can tell us only the limits of things that are likely to happen, rather than exactly what will happen. The flavor of the past does not set fate, but it hampers Lady Fortune's range of styles. Skeptics about the use of culture for social prediction emphasize the changeable quality of identities and vogues. Free choices among them are possible, but not infinite in range. Positivist skeptics claim that these are merely "residual" categories of explanation, always less acceptable than "structural" categories whenever the latter are available.[36] They suggest that external constraints on opportunities for action are the best guides to prediction because evidence about these can be tested independently. This is supposed to be especially true when the constraints are on individuals, not groups. But to justify this bias for situational and individual evidence as against data about intentions and large networks, it would be insufficient to show that such evidence is less ambiguous than cultural information (as it often is). Instead, it would be necessary to show that using *both types together* would not reduce the ambiguity of conclusions still further. Considering intentions along with situations does not reduce, at all, the validity of any good conclusions that can be derived from the latter alone. The problem with exclusive claims for the individualist-situational bias is that it leaves conclusions with less support because it a priori excludes many potential causes.

Yet some analysts claim that factors of habit and culture scarcely ever need to be considered because contexts alone "overdetermine" action. They are supposed to explain it well enough that norms or institutional habits among the actors can be ignored. This is just an assertion, and its frequent repetition does not make it generally true. The parallel claim of humanists, which is equally narrow, is that culture overdetermines anything that can really be learned from people being studied, so that knowing the culture is enough.

If contextual approach has an advantage, this is a matter of premises, not findings. Situational contexts can be modeled in a way the analyst surely understands because the scientist alone constructs the model. The danger with an exclusive preference for studying situations is narcissism. Why should the understandings and habits of a scientist determine the content of science, more than the understandings and habits of the people who are studied? The answer concerns clarity: The researcher can know his or her own mind better than the minds of those being studied. But any analyst who admits either lapses of self-clarity or interest in learning from the subjects (and most researchers do this in practice, whether or not the routine is confessed) has no reason to privilege the scientist's constructions over the subjects'. Writers can offer their own ideas more surely than the notions of others; but that is a rhetorical advantage, not an evidentiary one. An exclusive stress on it would privilege clarity over relevance, consistency over exploration. Why throw out half the job of science in this way? Both halves were always part of the project.

Culturalist thinkers, for their part, often reject causal argument altogether. Of course, it is possible to overspecify cultural traditions when drawing inferences from them. For example, in Chinese studies "tradition" is often simplified as merely Confucian, with short shrift given to Buddhist, Taoist-animist, and other local or lineage norms. Drawing conclusions from Confucianism alone can be chancy. Frederic Wakeman lists four similarities between Confucianism and Communism: First, "memory of the dynastic cycle" once gave the CCP hope that change was possible in China and now gives it uncertainty about its own permanence. Second, an emphasis on the ideal of ethical leadership, rather than mere expertise alone, is clear in both Confucianism and Chinese Communism. Third, Mencius and Mao both claimed faith in the capacity of the masses; they were in that sense populists. Finally, an intrusive moralism makes both Confucians and Communists inveterate sermonizers.[37]

It is possible to surmise that Chinese tradition, defined in this way, precludes Chinese liberalism. This could be said to follow from the four traits of the national culture, as described above: Cycles suggest that basic developmental progress, such as liberals espouse, is impossible. Reliance on generalist gentlemen delegitimates modern professionals. Chinese populism gives the masses a role in rebellions only to change leaders who are so corrupt that they threaten natural hierarchy. And moralizing is the opposite of listening to the voices of the democratic many.

It is equally possible, however, to take the same traits of Chinese tradition, as defined in this way, and suggest how a cultural entrepreneur could use them for change toward liberal or corporatist politics. The cycles could be seen as surges of enfranchisement among new groups of citizens.[38] The most important ethical generalists are common people, not technocrats or specialized theorists who tell people what to think.[39] The populism could be serious, not just sporadic or irrelevant to a growth of political diversity. Finally, Confucian moralism could be interpreted as liberal respect for the worth of each good person. Chinese tradition alone does not support or preclude liberalism. It also does not preclude a state that might take nonstate corporate power networks more seriously than most recent Chinese regimes have done (except on Taiwan). The only question is how Chinese leaders in many sizes of collectivity use their traditions.

Chinese meanings may be misread, and the only way to be sure of avoiding misinterpretation is to ignore cultural data. Foreign analysts of China are stuck with the job of balancing these two hazards. During the high reforms of 1989, for example, the man who stood in front of a line of tanks, and halted them, provided a riveting image from Tiananmen—but what did it mean? In the West, and for some in China, this man became a symbol of individual bravery in the face of a mechanical, repressive state apparatus. Yet the government's own central television station replayed the famous video with a caption: "If the soldiers had not exercised restraint, how could this man, hailed as a hero by some Western media, have been able to show off in front of these tanks?"[40] Like much else in reform China, the image admitted multiple interpretations. Those who stressed the premise that the state's power was inexorable and natural deemed the man foolish. But others, who stressed that they were more like the man than like the tanks, respected him.

Culture can cause events because the basic notion of cause may first have come from an idea of intention. Evidence of a person's wish to do something can be taken as a cause of it. Presuming so, even institutions of thought could bring social results. Weber, in the *Protestant Ethic and the Spirit of Capitalism,* attempted this kind of causal discussion. Despite whole bookshelves of cogent critiques of his thesis, other comprehensive explanations of the first germs of modern change are hard to find.

The bases of the anticulturalism of most contemporary social science lie in a particular philosophy, logical positivism, which early in the century was a healthy reaction against Victorian romantics. But the most thoroughgoing positivist thinkers changed their views radically later, as they realized that all languages in which propositions can be made are unavoidably cultural. Even the operations of mathematics are metaphors. The difference between early and late Wittgenstein, for example, is known to philosophers but seldom to social scientists. Another example is A. J. Ayer whose first book, *Language, Truth, and Logic,* became the main statement in English of the logical-positivist tenet behind mainstream social science: the idea that the meaning of a proposition is contained in the procedure for its verification.[41] This required expressing the statement, or a tautology of it, reliably in terms of sensations. This was not a wholly new idea—questioners from Socrates to Hume and beyond had suggested it—but it became a refining fire against metaphysics. It remains a major basis for social science.

Four decades after the publication of his book, however, a mellower Ayer confessed plainly that "the defect [of logical positivism] was that nearly all of it was false." The "spirit" of the movement remained valid; asking about how a conjecture might be proved was always interesting. But "no logically precise formulation" showing how to do this had ever been found, Ayer admitted, despite his youthful hopes. Languages and mathematics were subject to interpretation. All that was really left of the doctrine was that "a scientific hypothesis must have some [*sic*] relation to observation." This point was "wishy-washy." Furthermore, the idea that all scientific concepts could or should be "reduced" to sensations was "unworkable."[42] It remains unclear that a stark separation between logical-mathematical tautologies ("analytic" statements or pure models) and empirical propositions about the world is justified. "Conventions," which are arguably a logical parallel to social institutions, became far more important in positivists' late thinking than they had been earlier. It is difficult to show empirically that even the principles of mathematics are not conventions, generated within limits set by human brains and the kinds of things that they can conceive.

Wittgenstein's mellowing was at least as thorough as Ayer's. These epiphanies of realism were not just personal, because these two had earlier (often indirectly, through Karl Popper and others) provided the main criteria for accepting or rejecting projects in social research. What remains of logical positivism, after these recantations, is actually a fine basis for social science that accounts for both norms and situations. But most researchers still do not realize how much backtracking the most careful epistemologists in this genre had to do.[43]

The scientific method of proposing sentence hypotheses, then testing them, depends not at all on whether the data for the tests are intentional or situational. Culturalists use this method as much as naturalists do. Their only special problem is that words in their propositions (especially in the predicates, or in alternative predicates) may have meanings that are not unique, because these have been normalized in diverse uses of practical language and will continue to be used diversely. Humanists sometimes suggest they can do without propositions, and would-be social naturalists sometimes pretend they are the only thinkers to use them. But these pretensions are plain wrong. The difference between an interpreter's text and a modeler's proposition is in the kind of data that can make it significant. Both are words strung into sentences.

Scholars are often asked, like witnesses before an evangelist at a revival meeting, to stand up and declare themselves for either "hermeneutic interpretation" or "rationality," even "the public interest" or "methodological individualism." This is silly, since all practical research pays attention to each type of data. Old-style functionalism, despite its flaws, was less vulnerable to willful narrowness than is much contemporary social science. Its faults can be fixed by pushing functionalist logic to its conclusion, so that incoherent and concrete factors of action receive more attention than, for example, Parsons implied they should. Writers who tell stories about integration tend toward functionalism no more than those who write about conflicts and foils. No linkage is more obvious than a contrast. Cockfights, cat massacres, or political domination and resistance are as good grist for a circumspect kind of functionalist mill as are plans for the Tennessee Valley Authority, civic cultures, or the economic bases of democracy.[44]

Such stylistic choices are in principle arbitrary. It is unnecessary to claim that one method treats all social subjects, and it is useful to look around from several angles when treating social subjects.[45]

Centralizations and Decentralizations: State and Nonstate

The causes of revolution have generated far more attention than the causes of reform. Yet these topics are historical inverses. The means to study either would find both. Even in countries that were centralized by movements less rigidly disciplined than the CCP, unification occurred in nonstate institutions as well as in government—and between them.[46] Decentralization can be seen with the same lenses. The state–nonstate distinction may be important, especially for analysis of a short era if the boundaries of the state are defined for specified issues in terms of local leaders' actual responsiveness to central institutions, not just in terms of the state's organization chart. But for dynamic analysis to show increasing centralization or decentralization, nonstate power networks may not show the same trend as the state network. The hallmark of a revolutionary era, in

China from 1949 through the 1960s, is that state leaders induce more centralization in other networks to buttress their own power. The hallmark of a postrevolutionary era, as in China since 1970, is that nonstate leaders gradually augment their networks' influence over the policy and structure of the state.

However one evaluates revolutions or the states led by revolutionaries, such regimes try to centralize their countries in terms of fiscal revenues, police power, and sources of legitimacy for leaders. Use of the word "revolutionary" to describe the Meiji reformers, Franco, Hitler, or other rightist leaders can generate either heat or light; and "revolutionary" can be a debatable label even for the likes of Napoleon or Stalin.[47] The extent of apt comparisons—for example, whether Cromwell's England and Lincoln's America also centralized their "houses divided" in a similar revolutionary way—is arguable. But whether centralizations are viewed as good or bad, they have occurred. Leftists and rightists have both led them. They can be compared.

The violence that abets these broad centralizations splits a nation's previous elite into two parts. In the aftermath, as reforms begin, leaders in the political group that won need those in the families that lost. At least some notables from families that had opposed the centralizing regime become legitimated after the peak of state coercion. Such events seem to have occurred in China, during the middle or late 1970s; in Russia, about 1985; in Spain, about 1975; in the United States, over many years after 1865; in France, about 1815; and in England, between 1660 and 1690.[48] But notables who had supported the centralization still retained their positions, too. For example, when Charles II was invited back to England, the largely Puritan House of Lords also readmitted its members who had taken the Stuart side in the civil war. The new king selected a Privy Council that included former supporters of Cromwell, royalists, and men who had aided only some of the parliamentary regimes.[49] The late Stuart king "needed the cooperation of locally important people, both for the continuation of ordinary government at local level and to support his policies nationally. By 1688, his policies were seen by the people as an encroachment." Many localities now had more diverse leaders—the nobility, gentry, urban elites, and office holders—and these hinge leaders were "resisting the centralizing tendency of the Stuart monarchy."[50]

There is no hope or need here fully to show that the pattern of postrevolutionary reforms in China is like that in other countries. Many books have been written about revolutions, so many should also be written to explain the sequels. The question that needs to be asked comparatively is, "And then what happened?" The logics applicable to postrevolutionary truces might stir as much interest as those accounting for the earlier mounting violence. All the cases of decompression showed very quick economic growth, rampant and well-perceived corruption, comedy but also ambiguous "years of doubt" (as the English called them), some administrative decentralization, and reconciliation among different types of elites. Certain aspects of the syndrome that are very evident in the Chinese case (such as inflation) are absent in others. But economic growth, often driven by new industries, appears in them all.[51]

The relationship of hinge leaders to the state becomes crucial as they gain importance in the postrevolutionary decompression. The virtues and faults of state centralization become a public issue. As Tocqueville wrote: "Indeed, I cannot conceive that a nation can enjoy a secure or prosperous existence without a powerful centralization of government. But I am of the opinion that a central administration enervates the nations in which it exists, by incessantly diminishing their public spirit."[52] He claimed that centralization "perpetuates a drowsy precision in the conduct of affairs," and "in short, it excels more in prevention than in action . . . . If once the co-operation of private citizens is necessary to the furtherance of its measures, the secret of its impotence is disclosed." Local notables, partly coordinated by the state but now more autonomous from it, led modern revivals after spates of violence in each of these countries.

Revolutions make national networks and normative ideals more important, while reforms raise the profile of small power networks and situational contexts in politics. These dimensions are yardsticks for measuring the current Chinese trends:[53]

- Power is increasingly local during China's decentralizing reforms. Individuals, and especially small power networks, become more important than they were before 1970. These trends may be reversed again in the future, of course. But the rise of local networks during the reforms is mirrored by a relative decline of the main collective institution, the state.
- Unintended losses of resources weaken the state, and many official Chinese norms are now in disarray. A fiscal crunch, especially evident in deficits of official revenue and personnel for the regime, combines with unprecedented symbolic ambiguity about right and wrong. There are widespread reports of corruption and other perceived failures of norms. Nothing is especially new about people speaking in one way while acting in another, but more Chinese people today apparently say they are guided by unintended forces than ever before.
- Time is also crucial for thinking about causations, despite many social scientists' odd resistance to using it as a fully respectable analytic category. So part of the story is periodization: The Cultural Revolution mainly ended, and the reforms began, during the early 1970s (not in 1976 or 1978). There is evidence to show this in many fields, though not all; and there are current political reasons why such a periodization is avoided in official literature. At times after violent centralizations in other countries (after Cromwell in England, after Napoleon in France, after Stalin in Russia, after the Civil War in the United States), there have likewise been periods of normative ambiguity, individual initiative, economic growth, and political decompression.
- Space (not just administrative levels, but specific geographical places) is also far more important than official analyses of politics suggest. This book makes arguments for the Shanghai delta, some of which do not hold

true elsewhere in China. This broad delta with its hundred million people should not require much justification as an adequate place to study, but politics in other places was often different. Comparativists often admit geographical differences, mainly when comparing countries that have governments claiming sovereignty separately. But for study of a nation as large as China, distinctions within this subcontinent are also needed to organize many (not all) of the available facts.

Civil and Uncivil Institutions

This analysis privileges political networks, but not just the state, both as objects of study and as causal vehicles. It argues that Beijing was less important than its spokespersons generally pretended—but it does not broadly argue that *leadership* was less important. The only qualification is that the present approach also seeks to relate the power of nonhierarchical networks (e.g., markets) to the power of hierarchical ones; and this is certainly not to say that leaders are insignificant. Local leaders are the subjects of the most crucial sentences here. Traditions or neotraditions or ideologies (hierarchic or democratic, economic or voluntaristic) were effective only insofar as leaders adopted these in the situations that they faced. Top leaders Mao and Deng certainly shaped a great many local thoughts during their periods of fame, and local leaders framed even more. The difference between a too-broadly social approach to China's reforms and this specifically political tack is a stress on the importance of the agency of leaders, including but not restricted to the famous ones.

"Local power networks" are not the state power network, but they are also not "civil society." Segments of society provide resources, prestige, and space in which local power networks cause actors to do things that otherwise they would not do, but this does not make the two concepts identical.[54] Civil society is far more abstract because no usual definition of it requires the trait that it must be a structure in which power is wielded. So civil society is higher on "the ladder of abstraction" than political networks are; it may cover more because its required definitional traits are fewer (and by the same token, it is a vaguer notion).[55] Units of civil society may sometimes be discussed in this book; but the interest in them here focuses on their governing or following other similar entities, for example, structures of the Chinese government. For that, we need an institutional concept like the state, and local power networks provide it.

"Civil society" has had many interpretations, which are often quite indistinct. Antonio Gramsci wrote of it floridly as including "everything . . . that is not strictly part of the state."[56] But he also emphasized the state's chance for hegemony, which he thought could be planted even in people's minds. So he ended up using the term "civil society" as if all important aspects of it were linked to the state rather than just "not strictly part of the state." Marx had written, "The form of relations determined by the existing productive forces . . . is civil society. . . . It embraces the whole commercial and industrial life of a given stage."[57] In other words, civil society is superstructural, like the state. What Gramsci added to Marx's view of civil society was to include politics more clearly in normative and cultural life, not just commercial and industrial relations involving resources, and he suggested that "relations" outside the state can involve power. This much was fine, but Gramsci's many different uses of the term "civil society" confused the idea.

Gramsci, Foucault, Gaventa, Lukes, and other theorists have shown in various ways that political power cannot be isolated. Power exists in economic, sexual, religious, journalistic, artistic, educational, and many other institutionalized or habitual links between people—not just in formal government. This is a more realistic way to attempt political science than are narrower approaches. But two problems of so much emphasis on nonofficial forms of power must be admitted and overcome: First, a broad view of power presents a need to do research in many social realms that are not usually treated together, but that work is possible.

Second, it would be wrong to suggest that the state cannot control any specific, short-term situation that its leaders wish. For example, in China during reforms, the state is now being weakened by the power of many other institutions; but if the top PRC leaders are reasonably united for any feasible result at any specific place and time, they can obtain it. What they increasingly fail to achieve is many of their wishes at most places over long times. They are frustrated by the unintended results of their own previous policies, by the social effects of technical (including organizational) changes that they do not want to reverse, by local traditions, and by charismas and interests of both official and nonstate actors "below" them.

The strongest link between the state and local power networks in China is almost surely normative: the notion that the government is a good parent, so citizens should be filial children. This idea is ancient; the *Ritual Records* (*Li ji*, 26:1) of the Han calls a king "the father and mother of the people." Such concepts are further expressed in writings compiled by Confucius and Mencius. They distinguish the state and local polities, including families, only to show their parallel forms and harmonious links; state and nonstate power relations are supposed to be seamless.

Even in modern times, harmony rather than conflict—understandings of right principles rather than institutional habits of action to channel tensions—are deemed the basis of social progress. Sun Yat-sen, for example, disagreed with Marx's views of historical development; Sun claimed that China could not progress through struggle.[58] But to say, as statists do, that all of Chinese heritage encourages respect for leaders is to ignore parts of that culture, including some memorable recent parts. A major debate rages among modern China historians, especially Western ones, about whether concepts such as "civil society" can be useful in a country with China's traditions.[59] But too much of this debate on both sides implies that all politics are public, that all Chinese traditions are consistent, or both.

Some Westerners have been enchanted by what they take to be normal Chinese hierarchy. Harvard comparativist Samuel Huntington quotes John Fairbank that "an equal relationship has little precedent in Chinese experience." He quotes Lucian Pye that "in [Chinese] politics there are no equals, only superiors and inferiors." But then he leaps to a very Huntingtonian conclusion: "Government is of supreme importance in China."[60] Actually, families are the top priority for most Chinese. Localities are second to none, in that country as in others. Hierarchical frameworks exist outside governments, and nonstate power networks have been effectively coercive. Also, modern changes may make hierarchy separate from functional talent less important, although even very traditional lineages had clerk leaders who were chosen on the basis of ability, not just seniority.[61] Some functional differentiation is a tradition in Chinese politics. As Pye has elsewhere noted, "The very word 'pluralism' seems to provoke rage in some scholars."[62]

Western researchers such as William Rowe describe Chinese as having a sense of local autonomy, and this legitimates a great deal of local action. But other scholars such as Frederic Wakeman see in Chinese political traditions an overwhelmingly greater sense of obligations. The debate about whether early modern China had some kind of "civil society" and "public sphere" centers on this issue of rights or duties. It became a suspiciously dominant question among China historians during the PRC reforms.

In the "civil society" debate, both sides treat the differences between assumptions in abstract terms, as if, over time, "concepts of man" or "the psychology of the Chinese people" generate practice more than practice sires them.[63] Approaches like those of David Hume or Karl Mannheim, fastening consciousness to the context in which it arises, may be close enough to Confucius or even Lao Zi—and far from either the autonomy or obligation schools. Rights and duties both suggest an artificial deal, an agreement that never existed. Both presume a distinction between nature and society that is at least overdrawn for the sake of argument. The most lasting Chinese contribution to the discourse goes beyond these categories and concerns nature, not implicit contracts of autonomy or obligation.

Causal metaphors are more solid if they reason forward from current conditions, rather than backward from expected future states. Wakeman writes, "If we allow ourselves to be hobbled by teleology then neither concept ['civil society' or 'public sphere'] is going to fit the Chinese case very well. But as terms of social practice, which can be gingerly universalized, civil society and public sphere may afford a better understanding of recent events in China." Wakeman mentions Western intellectuals' underestimation of the potential for change in Eastern Europe during the late 1980s; he asks, "Could the same be true for China today?"[64] The current book argues that it could.

Several different forms of state structure could attain modern goals for China; and political scientists have developed taxonomies of such structures. Certainly not all are pluralist. There is a tentative consensus among comparativists that the historical record suggests certain modern nonliberal forms are basically transitional.[65]

They appear, they may reappear after a liberal or totalist interruption, but they do not last extremely long. Even if China's sometime future does turn out to be liberal, the forms of democracy are also many. As Wakeman points out, a problem with the idea of "civil society" is that it may be misread to imply that countries like China will somehow develop structures that closely resemble those in the United States. "American exceptionalism" is a question in the political science literature on this topic. The present book avoids the term "civil society" not because this misreading has been imputed to it, but because the political meaning of the term can be better captured in nonstate power networks that are often "uncivil."

The current book also avoids the term "public sphere." Habermas lyricizes "the domain of our social life in which such a thing as public opinion can be formed." Yet most of China's recent reform has come in nonpublic spheres, in changes that are more demonstrable by concrete situations than by expressed opinions, and among new entrepreneurial groups rather than among the ever-articulate intellectuals who have ruled China for centuries. Habermas restricts his concept to occasions on which citizens "deal with matters of general interest without being subject to coercion."[66] This definition is odd, in part because it is so explicit in its surrealism. "Matters of general interest" will practically always be at least somewhat "subject to coercion." This definition of the public sphere may well describe an empty set, even in democratic societies.

If there is anything like civil society in China, then many people's actions there show it better than documents written by intellectuals associated with the state. Official documentation, expressing government opinion as if it were all of public opinion, tends to overwhelm academic analyses of China. Outside analysts who want to balance this bias must seek what Suzanne Rudolph calls the "questions that the indigenous accounts [in China, too many of these are official and elitist] would like to let sleep."[67] Many of these, currently, are questions of elitism vs. populism—and many Chinese intellectuals associate elitism with reform and populism with the Cultural Revolution. Sun Liping explicitly cited Western ideas about a neotraditionalist structure in which workers were controlled by being made interdependent. This Beijing sociologist rued the "subconscious disrespect for authority ... in certain work units, where it is becoming almost 'legal' to refuse orders and where qualities of defiance are gaining new respect .... A crisis facing society, and in particular a real or imaginary threat to political power from an elitist group will give rise to populist methods of dealing with that threat."[68]

There are other, broader-based Chinese sources for understanding the PRC's political diversification. Many of the most revealing data come from evening newspapers, popular magazines, and inconsistencies over time in government claims. These are not the standard, signposted roads to comprehending Chinese politics, however. Government documents openly claim to cover the whole topic. A 1992 *Complete Book of Chinese Reforms,* for example, offers a four-thousand-page anthology of central state decrees—and practically no behavioral information about whether any of them have been followed. Seven thick volumes cover official orders from 1978 to 1991: laws, documents on regulations, speeches from politicians, policy chronologies, even hundreds of one-line mottoes of instruction from national leaders—all arranged by functional topic.[69] This is a useful source for some purposes. It suggests, however, that only a tiny part of the actual Chinese political system really exists.

Bureaucrats may be no more guilty of these problems than are academics. The great reluctance to discuss politics in small family-like units, as if these politics were real, may arise from the state's lack of control there. "New institutionalists" wanted to "bring the state back in" to studies of politics. This group often wrote in terms of "state–society" relations—but was slow to conceive of society, in that usage, as a set of power networks quite like the state. In a recent essay on the waning of the Communist state, one distinguished scholar substitutes a "regime-centered focus for the prevalent concern for state-society relations."[70] But politics can, and in China increasingly does, exist in nonstate organizations.

Scholars have had difficulties taking local politics seriously. Calling it "civil society" scarcely solves the problem because that concept depends so heavily on the open articulation of views. Those who like the idea "civil society" often like it because they hesitate to talk about power. Those who dislike it often do so because they think it supports an inaccurate discourse about power. The term is too vague because it stresses norms rather than resources, and highly educated people rather than other groups. Western intellectuals have sympathized with their Chinese peers, suffering at the hands of government in times like 1957, 1966–69, or 1989. They have been less ready to see the interest of dissident intellectuals in denying the quiet politics of unschooled masses, for example, rural industrialists who gain power without certified kinds of knowledge.[71]

Pluralization Without Protest

Expression is not the same as pluralization. If "civil society" means protest, then it was successfully repressed during most of China's reforms. But if "civil society" means pluralization, a growth of local and functional institutions, it occurred in spades. Nonstate institutions such as rural enterprises acquired more money, not more complaints; and this situational change was political. From 1981 to 1984, the number of common-interest associations that were registered at the municipal level in Shanghai quadrupled, from 628 to 2,627.[72] These were not "mass organizations," sponsored by higher levels, but groups organized unofficially and called "social clusters" (*shehui qunti*). The very speed of diversification hindered the PRC official habit of registering all of society's "circles." The high new numbers became simply too large to monitor effectively. "According to a 1985 statistic, there are already more than 5,000 circles in Shanghai, [but] not all parties and groups which participate in the Chinese People's Political Consultative Conference need to be registered."[73]

Shanghai by 1987 had thirty-seven chambers of commerce, covering fields as diverse as food, clothing, packing technology, construction metals, computer software, and electrical appliances. These associations did not restrict their operations to Shanghai; they had members in many other East China cities. For example, the Shanghai Electrical Equipment Association had 150 firms as members, including sixty-four from Jiangsu, Zhejiang, Jiangxi, Shandong, and Fujian.[74]

Two-thirds of these chambers of commerce at the end of 1987 were joined in an overall organization that was notionally guided by the Municipal Economic Commission. These chambers of commerce were all supposed to depend (*guakao*) on government agencies. But as an analysis of them pointed out, "both organizationally and economically, they are supported by enterprises; so in practice, the administrative agencies' hold over them was limited."[75] Between June 15 and 21, 1989, in Shanghai 126 members of "illegal organizations" were jailed. These included staff of organizations that were only vaguely reported, such as the "Higher Schools' Autonomous Federation," the "Workers' Autonomous Federation," and others.[76] They were apparently new groups, emerging at a politically unusual time, but they showed that the state had not advertised the extent of autonomy in other networks. There was some autonomy in new groups that did not advertise the fact.

In places outside Shanghai, where state control is more sporadic than in the metropolis, the proliferation of new organizations was even more dramatic. Local leagues created during the reforms in Xiaoshan, Zhejiang, included a Poultry Breeding Association, a Cement Industry Association, the Quality Management Association, the Accountants' Society, the Qigong Society, a local Red Cross, an Abacus Association, a Society of Patriotic Catholics, a Poets' Society, and the Friendship Association of Women Directors and Managers. Many of these began without the patronage of the local state, although most sought blessings from the CCP city fathers, and some included officers who were concurrently local cadres. The benefits of such linkages often outweighed the fear in associations that they could be controlled in any way not to their liking because the "state" cadres in these cases were hinge leaders, depending largely on local resources. Many such associations asked retired cadres or active local CCP leaders to take honorary seats on their committees. The idea, apparently for both the municipal government *and* for the associations, was to "issue orders through another's bugle" and "fight a battle with borrowed soldiers."

Some organizations were classed as "popular" (*minjian*). A small minority were "official" (*guanban*). Most were "semiofficial" (*banguan*). None described their goals as antithetical to the state's, of course—that option was not salient in the cultural lexicon. But by the same token, their members reportedly wanted to use local CCP leaders. In a town like Xiaoshan, by the late reforms, these could not directly be equated with "the state" at the national level. According to a careful researcher of Xiaoshan, "Aware that some social autonomy is necessary for innovation, creativity, and initiative, the [local] state is prepared to keep a distance from these social organizations. . . . Neither a civil society framework alone nor a state-centered approach can adequately explain these hybrid organizations."[77]

The problem with overemphasizing state patronage is the same as the problem with overemphasizing civil society: Each of these opposite views assumes more coherence than is real in the institutional structure whose importance it highlights. Each assumes a sharper distinction between those two "spheres" than is evident in the acts of Chinese people. "State" and "society" both tend to be interpreted in terms of ideal norms, but the situational context of action affects action too. When that element is added, most evidence suggests that the structure of the state is decreasingly important during reforms. This can occur even while statist ideals remain very important, *as* ideals, to most actors.

Uncivil Polities

Writers who like the term "civil society" include within it fewer elements of coercion and more factors that lead to modern convergence than do those who dislike it. Martin Whyte takes a middle view: "The essence of the term involved the idea of the existence of institutionalized autonomy for social relationships and associational life, autonomy vis-à-vis the state." He says it "implies fairly explicit . . . recognition by the state of the right . . . of civil society to proceed without substantial state interference or control."[78] This summarizes well most uses of the phrase by both its advocates and its critics.

Yet why should the presence of the state's intentional, explicit recognition of civil society's parts become the focus of debate? Why would a state elite find an interest in licensing all this, except to use and tax it? If the state politely refrains from controlling another organization, then what *is* controlling it? Is that not a distinctly political interaction, rather than a more generally social one, since it must involve some use of power? The things that actors do over time show what they do or do not recognize; and it is unclear why state leaders' recognition of elements in civil society should be taken as more crucial in a definition than anybody else's. The usable part of the "civil society" cluster of meaning soon becomes political. It is subject to contention, expressed or not, among different kinds of leaders. When it is seen by definition as uncoercive, as civil, then its units are misperceived as lacking exactly the quality of nastiness that in fact makes them comparable to the state.

Part of this problem is logical. Daniel Little, quoting Wittgenstein, shows that some concepts (including "state") are not defined by any entirely clear set of properties, but instead "through a series of family resemblances. . . . The concept is open-ended, defined in terms of a cluster of properties typically possessed by the organizations referred to as 'states,' without any of these properties being essential to the concept."[79] Civil society is also a "cluster term," but that does not make it sufficiently similar to the state to allow clear comparisons.

Weber defined the state as the social organization that claims a right to exercise legally legitimate coercion. But local nonstate power networks are similar: They actually have much legitimacy, and they often use sanctions. They do not in public usually claim the only legal right to do so; but from the viewpoint of the people whom they actually control, that is a minor point.[80] Generalizations may be advanced either on the basis of surreal definitions or on the basis of Wittgenstein's "family resemblance" definitions. The latter option is best in this case, since resemblances are very strong in China today between state and local power networks.

In substance, not just as a definitional matter, local tyrannies can be fierce. Many cases could be offered; but a dramatic example occurred in 1985 at Tongluo township, Wujiang, Jiangsu, on the Shanghai delta. This involved four local Chinese opera actresses, who became extremely popular and were funded for further training by the local government. They made the tiny Tongluo Cultural Station famous among opera buffs throughout the delta. They were welcomed by well-known actors in Hangzhou, Kunshan (whose local opera tradition is excelled by none), Shanghai, and elsewhere. The Cultural Bureau of the major city, Jiaxing, Zhejiang, decided to employ these actresses and arranged new household registrations for them in Jiaxing—a much bigger stage than Tongluo. But the local Tongluo government, backed by its Party committee, refused to let them move, saying their residence registrations would not be changed. It also demanded that they repay the local money spent for their training, in an amount greater than they could afford. The four actresses protested, in a letter to a national journal:

> We do not understand why the wife and children of the [Tongluo] Party secretary can easily leave the county to work in town, but he uses all kinds of methods to stop us from going to be formal actresses. Do we really owe a training fee? No! Tongluo Cultural Station had nothing originally.... Our opera became a byword in Zhejiang, Jiangsu, and Shanghai within three years. Indeed, we contributed a lot to our hometown.... We appeal to your journal to uphold justice, maintain socialist democracy, and remove this local mountain from our backs.[81]

Local politics in China remains more nasty and Hobbesian than empowered and Rousseauian for many members of many groups—even as local cadres take powers away from the state. Lawrence Stone, writing about another time and place, describes reform China when he portrays the life of ordinary people as "the very opposite of the life of security and stability depicted by nostalgic romantics."[82] This situation is slowly changing, as markets extend their reach and provide a basis on which a more representative state might later emerge. But such change is slow. Like other countries, China may take a long time about it.

Local Leaders, Elite Recruitment, Rights and Duties

Not all local cadres were reformist. Many were reactionary, autonomous, and able to disobey liberalizing mandates from the state. When they were conservative and determined to keep their current situations, they prevailed over Beijing policies just as surely as, in other places, reformist local leaderships did. In parts of Zhejiang where local leaders did not foster rural industry, for example, 15 percent of that province's agricultural workers as late as 1979 made less than 50 yuan per month; this was near subsistence for them and their families. A report concluded, "The main reason was that the [local] government carried out the leftist line." Central policies had changed, by then, to allow such an accusation. "Under the left line, diverse economic forms were not allowed; so surplus agricultural laborers could not get other jobs."[83] In these areas, socialist management, ownership, and monoculture were all fully intact. Hidebound local Party leaders were often able to resist changing them, even when reforms in adjacent jurisdictions were making peasants prosper. Local leaders followed their own lines. Just as many local cadres in Zhejiang during the early 1970s had ignored antimarket radicals in Beijing and Hangzhou, some after 1978 ignored a reformist Beijing. The constant element was the localism.

Policies are not conveyed smoothly from the high state into all jurisdictions because contexts and cultures in such a large country are variegated. The overemphasis by liberal analysts on "civil society" or "the public sphere" follows an intellectual's premise: that the main or only way to know why things happen is to perceive the consciousness of the people being studied, and that such an awareness is readily communicable. Frederic Wakeman ends an eloquent critique of "civil society" with the thought that "most Chinese citizens appear to conceive of social existence mainly in terms of obligation and interdependence rather than rights and responsibilities."[84] But things happen to people that nobody fully intends, because consciousness is not subject to sure laws of effectiveness or clarity. The ears that hear are at least as important as the mouths that speak. Also, any agent's exercise of influence can have unintended effects in unexpected contexts. Further, people with high official titles are often far less clear about what they want to do than their publicists imply. Even when they make decisions, their policies have different purposive and implementing aspects, which are often in some tension with each other. For example, Mao and his colleagues before 1966 often used administrative methods to mobilize or scare people—without any clarity about what the intermediate or eventual results of these quasi-violent political techniques might be.[85] Even if Chinese think mostly about obligations rather than rights—as they probably do—such devotion to duties will not always tell them exactly how to make their interdependence fruitful and their responsibilities well fulfilled. Should they, for example, carry out their duties to large or small groups? Local leaders are the crucial actors because their "hinge" status gives them extra legitimacy and resources to decide such issues. Some local leaders are now reformist, and others are reactionary.

Traditions of Speech vs. Traditions of Behavior

Various Chinese think usually in terms of interdependence and perhaps occasionally in terms of independence or other categories. But the way they think does not determine everything they do. Situations are not just different from norms; they affect norms. Local wealth, for example, or unintended results of policies in earlier decades have been crucial to the context in which local leaders' power has increased vis-à-vis more central authorities. This process is in part irrespective of the consciousness of either. Leaders of the many, not of the weak, have real weapons partly because of their common identities with their followers, and partly because of the concrete constraints they together place on state bureaucrats. This gives them some practical autonomy, although they have little need or interest to talk about it. Practically everybody, at least in China's reforms, says the state apparatus has more power than it objectively does.

The value of order, which Chinese often express, strains against many current patterns of behavior. This tension may eventually be resolved by Chinese who alter some of their previous values, as people have done in other countries more sharply than traditions of speaking commonly stress. But some analysts, especially historians who stress the great power of Chinese statist traditions, write as if there were a unique danger in using teleological concepts, especially the concept of modernization. This concept may encourage people to be too cocksure about what will happen in China's future. That danger is real, but there is just as much peril in taking "tradition" as a set of consistent premises for prediction.

A stress on tradition with an antiteleological analysis and a stress on context with a modernization analysis share an identical and fatal problem: Both begin with a coherent set of premises that would restrict Chinese people from dealing with the full array of norms and situations that they actually face. There is no theoretical reason to favor one of these interpretations over the other, especially as an account of Chinese political structure. There is no substitute for trying to look at all the available kinds of evidence about how the resources and ideas available to Chinese people affect the ways they dominate or influence each other. "Civil society" covers more than the meaning needed, which might be described in reform China as a network of postrevolutionary and often unstately polities.

Reconciliation vs. Memory in Postrevolutionary Politics

A slow epidemic of tolerance among groups that can produce political leaders spreads, as revolutions end. Part of the Restoration settlement in England was an "Act of Indemnity and Oblivion" of 1660, which gave a blanket pardon to almost everyone who had engaged in the Puritan Revolution (except those directly involved in the execution of Charles I). Fines were imposed, for three years, on anyone who after the Restoration criticized the conduct of anyone else during the previous two decades.[86] In France after Napoleon's demise, late Bourbon kings recognized both early Bourbon and Napoleonic titles of nobility. In Spain after Franco's death, both pro- and anti-Falange leading families became important. In the wakes of some one-party centralizations, notably after Stalin's thorough job, protoreformism was minimal though not entirely absent.[87] But in China, non-Communist local leaders were not totally extirpated or co-opted even in the radical years after 1957.

By 1978 in China, obviously unjust violence against people tagged with bad labels in the Cultural Revolution had already cast doubt in the minds of many about the wisdom of labeling. The public campaign to abolish labels began in April of that year, and the Third Plenum passed a resolution moving in this direction.[88] This movement—which meant the relegitimation of several kinds of previous local elites—was resisted by antirecruitment "lions" in the CCP and was supported by reformist "foxes" there. It could never be utterly complete, for the reason Pareto gives: Ruling cliques have to value their integrity. The administrative mechanism for discrimination thus did not disappear so quickly as the high-state decision to end discrimination would imply. Many local CCP leaders were deeply uninterested in rehabilitating people whom the state now said they had wronged.

Also, the sheer amount of paperwork was daunting, in the project of ending the revolution's comprehensive system of labels. The household registry form did not much change in Shanghai from the 1950s through the late 1980s.[89] But by the 1980s, new forms included new kinds of entries, and class status was usually dropped as a category (although local memories were not so short that anybody forgot, and many old papers were still on file). Applications to certain schools, to the youth league, or to the Party, for example, commonly asked about "hobbies" (*xingqu aihao*) and about foreign language abilities—topics that for different people carried both positive and negative interest after reforms were initiated.

Concern among those who would suffer from a revival of previous discriminations rose and fell, along with the cycle of lions and foxes. Not all were old elites. Worry affected many local Jiangnan ex-bourgeois families, but also those who had prospered in the early 1950s, or after 1970 as leaders in very rich collectives, or after 1980 as new entrepreneurs. A Shanghai paper admitted in 1988: "With their businesses booming, well-to-do individuals in the rural and urban areas are now afraid of change in the Party's policies, and reclassification of their social status." The newspaper tried to assure them that being a "socialist boss" was acceptable, and that there would be "no reclassification of class statuses" or any "irrational setting of quotas." But even this paper admitted that, whenever they thought about the possibility that labels might be revived, "the scene of settling scores with the landlords naturally flashes into their minds."[90]

"The traumatic memory of past conflicts . . . may either perpetuate conflict or cause parties to draw together," as Hans Daalder says.[91] For this reason, authoritarian ideologies do not automatically perpetuate themselves. If they legitimate regimes that create traumas—as occurred in China during the Cultural Revolution—then authoritarianism can teach antiauthoritarian, tolerant, liberal lessons.[92] In reform China and other postrevolutionary countries, dictatorship apparently scares local leaders in the short term, while also encouraging them to respect each other in the long term. Learning among groups of leaders is a mixed process, but comparative evidence suggests that it does occur.

Elites want to preserve their standing criteria for recruitment, but they also can face situations of change in which the recruitment of new talent is necessary to their continued standing. These are contradictory impulses, and they were both evident throughout China's reforms. Conservative leaders in 1989, for example, still considered "bourgeois liberals" to be the cause of disorder. Yuan Mu, head of the main hard-line think tank, the Research Office of the State Council, said in mid-May 1989, "It needs long and hard work for us to go against bourgeois liberalization, which could not be solved by any kind of campaign."[93] He was right, but he practically admitted the risks in his project.

A postviolence climate, as in China for several decades after 1970, breeds an ambiguous combination of nervousness and confidence among hinge leaders. A majority of Chinese people who could be interviewed in the late 1980s admitted they were "careful" in dealing with political subjects.[94] Dissidents, however, felt China had all too much "feeling of security" (*anquan gan*). They could mourn, in print then, that China had no "middle class" (*zhongchan jieji*), even though they did not explicitly mourn the lack of a "bourgeoisie." They felt China had a "psychology of officials and commoners" (*chenmin xinli*). Highly educated people could easily be induced to opine that history's bequest to China of a "special middle group," the intellectuals, was in this view the only hope of unifying society. But many Chinese intellectuals had less smugness and more ambition than a typical middle class. Only gradually did analyses cover the start of a true middle class, first in suburban and rich rural areas, from the 1970s through the 1990s.

Liu Binyan, one of the bravest of the intellectuals, projecting on others his own will to end political frustration, saw great changes in Chinese personalities. Liu said in 1989, "Since 1949, the Chinese people have never been as dynamic as they are now. I have lived through this whole period, and I have never seen common people so determined, with such a high degree of self-awareness—and independent awareness—that says 'I am a human being, you can't bully me.' "[95] Liu may have been hopeful; but he has seen more of China than most commentators, and popular moods shift over time, so he may prove to be right. The reconciliation of elites takes time.

Intellectuals, Intolerance, Patriotism, and Ambition

As the intellectual Chen Yizi once said, "The smart people caused all the problems."[96] Max Weber long ago thought that the special connection of literati to power in China created a structural impediment to modernization there.[97] If political progress is defined in simplistic terms as motion toward anything that resembles democracy, then it is easy to show that many Chinese intellectuals hold undemocratic attitudes. A spring 1989 survey of a group that nominally espouses democracy—Beijing university students—asked their opinions of the statement, "One of the most important principles in democracy is that the minority should submit to the majority, but the latter should also respect the interest of the former." Less than half the students agreed. More than one-third actively disagreed with this statement.[98]

A large-scale poll in 1989, before June 4, showed that only 31 percent of intellectuals thought the following statement could have an operational meaning in practice: "I firmly oppose your views, but I strongly protect your right to advocate them." Fully 42 percent of intellectuals thought this was a contradiction. Another 22 percent thought it was disagreeable or unfeasible.[99] Such attitudes are not conducive to behavior that makes the information behind decisions public, nor toward behavior that holds officials accountable. But two flaws haunt the argument that attitudes preclude democracy in China. First, many certifiable democratic countries also include citizens with similar views; yet these do not destroy the liberal tenor of their countries. Second, attitudes are practiced in the context of institutions, which come to affect their content.

The Chinese state for centuries has supported knowledge elites who try to justify their power by claims to specially defined moral virtues. Under this kind of regime, intellectual tolerance has often been repressed. If the structure for obtaining office changes from knowledge certification to electoral victory—even if this change is brief or temporary—it is difficult to be sure how such a new structure will affect attitudes. That it would do so somewhat (just as the old structures have done) is likely. Structure affects notions of what is feasible, not just the other way around. Ideas about political practicality can change quickly; they are less stable than most intellectuals admit.

Shanghai's 600,000 popularly labeled intellectuals (*zhishi fenzi*) in the 1980s were a prestigious group, whose talents the Party could obviously use. So a "large-scale seminar on ideological work among intellectuals" was addressed by Jiang Zemin in late 1987.[100] But intellectuals did not necessarily conceive of themselves as naturally separate from power such as Jiang represented. They did not think of themselves as mere tools of the state, even if they were to be well treated in that role.[101] The vulnerability of Chinese intellectuals comes partly from an old but dubious premise that their talents, which run to juggling ideas, are particularly useful in the state. This is true, but they are also useful in other institutions.

Many Shanghai intellectuals interviewed for this book bemoaned that young, educated, well-intentioned reformers—once they became officials (*zuo guan*)—found they could do little to implement their ideals. They were constrained not only by more conservative elders, but also by established bureaucratic structures and especially by the need to meet budgets so that no established perquisites would be reduced and no jobs lost. This is not the first reforming elite to discover that structures are difficult to change. Partly because of this problem with institutions, these thinkers understandably revert to the possibility of changing ideas. Intellectuals' stress on the crucial importance of personal reform may be explained as Confucian, but it may also tend to confirm educators' rights to rule. Individual-ideal change based on personal will is not, however, the only way to improve politics.

Su Xiaokang, who as director of the documentary *River Elegy* has been extraordinarily influential among PRC intellectuals, follows the May 4 spirit by calling for nothing less than a psychological reform of Chinese personalities:

> We cannot change the color of our skins, just as we cannot change the color of the Yellow River. And yet we must rebuild the culture of Chinese people—the structure of their minds. This will be an extremely difficult and complex piece of culturo-philosophical systems engineering.[102]

Such an approach seeks a magic idea that can transform people. Among exiled dissidents since June 4, conference after conference has been held to find the grand new philosophy that China is thought to need. This effort would be useful on the presumption that mind rules matter, that action is easy once knowledge is firm. If so, the intellectuals with the best ideas would have a right to rule.

The main problem with this notion is neither that it is undemocratic nor that it is easy to deconstruct into social interests. The difficulty is that it is based on a historically misleading view of how wealth and power have actually been achieved in the countries that most people agree are modern. If democracy and national solidarity are regarded as important aspects of development, there is scant evidence that ideas alone are what makes them grow. State policies, based on ideas and sometimes mass ideas, have been important for modernization in some respects, but they have clearly hindered it in others. Systems engineering sometimes works, but the dispersal of wealth and power away from elites (including intellectual elites) is the main story. Intellectuals, especially but not exclusively in China, overrate the influence of ideas as distinguished from the power of circumstances. This is not surprising in view of their abilities, but it is a reflexive fault that they could overcome. The kind of cultural change that is relevant in China, during the reforms, involves alteration rather than rejection of previous norms of Chinese culture.

Many urban Chinese intellectuals are dissatisfied with the slowness of reforms since 1978. They see their countrymen as having a feudal mind-set, fixated on a traditional need for obedience. But only a few after the Cultural Revolution see most of China's population as too fearful of discord. They are schizophrenic about whether their compatriots are overly respectful of emperor-like figures at the very center of their "central country." On the one hand, Mao gave them many reasons to see faults in their state. On the other, they are nostalgic for the imagined peaceable kingdom before Mao came to power, when intellectuals fared well. In smaller social units such as factories and families, the urban intellectuals who criticize this feudal mentality see petty emperors whom the masses continue to obey, even when these little tyrants are arbitrary and when more competent local leaders could do better. Interviewees occasionally express that the traditional stress on "sincerity" thwarts fair and predictable procedures. Although some modernists—not all intellectuals—see virtues in the nearly metaphysical old emphasis on prosperity and multiplicity, represented in many sons in a family or many oranges on New Year's trees, most current intellectuals downplay the value of even these traditions.

Some intellectuals have become so disillusioned by incivilities in Chinese tradition that, in effect, they eschew serious politics. The astrophysicist Fang Lizhi, even before his expulsion from the Party, called for "complete Westernization."[103] His deep pessimism about the possibilities in Chinese culture is not widespread among PRC leaders or people, and it is widely seen as impatient. In fact, China has changed much faster during and since the 1970s than any purely cultural analysis could imply. China's intellectuals are still angry about the Cultural Revolution, which was unfair to them, and about the many midlevel Party hacks who did not suffer at that time or owed promotions to witch hunts after the Antirightist Campaign. Although such anger is easy to understand, it hardly makes for circumspect observation of the current trends in China. Depressed feelings, especially those of intellectuals, are a very unreliable indicator of social progress or regress.[104]

Guardian Technocrats and Issues of Value

China's educated people have a common interest in maintaining the norm that intellectual attainment confers some right to rule. They want the state to support university exams that certify prospective office-holders. This is not a uniquely Chinese institution. Plato foreboded it. The British administered their empire with it; Oxbridge-certified district officers ran India with classical educations in Latin, Greek, and the importance of moral community.[105] In each case, education gave prefects connections and a social finish that was crucial to their later careers. There was no close relevance between their administrative work, on the one hand, and the specific content of the education that they received, on the other. A study of almost any major dead language would suffice. The combined studies Plato proposed, or Marxist theorizing, or Homer and Cicero, or Confucian "eight-legged essays" all justified power. The resulting organizations were status-based rather than class-based; their aim was rule, not production. An intellectual test, involving moral subjects, could sort talent and certify that each member of a state apparatus had studied something to claim dignity in power.[106] Many societies, including China, have carved the stamp of elite legitimacy in terms of some knowledge that most people are supposed not to have.

In the PRC during reforms, technical educations have been the most important basis for elite recruitment. China is developing, and development requires
engineers. But this connection does not undermine the consummatory, rather
than instrumental, gifts such training brings. Engineering was the subject of
study for over half of Shanghai's university-level students in the 1980s, with less
than 15 percent in teacher training and still fewer in all other major fields
together, including natural sciences and medicine.[107] China's engineering universities have been in the forefront, since the 1950s, of assuring that their most
promising graduates have political leadership abilities.[108] They are training not
just engineers, but politicians.

Science is linked with planning, and thus with modern government. Deng
Xiaoping in 1978 confirmed that science has "no class nature" but also (contra-
dictorily, in the same speech) that scientists should consider themselves "part of
the working class." Actually, they are an especially self-conscious part. They
responded to Deng's invitation with gusto. Returning to government offices,
groups quickly produced "strategy" (*zhanlüe*) documents on every conceivable
aspect of the future. They projected not only the Sixth Five-Year Plan (1981–
85), but also a putative Twenty-Year Plan (1981–2000). This last essay assignment went to think tanks for Premier Zhao in the early 1980s; but it took so long
to write that it could not be finished in time. The result was a Fifteen-Year Plan,
for 1986–2000.[109]

Democracy was, for conservatives, solely an instrument of centralization.
Deng Xiaoping and other stability-oriented leaders saw democracy as a means to
convey more information to executive organs. In May 1987, for example, Deng
reacted to political reform proposals from Zhao Ziyang's think tank by declaring,
"The main goal of our reform is to guarantee the efficiency of the executive
organs without too much further interference. . . . Dictatorship cannot be abandoned. Do not yield to the feeling for democratization . . . . We want a system
that can strengthen efficiency, streamlining governmental structure. Democracy
is only a means. Democracy should be discussed in connection with legality."[110]

The links between science and democracy are made even in the PRC's basic-
level practice, because science involves empirical investigation. This is sometimes translated into a notion that the government should listen to the views of
people whom it does not appoint. As a speaker at the end of a local political
consultative conference said:

> What function can the conference carry out? I think the conference can play
> an important role in the democratization and scientification [*minzhu hua,
> kexue hua*] of decision making . . . . A correct decision should undergo the
> following procedure: (1) establishing an agenda [by the government, appar-
> ently], (2) democratic discussion, (3) experts' corrections, (4) examination in
> practice, (5) legislative procedure. This is a democratic and scientific method.
> The conference can play a more important role in this procedure than any
> other organization.[111]

Democracy is thus conceived of as a scientific planning procedure. The link between science and democracy is justified this way even in rural China. A suburban Shanghai Party secretary told his listeners that,

> to study and establish a development plan is to facilitate the democratization and scientification of the leadership's decision making. Our comrades working in local government know their areas very well, and they also have local experience and can lead local development. . . . Many township leaders also take part in decision making. They make a lot of careful investigations in their areas, study and analyze their areas' situations. Based on this procedure, a plan can be said to be more democratic and scientific compared to past plans. . . . After all the townships raised questions and problems, the plan was modified and improved.[112]

This is a representative and information-gathering method. Setting agendas and making decisions is still, however, a top–down imposition under this very "scientific" view of democratic procedure. Questions of value—who wins and who loses, for example—are not addressed. Government is seen as a technical problem, best left to benign technocrats.

Not all political problems, however, can be solved by expertise. The argument for neoauthoritarian rule by scientists or technocrats is based on questionable ideas: that every human question has a correct answer, and that there is some unified method to find this answer. Confucian moral science and Marxist historical science both made this claim, when they were yoked to the task of providing Chinese regimes with legitimacy. Now, during reforms, a less specifically Chinese and less obviously ideological kind of science has inherited this elite-legitimating role. But the new pipe plays an old tune; it is still there to keep an identifiable, stable group in power. Its message now is that selected experts in the right arcana (which the masses will never understand) have a natural mandate to rule. This is an arresting notion; but it is not obviously correct quite aside from the fact that it is undemocratic. "Mr. Science," in his usually narrow moods, is an enemy of "Mr. Democracy."

As Richard Suttmeier writes, "Distorted policymaking, resulting from the primacy of technical advice and the illusion of the technical fix, are one manifestation of a larger problem . . . the 'cognitive conquest' of 'technicism.' "[113] Albert Einstein "was once asked why, if he could solve the secrets of the universe, he could not devise a plan for the prevention of war. His answer was that world politics was more complicated than the rules of physics."[114]

Efficiency, the Democratic Love of People, and an Alternation of Elites to Protect Them

Mr. Science cannot, despite the faith his adherents invest in him, solve all human problems. Some of his advocates, despite their obvious virtues, are also famed in China for their arrogance. They tend to neglect nonintellectuals who have political resources—and who thus can be mobilized by other groups (including more tolerant intellectuals) in political struggles. That kind of fighting, pluralization, and resource-seeking is a usual hallmark of protodemocratic evolutions, even though none of its participants may be mainly liberal. E.E. Schattschneider has urged a distinction

> between what amateurs know and what professionals know. The problem is not how 180 million Aristotles can run a democracy, but how we can organize a political community of 180 million ordinary people so that it remains sensitive to their needs. . . . The people are involved in public affairs by the conflict system.[115]

This stress on conflict, and this definition of democracy as coming not just from normative habits but also from struggles for concrete goods outside the state, is at odds with the notion that democracy arises when people are taught right values. This realist view shows competing elites trying to recruit resources from larger social groups, so that they can win against their rivals. In the process, ordinary people may get somewhat more chance to pick their leaders. Conflicting Chinese intellectual factions, despite their elitism, might in the future slowly broaden their interests, lose some of their obvious political hauteur toward other kinds of people, and become more effective in garnering support from farmers, businesspeople, clerks, workers, and soldiers. The intellectuals who do this stand a greater chance of long-term political success than the intellectuals who do not.

Rural entrepreneurs and farmers, who have done more than intellectuals during reforms to change the basic structure of the Chinese state, were barely represented at China's major democratic rallies in 1976, 1978–79, 1986, and 1989. Intellectuals, who did not realize how much other groups participate in stable democracies, nonetheless furthered their country's political evolution in these movements. Most of China's would-be democrats lacked any clear definition of democracy. Nonetheless, they promoted it not just as a temporary fad or a shadow. They began to explore new ideas and constituencies. Many people in Chinese cities remember this, and similar memories have brought later political openings in other countries previously. It is unclear exactly when or how this might happen in China, but it is possible to specify conditions that affect pluralization.

Many government and dissident intellectuals have argued that the Chinese masses are unready for democracy. Interests often lie behind this stance, which lessen its credibility from many who avow it. Elites' disbelief in the political capacities of others is easy to deconstruct, and Schattschneider on this subject is very pithy:

> It is profoundly characteristic of the behavior of the more fortunate strata of the community that responsibility for widespread nonparticipation is attributed wholly to the ignorance, indifference, and shiftlessness of the people. This has always been the rationalization used to justify the exclusion of the lower

classes from any political system. There is a better explanation. Abstention reflects the suppression of the options and alternatives that reflect the needs of the nonparticipants.[116]

Nonparticipation in a polity often comes from politicians' previous structuring of the political agenda, so that issues of interest to groups that might support their rivals cannot be addressed. It may not be inferred from the non-expression of political issues, however, that they do not exist.

Two kinds of problems stubbornly recur, so that even the most hidebound elites cannot ignore them forever. Governments in many countries, over long eras, have supported either the efficiency brought by businesses and markets, or else the protection of people from harsh effects of putting onto the market their own labor, earnings, and environment.[117] These two aspects of development are not easy to mesh. They are largely opposite, and their *laissez-faire* or regulatory functions—both of which all modern societies need—are arranged by business or labor leaderships, with different political bases, in different eras. Democratic systems, despite their faults, have done a fairly sensitive job of tackling both these aspects of development. Perhaps other regime types can do as well, to make societies more prosperous and more liveable at the same time. Good evidence to show decisively other regime types' abilities to further these two opposite aspects of modernization simultaneously has not emerged. Some authoritarian states seem to further efficiency *or* equality adequately, but not both together. As the liberal realist Schattschneider says, "We pass judgement on the most complex mechanisms on the basis of the *results* they produce." So "the reluctance of the public to press its opinions on the government concerning a great multitude of issues is really not as bad a thing as we may have been led to think. . . . The public is far too sensible to attempt to play the preposterous role assigned to it by the theorists. . . . The crisis here is not a crisis in democracy but a crisis in theory."[118]

Intellectuals, Constitutions, and Hierarchical Patriotism

As Mao Zedong often said, and inadvertently proved, Chinese intellectuals can be arrogant. Pride has been a hallmark of ruling groups, and self-congratulating leaderships have been usual during the development of many nations: The classic haughtiness of Roman citizens, British imperialist racism, Japanese samurai condescension, and many other examples all included some leaders' views that they had a right to rule the lower classes of their own countries, as well as foreign heathen. One reason why no major Chinese politician since Sun Yat-sen has leapt to advocate Western-style democracy is that such a regime type would be an import. Chinese patriotic elites have been partly shaped by the premises of the foreigners they had to fight.[119] There are many different kinds of Chinese leaders, of course; but many of them still vividly deduce, from their nation's past and current experiences with foreigners, a pressing need for arrogance with Chinese characteristics.

Educated people are essential for the growth of any state form that helps larger numbers, because they alone create organizational options for voters, as Chapter 4.3 argues. Writing constitutions requires a study of how and what to write. Comparative political science may not provide all the keys to wisdom about state forms, but it highlights pitfalls to avoid. Educated people are also good at expanding assemblages of quiet networks into open parties. Universities train them to be idea-jugglers; so they can provide new policy platforms, searching critical alternatives to whatever the current incumbents of power espouse. Education combined with ambition can bring new issues to the public agenda. Groups to which the government was previously irrelevant may then assist more promising leaders into power. Any state form, such as democracy or dictatorship or corporatism, is from this viewpoint a tactical habit of leaders, not mainly a set of values. Intellectuals can be crucial in the development of institutional democracy, for example, but only as they use their intellects to help other people as well as themselves. If high leaders can succeed in politics only when the interests of successively lower hinge leaders are served—and if, eventually, a larger number is served—the habit becomes a syndrome for greater sovereign choice by more people. Particularly strong Chinese traditions, like many traditions in other countries, militate against this process, so it will take a while. Educated people's immediate reasons to discourage such structures are as strong as their reasons to speed the change. But the resource infrastructure for it is quickly expanding in reform China. When some intellectuals realize that their own political prospects can benefit from that expansion, they may stoop to solicit more support from other people.

Many Chinese intellectuals' view of the world is still inseparable, however, from the traditional prowess in the Confucian bureaucracy, whose gatekeeping mechanism was scholarly exams based on moralistic texts. The empire lasted a long time on this basis. But it has bequeathed to some Chinese intellectuals great political haughtiness and an implicit assumption that hierarchy is almost always proper because they will almost always be the hierarchs. This is not a democratic attitude. It often comes in xenophobic or racist guises, although that may enhance its appeal within China. It may eventually change, both in its domestic and international aspects, if politicians who garner more support by shedding it win contests with alternative leaders. But less civil medium-term futures are possible, too.

The main problem of China, in the medium run, does not come from hubris about the inherent strengths of Communist organization. It comes, instead, from the link between the social pride of intellectual-politicians and their potential ability to win in political struggles if they hide their pride under nationalistic, xenophobic, or quasi-racist covers. In countries like Germany and France during this century and the previous one, intellectuals often compensated for their social marginality by becoming existential patriots.[120] This "treason of the intellectuals" to humanity is possible even in China. There is already evidence of it, despite elements of Chinese tradition that militate against praising cruelty.

In late 1994, Party Chairman Jiang Zemin circulated a fervently elitist and antiforeign book, entitled *Looking at China Through a Third Eye,* at a Party plenum.[121] He opined that it was a "good book" *(hao shu)*. In Shanghai, the *Economic Daily* in 1994 printed a series of articles about structural problems in market economies: labor disputes, competing companies that hide technologies, problems of enforcing debt repayment, and other difficulties.[122] These conservative questions about markets centered on the need for predictable reliability and trust. The main issue was state jobs for government intellectuals and their clients.

A group of young journalists in 1996 wrote a superpatriotic book, *China Can Say No,* to argue against Western and especially American views of China.[123] The book severely criticized American cultural influences. These thinkers deemed the film *Forrest Gump* to be particularly inane. The two authors who conceived and publicized the book, Song Qiang and Zhang Xiaobo, had been classmates at East China Normal University in Shanghai. In an interview, Zhang opined that American computers were "more dangerous than nuclear weapons," so that when computers have "taken control over all aspects of life, it will endanger our national interests. . . . This is a kind of network violence. So if you like, you could call us the New Boxers." This neo-Luddism was proudly xenophobic. It also mirrored earlier Western racism. As Song complained, "When the yellow races grasp Western rules and perform well, then the whites will change them. . . . The Westerners are really cowards."[124]

The authors merely implied, but did not specify, criticisms of their own government. When asked about the democracy movement, Zhang vaguely said it was "to some extent going down a blind alley. As for Tiananmen, I think we had better skip this topic."[125] Here was a conservative equivalent of *River Elegy,* though it was even more elitist and even less coherent. It had support from high-level conservatives, especially "princes" of the younger Party generation who hoped that their families' own proprietary revolution would not end. Some of these were in the military; but in Shanghai, one estimator guessed that almost 70 percent of "officials' sons" worked for trading companies.[126] The greatest supporters of these views were well educated. The first 50,000 copies of *China Can Say No* were sold out almost immediately. The book was "much discussed among young intellectuals in Beijing."[127]

China's cultural-political elite is not the first to resent the dilution of its power in a modern division of labor. Nor is China the first country in which intellectual politicians have resisted this trend by suggesting it is a wholly foreign invasion—all the more invidious, in their view, because the bullets are ideas. French elite discomfiture at Americanization has received particular attention, especially for the era of Servan-Schreiber and de Gaulle.[128] The same phenomenon is evident in many countries. Yet French or Indian or American or Russian or Chinese identities are actually not in danger of perishing. The real question is which group of French, Indians, Americans, Russians, or Chinese may set the national style. Does the cultural and political elite rightly determine this alone, irrespective of mass groups? The state, the necessarily coercive agency in any country, may not serve others best by making all the choices.

Other nations, in which many felt the state was too weak, have also seen the rise of nationalist theoretician-politicians together. The German case is best known, but aspects of the pattern can be found in most large countries of continental Europe, as in heavily populated parts of Asia and elsewhere.[129] Solzhenitsyn and Stalin, despite their differences, both propagated a particularist regard for the virtues of the Russian land and people. Japan has been through alternating stages of xenophobia and internationalism, but technocrats there still justify extensive rule by educated administrators on grounds of the importance of the national community.[130] China is the largest—and because of its eventual future military potential, the most dangerous—country in which intellectual-politicians might legitimate their domestic rule by acting on claims that China has a right to primacy among countries. This has been a pattern in several large states, where intellectual-politicians continue to try it.

This fate is, however, not foreordained. China is civilized. Confucian traditions are diverse enough to support several different results. Perhaps advocates of more universalist views will carry the day politically. But only in a few cosmopolitan Chinese environments have intellectuals sometimes suspended their social disdain for other groups—and then just partially. When they are in power, they can maintain the political-social structure that benefits them by claiming only they have the knowledge to make the Chinese race wealthy and powerful. In some periods of reform, especially after 1989, intellectual-politicians who won (as distinct from those who lost) stressed their nationalism up to the point that it threatened overseas investment. But in fact, China is now becoming appropriately stronger because of the activities of nonintellectual groups. The inherited social attitudes of intellectuals, who think they own the whole country, still create barriers to expression of the interests of all Chinese.

This problem, combined in China with memories of violence by imperialists, is heartily sustained by the image of Taiwan. Foreign protection of Taiwan continues in tacit forms, and the regime type on that island has already become democratic with Chinese characteristics. A minoritarian mainlander government there placated the subethnic majority Taiwanese by dispersing power to entrepreneurs. The resulting economic success, now well known throughout China though still disdained in a few northern educated and governmental circles, has challenged the right to rule of Chinese nonentrepreneurial intellectuals on the mainland. These concerns come from overseas, but for China's elite they engage domestic political claims. Both the foreign involvement and the state form on Taiwan challenge the efficacy of CCP rule in China.

A Western motto says that "patriotism is the last refuge of scoundrels." Real past injustices by foreigners to Chinese, combined with some millennia of the notion that the map of the world has a center, will for a long time make patriotism sound better there than it is. Also, many intellectuals are adept at not looking like scoundrels. Some from Beijing in particular have a mind-over-matter caprice that is highly compatible with ardent patriotism and strenuous claims to elite status. They tend to equate politics with philosophy, as if the only practical way to resolve any conflict of interests is through better understanding—and thus through making sure that the knowledgeable rule. This is a romantic and beautiful view of social life, but it does not admit that people have interests. It tends to classify any kind of noncerebral conflict as illegitimate, especially in domestic politics. People with skills of articulation are needed (along with others) to create modern decision frameworks that can take better account of the many different kinds of Chinese, but the willful kind of intellectualism nearly disables people from becoming democrats.

"Authority has always fascinated intellectuals," as Edward Shils once noted. Then he tried to justify this interest: "Authority is a manifestation of what is central in society, and it is in the nature of the educated intelligence to be concerned with the central, the essential, in existence."[131] A skeptic can point out that "the essential" seems pleasantly powerful, too. But much evidence shows that Shils is right to claim that authority appeals to intellectuals. Few Chinese thinkers have looked forward to the demise of scholars' special role in censoring the government. Chen Fangzheng predicted this change at a conference sponsored by the Chinese Academy of Social Sciences. Chen foresaw that intellectuals still have a special role, but at some future time there may be no need for them to serve as the "carriers of the word" (*daiyan ren*) for the masses, who will find their own voices.[132]

Different geographical places do not have exactly the same experiences in this respect, and non-PRC intellectuals have already pioneered new kinds of links between thinkers and bureaucrats. Taiwan's experience suggests that normalizing political conflict between groups in a Chinese context is not only possible, but the pro-state and pro-organization thrusts of Chinese culture may aid the process. There has been as much public articulation in Taiwan recently as any theorist advocating open political discourse could possibly want. The occasional violence has been symbolic, aimed to attract attention in electoral contests. The state on Taiwan has not just been respected, but avidly used by other power networks.

One reason to study Shanghai is its difference from Beijing. The capital has far more state and nonstate intellectuals—and despite its smaller population, more people with tertiary degrees. The number of students and universities in Shanghai is much lower. Technical and office jobs by 1982 employed 17 percent of Shanghai's labor, but 22 percent of Beijing's. Also, a higher portion of Shanghai's intellectuals come from worker, manager, or trader family backgrounds. The number of workers in Shanghai is greater, even as a proportion of the East China city's larger population. State-owned enterprises in Shanghai are fewer in absolute number, but on average they hire many more employees. Shanghai on a per-capita basis has fewer theaters, hospitals, retail stores, or other nonindustrial institutions—and much more residential crowding at any given distance from the city center. The 1985 density of central Shanghai was reported at nearly 20,000 persons per square kilometer, more than ten times the crowding in spacious central Beijing.[133] Cities are obviously important in politics; yet the differences between them are so sharp as to raise doubts whether words like "city" or "urban" have stable definitions. No sinologist has yet been able to link contextual differences between cities with political outcomes exactly, but perhaps too much attention has been devoted to intellectuals in the capital.

Even Beijing has changed as a result of the reforms. The surprising thing about Tiananmen in 1989 was not that thousands of students turned out for a few weeks to protest a corrupt and repressive government. Their predecessors had done this in the same place, many times in this century. Instead, the surprising thing about Tiananmen in 1989 was that millions of ordinary Beijing citizens came to the Square and barricaded streets to protect these intellectuals. For a few days only, there was a political coalition between some kinds of masses and intellectuals—of the sort that can make a credible opposition to other, Leninist intellectuals. Similar coalitions have overthrown such parties in several ex-socialist countries. These young intellectuals led the opposition to politician-engineers like Li Peng. Their connection to people without much education was temporary and weak. But more than any specific political symbols or platform they proposed, this connection was what made the government exile or jail them—and shoot many nonintellectuals who showed them sympathy.

The students never formulated their demands in a specific constitutional call for a new state form that could garner mass appeal. The intellectuals did not do this, because they were themselves oriented to presume the power of the state, not that of nonstate institutions. Interviews and surveys confirm that many in cities and in the countryside were so distressed by inflation and corruption that they did not mind seeing the Party given grief in 1989.[134] But the groups least affected by such problems—collective and private entrepreneurs, especially in the countryside—mostly chose to tend their shops and factories rather than protest. Students and state-sector employees, who did most of the demonstrating, were the groups most vulnerable to official sanctions. Few students in 1989 yet found a way to relate their own careers to local power networks outside the state.

This book could rightly be criticized if it were accurate in its descriptions but lacked policy recommendations. The text often tries to deconstruct the interest in power evident among modern mandarins. Many intellectuals are hesitant democrats. But this behavioralist perspective, which describes a growing weakness in the Chinese high state, runs a danger: Any country requires at least some government strength to let its people prosper; so it is not enough just to point out how weak Beijing has become. Deconstructing the pretensions of intelligentsias need not be the same as sharing Nero's nonchalance while Rome burned. The findings here imply a policy recommendation addressed mainly to China's intellectuals: Educated people in their country will serve it best only after most other Chinese, notably the new entrepreneurs, see intellectuals as constitutionally helpful.

University graduates could, even in some possible nationalist future after Communism, still continue to claim exclusive power on the basis of their "science." Or they could take the opposite approach, claiming less uniqueness, being more honest about what they do not know, becoming less proud, and making better connections with other kinds of people. The variety of China's local leaders is expanding, and the most truly patriotic intellectuals there will welcome this change, rather than resisting it. They can do so by writing charters to normalize links among the different sorts of chiefs in China, rather than continuing to spin nostalgic ideologies to claim anew their old authority.

Monism in Politics vs. Monism in Scholarship

Intellectuals deal with ideas. But as a reform economist said, "In a capitalist society, people talk about money, money, money. In a socialist society, it's power, power, power. With power, you're a goddess in a temple showered with gifts and cheques, in return for your blessings on their projects."[135] This zesty point misses the extent to which money can declare its independence of state power by undergirding nonstate power. Politics does not stop at the edges of government organization charts or editorial pages. Resource arrays in economic institutions have long been important causal factors in politics. The reforms' dispersion of resources strains against the old monist principle that there is some unique right policy, the discovery of which would validate a thinker's claim to power. In the reforming PRC, this issue is often discussed in terms of differences between capitalism and socialism. People want both efficiency and security, but nobody in China or elsewhere has yet figured out a single principle for organizing politics that brings them both.

The existence of different levels of political corporation in China ensures that state intentions will be mutilated by localities and vice versa. So the process of reform has been gradual and uneven, involving much random trial and error. Uniform, one-knife-cuts-all policy has been impossible, even though that is the kind intellectuals seek. Such policy can lead to disasters for large numbers of people, just as it can also lead to massive betterment of their lives. The PRC under Mao provided superb examples of both the successes and failures of monist policy, as can be shown by a contrast between its largest failure in food distribution and its largest success in medicine. China from 1959 to 1961 experienced the most murderous famine in all human history. But forceful, uniform state policies of the kind that created this disaster also allowed China to do far better than most poor countries in conquering infectious diseases. China had a terrible famine, but has usually avoided endemic hunger. India, by contrast, has experienced no very major famines since the late nineteenth century, but many Indians suffer endemic malnutrition.[136] The communitarian policies that created China's famine also created an infrastructure for benefits.

The trouble with monist policy ideals is that people benefit by having more than one type of politics. "Human organization" campaigns, for example, can develop mineral-intensive heavy industries and prevent endemic diseases. But "technical organization" policies develop labor-intensive light industries and cure chronic diseases. Regime elites typically claim power on either support-led or growth-mediated grounds, not both. So most people gain when elites inspired by symbols alternate in government with elites inspired by efficiency.

Ideology does not end; it cycles. Both the communitarian and entrepreneurial elites reappear to bring policy benefits that the other type downplays. This cycle is a more broadly social version of that between conservative lions and reformist foxes, which has as much to do with the coherence of elites as with their relations to other people. Shortly after the tumult of 1989, one of the best analysts of the Beijing leadership noted, "The apparent death of ideology in China and the perplexed and intensely aversive elite reaction to its consequences placed the entire future of reform in some question."[137] This seemed an apt conclusion at the time. But it is true only if reform is defined as a result of norms, not situations, and as a top–down affair controlled by high CCP leaders. Actually, the Party politicians at that high level did not begin the reform syndrome, and because of local resources, they cannot now end it. Quite the opposite: It may end them.

Against the regime, the main issue of any future opposition could well become excessive central taxation, corruption, and waste. The Party's main platform is likely to remain patriotism. As reforms begin to affect state structure more directly, southern and nonstate elites are likely to conflict even more openly with Communist conservatives. Neither of their basic platforms, concerning issues as basic as family income and national identity, will soon become irrelevant in China. Political conflict between such sides could last a long time.

Unless the Party resumes more regulatory socialist causes than it has in recent years, CCP might come to stand for Chinese Capitalist Party. As one sinologist argues, "The Chinese Communist Party's repudiation of revolutionary ideals . . . is only to be expected, since it starts to redefine its social function as the ruler of China's post-socialist society."[138] But if the Party survives for a long time, it might eventually become socialist in the usual sense: protecting people, their environment, and their earnings against the insults of the market. The word "socialist," as now used by most conservative Party leaders, means something different and simpler: the primacy of their particular political group. Since the state elite so often refers to socialism in this obviously self-serving way, its archetypal causes (such as wage protection, labor safety, environmental and market regulation) could well be left in the future to oppositionists, who might be less democratic than corporatist. This has hardly begun to happen yet, because opposition is disallowed. But the CCP is painting itself into a policy corner, and it may later be unable to return unstained to the rest of the room.

A Western Russianist wrote during the USSR's decline, "Gorbachev's policies continue to be obstructed not only by objective difficulties, but also by the legacy of the totalitarian past."[139] Not only was the country hurt, but so were the ways to think about it. The totalitarian legacy has inhibited Western scholarship on countries in which dictatorships declined. Before the CPSU fell, too few realized that such a thing could happen even to a Leninist party. Most intellectuals were so smitten by the elegant beauty of tight organizational principles—either praising or damning them—that they missed much else. A revolution can end, and coercive centralization is now ending even in China.

Cold Shower vs. Slow Reforms: Reactions to Communism's Demise

Specific policies for early postrevolution periods offer many options. Reforms can proceed quickly, as in the "cold showers" that East Germany and Poland experienced. Or they can be cautious, as Chinese say, "crossing the river by feeling the stones."[140] A cold shower to cleanse inefficiency requires that a government make many decisions quickly. Big questions—on the best sequence of reform among sectors, or the best methods of transferring property rights, for example—tend to be answered in central decrees by such regimes largely on the basis of market ideology. High policies for transitions to capitalism in Eastern Europe have often come pell-mell, based more on frustration with the old system than on information about the possibilities—with an overall result that has sometimes been chaotic. Market signals have not always or soon provided correct information to create efficiency. So a cold shower can soon become very hot, politically as well as economically. A protocapitalist policy group, as it quickly processes data crucial to its own success, can easily show the same defects of rashness that were evident under central planning.

More socialist alternatives imply big problems, too. In China, gradualism has been touted by the government largely for fiscal reasons and because the regime fears urban unrest if it threatens its wards with unemployment. Cadres and workers could become politically unquiet if state enterprises were forced to increase efficiency because of an end to their "soft budget constraint."[141] One analyst describes a regime afraid of the proletariat even in its own state factories: "Despite poor performance, massive overproduction and bulging warehouses full of overstocks, the government has sought to buy labor peace in urban industry by keeping workers employed producing goods no one wants, paying workers even when their enterprises are idled for lack of power, and regularly raising urban food and other subsidies to keep up with inflation."[142] Such policies are reactive. Top leaders clearly feared more turmoil in cities if the market had forced more efficiency on state firms. Actual power and policy were in the hands of local networks that disabled or enabled change toward cost-effectiveness, not in the hands of high state reformers who wanted more efficiency.

Yet aside from these fiscal and political causes of gradualism, production and sales in China during reforms have boomed. Whatever the causes or ideology may be, Chinese gradualism has a fine track record of aggregate growth. Compared to many desocializing countries, the PRC has made a relatively careful shift from information-poor plans to information-poor markets, producing enough goods along the way to help keep much of the populace quiet, if not always compliant. No consistent economic policy has carried the day, and the results of the mix have been admirable. Reformers like Zhao Ziyang sometimes have led the government; but even then, reform in the state sector has been slow despite many speeches. Nonstate and ex-state local networks have prospered, because they could avoid monitoring and imposts. They could often hide noncompliance with any official orders that did not serve their profits.

Conditions for Success with Quick, Slow, or Mixed Economic Reforms

On the premise that large firms need to be weaned from the security blanket of planning, the "cold shower" has seldom been tried for them in China, whereas gradual adjustment on a company-by-company basis has been the typical approach for old socialist firms. The argument for the slow method is that personnel, finances, and other infrastructure in many fields take time to build if corporations are to become efficient. Large enterprises need major infusions of capital, before they can compete well, especially on international markets. Smaller firms, on the other hand, have been able to experiment with many innovations that create intense "cold showers" in the sectors they dominate. The quick approach is really a decision to develop fast-return sectors at the expense of slow-return sectors, which socialists claim may prove more important for sustained growth.

After years of state protection, however, few managers or workers in large firms have much incentive to take the risks inherent in competitive markets. Entrepreneurs are likely to appear only in sectors where profits bode to be good. Slow change is thus arguably the best prescription for transforming large companies in postsocialist economies. In this view, which is official in China, economic stability and care for normative habits, not just external and situational incentives, are crucial for creating a new basis to sustain a change toward greater efficiency later. Whether or not this theory is correct in the abstract—neoclassical economists fundamentally disagree with it—the productive results in reform China at least through the mid-1990s indicated its wisdom.

Slow reforms also create a distinctive set of problems. They extend the period during which the state cannot make money from its own enterprises in practically any field where nonstate companies can make profits.[143] So they increase government debt, threatening factory closures and unemployment among urban workers. Slow reforms also prolong opportunities for economic corruption, when neither plans nor markets alone effectively set prices. They extend the dissatisfaction of politically dangerous intellectuals, who see *nouveaux riches* earning more. They threaten, because of these problems, the legitimacy of the government—just as they also protect that legitimacy if production remains strong. A central argument for slow reforms is that the difficulties created by fast reforms are as awful.

For large firms, the case for their quick decoupling from the state relies on the opposite assumptions about finance and personnel incentives. According to a reformist line of thought, the planned sector lacks a "hard budget constraint," and for political reasons it can never achieve one. Socialism can thus never achieve serious incentives for productivity of management or labor. The way to make reform would therefore be to support new work norms with external incentives that assure the old norms lead to the economic failure of firms that fail to change. "Cold shower" reformers see no need to dally. If old fiscal systems continue to put money into the hands of bureaucrats who waste it, then what the state needs is a budgetary crash diet (as the Chinese government has actually faced). Funds not paid in taxes do not disappear into thin air; on the contrary, nonstate agencies may well find better uses for such money. If politicized career systems have created lackadaisical managers, it is better to raze these structures and build anew. Only then will economic leaders and troops have a real stake in their firms' profits and in hard work.

Comparing China with Russia, the case for economic change along mixed principles in the PRC seems strong. This involves gradual adjustment in large firms, but acquiescence to the creation of a "cold shower" for new local firms. Central state financing may be replaceable in China, since in many sectors it was not overwhelmingly important even in the heyday of planning. Mass interest in the PRC's financial markets has been evident, despite the doubts of powerful conservatives about the resurgence of Chinese capitalism. Overseas and domestic investors, along the whole southern coast from Shanghai to Guangdong especially, continue to take capital market risks, often sustaining losses; yet they keep coming. Willing venture capital is even more obvious in late-socialist China than it is in protocapitalist Russia. So the financial infrastructure for the quick-changing parts of China's economy is in place. As for personnel, many jurisdictions in the 1980s have seen shifts toward more localist, more specialized, and better-educated leaders.[144]

PRC state policy is mostly gradualist, and the policies of local power networks are effectively "cold shower." The net result is something in between. The problem is not one of analytic principles, because normative and situational interests in many sizes of Chinese economic units remain powerful. This shower has a water-mixer. A 1987 attitude survey suggested that about one-third of Chinese citizens advocated experimental and careful reforms, another third were for bold reform, and the remainder was about equally divided between uncertainty and warnings against reforms.[145]

Distinctive Traits of Chinese Reforms in International Contrasts

Differences between Russian *perestroika* and Chinese *gaige* reform have been many.[146] It is useful, when thinking about this comparison, to separate facts from premises, because both affect common perceptions of what has happened.

First, economic change was sharp and early in China, while change in PRC political reform has been incomplete and halting. In the USSR, however, political change at all levels rushed ahead while the economy worsened so quickly as to threaten the political system. China's reform has thus been viewed as gradual, despite all the evidence not just in the economy that it has been fast. Most analysts presuppose political change at the top of the state somehow to be more real than local change of either the political or economic kinds. This view is plausible but arbitrary. The many differences between reforms in these two huge countries can be described more carefully than by adjectives of speed alone. Change has been partial in both countries. In the 1990s, it was more at the local level (both political and economic) in China and more at the national level (especially political) in Russia.

Second, China's reforms began mostly in rural areas, whereas Soviet cities were the first places affected strongly by currents of change. The Russian countryside still has not seen much restructuring.

Third, the Chinese approach to formal and legal change has been very conservative, especially as regards property rights. Until the mid-1990s at least, there was an almost exclusive practical retention of collective ownership, rather than property transfers to individuals. In Russia, however, many state assets were really sold.

Fourth, Chinese entrepreneurs have nonetheless created new companies and other corporate entities especially in the first stages of reform, while very extensive institutional creativity among Soviet managers came only after state policies licensed it.

Fifth, public welfare provisions were far more institutionalized for most Russians than for most Chinese; so political rigidities caused by entitlements to pensions and benefits have somewhat been less onerous in China.

Sixth and very important, overseas Chinese in Hong Kong and Taiwan have helped the PRC change. They have contributed the great bulk of overseas investment there. Russia lacks any comparable overseas analogue group; its reforms have suffered in comparison.

These and other differences between post-Communist reform in China and Russia tend to be overwhelmed by the first one: that China's reform has been more messy in principle, less tied to either markets or socialism. The leadership there has not been so blighted by threats of political collapse as have many in the ex-Soviet polities.

Mainstream Western economics supports uniformity in tax rates and in markets, not the pandemic of nonstandard contracting that has emerged in reform China. Yet regular price reform, to the extent it was attempted in Russia, did not quickly raise wealth there. Nor did it bring more legitimacy to politicians who proposed systems to get the prices right. Particularistic contracting and agency privileges seem to help, not harm, the most important kinds of reform, because these habits encourage agencies to be entrepreneurial. There is a link between "rule by consensus" in China and the avoidance of bumps on the long road to efficiency there.

This may well apply to politics, not just economics. The neoclassical market model neglects entrepreneurship and growth efficiency for the sake of specifying current allocation efficiency—and thus has created no theory that can predict growth anywhere over any substantial time. By the same token, political models that neglect local and national leaders' searches for opportunities, for the sake of explaining aggregations of standard kinds of preferences, have not offered any theory to explain the observable patterns of political development. They sometimes explain things other than change. But such models are insufficiently multicausal to be realistic.

Official styles, in both China and the West, downplay theoretical interest in mixed economies. Neoclassicists, when explaining the dangers of half-baked economic policies, point with glee to its inconsistencies and show the logical consequences of trying to be "half pregnant." In China, notions about a future convergence of socialism and capitalism have periodically been subjected to stinging critiques by cadre patriots who have a taste for theory. Social scientists there have been publicized on the continuing importance of "class relationships in capitalist societies." Chinese academics have sometimes been reported to doubt that "the labor–capital relationship in capitalist society had been basically transformed as a result of the widespread share-capital system and the increase of urban professionals."[147] Both the West and China provide much evidence that (irrespective of their actual behavior) elites like to announce themselves as either lovers or despisers of the market.

"Capitalism" and "socialism" are in reality imprecise as theories. They are not social sciences (even though some economists have practically failed to notice this). They are political platforms by which elites recruit support. A word like "capitalism" only describes vague policy tendencies designed to support the social efficiency that markets bring. "Socialism" may refer to any broad scheme to protect people from becoming ordinary commodities on the market. These are ideologies, policy preferences either to advocate the market for the real social benefits that it brings, or else to protect people and their surroundings and earnings from social threats that the market also brings. Capitalism and socialism mainly become excuses for leaders to claim larger power by trying to identify communal feelings—usually national patriotism—with one or the other of these broad policy biases.

Just as many U.S. politicians try to paint America as inherently capitalist, many Chinese politicians try to paint their nation as naturally socialist. But because no modern country has been willing to forgo *either* the benefits of efficiency *or* the benefits of protecting people from free markets, all such countries are in fact both capitalist and socialist. The Chinese Communist government would be absolutely delighted to have the high per-capita social welfare budgets that have been unflinchingly administered, for instance, by U.S. Republicans or British Conservatives. Some Western political elites maintain their claim to power partly by trying to link their nations' patriotisms with particular groups of rulers closely associated with markets. In the same way, the CCP in China uses "socialism with Chinese characteristics" as a way to claim continued power for its own leaders. Capitalism and socialism are political slogans used by elites to confuse nonelites; they are not philosophies, and they often obfuscate more than they reveal. All developed countries are, in behavioral terms, both more capitalist *and* more socialist than all underdeveloped countries—even though rulers try to hide this fact.

Predicting the Future

Septuagenarian playwright Wu Zuguang said bluntly in 1989, "We've got a bunch of old, weak, and crippled ex-soldiers running this country. Out of a population of 1.1 billion, is that the best we can do? . . . In any situation, the Communist Party is always wanting to take the lead. What a nuisance!"[148] Will this change?

Communist parties fell in many socialist countries during 1989, but in China the discipline imposed by top politicians after Tiananmen was, from their point of view, a success. The CCP elite is, however, not completely unified against structural changes in political institutions. In any case, changes proceed apace in local institutions that are powerful over the people in them. Leaders high in the government have shown they do not have enough sanctions or legitimacy to prevent this evolution. When the top of the regime is to change, it could do so quickly.

China's State Could Become Even Less Tightly Integrated

Many thinkers, both in China and the West, search for a single principle for the future of PRC politics—perhaps something like imperial rule or a leap for democracy, perhaps neotraditional socialism or market capitalism, perhaps some carefully guided smooth transition to political forms that are seen as more modern. But what happens is likely to be less neat. A bumpy, rachet-form pattern of pressures for and against change in China's political structure is evidenced by spurts of reform and reaction; fluctuation is the main constant.

In various years (e.g., 1974–75, 1976, 1979, 1986–87, and 1989), much the same course of events recurred: An opening was followed by a repression. Each of these periods, roughly speaking, saw a movement for democracy or modernization involving both local leaders and identifiable quasi-liberal high officials (who did not end up permanently purged, despite the sequel). In all cases since 1976, the movement has also involved students at the public centers of major cities, including Tiananmen Square in Beijing and People's Square and the Bund in Shanghai. These rallies were in each case put down, posters were washed off walls, and the quasi-liberal politicians were usually dismissed from their main offices. But none of these events or personalities is wholly forgotten, and in particular locations or occupational spheres the drama has been replayed similarly at a lower level of intensity. This is the cycle of China's expressive politics, which keeps repeating partly because the mute and local resources for political diversity have been increasing.

Each successive rally raises more demands for basic change. Many have been joined by high cadres. The winter 1986–87 and June 1989 events practically included, among the quasi-liberals, none other than the current heads of the Communist Party (Hu Yaobang and Zhao Ziyang). Yet after these public eruptions, structural reform in politics has usually been low on the top elite's agenda for a while, only to surface later in debates and sometimes in minor changes. After each crackdown, further demands (and a new generation of university students) create another demonstration against police and other centralizers, who by that time are always trying to defend an even less legitimate concentration of authority than they had in the previous round. The economy booms; but in each successive case the central government's debt, for example, is greater than in the previous case. This pattern is zigzag, but it also has a long-term trend. It amounts to political reform of a grand sort, although it is not policy.

In future cases, forces that are older than the young demonstrators will determine the outcome partly on the basis of their relations with student intellectuals, and partly on the basis of the Party-government's performance at that time. Military units have not—yet—ever joined such demonstrators. Influences from abroad are blamed or credited for China's trends, and the "opening" since the early 1970s has certainly been a spur to reform, but this relationship is diffuse. Hu Qiaomu in 1985 complained that Shenzhen is modeled after Hong Kong, Guangdong after Shenzhen, and China after Guangdong—so that the whole country is becoming "Hongkongized."[149] Because the domestic and foreign factors interact, there is probably no way to separate their importance in causing these events.

Many Party members—by one estimate 800,000—joined democratic rallies nationwide before June 4.[150] This was only about 2 percent of the total CCP membership (which is still mostly rural), but it was an important and educated group. Diversification of the kind of people in local and national CCP positions has been a continuing aspect of political change. This shift can be discussed as if it were ideological, although its contextual aspects are at least as important. Deng Xiaoping, in a conservative mood, said in 1986,

With regard to the question of opposing bourgeois liberalization, I am the one who has talked about it most often and most insistently. Why? First, because there is now a trend of thought—that is, liberalization—among the masses, especially among the young people. Second, because this trend has found support from the sidelines. For example, there has been some comment from people in Hong Kong and Taiwan. . . . If you have read some of the comments that have been made by the people in Hong Kong and by bourgeois scholars in foreign countries, you will see most of them insist that we should liberalize or that there are human rights problems in China. These commentators oppose the very things we believe in, and they hope we will change.[151]

Deng Xiaoping often received credit for being the main factor driving reform in China. He was indeed the most active top politician jumping to declare for modern reforms in 1974–75 and 1977–78. But in 1957, he had supported the Antirightist Campaign that began a spate of antiliberal violence that escalated in China for many years thereafter. In 1989, he authorized the Tiananmen crackdown. The very mixed evidence on Deng's ideology suggests that he was most interested in staying near the top of the political system. He claimed he knew what the Chinese people wanted; but if so, he did not always give it to them, because he also knew what his fellow power-brokers at or near the top wanted.

"Representative ideologies" dominate major historical periods, as Karl Mannheim wrote. These are notions advocated by important social groups. In China's reforms, the relevant groups expanded and diversified.[152] Near the top of the state, especially among intellectuals, their ideology tended to be conservative and technocratic. This affected state structure slowly during the 1980s promotions of young educated leaders, because both the old ideas approving moral hierarchy and those approving a modern technical basis for it could be used against the remnants of the revolution.

The change to technocracy has not been a change away from Party government, even though it has meant more variegated kinds of CCP members and has practically ended the importance of Communism as an ideology. Despite 1980s' speeches about a need to separate managerial and Party functions more strictly, and to make sure that CCP committees allow executives to do their proper jobs, a blurring of these roles is still completely normal in most Chinese local groups. This papal division of China's political world into separate spheres of Party and government has not been the most crucial reform in practice, and by the 1990s discussion of it was scarcely heard. Instead, the main change is that the basic purpose of politics is now different for most actors: first, to make the economy grow and, second, to mobilize political support under state auspices. This reverses the pre-1970s' priorities, not because a few leaders willed them reversed, but because very many Chinese leaders have done so. Decisions requiring specialized expertise have become more important, so many technical managers are brought into the Party. The CCP generalists have less to do now because mass mobilization no longer benefits most local leaders.

Seweryn Bialer in the late 1970s saw three widespread changes in the Soviet polity that boded basic change. First, the decisions that had to be made in the Soviet Union increasingly required expertise, so the roles of managers and Party secretaries became blurred. Second, there was simply a "disappearance of Party generalists." Even CPSU officials, as their Party began to decline, had to specialize in localities or functional agencies. In comparison with previous leadership generations, they seldom moved to new places or new roles during their careers, but instead were promoted in their old offices. Third, as the war generation died, the pre-*perestroika* advancements of some young specialists became extremely quick.[153] All three of these trends are currently manifest in China. Bialer made his analysis, and broad predictions from it, in Brezhnev's time before Gorbachev's rise, and well before any announcement of *perestroika*. It was an accurate augury.

In China, Party membership is something common to all high- and medium-level officials. If "where they sit determines where they stand," the nearly universal Party membership of high officials allows scant distinction between them. So their functional jobs become the basis of political conflict. Ministerial officials uphold the interests of their ministries, National People's Congress officials claim the autonomy of the NPC, and all leaders from fields as separate as journalism and industry follow this pattern of divisions by role, not unity because of their formal political organization. Leninism may hold out for a few years in China still, and certainly new leaders can emerge out of the current CCP. But it is getting late, and perhaps the Party is almost over.

China Will Not Become a
National Competitive Democracy Soon

The question of what happens after revolutions has not received much attention from comparativists. In general, the elite that led the movement for fiscal and police centralization then gives some political ground to other types of leaders. New coalitions have needed to shore up their authority by making connections with groups outside their original constituencies. In Soviet successions, for example, they did so largely by trying to adopt popular policies.[154] Will this bring democracy? That state form is likely to be, for some future high Chinese politicians, a vague platform to attract support from more local leaders. It has never, in any country, taken complete hold of the government.

Whenever an American scholar suggests that some form of democracy might emerge in a future China, traditionalist Western intellectuals and nationalist Chinese intellectuals leap to the criticism that such a notion is ethnocentric, neoimperialist, even cryptoracist, or just naive. Not until liberal countries are brought into a comparative political science, treating them along with other nations, including China, will there be a proper vocabulary for talking about their commonalties and exceptionalisms. Often it seems easiest to avoid that aim, perhaps by concentrating on models that apply only in some countries, perhaps by forgetting that middle-level generalizations depend on fully general terms, or most often by defining "politics" so narrowly that diverse peoples are not seen to face political questions of the same types. There is finally no way to choose between exceptionalism and generalization. Both are needed all the time.

Two main questions about possible democratic options in China may be asked: First, would democracy be good for most people there? Second, is a forecast of Chinese democracy in the foreseeable future accurate? Neither of these questions is very easy to answer. On comparative empirical grounds, the first is more tractable than the second. Democracy is a state form, and the particular specialty of states is coercion. A great deal of evidence from many countries shows that democratic regimes domestically tend to use less arbitrary force against ordinary people than do nondemocratic regimes.[155] There is also evidence that internationally they seldom go to war against each other.[156] Economically, democracies prosper; a great majority of them cause that group to be very much wealthier, per person, than any other class of states (except a few upon which Allah has bestowed oil). Their economies grow fairly well, even though generally already rich; democracies on average have as good growth records as other states; and they have statistically better records on income distribution.[157]

Any kind of stable democracy in China would almost surely lead to less capricious use of force both domestically and abroad. The economic comparison of more authoritarianism or more democracy in China is difficult to make, but the choice involves more variegated options: less unified authoritarianism, democracy, or a corporatist regime type. In terms of what large numbers of people want, however, the evidence suggests that liberal democracy brings these desired things. Democracy is not nearly as dumb as it looks. This need not be read as a prescription; it may be a statistical fact. If traditionalists or leaders of the CCP do not like this situation, there nonetheless seem to be good reasons for favoring Chinese democracy—whether one can predict it or not.

Possible Factors for Liberal Structure and Possible Missing Links

The second question is far more chancy to answer: Will an extensive Chinese democracy occur anytime soon? Dankwart Rustow's classic comparative analysis of this question finds that "certain ingredients are indispensable to the genesis of democracy." National unity is a basic background factor—and despite China's large size and lanky administrative structure, most Chinese now closely identify with their nation. A second cause is the long-term existence of social and economic conflicts between identifiable groups (such as China arguably has); if these need resolving, leaders may become interested in democratic procedures to fix them. The third and most crucial ingredient is a short-term "conscious adoption of democratic rules." A fourth condition for the stability of a liberal regime, not for its genesis, is that "both politicians and electorate must be habituated to these rules." Rustow claims that "these ingredients must be assembled one at a time" and "each of these four tasks has its natural protagonist."[158]

The crucial third stage, adopting liberal rules, would certainly involve intellectuals. They are the people who can write constitutions. Perhaps a reason why China is not liberal is that its intellectuals secretly believe the modern order disadvantages them, relative to their high traditional status. Political modernization of the democratic kind would not resolve their nostalgia for the traditional exams (not elections) as the proper road to power. Until both technocratic and humanist thinkers in China more fully realize that their country has really changed, many of them have reason to inhibit rather than aid "a conscious adoption of democratic rules."

Robert Dahl has explored the histories of many countries to seek causal factors of "polyarchy," which can be called democracy here. His summary list of seven broad causes includes the one that Rustow emphasizes: Democracy is more likely if political activists believe that competitive elections will bring legitimate and effective rule. None of the others are mainly connected with intellectuals:[159]

1. a historical sequence in which legitimated contest precedes the inclusion of masses;
2. dispersed land, money, weapons, factories, and capital;
3. a relatively high GNP/capita;
4. acceptably low and perceptibly decreasing relative deprivation among low-income groups;
5. low ethnic tensions or mutual guarantees of fairness;
6. weak or temporary domination by foreign powers; and
7. appropriate beliefs among political activists about the likely efficacy of democracy.

Each of these factors relates to an increase of trust among social groups. China's ratings on these dimensions, if they may be guessed, would be relatively favorable for democracy on items 5 and 6. As regards item 3, China's economy has been growing rapidly (by the World Bank's estimate, at the highest annual GNP/capita rate among all "low-income" countries over the quarter century before the 1990s, and quickly in that decade too).[160] On actual and perceived equality among groups, item 4, the high record of growth may delay the envy of people not yet sharing in it because they may expect to enjoy it later.[161] For item 2 on Dahl's list, the recent sudden dispersal of wealth to new local power networks, especially in South China, is reducing the government's monopoly of capital, and the record of dispersal among other groups is mixed.[162] Item 7 is more dubious, because many of China's political activists are intellectuals, from a stratum that traditionally had much governmental power without popular review. So aside from questions about the last item on the list, perhaps the main omitted factor for democracy is the first: a historical sequence that legitimates contest.

Some theorists, notably Samuel Huntington, argue that a particular sequence (elite contest first, mass participation later) is the most important factor for democracy.[163] Many Chinese still shy away from political contest. The first and last items on Dahl's list may overlap in the Chinese case because the main protesters there, who are intellectuals, hold their punches against any incumbent regime, lest the sequel destroy their own status. Repeated continuation of this pattern might reduce the chances for stable democratic evolution in China, because it delays the rise of conflict between elites.

The plot thickens further, because there may be a sufficient economic condition that strongly correlates with the democratic regime type, namely, high prosperity. In industrial countries with per-capita incomes of more than U.S. $5,000, it is easy to show empirically that dictatorships have extreme difficulty maintaining themselves.[164] China is not near that level yet—only about $500 by a recent estimate—but for some time it has been growing more rapidly than any other low-income economy.[165] The increasing division of labor seems to be the change that brings both greater wealth and a need for more regular ways to channel conflict. China's "middle class" by the mid-1990s numbered only about 60 million—still a small proportion of the people, although some liberal regimes have been sustained by smaller portions.

Chinese people usually think of democracy in terms of ideal and personal rather than structural and collective change. In casual conversations, they identify it with freedom (using the word *ziyou,* which has overtones approaching "selfish"). As political scientist Yang Baikui has said, Chinese are simply perplexed: "Democracy and liberty are often confused in many people's minds. When they address the matter of democracy, they are actually discussing liberty."[166] Comparative experience suggests that the main problem is not to define either democracy or liberty, but to structure institutions so that individuals and groups can benefit from both their communal similarities and their complementary differences. Competitive elections provide convenient means of alternating the two kinds of elites that make policies for these two kinds of benefits. Beyond that, democracy varies immensely.

As for liberty, the notion of freedom also comes in greater variety than most people realize. In early Massachusetts an "idea of collective liberty, or 'publick liberty' as it was sometimes called, was thought to be consistent with close restraints upon individuals."[167] But later, and farther from cities, other notions of liberty were less constrained because the contexts were different. In China too, there is some evidence of such variation.[168]

Looking Up from the Ground, Not Just Down from the Sky

This book adduces evidence to show that Chinese behavior is not always hierarchically ordered. Traditional Confucian and Communist values can be summed up largely in terms of peace, obedience, and command, but the story does not end with tradition. A stress on the Chinese legacy of tight rule is compatible with each of the following points, which have a nontraditional import for the state: First, behavior in China is in fact increasingly nonhierarchical, even though the language with which it is discussed retains the old form and changes far more slowly. In reforms, there is less compliance with official orders than in earlier decades; partly for that reason, the state bothers to mandate less. Although the presumption of an effective hierarchy was realistic to an extent in the 1950s, the situation has now changed. This book aims to show what Chinese people are doing, not just to recite traditional verities about how they are supposed to speak.

Second, and more important, there is more than one Chinese tradition. Official ways of talking about society, at least in the reform period, come mainly from intellectuals—such as were hired in great numbers to high positions of power in the 1980s.[169] They bear "neotraditional" burdens from Stalin's model of the educated professional bureaucrat and real tradition from the Confucian model of an intellectual who earns a state post. But most Chinese are not intellectuals, even if they have been affected by the ways in which intellectuals describe China. No single group in a society has any full monopoly on its culture. It would be circumspect, especially when discussing the state in whose majesty most Chinese intellectuals are very interested parties, to seek a greater variety of evidence than they provide. Rural entrepreneurs, religionists, and peasants, for example, write less. The national capital, Beijing, is still the main source of information. Most footnotes in the academic literature come from just one place—where more than a billion Chinese do not live. Most journalists, foreign officials, traders, and even academics are fixated on Beijing and what it can do. Even analysts on Taiwan, of all places, sometimes speak as if China had a single center rather than a rich diversity. Like all these, the present author and his gentle readers are almost by definition intellectuals. It may be healthy to ponder the problems that China's special linkage between state and intellectuals creates for obtaining something closer to a full view of this country.

A third reason to try nonhierarchical ways of describing Chinese politics is simply that the approach may add to what is known already. It may complement more usual versions of the story, which are still fine to describe important aspects of China. The new-mesh net may catch new fish. Specifically, writings about the PRC could more often stress that most local power networks are very illiberal. Often their members foster attitudes that are more hierarchical, and less tolerant, than most operational views in the state elite. When various networks of various sizes conflict, but none can destroy its rivals, each may best save costs and maximize resources by seeking tolerable accommodation. The narrative may be about pluralization, without clearly or surely being about liberalism.

Markets and Technocrats: Modernism Without Human Values?

Some scholars suggest that market discipline is even more repressive than were state impositions before modern reforms. Maoist policies unintentionally strengthened peasant resistance to central rules, as Vivienne Shue shows. She also suggests that China's market reforms may increase centralized power, relative to that of other political sectors, and that hypothesis is harder to sustain with recent data. In the long term, however, it may be true that economic prosperity and better communication will increase central state power. The road from here to there is long and indirect. More modern state control, pervasive but less arbitrary than past large or small tyrannies, could later emerge; discipline may finally replace punishment in China. But many Chinese individuals and political sets, not much restricted by the state, are now going their own ways. In that process, the main problem is in the near term: Strong and often arbitrary local power networks have conflicted during reforms with a state whose reach has shrunk. The possible future of centralized coordination by inhuman markets is not at hand.[170] The markets are callous, but not yet fully coordinated.

Technocrats try to coordinate them. The many new, well-educated appointees of the 1980s will in the long term raise the state's capability: "If the new economic and governmental elites . . . successfully negotiate this period of transition and find formulas for working in tandem, the resulting new state-corporate power structure could well prove a good deal more efficient," as Shue writes.[171] The cadre nodes in this new political web have already changed. But the state, too, would be transformed in the modern process. Its power may well become more rationalized and routine; and if so, it would also be less arbitrary than under Mao.[172] Markets now inform more people what to do, but small cellular tyrannies were important under Mao—and they are still important. Filmmaker Wu Tianming spoke in 1989, offering a semitruth about state leaders that applies equally to local cadres: "Those holding power will not, indeed cannot, change their ways. The fundamental contradictions are irreconcilable . . . . Please don't be prematurely happy."[173]

Many Chinese, especially intellectuals, are gloomy about the political possibilities in their future. If they nostalgically support politicians who want to restore discipline and recreate the Chinese empire run by intellectuals, rather than a modern Chinese state, they could prove their pessimism right. But larger groups in China also now interact in ways that might cause a more pluralistic but still authoritarian result. Local and contextual factors in recent decades have given strong impulses in that direction—which might well, for a period at least, take a political form that would be more modern but not very democratic.

Corporatism for a Spell?

Max Weber said that it was crucial for social scientists to raise "inconvenient facts," by which he meant facts inconvenient for "party opinions."[174] For Chinese, the main such fact is that states, in general, are not what they have been cracked up to be. For liberals, the main inconvenient fact is that the state remains so powerful as a symbol in the world's most populous country, a long time may pass before authoritarian regimes at many sizes of collectivity are replaced there by a more democratic form of management.

Vertical relations in China are weakening, and rules sent from high levels are commonly evaded. In previous authoritarian countries like Argentina, modern diversification has often led to politics structured around vertical "corporatist entities" that co-opt social groups. In the clearest examples of corporatist states, the political congeries are separate but each is well integrated internally. They represent identifiable functions: industrial labor, agricultural labor, domestic capital, often some symbolic institutions, foreign traders, and others. The police and the army are never far in the background, or are in the foreground. In the past, some states have articulated corporatist political sectors with great clarity.[175] Competition between the leaders of different social corporations may, in such cases, be only sporadic. Often important national policies are bargained behind closed doors, as already happens extensively in China.[176] These top elites join periodically to reconstitute the state. They do not compete for mass support from individuals in other corporate groups. By the same token, "the masses" remain politically passive cogs, for the most part, in the political machines run by their generally recognized functional leaders.

China is different in some respects. First, the corporate entities there have thus far been more often regional than functional—not unions, churches, business lobbies, and the like. China's current corporatism looks much like an evolving federalism, but without any benefit of federalist legal structures or ideals. It has often emerged in terms of relations between different places. The links between corporatism and federalism are intriguing and mostly unstudied.

Second, people in China speak respectfully about hierarchical relations, even though their behavior often shows a practical lack of such respect. China still has a single party, which is only slowly disintegrating and is inspired by the recent history of Eastern Europe to remain united and stay in power. Especially in small collectivities, leaders do not claim independent power; they simply take it. But most corporatism elsewhere presumes a publicly explicit normative legitimacy for the corporations as political actors. Such norms in China are developing slowly, if at all.[177] The PRC nonetheless already shows some aspects of the corporatist pattern. Corporatism is like interest-group politics in its rationality about external factors, but it is like clientelist politics in claiming to be collective.

Democracy, defined as a system that has competitive elections, is unlikely to be the first result of the evolution that has occurred in reforms. China is changing, and the strengthening of local power networks will affect the ways in which political interests are aggregated there. The current government is overloaded, and its normative and physical resources are in decline. Decentralization of many decisions is already a clear pattern, but democracy is not just decentralization. Many federal, consociational, and corporatist forms of interest aggregation need not be democratic. Federalism can take totalist forms, as Stalin's USSR all too amply showed. Consociationalism, as in Lebanon or Yugoslavia before the violence, or in Malaysia on a more steady basis, is an especially attractive alternative for elites wanting to experiment with tolerance. Corporatism is of so many types that the variations in Latin America alone have inspired a whole political science.[178]

The variations of corporatism also include lapses away from it, toward temporarily democratic or temporarily more authoritarian forms. Democratization has been a historically uneven process, coming in waves, sometimes ebbing.[179] The past record shows that even when a country establishes competitive elections, it stands a good chance of reverting to authoritarian rule—especially if it is poor or if it has scant previous experience with democratic procedures locally and nationally. This does not argue that democracy is impossible in China. The present author expects some Chinese form of it eventually. But interest aggregation can take many forms besides the democratic one. Which will Chinese use? The decision, perhaps to be made differently at different times, will depend on the interests of leaders both in Beijing and in localities. If guesses must be made concerning China's future political structures, the following oracles might possibly be right.

Many elements of the current situation, including the conservative elite and a status quo party, will not disappear totally. As for constitutional forms, explicit federalism is an unlikely ideal choice for Chinese leaders, even though a great deal of de facto decentralization has already taken place, and the mainland–Taiwan relationship could informally evolve in this way.[180] The provinces of China proper, where most people live, are overwhelmingly of the Han ethnic persuasion.[181] So consociational rules, most useful in multiethnic countries, are unlikely to have much appeal. But state leaders will find that their organization must become more tolerant of other institutions. They need support for public decisions from workers, entrepreneurs, intellectuals, farmers, and other groups that could become better organized and more openly corporate. In that case, a large-scale form of Chinese corporatism could emerge.[182] This would be consonant with a great variety of state forms at the top of the system, only some of which are democratic. But it would be a change from the Chinese official tradition that the state is utterly unified and need not take seriously any other domestic political institutions.

Philippe Schmitter makes distinctions between corporatist, syndicalist, pluralist, and monist systems. While describing these along a host of other dimensions, he studiously leaves open the question of whether the "corporatist" type is generated at state initiative, or at the behest of more local power networks.[183] But that is a question of interest for reform China. A national tradition that might incline the nation to corporatism may instead be overwhelmed by either syndicalist or monist patterns—until the regime recognizes politically that semiautonomous syndicates already exist there at local levels.

For Whom Is Democracy Dangerous?

Many urban Chinese suggest that democracy might be dangerous for China, and corporatist options are especially attractive to intellectuals. Under what conditions can electoral mechanisms produce antidemocratic results (as happened in Germany in 1933)? The answer seems to be that illiberals can win competitive elections when their popular appeal is based on ethnic or religious fundamentalism and when unemployment is high.[184] Nondemocrats often compete in democratic systems that suffer economic trouble and include fundamentalist minorities; unless these traits are very prominent, however, the illiberals do not win.

In China, *qigong* and some other fundamentalist fads exist, but they do not deeply affect a majority of the people. The economy has problems, and they might become worse; but in comparison with most Third World or ex-socialist countries, China's output growth and distribution of income are in relatively good shape. Unless these conditions change sharply, there is little reason to think that democracy in China would elect principled antidemocrats.

Incumbent Party elites have obvious reasons to raise objections against electoral procedures that would threaten their own power. The conditions under which democracy might be tried, but then might terminate itself, do not generally exist in China, although they might emerge there. Internationally, situations in which democratic procedures reconfirm themselves are quite common: Elected leaders gain legitimacy because they have won competitive votes. Winners in this process are, over time, more willing than losers to risk their political power by trying it again. The winners' personal interests (not just philosophical commitments or character changes among either masses or elites) are probably the main means by which democracies sustain themselves.

Democratic procedures and markets are similar in that both are socially rapacious: Once they begin, no intellectual planning process is required for them to garner further resources. A free market absorbs inputs anywhere it finds them. Decrees go down from intellectual planners in Beijing or provincial capitals, but by the time they reach localities, the resources that they planned to allocate have disappeared into market channels. Democracy, if it were started in China, might well take the same form. National patrons would still try to determine who had local power, but they could not control the process as fully as they control their current bailiwicks. The politicians who actually won local elections would favor the continuance of such procedures, whether or not they were tightly networked into the national scene at the beginning of the process. Electoral procedure, once started, does not inevitably maintain itself, but it stirs cumulative interests in continuance. Although democratic countries contain strong antidemocratic elements, it is difficult to find decisive reasons to think that China's illiberals will be stronger than elsewhere. Patriarchal traditions have in the past seemed overwhelmingly powerful in many countries—including many that are now liberal states.[185]

Will China Change to Totalism or Corporatism?

The long-term trend is that the end of China's revolution will not just strengthen the country, it will also strengthen the abilities of local hinge leaders to help their friends and relatives. This is the "inconvenient fact" for monists at a high level. It is still somewhat chancy for a Westerner to make this assertion. Western intellectuals have often looked in a "Chinese mirror" and seen positive examples to praise or else negative lessons to condemn. Their understandings often had more to do with their own situations than with anything in China. Quesnay saw a meritocracy based on civil service exams, and this was obviously better than feudal France. Voltaire saw that Confucian China lacked superstition, and this seemed better than what the Church propagated.[186] Romantics who liked China stressed its Daoism, while those who disliked China instead emphasized the repression of heroes by Confucian bureaucrats. In politics, by the 1930s and 1940s, many Americans thought that China must be democratic because it had a president. Many imagined that China was brave and efficient, because it was an ally.[187] By the 1950s, China was Communist and therefore a pit of evil. By the late 1960s, many thought China egalitarian and therefore a lesson in social good. In the early 1980s, China was becoming capitalist, "like us." Then in 1989, it suddenly became antidemocratic and therefore repugnant. The simplicity of these half-truths is not the point. A worse problem is that these images were mostly about Westerners, not about China. About China, they were largely wrong because they described the policies of top politicians and intellectuals, not the politics of most Chinese.

This resilient pattern of distortion makes a prediction possible: When after the 1990s a somewhat more liberal regime takes over from hard-liners in Beijing (as eventually it will), many Western and Chinese intellectuals may assume that a day of democratic judgment has finally arrived. In practice, however, this never fully happens to any country. All new regimes resemble their predecessors far more than they advertise. Is reform China still essentially totalitarian, has it become merely authoritarian, or is it really becoming democratic? A meaningful answer to such a question depends on definitions of the regime types. Juan Linz offers these along three dimensions: the scope of popular participation, the degree of legitimate contest, and the extent to which ideas legitimating the system are intellectually elaborated.[188]

Linz calls a regime "totalitarian" if it has three characteristics: "citizen participation . . . channeled through a single party," a "center of power [that is] mostly a political creation rather than an outgrowth of the dynamics of the pre-existing society," and a "more or less intellectually elaborate ideology." The PRC in the 1990s arguably has all three—but in much weaker form than before the 1970s. Most citizens' support for the regime by the 1990s was clearly less enthusiastic than in the PRC's first two decades. The state ideology became so flexible to meet new situations that few believed it any more. This was a very callow kind of totalitarianism, if it can be said to fit that mold at all.

"Authoritarian" regimes, according to Linz's definition along the same dimensions, are those with limited, not responsible, political pluralism, without elaborate and guiding ideology, with distinctive mentalities, without extensive nor intensive political mobilization, except at some points in their development, and in which a leader or occasionally a small group exercises power within formally ill-defined limits but actually quite predictable ones.

Reform China, then, is authoritarian. At least it is petty-tyrannical below the top of the state, where the belief in participation is greater, the faith in pluralism is less, and the belief in ideology may be still present. Linz adopts a distinction between totalitarian "ideology" and authoritarian "mentality." The latter is only a relatively unstructured and pragmatic way of "feeling," not a credence system that could justify extensive violence. Linz avows that "limited pluralism" is a hallmark of authoritarianism. That could serve as a description of many tendencies in reform China.

The old Aristotelian project of typing regimes easily becomes idealist and elitist. The notions of regime leaders are taken as the crucial data for the classification—not the concrete resources they have, nor the ideal or concrete resources of anybody else. None of Linz's dimensions is logically restricted in this way, but all adapt to easiest application by looking at elite intentions. If this happens, the typology does not really classify behavioral patterns of power. To be totalitarian, a state must be artificially concentrated, follow an exclusive ideology, and urge citizen participation. But the intentions and actions of top leaders do not tell us everything about a political system. To be authoritarian, by the same token, the legal sovereign has a different attitude: It is somewhat more tolerant of plural centers, more pleasantly muddle-headed about its ideology, and less demanding of subjects. But again, the center is not the whole, and intentions do not solely determine behaviors.

By these best-available definitions of totalitarianism and authoritarianism, China is different from both viewpoints. Since the availability of situational data is so intertwined with the position of a regime in this best taxonomy (totalitarian regimes divulge fewer reliable facts), the absolute positions of regimes in such a classification are harder to fix than are trends. The recent currents in China are certainly away from the totalitarian extremes. They will keep moving, sometimes in one way and sometimes in the other, because authoritarianism is generally temporary. As Linz sagely notes, "None of the authoritarian regimes has fired the imagination of intellectuals and activists across borders. None has inspired an international of parties. . . . Authoritarian regimes, whatever their roots in the society, whatever their achievements, are ultimately confronted with two appealing alternative models of polity [the totalitarian and the democratic], which limit the possibilities of full and self-confident institutionalization and give strength to their opponents." The authoritarian species is transitional.

So China is probably headed toward both more democracy and more authoritarianism in different stages as the population gradually pluralizes further. This country may well have passed the climax of its long and convulsive revolution about 1969, but other cases suggest the possibility of aftershocks. As Tocqueville said in 1848, "Here is the French Revolution beginning over again, for it is still the same one."[189] Revolutions generally have many peaks. For some countries, they seem to have lasted more than a century; for others, they change the state more decisively in a shorter time. China has seen many revolutionary heights, and each left a distinctive mark: 1898 for new ideas, 1911 for establishing a republic, 1919 and 1925 for urban mobilizations of intellectuals and new economic classes, 1927 for greater centralization, 1949 for quick state-building, 1957 for narrowing the elite constituency that the government served, and 1966–68 for a violent attempt to destroy old habits. In 1969, the summit of the pass was almost surely traversed. This did not mean that China's political history ended.

Some behavioral time series, tabulated in various chapters above, suggest very fast rates of local and structural reform in later years of reform through the mid-1990s. These changes had not, by press time, affected high politics in irreversible structural terms. But this book does not exclude the possibility that, cumulating with earlier reforms, they might more noticeably erode the coherence of the CCP in the medium-term future.

Nobody knows all the factors, including fortuitous ones, that will guide future Chinese political development. Those who expect a Chinese democracy can rightly point out that China is civilized. Its local networks and extended family systems have given many people extensive experience in nonpublic politics. After the Cultural Revolution, there was some hesitant mutual tolerance in public life between kinds of people who had earlier attacked one another. These factors pointed to the political openings that have hesitantly begun. But those who expect stronger Chinese authoritarianism, or even a renewal of totalitarianism, can also show that most local power networks in China are more patriarchal than in currently liberal countries. More ominous, the economic decline of intellectuals and state workers, as compared with new entrepreneurs, could lead many to support an autocrat who promises to restore part of an old order they recall as good. A depression would be politically dangerous.

Will democracy or a more partial liberalization come to China in the near term? If so, will it be stable? Any reply to such questions has to be based on causal logics that previous cases elsewhere have not normalized entirely.[190] Also, the accuracy of such predictions depends on factors (such as the personalities of future national leaders) that cannot now be known. The likeliest result, for a while, is what one analyst has called a "sporadic totalitarian state."[191] Tight rule at the center will wax and wane, as more complex information and decision systems develop in many smaller political networks.

As more stable democratic institutions emerge in Taiwan, and as Hong Kong, Guangdong, and Shanghai politicians variously use their wealth to affect Beijing politics, the amplitude of fluctuations between conservatism and reform could decrease. This would help stabilize the recent roller-coaster of Chinese politics. Crucial strides toward less half-hearted democracy were made in England during the nervous restoration of multiple state elites after Cromwell's Commonwealth, in France after the Bourbon restoration, and in other countries when previously conflicting types of leaders learned that they could get along. But political scientists and historians have a dismal record of failing to predict the beginnings of postcentralization democracies.

The Iberian peninsula has offered two astounding examples in recent decades. After the systems created by Franco and Salazar fell, most sensible analysts predicted successor dictatorships of either Left or Right. The cultural and economic arguments for authoritarian predictions in Spain seemed overwhelmingly strong. A study of militantly illiberal Catholicism in "Todas las Españas" (even if it skipped questions of intolerance between Basques, Catalans, Andalusians, and others) could then easily prove that Spanish democracy was a contradiction in terms. Also, a treatise on Portugal's poverty at that time could footnote a shelf of books, showing the unlikelihood of democracy there on many kinds of grounds. The same understanding for China would be easy to document. Yet in Iberia, none of that described anything important that happened.[192] Political and economic culture there were consistent with a more liberal result than most forecasters had predicted.

The arguments against serious political change in China are just as compelling. Large population size is one of the vaguest of these, although it can often be heard from the lips of urban educated people there. The 1.2 billion people probably do not preclude democracy, any more than strong hierarchical traditions or some poverty do. The United States is now the third most populous nation in the world, yet it is partially democratic, and many other countries with large populations still maintain competitive elections. Population density also does not rule out democracy; if it did, the Netherlands would certainly have to be a dictatorship.

Low per-capita production correlates with authoritarianism over a large sample of countries. But China is by no means the most impoverished country in the world—especially when the relative health, literacy, and income of most of its ordinary citizens are considered. The *Human Development Report* of the UN Development Program annually computes a "human development index" (HDI), based on three components: life expectancy at birth as a health indicator, years of education as a sociocultural indicator, and for economic well-being an index of real gross domestic product per capita (as adjusted to weigh heavily, but not exclusively, the average citizen's purchasing power for basic needs). China's HDI in the early 1990s ranked 82d among 160 countries. It thus had a "medium" level of human development (in contrast to countries such as Indonesia, Morocco, Kenya, and India, which all had considerably lower HDIs and were classified as having "low human development"). More important, China's HDI rank among all countries for a while exceeded its GNP/capita rank by more places than any other nation.[193] China is not yet a rich country on a per-person basis; but its basic school, health, and provision systems are in better shape (relative to those of other nations with similar GDP/capita) than most Chinese intellectuals realize. This could help future political development.[194]

Social scientists should admit plainly they have scant idea why democracies begin. Democracies have developed unevenly and slowly, in part because "founding fathers" had inconsistent ideals. When the U.S. Constitution was first written, for example, "the people" *if* they were rich, white, and male elected one-half of one-third of the government: the House of Representatives in the legislative branch. The rest was generated indirectly. Yet democracy grew in the popular mind and in the course of many decades of struggle and civil war.[195] Most citizens in democratic countries forget that they have had a social revolutionary centralization that follows the normal multi-peak pattern discoverable in the modern political histories of the United States, Britain, France, Russia, Germany, Italy, Japan, Spain, and arguably all other large industrialized countries. What will happen to China's state form, and at what various times different things will happen to it, cannot be surely known. But many elements of the postviolence syndrome have been evident in China for more than two decades: unprecedented local economic growth, ambiguous legitimacy and morality, irregular spurts of coercion, and constant struggle between clearly identifiable conservatives and reformers in government.

Ideas of democracy have often been extremely vague in the minds of the people who actually made democracy. If an academic political theorist polled a *sans-culotte* storming the Bastille, or a Minuteman at Concord Bridge, for their accounts of democracy, the answers would have been hazy and unsatisfactory. Chinese demonstrators in city squares, during 1976, 1978–79, 1986, and 1989 were not able to explain democracy very well either. Chinese entrepreneurs, who were not even in the city squares but continued to make money, generally liked the notion of freedom but had no further structured ideas about it. Yet all these people had good senses of what they were doing. The direction in which they hoped to push their society was often toward lower taxes, less corruption, less central control, and more sympathetic leaders.

Democracy draws previously uninvolved resources into conflicts channeled through the state. It "expands the sphere" of government by rewarding political actors who scout for support in previously private political networks. An unintended consequence of the process is usually that the state becomes more stable. But victory, not system stability, is the aim of rivals in the fray. Intellectuals such as Madison and Schattschneider have described this process theoretically.[196] They are more realistic than other intellectuals (including most in contemporary China and many sinologists in the West) who suppose that democratic institutions are built mainly from ideas other than memories of conflict.

Among high-level state leaders and many middle-level cadres in China, reform of the political structure is still an ideal. When they talk about it, that may be important for the future even when they fail to accomplish it. The top elite sporadically pushes in the opposite direction, to resist democracy. Many reactions—the 1975 resurgence of Jiang Qing radicals, the 1979 closure of Democracy Wall, the 1987 removal of political reformer and Party head Hu Yaobang, and 1989 at Tiananmen—show how angry rulers become when they discover they rule less. Despite this, the conservatives in such "Eighteenth Brumaires" almost admit that they are reactionary and transitional. Their main public argument is often that their society is not ready quite yet for a new political structure. They leave open, for the future, the possibility that the eventual legitimate condition might be democratic and involve competition. These leaders' definition of democracy is no clearer than that of their opponents in the public rallies, but both groups know the directions in which they are pushing.

Greater liberalism may come to China when memories of half-won, half-lost conflicts (not just the civil war and the Cultural Revolution, but also ongoing conflicts between reformers and conservatives) create a sense of tolerance among different elites. Values or science by themselves do not bring this tolerance, even though constitution-writers can temper institutions so that ordinary people can choose between elites. This does not mean that nonstate leaders will ever relinquish all their prestige or local power. Change to democracy is very partial everywhere. Liberalism often comes to countries after spates of authoritarian rule (Franco, Jaruzelski, George III, fascists), but not all authoritarians are succeeded by democrats. Most are followed by more moguls. Liberal states can rise in opposition to, or in memory of, tyrants who caused civil, religious, or international wars. But this also implies a definition of liberalism that is directional, not absolute. What the democratic regime type "is" may be better approached as a historical rather than a philosophical question. Evidence may be more useful for telling when liberalism is growing than for telling when some definition of it is satisfied. It has arisen differently in various nations. Parallels in development may be the whole story.

China will show its "national characteristics" in any state form its elites evolve, even if it becomes more democratic. Competitive parties vie for voters' support in Japan, India, Italy, the United Kingdom, and the United States. But these countries' democracies are in many ways different. So will the Chinese version be, if that country's multilayer leadership ever finds most to be gained by electoral procedures. CCP leaders and other Asian authoritarians often propagate the notion that democracy slows economic growth and enfeebles a country. Comparative empirical evidence does not confirm this view; economies in democracies grow in a quite stable way on average. In the international arena, domestically "weak" states with careful and divided governments can be very strong abroad. The United States apparently won the cold war because it was weak; its government was constrained by liberal ideology and many interest groups, so that it could not spend too much money on nonproductive armaments, as the strongly centralized USSR did.[197] Local power networks shape what a state can do—and they sometimes strengthen it, over time, by mobilizing their own resources better than officialdom could. "The passion of wealth takes the place of ambition," as Tocqueville said, "and the warmth of faction is mitigated by a sense of prosperity."[198]

Development is now the main ambition in China, but it is presented in terms that are very communal and political. Even Chinese who press the CCP for a change of elite structure often do so in stridently patriotic language. In mid-May 1989, students protesting on Shanghai's Bund carried banners saying, "It is better to love one's country than go abroad!"[199] In Hong Kong, placards in demonstrations immediately after the Tiananmen massacre and on its anniversaries declared, "Chinese do not beat up Chinese!"[200] This was an understandable sentiment, but it strengthened its claim by suggesting that there was no big problem in beating up other people. Democracy, like growth, is still often presented by educated Chinese people as instrumental to national strength. The country's intellectual elite, which has suffered so much from a lack of fair procedures in past years, still oddly neglects the benefits for small groups in devolutions of sovereignty to honor China's many parts.

Uncivil and unstately society could well make for national strength in China, and at the same time it could over many years sustain authoritarian nationalist leaders. They would try to replicate, throughout the nation, the solidarity of the Chinese family. This could be dangerous to other countries, to Chinese in Taiwan and Hong Kong, and to domestic Chinese liberals. This nationalist socialist appeal in PRC politics might not carry the day—and the chances that it will form a powerful government are reduced not just by memories of past violent centralizations, but also by decentralized resource arrays after reforms. But politicians will try this and any other tack that might lead them to power.

Corporatist evolution, leading to a later representative state form, is more likely than nationalist dictatorship to produce political winners in China's postcentralization climate. An old saying of Confucian scholars holds that "The gentleman is not a tool" (*junzi buqi*). This confirms integrity in leaders, and perhaps it will be gradually extended so that others are also not treated as tools. When all Chinese elites have to make serious connections with entrepreneurs, workers, and farmers—and when the competing elites who do this are the ones who win—China may well become more democratic.

Democracy and corporatist weak authoritarianism are not just state forms; they are also platforms. Rival leaders may espouse them to claim power. Democrats may be less different from authoritarians than either pretend. Both types ordinarily proclaim national prosperity as their main aim. Both tend to espouse state-directed economic strategies, using either markets or plans except insofar as international pressures and domestic structures modify this position. Both choose technocrats to head state organizations. Liberals and authoritarians could cooperate, in China's future as in many other countries, to support large-scale corporatist means of mediating interests.

The Uncertain Speed of the Future

In the late 1970s, long before *perestroika,* Seweryn Bialer, Stephen F. Cohen, Moshe Lewin, and a few other scholars virtually predicted that the accumulated change in local Soviet networks would end Stalin's legacy in the USSR. Bialer put this in terms of the likely effect of postrevolutionary generations on the top leadership, after a succession ratified what had already happened more widely in the Soviet population. Publishing in 1980, Bialer also raised a caveat: "I do not underestimate the powerful forces at work in the attitudes and behavior of self-replicating elites. Just because these forces are so strong, I see in the combination of a generational gap and succession the rare opportunity for their hold to be weakened if not broken."[201]

This change, when it came after 1985, moved faster and further—for more than a decade, at least—than had been presaged even by the minority of Soviet specialists who had earlier seen the essential flexibility of the system. The basis for change was, as it turned out, not just generational as Bialer had expected. It was not just grounded in the burgeoning social diversification that had grown for many decades, as Lewin had stressed. The cataclysm of the USSR ended not just Stalinism but also Leninism, whose continuing strength Cohen had implied. Scholars such as these had looked more clearly into their crystal balls than did most of their colleagues, but the speed and depth of the transformation outpaced them.

China is not Russia, and the CCP has been warned by a startlingly strong demonstration effect from the north. No student of China can be sure of the timing of future political change there, because no country's politics is wholly scrutable. But many scholars, having learned a lot about the place they study, have an investment in the premise that it will not change. They are like weather forecasters, whose safest prediction is usually that tomorrow will be much like today. But dramatic reforms have already occurred in China. The government did not start them. As the limited success of the post-1989 conservatives shows, it cannot stop them. State-level successions will be important for making a gradual accumulation of power in many local networks more obvious. Eventually, even the Beijing court will adjust.

No Chinese Yeltsin is likely to emerge very soon. China's military tank drivers have been warned not to provide vehicles because such people climb on top of them. But Gorbachev-like Chinese Communist leaders have already made appearances. Many more can be expected. The result will probably not be democratic, at least for a time, because of the historical role of intellectuals in China's politics; but it is already not monolithic. Change is coming, and it is in an ex-Leninist direction. The Communist Party of China has considerable trouble maintaining prestige and recruiting young elites now; and the trend, from its viewpoint, is becoming progressively worse. China will survive quite handily. In the long run, the CCP will not.

Can China fundamentally change? This question has occupied the best minds at the best academic institutions for a long time. It was for years the main sinological question at Harvard, as at Beijing University. Perhaps the time is coming to move to other questions, instead. "Change" and "continuity" are not always opposites, for at least three reasons: First, old Chinese patterns are diverse, often richly inconsistent with each other. This country's normative heritage offers enough basically different options to be useful in almost any new situation that may arise, even though powerful interests may prevent people from developing these options. Inconsistencies in the legacy explain why Chinese tradition has remained so lively for so long.

Second, the change/continuity conundrum leaves people out of the question. Individuals or groups take actions on many grounds, and only sometimes do they act traditionally. Often they set their course first; then, if they are conscious or explicit about heritage at all, they can justify an action on the basis of its "Chinese characteristics" (if they wish to appear particularist). They can as easily do so on grounds of the action's novelty (if they wish to appear modern). The notions of continuity and change are too abstracted from the contexts of political decisions. In their most common uses, these are norms on the basis of which people make claims, not historical truths that can be shown separately from those contexts.

Third, an overemphasis on the "can China change?" question may cause disregard for the corollary query, "change into what?" Proponents of the China-as-basically-continuous hypothesis tend to assume that other ideas (such as are argued in this book) must lead to some unambiguous form of a modern conclusion, for example, that China is basically becoming democratic and like the United States. Similarly, advocates of the China-as-basically-changing hypothesis may overspecify modernization and not admit a range of modern alternatives.

"Reform" is local, not just national, and some of it is substantively conservative. Intellectuals tend to think that "reform," defined as a protoliberal policy set, is the only really major thing that has happened in China during the past few decades. Most Chinese people, with less concern beyond their localities, see a tightening of controls in their immediate networks, now that the state is weaker there. Some of these trends are antireform, because they may restrict which local individuals enter and benefit from markets. As reforms spread, petty tyrannies may later diminish under new pressures from collective institutions such as the market or new media, which are somewhat displacing the state. Until that happens, reforms appear conservative to many Chinese.

If the state is no longer the main effective caretaker for the good of many Chinese, then what other institutions will do this job? The market, together with the separate entities that trade on it, creates another collective institution that serves part of this need. But it develops with support from many power networks (including the state), and its only forte is efficiency. The state is essential for future progress among most of China's people. This book criticizes past state predations and pretensions in the PRC, and it links these faults to continuing social arrogance among Chinese intellectuals. But nothing here should be read to imply that the largest of China's power networks has no vital future role—or that intellectuals have no past accomplishments or future mandates to help figure out how the state can more effectively serve the people.

Hierarchical hegemony can be a good thing when it helps groups overcome barriers to beneficial collective action. This book does not argue against hierarchy as such, only against the usual Beijing presumption that China's current state brings the benefits of hegemony. If data from China showed scant evidence of corruption, of "free riding," or of incentive-inefficient allocations within the state sector, then this book's argument that the state is unruly would be weak. But the Chinese political system now, after its centralizing revolution, again resembles the locally divided "heap of sand" that Sun Yat-sen bemoaned. The PRC government is not yet granting its whole people the benefits that hierarchy should bring.

In the future, perhaps a Chinese state will offer more collective benefits. Now local leaders are doing this instead, even though some are local tyrants. China's stately norms could bring real benefits to China's people. This would be a contribution to the happiness of the world that the Chinese elite, especially its intellectuals, have not yet achieved. The present author, like most of them, looks forward to a day when the Chinese government achieves wider popular influence.

A variety of futures could be in store. Even as a more popular "semi-sovereignty" emerges, it will come at different times in different forms. Continuity is like the clay, and change is like them molding. They are not opposites, but parts of the same process. Many sculptors vie to find the best shape for China's future. Already, reforms have enriched and empowered many. That is a good process, and it has not ended.

Notes

1. Quoted in *Wilson Quarterly* 19:4 (Autumn 1995), p. 92, italics in the original.
2. Quoted in *Times Higher Education Supplement,* London, February 4, 1994, p. 15.
3. This example of Weber's brutal honesty is quoted by the editors in John Stone and Stephen Mennell, eds., *Alexis de Tocqueville on Democracy, Revolution, and Society* (Chicago: University of Chicago Press, 1980), p. 27.
4. This *cri de coeur* is of a kind that China hands also sometimes want to utter—and of a kind very few Americanists in political science would be careful enough to utter. It was attributed to David Wilson in Benedict Anderson, "Studies of the Thai State: The State of Thai Studies," the manuscript of an article later published in Eliezer B. Ayal, ed., *The Study of Thailand* (Athens: Ohio University Southeast Asia Program, 1978). The partly democratic, still crucially monarchic polity of Thailand is indeed odd. But so is everyplace else.
5. On "tendencies of articulation," see H. Gordon Skilling, "Group Conflict in Soviet Politics: Some Conclusions," in *Interest Groups in Soviet Politics,* Skilling and Franklyn Griffiths, eds. (Princeton: Princeton University Press, 1971), pp. 379–416.
6. Central politics are the main application of these notions in Avery Goldstein,

From Bandwagon to Balance-of-Power Politics: Structural Constraints and Politics in China, 1949–78 (Stanford: Stanford University Press, 1991). They are borrowed from international relations theory, but they can apply to local politics, too.

7. Kenneth Lieberthal and Michel Oksenberg, *Policy Making in China: Leaders, Structures, and Processes* (Princeton: Princeton University Press, 1988), p. 3.

8. Rationality models and power models, with good lists of scholars who have used each, are followed by a less philosophical and more practical treatment of bureaucratic power models in ibid., pp. 11–18. See also David M. Bachman, *Bureaucracy, Economy, and Leadership in China: The Institutional Origins of the Great Leap Forward* (Cambridge: Cambridge University Press, 1991).

9. The word "modernization" is often avoided in this book, but not because it lacks verifiable content. It refers mainly to situational correlations, which some scholars reject only because they were unintended, not because they are undetectable. The main reason for advising care in using this word is that it has become such an anathema to some good humanists that its appearance might cause them to reject prematurely the chance that its content could be combined with topics in which they have been more interested—and there is no reason why this book should be inaccessible to them. What is happening in China is understandable partly on the basis of what has happened elsewhere. If that much creates no problem (and writing in English about any Chinese topic already implies such a project), then parallel patterns among nations may be named whatever the reader likes.

10. Quoted from a compilation by Geremie Barmé in James D. Seymour, "China's Democracy Movement: What the Agenda Has Been Missing," paper presented at a conference on "Rights in China: What Happens Next?" London, June 28–29, 1991, p. 2.

11. James C. Scott, *Domination and the Arts of Resistance: Hidden Transcripts* (New Haven: Yale University Press, 1990), pp. 13–14.

12. Ibid., pp. 202–3.

13. Daniel Kelliher, *Peasant Power: The Era of Rural Reform, 1979–1989* (New Haven: Yale University Press, 1993), p. 176.

14. Compare James C. Scott, *Weapons of the Weak: Everyday Forms of Peasant Resistance* (New Haven: Yale University Press, 1985).

15. An oral presentation long ago by Joel Glassman, concerning PRC education policies in the early 1960s, suggested this example to the author.

16. A striking example is the contrast between Mao's 1958 Great Leap Forward policies and his 1956 speech "On the Ten Great Relationships," trans. in Stuart R. Schram, ed., *Chairman Mao Talks to the People* (New York: Pantheon, 1974), pp. 61–83.

17. Dorothy Solinger, "China's Transients and the State: A Form of Civil Society?" *Politics and Society* 21:1 (March 1993), pp. 91–122.

18. David M. Lampton, "The Implementation Problem in Post-Mao China," in *Policy Implementation in Post-Mao China,* Lampton, ed. (Berkeley: University of California Press, 1987), p. 7.

19. Dorothy J. Solinger, *China's Transition from Socialism: Statist Legacies and Market Reforms, 1980–1990* (Armonk, NY: M.E. Sharpe, 1993), p. 10.

20. Zhou Xueguang, "Unorganized Interests and Collective Action in Communist China," *American Sociological Review* 58 (February 1993), p. 57.

21. The terms about organization are from Franz Schurmann, *Ideology and Organization in Communist China* (Berkeley: University of California Press, 1966); and those about two types of security are Amartya Sen's, from J. Dreze and A. Sen, *Hunger and Public Action* (Oxford: Clarendon Press, 1989).

22. On shifts between states' support of efficient and regulatory policies, the classic is Karl Polanyi, *The Great Transformation: The Social and Economic Origins of Our Time*

(New York: Rinehart, 1944). Social scientists' biases and fads have similar local coalition-building effects.

23. "Complexity" logics, to treat systems on the edge of "chaos" in which slight changes in one or a few initial variables creates indeterminate or nearly random outcomes, are still in their infancy but might later aid rather than hinder realism in analyses of these political shifts. See Arthur Stinchcombe, "Social Structure and Organization," in *Handbook of Organizations*, James G. March, ed. (Chicago: Rand McNally, 1965), pp. 153ff.; Daniel Kahneman, Jack L. Knetsch, and Richard H. Thaler, "Anomalies: The Endowment Effect, Loss Aversion, and Status Quo Bias," *Journal of Economic Perspectives* 5:5 (Winter 1991), pp. 193–206; Stephen Jay Gould, "What Is a Species?" *Discover* (December 1992), pp. 40–44; and James Gleick, *Chaos: Making a New Science* (New York: Penguin, 1987). Thanks to Professor Yang Dali for suggestions here.

24. The modern intellectual history of multiple causation in these three fields is treated in Peter M. Swire, "The Onslaught of Complexity: Information Technologies and Developments in Legal and Economic Thought" (Senior thesis, Princeton University, Woodrow Wilson School, 1980).

25. Charles C. Ragin, *The Comparative Method: Moving Beyond Qualitative and Quantitative Strategies* (Berkeley: University of California Press, 1987), p. xiii, and especially chap. 6, a simple introduction to Boolean algebra.

26. There is essentially just one mathematical relationship: addition. Subtraction is a negative form of it; multiplication, a repeated form of it; division, a negative form of that; exponents, a repeated form of multiplication; roots, a negative form of that; and the operations of calculus, factorials, and other summations are all variations on this theme. Addition is indeed a clear way to link amounts of similar things; but only a great leap of faith can undergird the notion implicit in much social science that quantities exhaust all predicates. A further problem arises because the variables used in mathematical approaches to politics often have fuzzier definitions than in other approaches. So the manipulations by these various forms of addition are often clearer than the meanings of the items being manipulated.

27. Charles C. Ragin, *The Comparative Method*, p. 101.

28. Harry Eckstein, "Case Study and Theory in Political Science," in *Handbook of Political Science*, vol. 7, F. Greenstein and N. Polsby, eds. (Reading, MA: Addison-Wesley, 1975), especially p. 123.

29. Especially notable is Richard Baum, *Burying Mao* (Princeton: Princeton University Press, 1994).

30. Daniel Little, *Understanding Peasant China: Case Studies in the Philosophy of Social Science* (New Haven: Yale University Press, 1989), p. 219.

31. Ibid., p. 233.

32. This book argues elsewhere that the logical opposition between symbols chosen for emphasis by Clifford Geertz (in Bali, not just the cockfight but also the Brahmana ordination ceremony) exhausts a logical field and is crypto-functionalist. Several of Geertz's books, e.g. *Agricultural Involution* (Berkeley: University of California Press, 1963) and *Islam Observed* (New Haven: Yale University Press, 1968), are superb examples of applied functionalism.

33. Daniel Little, *Understanding Peasant China*, pp. 219 and 228.

34. Donald Davidson, *Essays on Actions and Events* (Oxford: Oxford University Press, 1980), suggests that individuals' intentions for action may be taken as causes. Only in social science would this be such a surprise.

35. An example is explored in Lynn White, "Social Choice in China's Reforms," a review article about Susan L. Shirk's *The Political Logic of Economic Reform in China*,

in *Harvard International Review* (Summer 1994), pp. 60–61. Shirk uses a decision rule (explicitly part of a rational-action model) that not only explains immediate causations well, but also suggests interesting observations about Chinese political culture.

36. This claim for the word "structural" is like that for "formal." The implication that culture is unstructured is as careerist as the implication that the methods of good interpretive anthropology have no form. But the text above benefits from David Elkins and Richard Simeon, "A Cause in Search of Its Effect, or What Does Political Culture Explain?" *Comparative Politics* 11 (January 1979), pp. 127–46, with attention to their own crucial retreat on their argument in the middle of p. 136. It also relies on the very different but compatible arguments in Joseph Levenson, e.g., *Confucian China and Its Modern Fate: The Problem of Monarchical Decay,* e.g., vol. 2 (Berkeley: University of California Press, 1964), pp. 3–21.

37. This is based on Frederic Wakeman Jr., "The Chinese Mirror," in *China's Developmental Experience,* Michel Oksenberg, ed. (New York: Praeger, 1973), pp. 216–17.

38. Such surges have occurred in many modernizing countries. Reinhard Bendix, *Nation-Building and Citizenship* (New York: Wiley, 1964), is one of several classic treatments. Another is Karl Polanyi, *The Great Transformation.*

39. See E. E. Schattschneider, *The Semi-Sovereign People: A Realist's View of American Democracy* (Hinsdale, IL: Dreyden Press, 1975).

40. James Lull, *China Turned On: Television, Reform, and Resistance* (London: Routledge, 1991), p. 216.

41. A. J. Ayer, *Language, Truth, and Logic* (New York: Dover, 1952).

42. From a British Broadcasting Corporation interview with A. J. Ayer, March 1976 (videotape sold by the BBC), "Logical Positivism and Its Legacy" in the series *Men of Ideas: Creators of Modern Philosophy.*

43. This change in Ayer—or contrasts between the "clouds of meaning" in Wittgenstein's late *Philosophical Investigations* (New York: Macmillan, 1953) and his positivistic, earlier, less circumspect *Tractatus Logico-Philosophicus* (London: Routledge and Kegan Paul, 1974 [1922])—is not yet reflected by the main gurus of social science method. They have been very slow. Cf. the first epigram, at the head of this chapter. Karl Popper, particularly though inadvertently, has justified many professionals who prefer faith to research. It is high time that they come to terms with Ayer's and Wittgenstein's afterthoughts, as well as with the limitations of their own work. For students of politics, these last are catalogued in expert detail by Ian Shapiro and Donald P. Green, *Pathologies of Rational Choice Theory: A Critique of Applications in Political Science* (New Haven: Yale University Press, 1994).

44. The six examples refer, respectively, to Clifford Geertz, "Deep Play: Notes on the Balinese Cockfight," in *The Interpretation of Cultures,* Geertz, ed. (New York: Basic Books, 1973), pp. 412–53; Robert Darnton, *The Great Cat Massacre and Other Episodes in French Cultural History* (New York: Basic Books, 1984); James C. Scott, *Domination and the Arts of Resistance;* Neil J. Smelser and Talcott Parsons, *Economy and Society* (Glencoe, IL: Free Press, 1956); Gabriel Almond and Sidney Verba, *The Civic Culture* (Princeton: Princeton University Press, 1963); and Seymour Martin Lipset, *Political Man* (London: Heinemann, 1969).

45. The literature about "Function and Cause" is a large, often disembodied one. For a sensible survey, see (Asianist) Ronald Dore's chapter with that title in *The Philosophy of Social Explanation,* Alan Ryan, ed. (Oxford: Oxford University Press, 1973), pp. 65–81.

46. The largest banks in post-Meiji Japan, for example, recruit leaders among graduates from the same top universities as government ministries; so nonstate and state notables are socialized in cohorts to work together. Even provincial bankers are often ex-bureaucrats, humorously called "*amakudari*" (descended from heaven). Kent E. Cal-

der, "Elites in an Equalizing Role: Ex-Bureaucrats as Coordinators and Intermediaries in the Japanese Government-Business Relationship" (manuscript).

47. The analysis of Wang Xizhe, "Mao Zedong and the Cultural Revolution," in *On Socialist Democracy and the Chinese Legal System,* Anita Chan, Stanley Rosen, and Jonathan Unger, eds. (Armonk, NY: M.E. Sharpe, 1985), pp. 177–260.

48. Most English people are still not fully aware that their country ever had a real revolution. (State elites, even there, present the national history differently.) But it is one of the most interesting cases, partly because mainstream historians still treat the relatively peaceful "Glorious Revolution" as more than an aftershock to the Puritan capture of government, four decades earlier. Cromwell's regime, and the process that led to it, affected a greater portion of the people more deeply; and it began institutional changes that took much longer to stabilize. Hugh Trevor-Roper admits that the events after 1688 were merely a "conservative revolution." See his chapter in *The Anglo-Dutch Moment: Essays on the Glorious Revolution and Its World Impact,* Jonathan Israel, ed. (Cambridge: Cambridge University Press, 1991), p. 494. Editor Jonathan Israel's own essay, e.g., p. 128, makes clear that the Glorious Revolution was in large part a foreign invasion, carried out by the Dutch Republic to balance Louis XIV's military and economic power. William's Dutch army was militarily stronger than James's more dispersed forces. His invasion at Torbay and march on London caused little bloodshed in a politically divided England; so it was able to succeed without stirring local rancor—and without being widely seen as the foreign attack it actually was. Israel does not stress (as Eugen Weber might, on analogy to the nineteenth-century change of *Peasants into Frenchmen* [Berkeley: University of California Press, 1977]) that the sense of English identity may, even in the 1680s, not have been so widespread among local groups as apologists for London regimes long suggested. Successful invasions at that time, even after the Armada, were not yet as national as they later became.

49. Ronald Hutton, *The Restoration: A Political and Religious History of England and Wales, 1658–1667* (Oxford: Clarendon Press, 1985), p. 127.

50. Jennifer Carter in *The Restored Monarchy, 1660–1668,* J. R. Jones, ed. (London: Macmillan, 1979), pp. 92–93.

51. For example, the French case was not so inflationary, but although industry accounted for 18 percent of the French national product in 1789—and by 1815, this proportion had risen only to 22 percent—by 1825, the industrial proportion was already up to 26 percent, and then 30 percent by 1859. (In 1959, a full century later, the industrial contribution was, partly because of pricing at that time, still less than 50 percent.) See B. R. Mitchell, *European Historical Statistics, 1750–1975,* 2d rev. ed. (London: Macmillan, 1980), pp. 840 and 849. The quickest rise in the percentage contribution of French industry postdated the domestic violence and Napoleon's wars, in the decade 1815–25.

52. John Stone and Stephen Mennell, eds., *Alexis de Tocqueville* (Chicago: University of Chicago Press, 1980), p. 60; and, for the later quotation, p. 62.

53. These propositions are certainly meant to challenge the currency of opposite hypotheses, which are common. But they do not forever invalidate those contrary adjectives; no mere predicates could do such a thing, despite the popularity among scholars for suggesting that favorite adjectives or arguments can do this. The main purpose of the exercise here is to suggest better ways of thinking about reforms in China and in postrevolutionary situations generally. A secondary purpose, necessary to achieve the main one, is to suggest that writers distinguish analytic concepts from concrete things more faithfully when writing about such issues.

54. Philosopher-anthropologist Ernest Gellner suggests that segmentary society is at least one of the alternatives to civil society. The former, in Eastern Europe and East Asia,

has fostered growth; but Gellner suggests that it has not necessarily fostered democratic liberalism. The question is whether concrete modern growth merely precedes or under some conditions replaces some institutionalization of ideal tolerance. Is their disjunction ephemeral, just a lag, or a new order? The question is nicely raised, and not fully answered, in Gellner's *Civil Society and Its Rivals* (New York: Penguin, 1994). See also Alan Ryan's comment, "Why Democracy?" *New York Times Book Review,* January 1, 1995, pp. 8–9.

55. The logical need to specify concepts in polar fashion, distinguishing them from what they are not, is stressed in the classic article by Giovanni Sartori, "Concept Misformation in Comparative Politics," *American Political Science Review* 64:4 (December 1970), pp. 1033–53.

56. Antonio Gramsci, *Letters from Prison,* trans. Lynne Lawner (New York: Harper and Row, 1973), p. 42, in Dorothy Solinger, "China's Transients," pp. 91–122.

57. Marx citations in Solinger, ibid.

58. G. Kindermann, "An Overview of Sun Yat-sen's Doctrine," in *Sun Yat-sen's Doctrine in the Modern World,* C. Y. Cheng, ed. (Boulder: Westview, 1989), p. 57.

59. Important contributions to this debate are William Rowe, *Hankow: Conflict and Community in a Chinese City, 1796–1895* (Stanford: Stanford University Press, 1989); David Strand, *Rickshaw Beijing: City People and Politics in the 1920s* (Berkeley: University of California Press, 1989); and Frederic Wakeman Jr., "The Civil Society and Public Sphere Debate: Western Reflections on Chinese Political Culture," *Modern China* 19:2 (April 1993), pp. 108–38.

60. Samuel P. Huntington, *American Politics: The Promise of Disharmony* (Cambridge: Harvard University Press, 1981), p. 58.

61. Even in traditional lineage governance, administrators were chosen from the most capable sons in a major lineage. These became *zongzi,* and often they were at least thought to have the potential of passing official exams to become *shenshi* (gentry). Formally, the heads of major lineages, or *zuzhang,* had their status irrespective of talents; but in practice the *zongzi* administrators were also influential. See anthropologist Hu Hsien-chin, *The Common Descent Group in China and Its Functions* (New York: Viking Fund, 1948).

62. Lucian W. Pye, *The Mandarin and the Cadre: China's Political Cultures* (Ann Arbor: Center for Chinese Studies, University of Michigan, 1988), p. 6.

63. Donald J. Munro, *The Concept of Man in Contemporary China* (Ann Arbor: University of Michigan Press, 1977), p. 15, refers to a Chinese "case for man's social essence." Michael Harris Bond, *The Psychology of the Chinese People* (Hong Kong: Oxford University Press, 1986), p. 215, claims that "the Western starting point of the anomic individual is alien to Chinese considerations of man's social behavior, which see man as a relational being, socially situated and defined within an interactive context." But even Confucius, and certainly others including some Daoists, Legalists, and Yang Zhu, also spoke of individuals. For more, see Vitaly A. Rubin, *Individualism and the State in Ancient China,* Steven Levine, ed. (New York: Columbia University Press, 1976), and William Theodore de Bary, *The Liberal Tradition in China* (New York: Columbia University Press, 1983), especially pp. 91–108.

64. This seems an odd ending to the most powerful critique yet published of "civil society" approaches in modern Chinese history; but it is consistent with an aversion to teleology. Frederic Wakeman Jr., "The Civil Society," pp. 112 and 134.

65. On the main nondemocratic alternative, see Philippe C. Schmitter, "Still the Century of Corporatism?" in *The New Corporatism,* F. Pike and T. Stritch, eds. (South Bend: Notre Dame University Press, 1974).

66. Jürgen Habermas, *The Structural Transformation of the Public Sphere: An Inquiry*

into a Category of Bourgeois Society (Cambridge, MA: MIT Press, 1989), p. 398. As David Goodman suggests, however, Habermas would strictly deny the applicability of terms like "civil society" to China because they are connected with European culture. See *China's Quiet Revolution: New Interactions Between State and Society,* David S. G. Goodman and Beverley Hooper, eds. (New York: St. Martin's, 1994), p. xvii. But perhaps teahouses are as good for this as coffeehouses. Given the difference within and among European countries, it is unclear whether Habermas's reservations on this point should be given much credit.

67. Quoted in William T. Rowe, "The Problem of Civil Society in Late Imperial China," *Modern China* 19:2 (April 1993), p. 141.

68. Sun Liping, "Populism and Chinese Reform," *Strategy and Management* 2 (1995), pp. 5 and 8.

69. A considerable shelf in several libraries is occupied by the *Zhongguo gaige quanshu* (Complete Book of Chinese Reforms), separate editorial committee for each volume (Dalian: Dalian Chuban She, 1992).

70. Andrew G. Walder, "The Quiet Revolution from Within," in *The Waning of the Communist State,* Walder, ed. (Berkeley: University of California Press, 1995), p. 5.

71. See Li Cheng and Lynn White, "China's Technocratic Movement and the *World Economic Herald,*" *Modern China* 17:3 (July 1991), pp. 342–88.

72. *RMRB,* April 29, 1988. A slightly different report is in *CD,* November 1, 1989. Such groups were sometimes also called *shehui tuanti.*

73. Huang Ping in *Shanghai shangbao* (Shanghai Business News), January 13, 1989.

74. *SHJJNJ88,* Xiao Jun et al., eds. (Shanghai: Shanghai Renmin Chuban She, 1988), pp. 95–96.

75. Ibid., p. 97.

76. These organizations' names were abbreviated Gao Zi Lian and Gong Zi Lian. *RMRBHWB,* June 24, 1989.

77. The quotations are from Jude Howell, "The Poverty of Civil Society: Insights from China" (Norwich: University of East Anglia School of Development Studies, 1993), pp. 10–11 and 37–38. On Xiaoshan at the same time, see also Gordon White, "Prospects for Civil Society: A Case Study of Xiaoshan City," in David Goodman and Beverley Hooper, eds., *China's Quiet Revolution,* pp. 194–215.

78. Martin K. Whyte, "Urban China: A Civil Society in the Making?" in *State and Society in China: The Consequences of Reform,* Arthur Lewis Rosenbaum, ed. (Boulder: Westview, 1992), pp. 77–78.

79. Daniel Little, *Understanding Peasant China,* p. 192.

80. There are a very few cases during China's reform years when peasant "emperors" and *qigong* specialists have claimed sole sovereignty. This is discussed elsewhere in this book, and it is relevant to the decline of the PRC state even though it is a rare phenomenon. Weber's definition is formally unexceptionable because of words like "claim" and "legitimacy" and because he was always careful to distinguish concrete from ideal types. But he was an ardent patriot in a Germany that had been rather recently unified, and for once his vocation in politics may have affected his choices in science. Huge China, at a time of political decentralization, is not the context in which this particular definition of the state proves most relevant.

81. Another viable translation of *tushan* would be "mountain of dirt." *Minzhu yu fazhi* (Democracy and Law) (March 1985), p. 33; also another article in the previous (February) issue.

82. Quoted in Samuel L. Popkin, *The Rational Peasant: The Political Economy of Rural Society in Vietnam* (Berkeley: University of California Press, 1979), p. 88.

83. *Zhongguo renkou qianyi* (Population Shifts in China), Tian Fang and Ling Fatong, eds. (Beijing: Zhishi Chuban She, 1987), pp. 248–59.

84. Frederic Wakeman Jr., "Civil Society"; see also Wakeman, "Models of Historical Change: The Chinese State and Society, 1839–1989," in *Perspectives on Modern China: Four Anniversaries,* Kenneth Lieberthal, Joyce Kallgren, Roderick MacFarquhar, and Wakeman, eds. (Armonk, NY: M.E. Sharpe, 1991), pp. 68–102.

85. See Lynn White, *Policies of Chaos: The Organizational Causes of Violence in the Cultural Revolution* (Princeton: Princeton University Press, 1989).

86. Jennifer Carter in *The Restored Monarchy,* p. 82.

87. Evidence of reformism in Stalin's time can often be found associated with Bukharin, about 1934 with the name of Kirov, and about 1948 with Voznesensky. Any such tendency, whenever it arose, was skillfully and ruthlessly rooted out by the dictator. Despite him, other reformers arose again later, and they referred to their predecessors. The most important example in the ex-Stalinist state can be centered about 1956 and associated with Nikita Khrushchev. The author owes his colleague Stephen F. Cohen thanks for some of these ideas.

88. See *Zhongguo gongchan dang qishi nian* (The Chinese Communist Party's Seventy Years), Hu Sheng, ed. (Beijing: Zhonggong Dangshi Chuban She, 1991), p. 565.

89. This is based on interview information. The forms are not always filled out completely, however. "Class status" (*jieji chengfen*) is now not applicable or replaced by "family origin" (*jiating chushen*). Sometimes there is reference to "occupational status" (*benren chengfen*), a term referring to status as a cadre, worker, student, or intellectual.

90. *FBIS,* March 16, 1988, p. 28, reporting *SJJJDB* of February 29.

91. Hans Daalder, "Parties, Elites, and Political Developments in Western Europe," in *Political Parties and Political Development,* Joseph LaPalombara and M. Weiner, eds. (Princeton: Princeton University Press, 1966).

92. This idea is derived from a seminar led by my colleague Nancy Bermeo, whom I also thank for the reference in note 91.

93. *Post,* May 13, 1989.

94. *ZGQNB,* June 30, 1988, carries statistics on this to four decimal places, when counting responses to vague questions in attitude surveys (but with no information about the samples). The link between such data and behavior may be quite indeterminable. Nonetheless, many Chinese admitted that they were wary of politics in the 1980s. On both the substance and the surveys, much of the best writing has been done by Stanley Rosen. See his work with David Chu on *Survey Research in the People's Republic of China* (Washington: United States Information Agency, 1987); also his "The Chinese Communist Party and Chinese Society: Popular Attitudes Toward Party Membership and the Party's Image," *Australian Journal of Chinese Affairs* 24 (July 1990), pp. 51–92; and many other researches by Rosen.

95. *Post,* May 13, 1989.

96. Chen Yizi, at a conference sponsored by the Princeton China Initiative, May 5, 1991.

97. Max Weber, *The Religion of China* (Glencoe, IL: Free Press, 1951), and a talk by S. N. Eisenstadt at the University of Hong Kong, January 24, 1994.

98. Li Cheng, "The Rise of Technocracy: Elite Transformation and Ideological Change in Post-Mao China" (Ph.D. dissertation, Politics Department, Princeton University, 1991), p. 310, from a study by Wang Fuchun and Wu Xiaojian in *Zhengzhi xue yanjiu* (Political Science Research) 1 (1989).

99. Ibid., p. 311, from Min Qi, *Zhongguo zhengzhi wenhua* (Chinese Political Culture) (Kunming: Yunnan Renmin Chuban She, 1989), p. 123.

100. *FBIS,* December 30, 1987, p. 35, reporting radio of December 24.

101. A traditional aphorism holds that "the gentleman is not a tool" (*junzi bu qi*).

102. Su Xiaokang and Wang Luxiang, *Deathsong of the River: A Reader's Guide to*

the Chinese TV Series Heshang, trans. Richard W. Bodman and Pin P. Wang (Ithaca: Cornell University East Asia Program, 1991), p. 98.

103. Fang Lizhi, "Democracy, Reform, and Modernization," *China Spring Digest* (March/April 1987), p. 12.

104. A classic example is Japan in the mid-1950s. As Kent Calder says, "Japan's double-digit economic growth rarely evoked a clear sense of euphoria and confidence in Japan while it was actually occurring." Calder, *Crisis and Compensation: Public Policy and Political Stability in Japan, 1949–1986* (Princeton: Princeton University Press, 1988), p. 47.

105. See Rupert Wilkinson, *Gentlemanly Power: British Leadership and the Public School Tradition, A Comparative Study in the Making of Rulers* (Oxford: Oxford University Press, 1964).

106. Cf. Harry Eckstein, "The Idea of Political Development: From Dignity to Efficiency," in *Political System and Change,* Ikuô Kabashima and Lynn White, eds. (Princeton: Princeton University Press, 1986), pp. 311–46.

107. *Shanghai shehui xiankuang he qushi, 1980–1983* (Situations and Trends in Shanghai Society, 1980–1983), Zheng Gongliang et al., eds. (Shanghai: Huadong Shifan Daxue Chuban She, 1988), p. 196.

108. See Li Cheng, "University Networks and the Rise of Qinghua Graduates in China," *Australian Journal of Chinese Affairs* 32 (July 1994), pp. 1–32.

109. Information on these plans came to the author from Lyman Miller of Johns Hopkins University.

110. Notebook of Wu Guoguang, an associate of Zhao at the time, quoted in Wu Guoguang, "Hard Politics with Soft Institutions: China's Political Reform in 1986–1989" (Ph.D. dissertation, Politics Department, Princeton University, 1995), chap. 2, p. 31.

111. *Lianhe shibao* (United Times), April 28, 1989.

112. This is from a lecture by Shanghai County Party Secretary Shang Yafei at the 1987 Shanghai working conference on rural areas, in *Yige chengjiao xiangcun de jintian he mingtian* (A Suburban Village Today and Tomorrow), Ling Yaochu and Zhang Zhao'an, eds. (Shanghai: Shanghai Shehui Kexue Yuan Chuban She, 1988), pp. 1–6.

113. Suttmeier uses phrases from Manfred Stanley in "Science, Technology, and China's Political Future—A Framework for Analysis," in *Science and Technology in Post-Mao China,* D. F. Simon and M. Goldman, eds. (Cambridge: Harvard Council on East Asian Studies, 1989), p. 392.

114. James Forman, *That Mad Game: War and the Chances for Peace* (New York: Charles Scribner's Sons, 1980), p. ix.

115. E.E. Schattschneider, *The Semi-Sovereign People,* p. 135.

116. Ibid., p. 102.

117. This has been best documented for Britain in Karl Polanyi, *The Great Transformation;* but it is a general pattern. E.E. Schattschneider, *The Semi-Sovereign People,* provides essentially the same framework for the United States. Deng's government has clearly supported markets a good deal, as Mao's earlier supported some protection of people against their ill effects.

118. E. E. Schattschneider, *The Semi-Sovereign People,* quoted from pp. 134 and 131; italics in original.

119. John Fitzgerald, "In Pursuit of the Authentic Chinaman: Racism, Nationalism, and Ethnography in Modern China," paper presented at a conference, Hong Kong University, July 1, 1991, now part of *Awakening China: Politics, Culture, and Class in the Nationalist Revolution* (Stanford: Stanford University Press, 1996). Even Sun Yat-sen's constitution (an edition of which is currently used on Taiwan) adopted a five-part rather than a three-part separation of powers, citing older Chinese precedents. Frank Dikötter is

developing some contrarian refinements to Fitzgerald's point, however.

120. Julien Benda, trans. R. Aldington, *The Treason of the Intellectuals* (New York: Norton, 1969 [1928]).

121. See Joseph Fewsmith's review of "Leninger's" *Disan zhi yanjing kan Zhongguo* (Looking at China Through a Third Eye) in *Journal of Contemporary China* 7 (Fall 1994), pp. 100–104.

122. Alex B. Clavel, *Law and Authoritarianism in China, 1978–1995* (Senior thesis, Princeton University, East Asian Studies, 1995), p. 6, quoting *Asian Wall Street Journal,* October 4, 1994.

123. Song Qiang et al., *Zhongguo keyi shuo bu* (China Can Say No) (Beijing: Zhonghua Gongshang Lianhe Chuban She, 1996). The title of this tome is odd, considering the Chinese patriotic content, because it paraphrases the title of an earlier volume by distinguished Japanese xenophobes, which was translated into English as *The Japan That Can Say No.*

124. Interview with Zhang Xiaobo (whose pen name is Zhang Zangzang) and Song Qiang, *Post,* August 3, 1996. This article also quotes the book very concisely on these young intellectuals' appeal for PLA backing and on Taiwan: "We must prepare for war."

125. Ibid.

126. Jean-Louis Rocca, "Corruption and Its Shadow: An Anthropological View of Corruption in China," *China Quarterly* 130 (June 1992), p. 415.

127. *Economist,* July 20, 1996, p. 22.

128. Richard Kuisel, *Seducing the French: The Dilemma of Americanization* (Berkeley: University of California Press, 1993).

129. Few engage in such dismal comparisons now, perhaps because the problem has during the 1990s become somewhat less obvious in large (though not small) countries or perhaps because mainstream social science now tends to discount a priori the use of studying large-group norms such as patriotism. But Max Weber, by contrast, was ardently proud of his officership in the Prussian army reserve. His sufferance of "the antinomies of existence," e.g., between national identity and scientific objectivity, is treated in H. Stuart Hughes, *Consciousness and Society* (New York: Vintage, 1961), pp. 290–91.

130. There may be domestic structural reasons for the Japanese hypothesis that they are not much liked elsewhere. The xenophobia of Korean students may be understandable because their country is still divided, but it is inseparable from a claim by ex-Confucian intellectuals that international security and business concerns should not shape Korean identity so much.

131. Edward A. Shils, "Rulers and Intellectuals: Some General Observations and Some Particular References to India," in *Leadership and Authority: A Symposium,* Gehan Jayawardene, ed. (Singapore: University of Malaya Press, 1968), p. 310.

132. Chen is from the Chinese University of Hong Kong. Intellectuals in that city, having avoided a sense that the Cultural Revolution holocaust against them gives them special privileges now, may construct a relatively clear picture of what they can do for China in the future. Vera Schwarcz, "Memory, Commemoration, and the Plight of China's Intellectuals," *Wilson Quarterly* (Autumn 1989), p. 123.

133. Alice Goldstein and Guo Shenyang. "Temporary Migration in Shanghai and Beijing," *Studies in Comparative International Development* 27:2 (Summer 1992), p. 43.

134. Research by Andrew J. Nathan and Shi Tianjian on "China's Ideological Spectrum" (manuscript) using a careful opinion survey in 1990, shows much higher public concern about inflation, corruption, crime, and other livelihood issues than about any aspect of political or ownership system reforms.

135. *Asian Wall Street Journal,* January 31, 1989.

136. Dips in Indian food production have been caused by droughts or floods, but the most recent big disaster was the Great Bengal Famine of 1943, in which the excess

mortality was 3 million. Help with this section came from a Princeton graduate student originally from Chittagong, Elora Shehabbudin. This compares with the Dreze and Sen collation of estimates cited in Chapter 1.1 for China, 1959–61, ranging from 17 to 30 million above-normal deaths.

137. Lowell Dittmer, "Patterns of Leadership in Reform China," in *State and Society in China: The Consequences of Reform,* Arthur Lewis Rosenbaum, ed. (Boulder: Westview, 1992), p. 51.

138. Charles Burton, *Political and Social Change in China Since 1978* (New York: Greenwood Press, 1990), p. 93.

139. Geoffrey Hosking, *The Awakening of the Soviet Union* (Cambridge: Harvard University Press, 1990), p. 162.

140. "*Mozhe shitou guo he.*" For more on this contrast, see the *Economist,* November 28, 1992, p. 10. The best comparative treatment is Minxin Pei, *From Reform to Revolution: The Demise of Communism in China and the Soviet Union* (Cambridge: Harvard University Press, 1994).

141. This term is János Kornai's; see *The Road to a Free Economy: The Example of Hungary* (New York: Norton, 1990).

142. Richard Smith, "The Chinese Road to Capitalism," *New Left Review* 199 (May–June 1993), p. 68.

143. The main exceptions are legal state monopolies, such as cigarette production. In these fields, there is extensive illegal production.

144. See Li Cheng and David Bachman, "Localism, Elitism, and Immobilism: Elite Formation and Social Change in Post-Mao China," *World Politics* 42:1 (October 1989), pp. 64–94, and Li Cheng and Lynn White, "Elite Transformation and Modern Change in Mainland China and Taiwan," *China Quarterly* 121 (March 1990), pp. 1–35; and Li Cheng and Lynn White, "The Thirteenth Central Committee of the Chinese Communist Party: From Mobilizers to Managers," *Asian Survey* 28:4 (April 1988), pp. 371–99.

145. *FDXB,* June 1988, p. 64, reports *SJJJDB,* October 26, 1987.

146. *Gaige* is the Chinese word for reform. The section that follows is partly indebted to a 1993 oral presentation by the author's colleague, Professor Minxin Pei, who bears no responsibility for the interpretations here. See also Pei's book, cited above.

147. *CD,* August 8, 1989.

148. *Post,* May 13, 1989.

149. *Zhengming* 99 (January 1, 1986), quoted in *FBIS,* January 7, 1986, pp. W5–8.

150. Richard D. Baum, *Burying Mao,* chap. 12, cites *FEER,* August 3, 1990.

151. Quoted in Jane's Information Group, *China in Crisis: The Role of the Military* (Coulsdon, UK: Jane's Defense Data, 1989), pp. 65–66.

152. Mannheim does not follow Marx or Gramsci in specifying the groups as necessarily economic or even very intellectual. See his *Ideology and Utopia* (London: Routledge, 1936); and Howard Williams, *Concepts of Ideology* (Sussex, UK: Wheatsheaf, 1988).

153. Seweryn Bialer, *Stalin's Successors* (Cambridge: Cambridge University Press, 1980), pp. 117–24.

154. See Valerie Bunce, *Do New Leaders Make a Difference? Executive Succession and Public Policy Under Capitalism and Socialism* (Princeton: Princeton University Press, 1981).

155. On this point, see a book by the sometimes-reluctant predictor of democracy, Samuel P. Huntington, *The Third Wave: Democratization in the Late Twentieth Century* (Norman: University of Oklahoma Press, 1991). Michel Foucault would question the interpretation here. He may be right to suggest that a subtle kind of modern "discipline" replaces "punishment" in democratic "bourgeois societies," but even he would agree that the states

against which he rails use less straightforward coercion than did their predecessors.

156. The evidence is strong, although the underlying reasons are not obvious. This conjecture, tracing many international conflicts and finding that liberal systems can be very violent against nonliberal regimes but sharply avoid making war against each other, is in Michael Doyle, "Kant, Liberal Legacies, and Foreign Affairs," *Philosophy and Public Affairs* 12:3–4 (Summer and Fall 1983), pp. 205–35 and 323–52. It has later been challenged in some respects; but it seems nonetheless to hold as a general guideline, in the modest way it was originally proposed.

157. See Atul Kohli, "Democracy and Development," in *Development Strategies Reconsidered,* John P. Lewis and V. Kallab, eds. (New Brunswick, NJ: Transaction Press, 1986), p. 157.

158. Rustow describes his model as nonfunctionalist, but it is really a loose functionalist scheme, of a very sensible sort that considers concrete situations, not just consensus norms, and short-term requisites, not just long-term prerequisites, as well as chance factors. See Dankwart Rustow, "Transitions to Democracy: Toward a Dynamic Model," *Comparative Politics* 2:3 (1970), p. 361.

159. This list is rephrased from Robert A. Dahl, *Polyarchy: Participation and Opposition* (New Haven: Yale University Press, 1971), p. 203.

160. World Bank, *World Development Report, 1991* (New York: Oxford University Press, 1991), p. 204.

161. See the classic by Albert Hirschman, "The Changing Tolerance for Income Equality in the Course of Economic Development," *World Development* 1:12 (December 1973), pp. 29–36.

162. See Ma Guonan, "Income Distribution in the 1980s," in David Goodman and Beverley Hooper, eds., *China's Quiet Revolution,* pp. 19–40.

163. The classic is Huntington's *Political Order in Changing Societies* (New Haven: Yale University Press, 1968), which argues that raising political institutions prior to a rise of political demands is essential for democratic outcomes. On this basis, Huntington in 1984 wrote "Will More Countries Become Democratic?" in *Political Science Quarterly* 99:2 (Summer 1984), pp. 193–218. Since then, at least on the basis of 1991 data, many of Huntington's 1984 predictions have proved spectacularly wrong. But he has refined his theory—and added prescriptions for would-be democratizers to it—in his later book, *The Third Wave.*

164. See Barrett L. McCormick, "Democracy or Dictatorship?" *Australian Journal of Chinese Affairs* 31 (January 1994), p. 103. A survey of a World Bank list of countries by per-capita income, considering their political systems, shows that some long-lasting but somewhat shaky democracies (India, Sri Lanka, the Philippines, perhaps Peru) have incomes of less than $1,000 per person. *All* the sovereign states above $10,000 have clearly stable democracies (except the United Arab Emirates, some others with less than a million inhabitants, and arguably the philosopher-king's Singapore). So do most states in the $3,000–$10,000 range. The data are in the *World Development Report, 1994* (New York: Oxford University Press, 1994), p. 162.

165. The $470 per capita estimate for China in 1992 understates the provision of basic goods. But China's 7.6 percent annual growth, in 1980–92, was *more than twice* that of all but two (including Indonesia at 4.0 percent) of the other forty-odd low-income economies. Growth for India was estimated at 3.1 percent annually in that period. See World Bank, ibid.

166. *CD,* February 3, 1988.

167. David Hackett Fischer, *Albion's Seed: Four British Folkways in America* (New York: Oxford University Press, 1989), p. 200.

168. Well-defined contrasts between different kinds of freedom in Shanghai and Qinghai, late in Mao's time, emerge from a comparison of two essays in B. Michael Frolic, *Mao's People: Sixteen Portraits of Life in Revolutionary China* (Cambridge: Harvard University Press, 1980), pp. 144–56, and 224–41.

169. See for example, Li Cheng and Lynn White, "Elite Transformation," pp. 1–35; and Li Cheng and Lynn White, "The Thirteenth Central Committee," pp. 371–99.

170. Max Weber, predicting a "polar night of icy darkness and hardness," was also too quick to predict the rule of reason, so Shue is in very good company. See Vivienne Shue, *The Reach of the State: Sketches of the Chinese Body Politic* (Stanford: Stanford University Press, 1988). In comparative studies, the most thoroughgoing expression of this possibility Shue explores comes from Michel Foucault, but her version is much clearer.

171. Ibid., p. 152.

172. Michel Foucault, e.g., in *Discipline and Punish* (New York: Pantheon, 1977), may have led analysts astray by implying the comparability of "discipline" in professionalized societies and legal power in old regimes (not just for example the French one, where his ideas may apply too exclusively). The old form of power meets a classic definition: Power is evidenced when the influential algebraic character A wants something, and B does it but would not otherwise do it. In Foucault's modern form, however, adoption of Gramsci's concept "false consciousness" makes intentions hard to evidence; so what A wants becomes as hard to specify as what B would otherwise want. Discipline and punishment seem to be such different objects that moral comparisons between them are hindered. Foucault's theory seems to work only if its purpose is to chastise each of them separately. For more on related topics, see Laura Engelstein (with reactions from Rudy Koshar and Jan Goldstein, and a reply by Engelstein), "*AHR* Forum; Combined Underdevelopment: Discipline and the Law in Imperial and Soviet Russia," *American Historical Review* (April 1993), pp. 338–81.

173. *Post,* May 13, 1989.

174. Max Weber, "Science as a Vocation," in *From Max Weber: Essays in Sociology,* H.H. Gerth and C. Wright Mills, eds. (New York: Oxford University Press, 1958), p. 147.

175. Industrial labor in Argentina has been represented by the Confederación Général de Trabajo; agriculture by the Sociedád Rural Argentina; the national bourgeoisie by the Confederación Général Económica; and the international bourgeoisie by the Unión Industrial Argentina. See Davide Erro, "The Crisis of Argentine Political Economy and the Breakdown of Corporatism, 1966–1989" (Senior thesis, Princeton University, Woodrow Wilson School, 1991), p. 21, which notes that elite political alliances have been formed between agriculture and the international bourgeoisie, between the two bourgeoisies, and even between labor and the national bourgeoisie—but seldom for long in different combinations. Ethnic groups have often (e.g., in nineteenth- and twentieth-century American cities) been organized politically in a manner that strongly resembles corporatism.

176. See information about the periodic national economic conference that sets PRC localities' remittances, in Chapter 1.2 above. Much further information is in Ding Xueliang, *The Decline of Communism in China: Legitimacy Crisis, 1977–1989* (Cambridge: Cambridge University Press, 1994).

177. The author's formulation of these ideas came partly from one of his graduate students, Zheng Yongnian.

178. The literature on these subjects is huge, and there is no space or need here to summarize the relevant works by writers such as Nancy Bermeo, David Collier, Albert Hirschman, Juan Linz, Abraham Lowenthal, Guillermo O'Donnell, Philippe Schmitter, Paul Sigmund, Alfred Stepan, and Arturo Valenzuela. A partial but interesting statement, by one of the major comparativists who uses such ideas for policy, is Arend Lijphart,

"Consociation and Federation: Conceptual and Empirical Links," *Canadian Journal of Political Science* 12:3 (September 1979), pp. 499–515, with the immediately following "Comment" by Kenneth D. McRae, pp. 517–22.

179. See Samuel P. Huntington, *The Third Wave.*

180. See Zheng Yongnian, "Institutional Change, Local Developmentalism, and Economic Growth: The Making of a Semi-Federal System in Reform China" (Ph.D. dissertation, Politics Department, Princeton University, 1995).

181. "Persuasion" is the word here because, particularly in many southern provinces, Han migrants since the Tang dynasty absorbed (by religion, language, kinship system, and intermarriage) rather than liquidated other ethnicities. This process still proceeds apace in provinces such as Guangxi, Yunnan, and Inner Mongolia. Tibet is certainly the largest exception. It is followed by Xinjiang, whose habitable nonurban areas are the domain of Uighurs and Kazakhs, speaking closely related Turkic languages. Many Tibetans and Turkic Muslims, despite Beijing's hopes, have shown little inclination to be persuaded that they are Chinese.

182. A classic is Philippe C. Schmitter, "Still the Century of Corporatism?"

183. Schmitter's conclusion about the "century of corporatism" being a short one—and his suggestion, in his last sentence, that the next century may be "that of syndicalism"—meshes well with the upshot of this book about China. Most important about this analysis is the single dimension that it explicitly omits: whether the state or other (local or functional) units most crucially constitute the regime. See Philippe C. Schmitter, "Still the Century of Corporatism?" p. 98.

184. Hitler's votes came largely from rural Germans who thought that their communities had been hurt by modernization, by Jews, and by foreign countries that imposed the Versailles treaty. In Algeria's first free election in 1991, the Islamic Salvation Front won a majority of the votes—to the embarrassment of democrats throughout the world. Other recent cases might have included Le Pen in France and Duke in Louisiana, except that they did not win.

185. Contrast this with Andrew Walder, *Communist Neo-Traditionalism: Work and Authority in Chinese Industry* (Berkeley: University of California Press, 1986), and Barrett L. McCormick, *Political Reform in Post-Mao China: Democracy and Bureaucracy in a Leninist State* (Berkeley: University of California Press, 1990). These books may have underestimated the power of forces likely to alter Chinese politics.

186. Frederic Wakeman Jr., "The Chinese Mirror," pp. 208–19.

187. Joseph Stilwell and John S. Service tried to fill in this picture, but their efforts were unavailing. See Barbara Tuchman, *Stilwell and the American Experience in China, 1911–45* (New York: Bantam, 1971).

188. The presentation here schematizes Linz's ideas, in his nearly book-length essay "Authoritarian and Totalitarian Regimes," in *Handbook of Political Science*, vol. 3, Fred Greenstein and Nelson Polsby, eds.; the quotations here and below are on pp. 191, 264, 266, and 273–74.

189. See *Alexis de Tocqueville,* John Stone and Stephen Mennell, eds., p. 266.

190. See the attempt in Samuel P. Huntington, *The Third Wave.*

191. Liu Yia-Ling, "Reform from Below: The Private Economy and Local Politics in Wenzhou," *China Quarterly* 130 (June 1992), p. 313.

192. On the actual history, see Paul Preston, *The Triumph of Democracy in Spain* (London: Methuen, 1986); Raymond Carr and Juan Pablo Fusi, *Spain: Dictatorship to Democracy* (London: George Allen & Unwin, 1981); Kenneth Maxwell, ed., *Portugal in the 1980s: Dilemmas of Democratic Consolidation* (New York: Greenwood, 1986); and the interviews in Hugo Gil Ferreira and Michael W. Marshall, *Portugal's Revolution: Ten Years On* (Cambridge: Cambridge University Press, 1986).

193. This change of rank does not have any connection—or at least none that is obvious—to China's large population. See United Nations Development Program, *Human Development Report, 1991* (New York: Oxford University Press, 1991), p. 120, which generally uses statistics from 1990. Mahbub ul-Haq, the Pakistani economist behind this report, has presented a nice intellectual challenge to the premises of the similar annual development report from the World Bank, which computes its figures in ways less relevant to political analysis.

194. The socioeconomic conditions for democracy in Hong Kong, which has only one-two-hundredth of China's population but more than one-eighth of its wealth or cultural influence, place that small territory twenty-fifth on the HDI list. Every political unit in the world with a higher HDI is a clearly stable democracy with a good record on human rights. (So are many countries with much lower HDI ratings than Hong Kong has.) These statistics preclude any serious argument that Hong Kong lacks the socioeconomic makings for democracy. United Nations Development Program, *Human Development Report*, p. 119.

195. For more, see E. E. Schattschneider, *The Semi-Sovereign People.*

196. See also James Madison, "Federalist Paper No. 10," in *The Federalist Papers,* ed. Roy P. Fairfield (Garden City, NY: Anchor, 1961), pp. 16–23.

197. See Aaron Friedberg, *Creating Power: The American State and the Conduct of the Cold War* (Princeton: Princeton University Press, 1996).

198. John Stone and Stephen Mennell, eds., *Alexis de Tocqueville,* p. 60; and, for the later quotation, p. 74.

199. *Aiguo,* "love of country," rhymes with *waiguo,* "abroad." Joan Grant, *Worm-Eaten Hinges: Tensions and Turmoil in Shanghai, 1988–89, Events Leading Up to Tiananmen Square* (Melbourne: Hyland House, 1991), p. 126.

200. The author was at several of these demonstrations, in 1989, 1990, 1991, and 1994. The slogan "*Zhongguo ren bu da Zhongguo ren!*" appeared at each. This is unexceptionable, as far as it goes. Could intellectuals have missed its implication about violence to others?

201. Seweryn Bialer, *Stalin's Successors,* p. 101.

Sources

Bibliography

Most books cited in the footnotes are on the list below. Chinese newspapers and journals, especially those on the roster of abbreviations near the Table of Contents, were essential for this study because these are often less thoroughly censored than books. Other essential bases for this study were interviews in Shanghai, Beijing, Hong Kong, Taipei, Princeton, and elsewhere.

Many materials that would have been of great relevance to this study are available only in Chinese publications that are limited-circulation (*neibu*). But daily newspapers sometimes provide materials on topics similar to those covered in confidential sources. The contemporary China field is in any case not plagued by a dearth of materials; it suffers on the contrary from a surfeit. No one will ever read all the good materials about the Shanghai delta from the 1970s into the 1990s, because there are far too many.

Materials in languages other than Chinese

Aberle, D.F., et al. "The Functional Prerequisites of a Society." Indianapolis: Bobbs-Merrill reprint, 1966; from *Ethics* 60, pp. 100–110.

Aijmer, Göran, ed. *Leadership on the China Coast*. London and Malmö: Curzon Press for the Scandinavian Institute of Asian Studies, 1984.

Almond, Gabriel A., and James S. Coleman, eds. *The Politics of the Developing Areas*. Princeton: Princeton University Press, 1960.

Almond, Gabriel A., and G. Bingham Powell, Jr. *Comparative Politics: A Developmental Approach*. Boston: Little, Brown, 1966.

Almond, Gabriel A., and Sidney Verba. *The Civic Culture*. Princeton: Princeton University Press, 1963.

Anagnost, Ann S. "The Beginning and End of an Emperor: A Counterrepresentation of the State." *Modern China* 11:2 (April 1985), pp. 147–76.

Anderson, Benedict. *Imagined Communities: Reflections on the Origin and Spread of Nationalism,* rev. ed. London: Verso, 1991.

Anderson, Benedict. "Studies of the Thai State: The State of Thai Studies," consulted in manuscript but published in Eliezer B. Ayal, ed., *The Study of Thailand.* Athens, OH: Ohio University, Southeast Asia Program, 1978.

Andrews, Julia F. *Painters and Politics in the People's Republic of China, 1949–1979.* Berkeley: University of California Press, 1994.

Antier, Gilles. "New Planning Trends in Shanghai." Paris: Institut d'Aménagement d'Urbanisme de la Région d'Ile-de-France, 1993.

Arnold, Walter. "Japan and the Development of Shanghai's Pudong Area." *Pacific Review* 5:3 (September 1992), pp. 241–49.

Atkinson, A.B. *Unemployment Insurance and Economic Reform in China.* London: Development Research Program, 1990.

Aubert, Claude. "The Agricultural Crisis in China at the End of the 1980s." In Jørgen Delman et al., eds., *Remaking Peasant China: Problems of Rural Development and Institutions at the Start of the 1990s.* Aarhus: Aarhus University Press, 1990, pp. 16–37.

Ayer, A.J. *Language, Truth, and Logic.* New York: Dover, 1952.

Bachman, David M. *Bureaucracy, Economy, and Leadership in China: The Institutional Origins of the Great Leap Forward.* Cambridge: Cambridge University Press, 1991.

Bachman, David M. *Chen Yun and the Chinese Political System.* Berkeley: Center for Chinese Studies, University of California, 1985.

Bakken, Børge. "Crime, Juvenile Delinquency, and Deterrence Policy in China." *Australian Journal of Chinese Affairs* 30 (July 1993), pp. 29–60.

Bakvis, Herman, and William M. Chandler, eds. *Federalism and the Role of the State.* Toronto: University of Toronto Press, 1987.

Barlow, Tani E., and Donald M. Lowe. *Teaching China's Lost Generation: Foreign Experts in the People's Republic of China* [at the Shanghai Foreign Languages College]. San Francisco: China Books and Periodicals, 1987.

Barmé, Geremie. "Liu Dahong: Artist Laureate of China's Reform." *Far Eastern Economic Review* (March 4, 1993), p. 60.

Barmé, Geremie, and Bennett Lee, eds. *The Wounded: New Stories of the Cultural Revolution.* Hong Kong: Joint Publishing Company, 1979.

Barmé, Geremie, and John Minford, eds. *Seeds of Fire: Chinese Voices of Conscience.* New York: Noonday, 1989.

Bartke, Wolfgang, ed. *Who's Who in the People's Republic of China.* Armonk: M.E. Sharpe, 1981.

Bastid, Marianne, and Ruth Hayhoe, eds. *China's Education and the Industrialized World.* Armonk: M.E. Sharpe, 1987.

Bates, Robert H. *Markets and States in Tropical Africa: The Political Basis of Agricultural Policies.* Berkeley and Los Angeles: University of California Press, 1981.

Baum, Richard. *Burying Mao: Chinese Politics in the Age of Deng Xiaoping.* Princeton: Princeton University Press, 1994.

Baum, Richard, ed. *Reform and Reaction in Post-Mao China: The Road to Tiananmen.* New York: Routledge, 1991.

Bei Dao (Zhao Zhenkai). *Notes from the City of the Sun.* Bonnie S. MacDougall, trans. Ithaca: Cornell University China-Japan Program, 1983.

Belden, Jack. *China Shakes the World.* New York: Monthly Review Press, 1970.

Belich, James. *Victorian Interpretation of Racial Conflict: The Maori, the British, and the New Zealand Wars.* Montreal: McGill-Queen's University Press, 1989.

Benda, Julien. *The Treason of the Intellectuals* (La trahison des clercs). R. Aldington, trans. New York: Norton, 1969 [1928].

Bendix, John, Bertel Ollman, Bartholomew Sparrow, and Timothy Mitchell. "Going Beyond the State." *American Political Science Review* 86:4 (December 1992), pp. 1007–20.

Bendix, Reinhard. *Max Weber: An Intellectual Portrait.* Garden City, NY: Doubleday, 1960.

Bendix, Reinhard. *Nation-Building and Citizenship.* New York: Wiley, 1964.

Bendix, Reinhard, John Bendix, and Norman Furniss. "Reflections on Modern Western States and Civil Societies." *Research in Political Sociology* 3 (1987), pp. 1–38.

Benewick, Robert, and Paul Wingrove, eds. *Reforming the Revolution: China in Transition.* Basingstoke, UK: Macmillan, 1988.

Bennett, Gordon A., and Ronald N. Montaperto. *Red Guard: The Political Biography of Dai Hsiao-ai.* Garden City, NY: Doubleday, 1972.

Bergère, Marie-Claire. " 'The Other China': Shanghai from 1919 to 1949." In Christopher Howe, ed., *Shanghai: Revolution and Development in an Asian Metropolis.* Cambridge: Cambridge University Press, 1981, pp. 1–34.

Bernstein, Thomas. *Up to the Mountains and Down to the Villages: The Transfer of Youth from Urban to Rural China.* New Haven: Yale University Press, 1977.

Berry, Chris, ed. *Perspectives on Chinese Cinema.* Ithaca: Cornell University China-Japan Program, 1985.

Bertrand, Jacques. "Compliance, Resistance, and Trust: Peasants and the State in Indonesia." Ph.D. dissertation, Princeton University, Politics Department, 1995.

Best, Geoffrey, ed. *The Permanent Revolution: The French Revolution and Its Legacy, 1989–1989.* London: Fontana, 1988.

Bialer, Seweryn. *Stalin's Successors.* Cambridge: Cambridge University Press, 1980.

Binder, Leonard, James S. Coleman, Joseph LaPalombara, Lucian W. Pye, Sidney Verba, and Myron Weiner. *Crises and Sequences in Political Development.* Princeton: Princeton University Press, 1971.

Birnbaum, H. Philip, and Gilbert Y. Y. Wong. "Cultural Values of Managers in the People's Republic of China and Hong Kong." Hong Kong: University of Hong Kong, Department of Management Studies Working Paper 13, n.d.

Blecher, Marc, and Vivienne Shue. *Tethered Deer: Government and Economy in a Chinese County.* Stanford: Stanford University Press, 1995.

Blendon, Robert J. "Can China's Health Care Be Transplanted Without China's Economic Policies?" *New England Journal of Medicine* 300, pp. 1453–58.

Bond, Michael Harris. *The Psychology of the Chinese People.* Hong Kong: Oxford University Press, 1986.

Bonnin, M., and Y. Chevrier. "Autonomy During the Post-Mao Era." *China Quarterly* 123 (1991), pp. 569–93.

Boorman, Scott. *The Protracted Game: A Wei-ch'i Interpretation of Maoist Revolutionary Strategy.* New York: Oxford University Press, 1969.

Bosco, Joseph. "*Yi Guan Dao*: 'Heterodoxy' and Popular Religion in Taiwan." Unpublished manuscript.

Bosco, Joseph. "Faction Versus Ideology: Mobilization Strategies in Taiwan's Elections." *China Quarterly* 137 (March 1994).

Bosco, Joseph. "Taiwan Factions: *Guanxi,* Patronage, and the State in Local Politics." *Ethnology* 31:2 (1992), pp. 157–83.

Brady, James P. *Justice and Politics in People's China: Legal Order or Continuing Revolution?* New York: Academic Press, 1982.

Bramall, Chris. "Origins of the Agricultural 'Miracle': Some Evidence from Sichuan." *China Quarterly* 143 (September 1995), pp. 731–55.

Brewer, John, and John Styles, eds. *An Ungovernable People: The English and Their Law in the Seventeenth and Eighteenth Centuries.* London: Hutchinson, 1980.

Bunce, Valerie. *Do New Leaders Make a Difference? Executive Succession and Public Policy Under Capitalism and Socialism.* Princeton: Princeton University Press, 1981.

Bureau of Shanghai Urban Planning and Building Administration, ed. *The Comprehensive Plan of Shanghai.* [No title page, but Shanghai: Bureau of Shanghai Urban Planning and Building Administration, apparently 1986.]

Burke, Edmund. *Reflections on the Revolution in France.* Conor Cruise O'Brien, ed. London: Penguin, 1968.

Burns, John P. "China's *Nomenklatura* System." *Problems of Communism* (September–October 1987), pp. 30–41.

Burns, John P. "Rural Guangdong's Second Economy." *China Quarterly* 88 (December 1981), pp. 629–44.

Burns, John P., and Stanley Rosen, eds. *Policy Conflicts in Post-Mao China.* Armonk: M.E. Sharpe, 1986.

Burton, Charles. *Political and Social Change in China Since 1978.* Westport, CT: Greenwood Press, 1990.

Butler, Steven. *Agricultural Mechanization in China: The Administrative Impact.* New York: East Asian Institute, Columbia University, 1978.

Byrd, William A. *China's Financial System: The Changing Role of Banks.* Boulder: Westview, 1983.

Byrd, William A., and Lin Qingsong, eds. *China's Rural Industry: Structure, Development, and Reform.* Washington: World Bank, 1990.

Byres, T.J., and Peter Nolan. *Inequality: China and India Compared, 1950–70.* Milton Keynes, UK: Open University, 1976.

Calder, Kent E. *Crisis and Compensation: Public Policy and Political Stability in Japan, 1949–1986.* Princeton: Princeton University Press, 1988.

Calder, Kent E. *Strategic Capitalism: Private Business and Public Purpose in Japanese Industrial Finance.* Princeton: Princeton University Press, 1993.

Calder, Kent E. "The State and Selective Credit Programs in Japan, 1946–1986." Draft of book manuscript; Woodrow Wilson School, Princeton University, 1988.

Cannon, Terry, and Alan Jenkins, eds. *The Geography of Contemporary China: The Impact of Deng Xiaoping's Decade.* London: Routledge, 1990.

Carr, Raymond, and Juan Pablo Fusi. *Spain: Dictatorship to Democracy,* 2d ed. London: George Allen and Unwin, 1981.

Carrère d'Encausse, Hélène. *Stalin: Order Through Terror.* London: Longman, 1981.

Chai, Joseph C.H., and Chi-Keung Leung, eds. *China's Economic Reforms.* Hong Kong: University of Hong Kong, Centre of Asian Studies, 1987.

Chan, Anita. *Children of Mao: Personality Development and Political Activism in the Red Guard Generation.* Seattle: University of Washington Press, 1985.

Chan, Anita. "Dispelling Misconceptions about the Red Guard Movement: The Necessity to Re-Examine Cultural Revolution Factionalism and Periodization." *Journal of Contemporary China* 1:1 (1992), pp. 61–85.

Chan, Anita. "Revolution or Corporatism? Workers and Trade Unions in Post-Mao China." In David S.G. Goodman and Beverley Hooper, eds., *China's Quiet Revolution: New Interactions Between State and Society.* New York: St. Martin's, 1994, pp. 162–90.

Chan, Anita, Richard Madsen, and Jonathan Unger. *Chen Village.* Berkeley: University of California Press, 1984.

Chan, Anita, Stanley Rosen, and Jonathan Unger, eds. *On Socialist Democracy and the Chinese Legal System.* Armonk: M.E. Sharpe, 1985.

Chan, Joseph. "The Asian Challenge to Universal Human Rights: A Philosophical Appraisal." In James T. H. Tang, ed., *Human Rights and International Relations in the Asia Pacific Region.* London: Pinter, 1995.

Chan Ka Yan. "The Role of Migration in China's Regional Development: A Local Study of Southern China." M.Phil. thesis, University of Hong Kong, Department of Geography, 1990.

Chang, Arnold. *Painting in the People's Republic of China: The Politics of Style.* Boulder: Westview, 1980.

Chang Ta-kuang. "The Making of the Chinese Bankruptcy Law: A Study in the Chinese Legislative Process." *Harvard International Law Review* 28:2 (Spring 1987), pp. 333–72.

Chen Jialing. *Hua* (Transformation). Hong Kong: Plum Blossoms, 1990.

Chen, Nancy N. "Urban Spaces and Experiences of Qigong." In Deborah S. Davis et al., eds., *Urban Spaces in Contemporary China.* New York: Cambridge University Press, 1995, pp. 347–61.

Chen Ta. *Chinese Migrations: With Special Reference to Labor Conditions.* New York: Paragon, 1967 (orig. 1923).

Cheng Hsiao-shih. *Party-Military Relations in the PRC and Taiwan: Paradoxes of Control.* Boulder: Westview, 1990.

Cheng Kai Ming. "Reform in the Financing of Education in Mainland China." *Chinese Education: A Journal of Translations* 25:2–4 (1992), three whole issues.

Cheng Xiaonong. "The Structure of Economic Growth in China: An Approach to Measuring the Contribution of the Public and Non-Public Sectors, and Some Estimations." Unpublished paper, Princeton University, 1993.

Chesneaux, Jean. *The Chinese Labor Movement, 1919–1927.* Hope M. Wright, trans. Stanford: Stanford University Press, 1968.

Child, John, and Xu Xinzhong. "The Communist Party's Role in Enterprise Leadership at the High Water of China's Economic Reform." Beijing: China-EC Management Institute Working Paper, September 1989.

Childs, John. *The Army of Charles II.* London: Routledge & Kegan Paul, 1976.

Chirot, Daniel, ed. *The Crisis of Leninism and the Decline of the Left: The Revolutions of 1989.* Seattle: University of Washington Press, 1991.

Chomiak, Theodora B. "First Government, Then Power: The Lviv [L'vov] City Council, 1990." Senior thesis, Princeton University, Politics Department, 1991.

Chow, Gregory C. *The Chinese Economy.* New York: Harper & Row, 1985.

Chow, Gregory C. *Understanding China's Economy.* Singapore: World Scientific Press, 1994.

Chui, Victor Chi-leung. "Chinese Perception of Organization and Authority." M.B.A. thesis, University of Hong Kong, Department of Management Sciences, 1987.

Clark, Paul. "Official Reactions to Modern Art in China Since the Beijing Massacre." *Pacific Affairs* 65:3 (Fall 1992), pp. 334–52.

Clark, Paul. *Chinese Cinema: Culture and Politics Since 1949.* Cambridge: Cambridge University Press, 1987.

Clarke, Donald C. "Dispute Resolution in China." *Journal of Chinese Law* 5:2 (Fall 1991), pp. 245–96.

Clarke, Donald C. "Regulation and Its Discontents: Understanding Economic Law in China." *Stanford Journal of International Law* 28:2 (1992), pp. 283–322.

Clarke, Donald C. "What's Law Got to Do with It? Legal Institutions and Economic Reform in China." *UCLA Pacific Basin Law Journal* 10:1 (Fall 1991), pp. 1–76.

Clavel, Alex B. "Law and Authoritarianism in China, 1978–1995." Senior thesis, Princeton University, Department of East Asian Studies, 1995.

Cleverly, John. *The Schooling of China: Tradition and Modernity in Chinese Education.* Sydney: George Allen and Unwin, 1985.

Coady, Dave, et al. *Production, Marketing, and Pricing of Vegetables in China's Cities.* London: Development Research Program, 1990.

Coale, Ansley J., et al. "Recent Trends in Fertility and Nuptiality in China." *Science* 251 (1991), pp. 389–93.

Coble, Parks M., Jr. *The Shanghai Capitalist Class and the Nationalist Government, 1927–37.* Cambridge: Harvard University East Asian Studies Center and Harvard University Press, 1986.

Cohen, Jerome Alan. "Chinese Law: At the Crossroads." *China Quarterly* 53 (January–March 1973), pp. 138–43.

Cohen, Joan Lebold. *The New Chinese Painting, 1949–1986.* New York: H.N. Abrams, 1987.

Cohen, Michael, et al. "A Garbage Can Model of Organizational Choice." *Administrative Science Quarterly* (March 1972), pp. 1–25.

Cohen, Paul. "The Post-Mao Reforms in Historical Perspective." *Journal of Asian Studies* 47:3 (August 1988), pp. 518–40.

Cohen, Stephen F. *Rethinking the Soviet Experience: Politics and History Since 1917.* New York: Oxford University Press, 1985.

Coleman, D.C. *The Economy of England, 1450–1750.* Oxford: Oxford University Press, 1977.

Conner, Alison W. "To Get Rich Is Precarious: Regulation of Private Enterprise in the People's Republic of China." *Journal of Chinese Law* 5:1 (Spring 1991), pp. 1–57.

Connor, Walter D. *Deviance in Soviet Society: Crime, Delinquency, and Alcoholism.* New York: Columbia University Press, 1972.

Cook, Chris, and John Stevenson. *Modern European History, 1763–1985.* New York: Longman, 1987.

Cornelius, Wayne A. *Politics and the Migrant Poor in Mexico City.* Stanford: Stanford University Press, 1975.

Coser, Lewis. *The Functions of Social Conflict.* New York: Free Press, 1956.

Croll, Elisabeth. *Changing Identities of Chinese Women: Rhetoric, Experience, and Self-Perception in Twentieth-century China.* Hong Kong: Hong Kong University Press, 1995.

Cromer, Alan. *Uncommon Sense: The Heretical Nature of Science.* New York: Oxford University Press, 1993.

Cui Zhiyuan. "Getting the Prices and Property Rights Wrong? The Chinese Reform in the Schumpeterian Perspective and Beyond." In Gan Yang and Cui Zhiyuan, eds., *China: A Reformable System?* New York: Oxford University Press, forthcoming.

Cumings, Bruce. *The Origins of the Korean War.* Princeton: Princeton University Press, 1990.

Dahl, Robert A. *Modern Political Analysis.* Englewood Cliffs, NJ: Prentice-Hall, 1963.

Dahl, Robert A. *Polyarchy.* New Haven: Yale University Press, 1971.

Dahrendorf, Ralf. *Class and Class Conflict in Industrial Society.* London: Routledge & Kegan Paul, 1959.

Dai Houying. *Stones of the Wall.* London: Sceptre, 1987.

Dalai Lama (Tenzin Gyatso). *Freedom in Exile: The Autobiography of the Dalai Lama.* New York: HarperCollins, 1990.

Daniels, Robert V. *Soviet Communism from Reform to Collapse.* Lexington, MA: Heath, 1995.

Darnton, Robert. *The Great Cat Massacre and Other Episodes in French Cultural History.* New York: Basic Books, 1984.

David, Cristina C., and Keijiro Otsuka, eds. *Modern Rice Technology and Income Distribution in Asia.* Boulder: Lynne Rienner, 1994.

Davidson, Donald. *Essays on Actions and Events.* Oxford: Oxford University Press, 1980.

Davis, Deborah S. "Housing and Family Life in Shanghai." *China Update* 11:3 (Fall 1991), pp. 8–13.

Davis, Deborah S., and Ezra Vogel, eds. *Chinese Society on the Eve of Tiananmen: The Impact of Reform.* Cambridge: Harvard Council on East Asian Studies, 1990.

Davis, Deborah S., Richard Kraus, Barry Naughton, and Elizabeth Perry, eds. *Urban Spaces in Contemporary China: The Potential for Autonomy and Community in Post-Mao China.* Cambridge: Cambridge University Press, 1993.

deBary, William Theodore. *The Liberal Tradition in China.* New York: Columbia University Press, 1983.

Deng Xiaoping. *Fundamental Issues in Present-Day China.* Beijing: Foreign Languages Press, 1987.

Deng Xiaoping. *Selected Works of Deng Xiaoping, 1975–1982.* Beijing: Foreign Languages Press, 1984.

Derbyshire, Ian. *Politics in China: From Mao to Deng.* Cambridge: Chambers, 1987.

Des Forges, Roger, et al., eds. *China: The Crisis of 1989, Origins & Implications.* Buffalo: Council on International Studies, State University of New York, 1990.

Deutsch, Karl. *The Nerves of Government: Models of Political Communication and Control.* Glencoe, IL: Free Press, 1963.

Dicker, Richard. "A Law for Change—With Loopholes." *Human Rights Tribune* 3:2 (Summer 1992), pp. 7–9.

Dikötter, Frank. *The Discourse of Race in Modern China.* Stanford: Stanford University Press, 1992.

Ding Xueliang. *The Decline of Communism in China: The Legitimacy Crisis, 1979–1989.* New York: Cambridge University Press, 1994.

Dittmer, Lowell. "Ideology and Organization in Post-Mao China." *Asian Survey* 24:3 (March 1984), pp. 349–69.

Domes, Jürgen. *Socialism in the Chinese Countryside: Rural Societal Policies in the People's Republic of China, 1949–1979.* Margritta Wendling, trans. London: C. Hurst, 1980.

Donnithorne, Audrey. "China's Cellular Economy: Some Trends Since the Cultural Revolution." *China Quarterly* 52 (October–December 1972), pp. 605–19.

Donnithorne, Audrey. *China's Economic System.* New York: Praeger, 1967.

Dorfman, Robert, Paul A. Samuelson, and Robert Solow. *Linear Programming and Economic Analysis.* New York: McGraw-Hill, 1958.

Doyle, Michael. "Kant, Liberal Legacies, and Foreign Affairs." *Philosophy and Public Affairs* 12:3–4 (Summer and Fall 1983), pp. 205–35 and 323–52.

Dreyer, June Teufel. "The Demobilization of PLA Servicemen and their Reintegration into Civilian Life." In June Dreyer, ed., *China's Defense and Foreign Policy.* New York: Paragon, 1988, pp. 297–349.

Dreyfus, Hubert, and Paul Rabinow. *Michel Foucault: Beyond Structuralism and Hermeneutics,* 2d ed. Chicago: University of Chicago Press, 1983.

Dreze, J., and A. Sen. *Hunger and Public Action.* Oxford: Clarendon Press, 1989.

Du Ruiqing. *Chinese Higher Education.* New York: St. Martin's Press, 1992.

Duara, Prasenjit. *Culture, Power, and the State: Rural North China, 1900–1942.* Stanford: Stanford University Press, 1988.

Duke, Michael. *Blooming and Contending: Chinese Literature of the Post-Mao Era.* Bloomington: Indiana University Press, 1985.

Dutton, Michael R. *Policing and Punishment in China: From Patriarchy to "the People".* Cambridge: Cambridge University Press, 1992.

Duverger, Maurice. *Political Parties: Their Organization and Activity in the Modern State.* B. and R. North, trans. New York: Wiley, 1954.

Dworkin, Ronald M. *Taking Rights Seriously.* London: Duckworth, 1978.

Dye, Thomas. *American Federalism: Competition Among Governments.* Lexington, MA: Heath, 1990.

Eberstadt, Nick. "Population and Economic Growth." *Wilson Quarterly* 10:5 (1986), pp. 95–127.

Eckstein, Harry. "Case Study and Theory in Political Science." In F. Greenstein and N. Polsby, eds., *Handbook of Political Science,* vol. 7. Reading, MA: Addison-Wesley, 1975, pp. 79–137.

Eckstein, Harry. "The Idea of Political Development: From Dignity to Efficiency." In Ikuô Kabashima and Lynn T. White III, eds., *Political System and Change.* Princeton: Princeton University Press, 1986, pp. 311–46.

Eckstein, Harry, and David Apter, eds. *Comparative Politics: A Reader.* Glencoe, IL: Free Press, 1963.

Eftimiades, Nicholas. *Chinese Intelligence Operations.* Annapolis, MD: Naval Institute Press, 1994.

Eisenstadt, S.N., and René Marchand, eds. *Political Clientelism, Patronage, and Development.* Beverly Hills: Sage, 1981.

Elkins, David, and Richard Simeon. "A Cause in Search of Its Effect, or What Does Political Culture Explain?" *Comparative Politics* 11 (January 1979), pp. 127–46.

Engelstein, Laura (with reactions from Rudy Koshar and Jan Goldstein, and a reply by Engelstein). "*AHR* Forum; Combined Underdevelopment: Discipline and the Law in Imperial and Soviet Russia." *American Historical Review* (April 1993), pp. 338–81.

Erro, Davide. "The Crisis of Argentine Political Economy and the Breakdown of Corporatism, 1966–1989." Senior thesis, Princeton University, Woodrow Wilson School, 1991.

Etzioni, Amitai. *A Comparative Analysis of Complex Organizations.* New York: Wiley, 1961.

Evans, Grant. *Lao Peasants Under Socialism.* New Haven: Yale University Press, 1990.

Evans, Peter. *Dependent Development: The Alliance of Multinational, State, and Local Capital in Brazil.* Princeton: Princeton University Press, 1979.

Evans, Peter B., Dietrich Rueschemeyer, and Theda Skocpol, eds. *Bringing the State Back In.* Cambridge: Cambridge University Press, 1985.

Fabre, Guilhem. "Le réveil de Shanghaï: Stratégies économiques 1949–2000" (The Awakening of Shanghai: Economic Strategies, 1949–2000). *Le courrier des pays de l'est,* no. 325 (January 1988), pp. 3–40.

Faligot, Roger, and Rémi Kauffer. *The Chinese Secret Service.* Christine Donougher, trans. London: Headline, 1989.

Faure, David. "The Lineage as a Cultural Invention: The Case of the Pearl River Delta." *Modern China* 15:1 (1989), pp. 4–36.

Fei Xiaotong. *Small Towns in China: Functions, Problems, and Prospects.* Beijing: New World Press, 1986.

Feinerman, James V. "Chinese Constitutionalism." Unpublished paper, 1993.

Fenwick, Ann. "Equity Joint Ventures in the People's Republic of China: An Assessment of the First Five Years." *Business Lawyer* 40:3 (May 1985), pp. 839–78.

Fenwick, Ann. "Evaluating China's Special Economic Zones." *International Tax and Business Lawyer* 2:2 (Fall 1984), pp. 376–97.

Fewsmith, Joseph. *Dilemmas of Reform in China: Political Conflict and Economic Debate.* Armonk: M.E. Sharpe, 1994.

Fewsmith, Joseph. "Review of Leninger's *Disan zhi yanjing kan Zhongguo* (Looking at China Through a Third Eye)." *Journal of Contemporary China* 7 (Fall 1994), pp. 100–104.

Field, Robert Michael, Nicholas R. Lardy, and John Philip Emerson. *Provincial Industrial Output in the People's Republic of China: 1949–75.* Washington: U.S. Department of Commerce, Bureau of Economic Analysis, 1976.

Field, Robert Michael, Kathleen McGlynn, and William Abnett. "Political Conflict and

Industrial Growth in China, 1965–77." In *Chinese Economy Post-Mao*, vol. 1. Washington: Government Printing Office, 1978, pp. 239–83.

Finnane, Antonia. "The Origins of Prejudice: The Malintegration of Subei in Late Imperial China." *Comparative Studies in Society and History* 35:2 (April 1993), pp. 211–38.

Fischer, David Hackett. *Albion's Seed: Four British Folkways in America*. New York: Oxford University Press, 1989.

Fisher, Richard D., and Jason Bruzdzinski, eds. *U.S. and Asia Statistical Handbook, 1993 Edition*. Washington DC: Heritage Foundation, 1993.

Fitzgerald, John. *Awakening China: Politics, Culture, and Class in the Nationalist Revolution*. Stanford: Stanford University Press, 1996.

Forster, Keith. "The Politics of Destabilization and Confrontation: The Campaign Against Lin Biao and Confucius in Zhejiang Province, 1974." *China Quarterly* 107 (September 1986), pp. 433–62.

Forster, Keith. *Rebellion and Factionalism in a Chinese Province: Zhejiang 1966–76*. Armonk: M.E. Sharpe, 1990.

Fortescue, William. *Revolution and Counter-Revolution in France, 1815–1852*. Oxford: Basil Blackwell, 1988.

Foster, Frances Hoar. "Codification in Post-Mao China." *American Journal of Comparative Law* 30 (Summer 1982), pp. 395–428.

Foucault, Michel. *Discipline and Punish: The Birth of the Prison*. New York: Pantheon, 1977.

Frankenstein, John. "The People's Republic of China: Arms Production, Industrial Strategy, and Problems of History." In Herbert Wulf, ed., *Arms Industry Limited*. Oxford: Oxford University Press, 1993, pp. 271–319.

Fransman, Martin. *Technology and Economic Development*. Boulder: Westview, 1986.

Friedberg, Aaron. *Creating Power: The American State and the Conduct of the Cold War*. Princeton: Princeton University Press, 1996.

Friedman, Edward. "Deng vs. the Peasantry: Recollectivization in the Countryside." *Problems of Communism* (September–October 1991), pp. 30–49.

Friedman, Edward. "Reconstructing China's National Identity: A Southern Alternative to Mao-Era Anti-Imperialist Nationalism." *Journal of Asian Studies* 53:1 (February 1994), pp. 67–87.

Friedman, Edward, Paul G. Pickowicz, and Mark Selden. *Chinese Village, Socialist State*. New Haven: Yale University Press, 1991.

Frolic, B. Michael. *Mao's People: Sixteen Portraits of Life in Revolutionary China*. Cambridge: Harvard University Press, 1980.

Fu Gangzhan et al. *Unemployment in Urban China: An Analysis of Survey Data from Shanghai*. London: Development Economics Research Programme, 1992.

Fu Poshek. *Passivity, Resistance, and Collaboration: Intellectual Choices in Occupied Shanghai, 1937–1945*. Stanford: Stanford University Press, 1993.

Fu Zhengyuan. "The Sociology of Political Science in the PRC." In D. Easton, J. Gunnell, and L. Graziano, eds., *The Development of Political Science: A Comparative Study*. London: Routledge, 1991, pp. 223–51.

Fuegi, John, et al., eds. *Brecht in Asia and Africa: The Brecht Yearboook XIV; Brecht in Asien und Afrika, Brecht-Jahrbuch XIV* (in English and German). Hong Kong: University of Hong Kong, Department of Comparative Literature, 1989.

Gallin, Bernard. *Hsin Hsing, Taiwan: A Chinese Village in Change*. Berkeley: University of California Press, 1966.

Gannon, Martin J., et al. *Understanding Global Cultures: Metaphorical Journeys Through 17 Countries*. Thousand Oaks, CA: Sage, 1994.

Gargan, Edward. *China's Fate: Reform & Repression, 1980–90*. New York: Doubleday, 1990.

Gates, Hill. *China's Motor: A Thousand Years of Petty Capitalism.* Ithaca: Cornell University Press, 1996.

Geertz, Clifford. *Agricultural Involution: The Processes of Ecological Change in Indonesia.* Berkeley: University of California Press, 1963.

Geertz, Clifford. *Islam Observed: Religious Development in Morocco and Indonesia.* New Haven: Yale University Press, 1968.

Geertz, Clifford. *Negara: The Theatre State in Nineteenth-Century Bali.* Princeton: Princeton University Press, 1980.

Geertz, Clifford. *The Interpretation of Cultures.* New York: Basic Books, 1973.

Gelatt, Timothy A. "Book Review." *China Law Reporter* 7: 3–4 (1993), pp. 231–41.

Gellner, Ernest. *Civil Society and Its Rivals.* New York: Penguin, 1994.

Gerschenkron, Alexander. *Bread and Democracy in Germany.* Berkeley: University of California Press, 1943.

Gerschenkron, Alexander. *Economic Backwardness in Historical Perspective: A Book of Essays.* Cambridge: Harvard University Press, 1962.

Gipouloux, François. *Les cent fleurs à l'usine: Agitation ouvière et crise du model sovietique en Chine, 1956–1957.* Paris: Ecole des hautes études en sciences sociales, 1986.

Gleick, James. *Chaos: Making a New Science.* New York: Penguin, 1987.

Gold, Thomas B. "Urban Private Business and Social Change." In Deborah Davis and Ezra Vogel, eds., *Chinese Society on the Eve of Tiananmen: The Impact of Reform.* Cambridge: Harvard University Press, 1990, pp. 157–78.

Goldblatt, Howard, ed. *Chinese Literature for the 1980s: The Fourth Congress of Writers and Artists.* Armonk: M.E. Sharpe, 1982.

Goldman, Merle. *China's Intellectuals: Advise and Dissent.* Cambridge: Harvard University Press, 1981.

Goldman, Merle. *Literary Dissent in Communist China.* Cambridge: Harvard University Press, 1967.

Goldman, Merle. *Sowing the Seeds of Democracy in China: Political Reform in the Era of Deng Xiaoping.* Cambridge: Harvard University Press, 1994.

Goldstein, Alice, and Guo Shenyang. "Temporary Migration in Shanghai and Beijing." *Studies in Comparative International Development* 27:2 (Summer 1992), pp. 39–56.

Goldstein, Alice, Sidney Goldstein, and Shenyang Guo. "Temporary Migrants in Shanghai Households, 1984." *Demography* 28:2 (1991), pp. 275–91.

Goldstein, Avery. *From Bandwagon to Balance-of-Power Politics: Structural Constraints and Politics in China, 1949–1978.* Stanford: Stanford University Press, 1991.

Goldstein, Sidney. "Forms of Mobility and Their Policy Implications: Thailand and China Compared." *Social Forces* 65:4 (1987), pp. 915–42.

Goldstein, Sidney, and Alice Goldstein. "Population Movement, Labor Force Absorption, and Urbanization in China." *Annals of the American Academy of Political and Social Science* 476 (1984), pp. 90–110.

Goldstein, Sidney, and Alice Goldstein. "Varieties of Population Mobility in Relation to Development in China." *Studies in Comparative International Development* 22:4 (1987–88), pp. 101–24.

Goldstein, Steven M. "Reforming Socialist Systems: Some Lessons of the Chinese Experience." *Studies in Comparative Communism* 21:2 (Summer 1988).

Goodman, David. *Beijing Street Voices: The Poetry and Politics of China's Democracy Movement.* London: Marion Boyars, 1981.

Goodman, David. *China's Regional Development.* London: Routledge, 1989.

Goodman, David, and Gerald Segal, eds. *China at Forty: Mid-Life Crisis?* Oxford: Clarendon Press, 1989.

Goodman, David, and Gerald Segal, eds. *China Deconstructs: Politics, Trade, and Regionalism.* London: Routledge, 1994.

Gorbachev, Mikhail. *Perestroika: New Thinking for Our Country and the World.* New edition. London: Fontana, 1988.

Gramsci, Antonio. *Letters from Prison.* Lynne Lawner, trans. New York: Harper and Row, 1973. Another edition is *Prison Notebooks.* New York: International Publishers, 1971.

Granick, David. "China's Multiple Labour Markets." *China Quarterly* (November–December 1991), pp. 269–89.

Granick, David. *Chinese State Enterprises: A Regional Property Rights Analysis.* Chicago: University of Chicago Press, 1990.

Granovetter, Mark. "Economic Action and Social Structure: The Problem of Embeddedness." *American Journal of Sociology* 91 (November 1985), pp. 481–510.

Grant, Joan. *Worm-eaten Hinges: Tensions and Turmoil in Shanghai, 1988–89, Events Leading Up to Tiananmen Square.* Melbourne: Hyland House, 1991.

Habermas, Jürgen. *Legitimation Crisis.* Boston: Beacon Press, 1973.

Habermas, Jürgen. *The Structural Transformation of the Public Sphere: An Inquiry into a Category of Bourgeois Society.* Cambridge, MA: MIT Press, 1989.

Habermas, Jürgen. *Toward a Rational Society: Student Protest, Science, and Politics.* Boston: Beacon Books, 1970.

Hall, Peter A. *Governing the Economy: The Politics of State Intervention in Britain and France.* New York: Oxford University Press, 1986.

Han Minzhu (pseud.), ed. *Cries for Democracy.* Princeton: Princeton University Press, 1990.

Hankiss, Elemér. *East European Alternatives.* Oxford: Clarendon Press, 1990.

Hansen, Chad. "Chinese Language, Chinese Philosophy, and 'Truth.' " *Journal of Asian Studies* 44:5 (May 1985), pp. 491–520.

Hansen, Chad. "Do Human Rights Apply to China? A Normative Analysis in Comparative Ethics." Unpublished paper, University of Hong Kong, Philosophy Department, 1994.

Harding, Harry. *China's Second Revolution: Reform After Mao.* Washington: Brookings Institution, 1987.

Harding, Harry. *A Fragile Relationship: The United States and China Since 1972.* Washington: Brookings, 1992.

Harrell, Stevan. "Men, Women, and Ghosts in Taiwanese Folk Religion." In Caroline Bynum, Stevan Harrell, and Paula Richman, eds., *Gender and Religion: On the Complexity of Symbols.* Boston: Beacon Press, 1986, pp. 97–116.

Harsanyi, J.C. "Rational-Choice Models of Political Behavior vs. Functionalist and Conformist Theories." *World Politics* 21:1 (July 1969), pp. 513–38.

Hayhoe, Ruth. *China's Universities and the Open Door.* Armonk: M.E. Sharpe, 1989.

Hays, Samuel P. *The Response to Industrialism, 1885–1914.* Chicago: University of Chicago Press, 1957.

Henriot, Christian, ed. *Shanghai dans les anneés 1980: études urbaines.* Lyon: Université Jean Moulin, Centre Rhônalpin de Recherche sur l'Extrême Orient Contemporain, 1989.

Hicks, George, ed. *The Broken Mirror: China After Tiananmen.* London: Longman, 1990.

Hill, Christopher. *Reformation to Industrial Revolution.* Harmondsworth, UK: Penguin, 1969.

Hirschman, Albert. *Exit, Voice, and Loyalty.* Cambridge, MA: Harvard University Press, 1970.

Ho, Samuel. *Rural China in Transition: Non-agricultural Development in Rural Jiangsu, 1978–90.* New York: Oxford University Press, 1994.

Ho, Samuel P.S., and Ralph Huenemann. *China's Open Door Policy: The Quest for Foreign Technology and Capital.* Vancouver: University of British Columbia Press, 1984.

Hobsbawm, Eric J. *Primitive Rebels.* Manchester: University of Manchester Press, 1959.

Hobsbawm, Eric J. *The Age of Revolution, 1789–1848.* New York: Mentor, 1962.

Hodder, Rupert N.W. *The Creation of Wealth in China.* London: Belhaven Press, 1992.

Hodder, Rupert N.W. "China's Industry—Horizontal Linkages in Shanghai." *Transactions of the Institute of British Geographers* 15 (1990), pp. 487–503.

Hodder, Rupert N.W. "Exchange and Reform in the Economy of Shanghai Municipality: Socialist Geography Under Reform." *Annals of the Association of American Geographers* 83:2 (1993), pp. 303–19.

Hong Kong Trade Union Education Centre. *A Moment of Truth: Workers' Participation in China's 1989 Democracy Movement and the Emergence of Independent Unions.* Hong Kong: Hong Kong Trade Union Education Centre, 1990.

Honig, Emily. *Creating Chinese Ethnicity: Subei People in Shanghai, 1850–1980.* New Haven: Yale University Press, 1992.

Hood, Marlowe. "Mystics, Ghosts, and Faith Healers." *Los Angeles Times Magazine,* April 19, 1992, pp. 20–35.

Hood, Marlowe. "On the Use and Abuse of the Print Media by China's Leaders During the 1980s." Paper for a conference on "Voices of China," University of Minnesota, 1991.

Horgan, John. "Can Science Explain Consciousness?" *Scientific American* 271:1 (July 1994), pp. 72–78.

Hosking, Geoffrey. *The Awakening of the Soviet Union.* Cambridge: Harvard University Press, 1990.

Hoston, Germaine A. *Marxism and the Crisis of Development in Prewar Japan.* Princeton: Princeton University Press, 1986.

Howard, Pat. *Breaking the Iron Rice Bowl: Prospects for Socialism in China's Countryside.* Armonk: M.E. Sharpe, 1988.

Howell, Jude. "The Poverty of Civil Society: Insights from China." University of East Anglia, School of Development Studies, 1993.

Hsieh Chiao-min. *Atlas of China.* New York: McGraw-Hill, 1973.

Hsu Kai-yu. *Literature of the People's Republic of China.* Bloomington: Indiana University Press, 1980.

Hu Hsien-chin. *The Common Descent Group in China and Its Functions.* New York: Viking Fund, 1948.

Hua Junwu. *Cartoons from Contemporary China.* Beijing: New World Press, 1989.

Hua Sheng, Zhang Xuejun, and Luo Xiaopeng. *China: From Revolution to Reform.* London: Macmillan, 1993.

Huang, Philip C.C. *The Peasant Family and Rural Development in the Yangzi Delta, 1350–1988.* Stanford: Stanford University Press, 1990.

Huang, Philip C.C. "The Paradigmatic Crisis in Chinese Studies: Paradoxes in Social and Economic History." *Modern China* 17:3 (July 1991), pp. 299–341.

Huang, Philip C.C. " 'Public Sphere'/'Civil Society' in China? The Third Realm Between State and Society." *Modern China* 19:2 (April 1993), pp. 216–40.

Huang Weixin. *Economic Integration as a Development Device: The Case of the EC and China.* Saarbrücken: Nijmegen Studies in Development, Breitenbach Verlag, 1992.

Huang Yasheng. "Information, Bureaucracy, and Economic Reforms in China and the Soviet Union." *World Politics* 47:1 (October 1994).

Hughes, H. Stuart. *Consciousness and Society.* New York: Vintage, 1961.

Huntington, Samuel H. "Political Development and Political Decay." In Ikuô Kabashima and Lynn T. White III, eds., *Political System and Change.* Princeton: Princeton University Press, 1986, pp. 95–139.

Huntington, Samuel P. *American Politics: The Promise of Disharmony.* Cambridge: Harvard University Press, 1981.

Huntington, Samuel P. *Political Order in Changing Societies.* New Haven: Yale University Press, 1968.

Huntington, Samuel P. *The Third Wave: Democratization in the Late Twentieth Century.* Norman: University of Oklahoma Press, 1991.

Huntington, Samuel P., and Joan M. Nelson. *No Easy Choice: Political Participation in Developing Countries.* Cambridge: Harvard University Press, 1976.

Hussain, Athar. *Chinese Enterprise Reforms.* London: Development Research Program, 1990.

Hussain, Athar, et al. *The Chinese Television Industry.* London: Development Research Program, 1990.

Hussain, Athar, and N. Stern. *On the Recent Increase in Death Rates in China.* London: Development Research Program, 1990.

Hutton, Ronald. *The Restoration: A Political and Religious History of England and Wales, 1658–1667.* Oxford: Clarendon Press, 1985.

Imai, Hiroyuki. "China's Business Cycles." *China Business Review* (January–February 1994), pp. 14–16.

Inkeles, Alex, and David Smith. *Becoming Modern: Individual Change in Six Developing Countries.* London: Heinemann, 1974.

Ishida Hiroshi. *Chûgoku nôson keizai no kiso kôzô: Shanhai kinkô nôson no kôgyôka to kindaika no ayumi* (Rural China in Transition: Experiences of Rural Shanghai toward Industrialization and Modernization). Kyôto: Kôyô Shobô, 1991.

Israel, Jonathan I., ed. *The Anglo-Dutch Moment: Essays on the Glorious Revolution and Its World Impact.* Cambridge: Cambridge University Press, 1991.

Jameson, Fredric. *The Political Unconscious: Narrative as a Socially Symbolic Act.* Ithaca: Cornell University Press, 1981.

Jane's Information Group. *China in Crisis: The Role of the Military.* Coulsdon, UK: Jane's Defense Data, 1989.

Jia Hao and Lin Zhimin, eds. *Changing Central-Local Relations in China.* Boulder: Westview, 1994.

Jing Jun. "The Working Press in China." Unpublished paper, 1985.

Joffe, Ellis. *The Chinese Army After Mao.* London: Weidenfield and Nicolson, 1987.

Johnson, Chalmers A. *Peasant Nationalism and Communist Power: The Emergence of Revolutionary China, 1937–1945.* Stanford: Stanford University Press, 1962.

Johnson, Chalmers A. *Revolutionary Change.* Boston: Little, Brown, 1966.

Johnson, Kay. "Chinese Orphanages: Saving China's Abandoned Girls." *Australian Journal of Chinese Affairs* 30 (July 1993), pp. 61–87.

Johnston, Tess, and Deke Erh. *A Last Look: Western Architecture in Old Shanghai.* Hong Kong: Old China Hand Press, 1993.

Jones, Andrew F. *Like a Knife: Ideology and Genre in Contemporary Chinese Popular Music.* Ithaca: Cornell East Asia Series, 1992.

Jones, J.R., ed. *The Restored Monarchy, 1660–1668.* London: Macmillan, 1979.

Jose, Nicholas. "Next Wave Art." *Art and Asia Pacific Quarterly* 1 (1993), pp. 25–30.

Joseph, William, Christine Wong, and David Zweig, eds. *New Perspectives on the Cultural Revolution.* Cambridge: Harvard University Press, 1991.

Jowitt, Kenneth. "An Organizational Approach to the Study of Political Cultures in Marxist-Leninist Systems." *American Political Science Review* 68:3 (September 1974), pp. 1171–88.

Jowitt, Kenneth. "Soviet Neo-traditionalism: The Political Corruption of a Leninist Regime." *Soviet Studies* 35:3 (July 1983), pp. 275–97.

Jowitt, Kenneth. *New World Disorder: The Leninist Extinction.* Berkeley: University of California Press, 1992.

Kahneman, Daniel. "New Challenges to the Rationality Assumption." *Journal of Institutional and Theoretical Economics* 150:1 (1994), pp. 18–36.

Kao Mayching, ed. *Twentieth-Century Chinese Painting.* Oxford: Oxford University Press, 1988.

Kaple, Deborah. *Dream of a Red Factory: The Legacy of High Stalinism in China.* Oxford: Oxford University Press, 1994.

Karmel, Solomon M. "Capitalism with Chinese Characteristics." Princeton, New Jersey, August 1993.

Karmel, Solomon M. "The Neo-Authoritarian Contradiction: Trials of Developmentalist Dictatorships and the Retreat of the State in Mainland China." Ph.D. dissertation, Princeton University, Politics Department, 1995.

Kelliher, Daniel. *Peasant Power: The Era of Rural Reform, 1979–1989.* New Haven: Yale University Press, 1993.

Kelliher, Daniel. "The Political Consequences of China's Reforms." *Comparative Politics* (July 1986), pp. 480–81.

Kenyon, Daphen A., and John Kincaid, eds. *Competition Among States: Efficiency and Equity in American Federalism.* Washington: Urban Institute, 1992.

Kenyon, John P. *Stuart England.* 2d ed. Harmondsworth, UK: Penguin, 1985.

Key, V.O., Jr. *Southern Politics.* New York: Vintage, 1949.

Kim, Samuel S. *China, the United Nations, and World Order.* Princeton: Princeton University Press, 1989.

Kindermann, G. "An Overview of Sun Yat-sen's Doctrine." In C.Y. Cheng, ed., *Sun Yat-sen's Doctrine in the Modern World.* Boulder: Westview, 1989, pp. 52–78.

King, Richard. " 'Wounds' and 'Exposure': Chinese Literature After the Gang of Four." *Pacific Affairs* (Spring 1981), pp. 82–99.

Kinkley, Jeffrey, ed. *After Mao: Chinese Literature and Society, 1978–81.* Cambridge: Harvard University Press, 1985.

Kleinberg, Robert. *China's Opening to the Outside World: The Experiment with Foreign Capitalism.* Boulder: Westview, 1990.

Kohli, Atul. *Democracy and Discontent: India's Growing Crisis of Governability.* New York: Cambridge University Press, 1990.

Kohli, Atul. *The State and Poverty in India: The Politics of Reform.* New York: Cambridge University Press, 1987.

Kojima Reeitsu. *Chûgoku no keizai kaikaku* (China's Economic Reforms). Tokyo: Keisô Shobô, 1988.

Kojima Reeitsu. *Urbanization and Urban Problems in China.* Tokyo: Institute of Developing Economies, 1987.

Kojima Reiitsu. "The Growing Fiscal Authority of Provincial-Level Governments in China." *Developing Economies* 30:4 (December 1992), pp. 315–46.

Kojima Reeitsu, ed. *Chûgoku no toshika to nôson kensetsu* (Chinese Urbanization and Rural Construction). Tokyo: Ryûkei Shosha, 1978.

Kornai, János. *The Economics of Shortage.* Amsterdam: North-Holland, 1980.

Kornai, János. "The Hungarian Reform Process: Visions, Hopes, and Reality." *Journal of Economic Literature* (December 1986), pp. 1687–1737.

Kornai, János. *The Road to a Free Economy: The Example of Hungary.* New York: Norton, 1990.

Kornai, János. *The Socialist System: The Political Economy of Communism.* Princeton: Princeton University Press, 1992.

Kouwenhoven, Frank. "Developments in Mainland China's New Music." *China Information.* "Part I: From China to the United States," 7:1 (Summer 1992), pp. 17–39; "Part II: From Europe to the Pacific and Back to China," 7:2 (Autumn 1992), pp. 30–46.

Krasner, Stephen D. *Defending the National Interest.* Princeton: Princeton University Press, 1978.

Kraus, Richard. *Brushes with Power: Modern Politics and the Chinese Art of Calligraphy.* Berkeley: University of California Press, 1991.

Kraus, Richard. "China's 'Liberalization' and Conflict over the Social Organization of the Arts." *Modern China* 9:2 (April 1983), pp. 212–27.

Kuan Hsin-chi and Maurice Brosseau, eds. *China Review, 1991.* Hong Kong: Chinese University Press, 1991.

Kuan Hsin-chi and Maurice Brosseau, eds. *China Review, 1992.* Hong Kong: Chinese University Press, 1992.

Kueh, Y.Y. *Economic Planning and Local Mobilization in Post-Mao China.* London: SOAS Contemporary China Institute, 1985.

Kuhn, Philip A. *Soulstealers: The Chinese Sorcery Scare of 1768.* Cambridge: Harvard University Press, 1990.

Kuhn, Thomas. *The Structure of Scientific Revolutions.* Chicago: University of Chicago Press, 1964.

Kuisel, Richard. *Seducing the French: The Dilemma of Americanization.* Berkeley: University of California Press, 1993.

Kwan Ha Yim, ed. *China Under Deng.* New York: Facts on File, 1991.

Kwok, Daniel W.Y. *Scientism in Chinese Thought, 1900–1950.* New Haven: Yale University Press, 1965.

Kwok, Reginald Yin-wang. "Metropolitan Development in China: A Struggle Between Contradictions." *Habitat International* 12:4 (1988), pp. 201–12.

Kwong, Julia. *Cultural Revolution in China's Schools, May 1966–April 1969.* Stanford: Hoover Institution Press, 1988.

Laing, Ellen. *The Winking Owl: Art in the People's Republic of China.* Berkeley: University of California Press, 1988.

Lakoff, George. *Women, Fire, and Dangerous Things: What Categories Reveal about the Mind.* Chicago: University of Chicago Press, 1988.

Lam, Willy Wo-Lap. *The Era of Zhao Ziyang: Power Struggle in China, 1986–88.* Hong Kong: A.B. Books, 1989.

Lam, Willy Wo-Lap. *Toward a Chinese-style Socialism: An Assessment of Deng Xiaoping's Reforms.* Hong Kong: Oceanic Cultural Service, 1987.

Lamb, Franklin P. "An Interview with Chinese Legal Officials." *China Quarterly* 66 (June 1976), pp. 323–27.

Lampton, David M. *Paths to Power.* Ann Arbor: Center for Chinese Studies, University of Michigan, 1986.

Lampton, David M., ed. *Policy Implementation in Post-Mao China.* Berkeley: University of California Press, 1987.

Lane, Ruth. "Concrete Theory: An Emerging Political Method." *American Political Science Review* 84:3 (September 1990), pp. 927–40.

Langer, Suzanne. *Feeling and Form.* New York: Scribner's, 1943.

Langer, Suzanne. *Philosophy in a New Key: A Study in the Symbolism of Reason, Rite, and Art.* New York: Penguin, 1942.

Lanternari, Vittorio. *Religions of the Oppressed: Studies of Modern Messianic Cults.* New York: Knopf, 1963.

LaPalombara, Joseph. *Democracy, Italian Style.* New Haven: Yale University Press, 1987.

Lardy, Nicholas R. *Agriculture in China's Modern Economic Development.* Cambridge: Cambridge University Press, 1983.

Lardy, Nicholas R. "Consumption and Living Standards in China, 1978–1983." *China Quarterly* (1984), pp. 847–65.

Lawrence, Susan. "Democracy, Chinese Style." *Australian Journal of Chinese Affairs* 32 (July 1994), pp. 61–68.

Lee, Hong Yung. *From Revolutionary Cadres to Party Technocrats in Socialist China.* Berkeley: University of California Press, 1991.

Lee, Peter N.S. *Industrial Management and Economic Reform in China, 1949–1984.* Hong Kong: Oxford University Press, 1988.

Lee, Peter N.S. "Reforming the Social Security System in China." In Stewart Nagel and Mariam Mills, eds., *Public Policy in China.* Westport, CT: Greenwood Press, 1993, pp. 33–51.

Leeming, Frank. *Rural China Today.* Harlowe, UK: Longman, 1985.

Leung, Beatrice. *Sino-Vatican Relations: Problems in Conflicting Authority, 1976–1986.* Cambridge: Cambridge University Press, 1992.

Leung, Beatrice, ed. *Christianity in China: Foundations for Dialogue.* Hong Kong: University of Hong Kong, Centre of Asian Studies, 1993.

Leung Chi Yan. "The Politics of Economic Leap Forward and Readjustment: A Case Study of Economic Policy Making in China, 1977–1980." M.Phil. thesis, University of Hong Kong, Political Science Department, 1992.

Leung Yuen-sang. *The Shanghai Taotai: Linkage Man in a Changing Society, 1843–90.* Honolulu: University of Hawaii Press, 1990.

Levenson, Joseph. *Confucian China and Its Modern Fate: The Problem of Monarchical Decay.* Berkeley: University of California Press, 1964.

Levi, Carlo. *Christ Stopped at Eboli.* New York: Farrar, Straus and Company, 1947.

Levy, Marion J., Jr. *The Family Revolution in Modern China.* New York: Atheneum, 1948.

Levy, Marion J., Jr. "Structural-Functional Analysis." In *International Encyclopedia of the Social Sciences.* London: Macmillan, 1968, pp. 21–28.

Levy, Marion J., Jr. *The Structure of Society.* Princeton: Princeton University Press, 1952.

Levy, Marion J., Jr. *Modernization and the Structure of Societies.* Princeton: Princeton University Press, 1966.

Lewin, Moshe. *The Gorbachev Phenomenon: A Historical Interpretation.* Berkeley: University of California Press, 1988.

Lewis, W. Arthur. *Politics in West Africa.* London: Allen and Unwin, 1965.

Lewis, W. Arthur. *The Theory of Economic Growth.* Homewood, IL: Irwin, 1955.

Li Cheng. "The Rise of Technocracy: Elite Transformation and Ideological Change in Post-Mao China." Ph.D. dissertation, Princeton University, Politics Department, 1992.

Li Cheng. "University Networks and the Rise of Qinghua Graduates in China." *Australian Journal of Chinese Affairs* 32 (July 1994), pp. 1–32.

Li Cheng and David Bachman. "Localism, Elitism, and Immobilism: Elite Transformation and Social Change in Post-Mao China." *World Politics* 42 (October), pp. 64–94.

Li Cheng and Lynn White. "The Army in the Succession to Deng Xiaoping: Familiar Fealties and Technocratic Trends." *Asian Survey* 33:8 (August 1993), pp. 757–86.

Li Cheng and Lynn White. "China's Technocratic Movement and the *World Economic Herald.*" *Modern China* 17:3 (July 1991), pp. 342–88.

Li Cheng and Lynn White. "Elite Transformation and Modern Change in Mainland China and Taiwan." *China Quarterly* 121 (March 1990), pp. 1–35.

Li Cheng and Lynn White. "The Thirteenth Central Committee of the Chinese Communist Party: From Mobilizers to Managers." *Asian Survey* 28:4 (April 1988), pp. 371–99.

Liu Guisheng, ed. *Modern Western Ideologies and the May 4 Movement in China.* Beijing: Qinghua Daxue Chuban She, 1989.

Li Lianjiang and Kevin J. O'Brien. "Villagers and Popular Resistance in Contemporary China." *Modern China* 22:1 (January 1966), pp. 28–61.

Li, Linda Chelan. "Central-Provincial Relations in the People's Republic of China, Nature and Configurations: The Administration of Fixed Assets Investment in Shanghai and Guangdong Since 1978." Ph.D. dissertation, School of Oriental and African Studies, University of London, 1994.

Li Maoguan. "Why 'Laws Go Unenforced'." *Beijing Review* (September 11–17, 1989), pp. 17–19 and 26–27.

Li, Victor. "Law and Penology: Systems of Reform and Correction." In Michel Oksenberg, ed., *China's Developmental Experience.* New York: Praeger, 1973, pp. 144–56.

Lieberthal, Jane Lindsay. "From Cooperative to Commune: An Analysis of Rural Administrative Policy in China, 1955–58." M.A. thesis, Columbia University, Department of Political Science, 1971.

Lieberthal, Kenneth. *Governing China.* New York: Norton, 1995.

Lieberthal, Kenneth, and Michel Oksenberg. *Policy Making in China: Leaders, Structures, and Processes.* Princeton: Princeton University Press, 1988.

Lijphart, Arend. "Consociation and Federation: Conceptual and Empirical Links." *Canadian Journal of Political Science* 7:3 (September 1979), pp. 499–515.

Lin Bih-jaw and Fan Li-min, eds. *Education in Mainland China.* Taipei: Institute of International Relations, 1990.

Lin Bih-jaw and James T. Myers, eds. *Forces for Change in Contemporary China.* Taipei: Institute for International Relations, 1992.

Lin You Su. "Urban Migration in China: A Case Study of Three Urban Areas." Ph.D. dissertation, Australian National University, Department of Geography, 1992.

Lindblom, Charles E. *Democracy and Market System.* Oslo: Norwegian University Press, 1988.

Lindblom, Charles E. *The Policy-Making Process,* 2d ed. Englewood Cliffs, NJ: Prentice-Hall, 1980.

Lindenbaum, Bradley. "The Bifurcated State: Chinese Fiscal Structure and the Most Favored Nation Debate." Senior thesis, Princeton University, Woodrow Wilson School, 1992.

Link, Perry. *Evening Chats in Beijing: Probing China's Predicament.* New York: Norton, 1992.

Link, Perry. *Stubborn Weeds: Popular and Controversial Chinese Literature After the Cultural Revolution.* Bloomington: Indiana University Press, 1983.

Linz, Juan. "Authoritarian and Totalitarian Regimes." In Fred Greenstein and Nelson Polsby, eds., *Handbook of Political Science,* vol. 3. Reading, MA: Addison-Wesley, 1975.

Lipset, Seymour Martin. *Political Man.* London: Heinemann, 1969.

Little, Daniel. *Understanding Peasant China: Case Studies in the Philosophy of Social Science.* New Haven: Yale University Press, 1989.

Little, Daniel. *Varieties of Social Explanation: An Introduction to the Philosophy of Social Science.* Boulder: Westview, 1991.

Liu, Alan P.L. "Communications and Development in Post-Mao Mainland China." *Issues and Studies* 27:12 (December 1991), pp. 73–99.

Liu, Alan P.L. "The 'Wenzhou Model' of Development and China's Modernization." *Asian Survey* 22:8 (August 1992), pp. 696–711.

Liu Binyan. "People or Monsters." In Perry Link, ed., *People or Monsters.* Bloomington: Indiana University Press, 1983.

Liu Dahong. *Paintings, 1986–1992.* Hong Kong: Schoeni, 1992.

Liu Yia-ling. "Reform from Below: The Private Economy and Local Politics in Wenzhou." *China Quarterly* 130 (June 1992), pp. 293–316.

Lo, Leslie Nai-kwai. "State Patronage of Intellectuals in Chinese Higher Education." *Comparative Education Review* 35:4 (November 1991), pp. 690–720.

Lord, Bette Bao. *Legacies: A Chinese Mosaic.* New York: Knopf, 1990.

Lord, Bette Bao. *Spring Moon.* New York: Harper and Row, 1981.

Lü Xiaobo. "Organizational Involution and Official Deviance: A Study of Cadre Corruption in China, 1949–93." Ph.D. dissertation, University of California at Berkeley, Department of Political Science, 1994.

Lull, James. *China Turned On: Television, Reform, and Resistance.* London: Routledge, 1991.

Luo Zhufeng, ed. *Religion Under Socialism in China.* Armonk: M.E. Sharpe, 1991.

Lyons, Thomas P. *Economic Integration and Planning in Maoist China.* New York: Columbia University Press, 1987.

Ma Xia. "On the Temporary Movement of the Rural Population." *Chinese Society and Anthropology* 21:2 (Winter 1988–89), pp. 78–84.

McCormick, Barrett L. "Democracy or Dictatorship?" *Australian Journal of Chinese Affairs* 31 (January 1994), pp. 91–105.

McCormick, Barrett L. *Political Reform in Post-Mao China: Democracy and Bureaucracy in a Leninist State.* Berkeley: University of California Press, 1990.

MacDougall, Bonnie S., ed. *Popular Chinese Literature and Performing Arts in the People's Republic of China, 1949–1979.* Berkeley: University of California Press, 1984.

MacFarquhar, Roderick, ed. *The Politics of China, 1949–1989.* Cambridge: Cambridge University Press, 1993.

Machiavelli, Niccolò. *The Prince.* Luigi Ricci, trans.; Christian Gauss, intro. New York: Mentor, 1952.

MacInnis, Donald E. *Religion in China Today: Policy and Practice.* Maryknoll, NY: Orbis, 1989.

Mackerras, Colin, and Amanda Yorke, eds. *Cambridge Handbook of Contemporary China.* Cambridge: Cambridge University Press, 1991.

Macleod, Roderick. *China, Inc.: How to Do Business with the Chinese* [by an American businessman in Shanghai]. New York: Bantam, 1988.

Madison, James. "Federalist Paper No. 10." In Roy P. Fairfield, ed., *The Federalist Papers.* Garden City, NY: Anchor, 1961, pp. 16–23.

Madsen, Richard. *Morality and Power in a Chinese Village.* Berkeley: University of California Press, 1984.

Madsen, Richard. "The Public Sphere: Civil Society and Moral Community." *Modern China* 19:2 (April 1993), pp. 183–98.

Malhotra, Angelina. "Shanghai's Dark Side: Army and Police Officers Are Once Again in League with Vice." *Asia, Inc.* 3:2 (February 1994), pp. 32–39.

Manion, Melanie. *Retirement of Revolutionaries in China: Public Policies, Social Norms, Private Interests.* Princeton: Princeton University Press, 1993.

Mannheim, Karl. *Ideology and Utopia: An Introduction to the Sociology of Knowledge.* London: Routledge, 1936.

March, James G., and Johan P. Olsen. "The New Institutionalism: Organizational Factors in Political Life." *American Political Science Review* 78:3 (March 1984), pp. 734–49.

Martz, John. "Taiwanese Campaigning and Elections, 1991: An Outsider's View." *Studies in Comparative International Development* 27:2 (Summer 1992), pp. 84–94.

Marx, Karl, and Frederick Engels. *Manifesto of the Communist Party.* Beijing: Foreign Languages Press, 1965.

Marx, Karl. "The Eighteenth Brumaire of Louis Bonaparte." In Robert C. Tucker, ed., *The Marx-Engels Reader.* New York: Norton, 1972, pp. 436–525.

Mayer, Arno J. *Dynamics of Counterrevolution in Europe, 1970–1956.* New York: Harper Torchbooks, 1971.

Mayer, Arno J. *The Persistence of the Old Regime: Europe to the Great War.* New York: Pantheon, 1981.

Meaney, Connie Squires. "Market Reform in a Leninist System: Some Trends in the Distribution of Power Strategy and Money in Urban China." *Studies in Comparative Communism* 22:2–3 (Summer–Autumn 1989), pp. 203–20.

Meyer, John W., and Brian Rowan. "Institutional Organizations: Formal Structure as Myth and Ceremony." *American Journal of Sociology* 83 (1977), pp. 340–63.

Migdal, Joel S. *Strong Societies and Weak States: State-Society Relations and State Capabilities in the Third World.* Princeton: Princeton University Press, 1988.

The Military Balance, 1988–1989. London: International Institute for Strategic Studies, 1988.

Miller, H. Lyman. *Science and Dissent in Post-Mao China: The Politics of Knowledge.* Seattle: University of Washington Press, 1996.

Miller, Robert, ed. *The Development of Civil Society in Communist Systems.* London: Allen and Unwin, 1991.

Mitchell, Timothy. "The Limits of the State: Beyond Statist Approaches and Their Critics." *American Political Science Review* 85:1 (March 1991), pp. 77–96.

Moerman, Michael. "A Thai Village Headman as a Synaptic Leader." In Clarke Neher, ed., *Modern Thai Politics,* rev. ed. London: Schenkman, 1979.

Mok Chiu Yu and J. Frank Harrison, eds. *Voices from Tiananmen Square: Beijing Spring and the Democracy Movement.* Montreal: Black Rose Books, 1990.

Morgan, Stephen L. "City-Town Enterprises in the Lower Changjiang (Yangtze) River Basin." M.A. thesis, University of Hong Kong, Department of Asian Studies, 1987.

Mosca, Gaetano. *The Ruling Class.* New York: McGraw-Hill, 1939.

Moss, Hugh. *Some Recent Developments in Twentieth Century Chinese Painting: A Personal View.* Hong Kong: Umbrella, 1982.

Mote, Frederick W., and Lynn White. "Political Structure." In Gilbert Rozman et al., eds., *The Modernization of China.* New York: Free Press, 1981, pp. 255–351.

Mount, Ferdinand. *The Subversive Family: An Alternative History of Love and Marriage.* New York: Free Press, 1992.

Municipal Statistical Bureau of Shanghai. *Shanghai Statistical Yearbook, 1988: Concise Edition.* Beijing: China Statistical Publishing House, 1988.

Municipal Statistical Bureau of Shanghai. *Shanghai Statistical Yearbook, 1989: Concise Edition.* Beijing: China Statistical Publishing House, 1989.

Munro, Donald J. *The Concept of Man in Contemporary China.* Ann Arbor: University of Michigan Press, 1977.

Murphey, Rhoads. *Shanghai: Key to Modern China.* Cambridge: Harvard University Press, 1953.

Mushkat, Miron, and Adrian Faure. *Shanghai—Promise and Performance: Economic and Stock Market Review.* Hong Kong: Baring Securities, 1991.

Myers, James T. *Enemies Without Guns: The Catholic Church in the People's Republic of China.* New York: Paragon, 1991.

Nathan, Andrew J. *China's Crisis: Dilemmas of Reform and Prospects for Democracy.* New York: Columbia University Press, 1990.

Nathan, Andrew J. *Chinese Democracy.* Berkeley: University of California Press, 1985.

Nathan, Andrew J., and Shi Tianjian. "Left and Right with Chinese Characteristics." *World Politics* 48:4 (July 1996).

Nathan, Andrew J., and Shi Tianjian. "Cultural Requisites for Democracy in China: Findings from a Survey." *Daedalus* (Spring 1993), pp. 95–123.

Naughton, Barry. "Industrial Policy During the Cultural Revolution." In W. Joseph et al., eds., *New Perspectives on the Cultural Revolution.* Cambridge: Harvard University Press, 1991, pp. 153–81.

Naughton, Barry. "False Starts and the Second Wind: Financial Reforms in China's Industrial System." In Elizabeth J. Perry and Christine Wong, eds., *The Political Economy of Reform in Post-Mao China.* Cambridge: Harvard University Press, 1985, pp. 223–52.

Nee, Victor, and David Stark, eds. *Remaking the Economic Institutions of China and Eastern Europe.* Stanford: Stanford University Press, 1991.

Nicholas, Ralph W. "Factions: A Comparative Analysis." In Michael Banton, ed., *Political Systems and the Distribution of Power.* London: Tavistock, 1968, pp. 21–58.

Nolan, Peter. *Growth Processes and Distributional Change in a South Chinese Province: The Case of Guangdong.* London: SOAS Contemporary China Institute, 1983.

Nolan, Peter. *The Political Economy of Collective Farms: An Analysis of China's Rural Reforms Since Mao.* Cambridge: Polity Press, 1988.

Nolan, Peter, and Robert F. Ash. "China's Economy on the Eve of Reforms." *China Quarterly* 144 (December 1995), pp. 980–98.

Nolan, Peter, and Dong Fureng, eds. *Market Forces in China: Competition and Small Business, The Wenzhou Debate.* London: Zed Books, 1990.

North, Douglass C. *Institutions, Institutional Change, and Economic Performance.* Cambridge: Cambridge University Press, 1990.

Nozick, Robert. *Anarchy, State, and Utopia.* London: Blackwell, 1974.

O'Brien, Kevin J. *Reform Without Liberalization: China's National People's Congress and the Politics of Institutional Change.* New York: Cambridge University Press, 1990.

O'Brien, Kevin, Jr. "Chinese People's Congresses and Legislative Imbeddedness: Understanding Early Institutional Development." Draft of paper for *Comparative Political Studies.*

O'Brien, Kevin, Jr. "Implementing Political Reform in China's Villages." *Australian Journal of Chinese Affairs* 32 (July 1994), pp. 33–59.

Oi, Jean C. "Fiscal Reform and the Economic Foundations of Local State Corporatism in China." *World Politics* 45:1 (October 1992), pp. 99–126.

Oi, Jean C. *State and Peasant in Contemporary China: The Political Economy of Village Government.* Berkeley: University of California Press, 1989.

Oksenberg, Michel. "Chinese Policy Process and the Public Health Issue: An Arena Approach." *Comparative Studies of Communism* (Winter 1974), pp. 375–412.

Oksenberg, Michel, and Bruce Dickson. "The Origins, Process, and Outcomes of Great Political Reform: A Framework for Analysis." In Dankwart Rustow and Kenneth Erickson, eds., *Comparative Political Dynamics: Global Research Perspectives.* New York: Harper and Row, 1991, pp. 235–61.

Oksenberg, Michel, and James Tong. "The Evolution of Central-Provincial Fiscal Relations in China, 1971–1984: The Formal System." *China Quarterly* 125 (March 1991), pp. 1–32.

Orr, Iain, et al., eds. *China Reflected: An Anthology from Chinese and Western Sources.* London: Foreign and Commonwealth Office, 1986.

Orr, Robert G. *Religion in China.* New York: Friendship Press, 1980.

Paltiel, Jeremy T. "China: Mexicanization or Market Reform." In James A. Caporaso, ed., *The Illusive State: International and Comparative Perspectives.* Newbury Park, CA: Sage, 1989, pp. 255–78.

Pan, Lynn. *The New Chinese Revolution.* Revised and updated ed. London: Penguin, 1987.

Pareto, Vilfredo. *The Rise and Fall of Elites.* Hans Zetterberg, intro. New York: Arno Press, 1979.

Parish, William L., Xiaoye Zhe, and Fang Li. "Nonfarm Work and Marketization of the Chinese Countryside." *China Quarterly* 143 (September 1995), pp. 697–728.

Parish, William L., and Martin K. Whyte. *Village and Family in Contemporary China.* Chicago: University of Chicago Press, 1978.

Parker, Geoffrey. *The Dutch Revolt.* Rev. ed. Harmondsworth, UK: Penguin, 1985.

Parsons, Talcott. *The Evolution of Societies.* Jackson Toby, ed. Englewood Cliffs, NJ: Prentice-Hall, 1977.

Parsons, Talcott. *The Social System.* Glencoe, IL: Free Press, 1951.

Parsons, Talcott. *Societies: Evolutionary and Comparative Perspectives.* Englewood Cliffs, NJ: Prentice-Hall, 1966.

Parsons, Talcott. *The Structure of Social Action.* New York: McGraw-Hill, 1937.

Pas, Julian, ed. *The Turning of the Tide: Religion in China Today.* Hong Kong: Oxford University Press, 1989.

Pearson, Margaret M. "The Janus Face of Business Associations in China: Socialist Corporatism in Foreign Enterprises." *Australian Journal of Chinese Affairs* 31 (January 1994), pp. 25–46.

Pearson, Margaret M. *Joint Ventures in the People's Republic of China: The Control of Foreign Direct Investment Under Socialism.* Princeton: Princeton University Press, 1991.

Pearson, Veronica. "Law, Rights, and Psychiatry in the People's Republic of China." *International Journal of Law and Psychiatry* 15:1992, pp. 409–23.

Pearson, Veronica. *Mental Health Care in China.* London: Gaskell, 1995.

Pei Minxin. *From Reform to Revolution: The Demise of Communism in China and the Soviet Union.* Cambridge: Harvard University Press, 1994.

Peng Xizhe. *Demographic Transition in China: Fertility Trends Since the 1950s.* Oxford: Oxford University Press, 1991.

Pensley, Danielle S. "The Socialist City?" [about Neubaugebeit Berlin-Hellersdorf]. Senior thesis, Princeton University, Woodrow Wilson School, 1993.

Pepper, Stephen. *World Hypotheses: A Study in Evidence.* Berkeley: University of California Press, 1970.

Pepper, Suzanne. *China's Education Reform in the 1980s.* Berkeley: Center for Chinese Studies, University of California, 1990.

Perkins, Dwight, et al. *Rural Small-Scale Industry in the People's Republic of China.* Berkeley: University of California Press, 1977.

Perry, Elizabeth J. "Rural Violence in Socialist China." *China Quarterly* 103 (September 1985), pp. 414–40.

Perry, Elizabeth J. "Labor Divided: Sources of State Formation in Modern China." In Joel S. Migdal, Atul Kohli, and Vivienne Shue, eds., *State Power and Social Forces.* New York: Cambridge University Press, 1994, pp. 143–73.

Perry, Elizabeth J. *Rebels and Revolutionaries in North China, 1845–1945.* Stanford: Stanford University Press, 1980.

Perry, Elizabeth J. *Shanghai on Strike: The Politics of Chinese Labor.* Stanford: Stanford University Press, 1993.

Perry, Elizabeth J. "The Shanghai Strike Wave of 1957." (Seen in manuscript form.)

Perry, Elizabeth J., and Li Xun. *Proletarian Power: Shanghai in the Cultural Revolution.* Boulder: Westview, 1996.

Perry, Elizabeth J., and Christine Wong, eds. *The Political Economy of Reform in Post-Mao China.* Cambridge: Harvard University Press, 1985.

Phillips, Michael R., Veronica Pearson, and Ruiwen Wang, eds. *Psychiatric Rehabilita-*

tion in China: Models for Change in a Changing Society. Supplement 24 to the *British Journal of Psychiatry* 165 (August 1994), pp. 1–142.

Piven, Frances Fox, and Richard A. Cloward. *Poor People's Movements.* New York: Vintage, 1979.

Polanyi, Karl. *The Great Transformation: The Social and Economic Origins of Our Time.* New York: Rinehart, 1944.

Polumbaum, Judy. "In the Name of Stability: Restrictions on the Right of Assembly in the People's Republic of China." *Australian Journal of Chinese Affairs* 26 (July 1991), pp. 43–64.

Popkin, Samuel L. *The Rational Peasant: The Political Economy of Rural Society in Vietnam.* Berkeley: University of California Press, 1979.

Popper, Karl R. *Conjectures and Refutations: The Growth of Scientific Knowledge.* New York: Harper, 1965.

Portes, Alejandro, Manuel Castells, and Lauren A. Benton, eds. *The Informal Economy.* Baltimore: Johns Hopkins University Press, 1989.

Poston, Dudley L., Jr., and Saochang Gu. "Socioeconomic Development, Family Planning, and Fertility in China." *Demography* 24:4 (November 1987), pp. 531–49.

Potter, Pitman B. "Riding the Tiger: Legitimacy and Legal Culture in Post-Mao China." *China Quarterly* 138 (June 1994), pp. 225–58.

Potter, Pitman, ed. *Domestic Law Reforms in Post-Mao China.* Armonk: M.E. Sharpe, 1993.

Potter, Sulamith Heins, and Jack M. Potter. *China's Peasants.* Cambridge: Cambridge University Press, 1990.

Powell, Walter W., and Paul J. DiMaggio, eds. *The New Institutionalism in Organizational Analysis.* Chicago: University of Chicago Press, 1991.

Prime, Penelope B. "Industry's Response to Market Liberalization in China: Evidence from Jiangsu Province." *Economic Development and Cultural Change* 41:1 (1992), pp. 23–50.

Przeworski, Adam. *Democracy and the Market: Political and Economic Reforms in Eastern Europe and Latin America.* New York: Cambridge University Press, 1991.

Putnam, Robert. *Making Democracy Work.* Princeton: Princeton University Press, 1993.

Putterman, Louis. "Institutional Boundaries, Structural Change, and Economic Reform in China." *Modern China* 18:1 (January 1992), pp. 3–13.

Pye, Lucian W. *The Mandarin and the Cadre: China's Political Cultures.* Ann Arbor: Center for Chinese Studies, University of Michigan, 1988.

Rabb, Theodore K. *The Struggle for Stability in Early Modern Europe.* New York: Oxford University Press, 1975.

Rae, Douglas. *The Political Consequences of Electoral Laws.* New Haven: Yale University Press, 1967.

Ragin, Charles C. *The Comparative Method: Moving Beyond Qualitative and Quantitative Strategies.* Berkeley: University of California Press, 1987.

Rawski, Thomas. *Economic Growth and Employment in China.* New York: Oxford University Press, 1979.

Reynolds, Bruce. *Reform in China: Challenges and Choices.* Armonk: M.E. Sharpe, 1987.

Richman, Barry. *Industrial Society in Communist China.* New York: Random House, 1969.

Rigger, Shelley. "Electoral Strategies and Political Institutions in the Republic of China on Taiwan." *Fairbank Center Working Papers,* No. 1. Cambridge: Harvard University, Fairbank Center, 1993.

Riker, William H. *Federalism: Origin, Operation, Significance.* Boston: Little, Brown, 1964.

Rocca, Jean-Louis. "Corruption and Its Shadow: An Anthropological View of Corruption in China." *China Quarterly* 130 (June 1992), pp. 402–16.

Rocca, Jean-Louis. "Réprimer et rééduquer: Le traitement de la délinquance juvénile dans la municipalité de Shanghai." In C. Henriot, ed., *Shanghai dans les anneés 1980: études urbaines.* Lyon: Université Jean Moulin, Centre Rhônalpin de Recherche sur l'Extrême Orient Contemporain, 1989, pp. 106–44.

Roney, Jennifer. "Relaxing the Iron Hand: Crime Under Perestroika." Senior thesis, Princeton University, Politics Department, 1991.

Rosen, Stanley. "The Chinese Communist Party and Chinese Society: Popular Attitudes Toward Party Membership and the Party's Image." *Australian Journal of Chinese Affairs* 24 (July 1990), pp. 51–92.

Rosen, Stanley. "The Effect of Post-June 4 Re-education Campaigns on Chinese Students." Paper for the American Association of China Studies, 1992.

Rosen, Stanley, and David Chu. *Survey Research in the People's Republic of China.* Washington: United States Information Agency, 1987.

Rosenbaum, Arthur Lewis, ed. *State and Society in China: The Consequences of Reform.* Boulder: Westview, 1992.

Roseneau, Pauline Marie. *Post-modernism and the Social Sciences: Insights, Inroads, and Intrusions.* Princeton: Princeton University Press, 1992.

Rowe, William T. *Hankow: Conflict and Community in a Chinese City, 1796–1895.* Stanford: Stanford University Press, 1989.

Rowe, William T. "The Problem of Civil Society in Late Imperial China." *Modern China* 19:2 (April 1993), pp. 139–57.

Rozelle, Scott. "Decision-making in China's Rural Economy: The Linkages Between Village Leaders and Farm Households." *China Quarterly* 137 (March 1994), pp. 99–124.

Rozelle, Scott, and Richard N. Boisvert. "Quantifying Chinese Village Leaders' Multiple Objectives." *Journal of Comparative Economics* 18 (1994), pp. 25–45.

Rubin, Vitaly A. In Steven Levine, ed., *Individualism and the State in Ancient China.* New York: Columbia University Press, 1976.

Rudé, George. *Revolutionary Europe, 1783–1815.* London: Fontana, 1964.

Rueschemeyer, Dietrich, et al. *Capitalist Development and Democracy.* Chicago: University of Chicago Press, 1991.

Rustow, Dankwart. "Transitions to Democracy: Toward a Dynamic Model." *Comparative Politics* 2:3 (1970), pp. 337–63.

Ryan, Alan. "Why Democracy?" *New York Times Book Review,* January 1, 1995, pp. 8–9.

Ryan, Alan, ed. *The Philosophy of Social Explanation.* Oxford: Oxford University Press, 1973.

Saich, Tony. *China's Science Policy in the 80s.* Atlantic Highlands, NJ: Humanities Press, 1989.

Saich, Tony, ed. *The Chinese People's Movement: Perspectives on Spring 1989.* Armonk: M.E. Sharpe, 1990.

Saith, Ashwani, ed. *The Re-emergence of the Chinese Peasantry: Aspects of Rural Decollectivization.* London: Croom Helm, 1987.

Sangren, Stevan. "Traditional Chinese Corporations: Beyond Kinship." *Journal of Asian Studies* 43:3, pp. 391–415.

Sartori, Giovanni. "Concept Misformation in Comparative Politics." *American Political Science Review* 64:4 (December 1970), pp. 1033–53.

Saso, Michael R. *Taoism and the Rite of Cosmic Renewal.* Pullman, WA: Washington State University Press, 1989.

Schak, David, ed. *Entrepreneurship, Economic Growth, and Social Change.* Brisbane: Griffith University, Centre for the Study of Australian-Asian Relations, 1994.

Schattschneider, E.E. *The Semi-Sovereign People: A Realist's View of Democracy in America.* David Adamany, intro. Hinsdale, IL: Dreyden Press, 1975.

Schelling, Thomas C. *Micromotives and Macrobehavior.* New York: Norton, 1978.

Schmitter, Philippe. "Still the Century of Corporatism?" In F. Pike and T. Stritch, eds., *The New Corporatism.* South Bend: University of Notre Dame Press, 1974.

Schneider, Ben Ross. *Politics Within the State: Elite Bureaucrats and Industrial Policy in Authoritarian Brazil.* Pittsburgh: University of Pittsburgh Press, 1991.

Schoeck, Helmut, and James W. Wiggins, eds. *Scientism and Values.* Princeton: D. Van Nostrand Co., 1960.

Schoenhals, Michael. "The Organization and Operation of the Central Case Examination Group (1966–1979): Mao's Mode of Cruelty." *China Quarterly* 145 (March 1996), pp. 87–111.

Schoenhals, Michael. *The Paradox of Power in a People's Republic of China Middle School.* Armonk: M.E. Sharpe, 1993.

Schoppa, Keith. *Xiang Lake [N. Zhejiang]: Nine Centuries of Chinese Life.* New Haven: Yale University Press, 1989.

Schorske, Carl E. *Fin-de-Siècle Vienna: Politics and Culture.* New York: Vintage, 1981.

Schram, Stuart, ed. *Chairman Mao Talks to the People.* New York: Pantheon, 1974.

Schumpeter, Joseph. *Capitalism, Socialism, and Democracy,* 3d ed. New York: Harper, 1950.

Schurmann, Franz. *Ideology and Organization in Communist China.* Berkeley and Los Angeles: University of California Press, 1966.

Schwarcz, Vera. "Memory, Commemoration, and the Plight of China's Intellectuals." *Wilson Quarterly* (Autumn 1989), pp. 120–29.

Schwarcz, Vera. *The Chinese Enlightenment: Intellectuals and the Legacy of the May Fourth Movement of 1919.* Berkeley: University of California Press, 1986.

Scott, Ian. *Political Change and the Crisis of Legitimacy in Hong Kong.* Oxford: Oxford University Press, 1989.

Scott, James C. *Domination and the Arts of Resistance: Hidden Transcripts.* New Haven: Yale University Press, 1990.

Scott, James C. "Everyday Forms of Resistance." In Forrest D. Colburn, ed., *Everyday Forms of Peasant Resistance.* Armonk: M.E. Sharpe, 1989, pp. 3–30.

Scott, James C. *Weapons of the Weak: Everyday Forms of Peasant Resistance.* New Haven: Yale University Press, 1985.

Segal, Gerald. *China Changes Shape: Regionalism and Foreign Policy.* London: International Institute of Strategic Studies, Adelphi Paper, 1994.

Seligman, Adam. *The Idea of Civil Society.* New York: Free Press, 1992.

Selznick, Philip. *The Organizational Weapon: A Study of Bolshevik Strategy and Tactics.* New York: McGraw-Hill, 1952.

Semsel, George S., ed. *Chinese Film: The State of the Art in the People's Republic.* New York: Praeger, 1987.

Seymour, James D. "China's Democracy Movement: What the Agenda Has Been Missing." Paper presented at the conference on "Rights in China: What Happens Next?," London, June 28–29, 1991.

Seymour, James D. *China's Satellite Parties.* Armonk: M.E. Sharpe, 1987.

Seymour, James D., ed. *China's Fifth Modernization: The Human Rights Movement, 1978–1979.* Stanfordville, NY: Human Rights Publishing Group, 1980.

Shapiro, Ian, and Donald P. Green. *Pathologies of Rational Choice Theory: A Critique of Applications in Political Science.* New Haven: Yale University Press, 1994.

Shirk, Susan L. *Competitive Comrades: Career Incentives and Student Strategies in China.* Berkeley: University of California Press, 1985.

Shirk, Susan L. *The Political Logic of Economic Reform in China.* Berkeley: University of California Press, 1993.

Shortell, Troy. "The Party-Building Campaign in China." Senior thesis, Princeton University, 1991.

Shue, Vivienne. "Beyond the Budget: Finance Organization and Reform in a Chinese County." *Modern China* 10:2 (April 1984), pp. 147–86.

Shue, Vivienne. "Emerging State-Society Relations in Rural China." In Jürgen Delman et al., eds., *Remaking Peasant China: Problems of Rural Development and Institutions at the Start of the 1990s.* Aarhus: Aarhus University Press, 1990, pp. 60–80.

Shue, Vivienne. "Grasping Reform: Economic Logic, Political Logic, and the State-Society Spiral." *China Quarterly* 144 (December 1995), pp. 1174–85.

Shue, Vivienne. "State Power and Social Organization in China." In Joel Migdal, Atul Kohli, and Vivienne Shue, eds., *State Power and Social Forces: Domination and Transformation in the Third World.* Cambridge: Cambridge University Press, 1994, pp. 65–88.

Shue, Vivienne. *The Reach of the State: Sketches of the Chinese Body Politic.* Stanford: Stanford University Press, 1988.

Siddiqul, Kamal. "The Emergence of Local Self-Government in Rural China." *Journal of Social Studies* 64 (April 1994), pp. 48–72.

Silin, Robert, and Edwin A. Winckler. *China Provincial Economic Briefing Series: Guangdong.* Hong Kong: Consulting Group, BankAmerica Asia, Ltd., 1981.

Simon, Denis Fred, and Detlef Rehn. *Technological Innovation in China: The Case of the Shanghai Semi-Conductor Industry.* Cambridge, MA: Ballinger, 1988.

Simon, Denis Fred, and Merle Goldman, eds. *Science and Technology in Post-Mao China.* Cambridge: Harvard University Press, 1989.

Siu, Helen F. *Agents and Victims in South China: Accomplices in Rural Revolution.* New Haven: Yale University Press, 1989.

Siu, Helen F. *Furrows: Peasants, Intellectuals, and the State.* Stanford: Stanford University Press, 1990.

Siu, Helen F. "Recycling Rituals: Politics and Popular Culture in Contemporary Rural China." In Perry Link et al., eds., *Unofficial China: Popular Culture and Thought in the People's Republic.* Boulder: Westview Press, 1989, pp. 121–37.

Siu, Helen F. "Socialist Peddlers and Princes in a Chinese Market Town." *American Ethnologist* 16:2 (May 1989), pp. 195–212.

Skilling, H. Gordon, and Franklyn Griffiths, eds. *Interest Groups in Soviet Politics.* Princeton: Princeton University Press, 1971.

Skilling, H. Gordon. *Samizdat and an Independent Society in Central and Eastern Europe.* Houndmills, UK: Macmillan, 1989.

Skinner, G. William. *Leadership and Power in the Chinese Community of Thailand.* Ithaca: Cornell University Press, 1958.

Skinner, G. William. "Overseas Chinese Leadership: Paradigm for a Paradox." In Gehan Wijeyewardene, ed., *Leadership and Authority: A Symposium.* Singapore: University of Malaya Press, 1968, pp. 191–203.

Skinner, G. William, and Edwin A. Winckler. "Compliance Succession in Rural Communist China: A Cyclical Theory." In Amitai Etzioni, ed., *A Sociological Reader in Complex Organizations,* 2d ed. New York: Holt, Rinehart & Winston, 1969, pp. 410–38.

Skocpol, Theda. *States and Social Revolutions.* Cambridge: Cambridge University Press, 1979.

Smart, Alan. "Gifts, Bribes, and *Guanxi*: A Reconsideration of Bourdieu's Social Capital." *Cultural Anthropology* 8:3, pp. 388–408.

Smelser, Neil J. "The Rational Choice Perspective: A Theoretical Assessment." *Rationality and Society* 4:4 (October 1992), pp. 381–410.

Smelser, Neil J., and Talcott Parsons. *Economy and Society.* Glencoe, IL: Free Press, 1956.

Smil, Vaclav. *The Bad Earth: Environmental Degradation in China.* Armonk: M.E. Sharpe, 1984.

Smith, Karen. "In With the New: China's New Art, Post-1989." *Asian Art News* 3:1 (January–February 1993), pp. 32–39.

Smith, Richard. "The Chinese Road to Capitalism." *New Left Review* 199 (May–June 1993), pp. 55–99.

Solinger, Dorothy J. "China's Transients and the State: A Form of Civil Society?" *Politics and Society* 21:1 (March 1993).

Solinger, Dorothy J. "China's Urban Transients in the Transition from Socialism and the Collapse of the Communist Urban Public Goods Regime." *Comparative Politics* (January 1995), pp. 127–46.

Solinger, Dorothy J. *China's Transition from Socialism: Statist Legacies and Market Reforms, 1980–1990.* Armonk: M.E. Sharpe, 1993.

Solomon, Andrew. "The Fine Art of Protest." *Post Magazine,* January 23, 1994.

Solomon, Richard H. *Mao's Revolution and the Chinese Political Culture.* Berkeley: University of California Press, 1971.

Spruyt, Hendrik. *The Sovereign State and Its Competitors.* Princeton: Princeton University Press, 1995.

State Statistical Bureau, PRC, comp. *China: Urban Statistics, 1986.* Hong Kong: Longman, 1987.

Stavis, Benedict. *Agricultural Mechanization in China.* Ithaca: Cornell University Press, 1978.

Stavis, Benedict. *China's Political Reforms: An Interim Report.* New York: Praeger, 1988.

Stavis, Benedict, ed. *Reform in China's Political System* [special issue of *Chinese Law and Government*]. Armonk: M.E. Sharpe, 1987.

Stepan, Alfred. *Rethinking Military Politics.* Princeton: Princeton University Press, 1991.

Stepan, Alfred. *The State and Society: Peru in Comparative Perspective.* Princeton: Princeton University Press, 1978.

Stone, John, and Stephen Mennell, eds. *Alexis de Tocqueville on Democracy, Revolution, and Society.* Chicago: University of Chicago Press, 1980.

Stone, Lawrence, and Jeanne C. Fawtier Stone. *An Open Elite? England, 1540–1880.* Abridged ed. New York: Oxford University Press, 1986.

Strand, David. *Rickshaw Beijing: City People and Politics in the 1920s.* Berkeley: University of California Press, 1989.

Strecker, Erica. "The One-Child Campaign in Rural China: Limits on Its Implementation and Success." Thesis, Georgetown University, East Asian Studies, 1994.

Streeck, Wolfgang, and Philippe Schmitter. "Community, Market, State—and Associations? The Prospective Contribution of Interest Governance to Social Order." In Streeck and Schmitter, eds., *Private Interest Government: Beyond Market and State.* Newbury Park, CA: Sage, 1985.

Street, John. "Popular Culture = Political Culture? Some Thoughts on Postmodernism's Relevance to Politics." *Politics* 11:2 (1991), pp. 20–25.

Su Xiaokang and Wang Luxiang. *Deathsong of the River: A Reader's Guide to the Chinese TV Series "Heshang".* Richard W. Bodman and Pin P. Wang, trans. Ithaca: Cornell University, East Asia Program, 1991.

Suleiman, Ezra N. *Private Power and Centralization in France: The Notaires and the State.* Princeton: Princeton University Press, 1987.

Sung Yun-Wing. *Explaining China's Export Drive: The Only Success Among Command Economies.* Hong Kong: Chinese University, Hong Kong Institute of Asia-Pacific Studies, 1991.

Suttmeier, Richard P. "Party Views of Science: The Record from the First Decade." *China Quarterly* 44 (October–December 1970), pp. 146–68.

Swire, Peter M. "The Onslaught of Complexity: Information Technologies and Developments in Legal and Economic Thought." Senior thesis, Princeton University, Woodrow Wilson School, 1980.

Tai Hung-chao. "The Oriental Alternative: An Hypothesis on Culture and Economy." In *Confucianism and Economic Development: An Oriental Alternative.* Washington DC: Washington Institute Press, 1989.

Tai, Jeanne, ed. and tr. *Spring Bamboo: A Collection of Contemporary Chinese Short Stories.* New York: Random House, 1989.

Tanner, Murray Scot. *The Politics of Lawmaking in Post-Mao China: Institutions, Processes, and Democratic Prospects.* Forthcoming.

Tatlow, Antony, and Tak-Wai Wong, eds. *Brecht and East Asian Theatre.* Hong Kong: Hong Kong University Press, 1982.

Taylor, Charles. *Philosophy and the Human Sciences.* Cambridge: Cambridge University Press, 1985.

Thurston, Anne F. *Enemies of the People.* New York: Alfred Knopf, 1987.

Tian, G. "The Emergence of Shanghai's Role as an Entrepôt Centre Since the Mid-1980s." Unpublished manuscript.

Tidrick, Gene, and Chen Jiyuan, eds. *China's Industrial Reform.* New York: Oxford University Press, 1987.

Tilly, Charles. *Big Structures, Large Processes, Huge Comparisons.* New York: Russell Sage Foundation, 1985.

Tilly, Charles. *From Mobilization to Revolution.* Reading, MA: Addison Wesley, 1978.

Tilly, Charles, ed. *The Formation of National States in Western Europe.* Princeton: Princeton University Press, 1975.

Tillyard, E.M.W. *The Elizabethan World Picture: A Study of the Idea of Order in the Age of Shakespeare, Donne and Milton.* New York: Vintage Books, n.d.

Todaro, Michael P. "A Model of Labor Migration and Urban Unemployment in Less Developed Countries." *American Economic Review* 59 (1969), pp. 138–48.

Tong Yanqi. "State, Society, and Political Change in China and Hungary." *Comparative Politics* 26:3 (April 1994), pp. 333–53.

"Towards Dominance of Technocrats and Leadership Stability: The Shanghai Leadership Change, 1976–1993." Anonymous manuscript.

Towery, Britt. *The Churches of China.* Hong Kong: Amazing Grace Books, 1986.

Trimberger, Ellen Kay. *Revolution from Above: Military Bureaucrats and Development in Japan, Turkey, Egypt, and Peru.* New Brunswick, NJ: Transaction Books, 1978.

Tu Wei-ming, ed. *China in Transformation.* Cambridge: Harvard University Press, 1994.

Tucker, Robert C., ed. *The Lenin Anthology.* New York: Norton, 1975.

Tucker, Robert C., ed. *The Marx-Engels Reader,* 2d ed. New York: Norton, 1972.

Tucker, Robert C., ed. *Stalinism.* New York: Norton, 1977.

Turner, Victor. *The Forest of Symbols: Aspects of Ndembu Ritual.* Ithaca: Cornell University Press, 1967.

U.S. Congress, Joint Economic Committee. *China: A Reassessment of the Economy.* Washington DC: Government Printing Office, 1975.

U.S. National Foreign Assessment Center. *China: Gross Value of Industrial Output, 1965–77.* Washington DC: National Foreign Assessment Center, 1978.

United Nations Educational Scientific and Cultural Organization. *Chinese Paintings: Catalogue of the Thirteenth UNESCO Travelling Exhibition.* Paris: UNESCO, 1979.

Unger, Jonathan. "China's Troubled Down to the Countryside Campaign." *Contemporary China* (1979), pp. 79–92.

Unger, Jonathan. "The Decollectivization of the Chinese Countryside: A Survey of Twenty-eight Villages." *Pacific Affairs* 58:4 (Winter 1985–86), pp. 585–606.

Unger, Jonathan. " 'Rich Man, Poor Man': The Making of New Classes in the Countryside." In David S.G. Goodman and Beverley Hooper, eds., *China's Quiet Revolution: New Interactions Between State and Society.* New York: St. Martin's, 1994, pp. 43–63.

Unger, Jonathan, ed. *The Pro-Democracy Protests in China: Reports from the Provinces.* Armonk: M.E. Sharpe, 1991.

Unger, Jonathan, and Anita Chan. "China, Corporatism, and the East Asian Model." *Australian Journal of Chinese Affairs* 32 (January 1995), pp. 29–53.

Urban, Michael E. *More Power to the Soviets: The Democratic Revolution in the USSR.* Worcester, UK: Elgar, 1990.

Ure, John. "Telecommunications with Chinese Characteristics." Hong Kong University, Centre of Asian Studies, unpublished paper, November 1993.

Versenyi, Laszlo. *Socratic Humanism.* New Haven: Yale University Press, 1963.

Vogel, Ezra F. *One Step Ahead: Guangdong Under Reform.* Cambridge: Harvard University Press, 1989.

Wagner, Rudolf G. *The Contemporary Chinese Historical Drama: Four Studies.* Berkeley: University of California Press, 1990.

Wakeman, Frederic, Jr. "The Chinese Mirror." In Michel Oksenberg, ed., *China's Developmental Experience.* New York: Praeger, 1973, pp. 208–19.

Wakeman, Frederic, Jr. "The Civil Society and Public Sphere Debate: Western Reflections on Chinese Political Culture." *Modern China* 19:2 (April 1993), pp. 108–38.

Wakeman, Frederic, Jr. *History and Will: Philosophical Perspectives of Mao Tse-tung's Thought.* Berkeley: University of California Press, 1973.

Wakeman, Frederic, Jr. "Models of Historical Change: The Chinese State and Society, 1839–1989." In Kenneth Lieberthal, Joyce Kallgren, Roderick MacFarquhar, and Frederic Wakeman, Jr., eds., *Perspectives on Modern China: Four Anniversaries.* Armonk: M.E. Sharpe, 1991, pp. 68–102.

Wakeman, Frederic, Jr., *Policing Shanghai.* Berkeley: University of California Press, 1994.

Wakeman, Frederic, Jr. *Strangers at the Gate: Social Disorder in South China, 1839–1861.* Berkeley: University of California Press, 1966.

Wakeman, Frederic, Jr., and Wen-hsin Yeh, eds. *Shanghai Sojourners.* Berkeley: University of California, Institute of East Asian Studies, 1992.

Walder, Andrew. *Communist Neo-Traditionalism: Work and Authority in Chinese Industry.* Berkeley: University of California Press, 1986.

Walder, Andrew G., ed. *The Waning of the Communist State.* Berkeley: University of California Press, 1995.

Wang Hongying. "Transnational Networks and Foreign Direct Investment in China." Ph.D. dissertation, Princeton University, Politics Department, 1996.

Wang Shaoguang. *Failure of Charisma: The Cultural Revolution in Wuhan.* Hong Kong: Oxford University Press, 1995.

Wang Shaoguang. "The Rise of the Second Budget and the Decline of State Capacity in China." Unpublished paper, apparently 1993.

Wasserstrom, Jeffrey. *Student Protests in Twentieth Century China: The View from Shanghai.* Stanford: Stanford University Press, 1991.

Watson, Andrew. "New Structures in the Organization of Chinese Agriculture: A Variable Model." *Pacific Affairs* 57 (Winter 1984–85), pp. 621–45.

Waxman, Chaim, ed. *The End of Ideology Debate.* New York: Funk and Wagnalls, 1968.

Weber, Eugen. *Peasants into Frenchmen.* Berkeley: University of California Press, 1977.

Weber, Max. *From Max Weber: Essays in Sociology.* H.H. Gerth and C. Wright Mills, eds. New York: Oxford University Press, 1958.

Weber, Max. *The Protestant Ethic and the Spirit of Capitalism.* New York: Scribner's, 1958.

Weber, Max. *The Religion of China.* Glencoe, IL: Free Press, 1951.

Wei, Betty Pei-t'i. *Shanghai: Crucible of Modern China.* Hong Kong: Oxford University Press, 1987.

Wei Lin and Arnold Chao, eds. *China's Economic Reforms.* Philadelphia: University of Pennsylvania Press, 1982.

Weldon, Thomas. *The Vocabulary of Politics.* Harmondsworth, UK: Penguin, 1960.

Weller, Robert P. *Resistance, Chaos, and Control in China: Taiping Rebels, Taiwanese Ghosts, and Tiananmen.* Seattle: University of Washington Press, 1994.

Weller, Robert P. *Unities and Diversities in Chinese Religion.* Seattle: University of Washington Press, 1987.

White, Barbara-Sue. *Turbans and Traders: Hong Kong's Indian Communities.* Hong Kong: Oxford University Press, 1994.

White, Gordon. "Prospects for Civil Society: A Case Study of Xiaoshan City." In David S. G. Goodman and Beverley Hooper, eds., *China's Quiet Revolution: New Interactions Between State and Society.* New York: St. Martin's, 1994, pp. 194–215.

White, Lynn. "A Political Demography of Shanghai After 1949." *Proceedings of the Fifth Sino-American Conference on Mainland China.* Taipei: Kuo-chi kuan-hsi yen-chiu so, 1976; repr. serially in *Ming bao* (Bright News), Hong Kong, November 1976.

White, Lynn. "Agricultural and Industrial Values in China." In R. Wilson, S. Greenblatt, and A. Wilson, eds., *Value Change in Chinese Society.* New York: Praeger, 1979.

White, Lynn. "Bourgeois Radicalism in the 'New Class' of Shanghai." In James L. Watson, ed., *Class and Social Stratification in Post-Revolution China.* Cambridge: Cambridge University Press, 1984, pp. 142–74.

White, Lynn. *Careers in Shanghai: The Social Guidance of Individual Energies in a Developing Chinese City.* Berkeley and Los Angeles: University of California Press, 1978.

White, Lynn. "Changing Concepts of Corruption in Communist China." In Yu-ming Shaw, ed., *Changes and Continuities in Chinese Communism: The Economy, Society, and Technology.* Boulder: Westview, 1988, pp. 316–53.

White, Lynn. "Deviance, Modernization, Rations, and Household Registration in Chinese Cities." In R. W. Wilson, S. Greenblatt, and A. Wilson, eds., *Deviance and Social Control in Chinese Society.* New York: Praeger, 1977, pp. 151–72.

White, Lynn. "Joint Ventures in a New Shanghai at Pudong." In Sally Stewart, ed., *Advances in Chinese Industrial Studies: Joint Ventures in the PRC.* Greenwich, CT: JAI Press, 1995, pp. 75–120.

White, Lynn. "Leadership and Participation: The Case of Shanghai's Managers." In Victor C. Falkenheim, ed., *Citizens and Groups in the People's Republic of China.* Ann Arbor: University of Michigan Press, 1986, pp. 189–211.

White, Lynn. "Leadership in Shanghai, 1955–69." In Robert A. Scalapino, ed., *Elites in the People's Republic of China.* Seattle: University of Washington Press, 1972, pp. 302–77.

White, Lynn. "Local Autonomy in China During the Cultural Revolution: The Theoretical Uses of an Atypical Case." *American Political Science Review* 70 (June 1976), pp. 479–91.

White, Lynn. "Low Power: Small Enterprises in Shanghai." *China Quarterly* 73 (March 1978), pp. 45–76.

White, Lynn. "Non-Governmentalism in the Historical Development of Modern Shanghai." In Laurence J.C. Ma and Edward W. Hanten, eds., *Urban Development in Modern China*. Boulder: Westview, 1981, pp. 19–57.

White, Lynn. *Policies of Chaos: The Organizational Causes of Violence in China's Cultural Revolution*. Princeton: Princeton University Press, 1989.

White, Lynn. *Shanghai Shanghaied? Uneven Taxes in Reform China*. Hong Kong: University of Hong Kong, Centre of Asian Studies, working paper, 1989.

White, Lynn. "Shanghai's Polity in Cultural Revolution." In John W. Lewis, ed., *The City in Communist China*. Stanford: Stanford University Press, 1971, pp. 325–70.

White, Lynn. "Shanghai-Suburb Relations, 1949–1966." In Christopher Howe, ed., *Shanghai: Revolution and Development in an Asian Metropolis*. Cambridge: Cambridge University Press, 1981, pp. 241–68.

White, Lynn. "The Cultural Revolution as an Unintended Result of Administrative Policies." In W. Joseph, C. Wong, and D. Zweig, eds., *New Perspectives on the Cultural Revolution*. Cambridge: Harvard University Press, 1991, pp. 83–104.

White, Lynn. "The Liberation Army and the Chinese People." *Armed Forces and Society* 1:3 (May 1975), pp. 364–83.

White, Lynn. "The Political Effects of Resource Allocations in Taiwan and Mainland China." *Journal of Developing Areas* 15 (October 1980), pp. 43–66.

White, Lynn. "The Road to Urumchi: Approved Institutions in Search of Attainable Goals." *China Quarterly* 79 (October 1979), pp. 481–510.

White, Lynn. "Workers' Politics in Shanghai." *Journal of Asian Studies* 26:1 (November 1976), pp. 99–116.

White, Lynn, and Li Cheng. "China Coast Identities: Region, Nation, and World." In Lowell Dittmer and Samuel Kim, eds., *China's Quest for National Identity*. Ithaca: Cornell University Press, 1993, pp. 154–93.

Whiting, Allen S. *The Chinese Calculus of Deterrence*. Ann Arbor: University of Michigan Press, 1975.

Whitson, William W. (with Huang Chen-hsia). *The Chinese High Command: A History of Military Politics*. New York: Praeger, 1973.

Whyte, Martin K., and William Parish. *Urban Life in Contemporary China*. Chicago: University of Chicago Press, 1984.

Wickeri, Philip L. *Seeking the Common Ground*. New York: Orbis, 1988.

Wickham, Carrie Rosefsky. "Political Mobilization Under Authoritarian Rule: Explaining Islamic Activism in Mubarak's Egypt." Ph.D. dissertation, Princeton University, Politics Department, 1996.

Wilkinson, Rupert. *Gentlemanly Power: British Leadership and the Public School Tradition: A Comparative Study in the Making of Rulers*. Oxford: Oxford University Press, 1964.

Williams, Howard. *Concepts of Ideology*. Sussex, UK: Wheatsheaf, 1988.

Wittgenstein, Ludwig. *Philosophical Investigations*. London: Blackwell, 1953.

Wittgenstein, Ludwig. *Tractatus Logico-Philosophicus*. London: Blackwell, 1973 reprint.

Wolf, Margery. *The House of Lim*. New York: Appleton-Century-Crofts, 1968.

Wolin, Sheldon S. *Politics and Vision*. Boston: Little, Brown, 1960.

Womack, Brantly. "Editor's Introduction: Media and the Chinese Public." *Chinese Sociology and Anthropology* 18 (1986), pp. 6–53.

Wong, Christine. "Between Plan and Market: The Role of the Local Sector in Post-Mao China." *Journal of Comparative Economics* (1987), pp. 385–98.

Wong, Christine. "The Economics of Shortage and Problems of Reform in Chinese Industry." *Journal of Comparative Economics* (1986), pp. 363–87.

Wong, Christine. "Fiscal Reform and Local Industrialization." *Modern China* 18:2 (April 1992), pp. 197–227.

Wong Siu-lun. *Emigrant Entrepreneurs: Shanghai Industrialists in Hong Kong.* Hong Kong: Oxford University Press, 1988.

Woo, Margaret Y.K. "Legal Reforms in the Aftermath of Tiananmen Square." *Review of Socialist Law* (1991), pp. 51–74.

World Bank. *China: Revenue Mobilization and Tax Policy.* Washington DC: World Bank, 1990.

World Bank. *World Development Report, 1994.* New York: Oxford University Press, 1994.

Wright, Joseph J., Jr. *The Balancing Act: A History of Modern Thailand.* Oakland: Pacific Rim Press, 1991.

Wu Dingbo and Patrick D. Murphy, eds. *Science Fiction from China.* New York: Praeger, 1989.

Wu Guanzhong. *Painting from the Heart: Selected Works of Wu Guanzhong.* Chengdu: Sichuan Art Publishing House, 1990.

Wu Guoguang. "Hard Politics with Soft Institutions: China's Political Reform in 1986–1989." Ph.D. dissertation, Princeton University, Politics Department, 1995.

Wu, Victor. *Contemporary Chinese Painters 1.* Hong Kong: Hai Feng Publishing Co., 1982.

Xu Lilai. "China's Financial Reform in the 1990s: A Case Study of Financial Environment in Pudong New Area, Shanghai." *Journal of Asian Economics* 2:2 (Fall 1991), pp. 353–71.

Yabuki Susumu. *China's New Political Economy: The Giant Awakes.* Stephen M. Harner, trans. Boulder: Westview, 1995.

Yahuda, Michael B., ed. *New Directions in the Social Sciences and Humanities in China.* New York: St. Martin's Press, 1987.

Yan Yunxiang. *The Flow of Gifts: Reciprocity and Social Networks in a Chinese Village.* Stanford: Stanford University Press, 1995.

Yang Dali. "Making Reform: The Great Leap Famine and Rural Change in China." Ph.D. dissertation, Princeton University, Politics Department, December 1992.

Yang, Mayfair Mei-hui. "The Art of Social Relationships and Exchange in China." Ph.D. dissertation, University of California, Berkeley, Department of Anthropology, 1986.

Yang, Mayfair Mei-hui. *Gifts, Favors, and Banquets: The Art of Social Relationships in China.* Ithaca: Cornell University Press, 1994.

Yang, Richard H., ed. *Yearbook on PLA Affairs, 1987.* Kaohsiung: Sun Yat-sen Center for Policy Studies, 1987.

Yin Qiping and Gordon White. *The "Marketization" of Chinese Higher Education: A Critical Assessment.* Sussex, UK: University of Sussex, Institute of Development Studies, 1993.

You Longgong et al. "Cigarette Smoking in China." *Journal of the American Medical Association* 274:15 (October 18, 1995), pp. 1232–34.

Young, Iris M. *Justice and the Politics of Difference.* Princeton: Princeton University Press, 1990.

Young, Susan. *Private Business and Economic Reform in China.* Armonk: M.E. Sharpe, 1995.

Yu Jingjie et al. "A Comparison of Smoking Patterns in the People's Republic of China and the United States: An Impending Health Catastrophe for the Middle Kingdom." *Journal of the American Medical Association* 264:12, pp. 1575–79.

Yu Shiao-ling Shen. "The Cultural Revolution in Post-Mao Literature." Ph.D. dissertation, University of Wisconsin, Madison, 1983.

Zafanolli, Wojtek. "China's Second Economy: Second Nature?" *Revue d'études est-ouest* 14:3 (September 1983), pp. 103–51.

Zang Xiaowei. "The Fourteenth Central Committee of the Chinese Communist Party." *Asian Survey* 33:8 (August 1993), pp. 787–803.
Zhang Mingwu et al. *Chinese Qigong Therapy.* Jinan: Shandong Science and Technology Press, 1985.
Zhang Qingwu. "Basic Facts on the Household Registration System." *Chinese Economic Studies* 22:1 (1988).
Zheng Yongnian. "Institutional Change, Local Developmentalism, and Economic Growth: The Making of a Semi-Federal System in Reform China." Ph.D. dissertation, Princeton University, Politics Department, 1995.
Zhang Zhongli et al., eds. *SASS Papers.* Shanghai: Shanghai Academy of Social Sciences, 1986.
Zhang Zhongli et al., eds. *SASS Papers (2).* Shanghai: Shanghai Academy of Social Sciences, 1988.
Zhou, Kate Xiao. *How the Farmers Changed China.* Boulder: Westview, 1996 (and Ph.D. dissertation, Princeton University, Politics Department, 1994).
Zhou, Kate Xiao, and Lynn White. "Quiet Politics and Rural Enterprise in Reform China." *Journal of Developing Areas* 29 (July 1995), pp. 461–90.
Zhou Xueguang. "Unorganized Interests and Collective Action in Communist China." *American Sociological Review* 58 (February 1993), pp. 54–73.
Zweig, David. *Agrarian Radicalism in China, 1968–1981.* Cambridge: Harvard University Press, 1989.
Zweig, David. "Rural Industry: Constraining the Leading Growth Sector in China's Economy." In U.S. Congress, Joint Economic Committee, *China's Economic Dilemmas in the 1990s: The Problems of Reforms, Modernization, and Interdependence.* Washington DC: Government Printing Office, 1991, pp. 418–36.

Materials in Chinese

Bao Ligui. *Jinxian dai difang zhengfu bijiao* (Comparative Modern Local Government). Beijing: Guangming Ribao Chuban She, 1988.
Baoshan xian zhi (Baoshan County Gazetteer). Zhu Baohe, ed. Shanghai: Shanghai Renmin Chuban She, 1992.
Bo Fengcheng. "Zhonggong nongye xiandai hua zhengce zhi fenxi" (An Analysis of CCP Rural Modernization Policy). M.A. thesis, National Chengchi University, 1978.
Cao Linzhang, Gu Guangqing, and Li Jianhua. *Shanghai shengchan ziliao suoyu zhi jiegou yanjiu* (Studies of Shanghai Production and Ownership Structure). Shanghai: Shanghai Shehui Kexue Yuan Chuban She, 1987.
Chen Baoliang. *Zhongguo liumang shi* (The History of Chinese Hooliganism). Beijing: Zhongguo Shehui Kexue Chuban She, 1993.
Chen Benlin et al. *Gaige kaifang shenzhou jubian* (Great Change in the Sacred Land [China] During Reform and Opening). Shanghai: Jiaotong Daxue Chuban She, 1984.
Chen Dongsheng and Chen Jiyuan. *Zhongguo diqu jingji jiegou yanjiu* (Studies on the Structure of China's Spatial Economy). Taiyuan: Shanxi Renmin Chuban She, 1988.
Chen Minzhi et al. *Shanghai jingji fazhan zhanlüe yanjiu* (Studies of Shanghai's Economic Development Strategy). Shanghai: Shanghai Renmin Chuban She, 1985.
Chen Minzhi, Xue Chao, and Gu Jirui, et al. *Gaige de zuji: Nanjing jingji tizhi zonghe gaige jishi* (Footprints of Reform: Notes on the Comprehensive Reform of Nanjing's Economic System). Shanghai: Shanghai Shehui Kexue Yuan Chuban She, 1988.
Chen Yifei. *Chen Yifei huigu zhan* (Chen Yifei: A Retrospective). Hong Kong: Plum Blossoms, Ltd., 1992.

Chengshi he jingji qu (Cities and Economic Regions). Li Zhongfan et al., eds. Fuzhou: Fujian Renmin Chuban She, 1984.

Chengshi shengtai jingji lilun yu shixian (The Theory and Practice of Urban Environmental Economics). Chen Yuqun, ed. Shanghai: Shanghai Shehui Kexue Yuan Chuban She, 1988.

Chongming dongtan tanyu ziyuan kaifa liyong shishi guihua zonghe yanjiu baogao (Summary Research Report on the Plan to Realize and Opening and Use of Beach Resources on the Chongming East Coast). Shanghai Environmental Economics Society, ed. Shanghai: Shanghai Shi Shengtai Jingji Xuehui, 1990.

Chongming xian zhi (Chongming County Gazetteer). Zhou Zike, ed. Shanghai: Shanghai Renmin Chuban She, 1989.

Chuansha xian jianshe zhi (Chronicle of Construction in Chuansha County). Wu Side, ed. Shanghai: Shanghai Shehui Kexue Chuban She, 1988.

Chuansha xian zhi (Chuansha County Gazetteer). Zhu Hongbo, ed. Shanghai: Shanghai Renmin Chuban She, 1990.

Dalu hunyin jicheng fa (Mainland Marriage and Inheritance Law). Xu Penghua and Chang Feng, eds. Taibei: Weili Falü Chuban She reprint of a PRC case book, 1989.

Dalu ruhe jiejue minshi jiufen (How the Mainland Solves Civil Disputes). Chang Feng, Yang Jiandong, and Qiu Haiyang, eds. Taibei: Weili Falü Chuban She reprint of a PRC case book, 1988.

Dangdai Zhongguo de guangbo dianshi (Radio and Television in China Today), 2 vols. Li Hua et al., eds. Beijing: Zhongguo Shehui Kexue Chuban She, 1987.

Dangdai Zhongguo de guding zichan guanli (Fixed Asset Investments and Management in Contemporary China). Zhou Daojiong, ed. Beijing: Zhongguo Shehui Kexue Chuban She, 1989.

Dangdai Zhongguo de Jiangsu (Jiangsu in Today's China). Liu Dinghan et al., eds. Beijing: Zhongguo Shehui Kexue Chuban She, 1989.

Dangdai Zhongguo de jingji tizhi gaige (Reform of the Economic System in Modern China). Zhou Taihe et al., eds. Beijing: Zhongguo Shehui Kexue Chuban She, 1984.

Dangdai Zhongguo de nongye jixie hua (Agricultural Mechanization in Contemporary China). Wu Shaowen, ed. Beijing: Zhongguo Shehui Kexue Yuan, 1991.

Dangdai Zhongguo de renkou (Population in China Today). Xu Dixin et al., eds. Beijing: Zhongguo Shehui Kexue Chuban She.

Ding Richu. "Xinhai geming qian Shanghai ziben jia de zhengzhi huodong" (The Political Activities of Shanghai Capitalists Before the Xinhai Revolution). In *Jindai Zhongguo zichan jieji yanjiu* (Studies on China's Capitalist Class in Recent Times), Fudan History Department, ed. Shanghai: Fudan Daxue Chuban She, 1983, pp. 501–23.

Fahui guangrong chuantong, minrong shehui kexue (Develop the Glorious Tradition, Let Social Science Prosper). Guo Jiafu et al., eds. Shanghai: Shanghai Shehui Kexue Yuan Chuban She, 1985.

Fang Litian. *Zhongguo Fojiao yu chuantong wenhua* (Chinese Buddhism and Traditional Culture). Shanghai: Renmin Chuban She, 1988.

Fazhan zhong de hengxiang jingji lianhe (Horizontal Economic Links in Development). Bureau for Economic System Reform, State Economic Commission, ed. Beijing: Qiye Guanli Chuban She, 1986.

Fei Xiaotong and Luo Hanxian. *Xiangzhen jingji bijiao moshi* (Comparative Models for Rural and Township Economies). Chongqing: Chongqing Chuban She, 1988.

Fengxian xian zhi (Fengxian County Gazetteer). Yao Jinxiang, ed. Shanghai: Shanghai Renmin Chuban She, 1987.

Fengxian yanzheng zhi (Gazetteer of the Salt Monopoly in Fengxian). Liu Guolun, ed. Shanghai: Shanghai Shehui Kexue Chuban She, 1987.

Fudan Daxue de gaige yu tansuo (Reforms and Explorations at Fudan University). Fudan Daxue Gaodeng Jiaoyu Yanjiu Suo, ed. Shanghai: Fudan Daxue Chuban She, 1987.

Gaige mianlin zhidu chuangxin (The Reforms Are Faced with System Innovation). Development Research Institute, ed. Shanghai: Sanlian Shudian, 1988.

Gaige: Women mianlin de wenti yu silu (Reforms: The Problems and Options That Face Us). Research Institute for the Reform of China's Economic Structure, ed. Beijing: Jingji Guanli Chuban She, 1987.

Gaige zhong de funü wenti (Women's Issues in the Reforms). Zhang Lianzhen, ed. Nanjing: Jiangsu Renmin Chuban She, 1988.

Gaige zhong de shehui zhuyi suoyou zhi (Socialist Ownership Systems in the Middle of Reforms). Shanghai Economics Association, ed. Shanghai: Shanghai Shehui Kexue Yuan Chuban She, 1987.

Ge Xiangxian and Qu Weiying. *Zhongguo mingong chao: "Mangliu" zhenxiang lu* (China's Tide of Labor: A Record of the True Facts about the "Blind Floaters"). Beijing: Zhongguo Guoji Guangbo Chuban She, 1990.

Gonghui jichu zhishi (Basic Knowledge about Trade Unions). All-China Federation of Trade Unions, ed. Beijing: Jingji Kexue Chuban She, 1987.

Guangdong sheng tongji nianjian (Guangdong Province Statistical Yearbook), various years, Guangdong Province Statistics Bureau, ed. Beijing: Zhongguo Tongji Chubanshe.

Guangzhou jingji, 1988 (The Economy of Guangzhou, 1988). Survey Office, Guangzhou People's Government, ed. Guangzhou: Zhongshan Daxue Chuban She, 1988.

Guangzhou tongji nianjian (Guangzhou Statistical Yearbook), various years. Guangzhou Municipal Statistics Bureau, ed. Beijing: Zhongguo Tongji Chuban She.

Gufen jingji yanjiu (Studies in the Economics of Shares). Shanghai Economics Association, ed. Shanghai: Shanghai Shehui Kexue Yuan Chuban She, 1987.

Guomin shouru tongji ziliao huibian, 1949–1985 (Collected Statistical Materials on National Income, 1949–1985). State Statistical Bureau, ed. Beijing: Zhongguo Tongji Chuban She, 1987.

Hao Mengbi and Duan Haoran. *Zhongguo gongchan dang liushi nian* (Sixty Years of the CCP). Beijing: Jiefang Jun Chuban She, 1984.

Hengxiang jingji lianhe de xin fazhan (The New Development of Horizontal Economic Links). Shanghai Economics Association, ed. Shanghai: Shanghai Shehui Kexue Yuan Chuban She, 1987.

Hong Ze et al. *Shanghai yanjiu luncong: Di yi ji* (Papers on Studies of Shanghai: First Set). Shanghai: Shanghai Shehui Kexue Yuan Chuban She, 1988.

Hongliu zhong de renmin: Jiangsu qiye jia baogao wenxue ji (People in the Torrent [of Reforms]: The Report Literature on Jiangsu Entrepreneurs). Shanghai: Shanghai Shehui Kexue Yuan Chuban She, 1988.

Hou Jun. *Piruan de yulun jiandu* (The Worn-Out Guidance of Public Opinion). Beijing: Zhongguo Funü Chuban She, 1989.

Hu Fanzhu. *Yumo yuyan xue* (The Linguistics of Jokes). Shanghai: Shanghai Shehui Kexue Yuan Chuban She, 1987.

Hua Daming. "Xiangban chang dui nonggong de guofen bodu ying yinqi zhuyi" (The Overexploitation of Peasant Workers by Township-run Factories Calls for Attention). *Shehui* (Society) [Shanghai], no. 2 (1990), pp. 12–13.

Huadong tongji nianjian (Statistical Yearbook of East China), various years to 1993. Statistical Information Network of the East China Region, ed. Beijing: Zhongguo Tongji Chuban She.

Jiading xian shedui gongye zhi (Records of Industry in Communes and Teams of Jiading County [Shanghai]). Group to Edit the Records of Industry in Communes and Teams of Jiading County, ed. Shanghai: Shanghai Shehui Kexue Yuan Chuban She, 1988.

Jiading xian zhi (Jiading County Gazetteer). Yang Yubai, ed. Shanghai: Shanghai Renmin Chuban She, 1992.

Jiangsu jingji he shehui fazhan gaikuang (The Development of Jiangsu's Economy and Society). Jiangsu Sheng Renmin Zhengfu Jingji Yanjiu Zhongxin [Yang Jiaxiang et al., eds.]. Nanjing: Jiangsu Renmin Chuban She, 1984.

Jiangsu jingji nianjian (Jiangsu Economic Yearbook), various years. *Jiangsu jingji nianjian* Editorial Committee, ed. Nanjing: Jiangsu Renmin Chuban She, same year.

Jiangsu sheng dashi ji, 1949–1985 (Chronology of Jiangsu, 1949–1985). "Dangdai Zhongguo de Jiangsu" Editorial Committee and Jiangsu Provincial Records Bureau, eds. Nanjing: Jiangsu Renmin Chuban She, 1988.

Jiangsu tongji nianjian, 1991 (Jiangsu Statistical Yearbook, 1991), various years. Jiangsu Statistical Bureau, ed. Nanjing: Zhongguo Tongji Chuban She, 1991.

Jiangsu xiangzhen gongye fazhan shi (History of the Development of Jiangsu Rural Industry). Mo Yuanren, ed. Nanjing: Nanjing Gongxue Yuan Chuban She, 1987.

Jiaoyu jingfei yu jiaoshi gongzi (Educational Funds and Teachers' Salaries). State Education Commission, Educational Funds Research Unit, ed. Beijing: Jiaoyu Kexue Chuban She, 1988.

Jihui youxing shiwei fa jianghua (Talking about the Law on Assemblies, Parades, and Demonstrations). Propaganda Office of the Judicial Department of the People's Republic of China, ed. Beijing: Falü Chuban She, 1990.

Jindai Shanghai da shi ji (Chronology of Modern Shanghai [1840 to 1918]). Tang Zhijun, ed. Shanghai: Shanghai Cishu Chuban She, 1987.

Jingji fazhan zhanlüe wenti lunwen ji (Collection of Essays on Issues of Economic Development Strategy). Shanghai Municipal Economic Association, ed. Shanghai: Shanghai Shi Jingji Xuehui, 1984.

Jingji tizhi gaige tansuo wenji (Collection of Documents Exploring the Economic System Reform). Shanghai Municipal Economic Association, ed. Shanghai: Shanghai Shi Jingji Xuehui, 1985.

Jingji xue tansuo de fengshuo chengguo: Shanghai shi jingji xuehui 1979–1985 nian huojiang lunwen ji (Rich Fruits from Explorations in Economics: Collected Prizewinning Shanghai Economics Association Theses, 1979–1985). Shanghai: Shanghai Shehui Kexue Yuan Chuban She, 1988.

Jinshan xian zhi (Jinshan County Gazetteer). Zhu Yanchu, ed. Shanghai: Shanghai Renmin Chuban She, 1990.

Jiu Zhongguo de Shanghai guangbo shiye, 1923–1949 (Broadcasting Enterprises in the Shanghai of Old China, 1923–49). Liu Guangqing, ed. Shanghai: Zhongguo Guangbo Dianshi Chuban She, 1985.

Jushi zhumu de banian (1978–1986): Zhongguo fazhan yu gaige jishi (Eight Years Attracting Attention Worldwide [1978–1986]: A Chronicle of China's Development and Reforms). Chinese Economic System Reform Research Institute, ed. Chengdu: Sichuan Renmin Chuban She, 1987.

Lei Ge. *Fansi gongping* (Reflections on Justice). Beijing: Zhongguo Funü Chuban She, 1989.

Li Pan, Li Douheng, and Chu Zhongxin et al. *Gaige yu kaifang xin wenti yanjiu* (Studies of New Questions in Reform and Opening). Shanghai: Shanghai Shehui Kexue Yuan Chuban She, 1987.

Liao Mei. *Shinian lai Fudan daxue xuesheng shetuan de fazhan qi qushi* (The Development and Tendency of Fudan University Student Associations over the Past Ten Years), a proposal for academic exchange among Fudan University, Taiwan National University, and Hongkong University students, January 1989.

Lin Qibing and Chen Hua. *Fu-Ri de shengchan fangshi* (The Fujian-Japan Method of Production). Shanghai: Shanghai Shehui Kexue Yuan Chuban She, 1987.

Liu Gang et al. *Shanghai chengshi jiti suoyou zhi gongye yanjiu* (Studies of Shanghai's Urban Collective Industries). Shanghai: Shanghai Renmin Chuban She, 1980.

Liu Guoguang. *Zhongguo jingji fazhan zhanlüe wenti yanjiu* (Studies on Issues of China's Economic Development Strategy). Shanghai: Shanghai Renmin Chuban She, 1984.

Liudong renkou dui da chengshi fazhan de yinxiang ji duice (Policies on the Influence of Transient Population for the Development of Large Cities). Li Mengbai et al., eds. Beijing: *Jingji ribao* Chuban She, 1991.

Liuwu qijian woguo chengzhen jumin jiating shouzhi diaocha ziliao (Survey of Residential Families' Incomes and Expenditures in Our Country's Cities and Towns during the Sixth Five-Year Plan). State Statistical Bureau, Urban Survey Group, ed. Beijing: Zhongguo Tongji Chuban She, 1988.

Lu Feiyun. "Zhuanye chengbao zhe—Yige xin jieceng de quqi" (Specialized Contractors—The Origins of a New Stratum). *Shehui* (Society) [Shanghai], no. 3 (1990), pp. 30–31.

Luo Zhufeng et al. *Zhongguo shehui zhuyi shiqi de zongjiao wenti* (Problems of Religion in China's Socialist Period). Shanghai: Shanghai Shehui Kexue Yuan Chuban She, 1987.

Ma Hong and Sun Shangqing. *Zhongguo jingji jiegou wenti yanjiu* (Studies on China's Economic Structure). Beijing: Renmin Chuban She, 1980.

Min Qi. *Zhongguo zhengzhi wenhua: Minzhu zhengzhi nanchan de shehui xinli yinsu* (China's Political Culture: Social-Psychological Factors Inhibiting the Birth of Democratic Politics). Kunming: Yunnan Renmin Chuban She, 1989.

Minzhu shengyue duchang gequ xuan (Selection of Folk Music Solos). Shanghai: Shanghai Yinyue Chuban She, 1990.

Mubiao, zhongdian, duice—Tan Shanghai chuantong gongye de jishu gaizao (Goals, Keypoints, and Policies—On the Technical Reform of Shanghai's Traditional Industries). Shanghai Municipal Enterprise Management Association, ed. Shanghai: Shanghai Shi Qiye Guanli Xiehui, 1985.

"Pipan" Beijing ren?! ("Criticize" Beijing Man?!). Luo Shuang et al., eds. Beijing: Zhongguo Shehui Chuban She, 1994.

Qi Shaohua. *Guanliao zhuyi zhongzhong* (Various Kinds of Bureaucratism). Shanghai: Renmin Chuban She, 1988.

Qingpu xian zhi (Qingpu County Gazetteer). Feng Wenxue, ed. Shanghai: Shanghai Renmin Chuban She, 1990.

Qiye gaige yu fazhan xinlu: Shanghai gongye qiye hengxiang lianhe diaocha baogao ji (The Reform of Enterprise and the New Road to Development: A Collection of Investigation Reports on Horizontal Integration in Shanghai Industrial Enterprises). Fudan University Economic Research Center, ed. Shanghai: Fudan Daxue Chuban She, 1988.

Quanguo ge sheng zizhi qu zhixia shi lishi tongji ziliao huibian, 1949–1989 (Historical Statistical Collection on Provinces, Autonomous Regions, and Municipalities Throughout the Country, 1949–1989). State Statistical Bureau, ed. Beijing: Zhongguo Tongji Chuban She, 1990.

Shanghai dangzheng jigou yange, 1949–1986 (The Evolution of Shanghai Party and Government Organization, 1949–1986). Jiang Zemin, ed. Shanghai: Shanghai Renmin Chuban She, 1988.

Shanghai difang shi ziliao (wu): Xinwen, chuban (Materials on the Local History of Shanghai [5]: Journalism and Publishing). Shanghai Literary History House, ed. Shanghai: Shanghai Shehui Kexue Yuan Chuban She, 1986.

Shanghai dixia dangzhi yuan Huazhong kang-Ri genju di (Shanghai's Underground Party Branches Helping the Anti-Japanese Base Areas in Central China). Zheng Gongliang, ed. Shanghai: Huadong Shifan Daxue Chuban She, 1987.

Shanghai Duiwai Kaifang de "Kaifang Du" Yanjiu Keti Zu (Research Group on Shanghai's "Degree of Openness" to the Outside). *Shanghai duiwai kaifang de "kaifang du" yanjiu* (Study of the Degree of Shanghai's Openness to the Outside). Shanghai: Shanghai Shehui Kexue Yuan, 1988.

Shanghai: Gaige, kaifang, yu fazhan, 1979–87 (Shanghai: Reforms, Opening, and Development, 1979–87). Shanghai Statistical Bureau, ed. Shanghai: Sanlian Shudian, 1988.

Shanghai gaoji zhuanjia minglü (Who's Who of Shanghai High-Level Specialists). Liu Zhenyuan, ed. Shanghai: Shanghai Kexue Jishu Chuban She, 1992.

Shanghai gongan nianjian, 1988 (Shanghai Public Security Yearbook, 1988) (*neibu,* photocopy reprint sold in Hong Kong, 515 pages). "Shanghai Gongan Nianjian" Editorial Department, ed. Shanghai: Shanghai Shehui Kexue Chuban She, 1988.

Shanghai gongye jiegou lishi yange ji xiankuang (The Historical Evolution and Present Situation of Shanghai's Industrial Structure). Shanghai Statistical Bureau, ed. Shanghai: Shanghai Tongji Ju, 1987.

Shanghai guoji yinyue bisai, 1987 Zhongxi bei, Zhongguo fengge gangqin qu, huojiang zuopin ji (Shanghai International Music Competition, 1987 China-West Album of Prizewinning Piano Competitions in Chinese Style). Shanghai: Shanghai Yinyue Chuban She, 1989.

Shanghai Jiaotong Daxue guanli gaige chutan (Preliminary Research on the Management Reform at Shanghai's Jiaotong University). Shanghai Jiaotong University, Communist Party Committee Office, ed. Shanghai: Jiaotong Daxue Chuban She, 1983.

Shanghai jiaoyu fazhan zhanlüe yanjiu (Research on a Strategy for Shanghai's Educational Development). Task Force on Shanghai Educational Development Strategy, ed. Shanghai: Fudan Daxue Chuban She, 1988.

Shanghai jiaoyu fazhan zhanlüe yanjiu baogao (Research Report on the Strategy of Shanghai's Educational Development). Kang Yonghua, Liang Chenglin, and Tan Songhua, eds. Shanghai: Huadong Shifan Daxue Chuban She, 1989.

Shanghai jiaoyu, 1988 (Shanghai Education, 1988). Wang Shenghong, ed. Shanghai: Tongji Daxue Chuban She, 1989.

Shanghai jingji, 1949–1982 (Shanghai's Economy, 1949–1982). Xu Zhihe, Ding Richu, Jin Liren, Wang Zhiping et al., eds. (Shanghai Academy of Social Sciences). Shanghai: Shanghai Renmin Chuban She, 1983.

Shanghai jingji, 1983–1985 (Shanghai's Economy, 1983–1985). Xu Zhihe, Ling Yan, Gu Renzhang et al., eds. (Shanghai Academy of Social Sciences). Shanghai: Shanghai Renmin Chuban She, 1986.

Shanghai jingji, 1987 (Shanghai's Economy, 1987). Xu Zhihe, Ling Yan, Gu Renzhang et al., eds. (Shanghai Academy of Social Sciences). Shanghai: Shanghai Renmin Chuban She, 1987.

Shanghai jingji, neibu ben: 1949–1982 (Shanghai Economy, Internal [i.e. classified] Volume: 1949–1982). Shanghai Academy of Social Sciences, ed. Shanghai: Shanghai Shehui Kexue Yuan Chuban She, 1984.

Shanghai jingji nianjian (Shanghai Economic Yearbook, various years). Often Xiao Jun et al., at the Shanghai Academy of Social Sciences, eds. Shanghai: Shanghai Renmin Chuban She or "Shanghai Jingji Nianjian" Chuban She, published in the same year.

Shanghai jingji qu de jianli yu fazhan (The Establishment and Development of the Shanghai Economic Zone). *World Economic Herald* and Shanghai Economic Zone Research Society, co-eds. Shanghai: Zhongguo Zhanwang Chuban She, 1984.

Shanghai jingji qu fazhan zhanlüe chutan (Preliminary Research on the Development Strategy of the Shanghai Economic Zone). *World Economic Herald* and Shanghai Economic Zone Research Society, co-eds. Shanghai: Wuxi Branch of Shanghai Eighth People's Printers, 1986.

Shanghai jingji qu gongye gaimao (General Description of Industry in the Shanghai Economic Zone), 30 vols. Shanghai Economic Association, ed. Shanghai: Jiaotong Daxue Chuban She, 1985 and 1986.

Shanghai jingji qu qiye jituan gaixian (Summary on Enterprise Groups in the Shanghai Economic Zone). Shen Jianzheng, Tong Wensheng, and Dai Xianru, eds. Shanghai: Baijia Chuban She, 1988.

Shanghai keji, 1949–1984 (Shanghai Science and Technology, 1949–1984). Wei Hu and Fang Kaibing, eds. Shanghai: Kexue Jishu Wenxian Chuban She, 1985.

Shanghai liudong renkou (Shanghai's Floating Population). Shanghai Statistics Bureau, ed. Shanghai: Zhongguo Tongji Chuban She, 1989.

Shanghai nongcun shehui jingji (The Economy of Shanghai Rural Society). Shanghai Municipal Statistics Bureau, ed. Shanghai: Shanghai Shehui Kexue Chuban She, 1989.

Shanghai Pudong kaifa yu touzi (Development and Investment in Pudong, Shanghai). Hong Kong: Jingji Daobao Chuban She, n.d., apparently 1990.

Shanghai Pudong xinqu fazhan qianjing yu touzi zhengce (Development Prospects and Investment Policies in Shanghai's Pudong New Area). Economic Information Center, ed. Shanghai: Kexue Jishu Chuban She, 1990.

Shanghai Pudong xinqu tongji nianbao, 1991 (Annual Statistical Report of the Pudong New Area). Shanghai Municipal Government Statistics Bureau, ed. Shanghai: Shanghai Kexue Jishu Chuban She, 1991.

Shanghai qiye jia (The Shanghai Entrepreneur). Zhou Bi, ed. Beijing: Zhongguo Jingji Chuban She, 1987.

Shanghai qiye jituan: Jianli yu fazhan (Shanghai Enterprise Groups: Their Establishment and Development). Dai Jinde and Li Gengchun, eds. Shanghai: Kexue Puji Chuban She, 1988.

Shanghai quanshu (Shanghai Encyclopedia). Chu Dawei, ed. Shanghai: Xuelin Chuban She, 1989.

Shanghai shehui kexue (Social Science in Shanghai). Institute of Information Studies of the Shanghai Social Science Academy, ed. Shanghai: Shanghai Shehui Kexue Chuban She, 1988.

Shanghai shehui tongji ziliao, 1980–1983 (Statistical Materials on Shanghai Society, 1980–1983). Group on the Shanghai Social Situation and Trends, ed. Shanghai: Huadong Shifan Daxue Chuban She, 1988.

Shanghai shehui xiankuang he qushi, 1980–1983 (Situations and Trends in Shanghai Society, 1980–1983). Zheng Gongliang et al., eds. Shanghai: Huadong Shifan Daxue Chuban She, 1988.

Shanghai shengli de shinian, 1976–1985 (Shanghai's Ten Years of Victory, 1976–1985). Shanghai CCP Propaganda Department and Shanghai Municipal Statistics Bureau, eds. Shanghai: Shanghai Renmin Chuban She, 1986.

Shanghai shi 1985 nian gongye pucha ziliao (Materials from the 1985 Industrial Survey of Shanghai). Gu Delun et al., eds. Shanghai: Zhongguo Tongji Chuban She, 1988.

Shanghai shi di sanci renkou pucha ziliao huibian (Compendium of Materials from the Third Census in Shanghai Municipality). Shanghai Census Office, ed. Shanghai: Shanghai Renkou Pucha Bangong Shi, 1984.

Shanghai shi difang xing fagui huibian, 1980–1985 (Compendium of Local Laws of Shanghai Municipality, 1980–1985). Secretariat of the Standing Committee of the Shanghai People's Congress, ed. Shanghai: Shanghai People's Congress, 1986.

Shanghai shi duiwai jingji tongji nianjian, 1993 (Foreign Economic Statistical Yearbook of Shanghai, 1993). Shanghai Municipal Statistics Bureau, ed., *neibu ziliao*. Shanghai: Shanghai Tongji Ju, 1993.

Shanghai shi fagui huizhang huibian, 1949–1985 (Compendium of Laws and Regulations of Shanghai City, 1949–1985). Shanghai: Shanghai Renmin Chuban She, 1986.

Shanghai shi gaoxiao zhuanye jieshao (Introduction to the Professions in Shanghai's University-level Academies). Fang Ren, ed. Shanghai: Jiaotong Daxue Chuban She, 1988.

Shanghai shi jiaoqu gongye qiye daquan (Compendium on Industrial Enterprises in the Shanghai Suburbs). Gu Delun and Xie Jinhuai, eds. Shanghai: Zhongguo Tongji Chuban She, 1988.

Shanghai shi jingji dili (Shanghai Economic Geography). Cheng Lu, ed. Beijing: Xinhua Chuban She, 1987.

Shanghai shi liyong waizi gongzuo shouce (Shanghai Overseas Investment Utilization Handbook). Shanghai Municipal Foreign Economic Trade Committee, ed. Shanghai: Shanghai Fanyi Chuban Gongsi, 1985. (Also, a second edition in 1988.)

Shanghai shi nongye jixie hua fazhan zhanlüe yanjiu (Studies on Strategy for Developing Agricultural Mechanization in Shanghai Municipality). Xie Zifen, ed. Shanghai: Shanghai Kexue Puji Chuban She, 1991.

"Shanghai shi qingshaonian baohu tiaolie" lifa jishi (Record on the Legislation of the 'Rules for Protection of Youths and Infants in Shanghai'). Drafting Office for the "Rules for Protection of Youths and Infants in Shanghai," ed. Shanghai: Shanghai Shehui Kexue Yuan Chuban She, 1987.

Shanghai shi waishang touzi qiye gaikuang (Shanghai Enterprises with Foreign Investment). Shanghai Translation and Publishing Centre, ed. Shanghai: Shanghai Fanyi Chuban Gongsi, 1988.

Shanghai shi wenxue jiang huojiang zuopin ji (1982–1984 nian baogao wenxue shige) (Collection of Prizewinning Works in Shanghai Literature [Reportage and Poems, 1982–1984]), 2 vols. Shanghai: Shanghai Shehui Kexue Yuan Chuban She, 1986.

Shanghai shi wenxue jiang huojiang zuopin ji (1982–1984 nian duan bian xiaoshuo) (Collection of Prizewinning Works in Shanghai Literature [Novellas and Short Stories, 1982–1984]), 2 vols. Shanghai: Shanghai Shehui Kexue Yuan Chuban She, 1986.

Shanghai shi wenxue jiang huojiang zuopin ji (1982–1984 nian lilun pinglun) (Collection of Prizewinning Works in Shanghai Literature [Theory and Criticism, 1982–1984]). Shanghai: Shanghai Shehui Kexue Yuan Chuban She, 1986.

Shanghai shi Xuhui qu diming zhi (Gazetteer of Shanghai City's Xuhui District). Shanghai: Shanghai Shehui Kexue Yuan Chuban She, 1990.

Shanghai shi zixun fuwu gongsi minglü (Catalogue of Shanghai Consultancy and Service Companies). Jin Zixin, ed. Shanghai: Xuelin Chuban She, 1985.

Shanghai shimin banshi zhinan (Citizen's Practical Guide to Shanghai). Shanghai Municipal Government Administrative Office, ed. Shanghai: Shanghai Renmin Chuban She, 1989.

Shanghai tongji nianjian, various years to 1993 (Shanghai Statistical Yearbook). Shanghai Shi Tongji Ju, ed. Beijing: Zhongguo Tongji Chuban She.

Shanghai touzi zhinan (Shanghai Investment Guide). Shanghai Investment and Trust Corporation, ed. Shanghai and Hong Kong: Shanghai Fanyi Chuban She and China Information Source Co., 1984.

Shanghai wenhua (Shanghai Culture). Liu Zhengyuan, ed. Hong Kong: Jingji Daobao She, n.d. [1989?].

Shanghai wenhua nianjian, 1987 (Shanghai Culture Yearbook, 1987). Liu Zhenyuan et al., eds. Shanghai: Zhongguo Da Baike Chuban She, 1987.

Shanghai yu Xianggang de jingji hezuo (Shanghai–Hongkong Economic Cooperation). China Economic Research and Development Consultants, eds. Hong Kong: Zhongguo Jingji Yanjiu Zixun Gongsi, 1988.

Shanghai zhigong tiaojian ziliao shouce (Handbook on the Conditions of Shanghai Employees). Shanghai Statistics Bureau, ed. Shanghai: Shanghai Tongji Chuban She, 1985.

Shanghai ziben zhuyi gongshang ye de shehui zhuyi gaizao (The Socialist Transformation of Shanghai's Capitalist Industry and Commerce). Shanghai Academy of Social Sciences, ed. Shanghai: Shanghai Renmin Chuban She, 1980.

Shangpin jingji yu rencai ziyuan peizhi (The Commodity Economy and Allocation of Talents and Resources). Shanghai Municipal Personnel Bureau and Shanghai Municipal Scientific and Technical Cadres Bureau, eds. Shanghai: Shanghai Shehui Kexue Yuan Chuban She, 1988.

Shanguang de zuyi: Shanghai shi gongchan dangyuan xianjin shiyi xuan (Flashing Footprints: Selected Progressive Deeds by Shanghai Communist Party Members). Shanghai: Shanghai Renmin Chuban She, 1986.

Shehui zhuyi jingji wenti xinlun (New Ideas on Questions of the Socialist Economy). Shanghai Economics Association, ed. Shanghai: Shanghai Shehui Kexue Yuan Chuban She, 1987.

Shehui zhuyi shangpin jingji tantao (Inquiries into the Socialist Commodity Economy). Shanghai Economics Association, ed. Shanghai: Shanghai Shehui Kexue Yuan Chuban She, 1987.

Shenhua qiye gaige tansuo (Explorations on Deepening Enterprise Reforms). Shanghai Economics Association, ed. Shanghai: Shanghai Shehui Kexue Yuan Chuban She, 1987.

Shi Huanzhang et al. *Huadong Zhengfa Xueyuan faxue suoshi lunwen ji* (Collection of Master's Theses in Law from the East China Institute of Politics and Law). Shanghai: Shanghai Shehui Kexue Yuan Chuban She, 1988.

Shi Tianchuan. *Guangbo dianshi gailun* (General Outline on Broadcasting and Television). Shanghai: Fudan Daxue Chuban She, 1987.

Shidai de zuowei yu lilun de xuanze: Xifang jindai sichao yu Zhongguo "Wusi" qimeng sixiang (Theoretical Selections from a Time Out of Joint: Modern Tides of Thought in the West and the Enlightenment Thought of China's "May 4"). Liu Guisheng, ed. Beijing: Qinghua Daxue Chuban She, 1989.

Shijie shida zongjiao (Ten Great Religions of the World). Huang Xinchuan, ed. Beijing: Dongfang Chuban She, 1988.

Shijie xin jishu geming yu Shanghai de duice (The Global Revolution in New Technology and Shanghai's Policies in Response). Shanghai Economic Research Center and Shanghai Science and Technology Committee, eds. Shanghai: Shanghai Shehui Kexue Yuan Chuban She, 1986.

Shuiwu gongzuo shouce (Tax Work Handbook). Zou Yunfang, ed. Beijing: Nengyuan Chuban She, 1987.

Song Qiang et al. *Zhongguo keyi shuo bu* (China Can Say No). Beijing: Zhonghua Gongshang Lianhe Chuban She, 1996.

Songjiang nianjian, 1987 [and 1988] (Songjiang Yearbook, 1987 [and 1988]). Shanghai: Shanghai Shehui Kexue Yuan Chuban She, 1987 [and 1988].

Songjiang xian xianqing: Xiandai hua jincheng diaocha (The Current Situation in Songjiang County: An Investigation of the Modernization Process). Yao Xitang, ed. vol. II. Shanghai: no publisher but probably the Shanghai Academy of Social Sciences, n.d.

Songjiang xian zhi (Songjiang County Gazetteer). He Huimin, ed. Shanghai: Shanghai Renmin Chuban She, 1991.

Songjiang zhenzhi (Gazetteer of Songjiang Town). Che Chi et al., eds. Shanghai: Shanghai Renmin Chuban She, 1988.

Su Xiaokang, Wang Luxiang, and Xia Jun. *Heshang* (River Elegy). Repr., Hong Kong: Sanlian Shudian, 1988.

Sunan fada diqu jiaoyu fazhan zhanlüe huanjing yanjiu baogao (Research Report on the Environment for Educational Development Strategy in the Developed Region of Southern Jiangsu). Task Force on the Environment for Educational Development Strategy in the Developed Region of Southern Jiangsu, ed. and pub. Mimeographed "discussion draft" (*taolun gao*), n.p., 1991.

Tao Yongkuan et al. *Dali fazhan disan chanye* (Vigorously Develop Tertiary Industry). Shanghai: Shanghai Shehui Kexue Yuan Chuban She, 1986.

Tao Youzhi et al. *Sunan moshi yu zhifu zhi dao* (The South Jiangsu Model and Road to Prosperity). Shanghai: Shanghai Shehui Kexue Yuan Chuban She, 1988.

Tao Youzhi. *Jishu gaige xinlun* (New Ideas on Technical Reform). Shanghai: Shanghai Renmin Chuban She, 1987.

Tian Yinong, Zhu Fulin, and Xiang Huaicheng. *Zhongguo caizheng guanli tizhi de gaige* (The Structural Reform of Chinese Fiscal Management). Beijing: Jingji Kexue Chuban She, 1985.

Tianjin tongji nianjian (Tianjin Statistical Yearbook), various years. Tianjin Statistical Bureau, ed. Beijing: Zhongguo Tongji Chuban She.

Tongji cidian (Statistical Dictionary). Jia Hongyu, ed. Shanghai: Shanghai Renmin Chuban She, 1986.

Tongyi gongzuo shouce (Handbook of Unification Work). Office of Unification Studies and Voice of Jinling Broadcasting Station, eds. Nanjing: Nanjing Daxue Chuban She, 1986.

Tongzhan gongzuo shouce (Handbook of United Front Work). Ma Fen et al., eds. Shanghai: Shanghai Renmin Chuban She, 1989.

Wang Anyun and Bo Xiangyuan. *Shanghai Da Shijie* (Shanghai's Great World [entertainment center]). Wuhan: Changjiang Wenyi Chuban She, 1988.

Wang Hongxun et al. *Fenghuang sanshi nian, 1958–1988* (Thirty Years of Phoenix [Bicycle Factory, Shanghai], 1958–1988). Shanghai: Shanghai Shehui Kexue Yuan Chuban She, 1988.

Wang Yu et al. *Da juanbian shiqi* (The Era of Great Transformation). Shijiazhuang: Hebei Renmin Chuban She, 1987.

Wenhui bao dashi ji, 1938.1–1939.5, 1945.8–1947.5 (Record of Major Events at the *Wenhui Daily* [to 1947]). Wenhui Bao Baoshi Yanjiu Shi, ed. Shanghai: Wenhui Chuban She, 1986.

Wenhui bao shilüe, 1938.1–1939.5, 1945.8–1947.5 (Outline History of the *Wenhui Daily* [to 1947]). Wenhui Bao Baoshi Yanjiu Shi, ed. Shanghai: Wenhui Chuban She, 1988.

Wenhui bao wushi nian, 1938–1988 (Fifty Years of the *Wenhui Daily, 1938–1988*). Wenhui Bao She, ed. Shanghai: Wenhui Chuban She, 1988.

Wenzhou moshi de lilun tansuo (Theoretical Exploration of the Wenzhou Model). Lin Bai et al., eds. Nanning: Guangxi Renmin Chuban She, 1987.

Wenzhou qiye daquan, 1986 (Compendium of Wenzhou Enterprises, 1986). Wang Wence, ed. Wenzhou: Wenzhou Shi Qiye Guanli Xiehui and Wenzhou Shi Gongye Pucha Bangong Shi, 1986.

Wenzhou shiyan qu (The Wenzhou Experimental Zone). Pan Shangeng, ed. Beijing: Nengyuan Chuban She, 1988.

Wu Yantao et al. *Shanghai de gupiao he zhaijuan* (Shanghai Shares and Bonds). Shanghai: Shanghai Shehui Kexue Yuan Chuban She, 1988.

Xian de jingji yu jiaoyu de diaocha (Survey of County Economies and Education). Task Force for Research on China's Rural Education, ed. Beijing: Jiaoyu Kexue Chuban She, 1989.

Xiandai hua yu Zhongguo wenhua yantao hui lunwen huibian (Proceedings of the Conference on Modernization and Chinese Culture). Chiao Chien, ed. Hong Kong: Xianggang Zhongwen Daxue Shehui Kexue Yuan Ji Shehui Yanjiu Suo, 1985.

Xiandai Zhongguo de yibai xiang jianshe (One Hundred Projects in Modern China). "One Hundred Projects in Modern China" Editorial Group, ed. Beijing: Hongqi Chuban She, 1985.

Xiao Zhenmei. "Dalu huatan sishi nian" (Mainland Painting for Forty Years). *Zhongguo dalu yanjiu* (Mainland China Studies) 35:11 (November 1992), pp. 89–98.

Xiao Zhenmei. "Zhongguo dalu de xiandai hua" (Contemporary Painting on the Chinese Mainland). *Zhongguo dalu yanjiu* (Mainland Chinese Studies) 36:4 (April 1993), pp. 75–86.

Xiao Zhenmei. *Xian jieduan zhi dalu nongjing biange* (The Transformation of the Mainland's Rural Economy at the Present Stage). Taibei: Juliu Tushu Gongsi, 1988.

Xie Zifen et al. *Shanghai xiangzhen qiye jingji, keshu fazhan zhanlüe he zhengce wenti yanjiu* (Strategy and Policy Studies for the Economic and Technical Development of Shanghai Rural Enterprises). Shanghai: Shanghai Shehui Kexue Yuan, 1988.

Xie Zifen, Li Wuwei et al. *Quyu jingji yanjiu: Zhanlüe guihua yu moxing* (Regional Economic Studies: Strategies, Plans, and Models). Shanghai: Shanghai Shehui Kexue Yuan Chuban She, 1988.

Xin xiaoshuo zai 1985 (New Novellas in 1985). Wu Liang and Cheng Depei, eds. Shanghai: Shanghai Shehui Kexue Yuan Chuban She, 1986.

Xin Zhongguo gongye jingji shi (A History of New China's Industrial Economy). Wang Haibo, ed. Beijing: Jingji Guanli Chuban She, 1986.

Xin Zhongguo shangye shigao, 1949–1982 (Outline History of New China's Commerce, 1949–1982). Ministry of Commerce, ed. Beijing: Zhongguo Caizheng Jingji Chuban She, 1984.

Xinwen xiaoshuo zai '86 (News Novellas, '86). Wu Liang and Cheng Depei, eds. Shanghai: Shanghai Shehui Kexue Yuan Chuban She, 1988.

Xinwen ziyou lunji (Collection of Essays on Journalistic Freedom). Shanghai: Wenhui Chuban She, 1988.

Xu Chongqi and Tang Yanbo. "Shanghai Pudong jihua de fazhan he pinggu" (Development and Assessment of Shanghai's Pudong Plan). *Zhongguo dalu yanjiu* (Mainland China Studies) 36:8 (August 1993), pp. 29–44.

Xu Riqing et al. *Shehui zhuyi chengshi caizheng xue* (Socialist Urban Finance). Shanghai: Shanghai Shehui Kexue Yuan Chuban She, 1986.

Xu Yiren and Cheng Pu. *Falü de shixiao wenti* (Issues of Legal Prescription). Shanghai: Shanghai Shehui Kexue Yuan Chuban She, 1988.

Xu Yonglu, Chu Yugen, and Yu Zhuwen. *Jingji qiangren zhi lu* (An Economic Strong Man's Way). Shanghai: Shanghai Shehui Kexue Yuan Chuban She, 1987.

Xu Yuanming and Ye Ding. *Tangqiao gongye hua zhi lu* (The Way to Industrialization in Tangqiao). Shanghai: Shanghai Shehui Kexue Yuan Chuban She, 1987.

Xu Zhenliang. "Shanghai caizheng shouru 'huapo' de xiankuang, chengyin ji qi duice" (The "Slide" of Shanghai's Financial Income: Situation, Reasons, and Countermeasures). *Caijing yanjiu* (Financial and Economic Studies) (March 1988), pp. 18–23.

Yan Jiaqi. *Lianbang Zhongguo gouxiang* (Plan for a Federal China). Hong Kong: Mingbao Chuban She, 1992.

Yan Jiaqi and Gao Gao. *Wenhua dageming shinian shi* (Ten Years of the Great Cultural Revolution). Tianjin: Tianjin Renmin Chuban She, 1986.

Yan Tingchang, Cai Beihua, Xu Zhihe et al. *Shanghai lüyou ye de jintian he mingtian* (Shanghai Tourism Today and Tomorrow). Shanghai: Shanghai Shehui Kexue Yuan Chuban She, 1987.

Yang Dongping. *Chengshi jifeng: Beijing he Shanghai de wenhua jingshen* (City Monsoon: The Cultural Spirit of Beijing and Shanghai). Beijing: Dongfang Chuban She, 1994.

Yanhai jingji kaifang qu: Jingji yanjiu he tongji ziliao (Coastal Open Economic Zones: Economic Research and Statistical Materials). State Statistical Bureau, ed. Beijing: Zhongguo Tongji Chuban She, 1989.

Yao Shihuang. *Jin sanjiao de tansuo* (Search for the Golden Delta). Chongqing: Chongqing Chuban She, 1988.

Yige chengjiao xiangcun de jintian he mingtian: Shanghai shi Shanghai xian Meilong xiang jingji fazhan zongti guihua yanjiu (A Suburban Village Today and Tomorrow: Comprehensive Plan for the Economic Development of Meilong Town, Shanghai County, Shanghai). Ling Yaochu and Zhang Zhaoan, eds. Shanghai: Shanghai Shehui Kexue Chuban She, 1988.

Yu Ning and Li Deming. *Zenyang xie xinwen pinglun* (How to Write News Editorials). Beijing: Zhongguo Xinwen Chuban She, 1987.

Yu Tijun and Shi Hejun. *Baocheng, zulin, gufen zhi* (The System of Responsibility, Leasing, and Shares). Shanghai: Shanghai Fanyi Chuban She, 1988.

Yu Youwei. *Shanghai jindai Fojiao jianshi* (Concise History of Modern Buddhism in Shanghai). Shanghai: Huadong Shifan Daxue Chuban She, 1988.

Yuan Enzhen et al. *Wenzhou moshi yu fuyu zhi lu* (The Wenzhou Model and the Way to Affluence). Shanghai: Shanghai Shehui Kexue Yuan Chuban She, 1987.

Zhang Linlan. "Women de tansuo—jiefang hou de Shanghai 'Xinmin bao' " (Our Exploration—Shanghai's *Xinmin News* After Liberation." In Chen Mingde et al., *"Xinmin bao" chunqiu* (The Spring and Autumn of the *Xinmin News*). Chongqing: Chongqing Chuban She, 1987, pp. 405–30.

Zhang Shanmin, Li Xin, and Wu Zhangnan et al. *Zou xiang chenggong* (Marching to Accomplishments). Shanghai: Shanghai Shehui Kexue Yuan Chuban She, 1988.

Zhang Sui. *Zongjiao gujin tan* (Religion Yesterday and Today). Shanghai: Shanghai Shehui Kexue Yuan Chuban She, 1985.

Zhang Zhanbin et al. *Xin Zhongguo qiye lingdao zhidu* (Leadership Systems for New China's Enterprises). Beijing: Chunqiu Chuban She, 1988.

Zhang Zhongli, Zhu Qingzha et al. *Disan chanye de lilun yu shixian: Jianlun Shanghai disan chanye fazhan zhanlüe* (Theory and Practice of the Tertiary Sector: On the Development Strategy of Shanghai's Tertiary Sector). Shanghai: Shanghai Shehui Kexue Yuan Chuban She, 1986.

Zhangjiagang Bureau of Rural Industries. *Zhangjiagang shi xiangzhen gongye zhi* (Gazetteer of Zhangjiagang Rural Industries). Shanghai: Shanghai Renmin Chuban She, 1990.

Zhe Xiaoye. *Chengshi zai zhuanzhe dianshang* (Cities at a Turning Point). Beijing: Zhongguo Funü Chuban She, 1989.

Zhejiang jingji nianjian (Zhejiang Economic Yearbook, various years). Zhejiang CCP Committee Policy Research Office and Zhejiang People's Government Economic, Technical, and Social Development Research Center, eds. Hangzhou: Zhejiang Renmin Chuban She, same years.

Zheng Zu'an. *Shanghai diming xiaozhi* (Précis on Shanghai Placenames). Shanghai: Shanghai Shehui Kexue Chuban She, 1988.

Zhong-Ying duizhao Zhonggong changyong ciyu lubian (A Chinese English-Lexicon of Chinese Communist Terminology), Institute of Current China Studies, ed. Taipei: Institute of Current China Studies, 1993.

Zhonggong zhengquan sishi nian de huigu yu zhanwang (Recollections and Prospects on the Forty Years of CCP Power). Wu An-chia, ed. Taipei: Guoji guanxi yanjiu zhongxin, 1991.

Zhongguo 1986 nian 74 chengzhen renkou qianyi chouxiang diaocha ziliao (Sample

Survey Materials on 1986 Chinese Migration in 74 Cities and Towns). *Chinese Demography* Editorial Group, ed. Beijing: *Zhongguo renkou kexue* bianji bu, 1988.

Zhongguo 1987 nian 1% renkou chouxiang pucha ziliao: Shanghai shi fence (Chinese 1987 1% Sample Survey: Shanghai Municipality Volume). Shanghai City Statistical Bureau, ed. Beijing: Zhongguo Tongji Chuban She, 1988.

Zhongguo 1987 nian 1% renkou chouxiang pucha ziliao: Zhejiang sheng fence (Chinese 1987 1% Sample Survey: Zhejiang Province Volume). Zhejiang Province Statistical Bureau, ed. Beijing: Zhongguo Tongji Chuban She, 1988.

Zhongguo 1987 nian 1% renkou chouxiang pucha ziliao: Jiangsu sheng fence (Chinese 1987 1% Sample Survey: Jiangsu Province Volume). Jiangsu Province Statistical Bureau and Jiangsu Province Census Office, eds. Nanjing: Zhongguo Tongji Chuban She, 1988.

Zhongguo 1987 nian 1% renkou chouxiang pucha ziliao: Quanguo fence (Tabulations of China 1% Population Sample Survey: National Volume). Department of Population Statistics, State Statistical Bureau, ed. Beijing: Zhongguo Tongji Chuban She, 1988.

Zhongguo baike nianjian, 1990 (Encyclopedic Yearbook of China, 1990). Luo Luo, ed. Shanghai: Zhongguo Da Baike Quanshu Chuban She, 1990.

Zhongguo caizheng tongji, 1950–1985 (Chinese Fiscal Statistics, 1950–1985). Comprehensive Planning Office of the PRC Ministry of Finance, ed. Beijing: Zhongguo Caizheng Jingji Chuban She, 1987.

Zhongguo chengshi jiating (The Chinese Urban Family). Five Cities Family Research Project, ed. Jinan: Shandong Renmin Chuban She, 1985.

Zhongguo chengshi jingji shehui nianjian (Economic and Social Yearbook of China's Cities, various years). Zhongguo Chengshi Jingji Shehui Nianjian Lishi Hui, ed. Beijing: Zhongguo Chengshi Jingji Shehui Chuban She, various years.

Zhongguo chengshi jingji tizhi gaige xuexi wenxuan (Selected Studies of China's Urban Economic System Reforms). Shanghai Academy of Social Sciences, ed. Shanghai: Shanghai Shehui Kexue Yuan Chuban She, 1984.

Zhongguo chengshi tongji nianjian (Statistical Yearbook of Chinese Cities, various years). State Statistical Bureau, ed. Beijing: Zhongguo Tongji Xinxi Zixun Fuwu Zhongxin and Xin Shijie Chuban She.

Zhongguo chengshi tongji nianjian (Statistical Yearbook of Chinese Cities, various years). State Statistical Bureau, ed. Beijing: Zhongguo Tongji Xinxi Zixun Fuwu Zhongxin and Zhongguo Jianshe Chuban She, various years.

Zhongguo chuban nianjian, 1985 (China Publishing Yearbook, 1985). China Publishers' Association, ed. Beijing: Shangwu Yinshu Guan, 1985.

Zhongguo falü nianjian (China Law Yearbook, various years, 1986–90). Beijing and Chengdu: Zhongguo Falü Nianjian Chuban She, published the following year.

Zhongguo funü gongzuo shouce (China Women's Work Handbook). Editorial Group for the *China Women's Work Handbook,* ed. Shanghai: Shanghai Renmin Chuban She, 1988.

Zhongguo funü tongji ziliao, 1949–1989 (Statistical Materials on Chinese Women, 1949–1989). Research Institute of the All-China Women's Federation and Research Office of Shaanxi Provincial Women's Federation, eds. Beijing: Zhongguo Tongji Chuban She, 1991.

Zhongguo gaige da cidian (Dictionary of Chinese Reforms). Dictionary of Chinese Reforms Editorial Group, ed. Haikou: Hainan Chuban She, 1992.

Zhongguo gaige quanshu (Complete Book of Chinese Reforms). 6 vols., separate editorial committee for each. Dalian: Dalian Chuban She, 1992.

Zhongguo Gongchan Dang dangyuan da cidian (Dictionary for CCP Members). Cheng Min, ed. Beijing: Zhongguo Guoji Guangbo Chuban She, 1991.

Zhongguo Gongchan Dang qishi nian (The Chinese Communist Party's Seventy Years). Hu Sheng, ed. Beijing: Zhonggong Dangshi Chuban She, 1991.

Zhongguo Gongchang Dang renming da cidian, 1921–1991 (Who's Who of the CCP, 1921–1991). Sheng Ping, ed. Beijing: Zhongguo Guoji Guangbo Chuban She, 1991.

Zhongguo gongye de fazhan, 1949–1984 (China's Industrial Development, 1949–1984). Guojia Tongji Ju, Gongye Jiaotong Wuzi Tongji Si, ed. Beijing: Zhongguo Tongji Chuban She, 1985.

Zhongguo gongye jingji tongji ziliao, 1987 (Statistical Materials on China's Industrial Economy, 1987). Guojia Tongji Ju, Gongye Jiaotong Wuzi Tongji Si, ed. Beijing: Zhongguo Tongji Chuban She, 1987.

Zhongguo jianzhu ye tongji ziliao, 1952–1985 (China Construction Statistics, 1952–1985). Guojia Tongji Ju, Guding Zichan Touzi Tongji Si, ed. Beijing: Zhongguo Tongji Chuban She, 1988.

Zhongguo jiaoyu chengjiu: Tongji ziliao, 1949–1983 (Achievement of Education in China: Statistics, 1949–1983). Department of Planning, PRC Ministry of Education, ed. Beijing: Zhongguo Jiaoyu Chuban She, 1984.

Zhongguo jiaoyu chengjiu: Tongji ziliao, 1980–1985 (Achievement of Education in China: Statistics, 1980–1985). Department of Planning, PRC State Education Commission, ed. Beijing: Zhongguo Jiaoyu Chuban She, 1986.

Zhongguo jiaoyu tongji nianjian (China Education Statistics Yearbook). State Education Committee, ed. Beijing: Zhongguo Jiaoyu Chuban She, 1991 for 1990 edition, and 1992 for 1991–92 edition.

Zhongguo jiaoyu tongji nianjian, 1987 nian (Statistical Yearbook on Chinese Education, 1987). Guojia Jiaoyu Weiyuan Hui, Jihua Caiwu Ju (Planning and Finance Bureau of the State Education Commission), ed. Beijing: Beijing Gongye Daxue Chuban She, 1988.

Zhongguo jingji jiegou wenti yanjiu (Studies on Issues of Chinese Economic Structure). Ma Hong and Sun Shangqing, eds. Beijing: Renmin Chuban She, 1981.

Zhongguo jingji nianjian (China Economic Yearbook, various years). Compilation Committee for China Economic Yearbook, ed. Beijing: Jingji Guanli Chuban She, various years.

Zhongguo laodong gongzi tongji ziliao, 1949–1985 (Statistical Materials on Chinese Labor and Wages, 1949–1985). Beijing: Zhongguo Tongji Chuban She, 1987.

Zhongguo minzhu dangpai: lishi, zhenggang, renwu (China's Democratic Parties: Histories, Platforms, and Personages). Qin Guosheng and Hu Zhisheng, eds. Jinan: Shandong Renmin Chuban She, 1990.

Zhongguo qingshaonian fanzui yanjiu nianjian, 1987 (Yearbook on Chinese Juvenile Delinquency Studies, 1987). Chinese Juvenile Delinquency Studies Association, ed. Beijing: Chunqiu Chuban She, 1988.

Zhongguo renkou dili (Demographic Geography of China). Hu Huanyong and Zhang Shanyu, eds., *neibu*. Shanghai: Huadong Shifan Daxue Chuban She, 2 vols., *shang ce* 1984, *xia ce* 1986.

Zhongguo renkou nianjian, 1985 (China Population Yearbook, 1985). Population Research Center, CASS, ed. Beijing: Zhongguo Shehui Kexue Chuban She, 1986.

Zhongguo renkou qianyi (Population Shifts in China). Tian Fang and Ling Fatong, eds. Beijing: Zhishi Chuban She, 1987.

Zhongguo renkou qianyi yu chengshi hua yanjiu (Studies on Chinese Migration and Urbanization). Editorial Group for Studies on Chinese Migration and Urbanization, ed. Beijing: Zhongguo Shehui Kexue Yuan Renkou Yanjiu Suo, 1988.

Zhongguo renkou tongji nianjian (China Population Statistics Yearbook, various years). State Statistical Bureau, comp. Beijing: Zhongguo Zhanwang Chuban She, the same year.

Zhongguo renkou: Jiangsu fence (China's Population: Jiangsu Volume). Du Wenzhen et al., eds. Beijing: Zhongguo Caizheng Jingji Chuban She, 1987.

Zhongguo renkou: Shanghai fence (China's Population: Shanghai Volume). Hu Huanyong et al., eds. Beijing: Zhongguo Caizheng Jingji Chuban She, 1987.

Zhongguo renkou: Sichuan fence (China's Population: Sichuan Volume). Liu Hongkang et al., eds., Beijing: Zhongguo Caizheng Jingji Chuban She, 1988.

Zhongguo renming da cidian: dangdai renwu juan (Who's Who in China: Volume on Contemporary Personages). Editorial Group for Who's Who in China, ed. Shanghai: Shanghai Cishu Chuban She, 1992.

Zhongguo shehui tongji ziliao, 1987 (Chinese Social Statistics, 1987). Social Statistics Office, State Statistical Bureau, ed. Beijing: Zhongguo Tongji Chuban She, 1987.

Zhongguo shehui zhuyi chengshi jingji xue (Chinese Socialist Urban Economics). Zhu Linxing, ed. Shanghai: Shanghai Shehui Kexue Chuban She, 1986.

Zhongguo shinian gailan (Summary of China's Ten Years of Reform). Gu Changchun and Deng Derong, eds. Beijing: Zhongguo Zhanwang Chuban She, 1989.

Zhongguo shuiwu baike quanshu (Encyclopedia of Chinese Taxation). Encyclopedia of Chinese Taxation Editorial Group, ed. Beijing: Jingji Guanli Chuban She, 1991.

Zhongguo tongji nianjian (China Statistical Yearbook), each year, 1981–93. State Statistical Bureau, ed. Beijing: Zhongguo Tongji Chuban She, 1981–93.

Zhongguo tongji zhaiyao, 1986 (A Statistical Survey of China, 1986). State Statistical Bureau, ed. Beijing: Zhongguo Tongji Chuban She, 1986.

Zhongguo tongji zhaiyao, 1988 (A Statistical Survey of China, 1988). State Statistical Bureau, ed. Beijing: Zhongguo Tongji Chuban She, 1988.

Zhongguo wujia tongji nianjian (Statistical Yearbook of Chinese Prices, various years). Urban Society and Economy Survey Group, ed. Beijing: Zhongguo Tongji Chuban She.

Zhongguo xinwen nianjian (Yearbook of Chinese Journalism, various years). An Gang et al., eds. Beijing: Zhongguo Shehui Kexue Chuban She.

Zhongguo xinwen nianjian, 1982 (Yearbook of Chinese Journalism, 1982). News Studies Institute of the Chinese Social Science Academy, ed. Beijing: Zhongguo Shehui Kexue Chuban She, 1982.

Zhongguo xueshu jie dashi ji, 1919–1985 (Chronicle of Chinese Academic Circles, 1919–1985). Wang Yafu and Zhang Hengzhong, eds. Shanghai: Shanghai Shehui Kexue Yuan Chuban She, 1988.

Zhongguo yanhai diqu xiao chengzhen fazhan yu renkou qianyi (Migration and the Development of Small Cities and Towns on the China Coast). Liu Zheng et al., eds. Beijing: Zhongguo Caizheng Jingji Chuban She, 1989.

Zhongguo yinyue nianjian, 1990 [also 1988 and 1989] (China Music Yearbook, 1990). Jinan: Shandong Jiaoyu Chuban She, 1990; Beijing: Wenhua Yishu Chuban She for 1988 and 1989.

Zhongguo youhua zhan xuanji (Selection from an Exhibition of Chinese Oil Paintings), portfolios 1 and 2. Shao Chuangu, ed. Shanghai: Shanghai Renmin Meishu Chuban She, 1988.

Zhongguo Zhenjiang hezi, hezuo, buchang maoyi xiangmu mulu (A List of Projects for Joint Venture, Coproduction, and Compensation Trade in Zhenjiang, China). Zhenjiang Municipal Planning and Economic Committee and Zhenjiang Municipal Foreign Economic Trade Committee, eds. Zhenjiang, Jiangsu: no publisher, 1988.

Zhongguo zhuming daxue gailan (A Brief Overview of China's Famous Universities). Huang Zhanpeng, ed. Jinan: Shandong Renmin Chuban She, 1990.

Zhonghua Renmin Gonghe Guo jingji dashi ji, 1949–1980 (Chronicle of Economic Events in the PRC, 1949–1980). Fang Weizhong et al., eds. Beijing: Zhongguo Shehui Kexue Chuban She, 1984.

Zhonghua Renmin Gonghe Guo jingji guanli dashi ji (Chronicle of PRC Economic Management). *Dangdai Zhongguo Jingji Guanli* Editorial Dept., ed. Beijing: Zhongguo Jingji Chuban She, 1986.

Zhonghua Renmin Gonghe Guo renkou tongji ziliao huibian, 1949–1985 (Compendium of PRC Materials on Population Statistics, 1949–1985). Population Office of the State Statistical Bureau and Third Bureau of the Ministry of Public Security, eds., *neibu*. Beijing: Zhongguo Caizheng Jingji Chuban She, 1988.

Zhonghua Renmin Gonghe Guo tongji dashi ji, 1949–1991 (A Chronicle of Statistics in the PRC, 1949–1991). Zhang Sai, ed. Beijing: Zhongguo Tongji Chuban She, 1992.

Zhonghua Renmin Gonghe Guo xianfa (Constitution of the People's Republic of China [1982]). Beijing: Falü Chuban She, 1986.

Zhonghua Renmin Gonghe Guo xingzheng susong fa jianghua (Talking about the PRC's Administrative Litigation Law). Propaganda Office of the Judicial Department of the People's Republic of China, ed. Beijing: Falü Chuban She, 1990.

Zhongwai lishi renwu cidian (Who's Who of Historical World Figures). Wang Banghe et al., eds. Changsha: Hunan Renmin Chuban She, 1987.

Zhou Yongcai. *Jiang Zhe Hu mingtu techan zhi* (Special Products of Jiangsu, Zhejiang, and Shanghai). Nanjing: Nanjing Daxue Chuban She, 1987.

Zhu Linxing et al. *Zhongguo shehui zhuyi chengshi jingji xue* (China's Socialist Economics of Cities). Shanghai: Shanghai Shehui Kexue Yuan Chuban She, 1986.

Zou Yunfang et al. *Shui wu gongzuo shouce* (Tax Work Handbook). Shanghai: Nengyuan Chuban She, 1987.

Zuo Chuntai, Song Xinzhong et al. *Zhongguo shehui zhuyi caizheng jianshi* (Sketch History of China's Socialist Finance). Beijing: Zhongguo Caizheng Jingji Chuban She, 1988.

Some of the Interviewees

Chen Haowen, Chief, Materials Group, *Qingnian bao* (Youth News).

Chen Shenshen, Assistant Director, Institute of National Economy Research, Shanghai Academy of Social Sciences.

Chen Yuqun, Head, Shanghai Society of Ecological Economics.

Fu Qiangguo, Judge, Shanghai High People's Court.

Gu Mingyuan, President, China Society for Comparative Education.

Harris, Norma, U.S. Consul for Press and Cultural Affairs, U.S. Consulate General, Shanghai.

He Deyu, Researcher, Population Institute, Shanghai Academy of Social Sciences.

Li Wuwei, Shanghai Investment Consulting Corporation, and Deputy Director, Institute of National Economics, Shanghai Academy of Social Sciences.

Li Xuecheng, Reporter, Shanghai Radio and Television Bureau.

Lin Hao, Correspondent, *Shijie jingji daobao* (World Economic Herald).

Lin Lu, Chief Editor, *Shehui kexue bao* (Social Sciences Information).

Lin Quanshui, Associate Professor, Institute of Economics, Chinese Academy of Social Sciences.

Lü Zheng, Institute of Industrial Economics, Chinese Academy of Social Sciences.

Ma Da, Editor-in-Chief, *Wenhui bao,* and Standing Committee, Shanghai Municipal People's Congress.

Norris, John, U.S. Consul for Economic Affairs, U.S. Consulate General, Shanghai.

Orr, Iain, British Consul General, Shanghai.

Qin Jianxun, Correspondent, *Shijie jingji daobao* (World Economic Herald).

Shi Qingkai, Graduate Student in Economic Law, and Chief of the Academic Department of the Postgraduates' Union, Shanghai Academy of Social Sciences.

Shi Qingsheng, Researcher on Professionalization, People's Liberation Army, Beijing.

Shih, H.Y., Professor of Fine Arts, University of Hong Kong.

Shu Hanfeng, Journalist, *Shijie jingji daobao* (World Economic Herald).

Shu Renqiu, Chief Editor, *Xinmin wanbao* (Xinmin Evening News).

Song Jun, Director, Shanghai News Research Institute.

Su Songxing, Deputy Chief Editor, *Shehui Kexue bao* (Social Sciences Information).

Tatlow, Antony, Professor of Comparative Literature, University of Hong Kong.

Wang Chongfang, Assistant Professor, Department of International Politics, Fudan University.

Wang Shaoyun, International Department, Shanghai Television Station.

Williams, Adam, Jardine Mathieson, Shanghai.

Xia Jinxiong, Institute of World Economics, Shanghai Academy of Social Sciences.

Yan Chengzhong, Associate Research Professor, Shanghai Academy of Social Sciences.

Yang Sizheng, Member, Shanghai Committee of the Chinese People's Political Consultative Conference.

Yao Liang, Assistant Director, Institute of International Economics, Jiaotong University, Shanghai.

Yao Tinggang, Deputy Director, Institute of World Economy, Shanghai Academy of Social Sciences.

Yu Shutong, Vice-President, China Law Society.

Zhang Linlan, Deputy Editor, *Xinmin wanbao* (Xinmin Evening News).

Zhang Yongwei, Graduate Student in Political Sociology, Shanghai Academy of Social Sciences.

Zhou Ji, International Department, Shanghai Television Station.

Zhou Jianping, Deputy Director, Economic, Legal, and Social Consultancy Center, Shanghai Academy of Social Sciences.

Zhou Ruijin, Deputy Editor-in-Chief, *Jiefang ribao* (Liberation Daily).

Zhu Xingqing, Deputy Chief Editor, *Shijie jingji daobao* (World Economic Herald).

Zhuang Ming, Editor, *Shehui kexue bao* (Social Sciences Information).

Zou Fanyang, Former Director, Shanghai Radio and Television Bureau.

Index

Abortion, 255
Abstract art, 146, 147-148, 151-152
Action art, 155
Acton, Lord, 484
Adjudication, 335, 354
Advertising
    newspaper revenues from, 99-100, 102-103
    television revenues from, 104
Age
    at marriage, 219, 277n.16, 346
    in leadership selection, 487-490
Ai Qing, 167
Air pollution, 247, 284n.158
Alcohol consumption, 382-383
All-China Federation of Trade Unions
    (ACFTU), 398-399, 401-402, 404
Alley, The, 171
*American Politics: The Promise of
    Disharmony* (Huntington), 582
Amity Foundation, 67
Andrews, Julia, 157
Arbitration, 335, 354
"Ark, The" (Zhang Jie), 264-265
Army
    civilian control of, 325
    commercial activities/factories of, 327,
        330-332
    education and training, 327-328, 501
    and leadership succession, 467
    political appointments from, 324, 325, 326
    preuniversity year in, 428-429
    recruitment in, 327
    resistance to demobilization, 325
    and retirement policy, 325-327, 520, 521
    specialists in, 503
    state funding of, 328-330, 332

Aron, Raymond, 26
Artist (journal), 156
Arts, 141-203
    and aesthetic standards, 199-201
    censorship, 146-147, 150, 155, 161, 163,
        172, 175, 201
    lack of support for, 201-202
    modes of organization, 198-199
    salons, 202-203
    See also Film; Literature; Music; Painting;
        Theater
Association for Promoting Democracy, 559
Auden, W.H., 4
Authoritarianism
    characteristics of, 674-675
    corporatist, 594-596, 670-672, 680
    and economic growth, 591-592
    and goal change, 311-313
    monist, 596
    neoauthoritarianism, 581-584, 589-590
    and political culture, 584-588
    and population size, 593, 677
Authority, Weberian types of, 309,
        358-359n.62
Ayer, A.J., 627

Ba Jin, 162, 183, 563
Bai Hua, 172-173, 485
Bai Jingyi, 172
Bamboo Gang, 317
Bankruptcy law, 546
Bao Gong, 584, 606n.44
Baoshan Steel Plant, 342, 552
Bastid, Marianne, 415
Battle of Leopard Valley, The, 171
Bazin, André, 171

Lynn T. White III is a professor in the Woodrow Wilson School and the Politics Department at Princeton University, frequently visiting the University of Hong Kong's Centre of Asian Studies for research. His previous books include *Careers in Shanghai*, which mostly concerns the 1950s, and *Policies of Chaos*, dealing with the causes of the Cultural Revolution in the same city during the 1960s. *Unstately Power* follows these studies into the era of China's reforms and into Shanghai's hinterland. For each of these periods, White tries to explain political patterns by a combination of unintended and policy factors, both among individuals and at larger sizes of organization.

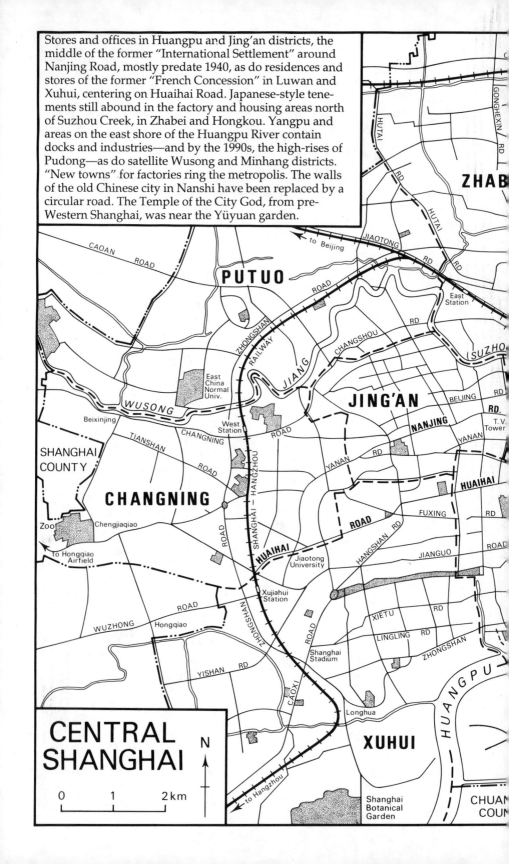

Stores and offices in Huangpu and Jing'an districts, the middle of the former "International Settlement" around Nanjing Road, mostly predate 1940, as do residences and stores of the former "French Concession" in Luwan and Xuhui, centering on Huaihai Road. Japanese-style tenements still abound in the factory and housing areas north of Suzhou Creek, in Zhabei and Hongkou. Yangpu and areas on the east shore of the Huangpu River contain docks and industries—and by the 1990s, the high-rises of Pudong—as do satellite Wusong and Minhang districts. "New towns" for factories ring the metropolis. The walls of the old Chinese city in Nanshi have been replaced by a circular road. The Temple of the City God, from pre-Western Shanghai, was near the Yüyuan garden.

GONGHEXIN RD

HUTAI RD

ZHAB

HUTAI RD

to Beijing

JIAOTONG

RD

RD

CAOAN ROAD

PUTUO

ROAD

East Station

ZHONGSHAN

RAILWAY

CHANGSHOU

RD

(SUZHO

East China Normal Univ.

JIANG

JING'AN

BEIJING RD

RD.

T.V. Tower

WUSONG

Beixinjing

West Station

CHANGNING

ROAD

NANJING

YANAN

SHANGHAI COUNTY

TIANSHAN

ROAD

SHANGHAI – HANGZHOU

YANAN

RD

HUAIHAI

CHANGNING

ROAD

FUXING

RD

Zoo

Chengjiaqiao

HANGSHAN RD

JIANGUO

ROAD

To Hongqiao Airfield

HUAIHAI

Jiaotong University

ROAD

Xujiahui Station

WUZHONG

Hongqiao

ROAD

XIETU

RD

LINGLING

RD

ZHONGSHAN

YISHAN RD

CAOXI

Shanghai Stadium

ZHONGSHAN

HUANGPU

Longhua

CENTRAL SHANGHAI

N

↑

XUHUI

0   1   2 km

to Hangzhou

Shanghai Botanical Garden

CHUAN COU

ECONOMIC SURVEY METHODS

John B. Lansing

and

James N. Morgan

ISR Code No. 3276

Library of Congress Catalog Card No. 71-633672
ISBN 0-87944-008-2 paperbound
ISBN 0-87944-009-0 clothbound

Published by the Survey Research Center
of the Institute for Social Research,
The University of Michigan, Ann Arbor, Michigan 48106

First Published 1971
Fifth Printing 1977

DEDICATION

We dedicate this book to the memory of John Lansing, a w
friend, creative colleague, and careful scholar. It was his sense of c
science, and of the need for system and order, which led us to un
writing task. His concern for methodological investigation and imp
while always pushing ahead with substantive research in the meanti
up throughout the book. And his willingness to look for something
useful in many alternative procedures has broadened its scope, has ke
being parochial. We shall miss him, and hope that those who benefit
book will appreciate his contributions.

James N. M

PREFACE

Economics is both a social and a behavioral science. It deals with the inter-relationships among economic units, the ways in which the decisions of house-holds, business firms, and legislatures interrelate and the outcome for the whole economy in terms of resource allocation, economic growth, employment and stability. It is becoming increasingly apparent that the sophisticated models currently being used require better behavioral information if they are to be useful for either prediction or policy making. And the behavioral relations must increasingly be at the level of individual households or firms where they can be investigated and understood. Hence the need for economic survey research, where economic behavior can be related to financial, demographic, psychological and sociological variables.

Survey research is multidisciplinary, since it focuses on understanding human behavior, but it can be organized to some extent on disciplinary lines according to the behavior being studied. And the problems and procedures do differ somewhat depending on the kind of behavior being studied. Although we are also concerned that surveys be economic in the sense of prudent with resources, this book focuses rather on economic survey methods, meaning using the tool of surveys to study economic behavior.

We felt this book had to be written, even though it adds to an already overwhelming flood of printed paper. As the amount of survey research on economic behavior expands, it becomes increasingly clear that old mistakes are being repeated, and methods are all the time being rediscovered. This is so primarily because the accumulated experience of the past has not been systematically summarized and therefore principles generalizeable from it could not be applied to future research. If the availability of this book assists people in avoiding the same old mistakes, if it perhaps reduces the number or seriousness of new ones, it will have served its purpose.

The authors started doing survey research more than twenty years ago when there was little experience to go on, and most of it in different substantive areas, particularly sociology. We have learned a great deal from our colleagues at the Institute for Social Research, as well as from our own mistakes and experiences. When we found ourselves occupied with training staff, trying to convince research sponsors about what was good study design, and teaching a graduate seminar on economic survey methods, the paucity of appropriate written material became painfully evident.

Leslie Kish's writings left the theory and practice of sampling in excellent shape; hence we include here only a few examples showing the implications of alternative sample designs. Statistical literature on data analysis is voluminous, but much of it is still in the hypothesis testing tradition, or focused on small data sets like time series, so that it tends to be not relevant or even misleading. The peculiar problems of searching large masses of data for the structure of relationships have been tackled, but often at scattered sites and with unconnected developments, and by procedures whose formal mathematical justification is incomplete. This book brings together in one place a discussion of several strategies for analyzing such data.

There are books on questionnaire design and on field procedures, which the present volume supplements and translates into the problems of economic surveys. The processes of content analysis, scaling, generation of conceptual variables, and analysis, are a warring battlefield of competing methods, none of them completely satisfactory and most of them poorly explained or justified. However, we do discuss methods and techniques that have proven satisfactory for us.

All in all, the field is neither systematic nor orderly enough so that a set of general principles will provide guidance. Yet a case-study approach is limited, and it induces uncritical imitation of less-than-optimal designs. So we try to steer a middle course, applying *some* general notions about resource allocation, and about the motivation of respondents, for instance, but also giving examples from which other generalizations may be drawn.

With the impending explosion of quantitative behavioral studies in economics, some parts of this book should soon get out-of-date, and the need to incorporate the new experience will increase with time. The reader is encouraged to supplement this book with the reports of both the methodology and substantive findings of current surveys, and ask himself whether they illustrate, add to, or contradict what we have said.

We are grateful to a large number of present and former colleagues, and in particular to George Katona, Charles Cannell, Leslie Kish, John Scott, and Angus Campbell. The Institute for Social Research and the University of Michigan funded assignments to off-campus duty for John Lansing in 1967-68 and for James Morgan in 1969-70 that allowed this to get written. Doris Thackrey edited the manuscript and William Haney saw it through the publishing. Anita Ernst typed most of it, several times.

TABLE OF CONTENTS

Chapter I

A NEW TOOL AND ITS USES

Historical Development

Although getting facts by interviewing people has a long history, starting with politicians and journalists, scientific survey research differs from this in very important ways. Simply asking someone questions tends to develop what Professor Daniel B. Suits refers to as "a man-who statistic," as in the phrase "I know a man who. . . ." This kind of survey, covering in some cases substantial groups of people, has been done for quite some time. Surveys were done in Germany in the 19th century on such things as the attitudes of workers in factories. Unfortunately, the political interests of those who conducted such surveys overwhelmed their scientific interests, and objectivity rapidly got lost.[1] Later on, largely in England and France, surveys were used to document the plight of the poor. Many of them focused on one industrial community, documenting the horrors of the industrial revolution and the urban slums. These were followed early in the 20th century by a number of surveys whose major purpose was to collect expenditure data. Such data were used largely for establishing the weights for cost-of-living indexes, but also for estimating income elasticities of various kinds of expenditures.[2] Starting in the 1940's, economic surveys expanded to cover a relatively wide range of subject matter.[3]

The Development of the Scientific Tool

It has only been in the last twenty-five years that survey research has become a scientific tool, that is, able to produce quantified, reproducible information that can be used to test hypotheses or to provide unbiased measurement of quantities or relationships. There were three scientific breakthroughs required for this. First was the development of techniques for selecting probability samples of human populations. This allowed inferences to be made about the whole population on the basis of the samples and allowed these inferences to be tested by computation of sampling variances. Second was the development of techniques for eliciting quantified reproducible information from people. And third was the development of techniques for analyzing fairly large, rich masses of data, mainly by computers.

1

The first two of these essentially involved tricks. Why was it so difficult to develop a probability sample of human populations? In the first place, in most cases there was no list or "sampling frame" from which one could sample people. Second, and perhaps more important, people are scattered all over the country. A purely random sample would have involved so much costly traveling to find the people that it would not have been feasible to do much survey research. What was necessary was some means of reducing travel cost while still preserving a sample that was basically a probability sample. The trick was to sample not people but the map. One can divide the map into sample areas and then fairly small subareas within those, and either interview everyone within small subareas or a sample within them of two, three, four, or five households.

Here we have an example of a straight economic problem in design: The larger the clusters in the sample, the less information per interview, but the less money one spends getting the interviews. There must be some point where the information per dollar reaches a maximum. The problem is complicated, of course, by the fact that the effect of clustering on the amount of information one gets depends on what one is asking. We shall return to this in Chapter III, where sampling is treated in more detail. Suffice it to say that sampling is a very complex science today, involving elaborate designs and interlaced controls to achieve the maximum information per dollar spent.

The second requirement was the development of procedures for eliciting information from people in such a way that one could have some confidence in it. These procedures are still being worked out, but certain important developments have vastly improved their quality. Perhaps the most important of these was the standardization both of the stimulus that was given to the respondent in the field and the procedures under central office controls for quantifying his replies. Interviewing looked at in this way is essentially a stimulus-response process where it is very important that the stimulus be controlled. In the case of attitudinal questions and even of factual questions, controlling the stimulus meant training interviewers to ask questions exactly as they were written (including questions which called for "open answers") and to write down the answers fully, and then having a controlled central office procedure by which those answers were interpreted. For attitudinal information, these procedures permitted some confidence that the proper frame of reference was being used by the respondent and that cases where he really was not answering the question could be discovered. For factual or demographic information also, open answers often revealed situations where the respondent was answering the wrong question. One example may suffice: in one pretest, a question was inserted, "Do you have any stock?" One respondent answered, "Yes, I have two cows and a horse." Clearly the question was inadequate. In more recent studies, we have had similar problems with questions about food stamps. To some people, food stamps are the commodity stamps issued to poor people by which they get food at less than market prices.

To others, food stamps mean S & H Green Stamps which they get when they buy food and which are exchanged later for premiums.

We return to the process of quantification in Chapter V in the discussion of data processing. But it is important to remember that science requires proper quantification, and proper quantification requires some kind of reproducibility. If answers are written down, at least the process of making them numerical and machine-readable can be rechecked at the time and again later if necessary. In the case of trends or reinterviews, it is possible to go back and requantify earlier information to make sure the procedures have not changed. So area probability sampling made reasonably sure that we had a representative sample of something and fixed-question open-answer procedures with central office control over the interpretation made reasonably sure that we had good information about what the respondent said.

But a rich matrix of information for a substantial sample of people would have been of very little use if we had not had computers to enable us to analyze the data. When we come to discuss analysis methods in Chapter VI, we shall discover that the most modern computers are freeing the researcher from various constraints more adequately than the previous generation of computers, allowing him to make flexible use of the matrix of data that he can collect in a survey. Actually the most recent improvements have been not so much in statistical analysis as in file management, the ability to generate new and complex variables, more in keeping with analytical models one may want to use. And, furthermore, computers have opened the possibility of using survey data in simulation to say more about their dynamic implications in elaborate economic models. It is important to keep in mind just how rich the set of data that one can get from a survey really is. Not only does one have a representative sample of families or individuals, but he also has a wide variety of information about each individual in the sample. This opens up elaborate possibilities for analysis, and also, of course, tempts the researcher into trying to collect too much information in any one interview.

For those sensitive to disciplinary boundaries, we should point out that much of the early development of survey research came from sociology rather than economics. In this book, however, we will focus on the development of the use of surveys in economics and on the possible future uses of survey research in economics.

Appropriate Purposes for Economic Surveys

Any new tool tempts us into what Abraham Kaplan in his book *The Conduct of Inquiry*[4] calls the law of the instrument, a law illustrated by the child who, given a hammer, discovers that a great many things need pounding. It is going to require continued restraint to use surveys only where they are appropriate.

While the ultimate purpose of survey research may often be prediction or explanation or evaluation, much of it seems to involve description or measurement. In a sense, description is subordinate to the other purposes. The analyst seeks to describe as a preliminary step toward subsequent prediction, explanation, or evaluation. Description is often a *necessary* preliminary. It may be necessary to know something about a phenomenon to consider what type of explanation may be appropriate. There is a tendency to regard description as a low level of professional activity and, hence, economists hesitate to admit that they are engaged merely in describing a phenomenon. Part of the low prestige associated with description results from a failure to distinguish between good and bad description. Description necessarily is based on some point of view. There is no such thing as describing a phenomenon without introducing the mind of the observer between the phenomenon and his report of it. He necessarily selects and organizes what he observes. He does the job well if he facilitates the subsequent processes of prediction, explanation, and evaluation. He does the job poorly if he fails to assist these processes. One description may be better than another, therefore, because of choice of point of view, it makes use of more relevant concepts to organize the report of the phenomenon described. The most useful method of description, however, cannot be ascertained until it is known how the description will be used. A description never used may be a mass of unrelated information, a sandpile of facts.

Much descriptive survey research is the responsibility of the government because it is needed not only for the nation as a whole but also for states and counties in some areas. The Census Bureau, in particular collects data on employment, distribution of income, home ownership, and frequency of moving. These descriptive data are useful not only to *measure* inequality or to look at differences in some parts of the population but also to analyze the impact of taxes or of other government policies on different groups in society. Furthermore, if such data are collected repeatedly over time, they produce information on *trends* in income, in inequality, in unemployment, in prices. Indeed, we are moving in the general direction of more such trend measurements, or "social indicators." There has been much interest recently in the problems and possibilities of improvement of "social indicators."[5] While some of the data for monitoring social change can come from public records, most of the improvements in and additions to social indicators will require surveys repeated with reasonably stable procedures so that the trends are valid.

Economists are often frustrated in their attempts to study alternative tax and spending policies by the lack of adequate distributional survey data from which they could infer the impact of these policies on different groups of individuals. Surveys with or without trend data can also study such things as the acceptance of innovation—the spread of TV, the use of seat belts, or early retirement.

But surveys lead immediately to the possibility of studying relationships. Who are the people who do one thing or another; who are the people with debt, or with high incomes; and what is the relationship between income and expenditures? Such analysis may sometimes lead immediately into explanations, but it may only be the search for relationships without attempting to provide elaborate explanations. Efforts to analyze the so-called "consumption function" made use of survey data particularly in attempts to estimate the marginal propensity to consume, the relation of consumption expenditures to income. Much was written over what now appears to be a technical issue—the discrepancy between cross-section and time series estimates of the marginal propensity to consume. It now has been seen that the permanent income hypothesis is just a statement about errors in variables, and the biases that were created when errors occurred in one explanatory variable.[6]

Economic experiments with human populations have been quite rare, because they are expensive and difficult to design. They often require the use of surveys to monitor the impact of the experiment. For instance, if one wants to know the effect of changing the welfare laws, as in a negative income tax experiment, it becomes necessary to follow the behavior of the experimental groups and of a control group over a period of time to find out how changes in the welfare laws affect people's behavior.

But, inevitably, almost any use of survey data ends with attempts to explain "why." It is not always obvious what constitutes a satisfactory explanation. Abraham Kaplan distinguishes two basic types of explanation which he designates as the deductive model and the pattern model.[7] In the deductive model an event is explained by subsuming it under general laws. An analyst knows the reason for "x" if he can deduce it from other facts. The other facts in turn may require explanation which the analyst may or may not be able to provide. Ability to explain "x" is not the same as the ability to explain the facts which explain "x." It is also possible, and in economics it is usually true, that the explanation is in probabilistic terms. What is known is that the *probability* of "x" depends on other facts in a certain manner. The pattern model is perhaps less familiar. An analyst knows the reason for "x" if he can put it into a known pattern. He relates "x" to a set of other elements so that together they constitute a unified system. No deduction is involved. Explanation consists in recognizing a pattern for what it is—it fits.

The broad purpose of most economic surveys is to explain or contribute to the development of explanations of economic phenomenon. Thus, results of the surveys are to be evaluated in terms of the quality of the explanation to which they lead. The quality may be evaluated in statistical terms. The analyst is concerned with the precision of his estimates, the absence of bias in procedures, and the like. There is sometimes disagreement about the importance to be attached to different statistical criteria. For example, how important is it for a statistician to estimate accurately the regression coefficient for income in an explanation of some expenditure, and how important to explain a high proportion of the variance of the dependent variable, or to estimate the probability that his hypothesis is false? Such choices, with the stress to be placed on specific criteria, clearly should depend on the purpose of the inquiry. We come back to this in Chapter VI when we discuss the analysis and interpretation of survey data.

The quality of explanation may also be considered in terms of the relation between the explanation and the general body of knowledge. At a minimum, explanation should be consistent with other knowledge.

Surveys are used in several ways to explain why something happened. Sometimes we ask people directly why they did something. And sometimes we use indirect projective questions, where we hope that a person will tell us indirectly what he thinks. For example, some people say that *other* people do not fly because they are afraid, while at the same time they might refuse to admit they are afraid themselves (even though they are).

It is often said that the ultimate purpose of any scientific inquiry is prediction. In the case of economic studies, this is the purpose as well. The simplest example is the attempt to predict the impact of changing aggregate income on the pattern of consumption by estimating different income elasticities from budget data, the Engel curves.[8] Or one may want to predict changing patterns in consumption by noting that more and more people are moving from the country to the cities, and when people move to the cities their consumption patterns change. One may also want to describe the impact of particular policies by simply knowing *who* is likely to be affected by them. But more important, one may want to predict the responses to policies by finding patterns in people's attitudes, preferences, or behavior. Indeed, in many cases of public policy, one may want both to monitor the current responses to an on-going policy *and* to understand and predict future responses on the basis of the same data.

Another kind of prediction from economic surveys is the prediction of discretionary expenditures. In an affluent society where large masses of consumers have a great deal of flexibility in their spending, they are able to postpone or speed up their expenditures, particularly those for durables bought to replace other durables. Hence it may well be that surveys can measure the current state of consumers' optimism, confidence, and willingness to spend their money. Moreover, the data from a series of such surveys can be used to investigate further what kinds of events and understandings of events caused consumers to change their propensity to consume over time.[9] Here, as in other parts of scientific endeavor, the purposes of prediction, explanation, and understanding all mingle together, and the same data that are used in the short-run for prediction can be used in the long-run for understanding and improving the predictions of the future.

A long-range possibility involves the use of survey data in simulation models to predict changes in whole systems. Major developments in this area were started some years ago by Guy Orcutt.[10] He pointed out that one way to go from information about the behavior of individuals to inferences about dynamic responses in the aggregate was to build a simulation model where representative groups of consumers moved iteratively month by month, the basic behavioral input being relations between initial state and subsequent behavior. The aggregate dynamic implications could then be dredged out of the computer in the course of the simulation. This process requires both a tremendous quantity of data and tremendous resources in computer and analytic expertise and is not moving very rapidly; but it does say something about the kinds of survey data that will be needed in the future. Survey data need to be collected which are at least dynamic enough to related initial states to subsequent actions, and to test whether such relations are stable over time.

The final purpose of economic surveys is evaluation, both of the impact of policies and of the potential uses of various kinds of new investments and, perhaps most important, of the need for certain kinds of collective consumption. There are a growing number of areas where government policies affect the individual and where voting is an ineffective way of deciding which of several policies is best overall. This problem is particularly crucial in the case of the provision of social goods like parks, hospitals, and highways. Surveys can provide important information on the patterns of individual preferences. How else can the technicians and policy makers compare the *benefits* to drivers of better highways and parking lots with the *losses* to those who use public transportation? The literature on urban problems is rife with assumptions about the relative importance of privacy, space, quick journey to work, and scenic beauty, without any evidence as to how people feel other than the author's casual empiricism. Therefore, surveys are needed to help evaluate the social benefits of such things as parks and clean air, things that cannot be priced and sold on the market. Even where a major investment results in something to be sold in the market place, surveys may avoid vast misallocations of resources by providing some evidence as to whether people are likely to be willing to spend their money on the new product or service when it is available.

It should be made clear, however, that surveys are *not* to be used to make public policy directly. They provide the basic input into discussions of public policy in the same way that they provide the input into the econometric models. They may keep policy makers aware of the existence of diverse groups, with strong desires requiring some diversity of public policy.

Inappropriate Purposes for Economic Surveys

Some years ago Leonard Salter wrote a book called *A Critical Review of Research in Land Economics*.[11] In it he pointed out that a very large number of research projects in his field, many of them involving surveys, were useless because they started with no particular hypothesis, went through no particular organized structure and, hence, could not come to any particularly useful conclusions. Salter was correct in asserting that it is inappropriate to conduct surveys unless there are some particular, explicit purposes connected with them beyond simply asking interesting questions. But even some clear purposes are not appropriate. Surveys are not good for estimating national aggregates, particularly of skewed distributions where a few people account for a large fraction of the aggregate. They are not useful for estimating total assets of a country, for instance, or even its aggregate income. They are not useful for studying illegal or illegitimate activities since, obviously, the respondents usually cannot be sufficiently sure of the confidentiality of their answers. They are clearly not appropriate for use in law enforcement since the respondent would have to be deceived about the purpose of the survey. Nor should surveys be used to collect data for the exclusive use of some particular client, whether government or private, since such data could be used to manipulate people without their knowledge. Although the whole popular controversy over privacy in survey research is focused on the issue of dossiers and the availability of such information to persons other than those for whom it was intended, another issue is equally important—the potential misuse of survey data when important facts about the attitudes, behavior, and preferences of masses of people are available only to some people and not to others. There is more opportunity to use surveys to manipulate people if the data are available to only certain people.

Surveys are also not useful to study uncommon phenomena. For instance, it is very difficult to use surveys to study fraud against consumers, not only because those who have been defrauded may not like to admit it, but because such fraud is a fairly rare thing and difficult to locate in a population. Surveys are probably not useful to estimate price elasticities or substitutional elasticities since prices do not change much in short periods and price differences in some areas are often associated with other differences. Nor are surveys useful to make precise estimates of income elasticities. For instance, there was a great deal of interest during the tax cut of 1964 in the possible measurement of what might be called the marginal propensity to spend the tax cut. This would have required measuring income during relatively short periods to the nearest percentage point and measuring consumption to the nearest 1/2 percentage point of the truth in order to be able to talk about a marginal propensity to spend part of a small change in income. What *is* possible in connection with such a change is to study the way people see such tax cuts, their level of information, whether they see themselves as having made major, discretionary expenditures either before their take-home pay actually went up or after they noticed they were accumulating the funds. One can study differential responses by people who did or did not have income increases other than those resulting from the tax cut.

can one say about the benefits of a proposed piece of survey re-
ldom will the result lead immediately to improved decisions that will
y outright. More often, a general case can be made that better knowl-
man behavior helps avoid futile, disruptive, or wasteful policies of gov-
business. If, for example, extended family financial responsibilities are
nal and reduce people's incentives to earn and accumulate, then policy
lic responsibility for the indigent can be better shaped to meet the fu-
know what pleases or displeases people about their housing and neigh-
we can allocate funds and make better design decisions about our cities.
is enthusiasm for the research he wants to do, the proposer may well
its benefits. What is less forgivable is for him to suggest benefits with-
g out what they are. *Why* is the topic of great national importance?
sions are being made which may involve costly mistakes if information
Will anyone do anything different on the basis of the results of the
ll the results contribute to a systematic and growing body of knowl-
end results of which may have some benefit?
f that the research team knows the substantive area also requires at
search of the literature and summary of the state of knowledge.
ometimes an unwarranted demand for excessive bibliographic work,
also true that sometimes research projects are started with inadequate
e of what has already been done.
common to suggest that there should be an advisory group of experts
ject matter to advise on the survey. It might be suggested that this ad-
up should also contain some experts in survey methodology since the
ocess of research design requires that the substantive needs and the sci-
ssibilities of surveys be merged.
second question, whether the topic can be studied at a reasonable
ally not independent of the first, since a cost is reasonable only in com-
ith the benefits it produces. Cost must first be related to the volume
sion of the information that will be produced. A common error in de-
search is to design a study too large and expensive for the purpose.
s the sample is larger than necessary for the precision required. More
amount and variety of data to be collected are far beyond what is
to study the main topics, and often beyond the point where the
t can be expected to provide good information. The tell-tale sign of
insufficiently informed about the technology of survey research is the
e of an excessively long questionnaire in advance of a carefully worked
ment of detailed objectives.
eed, an important question is whether there should not be several al-
designs, ranging from an inexpensive study to scout the field, narrow
, and check the feasibility of a larger study, to a full-blown definitive
t leaves no reasonable hypotheses unchecked.

Finally, surveys are probably not appropriate for testing elaborate hypotheses which require for their testing very high precision; indeed, as we shall see later, it is often unwise to think of a survey as testing a particular hypothesis rather than allowing the analyst to select among several alternative hypotheses. Very sophisticated methods of analysis assuming a particular causal structure prove to be nearly useless for determining the proper structural assumption.

Conclusion

Recent developments in scientific sampling, eliciting and quantifying information, and data processing have provided a new scientific tool to economists. It must be used with discretion. It has a wide range of potential purposes but also opens up temptations to use it where it is not appropriate. In using economic surveys, economists should keep in mind that in the process of explaining economic behavior, noneconomic variables may be important, and in the process of estimating and predicting the things economists are interested in, the same data may be very useful to other social scientists for purposes other than those for which the original survey was designed. There is a great deal of symbiosis possible in survey research, and a promising future for interdisciplinary cooperation.

A study design that proposes to test a single complex hypothesis is inappropriate, in most cases. There are usually a number of competing hypotheses and the design should allow one to rank them. At the other extreme are many studies which do not have enough theoretical structure behind them, and hence are not set up either to test one hypothesis or to select among competing explanations. Sometimes there is not even a single thing (situation, behavior) to be explained. The study may purport to study tenant farmers, or the poor, or home owners, but unless it is trying to explain something about the situation or behavior or plans of some group, the result is likely to be useless description.

How does one steer between the narrow rigidity of the "hypothesis testing" approach on the one hand, and the grab bag data collection with no structure on the other?

One way is to be sure there are clear answers to two questions:

What situation, or behavior, or set of them, is to be explained?
How will it be possible to show that the explanation given is superior to likely alternative explanations?

Footnotes to Chapter I

1. Anthony Oberschall, *Empirical Social Research in Germany 1848-1914,* Mouton and Co., Paris, 1964.

2. Faith Williams and Karl Zimmerman, *Studies of Family Living in the United States and Other Countries,* U.S. Dept. of Agriculture, Washington, D.C., December 1935. See also George Stigler, "The Early History of Empirical Studies of Consumer Behavior," *Journal of Political Economy,* 62 (April 1954) pp. 95-113.

3. James Morgan, "A Survey of Recent Empirical Research on Consumer Behavior," in *Consumer Behavior,* Lincoln Clark, Ed., Harper and Brothers, New York, 1958; James Morgan, "Repeated Surveys of Consumer Finances in the United States," in *Family Living Studies,* International Labour Office, Geneva, 1961.

4. James Morgan, "Contributions of Survey Research to Economics," in C. Y. Glock, editor, *Survey Research in the Social Sciences,* Russell Sage, New York, 1967, pp. 217-218.

4. Abraham Kaplan, *The Conduct of Inquiry: Methodology for Behavioral Science,* Chandler Publishing Co., San Francisco, California, 1964.

5. Raymond Bauer, Ed., *Social Indicators,* M.S.T. Press, Cambridge, Massachusetts, 1966; see also U.S. Dept. of Health, Education, and Welfare, *Toward A Social Report.* U.S.G.P.O., Washington, D.C., 1969.

6. Nissan Liviatan, "Tests of the Permanent-Income Hypothesis Based on a Reinterview Saving Survey," in *Measurement in Economics: Studies in Mathematical Economics and Econometrics in Memory of Mehuda Grunfeld,* Stanford University Press, Stanford, California, 1963.

7. Abraham Kaplan, *op. cit.* - Chapter IX.

8. S. J. Prais and H. S. Houthakker, *The Analysis of Family Budgets,* Cambridge Univ. Press, Cambridge, 1955. See also Harold Lydall, *British Income and Savings,* Oxford, Basil Blackwell, 1955.

9. George Katona, *Mass Consumption Society,* McGraw-Hill, N.Y., 1964.

10. Guy Orcutt and others, *Microanalysis of Socio-Economic Systems,* Harper, New York, 1960.

11. Leonard Salter, *A Critical Review of Research in Land Economics,* University of Wisconsin Press, Madison, Wisconsin (Reprinted) 1967.

Chapter II

THE DESIGN OF SUR

Three Requirements

Designing anything means ensuring that th
cannot focus on one aspect alone. And this fittin
tern, occurs at two stages. The first stage is the se

will produce some important benefits,
can be studied at a reasonable cost,
has some chance of being financed.

This requires familiarity with:

the state of knowledge in the substantive fie
the state of technology in survey research,
the state of mind of the fund-granting source

Since most surveys involve substantial costs,
other more individualistic forms of research, the c
costs of a proposed survey must be made somew
There are important topics which cannot be stu
sonant with their importance. There are things
worth it—readers of the results may fairly ask, "so

A thorough grasp of the state of knowledge
theory and fact, is not easy to come by, since theo
ments tend to go their own separate ways, and b
usually poor, particularly for quantitative researc
been done, but published in obscure places and ar
professional journals.

Knowledge of the possibilities of survey re
experience, but it is hoped that this book may a
ideas. Since people usually do not advertise their f
tions of the survey method in particular need to b
ond stage of design, to which we return below,
design decisions about the survey itself, decisions t

When we come to the interlaced set of decisions that must be made about any one design, however, it is a substantial task to work out one or two alternative designs, with cost estimates and some consideration of feasibility.

It is sometimes stated that a survey design should specify a formal theoretical structure that is to be tested. We maintain, on the contrary, that in the present state of knowledge in economics we are necessarily selecting among competing, alternative hypotheses. A good research design, then, must encompass a variety of alternative hypotheses or theoretical structures, and attempt to provide the critical information necessary to choose among them. The task is made more difficult by the loose connection between the theoretical constructs on the one hand, and the things that can actually be measured, on the other. The notion that it is efficient to test a single hypothesis has long since been obsolete in the field of experimental design, owing largely to the contributions of R. A. Fisher and others. And procedures for statistical analysis have been affected by the Bayesians who insist that any data analysis must implicitly or explicitly start with some *a priori* probabilities about what the world is like.

So, a good research design starts with a broad view of the various possible theoretical models that might explain. Some of these models will involve more complex structures than a single dependent variable (a state or a behavior), introducing chains of causation or a hierarchy of explanatory variables. Indeed, it is sometimes important to have a model where some of the variables are *dependent* variables in part of the analysis, and *explanatory* variables in another part. Studies of adoption of innovation characteristically use background factors and the input of persuasion to explain changes in information and understanding, and those in turn, to explain changes in attitudes, intentions and belief. They may then use changes in attitudes, etc. to help explain changes in actual behavior.

The third consideration in undertaking a survey topic was the availability of funds to support the research. Information about the state of mind of the foundations and the various government agencies with research funds is not easy to get, particularly since any given research team only engages in this exercise at scattered intervals. Funding procedures vary, and some agencies provide informal advice in order to avoid many formal refusals.

Given the substantial staff turnover, changes in structural divisions, and changes in stated policies in most grant-giving organizations, the researcher may have a difficult time knowing where to submit his proposal. Hopefully, however, a good proposal can somehow be made to fit in somewhere. In fact, the very variety of the funding sources gives new ideas a better chance than they would have at the hands of one monolithic source for all social science research funding.

An added difficulty, of course, is that survey research competes with other kinds of research which cost less per printed page of output. In between the very expensive detailed data collections of government, and the seemingly cheap small-scale individual research projects, small-sample survey research finds its uneasy place.

In these days of focus on "power," it is common to ask who decides on research design, the sponsors or the researchers. It is also common to assume that research focused on the immediate public problems of the moment is "problem oriented" not "basic" and will contribute little to the permanent body of knowledge. Less commonly heard in academic circles, but also widely believed, is a charge that social researchers left to their own devices, tend to study unimportant and esoteric problems of interest only to little "in-groups."

Our own experience of what actually happens is that it is usually a process of adjustment. Sometimes the process starts with a proposal being prepared by a researcher and then being refined and altered until it seems to meet some purpose seen as appropriate by some funding source, or by the experts consulted by that source. Sometimes a source of research funds specifies an area of research or a set of problems, and the researchers then design studies which attempt to focus on those problems while still contributing some basic knowledge of lasting value. The source of initiation is less important than the process of negotiation and fitting. It is our view that researchers need to justify their research in terms of some social benefits, but that it is possible to study real problems and still be contributing to basic scientific knowledge and to the development of improved methods.

Both extremes can lead to waste. There are examples of bad research, conducted under pressure of current issues or problems, often focused on some popular hypotheses, where the researcher seems to become the handmaiden of the particular views of the sponsor. There are also examples of research where the findings are of little relevance, either because the problem does not have any importance, or because the design tests some very particular theory while ignoring other possibilities.

As researchers, the authors have the feeling that too often administrators without much expertise in the design and conduct of research attempt to go beyond their legitimate concerns about importance and relevance of the research, and interfere with technical decisions about how the research should be conducted. On the other hand we have seen ourselves and others restrained from waste of resources by fund limitations or the demands of funding agencies for the justification of a broad design and its budget. One of the most common sins of survey researchers is to collect more information than they need, because "it would be interesting to know." This not only wastes resources but imposes a burden on respondents who are often annoyed by the obvious irrelevance to the main topic of many of the questions asked.

It is only fair to add that until very recently it was extremely difficult to get research funds to study racial problems. It is still difficult to get funds to study human attitudes and behavior in areas of international conflict, world peace, and arms control. Funds for developing and testing methods of measuring both economic and non-economic variables from theory have also been extremely difficult to get.

Some Questions to Answer

One way to look at overall design decisions is to frame a sequence of questions:

A. Is the goal or purpose clearly stated, with some potential benefits that would justify the expenditures involved?

While it is difficult to measure the economic value of information, it is still a useful exercise. Sometimes major policy decisions will depend on the answers, and the costs of error in those decisions can be assessed. Much information, however, is a public good, whose value depends on how many people use it. Some focus on why the information is needed will at least get away from studies which are done because "it would be interesting to know." Curiosity may be a good thing, but it is not enough to justify large expenditures.

B. Does the design fit the goals or purposes of the study?

The information needed must be at least potentially available from the respondents. The total scope of the objectives must be sufficiently bounded so that it can be handled in a single study, but not so narrow that some of the respondents' potential time is not used. We shall see later some examples where important objectives were not capable of adequate study with surveys.

C. Is there at least a rough working theoretical structure to guide the detailed design?

Is the level of analysis proper individual, family, or group? Are all the basic kinds of explanatory variables included: background factors, constraints, current outside forces, and motives of the respondents? Are the "intervening variables" also included in the design? For instance, background and recent events may affect people's attitudes, which in turn affect their behavior patterns, which then affect their incomes. To relate background or recent events to changes in income and omit the intervening variables is to fail to take the opportunity to study the whole process.

D. Is a survey really necessary rather than just an experiment?

A whole range of possibilities exists between a survey of a representative sample at the one extreme and a controlled laboratory experiment on the other. One might select extremes on a dependent variable for the sample in order to accentuate the possibility of explaining differences. One might manage to hold some things constant, by sample selection or manipulation. One might vary some things systematically, either for some group, or for a random subsample of a group. When a series of things are varied systematically with randomly selected subgroups, and other things are held constant for everyone, we are at the experimental-design end of the continuum. Semi-controlled experiments have a checkered history, but some fruitful ones may still be possible. Laboratory experiments may seem unreal, or expensive per person, but allow (a) a focus on crucial variables, (b) variation of things which may not move much or for very many at once in real life situations, and (c) an isolation of the effects of interest from the "noise" and confounding that otherwise cause difficulties.

E. Will a single survey suffice, or is it necessary to revisit and reinterview?

Economists need dynamic data, people's responses to changes in incomes, wage rates, prices, etc. At a minimum this requires data on the relation between an event or a situation and subsequent behavior. Given the limits of people's memories, this may well require panel studies. Yet panels raise difficult problems of shifting units, extensive costs, and require explicit justification and attention to detailed design problems.

F. Is the general allocation of resources an efficient one?

Is the allocation of time and money among the procedural steps optimum, that is, between design, sampling, data collection, processing, analysis, and writing and presentation? There is a tendency to shortchange design and planning in order to get into the field, and to shortchange writing and clarity of presentation in order to get the findings out and get on with the next piece of research.

Is the allocation of interviewing time optimal, (a) between measuring the dependent variables and the explanatory variables, (b) between more dependent variables and more precision in measuring each one—which usually takes more time and questions, and (c) between more variety and more precision in measuring the explanatory variables?

Finally, is the total magnitude of the study, including sample size, within a reasonable range of optimality? One can think of a "total benefits" curve which rises rapidly as one devotes enough resources to the study to make it efficient, then rises more slowly as the additional funds go largely to increased sample size, reducing uncertainty only by the square root of the increase, and increasing the problems of quality control. In the figure, total budgets less than OA might be cause to cancel the study as not worth the expenditure, while budgets larger than OC might be considered extravagant.

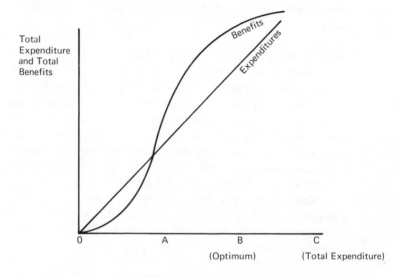

G. Are the basic outlines of the operational details proper, that is, the sample, kind of interview, designated respondent, and analysis plans?

These are taken up in more detail shortly, and again in subsequent chapters, but in the basic design of a study, they need to be considered sufficiently to be sure that they all fit together into an effective and operational pattern.

If we think of the basic design as the decisions made before a study is funded, in the process of writing the proposal, and the implementation as what is done after the funds are available, it turns out that a great many decisions must be postponed, and that the funds must be granted on the basis of a rather general outline of a design, often without proof that the procedures will work, or that respondents have the information or will reveal it. It is often suggested that a pilot study be conducted to check feasibility. The difficulty is that so much work must go into a properly designed pilot study that the proper economic decision about whether to go ahead may be altered in favor, while the sponsoring agency may well feel they have "the answer" from the pilot study and not want to do more. Furthermore, it is difficult to convince researchers to devote time and energy to something which may never come to fruition, particularly when after some past experience, they feel reasonably sure that a fruitful study is possible.

It is easy to state whether the margin of sampling errors on the dependent variables will be within some prescribed limits, but once the sample gets beyond the smallest sizes, the issue of response errors and non-response errors predominates, and is much more difficult to specify.

H. What are the basic limitations of the study?

Some things do not vary in a cross-section, such as prices, so that studies of price-elasticity of demand usually require some other design. Sometimes, particularly in special samples, an explanatory variable of interest is badly confounded (highly correlated with) some other variable or variables, so that one would never be able to decide which variable was really causal. Sometimes basically wrong assumptions are made, about who can report something, about whether people have ever thought about a subject and can talk intelligently about it, etc.

One way to think about basic design is that it attempts to avoid conceptual errors, whereas the more specific design decisions made in implementing the study attempt to avoid operational errors, or even mechanical errors.

I. Is some possible source of funds available?

Some of us like to try for the best, testing whether we can find funds for what we think is *most* important. But we may settle for second or third best. And the need for good survey research on economic behavior is so vast, compared with what has been done, that the third best may still be well worth doing.

It is often tempting to design a study around some enticing captive audience, or available sample frame, or other special circumstance. This frequently turns out to be a mistake—a smaller representative sample would have provided more appropriate information.

We might also distinguish studies according to whether they are intended to improve the design of a product or a public policy, or to figure out how to make an existing one more salable. It is our opinion that the former are not only ethically superior, but more creative and more productive. It is one thing to try to figure out how to sell the idea of supersonic transport to people in the path of the 100 mile wide sonic booms the planes trail behind them, and quite another to assess the relative importance of the various benefits and disadvantages of this transport to different groups in society, so that elected representatives can make intelligent decisions, or design the best options on which to let people vote.

Assembling the Elements of a Survey Design

The second stage of design, where many things have to fit together, is what is generally thought of as survey design, and much of it may have to be worked out before funds are assured, in order to convince some funding agency that the study is feasible. Consistent and appropriate decisions must be made simultaneously about:

> the unit of analysis,
> the dependent variables and their measurement,
> the kinds of explanatory variables,
> the sample size and design,
> the data collection procedures (mail, phone, or personal interviews; reinterviews; other outside data also?),
> required staff, resources, and advisory committee,
> kind of analysis (will it select among competing hypotheses?).

However difficult it is to discuss these one at a time, we shall try. The reader should also remember that many of them are only specified broadly at the design stage, the implementation requiring many more detailed decisions that will be discussed in later chapters.

The Unit of Analysis

Since it is economic behavior we are likely to be studying, a crucial problem is the locus of decision making. Immediately at the end of World War II there were many married couples living with their in-laws, keeping separate finances, planning to move out as soon as they could find or afford housing, and making many of their own decisions about a car, insurance, savings, etc. The concept of a "spending unit" or nuclear family made sense, and required taking more than one interview in households with secondary units, a difficult thing to do. There were also complications, when the secondary unit paid rent to the primary, for instance. On the other hand, today a hippie commune, if it is a genuine commune, might be considered a single economic unit making unified decisions.

But if one is studying unions, or cooperatives, or rural villages, why not think of the whole organization as a unit? Are the variables that explain union militancy, or cooperative efficiency, or acceptance of innovation all measurable at the organizational rather than the individual level? Actually, we tend to doubt it, and shall argue below that one can use both group and individual variables if the analysis is at the individual level, but not if it is at the group level.

At the other extreme, if one is analyzing purchases of durables, or vacation trips, it may be the particular incident that is the unit of analysis, even though some families account for none, and some for several. And to take only one incident per family where there are several would produce a biased sample of the incidents.

These decisions about the unit of analysis may affect the sample design, and will certainly affect the interviewing, editing, coding, and even sampling.

Dependent Variables and Their Measurement

Adequate measurement of the states or behaviors to be studied is of crucial importance. Random errors may cause no bias in the estimated relationship, but they may result in no significant findings either; and one cannot be sure they are random. In the case of economic behavior, the time dimension is a problem. Behavior over very short periods may be easier to remember, but is subject to more random variance as well as to errors and problems in specifying the time boundaries, such as including acts which actually took place before the reference period started.

The connection between things about which people make decisions and act on the one hand, and the concepts of economics on the other, is not always good. Economists may be interested in saving, or in spending (which is not the same as income minus saving), but the family may make decisions about some discretionary spending, and about some discretionary saving, which are easier to isolate, study, and even predict.

Good research is often organized around the *dependent* variables, the things to be explained. It is not functionally efficient to organize research around "age" or "race" or "the city." Some explanatory variables, or places, may be more interesting or more important to policy than others, but in order to study how age, or race, affect behavior, one must study everything that affects that behavior, in order to make sure the effects of age or race are not spurious. While the large city may be the focus of many problems, each of those problems may best be studied explicitly. It is not the city that is being studied, but human behavior, or human situations in the city.

Kinds of Explanatory Variables

A good design must include consideration of the kinds of variables necessary to evaluate the various competing hypotheses. This includes measures not only of the crucial variables involved, but also of other variables necessary to remove "noise," or to eliminate those who could not possibly respond to some theoretically interesting variable, or to allow for interactions that alter the effect of some other variable. In the early design stages, it is more important to list variables by type, rather than spell out all the details. The broad coverage, and the procedures for selecting among competing ones, are more important than details of how each is to be measured. At most, measurement errors may make us unable to see a relationship that exists, or distort our evaluation of the relative strength of different forces. They are unlikely to lead us to positive inferences that are wrong.

A major problem for economists is how to deal with the "non-economic" explanatory variables. Cooperation with other social scientists helps, but in fact the state of measurement of many psychological and sociological variables is not good. Even where some intensive development and testing of measures of some concept has taken place, it is often with captive audiences, or in studies where extensive blocks of time could be devoted to a single measure. The researcher may well find himself forced to alter some existing measure substantially, truncating the number of questions, eliminating irritating ones, etc. Or he may find himself inventing a new measure, and trying to test it before his main study starts. It is our belief that it is better to make some attempt to measure these other variables than to ignore them. And clearly a study design should consider them, even if attempts to measure them fail.

Sample Size and Design

We discuss sampling in more detail in Chapter 3, but the basic elements must be fixed, appropriate to the particular study. One must decide on the *unit* to be sampled, whatever the unit to be interviewed, or the unit to be analyzed. But where one is *analyzing* accidents, or purchases, or some other behavior, it may prove possible to *sample* the same kind of unit. On the other hand, one must always ask whether in sampling something, one has left out the other side of the picture, the control group, the sample of those who decided *not* to do something.

One may want to sample dollars rather than people, or employees when studying firms. This can be considered changing the unit of sampling, or varying the sampling fractions. One might, for instance, want to sample farms in proportion to their output of some crop, and this affects the presentation of the results, which are then in the form: "Farmers representing ____% of the aggregate wheat output, said that . . . . !"

In any case, the sample size is a critical decision. It affects costs and precision of data. One may prefer to spend the money on a smaller sample interviewed more than once. Or the choice might be a larger sample with a briefer questionnaire, using several forms so that some questions are answered only by subsamples. The sample size may be affected by existing facilities, the number of primary sampling areas with trained interviewers already present in them, plus the knowledge that it is inefficient for an interviewer to take fewer than 15-20 interviews on a single study.

Anyone proposing to depart from a single representative sample should openly answer the question about the groups oversampled: "Why is this particular group important out of all proportion to its numbers in the population?" One should also ask whether there are other purposes of the study for which this disproportionate sampling will produce a reduction in the amount of information per interview.

Design Decisions about Data Collection Procedures

Whatever the unit of analysis or of sampling, there may be a different unit for interviewing. For instance, one may want to analyze every individual in the family but only collect the data by talking to one person. There needs to be a decision about who is to be interviewed and the range of information to be asked of this person. There should also be decisions about reinterviews, about how much memory information is to be asked, and about the extent to which ancillary information is to be assembled about the area in which the man lives, or whether information is to be collected from records about him. There need to be decisions about the extent to which money should be invested in callbacks and other attempts to make the response rate as high as possible. Here again a decision must be made about whether some of the features are so novel as to require special pretesting in advance to be sure that they are practical. There needs to be some pretesting of the research instrument in any case. It is important to decide just how extensive this pretesting should be and the amount of time the pretesting process should spend on the field pretest itself, or on validating the information by some outside source. A very important design decision about data collection has to do with the length of the interview and the amount of material to be included in it. There are resource-allocation decisions about how many different dependent variables can fit into one interview and the number of explanatory variables to be used. Any particular construct can be measured with one question or five or ten or twenty, the added questions usually giving better precision on that particular variable. Clearly if one has ten or fifteen possible explanatory variables, the choice must be made whether to take all fifteen and use fewer questions on each one, or to take fewer explanatory variables and try to measure them more fully.

It is tempting to translate research objectives immediately into questions. But these questions are almost never appropriate when asked of the respondent.

How well does X understand what is expected of him in his job?

Does this retailer engage in the best approved business practices?

How much of his income did he save last year?

How much actual cooperation is there in this cooperative?

The process of getting to actual questions requires determining what reasonably exact and hopefully quantifiable information can be elicited by questions that bear on the research question. It may bear only indirectly. We may try to get at mutual understanding by looking at the extent of the communication.

The process can be thought of as a search for something *quantitative.* Cooperation in a cooperative village can be translated into the proportion of the land that is farmed cooperatively, or the proportion of people's working time they devote to the cooperative endeavors, or the fraction of the proceeds from selling the output that is not distributed among the members right away.

And in many studies of social change, the quantification can be either in terms of the inputs or the outputs, that is, one can measure the various programs designed to change things: time and money spent, the number of cattle-dips built, the amount of hybrid seed distributed, or one can try to measure the resulting outputs: increase in crop yields, healthier cattle, etc.

Even crude "quantification," categorizing people into groups, is better than nothing.

We go into data collection procedures and problems more fully in Chapter IV.

Required Staff, Resources and Advisory Committee

It is sensible of fund-granting agencies to require some evidence that those proposing a survey have access to the facilities needed to get the work done. The actual time commitments of the top staff must be presented, plus some statement of where the specialized skills and facilities are to be found. This makes life difficult for an individual who has an idea and wants to do a study. There are not always idle survey research stations ready to service his needs. Indeed, the requirements for team-work in survey research and for each specialist to understand enough about the other specialties to work with them, usually make it necessary for the subject matter specialist to find a survey methods specialist to work with. And since substantial funds are involved, some research advisory committee is usually required.

External Economies in Design

A major advantage of having a permanent organization, conducting whole sequences of surveys is that there are huge economies. The usual economies of scale are obvious—spreading the cost of a sample, of hiring and training interviewers, of getting a whole working organization together, over many surveys instead of one. But there are other kinds of economies. Topics which do not need a full interview, can share the costs of locating respondents and eliciting the background variables. Or a study with the same dependent variables (states, behaviors) may allow explanation in terms of the variables and interests of several disciplines.

A sample from one study can be revisited for a second, avoiding the need to ask the background information again, and allowing subselection to focus on or emphasize certain more interesting subgroups of the population. Previous studies in a sample using the same sub-areas until the addresses are exhausted, could be pooled to provide information about the area, as a kind of environmental variable richer than could be obtained from Census tract data.

Another kind of design makes two sets of data more useful by eliciting them from matched samples. One may have a sample of foremen and a sample of the workers they supervise, or a sample of politicians and of their electorates. It is often very useful to have information about how different groups look at the same situation.

Sometimes economies are possible because some list exists of a group of special interest, preferably with some additional information about them. This is particularly true where governments have form-filing requirements, but are interested in knowing more about the individual respondents from a small sample more intensively interviewed.

The technique of eliciting from a sample the names of those who form another relevant sample, is sometimes useful. It has its dangers, however, for when asked to name friends, people tend to name those a little better off than they are (their "best" friends). One study of tax compliance in Wisconsin asked a sample of tenants what rent they paid, and then checked the tax returns of the landlords to see if the rent was properly reported as income!

Where sequential processes, or sub-sampling do not work, and a special group needs to be sampled, it is frequently necessary to look for some bottleneck through which they all must pass, and try to find a method of sampling the flow. Tourist statistics, for instance, may be collected in the international departure lounges of a country's airports, or even in the planes themselves.

Analysis Design

It would be an ambitious researcher who thought he could specify in advance exactly how he was going to analyze the data. However, his design specifications require some statement about the kinds of constructs he is going to develop, the kinds of hypotheses he wants to choose between, and the kind of analysis that may allow him to decide that one or the other alternative

TABLE I

SUMMARY OF POINTS ABOUT WHICH CHOICES ARE MADE
IN THE DESIGN OF TYPICAL ECONOMIC SURVEYS

Specification of Objectives

    (Overall objectives and second level objectives)

Planning

    a. Selection of research staff
       (types of training and experience represented)
    b. Selection of methods for bringing relevant knowledge to the attention of the research staff
       (literature search, consultation, advisory group)
    c. Dependent and explanatory variables and how created from replies to questions
    d. Unit of analysis and unit covered by each respondent
    e. Preliminary investigations, if any
       (to estimate costs, to try out sampling procedures, to develop and test methods of measurement or analysis)

Sample Selection

    a. Type of sample
       (cross-section sample, experimental design, unit of sampling)
    b. Universe to be sampled and sampling frame
    c. Use of repeated interviews, reinterviews, or screening interviews
    d. Use of constant or variable sampling fraction
    e. Size of sample
    f. Procedure to select exact individuals to be interviewed
    g. Method of estimating sampling errors

Field Work

    a. Method of data collection
       (personal interviews, telephone interviews, mail questionnaires) (more than one per family?)
    b. Mix of types of questions
       (fixed alternative, free answer, use of observations by interviewers, use of non-interview data, use of complex systems of measurement)
    c. Length of interview
    d. Procedures for selection or special training of interviewers
    e. Number of callbacks and procedures for problem cases.

Analysis

    a. Method of selection among competing hypotheses
    b. Tests for universality of measured parameters or relationships

interpretations of data is the proper one. For instance, in a study of medical insurance and utilization of medical services there are two alternative hypotheses: one, that insurance leads to over-use and abuse of hospital facilities; and the other, that lack of insurance leads to inadequate medical care. Hence, the design needs to specify some procedure by which one can say which of these is more likely to be true. This might require either some outside assessment of the adequacy of the care, or some information from the individual about the extent of unmet needs or untreated symptoms. Sometimes lip service is paid to the notion that survey design starts out with one or two or three hypotheses which are then to be tested. This is not really what happens in practice. The hypotheses that exist are not specific, but general, having to do with the *kinds* of variables that affect the behavior in question, and most analysis discards a number of alternative hypotheses in the process. What is really required is the strategy of analysis and the specification of the kind of sequence of operations that may be used. Even if a main purpose is only to measure relationships (income elasticities, for instance) the analysis may have to check for different relations in different parts of the population.

It is useful to have a check-list of things about which decisions must be made in designing a study.

Privacy

One additional consideration needs to come into study design, particularly in view of the concern about privacy in behavioral research, and that is the specification of how the confidentiality of the data is to be preserved and the rights of the respondents to be respected. Actually, there are two issues here. One is the confidentiality of the data the respondent gives to a survey interviewer, and procedures need to be worked out for this purpose. Generally, this consists of separating the pages containing identifying information about the individual from the questionnaire material as soon as they arrive at the central office so that the processing of the data can proceed without any further identification of the individuals involved. The identifying information is, of course, necessary for checking out the sample and making sure that everyone has been contacted. An allied issue is whether the respondent's willingness to be interviewed was based on "informed consent," i.e. on reasonably clear information about the content and purposes of the survey. The second issue, however, is one not so fully discussed these days and has to do with the extent to which the findings of the research project are to be made generally available. It is undoubtedly quite dangerous for individuals to have information about them available only to one group in society. Potential use of such information for manipulation of people is fairly obvious. Therefore, one basic part of a study design should be some procedure for making the data generally available to the profession and, if possible, in summary form to the respondents themselves. Indeed the latter is often a very good way of inducing cooperation since many respondents would like to know what other people said about the same questions.

It is sometimes charged that survey research is too conservative, that it never really comes out with any exciting or dramatic conclusions. In a sense this is true. Quantitative facts about representative samples of the population usually turn out to be less dramatic than most of the hypotheses that have been advanced. There is a more meaningful sense in which this may also be true. Some social problems involve serious difficulties with very small groups of people and a sample of a representative population does not really provide adequate evidence. For instance, this is likely to be the case with problems such as frauds, extreme poverty, or extreme cases of mental illness.

Theoretical Constructs vs. Measurable Variables

It is a great temptation for an economist to want to collect all the components of some global construct, like total expenditures, or savings. Doing so puts such a burden on the respondent that it allows little time for any other explanatory or related variables. Furthermore, some components of the total may be very difficult for the respondent to remember. The design question, then, is whether some components which are accessible can be used as proxies for a more complete concept, and whether a focus on some aspects of behavior, with more attention to explanation, might not be more productive, than forcing the analysis into the formal mode of economic theory. Indeed, it seems likely that many of the concepts of economic theory, such as saving, may have little motivational meaning since they are the result of several different kinds of decisions which the consumer may not even see as related, and which may be differently motivated. The decision to buy a car, for instance, may be seen as an investment, but the decision to take a longer vacation as consumption, even luxury.

The collection of information about total expenditures or total consumption is very difficult. There is a common belief that in order to get it all, one must ask a great many detailed questions, and there is some evidence that asking more questions does get larger total amounts. What is not clear is whether these larger totals are more accurate, particularly in light of recent evidence on people's tendency to "telescope" expenditures forward into the period asked about (thus exaggerating them). Various devices have been suggested to take some of the burden off the respondent, but most of them exact a price—either collecting some expenditures from some sub-samples and the rest from others, restricting the period with the attendant problems, or going to the expense of reinterviews and even diaries. The question remains whether the basic problem that led to an interest in expenditure detail cannot be attacked better with other data, using house value or rent and size of dwelling as proxies for housing expense, miles driven and age of car as proxies for transportation costs, etc.

Advantages and Problems of Panel Designs

It is currently fashionable to argue that the dynamic data needs of economists call for panel (reinterview) studies. A summary of some of their advantages and disadvantages seems in order:

The main advantages of the panel study are a reduction in problems of recall, the ability to get data on changes in attitudes, expectations, and cash balances, and other things the respondent may forget over a period of time.

Improved rapport from revisits is also believed to lead to better data, in addition to the cumulative accrual of data and possible cross-checks for consistency and accuracy.

Validity studies are also possible by repeating questions to which the answers should not change. Triple measures on variables allow some tests for instability (measurement error).[1] Stable personality items which differ widely between people can be eliminated by relating changes to changes (using first differences), though with qualitative measures this is not so easy as it seems.

Most important, one may be able to uncover dynamic sequences: Did attitudes change before or after behavior changed? What was the time lag between an event and its influence?

Finally, there are some economies in locating people on revisits, and in the use of official records, etc.

What about the disadvantages? Cost is the main one. Reinterviews are expensive, requiring several interviews for information on one unit. The revisits often require extra travel because people have moved out of the geographic clusters in which they were originally sampled. Losses cumulate, since most panels cannot use cases where any one of the interviews is missing.

Changes in the composition of the units cause problems. What is the same unit, in cases of divorce, marriage, etc.? How does one replace the units which die, leave the country, or enter institutions? A partial solution is to treat the individuals of the original sample as the sample frame, and interview any family containing any of those individuals from then on. (Of course this soon becomes a non-representative sample of *families* overrepresenting those containing unstable individuals). And those same changes usually occur *during* the year, not on January 1, so measures of flows like income and expenditures require special editing adjustments, and must be related to family size, also adjusted in some way.

The cumulative improvement of information is itself a problem, since measures of real change are confounded with improved data, and multiple consistency checks may be required. Where inconsistencies occur and the truth is unknown, complex editing decisions are necessary.

Finally, there are even mechanical problems of handling the vast mass of information assembled for each individual (or family), and new computer procedures are still being developed to handle the problem. Unless one is willing to generate numerical indexes, the data on change in a set of five attitudinal questions can be a problem to analyze or to use in the analysis of other changes.

Perhaps the main reason why there have not been many panel studies is a more general problem for survey research, the lack of funding sources willing to commit funds for more than a year or two at a time. Panels need to be planned as panels, including informing the respondents and collecting information on how to find them if they should move. There needs to be enough agreement on the content so that major design decisions are not re-worked every year, leaving time for some analysis of one year's data before the press of the next wave of interviews is on the research staff.

But if panels require both substantial amounts of money, and long term commitments, then their justification and careful original design is even more important than with single surveys. Chopping out unnecessary or peripheral objectives becomes more important, too, since the cooperation of the respondents hinges on keeping the demands on them within reason.

Some Design Problems

We shall try now to put a little meat on these bare bones by giving some examples of actual or potential survey designs—good and bad—in an attempt to illustrate some of the principles. The difficulty, of course, is that it is much easier to illustrate examples of good or bad sample design or analysis design than it is to illustrate a good or bad case of specification of objectives or questionnaire design. Let us first give some examples of mistakes made in design, or designs that were not as good as they might have been, then go on to give some examples of design problems and ways they might be handled.

Suppose one took a sample of graduate students of a particular year and found them "x" years later, studied their incomes and the relationship between their field of study and how far they went in graduate school. This was actually done. The difficulty here is that there is an inevitable confounding between the amount of graduate education the man got and the number of years of experience on his job, so that there is no way really of sorting out these two influences. (Those who left school sooner have more job experience.) It would have been much better to take several cohorts of graduate students so that one could untangle these two influences.

Another example is a sample of personal bankruptcies. People who go into bankruptcy have to file a statement of their assets and their last three years' income. Researchers have taken samples of these statements and, in some cases, have also gone back and talked to the people. The difficulty here, of course, is that there is no way of comparing these people with others in equally bad circumstances who paid off their bills and did not go bankrupt.

The third example is a design that seeks to achieve minimum memory problems asking only about last week's expenditures. The only difficulty is that you cannot, from last week's expenditures, get *distributions* of monthly or annual expenditures. You can only get unbiased estimates of aggregates or means.

Another example is a study of farm housing which took the master sample of agriculture, sampled the segments and took three farms per segment. The problem here, of course, is that a segment with thirty small farms had only one farm in ten represented, whereas a segment with three large farms had them all represented. The result is a biased set of estimates which could have been corrected by weighting the data if someone had thought in advance about the problem.

Another study design problem involved getting information about the occupations and educations of respondents and their fathers in order to study the intergenerational transmission of education (or occupation). If one considers this as a Markov process, a set of transition probabilities which remain constant, one can extrapolate many generations into the future. The difficulty is, of course, that a sample of children (respondents) is not a representative sample of families (fathers), because the more children, the more respondents available to fall into the sample. What is worse, the transition probabilities (proportion of cases where father went to 6th grade and the son went to 8th, for instance) are probably affected by family size, the speed of upgrading being greater where there were fewer children for the family to support. One could weight inversely according to the number of brothers and sisters the respondent had, or do the analysis separately for different family sizes, or ask respondents about the completed education of their *children*. The latter raises other difficulties, since not all respondents have children who have completed their education, (and other parents are already deceased).

There was a study which inspected deed transfers to get a sample of home buyers. The difficulty was that not all transfers involved residential properties, and some real transfers were not recorded by deed transfers until years later. (They may have been transfers in the family, or conditional sales as with land contracts.)

In a study of industrial location, sampling fractions were varied from industry to industry to make sure that each of several industries was represented and could be discussed separately. It turned out that there were no appreciable differences between the industries, consequently the sample was quite inefficient.

Another study started out to be a panel, but in the initial interview respondents were asked to take part in the panel before any facts about them were ascertained which could have allowed an assessment of the bias from noncooperation. Since a substantial proportion refused, the bias could well have been substantial.

One study on farm housing, used an extremely long interview with a large number of questions about whether the respondent would like to have this or that housing feature. Without the discipline of a choice of alternatives, people could say they wanted many things. The reader of the report would have no way of knowing how poor the information was, nor how many interviewers quit in the middle of the project.

In a study of farm management, one objective was to study how farmers made decisions, but the implementation of this objective was a question fourteen lines long which really asked the farmers whether they used inductive or deductive reasoning. This was followed by a series of questions pushing the matter further. The polite farmers answered the questions but there is some doubt about the realism of the answers. It might have been better to have asked for details of some actual recent decisions, and then attempted in a central office to interpret the process.

Another study went to great lengths to get a sample of high income people, but was so concerned with getting accurate detail about their incomes and assets that this took up the whole questionnaire, and no questions were asked that could have thrown light on *why* people chose the portfolios they had. A similar study used a different design, asking about recent changes in portfolio and the reasons for them, purposes people had in investing their savings, their plans for the future, and their sources of information. This allowed more inferences about why people did what they did, even though the information on their actual incomes and assets was less precise.

A major study of poverty, revisiting addresses to measure changes in poverty, was revised after two waves, to introduce more questions about people's attitudes, plans, and actual behavior, so that it would be possible to say more about *why* some people stayed poor, and others improved their situations.

There have been a number of attempts in the past to start national studies of auto accident victims or work-injury victims. In both cases there are problems: auto accidents are reported locally, some not reported at all, and the reports are sometimes kept locally, or sometimes sent to the state offices. And in each state, Workmen's Compensation is a regime unto itself, each with its own system for filing work accident reports, and with varying levels of concern to see that all accidents are reported. A major analytical problem is whether the differences in state laws and state administration leads to differences in results, but the variety is such that a very large number of states would have to be investigated. It is possible that these problems could be solved by taking a national sample of hospitals, selecting a sample of their discharges, interviewing them about their experiences, costs, compensation, and whether they were in the hospital because of an auto accident, work injury, or something else. One would then have *three* representative samples, proper for studying three problems, at least as efficiently and economically as one could have studied one.

An elaborate study to assess the effects in several different areas of programs to educate farmers, concluded that while there were effects they differed from one place to the next. And it was difficult to tell whether this resulted from differences in the places, or differences in the quality of the local educational programs. In other words, in studies of "impact," it is essential to have some measurement of the *quality* of the inputs into programs designed to change things.

Another common problem is circularity, or uncertainty as to causal directions. Time sequences do not always solve the problem. For instance, if farmers who have had extensive visits from extension agents adopt a new practice more than other farmers, it is still possible that the extension agents visited them because they thought they were more likely to adopt the practice. In other words, the farmer's modernism led to the visits, rather than resulting from them. It may be possible to find out which is more likely, if the interviews with farmers and agents are designed with the problem in mind. Similar problems exist with studies of the effects of education, or geographic mobility.

The advantages of interviews should not blind the designer to the possibilities of other information. In a study of retail stores, for instance, a sample of observations at points of time, can provide quantitative data as to how much of the time there are too many clerks or too few, or as to how often displays are changed, etc. Samples of the cars in the parking lot may give indications of the kind of customers, etc.

It is much easier to give good or bad examples than to establish general principles. It is true that the respondent must have available in his memory the information we want, and that there should be some variation in the population that can be "explained." Information far in the past, not salient to the respondent, and not easy for the respondent to find in a record somewhere, is not a good candidate for survey research. Beyond this it is difficult to generalize. We turn now to a series of more detailed examples of research designs, first, some illustrations of things that have been done, and then a few which have not been carried out.

Detailed Examples of Research Designs

It is not possible in any brief review of the subject to include examples of research design that will cover anything like the full range of topics of inquiry, populations, and techniques of investigation in the field of economic surveys. The diversity of the field is extraordinary, and new investigations are continually being undertaken all over the world. What will be attempted here is simply to describe briefly the design of a few selected projects.

1950 and 1951 Surveys of Consumer Finances· Surveys of Consumer Finances have been undertaken annually by the Survey Research Center of the University of Michigan since 1947. They were developed from financial surveys inaugurated during the war years. Over the years there have been changes in the objectives and methods of these projects. The surveys of 1950 to 1951 are of special interest to economists because of the objectives pursued, the techniques employed, and what was subsequently learned about the techniques used at that time in special methodological projects.[2] This account, therefore, will be concerned with the surveys of that period.

The immediate objectives of these surveys were descriptive. The intention was to measure, for a national sample of households, the following: the income of each household, including considerable detail as to the components of total income and an estimate of federal income tax; the major assets, liabilities, and net worth of the household, with detail about the principal components both of assets and of liabilities; the annual saving of the household, also with detail as to the changes in its balance sheet; the principal outlays of the household, and the purchase of durable goods; and the attitudes, plans, and expectations of the household, especially those likely to influence or to reveal its propensity to consume in the immediate future. Given each of these items of information for each of a sample of households, together with measures of the demographic characteristics of the household, there were extensive possibilities both of descriptive tabulation and of analysis intended to explain or to predict consumer behavior. These possibilities, however, were not made explicit in a formal statement of objectives at the time each of these projects was planned. What was planned, however, was implied in part by reports of previous surveys in the *Federal Reserve Bulletin.*

The selection of research staff presents a less difficult problem on a continuing project than on a new survey. The staffs involved both at the Survey Research Center and at the Federal Reserve Board, which sponsored those surveys, had had the experience of work on earlier surveys in the series. No special efforts were made to bring relevant knowledge to the attention of the staff at this stage in the series. No preliminary investigations were undertaken, though there were pretests of each questionnaire. (There had been a pilot study some years before, prior to the first national survey.)

The sample was a cross-section of all households (spending units) living in private dwellings in the United States. (A precise definition of the empirical equivalent of the theorist's household will be considered in later chapters.) The dwelling units were chosen by methods based on the selection of small geographic areas for inclusion in the sample. In order to improve the accuracy of estimates of such statistics as mean income and mean assets, a variable sampling fraction was used. The method involved dividing the sample into three strata based on preliminary estimates of the economic level of each dwelling (estimated rent or house value). A higher sampling fraction was used in the "high" stratum than in the "medium" or "low" stratum. Another way of stating what was done was that half the medium dwellings in a sample were thrown out, and three quarters of the "low" economic level dwellings. (This technique, and the accompanying use of weights to prevent bias in the tabulated results, is discussed in Chapter III.) The total sample was about 3,000-3,500 households per year. Within households, the designated respondent was the head of each spending unit. Estimates of sampling error of means and percentages were made which allowed for the complexity of the sample design but stopped short of providing specific estimates of error for each statistic.

The field work relied on personal interviews using a questionnaire containing a mixture of open-ended and fixed alternative questions. Interviews averaged about one hour, and were conducted by the national staff of interviewers employed by the Survey Research Center. An interview was taken with the head of each economic unit (spending unit) in the household, covering the members of that unit. At that time there were still a considerable number of secondary spending units, usually children or parents of the main family head, who had their own income and kept their finances separate.

Analysis involved "editing" each questionnaire, a process which included calculation of a series of summary measures, prior to "coding," in which each answer was summarized by a numerical code on a transfer sheet. Processing then involved key-punching the data from coded sheets and the preparation of tables using punched cards and the I.B.M. machinery then available. Publication was initially in the form of a series of articles in the *Federal Reserve Bulletin,* with later special analyses published elsewhere.

Evaluation of the success of these surveys requires assessment of the usefulness and accuracy of the measurements made. While criticisms have been made of the choice of topics covered and definitions adopted, there has been little question of the usefulness of these surveys viewed as a whole. There have been serious questions raised, however, about the accuracy of some parts of the data. A considerable effort has been made to evaluate the accuracy, with complex results. A detailed discussion of this type of research is dealt with in Chapter IV. In brief, it is now possible to prepare a rough ranking of types of results according to the accuracy of the estimates in these surveys. Income was estimated with comparatively high accuracy, consumer debt with medium accuracy, and change in liquid assets (and, hence, saving) with comparatively low accuracy. Such findings have led to refinement in some measures and to de-emphasis or abandonment of others in subsequent surveys. Meanwhile, some of the major findings have been widely accepted.

Urban Income and Saving in India: A series of studies of income and saving in India was begun in 1958 by the National Council of Applied Economic Research, located in New Delhi. The starting point of this research was recognition of the importance of saving in a developing country. The program included work in compiling data from institutional sources and sample surveys. Both an urban and a rural sample survey were undertaken, but, for simplicity, only the urban survey is considered here.[3]

The broad purpose of the survey was to contribute to the overall goal of obtaining "a clear insight into the volume, composition, and motivation of saving." The topics of investigation included the demographic and socioeconomic characteristics of the population and income, as well as saving. Thus, the initial purposes of the survey were descriptive in the same sense as those of the Surveys of Consumer Finances. The general strategy of the project was also similar, except for the closer integration in India of the survey approach with the institutional approach to the study of saving.

The staff for the Indian project included a substantial investment in foreign consultants in addition to the Indian economists, and in this way foreign experience was directly brought to bear at every stage in the project. The investigators undertook a pilot study in Delhi in 1959, including interviews with 600 households, and its results were published.[4]

The national survey of urban India was intended to represent the population of India living in cities and towns of 10,000 or more population. As in the Surveys of Consumer Finances, the sampling procedure was based on the selection of small geographic areas, and a variable sampling fraction was used to oversample high income households. About 4,650 interviews were taken in addition to the 600 in Delhi. At the time of publication of the monograph, sampling error calculations which took into account the complexity of the design were in progress, but only limited results were available.

Data collection was based on personal interviews. The mix of questions included both fixed alternative and open answer questions. At the analysis stage extensive use was made of data from institutional sources, but these data referred to aggregates, not to individual households. Interviewers were trained as a group in the central office prior to the start of the survey, in contrast to American practice, in which training is done in or near the communities where the interviewers live. The questionnaires were prepared and printed in English and translated by each interviewer during the interview.

The analysis of the data involved editing, coding, key-punching, and the preparation of tables using punch card equipment. Publication was in the form of a series of monographs. No multivariate analysis procedures were reported in the monograph on *Urban Income and Saving.*

This survey achieved one of its objectives by making available many statistics which previously were unknown for urban India. Its success in providing information about saving which could be combined with the data from institutional sources was limited by conceptual differences and reporting biases. These two sources of discrepancy were separated in the report, but only on the basis of rough approximations. Essentially, the survey estimates were taken to be good approximations of gross investment in physical assets, but poor approximations of saving in the form of financial assets. (The survey estimate of the latter is 126.9 crores of rupees; the adjusted estimate, 340.5.) The estimates of income were believed to be reasonably accurate on the basis of what checks with non-survey aggregates could be made, and the demographic information also seemed reasonably accurate. In brief, on the basis of the published monograph, the survey seems to have been moderately successful as an instrument for obtaining new descriptive data on income and saving. Whether the total project, of which the survey is a part, will lead to the desired insights into saving and, hence, to more enlightened and effective economic policy is inherently more difficult to judge.

A Study of Capital Expenditures by Large Corporations: A study based on intensive interviews with business executives was published by Robert Eisner in 1956.[5] This project is of continuing interest because of the economic importance of knowing the determinants of capital expenditure. The work was a part of a larger study of "expectations and business fluctuations." To some degree, the objectives of the interviews were influenced by other parts of the larger study. The published statement of objectives of the specific project is as follows:

> In regard to capital expenditures, the interviewer was hunting in general for determinants of the level of expenditure.[6]

The entire project was under the direction of Franco Modigliani. This specific study was the work of Robert Eisner, who personally conducted the interviews, analyzed them, and wrote the resulting monograph. Some preliminary interviewing, "of a pilot nature," had been done by Modigliani and others in the spring of 1950.

The sample included fourteen large manufacturing corporations in six different industries. There was no attempt to select a random sample, but the firms were chosen to represent producers of both consumer and capital goods. Geographic convenience of accessibility to the interviewer was also a consideration. Several interviews were taken in most corporations, and in some cases reinterviews were undertaken in 1954-1955. The selection of respondents within the corporations was not systematic. Interviews generally commenced with a top executive and continued with subordinates. No sampling errors were calculated. Indeed, the report contains no tabulations.

The data collection began with a personal letter sent from the Dean of the College of Commerce at the University of Illinois. Further correspondence was undertaken by Eisner himself. No formal questionnaire was used. On the basis of the unstructured personal interviews, a "terminal letter" was sent to each corporation asking summary questions. Drafts of much of the final report, including case reports on the individual firms, were submitted for comment.

Analysis consisted in the preparation of a verbal summary based on Eisner's interpretation of the case studies. In addition fourteen reports on the individual firms were published. The latter vary considerably in length, occupying from two to twelve pages in the published report.

The conclusion which receives the most stress in the report is methodological. Eisner argues vigorously that what is important to individual firms may not be what is important in the aggregate. Changes in sales may influence many firms, but, conceivably, in ways which cancel in the aggregate. A factor such as an increase in the interest rate may be crucial only "at the margin" i.e. for a few firms where other forces are indecisive. Yet, those firms will be influenced in the *same* direction by a general increase in the rate. A "majority vote" is meaningless viewed from the standpoint of a theorist concerned with *marginal* considerations. This point is an important one, and will be further considered in Chapter VI, "Analysis."

Eisner is extremely cautious in what he says about substantive issues concerning the determinants of capital expenditures. Perhaps his most interesting findings concern "calculations," that is, various formal costs and earnings criteria. He found the methods used crude, frequently internally inconsistent, and subject to systematic bias. Fortunately, not all the biases operate in the same direction. These results are especially intriguing in view of the great interest, since Eisner's report, in "systems analysis" and "operations research." These areas involve the application of sophisticated methods of analysis to problems such as those with which he was concerned. If we take this view of his results, we must conclude that Eisner found something for which he was not looking, and underestimated its importance. He experiences considerable difficulty, however, in coming to definite conclusions about the topics he set out to investigate.

A Study of Job-Seeking Behavior: In late August to early October of 1964 a sample of unemployed workers in Erie, Pennsylvania, were interviewed in a project undertaken by Harold L. Sheppard and A. Harvey Belitsky of the W. E. Upjohn Institute for Employment Research. A monograph based on these interviews and ancillary data collection was published in 1966.[7]

The overall objective of the project was stated as follows:

> . . . to spell out in greater detail the widely accepted findings about the job-seeking behavior of unemployed workers and, in particular,

to explore the relationship of social-psychological and other factors, hitherto neglected in manpower studies, to job-seeking behavior.[8]

The study was intended more specifically to ascertain the social-psychological variables that affect "the nature and intensity of an unemployed worker's search for re-employment" and his chances of success. It was not intended to argue the primacy of social-psychological factors. Whether a worker *finds* a job will be "heavily influenced by basic economic processes." But job-*seeking* is open to explanation by social-psychological tendencies.

Three social-psychological measures were investigated—"achievement motivation," "achievement values," and "job-interview anxiety." The effect of each was sought on such measures of job-seeking behavior as how soon a worker starts looking for a new job, and the total number of job-seeking techniques that he uses.

While the above objectives were regarded as central by the investigators, there were a number of secondary objectives which are not easy to summarize concisely. It is fair to say that they amount to an attempt to describe the labor market in one urban area, with emphasis on the market for services of blue-collar male workers. In effect, the explanatory study using the social-psychological predictors was imbedded in a descriptive study.

The monograph is not explicit as to the training and experience represented by the research team, but it is clear that the effort was interdisciplinary and involved personnel with psychological training. They were able to supervise the administration and coding of picture protocols to obtain scores on need for achievement. The project itself, as noted above, was regarded as exploratory, and no preliminary investigations seem to have been undertaken.

The basic sample was a cross-section of workers unemployed at some time during a fifteen-month period, January 1, 1963 to March 31, 1964, in Erie, Pennsylvania. The sampling frame was the file of blue-collar workers who applied for jobs in the Erie office of the Pennsylvania Employment Service. From a cross-section sample drawn from this file certain marginal groups of workers were omitted (those with serious physical handicaps, recent entrants into the labor force, seasonal workers, those living at a distance). The sample designated for interview was a cross-section of the remainder whose names had been selected from the file. There was one round of interviewing, which produced 473 interviews. No attempt was made to follow those who had moved. Since the sample was essentially a simple random sample, no special calculations of sampling errors were needed.

Field work was undertaken by interviewers employed by National Analysts, Inc., of Philadelphia, who visited the workers in their homes. The questionnaire was unusual in that it included measures of the three social-psychological variables noted. Of these, the measures of achievement motivation and achievement values were taken from earlier work by David McClelland and Bernard Rosen. The measure of job-interview anxiety was adopted from measures developed by G. Mandler and S. B. Sarason in studies of the anxiety of students concerning the taking of tests. The questionnaire included some 156 questions including the four pictures and associated questions. No account of special training for the interviewers appears in the monograph.

The analysis consisted essentially in the preparation of tables of percentages without the use of formal multivariate procedures. As predicted, evidence was found of systematic association between achievement motivation and several of the measures of job-seeking behavior. The investigators seem to have expected to find that, since those who have high need for achievement search more diligently, they would be more likely to have found jobs. On this point the evidence for the hypothesis is marginal. Results for the second predictor, achievement values, are broadly similar, but the relationships seem somewhat weaker and are presented in less detail. Job interview anxiety seems to have had limited effects on job-seeking patterns but did have some effect, for example, in slowing the start of the search, and, for young people, in producing greater reliance on the Employment Service. In summary, the attempt to deduce differences in job-seeking behavior from social-psychological theory was reasonably successful.

The results of the descriptive portions of the study are not easily summarized. They included results of 48 interviews with industrial leaders, union officials, and community leaders, as well as results of small studies of Negro males and white-collar women. A considerable quantity of factual information is presented. The authors themselves refer in the final chapter to "the tree-like profusion of facts and statistics that comprise the preceding chapters,"[9] from which they emerge "at last." The difficulty is a common one: it is not easy to develop a description of something as complex as a local labor market in such a manner that the parts of the description form a whole which is well articulated and comprehensible.

A related difficulty is that the policy recommendations are not closely related to solid empirical results. For example, the first recommendation is for an extension of techniques used by McClelland and associates aimed at increasing achievement motivation and values among businessmen in other countries, and of programs of managerial technical assistance in areas of economic retardation in the United States. A similar recommendation is made for improving the job-seeking behavior of workers. Without prejudice to the merits of these policies, it must be said that the reasoning leading up to such recommendations is not carefully developed in this monograph. There is a considerable jump between a finding that need achievement relates to behavior in searching for jobs and the feasibility of a policy of increasing need achievement among workers—and, indeed, the monograph recommends experimental projects. The successful attempt at explanation of job-seeking behavior does not lead automatically to successful predictions or to a well-considered evaluation of probable consequences even if the proposed efforts to induce psychological changes were to succeed.

We turn now to some additional examples where only the unusual or crucial decisions are discussed, not the total design.

Effects of Lump-Sum Settlements on Insured Workers: The initial purpose of this study was to determine the effects of lump sum compensation settlements on the rehabilitation of injured workers.[10] Behind this were two conflicting hypotheses. One was that if an injured worker settles his claim against his employer and cannot count on any more weekly payments or medical care payments, he is more likely to get back to work. The competing hypothesis was that the worker is usually genuinely disabled and has a difficult time living on a weekly payment, so that if he settles for a lump sum settlement, he will merely pay off his back debts with the money, lose his right to decent rehabilitative medical care, and end up on the welfare rolls. An obvious way to discriminate between these two hypotheses is to take a sample of workers who have accepted lump sum settlements and see what happens to them. Workmen's compensation is administered differently in each of fifty states, and fifty separate samples would be impossible. Even in one state, like Michigan, there are several different files: A file of accident reports, a file of people currently being paid weekly benefits, and a file of actual redemption settlements. Clearly a sample of the file of current payments would not do. In the first place it is not a representative sample of accidents because the longer a man stays on weekly payments the more chance he has of being drawn in a sample.

If one samples accident reports one gets a very large number of accidents where very few weekly payments were made, and few where any settlement was ever made. So we took a sample of the actual redemption settlements, and then tried to find some kind of reasonably matched sample of people who stayed on actual weekly payments. Of course, it turns out to be impossible to do this matching cleanly because the kinds of accidents and kinds of people who stay on the weekly payment are different from the ones who settle.

How far back in time should one go to take a sample of settlements? This involves a substantive issue as to how long is required for the event to resolve itself. It would seem that it ought to be a year or so. But the longer one waits, the harder it is to find people, and the less they remember about what happened. We finally selected a sample of settlements about 1-1/2 years prior to interview date. In this particular study, it turned out that people who accepted these settlements were mostly not back to work a year and a half later, not even most of the "bad back" cases. The implication was that the settlements were being secured by people who were desperate for money to pay their bills, whose lawyers wanted to be paid, and where the insurance company was glad to get off the hook of an open-ended commitment. The settlements did not lead to rehabilitation and re-entry into the work force. Unfortunately, the practical results of this study were that the Workmen's Compensation Department simply made it more and more difficult for anybody to get a settlement. But the workers could hardly survive on the weekly payments at the level where they were fixed. It was not until a number of years later that the legislature finally raised the weekly payments so that people could survive on them.

A Study of Medical Insurance and Utilization of Medical Services: What is the effect of medical insurance on the utilization of medical services?[11] Here again there are two opposite hypotheses. One, that without insurance people will get inadequate medical care, and the other, that with insurance, they are over-cared for and stay in the hospital too long and use services they don't really need. Sometimes the hypothesis is that the doctor, knowing the insurance status, prescribes things unnecessarily. Others argue that the patient himself, being conscious of the economics of the matter, has some say about what goes on. Now, how should one design such a study? A major problem is that a very large number of people have little or no medical expense during the year, so that if one started with a simple cross-section sample, a lot of interviews would contribute little or nothing to the variance to be examined. How about a sample of hospital patients? Should one sample admissions, people currently in the hospital, or discharges? If we sample admissions, we have to go back in the past. Some of the people may still be in the hospital and some may be dead. If we sample people (patients) in the hospital, the sampling probabilities are in proportion to how long people stay in the hospital. But suppose we do take a sample of discharges? We still have the problem of the other people who were sick but did not go to the hospital. Furthermore, it is a rather complicated procedure. One would first have to take a sample of hospitals, secure their cooperation, sample their discharges, then look up the addresses and go interview the people. We certainly could not get the detailed hospital information about their illness or the amount of the bill. On the other hand, if we went to the individuals first, we could have them sign a release, and then go to the hospital and get the detailed billing information, provided we want to spend that much time and trouble to get detailed dollar figures from some source other than the respondent.

What was done to make the field interview more efficient was to take a large sample but then go to the door and ask some screening questions. Where the people had very little to report, we took only half or a quarter of those households. Two questions were asked. The first was whether there was anyone over 65 in the house, and the second was whether anyone in the household had been in the hospital in the last year. There is plenty of evidence that the incidence of the need for medical care skyrockets dramatically as people get older, so that people over 65 could be expected to have more to report, more choices to make, and perhaps more variance in their utilization of medical service, part of which might be explained by insurance coverage.

There were some problems with screening about actual hospitalization, however. In the part of the sample where we did no screening, but asked about hospitalization in the middle of a long interview, substantially more hospitalizations got reported than when we used an initial, screening, question. Of course, with any screening or subsampling it was necessary to weight the final data to maintain representativeness. Weights were adjusted so that they also took account of this "over-screening."

To test the hypothesis that the uninsured are using medical services less because they just cannot afford them and are undercared for, we asked people about treatments suggested by doctors they had done nothing about, and about untreated symptoms. (Things that might require going to a doctor but about which people had done nothing.) Of course other variables affect utilization of medical service too, such as differences in need and differences in attitude, so we also had to ask age and sex and whether people thought it was a good idea to go to the hospital or the doctor at the first sign of illness. Even taking into account age, sex, and attitudes, there was a relationship between lack of insurance coverage and reporting of unmet needs or untreated symptoms. Hence, the correlation between insurance and utilization was at least in part the result of inadequate care of the uninsured.

In this particular study we could not trust people's knowledge about what their insurance covered so we asked them the name of the company and the number of the policy. We were able to check a large number of these and make an estimate as to what fraction of a standard package of medical needs would be covered by these particular policies. This allowed us to use a scale variable of how well the person was insured, rather than a dichotomy; insured or not. We also checked some hospital records to see whether people were exaggerating their medical expenses and, of course, some of them were. This kind of validity study is one-sided, because we could only get expenses that people reported, and the hospital did not confirm the bills from doctors, other hospitals, or other hospital visits, which respondents failed to report. There is no way to find out where to look for such information.

Air Travel: How can the predictions of demand for air travel be improved? One approach is to find out why some people travel and some do not. What problems does this approach pose? First, many people *never* travel by air. Hence, in a probability sample of the population, we will have more non-travelers than needed to find out why some people do not fly and not enough of the people who do use air travel. On the other hand, suppose we take a sample of people in airplanes? Then we could get *only* the people who do travel by air, and the probability of selection would be proportional to the *amount* of travel. This is not necessarily bad if we weight the data appropriately. We may want more of the people who do a lot of traveling, particularly if we want to estimate the total demand for air travel, not merely the change in the proportion that do any traveling at all. Two samples could be spliced together: a cross-section sample and a sample of air travelers can be combined and the weights lowered for the people from both groups who do travel by air. The criterion for combining the samples and weighting them may be open to question, of course, because there may be response errors in people's reports.

Now suppose we have drawn some kind of sample. What might be a major reason why some people do not travel by air? Fear? How can we get people to admit they are afraid of flying? Some of them will admit it and maybe a few even exaggerate it, but the real problem is that at least some people will refuse to admit it. Studies designed by Lansing asked: "What might keep some people from traveling by plane?" More people mentioned fear in that situation than would admit they were afraid themselves.[12] There are dangers in these projection techniques, of course. Some people may really be saying literally that they think *other* people are afraid but that they are not. However, many psychologists argue that there is a lot of projection, and that if a man brings up fear in this kind of discussion, the chances are it has at least some relevance to his own situation.

Now, what else could we find out? We could ask some memory questions about when people first started to travel, and why. And we would have to separate pleasure from business travel. We could also find out some things about *where* people have some reason to travel, for example, where their relatives live. We can ask about car ownership, the size of the family, where they live in relation to airports, and the value of their time based on the husband's hourly earnings.

Then we can do some kind of economic analysis of what the actual cost of travel by various modes would be for such a family. We can determine whether some of the differences in travel are based on reasonable economic choices in each situation. We can also find out whether people know certain relevant facts. For instance, do they know what it costs to go by air, what it costs to get to the airport? It is difficult to believe that they are making careful economic calculations if they do not have the facts, or that they would even respond to changed air fares if they do not know what they are.

On the other hand, one must be careful with interpretation of the effects of ignorance because if and when air fares got to the point where they were really competitive, the news might travel very quickly.

A Study of the Decision When to Retire: A study of why people retire when they do has obvious importance in the future supply of labor. A representative cross-section sample contains many people too young to have thought much about retiring. Furthermore, it contains very few of those benefiting from private pension plans (few have qualified yet) or special supplemental early retirement benefits such as those available to auto workers.

A study designed to deal with these problems has been done.[13] It involved two samples: a cross-section sample, and a sample of workers in the automobile and agricultural implement industry 58-61 years old who were eligible for some special supplemental early retirement benefits.

The cross-section sample was in two waves, so that the retirement questions would be combined with other objectives, and those under 30 would not have to be asked about retirement. Those not retired were asked about their plans, how much retirement income they would have, etc. The retired were asked about their past decision to retire, whether they retired early or not, and whether the retirement was unexpected (precipitated by illness, unemployability, etc.). Interesting comparisons were possible between the plans of the first group and the retrospective reports of the second group on what they actually did. For example, the workers expected to do more community work when they retired, but the retired did not report doing more than before retirement.

The sample of UAW workers provided information about a group in a narrow age range and in rather special circumstances. It turned out that their working wages covered a very narrow range, but that the amount they were entitled to if they retired early (and even whether they were entitled to anything) varied widely, depending on how long they had worked for the company.

A screening questionnaire was sent out by mail to the UAW workers, allowing some analysis of who had already retired early, and provided a sample selection for personal interviews later. These interviews focused somewhat more on those who had retired early or planned to.

Later on, a check of the records revealed who had indeed retired early (after the interview), so that an analysis could be made parallel with that of planned early retirement, using actual early retirement as the dependent variable.

The design calls for an additional follow-up, perhaps by telephone, both to secure more data on the actual retirement decision, and to test a hypothesis that the joy of the early retirees will diminish as time goes on, inflation continues, and they reach 65, when, in some cases, their total retirement income will diminish. (The study has, however, already shown that the workers are quite well informed about the system, and about the change in income at 65.) Economic variables proved to dominate in the retirement decision, but perhaps more interesting was the appearance of a nonlinearity, a threshold retirement income (about $4000 a year) below which few planned to retire early (or even voluntarily). The implications for the aggregate labor supply are clear—only when private pensions push people's retirement income up *substantially*, will they cause any large volume of early retirement. It is the number pushed beyond the threshold, not the aggregate, that matters.

Two Study Designs Still on the Drawing Boards

Philanthropy: The following is a design for a study of philanthropy, a study which has not yet been done. Its purpose is to study people's contributions of time *and* money to worthy causes. Do some people contribute time, others money? Will the growth of government welfare systems cause private charity to decline? Does this seem like the kind of subject that could keep a respondent interested for 50 minutes? If someone is giving neither time nor money to anything, he will not have much to report and the interview might be relatively short. On the other hand, the attitudinal material and the background material need to be collected for these people too. Fortunately, a substantial number of people in this country give at least some time and money, if not to organized charity, at least to helping friends and relatives. This study is proposed to build on previous studies which have already collected partial data, one study on contributions of *money* to church, charity, and individuals. The other on *time* devoted to helping others.[14]

Suppose one wanted to define a single dependent variable for this study. First, how would one decide whether it was feasible to combine time and money gifts into a single dependent variable called philanthropic activity? One might want to find out whether the same explanatory variables were operating in roughly the same way to explain contributions of time, and contributions of money. The federal income tax law is neutral in respect to the choice of giving time or money, so long as a man has a possibility of earning more money by working more. He can either work longer, give the money away, and deduct the contribution from his income, for tax purposes, or he can devote the time directly to charity instead of to earning income. If we discovered that the effects of explanatory variables like income on the two kinds of contributions are roughly similar, we could then combine the two kinds of philanthropy into one dependent variable. How would we combine the different units? One is in hours and the other is in dollars. If we believe in marginalism, and if we think that the individual has some choice as to whether he works hard and earns more money on the one hand, or spends more time on charitable work on the other, we could argue that his wage rate measures his marginal time value. If he spends so many hours on charity he must think that the time he spent was worth that much in terms of his contribution. Now this theory does not work if he is under some kind of restraint, e.g., if he can work only 40 hours a week, or if he really does not want to do any more work. On the other hand, you cannot argue that people merely like variety, because this can be specified in the diminishing curve of the marginal utility of leisure, the increasing curve of the marginal disutility of work. One can also argue that the producers' surpluses are ignored by this marginal calculation, but they are ignored in evaluating people's work effort and their paid work too. So we would have, at least, some rough way of converting everything into dollars. What about a housewife? We do not have a dollar value for her time on any simple basis, but we could estimate what women of the same age and education make in the labor market. We can assume that most housewives could work for money (or at least that their skill levels are such that if they did not have children at home to take care of, they could make that much working at a job).

Finally, there is an analysis problem: We may explain philanthropy on the basis of current income, attitudes, and religious identification, of course. But we might want to find how a man's current attitudes depend on some past history, like his parent's beliefs, or religious activity, or philanthropy, his early church experience, and the gradual development of his interest in doing things for other people.

A Study of People's Preferences about Housing and Community: Finally let us look at another, more complex design, which also has not been carried out, but may well be if the concern about urban problems is implemented with research funds.

The purpose of such a study would be to find out, or infer, what people really want in their homes, neighborhoods, and communities. The results would not be used to make policy directly, but would be combined with information from engineers and urban economists, in order to help the elected representatives decide what ought to be done.

How should one go about such a study? We could ask people what they like or do not like about their neighborhood. This runs into a difficulty that is illustrated by the fact that there is a correlation between whether a man likes his neighborhood and whether he likes his wife. Some people just like everything and other people dislike most things. We could ask people who moved recently how they compare the neighborhood they moved to with the one they left, their reasons for moving, and why they were willing to spend more or less for the new place. This is subject to a second difficulty, namely, rationalization and memory error in remembering what the other neighborhood was like. This error can operate in both directions. Some people are nostalgic about an old neighborhood, and have difficulty getting used to a new one. On the other hand, most people tend to justify a decision they have made by remembering all the good things about the place to which they have moved and the bad things about the place they left.

If we remove the restriction of a single survey, we may try to set up a more elaborate design where we (a) interview people about their past and present neighborhoods, and the detailed things they like and do not like about each neighborhood, (b) then return several years later to the same dwelling and talk to the people who live there, (c) if the people have moved, we would also follow those people and interview them in their new dwelling.[15]

This allows several kinds of triangulation on the problem. For those who have not moved but whose neighborhoods have changed, we can find out how they currently see their neighborhood before and after the change, and also how they think back in the second interview on the changes that have taken place. Those who have moved are even more interesting because they can now describe the new neighborhood they are in, and we can compare those ratings with the concurrent ratings made of the old neighborhood. Most of the personality differences between people will thus be neutralized. We can also ask movers to think back about the neighborhood they used to live in as a check on what they told us earlier, and as part of the explanation of why they moved, and as a general methodological check on the kinds of biases one gets in using retrospective data about previous neighborhoods. Other people will have moved into the houses that the first people left, and they can be asked these same retrospective questions about the previous neighborhoods since we now have another group from which we tell what kind of biases exist. Finally, we also have, in the original houses to which new people have moved, both their attitudes about this neighborhood and the attitudes expressed earlier by another set of families who previously lived there. In this way we can develop some information particularly in unchanging neighborhoods about the variety of responses of different people with the same situation.

It might, of course be useful in a study like this to oversample areas where something is likely to happen, or oversample people who are likely to move, because the more neighborhoods change, the more information we would get from the revisits, and the more people move, the more they can tell us about actual decision-making processes and considerations. Scientifically, however, it must be remembered that we may want to compare those who move with those who did not move, since a critical dimension of action is moving or not moving, and it is very dangerous to look only at those who have made a decision one way, namely, to move, ignoring those who made the other decision, namely, not to move.

We may also want to cluster the sample somewhat more heavily, so that we can make better use of the averages of several people's responses in the same neighborhood. The average income, age, mobility, and evaluation of the neighborhood of a small sample of people in a neighborhood provides a set of variables of interest to sociologists as well as economists, and has less variance than the individual data, even though they would be used to help explain individual behavior and attitudes.

Design of Consumer Expenditure Surveys

We have not said much about the design of consumer expenditure surveys, which attempt to secure details about a great array of expenditures. Those who are interested can find a recent summary of the experiments and some suggestions in a monography by Robert Pearl.[16]

Much attention has been given to improving expenditure information by repeated visits, diary-keeping, allocation of part of the items only to subsamples, etc. Revisits at short intervals are proposed to improve the accuracy and get "bounded estimates" that do not bring two Saturdays into one week. Reinterviews at longer intervals are proposed to get better trend data.

Strangely enough, little attention has been given to reducing the respondent's task by doing the classification of expenditures in the central office, asking the respondent only to list how much he spent and on what. It is possible that the classification of expenditures could then be done by computer, the vast cost of getting an interpretative dictionary into the computer being amortized over the repeated expenditure surveys, and justified by the possibility of classifying expenditures in several ways. For instance, expenditure studies currently do not distinguish consumption expenditure from investment expenditure, e.g. the gasoline from the purchase of a car. Both are classified by general purpose, such as transportation, housing, food, etc. One might even want to allocate parts of some expenditures to different purposes, for instance part of the car to transportation and part to recreation. This seems like one of the few places where computer interpretation of words might be functional and economic.

Summary

We have tried in this chapter to say some general things about the designing of studies, and then to make these principles more realistic through a series of examples, some of specific problems and some of whole designs. It is easier to see what is wrong with a study, particularly after completion, than to state in general what good design is. Perhaps the one most important principle of all is that every aspect of a study, and every question asked, should have a clear justification and relation to the purpose of the study. The single most common design mistake is to become too diffuse, trying to cover too much ground and asking too many unnecessary questions. This leads to each topic being inadequately handled. Scientific judgement requires comparison, which means a control group for every behavior studied, and an alternative (opportunity cost) for every preference. The question one must keep asking is "compared with what?"

Finally, since the essence of science is quantification and measurement, the design should allow for some kind of quantification. This may range from the crudest use of dichotomies (dummy variables) through arbitrary scaling and the creation of indexes to elaborate calculation of factor weights. But it makes a difference in designing questions whether one has clearly in mind the necessity for quantified measurement of the theoretical concepts.

Footnotes to Chapter II

1. James Coleman, "The Mathematical Study of Change" in H. M. Blalock, Jr. and B. B. Blalock, *Methodology in Social Research,* McGraw Hill, New York, 1968.

2. See sundry issues of the *Federal Reserve Bulletin,* June 1950-Dec. 1951. See also "Methods of the Survey of Consumer Finances," *Federal Reserve Bulletin* and James N. Morgan," Repeated Surveys of Consumer Finances in the United States," in *Family Living Studies,* International Labour Office, Geneva, 1961, pp. 191-206.

3. *Urban Income and Saving,* National Council of Applied Economic Research, New Delhi, 1962. See also other publications of the N.C.A.E.R., e.g. *All India Rural Household Survey* (3 vols.) 1964; 1965, 1966.

4. *Delhi Saving Survey,* National Council of Applied Economic Research, New Delhi, 1960.

5. Robert Eisner, *Determinants of Capital Expenditure: An Interview Study,* University of Illinois Bulletin, Volume 53, Number 43; February, 1956. Published by the University of Illinois, Urbana.

6. *Ibid.,* p. 14.

7. Harold L. Sheppard and A. Harvey Belitsky, *The Job Hunt,* The John Hopkins Press, Baltimore, Maryland, 1966.

8. *Ibid.,* p. ix.

9. *Ibid.,* p. 211.

10. See J. Morgan, M. Snider, and M. Sobol, *Lump Sum Redemption Settlements and Rehabilitation: A Study of Workmen's Compensation in Michigan,* Survey Research Center, University of Michigan, Ann Arbor, 1954.

11. See Grover Wirick, Robin Barlow, and James Morgan, "Population Survey: Health Care and Its Financing," in McNerney, ed., *Hospital and Medical Economics,* 2 Vols., Hospital Research and Educational Trust, Chicago, 1962, Vol. 1, pp. 61-357.

12. John B. Lansing and Dwight M. Blood, *The Changing Travel Market,* Institute for Social Research, University of Michigan, Ann Arbor, 1964, pp. 83-87.

13. See Richard Barfield and James Morgan, *Early Retirement,* Survey Research Center, University of Michigan, Ann Arbor, 1969.

14. For money given, see J. Morgan, M. David, W. Cohen, and H. Brazer, *Income and Welfare in the U.S.,* McGraw Hill, 1962, and Helen H. Lamale and J. A. Clorety, "City Families As Givers," *Monthly Labor Review,* Dec. 1959, pp. 1303-1311. For time given, see J. Morgan, I. Sirageldin, and N. Baerwaldt,

Productive Americans, Survey Research Center, University of Michigan, Ann Arbor, 1966.

15. Panel designs are also useful when precise measurement of changes (in unemployment for instance) are desired, and then an overlapping panel may be best. For a sophisticated example see: U.S. Bureau of the Census, *The Current Population Survey, A Report on Methodology,* Technical Papers No. 7, U.S. Department of Commerce, Bureau of the Census, Washington, D.C., 1963.

16. Robert B. Pearl, *Methodology of Consumer Expenditure Surveys,* Working Paper 27, U.S. Department of Commerce, Bureau of the Census, Washington, D.C., March, 1968; see also W. F. F. Kemsley and J. L. Nicholson, "Some Experiments in Methods of Conducting Consumer Expenditure Surveys," *Journal of the Royal Statistical Society,* Series A, Vol. 123 (1960), pp. 307-328.

Chapter III

SAMPLING PROBLEMS IN ECONOMIC SURVEYS

There is a well-developed literature on survey sampling. The economist interested in sample surveys can turn to such books as Leslie Kish's *Survey Sampling* for an extensive account of the subject, or to any one of a number of excellent introductory accounts such as that in chapters V-VII of C. A. Moser, *Survey Methods in Social Investigation* or the U.S. Census' *Sampling Lectures.*[1] This chapter is focused, therefore, on certain limited aspects of the sampling problems of special concern to economists. Special attention will be paid to the choices of strategy in designing a survey. In giving formulas we focus on making clear the issues, not on such niceties as small sample corrections or how one estimates population values of variances or frequencies.

Choice of Type of Sampling Procedure

The types of sampling procedure in common use may be grouped into three broad categories: cross-section sample using probability sampling; experimental designs; and non-probability samples using methods of selection based on judgment, quota sampling procedures, and the like. In any proposed study, there is a basic choice to be made among the three.

Cross-section surveys using probability samples: The standard procedure in economic surveys is probability sampling. The crucial characteristic of probability sampling is that it is based on a method of selection designed so that every member of a specified population has a known non-zero chance of falling into the sample. The theory is simple, but in practice, dealing with real sampling problems in an efficient way requires great skill.

In probability sampling one does not usually select elements directly but makes use of a sampling frame, that is, a list of the elements in the population to be studied. The practical problems involved in the selection and use of a sampling frame will be considered below.

The population specified may be broad, e.g., all families in a nation; or it may be narrow, e.g., all families in a certain city who purchased a house in a specified period, or all establishments in a certain type of manufacturing industry employing over a minimum number of persons.

The unit or element sampled may be dwellings, families, transactions, automobiles, etc., and it is crucial that attention be paid to the relation between this
unit and the unit of analysis. If one samples car purchases, one can analyze families purchasing cars, but must remember that some families may have to be
counted more than once if they bought more than one car. If one samples dwellings and then selects only one adult in each dwelling, the result is only a representative sample of *adults* if one weights each respondent by the inverse of the
number of adults in his dwelling to allow for differences in the final probability
of selection.

The surveys discussed in Chapter II are all cross-section surveys using
probability sampling except for the pilot study by Eisner and the UAW part of
the retirement study. We return to the details of probability sampling later. The
remainder of the chapter is concerned with ways of developing and using this
type of sample design.

For projects whose basic purpose is unbiased estimates of facts or relationships, the usefulness of probability cross-section sampling does not need elaboration. A sample from a given population with suitable data collection procedures
will provide a miniature representation of the population, which can be manipulated to provide a great variety of information about the whole population.

When the purpose of a project is explanation, limitations of cross-section
samples may become more important. Isolation of the effects of variables may
prove difficult. Either independent variables or dependent variables may be distributed in a way that is not optimal for analysis. Experimental designs deserve
consideration here.

Experimental Designs: An "experimental design" for a survey involves a
sampling procedure which does not represent the full population. Such designs
fall into two broad groups, truncated cross-sections and experiments with randomized treatments.

Truncated Cross-Sections: A cross-section sample is selected as a first step;
in a second step, a probability of zero is assigned to certain elements in the sample. These sampling procedures may be classified according to the basis on which
elements are excluded. Information may be available from the sampling frame
either concerning the dependent variable in a study, or concerning an explanatory variable, or both. The truncation can also be done in the field, using screening equations at the time of the interview.

Experiments with Randomized Treatments: An experiment may consist in
the assignment of "treatments" to members of a specified population or subpopulation, the "treatments" being assigned to individuals by a method which
involves randomization. There are a limited number of possibilities for the use of
these methods in economics. It may be noted that it is sometimes possible to apply randomized treatments to individuals selected from a cross-section; such
projects will be considered along with others involving randomised treatments.

In some cases, the knowledge of the values of the principal *dependent* variable in a project is available for individuals in advance, and is used to exclude part of the population from the sample. An example of such a situation arose when a study of long-distance telephone calls was undertaken for a telephone company. The records of the telephone company included information on the frequency and cost of the trunk calls made by each subscriber in a certain period. This information was used in the selection of the sample. The distribution of all telephone subscribers by expenditure for long-distance calls is J-shaped. Many subscribers make no such calls in a period of a few months. A considerable number of subscribers make a few calls.

The procedure adopted was to interview only the extreme groups. Equal numbers were selected of frequent users, that is those whose spending was K or more, and non-users. The analysis consisted essentially in the comparison of these groups. In effect, the study was designed to answer the question, what variables distinguish frequent users from non-users?

This type of design has advantages. A simple random sample would have yielded very few frequent callers. The design used solved this problem by minimizing the sampling error of comparisons between the selected groups for a given number of interviews by making the groups equal in size.[2] This method selects groups which are known to be very different in behavior, and, hence, makes it probable that large differences will be found in the values of the explanatory variables between the groups. The sensitivity of the design is much greater than it would be if the groups were more similar in purchasing behavior.

This type of procedure also has limitations. Nothing can be said about the intermediate group except by inference from what is learned about the extreme groups. Also, behavior in a limited time period may not be typical. The underlying situation *may* be one in which certain people are persistently at the extremes of the distribution. Then the stable characteristics of those people which drive them to the extremes can be examined. But the true situation may be one in which every individual is as likely as any other individual to be found at any given place on the continuum. Events may lead anyone to make several long-distance calls. That is, people may do their long-distance calling in "spurts," say, when a young couple has its first child. Then the search for stable characteristics of people which predict their behavior will fail, and research can at best reveal the circumstances which produce frequent calling. If both models operate, each for part of the population, the length of the time period considered will be a matter of importance in distinguishing the two types of callers.

The importance of the length of the period may be illustrated by a hypothetical example. Suppose that it is desired to study the factors which lead some people to spend a great deal on cars and others to spend much less. A sample of those who bought new cars in any given month would include some people who buy new cars frequently and some for whom buying a new car is a rare event.

Only the former might be of interest for the project. A dramatic example from another field was a study of marriage announcements in the *New York Times.* The authors selected the month of June, and took that month each year for ten years. Finding disproportionately few Jewish names in the announcements, they concluded that the Times was anti-semitic or else Jews had low social status.[3] A critic pointed out that June comes between two important religious holidays in the Jewish calendar and that few orthodox Jews would consider getting married in June. Spreading the sample over ten years had not helped at all.[4]

The second type of situation is one in which a measure of one or more *independent* variables is available in advance. For example, a measure of family income may be available. It may be advantageous to use this information in selecting the sample by varying the probability of selection of individuals at different income levels. Variable sampling fractions are considered below. An extreme type of objective is to set aside the study of a cross-section of the population and consider only the objective of measuring the effect of income on some dependent variable (or variables).

Gains in statistical efficiency will result from selecting individuals who differ widely in their score on the predictor provided that the relation between the predictor and the predicted variable is monotonically increasing or decreasing. Consider the case of a linear relationship. The more widely separated the scores on the predictor, the smaller the sample that will be required to establish the existence of a relationship.

Suppose, however, that the problem is to estimate the *shape* of the relationship between the predictor in question and a dependent variable, and that nothing can be assumed about the relationship. The best procedure then would be to specify the range of the independent variable and select the sample so as to provide observations which are evenly spaced over that range. For example, there might be K interviews in each thousand dollar interval of income up to some level of income. (It would also be necessary to specify such a maximum level of income owing to the small number of families in the population at very high income levels and their inaccessibility to interviewers.) The range of greatest interest might well be above the range where most observations would be found in a straight cross-section. Incomes are rising in most parts of the world, and there is interest in studying the economic behavior of those now at the income levels which will contain the bulk of the population in the future.

This procedure, however, would be optimal only if the investigators were satisfied that the predictor as measured, e.g. income, was the variable of crucial concern, and that the effect of this variable could be considered without regard to the effects of other dependent variables or to the proportion of the population represented in each interval. In practice, the contrary is often the case.

A theoretically optimal design for some purposes is known as factorial design. Here, several predictors are taken into account, with equal numbers of observations for subgroups specified in several dimensions. For example, one would like to have an equal number of interviews from each of these populations, and within each of them an even distribution over the range of incomes. Practical considerations of the lack of availability of information prior to sample selection have tended to inhibit the development of designs of this type. Even where such prior information seems to be available, it frequently turns out to be of low quality, or to cover only *part* of the population. However, the possibility should not be ruled out. For example, when a two-stage inquiry is undertaken, it may be possible to use the first stage to select for the second stage subgroups defined on almost any desired basis. Such data form a kind of pseudo-factorial design which can be analyzed as such, provided there is not some other variable influencing which subgroup the individual is in.

There is a special class of independent variables which can be defined in geographic terms. That is, it may be possible to identify locations across which the variables of interest vary systematically. These situations lend themselves easily to experimental designs. For example, if one is interested in the effects of climate, he can select areas to represent the range of climates which are important to him. Or, there may be interest in the location of homes within a metropolitan area as a predictor, say, of the use of certain recreation facilities. Samples of homes at different distances from a facility could be used to study the effect of distance on use.

There is an interesting class of truncated cross-section designs in which information is available both about a dependent variable and one or more predictors. The information might come, for example, from a preliminary sample survey conducted on a large scale but with a limited number of questions. Then it may be possible to carry out a preliminary analysis of the relation between one or more predictors and the dependent variable. For example, in the study of long-distance telephone calls, if data had been available, a curve might have been fitted to estimate the relationship between family income and frequency of calling. Then the two groups selected for special study might have been those who made either a very large number of calls or a very small number *for their income group.* Those in the lowest income groups might even have been excluded from the study altogether. In principle, the method of selection could be based on a highly multivariate analysis, not just one predictor. All that is required is that the analysis yield a predicted score for each individual which can be compared with an actual observation on some dependent variable, making possible the selection of individuals with large positive and large negative deviations from predicted scores.

This hybrid design avoids a basic limitation of designs based only on the dependent variable. In a great many studies in economics one or two independent variables are obviously important. Income is a crucial variable in practically all studies of consumer behavior. An investigator is likely to find himself solemnly concluding that the major difference between those who spend a great deal on commodity X and those who spend very little is that the former have more income than the latter. Of course, the effect of income can be taken into account statistically in the analysis, but it would be more efficient if this effect could be taken into account in the design. In general, one would like to consider in the experimental design what is known about the effects of the predictors already studied.

A third type of experimental design is one which conforms to more familiar ideas about what constitutes an experiment. The essence is assignment of "treatments" to members of the population on a random basis. It is this type of experiment which is the subject, for example, of R. A. Fisher's classic, *The Design of Experiments.*[5] Experiments with randomized application of treatments are unusual in economic surveys but they are by no means unknown. The greatest number of examples of their use is in methodological studies. For example, a sample may be selected, and different methods of data collection may be used on a random basis. It can then be observed whether the results differ. Methodological studies of data collection will be considered in Chapter IV.

Experimental manipulations to investigate the effects of altering variables are sometimes undertaken, especially by business enterprises. The most interesting experiments are those concerned with the effects of variations in price. Two types of situations may be distinguished, those in which the commodity to be priced is new, and those in which it is already on the market.

If the commodity is new, the seller has the advantage that he has complete control over the supply. He may then introduce it at different prices in different markets, and observe the difference in his total revenue. The problem of designing the experiment becomes one of selecting areas of similar market potential, and weighing the extra information to be gained against the extra cost of including more areas and extending the study over a longer period. It is entirely possible, for example, that price is more important in repeat sales than for initial sales.

For a commodity already on the market, the problems are different. The effect of a change in its price on total spending for a given commodity may be thought of as a problem in estimating the substitution which will take place as the price is varied. Some substitutions may take place during an experimental manipulation, however, which would not occur if an actual price change occurred. The experiment will succeed in its purpose only if the manipulation can be prevented from producing such effects.

Substitution among competing firms will take place if one firm varies its price experimentally while its competitors do not. It may be expected that an actual price change would be met by changes in competitors' prices. In studying the effect of changing the price of a *commodity,* some method must be found of varying the price charged across the entire market. Perhaps all sellers will cooperate. Perhaps a market can be found in which one seller has a monopoly. In any case, a survey to find out what the customers are thinking would provide useful auxiliary information.

If the experimental manipulation is believed by the customers to be temporary, they may shift their purchases over time. A large cut in price, for example, may lead people to buy in advance of needs. It may be necessary to maintain the experimental price for some time in order to estimate more normal, long-run sales at the lower price.

How long a time is a difficult question. It is entirely possible that the response to a major price change may be slow. It may take time, for example, for people to increase consumption of a food when its price falls secularly. (Housewives may have to learn new recipes and/or convert conservative husbands.) There may be a "ratchet" effect on consumption. In the market for air travel there is evidence that, once people begin to fly, they are likely to continue. It may take time before such effects take place with any commodity.

There remains the special problem of how a change in price is to be brought to the attention of the customers. With a price increase, the information will be passed on more or less automatically at the point of sale. With a price cut, it is not clear how the new price may be brought to the attention of potential buyers. If an entire geographic area is to be involved, the advertising media may be used. If only a selected group of people are to be offered the reduced prices, special procedures may be needed. It will be important to design those procedures so as to convey the information without confounding the experiment by adding unusual selling procedures. For example, a personal visit to a potential customer may sell a commodity even without a price cut. If visits seem needed, perhaps a control group of customers can be used who receive a visit but are not offered a price reduction. This allows a measurement of the effects of price reductions, but not of the effects of visits.

Such experimental manipulations may be accompanied by special sample surveys with limited objectives. This is discussed in Chapter IV, "Surveys as Part of an Experimental Design." A probable objective is to study the processes of substitution among commodities in detail. For example, a fare cut may be followed by a survey of the customers of a transit company to determine if any increase in travel comes from people who used to drive themselves, from people who were members of car pools, or from people who formerly walked to work, and how much from an increase in total travel. It might also be desired to compare the income level of the users before and after the fare cut. What is the economic level of the new users? If a cut in fare leads to losses for a publicly owned or subsidized company, the economic level of both the new and old customers would be matters of interest.

Such factorial designs allow an elegant statistical analysis which tests not only for main effects of each of the classifying variables but also for each of the interaction effects. For instance, X1 may alter the effect of X2 on Y. With more than two classifying characteristics, one gets higher order interaction effects. The tendency of economists to focus on multiple regression for its efficiency and economy has tended to make us eager to assume additivity of the separate effects (no interaction effects), or at least a specific few that could be introduced explicitly. In fact, the real world seems to be full of interaction effects. The classic illustration of this is, of course, the search for the best unbiased estimate of the marginal propensity to consume, a foolish quest if there are indeed several different income elasticities depending on the values of other variables.

There remains an important problem with factorial designs. They give equal importance to each subgroup (possible combination of the explanatory classes), even though they may have widely differing size and importance in the population. Indeed, one rapidly comes to combinations which should not exist except for errors.

Furthermore, while statistical convenience might dictate equal-sized groups, economic considerations may not. In the case of experiments with the "negative income tax," the high cost of the experimental income subsidies led the analysts to decide that the control group should be much larger than the experimental groups, since it provided so much more information per dollar.

Finally, experimental designs focus on hypothesis testing, on significance, rather than importance. If one is primarily concerned with what will account for the real world variations in some behavior, or other dependent variable, then the only reason for disproportionate representation of any subgroup would be that it reflects forces which do not affect cross-section differences so much as aggregate changes over time (because the changes in that variable tend to be in the same direction for many people, and do not cancel out).

The considerations which may be involved in the decision whether to use an experimental design, then, include the following:

(1) The distribution of population on the dependent variable. (Is it J-shaped?)
(2) The distributions of the population on the independent variables.
(3) Measurement problems (for all variables).
(4) The variation over time of values of the dependent variable for any individual.
(5) The same, for independent variables.
(6) The problem of taking into account known relationships.
(7) The availability of sample frames allowing such selection for the experiment.

(8) The likelihood of uncontrollable events that would confound the whole experiment.

(9) Confidence that the manipulated variables are the ones that matter, i.e., tend to produce aggregate changes, by affecting many people in the same way.

(10) The need to manipulate in order to assure that x varies, or varies in a manner uncorrelated with other factors affecting y.

Judgment Samples and Quota Samples: There are many methods for selecting samples based on judgment or quota sampling procedures. It is easiest to define these methods negatively: they are *not* based on mechanical selection from a frame. Elements of personal choice, usually the choice of the interviewer, enter the process of selection. It is rarely claimed that these methods of selection lead to superior quality in terms of information per interview taken. They do seem to yield more information per dollar spent on data collection. As a result of the element of personal choice in the selection procedure, there is an inherent tendency to ambiguity and uncertainty as to exactly what is done.[6] Hence, there is uncertainty as to the merits of the claim of more information per dollar. It would take a good deal of trouble and expense to prove the claim to be false in a specific situation, and the job must be repeated for other specific procedures and specific objectives.

The usual procedure in quota sampling is to estimate, primarily from census data, the number of individuals in each of a set of subclasses of the population. These subgroups may be specified using such controls as geographic area, age, sex, race, and economic level. Interviewers are then assigned to quotas of interviews designed to produce a total sample which will match the population with regard to the control variables. One might think of discarding interviews afterward, or weighting to achieve quota distributions, but this would increase costs per unit of information and eliminate most of the economies.

Only those variables which are manageable from the interviewers' point of view are usable as controls. It must be possible for an interviewer to assign people quickly and with reasonable accuracy to the categories specified. Classification of potential respondents by economic level presents greater problems to an interviewer than classification by age, sex, race, or geographic area.

There are three difficulties with procedures of this type, which may be indicated briefly. First, the method may be biased. The quotas themselves may be wrong, and within quotas the interviewer is free to select the respondents. There is a tendency to select those most easily available, and they may differ systematically from those who are harder to locate. For the probable nature of the bias, see the comparison in Chapter IV of interviews taken on first call with those taken on second and higher order calls on probability samples. Second, the method may lead to an underestimate of the variability in the population.

Interviewers tend to select, within quotas, people who are similar to each other. For example, the number in the "low" economic status group may be correct, but there may be too few people with very low economic status. Excessive clustering may lead to larger variance between clusters and, hence, to a lower effective sample size. Third, it may be difficult to estimate correctly the variance of the sample estimates. It is possible, however; Moser and Stuart did so and concluded that one could not count on higher precision, even per dollar.[7] Such estimates are not usually made because procedures of this general type are often used in very small and informal studies, especially in pretests. When no statistical presentation is planned and it is desired only to try out a procedure, it may be useful to make a systematic effort to cover a broad range of situations with a few interviews. The pilot study by Eisner involved such a sample, with the 14 studies of companies distributed by industry. Also, in trying out a questionnaire, a special effort may be made to locate people of very different characteristics with different experiences to make sure that the questions fit the full range of situations. As will be discussed in Chapter IV, a common error in questionnaire design is to develop question sequences which fit most people—but not everybody.

When it is the purpose of a study to estimate such statistics as measures of central tendency and percentages which apply to a population, there is a presumption against methods of sample selection which may be seriously biased. A more difficult question, for the economist, is whether to analyze data already collected from a study which used quota sampling. Essentially the same question arises when an investigator must decide whether to take seriously results reported by others based on such a sample.

Bias in a selection procedure does not necessarily lead to bias in the estimation of a relationship. Suppose, for example, that a selection procedure is biased in such a way that the samples contain too few peoples at the top and too few at the bottom of the income distribution. It may still be possible to use the data to estimate the relation between income and, say, expenditure on commodities. The relative lack of data at the extremes will not in itself distort the estimated relationship in the range where the number of observations is adequate.

It may be that the relation between income and owning commodity X varies depending on the value of some third variable, Z. With Z present, the slope may be steep; with Z absent, it may be flat. The line fitted may be an average relationship. Then the estimated equation will vary depending on the distribution of Z in the sample. For example, the relation between income and travel for married couples aged 20-24 may be different depending on whether they have young children. Those without children may travel frequently or not depending on their income. Those with children may make one trip a year to visit the grandparents regardless of income.

It is possible for the sample estimate of the average income effect to be biased if there is a tendency to underrepresent those for whom $Z = 1$. For example, in the extreme, the interviewers might fill their quota for young couples entirely from those with children, for whom $Z = 1$. The average amount spent on X, however, might be estimated correctly. *In general there will be a bias in the estimate of the relationship between a predictor and a predicted variable if (1) there is an interaction between the predictor's influence and a conditioning variable, and (2) the sampling procedure is biased with regard to the conditioning variable.*

To demonstrate that there is a *risk* of bias is by no means the same as to demonstrate that there is in *fact* a bias in the estimate of relationship. In any particular problem it may be possible to test for a suspected bias. What is required is that all relevant variables be measured—in our example, income, X, and Z—and that a search for interactions be made. In the absence of measures of Z, it may be possible to test for bias by repeating the analysis for interviews obtained on different calls, for example, on first and second call—assuming at least two calls were made. If the relation estimated is not the same, the conclusions which can be drawn about the population must be carefully considered.

It should be noted that the above discussion concerns only the possibility of bias in the estimate of relationships. There is little doubt that the sampling errors of complex statistics will be much larger when the statistics are based on a sample of this type than the sampling errors of estimates based on a well-designed probability sample with an equal number of interviews. This statement seems justified even though to the best of the authors' knowledge no estimates have ever been made of the sampling errors of complex statistics based on quota samples using methods which take into account the actual nature of the sample design. The greater variance per element found by Moser and Stuart may be expected to lead to this result.

There is one final use of judgment or quota samples which deserves mention. There may be in existence no feasible method of sampling some special populations. Frequently an ingenious investigator can devise a scheme for selecting a probability sample. Yet, if he cannot, he may be better advised to use a judgment sample than to leave out the sub-groups entirely. The judgment sample may at least permit a preliminary assessment of the magnitude of the bias resulting from omitting the subgroup. For example, area probability samples ordinarily omit those with no permanent dwelling, such as migrant workers in the United States or sidewalk dwellers in India. In a study of extreme poverty, a poor sample of such groups might be better than no sample at all.

Summary of Quota Samples

Quota samples can mean anything from almost no instruction to interviewers to very highly structured directions that can get almost to the point where they are as good as probability samples, except that then they may cost more. The basic element is that they allow the interviewer some freedom in selecting the respondent. The more freedom the interviewer has, the more likely she might be able to cut costs, but the more likely also she is to introduce a bias and even higher variability. The difficulty in comparing quota samples and probability samples, is of course that there is no easy method of estimating the precision of a quota sample. The Moser-Stuart study compared paired interviewers and discovered that the between-interviewer variance was so high for quota samples that it cast doubt on the existence of any savings from the quota samples in terms of information per dollar. Quota samples are not the same thing as screening. One can take a probability sample, eliminate by some screening device those of less interest, and produce a probability sample of the selected subpopulation. It will have all the good characteristics of any other probability sample, so long as the screening operation works.

There may be times when it pays to take a little bit of sampling bias rather than very high costs, but this should be a conscious decision. If one decides not to take some cases because of their high cost, it is still important to a few of them to find out how much bias there is, even though it is costly and gives only an estimate of the bias with a fairly small number of degrees of freedom. For instance, one might eliminate ten interviews in scattered rural places. But, if one actually spent the money to go out and interview these people, one would have an estimate of bias based on ten cases.

If the quotas do not come out right, or there are other controls that cannot be used in the field, it is always possible to discard some interviews to improve the balance (reduce the bias). Even more efficient, one can weight the interviews. This assumes, of course, that the people who are interviewed, say at the ends of the income distribution are like (representative of) those high- and low-income families who were not interviewed. A difficulty from the reader's point of view is that if a quota sample is weighted properly, the overall distributions on most of the main explanatory variables will look correct, even though substantial biases may exist.

The use of weights allows a quota sample user to relax the rules for interviewers, since if they do not get exactly the right combinations, the weighting "makes up for it." But of course the efficiency per dollar spent falls if the interviewers get many interviews with the easy middle class groups, interviews which have to be weighted down, and hence add less to the precision of the final estimate.

Partly Probability Samples

It is tempting to compromise—to select a basic sample by probability methods, but leave some discretion in the field. This is usually a mistake; biases in the field selection undo all the good of the original sample.

It is not often that the biases become apparent. One dramatic case occurred in a rural development survey in an East African country. A probability sample of small rural areas was drawn, and interviewers instructed to interview the farmer on every second farm in each area. Three years later, another set of interviewers was sent back with the same instructions, so that data would reflect changes over the three years. Casual reports from the second interviewers indicated that about two-thirds of the interviews were reinterviews. (Half should have been by pure chance.) There were both "experimental areas" and "control areas," but in both, dramatic "changes" appeared:

| | Experimental Areas | | Control Areas | |
	1965	1968	1965	1968
Percent who:				
Were 45 or older	51	40	69	49
Had 2 or more wives	44	26	42	28
Were literate	39	55	47	54
Utilized mass media (5 or more on a scale)	21	42	22	48
Had fields at least partly divided	47	68	43	63

While the peasants might have divided their fields in the three-year period, and even started utilizing mass media, it is doubtful that they would become literate, drop their extra wives, or get younger.

When it was learned that the 1965 interviews were taken by civil servants, and the 1968 interviews by university students on vacation, the possibility that each group of interviewers selected respondents closer to their own age and degree of modernity seems likely. The biased selection might have been of the farms, or of whom to talk to on each farm selected. The report does not state whether the students knew which were the experimental areas where changes were supposed to have taken place. However, problems of bias in the substantive findings would also arise even if one merely compared the changes in experimental areas with those in control areas, hoping that the respondent-selection bias would operate evenly everywhere.

The obvious way of avoiding the sampling difficulty would have been to take smaller grids, and instruct the interviewers to interview the senior farmer on *every* farm, defining senior in some way, such as closest to age 60.

Clearly there is no point in elaborate sampling unless it carries through to the final unit, and a substantial proportion of those units are interviewed.

Avoiding biases when interviewers know which is the experimental group is much more difficult. Even if they are not told, and if groups fall into geographic areas, the clever interviewers will soon figure out which area is which. Or they may even find out from the early replies in the interview. Here the best one can hope for is that interviewers ask questions as they are written and write down answers as they are given. An experimental researcher might want to mislead subsets of the interviewers in opposite directions as to the hypotheses to see what biases would creep in! This would require randomizing the assignment of respondents to interviewers, always a difficult and expensive process. Or one might want to put the interviewers' notions into the analysis as part of the set of explanatory variables, hoping to remove the unwanted variation arising from that source.

Ratio Estimates

Estimates of means, aggregates, or proportions from a sample, whether a strict probability sample or not, can always be improved (given smaller sampling variance) by using subgroup estimates of the variable in question, weighted by outside estimates of the proportion of the population represented by that subgroup. Sample variability in the second of these is thus eliminated. There are various methods available to estimate aggregate income. These range all the way from multiplying the sample average income per family times the census estimate of the number of families (plus unrelated individuals in their terminology), to the use of many small sub-groups defined on several variables, weighted by outside estimates of their importance in the population. Of course, as one goes from simple to complex, it becomes more difficult to find outside estimates of population proportions, and they may be less reliable or less up-to-date. As a result, the sampling stability of the subgroup estimates from the survey also falls. There is a long debate in the literature about "ratio estimating bias" which seems to have ended with the discovery that there may actually be such a bias but that it will usually be so small that it may be ignored.

Sampling Frames and the Coverage Problem in Economic Surveys

Since the process of selection of a probability sample requires the use of a sampling frame, the characteristics of the frame and the methods adopted to remedy any deficiencies in it are matters of fundamental importance. The subject is especially important because weaknesses in a frame may pass unnoticed unless an explicit effort is made to locate and correct them.

There are two general types of sampling frames. The first type consists of actual lists of the elements to be sampled. For example: in Great Britain the adult population is listed in an electoral register; in Michigan the office of the Secretary of State maintains a file of vehicles registered in the state; a trade association will have a list of its members. The second type of frame does not involve a list of the elements to be selected but provides a systematic description of some intervening set of elements so that it is possible to associate the elements in the population to be sampled with the elements in the intervening set. The most important example is population sampling for which the frame is a set of locations on maps.

A perfect sampling frame of the first type would comprise a complete list of all elements in the population to be sampled. Each element would appear on the list once and only once. Nothing else would be included in the list. In addition, a sampling frame may include information directly useful in analysis about the characteristics of each of the elements, or it may include information useful for purposes of stratification but not for analysis. For example, the list of members of a trade association may include information on the total number of employees of each member. Or, a list of cars registered in a state may give make and year model, weight, and even the amount of any lien on the car.

A perfect sampling frame of the second type would be so constructed that the identification of elements from the intervening set with elements in the population under study was exact. Each element in the population would be identified with one and only one of the intervening elements. Each intervening element would be identified with one and only one of the elements in the population. None of the elements of the intervening set would be identified with anything else.

By preference, the task of associating elements in the two sets would be one which could be carried out easily and economically (by preference at zero cost) and without error. For example, it would be ideal to proceed from a set of selections based on maps to a set of families to be interviewed without ambiguity or risk of human error. The real world is not ideal, and investigators must concern themselves with how to locate weaknesses in sampling frames and with methods of remedying weaknesses and controlling errors in procedures.

Lists and Files as Sample Frames: There are three basic types of problems with list samples, each of which will be considered briefly.

(1) *Missing elements:* To check on whether there is a problem of missing elements, it may be necessary to investigate carefully the nature of a list and to ask, how do people get on the list? Under what circumstances might someone be

left off the list? How is the list kept up-to-date? The essential question is, does the list in fact represent all elements in the population which is to be studied?

Auto accident reports may be missing, and particularly so in areas where police are known to give a ticket to one or both drivers (for not having their car under control), or particularly at night when the police are busy on other things like catching thieves. Or those under litigation or prosecution may be temporarily out of the files.

If so, it will be necessary to judge whether the missing elements are numerous and whether they have special properties of such importance that a special supplemental sample should be selected. Some lists, of course, are obviously incomplete; for example, the list of telephone subscribers in any city will not be a list of all families. The usefulness of an incomplete list depends on the degree of incompleteness and on what methods can be devised to sample the population not included in the list.

(2) *Foreign elements:* There is usually no problem in identifying foreign elements selected from a list if the survey is one which uses personal interviews. For example, the interviewer can tell well enough that the address to which she has been sent is that of a dwelling recently destroyed by fire. There will be some marginal cases—is this building a seasonal residence now closed for the winter or will the people be back in a few hours? But usually she can tell. The difficulty is the trouble and expense involved in making the check. When the data collection does not involve personal interviews there may be some margin of uncertainty as to who replied, whether there were other units at the same address, and whether some of the non-response was really non-sample.

The correct procedure to allow for foreign elements is to select a large enough initial sample so that the foreign elements can be rejected and the desired number of interviews still obtained. It sometimes happens that inexperienced investigators substitute the next valid item on a list for the foreign element. This procedure will produce a bias and should never be used. To understand why there is a bias, consider what this procedure would do to the chances of selection of the one year-round dwelling in a group of summer cottages if all the cottages appeared on the list just ahead of the year-round dwelling. The next valid entry would be the year-round dwelling if *any* of the cottages were selected.

(3) *Duplicate listings:* A list may be so constituted that the same element appears more than once. For example, it may be desired to select a sample of auto owners from a file in which each owner appears once for each car that he owns. This type of duplication usually is obvious from the way the file was constructed.

There are two possible treatments. First, it may be possible to correct the file. A new file might be prepared based on the "first" car only. Similarly if "first" cars are somehow designated in the file, it may be possible to proceed as if the file had been corrected without physically correcting it. Second, it may be possible to select from the uncorrected file, but compensate for the unequal probability of selection by using the inverse of that probability as a weight. Those who own two cars will be given a weight of .5 in the final tabulations while those with one car are given a weight of 1.0. There would be twice as many two-car owners selected as there "should" be, compared to one-car owners, but the weight would lead to a correct estimate of such statistics as the proportion of two-car owners in the population. Facing this problem in advance would remind the investigator to ask respondents how many cars they owned.

An example of an ingenious system for solving a massive problem of multiple listings was one developed for a study of owners of record of common stock. The same person, of course, may own shares in many companies or be listed more than once on the company's lists. Yet, it was desired to develop a sample of owners of stock. The "Alph-Seg" method of detecting duplication was based on defining narrow ranges of letters of the alphabet and selecting people from each list with names in the ranges. Within ranges the problem of checking for duplication was manageable. This example illustrates a general technique: in correcting or checking a frame it may not be necessary to work with the complete frame. It may be feasible to develop a procedure for selecting part of the frame to be checked or corrected. If the frame to be checked is very large or if the process of correction is expensive, in cost per element checked, the economy of effort from this approach may be important.

Projects based on samples from lists or files may rely on the data in the files for purposes of analysis, as noted above. The completeness and accuracy of the data in the file then become matters of vital concern. It is not unusual for analysts to be disappointed in this respect. The people responsible for the creation and maintenance of a set of files are the usual sources of information about the files. They may be expected to have a natural tendency to think well of their files. It is also possible that the files are well adapted to their purposes but less well adapted to the purposes of an investigator. A methodological study by Ferber involving use of the files of a local credit bureau may illustrate how a set of files can fall somewhat short of expectations.[9]

A second type of problem concerns, not the data in the file, but the manner in which individuals are selected for inclusion in the file. It may appear that a file is reasonably representative of a broad population, but it may turn out that a hidden process of selection is at work. This problem may be illustrated by a methodological study of car debt in Chicago. It was thought that the people with evidence of debt listed in the file of chattel mortgages in Cook County would be reasonably representative of the larger population who buy cars on credit. It developed that the file contained primarily people who had bought on credit and later refinanced their debt, a highly selected sub-population.[10] The list was accurate enough, but much less satisfactory for the purposes of the project than had at first appeared. The limitation could have been foreseen only if the preliminary work on the project had included a more careful check on the nature of the population represented in the file.

Geographic Areas as Frames: Maps of geographic areas as a frame is a widely used approach to probability sampling in the absence of lists of the elements in the population to be sampled. If, as is usual, the sample is selected in two or more stages, the selection of the first stage may proceed without maps if a list of the elements is available for that stage. For example, one can select counties in the U.S. from a list of counties, or, in an underdeveloped country, there may be a list of villages or districts. After completion of the first stage (or stages) of selection it may be possible and not prohibitively expensive to obtain detailed maps or aerial photographs of the selected areas. Thus, detailed maps will be required of the selected counties, not of all counties. This approach to the development of a frame may be attractive compared to any available alternative. Indeed, there may be no practicable alternative.

The most serious potential departure from the ideal described above for this type of frame is that coverage may be incomplete. That is, the practical method of proceeding from the selections on maps to the individual elements in the sample may be such that some elements properly in the sample are missed. For example, if it is a sample of dwelling units, some dwelling units may be missed. It is also possible, if a dwelling unit contains two or more families, for one of them to be missed.

The fact that some dwelling units are missed is not a cause for great concern if the missed units closely resemble the units that are not missed. Unfortunately, the contrary is virtually certain. For example, an interviewer may be sent to a block in a city and instructed to prepare a list of all dwelling units in the block. She can hardly miss single family homes located on large lots which are complete at the time she prepares the list. She may miss small apartments tucked away in unlikely places, in the basement or attic of an old home, or the second floor of a commercial structure. There are likely to be systematic differences in the economic status between people living in the missed dwellings and people living in dwellings which are counted.

A serious problem of this type existed in the Survey of Consumer Finances for several years.[11] A procedure which was theoretically quite correct and should have worked still ended with fewer dwellings than would have been expected. The product of the inverse of the fraction of the areas taken (sampling fraction) and the number of dwellings found in the sample was less than the census estimates of the number of occupied dwellings. By adding some further procedures, largely involving the use of city directories and other listings in a seemingly duplicate operation, the end result was a substantial closing of the gap. One difficulty was that a theoretically adequate procedure of checking to the right of each address for any new construction between it and the next listed sample address— the half-open-interval technique—was not always correctly executed in practice.

The lesson is that some redundancy may be useful, particularly where procedures have to be carried out by many people far from the central office.

In view of the possibility of serious bias from imperfect coverage, it is important to check for this problem especially in any survey based on a geographic frame. There are two methods of checking. First, it may be possible to expand the sample using the inverse of the sampling fraction, as reported by Kish and Hess. The product of the number of dwelling units located and the inverse of the sampling fraction may be compared with the best available estimate of the number of dwelling units in the universe. This procedure is subject to a margin of error resulting from differences in definitions of universe and of sampling elements. It is good practice, therefore, to use in a sample survey definitions which match as closely as possible those used in other compilations, especially in censuses. For example, a "dwelling unit" should be defined in the same way. Adjustments of counts to the same date may also be troublesome. The Census Bureau modified their definition of occupied dwelling unit to a "housing unit" in the 1960 census, counting as a separate unit any room or set of rooms with a separate entrance *or* cooking facilities. This slightly increased the total number of units as some light housekeeping rooms became separate housing units. Needless to say, borderline cases are possible.

The second method of checking is to send at least two or more investigators independently to the same areas armed with the same instructions and compare the results.

Any disagreements in the resulting lists should be reconciled. There is the possibility, of course, that the two will repeat the same mistakes. It may be feasible, however, to minimize this risk by making intensive checks in a limited number of areas. This type of check can lead to a description of the errors made, which may then prove manageable.

The same three general types of problems arise with area sampling frames as with other frames:

(1) *Missing elements.* There may be some members of the population who have no dwelling unit. For example, in the Delhi Savings Survey sidewalk dwellers were omitted from the frame.[12] In the United States those omitted include migrant laborers, persons living in institutions, on military bases, abroad, and the like. New construction may be missing. The resulting bias may or may not be serious depending on the objectives of the project. The risks are particularly great in studies of extreme poverty and studies of highly mobile people.

(2) *Blanks or Foreign elements:* Addresses which are not dwellings may appear on a list. Ordinarily they can be excluded, if selected as noted above.

(3) *Duplicate listings:* There is a growing problem of seasonal residences. Each family should be identified with a single dwelling only. There may be uncertainty as to whether to treat college students as resident with their parents or at college. Similar questions arise when any individual is absent from his "permanent address" for an extended period.

One solution is to determine where the eligible respondent spent most of the time during some specified period, e.g., the interviewing period. He then belongs in the sample if during most of the interviewing period he was living in a dwelling unit selected in the sample, or at least was not living in some other dwelling where he could have been sampled. But if he was out of the country, in jail, or living in another home not in the sample during most of the interviewing period, then he does not belong in the sample, and the sample dwelling becomes "house vacant," a non-sample dwelling, not part of the non-response. Ambiguous cases occur when the man was in hotels the whole time. Does one consider them institutions, or quasi households, and say the man was not in the population living in private households? And of course, in many cases where the respondent is away during the whole interviewing period, there is no way to find out where he was, and he is conservatively treated as in the sample but part of the non-response.

The Basic Elements of Complex Designs: Clustering, Multi-Stage Samples, Stratification and Controlled Selection

In the development of sample designs there is a presumption in favor of simplicity. Before deciding to use a complex design it is appropriate to consider whether a simple design may not be satisfactory or even preferable.

In some situations it may be possible to avoid sampling altogether and include the entire population in the survey. For example, Donald T. Brash undertook a study of *American Investment in Australian Industry*.[13] He was concerned with companies which were American-owned and engaged in manufacturing in Australia as of June 30, 1962. The first stage of his project consisted in developing a list of such companies—he located 208 which met his criteria. He included all 208 in his survey. Problems of incomplete or unsatisfactory response remained to be solved, but at least he eliminated sampling error. Whenever a sample is an appreciable fraction, f, of the population, the sampling error is reduced by a factor $= (1-f)$.

When it is unreasonable to include the entire population, it may be appropriate to take a simple random sample. There are two advantages to this procedure. First, most of the estimates of sampling errors in common use are based explicitly or implicitly on simple random samples. If the techniques of statistical analysis to be used will be interpreted as if they had been applied to simple random samples, why not make the procedure match the interpretation? Second, when complex sample designs are developed and executed by people who are inexperienced in this type of activity, there is a risk that they will make mistakes, and pay a penalty in inefficiency or bias, or both. Experience shows that this risk is not negligible. It may be prudent to rely on a scheme based on simple random sampling and spend one's energies in making certain that the scheme is correctly conceived and executed.

The randomness in the selection of elements from a frame may be achieved by a lottery of some sort developed *ad hoc.* An investigator working with a list might number the entries on his list, prepare a set of strips of paper with matching numbers, place them in a hat, stir well, and instruct his research assistant to draw the required number. It is better practice, however, to rely on published lists of random numbers which have been painstakingly developed with precautions taken to ensure that they are, in fact, random.

It is common practice when a list is being sampled to determine the sampling interval, say, k, needed to select a sample of the required size and begin by selecting at random a number between 1 and k. Thereafter every k^{th} entry will be included. (If the first selection is a, where $1 < a < k$, the second selection is a + k; the third selection is a + 2k; etc.). This procedure may be as satisfactory as the repeated use of a table of random numbers for each selection provided there is no periodicity or trend in the list. But suppose, for example, that a list of business enterprises engaged in manufacturing is the frame, every 200th is to be selected, and that the list is arranged in order by total sales starting at the top. Then it will make a difference in the sample estimate of mean sales per enterprise whether firms 1, 201, 401, 601, etc., are selected, or firms 200, 400, 600, 800, etc.[14] It would be appropriate to consider a more complex design.

There may be compelling reasons not to use simple random sampling. There may be possibilities of substantial reductions in sampling error at little or no extra cost. And it may be difficult to impossible to develop a frame which could be the basis of simple random selection. The basic features of complex designs are clustering, multi-stage selection, stratification, and controlled selection.

Clustering: Clustering is usually a necessary evil. It is undertaken only to reduce data collection costs per interview; it cannot reduce the sampling error of estimates for a given number of interviews. It is obviously not efficient to scatter interviews with no geographic clustering, say, 1000 personal interviews representing the population of the U.S. Development of sampling materials and travel time per interview would be prohibitively expensive. Clustering reduces the dollar cost per unit of information, and it produces *no bias.*

The effect of clustering on sampling error is usually indicated by comparing the standard error of the mean under simple random sampling with the standard error of the mean in a cluster sample when each cluster is fully enumerated*

$$(1) \quad \text{var } \bar{y}_o = \frac{s^2}{n} \quad \text{(S.R.S.)}$$

*We ignore here and elsewhere the finite population correction, which is trivial for the type of problem with which we are concerned. We also assume equal-sized clusters.

where $\quad \bar{y}_0$ = mean of some variate y estimated from a simple random sample

S^2 = variance of the variate y

n = number of interviews in the sample

var = variance

(2) $\qquad$ var $\bar{y} = \dfrac{S_a^2}{a}$ $\quad$ (clustered sample with enumeration of cluster)

a = number of clusters

(3) $\qquad \dfrac{\text{var } \bar{y}}{\text{var } \bar{y}_0} = \dfrac{S_a^2/a}{S^2/n} = D = [1 + \text{roh} (B\text{-}1)]$

D = design effect

B = number of elements per cluster

roh = coefficient of intraclass correlation

Alternatively, we may write:

(3a) $\qquad$ var $\bar{y} = [S^2/n] \, [1 + \text{roh} \ (B\text{-}1)]$

$\qquad\qquad$ = var $\bar{y}_0 \, [1 + \text{roh} \ (B\text{-}1)]$

Note that we multiply the variability of a simple random sample mean (var $\bar{y}_0$) by a factor which is 1 plus a term which depends on, (a) the size of the cluster—the larger the adjustment—, and (b) the homogeneity of the cluster. If roh = 0, there would be no loss from clustering. If it were 1, the variability of a single random sample, [var $\bar{y}_0$], would be multiplied by B, the number of elements per cluster. From consideration of this formula it is apparent why sampling statisticians are concerned with the determinants of roh, and especially the relation between roh and B.[15] For an intuitive feel, consider clusters of addresses on the same street if the purpose is to estimate the proportion of non-whites. Given segregation, roh could be as high as 1 (either the whole cluster is white, or it is non-white) in which case the variance is a multiple of simple random sampling equal to the number in the cluster (because you have only one bit of information on race per cluster, the additional interviews told you nothing more). Roh is a large-sample modification of Rho omitting some minor adjustments for small samples and small numbers of clusters. Roh is equal to

$1 - \dfrac{\text{within-cluster variance}}{\text{total variance}}$, so it varies from 1, (when all the variance is between-clusters, none within clusters and the second term becomes zero), to 0, (when all the variance is within clusters and the cluster means are all the same).

In practice, it is not common for all elements in a cluster to be enumerated when there is only one stage in selection.

Multi-stage sampling: Multi-stage sample designs are those in which the clusters are subsampled. For example, in a sample of the population of the United States, the first stage may be the selection of counties, and the counties in turn may be subsampled. The effect of subsampling is to add another component to the standard error or variance of the estimate of any statistic in addition to the variance resulting from sampling at the first stage. Thus, the formula for the variance of the estimate of the mean is:*

$$(4) \quad \text{var } \bar{y} = \frac{S_b^2}{m} + \frac{S_w^2}{mn}$$

S_b^2 = variance of Y between clusters

m = no. of clusters selected at stage one

S_w^2 = variance of y within clusters

n = no. of interviews within each cluster

There is no limit in theory to the number of stages of selection which may be introduced. In practice, attempts are made to limit the number of stages in the interests of simplicity. Each stage of selection presents a new problem in sampling, an additional set of complications in every part of the work from the development of the frame to the estimation of sampling errors. Each additional stage also implies additional clustering of the sample, and, hence, at least a risk of an increase in the sampling error. Gains from stratification are, however, possible at each stage (see below). Most designs are limited to three or four stages. We may note that the number of stages need not be the same in all strata in the sample. For example, in a sample of the U.S., New York and other very large cities may be selected with certainty while rural counties will be sampled.

The sample may still be self-weighting, since different probabilities of selection at one stage can be offset by reversed differences at a later stage. What

---

*Again we ignore the finite population corrections and assume the same number of units are selected in each cluster. If the cluster n_i's vary, terms must be added for variance in the n_i's and for covariance between the cluster mean and the cluster size.

matters is that the product of all the probabilities (from each stage) for any individual be the same as for all other individuals.

Thus, a part of the development of a complex sample design is the specification of the number of stages of selection and the size of the clusters at each stage in each of the major strata of the sample. There are, in theory, an indefinitely large number of ways to select a probability sample of a given total number of interviews from a given population. While some of the theoretical possibilities can be ruled out quickly, there remain difficult problems involving: (1) the number of stages of selection, (2) the definition of the elements to be sampled at each stage, and (3) the number of elements to be selected at each stage.

In theory, it is a simple problem of maximizing the amount of information per dollar, or minimizing the cost of a body of information. The difficulty is that the facts are frequently not known precisely, and there may be a variety of kinds of information wanted, differentially affected by the choices made in sampling design. For instance, very local clustering may do damage to estimates of race, but clustering at county or state level may affect things which vary by government jurisdiction (treatment of people on welfare, for instance).

Stratification: Some use of stratification is made in all but the simplest sample designs. A major attraction of stratification is that it makes possible a reduction of the variance of the estimates, and often the gains may be realized at little or no additional cost. Stratification may also be used to divide the population into groups within which different procedures are employed. No bias is introduced, but the amount of gain in efficiency may depend on the wisdom of the stratification used.

The procedure is to arrange the population into subpopulations or strata and *then* select a random sample of each. For example, a list may be arranged in order and *then* every k^{th} individual may be selected from the list. The object is to arrange the population into strata which differ as widely as possible from each other but are as homogeneous as possible within each stratum.

The variance of the estimate of a mean within a stratum when simple random sampling is used is the same as if that stratum were a complete sample (See equation (1) above.)

$$(5) \quad \text{var}\,(\bar{y}_h) = \frac{s_h^2}{n_h}$$

The subscript h refers to stratum h.

Then the variance of the mean for the entire sample can be computed from the means for all strata:

$$(6) \quad \text{var}(\bar{y}) = \Sigma W_h^2 \frac{S_h^2}{n_h}$$

W_h is a weight assigned to stratum h, and $\Sigma W_h = 1$.

Note that only the variation within strata enters the sampling error. The gain from stratification can be seen more easily from the following expression:

Variance of $\bar{y}$ with proportionate stratified sampling = Variance of $\bar{y}$ with simple random sampling (var $\bar{y}_o$) - Weighted variance of stratum means $\left(\dfrac{\Sigma N_h (\bar{y}_h - \bar{y})^2}{\Sigma N_h}\right) / n$

Consequently, the gains from stratification are greatest when the strata means differ greatly, but not by finding very small strata. Unequal N's reduce the potential size of the last term, other things being equal.

It is important to understand the implications of errors or inefficiencies in the development of strata. Suppose, for example, that it is desired to stratify households by income but no actual measure of income is available. All that the investigator has at hand is estimates of economic level made by interviewers who have looked at the outside of the homes of the subpopulation being considered. Frequently, the interviewers will make mistakes. Yet, so long as their ratings have *some* correlation with actual incomes, it will be better to use them to stratify the population than not to stratify at all. The question is one of whether variability estimated from (6) is appreciably lower than variability estimated from (1), i.e. are the strata based on the interviewers' ratings more homogeneous inside than random subgroups of that size? The question of using such ratings in practice is not whether they are better than no stratification at all but whether they lead to sufficient improvement compared to other possible methods of stratification to justify the cost of preparing them. No bias is involved, only differences in efficiency. Whether to use such ratings as a basis for varying the sampling fraction is a different question—see below.

Note that at every stage in a multistage sample, stratification is possible. Moreover, the principles of stratification need not be the same across the entire sample at any stage. For example, if counties are to be selected in the first stage of a population sample of the United States, the list of all counties may first be stratified by region. Within the South, the further stratification may be based on different variables than those used elsewhere, e.g., percent of total agricultural land planted to cotton.

It is almost always advisable to stratify a sample. In sophisticated designs, stratification may be carried to the point where there is only one element selected per stratum.

It is practically impossible for stratification to increase the sampling variance, or to produce any bias. It seems likely that the substantial gains from even relatively simple stratification apply to a wide range of variables and study purposes, so that multi-purpose samples save more in spreading of sampling costs over many studies than they lose by not tailoring the stratification to the needs of each study individually.

Controlled Selection: Controlled selection is an ingenious solution to the problem of how to retain randomness of selection and yet exercise a greater degree of control over the selection than is possible through simple stratification alone. The essential principle may be illustrated for a Latin Square design. (See Table Y.) Suppose stratification has been carried to the limit of one selection per stratum for each of the three strata. It may still be desirable to take into account an additional variable. If no controls were introduced, there would be a total of 3 x 3 x 3—twenty-seven possible patterns of selection of three cells. Of the twenty-seven, three would be particularly undesirable, in that the selections for the three strata would all come from control class 1, or 2, or 3. But there are six especially desirable patterns because there is one selection from each control class. These patterns are indicated by the letters A through F in Table Y. A random number from one to six may select one of the six desirable patterns. The twenty-one less desirable patterns will be given zero chance of selection. (Pattern A selects a C1 from Stratum I, a C2 from Stratum II, and a C3 from Stratum III.)

TABLE Y: LATIN SQUARE DESIGN

	Control Classes Based on X_1		
Strata	1	2	3
I	AD	BE	CF
II	CE	AF	BD
III	BF	CD	AE

This method can be carried farther. An additional principle of control X_2, may be introduced. Instead of a 3 x 3 square we may have a cube, 3 x 3 x 3. (We are still assuming equal cell sizes.) Then there will be a new set of preferred patterns such that three elements will represent each stratum once, each control class on X1 once, and each control class on X2 once.

In practice controlled selection must take into account the inequality of stratum sizes[17] and a good deal of judgement is involved in deciding what the various controls should be. It is a matter of how *large* the gains in efficiency will be.

Economists who are not specialists in sample selection are unlikely to make use of controlled selection in drawing samples. They may well encounter data based on surveys which have been taken using this procedure, however. They should recognize that its use imposes limitations on the analysis of the resulting data. The extreme case is one in which an investigator wishes to examine the nature of the relationship among variables related to the characteristics used in the controlled selection without realizing what he is doing. For example, he might wish to see whether being in stratum I had an effect on whether an individual fell in 1, 2, or 3 on X-1. He would find that all those in I were in *one* of the three categories on X-1. He might further find that all those in I were in category C on variable X-2, which he might argue was unlikely to have arisen by chance. With sufficient diligence he might be able to reproduce exactly the pattern of controlled selection actually chosen—but he would have found nothing about the population.

This type of difficulty has arisen in practice when tabulations have been made for finer geographic breakdowns than were intended. For example, the sample might be so designed that three cities fall in strata I, II, and III, and X-1 might be income level of suburbs. Then the sample might include a high income suburb of city I, a medium income suburb of city II, and a low income suburb of city III. It might represent the three cities combined quite adequately, but it would be a poor sample of any one of the three in isolation. If the sample had been intended to represent each of the cities individually, it would have been selected in an entirely different way.

One need not understand the detail of Latin Squares or Graeco-Latin Squares; it is the principle that is important. That is, it is always possible to do better than simple random or even stratified random sampling if you are willing to forego inclusion of all possible combinations of strata in the sample. The limitation of this kind of procedure is, for example, that you may not have a genuinely representative sample of each of twelve metropolitan areas, although you may have a representative sample of the central city of each area.

Sampling Dwelling Units: Households and Quasi-Households: In the United States we have no sampling frame that lists all the families or adult individuals so dwelling units are used. The reason we exclude the institutional population and those in quasi-households is that they are difficult to interview, very badly clustered and represent only a very small fraction of the population. A decennial census counts everybody including the institutional population. Institutional populations as largely people in places where they cannot get out easily, like hospitals, mental institutions, jails, and the like, but there are also quasi-households such as flophouses, communes, residential hotels and some old peoples' homes, with a lot of people in one structure without separate entrances, or separate cooking facilities.

The Census changed its unit from a dwelling unit in 1950 to a housing unit in 1960, the housing unit being defined as having *either* a separate entrance *or* separate cooking facilities. Consequently an old hotel where people have cooking facilities in their rooms might now be considered several hundred housing units, rather than being a quasi-household. Quasi-households are included in the Census Current Population Survey, but not the institutional population. The Survey Research Center samples generally exclude the quasi-households as well as the institutional population. Other dwellings may, however, have roomers and boarders in them who are included and treated as separate families. Alaska and Hawaii are also generally excluded from most small samples.

When the interviewers actually go out to interview at the addresses selected to form a sample, they sometimes meet with surprises. The original field work in listing addresses and selecting the sample may have been correct, but in the meantime, dwellings may have been torn down, subdivided, converted to institutions, or newly built in large numbers. When the result is fewer dwellings than expected, some efficiency is lost, but there are no great problems. But when the buildings or the areas included in the sample suddenly have large unexpected clusters of dwellings (all of which belong in the sample), an alarming problem arises. If they are left out one has a large non-response, and a bias. If they are all taken, it is extremely costly and difficult, yet each interview adds little to the total information. The usual procedure is to take a fraction of the interviews and weight them up to represent the rest. The inefficiency remains, but at least the field costs have not been blown up, nor delays in completing the study encountered.

The Unit of Analysis: Families may also include members who are quasi-independent. The early Surveys of Consumer Finances used a "spending" unit in which even related people who kept separate finances and had an income of their own, were treated as separate units and interviewed separately.

After World War II there were a substantial number of people who lived doubled-up waiting for the housing shortage to ease, often with quite separate finances, quite separate purchase plans, and quite separate expectations about the future. As the proportion of these related secondary units dropped to less than ten percent, and they became more and more restricted to very old or very young people, it became less important to talk about them separately. Now the interviewing is done on a family basis, although in the SCF each year some tabulations are done on a spending unit basis by separating income between spending units within a family and asking who owns the cars so that one can prepare tables about what kind of cars people own, by income, on a spending unit basis. Of course there are also unrelated people in one or two percent of dwellings, who are separate families, and are usually interviewed separately.

In a national poverty study we became concerned about doubled-up families even when the people who were being housed by their relatives had no income of their own.[16] So, although we interviewed on a spending unit basis, and combined the data to create family information for some purposes, we also took families apart into what we called "adult" units. An adult unit consisted of a single adult or a married couple and their children. This required dividing the income and making some estimates of the extent to which aged relatives or adult sons or daughters were receiving free housing and free food from their children or parents with whom they lived. We wanted to include this as part of their real income. There is a very large amount of potential poverty hidden by doubling up in this country. As a result, anyone who wanted to establish a guaranteed income as a matter of right, with no relatives' responsibility requirements, would be faced with a much larger problem than he might think if he looked only at family income distribution.

Problems of Sample Selection of Special Concern to Economists

Self-weighting Samples: In the design of samples for economic surveys, there is an initial presumption in favor of equal probability of selection of the elements, which implies that the resulting sample will be self-weighting. That is, each interview will be given the same weight in analysis as any other interview. For the analyst it is convenient not to have to use weights in calculating statistics based on the sample, nor to have to shift from weights to number of interviews in getting degrees of freedom for significance tests. This consideration may be of minor importance, however, if the data are to be analyzed on a computer using programs which will accept weighted data. The presumption in favor of equal probability of selection rests more fundamentally on the proposition that interviews in each stratum are expected to cost about the same and that for the important statistics under study, estimates from different strata will have similar variance. It also assumes that units are important in proportion to their frequency in the population. If in some stratum interviews are known to be cheap, or the variance of important statistics is known to be large, or the people important for some policy reasons, oversampling in that stratum should be considered. In the absence of these conditions equal probability is preferable.

We may contrast this approach with one in which the design is planned by specifying a certain number of strata and taking an equal number of selections per stratum. For example, one might specify three strata of counties, those with high, medium and low income per capita, and select 10 counties per stratum. If there are unequal numbers of counties in the three strata, the result will be unequal probabilities of selection of families and of family units. If the same procedure is followed at each stage in a multi-stage sample, the final probabilities of selection may be extremely unequal.

Equal probability of selection can be achieved, however, by assigning to each element a probability of selection proportional to size, i.e. the number of basic units in it (housing units). One of the possible methods of achieving this result is to consider a list of elements $x_1 \ldots, x_n$ from which a sample is to be selected. For each element there is a measure of size. For example, we might have a list of 1000 city blocks, with an estimate of the population of each, the total being 30,000. Then the data may be arranged in the following format:

(1)	(2)	(3)
Block Number	Population per Block	Cumulative Population
1	572	1-572
2	409	573-981
3	51	982-1032
. . . .	. . .	. . .
1000	207	- 30,000

If ten blocks are to be selected, we use an interval of 30,000/10, or 3000. Then we apply an interval of 3000 to column 3, and with a random start select a sample of ten blocks. If the random start (a random number between 0 and 3,000) is 313, then one selects blocks which include the numbers 313, 3313, 6313, 9313, etc. The probability of selection of any block will be proportional to its population. *There is no need to assign equal probabilities of selection to the blocks.*

Use of Variable Sampling Fractions: It is sometimes efficient to use a sampling fraction which varies from stratum to stratum in a sample. It is useful to consider the formula for optimum allocation, and its implication. The optimum allocation requires that sampling rates within strata be directly proportional to the standard deviations within strata of the variable being studied and inversely proportional to the square root of the cost per element within strata:[18]

$$(7) \qquad f_h = \frac{n_h}{N_h} = K \frac{S_h}{\sqrt{J_h}}$$

where f_h = sampling fraction in stratum h

n_h = number of elements selected in stratum h

N_h = number of elements in the population in stratum h

K = a constant of proportionality

S_h = standard deviation (of a variate to be investigated) in stratum h

J_h = cost per interview in stratum h

This formula refers to the standard deviation of a single variable. Actual surveys involve the estimation of measures of many variables, often several hundred. For a practical decision to be taken with full information, some estimate would be needed of the optimum value of f_h in each stratum for each variable. The optimum may well differ from variable to variable. A low level of precision may be acceptable for some variables, and some judgments or perhaps some rough system of weighting, may guide the choice of sampling fractions to be used for the strata in the survey.

Gross differences in cost per interview (J_h) from stratum to stratum occur where a different method of data collection is used. For example, in one stratum it may be possible to collect data by telephone while in another personal visits must be made. There may also be geographic strata in which interviewing is very expensive because of the physical isolation of an area. In such cases an adjustment in the sampling fraction may be needed. Note that even a substantial adjustment will not destroy the representativeness of the sample, as would a decision to omit the expensive stratum entirely.

Differences in standard deviation per element from stratum to stratum (S_h) are ordinarily of more concern in the design of economic surveys than difference in cost. In general, for the estimation of percentages the gain from the use of variable sampling fractions is small, while for the estimation of the mean of a distribution, the gain may be substantial.

The gain in estimating percentages is small because the variance of a proportion is p(1-p). Within a stratum the standard deviation will be $\sqrt{P_h (1-P_h)}$.[19] For values of P_h from 0.10 to 0.90, $\sqrt{P_h (1-P_h)}$ ranges only from 0.3 to 0.5. It does not often happen that strata can be defined in which P_h will vary so widely.

For the estimation of means, however, the situation may be very different. In some situations it may be efficient to include in a sample *all* elements in a stratum. For example, in a sample of business enterprises in a certain industry, all enterprises in the largest category when ranked on a specific characteristic might be included, with sampling of the enterprises only in other strata.

A method of variable sampling fractions based on field ratings used for some years in the Survey of Consumer Finance illustrates the uses and limitations of variable sampling fractions. Interviewers listed the dwellings in a sample of blocks and estimated the income of the family in each dwelling by observation from the outside. Dwellings were divided into three groups, "low," "medium" and "high" (L, M, H). The following tabulation from Kish, p 414, summarizes the results of a study of the usefulness of this procedure:

TABLE 1

Variances at Three Economic Levels,

and Optimum Sampling Fractions

Variable	Mean			Standard Deviation			Optimum Loading			Efficiency of Optimum Compared to Proportionate
	L	M	H	L	M	H	L	M	H	
Mean income	$2800	$4200	$8000	$1700	$2800	$8100	1	1.6	4.7	1.36
Mean liquid assets	700	1800	5800	1700	3400	10,100	1	2.0	5.9	1.45
Percentage with income over 10,000	0.4	5	31	6.4	21	46	1	3.3	7.2	1.43
Percentage below median income	70	44	32	46	50	47	1	1.1	1.0	1.00

For mean income, the optimum sampling fraction for the High stratum is 4.7 times the fraction for the Low stratum, since the standard deviations are in the ratio 8100 to 1700 or 4.7 to 1. The ratio of the *mean* income in the High stratum to that in the Low, 8000 to 2800, is smaller. Yet the table shows there is a tendency for the standard deviation to increase as the mean increases.

Note that the potential gains in efficiency from optimal loading are substantial for the means, and also for the percentage with income over $10,000. Note too, that the optimal loadings vary, and that the optimum loading for estimating the percentage with income below the median is not loading, but a constant sampling fraction. Most items estimated in this survey were of the latter type.

This type of investigation has been carried much farther for single descriptive statistics (such as the mean of a distribution for the sample as a whole) than it has for complex statistics (such as regression coefficients from multiple regression equations). It is clear that the device of using variable sampling fractions may be extremely useful in studies intended to estimate the mean or aggregate of some financial quantity for the population of a geographic area. On the other hand, the more variances differ, the more likely the variable is skewed and not effectively estimated by a survey. And the gains in complex statistics are likely to be smaller, just as the clustering losses are smaller.

Of course, in designing a sample one often does not know the variances to be expected within strata. He may use estimated differences in strata means, assuming that the variances are proportional to the means, but even the means may not be known. High precision is not required, but unless the range among the variances is substantial (four to one or more) the gains are probably not worth the complications.

A special type of varying sampling fractions arises when they vary across sampling units because one wants the sample to represent something other than families, for instance, dollars of income. One might, given a list of people with their incomes, sample dollars of income—a sample which would contain many high-income people, and only a small fraction of the numerous low-income people. Without weighting, then, one could give results in terms of dollars of income represented. "People representing x% of the income say they like to invest in common stock."[20] Similarly, a sample of firms proportional to number of employees allows one to talk about employers representing some fraction of the employees in the state. If one sampled transactions, proportionately to their size, again it might make sense to report the information or intentions or backgrounds of people according to the volume of transactions they accounted for. This would be a self-weighting sample, but of dollars spent, not of people. Again it is important to remember that the unit of sampling, of interviewing, and of analysis need not be the same.

Point Sampling: Sometimes the desire to sample something other than people or dwellings leads to the necessity to sample some continuous stream, like time, or some continuous surface like area. One may want to determine in what fraction of time something happens, or what fraction of a land area is covered with a particular crop. In these cases, it is frequently simpler and more efficient to use pin-point sampling; that is, to take a large sample of points in time or space. If 50% of the points satisfy the criterion (the man was working, etc.) then 50% of the continuum does also. This procedure was probably first publicly suggested by an Australian agronomist who put a point on the tip of his boot and took a random walk around the pasture to estimate the proportion of the area covered by each of several grasses.[21] One recent study asked researchers to carry a random alarm mechanism, and report what they were doing every time it sounded.

Screening Interviews: It is not unusual in economic survey work for problems to arise which can be studied only by interviewing a narrowly defined population. One might be interested, for example, in interviewing people who had moved within a year from one county to another, in order to study the cost of such moves. Or one might wish to study the cost of college by interviewing the parents of undergraduates. While it sometimes happens that a list will be available which can serve as a sampling frame, often there is no such list. In this situation screening interviews may be useful.

This method of developing a sample will be successful if three criteria are met. First, the screening interviews must be cheap. One way to hold down the cost is to include the screening questions in an on-going survey with other purposes and content. Or it may be possible to screen a large number of families economically in some other way, perhaps a brief doorstep interview with questions which even neighbors can answer.

Second, the screening question must yield accurate information. Clearly the doorstep screening questions cannot involve sensitive information like income, assets, family planning, or some forms of disability or medical care. In a study of hospital utilization, doorstep screening for occupants 65 or older worked well, but for people who had been in the hospital in the last year it under-selected. Data from a parallel representative sample allowed weighting to reduce biases.[22] It is crucial that the number who are erroneously classified as *unsuitable for inclusion* in the sample be small. If some are erroneously *included,* the error could be detected in the subsequent intensive interviews and those cases eliminated.

Third, the original sample must be satisfactory (both in design and execution). Any loss from non-response in the screening interviews implies a corresponding loss in the sample for the intensive interviews. It may be that the probability of non-response on the screening interviews varies systematically and that the probability of non-response is somehow related to the probability that a unit will be eligible for the intensive interviews. (See the discussion of non-response in Chapter IV.)

When the three criteria are met, however, screening procedures can be extremely useful. The criterion used in screening need not be a simple demographic characteristic. An analyst, for example, might carry out a complex statistical procedure from which he emerged with a predicted score and an actual score for every member of a cross-section sample, as discussed above. He might then select for reinterview every individual for whom the discrepancy between these scores exceeded some absolute amount. This strategy is, in effect, a special type of reinterview.

Reinterviews and the Estimation of Changes over Time: For efficiency in sample design, reinterviews are especially useful for surveys intended to measure changes over time. The Current Population Survey, for example, is intended to measure changes in the unemployment rate over time with a high level of precision.

The problem may be regarded as one of estimating the difference between two means:[23]

$$d = \bar{x} - \bar{y} = \frac{\Sigma x}{n_x} - \frac{\Sigma y}{n_y}$$

where

d = difference between two means

$\bar{x}$ = mean from the first sample

$\bar{y}$ = mean from a second sample

n_x = no. of interviews in x

n_y = no. of interviews in y

If n_x and n_y are taken as given, the variance of the difference becomes:

$$\text{var }(d) = \frac{\text{var}(x)}{n_x^2} + \frac{\text{var}(y)}{n_y^2} - \frac{2 \text{ cov}(x,y)}{n_x \, n_y}$$

Thus, the variance of the difference is reduced by a factor which depends on the covariance of x and y. For many variables of economic importance, the covariance will be substantial with reinterviews. Labor force status, for example, does not change for most people over a one-year period. Hence, there will be gains from the use of reinterviews. However, repeated samples using the same sampling areas (down to small subareas) also have substantial covariances.

These gains must be weighed against the tendency of a sample to become unrepresentative over time because of problems of non-response, moving, and the appearance of new units in the population or changing of the units (divorce, for instance). These problems are treated at length in Chapter IV. There is the additional possibility that repeated interviewing of the same unit may in itself create a change in the behavior of the unit or in the completeness and accuracy of the report given. Any change in quality of report, even a change toward greater accuracy, may cause a bias in the estimate of the change taking place in the population. Continuing projects, therefore, use designs involving partial overlaps, with systematic periodic addition of new sub-samples and retirement of old ones. A sophisticated scheme of this type is used in the Current Population Surveys of the Bureau of the Census. Reinterviews are particularly useful where analysis of change is desired and where nuisance variables (such as stable personality characteristics which differ between individuals) need to be eliminated.

Highly Skewed Distributions: One way to check the validity of a study is by multiplying a mean by the inverse of the sampling fraction to estimate the aggregate and then comparing these aggregates with some national income statistics or other source of aggregate data. The items that seem to check out best are the ones that are not badly skewed, in other words, not concentrated in the hands of a few people. Also, they are something people are not terribly sensitive about, something regular like contractual payments, and things that are very likely to be *personal* assets, or debts, and not institutional or business accounts. Many of the aggregate statistics are assumed to be either individual or business, depending on their name or on some rough estimates from institutional reporters, when in fact we really don't know.

It would be very useful to do methodological studies which start out with a sample of the records on which the national income or other aggregate data are based, follow them back to their original source, and find out what the ownership, function, and purpose of that particular amount really was. This would help us to better understand the aggregate statistics and would also improve our notion of the comparisons with survey data.

In general surveys are not good to estimate aggregates of skewed distributions. It is not true, as intimated in many books on statistics, that the distribution of a sample of sample means is normal even though the basic distribution of the numbers is skewed. If the sample is badly skewed, even the distribution of sample means is skewed so that more than half of the samples would produce estimates below the true average. It is not hard to see how this would be true if you had samples of 1,000, and one man in 1,000 has an income of $1,000,000 and everybody else has an income of $6,000. You might take many samples before you found one with a millionaire in it and he would produce a sample with a very high estimate. The chances are that in dealing with skewed distributions, any estimates of means or aggregates should be done with an arbitrary cut-off point and stated to be estimates of the amounts excluding the extremes, e.g., those with incomes over $100,000 or assets over 1/2 million. These boundaries should be determined before reporting survey results, not after.

Effects of Non-Optimal Sampling on Analysis: A problem which sometimes presents itself to an economic analyst is whether or not to use an existing unrepresentative sample for analysis. For example, two well-known econometricians, H. S. Houthakker and John Haldi, carried out an extensive analysis of the demand for automobiles using data from a panel operated by J. W. Thompson on a commercial basis.[24] The panel was set up and replacements were made to it in such a way that the panel did not comprise a representative sample. Two elaborate studies have been based on very special samples of (a) subscribers to *Consumers Reports* (highly educated for the most part), (b) who sent in their ballot and annual mail questionnaire (still more select), and then (c) were willing to participate in further inquiries.[25]

The proposition that the representativeness of a sample can be ignored for analytic work has interesting implications. A good deal of money might be saved, for example, if unrepresentative samples could be used for analysis. There are two questions which must be raised about results based on such samples.

First, is it possible to measure accurately the variance of the estimates based on such a sample? It is certainly not justified to assume that the individual families were selected independently; clustering is virtually certain. Hence, the variance per element is likely to be substantially higher than with a simple random sample, and this variance will not be known unless there were special efforts made to design the study so that it could be estimated. For the ordinary non-probability sample no adequate basis for estimating sampling errors exists.

Second, will the estimates themselves be biased? For example, will the estimate of the relation between income and purchases be correct? There is no reason to suppose that the estimates will be biased *provided* there are no *interactions* between the variables whose predicting power is being investigated and the variables related to the probability of inclusion in the sample. How seriously this proviso must be taken cannot be considered in general; it will depend on the type of analysis being undertaken and the particular methods of selection actually used. It is certainly quite possible that people who are willing to participate in a panel—that is, willing to keep fairly detailed financial records and make periodic reports—may differ in the way they handle their money from those who are not willing to do so. There is consequently a possibility that, say, income elasticities of demand for some commodities will be different for panel members and non-members.

It does not follow that unrepresentative samples should never be used. They should be used with caution and efforts must be made to deal with the problems just described. A theory of panel selection would be especially useful—that is, a theory which specified the characteristics of panel members, including any variables likely to be related to subtle differences in their tastes and attitudes as well as their gross economic and demographic characteristics.

Sampling Errors for Complex Samples

In estimating the sampling errors of statistics based on complex samples it is necessary to consider the effects of the method used. There will be gains in efficiency from stratification and controlled selection, which ordinarily are more than offset by losses due to clustering. As mentioned above, it is useful to define a summary statistic called the "design effect":

$$D = \frac{S_c^{\,2}}{S_{srs}^{\,2}}$$

where $S_c^{\,2}$ = variance (for a given statistic) for a complex sample

$S_{srs}^{\,2}$ = variance for a simple random sample of equal n.

Use is often made of $\sqrt{D}$, sometimes written $\sqrt{\text{deff}}$, which is the ratio of the actual standard error to the standard error for a simple random sample of equal n. If an investigator knows $\sqrt{\text{deff}}$, he knows by how much to increase estimates of error computed using formulas appropriate for simple random samples.

The design effect need not be the same for all estimates. The system of stratification used may well produce larger gains for estimates of one variable than another. The system of clustering may also have different effects. But if it is reasonably similar, general purpose tables of sampling errors are possible without computing them individually.

The details of direct calculation of sampling errors for complex probability samples will not be given here. They are only possible for simple statistics such as means and proportions, not for complex statistics such as regression coefficients or proportions of variance explained by one variable or another. The procedure requires assembling strata in pairs (using random halves of the strata selected with certainty) and estimating components of variances associated with differences between the two items of each pair.

It would be expensive to compute sampling errors specifically for every statistic in a published report, and the publication of the sampling errors would multiply the complexity of the tables. In principle each table showing a column of percentages could be accompanied by another table showing the sampling error of each percentage in the main table, as well as tables showing the sampling errors of the differences between all possible pairs of percentages. This would take more space than the data themselves. Some simplification is necessary, but there is no substitute for the calculation and presentation of specific sampling errors when a high order of precision is important.

A common simplification for sampling errors of percentages is to present a table of general-purpose sampling errors showing an estimated range within which the sampling error may be expected to lie for a given 'n' and a given range of estimated percentages. (The sampling error of a percentage varies with the size of the subgroup for which it is calculated, as one can tell from the simple random sampling formula $\sqrt{P(1-P)/n}$.) But, since most users want to compare two percentages, a table showing the range of sampling errors of *differences* between two percentages for different levels of the two percentages, and different n's of the two subgroups, is even better. The width of the range (the amount of possible design effect) is greater, the *larger* the subgroup sizes, because the full impact of clustering is felt with the full sample. Subgroups often contain only one representative or none from each of the final clusters, and fewer in each of the larger clusters, so the main impact of clustering is felt with the items based on the largest fractions of the sample, where the larger number of cases reduces the sampling error to offset some of the clustering effect.

Such general purpose tables of sampling errors of percentages take care of these two effects (a) the subgroup size (more precision and more design effect), and, (b) the general level of the percentages (how close to 50% where sampling errors are largest), leaving the analyst to use his judgment about whether a particular item for particular subgroups is larger or smaller than average losses in efficiency from the sample design. Geographically clustered variables like home ownership, for subgroups which do not cut through clusters (like city size) are likely to have serious design effects, and high sampling errors.

For averages of numerical variables, which can have widely different variances, one can still provide the reader with some approximate notions of sampling errors by calculating and developing estimates of the design effects. The reader can then use the variance of a variable in the sample, the number of cases the mean is based on, and a range of design effects from none to x%, to put lower and upper limits on the sampling errors. $2\sqrt{\dfrac{VAR\ x}{N}} \times DEFF = $ Sampling error.

The usual way of interpreting such two-level sampling errors in a simple random sample is to say that anything below the lower level is clearly not significant, anything larger than the upper level is clearly significant, and that in between one should withhold judgement.

Beyond proportions and means, there are no formulas for calculating sampling errors from complex samples. Even for the median, one estimates the sampling error of the proportion below the median level and infers the sampling error of the median from that. In the case of regression, there are computer programs which produce sampling errors, based on the assumption of simple random sampling, which is not the case.

However, there are ways of estimating sampling errors for complex statistics, such as multiple regression coefficients, indexes, etc. The leading candidate among a number of similar methods is what Kish calls balanced repeated replication.[26] It requires arranging the sample strata in similar pairs as much as possible. Where there was only one primary selection per stratum, one can still pair the adjoining strata for the small ones, or develop pairs within the strata for the very large ones selected with certainty (the twelve largest metropolitan areas, for instance, in the Survey Research Center sample).

If there are k pairs of strata, there are 2^{k-1} possible ways of selecting one of each pair to form a proper half-sample that takes into account the sampling design. But almost all the information is contained in k + 1 half samples, selected by balanced controlled selection procedures. The squared differences of these half-sample estimates from the full sample estimate provide an estimate of the sampling variance of the estimate in question, although the variance of the squared differences is *not* an estimate of the variance of the variance estimates. Since each split-half provides an estimate of the sampling error with only one degree of freedom, however, we know that it is not a stable estimate, and a substantial number of half samples, say a dozen or more, are required for stability. A variant of this procedure involves dividing the sample into many replications and comparing an estimate based on each replication with one based on *all* the other replications. This is called "jackknifing," from the analogy of slicing a wedge out of an apple.

When the balanced repeated replication procedure is used to estimate sampling errors of multiple regression coefficients from the Survey Research Center's national sample, an average design effect of about 1.12 (standard errors 6% higher than simple random sampling) was found. This still means that using computer-supplied SRS sampling errors or t-ratios is dangerous and non-conservative, but it is a smaller design loss than people had feared, and smaller than for means or simple percentages. Perhaps the use of several predictors, cutting across the sample design in different ways, reduces the clustering effects somewhat.

A special possibility for simpler estimation of the sampling errors of regression coefficients of dichotomous (dummy) variables arises because they can be thought of as subgroup means (means of the dependent variable for the subgroup non-zero on that predictor) adjusted for intercorrelations (for the fact that that subgroup is not distributed like the population on the other predicting variables or characteristics). We return to this in Chapter VI.

Estimating Required Sample Size

One of the basic decisions in developing plans for a sample survey is the selection of the size of the sample. The penalty for too large a sample is economic—too much money will be spent on field work and data processing. The penalty for too small a sample is that the results of the project may be inconclusive.

Two examples may indicate the type of difficulties which arise when an analyst finds himself with too small a sample for his purposes. Sheppard and Belitsky conducted a study of job-seeking behavior of unemployed workers in Erie, Pa., in 1963-64.[27] Their basic sample of 450 blue collar workers was selected from the files of the State Employment Service. For most of their purposes the size of sample was sufficient. But they found themselves writing a chapter on the "Re-employment Status and Job-Seeking Behavior of Negro Blue-Collar Workers" essentially on the basis of thirty-one interviews with Negro males. Attempts to supplement this sample by non-random methods yielded an additional ten cases. Sampling errors of percentages based on thirty-one (or even forty-one) observations are so large that only very limited conclusions are possible concerning differences between whites and Negroes.

Lansing and Mueller conducted a study of the geographical mobility of labor.[28] A large part of the analysis consisted in the study of variables measured in a first interview which were believed to be possible predictors of whether or not a family moved between labor market areas during the interval between the first interview and a reinterview. About 948 families with the head in the labor force were covered by the reinterview. The importance of some variables as predictors of mobility was readily confirmed. There were other variables of analytical importance, however, whose importance could not be definitely confirmed nor rejected. For example, does home ownership inhibit mobility, other things being equal? In a regression equation in which the dependent variable was whether or not the family moved between interviews the coefficient for home ownership had a value of -.03 with a standard error of .02 and a T-ratio of 1.75. The estimate of the standard error should be increased by about 10 percent to allow for the design effect. The desired T-ratio was the conventional 1.96. Thus, data are inconclusive on the question of whether home ownership inhibits mobility. A larger number of reinterviews, which would have yielded a smaller error, would have contributed substantially to the analysis. This study, like that by Sheppard and Belitsky, is typical in that the sample was adequate for many purposes but not for all purposes which the analysts considered important enough to discuss in print.

The problem of estimating in advance the required sample size is somewhat different for simple and complex statistics and the discussion which follows treats only the former.

Required Sample Size for Simple Statistics: The problem of determining required sample size has been well developed for simple statistics such as percentages which are so widely used in descriptive surveys. For a simple percentage based on the sample as a whole, all that is required is a table of sampling errors such as Table 2. Note that the errors shown should be estimated taking into account the design effect. The analyst then need only know the approximate level of the percentage in which he is interested and the sampling error which he can tolerate in order to consult the table and select the required sample size. More often, he knows how big a sample he can afford and wants to state in advance how much precision can be expected from it.

Where the percentage to be estimated is from only a part of the sample, then the desired number for the base of the percentages has to be multiplied by the inverse of the proportion of the sample that is relevant for the calculation. For instance, if one wanted to estimate the proportion of women who were Republicans, within six percent, this would require interviews with 500 women, hence a sample of 1000, assuming half the respondents are women.

In most surveys no single statistic is of overriding importance. A common rule-of-thumb approach to the problem in cross-section surveys is what we may call the *crucial subgroup method.* The analyst may conclude that he needs enough observations to obtain reasonably accurate estimates for a crucial subgroup, say, those with incomes over $K; or, the top ten percent of families ranked by income; or, people who moved last year. In effect, he may make a

TABLE 2

Sampling Error of Percentages

Level of Percentage	Number of Interviews					
	2000	1000	700	500	300	100
50	3	4	5	6	8	14
30 or 70	3	4	5	6	7	13
20 or 80	2	4	4	5	6	11
5 or 95	1	2	2	3	4	

Source: Kish, p. 576. Sampling errors are twice the estimated standard error of a percentage. Based on calculations on the Surveys of Consumer Finances.

judgment that if there are enough interviews in that subgroup, in the cross-section survey, there will also be enough in any other important subgroups. For example, he may decide that the sampling errors associated with a subgroup of one hundred are tolerable.

A slightly different and more appropriate analytical approach is to focus attention on the sampling error of the difference between two percentages. A set of estimates of sampling errors is required which should incorporate the design effect. Table 3 shows such information. This table has been constructed assuming a certain design effect, that of the Survey Research Center's national sample. For example, if the difference between two groups in an important percentage is expected to be about six percent, the percentage is around fifty percent, and the two groups are each about thirty percent of the sample, then for the difference to be significant one would need about 700 in each group, or a sample of 700 x 100/30 = 2300.

An analyst may have in mind a more powerful statistical procedure than the comparison of two percentages. Yet, he may find it useful to carry out the simple type of calculation of Table 3 to help him make a rough estimate of the sample size which he will need.

Once desired sample size has been estimated, it remains to establish a sampling fraction. (See the Kish-Hess article on the Survey Research Center's National Sample of Dwellings[14]). The sampling fraction is given by dividing the desired number of interviews by a product of several items: the total number of occupied dwelling units, an estimated response rate, an estimated

Table 3

APPROXIMATE SAMPLING ERRORS[a] OF DIFFERENCES

(In percentages)

Size of Group	Size of group						
	3,000	2,000	1,400	1,000	700	500	200
For percentages from 35 percent to 65 percent							
3,000	3.5	3.7	4.0	4.4	4.9	5.5	7.9
2,000		3.9	4.2	4.6	5.0	5.6	8.0
1,400			4.5	4.8	5.3	5.8	8.1
1,000				5.1	5.5	6.1	8.3
700					5.9	6.4	8.6
500						6.9	8.9
200							11.0
For percentages around 20 percent and 80 percent							
3,000	2.8	3.0	3.2	3.5	3.9	4.4	6.3
2,000		3.2	3.4	3.7	4.0	4.5	6.4
1,400			3.6	3.8	4.2	4.7	6.5
1,000				4.1	4.4	4.9	6.7
700					4.8	5.2	6.9
500						5.5	7.2
200							8.5

(Table 3 continued on page 94.)

[a]The values shown are the differences required for a significance (two standard errors) in comparisons of percentages derived from two different subgroups of a survey.

Table 3

(continued)

Size of group	Size of group						
	3,000	2,000	1,400	1,000	700	500	200
For percentages around 10 percent and 90 percent							
3,000	2.1	2.2	2.4	2.6	2.9	3.3	4.7
2,000		2.4	2.5	2.7	3.0	3.4	4.8
1,400			2.7	2.9	3.2	3.5	4.9
1,000				3.1	3.3	3.6	5.0
700					3.6	3.9	5.2
500						4.1	5.4
200							6.4
For percentages around 5 percent and 95 percent							
3,000	1.6	1.7	1.8	2.0	2.2	2.5	3.6
2,000		1.8	1.9	2.0	2.3	2.5	3.6
1,400			2.0	2.2	2.4	2.6	3.7
1,000				2.3	2.5	2.7	3.8
700					2.7	2.9	3.9
500						3.1	4.0
200							4.8

Source: *1968 Survey of Consumer Finances*, S.R.C., Ann Arbor, Michigan, 1969.

coverage rate, and an estimate of the number of eligible respondents per dwelling. Estimates of the number of occupied dwellings in the continental United States are usually secured from the Census Bureau. But if one took dwelling units instead of occupied dwellings one would have to multiply this by an estimate of the occupancy rate as well. Response rates can be estimated on the basis of previous surveys, how difficult this one is, and how much money one is going to spend on call-backs. The coverage rate is an estimate based on the fact that in previous sample surveys the number of occupied dwelling units as discovered, was fewer than the number one would expect. By multiplying the inverse of the sampling fraction by the number of interviews, one should get an independent estimate of the number of occupied dwelling units. In other words, Census enumerators do a better job of finding every doorbell than interviewers concentrating on the subject matter of some substantive study. Therefore, it is necessary to take a larger sampling fraction than you might think in order to make sure you find enough dwellings. Finally, even if you are interviewing only primaries, secondaries are also to be interviewed, there may be more than one respondent per dwelling unit.

Summary

A great many problems may seem to call for a non-representative sample, focused on some special group. It is always wise in these cases to ask why some groups are important out of all proportion to their frequency in the population, or why it is not important to know something about the group that did not do something or is not in something, as a kind of "control group." Any fancy sampling intended to improve precision for one purpose may well make the sample substantially less efficient for many other purposes.

Scientific analysis and generalization calls for probability sampling. But this does not mean random sampling. Even the simplest type of stratification can do better than random sampling, with no bias. And if the stratification was for one purpose, it will usually leave the sample at least as good as a random sample for other different purposes. Where the sample is multi-stage, stratification can be imposed at each stage, using whatever information is available at each.

Economy, not increased precision per interview, is the reason for clustering. But in some situations, good control over field operations may require taking smaller or fewer clusters, and taking everyone in each cluster. This is particularly important where a series of surveys may be taken over time to assess changes, but where identifying individuals, or individual houses, is difficult or where assuring careful field work in locating all eligible respondents is difficult. (Migrant workers camps?)

It may seem that when a sample gets so complex (and efficient) that sampling errors can be computed only with difficulty and only for simple statistics by exact methods, it is not worth it. Our position is that efficiency and unbiasedness in the sample are more important than ease and precision in estimating sampling errors. Experience shows that design effects can be estimated, and approximate sampling errors used. Experience also seems to show that for the more complex multivariate statistics, the design losses become smaller, and the dummy variable regression coefficients are so dominated by differences in the sizes of the subgroups (not-zero on that dimension), that approximating the variance is not much of a compromise. There remains a question of the sampling error of subgroups isolated by more complex searching procedures like the Automatic Interaction Detector (See Chapter VI). So many things have been tried that there are clearly no degrees of freedom left. On the other hand, a subgroup defined in many dimensions, may cut across the clusters in such a way that the sampling error of its mean in a series of samples, might be close to that estimated by simple random sampling (overall standard deviation divided by the square root of the number of cases). The standard deviation within the group would clearly underestimate the sampling error of its mean, since the group was "found" by the program in such a way as to make it different from others, and homogeneous (low variance) inside the group.

We suggest, then, focusing on efficiency in sampling rather than on ease in estimating sampling errors, and on approximations rather than a heavy investment in computing or estimating sampling errors. The balanced-repeated-replication method provides a method of estimating sampling errors, and we need more experience in using it to see whether design effects are reasonably constant. But the purpose of most analysis is finding what matters, what helps explain something, and explanatory *power* is what counts. Almost anything that substantially reduces the unexplained variance in some dependent variable will be significant, or would be if the sample were a little larger. Indeed, what we are really interested in is the sampling stability of our estimates of the fraction of variance accounted for by an explanatory variable, or the stability of our ranking of a number of explanatory variables according to their importance (power in reducing the unexplained variance).

The preceding discussion of sampling has assumed that economists who are concerned with sample surveys will find themselves in one of two situations. They may undertake on their own projects which require only fairly simple sample designs or they may be involved in the design or the analysis of large-scale and expensive projects, involving specialists in sampling.

The merits of simplicity in sample design have been stressed for those in the first situation. In a great many situations it is possible to use simple random sampling, or simple random sampling modified only by the introduction of stratification. Especially for small scale or pilot studies there is a presumption in favour of self-weighting samples with equal probabilities of selection of the final elements in the sample. It should be kept in mind that many refinements have been developed in order to improve the *efficiency* with which simple descriptive statistics can be estimated. Such statistics may or may not be important in a given project. This presumption in favor of simplicity, however, does not extend to situations in which there are large potential gains from such techniques as the use of controlled selection or variable sampling fractions.

For economists concerned with the design or analysis of large scale sample surveys, it is important to understand the nature of the sampling procedures used to develop them. Such techniques as controlled selection impose limits on the possibilities of analysis which are not obvious to someone without knowledge of sampling. The use of complex designs complicates estimates of the variance of sample statistics and, hence, estimates of the sampling errors of estimates. The execution of sample designs is a potential source of bias, which is insidious because it is concealed. There is an initial problem of the specification of the basic type of sampling procedure to be used. Anyone concerned with the design of sample surveys should have a grasp of the full range of possibilities.

Footnotes to Chapter III

1. Leslie Kish, *Survey Sampling,* John Wiley, New York, 1965. C. A. Moser, Survey Methods in Social Investigation, Heinemann, London, 1958. For an excellent introduction, see *Sampling Lectures* (Supplemental courses for case studies in surveys and censuses), I.S.P. Supplemental Course Series No. 1, U.S. Department of Commerce, Bureau of the Census, Washington, D.C., 1968. ($1.00).

2. See any text on the design of experiments for the proof of the optimality of equal-sized groups, and for the efficiency of excluding the middle third of a distribution, e.g., W. G. Cochran and G. M. Cox, *Experimental Designs* (second edition) John Wiley and Sons, New York, 1957.

3. D. L. Hatch and M. A. Hatch, "Criteria of Social Status as Derived from Marriage Announcements in the *New York Times,*" *American Sociological Review* 12 (Aug., 1947) 396-403.

4. Cahnman, "Comment," *American Sociological Review* 13 (Feb., 1948) 96-97.

5. See R. A. Fisher, *The Design of Experiments,* 6th edition, Oliver and Boyd, London, 1953.

   and R. A. Fisher, *Statistical Methods for Research Workers,* 12th edition, Oliver and Boyd, Edinburgh, 1954, and the reference in note 2.

   For a neat design, see Bernard Berelson and Ronald Freedman, "A Study in Fertility Control," *Scientific American* 210 (May, 1964) 29-37.

6. See Kish, *op. cit.,* pp. 562-566.

7. C. A. Moser and A. Stuart, "An Experimental Study of Quota Sampling," *Journal of the Royal Statistical Society,* Series A, 116 (1953), 349-405.

8. The discussion follows Kish, *op. cit.*

9. Robert Ferber, *The Reliability of Consumer Reports of Financial Assets and Debts,* Bureau of Economic and Business Research, University of Illinois, Urbana, Ill., 1966.

10. John B. Lansing, Gerald Ginsburg, and Kaisa Braaten, *An Investigation of Response Error,* Bureau of Business and Economic Research, University of Illinois, Urbana, Illinois, 1961.

11. Leslie Kish and Irene Hess, "On Noncoverage of Sample Dwellings," *Journal of the American Statistical Association* 53 (June, 1958), 509-524.

12. National Council of Applied Economic Research, *Urban Income and Saving,* N.C.A.E.R., New Delhi, India, 1962.

13. Donald T. Brash, *American Investment in Australian Industry,* Australian National University Press, 1966.

14. Kish, *op. cit.* pp. 29 ff. For a full description of the Survey Research Center sample, see L. Kish and I. Hess, *Survey Research Center's National Sample of Dwellings,* Survey Research Center, University of Michigan, Ann Arbor, 1965.

    Moser, *op. cit.,* Chapter 6.

15. Kish, *op. cit.* p. 164 ff. See also U.S. Bureau of the Census: *Supplemental Courses for Case Studies in Surveys and Censuses,* Sampling Lectures I.S.P. Supplemental Course Series No. 1, Washington, D.C., 1968, pp. 52 ff.

16. James Morgan, Martin David, Wilbur Cohen, and Harvey Brazer, *Income and Welfare in the United States,* McGraw-Hill, New York, 1962.

17. For a method of treating this problem, see Kish, *op. cit.,* p. 493.

18. Moser, *op. cit.,* pp. 84-88.

19. Kish, *op. cit.,* p. 95.

20. See Robin Barlow, Harvey Brazer, and James Morgan *The Economic Behavior of the Affluent,* The Brookings Institution, Washington, D.C., 1966.

21. H. F. Huddleston, "Point Sampling Surveys for Potato Acreage in Colorado's San Luis Valley," *Agricultural Economics Research* 20 (Jan., 1968), pp. 1-4.

22. Grover C. Wirick, James N. Morgan, and Robin Barlow, "Population Survey: Health Care and Its Financing," in Walter J. McNerney, ed., *Hospital and Medical Economics,* Hospital Research and Educational Trust, Chicago, Illinois, 1962 (2 vols.), Vol. 1, pp. 61-357.

23. Kish, *op. cit.,* pp. 457 ff. See also U.S. Bureau of the Census, *The Current Population Survey: A Report on Methodology,* Technical Paper No. 7, Washington, D.C., 1963.

24. H. S. Hauthakker and John Haldi, "Household Investment in Automobiles: an Intertemporal Cross-Section Analysis," in Irwin Friend and Robert Jones, eds., *Consumption and Savings* (2 vols.), University of Pennsylvania Press, Philadelphia, 1960, Vol. 1, pp. 174-224.

25. F. Thomas Juster, *Anticipations and Purchases—An Analysis of Consumer Behavior* (National Bureau of Economic Research General Series No. 79), Princeton University Press, Princeton, 1964;

    Philip Cagan, *The Effect of Pension Plans on Aggregate Saving* (Evidence from a sample survey), Occasional Paper 95, National Bureau of Economic Research Columbia University Press, New York, 1965.

26. Kish, *op. cit.,* pp. 582-587; see also Philip J. McCarthy, *Replication: An Approach to the Analysis of Data for Complex Surveys,* National Center for Health Statistics, U.S. Public Health Service, U.S. Department of Health, Education and Welfare, Washington, D.C., April, 1966; and Leslie Kish and Martin Frankel, "Balanced Repeated Replications for Standard Errors," *Journal of the American Statistical Association,* 65 (Sept., 1970) 1071-1094.

    See also Walt R. Simmons and James T. Baird, Jr. "Pseudo-Replication in the NCHS Health Examination Survey," *Proceedings of the Social Statistics Section,* American Statistical Association, 1968, 19-30. They find larger design effects, presumably because their data come from more heavily clustered samples.

27. Harold L. Sheppard and A. Harvey Belitsky, *The Job Hunt,* W. E. Upjohn Institute for Employment Research, Johns Hopkins Press, Baltimore, 1966.

28. John B. Lansing and Eva Mueller, *The Geographic Mobility of Labor,* Survey Research Center, University of Michigan, Ann Arbor, Michigan, 1967.

29. See Kish, *op. cit.,* pp. 600, and T. Dalenius, *Sampling in Sweden,* Almquist and Wicksell, Stockholm, Sweden, 1957.

Chapter IV

METHODS OF DATA COLLECTION

Introduction

It is in data collection that economists who undertake sample surveys are most likely to find themselves in difficulties. In economics there is no well-developed tradition of methodology in data collection at the microeconomic level. The existing methodological literature on surveys has been written for the most part by non-economists, typically by sociologists, social psychologists, or statisticians. Often it is oriented toward problems which have little substantive importance to economists. Another difficulty is that there may be no neat answer to the question of how to handle a specific problem. Yet, it is possible to be wrong—and it is sometimes possible to prove that a particular method led to wrong results. Variables as measured may be poor approximations to the variables which an investigator meant to measure. In the extreme case, they may be so poor as to be useless.

We may contrast problems of data collection with those of sampling and analysis. Sampling is a specialized branch of statistics, but there is an extensive literature, and an economist with a good background in mathematical statistics is likely to find that he can learn what he needs to know about it without too much difficulty. In analysis he is likely to feel that he is on home ground. It is here that the work done by economists is often technically more sophisticated than that done by people from other disciplines. In data collection, however, this chapter will start from the beginning, assuming no special background of knowledge, and treat the subject in detail.

The Measurement of Economic Concepts: Introductory Remarks

The tension between economic theory and variables as measured in economic surveys becomes apparent when we recognize that economic theory for the most part is highly abstract. In the theory of the household, for example, one assumes initially the existence of a household. This household is conceived to have an income, and a set of preferences. It also will have a set of assets and liabilities and is thought of in any given period as dividing its income between

101

saving and spending, allocating the expenditure among a set of goods and services. It will have expectations (subjective probabilities) about the world and the
future. There is a tendency to think of the empirical referents of these concepts
as falling into two categories: "factual" and "psychological." The "factual"
variables would include income, prices, expenditures, assets and liabilities, while
the "psychological" variables are the preferences and the subjective probabilities.

This dichotomy is a useful starting point, but it has a tendency to break
down. It is not the objective magnitude, but what is perceived by the household
which often turns out to be theoretically relevant and useful for prediction. The
leading example of a construct now approached in this manner by economic
theorists is income: it is income taking into account income expectations, "permanent" income, or some such concept, which is now commonly used in the
theoretical literature, rather than a "factual" measure of income received in the
past. But even with last year's income, issues of non-money income, capital
gains, payroll withholding, or direct employer contributions to pensions, are
problems.

Factual concepts may be defined by economists in a highly sophisticated
manner. One thinks, for example, of the questions that must be resolved to determine the exact income of the owner of an unincorporated business. Or, of the
complications introduced by the concept of a flow of services given off by each
durable good owned by a family. The concept of "preferences" is highly abstract.
It incorporates the whole of the psychology of each of the several members of a
household, not to mention the psychology of their interaction with each other.

As a consequence, it is often difficult to define the empirical counterpart
of a theoretical construct. It is common to use in analysis variables which are at
best "proxies" for the theoretically relevant variables. For example, house value
has been used as a proxy for permanent income. Obviously, the two are not
identical, and it becomes a matter of judgment whether the one is a useful proxy
for the other in the context of a particular analysis.

There are two sides to the problem. Starting from a theoretical construct,
it may be difficult to find a satisfactory empirical counterpart. Starting from an
empirical variable as measured, it may be difficult to find a satisfactory theoretical counterpart. The problem is to develop methods of data collection that bring
the two as close together as possible. Of course, the gap may also be reduced by
the elaboration of appropriate theory.

While the above examples are drawn from the household sector, the same
type of problems also arise in studies of business enterprises. Problems of definitions for a business firm are particularly acute with such concepts as "research
and development" costs. Comparisons of a 1956 Bureau of Labor Statistics
study with a 1957 Census Bureau survey showed such large differences, that the
Census Bureau visited some of the firms to study the basis on which the figures
were reported.[1] In both areas it is important that an investigator have a thorough

knowledge of the problems with which he is concerned, preferably both theoretical and empirical knowledge.

Many economic concepts have been measured to a satisfactory level of accuracy using the survey method. A leading example is the measurement of the size of the labor force and the level of unemployment through the *Current Population Surveys*. It took years of development, under pressure from representatives from industry and labor who challenged the figures, for the present state to be reached, and problems still exist.[2]

A special set of problems arise in the collection of economic data because some are stocks or situational variables at some point in time and others are flows over a period of time. Theoretically one might like to use rates of flow at the same point in time, but in practice that is impossible with some flows which vary and need to be summed (averaged) over a period. In practice then, one may have data on a man's income for the previous year 1970 and his rate of payments on current installment debts as of February 1971. To compare one with the other and ask how many are paying more than twenty percent of their income on installment debt raises difficulties with people whose current rate of income differs from its average over the previous year, or whose debt payments will not continue for a whole year. Relating his current outstanding debt to his debt payments will at least tell one how many payments he is away from being out of debt, unless he has some complex mixture of debts, or balloon notes.

Similar problems arise with family composition, which may have changed during the year. If secondary earners have left the household, one is unlikely to have their earnings included in the family income reports for the previous year, but neither will they be counted as part of the family. If new income-earning members join the family, there is danger of getting their income only for the time they were with the family, but counting them as though they were in the family the whole year. Such problems are particularly difficult with budget studies, where elaborate editing may require putting in "partial people" as well as part of their annual incomes.

And if one is interested in an individual's total contribution to the flow of credit, it would be necessary to inquire about debts incurred during the previous year and already paid.

In general a problem may arise whether to measure a flow by asking for a flow, or by getting change in stocks. If there are many transactions, as with a savings account, one may want to ask the balance at beginning and end of the year, but with stocks or houses it may be better to ask about purchases and sales, unless one wants to include unrealized capital gains. Estimates of saving have traditionally been built out of a combination, some components being changes in stocks and some flows of saving (into retirement pensions, or mortgage repayments, or life insurance).

Other problems arise with unincorporated businesses and farms where it is difficult to distinguish the business from the private household. Even if one wanted to include the whole thing, problems of business accounting still intrude, since household accounts are largely on a receipts-expenditures basis, not appropriate for dealing with capital transactions and depreciation. In practice, we tend to ask about profits taken out of the business, and profits left in, as two components of family income. But poor accounting creeps in, when the respondent says there was no profit in the business because he had to pay for two new machines.

Ideally one could allocate the family income into such components as: contractual saving, discretionary saving in liquid form, other discretionary saving (stock purchases, etc.), investment in future consumption (in durables and house), regular "necessary" consumption, and discretionary consumption (vacations, etc.). But one could also measure everything in real—not monetary terms—taking into account of income in kind, irregular cash receipts, realized and even unrealized capital gains, etc. Attempts to get precise measures that fit the analysts' definitions may make the interviewing dull, difficult, and even irritating, sometimes out of proportion to the gains in accuracy.

An Overview of the Problem of Choice of Methods of Data Collection

There has been a proliferation of methods of data collection in the period since World War II and an increase in the sophistication with which methods are evaluated. It may be useful to review the range of choices and the criteria for selection of methods before considering details.

Basic Methods of Data Collection: There are three basic types of data collection: personal interviews, telephone interviews, and self-enumeration. Personal interviews are by far the most expensive method. Costs depend on a variety of characteristics, especially on the dispersion of the sample. Personal interviews are generally used where the material in the interview is complex or extensive, and where the sampling frame is such that personal visits are required to locate or select respondents. It is sometimes assumed that the quality of data from personal interviews is best, but this assumption is not always justified, especially when anonymity may be important.

Telephone interviews are much more economical than personal interviews. They have a basic limitation from a sampling point of view because some people have no phone, but the importance of this limitation is slowly declining, especially in the United States. Telephone interviews are advantageous when a sample is geographically dispersed.

Self-enumeration may be used with the questionnaire delivered to the respondent either by mail or in person by an interviewer. Mail questionnaires are *even* cheaper than telephone interviews but there is a major problem of non-response—people do not automatically return mail questionnaires. People may return partially filled-in replies. The wrong person may fill out the questionnaire and return it. The quality of the replies is also a matter of interest, but the most important limitations concern the length and complexity of the questionnaire.

The most satisfactory choice of technique may be a combination. For example, personal interviews may be followed up with telephone reinterviews. Again, a sample selected from a list may be approached by mail, with a follow-up in two stages of those who do not respond, the first follow-up on the telephone, and the second, in person. (Though telephone calls in advance have been known to *increase* refusal rates.)

Another possibility is to combine survey data with non-survey data about the individual in the sample. Sampling may be from a list which contains information in addition to the identification of the elements. It may be possible to find out more about the individuals interviewed, for example, by locating their homes on maps and reading information from the maps. Respondents may be asked for permission to release data in various records, such as social security.

Types of Questions: Questions may be classified according to the form of the stimuli presented to the respondent or according to the type of response desired. The stimulus is usually a fixed question intended to be asked or read precisely as written. It may be a form to be filled in accompanied by instructions rather than questions. It may be presented orally, or printed on a card which is shown to a respondent during a personal interview. Studies of attitudes make use of a variety of other stimuli: single words (in word association tests), pictures, incomplete sentences, and the like. The choice among stimuli depends primarily on what is to be measured, but, for a given objective, there may be a choice between a more or a less direct approach. It may be a little easier for a person to tell an interviewer that his income falls in the "G" range than to say, "It's about $9,000." Pointing to that range on a card may be still easier.

The response may be open or closed, that is, the respondent may be asked to answer in his own words, or to select from categories specified for him. It is cheaper and easier to process closed questions, but the risk of persistent misinterpretation of meaning is greater with closed questions. Closed questions may take many forms, including simple dichotomies (agree-disagree), multiple choice, numerical rankings, and scores indicated by the position of a mark, such as the position of a check mark along a line.

The problem of varying interpretation of the meaning of fixed alternatives is most serious where personal interviews are used and the interviewer does not read off the possible alternatives but tries to fit the respondent's answers into one of the categories. Not only is the variability of the interviewer's coding likely, but it may be persistent for each interviewer, leading to errors clustered geographically, and hence correlated with other variables.

Scales or indices may be constructed combining answers to several questions. For example, answers to a series of dichotomies may be combined in some way to place a respondent on a scale. There is an extensive psychological literature concerned with the methods of construction, interpretation, and validation of such scales. There is also much material in literature concerned with interviewing and questionnaire construction.

Use of Pretests and Pilot Studies: It is standard procedure in surveys to conduct a pretest of a questionnaire before it is used. Inexperienced investigators sometimes fail to realize the risks of error in using instruments which have not been adequately pretested. The difficulties which may be detected at this stage are legion, including ambiguities in questions, failure of questions to be understandable to respondents, and failure of questions to "fit" all respondents given their situations as they perceive them. How extensive a pretest is necessary, however, must be a matter of judgment. It is also a matter of judgment whether to carry an extensive pretest through the stages of tabulation, analysis, and the writing of a preliminary report.

A useful procedure in pretesting is to use many more questions in each area than will be retained in the final version, starting each area with the ones that may be used and adding a series of supplementary questions and probes in order to see whether the introductory question was getting the right information.

Criteria in Data Collection: The first criterion for a method of data collection is whether it can reasonably be expected to produce measures of the variables required for the objectives of a project. There may be only one method with any chance of success. For example, in surveys of illiterate peasants in underdeveloped countries there is no question of mail or telephone surveys. Some types of stimuli must be presented visually. Again, sheer length and complexity of an instrument may dictate the choice of personal interviews.

When there is a choice, two considerations apply, cost and quality of data. By data of good quality are meant data that will lead to correct conclusions concerning questions raised in the project.

Two broad classes of errors may arise, errors arising from non-response, and errors arising from inaccurate response. The relevant concepts have been developed most clearly for simple statistics such as the arithmetic mean. Consider, first, response accuracy. Suppose that there is conceptually for every element in a population a true score on some variable. Then there will also exist a true value for the arithmetic mean (and other parameters) for the population. We prefer methods of measurement such that, given a large enough sample, the mean for the sample would coincide with the population mean, i.e., no bias. We seek to avoid methods of measurement which would lead to understatements (or overstatements) even if we had very large samples. We *also* prefer methods which are accurate for each individual as well as accurate on the average for a large number of individuals, i.e. minimal random response variability. For a given sample we seek to minimize the sum of the squared discrepancies between true score and measured score.

The costs of the two types of "error" are different. If there is response variability but no particular bias, then we may fail to prove a relationship from the data when one really exists. On the other hand, if there is a persistent response bias it is always possible for it to lead to positive conclusions that are wrong, either about a measurement or, if the bias is correlated with some other variables, about a relationship. For instance, if people tend to understate their assets, particularly old people for whom they are a major source of security, then the survey will both underestimate consumer assets and also underestimate the correlation of asset accumulations with age.

Even if the methods of measurement were precise, the estimate of the true value for the population might be in error as a result of non-response. We may fail to obtain data from some elements in the sample, and these elements may differ in some systematic way from those we do enumerate.

What we seek to minimize is the discrepancy between our estimates of the statistics in which we are interested and the true values of those statistics (the parameters) in the population. We also need to know the probable magnitude of the discrepancies between the statistics we estimate and the corresponding parameter. There is a tendency to think of sources of error one at a time—response error, error of nonresponse, and sampling error. This tendency is natural, even necessary. But it should not distract us from our central concern, are conclusions we reach about the population correct?

Field Procedures

While all the decisions about a survey fit together into a pattern which must be consistent and appropriate, we cannot talk about everything at once, and have chosen to organize the discussion roughly according to the temporal order in which things happen. Regardless of the kind of instrument used, there are a set of field procedures which have to be worked out and designed. Getting a survey done is like organizing a major construction project or getting a banquet on the table while it is hot. Any little mistake may delay, or ruin, the whole process. There may be a limited time on the calendar when the field work can be done. Delays in completing the interviewing may hold up all subsequent steps and, since much of the cost of a survey is the salaries of the research and ancillary staff, delay means increased cost.

Assuming that some sample has been drawn, there is a considerable amount of work in getting procedures set up for checking out each sample address or identification. This is necessary first, to be sure that every address has been assigned to some interviewer; second, to monitor the field work and provide help where interviewers are falling behind; and third, to check out the sample and make sure some data are assembled on the nonresponse and nonsample addresses to allow an analysis of these problems. Where respondents are paid, or reinterviews are involved, even more elaborate records must be kept.

Procedures must be worked out to assure the privacy of respondent's replies. This means that the identifying information about the respondents should be capable of physical separation from the substantive replies, so that the latter can be processed without continual guarding. The general procedure is to have a separable cover sheet (often a double sheet) containing sample information, field experience reports, and whatever information the interviewer can be expected to report about nonsample cases. For instance, if the interviewer can estimate the rent level of dwellings where no interview was taken, the analyst can check whether the non-response come from more or less expensive dwellings than the response, i.e. whether there is that kind of non-response bias.

Some of the sampling information needs to be part of the analysis: city size, region, etc., which requires transfer of some information from the cover sheet to the questionnaire before they are separated. And for control purposes and later checks, it is usually essential to have a number identifying the location of the record in the sample books (and on the cover sheets), also on the questionnaire, and even coded as part of the information. This means that it would still be physically possible to isolate one record in the data file, go back to the sample books and identify the address (and even name if names were used). Such identifiability is impossible to avoid in reinterview surveys where the next wave's data must be connected case by case with that from the first wave. In single surveys once the sample has been checked the basic sample books can be locked up for a period, then destroyed. It is particularly important to do this if the information is such that someone might want to subpoena it later.

It is conceivable that one might still be able to identify individuals from the basic data in the data file by complex sorting, particularly if the local area information is quite detailed, but in most small sample surveys where the probability of selection is one in thirty thousand or so it is most unlikely.

There is also a problem when surveys are done for others because lawyers sometimes write into contracts that the basic data belong to the sponsor. It is essential to make clear in these cases that the phrase "basic data" does not include the information in the sample books. Indeed, there is another issue here, since survey data about individuals retained for the exclusive use of one group or agency (including the government) allows the use of that information to manipulate or exploit individuals. It is probably against good public policy for any surveys to be done and the data not made publicly available, at least after a brief period, not just for their utility in scientific analysis but to prevent their exclusive use by one group possibly to the detriment of another group. It is for that reason that survey organizations, like the Survey Research Center of The

University of Michigan, have charter provisions prohibiting them from conducting surveys unless the data will be made freely available.

Preparation of the basic sampling materials includes not only sample books and cover sheets (one for each address in the sample), but also control lists for the field supervisors, address labels for sending advance letters to respondents announcing the study and justifying it, and other materials for the interviews. Since it is often impossible to have extensive training sessions on each survey, the interviewers' instruction book for each study must contain material on the purposes of the study, and any special problems it may involve. The sheer magnitude of the problem of mailing out materials to interviewers (or sending out mail questionnaires) necessitates planning and organization if everything is to start on time. And it has to start on time if it is to end on time.

Whenever new *procedures* are involved, it may pay to pretest them, as well as the questionnaire itself. But in any case, pretests of the basic instrument, using regular interviewers and in a variety of circumstances, are essential. Given the natural propensity to keep changing and improving things, it is only too easy to have a questionnaire which has been changed considerably since the last pretest. It is a matter of judgment whether the changes require further testing, but the time schedule should allow it.

Mail questionnaires and other self-enumerated forms frequently show evidence of inadequate pretesting. A well-trained interviewer can sometimes get information even when the questionnaire is inadequate, but the main result in self-enumeration is either nonresponse or nonsense response.

If the interviewer's motivation is so important—as we shall see later that it is—how is it to be increased? Quick feedback as to good and bad interviewing is certainly important, whether from the field supervisor or from the analysis staff which looks over the interviews as they come in. Some sense of what happens to the interviews, both mechanically and scientifically, also helps the interviewer. Direct contact with both the central office administration and the research staff of each project is difficult when interviewers are scattered all over the country. Hence, the quality of the written material is crucial. It should have a personal touch, since interviewers, just as respondents, react as much to the desire to please *someone* as to a vague sense of scientific importance.

There is usually an interviewers' manual containing general instructions on procedures, preliminary sampling work, time and cost reporting procedures, etc. With each study there is also an interviewer's instruction book, giving procedural details, a general statement of purpose and how it is to be achieved, and question-by-question instructions. The latter often tend to become wordy and redundant, while failing to give instructions on how to handle difficult cases. Some also attempt to make up for an inadequate questionnaire by instructing the interviewer to "be sure to find out" without telling her how she is to do it. It is hard fact that if you want an answer, you have to ask the question. If you want to know whether the respondent is including in his reported food expenses the cost of milk delivered to the door, you have to ask him. It does no good to tell the interviewer to find out; she would only have to violate her general instructions by asking several questions not in the questionnaire.

There is one acceptable thing to tell interviewers to do when the questionnaire becomes inadequate, as the best of them do in such cases, and that is to find out a little more detail by asking a probe like "Tell me more about that" and writing down a story which the editor in the home office can then interpret.

Continuous monitoring during the course of a survey is very important. If flaws show up, interviewers can be warned about them or changes made. If individual interviewers are making errors—skipping sequences of questions, accepting inadequate answers, etc.—they can be told before they make the same errors on the rest of their cases. Extensive use of the long distance phone is often necessary, though the better the materials, and the better the interviewers' training, the less monitoring should be necessary.

In many studies it is essential that the preparation include securing the informed consent of various important interest groups. The local police and newspapers should know about the study, and the local bank or business community if it involves consumer finances. Often the local interviewer can do this but press releases help. Where the study involves some professional group or interest group, lawyers, doctors, labor unions, etc., problems are even more delicate. In one study of auto accident compensation, the state *Bar Journal* issued a statement before the study was even designed, asserting that no good could come from such a study. One study aborted completely because the medical association became hostile to one of the potential directors because he was associated with the field of public health, though he was a doctor. The usual objection of specialists is that the researchers do not really know the field and hence cannot do the study properly. Since studies often involve many specialties, even in a single study, the only solution seems to be research advisory committees and extensive efforts to consult with the "experts."

Decisions also have to be made about such field problems as call-backs and follow-up procedures. Standards of response rate levels are often used, but some rules about how many calls to make at any one place and what to count as a call (passing by and noticing no lights in the house?) are needed. This is the implementation of an economic decision, whether to get more interviews by taking a larger initial sample and restricting call-backs (with potential greater non-response bias) or whether to spend the money trying to get high response rates. We shall see later that there is some reason to believe that the reliability of the data from people difficult to find and interview is lower, so that the higher response rate may provide less non-response bias at the expense of some greater response bias.

Field procedures also involve preparations for feed-back to interviewers and respondents about the outcome of the study. Interviewers are usually interested in how their respondents compared with others and like materials so that they can talk intelligently with reluctant respondents about what happens to survey findings. Respondents, even if they are not to be reinterviewed, deserve to know the findings if only as a gesture of appreciation for their cooperation. The promise of such a report seems to be useful in inducing them to cooperate in the first place. In the case of reinterviews the mailing of a report between waves also serves as a check on the validity of mailing addresses and a way of finding who has moved in time to locate the new addresses.

The researcher's preoccupation with his study objectives may make it difficult for him to prepare a summary of results that would interest either interviewers or respondents. What is interesting to respondents may be such simple things as what kinds of people use seat belts or how long it takes other people to get to work, not elaborate interpretations of complex concepts.

A final problem is that while some respondents may want to secure a copy of the full report, it cannot be offered free on most budgets, and offering to sell it may irritate.

There is some doubt whether it is advisable to set up rules about procedures where interviewers may have to use their judgment, such as scheduling of interviews, when to call, etc. Sometimes, however, choices must be made which depend on the policy one seeks to implement. For instance, one study discovered that in interviewing employed persons there were ten to fifteen percent fewer not-at-homes if one called on week-day evenings, but also five to seven percent more refusals at those times.[3] The author's conclusion that the week-day evenings were better, is true only if one wanted to minimize costs, not if one wanted to maximize response rates.

Specific Methods of Data Collection

Personal Interviews and Telephone Interviews: There has been considerable interest in recent years in the use of interviews taken by telephone to replace or to supplement personal interviews. As previously noted, costs are much lower for telephone interviews. And the proportion of families who have a telephone is high and rising. How, then, do telephone and personal interviews compare?

The logical starting point of analysis is the lack of the personal presence of an interviewer in a telephone interview. Social motivation arising out of the presence of an interviewer is important in gaining the cooperation of respondents. In a telephone situation, since the interviewer physically is not present, one would expect the social motivation to communicate to be somewhat reduced. It is easier to say "no" over the phone. And the interviewer lacks the visual cues by which she may change her approach. In some degree, however, the social motivation should be found over the telephone.

It is also possible that the personal presence of an interviewer helps to communicate a sense of the importance of the research. It is more trouble to visit someone than to call by phone and respondents who accept the idea that a survey is important should be more likely to take trouble to answer carefully.

Another obvious limitation of telephone interviews is that visual stimuli cannot be used. The interviewer's credentials cannot be examined. Respondents cannot look at cards or place check marks and the like. For some purposes this limitation may be important, but most questions in personal interviews are presented orally. The lack of visual stimuli will also tend to reduce some of the subtler forms of communication that take place when two people meet face-to-face. Facial expressions, body movements, eye contact—all may play some part in the interpretation of what is said and of pauses in the verbal interchange. This loss no doubt would be serious for some types of interviewing, say, for a clinical diagnostic interview. It may be a small problem for routinized mass interviewing. There may even be some gain in standardization of interviewer behavior resulting from the elimination of visual contact.

There may also be some gains in how comfortable respondents feel.[4] There is a greater anonymity in a telephone interview, and a greater degree of control in the hands of the respondents, who knows he has the option of putting down the instrument. He may assume the interview will be brief.

The preceding observations are primarily deductions from what is known in general about interviewing, and should be checked by further research. There has not been as much research into the quality of data obtained by telephone as into the response rates by telephone which are comparable to those by personal interview.

There has been one extensive comparison by Jay Schmiedeskamp of data obtained by telephone reinterviews with data from a comparable sample of personal interviews taken at the same time with the same questionnaire.[5] The comparison was made as part of the Survey Research Center's regular quarterly survey of consumer intentions. Results from the telephone reinterview in general were similar to those from the personal interview. There were some differences, however, especially in the direction of less differentiated responses over the phone. This finding is consistent with the somewhat lower degree of motivation in telephone interviews suggested above.

There are a variety of ways in which telephone interviews can be used: entire studies can be conducted by telephone; preliminary interviews may be by phone; follow-up interviews may be by phone; and the phone may be used as part of a multi-stage approach, as in the study by Donald reported above. Follow-up interviews have been especially successful.[6] But preliminary telephone contacts have in at least one case *reduced* response rates substantially.[7]

There are two kinds of validity questions we deal with when we reinterview people by mail or telephone. One is the question of non-response bias and the other is the question of whether mail or telephone is getting different answers from what personal interviews would get. In the Schmiedeskamp data there is a third problem because reinterviews have two kinds of non-response: one because some people do not have telephones, and another because some people do not give the reinterview. In fact, there was an eighty-five percent response rate originally; then seventy-six percent of the people had telephones, ninety-one percent of them gave their numbers, and eighty-five percent of them agreed to an interview later when phoned. This gives a total non-response rate of fifty percent, starting from the initial sample frame. So when Schmiedeskamp compares the telephone reinterview with a new cross-section, he is combining various kinds of response biases from using the telephone with some non-response biases. But he does find that people tend to make more non-committal answers and are more likely to refuse to give sensitive financial information on the phone.

Mail Interviews, Self-Enumeration, and the Problem of Anonymity: The third general category of methods of data collection is characterized by the lack of participation by an interviewer in the process of recording answers to questions. Self-enumeration may take place after delivery of the questionnaire by mail or by an interviewer in person. Return of the questionnaire may be by mail, or an interviewer may call to collect it. If the interviewer calls, she may or may not check over the answers. In one variant the respondent places his response in a sealed envelope and the interviewer simply walks to the nearest postal box with the respondent and they mail the envelope together. A basic question concerning these techniques is the effect on the data of the partial or complete removal of the interviewer.

The most obvious loss is the reduction or elimination of social motivation to respond. As discussed earlier, low response rates often characterize mail questionnaires. Yet, as noted above, response rates vary widely depending upon three types of consideration: the nature of the inquiry and its auspices, the population being studied, and the techniques used. There are many situations in which reasonably good response rates can be obtained with self-enumeration procedures.

What, then, can be said about the quality of the resulting data? The removal of the interviewer from the communication process has one major consequence for the design of the questionnaire. Interviewers can be trained to make their way through contingencies. These contingencies may be important in a complex questionnaire for the purpose of adapting the questions to the respondent's situation. Whole blocks of questions may be meaningless for some people but not for others. Which sequence fits best may depend on answers not just to a single question but to two or more questions. "If A or B to Q.1 or Q.2 ask Q.3." An interviewer's job is like operating a set of switches to keep the interview on the right track. Respondents seeing a form for the first (and only) time cannot be expected to do this job as well.

It is also true that some respondents are illiterate and cannot handle a printed questionnaire at all. The difficulties of the semiliterate, however, may be exaggerated. Cannell and Fowler found in their study of accuracy of report of hospitalization that, contrary to expectation, level of education was more highly correlated with accuracy of report in personal interviews than in self-enumeration.[8] They suggest that people of low education may find it difficult to reply quickly to the sequence of questions in a personal interview. With a self-administered form at least they can take their time. The topic would bear further investigation.

Cannell and Fowler also suggest that the interviewer contributes to the quality of the data by evaluating the adequacy of responses. An interviewer can be trained to judge what constitutes a reply. She can wait for it and not proceed to the next item until she has it. (And she can at least try to cut off a flow of irrelevant material.) Cannell and Fowler do produce some evidence to support this contention, but, in their data, the differences are small. In reporting type of surgery in the personal interviews seventy-five percent reported replies which were coded in the same category as the report from the hospital records. The comparable percentage for the self-enumeration proceedings is sixty-nine percent.

Another difficulty is that one is not sure just who filled out the questionnaire. This is particularly bothersome with mail questionnaires to business establishments and with questionnaires dealing with plans, attitudes, expectations, or other matters likely to vary from person to person among those who might be replying.

The use of self-enumeration procedures, on the other hand, may lead to improvements in quality of data in some situations. First, a personal interview is ordinarily restricted to a limited time at one place. It may be advantageous to allow people time to check with other members of their families or to consult records. There were gains in the self-enumeration procedure in percentage of episodes reported by proxy respondents in Cannell and Fowler's project. Housewives could ask their husbands after the men came home from work. This advantage would be irrelevant, of course, if people responded only for themselves. In financial surveys, however, even if people speak for themselves they may not have all their records at hand when an interviewer calls.

Self-administered forms are sometimes used in the collection of data on household expenditures as a means of controlling the problem of memory error. Small outlays can easily be forgotten or recalled inaccurately. People may be asked, therefore, to keep a record book of some kind. This procedure is used by the Social Survey in Great Britain.[9] Interviewers re-visit the households periodically to supervise the record keeping.

There has been considerable interest in another potential advantage of self-administration, the possible gain in people's willingness to reveal information about their finances if they do not have to give the information to an interviewer.

There has been some research on the importance of anonymity in inquiries on a variety of subjects. Hyman summarized some of the findings in his monograph on interviewing.[10] Anonymity is clearly a matter of degree, and it is not obvious what constitutes anonymity as it is perceived by a respondent. The limiting case would be one in which a respondent was certain that the replies he gave could not be traced to him. He cannot be given this absolute assurance as long as he states his answers to an interviewer, who obviously associates the answers with the man who gives them. Yet there is some degree of anonymity in talking to an interviewer whom one has never seen before and never expects to see again. It may well make a difference whether or not the interviewer knows the respondent's name. If no interviewer is present, it may matter whether or not the name of the respondent is entered on the report form. Unsigned questionnaires administered to groups of people seem to meet the criterion of psychological anonymity, and there has been research on the difference between signed and unsigned questionnaires administered to groups. The subject matter of the studies, however, has not been economic.

The signature does make a difference in studies in the personality field. Unsigned instruments are more likely to elicit feelings associated with instability and physical symptoms with neurotic implications.[11] In studies among soldiers about attitudes toward military service those who signed their questionnaires gave more favorable attitudes toward officers and expressed more job satisfaction. In a study by Festinger of the voting behavior of Jewish and Catholic college girls in electing officers to an artificially created club, results were complex. Catholic girls always preferred Catholic officers. Jewish girls expressed preference for Jewish officers only when the girls were not identified by name and religion.[12]

Cannell and Fowler report no difference between personal interviews and *signed* self-reports in the completeness of report of "threatening" diagnoses. That is, there was no difference in the reporting of malignancies, venereal diseases, mental disorders, and the like. They infer that it was the signature which made the difference—unsigned self-administered forms might have been different. Of course it is difficult to do validity studies if there is *real* anonymity.

In a study of accuracy of reporting loans Lansing, Ginsburg, and Braaten experimented with use of a sealed envelope technique.[13] Results were inconclusive. There was some tendency toward greater reliability with the sealed envelope technique, but the difference was so small that it might have been the result of chance.

It is difficult to come to firm conclusions as to the importance of anonymity in financial surveys on the basis of the available evidence. There is convincing evidence that some types of economic information are underreported because people are not willing to reveal the answers. The worst biases are for bank accounts and other financial assets, and for income from property. People who are asked for such information are being asked for information which is not normally discussed. We may ask why they should persist in concealing this information and whether some degree of anonymity could overcome their reluctance.

It is possible that people withhold information for fear that it will come into the hands of the Internal Revenue Service. There is evidence that income tax is not paid on all income that is taxable. Recent improvements in enforcement procedures, such as the use of information returns from banks, should reduce evasion, and it will be interesting to see if survey reports improve correspondingly. To the extent that people evade taxes, the only chance of getting them to report the income in a survey would seem to be to provide absolute guarantees of anonymity. People cannot be expected to risk fines or imprisonment to help somebody's research project.

A second type of fear may be that financial information will somehow be used by people with opposing economic interests. The extreme case is a respondent who hesitates to admit he has large amounts of currency for fear the interviewer will steal it. It may be more common to be vaguely nervous about the interview—are those credentials forged? Is the interviewer really going to try to sell something after all? The suspicions aroused may be ill-defined, but they may lead people to be cautious. This type of difficulty should be soluble by procedures such as the sealed envelope technique and other devices for developing a solid identification of the research with an organization of impeccable reputation.

It may be that what is involved is a general sense of personal privacy, a feeling that certain things are nobody else's business. "Nobody else" may include the research organization. For people who take this view, anonymity may be a necessary but not a sufficient condition for accurate reporting.

Hyman has pointed out one additional consideration. Suppose that anonymity does tend to remove inhibitions about reporting. The removal of inhibitions may lead some people to report, not their actual situation, but the situation they would like to be in. Wishes and fantasies may lead to distortions. The desire to impress an audience may play a part, and the interviewer may provide the audience. This mechanism has been alleged to be at work in interviews on sexual behavior under Kinsey's auspices. We can only speculate about the psychological analogies between money and sex.

In the case of mail questionnaires, the gains from promised anonymity may be lost if one requires identification in order to check out the sample and to follow up those who have not responded. One way out of this is to ask the respondents to send in an anonymous questionnaire and, separately, a postcard with identification indicating that the questionnaire has been sent in.

A comprehensive analysis of research done on mail surveys, including comparisons with personal interviews, and with a bibliography of well over one hundred items, concluded:

"Despite the large amount of research reported on stimulation of response, the follow-up is the only technique which has been consistently found to raise response by a substantial amount—say over 20 percent. The evidence on the reliability and validity of mail survey response is meagre in quantity and poor in quality."[14]

The meager results of varying methods, even with elaborate factorial designs, was in spite of response rates which varied from less than twenty to more than ninety percent. Of course the quality of the instruments used varied and was not measured. The author, Christopher Scott, summarized the advantages and disadvantages of mail surveys admirably:

Advantages:
  Low cost
  No clustering in the sample
  No interviewer bias
  Respondent can consult others for information and take his time to consider his answers.

Disadvantages:
  Inadequate control over identity of respondent
  Inadequate control over whom he consults
  Inadequate control over date of response
  Inadequate control over order of questions (respondent can look ahead to see where you were going—you cannot funnel questions)
  Cannot use complex questions or complex instructions (skip sequences)
  Cannot secure spontaneous, first reactions
  Questionnaire design and coding are more troublesome
  Cannot be *sure* of an adequate response rate—they vary too much
  Cannot have the benefit of interviewers observations (race, neatness of house, type of neighborhood)

He might have added that it is difficult to separate non-response from bad addresses in mail studies, and that it is impossible to control the order in which the questions are actually answered.

Panels and Reinterviews: The choice of whether or not to use a research design involving reinterviews may depend upon the need to control response error and the cost of data collection as well as upon problems of non-response, discussed later in this chapter. There are also considerations related to analysis, which will be treated more fully in Chapter VI. (We may anticipate that discussion by noting that in the analysis of causal sequences it is an advantage to have observations for the same individuals at different points in time.)

There are advantages in the use of reinterviews from a sampling point of view. The cost of the preparation of a sample is less on a per interview basis when the same sample is interviewed more than once.[15] There are gains in statistical efficiency in estimating changes by the use of panels. Variation between successive samples does not enter the calculations. Thus, it is efficient for the Current Population Survey to use a rotating panel to estimate changes in labor force participation rates and unemployment rates. Each address is included in the sample a total of eight times.[16] Reference has been made earlier to reinterviews based on screening questions to select samples with special characteristics.

There is a corresponding disadvantage to the use of reinterviews which should be obvious but is sometimes overlooked. Repeated surveys can be combined to assemble large total samples for analysis which does not depend on the exact date of the interview. But an analyst may be better off with a total sample, say, 5000 interviews rather than five interviews with each of 1000 individuals. His sample of people in the top ten percent of the income distribution will be 500 people, not 100, and his opportunities for analysis of that group will be greatly increased.

There are economies in interviewing the same people repeatedly. The number of calls necessary to find people at home can be reduced. It may not be necessary to repeat all the questions asked in the first interview. For example, some of the background data of the family will not change. It may be possible to use cheaper methods of interviewing, especially the telephone, for interviews after the first.

There are important uses of reinterviews to control response error. First, in order to compare measurements of two dates, it is an advantage to reduce memory error by making the measurements close to the dates in question. Withey has shown the importance of this point for change in liquid assets and change in income over a period of twelve months.[17]

Second, it is possible only through reinterviews to use the important technique of "bounding" to prevent people from shifting events to points in time closer to the date of interview than the dates when they actually took place. This technique has been developed by the Census Bureau.[18] It consists of obtaining a detailed description of a particular event, such as a particular expenditure, in the initial interview. In the second interview reference is made to this information. It is not possible for the respondent to assign to the expenditure a date subsequent to the first interview. Some degree of control may also be gained over shifts in time in the opposite direction, to dates earlier than the first interview. If the event had already taken place, the interviewer may say, "you did not tell me about it in the first interview." In general any overlapping measurements offer possibilities of asking for reconciliation of differences.

Third, there may be some increase in accuracy of report associated with the longer experience of the respondent with the interview situation. This gain is more speculative, but the respondent may be better satisfied as to the good faith of the interviewer, and may have developed a more positive feeling toward the various aspects of the interview situation. This advantage did not prove to be important, however, in a validity study of savings account balances.[19]

There is a possible disadvantage to be set against these reductions in response error. There may be negative "conditioning" effects on the panel members. In the Current Population Survey, for example, conditioning is a problem. Families interviewed for the first time show a higher rate of unemployment, a score of 107.3, if the average for all groups is taken as 100.[20]

This reason for this phenomenon is not known. It could be that interviewers are more careful on the initial interview, or that new respondents report more fully. Or respondents may find it harder to maintain that they are looking for work when month after month they are still reporting no work. Conditioning may also influence the attitudes and behavior of respondents outside the interview situation. For example, people who are asked repeatedly for their opinions on some topic may develop opinions on that topic more fully than if they had not been interviewed about it.

There is also a potential non-response problem from the panel losses of people who move and there is, of course, an economic decision to make in a panel study of how far to follow movers. Since three-fourths of movers will move within the same county, it is easy to decide to follow some of them. On the other hand, if they move out of the county, following them becomes very expensive and you might prefer to trade a little bit of bias for a larger sample of the rest, and more precision.

We tend to lose from panels the young people, and we may also lose some people for whom the subject matter is basically completely unpleasant. Sobol reports losing more pessimists.[21] Pessimistic people are usually having financial difficulties or expect them, and it seems logical that they would not want to keep on granting financial interviews year after year if their financial situation were grim. In an extended panel study it is fairly clear that total losses can become substantial.

Another difficult problem with panels arises from changes in the composition and even identity of the unit (family, etc.). A sample of individuals can be followed, and the only sampling problem arises because older ones die and should be replaced with young ones coming in at the other end. If one starts with this in mind, however, it is possible to keep track of all those under eighteen in an original sample and bring them in as they become eighteen, to make up for those leaving the population. But if the unit of analysis is a nuclear family, or a regular family, or a household, then more serious problems arise. Suppose a couple gets divorced and each of them remarries. If one retains only the husband or the original wife in the sample, the panel develops a sex bias and some confusion as to whom to interview in later waves—the original person, or the new head of the family. If one decides to follow and interview *any* family containing *anyone* in the families originally interviewed, the sample gets larger, and biased in favor of larger unstable families, though it remains an unbiased sample of individuals.

To assess the extent of panel bias one can always compare what happens to a panel with an independent cross-section but, in a sense, a simpler, cheaper, and more advantageous procedure is to revisit the address of the original sample and interview people who moved in or were non-response of the previous year. This gives an independent cross-section sample, of which a very large fraction, say eighty percent, will be the same people as the members of the panel. The panel will include the people who did not move and were reinterviewed and also people who moved and were reinterviewed after they moved. The differences between these two overlapping samples, the interviews with all the people at the old addresses, and the reinterviews with people who did or did not move, consists in differences in the non-overlapping parts of the samples, and there is no simple sampling variation on the other part to "noise up" the estimates. The non-overlapping part of the new cross-section consists of some people who moved in and some people who were non-response last year but were willing to give an interview this year.

The non-overlapping part of the panel consists of people who moved and were followed and interviewed. What is missing in the panel, of course, are those who moved and could not be followed and the non-response of people who did not move. If we think carefully, there is one difficulty with this comparison. That is by going back to the old addresses there will be some non-response among people who did not move and were supposed to be interviewed, who may be slightly different from ordinary non-response in a brand new sample of addresses.

Selection of the Respondent

When information is to be collected about a unit consisting of more than one individual, there is a choice as to who will be designated as the respondent. There are four main possibilities in a general cross-section survey: (1) any responsible adult may reply; (2) there may be a random selection within the household or a random selection of husband or wife; (3) the head of the unit may be designated (i.e., the husband, if he is present); (4) each adult may be interviewed, either separately, or, possibly, together. The cost of data collection is probably lower when the interviewer can interview any adult. It is certainly more expensive to interview two or more adults per family. (It would be useful to know these exact cost differences.) On the other hand, the quality of data may vary according to who reports.

When information is to be collected involving people as individuals, there is clearly a risk of loss of accuracy when one person replies as a proxy for others.

In the validity study based on hospital records previously mentioned Cannell and Fowler found that the percentage of episodes not reported was twice as high when one adult was being interviewed about another as when the adult was reporting for himself.[22] It has been shown that the use of a self-enumeration procedure practically eliminated the difference, and it would be valuable to have comparable measures for other kinds of data.

When information is to be collected about the family as a unit, the selection of a respondent becomes essentially a question of whether husbands and wives give similar reports and, if they differ, which is more accurate. In a study by Haberman and Elinson of 645 marital pairs in New York it was found that the husbands do report higher total family income, $7377 versus $7179, and since income is commonly understated, there is a presumption that the husbands report somewhat more accurately.[23] The husbands in some families seem to have omitted or understated their wives' employment incomes. In the same study rent was asked in six class intervals. In 89.5 percent of the 612 families for which there were two reports, the reports were in the same category. As to the number of income earners, 90.1 percent agreed. With respect to these two variables, then, there is approximate agreement but by no means perfect consistency.

Wohlgast has reported a series of comparisons of data from husbands and wives.[24] Hers is the only study that finds out who actually predicts what happened. All the other studies are based on reports by husband or wife, or both, on who "usually decides" or who "has the most to say," or even who decides at each stage in the process. One gets a lot of role stereotypes in studies asking people who decides, but the Wohlgast study shows that in most cases, the wife is a somewhat better predictor than the husband, even for things like automobiles. The reason for this finding is not clear. Perhaps wives really and subtly dominate family decisions, or perhaps they are more realistic about what may happen, or perhaps they have a better sense of the desires of their husbands than husbands have of their wives' desires. It may be misleading to think of the husband-wife problem as one of power when it may be one of communication, consensus, and mutual understanding.

One small study throws some light on the possibility that wives may have better perception of the wants of husbands than the reverse.[25] Husband and wife were interviewed separately, hopefully simultaneously, and asked not only about their own attitudes, desires and plans, but their perception of how their spouse felt about each of these things. A whole series of comparisons is possible with such data.

There is a more general problem in that there is no theory about decision making in the family. Arrow's famous book shows that there *is no* set of criteria by which one can define the social optimum and maximize social welfare.[26] This is true for a family as well as for the whole society, so not only do we have very few descriptive findings about what happens in the family, we do not even have a deductive theory about what *should* happen. Psychologists have tried to develop something like an international trade theory of interpersonal relations. It assumes that people bring various goods and services and trade them for other goods and services, including affection.[27] However, there are problems with that theory if the different taste patterns are too disparate or, what is worse, if each party places a very high value on the other person's affection and doing what the other person would like. There is a funny passage in C. S. Lewis' *Screw-Tape Letters*[28] entitled "The Tea in the Garden Episode" where a family is being tricked by the devil's agent into sending themselves to Hell by getting very angry with each other. The whole process starts when each person sets out to try to do what the other person wants to do, and this "after you, Alphonse" process ends up with everybody angry.

A study by Sirken, Maynes, and Frechtling also contains data relevant to the evaluation of the accuracy of income reports from different respondents.[29] This project involved reinterviews by Census interviewers in August and September 1950 of about half the respondents from the Survey of Consumer Finances of January-February 1950. The project was part of the Census Quality Check (CQC). Identical, or virtually identical, sampling instructions were issued to the two sets of interviewers, and the resulting interviews were carefully matched so that it could be determined when the same families had been interviewed. In the SCF study "first quality respondents" were defined as heads of spending units. In seventy-six percent of the interviews the actual respondent was first quality. In the CQC a "first quality" respondent meant that all income recipients reported for themselves. In eighty-seven percent of the interviews the respondents were first quality. There was an initial expectation that reports of total income for a given family would agree more closely when first quality respondents were used in both surveys for that family. The reports did in fact agree more closely when first quality respondents were interviewed in both surveys. Under those conditions 62.6 percent of families reported incomes which fell in the same class interval. When other than first quality respondents were used in one survey or the other, 53.3 percent of the families reported incomes in the same class interval.

These results are consistent with those reported by Wohlgast and by Haberman and Elinson. In obtaining data on family income if a single individual is to report it is preferable to interview the husband. It is probably still better to interview each income receiver separately, if funds permit. Results for secondary earners were considerably improved in the later Surveys of Consumer Finances, however, on the basis of the study just mentioned without interviewing each person separately. A separate question was introduced in which the head was asked limited, specific supplemental questions about the income of his wife and other earners. In theory, that questionnaire had required that a long list of income questions be repeated for income receivers other than the head. The form was clear on the point—a column was provided for the answers—but it was less clear what the interviewer was supposed to do. The revised procedure, adopted in 1954, increased the percentages of spending units with more than one income receiver from 25.7 percent to 31.7 percent in one year. This experience illustrates a general point: it may be possible to reduce or even eliminate errors arising from the use of proxy respondents if the questionnaire is carefully designed with the problem in mind.

Problems of selecting respondents in business enterprises are not so easily reduced to precise rules. Different organizations have different internal divisions of labor and different systems of titles. It is especially difficult to apply the same rules to small firms as to very large ones. There may also be problems as to who is willing to respond. One cannot always go to the top. Instructions for selection of respondents, therefore, tend to be in more general terms, and to specify a function rather than a position—they specify the person concerned with and informed about a certain topic of inquiry. It may be useful to interview more than one person. On the other hand, where the respondent is extremely verbal and quick, it may be useful to have two interviewers or an interviewer and someone else to write it all down.[30]

What can one conclude about these joint decisions as to the mode of getting information and the selection of respondent? Those engaged in financial and economic surveys have concluded that even though the wife may have better overall view of the family's needs and desires, the husband is more likely to be able and willing to talk about financial matters. And in most families the degree of consensus on general goals (or at least mutual understanding on them) is sufficient so that the cost of interviewing more than one person has not seemed justified. On explicit purchase plans, however, some further attention to this problem may be required—the optimal outcome varying from attempts to interview the family together if possible, through random selection of head and wife, to separate interviews with each. Studies of details of family consumption (or expenditures) usually take any responsible adult (which means usually the housewife). Of course, for trend measurement, as distinct from analysis, there is little advantage of interviewing both over a random selection of husband or wife in a large sample. And for any intensive study, it seems clear that some personal contact from an interviewer is preferable. Extensive telephone interviews have been successfully done but usually with people previously interviewed in person.

Special Problems with Studies of Expenditure Details

While the calendar year is an excellent time period for studying income and saving and major expenditures, consumer expenditure studies which seek to secure detail on expenditures by categories or subcategories, face problems of deciding on the period of time for which to ask for each type of expenditure. If a very short time period, yesterday or last week, is used; then it is difficult to avoid double counting (telescoping, or bringing into the period things bought just before or just after), or omission of borderline or ambiguous items. If the period is too long, then memory errors are more likely. One expensive way out of this problem is to revisit a sample regularly and get reports of expenditures over a series of short periods covering the longer period (or to ask them to keep records over a series of short periods). An extensive discussion of these problems and of experiences in various countries with various methods, plus an extensive bibliography, was prepared by Robert Pearl as part of a proposed design for a continuous consumer expenditure survey (rotating panel) in the United States.[31]

Actually the experience is rather inconclusive, for one trades a smaller error variance (and perhaps less bias) with short period reporting for a larger sampling variance at least between families. Indeed, one cannot add up expenditure reports given for different periods and then look at the distribution of total expenditures, for although fifty-two times the average weekly expenditure is a good estimate of annual expenditure if one can eliminate seasonal bias, fifty-two times an individual's weekly expenditure is not a good estimate of his annual expenditure, nor is a distribution of such products a decent estimate of the distribution of annual expenditures. At least one major study did not consider this problem until the data were collected, probably because the objectives were not clearly spelled out and the focus had been on overall expenditure data for use in weighting cost of living indexes, rather than studies of interfamily differences.

The use of flows measured over short periods also exacerbates the problem of distinguishing between consumption, acquisition (purchase) and payment, and of trying to use one as an approximation for one of the others. The shorter the period, the more likely for the purchase to happen in one period, the acquisition (delivery) in another, the payment in a third, and perhaps the consumption in a fourth or over several periods.

In fact, it often turns out that diaries and records show less total expenditure than interview questions covering longer periods (and often more global groupings of expenditures). Most of the discussion is about telescoping, people getting tired of writing things down, etc., but it is entirely possible that some of the missing or shifted items were ambiguous as to just when they occurred, or as to which category they belonged to and, hence, were omitted.

One major technological possibility in this area, not used yet as we have pointed out in Chapter II, is to ease the load on the respondent and perhaps reduce the problem of his omitting items which do not fit the categories, by the machine coding of expenditures into categories. One expenditure study (Israel) let people put down just their expenditures in journal (list) form, but most of the others expect people to put them in categories, deciding whether telephone is utility or communication and transportation, and whether liquor for a company dinner is gifts, recreation, or consumption of liquor. Modern computers can store a very extensive English list of words with decisions as to the categories to which they belong. Only words missing from the machine dictionary would have to be hand-coded. Then the analysis of the data could be flexible as to where items were put. For instance, for trends one could put mortgage payments into expenditures, but for a more sophisticated analysis, the mortgage interest payments would go there, plus some fraction of the net equity in the house as imputed interest cost, while the rest of the mortgage payments would go into saving where they belong.

A major problem with expenditure surveys is the multiplicity of their purposes and the vast load they place on respondents. A reconsideration of the purposes might well lead to proposals for separate designs for each of several purposes, or at least some priority order among the various demands being put on the respondent.

If one were interested in getting short-run changes in consumption expenditures with details on categories, prices, and quantities, of secondary importance (or to be collected later after respondents get involved and motivated), then it might be useful to start with a sequence of topics which help the respondent understand the procedures. If one asked first only for cash receipts during a recent short period plus decrease (or increases treated as negative) of cash on hand, one could then explain that the sum represented what the family must have expended during the period. It would be an easy step then to ask about some expenditures which might have taken place which were not really expenses: money invested or loaned, use of expense account or gift money, investments in durables or home. After these corrections, the respondent should find it easy to remember fixed items like rent or installment payments or utilities, and large irregular items like trips, gifts, or repairs. Asking him to account for the rest presents him with a problem he has probably faced for himself and one which makes sense. Then, if he tries to build up from components the food, clothing, etc. expenses and they do not account for the total, he is motivated to search his memory for the missing items. But the expenditure total is reasonably accurate even if the allocation is not, and a repeated call for information on receipts since the last point in time, and change in cash, puts very little burden on the respondent.

If one then wanted to move toward saving estimates, one would have to ask about specific payroll withholdings, the value of the house and car (for depreciation estimates), and the details of any debt or insurance payments to separate insurance or interest costs or interest receipts from increases in equity (saving). And one would have to ask about financial investments—money put into or taken out of them and, if sales, whether there were capital gains.

The basic problem with the call for details of expenditures is that the ordinary person does not have all the information. As anyone knows who has tried to keep track of expenditures, they never add up to the correct total (receipts plus decrease in cash).

Surveys as Part of an Experimental Design

Whenever anything happens that may cause a change in people's attitudes or behaviors, the possibilities of securing revealing data from surveys are increased. Surveys before and after, particularly if they are with the same individuals, at least assure that one of the independent variables will change, whether it be the tax laws, the welfare laws, employment possibilities (if a plant shuts down, or opens), or some purposeful campaign by government or business designed to inform or convince people. Of course most such "experiments" are confounded, in the technical sense, both by other things which also just happen, and by the fact that most changes affect some people more than others (aside from their own responses). And being limited usually to one locality, such designs do not permit easy generalization.

There is also a possibility of designing such studies to cover a variety of areas where different things may happen.

As we pointed out in Chapter II, the situation is much better if the "treatments" or changes can be allocated to people or areas according to some experimental design, randomly, or better than randomly. There have been very few such experiments reported in the literature, though it seems likely that a certain amount of market research experimentation may never have been reported. One of the most intriguing such designs was in Taiwan where family planning educational and promotional programs were assigned, in varying intensity, to small districts, and the follow-up survey on the spread of information and acceptance covered the whole area, so it was possible not only to see what influence this program had locally but the spread of such influence to neighboring areas.[32]

One experiment allowed consumers to choose beef of various grades, all at the same price, and interviewed them later about how it tasted. They tended to select inferior grades because they had less fat, but their reports of taste correlated with the USDA quality ratings.[33]

There was one study of pricing and packaging of apples which used a very sophisticated Latin square design but no detailed data from the consumers. Another manipulated the price of milk.[34]

An elaborate attempt to compare those who moved into a housing project with those left behind, illustrated the difficulties: confounding in the selection of applicants, other events unevenly affecting people, etc.[35]

There is a great temptation to localize experimental studies in order to "control" over variables and reduce the variability of other forces. But such localization *increases* the possibility of some unique events particular to that area, spoiling the experiment and/or reducing its generalizability. It may well be better to take some probability sample of areas so that special local conditions are "randomized out," and indeed so that one can also study the effects of things that vary from area to area.

The design of experiments is a vast area of statistics which has gone through a great deal of development since R. A. Fisher's work, but the experience is frequently neglected or ignored when people first move from non-experimental designs to those which allow some manipulation. Or they make the other mistake of using such complex experimental designs that nothing about the results is firmly established. The subject is not simple and, since our concern is with the design of the surveys which accompany such designs rather than the designs themselves, we refer the reader to recent texts on experimental design.

The one thing that must always be kept in mind in experiments is that designing an experiment to test only one hypothesis is usually very inefficient and unnecessary. It may even be misleading if there are complex interaction effects present.

The focus of most "effects studies" has been more on the design of the programs whose effect was to be studied and their distribution over populations rather than on the surveys which determined the impact. A comprehensive investigation of the design of such studies in the communications industry reveals a good deal of poor design and also an overwhelming lack of significant effects, or impact of the media.[36]

The Use of Non-Survey Data about Individuals

Many successful research projects make use of non-survey as well as survey data for purposes of analysis. (All projects necessarily use non-survey data for purposes of sampling.) One basic reason for using non-survey data is that it may be useful for error control. The outside data may be more accurate than interview data. Where it is of equal accuracy it will still be valuable to have independent measurements of variables measured in the survey. It may be true that the outside data measure a construct which cannot be measured in a survey. The juxtaposition of the outside data and the survey data may be enlightening. It may be economical to add information from outside sources to the body of materials to be analyzed.

A study of attitudes toward government guarantees of employment found a correlation, other things considered, between support for such guarantees and the level of unemployment in the county several years earlier, even among those who had not experienced the unemployment themselves.[37]

From an analyst's point of view, there is nothing to be lost by increasing the information at his disposal. The only loss will be the trouble and expense of collecting the data. There are sometimes problems of confidentiality which limit access to non-survey data about individuals. Often, however, the real limitation is the lack of imagination and insight of the researchers. All that can be done here is to raise the subject, list some examples of possible sources of data, and suggest that on every project the question should be asked: Are there non-survey data which could be made available which would make a contribution to this research?

Examples of sources of such data include the following:

1. *Census data.* An area sample implies a sample of people located in a set of different areas which can be characterized using Census data for the block, tract, city, county, or other unit. It is a characteristic of an individual that he lives in areas with certain average income, racial composition, mix of types of housing, etc.

2. *Maps.* It will usually be possible to locate the place of residence of a person on a detailed map, and perhaps also to locate other places of importance to him. Measurements may be made, for example, of his journey to work.

3. *Observers.* The interviewer may observe characteristics of a location, or others may observe it. For example, professional appraisers may observe people's homes.

4. *Photographs.* The interviewer or other observer may photograph a dwelling and its surroundings, and the photograph may be used for analysis.

5. *Public records.* A variety of public records exist and may be consulted either for selecting a sample or for later collection of supplemental data. For example, there are records of real estate transactions, automobile registration, building permits.

6. *Special files.* Many files are kept by public and private organizations which may be made available for research under the proper conditions. They include police files of accidents, records of the Social Security Administration, records of sales, school records, records of people who have participated in some program or belong to some organization.

7. *Mail inquiries of those with access to records, or special knowledge about an area.* In a longitudinal study of income and income changes a simple mail form was sent to the directors of state unemployment compensation to be relayed to those in charge of unemployment compensation in selected counties (one for each selected county) asking for the unemployment rate, the hourly wage for casual unskilled labor, and the tightness of that casual labor market.

An important source of non-survey data is the interviewer herself. She saw the house and the neighborhood, even if she did not secure an interview, and having been interviewing in these areas for some time, is able to provide some rough data about the house values or rents in the neighborhood. She can report the kinds of structures, the size of the city, the distance to the nearest large city, etc. And where there is an interview, she can report such things as the race of the respondent (or his obvious color at least), the visual impact of the respondent and the interior of the dwelling, and who was present during the interview. In addition, she can provide a description of the situation and such other ancillary information that may help understand the answers to the structured questions. For instance, most surveys do not ask about emotional or physical disabilities but having a disabled or senile person in a household can affect a family's economic situation or make sense of otherwise unusual responses.

Design of Instruments and Interviewing Procedures

It may seem like putting the cart before the horse to discuss practice first, and the theory of interviewing second, but theory is built by testing it against reality in a series of revisions.[38] Following are some examples of the most obvious kinds of errors that are made in interviewing.

A common kind of mistake made in questionnaires is to ask "IFFY" questions. "If you had a million dollars, what would you do?" "If your taxes were cut ten percent, would you spend the money, and on what?" It is very tempting to do this because many study objectives are originally stated in this form, but it very seldom gets realistic responses, except in the rare cases where the phrase that comes after the "IF" is something a man has actually experienced in the past or expects to experience and can speak realistically about.

A second kind of bothersome question is the suggestive question. "Will you promise not to move your factory out of the state if we do not raise your property taxes?" People tend to give the answers that they are expected to give, particularly if they see some way in which it will benefit them.

In general, any question which asks the respondent to agree or disagree with something, tends to get more agreement than disagreement and, what is worse, the agreement comes from people of a particular sort—those who score high on scales of authoritarian personality and are less educated. It is necessary to balance questions. On the other hand, sometimes when people try to balance questions, they make them confusing. "Are you in favor of A or against A?" To this the respondent can reply, "Yes." Or, "Are you in favor of A or against B?"

There is a body of literature on response set, the most striking manifestation of which is the "acquiescence factor" just described, a tendency to agree with statements rather than disagree. This tendency is correlated with low education and high ratings on an authoritarian personality scale, so misinterpretations and substantial biases are possible.[39]

Then there is a type of questions known as "flabbergasters" which are long, complicated, and nonunderstandable. A classic example is a thirteen line question asking farm managers whether they used mostly inductive or deductive logic. It was actually used in a study of farm management and followed by a series of questions on which of these thinking methods was most natural, can you use one method without using the other, what proportion of your thinking is like the first method, what proportion of your thinking is like the second method, then could you give me an example of the first method, etc. The one thing that was done in this sequence that does make some sense is the check-up question asking a person for an example. It is often useful to ask for details, or for an example in order to be sure the general answer was meaningful. If a man says he reads a lot of magazines, he ought to be able to name a few of them. If he says he plans his vacations far in advance, he ought to be able to say something about his next vacation.

There is a general technique often used in questionnaires to determine both the salience and importance of the reason for doing something. It might be described as the "funnel technique." One starts with a series of very general questions about what is important or why in a certain area and gradually focuses on the thing one is really after. The final question might be, "Well, does the interest rate really have any effect on this?" If the respondent only mentions the interest rate at that point, you know it is not very salient, and you have doubts about its importance. On the other hand, it can be non-salient and still be important. He might say, "Oh yes, that's the most important thing of all. . . . I just didn't bother to mention it." Indeed, studies asking people what is necessary for a good diet finds people frequently failing to mention milk altogether because they spend all their time talking about leafy green vegetables and fresh fruit.

Then there are questions that threaten people, "Do you worry?" To which they often answer, "I'm not supposed to worry." And questions which have an indefinite comparison involved, "Is the world better?" Are you the kind of guy who worries?" "How is your wife?" All of which leave the respondent, if he is smart, with a feeling that he should reply: "Compared with what?"

The real problem with much questionnaire design, particularly mail questionnaires, is that people who designed them have never really tried them on a live victim and watched him squirm. Even with a mail questionnaire it is possible to let a man sit down and fill it out while you stand there listening to him complain, and noticing the questions where he has to hesitate for a long time.

Validity studies are extremely expensive and complex. They are really only worth doing if there are some fairly explicit hypotheses or real alternative procedures to be used. Methodological studies without validity data similarly are very complicated and often tell very little about "WHY" the particular results appeared. Consequently, one should think carefully about the kind of pretesting and pilot study work that goes on in a survey. It may be far more important to spend time developing the best instrument, than designing a fancy experiment to test various things without much evidence as to what might work and what might not, or any real willingness to shift the design depending on what happens. It is quite crucial for the researcher, himself, actually to take an interview or two, just to see how the process goes and discover how difficult it is to ask some questions. Sometimes a fairly small number of pretest interviews is enough to show that some attitude or event being examined is so rare in the population that it is hardly worthwhile asking about in a representative sample.

On the other hand, it is *not* possible in a pretest to *prove* that some questions are not good, because people will answer even when they do not have a real attitude or opinion. In political behavior studies, researchers are concerned with the possibility that they may get a substantial fraction of the sample for whom a question is either meaningless or uninteresting, the answers forming a random distribution. The rest of the people may be giving meaningful answers, which should correlate with other things and predict their behavior. But in analyzing the data, how does one distinguish the meaningful replies from the meaningless ones? Perhaps the best way is to collect additional information on people's information level and their interest level in the areas being talked about. Then one can analyze separately the informed, interested people.

Sometimes it is a question whether the respondent understands what the issue is. One could ask people whether they believed in the Mosaic Authorship of the Pentateuch. The fundamentalists would know exactly what was meant—you wanted to know whether they believed that Moses wrote the first five books of the Bible. On the other hand, you could ask perfectly understandable questions where some respondents really do not care, like, "What is your opinion of the XYZ corporation?" The person may not really have *any* opinion of the XYZ corporation, so he will give you a random response or his notion of what the interviewer wants.

A great deal can be learned in pretesting and development work. Hopefully one will end up with an instrument to which people respond, which they seem to understand and enjoy, and which does not take too long.

There is a kind of a natural time period for Americans—one hour. When an interview runs longer than that, the interviewer gets nervous, talks fast, and does not allow the respondent enough time to talk. Indeed, she may get a refusal at the doorstep, if she is unable, with confidence, to tell the man he is going to enjoy the interview and that it will not take very long. There are very few refusals once the interview is started, but that does not mean that length is not important, because length *is* correlated with refusals at the beginning. It takes pretesting to find out what the length really is, but pretests usually run faster than real interviews. When she does not dare take a chance of losing the interview, the interviewer has to spend a little more time on developing and maintaining rapport. Consequently, pretest interviews usually underestimate the length of time the real interviews will take. There are articles and books on interviewing, ranging from cook-book descriptions of details to theoretical discussions of the process.

In fact, a great deal of what is known about good techniques is not in the published reports. One can tell a great deal about the quality of an interview from the ease or difficulty in coding it, from interviewers' reports, and from the correlations which should exist among variables. Ambiguous questions are difficult to code, threatening questions usually result in no answer or an uncodable answer, double-barreled questions lead to dichotomous answers—some people answering one part, some the other. Questions forcing the respondent to accept the researcher's definitions of some complex concept of economic measure produce enough marginal interviewers notes, or replies inconsistent with other information in the interview, to raise doubts about what is really being answered. A major advantage of the fixed question-open answer technique is that the dropping jaw when a flabbergasting question is asked, can be reported by the interviewer.

Some other generalizations have come to be accepted by those with extensive experience in interviewing: People's views of themselves are subject to all kinds of distortions and distorted again by the impression they have of what the interviewer approves or expects. Furthermore, their statements about themselves in general terms do not agree with the impression derived by asking about explicit past behavior. For instance, questions about whether the respondent liked new products and bought them early or waited until others had tested them, and whether he thought most new products were good rather than just a way to get one's money, did not correlate with an index of reported actual use of new products.[40]

Questions need to be simple, brief, and focused. People have difficulty keeping long questions in their minds, particularly those which seek to redefine a concept to suit the investigator: "Do you have any debts—I mean debts to institutions on which you make regular payments that include interest or revolving accounts, but not debts to friends?" Faced with such a question, the respondent, who may think of installment credit as buying something bit by bit, not as a debt at all, may think only of the one hundred dollars he owes his uncle as a real debt, is asked to restructure his whole view and language. It may take longer, and require more questions, but it is ultimately easier on the respondent and provides better information, to ask a series of short explicit questions from which the concept can be built. Sometimes this requires asking a sequence of questions to determine in which category some set of payments belongs.

A concrete example, with both good and bad aspects, may help. The two pages reproduced here are from a panel study of changes in family well-being.

(ASK EVERYONE)

G22. How much do you (FAMILY) spend on the food that you use <u>at home</u> in an average <u>week</u>?

$_____ PER WEEK

G23. Do you have any food delivered to the door which isn't included in that?

[ ] YES ──► G24. How much do you spend on that food? $_____ per _____
                                                                (WEEK, MONTH)

[ ] NO (GO TO G25)

G25. How about alcoholic beverages -- how much do you (FAMILY) spend on that in an average <u>week</u>?

$_____ PER WEEK   [ ] NONE (GO TO G27)

G26. Is that included in the food bill?   [ ] YES   [ ] NO

G27. Do (any of) you smoke cigarettes?

[ ] YES   [ ] NO (GO TO G30)

G28. About how many cigarettes do you (FAMILY) smoke in a day or week?

_____ per _____
(CIGARETTES, PACKS, OR CARTONS)   (DAY, WEEK)

G29. Is that included in the food bill?   [ ] YES   [ ] NO

G30. Do you (or your family) get meals at work or at school?

[ ] YES   [ ] NO (GO TO G34)

G31. About how much do all these meals cost you (FAMILY) in an average <u>week</u>?

$_____ PER WEEK   [ ] NOTHING, FREE
                                  (GO TO G33)

G32. Were any of these meals free, or at reduced cost?

[ ] YES   [ ] NO (GO TO G34)

G33. About how much do you think these free meals saved you last year -- was it about $25, $50, $100, $200, or what?

[ ] ABOUT $25   [ ] $50   [ ] $100   [ ] $200   [ ] OTHER _____
                                                                (SPECIFY APPROX. AMT.)

G34. About how much do you (FAMILY) spend in an average <u>week</u> eating out, <u>not counting</u> meals at work or at school?

$_____ PER WEEK

G35. Did you (FAMILY) raise any of your own food during 1968, or do any canning or freezing?

[ ] YES   [ ] NO (GO TO G37)

> G36. About how much did that save you in 1968 -- was it about $25, $50, $100, $200, or what?
>
> [ ] ABOUT $25   [ ] $50   [ ] $100   [ ] $200   [ ] OTHER _____
>   (SPECIFY APPROX. AMT.)

G37. Did you (FAMILY) get any help buying your food with government food stamps (commodity stamps)?

[ ] YES   [ ] NO   [ ] NOT ASKED: FAMILY CLEARLY INELIGIBLE

                     (GO TO G41)

> G38. How much would you say that saved you (FAMILY) in an average <u>month</u>?
>
> $_____PER MONTH (GO TO G41)
>
> (IF   G39. Tell me how you use the stamps. _____
> DON'T
> KNOW)   _____
>
>   _____
>
>   G40. How much do you pay for the stamps?
>
> $_____ per _____

G41. Did you (FAMILY) get any (other) free food during 1968?

[ ] YES   [ ] NO (GO TO G43)

> G42. About how much would you say that was worth in 1968 -- was it about $25, $50, $100, $200, or what?
>
> [ ] ABOUT $25   [ ] $50   [ ] $100   [ ] $200   [ ] OTHER _____
>   (SPECIFY APPROX.
>   AMOUNT)

(ASK IF 2 OR MORE PEOPLE IN FU -- OTHERWISE TURN TO H1, PAGE 21)

G43. How many days a week does the family sit down and eat the main meal of the day together?

_____

The study design called for an estimate of family food consumption, but could devote only a few minutes to it:

G22 starts with what the respondent may know best—the weekly bill at the market, though it does force a definition (at home) on him and ask him for an average week, which may be biased.

But people may easily forget the milk bill, or other extras, so G23-24 asks about that, and whether it is included in the first figure given. Again G23 is not an easy question because it is double-barreled—the answer is yes only if two things are true: there is food delivered to the door, *and* it was not included.

And people may get their beer and cigarettes at the supermarket and forget that they are included in the weekly bill. Hence, the next series asks about them. We ask about number of cigarettes, and in editing we use data on cigarette taxes and prices to calculate dollars, differently in different states.

Again a strategy decision was made to exclude cigars and other tobacco products, because they are less common and less likely to be bought in food stores. And we also excluded cleaning supplies and other non-food items which may have been included because they would not vary much between families and would be difficult to separate anyway.

Then, people may pay for food at work or school, so the next sequence asks about that. But since we are after food consumption, not merely expenditures, a sequence asks about free or subsidized meals. To save the respondent from unnecessary work, the savings from such subsidies are asked in Question G33, which informs the respondent that we only want a rough estimate. After all, these items will be added to a much larger amount and need not be more precise than those other amounts.

When we come to eating out in restaurants it is necessary (G34) to make the respondent follow our definitions and not double-count by including the cost of meals at work or school again. Some such defining of terms is often unavoidable.

While only a few families grow their own food or get it free or with government food stamps, the amounts may be so substantial that we must ask about them, particularly in this study which oversampled the poor.

The question about raising food or preserving it (G35) again adds the phrase about canning or freezing so the respondent knows it is included, and it is followed by a question on amount which gives the respondent an easy selection, rather than the difficult job of estimating an exact amount.

In asking about amounts saved through the use of government food stamps (G37), we use a month rather than a week, knowing that the administrative procedures make this a more appropriate period. We could have asked how much the respondent paid for the stamps and how much food they got with them. We elected to use a single question for those who can say what the difference was, but ask the others for details. One reason for this procedure is that asking for amounts spent on stamps would have confused the respondent who had already included that in his food expenditures earlier, whereas the extra saving was not included.

Finally there was a general question on other free food, the interviewer using the "other" where appropriate. Such "mop-up" questions are common.

Similar problems of clearing up definitions arise with rent where it may be necessary to find out whether the utilities are included and, if not, how much they are. Or if you want rent exclusive of utilities, you would ask how much they were when they were included, so you could subtract them. And it might be necessary to ask whether the place was rented furnished or not.

The realism of people's replies can often be assessed by asking for details, or examples, or evidence of information or activity. If a man claims to be looking for work, questions about where he has applied may be useful, or questions about how much he expects to earn, or what kinds of jobs are available.

Evaluative questions are still more difficult. The respondent needs some standard of comparison: a question from the same panel study was:

Is there public transportation within walking distance of here?
[ ] YES   [ ] NO—go to Question _____

↓

Is it good enough so that a person could use it to get to work?

While vague, this sequence still provides an evaluation in the relevant framework, and perhaps more relevant than one would get by asking for actual frequency and directions and *assuming* which situations allowed people to ride public transportation to work. The open answer may pick up a number of unsuspected reasons why it is not good enough—though they should not be coded because this is volunteered information. If one suspected a variety of reasons and wanted quantification, it would be necessary to ask "WHY" to those who replied "NO" to the second question.

In asking respondents to rate themselves, some pairing, selected so that substantial numbers place themselves on each side, is helpful: "Are you the kind of person who plans his life ahead all the time, or do you live more from day to day?"

Sometimes it is useful in clearing up what is to be included to read off a reminder list, but, while this increases the chance of any item in the list being included, it may well lead to poorer reporting of items not explicitly on the list. A broader definition of the category, with a repeating of "Anything else?" until the reply is "NO," may do better, unless the list is limited and complete.

The wording of individual questions and the procedures used in the field are not all that matters. Certain general procedural suggestions follow: The sequence and structure of the interview matters. It is customary to start with easy,

inoffensive and, hopefully, even interesting things, and work up to the more difficult or sensitive items. On the other hand, the early questions should suggest
the general topic area for the interview, or else the later transitions will be difficult and seem like trickery. There should be some variety or change of pace.
Respondents seem to like to be given something to hold, or to have some short-
answer questions in between those which may take thought and require extensive answers. On the other hand, they resist things which seem to test them,
questions to which there are right or wrong answers. Yet if tests of information
or ability are to be given, it seems best to be frank as to what they are.

When there are transitions to a new aspect of the subject, or a new subject,
some transition statement is often useful, but it cannot be very long. Remember
that the interviewer is supposed to read everything word for word. It is very difficult to read more than a few lines to someone, and the respondent doesn't want
a long justification anyway, just a warning that some different questions are
coming.

As we shall see later, the motivation of the respondent is crucial. He will
sense the interviewer's enthusiasms and dedication, and that helps; but the more
the interviewer can provide emotional rewards, indications that the respondent is
doing a good job, the better. There may be indirect rewards that motivate some
sophisticated respondents with broad horizons, e.g., contribution to science, or
the possibility of receiving a report about how others respond to the same questions, or assurance that people like him are being properly represented in the results, etc., but the pleased reaction of the interviewer and the sense that he is
helping her do her job properly are probably more motivating for most people.

The archives of any survey center are full of stories about situations which
no structured questionnaire could handle properly: unrelated missionary ladies
living together in Christian communism sharing everything, hippy communes
with rotating and uncertain occupancy, the man who spent more than his income
on additions and repairs because the gasoline company bought his lot and moved
his house for him providing him with a large capital gain, or the man with fifteen
Cadillacs because he was going into the limousine rental business.

The number of objectives reflected in a questionnaire should be severely
limited to those essential to the study design. The most common fault of anyone's first study is to include too much. No questions should be included because "it would be interesting to know." A good study design, with each question linked to some specific objective, will soon tell whether some variables are
represented by too many different questions, and others by too few or none.
The problem becomes particularly acute when one wants to measure attitudes or
personality dispositions, and has available extensive scales developed and used
with captive audiences of college students or paid subjects. In fact, there is usually some subset of items which correlates well with the total. It is also frequently
necessary to select items that still have some face validity or appropriateness to a

voluntary interview situation with a wide range of ages and education levels.

A general principle in questionnaire design is to postpone to later stages anything which can be postponed. For instance, if one is asking about components of income, so long as the questions are reasonably well designed to avoid double counting or omissions, there is little point in asking the interviewer to add total income and check the result with the respondent. Interviewers, focused on maintaining rapport with a respondent, frequently make mistakes in addition, and respondents, not knowing what the total should be anyway in many cases, will agree with the number the interviewer reports back, even if it is added up incorrectly.

Similarly, precoding, or arranging questionnaire format to make direct keypunching easy, or having the interviewer mark little boxes that can be read by a machine like a test-scoring machine, all increase the interviewer's work, lead to errors, and save relatively little cost. What is worse, if the interviewer marks the wrong box, there is no way to find it out, but direct coding and keypunching *can* be checked for reliability, and reforms instituted if needed. Paper is cheap, particularly when several thousand questionnaires are to be printed, and good open format with space for comments is likely to ensure that every question is read, comments noted, and skip-sequences properly used.

Redundancy is also helpful. Complex sequences where some respondents answer one set of questions, some another, are aided both by boxes and indentations, and by explicit instructions at the answer boxes of any question which may lead to a skip, telling the interviewer where to go. The interviewer should never have to read any long statement or instruction before deciding what to do next. If it is necessary for her to recall later whether the respondent is married, then one can instruct her to check one of two boxes (married, not married), each of which is followed by an instruction where to go.

In some cases, one group is asked one set of questions, another group a set which is partly different. In this case it is frequently best to print all questions in both sections. Again, paper is cheap, and a full sequence of questions in each section may be important.

A general issue which arises in many areas is how direct and blunt to be about things. If one wants to know whether people are thinking of spending a lot of money in the near future, one can focus on explicit purchase plans, or ask more indirectly about their expectations about their own and the country's economic future and whether the present seems like a good time to buy things. On the surface the more explicit questions may seem safer, but in practice the more open questions are often better (including more open questions about plans to spend in the next twelve months *or so,* rather than shorter-run intentions).[41] One reason is that the more explicit one gets the more some relevant things might be omitted because they were not asked about or did not fit neatly into any one category. The experience with detail varies. One case trying alternative methods secured larger total expenditure reports (presumed better) using more detailed questions.[42]

On the other hand, a very detailed set of questions about both sources and purposes of consumer debt secured less total debt than somewhat more condensed questions in surveys in a repeated series of national studies (Surveys of Consumer Finances).

A similar issue arises in attempting to measure people's basic predispositions (personality types) or goals. One can think of a continuum from very vague projective questions asking what others, or most people, etc. want or feel, at one extreme, to very explicit questions about actual behavior in relevant situations, at the other. In between are other alternatives: asking respondent for a self-assessment, asking for attitudes which may reveal his goals or motives, asking for more specific attitudes or reactions in situations calculated to be revealing. Experience and opinions vary. One major study concluded:

"Our own experience with projective methods as a means of getting richer data on opinions was anything but successful. . . . Rather, it was our experience that the best method of getting richer material about a man's opinion was by the rather naive and direct device of asking him to talk about those things that mattered most to him as far as the world was concerned and then to direct him from general values to the specific topic under discussion."[43]

It may seem that goals and attitudes should not be very important in economic surveys, but economists concerned with the real world are seeing the need:

"Decisions must relate to initial conditions and expectations of the future. And here is where the most intractable difficulties develop. It is very difficult to find a stable relation between expectations of the future and observable past variables or initial conditions. Changes in taxes, government expenditures, monetary policy, consumer demand, and income may all have quite different effects as they relate differently to expectations of the future. Analysis and prediction of business cycles will remain sharply limited in their power as long as this nexus from past to present to future is so incompletely specified.[44]

The choice of broader or more explicit questions and of questions more personally or more generally oriented involves, as usual, a trade-off. The more personal, the more likely the question is to arouse defenses or the need to preserve some self-image, or the desire to please the interviewers; while the more impersonal, the more likely the responses to be not the specific feelings of the respondent.

Similarly, the more general the reference, the less it may reveal about the respondent, but the more explicit the situation he is asked to talk about, the more likely that that situation is not relevant for *that* respondent. It is tempting to argue that a series of explicit reports on the respondent's own past behavior, in situations calculated to reveal his goals or personality or attitudes, is best, but each of the specific situations may be irrelevant for some respondents (never happened, etc.) or his behavior may have been dominated by some other constraint or consideration.

For example, take risk avoidance. One can ask individuals to characterize themselves as cautious or bold, but people may well have distorted images of themselves. What is worse, they are rating themselves against some unknown and probably variable norm. The attempts to devise scales that are "self-anchoring" may or may not succeed. Alternatively, one can ask some attitudinal questions about specific kinds of risks and what it is best to do. Or one can ask what the individual really does: Does he fasten his seat belts, carry medical insurance, lock his car, etc. But he may not have a car, or it may not have seat belts, or he may get free medical care as a veteran, or be unable to get medical insurance. One way out of these difficulties is to select a set of such behaviors and neutralize the scoring for those for whom that item was irrelevant or constrained, hoping that at least some will apply to any one respondent. Optimal neutralization requires assigning to the irrelevant cases the mean score among those for whom the item is relevant, but even rough procedures assigning some mid-value will go a long way. An index can then be created and if it works (helps explain other behavior), one can dissect it to see which components do the most good.

Some studies have tried both the attitudinal and the behavioral approach to assessing motives and goals. When the two scales do not correlate with one another, however, it still becomes necessary to select one, and the authors find themselves more comfortable with behavioral revelations of goals or attitudes than with self-evaluations.

The Logical Sequence of Steps in Questionnaire Development

There is a logical order of steps to be taken in the development of a questionnaire or any research instrument. These steps are the preparation of a series of written statements as follows:

1. General Objectives
2. Specific Objectives and Analysis Plan
3. Specifications of Data
4. Questionnaire

We will consider each in turn. The general objectives are part of the basic re-search design, which should set forth the purpose of the project and the means by which that purpose is to be achieved.

The specific objectives should flow directly from the general objectives, but they will be much more detailed. They should include an outline of the strategy which is to be followed in analysis. For example, it might be stated that major dependent variables in the analysis will include Y-1 and Y-2, and that the predictors will include especially X_1, X_2, etc.

The specifications of data represent a list of variables to be measured with an indication of any special requirements or problems in regard to each. For ex-ample, precise measurement of variable Y_1 might be of critical importance, while X_1 may be peripheral in terms of the objectives as developed, and a rough ap-proximation may be adequate. When the questionnaire itself is developed, it should be possible to refer back to the Specifications of Data and the Specific Objectives for each question. Conversely, each Specific Objective and Specifica-tion of Data should have its counterpart in the questionnaire.

There is a tendency on the part of many investigators to go directly from a statement of objectives, even a statement of General Objectives, to a question-naire. This tendency is natural because the investigator must always have in the back of his mind the thought that he is planning a survey, and, ultimately, a sur-vey consists in asking people questions. What objectives are possible to achieve depends on what question can be asked. In effect, he keeps the intermediate con-siderations in his head.

There is no necessity, however, for the chronology of the development of a questionnaire to match the logical sequence from the general to the specific as outlined above. An investigator may do well to consider in detail what questions he can ask, and have satisfactorily answered, before he freezes his statement of specific objectives. Yet, there is often a good deal to be gained by working out the full logical sequence at *some* time before the questionnaire is complete. Errors of omission can be detected. Questions without objectives can be elimi-nated. Importance can be assessed, so that it does not turn out that major vari-ables are measured in a casual way while peripheral topics fill the questionnaire. It may also be useful to set down on paper what is in the mind of the principal investigator, to permit its examination by others. Later on it may be useful to attempt to label the specific objectives of *each* question.

The reader should not get the idea that we know conclusively about the relative merits either of various modes of data collection or about the best meth-ods of asking the questions. A great deal of the published findings have been on small special groups, with a wide variety of techniques, of interviewer training, *and* of subject matter. There is just enough disparity in the results that do exist to cast doubt on their generality. It seems likely that the quality of any data col-lection procedure depends on the whole mix of procedures, that *everything* must be right if the results are to be good, and that there are *combinations* that are right. For instance, a brief mail questionnaire using mostly check boxes, may work beautifully with simple and limited information easily accessible to the respondent. Telephone reinterviews, where the legitimacy of the study has been established by mail or personal visit, may be excellent for questions on what has changed, or on current expectations and attitudes.

It is our general impression that not enough time and energy goes into developing instruments in most studies, but the problem may be less in the level of investment than in its direction. For proper improvement, perhaps a better theory is more important than a lot of rules developed from experience.

The Theory of Interviewing

The central problem of data collection in surveys is how to obtain the information required by the objectives of the project from the individuals selected by the sampling procedures. A simple view of the problem is that all that is required to obtain information from people is to ask them whatever one wants to know. Experience has shown that this view may be too simple. Sometimes investigators obtain the data they require easily, but sometimes they find themselves in difficulties, either because they cannot obtain information, or because they mistrust the information obtained. The purpose of a theory of interviewing is to develop generalized knowledge of the interviewing process to guide the development of technique and to improve the quantity and quality of data.

Most of the relevant theory represents applications of theory developed in psychology, social psychology, or sociology. Most of the work in the field has been done by members of those disciplines. There are several ways to look at the interviewing process which have been emphasized by different investigators. These approaches are not mutually exclusive. In spite of the overlap, it may prove useful to look at the interview from each stance in turn.

Focus on the Interviewer: In much of the work on interviewing, especially the earlier work, the focus has been on the interviewer. This emphasis is understandable. The process of data collection by personal interview consists essentially in selecting and training a group of interviewers and sending them out to collect data. If they are carefully selected and well trained, and if they go about their work conscientiously, one might suppose they would do the job satisfactorily. If the results leave something to be desired, then one should re-examine interviewer selection and training, and devise checks to prevent sloppy work or cheating.

There have been a number of studies which have investigated whether the interviewers' own opinions influence their report. There are several such studies mentioned by Hyman[46] in his monograph on interviewing written in 1954. The evidence concerns such matters as accuracy in recording opinions. For example, Fisher found some evidence that interviewers tend to record more material which conforms with their own attitudes on controversial issues.[47] There is also evidence that interviewers vary in their probing habits. Those interviewers who probe fully may not be evenly distributed over the sample.[48] Hence, certain groups of respondents will be better reported. Hyman also reports a study of the effects of whether interviewers themselves held the majority opinion on how they pre-coded answers to opinion questions when the neutral category was omitted, so that respondents had to be classified as leaning either pro or con or as "don't know." Those interviewers holding the majority view pushed answers in that direction. Those holding the minority view pushed answers to "don't know.[49] Thus, there is evidence that interviewers' opinions can influence results, at least to some degree, even when there is no gross distortion.

Hyman was not overly impressed with the importance of these effects in well-conducted surveys, and argued that the beliefs of the interviewer *about the respondent* may be more important than what the interviewer herself thinks about matters of public controversy. The interviewer, he argues, may develop a stereotyped view of a particular respondent. This stereotype may make the interviewer insensitive to any aspects of the respondent's attitudes or behavior which do not fit the stereotype. Thus, the interviewer may make systematic errors of probing or of recording certain sorts of material which have nothing to do with his own personal opinions. Note that this type of error could apply to any kind of question. For example, an interviewer might decide (prematurely) that a respondent was a poor man, and neglect to ask him questions about his ownership of some kind of assets even though the questionnaire included such questions. Or she might decide that a widow with small children could not take a job, so not ask about whether the respondent was looking for work.

Hyman did not have great success, however, in demonstrating the practical importance of this mechanism. The most reasonable conclusion seems to be that it may operate in some situations, but is probably not serious. Methods of control would include training interviewers to ask questions conscientiously and asking interviewers to write down answers, not precode them into categories. In designing questionnaires to prevent the development of situations in which interviewers are forced to ask questions which obviously do not apply to some respondents, there should be reasonable rules for the omission of questions, rules which can be insisted upon.

In addition to their opinions and attitudes, interviewers are members of social groups. They may be characterized by sex, race, social status, and the like. There is evidence that *disparities* in group membership between interviewer and respondent may be important: they will be considered in the discussion of the interview as a social situation. But it is much less clear that *in general* members of certain social groups make better interviewers. Minimum standards of education, intelligence, and social skills seem to be what are required, as will be discussed under administration of field work. Efforts to discover measurable characteristics or combinations of characteristics which will predict success in interviewing in social surveys have not been successful.

The research on this subject has been handicapped by lack of satisfactory criterion variables. A leading study is that by Axelrod and Cannell.[50] They used three measures of effectiveness: ratings by field supervisors, by office administrative staff, and by coders. The latter rated individual interviews. From the ratings of a number of her interviews, ratings of each interviewer were constructed. Note that not one of these three groups was in possession of data on accuracy of response. They did have data on such matters as satisfactory completion of assignments and completeness of the reports submitted.

The predictors used in the project were standard socio-economic background variables and three well-known psychological tests: the Strong Vocational Interest Inventory, Kerr-Speroff Empathy Test, and Guifford-Zimmerman Temperament Survey. The population studied was interviewers employed by the Survey Research Center—that is, a group already presumably screened to remove obvious misfits. The analysis did reveal some differences in the measures of performance associated with difference in scores on the predictors, but the differences were small. It may well be that it is the *combination* of interviewer and respondent characteristics that matters.

Others concerned with the selection of interviewers have reported similar types of work. Sudman of the National Opinion Research Center has published a systematic scheme for rating interviewers, which indicated the type of evaluation which can be made.[51] His system is as follows:

Errors Forming Criteria for Rating of Interviewers

Error Weights	Type of Error
	1. Failure to probe initial response
5	a. Don't know
4	b. Vague answer
5	c. Irrelevant answer
5	d. Uncodeable
	2. Use of
1	a. Dangling probes
1	b. Unpreceded probes
	3. Improper probing
3	a. Accept partial answers
4	b. Use encouraging probe without using clarifying probes

Errors Forming Criteria for Rating of Interviewers—Continued

Error Weights	Type of Error
2	c. Accept first clear answer without probing for additional ideas.
5	d. Probe irrelevant answer instead of probing for a relevant answer, which results in irrelevant response.
5	e. Leading probes
1	4. Unexplained changes of code or answers (including erasures)
	5. Circling errors
5	a. Contradictions
1	b. Failure to code reply when codeable comment exists
5	c. Multiple coding
1	6. Answer recorded in wrong place
	7. Failure to complete
5-10	a. Omitting any part of classification. If race, sex, age, or marital status is omitted along with other omission, score in 10.
5	b. Enumeration and/or sampling table.
5	8. Evidence of paraphrasing (Always check other interviews. Give per interview, not per question.)
1	9. Unclear parenthetical notes
	10. Omission and superfluous notes
5	a. Omitting questions or portions of questions
1	b. Excess questions (or portions of questions)

This system of rating interviewers obviously rests on close scrutiny of completed interviews.

Another recent study of interviewer performance in studies of income and saving has been reported by Hauck and Steinkamp.[52] They attempted to relate characteristics of the interviewer to measures of performance in a series of panel surveys. Their results are of little interest for present purposes because of difficulties in obtaining a sufficient number of cases in which reported data could be checked for validity, but they propose methods of measuring performance which are of interest. They suggest that it is useful to distinguish four aspects of performance:

1. *Contact rate.* The contact rate measures the percentage of addresses in which the interviewer makes contact with a person eligible to be interviewed.
2. *Response rate.* The response rate they define as the ratio of the number of interviews to the number of contacts.
3. *Completeness rate.* The completeness rate for a given item under investigation is the percentage of interviews with respondents known to have the item (e.g. the percent known to own a particular asset) in which the item is reported.
4. *Accuracy rate.* The accuracy rate is measured for a given financial item for those interviews in which the item is reported. It measures the percentage of such interviews in which the reported magnitude is within some predetermined range from the true value, say, plus or minus ten percent.

Their proposed distinction between "contact rate" and "response rate" differs from conventional usage and will not be adopted here. As previously discussed, the distinctions among types of non-response are difficult to make and the most useful distinction is that between refusal and other forms of non-response. But the "completeness rate" and "accuracy rate" would be most useful measures. They amount to a method of breaking down total response error into two parts for purposes of analysis.

The U.S. Census Bureau has conducted extensive and well-designed studies of interviewer effects on the types of data collected in the Censuses of Population and Housing.[53]

Finally, the motivation of the interviewer, her belief in the importance of the study and the appropriateness of the instrument, must matter since there are large differences between studies in their refusal rates, and most refusals come before the respondent really knows what the study is about—certainly before he has heard the actual questions.

Focus on the Respondent: A second basic approach to the analysis of the interview is to focus attention on the respondent. One may seek to explain his response to the interviewing situation in terms of his perception of the situation and his motivations. In a sense this approach to the subject is indirect. The investigator cannot exert the degree of control over respondents that he can over interviewers. He must take his respondents as they are. Yet, he may hope to influence respondents through his control over those aspects of the interviewing situation which he *can* change.

For a respondent to participate in a survey at all, he must have some motivation to respond. In general, however, the motivation to respond is weak. A small pilot study reported by Cartwright and Tucker may illustrate the point.[54] They proposed to inverview sixty-three people from each of two parliamentary constituencies in London. A sample of names and addresses was drawn from the electoral register. Alternate respondents were sent a courteous note asking for their help in a study about people's health and the use of doctors and requesting that they return a form showing "which times you are most likely to be in and able to be interviewed." Only eleven percent replied giving suitable times to call, but fourteen percent wrote saying they did not wish to be interviewed. The pilot study was pushed through to completion, omitting those who had so requested, with a final response rate of eighty-two percent for those who had been sent no letter and only fifty-three percent for those to whom letters had been sent. The main study, when completed, had an eighty-six percent response rate. As this experience indicates, people's initial response to the idea of being interviewed is often unenthusiastic.

What, then, are the motives which may be aroused by an interview? It is usual to distinguish three broad groups of motives. People may respond to the content of the study or its stated purposes; they may respond to the sponsorship of the study; and they may respond to the social situation created by the presence of an interviewer. Their response may be positive or negative. Thus, the content of the study may interest them or may not be something they want to discuss; they may be sympathetic to the purposes of the study or they may be unsympathetic or suspicious; they may be positively disposed to the sponsor or research agency, or negatively disposed; they may respond positively or negatively to the social situation. In personal interviews, of course, the social situation involves the physical presence of an interviewer; in telephone interviews the interviewer is not physically present; and in self-administered procedures no interviewer is present and the social motives are altered or eliminated.

We note immediately that there is likely to be a dramatic contrast between the attitude of the respondent toward the topic of inquiry and the attitude of the investigators. The investigators are almost certain to be interested in the topic they are studying. Many respondents, however, may have paid little attention to the subject, and may be quite disinterested in it. They may even feel it is not appropriate to talk about.

The importance of variations in motivation toward a sponsor in explaining variations in willingness to respond may be illustrated by a study done for the League of Women Voters among its membership reported by Donald.[55] This study involved a questionnaire which covered nineteen pages, asked for 198 separate responses, and took an hour or more to fill out. It was, in a word, a formidable instrument. The procedure in data collection was sequential. First, a questionnaire was sent by mail to a sample of 2768 dues-paying members of the League. Second, a follow-up letter was sent to those who failed to reply. Third, a second letter and another copy of the questionnaire was sent. Fourth, personal telephone calls were made to those still not replying.

The response was as follows:

Responded to:	Percent of Sample	
First mailing	46.2	
Reminder letter	12.2	
Additional letter and questionnaire	8.8	77.3
Telephone call	10.1	
Non-response	22.7	
Total	100.0	

We may note, first, that a sixty-seven percent response rate was achieved entirely by mail, which is very high for so demanding a study. It appears that the average motivation to respond was high. Donald also made extensive comparison of the replies received at different stages. She found a strong tendency for those most involved with the organization to answer earlier. For example, officers of local chapters replied promptly. On the other hand a follow-up study showed that those who never turned in a questionnaire were often not involved at all, or barely involved. Half of the non-respondents were zero or marginal participators in the League.

Another example of a special group of respondents are the professionals, where both in Great Britain and in the United States, mail questionnaires have been used to secure information about their occupations and earnings, with high response rates (but declining if the survey is repeated several times).[56]

An extreme example of a situation in which people respond to sponsorship was reported by Boek and Lade.[57] They report a mail study undertaken for the Commissioner of Health of the State of New York among his own staff of 178 people. The commissioner was interested in what people said they would do in case of atomic attack. The staff had been given instructions about what to do—the study was directed to whether they accepted these instructions as practical guides to their personal planned behavior. The method of inquiry was to send to the staff members two items—a questionnaire, which was to be anonymous, and a postcard to be returned separately but at the same time as the questionnaire, which respondents were expected to sign, thus indicating that they had returned the questionnaire. The response rate was not quite one hundred percent—it seems the Commissioner did not fill out his own questionnaire, and somebody else was sick.

A mail questionnaire to Michigan deer hunters achieved a response rate in the nineties, perhaps because the hunters thought it might affect their chances of getting a special doe-hunting license, but also because they were interested in the subject. An intriguing study which mailed out a container into which respondents were to put their cigarette butts for a week before returning it, achieved a return rate above ninety percent.[58] Perhaps people liked the idea of having a portable ash tray.

Social Situation: There is evidence, however, that often it is the third type of motivation to respond which is most important, the motivation which arises out of the social situation created by the interviewer's presence. The experience of Cartwright and Tucker illustrates the point. As we have seen, when they wrote and asked for an appointment for a particular project, the response was often apathetic or negative. Yet, their main survey, with identical sponsorship and subject matter, reached a response rate of eighty-six percent. The personal presence of the interviewer made the difference. Similarly, Donald was able to obtain cooperation by telephone from people who had not responded to repeated approaches by mail.

Emphasis on the social aspects of interviews is also prominent in post mortem reports by respondents about the experience of being interviewed. This interpretation has been stressed by Cannell and Axelrod.[59] They sent a follow-up postcard to respondents on national sample surveys. Respondents were asked if they wanted a report, and a space was provided for comments. People's comments were primarily about the interviewer and their relation to the interviewer, not about the content of the study. Personal interviews in Detroit in which respondents were asked about their experience in the initial interview also led to comments about the interviewer, not the content. People almost always rated the interviewer as "friendly" in postcard follow-ups to personal interviews. In four such surveys, about eighty-five percent rated the interviewer as "very friendly."

Axelrod and Cannell also suggest that many people enjoy being interviewed. They interpret this reward to respondents as similar to the cathartic element in psychotherapeutic interviews. People often like to talk to someone who is friendly and supportive, interested in what they say, and who never criticizes them or disagrees with them. This sense of freedom to express one's self may be reinforced when the interviewer assures the respondent that his replies are anonymous.

The importance of the social aspect of the interview has been demonstrated indirectly by Gergen and Back. They start from a theory of aging, whose central theorem is that the transition from middle age to senescence is a process of progressive disengagement of the person from other members of society. Hence, they predict a lack of interest by older people in many topics and a lack of responsiveness to social pressure generally and social pressure from interviewers in particular.[60] They predicted specifically that older people would express fewer opinions and give more "no opinion" answers. Further, in expressing opinions they would avoid finer gradations and intermediate response categories and select undifferentiating or extreme answers. To test these ideas Gergen and Back analyzed an extensive body of material, primarily reports from a series of Gallup polls. The data supported the hypotheses for the most part. The one major exception was that among those with less than a high school education the tendency to express opinions rises rather than falls with age. (Perhaps, they suggest, because these people make up for low formal education as they age.) Measures of extremism and frequency of "no difference" replies do fit the hypotheses. The "no opinion" reply was more frequent for "old" than "middle aged" people for 38 of 46 items investigated, from four different surveys.

It is sometimes impossible to distinguish which motives operate in respondents, yet it may be possible to show that total motivation of respondents is important. Cannell and Fowler conducted a validity study in which they worked with a sample of hospital discharges and enjoyed access to the hospital records.[61] A subsample of respondents were asked to fill in a form left by the interviewer and mail it to the regional office of the Census Bureau. If the form was not returned in seven days, there was a mail follow-up. If that failed, a telephone call was made as a reminder, or a personal visit if the respondent had no phone. Cannell and Fowler argue that motivation of respondents must fall as one compares those who sent in the form on their own with those who required a mail reminder and with those who required a telephone or personal visit. They compare for these three groups the percent of known episodes not reported. The differences were substantial:

| | How the Reply Was Obtained | | | |
	First Mail Form	Second Mail Form	Telephone or Personal Visit	All
Percent of episodes not reported	13	15	22	16
Percent of hospital stays in which length of stay was correct	60	53	33	57
Number of hospital records	394	75	77	546

Focus on the Interaction Between Interviewer and Respondent: There is a substantial body of evidence that what happens in an interview may be influenced by major discrepancies between the group membership of interviewer and respondent. Within the United States the evidence is especially clear that racial differences are important, at least for some topics of investigation. There also seem to be differences in response attributable to discrepancies in social status, age, and sex. The importance of these discrepancies, however, seems to depend upon the topic of inquiry.

In his monograph on interviewing published in 1954 Hyman reviewed a series of studies on disparities in group memberships between interviewer and respondents.[62] The results were especially clear with regard to race. During World War II it was found by Stouffer that there were substantial differences in responses of Negro troops to Negro versus white interviewers. In 1952 the National Opinion Research Center conducted 1000 interviews with Negroes in Memphis, Tennessee. Half were interviewed by white, and half by Negro interviewers. There were large differences in response. The white interviewers tended to be given "acceptable" answers.[63]

Status differences can also be important. A study by Katz in a low-income area in Pittsburgh found differences in radicalism of response depending on whether the interviewer was middle class or working class.[64]

These projects were concerned with subject matter of little intrinsic relevance to economics. The importance of the relative status of interviewer and respondent was emphasized, however, by Hund in a study of business executives.[65] Hund personally conducted interviews at three levels of business executives in connection with two research projects. He reports a sharp difference in relative status of himself and his respondent which influenced the conduct of his interviews. At the highest level, the men were asked, not directed, to take part in the project. They did not submit passively to being interviewed. Hund was placed in an inferior position. One of the devices used seems to have been an insistence by respondents on maximum eye contact. He found it difficult to record the interview as it progressed. In thinking about this situation, it should be kept in mind that it is not easy to get cooperation at all at this level. At the middle level Hund felt he had rough equality of status, and at the third level, superiority, and he felt much more in control of the situation.

Ehrlich and Riesman have shown that the age and authority of the interviewer do influence the responses of adolescent girls.[66] They conducted a secondary analysis of data obtained in 1956 by Elizabeth Douvan in a study of girls undertaken for the Girl Scouts. On this project only female interviewers were used. The data analyzed concerned willingness to give "unacceptable" responses to projective questions concerning behavior of girls in relation to their parents and their evening social activities. The age of the interviewer did make a difference: older women (aged fifty-three or above) reported fewer unacceptable responses. More psychological measures of interviewer characteristics were available. "Ascendance" and "objectivity" of the interviewers also seemed to influence response. The highest percentages of unacceptable responses were obtained by women interviewers under fifty-two years of age with low scores on "ascendance" and "objectivity."

These findings do not apply directly to surveys on economic topics. They do suggest, however, that similar phenomena may be found there. It may be that the closest similarity will be to economic surveys in underdeveloped countries, which are discussed below.

Note the consistency between the above argument that people respond to the social aspects of the interview situation and the findings that the group memberships of interviewers sometimes influence responses.

Finally, while there is no solid evidence, there is reason to believe that respondents are interested in the results of some surveys and would like to know what others say to the same questions. Hence letters announcing that an interviewer will call often promise that a summary of findings will be sent to respondents. When offered an option, *many* ask for reports.

Another useful way of looking at the interview is to think in terms of interviewer and respondent as both having socially defined roles. The interviewer, according to this view, has a role into which she can be trained. The ideal, from the point of view of comparability on a project using several interviewers, is to develop a standardized pattern of behavior for interviewers so that each interviewer will obtain similar responses. The interviewer becomes a scientific measuring instrument. The more tightly the role of the interviewer is defined, the less reason will remain for variations in response among interviewers. If the respondent is precisely selected in advance, the questions are exactly specified, and probing is standardized, differences among interviewers are less probable.

Note that there is a conflict between an approach which emphasizes standardization of roles among interviewers and one which emphasizes the more subtle interviewing skills. The tendency in recent years has been toward standardization, at least in large-scale data collection. Role theory suggests the usefulness of role playing as a training device for interviewers. This technique is widely used.

Role theory also raises questions or role overload. There seem to be definite limits to the number of functions which interviewers can carry out successfully. The practical difficulties experienced by the Survey Research Center in getting interviewers to use the "half-open interval" technique to check for missing dwellings illustrate the point. (See Chapter III)

Respondents as well as interviewers have a role, and it is sometimes suggested that one of the most important jobs of the interviewer is to train respondents in that role. It is the general experience of survey organizations that once respondents start an interview they almost always carry through to the end of the interview. Experience on panel surveys is that people who are going to refuse to participate usually do so either before the first interview or before the second interview. Once the second interview is safely started, the chances are good for continuation for more interviews.

There are some people for whom the role of respondent is difficult or even impossible, but they are more likely to be found in underdeveloped countries.

Some may also consider an interview as a process of communication. From this viewpoint the central question is, what are the conditions under which effective communication will occur? It is not difficult to specify the logical requirements: (1) The respondent must understand correctly the questions which are being put to him. (2) The respondent must, himself, possess the information required. (3) The respondent must be able and willing to communicate the information. (4) The system of receiving and recording the information must function correctly. That is, in a personal interview the interviewer must hear correctly and write down correctly the answer as given: in a self-administered procedure the respondent must do the job correctly himself. Any one of these requirements may not be met.

(1) It is not easy to state questions precisely, and it is not sufficient for a question to be precisely stated for it to be precisely understood. Economists venturing into the conduct of surveys often underestimate the importance of this difficulty. Changes in a research procedure which do not change the logical content of questions may yet change the comprehension of the questions by respondents.

For example, Bauer and Meissner report the results of a mail survey of business enterprises in Germany.[67] They asked three questions only. These questions concerned changes in "basic" orders, changes in "re-orders," and changes in "total" orders, this month versus last month. Three answers were allowed for each: increase, no change, or decrease. Note that, since all orders must be basic orders or re-orders, some combinations of answers are logical impossibilities. It is not possible, for example, for each of the *types* of orders to increase while the total decreases. From July to December 1952 Bauer and Meissner used a format in which the three questions were printed on one page. They found 1.5 percent nonsense answers (of 198 replies). In 1953-1954 they printed the same question on two pages. They found 5.0 percent nonsense replies (of 765 replies). The inference seems reasonably safe that respondents had a better grasp of the meaning of the questions when they were printed on a single page.

Haberman and Elinson report a study in which separate personal interviews with husband and wife were taken with each of 645 marital pairs in New York City.[68] The study concerned "The Public Image of Mental Health Services," but it included a question on family income. Each respondent was shown a "flash card" which had printed on it sixteen income intervals identified with letters. Both weekly and equivalent yearly ranges defined each interval.

The question states:

> The figures refer to the total income of the entire family living here before any deductions, as for taxes or social security. Include income from all sources—wages and salaries of all family members, rents, pensions, etc.

Only 59.6 percent gave reports in the same interval, but on the average the reports were fairly close, with the median reported by the husbands $7377 and by the wives, $7179, or about $200 less. One aspect of the findings is of special interest in the present context: wives on the average reported *higher* total family income than husbands in those families in which the wife was working. The comparison of the two reports of income varies depending on the wives' working status as follows:

Comparison of Reports of Income for the Same Family	Wives' Working Status	
	Housewife	Some Occupation
Spouses the same	60.6%	57.9%
Husband's report higher than wife's	27.7	19.6
Wife's report higher than husband's	11.7	22.4
Total	100.0	99.9
Number of interviews	386	214

Thus, the wives' reports are higher than the husbands' in 22.4 percent of the families where the wife is employed compared to 11.7 percent where she is a housewife.

The question asked was perfectly explicit and even repetitive. It calls for income of the "entire family" and the wages and salaries of "all family members." Yet it seems highly probable that some husbands neglected to include their wives' incomes. It illustrates one of the problems of forcing a definition on the respondents, rather than asking the pieces and developing one's own measure.

Experience in asking income at the Survey Research Center has been similar. The remedy adopted has been to ask a separate additional question such as: "Does that include the income of everyone in the family?" Often enough, people then remember that there was an omission.

We repeat, it is difficult to communicate complex definitions all in one question. It may be more effective to start with a concept which comes easily to the respondent, and then correct or adjust it, step by step.

(2) Respondents may not have the required information, or they may be able to produce it only with some degree of difficulty. There are several possible reasons: (a) The information may be known to one family member but not to all. (b) The information may not be easily accessible to the respondent because he finds it related to something painful to think about—he has repressed it. This

possibility is more obvious for psychological inquiries in depth than for economic studies, but it may arise. (c) The information may not be easily accessible because it refers to something which the respondent has forgotten because it is remote in time, or because it is trivial to him.

To illustrate the importance of memory error we cite recent work done at the United States Census and reported by Barbara A. Powell.[69] She was concerned with reinterviews as a means of investigating the correctness of responses from initial interviews, an approach which has been developed extensively by the Census. She reports that a lag of three months between interview and reinterview is preferable to six months for reports of income and mobility, but that there is no difference for reports of ages, number of children, or children in school.

(3) The respondent must be able and willing to communicate the data. An interesting example of the difficulty which can arise in persuading respondents to communicate has been described by Jung.[70] He has been concerned with the problem of collecting reliable price data on goods and services for which the market price is different from the posted price, such as new automobiles. His basic method is to send out shoppers who, to be successful, must succeed in convincing salesmen that they are definitely in the market and will buy if the price is acceptable. The salesman is undoubtedly well informed about the price—the problem is to get him to state it. Jung has developed a complex standardized procedure which his shoppers follow. They pose as sophisticated shoppers. The routine involved includes: asking for a specific popular model with a standardized list of accessories; always rejecting the salesman's initial price as more than the customer had planned to pay and suggesting in reply a price approximately equal to the dealer's invoice; listening sympathetically to the complaint that this price was impossible; and then taking the next offer by the salesman as the market price. This system, Jung stresses, works only if the salesman is convinced the shopper will buy if the price is right; otherwise he may quote a "lowball" price which is lower than that at which he actually will sell.

There have been several investigations of the quality of interviewers' work in recording what takes place in an interview. The usual technique of investigation is to "plant" respondents, who are not known to the interviewers to be "stooges." Hyman has reported such a study done by the American Jewish Congress in cooperation with N.O.R.C.[71] For this study fifteen interviewers were hired, mostly with no experience. Each interviewed one to four "planted" respondents as well as actual respondents. There were fifty questions per interview, and an interviewer could make several errors per question. The study concerned race relations. At least one of the planted respondents, the "hostile bigot," was extremely difficult to interview. Under pressure, these inexperienced interviewers made mistakes. They averaged eight recording errors per schedule. They also made errors in asking questions—omitting questions or changing wording—averaging thirteen errors per schedule. And they committed thirteen probing errors, failures to probe when appropriate, or use of "bad" probes.

(4) Recording errors may be expected to increase in proportion to the difficulty of the interviewer's task. Verbatim recording of lengthy answers to open questions is more prone to error than the mere marking of answers to questions with fixed alternatives.

Focus on the Instrument and Clarity of Questions: There has probably been more work done, and less said, about the problem of the questionnaire itself, than the other issues. Yet when one looks at surveys with low response rates, and other problems, one has the impression in many cases that they were using a crude and confusing set of questions. There is very little which can be said in a general way except to note that pretesting is usually inadequate, and that changes are often incorporated after the last pretest. The mere fact that changing the questions produces different answers does not tell us which is correct, although we tend to assume that more assets or expenditure or debts reported is usually better (more nearly correct).[72] The discussion earlier in this chapter on response set (acquiescence factor or social desirability) is also relevant in designing an instrument. If it is impossible to remove biases from attitudinal questions, one can at least do a better job of interpreting them if there are ancillary questions determining the respondent's information level, his understanding of the necessary insights, his level of interest, and how strongly he says he feels about something.

Conclusions: The accumulating body of evidence, inadequate as it is, seems to focus on the interviewer as crucial. Little can be done about the respondent, and once well-pretested protocols have been developed, there is little evidence that further manipulation of procedures or wording will pay off. But there has been recent evidence not just that interviewer's motivation and behavior matters, but that purposeful changes in interviewer behavior can affect the results. This is more exciting than merely finding interviewer differences, since one might not be able to do anything about such differences except attempt to randomize interviewer assignments (at great expense) and reduce the scope of interviewer judgment (no interviewer selection of the proper response category).

In general, these recent studies seem to show that purposeful procedures by the interviewer to "reward" the respondent for working at his task, lead the respondent to work harder. This is not a matter of looking the respondent in the eye, but in actual expressions, "Good, that's the kind of information we are after," and the like.[73]

In the process of development of such techniques, the problem arose of measuring what went on. Techniques are now being developed not only to measure the interviewer's behavior, but also to assess quantitatively the quality of the interaction, by counting the number of times questions have to be repeated, probes have to be used, etc. Such measures may allow an assessment of the quality of questions, too. A question commonly followed by long pauses, requests that the question be repeated, inquiries as to its meaning, need for additional probes ("Tell me more about that" "How is that?") to secure an adequate answer, is clearly either a bad question, or searching for something difficult to elicit or both.

There is reason to believe that the best interviewers already engage in a great deal of the emotional-reward-giving behavior we have described. They may be very ingenious at tailoring it to the particular respondent, so that training interviewers to do better may require much more than giving them a few tricks. It probably requires giving them a real understanding of the needs of respondents, and the character of the interaction. One additional casual bit of information in this matter is that whenever professionals in some substantive field have tried to do interviewing, they have generally done much worse than professional interviewers even when the latter do not understand the subject matter. The reason is at least in part, that the "experts" are focusing on the subject matter, not on the respondent. Indeed, they have great troubles even getting interviews.

The Problem of Non-Response

In view of the importance of minimizing errors in data collection, we shall consider systematically the problems of non-response and response error. A final section of the chapter will consider the special problems of data collection in developing countries.

A Statement of the Problem of Non-Response: We may define non-response as failure to obtain a usable report from an individual who properly falls into the sample on a survey. There may be a margin of doubt as to what should be classified as a "usable" reply. If many items are missing from a questionnaire, or if a few crucial items are missing, it may lead to better results to reject the report than to retain it for analysis. For example, in the Surveys of Consumer Finances in the 1950's schedules which contained neither income nor liquid assets were rejected, but those with one of the two were accepted. The underlying criterion is whether the report in question contains enough useful information so that the estimates will be better if it is included.

There is also room for uncertainty as to whether an element is properly in the sample. For example, on a personal interview survey based on a sample of occupied dwelling units, a vacant dwelling should not be considered a non-response: it should be classified as a non-sample address. But a dwelling with nobody at home (after repeated calls) should be classified as non-response. Interviewers, however, may not be able to distinguish between the two with precision. On a mail survey the distinction between a non-response and an incorrect entry on the list may present problems. The investigator may never know which forms actually were delivered. There may be a tendency not to bother with the distinction. From the point of view of what can be done to improve the survey, however, a failure to respond is obviously different from a faulty address. Comparisons in response rate across mail surveys also are more satisfactory if isolated from differences in the quality of the lists used. The same is true with telephone surveys.

From the point of view of the cause of the failure to obtain a useful report we may distinguish the following categories:

Type of Non-report	Examples from Samples of Dwelling Units
I. Non-sample elements Includes any element selected in the sample which is found not properly to be in the sample.	Address is not a dwelling, address has been destroyed, address is vacant.
II. Non-response	
A. Refusal	R Refuses altogether,
B. Not-at-home	Nobody at home, Somebody at home but not the designated R.
C. Other	Address inaccessible (because of weather), Report lost (in the mail or the office), R unable to cooperate (because of serious illness, inability to speak any language known to interviewer).

The response rate (or non-response rate) should be calculated after subtracting from the original number of elements in the sample those elements found not to be properly in the sample, and adding any additional element found to belong in the sample not separately counted on the original list of elements. For example, in a sample of families based on a list of addresses if a sample address contains not one family but two, both should be included in the adjusted count of families who should be interviewed. The percentage of non-response should be computed using as a base the corrected count of the number of elements properly in the sample, even if the latter must be estimated.

The "not-at-home" rate can be reduced by persistent efforts by interviewers. There will be some point at which the extra interviews will not be worth the extra expense and delay in completion of the field work. One possible rule is to tell interviewers to keep calling until their response rate reaches a specific level. Another is to set a maximum number of calls. Efforts to push the not-at-home rate to zero are likely to approach this result in part by converting some "not-at-homes" to refusals. For example, there is a rather fine distinction between a respondent who breaks an appointment, i.e. who is not at home even though he made an appointment with the interviewer, and a respondent who refuses. If the interviewer keeps trying, it may turn out that the respondent was accidentally away from home or that he did not wish to be interviewed. Even after making some allowance for the presence of concealed refusals among the not-at-homes, we return to the point that the "true" not-at-home rate can be reduced by persistent calling. It is sometimes useful to distinguish between an address with nobody at home and one with somebody other than the respondent. In the latter situation the interviewer often can obtain useful information. For example, she may be able to remove any doubt as to whether the address is properly in the sample.

The refusal rate is another matter. It may be possible by persistent effort to reduce the number of refusals on a study. A second interviewer may succeed where the first failed. Added letters of persuasion may help. Success is likely to be the result of sensitive adaptation of the approach to the respondent. It is not simply a question of repeated calls.

The other forms of non-response are less common in cross-sections in the United States. The remedies which can be applied vary according to the problem —they range from improving handling techniques to prevent the loss of completed schedules in the office, to hiring Spanish-speaking interviewers to talk to recent immigrants from Puerto Rico. (A memo showing the details of the calculation of response rates for a Survey of Consumer Finances appears as an appendix to Chapter V.)

Non-Response Rates under Varying Conditions: The range of non-response rates in surveys is very wide. For the Current Population Surveys it is about five percent.[74] For personal interview surveys of the general population conducted by the Survey Research Center it is in the range of ten to twenty-five percent. For mail surveys losses may be anything up to ninety percent. For telephone surveys non-response rates are roughly comparable with those for personal interviews. In a follow-up primarily by telephone of a sample of married women in the Detroit area, the non-response rate was held to about two percent of those originally interviewed.[75]

It is obvious that the risk of bias in the findings resulting from non-response is serious in surveys where the losses are enormous, and small or even trivial where the losses are only a few percent. It is also obvious that a high loss rate will present problems to the analyst only if those who are not interviewed are systematically different from the respondents. We shall consider the determinants of response rate, and then the problem of bias.

First, the large variations in response rate seem to be attributable to differences in the willingness of people to respond. Accordingly, we may classify survey situations according to the types of motivation which operate. The usual starting place is the type of data collection:

Method of Data Collection	Motivation of R
Personal interview	Social motives present
Telephone interview	Social motives absent or weaker
Mail interview	No social motives

We have noted the importance of social motivation for many respondents; these motives are absent in mail surveys. Experience has shown that there is a difference between initial interview and reinterview in response rate. An initial personal interview seems to make for high returns from later mail or telephone interviews. A more complete classification, then, would be as follows:

Method of Data Collection

Initial interviews:
   Personal
   Telephone
   Mail

Reinterviews following personal initial interviews:
   Personal reinterview
   Telephone reinterview
   Mail reinterview
Supplementary forms to be completed after a personal interview
   (drop-offs)

Various combinations of methods became possible; the above classification is by no means exhaustive.

A second basic principle of classification is according to the intrinsic interest of the content of the survey for the population being interviewed. As we have seen already, people are more ready to respond to questions about something in which they are interested. Since some topics are interesting but people do not like to talk about them because they are too personal, perhaps we should speak of people's readiness to discuss topics as varying. This principle of classification is clearly independent of the first—readiness to discuss certain topics relates to the state of mind of the people being surveyed, while the choice of method of data collection is in the hands of the investigator.

A third dimension of the problem concerns variations in the details of the techniques used, basic type of data collection being held constant. There is a considerable literature on this subject, especially for mail surveys, where experimentation is comparatively easy. Some specific techniques seem to be useful, while others are of secondary importance. For example, Jeanne E. and John T.

Gullahorn experimented with different techniques in a mail survey of former Fulbright and Smith-Mundt grantees.[76] They had a response rate of about fifty percent. They found that when they used a standard return envelope rather than a business reply form the response rate was fifty-two percent rather than forty-eight percent. There is a difference but it is trivial.

We have offered at least some insight into the reasons for variations in response rate by type of data collection and content of the survey in terms of the motivation of the prospective respondents. Why should detailed variations in technique make a difference? Partly they may operate through getting people's attention. Partly it may be through leading people to distinguish between the data collection and other situations, e.g., advertising and selling efforts. Partly it may be through conveying to the potential respondent a sense of the importance of the project and its relevance to some goal which he has or some organization which he values. Unfortunately, most of the literature concerns what techniques work, not why.

There is, of course, a difference among interviewers in response rates, as well as in the quality of the responses they secure. Experienced interviewers often get lower response rates but tend to get biased samples (they do not lose respondents at random).[77] It is difficult to document this because it is generally difficult and costly to assign interviewers randomly to respondents.

Non-Response and Number of Calls: One standard method of examining the effects of increasing the number of calls made (or the number of mailings) is to compare results from successive calls. This method is most satisfactory when enough calls have been made to reduce non-response to a small percentage. One can then consider what the result would have been if the field work had been cut off after the first call, second call, or at any other specific point.

In economic surveys of the population of the United States people interviewed on different calls differ substantially. In one survey in 1963 conducted by the Survey Research Center with sixteen percent non-response rate the median income of those interviewed at different calls was as follows:[78]

Number of Call at Which Interviewed	Median Income	Number of Interviews
First	$4188	427
Second	5880	391
Third	6010	232
Fourth	6200	123
Fifth	6010	77
Sixth or higher	7443	59
All	$5598	1309

A survey with no call-back (i.e. one call only) using similar methods would have resulted in an estimate of $4188 for median family income compared with

$5598. The difference between people reached on first and later calls, in other words, is far from trivial.

Deciding how many calls should be made is a problem in economics, the only difficulty being that all the cost and benefit functions are not known. For instance, call-backs are somewhat more likely to produce an interview than original calls because interviewers have learned things about when the people are not home, and sometimes have even made appointments. But as one gets to respondents who were not only not home but reluctant, the probability of a call resulting in an interview drops. The expected quality of the information may also drop. So much for the cost side, but the benefit side requires the application of marginalism too, since the higher the response rate, the less additional responses will change estimates based on an incomplete sample, so the smaller the reduction in bias. And of course the smaller the increase in precision, since it goes up with the square root of the number of cases.

What the investigator needs to know is the extent to which the later calls will produce data which differ from early calls, how the cost per interview secured increases, and how the benefit of the information per added interview decreases. Our investigations leave the impression that after four or five calls, and a response rate in the eighties, the remaining non-response are widely scattered rather than systematically biased, costly or impossible to get, and likely to produce inadequate or incomplete information. But this may well depend on the content of the questionnaire.

The Reinterview Approach to the Study of Non-Response: A second basic method of studying the non-response problem is to seek to reinterview people about whom a good deal is known from an initial interview. One can then analyze the losses subsequent to the first interview. This type of inquiry is a necessary part of the most panel studies. Losses tend to cumulate, and it may be vital to know whether the individuals who remain in a panel are still reasonably representative of the population for purposes of the particular inquiry.

An example of such a check on a panel was reported by Sobol.[79] The study involved five waves over three years, 1954-1957, and the cumulative losses were substantial, as the following tabulation shows:

	Panel Mortality		Interviews Taken as a Percent of:	
	Interviews Taken	Lost	Addresses	Interviews in Wave I
Addresses sent out	(1358)		100%	
Wave I June 1954	1153	205	85	100%
Wave II Dec. 1954	958	195	71	83
Wave III June 1955	856	102	63	74
Wave IV Dec. 1955	819	37	60	71
Wave V Mar. 1957	707	112	52	61

Thus, in Wave V interviews were taken at only fifty-two percent of the addresses originally sent out. The original response rate on Wave I, however, had been eighty-five percent.

Sobol provides a breakdown of the losses which is as follows:

	Movers Not Followed		Refused		Unavailable	
Wave	Number	Percent	Number	Percent	Number	Percent
I	-	-	95	7	110	8
II	68	5	97	7	30	2
III	41	3	40	3	21	1
IV	12	1	13	1	12	1
V	41	3	35	2	36	3
Total	162		280		209	

Note that in this panel movers were not followed unless they moved to an address which was readily accessible to an interviewer. Note also that refusals were especially numerous in Waves I and II.

Converse has reported loss rates on a political panel study involving five waves also conducted by the Survey Research Center. They are remarkably similar to Sobol's in spite of the fact that the political panel extended over a longer period, 1956-1960:

Wave	Percent Response
I	100%
II	91
III	70
IV	63
V	61

Both projects ended with sixty-one percent of respondents in Wave I still in the panel for Wave V.[80]

Sobol compared those remaining in the panel with panel losses on a variety of socio-economic characteristics (degree of urbanization, age of family head, education, occupation, home ownership, income, sex of family head). She found some differences. For example, movers tend to be young. Home owners are less likely to move than renters. In general, however, considering the extent of the losses, the bias was remarkably small. Her results on family income were as follows:

1954 Family Income of Panel Members and Panel Losses

Income	Wave I	All Panel Members	Panel Losses			
			All	Movers Not Followed	Refused	Un- available
Under $2000	12%	10	14	20	11	14
$2000-4999	43	44	43	47	37	47
$5000-7499	25	27	22	21	25	17
$7500+	15	16	12	8	15	13
Not ascertained	5	3	9	4	12	9
Total	100%	100	100	100	100	100
Number of families	1153	707	446	162	190	104

Note that twelve percent of those who eventually refused had not disclosed their income in Wave I, while only three percent of the panel members who stayed for all five waves had income "not ascertained" in Wave I.

Another aspect of Sobol's results is of interest for the light it sheds on non-response. This project concerned people's economic attitudes. She found that those who said they did not follow business news in Wave I had a tendency to drop out. Thirty-three percent of losses fell in this group compared to twenty-six percent of persistent panel members. People differed in their willingness to remain in the panel, evidently, because of differences in interest in the topic.

Converse reports much the same thing. By 1960, he found, the political panel was overrepresenting people who had described themselves as politically involved in 1956. Converse was also concerned about the effect of panel membership on those who remained—"contamination" or "conditioning," as it is called. After 1960 he found he had five percent more people saying they had voted than in a new sample. The cumulative effect of five interviews, he felt, might have been to sensitize people to politics. Conditioning effects have also been found in panel studies of home repairs, as will be discussed later.

A study of refusals under special circumstances has been published by Robins.[81] He followed up thirty years later a group of 524 patients in a child guidance clinic plus 100 matched normal control subjects. He found some tendency for people to refuse more often if they were in routine white collar occupations, had low education, or came from foreign born parents. His most interesting finding is that those who had moved away to another city were much more likely to respond. Robins suggests that these respondents may have felt the interview was more important—they were told in advance that an interviewer was traveling to see them. The importance of the visit may have seemed greater also to the interviewer. And the distance may have lent anonymity.

In summary, the analysis of panel losses shows them to be not so bad as one might think. When one compares, on the basis of what was found in the original interview, those who got lost with those who did not in the succeeding waves, the differences seem to be small. Note, however, that this does not prove that there may not be substantial biases. Suppose, for example, that the people whose incomes fell since the first interview do not like to be reinterviewed. None of the analysis of the non-response would show this. Only comparing a panel sample with a total cross-section later, and asking about changes in income, would uncover this even in a rough way. On the other hand, spending a lot of time, energy, and money trying to locate the panel losses may turn out to be wasteful. For one thing, the easiest ones of the non-response to find are the ones the most likely to be like the response and the least like the rest of them. For another thing, even if one find some subset of the non-response, what does one do with this information?

There is a choice between adding them to the original panel, with very large weights so that they represent the rest of the non-response, or using them as an independent estimate of the size of the bias, but not putting them in. Or one might compromise and put them in as part of the original sample without weighting them up, claiming that they do not really represent the rest of the non-response anyway. If one puts them in and weights them, they may have such large weights that they increase the sampling variance, causing more troubles than the small reduction in bias is worth. If one puts them in unweighted, they will not change things much and may delay analysis and create a lot of confusion. If one leaves them out, then the estimate of biases is based on a very small sample and may not be a true estimate of the bias anyway. It must be kept in mind that a total bias is essentially the difference between two weighted estimates and that weighted estimates are relatively insensitive to fairly substantial variation in weights.

The Frame as a Source of Data about Non-Response: The third basic method of investigating non-response is to use data available from the sampling frame itself. Mayer and Pratt were able to use the frame in this manner in a study of individuals listed on personal injury auto accident reports.[82] They had considerable information about the accident as well as the age, sex, race, and occupation of the people listed on the report in the police files. Their methods of data collection and the resulting response rates were as follows:

Method	Percent of Sample Responding
1. Mailed questionnaire with cover letter	23.5%
2. Second mailing	23.2
3. Telephone	27.7
Total	74.4%

They found approximate similarity in many characteristics among those responding at each of the three stages and the non-respondents. There were differences in social status—those in low-status occupations and Negroes were considerably underrepresented on the first wave. They found a tendency for the refusal rate to be higher for drivers than passengers. The reason, they suggest, is that drivers might fear that they would be found at fault—with unpleasant consequences. Passengers could respond since they were merely spectators who could not be blamed for the accident. This interpretation, of course, is consistent with the emphasis in this discussion on the importance of the degree of readiness people have to respond to questions about the topic being studied.

Unfortunately, the amount that is known about non-response simply by knowing the geographic location of their residences, is relatively small. In general it appears to be both ends of the income distribution, families where all members are working (and hence seldom home), and people in congested areas (less trusting?) who are non-responses.[83]

The early Surveys of Consumer Finances were weighted to offset differences in response rates (as well as sampling rates), but it turned out that with response rates in the eighties, no appreciable difference was made in the results (hence no appreciable gain). This may, of course, have reflected only the lack of information about the non-response.

Other Methods of Reducing Non-Response: Two other methods have been used to "reduce" non-response, one illegitimate and the other legitimate. They both attempt to substitute someone like the original non-response. The illegitimate way to do this is to substitute someone next door. The Gallup organization did this during World War II and came up with a very high estimate of the proportion of families with victory gardens. When the Division of Program Surveys of the Department of Agriculture, using a probability sample and making callbacks, came out with a much lower estimate, they looked at their data according to the number of calls required, and of course, the more calls it took (the less the man was home) the less likely he was to have a victory garden. There was a characteristic, on which people differed, which might be called the "tendency to be at home," and it was highly associated with having a garden.

A more appropriate technique is to focus directly on the matter of not-at-homeness. The technique is a replacement technique which is possible if one has done previous surveys recently. *If* one can assume that those not-at-home in a previous survey, who can be interviewed in this survey, share with the not-at-homes in the current survey, the characteristic of not-being-home-much, *then* they can be treated as substitutes for the current not-at-homes. There is a chance of introducing bias this way, but also a chance of reducing bias. They are expensive interviews, usually taking more calls even the second time, and there are usually not enough of them to test the initial hypothesis that justified their use. They should clearly not be weighted up to substitute for all the not-at-homes.

Methods of Dealing with Non-Response in Analysis: The simplest procedure is to "do nothing" and prepare tabulations on the basis of the completed
reports. In effect, to do nothing amounts to assuming that the non-respondents
are like the rest of the population. The second possibility is to assume that the
non-respondents resemble, not the whole population, but some specified subpopulation. For this purpose one needs to know how many of the non-
respondents (and of the respondents) belong to that subgroup. Such information
may be available, say, from the sampling frame. One may know, for example,
the distribution of the population by size of place of residence. For example,
non-response tends to be higher in urban areas than in the rural parts of the
United States, and income is higher in urban than in rural areas. The assumption
that non-respondents resemble the entire population with regard to location is
less reasonable than the assumption that they resemble the other residents of
places of similar population.

The analyst, therefore, may decide to assign unequal weights to interviews
from different strata in the sample. He may estimate the fraction of the total
population which should be represented by stratum K, and assign a corresponding total weight to stratum K. It may be convenient to let the total weight of all
interviews in all strata equal 10,000 or to make the weights run only up to 9 or
to 99. Then the total weight for stratum K will be Wk, where $0 < Wk < 1$. The
weight for each interview in stratum K will be Wk/Nk, where Nk is the number
of interviews actually completed in the stratum. With modern data processing
equipment there should be no special problems in using the weighted data in
tabulation instead of simple counts of responses, except in tests of significance.

In analytic surveys the problem is somewhat different. The issue is not
whether means, medians, or percentages based on the full sample are biased, but
whether measures of relationship such as regression coefficients are biased. The
answer depends on whether there is an *interaction* between the variables in the
relationship and some factor systematically associated with non-response.

Suchman has published an example of a survey in which such an interaction exists.[84] He was working with a panel study of a presidential campaign.
Low-education people tended to have a low interest in politics and to drop out
of the panel. He found that the relation between reading and looking at TV
varied between panel members and those who dropped out as follows:

	Percentage Looking at TV Often			
Reading	Respondents to Both Waves		Non-respondents to the Second Wave	
Often	37	(907)	56	(461)
Sometimes	40	(303)	57	(221)
Hardly ever	59	(79)	59	(128)

Thus, among the non-respondents to the second wave (who were low-education people) there is not much substitution between reading and looking at TV often. Among respondents to both waves, there was such a substitution.

How can one search for such interactions? What is required is to consider, first, what are the factors associated with non-response on a project? Then one can check specifically to see whether the relationships in which one is interested are any different for those with different scores on the variables associated with non-response. Mayer and Pratt, for example, might have checked for differences in relationships within the two groups, passengers and drivers. Since respondents and non-respondents may differ in attitudes and motives relevant to the topic being studied, such searches may well be rewarded.

One difficulty is that we know very little about the non-response in most surveys. If and when good data become available in several dimensions on what the national population is like, it should be possible to devise weights not on the basis of evidence from a small study, but from a large sample survey with high response rates like the C.P.S. One would then divide the small sample into subgroups, say by age, education, sex of head, race, and city size jointly, and assign weights to the members of each subgroup so that their sum was appropriate for the proportion of the population represented by that group. What this requires is the basic population estimates, which must be in several dimensions, recent, use identical measurement of the variables, and use a selection of variables appropriate for the maximum reduction in bias.

Assuming that weighting may be needed, the problem is how to select the groups on which to compute the response rates to be used for weighting. One criterion, of course, is groups that differ as much as possible in terms of response rates. But another criterion equally important, is that the groups should differ on things you are trying to measure. You might find substantial differences in response rates between those who live in vertically stacked duplexes and those who live in horizontally connected duplexes, but this may well not make any substantial difference in the variables of the survey, and may be neglected. On the other hand, if there are different response rates according to family size, income, or home ownership, one might very well want to weight on these bases. Clearly by defining groups in several dimensions, you can find small groups that are substantially different from one another both as to response rates and as to their responses.

The question then is, how small should you make these groups? The smaller you make them, the more they differ from one another and the more you eliminate bias. But the smaller you make them, the more unstable the estimates of the groups and the larger the weights and you introduce potentially large sampling variance. In a group that is fairly small, there may turn out to be *no* response, so the theoretical weights would be infinite. But even if you take a group that had one hundred in the beginning, and you had only five responses, then you would have to assign weights of twenty to each of those five. Any idiosyncrasies in those five would be vastly exacerbated in the final results. So there is a optimization problem here, a strategy problem in making the groups big enough to be stable and not have too much difference in weights but small enough and well enough defined to be quite different so that you do as good a job as you can in reducing potential non-response bias.

There have been some other less adequate methods suggested for adjusting for non-response. One is to look for trends according to the number of calls it took to secure each interview, and extrapolate, assuming that the non-response is different in the same direction, only more. This can only be one item at a time, and it makes an unlikely assumption. The chances are that the final non-response are at least half refusals, who may be quite different from the people who were busy or not home much and required many calls to get.

Another scheme, associated with the Politz organization, is to ask the respondents who are interviewed whether they were at home at specified other times, and weight up those who were not home much, as a kind of replacement for others who were presumably not home and were not interviewed. One then cuts the number of call-backs. This is only really legitimate if you can randomize the time of the first call, if the reports people give on when they are home are accurate, and if you assume that not-at-homeness is a major source of bias, not refusals. Furthermore, the weights tend to be widely different and to increase variance while reducing bias. Finally, it costs time and money to tabulate the information and design the weights.

Item Non-Response: A special form of non-response is lack of response to particular items on a questionnaire. The omission may be the result of an oversight on the part of the interviewer or, in a self-administered procedure, an oversight by the respondent. One of the goals of questionnaire design is to minimize these inadvertent lapses. Omissions may also be deliberate. Respondents may be unwilling to respond to certain sensitive questions, or they may be unwilling to take the trouble to fill out all of a long, complex form.

Ferber has analyzed the number of omissions in a survey of the membership of Consumers Union.[85] This survey had an overall non-response rate of thirty-six percent. It involved a four-page leaflet with some seventy-one questions—an unusually lengthy form for a mail questionnaire. The omission rates were as follows:

Number of Omissions	Percent of Respondents
0	37.5
1	24.8
2-5	21.0
6-10	6.8
11-15	3.7
16-25	4.5
26 +	1.7
Total	100.0

While comparable data are scarce, it seems probable that the omission rate on this study is unusually high. There may well have been a marginal group of people who were fairly willing to respond, yet found seventy-one questions tedious.

Ferber conducted an elaborate analysis of the omissions. His main finding is that the omission rate is much higher for aged respondents, a result which is consistent with the findings of Gergen and Back. Low-education respondents omit more items—the task may well be more difficult for them. It is less obvious why women were found to omit more items than men.

Treatment of omitted items in analysis may be a considerable nuisance. As with non-response the simplest procedure may be to "do nothing," either showing "not ascertained" as a category in tables, or recomputing tables on the basis of those for whom data are available. The assumption that those who omit items are similar to the rest of the population, however, is dubious. As just shown, it is definitely false for the Consumers Union survey. It may be useful, therefore, to assume instead that those who omit items should have responded in the same way as others of similar socio-economic characteristics. A possible procedure is to "assign" for each omission a value equal to the mean for respondents with similar characteristics. More elaborate procedures may be worth the trouble in some situations. For example, one might base the assignment of family income on a multiple regression with income as dependent variable. Or, one might use a procedure which assigned the mean plus a random component so that the assigned values would be reasonably distributed instead of clustered at a limited number of incomes. Such procedures have two purposes: to remove bias from sample estimates and to simplify tabulating procedures for later work. These gains are purchased at the price of some delay in processing the data plus the cost of developing the assignment procedure. With a continuing program of surveys, a previous survey can provide the data for assignments. In case of variables which are zero for substantial numbers (expenditures on durables) the procedure may be first to assign whether any expenditure was made (on the basis of variables like age and income) and then if the first assignment is "Yes," to assign the amount on the basis of past expenditures of those who spent something, within income, etc. groups. This two-stage procedure is particularly useful when some cases are known to have spent something and only the amount has to be assigned. We return to this topic in Chapter V.

The Problem of Response Error

Even with a completed interview schedule in hand, we cannot proceed to analysis without some concern for the quality of the information. It is not easy to answer questions about response error, for if the data were easily available elsewhere, there would be no need for a survey. Evidence as to quality of data comes from several sources: The schedule itself may have evidence of respondent confusion, internal inconsistencies, substantial item non-response, or the need for substantial probling by the interviewers to build up an answer.

But the most startling and disturbing evidence of problems of response error in economic surveys comes from comparisons with aggregate data. Many economic magnitudes are estimated in the aggregate from published records, but a survey may be required to secure information on distributions, and on relationships at the micro-level with other magnitudes. We can estimate aggregate personal incomes, or savings accounts, but we may want to know how concentrated they are, and whether the low-income people also have little or no savings to fall back on. If a survey produces an estimate of the mean per family, one can multiply by an inside or outside estimate of the aggregate number of families to get an estimate of the aggregate amount.

There are of course various conceptual and coverage problems which require adjustments: the institutional population, non-personal incomes or assets belonging to unincorporated businesses or non-profit foundations, or universities, etc. But some general impressions remain from such aggregate comparisons: Asset holdings seem to be underreported by the widest margin. Consumer debt is better, particularly installment debt which is usually connected with purchases and involves regular payments easy to remember. Income is still better, particularly if enough time and attention is given to it in the interview.

Such comparisons leave one in the dark, of course, about the distribution of response errors—are they all concentrated in a few large amounts not reported, or held by those who were non-response in the survey, or widely distributed? In practice, such aggregate discrepancies, without any real evidence as to how damaging they were to distributions or correlational analyses, have led to the discontinuance of financial surveys, and to uncertainty as to the validity of analysis based on them. Yet, forgetting the few with very large amounts, survey analysis would only be badly biased if the errors were concentrated in a way correlated with one or more of the explanatory variables used. If every tenth person was just unwilling to admit he had a savings account, the result is noise and lower correlations, but not positive findings that are erroneous.

Hence, we are in serious need of better assessment of response error. The difficulty is, as we shall see, that this is expensive. When we turn to less quantitative measures—attitudes, expectations, plans, or classifications like occupation, the very concept of response error gets more complex.

Preliminary Statement of the Problem: It is useful to postulate the existence, for any individual respondent in a survey, of a "true value" representing the correct score for that individual on some characteristic measured in the survey. For example, the "true value" might be the actual amount of wages paid to an individual by his employer in a calendar year. Then the response error for that individual for that characteristic may be defined as the difference between the reported value and the "true value." It would be possible to think of the "reported" value as the value as entered on the interview report form. The term will be used here, however, to mean the value as used in the tabulating of the results of the survey. Response error, thus, is equivalent to total measurement error, including both collection and processing errors.

The assumption that there is a "true value" is not the same as assuming that the "true value" is measurable. Whether or not it is possible to measure something reasonably close to a "true value" varies according to the nature of the variable. For simple factual variables, the estimation of a "true value" is often possible. In economic surveys it is reasonably easy to define an acceptable true value for assets and debts with fixed money values and for financial flows. There exist, as a rule, institutional records where these amounts are recorded. For example, employers record the wages paid.

As one moves away from items of fixed monetary magnitude, problems of valuation and imputation become increasingly serious. The "true value" of the income of the owner of an unincorporated business is an elusive concept. It depends, of course, on such matters as how one estimates the annual depreciation of the assets of the business and how one values any income in kind the owner may have received. An investigator must adopt some set of definitions; for example, he may speak of income as defined for tax purposes by the Bureau of Internal Revenue. Even families which have no entrepreneurial income are very likely to own houses or at least durable goods which last beyond the period in which they are purchased. Economists may wish to take into account the flow of services received, say, by a home owner from his place of residence. The "true value" of that flow is a sophisticated concept, nowhere recorded in a set of reliable records. We may think of methods, however, for estimating the accuracy of reports of magnitudes which will enter into estimates of the imputed flow—we can seek to assess the accuracy of reports of house value, for example.[86]

It is when we turn to psychological variables that the measurement of a "true value" becomes most elusive and even the concept of such a value presents difficulties. There is, however, a literature on the subject of the validity of psychological constructs, especially of scores on psychological tests.[87] Cronback distinguishes four types of validation:

1) *Predictive* validity. Do the scores on a certain variable, as measured, predict future performance? In economic surveys one may investigate whether scores on some measure taken in one interview predict behavior at a later date as measured in a second interview. For example, one may investigate whether plans to buy cars are fulfilled.

2) *Concurrent* validity. Do the scores on a certain variable, as measured, correlate with performance measured at the same time? In economic surveys one may investigate whether scores on some measure taken in

one interview are associated with behavior as measured in the same interview. For example, one may investigate whether plans to send children to college are accompanied by saving money for the purpose.

3) *Content* validity. Do the items which enter into a measurement bear a reasonable relationship to the content to be measured? This requirement is for a logical study of the items in relation to the concept.

4) *Construct* validity. How can the scores on a measure be explained in terms of psychological theory? The test consists in setting up hypotheses and checking them by any suitable empirical procedure. For example, reasoning from the fundamental nature of a construct, one may deduce that people who have certain scores on this measure should have certain scores on related measures of their attitudes or behavior.

Cronback states that the validation of a test involves a long-continued interplay between observation, reasoning, and imagination. Imagination plays its part in suggesting what construct might account for test scores. Or, we may add, might be accounted for by such scores. Reasoning enters in deriving testable hypotheses from the theory surrounding the construct. And empirical work enters to test the hypotheses.

We may think of the "true" score of an individual on some psychological dimension, then, as the score which we would assign to him if we could apply a test, or a process of measurement, which had been validated as a result of careful, painstaking work of the type just described.

There is an unfortunate tendency for economists who work with constructs which are essentially psychological to be satisfied with elementary efforts at validation. For example, they may be satisfied to measure income expectations with a question which simply asks whether people expect their income to go up, stay the same, or decline. One may simply look at the content of such a question, note that on its face it has to do with what economists mean by income expectations, and proceed with the analysis. And the results may well be meaningful. But a sophisticated validation of the measure would require much more.

Methodological Studies: While it is possible to assemble an impressively long bibliography of reports on methodological studies of data gathering processes, a careful perusal shows that very little good-quality, reasonably conclusive work has been done. The best work has been on relatively simple variables where there was great concern with accurate estimates: morbidity, housing, unemployment, and population counts.

It is useful to distinguish various kinds of methodological studies:

1) One kind is studies of interviewer differences, that is, of apparent effects of the attitudes or social class of the interviewer, on the responses she reports. In many such studies, interviewers are not randomly

assigned to respondents, so that the effects are confounded with real differences between respondents, differences which can only crudely be controlled statistically.

Where there has been an experimental design, some interviewer effects have been found, mostly on attitudinal questions, of course. It is not clear what one does with the results, except to try to minimize the opportunities for interviewers to affect the results, by carefully training them to read the questions as written and write down the answers as closely to verbatim as possible. Or, if a limited set of choices is allowed, to have the interviewer read off the choices and let the respondent repeat one, rather than attempting to code a reply into some category in the field. And in view of differences in the number of responses given (e.g. reasons), some control over the probes is called for, such as repeating the phrase "anything else" until the answer "no" is reached.

2) Studies of differences depending on who is the respondent are much rarer. Most of these are, of course, husband-wife studies, and some are as concerned with who makes the decisions as with who is the best respondent—the two may not be the same.[88] Indeed, there is some reason to believe that wives may be better *predictors* of future family decisions, even in areas where both of them agree that the husband makes the decision.[89]

3) There are studies of differences between the findings of different surveys, or between survey data and outside aggregates, or studies based on demographic checks. These studies are generally inconclusive sometimes as to which is the correct figure, and generally as to why the errors exist. Over the years, various changes were made in the schedule and procedures of the Surveys of Consumer Finances sometimes in split half samples, and sometimes from year to year since the distributions were not expected to change much. In general the differences were small and, occasionally in an unexpected direction. We have already mentioned the case where a much more elaborate and detailed schedule of questions elicited less aggregated debt than the simpler procedures used the previous and the following years.

4) Studies of non-response bias should be included in this catalogue of methodological studies, even though they do not study response error. Indeed, by working to increase the response rate, one may be trading less non-response error for more response error, from those unwilling and uncooperative respondents.

5) There are somewhat more elaborate designs, allocating different procedures to separate samples or part samples, including varying the data collection between mail, telephone, and personal interview. Again differences may appear, though they have often been small, without

evidence as to where the truth lies, and little clue as to why there were differences. With reinterviews it is possible to study reliability by asking again for information that should not change, such as when the respondent was born, or his education. Or one can reconcile information by tracking back reported car transactions to see whether one can get back to the car reported the year before.

Reinterviews also allow elaborate designs to check on the reports of transactions where dating may be a problem, as with additions and repairs to homes. Questions in several waves may cover the same time period, and by identifying the particular transaction, one can see whether it was dated consistently. The most impressively elaborate such study was done at the United States Census Bureau and reported by Neter and Waksberg.[90]

Neter and Waksberg studied the accuracy of household expenditures for additions and repairs. They found that reported expenditures during a period of one month as given in a single interview seriously overstated actual expenditures, probably by about fifty-five percent, largely because of telescoping in time the dating of these expenditures, where the exact timing is often ambiguous. This error could be reduced if not eliminated, they found, by a procedure using two interviews, one at the start as well as one at the end of the period.

They used an unusually sophisticated design, and the study is a classic of careful analysis. However, it is unlikely that the results can be generalized to other consumer expenditures. The study dealt with a kind of consumer expenditure that is difficult to assign to one date. Often a long time span passes from the time someone first calls someone to do something around the house, or starts buying the materials, to the time that the job is commissioned or started, to the time when it is almost finished or a bill is rendered, or a bill is paid. It is doubtful that the amount of telescoping or shifting of time would be as large as most other consumer activities as it is in this one. Notice, however, that their problem was to estimate aggregates as accurately as possible, on a quarterly basis preferably, and not necessarily to provide for a detailed cross-section of information, which could be used to explain differences between people or over time, in people's behavior. It is quite possible that if one wanted to do the latter, one would insist on asking about annual expenditures, do the best job one could of getting it reasonably accurately, follow a panel over time to get changes from one year to the next, and mostly be concerned that the year-to-year changes in individual's reported expenditures were reasonably good.

In discussing needs for future research, the authors do *not* talk about experimenting with different specifications. Which date is relevant for these expenditures? They might very well ask the date that the first piece of work was actually started. It would be the easiest thing to remember, and yet this would cause problems if you wanted expenditure data, because people might have all kinds of things started in one period but paid for in another.

6) Finally there are genuine validity studies which check an individual item from an interview against some outside source, usually some record assumed to be correct.[91] Such checking is expensive, and in any case cannot cover more than a few items. It is not easy to secure access to records anyway.

An additional difficulty is that most validity checks are directional, that is they start with a list of people known to have been in the hospital or used a library, or had a bank account, and see whether they report it in an interview. Or they secure reports from an interview, and check a source to see if they also exist in the records. Such validity tests are biased in the sense that they mostly pick up one type of error and not the other. Starting with record information, one mostly picks up underreporting. If the respondent also reported an account in another bank, he might be over-reporting but that would not be discovered.

Similarly, if one starts with respondent reports, then it is only possible to find some that do not exist in records, presumably over-reports.

But a worse problem is that one is often not sure whether the amount is in error, or the name of the bank or hospital, or the date of the illness.

Finally, validity studies still do not go far toward providing notions as to why the errors exist. One can infer a little from the types of people who report well or badly, including their attitudes. In some of the best studies, validity checks have been combined with experimental variations in procedures, so that one at least knew which procedure was best, not just that they produced different results.

Mismatches in validity checks are always a possibility, and unfortunately they systematically distort estimates of error.[92]

In order to reduce mismatches, it may be necessary to ask for additional information in the interview, such as the name of the bank and in whose names the account is held, and the exact date for the amount given. Then the respondent may have to give permission for release of the records and in many cases, it is a complex task to get the right information out of the records. In the case of checking accounts, for instance, some adjustment must be made for the float of uncleared checks, already deducted in the owner's check book, but not yet subtracted from his account at the bank.

What is worse, having to rely on cooperation of both individual and institution, one may have a biased sample of both, so the results may not generalize, and the very detail asked to allow the check means that one does not have a validity test of the kind of procedure that would be used in a major study without a validity check.

One unpublished study in Detroit asked about property taxes, and using the address, checked the tax rolls. Most respondents were precise in reporting their taxes, but there were a few very large errors, mostly two-family houses where it was not clear whether the taxes were supposed to refer to the whole house or half of it, or people who gave their city taxes only rather than city, county, and school taxes.

An attempt to assess the coverage of individuals' health insurance policies by asking the name of the company and the policy number revealed problems of identifying companies when several had similar-sounding names and the fact that some people counted their auto insurance medical payments clause as medical insurance.[93] The same study compared people's reports of their medical costs after an accident with hospital records, finding as might have been expected, somewhat more overreports than underreports.

Given all these difficulties it is easy to see why people look for some cheaper or easier method to assess the validity of their data, or ignore the problem altogether. When one considers that a fifty-minute interview may contain some 400 items of information, each one of which may be potentially capable of some comparison with other information, or even verification, the magnitude of the problem is staggering. And when one considers that the other sources of information, even ignoring the conceptual and matching difficulties, may themselves be subject to error, and the final fact that there is not much use merely measuring error if one does not know why it arose or what to do about it, it may seem more profitable to invest the time and energy in better pretesting, reinterviews, investigation of consistency of people's reports, etc., rather than experimental validity studies.

Mathematical Models of Response Error: A substantial body of work has been done on the development of models of response error, primarily by statisticians who have approached the subject with a background in sampling. A center of work on the subject has been the United States Bureau of the Census. The purposes of the work of the Bureau evidently have been to assist in the formulation of policy in data collection and to provide information concerning the accuracy of Census' statistics for the guidance of users of the results. The focus of interest, therefore, has been on the accuracy of total counts and of estimated means and percentages. It has not been on the accuracy of estimates of analytical statistics, such as correlation coefficients and regression coefficients. This latter topic, which is of concern to economists who work with sample surveys, will be considered in Chapter VI.

The nature of the work done at the Census may be indicated by a brief treatment of a model of response error developed there. A more extended discussion will be found in publications by Census staff.[94]

Measurement error is defined by Hansen, Hurwitz, and Bershad to include both collection and processing errors. They consider surveys, including censuses, as conceptually repeatable. The particular results in one survey are the results of one trial. The value observed even for a particular measurement on a particular individual is only one of a universe of many values which might have been obtained if the same measuring process had been repeated many times for the same individual.

Consider the problem of estimating a proportion. For a member of a population under study, say, the jth individual, it would be possible ideally to measure without error whether or not he falls in some category. We may say that $U_j = 1$ if he falls in the category, and $U_j = 0$, if he does not. Then it is possible to define the "true value" of the proportion for the population:

$$(1) \qquad U = \frac{1}{N} \sum_{j=1}^{N} U_j$$

For example, if ten percent of the population fall in a certain income group, then for those individuals U_j will be 1, and for all others, zero. The average value of U, or $\bar{U}$, will be .10. It is this hypothetical "true value" that we seek to estimate.

The data that we actually have will be observations for individuals, say, individual j is typical; for a particular trial, say, a certain survey, survey t; taken under certain (uncontrollable) conditions according to certain specified procedures, say, conditions and procedures G. Thus our observations may be said to be of the form X_{jtg}.

Our estimate of $\bar{U}$, then, will be:

$$(2) \qquad P_{tg} = \frac{1}{n} \sum_{j=1}^{n} X_{jtg}$$

That is, we will estimate the mean of the values of X which we observe for the n individuals in the particular sample, t, taken under the particular conditions, g. (For a census, n = N.)

The expected value of P_{tg} over many repeated surveys (under conditions and procedures G) may be defined as follows:

(3) $\quad P_G = E_{PtG}$

It is not necessarily true that P_G will *equal* $\bar{U}$. There may well be some bias in the procedure which will persist regardless of the number of repetitions of the survey or census. This bias may be defined:

(4) $\quad B_G = P_G - \bar{U}$

The bias carries the subscript G since it will depend upon the conditions and procedures used.

The total variance of the estimate, P_{tG}, will depend upon the distribution of the values of P_{tG} around their expected value, P_G:

(5) $\quad \sigma^2 P_{tG} = E (P_{tG} - P_G)^2$

The mean square error of the estimate takes into account the bias in the estimate of P_{tG} as well as the variance in the estimate. It is, therefore, the basic measure of the accuracy of P_{tG}:

(6) $\quad MSE_G = E (P_{tG} - \bar{U})^2 = \sigma^2_{PtG} + B^2_G$

The mean square error, or its square root, is conceptually the best measure of the accuracy of any estimate. Of course, in practice the mean square error is unlikely to be known. Useful approximations, however, are possible.

For one individual, individual j, over many trials, there will be an expected value:

(7) $\quad E_j X_{jt} = P_j$

This expectation should be understood to assume that the conditions and procedures, G, are constant over all the trials.

There will be, then, a difference between the observed and expected value for unit j on trial t:

(8) $\quad d_{jt} = X_{jt} - P_j$

Estimates of this difference, the response deviation, play an important part in practical work on response error. Note that the response deviation is measured from the expected value for the individual in question.

It is possible that the expected value for individual j should be thought of as depending not only on conditions and procedures G but also on the other particular individuals who happen to be selected in the sample. The presence of these other individuals may influence the interviewer's approach to individual j. She may develop expectations about respondents as a result of her experience with these individuals. Hence, it may be necessary to think of an expected value for individual j over many repeated surveys with an identical sample:

$$(9) \qquad E_{js} X_{jt} = P_{js}$$

If it turns out that the effect on the estimate for j of the composition of the sample is close to zero, equation (7) will be all that is required.

The total variance of a survey will include contributions from response deviation and from sampling deviation as well as, possibly, from the covariance of the two. It may be stated:

$$(10) \qquad \sigma_{P_t}^2 = E (p_t - P)^2 = E [(p_t - p) + (p - P)]^2$$

$$= E (p_t - p)^2 + 2 E (p_t - p) (p - P) + E (p - P)^2$$

where $(11) \ p = \dfrac{1}{n} \sum_{j=1}^{n} p_j .$

Since P_j is the expected value for one individual (see equation (7)), p is the average for n individuals over many trials.

The first component is the average of the response deviations for the sample:

$$(12) \qquad \sigma_{d_t}^2 = E (Pt - P)^2 = E (\frac{1}{n} \sum_{j}^{n} d_{jt}) = E (\bar{d}_t)^2$$

The third term represents the sampling variance of P_t:

$$(13) \qquad \sigma_p^2 = E (p - P)^2 = E [\frac{1}{n} \sum_{j=1}^{n} (p_j - P)]^2$$

In a census there is no sampling variance; this term will have a value of zero.

This model has been developed in work on a number of problems. Topics considered include the effects of correlations among response deviations on a survey and methods of estimating interviewer variability (in 1950) and the effects of interviewer, supervisor, and processing variability (in 1960). Findings concerning the magnitude of individual response deviation for proportions (σ_d^2) are presented in the form of ratios to PQ, i.e. ratios to the variance of a proportion of the observed magnitude assuming the magnitude had been found in simple random sampling without response deviations. It turns out that the estimates of σ_d^2 are of the order of three to ten percent of PQ for items such as age which are regarded as measured with high reliability, but on the order of fifty percent of PQ for items measured with low reliability such as condition of housing in a census of housing, or unemployment in a census of population. In the Current Population Survey the estimates of σ_d^2/PQ are on the order of half the value in the decennial census.

Estimates of the bias in the 1950 Census have been made using the Current Population Survey as a standard. For some items, for example, the percent of persons who are classed as farmers or farm managers, the estimates of bias are on the order of magnitude of seven percent of the estimate from the Current Population Surveys. Such findings have led the Census Bureau to reconsider the allocation of resources between complete enumeration and sample surveys using more refined methods of data collection.

Kish has developed a model for the analysis of response error in a situation in which two estimates of a quantity are available for every individual in a sample and there is reason to consider one of the estimates to be preferable, but neither can be accepted as a close approximation of the "true value."[95] The data consisted in estimates of the market value of each of a sample of owner-occupied homes made by the owner and by a professional appraiser. The model considers the relationships among the variances and covariances of these estimates and the (unknown) "true value." In contrast to the previous model, only one estimate is considered for each respondent and each appraiser.

Let: r_i = response by the resident owner of home i
         a_i = estimate by the appraiser for home i
         y_i = "true value" for home i

We may estimate the mean of each:

(1) $\bar{R} = E(r); \quad \bar{A} = E(a); \quad \bar{Y} = E(y)$

We may also define the variances:

(2) $V(r) = E(r - \bar{R})^2; \quad V(a) = E(a - \bar{A})^2; \quad V(y) = E(y - \bar{Y})^2$

We may also define the difference between the estimates:

(3) $d_i = (r_i - y_i) - (a_i - y_i) = (r_i - a_i)$

Then $(\bar{R} - \bar{Y})$ will be the response bias, and $(\bar{A} - \bar{Y})$ will be the appraisers' bias. These are unknown, but we can estimate:

$$(4) \qquad \bar{D} = (\bar{R} - \bar{A}) = (\bar{R} - \bar{Y}) - (\bar{A} - \bar{Y})$$

We can also estimate the mean-square difference of the measurements:

$$(5) \qquad \text{M.S. } (d) = E(d^2) = E(r - a)^2$$

Finally we may write an expression for the covariance between the difference in measurements and the appraisers' values:

$$(6) \qquad \text{Cov. } (da) - E(d - \bar{D})(a - \bar{A})$$

The basic equation of the model is the following:

$$(7) \qquad V(r) + \bar{D}^2 = V(a) + \text{M.S. } (d) + 2 \text{ Cov } (da)$$

Or in terms of expected values:

$$E(r - a)^2 = E(r - y)^2 + E(a - y)^2 - 2E(r - y)(a - y)$$

The first term (left side of the equation) is available, and is larger than the next term (the true response error) by an amount composed of two other items: the third term which is the mean square error of the appraisers' estimates, and the four covariance term which is likely to be small. So the model tells us that the variance of the discrepancies between the two reports exaggerates the response error unless the check-source, here appraisers, is totally free of error. Hence a big improvement would be a double appraisal to provide evidence in the appraisers' errors.

The terms in the equation could be estimated in different situations in order to obtain further insight into the errors of estimation. For example, where the respondent had purchased the home recently his estimate of market value might be assumed to be better informed and the mean square difference should be smaller.

Ferber has developed a method of estimating the importance of contributions from different sources, including response error, to the bias in survey estimates of means. This procedure is descriptive.[96] He applied the method to the small sample of results from a study of farmers for whom data for validation of demand deposits was available, names having been selected from a list. The method consists essentially in estimating the proportion of the sample in each of four groups: (1) non-respondents (including all those not interviewed who should have been interviewed); (2) respondents who failed to report the existence of the deposit; (3) respondents who reported the existence of the account but refused to estimate the balance, and (4) respondents who reported a balance. For each group an estimate of the "true value" could be made and compared with the estimate that would have been made from the survey without the validation procedure to yield an estimated bias. The bias for the sample as a whole becomes an average of the biases for the four groups, weighted by the number of sample members in each group.

In Ferber's notation:

$$E = P_s(A_s - X_s) + P_o A_o + P_1 (A_1 - X_2) + P_2 (A_2 - X_2)$$

where:

P_i is the proportion of sample members in the ith category;
A_i is the average actual balance of sample members in category i;
X_i is the average recorded balance for category i.

Subscripts have the following meanings:

S non-respondents
0 respondents, account not reported
1 respondents, account reported but balance refused
2 respondents, account reported and balance given

Ferber also develops estimates of the effect of non-sampling errors on estimates of the reliability of the mean. His expressions for the mean square and sample variance, respectively, are as follows:

$$MSE_{\bar{y}} = (1 + k^2) \, \sigma_{\bar{y}}^2$$

$$\sigma_{\bar{y}}^2 = \sigma_{\bar{x}}^2 + \sigma_{\bar{e}}^2 + 2r^2 \sigma_{\bar{x}}^2 \sigma_{\bar{e}}^2$$

where:

x_i is the true size of account i
y_i is the reported size
bars denote means
$\bar{e} = \bar{y} - \bar{x}$
r = correlation between x and e

In the example based on the farm study, results were as follows:

k   .78
r   -.67
apparent standard errors of mean $(x_{\bar{y}})$ $317
true standard error of mean (MSE) $403
response-error-free standard error of the mean $413

Problem of Data Collection in Underdeveloped Countries

There has been a very considerable amount of effort devoted to survey research in underdeveloped countries since World War II, and there has begun to accumulate a literature describing the experiences of those who have undertaken these projects. In a sense nothing new has emerged from these reports—the problems encountered all have their analogues in the United States and other developed countries. Yet some problems which are easily handled or even trivial in developed countries are very much more serious in other parts of the world, so serious as to suggest that the limitations as to what can be done with sample surveys are quite different. It will require a further accumulation of knowledge before there is a reasonable degree of consensus as to what methods are optimal, what projects are and are not feasible. But it certainly is proving true that the possibilities and limitations of sample surveys are very different in different countries.

The Need for Data: There is reason to believe that data of the types obtainable from sample surveys in developed countries would be useful for many problems in underdeveloped countries. Freedman has published a list of conditions which make surveys related to family planning especially helpful in developing countries where there is a problem of high fertility.[97] His conditions also may have broader applicability:

1) In the context of a desire for massive social change there is little information about how much change has already occurred.
2) There is likely to be a gap of understanding between the leadership and the masses which is much greater than in developed countries. The mass media all communicate in one direction, to the masses, and feedback is poor.
3) Traditional ideology exists about family planning. The ideology may not fit the facts.
4) There may be many people in favor of a program who do not realize that others are too.
5) There is a need for surveys to check on the effectiveness of the programs.

One might find that a similar set of conditions applied, say, to the introduction of improved agriculture methods.

Controversy Over the Usefulness of Survey Methods: There have been attacks on the usefulness of survey from an anthropological standpoint. Such an attack by Thomas Rhys Williams was published in the *Public Opinion Quarterly* in 1959.[98]

Williams objected to two assumptions which he attributed to survey research. First, he objected to the assumption of the validity of a survey response as a social datum. There may be institutionalized patterns of saying one thing and doing another. People may describe their actions as they ought to have been, not as they actually were. Williams, in a word, is highly sceptical of what people say. He urges detailed empirical observation of social behavior.[99]

Second, Williams objects to the assumption of dynamic equivalence among survey responses as well as to equivalence between such responses and actual social behavior. Responses may be far from equivalent in different contexts. They should be interpreted in the context of the behavior of a specific social group. Presumably, while Williams might object to any comparisons across social groups, the more diverse the groups, the greater the force of the objection.

Surely, it would be going too far to urge that people *never* report their actions and their attitudes correctly or that responses are *never* comparable across social groups. It is entirely proper to raise questions on these points, however. Skepticism on these matters is a better general approach than a simple faith in the validity and comparability of responses to any and all questions.

Problems in Sampling: The problems of developing a satisfactory sample frame in underdeveloped countries were reviewed briefly by Wilson in 1958.[100] There may be a lack of census data. Existing statistics may be unreliable. There may be a lack of estimates of size at the local level, for example, of city blocks. There may not be adequate maps. Listing may be difficult because of makeshift housing arrangements. Random selection within households may clash with custom—it may be difficult to interview anyone but the accepted spokesman for the household.

These difficulties are not necessarily permanent. Frey, for example, reports that a study in rural Turkey was greatly facilitated by a 1960 census, which provided data on all 35,000 villages in the country, including especially measures of size, so that it was possible to select villages with probability proportional to size. Frey also found that it was possible to develop lists of villagers on the spot, relying on several sources of names, including lists of eligible voters and the fact that in small villages the leaders know every adult personally.[101]

It has been argued that the unit of opinion is not the individual in places such as rural Madras in India. The unit, it is argued, is communal, an extended family, sub-caste, or village.[102] This argument, however, need not imply a change in sampling. Presumably, the importance of an opinion can be gauged by how many people hold it, regardless of its origin. It is also argued that it is difficult to interview people in isolation. Groups gather automatically. The arrival of a visitor is a great event in some villages. The person selected may feel it is not his role to respond—that is the responsibility of the leader, who is the one who has opinions. It is not easy to insist on following through with a random sample of individuals. Carried to its logical conclusion this argument would imply that the population sampled should not consist of individuals or families but of some larger units. There may be situations in which such an approach should be considered, perhaps in combination with a more standard procedure. In Turkey, Frey reports that on his project the sample in each village included the political leader and his wife and the religious leader and his wife, as well as a random sample of other villagers.

Roe Goodman has suggested that problems of sampling and interviewing overlap, that if one wants to make sure the interviewer interviews each person in the sample, it may be better to go so far as to take fewer villages and include everyone in the village, so that the interviewer and the villagers both know that everyone is to be included. This also avoids the necessity for explaining principles of sampling so people will know why not everyone was interviewed.[103] It may also reduce field problems where roads and overnight accommodations are primitive or absent.

Problems in Interviewing: There is always a need for social acceptance of a project involving interviewing. In underdeveloped countries this acceptance is not necessarily automatic. It may be essential to obtain political support at levels which seem unreasonably high to an American. For example, Carlson found that in order to carry through a survey of mass media and communication behavior for Columbia University in Jordan he had to talk personally to the King.[104] The King responded favorably, and the project was successfully completed. In Turkey Frey reports it was essential to have top level political support, which was provided by the Turkish State Planning Organization. In India the National Council of Applied Economic Research, which carried out the project described in Chapter I, had the benefit of being an established Indian organization with close ties to the Planning Commission, which was one of the most powerful agencies of government. Working from the top down it becomes possible to obtain the necessary political support at the local level. Questions raised by local officials as to the legitimacy of an inquiry can be answered. Of course they may have to be educated in the process. In a number of countries *any* research project requires approval by the relevant government official.

An excessive display of political support can be disastrous, however. Frey reports a pilot study in Turkey (on another survey) in which interviewers dressed like officials and behaved like officials, summoning certain peasants to be brought before them. The peasants came, and lied in the manner demanded by the occasion. It seems likely that the social status and perceived role of the interviewer may cause trouble in many underdeveloped countries. Law enforcement may be lax, so that many people have something to hide. If they are squatters on the land, they may want to hide their very existence. If they have income too high to justify staying in a subsidized housing project, or are illegally converting part of a housing subsidy into cash by renting out some of the space, they are not likely to report income or household composition accurately. They may well distrust the government, or respect the higher social status of the interviewer, and hence give socially acceptable answers, or answers which agree with anything the question suggests, or that they think the interviewer would approve. Particularly where adopting new ways is promoted by the government as not only economically superior, but a patriotic duty to one's country, reports on adoption of, or the experience with, some new practice are likely to be biased.

The problems of communication in underdeveloped countries often begin with problems of language. Some countries, like Korea, are fortunate enough to have a common language.[105] In others there may be more than one language, and there may be dialects within main languages. A common reliance is on bilingual interviewers. This method was necessarily used in Turkey to reach people who speak Kurdish, a language which is unwritten. The standardization of questions becomes hard to enforce in such circumstances. When languages are written, it is possible to translate questionnaires, and check on accuracy by independent re-translation back into the original language. In the United States subtle differences in questions do make a difference in replies even concerning factual information, as was shown earlier in this chapter. (See the discussion of questions about income.) There is no reason to suppose that this problem is peculiar to the United States.

There may be difficult problems of finding generally understood equivalents for particular words, even when, as in Turkey, a single language is widely spoken. Frey reports difficulties with "problem," "prestige," and "loyalty." The choice is between synonyms, which may not have identical connotations, and explanations, which may introduce bias or become elaborate and formidable.

Even if we stick to "factual" material, there may well be problems with the definitions of terms. "Sorghum" may mean a grain meal or a molasses. Questions about ownership of livestock may cause trouble where cattle are commually owned, or frequently rented, so that possession and ownership do not jibe. The concept of depreciation may or may not exist, nor the notion of distinguishing current expenses from investments in capital improvements. Patterns of interfamily transfers may differ, particularly as to whether they incur obligations like loans or are genuine transfers. And the whole notion of careful definitions of boundaries or exact measurement or enumeration may be foreign to the culture and even regarded as improper or dangerous. In short, the appraisal of what one can expect to secure with reasonable accuracy in an interview requires an intimate knowledge of the culture as well as a good theoretical grasp of the concepts that would need to be measured for a particular study.

A different related problem of communication arises out of social divisions and factionalism. Extreme difficulties of this type were found by Hanna and Hanna in Nigeria and Uganda.[106] They spent three months in 1963 in each of two small urban centered communities, one in each of these countries. They interviewed probability samples of one hundred adults in each. In the community in Nigeria the population was almost all from the Ibo people, but they were divided into five clans with marked differences in dialect and feelings of social distance. In the Uganda community the population was split into two districts, one further divided into six distinct ethnic groups and the other with three clans. To these splits were added the problems in the town of an Asian minority comprising a third of the urban population but split into three religious groups, Hindus, Muslims, and Catholic Goans. In addition there was another category of "stranger" Bagandi families. And age and sex differences were much greater in both Nigeria and Uganda than in the United States. Interviewing had to be done by natives who knew the dialects, and each interviewer could reach only a few people. The Hannas calculated they should have had at least eighteen assistants in Uganda and fourteen in Nigeria so that each respondent could be approached by someone with whom he would communicate freely. We can compare these problems with the problems found to exist in the United States in interviews with Negroes and, on some subjects, in interviews with people of much lower socioeconomic status than the interviewer or wide disparity in age.

A familiar set of problems in the United States concern response variability and response set. There is evidence from a study by Landsberger and Saavedra that these problems are serious among lower-status, less-educated people in Chile, much more than among the better educated in that country.[107] They were especially concerned with acquiescence set—that is, with the number of "Yeasayers." They argue that, in general, response set is greater the greater the ambiguity of an item. Hence, individuals to whom a given item appears more ambiguous will have more response set.

The experiment concerned a well-known psychological measure, the California F scale. The method consisted essentially in reversing the content of the items, as in the following examples:

Form A	Form B
1. Human nature being what it is, there will always be war and conflict.	1. The existence of war and conflict is not due to man's nature.
2. The most important thing to teach a child is to obey his parents.	2. In a child's education, it is least important that he learn to obey his parents.

There were two types of respondents: (1) university students (N = 230); (2) working class groups, including (a) mothers attending discussions in community centers in a purely working class area (N - 140), and (b) housemaids attending adult-education classes in their trade-union center (N = 144).

The experiment involved two observations on each subject. All four possible sequences of forms were used: A form twice, B form twice, A then B, and B then A. Length of time between measurements was also varied.

For the students when the same form was repeated the scores were correlated in the range r = .72 to r = .93. When the forms were reversed the scores (corrected for the reversal) were still positively correlated r = .19 to r = .88. For both working class groups a reversal of forms actually led to negative correlations between scores: for the mothers, r = -.19; for the housemaids, r = -.33 to r = -.56. When the same form was repeated scores for the mothers were positively correlated at about the same level as for the students, r = .73. For the housemaids even when the same form was repeated the scores were correlated only r = .23 to r = .31. Landsberger and Saavedra are not quite so blunt, but we may go so far as to say that for the housemaids the form was worthless. The California F scale is of little intrinsic interest to economists, but acquiescence set can be a problem with any type of subject matter.

There is an assumption in survey research that when people reply to questions they will tell the truth. Errors are often regarded as the result of ambiguity, misunderstanding, inappropriateness of the questions, and the like. It is assumed that people will tell the truth, unless, perhaps, there is some special reason for them to conceal it, say, because the question concerns illegal or immoral activity. In some cultures, however, untruth may be tolerated much more than in others. Gastil has asserted that among the "modern middle class" in Iran in many circumstances telling the truth is regarded as foolish and stupid.[108] Gastil, who speaks Parsi, spent eleven months in Shiraz and wrote a dissertation on *Iranian General Belief Modes as Found in Middle Class Shiraz* (Harvard 1958). He regards this tolerance for untruth as associated with a general tendency for members of the "modern middle class" to distrust those around them. The evidence he cites in the article referred to above is essentially impressionistic, but it does grow out of personal experience of the society in some depth. We must agree that at least it raises a question of potential importance in economic surveys: who will tell the truth concerning economic matters in different situations in different societies?

A final comment about interviewing in underdeveloped countries is that unconventional methods of data collection may be developed which will prove helpful. For example, Stanton, Back, and Litwak report successful use of role-playing techniques in interviews in Puerto Rico.[109] Respondents entered into the role-playing readily in spite of the use of tape recorders. Such methods may be useful for some types of data as an intermediate method between conventional interviews with random samples and direct observation of behavior as it occurs naturally as proposed by such writers as Williams.

Problems of Research Design: As the preceding section suggests, there is an increasing body of experience about data collection in underdeveloped countries. The problems are identified, if not solved. There is little very written on the subject of research design. Yet we may at least point out the critical importance of the question, what research designs can be carried through to successful completion and what designs are unlikely to lead to useful results? There is reason to think the choice of projects will be particularly difficult. Investigators arriving from developed countries will be unable to rely on their own personal observations and prior experience to the degree to which they can do so in their own cultures. They will be tempted to apply directly the procedures which have worked elsewhere. For adaptation of these procedures to the society in which they are working they will tend to rely on the local intelligentsia, the people with whom they will have the most personal contact. There is reason to be cautious about excessive reliance on these people, however. They may be only too ready to adopt the "symbols and ceremonials" of research without adequate grasp of its essential character.[110] They are likely to come from the top strata of their own society, and, as previously discussed, the social distance between them and other members of the society may be much greater than in countries like the United States.

The danger is that projects will be undertaken which appear to be better designed than they really are because they do not adequately take into account the situation as it exists in the society where they will be conducted—either the situation in terms of the potential usefulness of the research or in terms of what research can be completed successfully. In view of these uncertainties and risks, perhaps the best policy is one of caution, with unusual emphasis on simplicity and limited objectives in the basic design, and on preliminary pilot investigations.

A knowledgeable anthropologist sensitive to economic matters can be very useful in survey design if social incentives, or social constraints are important in affecting people's behavior. Some paths to economic goals may be closed by cultural or institutional barriers.[111]

APPENDIX A

A List of Some Reports of Economic Surveys in Other Countries
(including broadly economic items like family planning and economic
attitudes but not strictly methodological discussions)

Accra, Office of the Government Statistician, *Surveys of Household Budgets in Accra, Akuse, Sekondi and Kumasi.*

Ione Acqua, *Accra Survey: A Social Survey of the Capital of Ghana, Formerly Called the Gold Coast, Undertaken for the West African Institute of Social and Economic Research 1953-56,* University of London Press, London, 1958.

Peter Russell Andersen, *Discretionary and Contractual Saving in Canada, a Cross-Sectional Study,* Harvard University Ph.D. Thesis, Cambridge, Mass., 1967 (based on Canadian Dominion Bureau of Statistics 1959 family expenditure survey of 3,031 families in urban areas of 15,000 or more).

Joseph R. Ascroft, Niels G. Roling, Graham B. Kerr and Gerald D. Hursh, *Patterns of Diffusion in Rural Eastern Nigeria,* Diffusions of Innovations Research Report II, Department of Communication, Michigan State University, East Lansing, Michigan, Feb. 1969.

A. Asimakopulos, "Analysis of Canadian Consumer Expenditure Surveys," *Canadian Journal of Economics and Political Science,* 31 (May 1965), 222-241.

Bernard Berelson and Ronald Freedman, "A Study in Fertility Control," *Scientific American,* 210 (May 1964), 29-37 (in Taiwan).

Gunilla Bjeren, *Makelle (Ethiopia) Elementary School Drop-Out 1967,* Research Report No. 5, Scandinavian Institute of African Studies, Uppsala, Sweden, 1969.

Robert O. Blood, Reuben Hill, Andree Michel and Contantina Safilios-Rothschild, *Comparative Analysis of Family Power Structure: Problems of Measurement and Interpretation* (Paper at 9th International Seminar on Family Research, Tokyo, 1965) printed in *International Yearbook of Sociology.*

J. L. Boutillier and J. Causse, "Les budgets familiaux, mission socio-economique du fleuve Senegal," Dakar, 1958.

J. C. Caldwell, "Fertility Attitudes in Three Economically Contrasting Rural Regions of Ghana," *Economic Development and Cultural Change* 15 (Jan. 1967), 217-238.

Dominion of Canada, Royal Commission on Banking and Finance, *Consumer Survey* (Conducted by McDonald Research Limited in spring 1962 and published by them).

Dominion of Canada, Dominion Bureau of Statistics. *Farm Family Living Expenditure: 1958,* (Catalogue N 62-523 Occasional) Dominion Printer, Ottawa, Jan. 1966.

Dominion of Canada, Dominion Bureau of Statistics. *Urban Family Expenditure: 1959,* (Catalogue No. 62-521, Occasional) Dominion Printer, Ottawa, March, 1963.

Dominion of Canada, Dominion Bureau of Statistics, *Urban Family Food Expenditure, 1962* (Catalogue No. 62-524 Occasional) Dominion Printer, Ottawa, December, 1965.

Central Treaty Organization, *Symposium on Household Surveys,* Dacca, East Pakistan, 1966 (reports on surveys in Turkey, Pakistan, Iran).

Ceylon, Central Bank, *Survey of Ceylon's Consumer Finances, May, 1953,* The Central Bank, Colombo, Ceylon, 1954.

Michael Chaput and Ladislav Venys, *A Survey of Kenya Elite,* Occasional Papers No. 25, Program of East African Studies, Syracuse University, May 1967.

University of Chile, *Family Incomes and Expenditures in Greater Santiago-Experimental Survey,* Santiago, Institut de Econ. Econ Pub No. 85, 1966.

Paul Clerc, *Grands Ensembles. Banlieues Nouvelles, Enquête Démographique Et Psycho-Sologique,* Presses Universitaires De France, Paris, 1967.

George E. Cumper, "Expenditure Patterns, Kingston, Jamaica, 1954" in *Social and Economic Studies* 7 (June 1958) 166- (N = 1180, a later 1957-8 study appears only as a government document, N = 355).

Thomas Dow Jr., "Attitudes Toward Family Size and Family Planning in Nairobi" *Demography* 4 (1967) 780-797.

J. M. Due, "Post War Family Expenditure Studies in Western Europe," *Journal of Farm Econ.,* 38 (Aug. 1956), 846-856.

East African Statistics Department, *The Patterns of Income, Expenditure and Consumption of African Unskilled Laborers in Kampala, Sept. 1953,* 1954; - - - - - - *The Patterns of Income, Expenditure, and Consumption of Africans in Nairobi 1957/58,* 1959; - - - - - - *"Patterns of Income, Expenditure, and Consumption of African Unskilled Workers in Kampala, February, 1957,* 1957; - - - - - - *The Patterns of Income, Expenditure, and Consumption of African Unskilled Workers in Mbale, Feb., 1958,* 1958; - - - - - - *The Patterns of Income, Expenditure and Consumption of Agrian Unskilled Workers in Gulu, Feb. 1959,* 1959; - - - - - - *The Patterns of Income, Expenditures and Consumption of African Unskilled Workers in Fort Portal, February, 1960,* 1960 (all Nairobi).

Europe, Office Statistique Des Communautés Européenes, *Budgets Familiaux,* 1963-64, No. 1, Luxembourg, No. 2. Belgique, No. 3 Nederland, No. 4, Italia, No. 5 Allemagne, No. 6 France, No. 7, Bruxelles, Belgique, 1966 or later.

European Coal and Steel Community, "Budgets familiaux des ouvriers de la C.E.C.A. 1956-7," *Informations Statistiques* Serie "Statistiques socials" No. 1, 1960. (See also *Informations Statistiques,* May-June 1959 and November, 1959 for results of a housing survey of 40,000 workers.)

Abdul Farouk, *Irrigation in a Monsoon Land,* University of Dacca, Bureau of Economic Research, Dacca, East Pakistan, 1958 (Economics of Farming in the Ganges-Kobadak).

Frederick C. Fliegel, Prodipto Roy, Lalit K. Sen, Joseph E. Kiflin, *Agricultural Innovations in Indian Villages,* National Institute of Community Development, Hyderabad, India, 1968.

Food and Agriculture Organization, *Review of Food Consumption Surveys,* FAO, Rome, 1958.

Phillips Foster and Larry Yost, "A Simulation Study of Population, Education, and Income Growth in Uganda," *American Journal of Agricultural Economics* 51 (Aug. 1969), 576-91.

Ronald Freedman, "Sample Surveys for Family Planning Research in Taiwan," *Public Opinion Quarterly* (Summer 1964), 373-382.

M. P. Gavanier, *Budgets Familiaux des Ouvriers de la Communaute Europeenne du Charbon et de L'Acier, 1956-7.* Luxembourg: C.E.C.A., December, 1959 (similar data for 6 countries, much attention to income in kind).

Ghana, Office of the Government Statistician, *Statistical and Economic Papers* (various surveys reported 1953-1960).

Great Britain, Ministry of Labour, *Family Expenditure Survey; Report for 1962,* Her Majesty's Stationery Office, London, 1962 (also reports for 1957-9, 1960-61, and individual years from 1963). See Ministry of Labour Gazette.

Greece, National Statistical Service, *Household Survey—Carried out in the Urban Areas of Greece, 1957-58,* Athens, 1961 (See also the NSS's *Monthly Statistical Bulletin,* IV (April 1959, 9-25 and July 1959, p. 9, 9-24. (Continuous surveys starting with 1958;9, 300 households, to be raised to 600).

Greece, National Statistical Service, *Preliminary Report on the 1963-64 Household Survey—In the Semi-Urban and Rural Areas of Greece,* Athens, 1965.

S. C. Gupta, *An Economic Survey of Shamaspur Village* (University of Delhi, Delhi School of Economics, Continuous Village Survey Series No. 2), Asia Publishing House, New York, 1959.

Peter C. W. Gutkind, *African Urban Family Life* (Publications of the Institute of Social Studies, Serios Minor Vol. III) International Institute for Social Studies, 's-Gravenhague. Mouton and Co, The Hague, 1963.

M. Habibullah, *Some Aspects of Productivity in the Jute Industry of Pakistan* Bureau of Economic Research, University of Dacca, Dacca, East Pakistan, 1968 (Interviews with workers and supervisors).

Donald F. Heisel, "Attitudes and Practice of Contraception in Kenya," *Demography* 5 (1968), 632-641.

Hungarian Central Statistical Office, *The Twenty-Four Hours of the Day* (Analysis of 12,000 time-budgets) English, summary, Budapest, 1965.

Gerald D. Hursh, Niels R. Roling, Graham B. Kerr, *Innovation in Eastern Nigeria, Success and Failure of Agricultural Programs in 71 Villages of Eastern Nigeria*. Diffusion of Innovations Research Report 8, Department of Communications, Michigan State University, East Lansing, Michigan, Sept. 1968.

Gerald D. Hursh, Allan Hershfield, Gramam B. Kerr, Niels G. Roling, *Communications in Eastern Nigeria: An Experiment in Introducing Change*, Diffusions of Innovations Research Report 14, Department of Communications Michigan State University, East Lansing, Michigan, July, 1968.

Alex Inkeles, "Making Men Modern," *American Journal of Sociology*, 75 (Sept. 1969) 208-225 (six countries).

International Labour Office, *Family Living Studies*, I.L.O., Rome, 1961 (reports in 14 surveys in 12 countries).

I.N.S.E.E. (French Statistical Office) "Un enquete sur les dépenses des menages des exploitants agricoles en 1952," *Bulletin mensuel de statistique*, Paris, Presses Universitaires de France) Nouvelle série, supplément July-Sept. 1954, pp. 45 ff.

Israel, Central Bureau of Statistics, *Family Expenditures Survey 1963-4*, Jerusalem 1966; see also *Statistical Bulletin of Israel:* English Summary, April-July 1958 for 1956-7 survey; and Bank of Israel, Savings Survey 1963-64, Jerusalem, 1967.

Israel, Central Bureau of Statistics and Bank of Israel, *Saving Survey 1963-4*, Jerusalem, 1967.

Ivory Coast, Service de la Statistique et de la méchanographie de la Cote d'Ivorie *Enquete nutrituion-niveau de vie, Subdivisionde Bongouanou*, Paris, 1958.

Italy, Institute Centrale di Statistica, *Primi Risultati Dell' Indagine Sui Bilanci Di Famiglia*, Anni 1963-4, Roma, Aprile, 1966.

Jamaica, Department of Statistics, *Household Expenditure Survey 1957-8*, Government Printer, Kingston, 1959.

Japan, Bureau of Statistics, Office of the Prime Minister, *Family Income and Expenditure Survey*, Tokyo, yearly.

Joseph A. Kahl, *The Measurement of Modernism: A Study of Values in Brazil and Mexico*, University of Texas, Austin, 1968.

Kenya, Republic Of, Ministry of Economic Planning and Development, Statistics Division, *Economic Survey of Central Province* 1963-4, Nairobi, 1968.

Kenya Government, Ministry of Finance and Economic Planning, *The Patterns of Income, Expenditure, and Consumption of African Middle Income Workers in Nairobi, July, 1963, 1964*, Nairobi.

Joseph E. Kivlin, *Correlates of Family Planning in Eight Indian Villages*, Research

Report 18, Project on the Diffusion of Innovations in Rural Societies, National Institute of Community Development, Hyderabad, India, May, 1968.

J. B. Knight, "Earnings, Employment, Education and Income Distribution in Uganda," *Bulletin of the Oxford University, Institute of Economics and Statistics* 30 (Aug. 1968) 267-297.

Korea, Ministry of Public Information, *Report of the First Nation-Wide Public Opinion Survey,* by Ministry of Cabinet Administration, December, 1960; *Report of the Seoul City Public Opinion Survey,* June 1961; *Final Report of the Second Nationwide Public Opinion Survey,* August, 1961.

Irving Kravis, "International Differences in the Distribution of Income," *Review of Economics and Statistics,* 42 (Nov. 1960), 408-416, extensive bibliography.

Simon Kuznets, "Quantitative Aspects of the Economic Growth of Nations: Parx VIII Distribution of Income by Size," *Economic Development and Cultural Change* 11 (Jan. 1963) 80 pp. (summarizes international data from 16 countries).

Nissan Liviatan, *Consumption Patterns in Israel,* Falk Project for Econ. Res. in Israel, Jerusalem, 1964.

Nigeria. *Urban Consumer Surveys of Nigeria,* Government Printer, Lagos, 1959, 1963.

Malawi, *Housing Income Survey for Major Urban Areas,* Government Printer, Zomba, 1967.

Benton F. Massell, "Consistent Estimation of Expenditure Elasticities from Cross-Section Data on Households Producing Partly for Subsistence," *Review of Economics and Statistics* 51 (May 1969), 136-142.

Benton F. Massell and Judith Heyer, "Household Expenditures in Nairobi: A Statistical Analysis of Consumer Behavior," *Economic Development and Cultural Change* 17 (January 1969), 212-233.

P. K. Mukherjee and S. C. Gupta, *A Pilot Survey of Fourteen Villages in U.P. and Punjab,* Asia Publishing House, New York, 1959.

National Council of Applied Economic Research, *All India Rural Household Survey,* Vol. I, Methodology, August, 1964; Vol. II, Saving, Income and Investment, July 1965; Vol. III, Basic Tables with Notes, January 1966; and *Urban Income and Saving,* New Delhi, 1962.

Netherlands, Central Bureau of Statistics, *Savings Survey of the Netherlands, 1960,* Part I, Methods and Definitions, and Part II Results and Specifications, Zeist, Amsterdam, 1963.

W. S. Mann and J. C. O. Nwanko, *Rural Food Consumption Surveys in Eastern Nigeria* (mimeo), Ministry of Agriculture, Enogu, Eastern Nigeria, 1963.

K. S. Palda, "A Comparison of Consumer Expenditures in Quebec and Ontario," *Canadian Journal of Economics and Political Science* 33 (February 1967), uses 1959 government budget survey data).

J. O. Retel, *Logement Et Vie Familiale* (2 Tomes) Centre D'Etudes Des Groupes Sociaux, Paris, 1965.

J. Reyer and L. Goreau, *Review of Food Consumption Surveys,* F.A.O., Rome, 1959 (45 post-war surveys).

H. Riedwyl and F. Thomet, "On the Determination of Saturation Levels" (Zem Problem der Sättingung), *Schweiz. Zeitschr. f. Wolkwirtschaft und Stat.* 102 (June, 1966), 157-178. (Cross section of Swiss households in 1963).

Everett Rogers, *Modernization Among Peasants,* Holt, Rinehart and Winston, New York, 1969 (Summarizes a variety of data, some previously unpublished).

Everett M. Rogers and Ralph E. Neill, *Achievement Motivation among Colombian Peasants,* (Diffusion of Innovations Research Report 5), Department of Communication, Michigan State University, East Lansing, Michigan, 1966.

J. Ross and S. Bang, "Predicting the Adoption of Family Planning," *Studies in Family Planning* 9 (January 1966), 8-12.

Prodipto Roy, Frederick B. Waisanen, and Everett M. Rogers, *The Impact of Communication on Rural Development,* U.N.E.S.C.O., Paris, 1969.

Harold T. Shapiro and Gerald E. Angevine, "Consumer Attitudes, Buying Intentions and Expenditures: An Analysis of the Canadian Data," *Canadian Journal of Economics* 2 (May 1969), 230-249.

James R. Sheffield, Ed., *Education, Employment and Rural Development* (Conference at Kericho, Kenya, Sept. 1966), East African Publishing House, Nairobi, Kenya, 1967 (especially chapters by H. E. Ijnen, Koff, Moris, Somerset).

Miyohei Shinohara, *Growth and Cycles in the Japanese Economy,* Kinokuniya Bookstore, Tokyo, 1962. (Includes some survey data not generally available in English).

Andrzej Sicinski, "Public Opinion Surveys in Poland," *International Social Science Journal* 15 (1963), 91-110 (Includes surveys of leisure and recreation, attitudes to work and private property.)

Stanislaw Skrzypek, "The Political, Cultural, and Social Views of Yugoslav Youth," *Public Opinion Quarterly* 29 (Spring, 1965), 87-106.

R. H. Stroup and R. G. Marcis, "Analysis of Income and Expenditure Patterns in Rural South Vietnam," *Western Economic Journal* 6 (December, 1967), 52-64. (1964 AID survey).

Burkhard Strumpel, "Preparedness for Change in a Peasant Society," *Economic Development and Cultural Change* 13 (January 1965), 203-216.

Thailand, *Household Expenditure Survey* (Done in 1962-3) Published, no date, in 1968 with English subtitles.

Suresh D. Tendulkar, "Econometric Study of Monthly Consumption Expenditures in Rural Uttar Pradesh," *American Journal of Agricultural Economics* 51 (February 1969), 119-137.

Sten Thore, *Household Saving and the Price Level,* National Institute of Economic Research (Konjunctur Institutet) Stockholm, 1961.

M. A. Tremblay, G. Fortin and M. LaPlante, *Les Comportements Economique de la Familie du Quebec.* Les Presses de L'Universite Laval. Quebec, Canada, 1964.

K. Tsujimura, "Family Budget Data and the Market Analysis," *Bulletin of the International Statistical Institute* 38 (1961), 215-242.

Uganda Government, *The Patterns of Income, Expenditure and Consumption of African Unskilled Workers in Kampala, February, 1964,* Statistical Branch, Ministry of Planning and Community Development, Entebbe, Uganda, 1966.

Uganda Government, *The Patterns of Income and Expenditure of Coffee Growers in Buganda, 1962/3,* Statistics Division, Ministry of Planning and Economic Development, Entebbe, Uganda, January, 1965.

M. Upton, "Socio-Economic Survey of Some Farm Families in Nigeria," *Bulletin Rural Econ. Sociol.* 2, 127-183.

F. B. Waisanen and Jerome T. Durlak, *A Survey of Attitudes Related to Costa Rican Population Dynamics,* Program Interamericano de Informacion Popular, American International Association for Economic and Social Development, San Jose, Costa Rica, 1966. (AID funded) (Has annotated bibliography of 62 similar items.)

U.S. Department of Commerce, Bureau of the Census, *The Soviet Statistical System: The Continuous Sample Budget Survey,* International Population Reports Series P-95, Washington, January, 1965.

Ursula Wallberg, *Hushållens Sparande år 1957,* Konjunkturinstitutet, Stockholm, 1963 and same in 1958, published in 1966, also a 1955 pilot study publ. in 1959.

Gordon C. Whiting, William A. Herzog, Gustavo M. Quesada, J. David Stanfield and Lytton Guimaraes, *Innovation in Brazil: Success and Failure of Agricultural Programs in 76 Minas Gerais Communities,* Diffusion of Innovations Research Report 7, Department of Communications, Michigan State University, East Lansing, Michigan, January, 1968.

Gordon C. Whiting and John A. Winterbon, *Methodological Background of the Phase 1, MSY-AID Brazil Diffusion Project,* Technical Report 6, Department of Communications, Michigan State University, East Lansing, Michigan, May, 1968.

Gordon H. Wilson, *An Evaluation of Three Years of Rural Development and Change at Samia-Kabondo-Bomet, Rural Development Survey* (prepared for Ministry of Cooperatives and Social Services Dept. of Community Development) Nairobi, 1968. (Changed interviewers and selection of final units led to biases).

F. C. Wright, *African Consumers in Nyasaland and Tanganyika,* H.M.S.O., London, 1955. (Inquiry carried out in 1952-3.)

Charles Y. Yang, "An International Comparison of Consumption Functions," *Review of Economics and Statistics* 46 (Aug. 1964), 279-286.

Footnotes to Chapter IV

1. See *Statistical Reporter,* July, 1959.

2. For some history, see Gertrude Bancroft, "Current Unemployment Estimates of the Census Bureau and some Alternatives," in *Measurement and Behavior of Unemployment,* Princeton University Press, Princeton, New Jersey, 1957.

   For a report on difficulties when a sample was changed, resulting not from sampling but from interviewer training and procedures, see Robert W. Burgess, "Report of Special Advisory Committee on Employment Statistics," *American Statistician* 8 (Dec. 1954), 4-6 and Stanley Lebergott, "Measuring Unemployment," *Review of Economics and Statistics* 36 (November, 1954), 390-400.

   For a report on the current definitions, see U.S. Congress, Joint Economic Committee, Subcommittee on Economic Statistics, *Unemployment: Terminology, Measurement, and Analysis,* U.S. G.P.O., Washington, D.C., 1961; and also U.S. Department of Labor and U.S. Department of Commerce (Bureau of Labor Statistics and Bureau of the Census), *Concepts and Methods Used in Manpower Statistics from the Current Population Survey,* B.L.S. Report No. 313, Current Population Series P-23, No. 22, U.S. G.P.O., Washington, D.C., June, 1967.

3. G. Allen Brunner and Stephen J. Carroll, Jr., "Weekday Evening Interviews of Employed Persons are Better," *Public Opinion Quarterly* 33 (Summer, 1969), 265-7.

4. One study of unwed mothers found more "public answers" in personal interviews, particularly from low-status respondents replying to middle-status interviewers: Dean D. Knudson, Hallowell Pope, and Donald P. Irish, "Response Differences to Questions on Sexual Standards: An Interview-Questionnaire Comparison," *Public Opinion Quarterly* 31 (Summer 1967), 290-297; see also Ralph H. Oakes, "Differences in Responsiveness in Telephone versus Personal Interviews," *Journal of Marketing* 19 (October 1954), 169 (more suggestions given in person than on phone).

5. Jay Schmiedeskamp, "Reinterviews by Telephone," *Journal of Marketing,* Vol. 26, No. 1, January 1962, pp. 28-34.

6. There is some evidence that preliminary phone calls improve response rates for mail surveys. See Neil M. Ford, "The Advance Letter in Mail Surveys," *Journal of Marketing Research,* Vol. IV, May 1966, pp. 202-204.

7. G. Allen Brunner and Stephen J. Carroll, Jr., "The Effect of Prior Telephone Appointments on Completion Rates and Response Content," *Public Opinion Quarterly* 31 (Winter 1967-68), 652-4.

8. Charles F. Cannell and Floyd J. Fowler, "Comparison of a Self-enumerative Procedure and a Personal Interview: A Validity Study," *Public Opinion Quarterly* 27 (Summer 1963), 250-264. See also Charles F. Cannell *Comparison of Hospitalization Reporting in Three Survey Procedures,* U.S. Dept. of Health, Education and Welfare, National Health Survey, P.H.S. Publ. No. 584-D8. Washington, D.C., 1963.

9. W. F. F. Kemsley, "Interviewer Variability in Expenditure Surveys," *J.R.S.S.,* Series A, Vol. 128, 1965, pp. 118-137. See also Life Magazine, *Life Study of Consumer Expenditure,* Time, Inc., New York, 1952.

10. Herbert N. Hyman, *Interviewing in Social Research,* University of Chicago Press, 1954, pp. 182-185.

11. See Hyman, *op. cit.,* for citations.

12. Leon Festinger, (cited by Hyman, pp. 182-185).

13. John B. Lansing, Gerald Ginsburg, and Kaisa Braaten, *An Investigation of Response Error,* Urbana, Bureau of Business and Economic Research, University of Illinois, 1961.

14. Christopher Scott, "Research on Mail Surveys," *Journal of the Royal Statistical Society,* Series A, Vol. 124 (1961), 143-195, The discussion on pp. 196-205 contains additional experience by other researchers who were the discussants.

15. See the discussion in Joseph Waksberg and Robert Pearl, "The Current Population Survey: A Case History in Panel Operations," *Proceedings, Social Statistics Section, American Statistical Association,* 1964, pp. 217-228.

16. *Ibid.* See also U.S. Bureau of Census *The Current Population Survey, A Report on Methodology,* Technical Paper No. 7, U.S.G.P.O., Washington, D.C., 1963.

17. Stephen B. Withey, *Consistency of Immediate and Delayed Report of Financial Data,* Ph.D. Thesis, University of Michigan, Ann Arbor, Michigan, 1952.

18. See John Neter and Joseph Waksberg, *Response Errors in Collection of Expenditure Data by Household Interviews: An Experimental Study,* U.S. Dept. of Commerce, Bureau of the Census, Technical Paper No. 11, U.S.G.P.O., Washington, D.C., 1965 (contains an extensive bibliography).

19. Lansing, Ginsburg, and Braaten, *op. cit.* See also Robert Ferber "Does A Panel Operation Increase the Reliability of Survey Data? The Case of

Consumer Savings," *Proceedings of the Social Statistics Section,* American Statistical Association, 1964, pp. 210-216; see also Robert Ferber, *Collecting Financial Data by Consumer Panel Techniques,* Univ. of Illinois, Bureau of Economic and Business Research, Urbana, Ill., 1964.

20. Waksberg and Pearl, *op. cit.*

21. Marion Sobol, "Panel Mortality and Panel Bias," *Journal of the American Statistical Association,* 54 (March, 1959), 52-68.

22. Cannell and Fowler, *P.O.Q.,* 1963.

23. P. W. Haberman and J. Elinson, "Family Income Reported in Surveys: Husbands Versus Wives," *Journal of Marketing Research* 4 (1967), 191-194.

24. E. Wohlgast, "Do Husbands or Wives Make the Purchasing Decisions?" *Journal of Marketing* (Oct. 1958), 151-8. See summary of this and others in Morgan, "Household Decision Making," in *Household Decision Making,* Nelson Foote, ed. New York University Press, 1961.

25. James N. Morgan, "Some Pilot Studies of Communication and Consensus in the Family," *Public Opinion Quarterly* 32 (Spring, 1968), 113-121; see also John A. Ballweg, "Husband-Wife Response Similarities on Evaluative and Non-Evaluative Survey Questions," *Public Opinion Quarterly* 33 (Summer 1969), 249-254; Robert Ferber, "On the Reliability of Responses Secured in Sample Surveys," *Journal of the American Statistical Association* 50 (1955), 788-810; John Neter and Joseph Waksberg "Effects of Interviewing Designated Respondents in a Household Survey of Home Owners Expenditures on Alterations and Repairs," *Applied Statistics* 12 (1963), 46-60; and Shirley A. Star, "Obtaining Household Opinions from a Single Respondent," *Public Opinion Quarterly* 17 (Fall 1953), 386-391.

26. Kenneth Arrow, *Social Choice and Individual Values,* John Wiley and Sons, New York, 1951.

27. George Levinger, personal communication.

28. C. S. Lewis, *The Screw-Tape Letters,* Macmillan, New York, 1944.

29. Monroe G. Sirken, E. Scott Maynes, John A. Frechtling, "The Survey of Consumer Finances and the Census Quality Check," in *Studies in Income and Wealth,* Vol. 23, *An Appraisal of the 1950 Census Income Data,* Princeton University Press, 1958, pp. 127-168.

30. Harry V. Kincaid and Margaret Bright, "Interviewing the Business Elite," *American Journal of Sociology* 63 (Nov. 1957), 304-311.

31. Robert B. Pearl, *Methodology of Consumer Expenditure Surveys,* Working Paper 27, Bureau of the Census. U.S. Department of Commerce, Washington, D.C., March, 1968.

32. Bernard Berelson and Ronald Freedman, "A Study in Fertility Control," *Scientific American* 210 (1964), 29-37.

33. Frederick G. Lasley, Elmer R. Kiehl and D. E. Brady, "Consumer Preference for Beef in Relation to Finish," *Research Bulletin* 580, Missouri Agricultural Experiment Station, University of Missouri, Columbia, Missouri, March 1955.

34. Donald J. Baker and Charles H. Berry, "The Price Elasticity of Demand for Fluid Skim Milk," *Journal of Farm Economics* 35 (February 1953), 124-129.

35. R. N. Morris and John Mogey, *The Sociology of Housing,* Routlege and Kegan Paul, London, 1965.

36. B. P. Emmett, "The Design of Investigations into the Effects of Radio and Television Programmes or Other Mass Communications," *Journal of the Royal Statistical Society* 129 (1966), 26-49, with discussion on pp. 50-60.

37. Philip Converse, "The Shifting Role of Class in Political Attitudes and Behavior," in *Readings in Social Psychology,* Eleanor Maccoby, Theodore Newcomb and Eugene Hartley, Eds., 3rd Edition, Henry Holt and Co., New York, 1958, pp. 388-399. See also Angus Campbell and Warren E. Miller, "The Motivational Basis of Straight and Split Ticket Voting," *American Political Science Review,* 51 (June, 1957) 293-312 (Effect of State Laws).

38. For the best statement yet, see Charles F. Cannell and Robert L. Kahn "Interviewing" in Gardner Lindzey and Elliot Aronson, eds., *Handbook of Social Psychology* Vol. II, Addison-Wesley, New York, 1968 (526-595) or the earlier more extensive books: Robert Kahn and Charles Cannell, *The Dynamics of Interviewing,* Wiley, New York, 1957; and Herbert H. Hyman and others *Interviewing in Social Research,* University of Chicago Press, Chicago, 1954.

39. B. M. Bass, "Authoritarianism or Acquiescence?" *Journal of Abnormal and Social Psychology* 51 (November 1955), 616-623.

Raymond A. Bauer and Stephen A. Greyser, *Advertising in America: The Consumer View,* Cambridge, Harvard University Press, 1968 (demonstrated by a number of conflicting statements, both agreed to).

I. A. Berg and G. M. Rapaport, "Response Bias in an Unstructured Questionnaire," *Journal of Psychology* 38 (Oct., 1954), 475-581.

Urie Bronfenbrenner, "Personality and Participation: The Case of the Vanishing Variables," *Journal of Social Issues* 16 (1960), 54-63.

Donald T. Campbell, Carole R. Siegman and Matilda B. Rees, "Direction-of-Wording Effects on the Relationships between Scales," *Psychological Review* 68 (November 1967), 293-303.

A. Couch and K. Keniston, "Yeasayers and Naysayers: Agreeing Response Set as a Personality Variable," *Journal of Abnormal and Social Psychology* 60 (1960) 151-174.

A. Paul Hare, "Interview Responses: Personality of Conformity?" *Public Opinion Quarterly* 24 (Winter, 1960), 679-685.

Harry A. Landsberger and Antonio Saavedra, "Response Set in Developing Countries," *Public Opinion Quarterly* 31 (Summer 1967), 214-229.

Gerhard Lenski and John Leggett, "Caste, Class and Deference in the Research Interview," *American Journal of Sociology* 65 (March 1960), 463-467.

Samuel Messick and Douglas N. Jackson, "Acquiescence and the Factorial Interpretation of the MMPI," *Psychological Bulletin* 58 (July 1961), 299-304.

David Horton Smith, "Correcting for Social Desirability Response Sets in Opinion-Attitude Survey Research," *Public Opinion Quarterly* 31 (Spring 1967), 95-102.

Hans J. Eysenck, "Response Set, Authoritarianism, and Personality Questionnaires," *British Journal of Social and Clinical Psychology* 1 (1962), 20-24.

J. B. Knowles, "Acquiescence Response Set and the Questionnaire Measurement of Personality," *British Journal of Social and Clinical Psychology* 2 (1963), 131-137 (argues against "balancing" questions).

John Martin, "Acquiescence—Measurement and Theory," *British Journal of Social and Clinical Psychology* 3 (1964), 216-225 (distinguishes between sets for acquiescence and social desirability).

40. James Morgan, Ismail Sirageldin and Nancy Baerwaldt, *Productive Americans,* Survey Research Center, University of Michigan, Ann Arbor, 1966; see also Alan C. Kerckhoff, "Nuclear and Extended Family Relationships: A Normative and Behavioral Analysis" in Ethel Shanas and Gordon Streif, eds., *Social Structure and the Family; Generational Relations,* Prentice-Hall, Englewood Cliffs, N.J., 1965, p. 112.

41. George Katona, *Mass Consumption Society,* McGraw Hill, New York, 1964.

42. Barbara B. Reagan, *Condensed v. Detailed Schedule for Collection of Family Expenditure Data,* U.S.D.A., Agricultural Research Service, Home Economics Research Branch, March 1954, Washington, D.C.

43. M. Brewster Smith, J. S. Bruner and R. W. White, *Opinions and Personality,* Wiley, New York, 1956, p. 286. (A study of ten men.)

44. Robert Eisner, Review of Robert A. Gordon and Lawrence R. Klein, ed., *Readings in Business Cycles,* Richard D. Irwin, Homewood, 1965, in *American Economic Review* 56 (Sept. 1966), p. 928.

45. See Kahn and Cannell, "Interviewing," in Gardner Lindzey and E. Aronson, *Handbook of Social Psychology,* Addison Wesley, New York, 1968, pp. 526-595; A. N. Oppenheim, *Questionnaire Design and Attitude Measurement,* H. Cineman, London, Herbert Hyman, and others, *Interviewing in Social Research,* University of Chicago Press, Chicago, 1954;

    Robert Kahn and Charles Cannell, *The Dynamics of Interviewing,* Wiley, New York, 1957.

46. Herbert H. Hyman, *op. cit.*

47. Cited by Hyman, p. 197. (See *International Journal of Opinion and Attitude Research,* IV, 1950, p. 391.)

48. See Hyman, *op. cit.,* p. 199.

49. Hyman, *op. cit.,* p. 218.

50. Morris Axelrod and Charles F. Cannell, "A Research Note on an Attempt to Predict Interviewer Effectiveness," *Public Opinion Quarterly,* Vol. 23, No. 4 (Winter 1959), pp. 571-575.

51. Seymour Sudman, "Quantifying Interviewer Quality," *Public Opinion Quarterly,* Vol. 30, Winter 1966, pp. 664-667.

52. Matthew Hauck and Stanley Steinkamp, *Survey Reliability and Interviewer Competence,* Bureau of Economic and Business Research, University of Illinois, Urbana, 1964. See also S. Steinkamp, "The Identification of Effective Interviewers," *Journal of the American Statistical Association* 59 (December, 1964), 1165-1174.

53. U.S. Department of Commerce, Bureau of the Census, Evaluation and Research Program of the U.S. Censuses of Population and Housing, 1960 Series ER 60 No. 7 *Effects of Interviewers and Crew Leaders,* Washington, D.C., 1968.

54. Ann Cartwright and Wyn Tucker, "An Attempt to Reduce the Number of Calls in an Interview Inquiry," *Public Opinion Quarterly* (Summer 1967), pp. 299-302.

55. Marjorie N. Donald, "Implications of Nonresponse for the Interpretation of Mail Questionnaire Data," *Public Opinion Quarterly,* Vol. 24 (Spring 1960), pp. 99-114.

56. See W. F. F. Kemsley, "Some Technical Aspects of a Postal Survey into Professional Earnings," *Applied Statistics* 11 (June 1962), 93-105; *Salaries and Selected Characteristics of U.S. Scientists* (preliminary report based on 1968

National Register of Scientific and Technical Personnel, U.S.G.P.O., Washington, D.C., Dec. 1968.

57. Walter E. Boek and James H. Lade, "A Test of the Usefulness of the Post-Card Technique in a Mail Questionnaire Study," *Public Opinion Quarterly,* Vol. 27 (Summer 1963), pp. 303-306.

58. Percy S. Gray and Elizabeth A. Parr, "The Length of Cigarette Stubs," *Applied Statistics* 8 (June 1959), 92-103.

59. Charles F. Cannell and Morris Axelrod, "The Respondent Reports on the Interview," *American Journal of Sociology,* Vol. 62 (September 1956), pp. 177-181.

60. Kenneth J. Gergen and Kurt W. Back, "Communication in the Interview and the Disengaged Respondent," *Public Opinion Quarterly,* Vol. 30 (Fall 1966), pp. 385-398.

61. Charles F. Cannell and Floyd J. Fowler, "Comparison of a Self-enumeration Procedure with a Personal Interview: A Validity Study," *Public Opinion Quarterly* 27 (Summer 1963), 250-264.

62. Herbert H. Hyman, *Interviewing in Social Research,* The University of Chicago Press, 1954. See page 155 ff.

63. But, Martin David found black respondents more likely to admit to white interviewers that they were on welfare, see Martin David "The Validity of Income Reported by Families Who Received Assistance During 1959," *Journal of the American Statistical Association* 57 (September 1962), 680-685.

64. Dan Katz, "Do Interviewers' Bias Poll Results?" *Public Opinion Quarterly* 6 (Summer 1942), 248-268.

65. James M. Hund, "Changing Role in the Interview Situation," *Public Opinion Quarterly,* Vol. 23, No. 2 (Summer 1959), pp. 236-246.

66. June Sacher Ehrlich and David Riesman, "Age and Authority in the Interview," *Public Opinion Quarterly,* Vol. 25 (Spring 1961), pp. 39-56.

67. Rainald K. Bauer and Frank Meissner, "Structure of Mail Questionnaires: Test of Alternatives," *Public Opinion Quarterly,* Vol. 27 (Summer 1967), pp. 307-311.

68. Paul W. Haberman and Jack Elinson, "Family Income Reported in Surveys: Husbands Versus Wives," *Journal of Marketing Research,* Vol. 14 (May 1967), pp. 191-194.

69. Barbara A. Powell, "Recent Research in Reinterview Procedures," *Proceedings, Social Statistics Section, American Statistical Association,* 1966, pp. 420-433.

70. Allen F. Jung, "Shopping Techniques for Collecting Price Data," *Public Opinion Quarterly* (Summer 1964), pp. 303-311.

71. Herbert H. Hyman, *Interviewing in Social Research,* The University of Chicago Press, 1954, pp. 228-242.

72. See U.S. Department of Agriculture, *Response Variation Encountered with Different Questionnaire Forms,* Marketing Research Report No. 163, U.S.D.A., Washington, D.C., 1957.

73. Kent Marquis, "Effects of Social Reinforcement on Health Reporting in the Household Interview," *Sociometry* 33 (June 1970) 203-215. For a development of theory toward this, see Kahn and Cannell, in Festinger and Katz, *Research Methods in the Behavioral Sciences,* Dryden, N.Y., 1953, then in *Dynamics of Interviewing,* Wiley, New York, 1957, and finally in their chapter in the *Handbook of Social Psychology,* Lindzey and Bronson, Ed., Addison Wesley, New York, 1968.

74. Joseph Waksberg and Robert B. Pearl, "The Current Population Survey: A Case History in Panel Operations," *Proceedings, Social Statistics Section, American Statistical Association,* 1964, pp. 217-228.

75. Lolagene Coombs and Ronald Freedman, "Use of Telephone Interviews in a Longitudinal Fertility Study," *Public Opinion Quarterly,* 28 (Spring 1964) 112-117. The women interviewed were recently married or had one, two, or four children.

76. Jeanne E. and John T. Gullahorn, "An Investigation of the Efforts of Three Factors on Response to Mail Questionnaires," *Public Opinion Quarterly,* 27, (Summer 1963), 294-296. But see Scott, op. cit. for a discouraging summary of varying methods of using mail.

77. Durbin and A. Stuart, "Differences in Response Rates of Experienced and Inexperienced Interviewers," *Journal of the Royal Statistical Society,* A114 (1951), 163-205; W. F. F. Kemsley, "Interviewer Variability a Budget Study," *Applied Statistics* 9 (June 1960), 122-128.

78. For other data on differences according to number of calls required, see Leslie Kish, *Survey Sampling,* Wiley, New York, 1965, pp. 532-547, and S. S. Zarkovich, *Quality of Statistical Data,* F.A.O., Rome, 1966, pp. 145-151, 167, and pp. 173-180.

79. Marion Gross Sobol, "Panel Mortality and Panel Bias," *Journal of the American Statistical Association* 54 (March 1959), pp. 52-68.

80. Philip E. Converse, "Discussion," part of a session on "Evaluation of Panel Operations," *Proceedings, Social Statistics Section,* A.S.A., 1964, pp. 229-231. For another report on panel losses, see R. Kosobud and J. Morgan, Eds., *Consumer Behavior of Individual Farmers over Two and Three Years,*

Institute for Social Research, University of Michigan, Ann Arbor, 1964, Appendix B by A. M. Marckwardt.

81. Lee N. Robins, "The Reluctant Respondent," *Public Opinion Quarterly* 27, (Summer 1963), 276-286.

82. Charles S. Mayer and Robert W. Pratt, Jr., "A Note on Nonresponse in a Mail Survey," *Public Opinion Quarterly* 30 (Winter 1966), 637-646.

83. See Hazel Gaudet and E. C. Wilson, "Who Escapes the Personal Investigators?" *Journal of Applied Psychology* 24 (1940), 773-777;

    T. P. Hill, "A Pilot Survey of Incomes and Savings," *Bulletin of the Oxford University Institute of Statistics* 22 (May 1960), 131-142;

    T. P. Hill, L. R. Klein and K. H. Straw, "The Savings Survey of 1953, Response Rates and Reliability of Data," *Bulletin of the Oxford University Institute of Statistics* 17 (Feb. 1955), 89-126;

    Lee N. Robbins, "The Reluctant Respondent," *Public Opinion Quarterly* 27 (Summer 1963), 276-286;

    H. Lawrence Ross, "The Inaccessible Respondent: A Note on Privacy in City and Country," *Public Opinion Quarterly* 27 (Summer 1963), 269-275;

    Frederick J. Stephan and Philip J. McCarthy, *Sampling Opinions,* Wiley, New York, 1963, pp. 235-272;

    Edward A. Suchman, "An Analysis of Bias in Survey Research," *Public Opinion Quarterly* (Spring 1962), 102-111.

84. Edward A. Suchman, *op. cit.*

85. Robert Ferber, "Item Nonresponse in a Consumer Survey," *Public Opinion Quarterly* 30 (Fall 1966), 399-415.

86. L. Kish and J. Lansing, "Response Errors in Estimating the Value of Homes," *Journal of the American Statistical Association* 49 (Sept. 1954), 520-538. For estimates of non-money incomes, see J. Morgan, M. David, W. Cohen and H. Brazer, *Income and Welfare in the U.S.,* McGraw-Hill, New York, 1962; and J. Morgan, I. Sirageldin, and N. Baerwaldt, *Productive Americans,* Survey Research Center, University of Michigan, Ann Arbor, 1966.

87. See Lee J. Cronback, *Essentials of Psychological Testing,* second edition, Harper and Bros., New York, 1960.

88. John A. Ballweg, "Husband-Wife Response Similarities on Evaluative and Non-Evaluative Survey Questions," *Public Opinion Quarterly* 33 (Summer 1969), 249-254.

    P. W. Haberman and J. Elinson, "Family Income Reported in Surveys: Husbands Versus Wives," *Journal of Marketing Research* 4 (May, 1967), 191-194.

Robert Ferber, "On the Reliability of Responses Secured in Sample Surveys," *Journal of the American Statistical Association* 50 (Sept., 1955), 788-810.

James Morgan, "Some Pilot Studies of Communication and Consensus in the Family," *Public Opinion Quarterly* 32 (Spring 1968), 113-121.

John Neter and Joseph Waksberg, "Effects of Interviewing Designated Respondents in a Household Survey of Home Owners Expenditures on Alterations and Repairs," *Applied Statistics* 12 (March, 1963), 46-60.

Shirley A. Star, "Obtaining Household Opinions from a Single Respondent," *Public Opinion Quarterly* 17 (Fall 1953), 386-391.

Elizabeth H. Wolgast, "Do Husbands or Wives Make the Purchasing Decision?" *Journal of Marketing* (October 1958), 151-158.

89. Wolgast, *op. cit.*

90. John Neter and Joseph Waksberg, "A Study of Response Errors in Expenditure Data from Household Interviews," *Journal of the American Statistical Association* 59, 1964, pp. 18-55. J. Neter and J. Waksburg, *Response Errors in Collection of Expenditure Data by Household Interviews,* U.S. Bureau of the Census, Technical Paper No. 11, Washington, D.C., 1965.

91. Robin Barlow, J. Morgan and G. Wirick, "A Study of Validity in Reporting Medical Care in Michigan," *Proceedings of the Business and Economics Statistics Section,* American Statistical Association, Aug. 1960, pp. 54-65.

Nedra B. Belloc, "Validation of Morbidity Survey Data by Comparisons with Hospital Records," *Journal of the American Statistical Association,* 49 (December, 1954), 832-846.

Michael E. Borus, "Response Error in Survey Reports of Earnings Information," *Journal of the American Statistical Association,* 61 (Sept. 1966), 729-738.

Gerhard Brinkman, *Berufsausbildung und Arbietseinkommen,* Duncker und Humblot, Berlin, 1967 (grades in school).

Arthur L. Broida, "Consumer Surveys as a Source of Information for Social Accounting," in *The Flow-of-Funds Approach to Social Accounting,* (Studies in Income and Wealth, Vol. 26), Princeton University Press, Princeton, 1962, pp. 335-381.

Charles F. Cannell, Gordon Fisher, and Thomas Bakker, *Reporting of Hospitalization in the Health Interview Survey* (Health Statistics, Series D, No. 4), U.S. Public Health Service, Washington, D.C., May 1961.

Martin David, "The Validity of Income Reported by a Sample of Families Who Received Welfare Assistance During 1959," *Journal of the American Statistical Association,* 57 (Sept., 1962), 680-685.

Robert Ferber, "The Reliability of Consumer Surveys of Financial Holdings: Demand Deposits," *Journal of the American Statistical Association,* 61 (March, 1966), 91-103.

Robert Ferber, *The Reliability of Consumer Reports of Financial Assets and Debts,* University of Illinois, Bureau of Economic and Business Research, Urbana, June, 1966.

Gordon Fisher, "A Discriminant Analysis of Reporting Errors in Health Interviews," *Applied Statistics,* 11 (Nov. 1962), 148-163.

Percy G. Gray, "The Memory Factor in Social Surveys," *Journal of the American Statistical Association,* 50 (June, 1955), 344-363.

Harold M. Groves, "Empirical Studies in Income Tax Compliance," *National Tax Journal,* XI (December, 1958), 291-301 (Reverse purpose—to check official records accuracy).

Lawrence D. Haber, "Evaluating Response Error in the Reporting of the Income of the Aged: Benefit Income," *Proceedings of the Social Statistics Section,* American Statistical Association, 1966, 412-419.

Einar Hardin and Gerald L. Hershey, "Accuracy of Employee Reports on Changes in Pay," *Journal of Applied Psychology,* 44 (Aug., 1960), 269-275.

W. Horn, "The Milli-RPS," an Investigation into the Nature and the Behavior of RPS Savers," transl. from HETP.T.T. bedrift, Vol. VIII (Aug., 1957).

David L. Kaplan, Elizabeth Parkhurst, and Pascal K. Whelpton, "The Comparability of Reports on Occupation, from Vital Records and the 1950 Census," U.S. Dept. of Health, Education and Welfare, Public Health Service, Office of Vital Statistics, *Special Reports,* 52 (June, 1961).

E. Keating, D. G. Paterson and C. H. Stone, "Validity of Work Histories Obtained by Interview," *Journal of Applied Psychology,* 34 (Feb., 1950), 6-11.

Leslie Kish and John Lansing, "Response Errors in Estimating the Value of Homes," *Journal of the American Statistical Association,* 49 (Sept., 1954), 520-538.

John B. Lansing, Gerald Ginsburg, and Kaisa Bratten, *An Investigation of Response Error,* University of Illinois, Bureau of Economics and Business Research, Urbana, June, 1961.

E. Scott Maynes, "The Anatomy of Response Errors: Consumer Saving," *Journal of Marketing Research,* 2 (November, 1965), 378-387.

E. Scott Maynes, "Minimizing Response Errors in Financial Data," *Journal of the American Statistical Association,* 63 (March, 1968), 214-227.

Joseph F. Metz, Jr., *Accuracy of Response Obtained in a Milk Consumption Study,* Methods of Research in Marketing, Paper No. 5, Cornell University, Agricultural Experiment Station, Storrs, July, 1956.

Saad Nagi, "Congruency in Medical and Self-Assessments of Disability," *Industrial Medicine and Surgery,* 38 (March, 1969), 22-33.

Twila E. Neely, *A Study of Error in the Interview,* Ph.D. Thesis, Columbia University, New York, 1937 (Summary of older data).

Robert C. Nuckols, "The Validity and Comparability of Mail and Personal Interview Surveys," *Journal of Marketing Research,* 1 (February, 1964), 11-16, (life insurance).

Mistuo Ono, George F. Patterson, and Murray S. Weitzman, "The Quality of Reporting Social Security Numbers in Two Surveys," *Proceedings of the Social Statistics Section,* American Statistical Association, 1968, p. 197-205.

Fred Østergård, *De Aeldres Levelilkar, I, Indkomsterne,* Socialforskings-instituttets, Publikationer 17, København, 1965 (Danish National Institute for Social Research). (A check of incomes of aged against tax returns.)

Alfred Politz, *Description of Operational Design and Procedures,* Vol. 4, Life Study of Consumer Expenditures, 1958 (Recall of supermarket bill that evening).

Lee N. Robins, *Deviant Children Grow Up,* Williams and Wilkins, Baltimore 1966, Chapter 12, reports on past behavior).

Barkev S. Sanders, "How Good Are Hospital Data from a Household Survey?" Paper at Statistical Section, American Public Health Association, October, 1958. (See other publications of this author.)

M. G. Sirken, E. S. Maynes, and J. A. Frechtling, "The Survey of Consumer Finances and the Census Quality Check," in *An Appraisal of the 1950 Census Income Data* (Studies in Income and Wealth, Vol. 23) Princeton University Press, Princeton, 1958.

Kaare Svalastoga, "Interviewets gyldighedsproblem: En Prøve" *Sociologiske Meddeleser* 5 (1960) 64-67 (Danish) Income checked by records.

U.S. Bureau of the Census, Evaluation and Research Program of the U.S. Censuses of Population and Housing; *Record Check Studies of Population Coverage;* Series ER 60 N' 2, Washington, D.C., 1964.

- - - - - - *Accuracy of Data on Housing Characteristics,* Series ER60, No. 3, Washington, D.C., 1964.

- - - - - - *Accuracy of Data on Population Characteristics as Measured by CPS-Census Match,* Series ER 60, No. 5, Washington, D.C., 1965.

- - - - - - *The Employer Record Check,* Series ER 60, No. 6, Washington, D.C., 1965.

Carol Weiss, *Interviewing Low-Income Respondents,* Columbia University, Bureau of Applied Social Research, Oct. 1966 (A survey of the literature).

David J. Weiss, Rene V. Davis, George W. England and Lloyd H. Lofquist, *Validity of Work Histories Obtained by Interview,* (Minnesota Studies in Vocational Rehabilitation XII), University of Minnesota, Industrial Relations Center, Minneapolis, 1961.

92. John Neter, E. Scott Maynes, and R. Ramanathan, "The Effect of Mismatching on the Measurement of Response Errors," *Journal of the American Statistical Association* 60 (December, 1965), 1005-1027.

93. Grover Wirick, *op. cit.*

94. Morris H. Hansen, William N. Hurwitz, and Max A. Bershad, "Measurement Errors in Censuses and Surveys," *Bulletin of the International Statistical Institute,* Vol. 38, part 1, 1961, pp. 359-374.

95. Leslie Kish and John B. Lansing, "Response Error in Estimating the Value of Homes," *Journal of the American Statistical Association,* 49 (Sept. 1954), pp. 520-538.

96. Robert Ferber, "Reliability of Consumer Surveys of Demand Deposits," *Journal of the American Statistical Association,* 61 (March 1966), pp. 91-103.

97. Ronald Freedman, "Sample Surveys for Family Planning Research in Taiwan," *Public Opinion Quarterly,* 28 (Summer 1964), pp. 373-382.

98. Thomas Rhys Williams, "A Critique of the Assumptions of Survey Research," *Public Opinion Quarterly,* Vol. 23, Spring 1959, pp. 55-62. See also L. Rudolph and S. H. Rudolph, "Surveys in India: Field Experience in Madras State," *Public Opinion Quarterly,* 22, (Fall 1958), pp. 235-244. See also the above issue of *Public Opinion Quarterly,* Fall 1958 and *Journal of Social Issues,* 1959-63, especially E. C. Wilson, "Problems of Survey Research in Modernizing Areas," *Public Opinion Quarterly,* 22 (Fall 1958), pp. 230-234, and A. G. Jones, "The Survey Methods in Under-Developed Countries," *International Social Science Bulletin,* 5 (1953), pp. 530-531.

99. For a description of interviewing difficulties in a Pakistan industrial setting, see M. Habibullah, *Some Aspects of Productivity in the Jute Industry of Pakistan,* Bureau of Economic Research, University of Dacca, Dacca, East Pakistan, Sept. 1968, pp. 19-21.

100. Elmo C. Wilson, "Problems of Survey Research Modernizing Areas," *Public Opinion Quarterly,* Vol. 22, Fall 1958, pp. 230-234.

101. Frederick W. Frey, "Surveying Peasant Attitudes in Turkey," *Public Opinion Quarterly,* Vol. 27, Summer 1963, pp. 335-355.

102. Lloyd and Suzanne Rudolph, "Surveys in India: Field Experience in Madras State," *Public Opinion Quarterly,* 22, Fall 1958, pp. 235-244.

103. Roe Goodman, "Survey Sampling and Implementation for Development Programs," *Proceedings,* Social Statistics Section, American Statistical Association, 1960, pp. 2-4.

104. Robert O. Carlson, "To Talk with Kings," *Public Opinion Quarterly,* Vol. 22, (Fall 1958), pp. 224-229.

105. Ralph Lewis and Helen M. Crossley, "Opinion Surveying in Korea," *Public Opinion Quarterly,* 28 (Summer 1964), pp. 257-272.

106. William John Hanna and Judith Lynne Hanna, "The Problem of Ethnicity and Factionalism in African Survey Research," *Public Opinion Quarterly,* Vol. 30 (Spring 1966), pp. 290-294.

107. Henry A. Landsberger and Antonio Saavedra, "Response Set in Developing Countries," *Public Opinion Quarterly,* 31 (Summer 1967), pp. 214-229.

108. Raymond D. Gastil, "Middle Class Impediments to Iranian Moderization," *Public Opinion Quarterly,* Vol. 22 (Fall 1958), pp. 325-329.

109. Howard Stanton, Kurt W. Back, Eugene Litwak, "Role-Playing in Survey Research," *American Journal of Sociology,* Vol. 62, (Sept. 1956), pp. 172-176.

110. On this point, see Lloyd and Suzanne H. Rudolph, *op. cit.*

111. See Raymond Firth, *Elements of Social Organization,* Watts and Company, London, 1951.

Chapter V

GETTING DATA READY FOR ANALYSIS

Introduction: Strategy

The most neglected and often the most unscientific part of the whole survey process is the quantification of the information and its preparation for analysis. While many economic magnitudes are already quantified, others are not, and many of the explanatory variables introduce problems of quantification. As we see in Chapter VI, new computer methods of analysis reduce the need for making all the variables into numerical scales, but many problems still remain.

We have already suggested that since the time and cooperation of the respondents is the scarcest resource, it should be economized, by postponing to a later stage any work that can be postponed. It is also wise to limit the time, attention, and work of the interviewer in the same manner.

In fact, one can argue that as one progresses from respondent to the computer, each stage is more specialized but less expensive, so that the basic strategy should be that wherever a task is simple enough to move forward to a more specialized and cheaper operation (and resource-demand), it should be moved. Respondents vary but are in possession of the basic information. Interviewers have been trained to handle a wide variety of different problems intelligently, including motivating respondents to cooperate, knowing how much to probe, organizing travel, developing and using sampling materials, etc. Editors, coders, keypunchers, and computers, are each in succession less broad in their outlook and decision-making powers, but speedier and more efficient in doing simpler and simpler things.

Technical considerations urge us to push tasks closer and closer to the respondent where they can be handled more intelligently and with more discretion; but economic considerations urge us to push tasks closer and closer to the computer where they can be handled rapidly, systematically, and with minimum cost. The final decision depends also on the volume of work, the number of interviews, and whether there will be other studies that can use the same procedures, since heavy investment in developing more mechanical procedures must be amortized. Pushing a task to a later stage without adequate planning and development can lead to major breakdowns.

An additional strategic consideration has to do with the cost of errors. Since each step builds upon the work of the preceding steps, any errors not found until after later steps have been completed will require repeating all those steps. There is a great premium on knowing that each step is working properly before proceeding to the next. But since it would be time-consuming, hence expensive, to wait till one step is done before going on, one must engage in immediate and continuous checking of each step, often tailored to the parts of the task most likely to be error-prone, or most likely to cause later trouble if they are wrong.

So, we try for the advantages of division of labor and specialization, and at the same time by dividing up the tasks attempt to accomplish each by the most systematic and specialized resources consistent with intelligent and proper handling of the data. The larger the study and the more similar studies to come, the greater the payoff to specialization. A small, one-time study might well be better handled with the researcher himself doing a great deal of the editing and coding, and, as we shall see, even generating his analysis variables as he codes so that the data are immediately ready for analysis.

For example, if it were important to know how far each respondent lived from the center of the nearest Standard Metropolitan Statistical Area (city of 50,000 or more), it would be unwise to use interviewing time and respondent energy by asking it directly. The interviewer, with her less precious time before or after the interview, and her knowledge of maps and the area, could easily estimate it along with the other observational items she adds to the questionnaire. Indeed, since the interviews come in clusters, the same estimate will apply to several other respondents.

Another example is the adding of income components to get total income. One might ask the interviewer to add them and check the total with the respondent. But interviewers are often not good at addition, and do not like to interrupt the flow of the interview. And respondents often do not know what the total should be, and will agree that a total is right even when it was added incorrectly. The whole process was wasteful of scarce resources with little or no gain. Editors in the central office can do it more efficiently while they are estimating income taxes.

Strategy in data handling once the interviews arrive at the central office depends, of course, upon the kind of computer equipment that is available, and the kind of manpower available. If the computer facilities are primitive, and there is great need to get results in a hurry, then the editing and coding of data can be designed to prepare the data fully, so that they are ready for analysis as soon as they are machine-readable. Assuming the study is small, or competent editor-coders are available, it should be possible to keep almost up to date with the field work. If there is no need for weighting the data, or getting rid of all the bad codes or discrepancies, one could get tables only a few days after the last interview comes in.

On the other hand, if one wants to do a careful job of editing and cleaning data or generate complex variables, it may be best to postpone some tasks to the computer, saving the time and energy of editors and coders. Coding things the way one wants to use them often means complex codes which slow down the coders and multiply the coding errors. (We already pointed out that questionnaires which make the respondent or the interviewer do their own coding also slow them down and multiply their errors.)

In the historical development of computers, perversely enough, the more powerful computers that first started using tape input rather than cards, were much less flexible when it came to data manipulation, particularly generating new variables or correcting errors. It was fairly simple to sort out cards with errors and correct them, or to select subgroups of cards and gang-punch new codes for them. But for many years it was difficult to change tapes. It is still true that even the smallest change usually requires rewriting the whole set of data on a new tape reel. The situation is now changed in the newest computers with adequate software, so that a very large number of fairly complicated tasks can be postponed and done on the computer. The computer is excellent for simple tasks that have to be repeated over and over again, such as adding up components, computing ratios, or looking for inconsistencies. It is also good for tasks which are only relevant and required for small sub-parts of the sample, where it does not seem profitable to train a whole set of editors to watch for the few cases they may come across.

On the other hand, there are some things that must still be done by editors because they require judgment, or complex decisions, or using look-up-tables where interpolation or extrapolation may be necessary. For example, assigning values where information on minor components of a total are missing, or calculating income taxes, or using tables where the number of items to be looked up for one interview varies and must be kept open-ended, are still done more efficiently by human beings.

One recent development in computers means that postponing complex tasks to the computer may not create as much delay as one might think. Modern computers are card-programmed. Hence it is possible to take small batches of data through each of the steps as they come in, including cleaning and variable generation. Each step then gets improved, debugged, and ready to apply very rapidly and efficiently on the last few interviews when they come in. The major delay is the time it takes to look up cases and correct errors, and that goes rapidly with the few final cases. Hence, batch-processing of material as it comes in greatly reduces the delay in getting the data ready after the last interview is in, and allows more time in the field to get those last difficult interviews.

We turn now to a discussion of the steps that must take place once the interviews arrive in the central office. The steps are:

1. Field controls, check-in and initial quality-check
2. Editing and check editing
3. Coding and check coding
4. Cleaning of wild codes, inconsistencies, and extreme cases
5. Generating new variables
6. Response rate analysis and weighting

Field Controls

Any probability sample requires a check to make sure that the sample is properly accounted for. This requires a set of sample books with each sample address or designation as a separate item in the book with an identifying number. In the case of area probability samples these books are usually arranged alphabetically by county, or by region of the country and by county within it. The interviewer has a copy of her pages from the sample book. The sample book number can be so organized that one of its digits represents the region, another the city size, and another whether or not the particular location is within a standard metropolitan statistical area or not. As the questionnaires come into the office the sample book number is generally on the cover sheet attached to the questionnaire, but is transferred to the questionnaire before they are separated. The questionnaire is also given a serially-assigned interview number. This number is used for control purposes, checking, putting interviews in batches for coding and editing, and generally for identifying each interview from this step forward. One might think the sample book number could be used for these purposes, but it turns out to be very useful to have a sequence number also. At the same time, a certain amount of pre-editing is done. This needs to be kept right up-to-date: making sure that the questionnaire is properly filled out, that it does not have to be sent back to the field for more work, that it is indeed a response and not a non-response. This requires some strategy in deciding how much information has to be available in order for a questionnaire to be considered a response, rather than thrown out as a non-response.

At the same time, a certain amount of other sample information is transferred from the cover sheet or the sample book to the questionnaire form so that the cover sheet, which has identifying information, can be physically separated and locked up—preserving the confidentiality of the information.

Some cover sheets will come in for non-response, refusals, not part of the sample, and no one at home. The information about them has to be coded from the cover sheet for an analysis of the non-response, which we shall discuss later. A different set of serial numbers is usually assigned these non-response cases. If it does not upset the coding too much, it sometimes turns out to be simpler to code a single card for each of the valid interviews, containing the same kind of information that is available for the non-response, so that it is very easy to compare the response and the non-response on the variables that are available for both of them. In any case, as we shall see later, it is also necessary to be able to list the response and non-response cases in order by sample book number in order to check out the completion of the sample and make sure there are no addresses unaccounted for.

If a *limited* amount of information about the local area (county, census tract, school district) is to be used, it may pay to transfer it from sample books to questionnaires at this stage. It is essential to do it at this stage if the areas are too detailed to be identified by the sample book number alone.

Editing

In most complex interviews division of labor is still an important advantage. It pays to do an editing operation before one tries to code the questionnaires. This is particularly true of economic surveys where there may be components of the economic measures that are wanted scattered throughout the questionnaire. They need to be combined or added. The editors scan the interview again for problems and once more decide whether, even after the first screening, it is a non-response case rather than an interview. Where the wrong respondent is accepted, e.g. wife when the head is called for, the editor must decide whether to accept her answers to attitude questions or treat them as "not ascertained," and check that the work and income of "head" and of "wife" are properly recorded.

Where only certain items are missing, the editors assign them unless they are to be left as "not ascertained" in the coding.[1] Assignment is important where there are very few missing values for a particular variable and where the variable is a major explanatory variable often used on controls of stubs of tables. It is also important where many components are added together to make a total and any one of the components may be missing. One does not want to throw away the total simply because some minor component is not there. The best source of assignments is previous similar surveys, particularly if things are not changing very rapidly. Building assignment tables or estimates from the same survey tends to slow down processing. In the Surveys of Consumer Finances it has been customary to use a number of previous surveys, indeed, in a distributed-lag function created by averaging the most recent survey averages for assignment groups with the previous *assignment* values, which means that preceding surveys are each weighted half of the one that follows. Hence, half of the weight of assignments come from the previous year and a quarter from the year before that and an eighth from the year before that and so on. The strategy problem here is to develop assignment tables which are based on enough cases from previous surveys to be stable and not increase the sampling variance too much, but which are small enough groups to be reasonably precise in estimating what the number should be for the case in which it is missing, that is similar to the missing case.

A number of problems arise in assignments; for instance, if there is both a question of whether a man has a particular item at all and if so how much it is, it is usually necessary to make two separate assignments. If he does not answer either question, one goes first to a probability table and some random numbers to assign whether or not he has a car, for instance, and if the assignment is that he has a car, one goes to a second table to assign its value. The reason for this, of course, is that if one took only the average value of all people in a particular sub-group including the non-owners, it would be very difficult to know what to do in cases where you knew the man was an owner. If one assigned the average value including non-owners, yet in other cases where it was clear the man did not own, you assigned zero, the result would be a set of biased estimates.

Similarly, when an important concept like income is made up of a whole set of sub-components, strategy decisions are necessary as to whether to assign the total or to assign each component. If one assigns the total only, then in many cases known complements will add up to more than the assignment. If one then succumbs to the temptation to use the known total whenever it is larger than the assignment, but the assignment whenever it is smaller, again one ends up with biased estimates. Consequently, it is much better to have assignment procedures for each of the components so that one assigns whatever components are missing and then adds together all the given and assigned data to get the total. No matter how careful one is there is always a problem of whether to use certain side information that may be available. Sometimes it is quite obvious from other information in the interview that the man could not possibly own a car. The thing to keep in mind in any such use of outside information is to reduce the possibility that it will produce bias, e.g., by only allowing corrections in one direction.

Sometimes it makes sense to assign only a class interval value for a variable, so that the bracket code can be used in tables without having a "not ascertained" group, while the missing information is not used when the variable is used as a dependent or independent variable in an analysis (where the assignments would spuriously increase the correlation with the variables used in the assignment process, but not with other variables). Sometimes it makes sense to do the reverse: assign the detailed amount, so that optimal estimates of means and aggregates can be made, but keep the "not ascertained" code in the class interval code as a record of how many assignments were required, as a method of eliminating them from any analysis, and because some statistical procedures allow them to be treated as a separate group.

In general, whenever complex information must be added or assembled from various parts of the questionnaire, it is useful for editors to use a worksheet designed so that the numbers entered on it can be keypunched directly rather than going through a separate coding operation. We have provided here one example of a fairly complicated four-page worksheet which puts together components, sub-totals, and totals of work hours, income, food consumption, calculation of food-need standards, and certain other items about housing and the journey to work.

These worksheets illustrate some decisions about the kinds of things that are properly done at the editing stage. In particular where there are components, many of which are zero for substantial parts of the population and where only the total is relevant, it is often useful to add them together and code only the total. The food-need standard is another kind of situation where one must enter a complex table based on age and sex for each individual in the family, but where the number of people in the family may vary from one to thirteen or more. It would be very cumbersome and expensive to do this by machine because one would have to have coded in the main file the ages and sexes of whatever maximum number of people one would expect, and then would have to engage in a machine table-look-up operation. On the other hand, after once estimating the total unadjusted food needs for the family, the computer was used in this case very effectively to make adjustments for family size (economies of scale) and for farm-nonfarm differences. Note that no missing data are allowed—assignments are made wherever necessary—but each variable has next to it a separate indicator of its accuracy, including whether it was assigned.

Another example on these same worksheets is the estimation of income taxes for the family—a very complex procedure that has so far proved intractable to economical machine programming, (particularly since tax rules change every few years). In other economic surveys expenditure on durables, total debt, and total debt payments have been added by the editors. They are thus not only able to make sure the numbers look reasonable and to avoid double counting, but can add up a variable number of items without leaving space in the computer tape record for an unlimited number of separate items, many of which would be a zero.

Another example, of course is entering the values of people's cars. Not only does one usually want the value of all cars owned by the family but sometimes having a simple set of tables available requires one to interpolate or extrapolate to estimate the value of cars that are quite rare or do not fit the usual categories. In general, it is useful to use a worksheet where some of the components of a total are useful and are to be analyzed, and the total is useful and needs to be analyzed, but some of the minor components are not. In this case one can make the important components and total machine-readable from the worksheet but does not have to use up space, time, and energy with all the minor components.

The editors have a major advantage in that they have looked through the whole questionnaire, have assembled the information, and made sure that it was

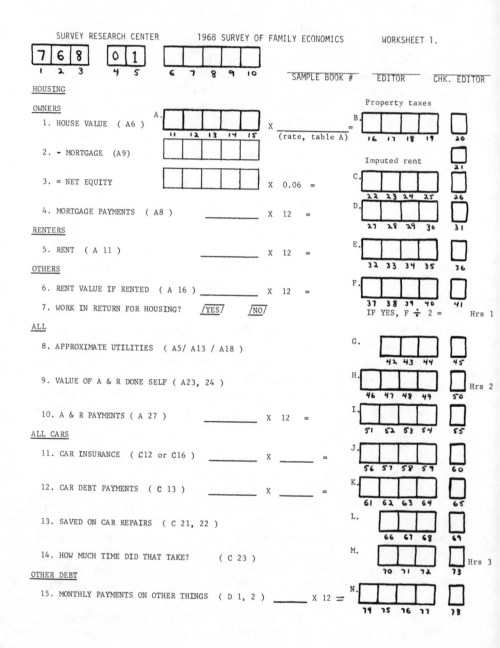

SURVEY RESEARCH CENTER   1968 SURVEY OF FAMILY ECONOMICS   WORKSHEET 1.

7 6 8   0 1   [   ][   ][   ][   ][   ]
1 2 3   4 5   6 7 8 9 10   SAMPLE BOOK #   EDITOR   CHK. EDITOR

HOUSING

OWNERS   Property taxes

1. HOUSE VALUE (A6)   A. [   ][   ][   ][   ][   ]   B. [   ][   ][   ][   ]   [   ]
                             11 12 13 14 15   X ——————————— =   16 17 18 19   20
                                                      (rate, table A)

2. - MORTGAGE (A9)   [   ][   ][   ][   ]   Imputed rent
                                                                                          [   ]
                                                                                           21
3. = NET EQUITY   [   ][   ][   ][   ]   X 0.06 =   C. [   ][   ][   ][   ]   [   ]
                                                                    22 23 24 25   26
                                                                 D. [   ][   ][   ][   ]   [   ]
4. MORTGAGE PAYMENTS (A8)   ————————— X 12 =   27 28 29 30   31

RENTERS

5. RENT (A 11)   ————————— X 12 =   E. [   ][   ][   ][   ]   [   ]
                                                                    32 33 34 35   36
OTHERS

6. RENT VALUE IF RENTED (A 16) ——————— X 12 =   F. [   ][   ][   ][   ]   [   ]
                                                                    37 38 39 40   41
7. WORK IN RETURN FOR HOUSING?   /YES/   /NO/   IF YES, F ÷ 2 =   Hrs 1

ALL

8. APPROXIMATE UTILITIES (A5/ A13 / A18)   G. [   ][   ][   ]   [   ]
                                                                    42 43 44   45

9. VALUE OF A & R DONE SELF (A23, 24)   H. [   ][   ][   ][   ]   [   ] Hrs 2
                                                                    46 47 48 49   50

10. A & R PAYMENTS (A 27)   ————————— X 12 =   I. [   ][   ][   ][   ]   [   ]
                                                                    51 52 53 54   55
ALL CARS

11. CAR INSURANCE (C12 or C16)   ——————— X —————— =   J. [   ][   ][   ][   ]   [   ]
                                                                    56 57 58 59   60

12. CAR DEBT PAYMENTS (C 13)   ——————— X —————— =   K. [   ][   ][   ][   ]   [   ]
                                                                    61 62 63 64   65

13. SAVED ON CAR REPAIRS (C 21, 22)   L. [   ][   ][   ]   [   ]
                                                                    66 67 68   69

14. HOW MUCH TIME DID THAT TAKE?   (C 23)   M. [   ][   ][   ]   [   ] Hrs 3
                                                                    70 71 72   73
OTHER DEBT

15. MONTHLY PAYMENTS ON OTHER THINGS (D 1, 2) ———— X 12 =   N. [   ][   ][   ][   ]   [   ]
                                                                    74 75 76 77   78

SURVEY RESEARCH CENTER   1968 SURVEY OF FAMILY ECONOMICS   WORKSHEET 2.

7	6	8		0	2						

1   2   3   4   5   6   7   8   9   10

INDIVIDUAL FOOD COSTS:
USE LISTING BOX AND TABLE B

TABLE B. INDIVIDUAL FOOD STANDARD   (LOW COST)

AGE	MALE	FEMALE
Under 3	3.90	3.90
4 - 6	4.60	4.60
7 - 9	5.50	5.50
10 - 12	6.40	6.30
13 - 15	7.40	6.90
16 - 20	8.70	7.20
21 - 35	7.50	6.50
35 - 55	6.90	6.30
55 +	6.30	5.40

1. _____
2. _____   SAMPLE BOOK #
3. _____
4. _____   _____
5. _____   EDITOR
6. _____
7. _____   CHK. EDITOR
8. _____
9. _____
10. _____
11. _____
12. _____
13. _____

A. [ ]
FAMILY SIZE   TOTAL UNADJUSTED _____
        11

SEE TABLE FOR FOOD AND NEED STANDARDS FOR THE ABOVE FAMILY SIZE AND UNADJUSTED FOOD TOTAL

B. [| | |]   C. [| | | | |]
ANNUAL FOOD STANDARD   12 13 14 15   ANNUAL NEED STANDARD   16 17 18 19 20
                                                            ANNUAL AMOUNT

FOOD EXPENDITURE
1. SPENT EATING OUT (E 2)   _____ X _____ = _____
2. COST OF MILK (E 4)   _____ X _____ = _____
3. OTHER FOOD   (E 5)   _____ X _____ = _____
4. FOOD BILL SUBTOTAL (1 + 2 + 3)   _____

5. ALCOHOL (E6) _____ X _____ = D. [| |] IF INCLUDED(E7) _____ [ ]
                                      21 22 23   ENTER AT RIGHT   24

6. CIGARETTES (E9) _____ X _____ = E. [| |] IF INCLUDED (E10) _____ [ ]
                                      25 26 27   ENTER AT RIGHT   28

CORRECTED FOOD BILL
7.   SUBTRACT 5, 6, FROM FOOD BILL IF INCLUDED   F. [| | |] [ ]
                                                          29 30 31 32   33

NON MONEY FOOD
8. HOME GROWN FOOD (E12) SEE SUPERVISOR   G. [| |] [ ] Hrs 4
                                                34 35 36 37
9. CLOTHES MADE AND MENDED (E17, 18)   H. [| |] [ ] Hrs 5
                                                38 39 40 41
10. FOOD RECEIVED ON THE JOB (J30, page 24) I. [| |] [ ]
                                                42 43 44 45
11. SAVED ON FOOD STAMPS (J32, page 24)   J. [| |] [ ]
                                                46 47 48 49

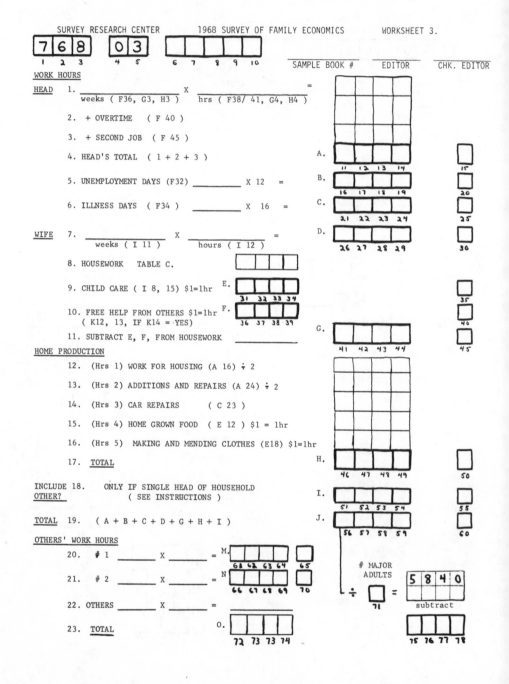

SURVEY RESEARCH CENTER   1968 SURVEY OF FAMILY ECONOMICS   WORKSHEET 3.

7 6 8   0 3   [ ][ ][ ][ ][ ]
1 2 3   4 5   6 7 8 9 10   SAMPLE BOOK #   EDITOR   CHK. EDITOR

WORK HOURS

HEAD   1. _____ X _____ =
          weeks (F36, G3, H3)   hrs (F38/ 41, G4, H4)

       2. + OVERTIME   (F 40)

       3. + SECOND JOB   (F 45)

       4. HEAD'S TOTAL   (1 + 2 + 3)   A.
                                                    11 12 13 14   15
       5. UNEMPLOYMENT DAYS (F32) _____ X 12 = B.
                                                    16 17 18 19   20
       6. ILLNESS DAYS   (F34) _____ X 16 = C.
                                                    21 22 23 24   25

WIFE   7. _____ X _____ =   D.
          weeks (I 11)   hours (I 12)   26 27 28 29   30

       8. HOUSEWORK   TABLE C.

       9. CHILD CARE (I 8, 15) $1=1hr   E.
                                               31 32 33 34   35
      10. FREE HELP FROM OTHERS $1=1hr F.
          (K12, 13, IF K14 = YES)   36 37 38 39   40

      11. SUBTRACT E, F, FROM HOUSEWORK _____ G.
                                                    41 42 43 44   45
HOME PRODUCTION

      12. (Hrs 1) WORK FOR HOUSING (A 16) ÷ 2

      13. (Hrs 2) ADDITIONS AND REPAIRS (A 24) ÷ 2

      14. (Hrs 3) CAR REPAIRS   (C 23)

      15. (Hrs 4) HOME GROWN FOOD (E 12) $1 = 1hr

      16. (Hrs 5) MAKING AND MENDING CLOTHES (E18) $1=1hr

      17. TOTAL   H.
                                                    46 47 48 49   50
INCLUDE 18.   ONLY IF SINGLE HEAD OF HOUSEHOLD
OTHER?   (SEE INSTRUCTIONS)   I.
                                                    51 52 53 54   55
TOTAL 19.   (A + B + C + D + G + H + I)   J.
                                                    56 57 58 59   60
OTHERS' WORK HOURS

      20. # 1 _____ X _____ = M.
                                      61 62 63 64   65   # MAJOR
      21. # 2 _____ X _____ = N.   ADULTS
                                      66 67 68 69   70   ÷ [ ] = 5 8 4 0
      22. OTHERS _____ X _____ =   71   subtract

      23. TOTAL   O. [ ][ ][ ][ ]
                                   72 73 73 74   75 76 77 78

SURVEY RESEARCH CENTER   1968 SURVEY OF FAMILY ECONOMICS   WORKSHEET 4.

```
| 7 | 6 | 8 |   | O | 4 |   |   |   |   |   |   |
  1   2   3      4   5      6   7   8   9   10
```

HEAD'S LABOR INCOME

1. LABOR PART OF FARM INC. (J4*)
2. LABOR PART OF BUS. INC. (J7*)
3. WAGES   (J 8)
4. BONUS, OVERTIME, COMM. (J10)
5. PROF., PRACTICE, TRADE (J11a)
6. LABOR PART OF ROOMERS ETC. (J11b*)

7. TOTAL   (SUM OF 1 to 6)   A
                                11 12 13 14 15

WIFE'S LABOR INCOME

8. WIFE'S INCOME FROM WORK (J15*)   B
                                    16 17 18 19 20

CAPITAL INCOME, HEAD AND WIFE

9. ASSET PART OF FARM INC. (J4*)
10. ASSET PART OF BUS. INC. (J7*)
11. ASSET PART OF ROOMERS ETC.(J11b*)
12. RENT, INT., DIV., ETC. (J11c)
13. WIFE'S INCOME FROM ASSETS (J15*)

TAXABLE INCOME OF HEAD AND WIFE   C
14. (A + B + CAPITAL INC.)
                                     21 22 23 24 25

TAXABLE INCOME OF OTHERS (J19 + J22)   D
15. OTHER WITH HIGHEST INCOME
                                         26 27 28 29 30

16. NEXT HIGHEST INCOME   E
                                     31 32 33 34 35

17. STILL OTHERS WITH INC. ?

OTHERS' TOTAL INCOME

18. (15 + 16 + 17)   F
                                     36 37 38 39 40

TRANSFERS (TOTAL FAMILY)   G

19. A.D.C. A.D.C.U.   (J11d)
                                     41 42 43 44 45

20. OTHER WELFARE (J11e)
21. SOCIAL SECURITY (J11f)
22. OTHER RETIREMENT (J11g)
23. UNEMP., WORKMENS' COMP. (J11h)
24. ALIMONY (J11i)
25. HELP FROM RELATIVES (J11j)
26. ANYTHING ELSE? (J11k*)
27. WIFE'S TRANSFER INCOME (J15*)
28. OTHERS' TRANSFER INCOME(J19,22*)

TOTAL FAMILY MONEY INCOME   H
29. (C + F + G + OTHER TRANSFERS)
                                     46 47 48 49 50

TAX EXEMPTIONS
OF HEAD AND WIFE

   □ ADULTS

 + □ CHILDREN

 + □ BLIND,
     65 & OVER

 + □ OUTSIDE FU ____ ENTER DOLLAR
     (J45)   AMOUNT (J46)

ENTER TOTAL
EXEMPTIONS
                 51 52 53 54

HEAD & WIFE
      │
      │── OTHERS
              CIRCLE
              TABLE USED

                       TAX FROM TABLE

   □   M   J
           S HH
   □   M   K
           S HH
   □   M   L
           S HH

                       - - - - -

                       - - - - -

TOTAL FAMILY TAX   M
   (J + K + L)
                       55 56 57 58 59

CHILD CARE (I8,15)   N
(SEE BOX E, SHEET 3)

UNION DUES (K18)   O

COST OF INCOME   P
  (M + N + O)
                       60 61 62 63 64

SAMPLE BOOK #
_____

    EDITOR
_____

  CHK. EDITOR
_____

ASSIGNMENTS
0 none / 1 minor / 2 major

A □   B □   C □   D □
  65   66   67   68

E □   G □   I □
  69   70   71

consistent and meaningful. Generally, the first thing the editors do is to read a little description—called a "thumbnail sketch"—in the back of the interview which describes the situation and anything about it the interviewer thought would be useful in interpreting what went on.

A final thing that editors may be called upon to do occurs when the analysis is not all to be done with the same unit of analysis. Sometimes one interviews spending units but wants to do some analysis on a family basis. In this case it may be important to combine the information from more than one questionnaire into family totals. Some of this can be done by machine, but in some cases—particularly for consistency and to avoid double counting—it is useful to have a family editing operation. The definition of family head and coding his age, is an example. Problems arise, of course, where one spending unit within a family was a non-response. This can become a very difficult matter to handle.

A more usual problem, however, has to do with subunits where one may want to do some analysis that treats each individual in the family, or each nuclear family in a larger family, as a separate unit. Indeed, the unit may not be a person but a transaction or an event or an object owned. Analysis has been done, for instance, of all the disabled individuals in a sample, or of all the purchases of durables (where one may want a price distribution of individual durables run against the income of the family that bought the durable), or all the cars owned in a family, or all the hospitalization experiences, or all the auto accidents. Indeed, wherever there is a problem of a varying number of items per interview, it may be useful to consider whether some analysis should not be done with each of these items as the unit of analysis. One may want to ask people about airplane trips, but some people would have one trip, and some two, and some ten. It would be very cumbersome to leave space on each record in a computer tape for an indefinite number of trips, particularly if one wanted to analyze the characteristics of trips by the people who took them and separately to analyze people according to how many trips they took. If there is to be a separate analysis by a different unit, then the editors may have to have worksheets—one for each of these units—where the material is entered to facilitate or bypass the coding operation. We will come back to this when we discuss coding.

At the end of editing there will be a complete questionnaire with assignments made of missing information, with some worksheets filled out, and with a general agreement that these are acceptable questionnaires. There is then usually a check-editing procedure which starts with very thorough check-editing at the beginning of the editing period. As the evidence that things are under control increases, check-editing is gradually reduced to the point where it is done only on a sample of the interviews, or only on some troublesome items. Check-editing needs to start early in order to correct procedures and reduce future errors. It needs to continue in order to detect diverging procedures or other, rarer, errors.

Much more complex editing may be in order in the case of reinterviews or panels, where one not only wants to analyze changes in many things, but may want a prior look at their reasonableness. Some combining of information from the two questionnaires may reveal discrepancies which one does not want to leave in the data, or even cases where the wrong person was obviously interviewed the second time.

When three or more interviews have been taken with the same family, the need for some flexible look at how the information fits together is obvious. If an income is reported for a secondary earner in some years and not others, but no mention is made of any change in his status, one is tempted to assume that there has been response error, rather than change in income.

What one never does in any editing operation, however, is to impose the editor's judgement to change answers, unless there is persuasive evidence not only that there was an error, but also what a better answer would be. One of the experiences with reinterviews has been that first-year answers which seemed odd, turned out, upon assembling the additional information, to be not only correct but meaningful—once one understood the situation.

If one should not change answers much, why edit? For one thing, errors in interpreting data can be avoided. In addition, it is possible to add some new variables representing the editor's judgement as to the quality of the data as was done on the worksheets reprinted here. Then analysis can be run excluding cases judged to be dubious, whenever the precision of the data is important, that is, when one is estimating amounts or the shapes of relationships, rather than looking for patterns.

There is very little printed material about the editing of survey data. There is one article by Walter Stewart on the experience with Bureau of Labor Statistics.[2] The Census Bureau uses a complex machine called FOSDIC in editing the Current Population Surveys. The machine reads microfilms of pre-coded questionnaires. The microfilms are done at several locations in the field to avoid bottlenecks. FOSDIC not only converts them to machine-readable form but edits the material and assigns missing information at the same time. This seems to work very well with the Standard Current Population Survey. It sometimes breaks down seriously when used on new and more complex questionnaires. Experience in the Survey Research Center has been a gradual movement from hand editing to computer work as the computer seems to be able to handle it, but a great deal is still done by editors because the sample sizes are small enough to make this feasible and the material is complex enough to make it essential. It may even pay to postpone to the computer editing operations that only need be done on a very small fraction of the cases, to reduce the number of different things editors must keep in mind.

Coding

The coders have now had their work very much simplified, both by the worksheets (with which they do not have to do anything at all) and by the editor's careful work on the questionnaire and assigning of missing information. The process of developing codes is a complex one which should be done in advance on the basis of the pretest questionnaires, even though some changes and additions may have to be made along the way.

Some specialization may be useful even within the coding operation. The classic example is "occupation" which is so complex that it is often coded for all the questionnaires by a single person who has memorized the Census Standard Occupation Code.

For purposes of easing the coder's job it is very important to have conventions and standards which are uniform, not only within a survey but from one study to the next. For instance, it is very useful to use the code "0" uniformly when the particular item is inappropriate or inapplicable for that person and to use "9" for N.A. (not ascertained) or missing information. This not only simplifies the coder's job but it makes possible computer software which automatically takes account of these two kinds of situations. In the case of yes/no questions it is useful to choose some uniform convention such as "1" for yes and "5" for no, so that the coders gradually memorize many of the simpler codes. Similarly with attitude or reasons codes, it is often useful to use a standard five-point Likert scale:

> "1" is unqualifiedly favorable or positive,
> "2" is positive with qualifications,
> "3" is a pro-con (on the one hand, on the other hand, kind of answer),
> "4" is a negative or a con answer with qualifications,
> "5" is an unqualified negative,
> "9" is uncodable answer or answer in the wrong frame of reference,
> "0" means the question was inapplicable to this particular person.

Once again, the general principle of postponing work to the point where it can be done at least expense applies in coding where one might be tempted to combine the answers to two questions, "Do you have one?" and "How much is it worth?" in a single code, because that is what is needed in the analysis. But it is much easier and faster for coders to code an answer for each question: "yes" or "no" to the first question and an amount for the second. Later the computer can combine this in the form it is to be used in the tables. There is not much on coding in the published literature. Perhaps the best treatment is that by Cartwright in the Festinger-Katz Book.[3] We do not need to pay too much attention here to the problems of quantifying the answers to relatively unstructured questions. But even in economic surveys there are going to be questions about reasons or attitudes or expectations about the future which raise coding problems. Cartwright gives two general characteristics that any code has to satisfy. First, the categories need to be exhaustive; and secondly, they need to be mutually exclusive. Many people set up categories that do not meet these criteria. Cartwright gives an example where people were asked where they were solicited to buy war bonds. The categories include: work, home, store, bank, and post office. If a man works in a bank, what does he do? Or, if he were solicited on the way to work what does he do? A more recent example is a mailed questionnaire where people were asked about breakdowns of their washing machines. They were asked to indicate why the washing machine broke down by checking categories like: it made a noise, fan belt broke, it did not pump out the water, man replaced the motor. Some of these are symptoms and some are diagnoses, some are repairs and, of course, sometimes two or more of them apply.

In the case of "reasons" codes, there are two kinds of problems. First, how many categories should be used; and second, how many different reasons should be coded for each person? In categorizing anything, one can try to impose structure by categorizing reasons into "reasons for" and "reasons against" or into economic and non-economic reasons. Of course, it is a mistake to code so much detail that there are codes into which almost no one falls. It is very useful to be able to specify in advance the combinations of reasons the analysis will use and group them together. Any reduction of the total number of categories, of course, involves imposing some structure and, if the structure has too many dimensions, trouble ensues. For instance, if one wanted to categorize reasons into economic and non-economic reasons, then one would have to leave a third category for reasons that are not clearly economic or non-economic. And if one wants to code reasons for and reasons against, it is necessary to leave another category for cases where it is not clear whether they are for or against, and the combination of these two triplets already requires nine categories into which reasons fit. One way to deal with this, of course, is to leave one place in the record for each of these nine categories and then code components within each one. The difficulty, of course, is that the same answer or something that seems like the same answer may appear in any one of the nine places.

Sometimes it is possible to use a code with no particular structure to it and only a few categories by simply putting the stereotyped answers into the main groups in which they fall. With some questions where people seem to give *only* stereotyped answers this may be the best thing to do. In the early days when we asked people how they felt about installment credit there were many who said, "It is the only way to buy things," others, "It is the way to establish your credit," and others gave more moralistic answers, "It is bad because you tend to spend too much." Nobody gave moralistic answers in favor of it, and very few gave institutional answers against it; so there would be no point allowing all the combinations. Sometimes after a code is put into use a large number of cases are in the category labelled "other"—it does not fit anywhere else. When this happens, it may be necessary to go back and reread these answers to see whether there is some important new category that should be established.

Whenever one wants to allow more than nine different kinds of reasons, there is a strategic question whether to use a two-digit reasons code, which often causes trouble in the computer, or whether to try to break the reasons up into two categories, code them separately, and then combine them later. The latter is usually better.

A second problem, of course, is how many different reasons to allow any one person to give. Allowing for many reasons per case greatly increases the amount of space that is taken up and it is particularly annoying if only a few people give more than one or two reasons. The result is a lot of 0's, just to get a few non-0's cases handled.

One way to avoid the need to code all reasons given is to put them in some kind of priority order. In a study of the affluent a major question was whether or not the individual used tax considerations as a reason for any one of a number of things he did. A priority rule was used. If taxes were mentioned as a reason they were always coded first. If they were not mentioned, then a number of other things were eligible to be mentioned. In this way, even if a man gave four reasons and we left room for only one or two or three, we still did not lose the fact that he mentioned taxes.

Another example of a priority code was a situation where respondents were asked what kind of things they did when they repaired their own car. The study was concerned with the level of difficulty of the things they did, not with categorizing specifically what part of the car was repaired or what was done. Consequently, a priority code was used. If a man did something very difficult or complicated he was coded "1," if he did something somewhat complicated requiring a certain amount of skill, he was coded number "2," and so on down to the code at the very bottom which was very simple things like washing and waxing. (See Appendix A to this chapter.)

Sometimes people are tempted to code combinations of things—a kind of a geometric code—where if there are three things that can be mentioned, whether they are reasons or things owned, the "1" code is for a, "2" code for b, "3" code for c, "4" code for a *and* b, "5" code for b *and* c, "6" code for a *and* c, and a "7" code for a *and* b *and* c. So:

1. a only   5. b and c
2. b only   6. a and c
3. c only   7. a, b, and c.
4. a and b

These codes often turn out to be cumbersome and difficult to handle. Ordinarily one wants to know how many of the three things were true, or whether any one of them was true, rather than all the combinations. This is a case of saving space on the record in a way that may make things more complicated instead of easier.

It is often tempting to try to build other kinds of pattern codes out of several variables. This turns out to be dangerous if it gets very complicated or has too many dimensions, and it is prone to coding error. We know it is prone to error because if we code the components too, and then by computer find out how many people have each of the combinations, the results do not agree very well with the "pattern coding" that was done. On the other hand, there are some simple examples where it is fairly easy. One can combine sex of head and marital status because there are only three categories—married couples, single females, and single males. This is a mutually exclusive code that exhausts the population.

When analyzing data, of course, one wants codes where there are a reasonable number of cases in each category. Sometimes it may be useful to allow somewhat more categories than necessary and then collapse the code by computer, combining adjoining items that have very few cases. With quantitative material such as income or values of assets, one can wait until after he has seen the data before generating brackets (class intervals) that spread the sample fairly evenly. On the other hand it is often very useful to have codes at either end of the scale which distinguish a fairly *small* part of the population—say five or ten percent—since they may turn out to be quite different from the rest of the population. One thing that should be avoided if possible is coding dichotomies when one can code three, four, or five groups, since it is a known statistical fact that you can maximize the chance of showing a significant effect of a particular variable if you compare the one-third of the group at one end with the one-third at the other end and leave out the middle. The middle may contain a lot of people for whom the question is meaningless anyway.

There is a great temptation to code everything the first time through just in case anybody wants it. In the case of economic surveys this often leads to the absurd situation of coding five- and six-digit dollar fields for things which are zero for ninety-five or ninety-eight percent of the population. Such a variable cannot be used as a dependent variable and probably not even as an explanatory variable since it is badly skewed and dominated by a few cases. One is far better off in situations like this with an interval code that distinguishes zero, small amounts, and large amounts. When anyone wants to look at the large amounts, he can look them up individually and write case studies on them. Even where five to twenty percent are non-zero it may be more sensible simply to code a crude bracket code, rather than try to preserve all the detail. Or one may decide to code one card only for some subgroup who were asked certain questions. A special smaller sample analysis can be done with them after transferring to that card some of the other information.

Another general strategy problem is whether to code several things which must be internally consistent, rather than build one of them out of the others. For instance, in the case of dollar fields and brackets one could code both the dollar field and the bracket code and then check by machine to make sure they agree. This may reveal some errors. In practice it turns out that for the most part the errors are errors in the coding of the bracket code, so that the gain was negligible, hence we have generally given up this practice. Similarly, when one has income taxes, total income, and income after taxes, one could code all three. It then becomes necessary to check to make sure that income after taxes plus taxes is equal to income before taxes. Unless there is some particular reason to believe that this will help uncover errors, it makes more sense to code only two of the components and get the third one by computer later on. On the other hand, where a very large number of components are to be added up later, it may pay to have the editors add that sum and code it as a single sum to check the accuracy of coding of all the components, particularly where each of the components is assigned where necessary so that the addition always holds.

Another temptation is to code the answers to questions which were not asked. It is difficult to interpret volunteered information since it is only volunteered by some people and one really does not know about the others. For instance, one might ask a question, "How many hours during a week day do you spend watching television?" Some people will reply, "I do not have a television." Now this *implies* that they do not watch it, but it also gives an additional piece of information—that they do not have one. The problem is that we did not ask the other people whether they had a television set or not, and we cannot really infer it from whether or not they watch television. Someone else who said he watched several hours a night may not own a television; he may watch it in the bar. Another man may simply say he does not watch television even though he owns one. Consequently, in general it does not pay to code information for which there is not an explicit question.

An allied problem is the temptation to write in the Interviewers' Instructions requests for information that is not included in the questions the interviewers are to ask. This puts the interviewer in an intolerable situation since she is asked to find out whether the man owns a television set, for instance, and there is no question in the questionnaire. She must either guess, invent a question, or not provide the information.

In general, the code should reflect the purposes of the study just as the questions should, and a question should not be asked if it is not necessary. Therefore, there should not be any uncertainty about whether to code the answers. There are, however, some exceptions where a question is simply asked to introduce a subject. In practice, however, such questions are often coded just in case someone may want the information, or simply to make the coder's life simpler because he has a general rule of coding one answer to every question.

The actual process of coding usually begins with a discussion of one or two examples of the completed questionnaires and codes. Then there is a process of check-coding, again done very heavily at first and less heavily later on, as the consensus develops about how to handle things and that things are under control. But at least some partial check-coding is continued right through the whole process. Sometimes problems arise later on or arise in fairly rare cases but need to be communicated to the other coders.

One advantage of both check-editing and check-coding is that records can be kept of the percent disagreement, even if one does not want to worry about who is right. There are, of course, problems as to the meaning of the number of such disagreements, because the more categories a code has, the more possibility there is for disagreement; and, of course, some disagreements have to do with whether the answer should be coded "not ascertained" or "don't know" or whether it actually is a codable reason. In general, a question with a high percent of disagreement is a troublesome question. It is either a bad question, a question that is answered in several frames of reference, or a question the interviewer is not handling properly.

On the other hand, one may keep a question year after year that has problems in coding, because it fits some theoretical objectives and for at least a substantial part of the population is bringing meaningful responses. Perhaps the classic example is one of the questions used by George Katona to assess the state of consumer confidence. It reads,

Now about the big things people buy for their homes—such as furniture, house furnishings, refrigerator, stove, television, and things like that. *Generally speaking,* do you think now is a good or bad time for people to buy major household items?

This question attempts to tap the state of people's feelings and, although it is flabbergasting to some people and some give funny kinds of answers, there is clearly something being asked that is important. A question which seemed to be clearer or easier to code might fail to get what one was after in this kind of situation.

We have pointed out that sometimes when there are variable numbers of things to be reported one may want to do a separate analysis with each of them as a separate unit: each person, each child, each appliance, each hospitalization, etc. On the other hand, even in this case, one may want some kind of summary codes to describe the whole family situation. Take the composition of the family, for instance. One may not want to code the age, sex, relation to head, etc. of each member of the family where this number may vary from one to fifteen but may want to economize by coding some summaries such as the total number of people in the family, the number of children eighteen or under, the age of the youngest child, the age of the oldest child, the number of children in school, whether any of the children are *not* the natural children of the head and wife, etc. The age of the youngest child is of particular relevance in economic surveys because it indicates whether someone needs to be home during the day to take care of children, or whether they are all in school, or whether they are all old enough to take care of themselves. And if the youngest is 12 or older, the family is unlikely to have any more children in the future. Similarly, one may ask someone to list the organizations he belongs to and what kind they are but may be content to code the total number of organizations and/or the total number of organizations that are other than sheer amusement organizations. Sometimes when people come up with this problem it results from the fact that they have failed to cut out of a questionnaire things they really do not need. If it is only necessary to know *how many* different organizations the man belongs to, it wastes his time to ask him to list them all and describe what they do.

Numerical fields require decisions about the treatment of missing information (if not assigned) and about cases which exceed the field width. The indication of missing information depends on the computer software available. It is often a series of nines, but that is dangerous if someone innocently ignores the code and the missing cases are treated as the largest possible value. Cases that exceed the field raise more substantive issues, that is whether they should not be truncated to a number within the field anyway, given their rarity in a sample, and the damage they would do to any least-squares statistical analysis. We suggest that one should not attempt to use the detail on extreme amounts, and should truncate them, even at the expense of some distortion of means and aggregates, in most analytic surveys.

There is also a question whether to code "don't know" separately from "didn't answer." Separation certainly seems called for with attitudes and expectations.

In summary then, the basic strategy in coding is to code things that are relevant to the analysis of the study and to keep the level of accuracy up. If errors are made, they may never be found unless they are caught either in check-coding or in later inconsistency checking. Consequently, all the expensive field work can be lost if poor work is done in quantifying the answers. It helps to standardize codes; it helps to keep them as simple as possible; and, as we will see below, it also helps to check up later on things that obviously are inconsistent. It is probably best to do a good deal of recoding and variable generation in the computer and keep the coders work as simple and straightforward as possible in order to reduce errors and increase speed. This depends very much on the computer facilities available and how complex the material is.

There have been various attempts to make the initial questionnaire easier to code, or suitable to be sent directly to keypunchers, or even machine readable (by putting black marks in boxes). We have argued that this puts a burden on interviewers and even on respondents, for a relatively small gain later, except where a relatively simple set of answers, mostly quantitative, is asked repeatedly of rather large samples (as with the Current Population Survey). The formats of such questionnaires almost always are more difficult to read and follow, and errors are likely to creep in. Faced with the problem of holding down the costs of a labor-intensive operation, the survey director will be under increased pressure to bypass the coding and/or keypunching operation; but he may merely find himself spending more on the costly labor involved in correcting errors, or the costs of lower response rates. Worksheets are another matter. They can be designed to be easy for editors and still suitable for direct keypunching. When machines allow keypunchers to write directly on tape, records of unlimited length, this will be a major improvement, obviating the need for match-merging decks of cards.

Treatment of Non-Response

We have already seen that the editors can assign missing items of information, and have pointed out the strategy problem: whether one uses a large group on which to base the assignment, making it somewhat less precise in terms of the individual being assigned, but more stable in terms of sampling variability. Sometimes assignments are made by actually copying a number from another interview with a similar "matched" family. This, of course, makes the assignment very explicit and appropriate for the individual, but subject to amplified sampling variance.

There are also situations where the whole interview is missing. In the flow chart presented here notice that information on the non-response is coded, keypunched, and verified, not only to check out the sample books but also so that one can compare distributions fo the response and the non-response on whatever kinds of information are available for both, to see whether the non-response are systematically different from the response cases. If they are, it may be necessary to weight the data, weighting up subgroups of the population that are more underrepresented than others in the sample. Whether such weighting for differential non-response is needed depends on the purpose of the survey. If the purpose is to make estimates of amounts or distributions or proportions, then weighting is necessary if the non-response are different from the response on the items which are to be estimated. On the other hand, if the purpose of the survey is analytical, estimating relationships between variables, then one needs to worry about non-response bias only if the non-response are systematically different in terms of these relationships, in other words, if there are things associated with non-response which interact with the explanatory variables of the study, altering their effect on the dependent variables. For instance, if the non-response is biased

Processing Flow—From Receipt of Questionnaires to Data Ready for Analysis

Decision whether to accept,
reject, or return to field
↓

Sample information   Sample book   Sample information
onto non-response   entry as   onto questionnaires
forms   response ↗   ↓
Assign serial   ←———   or non-resp.   Assign serial
 numbers   numbers
↓   ↓   ↔   Editing of
Coding   Editing   subunit information
Check-coding   Check-editing   Check-editing
                          ↓   ↓
                          Coding   Coding
                          ↓   ↓
                          Check-coding   Check-coding
                          ↓   ↓
Keypunching   Keypunching   Keypunching
Verifying   Verifying   Verifying
↓   ↓   ↗   ↓
List in order   List in order   Merge card   Merge card
by sample book   by sample book   files   files
number   number   onto tape   onto tape
                                           ↓   ↓
         ↘   ↙   Wild code check   Wild code check
         Compare listings   ↓   ↓
         with sample books   Corrections   Corrections
         Every address   Rerun check   Rerun check
         accounted for?   ↓   ↓
         ↓   Consistency   Consistency
         Corrections   check   check
                                           ↓   ↓
   ↙   ↘   Corrections   Corrections
Distribution of   Distribution of Rerun check   Rerun check
non-response by   of response   ↓   ↓
all available   by all information Extreme case check Extreme case check
variables   available also   Corrections   Corrections
                          for non-response ↓   ↓
     ↘   ↙   Add dictionary   Add dictionary
         Non-response ←   ↓   ↓
         analysis.   Generate new   Generate new
         Computation of   variables   variables
         weights if   (brackets, deciles,
         necessary   combinations,
                          ↘   county data,
                                             indexes)
                                            ↓
                                           Transfer in weights   Transfer in
                                                                 weights and
                                                                 variables from
                                                                 larger unit
                                            ↓   ↓
                                           Main file ready   Subunit file
                                            ↓   ready
                                           Analysis   ↓
                                                                 Analysis

in terms of income, but one is using income to predict or explain some expenditure, then the mere fact that there are too few people in some income groups should not bias that relationship. On the other hand, if the response underrepresents the single people or the old people and they have different income elasticities, then some weighting for differential non-response may reduce the bias of these estimated relationships.

The same kind of strategy problem involved in assigning individual items of missing information arises in assigning weights for non-response. If one uses very small groups, then the people whose weights are increased to take account of the non-response are more like the non-response because they are more carefully specified, *but,* if one gets widely varying weights this way, one may increase the sampling variance and trade a small reduction in bias for a large increase in sampling variance. This may not be wise. The extreme procedure again is to find *one* other family matched as much as possible to the one who is missing and simply duplicate his record. If this person turns out to be a millionaire or is unusual in some other way, of course, one can see what potentially disastrous results might occur. On the other hand, if one is very concerned with preserving not only unbiased estimates of means and proportions but unbiased estimates of the variances, one may want to make individual assignments with the greater variance. Taking a whole group and weighting them up may tend to reduce the variance of the sample in the same way that using an average of some other group to assign missing information may reduce that variance. The general experience has been that unless response rates vary quite widely and systematically, weights often make very little difference and are probably not worth the trouble. They create problems not only in simple analysis but also in complex analysis where one may want to apply significance tests, because the sum of the weights is different from the number of degrees of freedom. But an analysis of response rates is called for in any case. An example is given in Appendix B to this chapter.

The only analysis of response rates that can be done is for characteristics that can be measured for both the response and the non-response. This usually means locational items (city size), type of dwelling, and things the interviewer can guess: race, house value, or rent level. On the other hand, given good national data in several dimensions on the numbers of families, it might be possible with national samples, to estimate response rates without any direct information about the individual addresses where no interview was taken, and to produce weights on that basis.

There is a final kind of missing information which occurs when the sample does not cover the population properly. One may miss whole dwellings in a sample of dwelling units, either because of new construction or because of hidden dwellings in basements or above garages or without an outside door. A solution to this problem, which largely affects estimates of aggregates but may also affect other things, is to use outside data to estimate the total number of households for expanding from survey averages to estimates of aggregates. There may be situations where it is useful to develop the weighting procedures from outside estimates of the population distribution where one is particularly concerned about potential biases from missing whole dwellings plus potential biases from non-response.

Where different sampling fractions were used, or where one develops some data on a larger unit than that sampled (where the probability of selection varies with the number of elements combined) then weights are essential, of course.

Cleaning the Data

We have already discussed several processes intended to maintain the accuracy of the data: check-editing, check-coding. With each succeeding step of the process additional checks should be built in to maintain this quality. Here again, of course, there is a strategy problem and a problem in resource allocation. It may or may not be wise to invest very large amounts of money getting rid of a few small random errors. Sometimes it seems as though we pay attention to them out of all proportion to their real importance simply because they are so annoying or, in the final report, so embarrassing. On the other hand, there are a number of instances where people have gotten half way through the analysis stage and decided they had to go back, throw out all they had done, clean out the data first, and start over again.

Once the coding is done the data go to the keypunching operation, and the keypunching is verified by redoing it on a similar machine. Keypunching is a very straight-forward, rapid, and reasonably error-free procedure, but the verifying reduces the errors still more. Then in a major study where quality is important there follows a series of procedures for cleaning the data. Under present technology this is often done after the data are merged and put on tape. In a major study there may be anywhere from two to ten or fifteen computer cards full of material for each interview and the computer technology still requires putting the material on cards first. These decks then have to be put in order by some serial (interview) number, merged, and written on tape before one can use the data easily. It pays to do this before the cleaning process starts, *if* it is easy to make tape corrections.

The first step is usually to get rid of "wild codes," codes that are not in the original list of codes and thereby unacceptable. Sometimes, of course, codes have been added or altered during the coding process and one has to be careful to allow them. The process of finding wild codes is quite easy with a computer, but the process of looking up all the cases, deciding what the code should be and ordering the corrections is time consuming. In recent years the procedure has been to take the first few hundred interviews, do the wild code check and make corrections, and then continue to do wild code checks in batches as the data come in, rather than wait until the very end and have all the work piled up. This also leads to improvements in the coding process, since wild codes sometimes arise because the coders are doing something wrong. It is worth rerunning the wild code check after the corrections have been made. Sometimes the corrections are not made properly. Sometimes new errors are created in the process of making corrections. And once the program is ready to go, it is very simple and fast to rerun it.

The next step is "consistency checking" where one makes sure that if a man has a mortgage he has a house on which to have a mortgage, for example. One of the problems in writing requests for consistency checks is that some consistencies are one-way and some are two-way. Sometimes B is true *if and only if* A is true; sometimes B has to be true if A is true, but the reverse need not hold. This means that writing computer language for making such consistency checks is quite complicated, and only a fairly sophisticated set of computer software allows it to be done with ease. The problem arises, of course, even if the consistency checking is being done on a sorter; one has to remember to specify in advance exactly what the consistency is. In many cases, things that are thought to be inconsistent when writing the specifications turn out to be perfectly legitimate. On the other hand, sometimes things show up which are inconsistent because there are some real problems with the conceptual definitions or with the editing procedures. This often leads to real improvements in the data. Again, once the corrections are made, it pays to rerun the check to make sure they have been done right. When possible, it pays to do consistency checking in batches because it is a time-consuming process because sometimes improvements can be made in the interviewing, editing, or coding process on the basis of information secured during the early batches of consistency checking.

It also pays to look up the extreme cases to see whether there is something wrong with them. This used to be done as part of the regular consistency checking, but it is often better to hold it as a separate operation, because only a small fraction of the selected cases need correcting, but the listings need to be preserved. Any case that is extremely large or extremely small or unusual in the sense that it is possible but very unlikely is looked up to see whether there is something wrong.

One kind of check that has not traditionally been done but theoretically could be, particularly as computers get more powerful, is to run a multivariate analysis on each of the major dependent variables and sort out the cases that deviate substantially from what might be expected on the basis of three or four explanatory variables. One would then look them up to see if there was something wrong with them—either absolute errors or conceptual problems. Since in a later multivariate analysis the extreme cases might either have to be eliminated, or handled specially, this may save some later problems. It may also uncover some real errors. There is the theoretical difficulty that it might introduce certain biases by eliminating some kinds of errors and not others, and it would certainly spuirously increase a correlation if the errors were actually distributed up and down the range but the only ones that were discovered were the ones that reduced the correlation with certain explanatory variables.

At about this stage in the processing it may be useful to add a dictionary at the head of the set of data, naming the variables, specifying their tape locations, and perhaps specifying certain "inapplicable" or "missing data" codes for the convenience of the computer. Computer programs now exist which will actually pick up twenty-four letters of alphabetical description of each variable and print it along with the machine output in analysis runs. Also the dictionary allows a very easy way of designating variables by number in ordering a computer run without having to specify their dictionary titles every time. It also keeps the names of variables consistent.

Another decision that has to be made all the way through the processing stages is how many safety precautions to take in terms of back-up tapes or extra decks of computer cards. Since every time corrections are made to a tape, a whole new tape is written, the back-up tape then gets out of date and it would have to be rewritten too. Clearly, there must be some compromise between continually writing two tapes, and letting the back-up tape get so out-of-date that if anything happens to the main tape it would be very costly to redo it. Even the sheer record-keeping gets difficult, since any minor change in a tape requires writing a new tape, so that the identifying number of the tape reel changes many times.

Where the number of variables and required consistencies are small, it may pay to check for wild codes, inconsistencies, and extreme cases all in one operation. In general, however, trying to do too many things at once leads to trouble, even though sequences of steps seem cumbersome.

Variable Generation or Creation

Once the originally coded data have been cleaned up and are on a computer tape, it is generally necessary to create some new variables and add them to the tape. First there are variables containing information not collected in the interview or inserted by the interviewer, but having to do with the area in which the respondent lives (assuming they were not put on the questionnaire when checking it into the sample books). These tend mostly to be data about the country or the state or the region usually taken from the United States Census Bureau or other government agencies. Knowing which county each respondent lives in, one can add information about the employment level, median level of education, etc., in his county.

A second kind of added variable consists of class interval or bracket codes or deciles on quantitative information. It is generally useful to have the family income in dollars, but for many purposes when one wants to use income as the stub of a table or even in multivariate analysis, one may want eight or ten income brackets, or ten deciles (breaking up the population into ten equal groups arranged in order according to the size of their income). Deciles are difficult and complex to build because the data must be sorted in order by size of the variable to be "deciled." It requires a separate sorting for each variable. Even on a modern computer sorting several thousand cases on a five-digit variable is not a simple matter. Then one must allocate cases tied at the boundaries to one subclass or the next, in an unbiased way.

A third kind of variable to be generated consists of combinations of other variables. The classic example, of course, is stage in the family life cycle which combines information about age of the head, marital status, presence of children, age of the youngest child, and sometimes, whether the head is still in the labor force. With modern computer programs that look for interactions, it is somewhat less necessary than it once was to build variables containing interaction possibilities in them, but they are still very useful where there is a good theoretical base for them.

A fourth kind of variable that is often generated is what might be called an "aggregated variable," such as the mean of some characteristic for a whole subgroup of the population (or sample) to which the respondent belongs. These can be created right out of the sample. Or one might generate a residual from this mean indicating by how much the individual was above or below the rest of some group. The group might be expected to be a reference group for him. There are difficulties, of course, in the interpretation of such variables. Take the classic case in economics where one may want to separate a man's income into three components. One might first introduce a variable which is the mean income of people in the same education, race, and sex group as the respondent, a kind of proxy for a permanent lifetime income. One might add a second variable representing the deviation of the mean income of people in his age, education, race, and sex group from the first variable, representing the extra earnings or lower earnings that might be expected because he is in a particular age group too. And then one could add a third variable, the deviation of the individual's own income from the composite of the first two. The difficulty with assuming that these three represent expected lifetime earnings, extra expected current earnings of his reference group, and his own deviations from the sum of these two, is that they are basically representations of race, age, education, and sex. Several other interpretations can be given to them. And it can be argued that one should introduce all these variables into an analysis directly, find out which combinations matter in explaining the behavior to be studied, and then try to interpret whether the permanent income notion makes more sense than several other alternative explanations of what education and age and race mean. Furthermore, the individual deviations from expected income may represent *not* "transitory income" but permanent differences based on differential skill or motivation. There are many other possibilities of introducing as variables either the group average of some characteristic or the individual's deviation from that average. There are still difficult computer problems in creating such variables and adding them to each individual record, however.

Finally, and perhaps the most troublesome of all, one may want to generate various *indexes* combining a set of attitudinal questions or several different evidences of a particular behavior pattern. (See Chapter IV.) The literature in psychology is full of very complex procedures for getting a reduced set of variables out of several hundred, based largely on their intercorrelations. Factor analysis is perhaps the most commonly known of these but there are others of more modern variety such as "Least space analysis." All of them involve a great deal of computer work. All of them are based almost entirely on the intercorrelations among the items. None of them pay any explicit attention to the effects of these components on some variable that one is trying to explain. At the other extreme from this inductive approach are indexes built up with a great deal of theoretical structure giving a man points for various things and adding them up or perhaps putting on even more complicated weighting schemes.

One should view the problem differently depending on whether one is combining various bits of information to generate a *dependent* variable or an *explanatory* variable. In the case of a dependent variable it may be quite essential to do some thorough investigation before combining variables. There may even be some justification for a factor analysis, generating some weights to be applied to build a new dependent variable for analysis. In the case of explanatory variables, however, there are differences. For one thing, one may not want to be combining two or three things because they are correlated, if they have effects on the dependent variable in opposite directions from one another. Secondly, one certainly does not want to combine things that are negatively correlated with one another. But that does not mean that it is necessary to go through an elaborate procedure of weighting according to the size of correlation.

A strong case can be made for building fairly simple additive indexes to be used as explanatory variables. Once such a simple additive index is built out of components that are not negatively correlated (so that they will not offset one another) one can then use the bracket levels of this index as a set of dummy variables in an explanatory analysis, and look to see whether the effect is linear or not. If the effect is linear, then the assumption of additivity is maintained. If the effect is curved and concave from above so that nothing happens to the dependent variable until the index is very high, the assumption is justified that the components to the index are complementary because it takes many of them before anything happens, that is, they reinforce one another. If, on the other hand, the effect is curvilinear and convex from above, the implication is that the components are substitutes for one another. Any one or two of them will have as much effect as all of them together. In any case, there is great scanning efficiency in building such an index because if it has no effect at all and the components are all zero or mildly positively intercorrelated, one can be reasonably sure that none of the components have any effect either. If it has a strong effect, one can first check to see whether the components are additive, complementary, or substitutes, and one can also go back and search the detail to see which of the components is really having most of the effect.

There are great efficiencies in generating variables all in one batch on the computer with some preplanning rather than doing them as one goes along. Every time one generates a variable in a computer it is necessary to rewrite the whole tape. This means that the operation is rather expensive. It costs little or nothing more to generate a whole set of variables.

When new variables are generated, they are likely to be at least as important as the ones originally coded, and should be subjected to many of the same checks. Extreme cases should be looked up, and the distribution examined. This is doubly important if some variables are generated, from which still others will be created. It may be useful to get a distribution or average of each new variable, tabulated against one or more explanatory variables to see whether the results look reasonable.

How does one keep track of all these variables, so that it is easy to find where they are (on which tapes), or even against what other variables they have been run? Extremely elaborate and costly indexing systems could be devised, but they are quite likely to break down. Some try for an alphabetic card-file of variables by name, on which is entered all the data tapes where that variable exists, and even all the computer runs (by number) in which it was used. A sequential file of tabulation requests, with attached lists of the variables involved has proven the most useful way of keeping track at least during the main processing. Sometimes the tabulation requests are given different sequences of numbers depending on their purpose, i.e. whether file building, or which type of dependent variable.

In panel studies the process of variable generation is a great deal more complicated, because one generates a set of variables for each year, but when the next wave comes along a very large number of possibilities open up for generating variables which reflect changes from one year to the next, either absolute difference or percentage changes. If one wants to analyze changes, the change is always correlated positively with the second year's value and negatively with the first year's value. So, it may seem important to generate the average of the two years as a second independent variable (uncorrelated with the first) so that one can find out whether it is the over-all level, or the change, in this particular variable that is doing the work. For numerical variables these change variables and average level variables are not too difficult except for the amount of space they take but, if one wants to generate measures of changes in categorical variables, the problems are much more complicated. How does one develop a new variable reflecting change in occupation for instance?

Finally, a mechanical problem results from the fact that most computer software has been developed to handle records of a length up to a thousand variables. Any one survey may have several hundred variables. A panel study may easily reach the thousand limit with the first reinterview when the "change variables" are added. After that one has the same problem that existed with IBM cards i.e., the necessity for generating a *lot* of work tapes once one runs over the limit for a single file. This requires a good deal of planning, and some restriction on the total number of variables one wants to carry, from the sheer mechanics of staying within the restraints of the machinery.

The same process of consistency checking, corrections, and generating new variables may take place on the other files if they are separate files of subunit information. It is also possible to transfer information from one file to another, e.g. put family income on the record for each individual in that family.

At this point we are still not ready to analyze the data. There may be weights necessary to allow for variations in either sampling rates or response rates or both. As one can see from the flow diagram, a whole side process has been going on during the consistency check operations, checking the variations in response rates to see whether weights are necessary to allow for variations in response rates. If there were variations in the sample rates, weights would be necessary in any case. A simple way to put the weights on is to put them onto the unit that was sampled, namely a household or a family, and then transfer them into the subunit files from there. This has a certain efficiency because at the same time one can transfer *information* about the larger unit into each of the subunit records as well. For instance, if one has a record for each individual in the sample, one will want to have available alongside each individual's record, his family income and perhaps other information about the family. This information, together with the proper weights, can be transferred in at the same time. It should be fairly clear to those who understand sampling that whatever weight is appropriate for a family is appropriate for each of its members because it was the family that was sampled, not the individual members.

We now have one or more files of data ready for analysis, perhaps with a dictionary at the beginning, certainly with the data all cleaned up, and probably with a set of additional variables, brackets, indexes, etc., added at the end to make the analysis easier. We turn in the next chapter to the description of some of the problems of analysis and interpretation of the survey data.

A final note of warning: The importance of meticulous care and proper record keeping through the data cleaning and variable generation process cannot be exaggerated. One result of the process should be a code for each of the variables, including the newly generated ones, with notes on conceptual problems or extreme cases discovered in the cleaning process, and ideally with distributions of the categorical variables and means and variances of the numerical ones. At this stage, one or more back-up tapes should be written, hopefully with some mechanism to prohibit anyone from writing on them by accident. Any errors in the weights or in the generated variables will affect all the subsequent analysis, and if discovered later may require redoing a great deal of work.

Particularly since the data may well be used by other people, the codes and attached documentation should be sufficient to guard against most errors. Most surveys of any size are the joint work of a number of people, so procedures that assure that each of them knows what the other has done are important. A single master code is probably better, for this reason, than separate copies for each researcher, at least until the data are ready for analysis.

Records of the Process

Part of the documentation of any study should be a summary of the experience in editing, coding, and cleaning. A list of the codes for which the percent disagreement in check-coding was the highest is useful. Some account of the distribution among interviews of the number of uncodable answers per interview also helps, as well as some notion how many cases had to be assigned—unless a special code was added indicating assignments. Sometimes a bracket code is used with a category for missing information, even though the amount field contains assignments for those cases. Where no assignments are made, there is usually a code for missing information and a distribution of each code tells the reader how much of a problem there was with missing data.

Similarly, there should be a report from the editors on the areas of greatest difficulty in check-editing, and the kinds of problem cases or conceptual difficulties that were encountered.

If the checks for wild codes, inconsistencies, and extreme cases, were done by computer, there should at least be information on the number of corrections required, and perhaps a discussion of the kinds of codes which seemed to lead to trouble.

Under the pressure of work, it is often difficult to insure that proper notes are made of problems, hence it is even more important that the account be written as soon as possible after the end of the process. Presentation of such material in survey reports should not only improve the understanding of each report, but provide the base on which to improve the processing of future surveys.

Even narrative accounts of problems may be worth preserving. A brief list of some irritating and vexing problems we have faced may be useful here:

Corrections that were not properly made, or that introduced further inconsistencies or errors.

Difficulties and delays because of coding errors in interview numbers, scrambling data from two different interviews.

Discovery of errors after variables had been used to create other variables, or had been transferred to other decks or tapes, requiring multiple corrections, and redoing of later steps.

Picturesque variable names that misled or confused, like "remaining installment debt" for the total amount left to pay, including service charges, or "debt payments" including only installment debt payments to institutions.

Work decks or tapes not adequately documented, but not destroyed either.

Creation of a sequence of data tapes, each altering the tape location and variable number of each variable, but without creating a new code for each or maintaining in the variable name a reference to its original code location, so that locating the code detail requires translating through several transformation lists—those lists not with the codes but buried in piles of machine output.

Retention of the same variable name after the variable has been altered, truncated, corrected, etc., but with the old variable still on other tapes or cards.

Failure to date the completion of each step, so that one cannot tell whether an analysis run was done before or after certain corrections or changes in variables.

Regressions or other least squares analyses run with variables containing extreme cases, because the distribution had not been examined in advance.

Failure to save the computer instruction cards, so that one cannot tell which subgroup was selected (by filters, or sorting) for the analysis.

A decision to postpone one operation from editing to the computer was forgotten, and only noticed when some tables were run, partly because the master code did not contain a note, or a label for the variable indicating that it had not had one final adjustment made to it.

Footnotes to Chapter V

1. John Lansing and Thomas Eapen, "Dealing with Missing Information in Surveys," *Journal of Marketing,* 24 (Oct. 1959), pp. 21-27.

2. Walter J. Stewart, "Computer Editing of Survey Data—Five Years of Experience in BLS Manpower Surveys," *Journal of the American Statistical Association* Line 61 (June 1966), pp. 375-383.
   See also: Kenneth Janda, *Data Processing* (Applications to Political Research), Northwestern University Press, Evanston, Illinois, (second edition) 1969.

3. Dorwin Cartwright, "Analysis of Qualitative Material," in Leon Festinger and Daniel Katz, *Research Methods in the Behavioral Sciences,* Holt, Rinehart, and Winston, New York, 1953.

   See also A. N. Oppenheim, *Questionnaire Design and Attitude Measurement,* Basic Books, New York, 1966.

SOME EXAMPLES OF HOW RESPONSES FROM THE
COMPLETED INTERVIEWS ARE PROCESSED

Specifically, we shall follow the step-by-step processing of a series
of question on car repairs and food expenditures.

Car Repairs

The first section to be discussed is that on car repairs. The first
question in this series (C19), "Do you (or your family) do any of your own
repair work on your car(s)?" is merely a screening question separating those
who do repair work on their cars from those who do not.

The code for this question is also shown on the next page. Code categories "1" and "5" are, through convention at the Survey Research Center, used
for "Yes" and "No" replies respectively. The "9" category is traditionally used
for the "not ascertained" category. Usually, for a question so simple as this
one is, the "not ascertained" category is used when the question is inadvertantly
not asked when it should have been asked. The "0" category is used for those
cases where the family does not own a car, and hence not asked whether or not
they made repairs to their car.

The replies to the second question about car repairs, "What kinds of
things have you done on your car(s) in the last year?" are classified into
categories fitting the conceptual scheme of the study. Note that for this code
(next page) Col. 35 the phrase "PRIORITY CODE," appears. This means - in the
given example - that if a respondent gives a reply that fits into both categories
1 and 2, that we would code it into the 2 category, indicating that he had done
some work on his car requiring some skill and ignoring the fact that he may have
done some work requiring little or no skill.

A response we received such as "I owned different cars, and so did lots--
1st one overhauled engine 4 times--always grease car; tune it up;" would be coded
in "5" category on the grounds that the fact the respondent overhauled the engine
4 times takes priority over the fact that he also greased and tuned up the car.
since overhauling the engine takes more skill than greasing the car or tuning it
up. Another response such as "minor motor tuneup" would be coded 3.

The next 3 questions in this sequence (Qs. C21, C22, and C23) are
handled in the editing stage. The amount of money saved is considered one
of the nonmoney components of income.

Once the data from each of these interviews has gone through the editing
and coding stages, key punched onto IBM cards and put onto tape. it can be
utilized for analyses.

One of the most common ways of presenting the data we collect is in table
form. Still using the information on car repairs, the table on the following
page shows the difficulty of car repairs by family income. You will note that
the categories indicating the degree of complexity come from the code.

C19. Do you (or your family) do any of your own repair work on your car(s)?

☐ YES   ☐ NO (GO TO D1)

(IF YES)

C20. What kinds of things have you done on your car(s) in the last year?

_____

_____

C21. In the last year do you think you saved more than $50 that way?

☐ YES   ☐ NO (GO TO D1)

C22. (IF YES) About how much do you think you saved? $_____

C23. About how much time did that take you altogether? _____

(HOURS)

34

C19 Do you (or your family) do any of your own repair work on your car(s)?

1. Yes

Code 0
in Cols. ──5. No, or none in the last year
35-39

9. N.A.
0. Inap., family does not have car (Coded 0 in Col. 16)

35

C20 (If yes) What kinds of things have you done on your car(s) in the last year?

PRIORITY CODE - highest number

5. Yes, complex repairs that usually take a skilled mechanic (rebuilt engine or transmission)
4. Yes, extensive repairs, taking much skill (rings, valves, bearings, install factory rebuilt engine, king pins, ball joints, transmission work, motor work, or "I do anything that needs doing"
3. Yes, some skill required, (brakes, wheel bearings, exhaust system, starter)
2. Yes, some skill (tune-up, points, plugs, adjust carburetor, fuel pump)
1. Yes, little or no skill, mostly maintenance (oil change, greasing, tire switching) (touch-up painting)
9. N.A. whether or kind of repairs
0. Inap., family does not have car, does no repair work
7. Yes, but not in the last year.

Dollars saved put on worksheet 1, and become part of non-money income.

Hours spent go on worksheet 3, and become part of total work hours, and reduce estimated leisure time.

DIFFICULTY AND COMPLEXITY OF CAR REPAIRS BY TOTAL FAMILY MONEY INCOME

Difficulty and Complexity of Car Repairs	Total Family Money Income								
	Less than $1000	$1000 -1999	$2000 -2999	$3000 -3999	$4000 -4999	$5000 -7499	$7500 -9999	$10,000 -14,999	$15,000 or more
Complex repairs requiring a skilled mechanic	1%	1%	1%	2%	1%	2%	2%	3%	2%
Extensive repairs taking much skill	1	3	4	5	7	6	9	7	4
Repairs requiring some skill	3	2	2	3	6	8	12	10	5
Repairs requiring some skill of a lesser amount	1	2	3	5	6	11	17	15	13
Repairs requiring little or no skill	0	1	1	1	2	4	5	4	4
Not ascertained	1	1	1	1	1	2	1	1	1
No repair work	93	90	88	82	76	66	53	58	69
Made repairs but not last year	0	0	0	1	1	1	1	2	2
Total	100%	100%	100%	100%	100%	100%	100%	100%	100%
Percent who own no car	78	67	57	45	36	22	10	5	4
Percent of those with a car who repaired it	27	27	26	27	34	40	50	41	29

Expenditures on food

The calculation of expenditures on food involved an editing stage, which we will illustrate in the next few pages.

From the listing box of the interview we determine the weekly food requirement for each individual in the FU according to his age and sex. We then total this for all individuals in the FU and convert this total to an Annual Food Standard which also makes allowances for economics in feeding large families. Assuming that a family spends 1/3 of its total income on food, we then multiply the Annual Food Standard by 3 to get the annual income need standard which we label the "Annual Need Standard." Thus, we have arrived at our standards.

Having arrived at our standards, we can now see how our FU compares with our standards. To do this we need the FU's total food consumption. Total food consumption consists of the total Food Expenditure plus the total Non-Money Food consumed. Under Food Expenditure we have:

1. (Amount) Spent Eating Out taken from Question E2 of last year's questionnaire

2. Cost of Milk from E3

and 3. (Cost of) Other Food from E5.

The total of these three expenditures gives us the Food Bill Subtotal.

To obtain the total food expenditure labeled the "Corrected Food Bill" we must subtract any alcohol or cigarette expenditures which may have been included in the Food Bill. We now have the total Food Expenditure and must add to this the Nonmoney Food consumed to obtain total food consumption.

Nonmoney Food consists of:

1. Home Grown Food taken from E12 of last year's questionnaire

2. Food Received on the Job from J30

and 3. (Amount) Saved on Food Stamps from J32.

Adding the total of these three items to Food Expenditure, we finally arrive at total consumption figure which is in dollars. All of this information is edited on Worksheet 2, except the total Food Consumption, which is assembled in the computer.

We can now compare our FU's actual total Food Consumption with its Annual Food Need Standard. We do this in ratio form by placing Food Consumption over Food Need Standard. If this ratio is less than one, then this implies that the FU's Food Consumption in below the Standard. If the ratio equals one, then the Standard is just met. If the ratio is greater than one, then it means that the FU's Food Consumption is above the Standard.

However, this ratio is used for more than just comparisons. This ratio as well as other items (measures) are conveniently used in tables as summary statements of our data. These tables are very important in the analysis of our data and are used to make crucial policy decisions by policy makers. We have two such tables using this food consumption data for you to scan today. The table summarized the relationship between Family Size and Ratio of Food Consumption to Food Standard. We see that smaller families spend more on food, especially one person families - probably single men. The chart also indicates that larger families economize more; but we find that these larger families have a higher percentage of those who consume less food than the standard.

4

SECTION B

B1. How many people live here altogether? _Four (4)_

(LIST ALL PERSONS, INCLUDING CHILDREN, LIVING IN THE DU, BY THEIR RELATION TO HEAD)			(ASK B3 FOR THOSE AGED 5-25 (EXCEPT HEAD AND WIFE)		(ASK B4 IF ANSWER TO B3 IS "NO")
B2. How old are they and how are they related to you?	Age	Sex	B3. Is (he/she) in school?		B4. How many years of school did (he/she) finish?
1. HEAD OF DWELLING UNIT	26	M			
2. Wife	25	F	☐ YES	☒ NO ⟶	12
3. Son	5	M	☐ YES	☒ NO ⟶	00
4. Daughter	3	F	☐ YES	☒ NO ⟶	00
5.			☐ YES	☐ NO ⟶	
6.			☐ YES	☐ NO ⟶	
7.			☐ YES	☐ NO ⟶	
8.			☐ YES	☐ NO ⟶	
9.			☐ YES	☐ NO ⟶	
10.			☐ YES	☐ NO ⟶	

B5. Anyone else? (LIST ABOVE)

8

_____

E2. About how much do you (FAMILY) spend in a week eating out, including lunches at work (or at school)?

$ _00_

E3. Do you have any of your milk delivered to the door?

☒ YES   ☐ NO - (GO TO E5)

E4. About how much do you (FAMILY) spend on that milk in a week or month?

$ _5_   per _month_

E5. About how much do you spend a week on all the (other) food you use at home?

$ _20_

E6. How about alcoholic beverages -- how much do you (FAMILY) spend on that in an average week?

$ _____   ☒ NONE - (TURN TO E8)

E7. Is that included in the food bill?

☐ YES   ☐ NO

9

E8. Do any of you smoke?

☒ YES   ☐ NO (GO TO E11)

> E9. (IF YES) About how many cigarettes do you (FAMILY) smoke in a day or week?
>
> _4 Packs_ per _Week_
>
> (CIGARETTES, PACKS, OR CARTONS)   (DAY, WEEK)
>
> E10. Is that included in the food bill?   ☒ YES   ☐ NO

E11. Are there any special ways that you try to keep the food bill down?

☒ YES   ☐ NO (GO TO E14)

E12. (IF YES) What special ways do you have for keeping the food bill down?

We try to catch sales. We clip Coupons from the paper.

E13. Anything else? _No_

E14. (ASK IF 2 OR MORE PEOPLE IN FAMILY) How much of the time does the family sit down and eat the main meal of the day together? _Once every day_

24

J30. Did anyone here get more than $50 worth of food or clothing as a part of their pay?

$5 per week (food)

☒ YES   ☐ NO (GO TO J32)

J31. (IF YES) About how much would that be worth? $ _250_

J32. Did you (FAMILY) get any free food, clothing, or food stamps worth $50 or more in 1967?

☐ YES   ☒ NO (GO TO J34)

J33. (IF YES) About how much did that save you last year? $_____

SURVEY RESEARCH CENTER   1968 SURVEY OF FAMILY ECONOMICS   WORKSHEET 2.

7	6	8		0	2		0	0	0	0	0
1	2	3		4	5		6	7	8	9	10

INDIVIDUAL FOOD COSTS:
USE LISTING BOX AND TABLE B

TABLE B.   INDIVIDUAL FOOD STANDARD   (LOW COST)

AGE	MALE	FEMALE
Under 3	3.90	(3.90)
4 - 6	(4.60)	4.60
7 - 9	5.50	5.50
10 - 12	6.40	6.30
13 - 15	7.40	6.90
16 - 20	8.70	7.20
21 - 35	(7.50)	(6.50)
35 - 55	6.90	6.30
55 +	6.30	5.40

1. _3.90_
2. _4.60_
3. _7.50_
4. _6.50_
5. _____
6. _____
7. _____
8. _____
9. _____
10. _____
11. _____
12. _____
13. _____

SAMPLE BOOK #
_____

EDITOR
_____

CHK. EDITOR

FAMILY SIZE   A. | 4 | TOTAL UNADJUSTED _22.50_

SEE TABLE FOR FOOD AND NEED STANDARDS FOR THE ABOVE FAMILY SIZE AND UNADJUSTED FOOD TOTAL

ANNUAL FOOD STANDARD   B. | 1 | 1 | 9 | 6 | ANNUAL NEED STANDARD C. | 0 | 3 | 5 | 8 | 8 |
                           | 12 | 13 | 14 | 15 | | 16 | 17 | 18 | 19 | 20 |
                                                                                    ANNUAL AMOUNT

FOOD EXPENDITURE

1. SPENT EATING OUT (E 2)   — X — = —

2. COST OF MILK (E 4)   _5_ X _12_ = _60_

3. OTHER FOOD (E 5)   _20_ X _52_ = _1040_

4. FOOD BILL SUBTOTAL (1 + 2 + 3)   _1100_

5. ALCOHOL (E6) _____ X _____ = D. | 0 | 0 | 0 | IF INCLUDED(E7)   — | 0 |
                                      21 22 23   ENTER AT RIGHT   24

6. CIGARETTES (E9) _____ X _____ = E. | 0 | 8 | 3 | IF INCLUDED (E10)   83 | 1 |
                                       25 26 27   ENTER AT RIGHT   28

CORRECTED FOOD BILL

7.   SUBTRACT 5, 6, FROM FOOD BILL IF INCLUDED   F. | 1 | 0 | 1 | 7 | | 0 |
                                                        29 30 31 32   33

NON MONEY FOOD

8. HOME GROWN FOOD (E12) SEE SUPERVISOR   G. | 0 | 0 | 0 | | 0 | Hrs 4
                                                 34 35 36   37

9. CLOTHES MADE AND MENDED (E17, 18)   H. | 0 | 0 | 0 | | 0 | Hrs 5
                                              38 39 40   41

10. FOOD RECEIVED ON THE JOB (J30, page 24)   I. | 2 | 5 | 0 | | 0 |
                                                     42 43 44   45

11. SAVED ON FOOD STAMPS (J32, page 24)   J. | 0 | 0 | 0 | | 0 |
                                                 46 47 48   49

Table I

RATIO OF FOOD CONSUMPTION TO FOOD STANDARD
BY NUMBER OF PEOPLE IN FAMILY

Ratio of Food Consumption to Food Need Standard	Number of people in family								
	1	2	3	4	5	6	7	8	9 or more
Less than .75	6%	3%	5%	6%	6%	8%	18%	25%	41%
.75 - 1.24	21	20	31	33	39	46	45	57	42
1.25 - 1.74	25	27	33	36	33	32	30	19	14
1.75 - 2.24	19	25	18	17	15	10	6	4	3
2.25 - 3.74	22	21	12	8	6	4	1	0	0
3.75 - 6.24	6	4	1	0	0	0	0	0	0
6.25 - 9.74	1	0	0	0	0	0	0	0	0
9.75 - 14.24	0	0	0	0	0	0	0	0	0
14.25 or more	0	0	0	0	0	0	0	0	0
Total	100%	100%	100%	100%	100%	100%	100%	100%	100%
Number of Cases	791	1103	731	671	565	348	224	153	211

RATIO OF FOOD CONSUMPTION TO FOOD NEEDS STANDARD BY TOTAL FAMILY MONEY INCOME

Ratio of Food Consumption to Food Needs Standard	Total Family Money Income								
	Less than $1000	$1000 -1999	$2000 -2999	$3000 -3999	$4000 -4999	$5000 -7499	$7500 -9999	$10,000 -14,999	$15,000 or more
Less than .75	21%	18%	13%	10%	12%	6%	3%	1%	0%
.75 - 1.24	42	38	37	42	36	35	27	18	9
1.25 - 1.74	24	23	27	30	28	31	33	33	24
1.75 - 2.24	7	13	12	11	13	16	22	25	25
2.25 - 3.74	6	7	10	6	8	10	13	21	34
3.75 - 6.24	0	1	1	1	3	2	2	2	7
6.25 - 9.74	0	0	0	0	0	0	0	0	1
Total	100%	100%	100%	100%	100%	100%	100%	100%	100%
Number of Cases	154	496	510	507	419	998	649	707	344

APPENDIX B

AN EXAMPLE OF A RESPONSE RATE ANALYSIS

Survey Research Center   1967 Survey of Consumer Finances
Economic Behavior Program   Project 763
                                                October 1967

THE RESPONSE RATE OF THE 1967 SURVEY OF CONSUMER FINANCES[1]

by Alice Pruss and John Sonquist

This memorandum reports the analysis of the response rate statistics

for the 1967 Survey of Consumer Finances (first Debt Panel wave). The prelim-

inary response rate was revised and made higher by the NAH replacement proce-

dure described in P. 763 memo of September 6, 1967, "Response Rate Revisions,

1967 SCF:" Selected tables were rerun with the revised data.[2]

---

[1]This memo supersedes the September, 1967 memo with this same title.

[2]There were 91 households of P. 753 (1966 Survey of Consumer Finances)
where no member of the dwelling unit was contacted at any time during the interviewing period or some member of the dwelling unit was contacted, but the
financially responsible member of the family unit was not contacted and no
interview was obtained. These households were visited as part of the P. 763
sample; 45 interviews were obtained. There were 46 non-interviews, some of
which were refusals, no one at home, non-sample and non-eligible respondents.
The 46 non-interviews should never have been included in the non-interviews
for P. 763. Their non-interview number was obtained from Sampling and they
were removed from Deck 99.
        Replacement of 45 non-interviews of P. 763 by the 45 interviews obtained
was as follows: P. 763 non-interviews where no one was at home were listed
in order of PSU (P. 763, MTR 106). The PSUs where the 45 interviews were
taken were obtained from Sampling. One-to-one replacement was attempted;
that is, a NAH non-interview in a particular PSU was replaced by an interview
in that PSU. The random half indicator (circled line) was chosen to be identical for both. If there was no way of replacing a non-interview in a PSU by
an interview in the same PSU preserving the random half indicator, then one
from a nearby PSU in the same region was substituted. Similar regions were
substituted if the same region could not be used. About half of the 45 substitutions involved judgements. (See P. 763, MTR 107 for an 80 x 80 listing
of non-interviews removed from Deck 99.)
        In conclusion, all 91 of the P. 753 NAH's are accounted for by removing
Deck 99 cards. The overall revised response rate is accurate. However,
response rate by belt (P. 763, MTR 106) or other variables may be of
questionable accuracy due to the "fudging" necessary to replace the non-
interviews.

Computation: NER's (7000 series, non-eligible respondents) were considered like non-sample (9000 series) for both response rates and subtracted
from all addresses to give interviews and non-interviews. The computations
are as follows:

	Preliminary	Revised[3]
Addresses	5234	5163
Secondaries	56	56
Addresses & Secondaries	5310	5219
Non-sample (9000 series)	710	703
NER (7000 series)	667	659
Actual interviews	3165	3165
Non-interviews (8000 series)[4]	768	692
To compute response rate:	5310-710-667 = 3933	5219-703-659 = 3857
	$1 - \frac{768}{3933} = 80.5\%$	$1 - \frac{692}{3857} = 82.1\%$

The preliminary response rate of 80.5% and the revised rate of 82.1%
for the 1967 Survey of Consumer Finances represent a slight, but continued
decline over the past few years. As in past years the rates tend to be lowest in the big city metropolitan areas. However, the response rate differentials do not appear to require assigning weights to compensate for the slight
under-representation of big-city respondents. Table 1 shows the preliminary
response rates by PSU. The following PSU's had rates less than 60%:

>   San Francisco and Oakland Cities
>   St. Louis City
>   Washington City

In addition, the following PSU's had response rates between 60% and 70%:

---

[3]Takes account of replacement NAH's, Respondents Absent.

[4]All respondents that refused to give information for the listing box
on the face sheet were coded as refusals (8000 series) regardless of whether
they occurred on circled line numbers or not. Hence, there may have been a
few FU's with the head aged 60 or over in the "circled" half of the sample
who were classified as sample refusals rather than as NER's.

Chicago City North
Chicago City South
Cleveland City
New York suburbs in New York State
Jersey City and Newark, New Jersey

Philadelphia City
Baltimore suburbs
Harris, Texas

Santa Clara, California

Mercer, New Jersey
Worcester, Massachusetts
Onondaga, New York

Table 2 indicates that the preliminary response rate varied by region, ranging
from 76.1% in the Northeast to 83.1% in the South. The North Central, South,
and West regions were almost identical. The Northeast was slightly lower.
Revisions to Table 2 increased the response rate in the South and North Central
regions by about 2% as compared to about a 1% increase in the West and Northeast. Variations were somewhat greater when tabulated by size of place
(Tables 3 and 4). As in previous years, the highest response rates occurred
in rural areas. The next highest rates occurred in urban places ranging from
2500 to 50,000 in population. The lowest response rates occurred in the
central cities of the twelve largest SMSA's. These areas had a preliminary
rate of only 70.2%, and a revised rate of 72.7%. Revision increased the rates
in the central cities more than it did in other areas. The other large cities,
of population 50,000 and over exclusive of the twelve largest SMSA's had preliminary response rates of 74.8% and revised response rates of 77.1%. The
urban-rural differential in response rates is reflected when the statistic is
tabulated by Belt Code. The suburban areas of the 12 largest SMSA's can be
seen to be lower in response rate than the suburban areas of other SMSA's.
The relevant preliminary statistics are 78.5% and 85.1%, respectively; the
revised rates are 79.0% and 86.5%. The central cities of the twelve largest
SMSA's, as indicated before, had a preliminary rate of only 70.2%, compared

with 73.8% for the central cities of other SMSA's. The revised rates are

72.7% and 76.3% respectively. Distance from the center of a central city is

another variable used to explain the response rate for addresses which are in

SMSA PSU's but not inside the central city. The lowest response rates tend

to be within eight miles of the center of the central city. Higher response

rates are found between eight and 15 miles, and then the response rate drops

off again between 15 and 25 miles from the center of the central city. Re-

vision increased the rate fairly equally throughout. Differential preliminary

response rates by household composition existed, but are difficult to interpret.

When divided in this fashion, rates range from 82% to 100%; however, almost all

of the non-interview situations occurred in households in which it was not

possible to ascertain the household composition. Therefore, it is not clear

whether these households have the same composition as others for which inter-

views were obtained.

When broken down by interviewers' estimates of the family income, the

preliminary response rates range from 80.1% to 93.2%, the revised rates range

from 81.5% to 93.7%. Those having an estimated income of $10,000 or over

have the highest response rate. This might be expected in view of the distri-

bution of interviews over urban-rural areas. A large fraction of the refusals

occurred in households in which the interviewer was not able to obtain enough

information about the family to make an estimate of their income. There was

no significant variation in response rate by race. Revision increased the

rate the most for Negros. The preliminary rate is 84.3%, the revised rate

is 86.5%.

Though there is slight variation in response rates by age, the prelim-

inary ranging from 81.3% to 88.0% and the revised rate ranging from 81.9% to

89.1%, there is not enough to warrant compensation by weighting. The response

rate of young people under 25 increased from a preliminary rate of 87.5% to a
revised rate of 89.1%. When preliminary response rates are computed for
households living in various types of structures, considerably more variation
is apparent. Less than 70% of the families living in apartment houses of four
or more stories and containing five or more units were interviewed successfully.
On the other hand, 88% of those living in two family houses with two units
side by side were interviewed. The response rate problems clearly occur in
multiple-family dwellings (see Table 5).

The preliminary response rate by number of calls was tabulated. The
probability of obtaining an interview drops off very rapidly after the fourth
call. The number of calls made by interviewers was tabulated according to
the belt code location of the household. Getting the response rate in the
central cities of the twelve largest SMSA's up, even to the point where it is,
requires an extremely large number of calls. Of the interviews obtained in
these areas, some 43% were obtained after making four or more calls.

Types of non-sample addresses were also tabulated. There are no significant differences from data obtained in the previous year's Survey. About
80% of the non-sample addresses turned out to be unoccupied dwelling units.
Another seven or eight percent of the non-sample address classifications
resulted from dwellings which were either non-habitable, destroyed, or damaged,
or a trailer moved. There was a slight decline in the proportion of addresses
not occupied because of new construction. In 1966 this was 5.6% of the non-
sample addresses; in 1967 it was only 3.9% (preliminary rates). Changes in
the amount of new construction resulting from increased mortgage interest
rates during the past year do not appear to have affected sample characteristics noticeably.

The non-interviews were tabulated according to the reason for disposition of the schedule as a non-interview (Table 6). From 1964 to 1967, the

percentage of refusals has increased from 11.5% in 1964 to 12.6% in 1967.

In 1967, 2.7% of the non-interviews resulted from no one being at home during

the entire study period.   The percentage was 2.8% in 1964.   In 1965 and 1966,

the proportion dropped to about 2%.   In 1966, 1.3% of the non-interviews

occurred because the interviewers could not contact any of the financially

responsible adults in the family.   This proportion increased to 2.0% in 1967.

There are no significant differences in reasons for non-response between the

two years.

Taken together, these data appear to indicate that though we continue

to have some troubles with our response rates in the central cities of the

large SMSA's, these do not yet appear to be sufficiently bad as to warrant

compensatory weighting.

Table 1

RESPONSE RATE BY PSU

Preliminary

P S U	All addresses N	Ints. + Non-Ints. N	Interviews N	Response Rate (1) %	Response Rate (2) %
Los Angeles City	81	60	49	60.5	81.7
Los Angeles Suburbs	123	99	86	69.9	86.9
San Francisco and Oakland Cities	36	23	13	36.1	56.5
San Francisco Suburbs	50	42	34	68.0	81.0
Chicago City, North	85	66	41	48.2	62.1
Chicago Suburbs	93	69	56	60.2	81.2
Chicago City, South	42	30	19	45.2	63.3
Cleveland City	32	25	16	50.0	64.0
Cleveland Suburbs	30	26	20	66.7	76.9
Detroit City	55	41	32	58.2	78.0
Detroit Suburbs	68	59	49	72.0	83.1
St. Louis City	19	15	8	42.1	53.3
St. Louis Suburbs	36	27	21	58.3	77.8
New York City, Bronx, Queens, Brooklyn, Manhattan	221	174	131	59.3	75.3
New York Richmond	6	4	4	66.7	100.0
New York Suburbs (in New York State)	79	66	46	58.2	69.7
Jersey City & Newark, N.J.	15	13	8	53.3	61.5
New York Suburbs (in N.J.)	107	89	65	60.7	73.0
Boston City	22	14	12	54.5	85.7
Boston Suburbs	66	51	41	62.1	80.4
Philadelphia City	71	51	32	45.1	62.7
Philadelphia Suburbs	53	41	32	60.4	78.0
Pittsburgh City	17	14	10	58.8	71.4
Pittsburgh Suburbs	48	37	27	56.3	73.0
Baltimore City	30	20	17	56.7	85.0
Baltimore Suburbs	36	29	20	55.6	69.0
Washington City	27	25	11	40.7	44.0
Washington Suburbs	33	31	27	81.8	87.1

Table 1 - continued

P S U	All ad-dresses N	Ints. + Non-Ints. N	Inter-views N	Response Rate (1) %	Response Rate (2) %
Harris, Texas	83	72	44	53.0	61.1
Atlanta, Georgia	66	51	39	59.1	76.5
Jefferson, Kentucky	41	34	25	61.0	73.5
Dade, Florida	51	37	33	64.7	89.2
Tulsa, Oklahoma	49	41	30	61.2	73.2
Richmond, Virginia	59	48	41	69.5	85.4
Pulaski, Arkansas	56	43	30	53.6	70.0
Taylor, Texas	53	36	31	58.5	86.1
Montgomery, Alabama	50	39	31	62.0	79.5
Richland, South Carolina	48	37	33	68.8	89.2
Orange, Florida	48	38	28	58.3	73.7
Fayette, Kentucky	52	42	36	69.2	85.7
Sarasota, Florida	112	61	56	50.0	91.8
Pitt, North Carolina	55	46	45	81.8	97.8
Pulaski, Virginia	47	36	33	70.2	91.7
Mississippi, Arkansas	46	35	31	67.4	88.6
Erath, Texas	91	50	45	49.5	90.0
Clark, Arkansas	66	47	46	69.7	97.9
East Carroll, Louisiana	52	32	26	50.0	81.3
Rankin, Mississippi	50	36	30	60.0	83.3
Muhlenberg, Kentucky	86	56	52	60.5	92.9
Hickman, Tennessee	64	39	36	56.3	92.3
Watauga, North Carolina	55	36	34	61.8	94.4
Currituck, North Carolina	83	55	48	57.8	87.3
Franklin, Nebraska	58	37	31	53.4	83.8
Stoddard, Missouri	58	39	32	55.2	82.1
Crawford, Iowa	73	51	44	60.3	86.3
Marshall, Indiana	74	53	40	54.1	75.5
St. Joseph, Michigan	52	44	42	80.8	95.5
Adair, Missouri	62	50	45	72.6	90.0
Logan, Illinois	41	26	21	51.2	80.8
Knox, Ohio	75	54	47	62.7	87.0
Hancock, Ohio	62	45	36	58.1	80.0
Sheboygan, Wisconsin	57	35	32	56.1	91.4

Table 1 - continued

P S U	All addresses N	Ints. + Non-Ints. N	Inter- views N	Response Rate (1) %	Response Rate (2) %
Minnehaha, South Dakota	46	26	23	50.0	88.5
Butler, Ohio	44	35	30	68.2	85.7
Black Hawk, Iowa	57	51	45	78.9	88.2
Genessee, Michigan	56	46	39	69.6	84.8
Toledo, Ohio	55	41	33	60.0	80.5
Marion, Indiana	54	43	36	66.7	83.7
Hennepin, Minnesota	86	74	58	67.4	78.4
Montgomery, Ohio	77	66	48	62.3	72.7
San Diego, California	31	23	20	64.5	86.9
San Bernadino, California	30	20	19	63.3	95.0
King, Washington	44	36	28	63.6	77.8
Salt Lake, Utah	66	50	44	66.7	88.0
Maricopa, Arizona	54	40	33	61.1	82.5
Santa Clara, California	33	28	19	57.6	67.9
Lane, Oregon	63	54	44	69.8	81.5
Whatcom, Washington	64	44	38	59.4	86.4
Tulare, California	58	39	30	51.7	76.9
Logan, Colorado	50	31	29	58.0	93.5
Plumas, California	108	57	45	41.7	78.9
Susquehanna, Pennsylvania	53	30	27	50.9	90.0
York, Maine	98	53	49	50.0	92.5
Ulster, New York	49	34	28	57.1	82.3
Lycoming, Pennsylvania	65	44	37	56.9	84.1
New London, Connecticut	39	29	25	64.1	86.2
Luzerne, Pennsylvania	61	42	35	57.4	83.3
Mercer, New Jersey	44	42	29	65.9	69.0
Fairfield, Connecticut	44	34	26	59.1	76.5
Worcester, Massachusetts	59	43	29	49.1	67.4
Onondaga, New York	66	56	39	59.1	69.6
TOTAL	5310	3933	3165	59.6	80.5

NOTE: Response Rate (1) = Interviews divided by all addresses (if secondary FU in DU, address counted twice, etc.).

Response Rate (2) = Interviews divided by (Interviews + Non-Interviews), NER's are treated as non-sample (9000 interview series).

P. 763: MTR 4 and F. O. Memo.

Table 2

RESPONSE RATE BY REGION

(percentage distribution of family units)

Preliminary and Revised

Region	Interviews + Non-Interviews		Interviews	Response Rate (2)	
	Preliminary	Revised[a]		Preliminary	Revised[a]
	N	N	N	%	%
Northeast	961	945	731	76.1	77.3
North Central	1174	1149	944	80.4	82.1
South	1152	1125	958	83.1	85.1
West	646	638	532	82.3	83.4
TOTAL	3933	3857	3165	80.5	82.1

NOTE: Response Rate (2) = Interviews divided by (Interviews + Non-Interviews).

[a]See P. 763, MTR 107.

P. 763: MTR 18

Table 3

RESPONSE RATE BY SIZE OF PLACE

(percentage distribution of family units)

Preliminary and Revised

Size of Place (1960 Census Classification)	Interviews + Non-Interviews			Interviews		Response Rate		
	1966 N	Reviseda 1967 N	Prelim. 1967 N	1966 N	1967 N	1966 %	Reviseda 1967 %	Prelim. 1967 %
Central Cities of 12 largest SMSA's	442	557	577	324	405	73.3	72.7	70.2
Cities 50,000 & over (except central cities of 12 largest SMSA's)	654	863	889	500	665	76.5	77.1	74.8
Urban Places 10,000 - 49,999	474	665	672	409	550	86.3	82.7	81.8
Urban Places 2500 - 9999; urbanized areas not included above	569	818	827	488	688	85.8	84.1	83.2
Rural, in an SMSA PSU	175	183	187	147	160	84.0	87.4	85.6
Rural, not in an SMSA PSU	612	771	781	551	697	90.0	90.4	89.2
TOTAL	2926	3857	3933	2419	3165	82.7	82.1	80.5

NOTE: Response Rate = Interviews divided by (Interviews + Non-Interviews)

aSee P. 763: MTR 107.

P. 763: MTR 18

Table 4

RESPONSE RATE BY BELT CODE

(percentage distribution of family units)

Revised

Belt Code (1960 Census Classifications)	Interviews + Non-Interviews		Interviews		Response Rate[a]	
	1966 N	1967 N	1966 N	1967 N	1966 %	1967 %
12 largest SMSA's						
Central Cities	442	557	324	405	73.3	72.7
Suburban Areas	448	604	371	477	82.8	79.0
Other SMSA's						
Central Cities	521	689	401	526	77.0	76.3
Suburban Areas	436	621	355	537	81.4	86.5
Other Areas						
Adjacent Areas	499	671	447	580	89.6	86.4
Outlying Areas	580	715	521	640	89.8	89.5
TOTAL	2926	3857	2419	3165	82.7	82.1

NOTE: Response Rate = Interviews divided by (Interviews + Non-Interviews).

P. 763: MTR 106.

Table 5

RESPONSE RATE BY TYPE OF STRUCTURE

(percentage distribution of family units)

Preliminary

Type of Structure	Interviews + Non-Interviews		Interviews		Response Rate[a]	
	1966	1967	1966	1967	1966	1967
	N	N	N	N	%	%
Detached single family house	2014	2711	1705	2245	84.7	82.8
2-family house, 2 units side by side	132	150	113	132	85.6	88.0
2-family house, 2 units one above the other	113	227	94	171	83.2	75.3
Detached 3-4 family house	95	116	75	84	78.9	72.4
Row house	106	147	75	114	70.7	77.5
Apartment house (5 or more units, 3 stories or less)	173	245	137	172	79.2	70.2
Apartment house (5 or more units, 4 stories or more)	127	149	87	102	68.5	68.5
Apartment in a partly commercial structure	48	66	40	50	83.3	75.7
Trailer	83	80	75	65	90.4	81.3
Other	25	42	18	30	72.0	71.4
Not Ascertained	-	-	-	-	*	*
TOTAL	2926	3933	2419	3165	82.7	80.5

[a]Response Rate = Interviews divided by (Interviews + Non-Interviews).

*All Not Ascertained cases were assigned.

P. 763: MTR 18, 18a step 1.

Table 6

REASONS FOR DISPOSITION AS NON-INTERVIEW

(percentage distribution of interviews and non-interviews)

*	1967[a] N	1967[a] %	1966 N	1966 %	1965 N	1965 %	1964 N	1964 %
Refusal[b]	495	12.6	350	12.0	187	11.6	213	11.5
No one at home	107	2.7	58	2.0	30	1.9	52	2.8
Respondent absent	80	2.0	39	1.3	17	1.1	21	1.1
Other	86	2.2	60	2.0	24	1.5	30	1.6
Total non-interviews	768	19.5	507	17.3	258	16.1	316	17.0
Total all interviews and non-interviews	3933	100.0	2926	100.0	1607	100.0	1856	100.0

[a]Figures for 1967 are preliminary.

[b]Includes partial refusal i.e. respondent answered some interview questions, but not enough to be considered by the analysis staff as an interview.

P. 763: MTR 18.

Chapter VI

ANALYSIS

It is appropriate at the start of the analysis of survey data to refer back to the objectives of the project. As set forth in Chapter I, there are four general categories of purposes for a project: prediction, explanation, evaluation, and description. A particular investigation will include some combination of these four types, and analysis plans should be developed with that in mind. It is also useful to be as clear as possible about any potential social usefulness of the findings, whether they are expected to be relevant to the management of the economy as a whole, to some broad social problem, or to some specific policy.

The discussion which follows is divided into three parts. The first concerns the construction of variables and the second, the estimation of statistical relationships within analytical models. The third section considers the organizational aspects of analysis and the practical problems of manipulating survey data.

It is not possible nor would it be useful to present here a complete discussion of the topics mentioned. Much important material is covered in textbooks on statistics or elsewhere in the literature. We will indicate what topics are of particular importance for the analysis of economic surveys and why. For a systematic and detailed coverage of most of the topics the reader will be referred to the appropriate specialized literature. An attempt will be made to refer both to introductory and advanced discussions of each topic to allow for differences in readers' backgrounds and interests.

Construction of Variables

Theoretical Variables and Measured Variables: The analyst confronted with the data obtained from a sample survey has at his disposal a set of measurements on a certain number of variables, operationally defined. He knows, in principle at least, the precise methods which were used to obtain those measurements. If the project was well designed and well executed, he knows what was done by the people who drew the sample, took the interviews, and coded the answers.

The analyst also has in mind a theory, a set of theoretical concepts and propositions concerning the relationships among those concepts. The theory may be more or less completely worked out. It may be exclusively economic theory, or it may include elements from psychological or sociological theory. Even in descriptive studies, there will be some consideration given to conceptualization, to organizing the data in ways which have potential theoretical meaning.

It is important to recognize that there will always be a gap between the measured variables and any theoretical variable. The two are never identical.[1] The analyst, however, should seek to reduce the gap to a minimum. He should try to arrange the data at his disposal so that the measured variables are close approximations to theoretical variables.

The importance of these considerations has been brought home to economists by the discussion of "permanent income," "temporary income," and "measured income."[2] It has been argued that the theoretically relevant variable, "permanent income," is poorly approximated by "measured income." It has also been argued that close attention should be paid to what is sometimes called "non-income income." That is, one should consider the total flow of resources which become available to a household including such items as goods and services provided by employers, gifts, and capital gains, as well as those flows more commonly counted as income. A single theoretical variable may well be constructed from answers to several questions. A clear distinction should be drawn between a "variable" in the sense of answers to a question and a "variable" in the sense of the closest operational approximation to a theoretical variable. For example, answers to many questions may be combined to produce estimates of a single variable, income. The answers may simply be added together, as one adds income from interest to income from wages. But simple addition by no means exhausts the logical possibilities of combination. Whether or not a receipt is counted as income, for example, may be decided on the basis of a question about its origin.

The same kinds of consideration apply to consumption, to saving, to net worth, and so forth, as well as to income. In each case it will be appropriate to consider carefully the exact nature of the theoretically relevant construct and to raise the question of how the measured variable may be brought as close as possible to the theoretical variable.[3]

These considerations also apply to non-economic variables. For example, stage in the family life cycle is a single variable from a sociological point of view. The variable represents the stages through which individuals pass, defined in terms of the formation, changing composition, and dissolution of nuclear families. The stages may be defined in more or less detail according to the purpose: for example, one may or may not wish to distinguish families with a single child from those with two or more children. But it will remain true that families are being placed on a continuum which originated in sociological theory.

Psychological theory also provides examples. The sense of personal effectiveness is a psychological construct developed from the theory of ego-strength. Several questions or items may be used to develop an operational variable intended to measure personal effectiveness. That variable will be more satisfactory the stronger the evidence that it does in fact measure to a close approximation the theoretical construct. Yet, philosophically, a gap will always remain: the measurements are not the constructs which they represent.

They may even represent more than one thing. Take "ability to pay," and "need for housing," for instance. The more people there are in a family the more housing they need, but the less income per capita they have for any given family income. We might build an "ability-to-pay" variable by dividing family income by the number of people in the family. And we might use the number of people in the family as another variable indicating the need for housing. The only trouble is that these two variables are highly negatively correlated with one another since one of them is in the denominator of the other. Family size represents two conflicting forces.

Another example is the attempt to decompose the income into expected average lifetime income, expected current income deviation from the lifetime average, and transitory deviations from the sum of the other two. We can obtain such a measure by developing estimates of lifetime incomes for people according to education, race, sex, and then we can develop expected income for a group of this *age* by using education, sex, and race *and age.* Then we can get a measure of the deviation of actual income from that estimate which we could then call transitory income. The difficulty is that each of these concepts has used other variables which have effects of their own. It may be misleading to label these variables: "Permanent income," "permanent short-run income," and "transitory income." If a man is making $1000 more than his group, perhaps he is the kind of person who makes that much *more* all the time. Hence there may be more variation from year to year in terms of general lifetime changes in income than there are in the so-called transitory effect.

The problem of measurement and variable generation is different for dependent variables and for explanatory variables. It is absolutely essential that the dependent variable be well-measured, well-distributed, and have enough variance so that it can be explained, and relate to some theoretical construct with minimal error. With the possible exception of canonical correlation with dummy variables, it is not possible to scale the dependent variable in the process of the statistical analysis, as it is with the explanatory variables. Hence, much of what we say in the next pages about scaling applies largely to dependent variables. And since in economic surveys, the dependent variables are often numerical magnitudes which require no scaling, the whole issue is less important than in the other behavioral sciences. There are, however, economic behaviors which one may want to study and which would require the generation of variables: e.g., interest in early retirement, receptivity to change, or leadership in acquiring new products.

Level of Measurement: The discussions of cardinal versus ordinal utility have familiarized economists with one of the basic distinctions in the theory of measurement, the distinction between an *ordinal* scale, in which rank orders are known, and an *interval* scale, in which the distances between positions on the scale are also known. There are additional levels of measurement, however, which it is useful to distinguish.[4]

The simplest type of measurement consists in the construction of *nominal* scales, that is, the mapping of objects into categories. What is required is the ability to distinguish between objects which belong to a certain category and those which do not. Some variables of interest in economic surveys are such simple dichotomies. For example, an individual may be classified as a Negro or not a Negro. Many classifications, such as occupation, region of the country, or marital status, have neither order nor quantitative measure.

Between nominal scales and fully ordered ordinal scales Coombs introduces a category of partially ordered scales. In such a scale the members of one class *may* bear some relationship to the members of another class. One position may be "more than" or "greater than" another position. A complete ordering, however, is not possible. This situation may arise when there are two or more fully ordered scales which underlie the scale under consideration, but there is no exact set of equivalences between the underlying scales. Coombs' example is a scale of socio-economic status based on measures of income and education. If A has both more income and more education than B, his status is higher; if he has less of both, his status is lower; but if he has, say, more income but less education, his relative status is not clear. Only a system of equivalence between education and income will produce an answer to the question.

It is possible, of course, to introduce an arbitrary system of equivalences. One might say that one year of education is equivalent to $2000 in income. The resulting ordinal scale, however, would contain a corresponding arbitrary element.

There is a strong tendency for analysts to make such assumptions. Manipulation of the data is greatly facilitated if it is in the form of ordinal scales, or, better, interval scales. It may be possible to find some theoretical or empirical basis for the methods used to specify equivalences.

The risks involved, however, may be serious. It is very easy to become accustomed to the use of imperfect scales and to forget their weaknesses. Consider, for example, level of education. The number of years of formal education which a person has received is a variable which is not only an *interval* scale but, in Coombs' terminology, a *ratio* scale, since it has a meaningful zero point. Suppose it is desired to analyze the effect of education on income and to examine whether income has the same effect on the income of Negroes as of whites. There might be interest in whether Negroes earn lower incomes than whites of the same level of education as a result of discrimination in the job market. One might, therefore, propose to look at the relation between education and income for each racial group separately, and compare the results.

The proposed analysis, however, rests on the assumption that years of education are equivalent. The underlying social reality, unfortunately, does not support the assumption. The data actually represent two scales, one of which refers to years of formal education in one set of schools, and the second, to years of formal education in a second set of schools. What the analyst has at his disposal is two scales, a quantity scale and a quality scale. He must face the problem of equivalence between them.

If he does not do so he will then discover that Negroes earn less than whites of the "same" education. He may infer discrimination in the job market. If he does, he may be wrong. The market might be valuing people's services impartially when the quality as well as quantity of education is taken into account. Or, of course, lower incomes of Negroes than whites with the same number of years of education may be partly the result of job discrimination and partly of educational quality.

This line of reasoning may be applied more generally. School systems are not identical in different regions of the country, in different states, or even in different parts of the same city. They certainly differ over time: there are considerable differences between the instruction represented by a high school diploma in 1928 and 1968. Also, colleges and universities vary in quality. Closely considered, number of years of formal education is not a ratio scale, an interval scale, or even an ordinal scale: it is a partially ordered scale.

The same general considerations apply to other measurements familiar to economists. The entire discipline of accounting represents essentially a set of rules and procedures for reducing widely different situations to sets of numbers in the form of ratio scales.

One of the important implications of the existence of variables with different levels of measurement is that the statistical methods appropriate for analysis depend upon the level of measurement. We shall not attempt a detailed discussion of this subject here. In general, however, such techniques as rank-order correlation methods have been developed for use with ordinal scales.[5] Multiple regression was originally restricted to variables measured as interval or ratio scales, but has been extended even to nominal scales for the explanatory variables through the use of sets of dichotomous or "dummy" variables. Measurement theory also has implications for the development of practical techniques of measurement and the construction of variables.

Dummy Variables: Dichotomous or "dummy" variables have come into wide use in survey analysis in working with predictors (explanatory variables) which are not interval scales or which have a non-linear relation to the dependent variable. Specifically, dummy variables are frequently used as predictors in regression analysis. Analogous techniques also exist for the treatment of dependent variables. One of the basic attractions of the method of dummy variables is that the level of measurement required is only that represented by a nominal scale. That is, what is required is that "likes" be grouped together. The method is flexible enough so that the "likes" may be defined on two (or more) dimensions. For example, the individuals to be placed in one category might be college graduates who live in the Northeast.

It should be recognized that even these minimal conditions are not always easily met. For example, there is some question, as suggested earlier, as to the appropriateness of grouping together graduates of all colleges. A man who spent three years at a first rate institution but did not graduate may be better educated than one who spent four years at a marginal institution and did graduate. In practice one cannot expect to be perfectly successful in grouping "likes" into one category and "unlikes" into another, and the results must be interpreted accordingly.

When a dummy variable is used to represent a simple dichotomy, the procedure is simply to define a variable which takes the value 1 for all individuals falling into the category, and 0 for all others. For example, the variable might be sex, with all females assigned a score of 1, and all males, 0.

The method has been extended to classifications in which there are three or more categories. The usual procedure then is to define a *set* of dummy variables, the number of variables being one less than the number of categories. The reason for this is the k-1 dichotomies contain all the information. If the individual is known to be, or not be, in each of three regions, we know whether he is in the fourth. A fourth dummy variable would be identical to a linear function of the other three, so the four would give a determinant =0 in the denominator in solving the normal equations of regression. Like any case of perfect correlation among predictors, the system is insoluble. Consider, for example, a system of classification into four regions and the values which would be taken by each of the three dummy variables needed to represent the regions each individual:

	Dummy Variables		
Region	X_1	X_2	X_3
Northeast	1	0	0
Northcentral	0	1	0
South	0	0	1
West	0	0	0

When these three dummy variables are introduced as predictors in a regression, a regression coefficient for each will emerge from the calculations. These coefficients will measure for any individual the effect on the score on the dependent variable of being in a category *rather than the omitted category.* For example, the coefficient for X_1 would measure the effect of living in the Northeast *rather than the West.* For the West, of course, the coefficient is zero. The predicted scores for individuals in the West, however, will be included in the constant term. If a different region had been omitted the calculations would have yielded different regression coefficients and a different constant term, but the predicted score for any individual would have been identical. A simple linear transformation can be used to create *four* adjusted coefficients so that the weighted sum of the *four* coefficients (one for each region) is =0. Four such coefficients are easier to interpret than three where the fourth is constrained to zero. (See below) Thus, this procedure in effect makes it possible to introduce into a regression a system of classification without requiring a level of measurement even as high as a partially ordered scale.

The dummy variable technique also may be used in working with variables which are measured as interval or ratio scales to allow for curvilinearity in the relationship. In effect, the dummy variable can approximate a curvilinear relationship by a step function. If there is reason to believe that the true relationship actually is a step function, so much the better. For example, the exact age of an individual may be known, and it may be desired to include age as a predictor, say, of income. Age is a variable measured at a high level—age in years forms a ratio scale. But there is every reason to believe that the effect of age on income is not a straight line—people's incomes rise after they leave school but decline after retirement. Age in years can be divided into a set of dummy variables and treated exactly as in the above example for region. The regression coefficients will then be free to reflect the curvilinearity in the relationship. For a more comprehensive discussion of the technique, see the writings of Daniel B. Suits and Arthur Goldberger.[6]

The success of this device has reduced the interest of economists in scaling, a subject to which a great deal of attention has been given by psychologists. It is less important to achieve a higher level of measurement if one has available techniques which give reasonably good results with a lower level of measurement. The problem of dimensionality, however, to which reference has been made above, arises at any level of measurement. And, in addition, there is a gain in information and, hence, in predictive power when it is possible to place individuals on a finely graduated scale. For example, there is an advantage in knowing the income of a family to the dollar compared to knowing only in which of five classes their income falls. The importance of this advantage will depend upon the shape of the relation of income to the particular dependent variable under consideration. Compare expenditures on goods A, B, and C in the graph on the following page.

For analysis of A, the exact income would be useful. For analysis of B, at low levels no detail is needed but at high levels of income detail is essential.

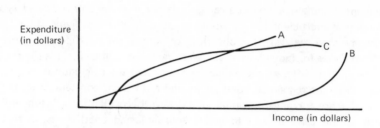

C, there is no need of detail at high levels of income. For other predictors presumably similar considerations apply. Consider the effect of substituting on the graph, "psychological attribute" for income. The vertical axis may be left "expenditure in dollars" or, more generally, may measure any type of economic behavior. It might read, "probability of buying a new car in a given period." Without knowledge of the nature of the relationships under study it is not possible to say how fine a system of classification is needed for a problem. However, the extent to which one loses precision by categorizing a numerical variable into a set of classifications is usually exaggerated. If, for instance, a predictor has a linear relationship with some dependent variable, accounting for some M percent of its variance, then dummy variables representing as few as five subclasses of the explanatory variable will account for ninety-five percent of that potential M percent, and ten subclasses will account for ninety-nine percent of the total possible.[7] And if in fact the relationship is not linear, a set of dummy variables may easily account for *more* of the total variance than a linear regression using the full numerical detail.

An additional advantage of dummy variables is that they allow flexible handling of missing information. A separate dummy variable accounts for the "not ascertained" cases of each classification or interval code. This saves all the other information available about these cases, and even indicates whether there is something peculiar about those who did not answer a particular question.

Note that the use of dummy variables as discussed above is as *predictors.* Economists are likely to use psychological or sociological variables as predictors. When the dependent variable is a dummy variable, other problems arise. Yet it *is* possible to have sets of dummy variables on both sides of an equation, as we see below when discussing canonical correlation.

Cumulative Dummy Variables: Where the classes represent an ordered scale, then it is possible to define a set of dummy variables representing "this level or less."[8] For instance, with education one could define the following variables:

Variable	Value = 1 if:	Years
X1	Less than 5 years of education	(0-4)
X2	Less than 9 years of education	(0-4 + 5-8)
X3	Less than 12 years of education	(0-4 + 5-8 + 9-11)
X4	Less than 16 years of education	(0-4 + 5-8 + 9-11 + 12-15)
X5	Not college graduate	(16 or more, no degree, or less)
X6	No advanced degree	(College graduate or less)
X7	Advanced degree or less	Everyone

Anyone coded 1 for variable X7 would also be coded 1 for variables X1 through X6, i.e. the variables form a Guttman scale.

Algebraically the results can be translated back into the other kind of dummy variables where each one represents a mutually exclusive group (level of education), though the intercorrelations among the dummy variables are higher and positive, where with the exclusive dummies they are smaller and negative.

One might think that the differences between the incremental dummies would be better indicators of the marginal effects of moving to the next step, but in fact they would seem to mask the true marginal effect. Suppose, for instance that the true effects of each level of education were as given in the first column of the table below. If the population were evenly spread, twenty percent in each group, then the cumulative coefficients would be as given in the second column, and the differences would understate the true payoff to additional education:

Educational Achievement	Income Coefficient (adjusted by regression)	Income Coefficient	
		(for that level or less)	(for that level or more)
0-6 grades	$ 2,000	$2,000	$ 6,000
7-11 grades	4,000	3,000	7,000
High school (12)	6,000	4,000	8,000
Some college	8,000	5,000	9,000
College degree	10,000	6,000	10,000

The "cumulative" coefficients are not themselves marginal payoffs to more education, nor are their first differences.

If the cumulation were defined the other way, so much education or *more,* the marginal payoffs would still be underestimated, except under the argument that the advantage of each level should include the option value of allowing further education. That is, finishing the first level has a value which includes the value of going on times the probability of doing so. It is not a convincing argument.

Hence, even though the regression coefficients and the calculated standard errors are a mathematical translation of those with the usual dummy variables, the data are in less usable form. Indeed, one might easily decide that the differences were not significant, as Rogers' dissertation seemed to do.

We return to a more detailed consideration of dummy (dichotomous) variables in regression later in this chapter.

Introduction of Measures of Price: A technique of special interest to economists is the introduction of data about prices with the purposes of converting variables which are measures of quantity into new variables which are measures of value. The survey may be used to provide the measures of quantity while other sources may provide the measures of price. For example, Houthakker and Haldi used published price data on cars to develop measures of households' inventories and investments.[9] The same technique has been used for years in the Surveys of Consumer Finances. Its usefulness arises from the added information gained. For example, one knows more about a family's situation if he knows that its stock of cars is worth $100 than if he knows only that it posseses one car.

The procedure requires a known set of prices which can be mapped into the data about quantities. The goods in question may have values which vary depending on their characteristics, e.g. the make, year, model, body style, and equipment of a car. The survey must contain information about the commodity which corresponds at least approximately to the data required to enter the price list. Inaccuracies in the price information, of course, will be reflected in the newly calculated variables and reduce correlations. Systematic variations in prices not taken into account can introduce systematic error in these variables. One must also be clear that it is market price he wants, not use value.

The possibilities of this type of procedure are best, therefore, when complete information about prices is published and the published prices are the actual prices. Also, the simpler the price structure, the easier the estimation. Price data for airline tickets, for example, meet the criteria of publication and close agreement between published and actual prices. To estimate the cost of particular trips, however, would present problems arising from the need to distinguish among classes of service and various types of special fares as they may apply to particular origins and destinations. In some situations one might ask about expenditures, and use price information to estimate quantities.

For goods and services subject to wide variations in price from customer to customer, from time to time, from place to place, and the like, an investigator may prefer to obtain his price data by developing questions to obtain it directly from the respondent. Alternatively, he may proceed by obtaining information about prices both from the interview and from outside sources.

Variables Representing an Individual's Subgroup: Another kind of variable often generated after the data are assembled, represents the mean of some characteristic measured over some subgroup to which the individual belongs. The rent level of his area, if there are large enough sample clusters to allow its estimation, is an example, or one might want to know the average value of cars owned by people in a person's age, education, income, and city size group, and each individual's deviation from that group average. Sometimes outside data about the subgroup may be available, e.g. median income in the county.

Panel Variables Representing Change versus Level: With reinterviews, possibilities open for generating variables representing change, absolute or relative, in some measure, such as the family income. Since the initial state (in the case of debt, or assets) is important as well as the change, problems arise because of the negative correlation between the two. As we have suggested, one solution is to generate two orthogonal (uncorrelated) variables: the average level (sum of the two measures) and the change (difference).

Scaling

When we have a number of measures each of which may be an imperfect measure of some theoretical construct, we may prefer to combine them rather than rely on any one. And if a set of measures are thought in various combinations to measure several theoretical constructs, we may seek some optimal way of developing several combinations, each uncorrelated with the others. The first problem is generally called scaling, and the second, factor analysis.

Scaling has a long history in psychology and sociology. It will be possible to include here only the bare elements of the subject.[10] The more complex procedures have in common the use of a battery of questions or scale items. There are problems, then, of constructing the individual items, and of selecting the best possible items from those that may be suggested for inclusion in the final scale. There are also problems of how best to combine the information from the items into a single scale.

The earliest of the basic approaches was developed by L. L. Thurstone. The first step in this procedure is to collect a large number of statements about a given subject. Each judge then independently sorts the statements into eleven piles. The piles are to be equal distance apart and to range from most favorable to least favorable. Since there are many judges, it is possible to compute for each item a median rank, and a measure of the dispersion of the assigned rankings, such as the interquartile range. The smaller the dispersion, the better the item. The final scale, then, can be constructed from the twenty or so best items. Respondents then express agreement or disagreement with each item. They should agree only with those in a limited range. The score on the scale for any respondent is the average of the scale values with which he agrees.

This procedure is open to objections. It rests upon the doubtful ability of the judges to perceive equal distance between items. It also rests upon the assumption that respondents and judges have the same frame of reference. Empirically it has been shown that some respondents when given Thurstone scales agree with statements that have widely different scale values. In such situations the meaning of average scores is doubtful.[11]

A second basic type of scaling procedure was originally developed by Likert and is now widely used. People are asked to respond to each item, not simply by agreeing or disagreeing, but by indicating the degree of agreement or disagreement. Typically, five steps are given between extreme agreement and extreme disagreement. No judges are used. In the development of a scale, people similar to the eventual respondents are the subjects.

The method of combining items is to add the scores for the items without regard to whether one item may appear to be different from another. A score of +1 may be assigned to extreme agreement, and +5 to extreme disagreement, on any item. Such scores are summed to give a total score for the test. The procedure is fast and simple.

The items used in the test may be selected from all items suggested for inclusion on the basis of correlation analysis. The criterion may be selection to yield high intercorrelation among the items. Alternatively, items with low intercorrelation with each other but high correlation with an outside criterion may be selected.[12]

These procedures remove some of the disadvantages of Thurstone scales, but also are by no means ideal. There is an arbitrary element in the system of weighting. The criterion of a high degree of agreement among items is imperfect in view of the possibility that the items may differ in their position on some underlying continuum. Again, the items may indeed be correlated, but this correlation is not in itself enough to establish that they belong on the same underlying continuum.

A third type of scale has been developed by Guttman. Guttman's scalogram analysis was developed to deal especially with the problem of unidimensionality.[13] He seeks to use the data obtained from a group of respondents to solve the two problems of ordering the items and ordering the respondents. The test of unidimensionality is whether the answers given by respondents do in fact order themselves systematically. Ideally, when the work is complete, respondents at a given scale position will give favorable replies to all statements up to that position and unfavorable replies to all statements farther along the continuum than their position. In preparing a test, items are selected which tend to fit into such a pattern. Stress is laid on achieving a high "coefficient of reproducibility." This coefficient is the proportion of responses to items which can be predicted correctly knowing the scale position of the respondents. The difficulty with this coefficient is that it tends to look too good—it can seldom fall below .80 and is affected by extreme marginals or large numbers of items.

In the development of a Guttman scale the procedure is to prepare a matrix with a column for each item and a row for each respondent. The entry in each cell may be a + or - sign, depending on whether that individual responded positively to that item. The analyst then rearranges the rows in optimal order, and also the columns in optimal order, optimal order being defined as that which yields the highest coefficient of reproducibility. It is possible, of course, that there is no arrangement which will produce a higher coefficient than should be attributed to chance. One would expect that result either if the items do not belong on a single continuum or if the respondents have no attitude on the topic.

There has been a considerable amount of attention to the question of circumstances in which a high coefficient of reproducibility might be achieved but the procedure might still be unsatisfactory, and Guttman has suggested taking into account additional considerations as well as the value of the coefficient. It is particularly desirable that some items which divide the population about evenly should be included instead of just items which almost everyone accepts or rejects. Also, the *pattern* of errors should be random and not systematic.

Guttman further proposes that intensity of feeling should be asked for each item. He suggests that a natural zero point on the scale may appear where intensity of feeling is low. The scale itself is an ordinal scale.

This procedure also has limitations. It may prove difficult to construct items which will "scale" satisfactorily unless the items are very similar. One approaches a procedure which may not be so very different from the Likert-type technique of asking people to place themselves in one of five categories from "agree strongly" to "disagree strongly" with a single statement.

It is by no means certain that people will feel strongly about something only if they hold an extreme position. A person might believe passionately that a middle position was correct. In such a situation no zero point could be discovered by Guttman's procedures.

The procedures reduce but do not eliminate the subjective judgment of the investigator. The rearrangement of rows and columns and the choice of items for elimination in the preparation of the test might be done differently by different researchers. It is possible that a scale will be satisfactory for one type of respondent but unsatisfactory for other respondents at another time or place or from a different socio-economic category.

An example of a Guttman scale comes from replies to a question we ask about whether it is all right for someone "like yourself" to borrow money for each of several purposes: eighty percent thought it was all right to borrow to cover illness expenses, seventy-seven percent to finance educational expenses, sixty-five percent to finance purchase of a car, fifty-two percent to finance the purchase of furniture, forty-three percent to pay piled up bills, forty percent to cover living expenses when income is cut, nine percent to cover vacation expenses, and four percent to finance purchases of a fur coat or jewelry.

When such a wide differentiation appears, the problem is, is there anyone who would approve of credit for jewelry but not for illness? There are very few. The coefficient of reproducibility indicates essentially how many people violate the proper ordering of a scale like this. But one must remember that this coefficient can get fairly high, when there is still a fairly bad scaling.

Scaling techniques are universally based on the interrelations among the components or potential components, usually with the imposition of assumptions of additivity and linearity. This is acceptable when the new variable is to be used as description (a measure of intelligence) or as the dependent variable in analysis. But where the new variable is to be used as an explanatory variable, there are problems:

1. The components may not operate additively, but in some more complex fashion.
2. Regardless how they are correlated with one another, the components may have opposite effects on the dependent variable. Combining two factors positively correlated with one another, but with opposite effects on the dependent variable, will produce a scale or index which will have no effect at all.

Of course, combining two factors negatively correlated with one another but both with positive effects on a dependent variable, will also produce an index with no apparent effect on the dependent variable.

A simple test should be considered prior to any elaborate scaling operations of an explanatory variable: First examine the gross relationship of each element with the dependent variable to be sure its effect is in the expected direction. Then build a simple additive scale by adding one to a sum for each component element that is positive. This produces an index ranging from zero for those who give positive responses to none of the items to a number equal to the number of items.

If one then looks at the *shape* of the relationship of this new index or scale with the dependent variable, one can tell whether the additivity assumption is valid.

1. If the relationship is linear, then the components are probably additive. Whether they occur in an ordered sequence can only be tested by some Guttman-like procedure, but may not be crucial anyway.
2. If the relationship is convex from above, then the components are probably substitutes for one another, any two or three of them

produce the effect. In this case it makes sense to ask whether it is the same two or three—which is not the same as asking whether a Guttman scale exists, for effects only of a subset could exist without any ordering of the items.

3. If the relationship is concave from above, then the components are complementary—it takes all or nearly all of them before any effect appears.

A final consideration is that, provided one combines items which are not negatively correlated with one another, and seem to have effects on the dependent variable in the same direction, the weighting of the components will make very little real difference. If any of them have an effect, the weighted sum will have effect. One might do better to think of indexes or scales as rapid ways of testing whether *any* of a set of items have any impact, returning to the details only if there is some indication that it will be useful.

On the other hand, if the problem is to develop a *dependent* variable to be explained, then a great deal more attention may have to be paid to its proper scaling.

The possible procedures in developing scales are by no means limited to those discussed above. An example of a sophisticated approach to the subject is Coombs' Unfolding Technique.[14] This method, unlike Guttman's scalogram, is designed to produce information about the *distance* between scale positions as well as an ordering of the positions. It is included here for its intrinsic interest although it has been rarely if ever used by economists. The method will be described in two stages: data collection and analysis.

The underlying hypothesis, in simple uses of the approach, is that there is a single underlying continuum and that there are, say, five stimuli ranged along it, probably at unequal distances from one another. We may think of people as each having a unique preferred position on this continuum, which probably will not exactly coincide with that represented by any stimulus. Still, each person will feel that the stimuli differ in how closely they are to his true feelings. The problem is to find how the five are arranged on the *true* scale.

There are different tasks which we can ask people to perform for us. We might ask, simply, that each person tell us the statement closest to his own position. We might ask for the two closest statements, or the three closest. The unfolding technique requires that we ask him both to select and to rank them according to how close they are to his position. If there were five items, in effect we have asked the respondent to omit two and order the others. Coombs calls this method "Order 3." (We might have asked the respondent to "Order 4," but here we restrict attention to the simpler task.)

The crucial point about this method is that the information thus collected includes information about metric relations—about distances on the underlying continuum—as well as about rank order. We may observe, for example, that some people pick position BCA but nobody picks BCD.

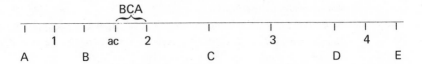

The implication is that the distance between A and the region in which B is first choice and C is second choice is less than the distance between D and the region in which B is first choice and C is second choice. On the above scale B is first choice anywhere between 1 and 2. B is first *and* C is second only for a person located between 2 and a point half-way between A and C, indicated by ac. People who pick B and C will always select A rather than D as third choice only if A is closer than D to the BC range.

The rank order of the stimuli to a respondent will depend on the distance they would be from his position if the scale were folded at his exact location. Hence, the name of the procedure, the "unfolding technique."

The important notion is that there is one true but unknown linear ordering of the stimuli. If all individuals accept that ranking, their ranking of the items shows where they are on the scale, but more important, analysis of many individual rankings will reveal what the basic ordering is, and even some of the metric.

The analysis consists, first, in the arrangement of the data in rows and columns as in the Guttman method, except that numbers, 1, 2, or 3, or a blank, appear in the cells for the items rather than + or -. Also as in the Guttman technique, the rows and columns are permuted until a matrix with desirable properties is achieved. These properties Coombs specifies as follows.[15]

1. The entries in the rows (i.e. for each individual) and in each column (i.e. for each stimulus), must be adjacent with no blanks.
2. The entries in the first row and first column must monotonically increase from left to right and top to bottom, respectively.
3. The entries in the last row and last column must monotonically decrease from left to right and from top to bottom, respectively.
4. The entries in all other columns must monotonically decrease and then increase from top to bottom.

The method provides the necessary information for a much more detailed ordering of individuals than is possible if all that is known is their first choices. For example, it distinguishes, among those for whom B is first choice, those who prefer A to C from those who prefer C to A. Thus, the group with B as first choice can be divided. Similar divisions are possible among those who select C or D as first choice. It is unlikely that actual data will satisfy these stringent requirements exactly, and there will be problems of how much deviation from the correct pattern to tolerate. The method calls attention to the individuals with patterns of response which do not fit the general pattern for the group as a whole. The question can be examined whether such individuals are very frequent in some subgroups of the population. One might conclude, for example, that a scale was satisfactory for people with high education but not for people of low education. This conclusion could not be drawn from responses to a simple Likert scale since the data do not contain enough information.

Coombs also suggests an ingenious way of checking whether there is indeed a single underlying continuum on which people find themselves. The trick is to ask people to name the choice the *farthest* from their position. That choice should be at *one end or the other* of the true scale, depending on the individual's position, hence there should be only two choices, representing the two ends, which get all the votes as least preferred. If the choices scatter all over, there is presumably no underlying continuum and one need not bother with unfolding, or scaling.

In building any kind of index, arbitrary or not, there is a question whether to rely on attitude questions or on reported behavior. When people were asked about their attitudes toward new products, and their self perception of whether they use them or not, their answers did not correlate very well with how many of ten specific new products they actually used. In another study nine normative items about task sharing in the family did not correlate well with an index based on actual task sharing. The author concluded that there is considerable deviation between normative definitions and actual behavior of the family studied.[16]

Finally, another way to build a scale is to order how *salient* a particular response is by designing a series of questions which lead into the subject gradually. The individual is then scored on how far one must push him before he responds. One might ask a sequence of questions about whether it was a good idea to have bought bonds in World War II and then mention the fact that price levels have gone up and say, "How about that?" and finally say, "How about common stock?" Then one can use, as an index of awareness of inflation and of the need for hedging against it, the stage in this process where a man says that buying something whose value would go up with the price level (like common stock) would have been a better idea. This gives some notion of how *salient* the notion of hedging against inflation is to the individual and may be a good predictor of whether he is likely to buy stock. However, an old finding in nutritional studies is that if you ask people what is needed for good nutrition they often fail to mention milk first because it is so obvious. So this technique of salience may be misleading in some cases. Another method is to ask for reasons and then say, "Well, which of these is the most important?" In a very large number of cases, it was the second or third reason given that turned out to be the most important by the man's own statement, not the first one.

This introduction to the subject of scaling is far from complete. No attempt has been made to cover all techniques in common use. Such topics as Lazarsfeld's latent structure analysis and the semantic differential have been omitted entirely. The reader is referred to the references cited above.

A brief word may be added in conclusion concerning basic methods of assessing scales. It is common to assess the reliability of a scale by the "split-half" technique. The procedure is to divide the items into two groups, compute scores for each half, and estimate the correlation coefficient. It is especially adapted to scales based on substantial numbers of items which are combined by simple addition of scores. The objection is sometimes made that a low correlation between halves may indicate either unreliability of the test or lack of unidimensionality.

Reliability may also be assessed by repetition. The assumption must be made that the observed changes over time measure the unreliability of the instrument rather than actual changes in the true position of the individuals on the scale. This assumption can best be defended when there is theoretical reason to expect stability and when the time interval is short. For example, psychologists would not expect intelligence to change over short periods.

Validity is sometimes checked against behavior. The behavior may be in the future, so that a measure of attitudes at one date is used to predict subsequent behavior. This type of check is especially relevant when the principal purpose of the attitude measurement is prediction. There is a sense, however, in which it begs the question of the relation of attitudes to behavior. To examine that question, strictly speaking the validation of the measurement of the attitudes should be made independently of the behavior. Otherwise one assumes that the attitude cannot exist unless it predicts behavior.

Factor Analysis: Extensive use has been made in psychology of principal components analysis or factor analysis. There has been some interest in the application of the procedures to problems of interest to economists, but little work actually has been done. The subject will be treated here only briefly.

The method was developed by Hotelling.[17] A systematic discussion of the theory may be found in Anderson, and for an application of the method to an economic problem see Stone.[18]

The purpose of principal components analysis is the compression of information. For example, a psychologist might have information on the replies to a large number of test items by a sample of individuals. He might seek to characterize those persons in terms of a limited number of attributes or factors.

The method begins with the covariance matrix measuring the relationship between each item and every other item. Mathematically, the principal components are the characteristic vectors of the covariance matrix.

The usefulness of statistical procedures for developing principal components is likely to be greatest at an early stage in the development of a field when there is little available theory. When the theory is better developed, an investigator is likely to be able to specify in advance the variables he wishes to measure rather than to discover them as a result of principal components analysis. His problem, then, becomes one of measurement, and he will devote his energies to the construction of variables which he has reason to believe are relevant to his analysis. He will not invent a large number of items more or less at random and later seek to sort them out.

There may be areas of inquiry at an early stage of development, however, with a plethora of measurements believed to be of independent variables. For example, one might have data on accident rates for each of fifty states, and measures of, say sixty characteristics of the states believed to be possible causes of accidents. Principal components analysis might then be considered as one way of compressing the sixty characteristics into a manageable number of variables. There is one difficulty with the technique which may be mentioned. The results will depend on the units in which the initial measurements are expressed. It is possible to make an arbitrary decision to divide each measurement by its own standard deviation and work with data thus standardized. A corresponding arbitrary element will enter the results.

Factor analysis was originally designed not just to economize on variables but to find out whether a large set of items could be broken down into a smaller set of components that had some meaning. For instance, the items in an intelligence test could be analyzed and they might fit into clusters which could then be considered components of intelligence: things like verbal facility, abstract reasoning, mathematical abilities, etc.

What factor analysis really does is to *assume* linear additive combinations. Start with the simple matrix of correlations among a whole set of items. There is no dependent variable and nothing is said about the relations of any of them to a dependent variable. There is then a statistical method by which clusters are identified and a set of weights determined so that a weighted sum of the items in any one cluster, forms a new variable or factor. These weights are called factor loadings. The factors can be derived so that they are uncorrelated with one another. This means that one can regard factor analysis as a method of taking fifty attitudinal items and converting them into three or four new variables that are nicely uncorrelated with one another and easy to put into an analysis to explain something.

There are the same two major difficulties. One is the assumption of additivity in the components of these factors, and the other is that in building them, no attention is paid to the relationships they have with the dependent variable. It is quite possible to have two items which are highly correlated with one another, and end up with large positive weights on one of these factors, but they have opposite effects on the dependent variable. In this case, this factor would have no correlation with the dependent variable since it is made up of two things which have opposite effects, and information is thrown away.

There has been very little use of factor analysis in economic surveys because by the time one collects the basic economic information (which is easy to combine by adding) there is not enough interviewing time left to ask fifty attitudinal questions. Consequently we are more likely to rely on five or ten.

Arbitrary Indexes of Attitudes or Behavior: In many economic studies the legitimate components of some index are relatively obvious and the number of candidates so small, that it is doubtful that elaborate and time-consuming methods of scale construction are justified. In a study of deliberation in purchase decisions, Mueller made use of several indexes created by giving the respondent a point for each of a list of activities, and then created a summary index as the sum of the component indexes.[19]

In a study of a number of aspects of economically adaptive or progressive behaviors, a number of indexes of attitudes or behavior were created, again as arbitrary sums of points given for various forms of behavior or of attitudinal (or self-assessing) responses.[20]

The logical basis of this procedure is partly theoretical and partly empirical. The theoretical basis is an argument, more or less carefully worked out, that the specific items in question are similar, or form a coherent typology or syndrome. There is an assumption that the set of behaviors can be used to predict other things, or can as a set be efficiently predicted, or both.

The empirical basis is that each of the components is related in the same direction to the other variables to which the index is to be related, whether explanatory or dependent, *and* that the components are not negatively correlated with one another. If either of these were in fact violated, the index would not work, that is it would not be easy to explain as a result of other variables, or be useful as a variable in predicting another variable.

It is not, however, necessary that an index combine things which are *strongly* positively correlated with one another. Indeed, if the components are *very* strongly positively correlated, one might use fewer of them, whereas one might very well want to combine into one index a number of statistically unrelated but theoretically similar things. Hence all that is required is that components not be negatively correlated, so that they will not cancel one another out, and that they have effects in the same direction.

A common reason for combining several items is that each one may be relevant, and revealing, for some part of the population, but provide no information for others. Indeed some of the components may actually be *alternatives* where it would be difficult to do both. For instance the husband might get a second job *or* let the wife go to work in the evening while he watched the children. The index, hopefully, contains at least some items relevant to each member of the population. It is a problem, however, to deal with the respondents for whom an item is inappropriate. Ideally, one should assign them the mean value for the rest of the sample. For instance, if a risk avoidance index gave a point for fastening seat belts, what about people with no car, not asked the question? If fifty percent of the car owners fastened their seat belts, the non-owners could be neutralized by giving them half a point. Or one could use even digits by giving two points to those who fastened belts, one point to those with no car, and no points to those with cars who did not fasten their seat belts. (This is the same as giving 0 to the non-owners, and -1 and +1 to the owners who did not or did fasten.) In practice, with digits added for indexes, it is tempting to use the 0, 1, 2 sequence even though 1 is not really the average of the other two groups. In this case the neutralization is not quite precise.

A second problem arises when some components are felt to be more important than others. Here again, it is possible to assign them larger weights in an index, remembering that the weighting of any index has relatively little effect.

Such indexes are, of course, arbitrary, and no better than the judgment that went into their composition. And it is difficult to describe them briefly without seeming to imply a great deal more theory than one wants.

An important justification for such arbitrary indexes, however, is their economy and efficiency. If the components are not negatively correlated with one another, and have effects on the dependent variable in the same direction, then either the index helps predict the dependent variable or it does not. If it does not, we can be reasonably sure that *none* of its components would have much predictive value separately. If it does have some effect, then we can pursue it further as we suggested earlier:

Treat the index as a set of dummy variables, and see whether its effect is linear or not. If it is linear, then presumably the components are operating additively, and one may only want to look at them separately, to sort out which ones are most useful. One might then, for instance, put each component into a regression as a separate dummy variable.

But if the effect is non-linear, it may mean that the components operate either as substitutes or in complementary fashion accentuating one another. If the relationship is concave from the top, the index having little effect until it reaches substantial values, then the implication is that it takes all the components or a large set of them, to have any effect, that is that they operate multiplicatively. If it is convex from the top, the implication is that any one or two of the items are enough to produce an effect, the others adding little, i.e. that the components are substitutes for one another. In any case, further decomposition of the index would then seem worth while, but in the non-linear case, only with techniques which allow for interaction effects now known to exist.

Frequently however, indexes made up either of attitudes, or of self-reports, or of supposedly revealing behavior, do not predict the dependent variable at all, and the rapid creation and use of a relatively arbitrary index serves to eliminate a whole set of hypotheses quickly and efficiently.

There is, of course, a problem if one wants to assess the relative importance of a number of indexes and other explanatory variables by looking at their contribution to reduction in the unexplained variance of some dependent variable. Some variables may be measured better than others. One might think, for instance, that if he had used factor analysis or some other technique to build an index, it might have explained more of the variance. This problem exists even in comparing simple variables for their relative power, of course. And again it is possible to exaggerate its importance. A variable or an index that is really important in explaining behavior, will show through some relatively bad measurement errors.

Estimation of Relationships

Given a set of measured variables, loosely connected with some theoretical constructs, how do we proceed with the analysis?

The process is really a search for structure of relations among the measured variables, and an interpretation in terms of the theoretical constructs that they represent. There may be situations where one should follow the conventional wisdom: embody the explanatory hypotheses in a model and test it, but we submit that this is rare. There are usually a substantial number of competing hypotheses, even at the theoretical construct level, and when we move to the measured variables, adding uncertainty about what represents what, the credibility of any one *a priori* model is rather low, and the need for showing that it is more credible than a number of competing alternatives is high.

We say this in the face of a burgeoning literature in both econometrics and in sociology that works out elaborate procedures for measuring relations or testing hypotheses, both because of the relatively primitive state of our knowledge and theory about human behavior, and because of the demands that the assumptions of these methods put on the data and the theory. They nearly all require at least some of the following assumptions:

> Sampling and measurement errors reasonably small, uncorrelated, normally distributed, and without too heterogeneous variances
> Measurability of variables (no scaling problems)
> Linearity of effects
> Additivity of effects (or very simple easily represented cross-product effects)
> Ability to specify causal directions
> A recursive system

> All the relevant variables are included
> The system is just identified.

Of course the last two compete with one another, and one is tempted to leave out variables or invent some in order to make the system tractable. Recently some have suggested checking for inconsistency of the separate estimates in an over-identified system as an indication of distortions caused by different and imperfect proxies for the real variables. (See Costner, Note 73.) It is doubtful that survey data have the characteristics, particularly the precision, to hold up the elaborate structures of many of these procedures.

Indeed, it is not obvious that the least-squares criterion on which *all* the statistical procedures are based, is appropriate. Are errors important in proportion to their square? Errors in survey data are often not so much normally distributed as rectangular—a large error being about as likely as a small one, say from misplacing a decimal. And the larger the discrepancy, the more likely that there is some conceptual difficulty or misunderstanding, such as mixing up a man's business affairs with his household accounts.

All this is not to say that one is not to use whatever theory he can, and whatever reasonable assumptions will make things easier. Whenever there are clear one-way causal directions or intermediate stages in the causal process, a basic structural model must take account of them. But within those broad bounds, we are really searching for better evidence about the structure of relationships, and about which variables really account for the variation in others. And beyond that we are attempting to interpret this structure and these relationships in terms of relationships among the theoretical constructs for which the measured variables serve as proxies.

Analysis of One Dependent Variable with One Level of Explanatory Variables

A great deal of analysis can be systematically organized and done in terms of what it is that is being described, explained, evaluated, or potentially predicted. Conversely, it is not usually efficient to organize research or analysis around an *explanatory* variable. Anything that is learned about one explanatory variable must be learned separately for each dependent variable, and in a multivariate context if we are to be sure it is not spurious.

The first step, often overlooked in the analyst's haste to get this multivariate analysis done, is to examine the distribution of the dependent variable. Two-way tables against the more important explanatory variables will reveal whether there are problems. The two main problems are kurtosis and heterogeneous variance. Skewness is less of a problem, and if it appears can usually be handled by some transformation, or even ignored. But extreme cases (leptokursis) play havoc with any least squares analysis.

Extreme cases should be examined in detail. They may be errors, for the distribution of errors made in processing data is not a normal distribution—very large errors are as likely as small ones. Extreme values may represent conceptual or measurement difficulties which would justify their elimination from the sample, or truncation to some large but not extremely large value. Or, one may take the square root or the log of the dependent variable, if there are no zeros or negative numbers.

Even a reasonably well-distributed dependent variable might have widely different variances in different parts of the population. In practice this has not turned out to be much of a problem, and in any case it affects significance tests most, parameter estimates somewhat, and analysis of variance (which explanatory variables account for the most variance) least of all. G.E.P. Box uses the term "robustness" for a procedure which is not badly affected by departures from its assumptions. He refers to tests for homogeneity of variance as rather like putting to sea in a rowboat to see whether it is safe for an ocean liner to set sail.[21]

Most distributional problems with the dependent variable can be located by inspection of tables. This does mean that even if the variable is numerical, a categorical (bracket) code should be created in order to investigate its distribution, overall, and in tables against the main explanatory factors.

The layout and labeling of tables is a matter of importance if readers are to see the results easily and clearly. Any table is a distribution of some kind of *unit* (families) according to some *dependent variable* (food expenditures per person) within subgroups classified by some *explanatory characteristic* (family size, income etc.), for the whole *sample* or some subpopulation thereof. Perhaps the best procedure, since the unit and often the subpopulation remain constant over many tables, is to put the variable of interest, and the classifying variable in the title, and the unit and subpopulation in the subtitle: Food Expenditures Per Person by Family Size (For Urban Families).

Such a convention, combined with consistency in the words used to label each variable, will be a great help to everyone concerned. It is also useful to have tables right-side-up on the page, not turned sideways, so that the percentages add to 100 percent at the bottom, and the number of cases is always easily found below the row of 100 percent's. The stability of a percentage depends on the number of cases on which it is based, so those numbers should be easily available. Sometimes where the same classifying variables are used many times and for the same sample, the frequencies can be relegated to an appendix.

A final convention, irritating to purists but nonetheless necessary, is to "fudge" the figures so that the percentages in each column add to 100 percent or 100.0 percent. (It is doubtful that in most surveys, carrying data beyond the nearest percentage is justified except where there is a large inappropriate group and someone may want to repercentagize the table omitting them.) The general rule is to force up, or down as necessary, the percentage closest to xx.50, but where several are very close, one may prefer to shift the larger of the two per-centages so that the *relative* error is kept small.

The purposes of examining a table are to observe the shape of the distribu-tion of the dependent variable, and whether that shape persists in subgroups, and second to see whether there is an association between the classifying variable (family size) and the dependent variable (food expenditure per person). If the dependent variable is reasonably well distributed, then one can move to using its average, or "whether the respondent is in a selected set of subclasses" as a vari-able, vastly simplifying the subsequent analysis. It is much easier to present a table of *average* food expenditure per person for families classified jointly by both income and family size, than to present the full distribution.

But there may also be substantive interest in the degree of association in the cross-classifications. It should be possible to state in a single sentence what a table shows, and sometimes to state in a second sentence something which indi-cates the magnitude of the relationship. First, the table is scanned to find the di-vision of just two classes of the explanatory characteristic for which the differ-ences in the dependent variable are the greatest, then again to find the level of the dependent variable at which the proportions differ the most. For instance, one might find that the greatest difference in food expenditure per person was between single person families (who eat out a lot) and all other families:

Weekly Expenditure Per Person by Family Size
(For All Families)

Food Expenditure Per Person Per Week	Actual		Cumulative		
	Single Persons	Families of Two or More	Single Persons	Families of Two or More	Difference
Under $2.00	5	10	5	10	5
$2.00-3.99	5	15	10	25	15
$4.00-5.99	5	25	15	50	35
$6.00-7.99	10	15	25	65	40
$8.00-9.99	10	10	35	75	40
$10.00-11.99	15	10	50	85	35
$12.00-13.99	25	5	75	90	15
$14.00-15.99	15	5	90	95	5
$16.00 and over	10	5	100	100	0
	100	100			
Number of cases	200	1800			

The difference can then be stated simply as follows: Three-fourths of the single people spend eight dollars a week or more on food, but only a little more than a third of the families of two or more spend that much.

Since a search took place for the largest difference in such a pair of percentages, one cannot simply apply a significance test to the difference between two percentages. And since in practice one first selects the two subclasses with the maximum difference in cumulative percentages, even the Kolmogorov-Smirnov test is not quite appropriate, though it is better.[22]

Actually it is not significance that matters, but importance (how much does it matter?), and the investigator's problem is really which classifying variable produces the greatest differences in the dependent variable. For this purpose, a comparison of the differences in cumulative percentages is a fast approximation.

There is a great deal of discussion in the literature about more sophisticated measures of association for cross-classifications. Where the two "variables" or characteristics have natural ordering, and one expects a monotonic relationship, then various kinds of rank correlation coefficients are appropriate, the best probably being Kendall's Tau beta.[23]

Kruskal's Gamma, and Kendall's three Tau measures of rank correlation are all based on a kind of trick: one considers *all possible pairs,* and asks which of them are concordant with the notion of a positive association, which discordant, and which are tied on X or Y or both. A simple diagram will show how these are computed:

The small letters represent proportion of the table total in that cell:

	X_1	X_2	X_3
Y_1	a	b	c
Y_2	d	e	f

Proportion concordant: $a(e + f) + b(f) = P$ $\left\{\begin{array}{l}\text{i.e., number of pairs where if second is} \\ \text{higher X class, then also higher Y class.}\end{array}\right.$

Proportion discordant: $c(d + e) + b(d) = Q$

Proportion tied on X: $ad + be + cf$ $= Xo$ Pairs where X is same.

Proportion tied on Y: $a(b + c) + bc + d(e + f) + ef = Yo$

Proportion tied on both $1/2\,[a(a - 1) + b(b - 1) + c(c - 1) + d(d - 1) + e(e - 1) + f(f - 1)]$

$$\text{Gamma} = \frac{P - Q}{P + Q} \qquad \text{Tau}_\alpha = \frac{P - Q}{n\,\dfrac{(n - 1)}{2}} \qquad \text{Tau}_\beta = \frac{P - Q}{\sqrt{(P + Q + Xo)\,(P - Q + Yo)}}$$

$$\text{Tau}_y = (P - Q)\,\frac{2n}{n^2\,(m - 1)} \quad \left\{\begin{array}{l}\text{where m = number of rows or columns,} \\ \text{whichever is smaller}\end{array}\right.$$

It is clear that Tau gamma is intended to deal with cases where one or the other characteristic has very few classes, that Tau alpha is to deal with very small samples, and that Tau beta, which is intended to deal with tied rankings, is probably the most appropriate to use with survey data. It is probably better than

Gamma since there can be vast differences in the number of ties in different cross-classifications.

Where one does not want to assume order and a monotonic relationship, the problem becomes more complicated, and the best judgment is that the method of choice depends on what you want to do.[24]

The most commonly used measure in the past has been chi-square, the sum of squared deviations of actual from expected frequencies divided by the sum of expected frequencies, but it has a number of disabilities, including instability when frequencies get small. Cramer proposed a measure "V" which adjusts for this: $V = X^2/N$ divided by R-1 or C-1 whichever is smaller.[24]

As another example of difficulty, there is Kruskal's Lambda, which is based on the relative reduction in the probability of predicting wrong a single case selected at random. If one knows only the overall distribution, one has to predict the modal value, which may contain m% of the cases, and has a probability of being wrong of (100-m)/100. If one knows which subgroup on some explanatory characteristic the individual is in, then one uses the modal value of the dependent characteristic for that subgroup. The sum of the fractions of the total sample in those modal subgroups, $\Sigma m_i n_i$ may be greater than m (it can never be smaller), and the gain is measured by $(\Sigma m_i n_i - m)/(100 - m)$, the increase in the probability of a correct guess, as a fraction of the original probability of a wrong guess. But sometimes even when there is a clear association the modal group is the same for each classifying group. For instance, the modal hourly earning rate is the same for whites and blacks in the United States, yet the distributions are skewed in opposite directions. Lambda would be zero, when there is clearly an association because the focus on predicting a single case is not proper. We want to know the error in predicting a random sample of cases. The stochastic element must be preserved. In fact, for most purposes where it is the predictive *power* that is wanted, the ideal measure would seem to be the size of a canonical correlation coefficient, treating the subclasses of the two classifications as a set of dichotomous (dummy) variables on both sides of an equation. (Canonical correlation estimates the coefficients of the variables on both sides such as to maximize the correlation between the two weighted indexes. It is not the coefficients that matter, but the ability to predict one distribution [set of coefficients] from the other distribution [set of coefficients].) One article has actually presented such a set of canonical correlation coefficients among the pairs of the explanatory characteristics used in its analysis as a guide for the readers as to the extent to which the explanatory power of one might be imbedded in another, but more recently, it turns out that Cramers V is identical in the limit (for large samples) with the mean square of all the canonical correlations.[25]

This means that the computational problems are simpler, since Cramer's V is based on a chi-square computation, whereas the calculation of a whole series of canonical correlations (each orthogonal to the rest) is quite a task. (Canonical correlations are computed sequentially so long as one more orthogonal set of co-efficients adds anything, much the way factor analysis proceeds to weaker and weaker factors.)

Limited Dependent Variables: Any truly multivariate analysis must neces-sarily compress the dependent variable to a number, though it may take only the values 1 and 0. For example, a household owns its home, or it does not. It may be a qualitative variable which can assume one of only three or more values. For example, workers in a certain area may be able to make the journey to work by car, bus, or train, but no other method of transportation may be possible. It may be a variable which has the value 0 for a large segment of the population, but may take any of a wide range of values for the remainder. For example, value of owned homes is 0 for non-owners but for owners may take any of a large number of values. It is, indeed, about as common to work with such de-pendent variables in survey analysis as with variables which are normally dis-tributed, or nearly so. The classical normal linear regression model, however, as-sumes that the distribution of the error term is homoscedastic. This assumption is clearly violated when y can no longer take on any value. Questions arise as to what are the most appropriate statistical procedures in such circumstances.[26]

The most widely used method with a dichotomous dependent variable is to proceed as in an ordinary regression analysis. The calculated value of y is treated as a conditional probability, and the regression equation is referred to as a linear probability function. Thus, the predicted score on the dependent vari-able, for individuals with a particular set of scores on the independent variables, might be, say, .75. The interpretation would be that 75 out of 100 such individ-uals would be expected to have a score of 1 on the dependent variable, and the remaining 25, a score of 0. It is safest if the proportions for most subgroups are between .20 and .80 where departures from normality of subgroup proportions are least.

This procedure is also open to the objection that some of the predicted scores, hopefully only a few, may fall outside the range from 0 to 1. Probabilities of less than 0 or more than 1 are embarrassing. To see how this situation can arise, consider the following diagram, which is a graph of a possible sample of actual observations with the straight line of best fit. (We assume that the inde-pendent variable is continuous. It might be income.)

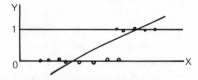

All the observed points necessarily fall on either the horizontal axis or the line parallel to it corresponding to y = 1. The regression line is very likely to intersect both of the "railroad tracks." Hence, there will be values of X for which the predicted value of y is negative or larger than 1.

One method of dealing with this difficulty has been proposed by Orcutt. He develops a transformation from expected values to probability estimates. The method is designed essentially to plot the average expected proportion who have a characteristic against the average observed proportion. The results may appear somewhat as follows:

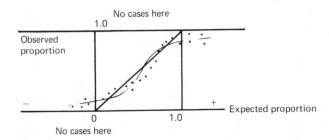

We would expect the straight line of best fit to be a ray from the origin with a slope of forty-five degrees. The observed proportions, however, may differ systematically from the expected proportions, since the latter can be less than 0 or greater than 1.0. These discrepancies can be computed by grouping the sample observations according to the expected proportion, computed from the regression equation (or related technique), and calculating the observed proportion for each group these formed. (Alternatively, if the residuals are computed for each sample observation, the sum of the residuals can be computed for each of the groups.) If the departure from linearity is systematic, as in the above graph, an appropriate S-shaped curve can be fitted.[27] Predictions, then, can be made on the basis of the expected proportion as adjusted. Note that this method will not lead to any adjustment in the regression coefficients, which also retain their usual interpretation. Even when there is no intention to adjust the predicted values, the procedure may be enlightening as to the quality of the fit of the linear equation.

There are other approaches to the problem which introduce the transformations earlier in the calculations and lead to different equations to estimate the relationship. Two such methods are the use of probits and logits.

The probit method has a long history in biological research. It has been discussed in detail by D. J. Finney.[28] It has been used in studies of the effects of insecticides, where it is known that a sufficiently large dose of poison will kill all of a batch of insects and it is desired to estimate the percentage kill for different doses. Interest attaches both to the *median* effective dose, that is, the dose that will kill half the insects, and to the *variance* of the resistance to the poison. The method involves the transformation of percentages into probits, which are based on the standard normal cumulative distribution. Instead of a linear relation between the concentration of the poison and the percentage kill, the transformation leads to a linear relation between the concentration of the poison and the probit, which in effect is equivalent to fitting a S-shaped curve to the raw data rather than a straight line. The probit of a proportion, P, is defined as the abscissa which corresponds to the probability, P, in a cumulative normal distribution with mean .5 and variance 1. It is y where:

$$P = \frac{1}{\sqrt{2\pi}} \int_{-\infty}^{y-5} e^{-1/2\mu^2} d\mu$$

The logic of the method may be sketched by outlining the graphic procedure described by Finney. The first step is to assemble the basic data, which include the percentage kill for each dose. The percentages are then converted to probits, using tables which have been calculated and published for the convenience of those using the method. The probits are plotted against the dose. (Actually, the log of the dose is ordinarily used.) A straight line then may be drawn to fit the points as plotted. It is possible to estimate graphically the slope of the line and other measures as desired, such as the dosage at which $y = 5$, corresponding to a fifty percent kill. It should be mentioned that the procedures for calculation require iterative methods of estimating the probits corresponding to each dose. For a more complete account including the statistical theory which underlies the method and computational procedures to obtain more exact results the reader is referred to Finney.

The statistical theory underlying probit analysis is based on maximum likelihood. Berkson has advocated the use of the logistic function rather than the integral of the normal curve, and the least squares criterion rather than maximum likelihood.[29] The logistic curve will also produce an S-shaped relation between the dose and the mortality rate. Berkson proposes that for each dose the logit should be evaluated, i.e. the natural logarithm of the percentage kill. He then fits a straight line by least squares to estimate the relation between the dose and the logit of the mortality. Each observation is weighted in the calculation by a factor $W_i = N_i P_i Q_i$, where N_i is the number of insects in batch i, P_i is the proportion killed, and $Q_i = 1 - P_i$. The result is a close approximation to a least squares solution of the logistic function, $Q = \dfrac{1}{1 + e^{a-bx}}$, where Q is the estimated mortality, and a-bx is the equation of the line of relationship. A closer approximation can be obtained by successive approximations. Berkson compares results from fitting probits and the logistic curve for several studies, and shows that the findings are similar.

Warner has compared results from calculations using several different methods applied to the problem of choice of mode for the journey to work, and Theil has proposed and illustrated the use of logit specifications with an information-theory interpretation.

Theil has pointed out the nice transformation provided by the natural log of the odds (that is, of p/1-p). It approaches minus infinity as p approaches 0, and it approaches positive infinity as p approaches 1. (One must be dealing with proportions or probabilities, of course.)

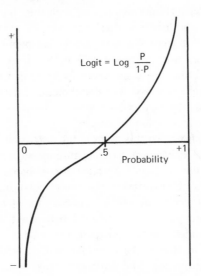

Theil then suggests that the measure of explanatory power be the "average conditional entropy," a concept from information theory, defined as minus the log of the probability, weighted by the probability of being in that row or column, summed over the marginal distribution of probabilities.

Warner recommends the use of the function:

$$Pn(X) = E^{L(X,N)}/(1+e^{L(X,N)})$$

Where Pn (X)   is the probability that an observation at X from a sample of size N is from population 1, X being an explanatory row vector;

and   L (X,N)   is a function which may be estimated with a limited amount of computation, given the results of the usual calculation of a linear probability function.

This approach is much easier from a computational point of view than the use of logits or probits since the solution is reached without procedures requiring iteration. The estimated probability approaches zero as $e^{L(X,N)}$ becomes small, and approaches one as that expression becomes large.

Work has been done by Tobin on the problem of how to handle in one calculation the analysis of mixed dependent variables of the class represented by the value of owned homes. He proposes a combination of probit analysis and multiple regression analysis.[31] Most analysts have approached this problem by splitting it into two separate problems, and analyzing, first, the factors which determine whether a unit does or does not own its home (or whatever the dichotomy may be), and second, the factors which determine for owners the value of the home. More widespread use of Tobin's approach may follow the increasing availability of high speed computers with large capacities and the development of appropriate software. But the choice also depends on which is the appropriate model—are the factors leading to home ownership different from those which determine house value for owners?

Discriminant Analysis: To this point in the discussion we have emphasized the approach to limited dependent variables through regression analysis. An alternative approach to the problem is through discriminant analysis. The logic of discriminant analysis is quite different but the calculations are the same. The starting point is the problem of assigning individuals to categories on the basis of their characteristics. In regression analysis the independent variables are regarded as fixed, while the dependent variable is regarded as fixed in discriminant analysis.

The procedures in discriminant analysis are developed on the basis of standards of good classification. The statistician seeks to make as few errors as possible. He may take into account the cost of different errors, as well as the number of errors, and seek to minimize the cost of misclassification.[32] Anderson's example of a discriminant problem is the selection of students for a college with a limited number of openings. There may be a battery of tests administered to each prospective student. The problem is to sort the prospects into two groups, those who will complete college training successfully and those who will not. We may note that the two possible errors of misclassification need not be evaluated as equally costly. That is, the college administration might not be concerned about rejecting applicants who should have been admitted, arguing that they could go elsewhere, but it might wish to be quite sure to accept only applicants who would succeed.

It is a noteworthy result that the linear discriminant function which minimizes the errors of classification is proportional to the function which is the result of application of the method of least squares, that is the statistical results are the same as regression with a 1-0 dependent variable.[33]

Discriminant analysis has been extended to cover the situation in which there are more than two possible values of the dependent variable. Regression analysis is not able to handle this situation except when the dependent variable is an interval scale. The problem of classifying individuals into one of three or more groups has been discussed in detail by Rao, who includes examples drawn from biometrics.[34] The procedures have been little used in economics, but would seem to be of potential value for survey data when the dependent variable is essentially a system of classification, a nominal scale.

Since the method is not in general use the logic of the procedures for the three category problem will be described briefly. (For a complete discussion, see Rao or Anderson.) The method requires calculation of the discriminant functions for any two pairs of categories. If the categories are A, B, and C, the function might be calculated for A vs. B, and for A vs. C. An indefinite number of separate measurements of characteristics for each individual may be available for use in these equations. Let X and Y, respectively, be the discriminant scores obtained from these equations.

Using these X and Y scores it is possible to define three regions whose boundaries are defined in terms of values of X and Y, as in the sketch below.

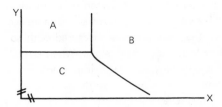

The boundary between A and B is based on scores on X; the boundary between A and C, on scores on Y; between B and C, on scores on X plus Y. Specifically, the average of the mean score on X for groups A and B is the boundary between A and B, and similarly for the other boundaries. It is also of interest to plot on the diagram the point representing the mean X and mean Y for members of category A, and similarly for the other categories.

This approach has been extended to allow for calculation of the boundaries of doubtful regions. The procedures just sketched make it possible to allocate any individual about whom the necessary measures are available to one of the three regions. It is also possible to define three regions specifying three constraints which limit the proportion of the population classified in each region in error. Thus, within region A, there will be a region A' in which the constraint is satisfied. There will also be a doubtful region, A'', containing that part of region A not included in A'. This method of analysis has not been applied to economic surveys, but it might well prove enlightening to know the equations which specify the boundaries of regions such as A and A'.

It may be useful to create categories A, B, and C out of the extreme ends and the middle of a measured dependent variable. The analysis of A vs. B and B vs. C may then reveal an assymetry of the causal force.[35]

Sometimes the dependent variable is unevenly distributed because it really represents the result of a set of decisions which need to be analyzed separately. We return to this problem near the end of this chapter.

Selection of Explanatory Variables: The analysis of survey data involves both the selection of explanatory variables to consider and the specification of the relationships among these variables. The two processes are interrelated, but may be separated for discussion.

The selection of variables is in large part a problem of survey design. Yet, even the analyst who is confronted with an existing body of data and has a restricted set of variables from which to choose may be able to create from the mass of data at his disposal a wide variety of analytical variables. The range of choice confronting him is still broad. The same general considerations apply as at the design stage.

The criteria for selection of variables must be based upon the objectives of the project. Four considerations may be relevant.[36]

(1) *Accuracy of measurement.* Between two variables of equal merit from other points of view, the variable which is measured more accurately is preferred. There may be some variables which are measured with so little accuracy that they must be discarded for that reason alone. When errors of measurement do occur in a variable, it will be particularly important to ask whether there are errors of measurement in other variables to be included in the analysis and whether the errors of measurement in these variables are correlated. In forming sets of variables for inclusion in a relationship, that set is to be preferred for which there is least correlation among errors of measurement. (The subject of errors in variables is further considered below.)

(2) *Availability for prediction.* Between two variables of equal merit from other points of view, the variable which is more likely to be available for prediction is to be preferred. In work whose principal purpose is prediction, this consideration may be of overriding importance. It is not of much practical help in such a situation to know that one could predict accurately if one knew something which one does not know. For making predictions which are conditional upon other basic predictions, it will be necessary to select variables which can be fitted into the framework of the basic prediction. For example, if a forecast is to be contingent upon a basic forecast of the level of income, the variable should be consistent with those used in that basic forecast. Of course the explanatory variable must also be expected to change over time, so some change can be predicted.

(3) *Theoretical appropriateness.* Between two variables of equal merit from other points of view, the variable which has the greater theoretical relevance is to be preferred. Theoretical relevance may be defined as appropriateness in terms of the best available theory concerning the causal processes which produce the phenomena under consideration. The subject of causal sequences will be further

considered below. An example of a situation in which one variable would be preferable to another is one in which the theory indicates that variable X causes Y and Z. In that situation in order to explain Y, the analysis should include X in preference to Z.

(4) *Parsimony.* The simplest possible explanation of a phenomenon using the least number of variables is to be preferred. The inclusion of large numbers of measured variables without close consideration of the theoretical meaning of the variables and of the logical interrelationships among them may produce results which defy comprehension and are equally useless for prediction. In an investigation in which the purpose is explanation, it may be argued that completeness is a virtue, in the sense that attention should be paid to the complete set of known interrelationships among the variables related to the phenomenon under consideration. Once the theory and the measurements are developed to the point where the underlying causal mechanisms are understood, however, it may be possible to simplify the model. For example, in the simple model above, it would be possible to eliminate Z from consideration and consider only the effect of X on Y.

Data Analysis: Having selected a set of explanatory variables, and assuming that they are all at the same causal level so that we can think of a single-level multivariate analysis, there is the problem of discovering just which variables, in what pattern, explain (and hence presumably predict) best. While the problem is often stated initially as though all the variables were cardinal scales (numbers), it is really more common to think of all the explanatory factors as sets of subclasses, ordinal scales.

Once there is a single valued dependent variable without some of the problems just discussed, analysis can most simply be thought of as reducing the unexplained variance, or the summed squared errors in predicting the dependent variable for each of a sample of cases. One can argue that it is the absolute errors that matter, not their squares, that an error of 100 is not 10,000 times as bad as an error of 1, but squaring produces nice statistical properties. If one tried to outwit the usual statistical procedures by using the square root of the dependent variable, one minimizes the absolute errors, but at the expense of fitting parabolic functions to it:

$$\sqrt{Y} = a + bX$$
$$\text{implies: } Y = a^2 + 2abX + b^2X^2$$

Any text in statistics can give the justifications for mean square error analysis.

It is instructive to avoid skipping to numerical fitting of functional forms and calculating of regressions, since that already imposes assumptions which may not be appropraite. Let us start more simply:

If we knew only the average of the dependent variable we should predict average for everyone and our errors in predicting the individuals in our sample would be:

$$\sum_{1}^{N} (Y - \overline{Y})^2 \equiv \Sigma Y^2 - 2\overline{Y}\Sigma Y + N\overline{Y}^2 \equiv \Sigma Y^2 - 2\overline{Y}\left(\frac{\Sigma Y}{N}\right)N - N\overline{Y}^2$$

$$\equiv \Sigma Y^2 - 2\overline{Y}^2 N + N\overline{Y}^2 \equiv \Sigma Y^2 - N\overline{Y}^2 \qquad \text{(a)}$$

For large samples this is also an estimate of the error variance in predicting the population not just the sample, for small samples one multiplies it by $N/(N-1)$.

The simplest application of information to reduce predictive error is to know which of two subclasses each individual is in. In this case, there are predictive errors around the *two* group means which are used for prediction:

$$\Sigma Y_1^2 - N_1\overline{Y}_1^2 + \Sigma Y_2^2 - N_2\overline{Y}_2^2 = \Sigma Y^2 - N_1\overline{Y}_1^2 - N_2\overline{Y}_2^2 \qquad \text{(b)}$$

and the gain over using one overall mean is:

$$N_1\overline{Y}_1^2 + N_2\overline{Y}_2^2 - N\overline{Y}^2 \qquad \text{(a)-(b)}$$

This is known as the "between sum of squares," and the first term above, (a), as the "total sum of squares," the phrase "around the mean" being understood. And (b) is the "within group sum of squares." The ratio of the additional explanation (a-b) to the original unexplained variance (a), is the square of the correlation ratio, eta, or the proportion of the variance (in the sample) explained by knowing which of two groups the individual is in. This is easily expanded to k groups and put in a form known as analysis of variance, and of variance components.

The total sum of squares (around the mean) is the same, and the gain or "explained sum of squares," or "between group sum of squares" for k subgroup means is:

$$\sum_{1}^{K} N_2\overline{Y}_i^2 - N\overline{Y}^2,$$

the weighted sum of squares of the subgroup means minus the standard correction factor. The simple one-way analysis of variance with k subclasses is given in Figure G-1. The divisor $\bar{n}$ is an adjustment for unequal group sizes, an approximation provided by Ganguli, which *is* the group size if they are all equal but progressively smaller if they are unequal:

$$\bar{n} = \frac{1}{K-1}\left[N - \frac{1}{N}\Sigma n_i^2\right]$$

so
$$\sigma_B^2 = \frac{\dfrac{B}{K-1} - \sigma_{\mathcal{E}}^2}{\bar{n}}$$

What this means is that the proportion of the population variance accounted for by groups, $\sigma_B^2/(\sigma_B^2 + \sigma_{\mathcal{E}}^2)$, can be estimated from the sample as:

$$\frac{\left[\dfrac{B}{K-1}\right] - \left[\dfrac{W}{N-K}\right]}{\left[\dfrac{B}{K-1}\right] - \left[\dfrac{W}{N-K}\right] + \bar{n}\left[\dfrac{W}{N-K}\right]} = \frac{1}{1 + \bar{n}\dfrac{W}{N-K}}$$

which is different from the proportion of the *sample* variance explained. It is lower, the larger the error variance, and lower, the more varied the subgroup sizes. The explained sum of squares in a sample, in other words, is biased upward by containing an error component itself, and upward by unequal subgroup sizes.[37] Figure G-1 summarizes all this.

We have focused on components of variance, estimates of which are relatively robust under departures from normality and homogeneity of variances. Tests of significance consist of treating the mean squares as estimates of the variance, equal if the groups were all the same, and computing the F-ratio B/(K-1) divided by W/(N-K), which is not only more sensitive to the basic assumptions, but also assumes simple random sampling which is rare in surveys.

At this level, the investigator's interest is often not so much in significance, or in predicting back to the population, as in comparing the explanatory power of the K subgroups of one classification with the L subgroups of some other classification, representing a different explanation. For this purpose, the total sum of squares remaining the same, all that need be compared is the "between group" sum of squares, or the mean square, adjusted for the number of subgroups. If one has a reasonably equal number of subgroups, it is only the size of $\sum_1^L n_i \bar{Y}_i^2$ that matters, which requires knowing only the subgroup means and the number of cases in each.

Where the dependent variable is a dichotomous variable taking only the values 1 and 0, the same relations hold, although some of the formulas simplify and look strange:

$$\text{Total} = NP(1 - P)$$
$$\text{Between groups: } \sum_1^k n_i P_i (1 - P_i)$$

But a computer program designed to handle a numerical dependent variable can take one with values 1 and 0, without altering the terminology.

FIGURE G-1

ONE WAY ANALYSIS OF VARIANCE AND COMPONENTS OF VARIANCE

	Sum of Squares	Degrees of Freedom	Mean Square (Estimate of Variance)	Mean Square is an Estimate of the Population Value of:
TOTAL (Around the Mean)	$\sum_1^N Y^2 - \frac{(\sum Y)^2}{n} = T$	$N-1$	$\frac{T}{N-1}$	$\sigma^2 Y$
BETWEEN GROUPS (Accounted for by Group Means)	$\sum_1^K N_i \overline{Y}_i^2 - \left(\frac{\sum Y}{n}\right)^2 = B$	$K-1$	$\frac{B}{K-1}$	If No Effect: $\sigma^2 Y$ — Otherwise: $\sigma_\varepsilon^2 + \overline{n}\sigma^2 B$
WITHIN GROUPS ("Error") or "Unexplained"	$T-B$	$N-K$	$\frac{T-B}{N-K}$	If No Effect: $\sigma^2 Y$ — Otherwise: σ_ε^2

No-Effect Hypothesis $\dfrac{B}{K-1} = \sigma_y^2 = \dfrac{T-B}{N-K}$; F-Ratio $= \dfrac{\frac{B}{K-1}}{\frac{T-B}{N-K}}$

Components of Variance: $\sigma_{Total}^2 = \sigma_{Between\ groups}^2 + \sigma_{Error}^2$
—in population

Sample Estimates: $\sigma_\varepsilon^2 = \dfrac{T-B}{N-K}$

$$\sigma_B^2 = \frac{\frac{B}{K-1} - \sigma_\varepsilon^2}{\overline{n}} \quad \text{where } \overline{n} = \frac{1}{K-1}\left[N - \frac{1}{N}\sum N_i^2\right]$$

$$= \frac{\frac{\sum N_i \overline{Y}_i^2 - \frac{(\sum Y)^2}{N}}{K-1} - \frac{\sum Y_2 - \frac{(\sum Y)^2}{N} - \left[\sum N_i \overline{Y}_i - \frac{(\sum Y)^2}{N}\right]}{N-K}}{\frac{1}{K-1}\left[N - \frac{1}{N}\sum N_i^2\right]}$$

Addendum: For most survey data, a fixed-effects model is more appropriate than the random-effects model requiring the complications above. Hence the proportion of the population variance accounted for requires only an adjustment for degrees of freedom:

$$= 1 - \left(1 - \frac{B}{T}\right)\left(\frac{N-1}{N-K}\right)$$

The analysis of subgroup means need not take only means classified according to a single explanatory variable at a time. If one were analyzing food expenditure, per family not per capita, then the explanatory power of income groups, or family size groups, or even the sum of the two would be considerably lower than that of the KxL groups classifying people *both* by income and family size. Indeed, comparison of the explained variance using the KxL subcells with that explained by the K plus that by the L subgroups provides a rough indication of the extent of interaction effects, although the former can be smaller than the latter sum if the two characteristics are highly correlated, their explanatory power overlapping.

We have departed from the usual approach of using numerical explanatory variables and then discussing possible problems, on the grounds that with surveys it makes more sense to treat all the variables, or nearly all, as sets of discrete classes rather than continuous numbers. Most of the statistical literature, however, is written as though all the variables were numerical, and some of our discussion of problems will have to be in these terms, even though the regression coefficient for a numerical variable may in practice be the shape of a set of dummy variable coefficients.

We turn now to a series of problems in multivariate analysis, and various ways of dealing with them.

Non-linear Relations: Non-linear relationships present no problem with dummy variables, as we shall see below. With numerical variables there are, broadly speaking, two statistical approaches to the problem of detecting non-linearities. The first strategy is to go ahead and fit a linear relationship, and then check to see whether the straight line fits the data. The second strategy is to proceed as if the relationship were non-linear and check to see whether evidence of the non-linearity does appear. The choice between the two approaches usually depends on what the investigator knows about the matter before he starts his analysis, and on the importance of departures from linearity for the problem at hand. He may believe that, while there no doubt is some departure from linearity, a linear relationship is a good approximation.

The basic procedure, if the first strategy is followed, is to analyze the residuals. That is, one fits the relationship, calculates for each individual in the sample the predicted score and the actual score on the dependent variable, and subtracts. Predicted scores, of course, may be estimated using multiple regression or any other procedure which yields an estimated relationship. If a linear relation has been erroneously assumed, there will be a systematic relationship between the independent variable and these residuals. The situation might be as sketched below:

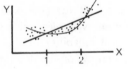

In this situation the average of the residuals below X = 1 will be positive, from X = 1 to X = 2 negative, and above X = 2, again positive. The analyst could detect this situation by dividing the data into groups according to the value of X and computing the mean residual for each group of observations. Or he could simply plot the residuals, or a sample of them, as in the sketch.

It may be possible to come to a conclusion on the question of linearity without using a formal statistical test. Such tests are available, however: Prais and Houthakker propose use of a statistic more familiar in time series analysis, the Durbin-Watson d. This statistic will provide a test of the degree of serial correlation between residuals when the residuals are arranged according to the magnitude of the determining variable, rather than by data as in time-series analysis where it originated.[38]

If an analyst follows the second strategy, proceeding as if the relationship were known to be non-linear, he has several options. He can transform one or more of the variables, using, for example, the log of income instead of income, he can fit a polynomial using, say, the square and the cube of the independent variable, he can introduce dummy variables, or he can break up the data, sorting on the independent variable, and fitting his entire equation separately for different ranges of values of the independent variable. He may also use a combination of these approaches.

The most common transformation of a variable is the use of its log. The log of a variable like income is particularly convenient because the original variable is highly skewed. The use of a complete multiplicative model, in which all variables are converted to log form is not necessary to cure non-linearity in a single variable. Another transformation which is sometimes used is to divide the individuals in the sample into groups of equal size and assign a score to each individual according to the tenth or decile of which he is a member, or even according to the mean of the dependent variable for that subgroup. Ratios are also commonly used, for example, the ratio of assets to income.[39]

In principle, any power of an independent variable can be introduced into a regression. It is unusual, however, to use higher powers than the square and the cube. Guthrie has provided an example of several methods to deal with non-linearity in the relation of liquid assets to income. The basic facts are that liquid assets are high in relation to income at low income levels and also at high levels but not at intermediate levels. Guthrie used as dependent variable the liquid asset-income ratio. As independent variables he used the income decile score of each unit and the square of that score.[40]

The use of dummy variables has been discussed earlier and will be treated fully later. Essentially, they permit the approximation of any curve by a step function. The number of dummy variables which can be used is limited only by considerations of the statistical reliability of the estimates. If a close fit is required, it may be possible to improve on the step function by fitting a continuous curve once the general shape of the relationship is known from the calculations using the dummy variables. How much improvement is possible could be estimated by the use of residuals in the manner outlined above for checking for departures from linearity.

To fit the entire relationship—the complete regression equation—for each of several ranges of the values of an independent variable will reveal non-linearity in the relationship between that variable and the dependent variable. The dummy variable technique, however, is more economical if non-linearity is the only problem. The complete re-fit is needed only when there are interactions in the data, as will be discussed below.

Much of the historic treatment of non-linearity was with time series data where there were very few degrees of freedom, and it was necessary to impose restrictive assumptions on the data. With survey data, there are enough cases so that even for numerical variables the most appropriate method in most cases is to convert each predictor into a set of dummy variables and let the output of a multiple regression indicate whether the effect is linear or not. There may be exceptions to this when some strong theoretical reasoning specifies the shape of some relationship, or when measurement of an elasticity is sought, but in general it would appear unwise to assume linearity or any other functional form when it is so easy to let the regression analysis decide the issue. The non-linearities in survey data are frequently bothersome: (a) discrete jumps, where completion of some type of schooling is more important than the number of years completed, (b) extreme effects of the extremes, where residence does not matter, except for the genuinely rural areas, and the very centers of the largest cities, or (c) non-monotonic effects, where the middle-aged earn more than the young *or* the old.

Errors in Variables and Their Effects on Relationship: The evidence is clear that there are substantial errors of measurement of some of the variables in survey estimates. Therefore, it is necessary to consider what effect these errors may have on the estimation of relationships. Fortunately, the relevant econometric theory has been worked out reasonably well. The theory, however, is rarely taken into account in the literature reporting the results of sample surveys. This compartmentalization of knowledge has produced a situation in which users of survey results are left uninformed as to whether reported regression coefficients (or related statistics) are biased as a result of errors in measurement of the independent variables. The simplest statement found in many statistics books, is that errors in the dependent variable can reduce the correlation but do not cause bias in the estimate of the relationship. But errors in an explanatory variable produce a downward bias in the regression coefficient (slope of the regression line). Actually, the problem is more complicated than that.

The reader is referred for a more complete treatment to J. Johnston's *Econometric Methods* or to Kendall and Stuart.[41] Johnston calls attention to a parallel between the theory of errors in variables and Friedman's analysis of the consumption function, a comparison which may assist economists to an understanding of the subject.

Consider a situation in which there are two variables, each of which is observed with error. If x and y are the true variables, the observed variables, X and Y, are equal to the true variables plus errors:

(1) $X = x + u$

(2) $Y = y + v$

The true variables are assumed to be related to each other in a simple linear relationship:

(3) $y = \alpha + \beta x$

We may then find the relation between the observed variables by substitution:

$$Y - v = y$$

$$X - u = x$$

(4) $Y - v = \alpha + \beta (X - u)$
      $Y = \alpha + \beta X - \beta u + v$

Hence,   (5) $Y = \alpha + \beta X + w$, where $w = v - \beta u$

But w is not independent of X. It includes the term, -Bu, and u is a component of the observed value, x. Thus, ordinary least squares procedures will yield biased estimates of α and β even if the sample is infinite and even if the mean values of the error terms are zero.

More generally:

(6) $\varepsilon\{w[x - E(x)]\} = \varepsilon(uv) - \beta u^2$

Thus, the covariance of X and w depends upon—(1) the covariance of the errors of observation, and (2) a factor which is the product of the true regression coefficient and the variance of the errors of observation for X. It is not surprising that the covariance of the errors of observation enters the expression. Any systematic relationship between the errors might well distort the estimate of the true regression coefficient.

It is instructive to consider the effects of the errors on the estimator of β from a sample of size n. The estimate of β would be as follows:

$$(7) \quad \beta_n = \frac{\sum_{i=1}^{n} (X_i - \bar{X})(Y_i - \bar{Y})}{\sum_{i=1}^{n} (X_i - \bar{X})^2}$$

If we introduce the error terms, the expression becomes:

$$(8) \quad \beta_n = \frac{\Sigma(x-\bar{x})(y-\bar{y}) + \Sigma(x-\bar{x})(v-\bar{v}) + \Sigma(y-\bar{y})(u-\bar{u}) + \Sigma(u-\bar{u})(v-\bar{v})}{\Sigma(x-\bar{x})^2 + 2\Sigma(x-\bar{x})(u-\bar{u}) + \Sigma(u-\bar{u})^2}$$

The estimate of β_n, therefore, will depend upon the following:

(a)   Whether u and v are independent of one another. (See the last term in the numerator.)
(b)   Whether each of the true variables is independent of the error in the other variable. (See the second and third terms in the numerator.)
(c)   Whether x is independent of the error in x. (See middle term in the denominator.)
(d)   The magnitude of the variance of the errors of observation of x. (See the last term in the denominator.)

It is, therefore, not possible to say in general whether β will be biased upward or downward. One must know the sign and the magnitude of each of the five terms in (8) which involve u or v or both.

We can, however, consider what is known about errors in sample surveys and its probable implications for these terms.

(a)   In sample surveys there is reason to expect u and v not to be independent. The same individual is reporting under identical circumstances. We would expect him to report both x and y accurately, or to report neither accurately. If u and v are *positively* correlated, the effect will be to *increase* β_n. This situation is likely to be a common one: for example, both income and savings may be understated. If, however, u and v are *negatively* correlated, the effect will be to reduce β_n. For example, income might be understated and charitable contributions overstated.
(b)   In sample surveys there may well be association between the true value of one variable and the error in the other. There is reason to believe, for example, that high income people report savings accounts more completely than low income people. If there is a *positive* correlation between a true

variable and the error in the other variable, the effect will be to increase β_n. If the correlation is *negative,* the effect will be to *reduce β_n.*

(c)   In sample surveys there may well be association between the true value of an independent variable and whether that variable is reported accurately. For example, in the measurement of total income, high income people tend to have income from property, which is typically underreported, while low income people have only income from wages, which is reported correctly. If there is a *positive* correlation between the true value of x and its error of measurements, β_n will be *reduced;* if there is a *negative* correlation, β_n will be *increased.*

(d)   In sample surveys the error of measurement in the independent variable may be substantial. The *larger* the squared error of measurement of x, the *smaller* the estimate of β_n. This may well be the most important problem.

As the preceding comments suggest, it may be possible to obtain estimates of the terms of equation (8) by conducting validity studies.

Johnston proposes three general approaches to the problem of how to conduct statistical analysis of data subject to errors of measurement. The first, or "classical," approach, involves stringent assumptions about the error terms. The specific procedure depends upon what is known about the errors. It will be discussed briefly below. The second approach involves grouping the data, plus making less stringent assumptions about the error terms. We admit to some uncertainty as to whether this method is as effective as it appears, and will simply refer the interested reader to Johnston and the references there cited. The third approach, the method of instrumental variables, will be discussed below.

The first approach is developed more fully by Kendall and Stuart, who discuss four cases which differ according to what is known or can be ascertained about the errors. The "classic solution" requires knowledge of the ratio of the variance of the errors. Given this information, and zero covariance terms, the problem becomes manageable. Instead of the ratio of the variance, the available information may be the actual variance of one or the other of the error terms, or, it may be that the variances of both error terms are known. We emphasize that it is generally impossible to know the covariance terms of equation (8) above, or even the distributions of the errors of each variable considered separately.

The method of instrumental variables may prove to be of practical value for some problems of survey work, and we shall discuss here the nature of the requirements it places on the process of data collection. Consider again the situation in which the following expressions apply:

(9) $Y = \alpha + \beta X + w$

$w = v - \beta u$

We introduce a variable Z, which is independent of both errors, u and v. We use as an estimator:

$$(10) \quad \hat{\beta} = \frac{\sum_{i=1}^{n} Y_i Z_i}{\sum_{i=1}^{n} X_i Z_i}$$

where X, Y, and Z are defined as deviations from their own means.

Note that:

$$(11) \quad \hat{\beta} = \frac{\beta \Sigma Y_i Z_i + \Sigma Z_i (w_i - \bar{w})}{\Sigma X_i Z_i}$$

The second term in the numerator will tend to zero as n becomes large because Z is not correlated with the errors u and v. Note that Z must have a fairly high correlation with x. If it does not, the denominator in (10) will be near zero, and the estimate of β will be near infinity.

The logic of the method requires that we estimate the relation between y and x by taking the ratio of the relation between y and z to that between x and z. There may be other independent variables at work, which influence the relationship, but in principle we can take them into account in a multivariate calculation.

Johnston noted three major problems with the method of instrumental variables. First, the choice of instrumental variables is arbitrary, and there is a possibility of variations in the resultant estimates as a consequence. It would be desirable to try two or more instrumental variables and compare the results to check this possibility. Second, there is the difficulty of checking that the instrumental variables actually are independent of the errors of observation, and that they are exogenous, not dependent on X or Y. We may note that in survey work some variables are measured a great deal more accurately than others. It is also possible, on occasion, to introduce into an analysis variables which are measured outside the survey. Third, Johnston notes that the approach places great stress on the importance of consistency of the estimate. This stress may prove warranted in surveys—one needs more information to be sure.

Another interpretation, suggested by Theil, focuses on the problem of shocks affecting both X and Y and producing an extraneous relationship rather than an over-determined system.[42] He proposed removing the error or random element from X by regressing it on some exogenous variable Z and treating the residuals from that regression as the random shock elements. In fact this amounts to using the predicted value of X from that regression, instead of the actual X, in finding its relation to Y, and is algebraically equivalent to the method of instrumental variables.

$$\hat{X} = a + bz$$

$$Y = c + dx$$

Again there is the problem of finding something which affects X but is not affected by either X or Y, and a question whether different Z choices would produce different estimates. The method is called "two-stage least squares" but should be carefully distinguished from analysis of residuals, and from step-wise least squares procedures.

These two solutions, instrumental variables, and two-stage-least-squares, assume that the focus is on the best estimate of *the* relationship between two variables, though others may be in the model additively. If there are interaction effects then there is no single relationship anyway. And if we are assessing the relative power of a number of explanatory variables, extending the methods is cumbersome.

The remaining problems in the one-level analysis of a dependent variable have to do with the multivariate nature of the problem—the fact that one is attempting to sort out the effects of a number of variables simultaneously, not just get the best unbiased estimate of the effects of one of them. These problems can be categorized into three main parts, intercorrelations among the predictors, interaction effects, and the "one dominant variable" problem.

Intercorrelations among the Predictors: If the predictor variables are completely uncorrelated with one another, then their simple correlations and regression coefficients are all that is needed. If any one predictor, at the other extreme is perfectly correlated with one of the others, or any linear combination of the others, then clearly there is no way at all to separate their influences, or attribute the explained variance to one or the other of them. (In solving the normal equations of multiple regression, a determinant in the denominator of one expression becomes zero, and the computer stops.) In between, the usual procedure for sorting out separate effects is that of multiple regression. Although the usual computing procedure for estimating multiple regression coefficients is by solving a set of so-called normal equations, it is easier to see what is really involved by describing an algebraically equivalent process in which they are estimated in a series of iterations. This process is itself most easily described when the explanatory variables are categorical—sets of dummy variables.

Suppose one had a dependent variable, income, and two explanatory characteristics: age and education. One could estimate a relationship between age and income (mean income for each age group) and one between education and income (mean income for each education group). These means are expressed as deviations from the overall mean. The coefficient (deviation) for the young, say, is adjusted for the fact that a smaller proportion of young than old are uneducated. This is done by multiplying the proportion of young uneducated by the income deviation for uneducated and the proportion of young educated by the income deviation for educated, dividing by the sum of the proportions, and subtracting the result from coefficient for young (that much being accounted for by the fact that a larger proportion of the young are educated and get paid more for that reason). Similar adjustments for the old would be smaller and in the other direction since more of them are uneducated. One then goes to the coefficients for educated and for uneducated, adjusting them for the disproportionate age compositions. The result is four new coefficients, adjusted once for intercorrelations among the predictors (the fact that a subclass of one is not distributed across the other in the same way as the whole population). The process can then be repeated, until the marginal adjustments are so small as to be negligible, and the resulting coefficients are now an additive set which will predict income with minimum error variance.

Note that we actually started with a set of subgroup means and adjusted them for possible distortion by the effects of disproportionality on other factors. If two predictors (subclasses) are identical (two subclasses one from each of two predictors) then the process does not converge, but goes into a set of oscillating, reversing corrections, the analogue of the zero denominator in the determinant solution of the normal equations.

With numerical predictors, one can think of plotting the scatter diagram, fitting a simple regression line, taking the residuals case by case and plotting (or running) them against the second predictor, taking those residuals in turn and running them against the first predictor again, and so forth until there is no relation left. This can be done graphically with small data sets, to get the feel for what happens.[43]

The price one pays for the powerful simultaneous determination of the effects of many variables in multiple regression is the required assumption of additivity and universality. That is, any variable which affects the dependent variables does so with the same impact in all subparts of the population, so that its effect can be added, across the whole population, to the effect of each of the other variables. But if this assumption is met, or can be approximated by judicious redefinition of variables, and if the intercorrelations among the predictors are not so high as to lead to unstable estimates of the regression coefficients, then multiple regression is a powerful tool indeed.

Furthermore, as we have said, it is not necessary to assume linearity of the effects of each predictor in order to use regression, provided one has enough cases to allow the use of dummy variables.[44]

If the direct algebraic solution to the normal equations of regression is to be used, one must either constrain the coefficients of each set of dummy variables so that their weighted sum is zero, or constrain one of them to zero. The latter is easier with computer programs already written. One merely omits one of each set. The result is that remaining coefficients are all in terms of differences from the excluded group, and the effects of being in the excluded groups are pooled into the constant term.

In the simple example with two predictors, of two classes each, Age (young and old) and Education (Uneducated or Educated), and a dependent variable, Income, the computer regression then becomes:

Income = Constant + A (if young) + B (if uneducated)

The only information an additive regression model needs is the simple variances and covariances (correlations) among all the variables including the dependent one. Where the explanatory variables take only the values 1 and 0, however, their covariances with the dependent variable are simple functions of the mean of the dependent variable for the subgroup that is non-zero on that dummy variable. And the covariances among the predictors when they only take values 1 and 0 are the two-way frequency tables of the pairs of explanatory characteristics. The data needed for the example are:

Mean Incomes				Frequencies		
By Age		By Education			Uneducated	Educated
Young	$6200	Uneducated	$4600	Young	10	40
Old	$5800	Educated	$7400	Old	40	10

All: $6000

Variances: Of dummies, NPQ where P is proportion non-zero; Q = (1-P)
        Of income, calculated from data. For our example we assume there is no "error" variance, that is, that the basic data are as follows:

Mean Incomes		
	Uneducated	Educated
Young	$3000	$7000
Old	5000	9000

(No variance within groups)

But the regression model does not use this information, being content with the one-dimensional subgroup means and the overall variance of the dependent variable.

If one actually calculates a regression using the subgroup means and the two-way frequency table, it will come out:

Income = $9000 - $2000 if young - $4000 if uneducated; R = 1.00

This is the form in which dummy-variable regression is usually presented; unfortunately so, since it is most misleading. The coefficients are in terms of differences from the excluded group, not from some known and stable base. If the excluded group is small, say the non-ascertained cases, all the other coefficients can have a very large, and somewhat erratic shift when the excluded group has a widely deviant mean. And the constant term can also be erratic. It is a bit like standing a triangle on its end.

A much better form, mathematically identical is:

$$\text{Income} = \text{Average income} \begin{array}{ll} + a1 \text{ if Young} & + b1 \text{ if Uneducated} \\ + a2 \text{ if Old} & + b2 \text{ if Educated} \end{array}$$

The transformation for each set of dummies is by simply adding a constant (C or K) to each coefficient (including the zero one) so that their weighted sum will equal zero, subtracting the same constant from the constant term:

Age	Education
50 (-2000 + C) + 50 (0 + C) = 0	50 (-4000 + K) + 50 (0 + K) = 0
100C = 100,000	100K = 200,000
C = 1,000	K = 2,000

so: Income = 9000 - 1000 - 2000

	- 1000 if Young	- 2000 if Uneducated
	+1000 if Old	+2000 if Educated

Another advantage of this form appears when one wishes to compare similar regressions computed for another sample or a different time or place. One can observe changes in the mean, and then check to what extent they can be attributed to:

(a) Changes in the proportions in each subgroup with no change in the *effects* of subgroup belonging (the coefficients).

One multiplies the original a and b coefficients by the new population proportions in those groups to see how far the result departs from zero. Perhaps changing incomes simply result from more college graduates and more older people, with the payoffs to education and experience remaining unchanged.

(b) Changes in the structural relations, which may be behavioral responses, or effects of background conditions.

One multiplies the original population proportions times a new set of a and b coefficients, again to see how far the sum departs from zero.

These two experiments can be done separately for each explanatory characteristic (set of dummy variables) since the model assumes independent additive effects.

When the number of predictors, and the number of subclasses of each, becomes large, presentation of the results becomes a problem. In order to see the effects of adjustments for intercorrelations among the predictors carried out by the regression analysis, the following form is useful:

INCOME

Predictors	Unadjusted		Adjusted (by regression)		Number of Cases
	Means	Deviations	Deviations	Means	
Young	$6200	+200	-1000	5000	50
Old	5800	-200	+1000	7000	50
Uneducated	4600	-1400	-2000	4000	50
Educated	7400	+1400	+2000	8000	50

What has happened is that the negative correlation between education and age (experience) has led to spurious reductions in the apparent effects of each, which the regression then eliminated. We made this an extreme case, where the apparent effect of age was actually reversed. The young seemed to be making more, but it was only because they were so much better educated. Taking account of education, they made less. In terms of simple correlations we have:

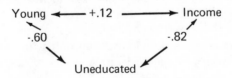

The small positive correlation is a classic example of spurious correlation resulting from the positive product of two high negative correlations with lack of education. (If we had defined a dummy variable "educated," rather than "uneducated," we should then have talked about two high positive correlations with
being young and with high income.)

By adding the mean to the adjusted deviations we can say what the mean
income of that group would have been if it were like the whole sample on all the
other dimensions.

It is also important to present the column of frequencies, since the sampling
variances of the means and deviations, unadjusted or adjusted, are mostly affected
by the varying sizes of the subgroups on which they are based. If the predictors
are perfectly uncorrelated, each subclass of each predictor being distributed like
the population across the classes of every other predictor, then the simple regressions, or the subgroup means in the case of categorical variables, are unbiased
estimates of the effects, and multiple regression is unnecessary. In the iterative
process, not even the first iteration would make any adjustments. If the young
were exactly half uneducated and half educated, the weighted product of their
deviations by education subclass would be zero. In fact, however, they are mostly
educated, so the weighted sum is a substantial positive number which is then
subtracted from the estimated deviation for "young," since it is attributable to
education, not youth. The same adjustments are made for each subclass of each
predictor, producing a set of first-adjusted deviations. The process is then repeated using these deviations to calculate new adjustments, and second-adjusted
deviations. The process is continued until no adjustments show more than some
very small amount (absolutely not relative to the size of the coefficient itself
since some adjusted deviations will be close to zero). The resulting final-adjusted
deviations are, as we have said, algebraically identical with the results of the
dummy variable regression calculations, except that they are already in the more
meaningful form, with no subclasses omitted. Each adjusted deviation is a departure from the overall mean attributable to membership in that subclass, and
not to the fact that the subclass differs on some of the other characteristics.

Usually the adjusted coefficients are smaller than the unadjusted ones, because the variables are usually positively correlated with one another, and with
the dependent variable. But if two explanatory variables positively correlated
with each other have opposite effects on the dependent variable, then simple relations understate both effects and multiple regression should produce more
striking regression coefficients. Similarly if two variables each positively affecting the dependent variable are negatively correlated with one another (age and
education on earnings), then again each effect would be underestimated by the
simple unadjusted subgroup means or simple regressions.

If the regression must be run on a standard program, forcing one of each
set of dummy variables to have a coefficient of zero, the chances are also that

the program will *not* give the mean of the dependent variable for each subgroup (not = 0 on that dummy variable). Yet an interpretation of the regression is improved if one sees just what the adjustment for intercorrelation among the predictors did. Hence, having gotten the regression coefficients expressed as subgroup deviations from the grand mean (adjusted by regression), one would like to compare them with the deviations of the unadjusted subgroup mean from the grand mean. Most regression programs do not provide this information, but they do provide data from which it is derivable, namely the simple correlations among all the variables, the means of all the variables, and the number of cases.

What we want is the mean of Y for the group where x_i = 0, which is: $\dfrac{\Sigma X_i Y}{\Sigma X_i}$

since X_i is = 1 for cases in the subgroup, otherwise = 0. What we have is:

$$r^2 = \frac{\text{cov } X_i Y}{(\text{var } X_i)\,(\text{var } Y)}$$

where

$$\text{cov } X_i Y = \Sigma X_i Y - \frac{\Sigma X_i\,\Sigma Y}{N}$$

$$\text{var } X_i = \sigma^2_{X_i}$$

$$\text{var } Y = \sigma^2_Y$$

So

$$\frac{\Sigma X_i Y}{\Sigma X_i} = \frac{\left(\Sigma X_i Y - \dfrac{\Sigma X_i\,\Sigma Y}{N} + \dfrac{\Sigma X_i\,\Sigma Y}{N}\right)}{\Sigma X_i} = \frac{\text{cov } X_i Y + \dfrac{\Sigma X_i\,\Sigma Y}{N}}{\Sigma X_i} = \frac{\text{cov } X_i Y}{N\overline{X}} - \overline{Y}$$

$$= \frac{\dfrac{\text{cov } X_i Y}{\sigma^2_{X_i}\sigma^2_Y} \cdot \sigma^2_{X_i}\sigma^2_Y}{N\overline{X}} - \overline{Y}$$

$$= \frac{r^2_{X_i Y} \cdot \sigma^2_{X_i}\sigma^2_Y}{N\overline{X}} - \overline{Y} = \text{mean of Y for } X_i \neq 0.$$

If the covariances are available, the next to last term provides the mean of the dependent variable for the subgroup not = 0 on x_i, but if only the correlations are available, the last term provides it.

This mean can be compared with the "adjusted mean," or one can subtract the grand mean from it and compare it with the "adjusted deviation," the multiple regression coefficient for x_i when they have been adjusted so that the weighted sum of each set of coefficients is equal to zero.

The use of standard regression packages with dummy variables entails a considerable amount of hand work for the results to be ready for easy interpretation by the reader. He needs the effects of each dummy variable (membership in some subgroup in the population) expressed as deviations from the grand mean (not from other subgroup arbitrarily selected to have its coefficient zero). And he needs to compare this with the subgroup's deviation from average, unadjusted by any consideration of its disproportionate membership in other subgroups. Or he may want both numbers expressed as averages, not deviations, i.e. with the grand mean added to both of them.

Let us take a somewhat more complex example, with less symmetry and with three subclasses, so that one uses two dummy variables, for each of two predicting characteristics. Again, all the regression uses is the one-dimensional subgroup means, and the two-way frequency distributions of the predictors, are the overall variance.

Means		Frequencies				
	Income		Uned	H.S.	College	
Young	$ 8,000	Young	5	10	15	30
Middle-aged	10,571	Mid.	10	15	10	35
Uneducated	4,200	Old	20	15	5	40
High School	6,750		35	40	30	105

(We have made the data realistic, if rounded, and with additive effects.)

If one uses a regular regression program, again one must eliminate one subgroup of each classification (since it is totally predictable from knowing whether each individual is in either of the other two subgroups). Suppose we eliminate the middle groups, and use four dummy variables, called Young, Old, Uneducated, and College. From the subgroup means one can calculate the simple correlations of each predictor with income:

	r
Correlation of income with "Young"	= .1456
"Old"	= -.7000
"Uneducated"	= -.6513
"College"	= .7282

And from the two-way frequency tables, one can calculate the simple correlations among the pairs of predictors:

	Old	Not
Young	0	30
Not	40	35

r = -.4961

	Uneducated	Not
Young	5	25
Not	30	45

r = -.2236

	College	Not
Young	15	15
Not	15	60

r = +.3000

	Old	Not
Uneducated	20	15
Not	20	50

r = +.2774

	College	Not
Uneducated	0	35
Not	30	40

r = -.4472

	College	Not
Old	5	35
Not	25	40

r = -.2791

Using only this information, and assuming additivity, the regression analysis might produce the following:

$$\text{Income} = 10,000 \quad \begin{array}{ll} -4,000 \text{ if Young} & -3,000 \text{ if Uneducated} \\ -6,000 \text{ if Old} & +5,000 \text{ if College} \end{array}$$

These coefficients represent deviations from the excluded groups (middle aged, or high school graduates) not from the mean, and the constant term is not the mean, but the mean plus the effects of the two excluded groups. Again a linear transformation, to make the weighted sum of the three coefficients equal to zero for each of the two explanatory characteristics gives a better equation.

If C is an adjustment added to each of the three age coefficients to make them have a weighted sum of 0, we have:

$$\begin{array}{ccc} \text{Young} & \text{Old} & \text{Middle Aged} \end{array}$$

$$0 = \frac{(C - 4000)\ 30 + (C - 6000)\ 40 + (C + 0)\ 35}{105}$$

(See Frequency Table for Weights)

  C = 3429

So we have - 571 if young
    +3429 if middle aged
    -2571 if old

   A similar process for education gives a constant of -429, and we have the "adjusted deviations" in column 3 of the table below. Note that if the two adjustments are also made to the constant term, it becomes the overall mean: 10,000 - 3429 + 429 = 7,000, and we have the more meaningful predicting equation:

$$\text{Income} = 7000 \quad \begin{array}{l} -\ 571 \text{ if Young} \\ +3429 \text{ if Middle Aged} \\ -2571 \text{ if Old} \end{array} \quad \begin{array}{l} -3429 \text{ if Uneducated} \\ -\ 429 \text{ if High School} \\ +4571 \text{ if College} \end{array}$$

And for each group, using the next-to-last column of the table, we can say what their average income would be if they were "average" on the other characteristic.

	Unadjusted		Adjusted		
	Means	Deviations	Deviations	Means	Number of Cases
Young	$ 8000	$+1000	$- 571	$ 6429	30
Middle Aged	10571	+3571	+3429	10429	35
Old	3125	- 3875	- 2571	4429	40
Uneducated	4200	- 2800	- 3429	3571	35
High School	6750	- 250	- 429	6571	40
College	12000	+5000	+4571	11571	30

   The regression coefficients came out as they did because we built the model into the data without any interaction effects (non-additivities) as in the data table below. We also allowed no (error) variance within any of the nine groups, so the multiple correlation coefficient came out 1.00.

MEAN INCOMES AND FREQUENCIES

	Uneducated	High School	College	All Educations
Young	$3,000	$ 6,000	$11,000	$ 8,000
	5	10	15	30
Middle Aged	7,000	10,000	15,000	10,571
	10	15	10	35
Old	1,000	4,000	9,000	3,125
	20	15	5	40
All Ages	4,200	6,750	12,000	7,000
	35	40	30	105

The differences between the unadjusted and the adjusted deviations in the prior table are of course the adjustments for intercorrelation among the predictors (unequal frequency distributions). Notice that three of them are smaller in absolute amount, indicating the elimination of some spurious correlation, while two are larger, indicating the elimination of some spurious lack of correlation, and one even changes direction! Take the sign reversal for illustration, and use correlation diagrams:

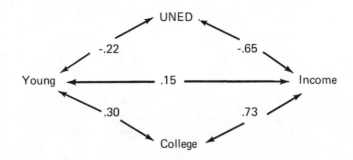

The simple small positive correlation between being young and having a high income is the spurious result of high positive products of correlations of the two through the two education variables. Young people have higher incomes because they are less likely to be uneducated (they avoid that negative effect), and more likely to have a college degree (they get that positive effect) but if they were only average on education, their incomes would be lower than average. The unadjusted effect of being young is distorted up by their high education (multiply the education deviations by the proportions of young in each educational class).

The question often arises whether one does not lose information by converting a numerical predictor into a set of subclasses which are assigned dummy variables. Actually the flexibility (non-linearity) allowed is achieved with very little loss in precision. As few as eight subclasses will explain almost all the variance the full detail will explain, and even more if there is non-linearity. Indeed, with most survey data, errors of measurement are sufficiently large so that some of the "lost precision" is spurious, and the extreme cases which tend to dominate the results of numerical least-squares estimates, are particularly likely to contain either conceptual or measurement errors. For example, using a single dummy variable for everyone whose house is worth more than $30,000 may keep some one person coded as having a house worth $500,000 (perhaps erroneously) from dominating the estimates.

In interpreting the results of dummy variable regression, one is usually interested in the relative *importance* of the various predictors, thought of as characteristics like age, education, and the like, and not interested in the importance of each subgroup by itself. The same is true with questions of statistical *significance*, though we argue that with substantial samples (1,000 or more) of the size to allow dummy variable regression, anything worth looking at (in terms of importance) will be significant anyway, and the crucial issue is the explanatory *power* of the predictors.

How then can we assess the explanatory *power* of a whole set of dummy variables associated with one characteristic, like education? There is a relatively simple answer by analogy with the partial beta coefficient of numerical regression, often used as an approximate indicator of the relative power of the predictors. The ideal indicator of course is the partial correlation coefficient, or the increase in the multiple correlation (squared) achieved by adding the predictor in question (the *set* of dummy variables) after all the others are already in. The true partial correlation coefficient can best be thought of as the simple correlation between two sets of residuals, residuals of the dependent variable after removing the effects of all the other explanatory variables except X1, and residuals of X1 after removing the effects from it of all the other explanatory variables. There is a great deal of confusion generated by the terminology and by the fact that the simple *regression* coefficient using these two sets of residuals is mathematically identical with the "partial beta coefficient" of a single multiple regression. However, the simple *correlation* coefficient between the two sets of residuals, which is equal to the partial *correlation* coefficient, cannot be derived from a single multiple regression analysis, unless the analysis also estimates the standard errors of the regression coefficient (b's) in which case:

$$r^2_{12.345} = \frac{(b_{12.345})^2}{(b_{12.345})^2 + (\sigma_{b12.345})^2 (D/f)}$$

$$= \frac{t^2}{t^2 + D/f}$$

where $D/f = N - K - 1$ with N cases and K predictors.

The regression coefficients of a numerical multiple regression become "partial beta coefficients" when multiplied by the standard deviation of the explanatory variable in question and divided by the standard deviation of the dependent variable:

$$\beta = \frac{b_i \, \sigma_{X_i}}{\sigma_Y}$$

They are a kind of "standardized" regression coefficient, in standard deviation units, i.e. How many standard deviations ones the dependent variable move when the explanatory variable changes by one standard deviation?

The analogue to the partial beta coefficient in the case of dummy variables is simple and obvious. The dummy variables can be thought of as a new scale, new sets of numbers. If each individual were assigned the coefficients instead of the 1-0 dummy variables, and a regression computed with the same dependent variable, the regression coefficients would be 1.00 for each of these new "variables." The partial beta coefficients are then simply 1.00 times the standard deviation of the new "variable" (square root of the weighted sum of squares of the dummy variable coefficients in the set) divided by the standard deviation of the dependent variable which is known. Therefore the "partial beta coefficient" for a set of coefficients, Ai is:

$$\beta_A = \frac{1.00 \sqrt{\frac{\Sigma \, n_i A_i^2}{\Sigma \, n_i}}}{\sigma_Y}$$

The main difference is that the signs of the A's have already taken account of direction of effects so this analogue beta is always positive.

It is useful in presenting the results of a regression using sets of dummy variables, to first list the predicting characteristics, in order of their "partial beta coefficients," then to present the tables of unadjusted means and deviations and adjusted deviations and means, for the more important predictors.

Readers are often interested not only in the power of each set of dummy variable in the multivariate context, but also its power if used alone. Again it is possible to use a standard statistic, Eta, the correlation ratio, which is directly comparable with the partial beta, except that it is calculated using the unadjusted deviations rather than the adjusted ones.

$$\text{ETA} = \eta = \sqrt{\frac{\frac{1}{n}\sum_{i=1}^{K} N_i (\bar{Y}_i - \bar{Y})^2}{\frac{1}{n}\sum_{j=1}^{N} (Y_i - \bar{Y})^2}} = \frac{\sqrt{\frac{\sum_{i=1}^{K} N_i (\bar{Y}_i - \bar{Y})^2}{\sum N_i}}}{\sigma_Y}$$

Indeed, eta is really the result of a one-way analysis of variance, using subgroup means, and relating the "explained sum of squares" explained by those means to the total variance (total sum of squares around the mean). Using the example on pp. 4-6, we can calculate η and β for "age" as follows: (remember we allowed no variance within the subgroups)

$$\eta = \sqrt{\frac{\frac{(200)^2 \cdot 50 + (-200)^2 \cdot 50}{100}}{\frac{(-3000)^2 \cdot 10 + (1000)^2 \cdot 40 + (-1000)^2 \cdot 40 + (3000)^2 \cdot 10}{100}}} = \sqrt{\frac{40,000}{2,6000,000}} = \sqrt{.0154} = .124$$

$$\beta = \sqrt{\frac{\frac{(-1000)^2 \cdot 50 + (1000)^2 \cdot 50}{100}}{\frac{(-3000)^2 \cdot 10 + (1000)^2 \cdot 40 + (1000)^2 \cdot 40 + (3000)^2 \cdot 10}{100}}} = \sqrt{\frac{1,000,000}{2,600,000}} = \sqrt{.3846} = .620$$

It is unusual to have β larger than η, because spurious correlation is more common than spurious lack of it.

Ideally, then one would present the etas and "partial betas" indicating the explanatory power of each predictor (set of subclasses) separately and in a multivariate analysis.

Purists from the regression school may ask what about the assumptions of normally distributed explanatory variables. How can something which takes only the values 0 and 1 be normally distributed? Actually regression, particularly if interpreted in terms of power in reducing unexplained variance, not as a set of significance tests, is relatively robust under departures from this normality assumption. Trouble arises when for some subclass almost everyone is either 0 (no cases, so high sampling variability) or 1 (no variance so no explanatory power), but these problems become obvious if the tables give the number of cases.

Regression can also be used where the dependent variable is a dichotomy, such as whether or not the person owns a home. Again the depatures from normality are most serious when the average proportion is close to zero or to one hundred percent. Otherwise, the analysis can proceed, and the calculations are the same as though one were conducting a discriminant analysis, though the assumptions about errors are different. It is best to think of the final equation as predicting a probability, rather than classifying a whole group "Yes" or "No" as discriminant analysis does.

Indeed, it is often useful to create dichotomous dependent variables, even when there is a well distributed dependent variable. For instance, one might want to check whether the things that make a man more likely to be at one end of the distribution (on the dependent variable) are different from those that put him at the other end.[45]

Where dichotomous dependent variable possibilities do not seem appropriate, but the dependent variable is still not normally distributed, then as discussed earlier various solutions have been proposed:

Transformations, such as logs or square roots, to reduce skewness, or allow elasticity interpretations of coefficients, or reduce the impact of extreme cases.

Probit analysis, where one posits a normally distributed resistance to the explanatory forces, and wants to estimate both the mean and the variance of that distribution.

Actually one of the main problems with a dichotomous dependent variable is that it is often based on a single bit of information (answer to one question) and has relatively little real variance, and substantial error variance (reporting errors, etc.). In many cases, it pays to get some additional dimensions with other questions, build an index combining the answers to several questions (however arbitrary the index), so as to have some additional variance to explain and also to average out some of the error variance. When this was done with early retirement, adding three other indicators, and giving an extra point for planning to retire *very* early, the correlation with expected cash retirement income quadrupled (from $r^2 = .04$ to .15) and the relationship become much more nearly linear.[46]

One difficulty with the additivity assumption of regression appears at this stage, because the predicted value of some of these subgroups may be impossible, less than zero, or in the case of dichotomous dependent variables treated as probabilities, an expected probability greater than one.

Of course, such impossible cases appear even more easily if one uses the multiple regression coefficients to predict individual cases. It is easy to make such predictions if the output is in the form suggested: One starts with the grand mean and for each predictor adds or subtracts an amount depending on which subclass of that predictor the individual is in. An individual who is in the group on each predictor with the largest negative coefficient, may well end up with a predicted value less than zero for some quantity which cannot be negative.

The sampling errors of dummy variable regression coefficients have some special properties which make it somewhat easier to approximate them. Suppose we consider them as subgroup means, to which some adjustments for intercorrelations have been made. Then their stability certainly depends directly on the square root of the number of cases in the subgroup that was not zero on the dummy variable, i.e. the group that provided the mean. When sampling errors were calculated for dummy variable regression coefficients by the method of balanced repeated replication discussed in the previous chapter on sampling, they did fit $\sigma\sqrt{N}$ rather well. In other words, differences in variance among subgroups were much less important than differences in their sizes. Hence, it is very important that one present the subgroups sizes as well as the unadjusted and adjusted coefficients, enabling the reader to discard the non-significant ones. Indeed, one could, in a well-designed survey, assume some design effect, perhaps 1.05 to be conservative, and then use the following approximations:

$$\text{Sample error of unadjusted deviations (subgroups means)} \doteq \frac{(1.05)\,(\sigma_Y)}{\sqrt{N_i}}$$

$$\text{Sampling error of adjusted deviations (dummy variable coefficients)} \doteq \frac{1.05\,\sigma_Y\sqrt{(1 - R^2)}}{\sqrt{N_i}}$$

When there is no previous work on the design effects of the sample being used for the dependent variable in question, then a number of sampling errors can be calculated using balanced repeated replication, in order to establish an approximate design effect, to replace the 1.05 above.

So multiple regression with dichotomous variables handles the problems of intercorrelations among predictors (if they are not too high) and non-linearities in their effects. It does *not* handle non-additivities. If the effect of one explanatory factor depends on the level of another, we are unlikely to find it by regression. If we wanted to check for a limited number of such effects, we could build them in, but the total possibilities are astronomical, particularly if one allows for higher-order interactions. The figure on the next page shows a dramatically different "effect" of income on home ownership depending on age and family size among the young, or living in central cities (with apartments but few private homes) among the old. There was also so much stepwise non-linearity, that the particular groups account for most of the potential variance. Separate dummies for each of the ten groups would work out well, if one knew in advance to define them that way.

In other words, multiple regression is not really multivariate analysis. It throws away the rich matrix of information, keeping only the simple correlations among pairs of variables. The assumption of additivity is very powerful statistically in reducing complexity, but it is commonly violated in the real world. Running separate regressions on subgroups of the sample is a cumbersome way to look for these non-additivities, but is a useful first step. Prior analysis with more flexible data searching programs may be more efficient.

Figure 1

Percentage Who Own Their Own Home, by Income Decile, for Four Subgroups

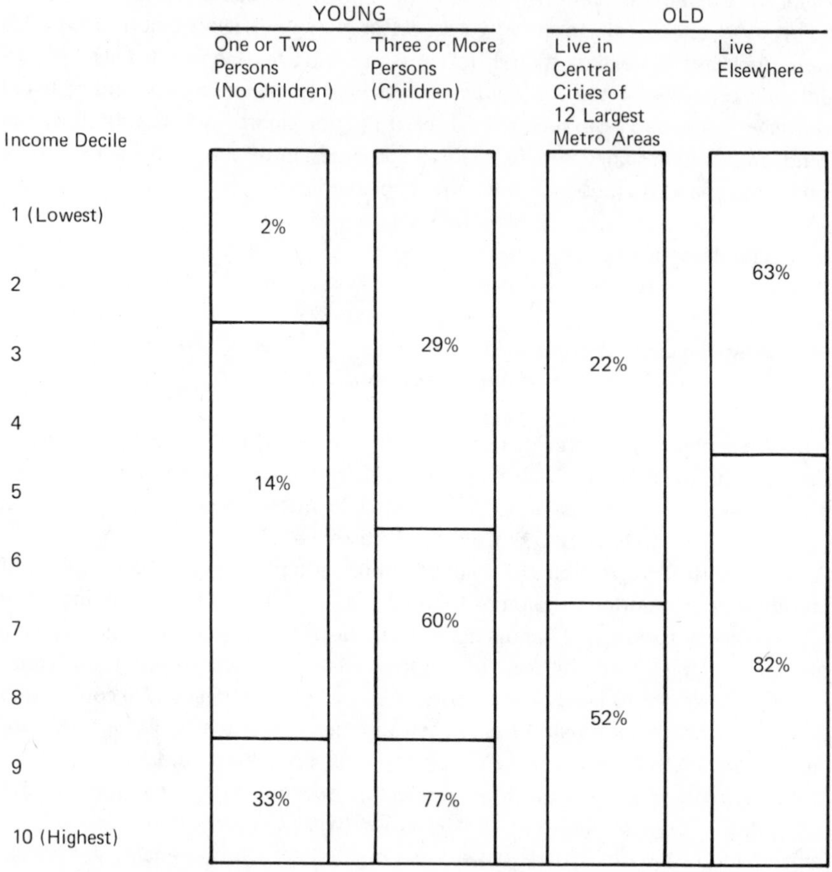

Source: George Katona et al 1967 Survey of Consumer Finances, Survey Research Center,
         The University of Michigan, Ann Arbor, Michigan, 1968.

As we shall see, these searching strategies deal with intercorrelation in a different way: sequentially. What influence is left to other predictors after one actually removes some of the effects of one predictor (by dividing the sample, and hence implicitly only looking at deviations from the means of groups defined according to that predictor)? Where prediction is more important than untangling the causal structure, such a sequential approach may make sense even for the intercorrelation problem. One may want to know the cheapest (in terms of variables) way to predict (optimal disaggregation), and if one variable incorporates the influence of another, the second can be omitted.

Stepwise Procedures: There are many ready-made multiple regression programs which have "stepwise" procedures, for adding variables according to some strategy. This does not make much sense with dummy variables, or even with numerical variables. If one merely wants to know how much each variable would add to the total explanation, if it were added after the others were already in, then one needs only the partial correlation coefficients, and these are easily derivable from the multiple regression coefficients and their standard errors.

It would seem preferable to eliminate variables on the basis of this statistic rather than on some earlier determination. Certainly one should not eliminate variables on the basis of their simple correlations with the dependent variable. There is always the possibility of spurious lack of correlation. Suppose for instance that both A and B really have effects on Y, but in opposite directions, and are highly positively correlated with each other. Then the simple correlations might be:

$$r_{AB} = +.70$$

$$r_{YA} = .00$$

$$r_{YB} = .00$$

Both variables would be eliminated by a researcher focusing on reducing the number of explanatory variables. It might have been better to combine A and B somehow, if it were really essential to cut the number of variables. With samples of 1000 or more, the whole need for restricting explanatory variables is considerably reduced anyway.

The same logic that led to the proposed "partial beta coefficient" measure of the power of a whole set of dummy variables reflecting a single characteristic, might be thought to lead to a method for measuring this marginal contribution more directly. Suppose one treated the coefficients of the subclasses as a new variable, assigning to each individual a value for that variable equal to the coefficient for the subgroup to which he belongs. One could then recalculate the regression using not r sets of characteristics with k_i subclasses each, but with r new "variables." The regression coefficients must all come out to be 1.000, but the standard errors provide a measure of the partial correlations using the following relationship:

$$R^2yx.wz = \frac{(b_{yx.wz}/\sigma_{b_{yx.wz}})^2}{(b_{yx.wz}/\sigma_{b_{yx.wz}})^2 + N - K - 1}$$

With:
N = cases
K = predictors
So:
N - K - 1 = Degrees of Freedom

    With simple numerical multiple regression, this formula provides a way of getting the partial correlations without actually recalculating the regression K times, each time leaving out one of the predictors. But with dummy variables, repeating the regression with the new scales, the formula exaggerates the marginal contribution of each, because it is equivalent to rerunning the regression leaving out one set of dummies, but *not allowing the coefficients for the others to change within the sets.* (The new regressions would only allow a uniform shift up or down in a whole set.)* In practice, however, these partial correlations using the new scales turn out to provide a closer approximation to the true partial correlations than the betas.

    When we have actually rerun the regressions leaving out each set of dichotomes separately, the reductions in the multiple correlation which are the true measure of the partial correlations, turn out to be closely approximated by the set of estimates from a single recomputation using the new scales, and fairly well approximated by the partial beta coefficient described earlier.

    Interaction Effects: It is important to be clear about the difference between interaction effects on the one hand, and intercorrelation among the predictors on the other. We simplify the discussion by making one of the two

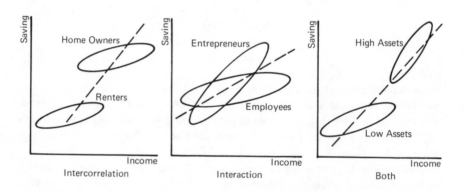

    explanatory variables a dichotomy. Where the two groups on that dichotomy have different levels but the same slope (intercorrelation only), the simple saving-income regression would be spuriously high, but a multiple regression would introduce a shift-variable for home-ownership and give the proper income effect.

    Where the two groups do not differ on income, but do have different income elasticities of saving (interaction effect) the simple saving-income regression is a compromise and adding a "entrepreneur or not" variable to make a

*We are indebted to W. H. Locke Anderson and Daniel Suits for this warning.

multiple regression would have no effect, self-employment appearing to have no influence. Only a covariance search, or a search for groups with different means (using income groups) would uncover the truth.

Where we have both intercorrelation and interaction effects, multiple correlation will measure neither of them properly. Only the more flexible search procedures will find the two effects, unless of course one suspects them and builds a linear model that incorporates them. But the number of possible interaction effects is almost unlimited and they are often higher order—for instance the people who do the most home-production (do-it-yourself work) are those who are home-owners *and* well educated *and* live in the country *and* have children *and* do not have any babies in diapers.[47]

With cardinal variables, interaction means that the relation between X1 and Y is different for different values of X2 (in which case the relation between X2 and Y will differ for different values of X1). Hence describing interaction effects is difficult since they can be stated either way, and it is impossible to know in most cases which way the causal influence goes (or whether it goes both ways).

In numerical regression, a common practice when interaction is suspected is to put in cross-product terms such as X1X2. This is a very restricted expression which may not fit the particular interaction that exists. It has the statistical disadvantage that it is highly correlated with both X1 and X2, and the substantive disadvantage that if there really is an interaction effect, then the meaning of the coefficients of X1 and of X2 is unclear, if not misleading. The interested reader would do well to read the literature on design of experiments and the testing for interaction effects in factorial designs.

The meaning of interaction effects is easier to see with categorical predictors, and a simple test for their presence easier to understand. Take a simple case without any interaction effects:

		X1		
		0	1	
X2	0	$1	$3	$2
	1	$3	$5	$4
		$2	$4	$3

Assume equal numbers exist in each of the four possible combinations, (no intercorrelation among the predictors), so that the overall average, and the X1 and X2 averages are simple to relate to the subcell averages. The test for interaction is whether one can predict the interior of the distribution from the marginals. For instance the X1 = 0, X2 = 0 combination is predicted by noting that for X1 the 0's are $1 below average, and for X2 the 0's are $1 below the average of $3, so $3 minus 1 minus 1 is $1. This is the technique for estimating data from missing cells in factorial designs in experimental work often called the "Yates missing plot technique."

Now suppose, in fact, that in addition to the separate effects of X1 and X2 there is an extra twelve dollars resulting from having both positive, then the inside of the table is not derivable from the marginals:

X1

		0	1	
	0	1	3	2
X2				
	1	3	17	10
		2	10	6

Using the marginals to make an additive prediction of the interior of the table would have the following expected values:

	0	1
0	-2	7
1	7	14

and the following residuals from expected (additive) values:

	0	1
0	+3	- 3
1	- 3	+3

which are systematic and large, revealing that there is an interaction effect.

Now a dummy variable regression using X1 and X2 would still leave a substantial unexplained variance of 36, from the last figure. Suppose we had put in a cross-product term X1X2 which had the value 1 when X1 and X2 were both 1? We could not also put in X1 and X2, since either one along with X1X2 would determine the other (perfect intercorrelation among the predictors). If we put in one of the main effects, say X1, and the corner term, we still do not uncover the original model. Indeed, there are three chances out of four of getting the wrong corner. Now one might say, why not put in dummy variables for three of the four subcells, that would reproduce all the information exactly, and one could tell everything? This is true, but in the real analysis of survey data, where we have many predictor classifications and many subclasses of each, to put in a dummy variable for each subcell (except one) of each K_1 by K_2 table for each pair of predictors, rapidly exhausts even the capacity of present day computers, to say nothing of the patience of the person examining the output. If one thinks of attempting to select a few cross-product terms, then the probability of getting the right one is clearly one in four for two dichotomies, and one in nine for two trichotomies, one in twenty-seven for three trichotomies, and one in a hundred for two decile codes!

Furthermore, we have been talking only about first-order interaction effects. There is no reason why the effect of X1 should not depend on the joint distribution of X1 and X3.

In other words, the initial specification of each interaction as a separate variable so that one can stick to a linear model and use regression, is extremely difficult because there are so many possible kinds of interactions. The cross product of two numerical variables assumes that a particular form of synergism occurs, but it is equally possible to have the reverse, that is, a very low value of Y only when both X1 and X2 are small, and this would require a different specification of the interaction variables.

Systematic Search for Interactions: In practice, careful investigators searching a body of data for interactions have traditionally done so by sequential steps, separating the sample according to some important main effect variable, and seeing whether the two parts responded differently to some third variable. This procedure has been formalized in a computer program, with the advantage that the search analysis, usually thought of as idiosyncratic and artistic, can be specified as a strategy and replicated on the same or a different set of data.[48]

A brief description of the computer program's algorithm may be useful: There is a dependent variable and a set of explanatory predictors (each a set of categories or subclassifications). For each explanatory classification, the computer examines the explanatory power achievable by using it to divide the data into two subgroups. Power means reduction in unexplained variance, indicated by the "between sum of squares" of a simple analysis of variance with one degree of freedom (the weighted sum of squares of the subgroup means minus the usual correction factor, $N(\bar{X}^2)$. For a predictor with K classes, maintained in some logical or optimal order, there are k-1 possible ways to use it to dichotomize the sample, and the one with the greatest explanatory power is retained, while the computer goes on to repeat the process with each of the other predictors. The best overall division is then the best of the best (best split on the best predictor). That split is actually carried out, and the process repeated separately on each of the two subgroups thus formed.

Whether a predictor is maintained in its original order, or reordered optimally depends on whether it has a natural order. If not, then the optimal ordering is one according to the mean of the dependent variable for that subgroup. Of course this vastly increases the possibilities for idiosyncratic splits and is generally to be avoided.

Hence at each stage, the group with the largest remaining internal sum of squares is examined and if possible, divided again. The sample is divided by sequential branching into a series of mutually exclusive subgroups like the roots of a tree, with no assumption of symmetry (universality of effect) nor of equal effects (interaction effects absent). The process can be stopped when there are a stated number of final groups, or when no group contains more than some small percentage of the original total sum of squares, or, best, when no further split could reduce the unexplained variance by as much as some small fraction of the original sum of squares, say .005.

Even if predictors are maintained in order, there are $\sum_{i=1}^{n} (K_i - 1)$ possible divisions at each split, with n predictors of k subclasses each, so that it is useless to talk about tests of significance. If a predictor is reordered, there are of course, k! possible orders, times k-1 ways of splitting into a dichotomy after the reordering. So the computer is selecting a branching diagram in many cases among as many as a trillion possibilities. What can one say about the stability properties of such results—the possibilities of getting a similar result from a different sample?

The best way to look at this question is to note that the selection of a particular split competes with splits on each of the other variables, and clearly the closer the nearest competitors in terms of their explanatory power, the more likely that in another sample one of the others would win out. So it is a matter of the difference between variances (or sums of squares) relative to the standard error of that difference. (There are also competitive splits on the same predictor using different groups on each side, but such differences are minor and unimportant compared with using an entirely different predictor.) The probability of getting a different split is then the sum of the probabilities of getting each of the various alternative splits. In practice most of the competitors are not within twenty percent of the same sum of squares, but a sum of small probabilities can still be important. And the probability of getting the same branching diagram is the *product* of the probabilities of getting the same split at each stage:

(1 - probabilities of getting a competitor at first split)
(1 - probabilities of getting a different split at second stage)
(1 - probabilities of getting a different split at third stage) etc.

Clearly this can be very small for a complex branching using many predictors, if there are many close competitors.

In a sense the greatest power of the program is its ability to eliminate a variable as not important. If the variable has no effect on the whole sample, nor on any of the various subgroups generated because they differ on the dependent variable, then it can be said with some confidence that that variable does not matter. Actually the output produces the means of the dependent variable for each subclass of each predictor, for each subgroup which it generates, so one can see how the apparent effect of a variable is altered, accentuated, or attenuated, as other variables are taken into account by dividing the sample by them.

It might seem inefficient to "take account" of a variable by making a single dichotomous split on it, but the process can easily proceed to make several splits in a row on the same predictor, and as we have seen, a relatively few divisions on a variable will have nearly as much variance-reducing power as its full detail.

Experience has shown that many interesting variables do not affect the whole population, but only some susceptible (or unconstrained) part of it. A measure of achievement motivation, for instance, proved to be powerfully related to hourly earnings of the individual, but only for middle aged college graduates, presumably the group most able to alter its own earnings.[49] Again, the utilization of medical and hospital services proved to be related to insurance coverage, but only for middle-aged women, the others presumably having less discretion (particularly the children).[50] Perhaps the most startling example of non-additivity is one where the forces keeping people from engaging in home production appeared to be substitutes for one another, only those for whom everything was favorable engaging extensively in the activity.[51] Another analysis revealed that the effect of family size on food expenditures was different in rural and urban areas.[52]

There are certain balanced offsetting interaction effects which this search program could still miss, as when young women and old men go to the hospital more often:

Percent Who Go to the Hospital

	Men	Women	Both Sexes
Young	2%	4%	3%
Old	4%	2%	3%
All ages	3%	3%	3%

Having no incentive to split the sample on either age or sex, the program would have no way to discover this interaction. A new option is being developed which looks ahead a step or two and would find such things. It actually makes the best split on each predictor, however useless it looks, and then makes one or two more splits, looking for the largest explained sum of squares for the two-split or three-split sequence.

One might also prefer a symmetric branching diagram, unless the loss in explanatory power was severe (defined as an option) since it is so much easier to discuss and understand things which affect more than one subgroup. Again an option is being developed which, if one of a pair of groups has been split on a certain predictor using certain categories, will split the other group the same way (down to the subclasses on each side) so long as the symmetry does not explain less of the variance by as much as X percent.

A Simple Test for Non-Additivity: There are an extremely large number of possible interaction effects, even with relatively few predictors. With modern computers it is also easy to determine not only the shapes of the main additive effects of many predictors, but the proportion of the variance such an additive "multivariate" analysis explains. What is being omitted are the details of the interior of the tables, since multiple regression uses only the marginals, and the interrelationships among the predictors, throwing away all information except that imbedded in the table of all possible simple correlations. Consider a case with three predictors, with four, five, and eight subclasses respectively. Regression will provide estimates for the seventeen coefficients (provided each set is constrained to a weighted mean of zero rather than making one of each set zero). But we actually have information on 4 x 5 x 8 or 160 subcells in a three-dimensioned table. We can consider the 160 subgroups in a one-way analysis of variance, and ask how much of the variance we could explain if we used those 160 subcell means to predict. The answer is simple, the explained variance is $\sum_{i=1}^{160} N_i \overline{Y}_i$ around zero, or in more usual form $\sum_{i=1}^{160} N_i \overline{Y}_i^2 - N\overline{Y}^2$ around the grand mean.

Or as a proportion of the variance around the mean, the 160 groups account for:

$$\frac{\sum N_i \overline{Y}_i^2 - N\overline{Y}^2}{\sum \overline{Y}^2 - N\overline{Y}^2} = \eta^2$$

This can be compared directly with the R^2 from the additive multiple regression to see whether the 160 subcells do better than the seventeen coefficients. If they do considerably better, then clearly the additivity assumptions are incorrect. One must be careful, however, to take account of the degrees of freedom used. F-ratios are more appropriate. After all, with sufficient subclassification one might end up with only one case per subcell, and could then predict the sample perfectly.

The F-ratio is the ratio of two variance estimates, one based on grouping by predictors, one on the variance within groups. For computational simplicity the following is most useful:

Multiple regression:

$$F = \frac{\dfrac{R^2}{K-1}}{\dfrac{(1-R^2)}{N-K}} = \frac{R^2}{1-R^2} \cdot \frac{N-K}{K-1}$$

where there are N cases and k predictors (including those constrained to zero)

A set of subcell means:

$$F = \frac{\dfrac{\Sigma N_i \overline{Y}_i^2 - N\overline{Y}^2}{K-1}}{\dfrac{(\Sigma Y_i^2 - N\overline{Y}^2) - (\Sigma N_i \overline{Y}_i^2 - N\overline{Y}^2)}{N-K}}$$

where there are N cases and k subcell means

each with K-1 and N-K degrees of freedom. The F-test here is not considered a significance test, to be compared with a null hypothesis, but a measure of importance or power of an analysis corrected for degrees of freedom used.

With a modern computer it should be very simple to impose a multiple sort and generate the weighted sum of squares of the subgroup means (or the equivalent $\dfrac{(\Sigma Y_i)^2}{n_i}$). All that is needed in addition is the total sum of squares, which is available from any of the additive regressions that may have been computed.

One Dominant Variable: A common problem arises when there is one variable which is of overwhelming importance, either because of its power, or because it is of substantive importance. In economic studies, it is usually income or education which fits this description, particularly income because the economic analyst or policymaker is primarily interested in the effects of income (or income elasticities). In studies of change, growth, or development, the initial state may be such a variable. The problem then is whether the relationship with this dominant variable is the same for all subgroups in the sample.

The traditional procedure in such a case is the analysis of covariance. Simply put, the analsyis of covariance fits a simple regression of the dependent variable against the dominant or control variable, separately for each of a set of subgroups of the sample, and partitions the variance into that accounted for by differences in the levels of the regression lines (subgroup means), that accounted for by differences in their slopes, and the remaining unexplained deviations from the regression lines. But in practice, one may want to *search* for which subgroups would be most useful in having the largest differences in regression slopes, for instance, which subgroups had the greatest differences in income elasticities of expenditure on cars.

For any single group, we have a total sum of squares which represents errors of prediction if one knows nothing. If one knows the grand mean, and predicts that for each case, the errors squared are then what is usually called the variance, or sum of squares around the mean:

Total sum of squares $\quad\quad\quad\quad\quad\quad \Sigma Y^2$

Sum of squares around the mean $\quad\quad \Sigma(Y - \overline{Y})^2 = \Sigma Y_i^2 - N\overline{Y}^2$

Reduction in error sum of squares
from knowing the mean: $\quad\quad\quad\quad N\overline{Y}^2 \equiv \dfrac{(\Sigma Y)^2}{N}$

If one adds information about the value of X for each case, and about the regression of Y on X, the error is reduced by a *fraction of the total sum of squares around the mean* equal to r^2. In more convenient computational form, the remaining error sum of squares knowing the regression x is:

$$[1 - r^2]\,[\Sigma Y_i^2 - N\overline{Y}^2] = \left[1 - \frac{\left(\Sigma XY - \frac{\Sigma X\,\Sigma Y}{N}\right)^2}{(\Sigma X^2 - N\overline{X}^2)\,(\Sigma Y^2 - N\overline{Y}^2)}\right][\Sigma Y^2 - N\overline{Y}^2]$$

and the gain, or explained sum of squares from knowing the regression, is:

$$r^2(\Sigma Y_i^2 - N\overline{Y}^2) = \frac{\left(\Sigma XY - \frac{\Sigma X\,\Sigma Y}{N}\right)^2}{(\Sigma X^2 - N\overline{X}^2)\,(\Sigma Y^2 - N\overline{Y}^2)} \cdot (\Sigma Y^2 - N\overline{Y}^2) = \frac{\left(\Sigma XY - \frac{\Sigma X\,\Sigma Y}{N}\right)^2}{\Sigma X^2 - N\overline{X}^2}$$

As a next step, having explained what we can knowing the mean of Y, its relationship with X, and the values of X, we break the sample into two groups, with different means, and different regressions on X. The gain in explanatory power (reduction in unexplained sum of squares) is in two parts: a gain from using two subcell means instead of one grand mean, and the gain from using two different regression *slopes* on X instead of one.

The error variance using two means instead of one is:

$$\Sigma Y_1^2 - N_1\overline{Y}_1^2 + \Sigma Y_2^2 - N_2 Y_2^2 \text{ but } \Sigma Y_1^2 - \Sigma Y_1^2 - \Sigma Y_2^2 = \Sigma Y^2$$

so the error is less than with one overall mean by:

(a) $\qquad N_1\overline{Y}_1^2 \quad + \quad N_2\overline{Y}_2^2 \quad - \quad N\overline{Y}^2$

Expl. by	Expl. by	Expl. by
Mean of	Mean of	Grand
Group 1	Group 2	Mean

The error variance using two subgroup regressions instead of one overall regression is: $[1 - r_1^2][\Sigma Y_1^2 - N_1\overline{Y}^2] + [1 - r_2^2][\Sigma Y_2^2 - N_2\overline{Y}_2^2]$

which is a gain of:

(b)
$$\frac{\left[\Sigma X_1 Y_1 - \dfrac{\Sigma X_1 \, \Sigma Y_1}{N_1}\right]^2}{\Sigma X_1^2 - N_1\overline{X}_1^2} + \frac{\left[\Sigma X_2 Y_2 - \dfrac{\Sigma X_2 \, \Sigma Y_2}{N_2}\right]^2}{\Sigma X_2^2 - N_2\overline{X}_2^2} - \frac{\left[\Sigma XY - \dfrac{\Sigma X \, \Sigma Y}{N}\right]^2}{\Sigma X_2 - N\overline{X}^2}$$

Explained by	Explained by	Explained by
Regression of	Regression	Overall Regression
Group 1	of Group 2	Before Splitting
		Into Two Groups

The thing to keep in mind is that in discussions of explanation by regression, it is the sum of squares *around the mean* that is being decomposed into an explained and unexplained part indicated by r^2 and 1-r^2. Hence the gain in going from one group to two is easily decomposible into a gain from using two means instead of one, and a gain from running regressions of two different slopes through those two different means, on the other. In comparing various pairs as candidates for splitting a sample, the third terms in expression (a) and (b) are constant over all possible splits and can be ignored. One seeks only for the division which makes the first two terms as large as possible.

The original computer search program maximized (a) at each split. It is easily possible to maximize (b) instead, or to maximize (a) plus (b).

If X is income, and Y is some expenditure (in logs if one likes to talk of elasticities), then splitting the sample to maximize (b) is a search for groups with the greatest differences in their responses to income, perhaps to find the optimal disaggregation. In that case one would argue that differences in level (means) between subgroups do not matter, only differences in their responsiveness to income.

On the other hand, there may be situations where one wants to locate groups which differ, whether by level (of Y) or slope (relationship to X), and that is also possible.

This modern variant of the analysis of covariance is much more flexible and makes use of the computer's capacity to carry out a programmed routine of investigative strategy tirelessly, and in a way which can be repeated on different data, or on the same data to check for errors or instabilities. Science seems likely to be best served by analysis strategies which are reproducible, just as is the rest of the research design.

The use of covariance analysis in the case of income elasticities is one approach to a problem which economists have struggled with for some time. Its most dramatic expression arose when it became obvious that income elasticities of total consumption expenditures calculated from cross-section data were substantially lower than those estimated from time series data, and always underestimated the growth of consumption over time as income increased. As we shall see below, one popular explanation advanced by Friedman, the "permanent income" hypothesis, essentially argued that there were errors in the measurement of income, the explanatory variable, which would have led to a downward bias in the regression slope. Permanent income, free from those short-run errors, would provide a better estimate of the true income elasticity of consumption. We shall return to this but it may be worth noting here that if the purpose is to predict the expenditure responses to changes in income, then a search for subgroups with differential responses does double duty—it allows one to find different responses according to conditions which may be token differences in permanent income, but it also allows one to find real differences in people's propensity to spend, for people in different situations. Prediction would then be improved by optimal disaggregation, asking to whom the income increases were going where it mattered.

In deciding on the best division of a sample or subsample, using differences in slopes only, a new problem arises, however. If the means of X and/or Y differ, and one is combining some of the k subclasses on a predictor into one group and the rest into another, it is possible for uniform slopes of several subgroups to be hidden by differences in their means. In the figures below, in both cases group B should certainly be isolated from the other two, yet the *pooled* slope through the clusters of A and C combined would not differ much from the slope for B alone, and the pooled slope criterion might easily segregate either A or C from the other two groups. Hence the computer program now being developed and

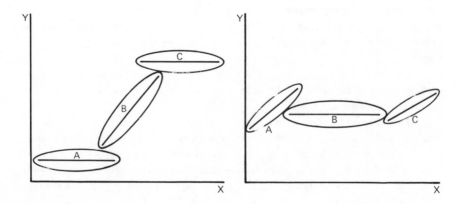

tested uses *weighted average* slopes as a criterion if one wants to focus on slopes, not full regressions.

The use of weighted average slopes for combinations of subgroups increases the possibility of idiosyncratic findings, however, since small subgroups can have their regression slopes dominated by a few cases. Hence we are finding that the search for different slopes must usually maintain the order of the subclasses of the predictors (allowing only the k-1 possible divisions along that ordering), and should also insist on a rather large minimum group size.

Special Problems in Estimating Income Elasticities: There has been more interest among economists in using sample surveys to estimate the effect of income on consumer behavior than the effect of any other independent variable. As a result of the close attention paid to income elasticities and related measures, the difficulties in estimating the theoretically relevant measures from survey data have been thoroughly discussed in the literature.

We may consider first the simple situation in which only two variables are involved, income and a measure of expenditures. From a theoretical point of view the simplest formulation is one in which both variables are in logarithmic form. The regression coefficient for income is then itself the income elasticity. This formulation assumes constant elasticity over the full range of income. It is doubtful whether this assumption can be defended in general—there are both theoretical and empirical objections—but it may be appropriate for some categories of expenditure.[53] Prais and Houthakker, after careful consideration, prefer a semi-log formulation for foodstuffs. It is also common to use income without a log transformation but to allow for curvilinearity in one of the manners discussed above.

When elasticity is permitted to vary, it is sometimes estimated at the mean, as a method of compressing the relationship of income to the dependent variable in a single statistic. There are theoretically any number of curves with the same slope at the mean, however, and it can be argued that the best procedure is simply to estimate and present the equation for the entire curve. It is also possible, of course, to calculate the elasticity at several points, depending on what one needs to know for the problem at hand. When the effect of the income is approximated by a step function, the calculation of point elasticity obviously requires curve fitting as an intermediate step.

The more fundamental problems in estimating income effects, however, concern the isolation of the effect of income from the effect of other variables. In the first place, the measurement of the effect of income on consumption requires the measurement of the effects of household size on consumption. This problem was carefully considered by Prais and Houthakker in the early 1950's by which time there was already a literature on the subject, and they were led to the development of unit-consumer scales. The objective was to adjust for the effect of household composition so that income effects could be isolated.[54]

An alternative to the use of equivalent adult scales is the separate analysis of families with different composition. For example, one might have a separate equation for married couples with one child, and estimate the effect of income on the consumption of some commodity for that segment of the population only.[55]

More recently attention has been drawn to the problems of isolating the effect of income from that of variables other than household composition. In particular, it is difficult to determine how to treat variables which may be correlated with "permanent" income. The problems are posed by the contention of Friedman that measured income is not a satisfactory approximation of the theoretically relevant income, nor, for that matter, is measured consumption satisfactory. The relevant income variable, he urges, is "permanent" income. Permanent income, empirically, is correlated with such variables as age and education. The analyst, therefore, is in an awkward position. If he chooses to think of age and education as essentially measures of tastes, or measures of factors which cause difference in tastes, then he should try to hold them constant since he would like to examine the effect of income for constant tastes. But if he thinks of such variables as related to permanent income he should not hold them constant. He must permit permanent income to vary if he wishes to measure its effect on consumption. If he thinks of these variables partly in the one way and partly in the other, he is faced with the problem of how to partial out their effects.[56]

One approach to the problem would seem to be to estimate permanent income directly. If income considerations other than those relating to current assets and current income influence how that income is allocated by consumers, logically these considerations must be in the nature of expectations. We may proceed by measuring these expectations and introducing them explicitly into the analysis. Then we may assert that any effect of, say, education, remaining after income expectations have been taken into account can be interpreted as the effect of education on tastes. This assertion, of course, is defensible in proportion to our ability to measure both education and the relevant expectations correctly. As an empirical fact, however, people's notions about their own future incomes are quite vague, and questions dealing with it elicit a large proportion of "don't know" answers. At any rate, if we are trying to measure a man's long-run economic status, expectations about future family obligations may be both more real and more powerful differentiators than differential income expectations.

Another possible strategy is to avoid asking questions about expectations and seek instead to approximate "permanent" income by using average measured income for several years. We may also prefer such an average measure for the entirely different reason that we hope the errors in our estimates of income will cancel out in the averaging process. This dual interpretation suggests again the close parallel between Friedman's analysis and the errors-in-variables problem discussed above.

In the same year that Friedman published *A Theory of the Consumption Function,* 1957, an article by Kuh and Meyer also analyzed the use of income coefficients from cross-section studies.[57] They were concerned in part with the types of consideration mentioned above, such as the problem of choice of functional form for the estimating equations. They also considered systematically the problems which arise in one important use of income coefficient from surveys, their inclusion in composite equations which combine cross-section with aggregate data.

The reasons for the development of this type of combined equation may be simply stated. In the analysis of consumer expenditure time series, estimates of price elasticity have been reasonably successful. Prices do vary over time; some prices vary considerably. It is more difficult, however, to estimate income coefficients from time series. Aggregate income changes slowly, and in a manner which may be hard to isolate from the effects of trends in other variables, such as trends in tastes, and is itself affected by changes in consumption. Income varies widely among families at a given point in time, however; while prices at any one time are likely to be the same for people at all incomes. Investigators have sought to use that variation to estimate income coefficients. Kuh and Meyer note, however, that the cross-section estimates of income elasticities of saving, usually have been lower than those obtained from time series. (This observation, of course, parallels Friedman's about the consumption function.)

Kuh and Meyer raise the question of whether people have adjusted their expenditure behavior to their income. There may be rigidities in spending behavior which lead to lags in adjustment, so that the relation between income and consumption may be a short run one for aggregate data but a long run for cross-section data.

We must conclude that satisfactory measurement of income elasticities from cross-section data requires more than simple bivariate calculations relating annual income and annual expenditures. We must also expect that similar close attention to other variables may reveal similar complications. It is quite possible that the imaginative application of the covariance search process described above particularly if used with panel data on changes in income and on spending will at least indicate where the differences are, from which a more realistic theory can be developed.

Analysis of Repeated Surveys: As the period for which sample surveys are available lengthens, there is increasing interest in the potentialities of analysing data from repeated surveys. For simple descriptive statistics it is possible to prepare measures of trend. One may examine, for example, the trend in the percentage of the population with income over a fixed level. Such comparisons require strict comparability of the survey procedures over time. Subtle differences in the questions asked, the method of sample, interviewer training, and the like, may influence the trends especially over periods of many years. It is also necessary to take into account changes in price levels. A twenty-year trend in median income, for example, obviously must take into account changing prices. And over long periods there are also changes in the demographic composition of households, including the average number of people per unit—such as the secular decline in the proportion of families containing two or more spending units. Careful comparisons must take these shifts into account.

One might think that the best way would be to measure all the variables in relation to the average levels that current year, but even aside from problems of calculating deciles of categorical items, this procedure would wipe out both changes in prices and changes in real incomes and expenditures. On the other hand, adjustments for price alone must face the fact that our ability to measure prices and price changes, particularly for components of expenditure, is not very good. The notion of calculating each year a measure of "real expenditure on cars" is likely to remain just an idea.

Repeated surveys allow somewhat better interpretation of age-related differences in behavior. If younger people in one survey are more receptive to the use of credit, is this because they are younger, or because they represent a new generation with new ideas which they will still hold when they are older; or do they represent a period of history in which they grew up so that their generation may be unique?

We can, with repeated surveys, sort out some of this, but not all. Suppose, for instance, that ten years later, the forty-five year olds, who were thirty-five ten years ago and favorable to installment credit, are now opposed to it. And suppose that the new group of thirty-five year olds are favorable to the use of credit. Then one might decide that it was age that made the difference. The age group, or generation, or cohort to use the demographer's word, did not have a stable attitude toward credit.

One should not count too much on the analysis of cohorts or generations in repeated surveys, because there are *three* hypotheses not two, and the three variables they imply are tightly interrelated: Is it the man's actual chronological age, his generation (when he was born), or the particular year of history that explains his attitude or behavior? One cannot sort out the relative influence of these three even with multiple regression, because any one of them is a strict linear function of the other two:

Age = Present year of history—Year born.

Only if one can assume that one of the three does not matter, is it possible using repeated survey data to separate the influences of the other two.

There has also been increasing interest in the comparison of relationship estimated at different dates. Miner has compared regression equations on consumer debt computed from repeated surveys.[58] Miner notes that there are three possible types of change in such an analysis: changes in the constant term in the regression equation, changes in the regression coefficients, and changes in the means of the predictors.

Changes in the *coefficients* reflect basic changes in behavior patterns. Multiplied times the original mean values of the explanatory variables, they provide an estimate of the aggregate or mean change that would have taken place if nothing but behavior patterns had changed.

Changes in the *means* of the predictors reflect changes in the situations people face, and multiplied by the original behavioral coefficients, provide an estimate of the overall change that would have taken place had nothing changed but the conditions people faced.

Residual changes in the grand mean, that is change in the mean minus the two estimates of changes accounted for by changes in behavior relations or in the situations measured, reflect changes unaccounted for in the analysis, often casually called "changes in taste." They are very difficult to interpret whether between years or between countries or between subgroups analyzed this way, because there are many hypotheses and only one degree of freedom.

Where dummy variables are used, the same analysis is possible, except that it is the proportions in subclasses which change rather than means of predictive variables, i.e., one deals with changing proportions in each income class rather than change in mean income. It is important, however, to have the data in the form suggested earlier, with coefficients for each subclass of each predictor, their weighted mean being zero, and the constant term being the overall mean. Otherwise the constant term has little meaning, being a composite of the means of the groups whose coefficients were forced to zero plus the grand mean; and changes in the other coefficients might well reflect not changes in behavior of that group, but in the behavior of the omitted group.

Such multivariate analysis of what accounts for overall differences in some dependent variable can be done not only with surveys at different points in time, but also with surveys in different countries, asking whether overall differences can be accounted for by differences in, say income or education levels, or differences in the effect of income or education on behavior, or are left to some other more global explanation (or to unmeasured variables). Similarly, one can analyze subgroups from a single survey in the same manner.

With expenditure analysis, one might want to regard the unexplained changes in the overall average as reflecting changes in the supply side of the market, including changes in price. But such changes might well affect different groups differently, so the problem would seem to require a more complete model.[59]

There is, of course, always the problem whether all the variables have been measured in the same way in successive surveys, and whether shifts in the other details of procedure have not introduced spurious changes. Strict probability sampling fully carried out is clearly essential. One study went back to the same geographic grids but allowed the interviewers to select every other dwelling "at random." The interviewers on the second wave were college students, and they interviewed younger, better educated people with larger farms, introducing all sorts of spurious change.

Where the repeated surveys use the same basic sample down to the rather small areas, added precision is provided for estimates of change even without re-interviews, because the correlation between first interview and second in demographic characteristics, etc. is higher than chance, and the negative covariance term in the formula for sampling error of the difference between two means (or two percentages) is larger, and so the sampling error is smaller than with two completely different random samples.

It is also possible to develop some semi-aggregated time series from a series of repeated surveys. One defines subgroups on characteristics that do not change much, and treats the mean income, saving, etc. of these subgroups as trends over time for the whole subgroups represented. The data are then subjected to econometric analysis like any set of time series. (Zellner forthcoming)

In a more general sense, analysis is possible on a within-year, between-year basis, where each variable is expressed as deviation of its actual value from its mean for all families that year, plus the overall deviation of the average that year for all families, from the average over all. By thus removing shifts attributable to the year, and to the individual family, what is left is presumably the revelation of short-run dynamic influences.[60]

Analysis of Reinterviews and Panels: There has been increasing recognition that reinterviews have important advantages for the analyst. The uses of reinterviews are diverse, and we shall keep clearly in mind that reinterviews may be undertaken for quite different purposes, and that it may be necessary to make a choice as to how a particular set of reinterview data is to be interpreted. If reinterviews are used primarily as a means of data collection, as in the work of Neter and Waksberg, the first interview may be used for purposes of "bounding" time intervals. Data from that first interview concerning the variable for which bounding is necessary cannot be used in analysis. Data from that interview on other variables, of course, may be used. It will be recalled that reinterviews may also be undertaken for purposes of sampling, such as reducing the sampling error of estimates of changes from repeated surveys. (The sampling error of a mean difference is about forty percent smaller than the sampling error of the difference between two means, though the gain over the surveys using the same sample structure is not that large.) Any gains in analytic potential which may result will be essentially by-products.

Reinterviews also may be undertaken primarily for the purpose of increasing analytic potential. The potential gains are of two basic types. First, the use of reinterviews makes it possible to focus attention on changes over time, and thereby to abstract from the stable characteristics of a unit. The resulting simplification may be advantageous. For example, Houthakker and Haldi were interested in the investment of families in automobiles. They set up an equation in which gross investment in a year is a function of income, initial stock, family characteristics, and an error term:

$$G_j = a + b\,Y_j + c\,S_j + d\,F_j + W_j$$

Where G_j = gross investment (for the j-th family)

Y_j = income

S_j = stock of cars (valued in dollars)

F_j = characteristics of the family

W_j = error.

They proceeded by setting up two such equations, one for each of the years under consideration, and subtracting the two. The F_j terms drop out.[61]

This method depends upon the assumption that the effects of the F_j terms, i.e., the family characteristics, are additive. If in fact there are interactions between these terms and the effects of income or stocks, the model is inappropriate. Whether there are such interactions is a question which must be considered for each model separately. But it seems unlikely that there will be important interactions. In principle one could include in such a model any such interactions, and any remaining stable characteristics of the family would still drop out.

It is possible that there may be *changes* over time even in the F_j, which will have additive effects. If such changes do occur, they will be reflected in changes in the constant term. The factors which drop out might be related to the location of the place of residence of a family for example. Over a period of two or three years, it seems reasonable to suppose that the characteristics of a location will not change. People who live in Manhattan will continue to be less likely to own cars than those who live in Connecticut. It is also quite reasonable that some people will continue to have a weakness for cars and allocate their income accordingly, while others are comparatively uninterested. Whether the income elasticity of the demand for cars is the same for these two groups seems more open to question.

The second basic way in which reinterviews may increase analytic potential is by their contribution to the problem of sorting out the sequence of causation. Several possible patterns may be used in analysis. In one pattern, conditions as measured in interview (1) are viewed as causes of one or more events in period (A) which is the period between interview (1) and interview (2). Interview (2) is needed only to measure the dependent variable. It may be brief. For example, in a study of the geographic mobility of labor, a major dependent variable was a measure of migration between an initial personal interview and a reinterview about a year later by telephone. The second interview was devoted essentially to ascertaining one fact, whether or not the family had migrated. Note that the analysis is based on two assumptions: (1) that the important causes of migration can be measured in advance, on the average, six months in advance. Causes that may operate close to the date of the move are ignored; (2) that the important causes can be measured at a single date. This type of analysis can be used either when the dependent variable is a discrete event, like moving to a new home, or a series of events, like saving money. Finally, note that any variable measured at interview (1) meets one logical requirement needed to qualify as a cause of events in period (A), the requirement of priority in time.

In the second two time periods are considered, (A) and (B). Events in (A) are measured in interview (1); events in (B), in interview (2). For example, Houthakker and Haldi examined the effect of income in (A) on investment in cars in (A), and the effect of income in (B) on the purchase of cars in (B). They found it useful, as noted above, to subtract the two equations to form a single equation involving the difference in value of the variables. The analysis relates changes in the variables.

This type of analysis assumes that the causes and effects are contemporaneous—e.g. income in a period influences outlay in that period. It is also possible to introduce stocks at the beginning of the period, relying on memory data. A variant on the scheme would measure the stocks in a preliminary interview at the start of the period (A). Then initial conditions plus contemporaneous events determine the dependent variable.

Wherever *change* in initial conditions (including attitudes and expectations), is supposed to cause *change* in subsequent behavior (a flow) then a third pattern involving three interviews is essential; (1) and (2) measuring initial conditions, and (2) and (3) measuring behavior (e.g., expenditures). It may be that the model believed to be relevant is one in which: (1) the crucial predictor or predictors are believed to operate with lags; and (2) the change in the value of the predictor is believed crucial. For example, a family which has experienced a decline in income may make a delayed adjustment. Then income may be measured for periods (A) and (B), and consumption for (B) and (C). The change in income from (A) to (B) may predict a change in consumption between (B) and (C). Then initial conditions plus events in the preceding period determine the dependent variable. This type of analysis obviously will be more or less revealing depending on the correctness of the assumptions as to what are the appropriate lengths of time periods and what are the appropriate lags. Periods often used are six months or a year, but either shorter or longer periods deserve consideration.

These three patterns, of course, by no means exhaust the possibilities. More complex schemes can be developed. This discussion is also incomplete in that it stresses only initial causes. An additional field for analysis is the causes of continuation of behavior, once initiated. It is widely believed that there are "ratchets" in consumer behavior—certain patterns of behavior, once established, tend to persist. (Compare, for example, the data on the effect of an initial experience on the propensity to travel by air.) We may expect increasing elaboration of analysis based on reinterviews.

Cagan has approached these problems in a different manner, relying on data from a single survey only.[62] His method is to use measures of wealth at time of the interview to estimate the average savings-income ratio in the past. The method requires an estimate of the relevant length of period, an estimate of the current value of net worth and an estimate of variations over time in the major independent variables, notably, in income. It also requires some method of dealing with changes in the price level and the associated capital gains (or losses). The method will tend to average out the effects of variables which fluctuate in the short run. Other factors which operate through their effect on the relevant lengths of period can also be omitted from explicit consideration. For example, some factors may operate through their influences on the data at which the family becomes the owner of its home. The essential idea implicit in the method is that careful consideration of the position of a family at a given point in time should be revealing as to the behavior of the family up to that date. In principle such information is available both to analyze the past and to predict the future. Hence, we may consider this method as a possible elaboration of the first pattern above.

In general before going to the vast expense and difficulty of reinterviews and panels, one should ask whether more extensive questioning in a single survey about events in the past would not produce as good a set of dated data for dynamic analysis. Substantial possibilities would seem to exist in studying the dynamics of changes in people's residences, and perhaps their cars, relying on their memories of past events.

It is quite possible for patterns of association found in static cross-sections to be the reverse of dynamic relations. For instance, various forms of economizing behavior are associated with lower than average incomes, presumably because people feel forced to adopt them. But over time, it may well be that those who do economize end up with increased incomes, a positive relation between an initial activity and the change. Or those who economize more than others in similar circumstances may end up with bigger income increases.

All this serves to dramatize another aspect of panels: some of the data are situations at time of interview: attitudes, rates of flow, but others are cumulative flows measured over a past period, such as last year's income and expenditure on durable goods. If one then has a hypothesis that changes in initial attitudes lead to changes in subsequent expenditures, we have already noted that it takes three interviews with the same people to provide the data to test this. The first two waves provide the initial stock and attitude data at the beginning of two years, and the second and third wave provide the after-the-period reports on actual behavior during the two years. A further difficulty with pursuing such dynamic analysis is the periodicity and lumpiness of many consumer decisions by which a powerful negative autocorrelation may be piled on top of a spurious positive cross-section correlation (through association of all variables with stage of the family life cycle), both of which make it difficult to find the dynamic correlation one seeks to measure.

When the data are for two different points in time for the same individuals, it is possible to convert an equation explaining the rate of change in some variable X_1 as a function of X_1 and X_2 to one which regresses its value at the second point in time on its value at the first point, and the value of other explanatory variables at that time. And the coefficients of such an equation can be related to the relationship between the dependent variable and the other explanatory variable in a static cross-section, if one is willing to assume that all the causal processes have resulted in an equilibrium state.[63]

Furthermore, given the regression of a dependent variable at the second time point on its value and the value of other variables at an earlier time point, if one takes a third wave of interviews, and uses only the third and first time points, then the mathematical model posits a difference between these coefficients and those using the time interval half as long. If there is nothing but measurement error, however, then the coefficients will be identical for the two time periods. In other words, one can estimate how much of the previously estimated dynamic relationship was pure measurement error and how much was a genuine dynamic relationship. Of course one must assume the basic relations have not changed, but at a minimum, this mathematical model suggests the importance of a third measurement on the same people in any study of change.

One way to deal with autocorrelation in panel studies is to use covariance analysis, treating the initial state or previous year's flow as the X variable, and searching for differences among subgroups in the regression slopes (rates of change). If, instead, one uses the change directly as a dependent variable, there will be a spurious negative correlation with the initial state if it is used as one of the explanatory variables:

$$(Y1 - Yo) = a + bYo + \ldots$$

or
$$Y1/Yo = a + bYo + \ldots$$

A similar problem arises with explanatory variables where one may want both the level and the rate of change in, say, income. The easiest way here is to generate two orthogonal (uncorrelated) variables (X1 + X2) and (X1 - X2) the first representing the level and the second the change. The same method can be used with two such highly correlated variables as the age of the head and wife. The mean and the difference make two better variables than the head's age and the difference, since the latter two are correlated.

The first step in looking at panel data would seem to be to generate as many first differences as possible, and find how they are related to one another. But ultimately some theoretical model is needed, such as the following, from a study of the dynamics of income change:

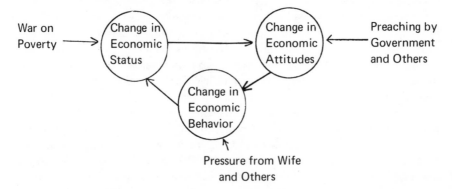

Such a working model allows flexibility and experimentation in the measurement of the major variables, and even if one can never really prove which way the causation runs, enough focus is put on how to look at the data, so that the model is helpful.

"Experiments" Natural and Real: The possibilities of experimenting with human populations are limited. Yet events occur spontaneously, and it may be possible for an investigator to obtain useful information from them as if he had instigated them. There are two types of events which have been studied, those that affect an entire population, and those that affect a part only of it. Study of the former requires measurement of the situation before and after the event, the investigator seeking to isolate the impact of the event from the consequences of any other forces which may have been operating. When the event affects only part of the population, there is the additional possibility of using the remainder as a control group.

There are three difficulties associated with the use of "natural experiments": (1) The "event" itself may not be equivalent to an experimental manipulation of the variables of theoretical interest. (2) Other forces may be operating whose consequences may be difficult to separate from those of the "event." (3) When the "event" affects only part of the population those affected may differ systematically in some important respect from those who are not affected. It may then be difficult or impossible to distinguish between the consequences of the event and the consequences of the factors which select those who experience it.

An example of an event which affected an entire population was the break in prices in the commodity markets which took place in the first week of February 1948. This event took place about the middle of the interviewing period on the 1948 Survey of Consumer Finances. The study had not been planned to include two halves which were random cross-sections, but an additional three hundred interviews, taken on short notice after the price break, were so distributed that the two halves were roughly comparable. It was possible, therefore, to compare the attitudes and expectations of consumers before and after the event. As would be expected, price expectations did shift. The percentage expecting prices to rise fell from fifty percent to fifteen percent. It turned out that the same proportions as before expected their own income to rise and expected good times to prevail.[64]

An example of an event which had a selective impact was the windfall of a refund or dividend on National Life Insurance policies of veterans. (This windfall resulted from unexpectedly low mortality experience.) The event was analyzed by Ronald Bodkin using data from the 1950 Consumer Expenditure Survey of the Bureau of Labor Statistics.[65] Bodkin was able to use data from this survey on income, expenditure, and saving to estimate the marginal propensity to consume out of the windfall. His conclusion was that this marginal propensity was about the same as that for all income—contrary to what might have been expected on the basis of Friedman's theories of consumer behavior.

Friedman took two of the logically possible positions to refute the conclusion. He argued that a hidden factor was at work in selecting those who received the windfall. Specifically, he argued that only those who kept up their policy after World War II received the dividend and whether the policy were kept up might well vary systematically depending on the economic position of the veteran—specifically, on his permanent income. Second, he argued that the dollar amount of the dividend as measured was not a satisfactory measure of the windfall since in later years annual dividends continued (even though these later dividends were not accumulative as was the first large payment). We are not here concerned with the force of these arguments; we note only that they are typical of the objections likely to be made to "natural experiments"—i.e. that they are "confounded."

The issue is not whether the groups exposed and not exposed to something differ as to their composition, age, etc., but whether they differ systematically according to the variable to be explained, and for some extraneous reason. For instance, two studies of the impact of private pensions (added to Social Security) on saving, were able to show an effect (the reverse of the economist's hypothesis) by arguing that individuals had no choice about whether they were included in such a plan, and had not had time to move to a job which suited their personal preferences about retirement provisions—the plans mostly being put in over a short period unilaterally or by union negotiations.[66] Differences in the earnings levels, ages, etc. of individuals could be taken care of by multiple regression or other multivariate analysis, leaving the effects of residual differences in saving associated with having or not having a private pension plan to be interpreted as the effects of plan or no plan.

As we indicated earlier in the chapter on design, there have been very few purposeful experiments designed to determine the effects of changes in explanatory variables. It is difficult to change things, and there are always other things not subject to control, so the result is not a controlled experiment but a semi-controlled one. Whether the statistical analysis can remove the effects of variations in the uncontrolled factors in order to see clearly the effects of those being manipulated, is always in doubt. But the analysis problem is clear. One has a whole set of explanatory variables, some with more than natural variation because of sampling to achieve that, or because of actual manipulation of the environment, and one desires to estimate the effects of these variables more precisely than in a representative sample in its natural situation, where the variables of concern may not vary much, or may vary too systematically with other things.

What must always be kept in mind in ranking the importance of different explanatory variables, is that variables which dominate the explanation of cross-section differences in behavior, may cancel out in the aggregates, or not move over time at all, and contribute very little to economic analysis which is essentially dynamic.[67]

Grouping as a Method of Dealing with Badly Distributed Dependent Variables: Particularly with expenditure data, we frequently have a large number of zeros, people who spent nothing during the period. This is true even for periods as long as a year, with durable goods. One way to average over a longer period of time, is to average over a group of people, on the argument that a random group of a particular type of family will contain those who just bought before the period started, those who bought during the period, etc., and that the proportion who bought measured the probability appropriate to the group, and the mean expenditure for all, the expected value. Indeed, with dichotomous dependent variables, only grouping converts to a proportion which can have a reasonable distribution for analysis.

The difficulty, of course, is that no matter how the groups are created, they average out certain variability which may be desired left in. If one averaged out much of the variability in family size, or age, or some other explanatory variable, then one reduces the possibility of finding the true effect of that variable, and increases the likelihood of erroneously concluding that it is not as important as some other variables.

Ideally one would want to group according to every explanatory variable jointly so that all their variance would be preserved. Of course one should not group by the dependent variable; this reduces the variation between groups of other unknown variables and raises the correlation and the regression slopes deceptively. Grouping on the explanatory variables can also reduce errors of measurement in them, and hence increase the regression coefficients.[68]

Since it is usually impossible to group on all the variables, one must at least be aware of the fact that those not used in the grouping will have much of their variance and explanatory power removed. If one groups by income, and regresses expenditure on income and family size, the latter will seem unimportant because the *average* family size in each income group varies little and effects of varying family size within the income groups have been averaged out and hidden. One must also keep in mind that any grouping hides some of the variation of the dependent variable and produces deceptive correlation coefficients. One can explain most of the variance of a set of *means* without explaining much of the basic variance of the variable.

Sometimes grouped data are used on the grounds that many of the explanatory variables actually operate on whole groups. For instance, one may study a number of villages, and be concerned with reasons why one village seemed to respond so much faster than another. Actually, it is often a mistake to use a larger unit of analysis on such grounds. One can always put into an analysis of family units, variables which are constant for the whole village. The only precaution, if one is using numerical variables measuring things affecting whole groups, is not to have them so detailed that knowing one specifies a sub-unit, and hence the value of all the other subunit information—this would mean perfect correlation among some predictors. But with some overlap to avoid this, it is possible to analyze data using variables at different levels of aggregation as explanatory variables. It is not necessary as studies of acceptance of innovation have sometimes done, to do one analysis at the village level, and another at the individual level that ignores the village variables.

Markov Processes: Whenever it is possible to assume some stability in survey-estimated relations between initial condition and subsequent change, the findings can be extrapolated over a number of periods into the future. One fascinating characteristic of the limits of such Markov processes is that they depend on the transition probabilities but not at all upon the initial states.[69]

For instance, if the probability of going from not owing a car to owning one is P, and the probability of a car owner becoming a non-owner is D, then whatever the initial proportion of car owners, the final proportion will be:

$$\frac{P}{P + D} \text{ owners}$$

because D% of the owners will drop out, replaced by P% of the non-owners:

$$D\left(\frac{P}{P+D}\right) = \frac{PD}{P+D} \text{ , and}$$

$$P\left(1 - \frac{P}{P+D}\right) = P\left(\frac{P+D-P}{P+D}\right) = \frac{P \cdot D}{P+D}$$

so the system is stable.

As an example, one can take a sample of adults, and relate their fathers' education to their own, and use this two-way table as an estimate of the matrix of transition probabilities.[70] Essentially one takes the marginal distribution of adults as a new set of fathers, estimates the distribution of their children's education, adds these distributions to get a new overall distribution of education for that generation, and so on. It is crucial to use adults and their fathers, not their children, to get the basic transition data since an adult has only one father, but a father can have several children. However, one might also want to improve the analysis by using different transition probabilities for families of different sizes.

If the transition probabilities vary for different but separate parts of the population, one can estimate the limit proportions separately and add. If the transition probabilities vary depending on other circumstances, then one has to move to a simulation model. Another example is suggested by Maisel in an analysis of the housing market.[71]

Maisel worked with data from the "1-in-1000" sample from the 1960 Population and Housing Census. The units are households. Each household faces a decision to move or not to move. If it moves it faces a decision to purchase or not to purchase. Estimates of choices made can be presented in the form of a probability tree. Trees can be estimated for the whole population, in Maisel's study the whole population of western Standard Metropolitan Statistical Areas over 1,000,000 in population. Estimates can also be made for those who at the start were owners, renters or new households. Maisel further breaks down the data by age, and also experiments with breakdown of the sample by income and by size of family (1 person, over 1 person). He reports the use of a form of matrix to project the state of households in Los Angeles at the next Census. He also notes that a satisfactory projection must include, in addition to a matrix which specifies choices by size of family, age, income, and tenure, a matrix which specifies demographic and income movements. The same type of analysis may be useful for other economic problems.

Actual simulation of livestock herds, or whole economies, can be done this way, with basic behavioral relations, and initial states, estimated from survey data (the former using reinterviews or memory to relate initial state to subsequent change or action). By then changing some of the relationships, such as a birth or death rate, one can quantify the effect of that change on the whole aggregate dynamics, such as the growth rate in Gross National Product.

The Problem of Aggregation: Many of the questions in economics have to do with the relation between two aggregates, such as disposable personal income and total consumption expenditures. The problem of how to go from micro-data about individual households to such aggregate data has been extensively discussed in the literature. Even where the individual micro-data are properly dynamic, there are problems, because a ten percent increase in income does not mean that each family's income increases ten percent. Even if it did, unless the income-expenditure relations are all linear, aggregate relations bear no simple relation to micro-relationships. Suppose, for instance, that whenever a family could count on $4,000 a year retirement income at age sixty-two, they would plan to retire early—a relationship which seems to appear in studies of people's retirement plans and behavior. Then increases in pension plan reserves, even if universally and equally distributed, would not relate to the amount of early retirement. One would have to know how many people's pension rights (combined with their Social Security) were passing the $4,000 per year threshhold.

The same problems exist, in spite of the elaborate algebra often presented, with attempts to use Engel curves from cross-section data to extrapolate and predict consumption patterns as national income rises. Changing income distribution (unequal distribution of income increases) or any non-linearities in the income-spending relations, will cause trouble. In addition, of course, there are the usual feed-back problems which have driven economics into structural equation models, so that going from micro-relations to aggregate dynamic systems requires complex simulation of the whole system.

Multi-Level Analysis of One Dependent Variable: All the preceding discussion operated on the assumption that the explanatory variables were at the same level of the causal process, that there were no one-way causal relations among them. If, however, one has two predictors one of which can affect the other but not vice-versa, there are difficulties with treating them at the same level in a multi-variate analysis. For example, one analyst used high school grades and whether the students said they planned to go to college to predict college attendance. In a mUltiple regression, the plans explained everything and it looked as though high school grades had nothing to do with going to college. Clearly the causal model was

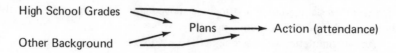

High School Grades

Plans ———→ Action (attendance)

Other Background

Only a true partial correlation, removing the effects of grades and parental background from both plans and acts and correlating the residuals would tell whether "plans" added anything not already in the other variables. This is difficult with classificatory variables. Correlating actual plans with residual actions not explained by grades and background, has a downward bias proportional to the correlation between plans and the background variables, but may sometimes be done for speed and economy.[72]

A similar problem of the explanatory structure arises when some of the explanatory characteristics are constraints or outside pressures, and others are motives or incentives.

In either case, one may want to engage in a two-stage analysis, first removing the effects of the causally prior variables, or the constraints, then entering into each individual's record the difference between his actual and expected value of the dependent variable, and then analyzing those residuals against another more immediate set of variables. Indeed, it is sometimes useful to make a third step, using the residuals from the residuals, and analyzing them against a new set of variables, held till this stage, because it is not even clear whether they affect the dependent variable or are affected by it. For those variables, one is still interested in their relationship, but does not want to let them dominate the explanation of the dependent variable.

The basic problem is not solved by such techniques as path analysis, which merely calculates a set of coefficients on the *assumption* of some particular pattern of causal forces, but does not really allow one to select among alternative models, except possibly by some "reasonableness of the coefficients" criterion. And things get much worse if we measure the theoretical variables only poorly or indirectly, particularly those at the middle or intermediate stages of causal paths.[73]

The structural models of econometrics should theoretically apply, but success in finding reasonable *and* identified models has been limited. One problem is too many explanatory variables. Another is the limited dynamism of the data.

Causal Sequences: The central problem in the analysis of survey data is how best to detect and exhibit complex causal patterns. As an introduction to the discussion of this problem, consider the possible patterns of relationship among three variables. There are five possible basic patterns, not counting the possibility that two, or all three, of the variables are unrelated. We also abstract from the problem of determining which variable fits at which point in each pattern. The five are as follows (arrows designate causation, not correlation):

(1)   *Spurious correlation.*

In this pattern B is a cause of A and also a cause of Y. A and Y will be correlated if considered as a pair. If the analyst has no knowledge of the part played by

B in the pattern, he may mistakenly conclude that there is a causal link between A and Y. There is always some danger that a new variable not heretofore considered will be found to be in the position of B in this sequence. It is also possible for a *real* effect of A only to be wiped out by a relation through B in the opposite direction!

(2)   *Causal sequence.*

$$A \longrightarrow B \longrightarrow Y$$

In this pattern A causes B, and B in turn causes Y. There is no effect of A on Y *except* through B. Note, however, that in this situation A does operate as a cause of Y. Analysts sometimes make the mistake of coming to the conclusion that A has nothing to do with Y—that is, they confuse this pattern with pattern (1) above. This confusion is easy because in both cases when B is taken into account statistically there is no remaining association between A and Y.[74]

(3)   *Compound causal sequence.*

In this pattern A is a cause of B which is in turn a cause of Y, just as in pattern (2), but in addition A has a direct effect on Y. For example, education has an effect on income and income has an effect on the consumption of a certain commodity; in addition, education may form a taste for the commodity and influence its consumption directly. We may note that, in principle, it is possible that B influences A as well as A influencing B.

(4)   *Separate causation.*

$$A \searrow$$
$$ Y$$
$$B \nearrow$$

It is possible for A and B both to influence Y. The simplest case is the one in which A and B are entirely independent of one another. It is this pattern which is the easiest for the analyst to discover.

(5)   *Interaction*

The relation of A to Y depends upon the value of B. This pattern is not easy to show with arrows. The pattern may be more easily illustrated by a graph showing one possible type of dependence:

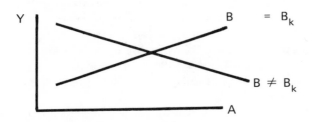

The slope of the line relating A to Y in this example is positive if $B = B_k$, but negative, otherwise. A great deal of elaborate discussion about causal paths starts out by assuming additivity (the absence of interaction effects), yet there is reason to believe that such interactions are quite important. And if both they and some one-way relations among the predictors exist, it often appears nearly impossible to tell from the data which causal model is appropriate.

The problem of the analyst is to discover *which* of these basic causal patterns is the appropriate one for his data. He is quite likely to have to concern himself with more than three variables, of course, but, as we see, he may have difficulties with only three. There are two basic strategies: he may rely on theory for guidance, or he may seek to learn from his data which causal pattern is the right one. It is possible to try both strategies, of course. The approach via theory emphasizes the attempt to construct a model which is consistent with what is already known to be true or believed to be true about the relationships under scrutiny. The approach via the data may involve an attempt to use the data to specify a more complete causal model or it may involve a special examination of timing. The specification of timing is extremely important for many problems, and we shall consider it first.

The central idea is the simple proposition that A cannot be a cause of B if B preceded A in time. There is a difficulty with this facile assumption in the case of dynamic (change) data. If in fact Y depends on the rate of change in X, then as X moves up and down in sinusoidal fashion, Y will always change direction *first* responding to the rate of change in X. This is a common problem with economic time series, but could occur in survey data too. In any case analysts turn their attention to the empirical question of which variables come first. For some, the answer is obvious. For example, the chronological age of an individual must be the result of the date of his birth and cannot be a consequence of anything that happened later. Events can influence whether he survives or not, but not his age.

For some variables it is possible to reconstruct timing on the basis of the data gathered in the interview. Special questions can be asked about the dates at which events take place. For example, we know that in a certain family the wife is working, and the family owns two cars. We set up the hypothesis that the second car was purchased *because* the wife needed it to get to work. We ask about timing, and are informed that the family has had two cars for five years, but the wife only started work last month. The hypothesis is greatly weakened. It is still barely conceivable that the wife bought the car in the expectation of going to work and has been on the verge of going to work for five years—but the suggestion strains our credulity.

There is always the possibility that the time of an event as reported in an interview is not precise. We may not be willing to accept the reported time as accurate enough to help us determine the causal pattern in which we are interested. It may then be necessary to establish time sequences through the use of reinterviews.

We return to the alternative use of data to help establish causation: the specification of a more complete causal model. A basic possibility is the addition of steps in the proposed causal sequence. The process by which, say, B causes Y, may be examined in detail. More detailed knowledge of the process will strengthen the interpretation that the causation is as hypothesized. It will reduce the possibility that the relationship may be found to be spurious.

The introduction of additional steps may be accomplished by adding psychological variables to the model. We may have an initial model in which the types of variables are as follows:

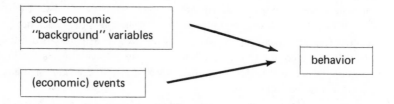

The more complete model may be as follows:

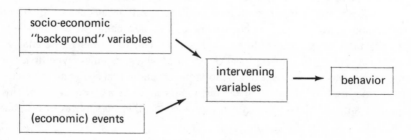

For example, the behavior may be the purchase of airline tickets by a family. The relevant background variables may be the demographic composition of the family. The "event" may be an increase in family income. We may observe repeatedly in successive surveys the relation between income change and purchases of tickets. It turns out that this relation is not constant—it shifts over time. We find that people's attitudes toward air travel can be measured. They are found to be shifting systematically as people shift from "non-fliers" to "fliers," that is, from the category of those who never have taken an air trip, to those who have done so. People who are "fliers" have a higher propensity to fly again. Knowledge of this shift helps us to understand the shift in the relation between income (and probably also, price) and the behavior.

Remember that we are still dealing with a situation where there is a single dependent variable to be explained, and the problem is that the explanatory variables are not all at the same stage in the causal process. The critical revelation of difficulty is that there are some pairs of predictors where one could be a cause of the other, but the reverse is not true. It is not simple intercorrelation that causes difficulty, but the one-way nature of the relationship.

In most survey work, for instance, there are some clearly exogenous variables whose relationship to one another cause no problems, but whose relationships to a second set can only be causal, not resultant: Year born, race, where grew up, can each affect a man's education, but cannot be changed by his education. His education in turn can affect his occupation, but a later occupation seldom changes the amount of formal education a person gets. How then can we take account of all this in accounting for a man's current wage rate?

One simple solution is to eliminate the variables except the most immediate proximate causes, and argue that the past is incorporated into occupation. But it is usually the case that we also believe that education, race, and age have direct effects on current earnings as well as the indirect effects through occupation. If that were all, one could do a stepwise analysis, first removing the effects of age, race, and where grew up, then relating the residuals to education, and relating the residuals from that analysis to occupation. But if the effect of occupation depends also on age, such a stepwise analysis which assumes additivity, at least between steps, is inappropriate. (Non-additivity at each stage can easily be handled by some variant of the sequential search strategy.)

And of course, one must believe the model. The use of residuals from one analysis in a second analysis, where the model is *not* sequential, produces a downward bias in the second-stage estimates, proportional to the degree of correlation between step one variables and the step two variables.[75] But one can still do a stepwise analysis where some causal directions are clear, putting in at later stages variables like age which may interact with later stage variables in their effects on the dependent variable.

The question becomes, how one selects the first stage variables, are they prior in time, clearly exogenous (not in turn affected by the dependent variable) unlike some of the other predictors, or what? Our preference is to eliminate at a first stage those clearly prior in time.

There are also constraints or overwhelming pressures, which one may want to consider eliminating before examining the effects of the more motivational (economic or psychological) variables. For instance, a man may be disabled, or a woman unable to work because she has small children and no husband. In these cases, an alternative procedure is to eliminate such cases from the sample for further analysis, since these constraints may affect not only the individual's earnings, but his capacity to have his earnings affected by any of the other variables.

Indeed, a common problem in survey research is that hypotheses about behavior really apply to those who are free to make choices, whereas a substantial part of the population may not be free. In that case, any real effect for the first group may be diminished by combining them with the constrained group.

It would be nice to recommend a simple recursive system, in place of stepwise analysis of a dependent variable, with the predicted values of each stage used in place of actual values, to predict a different dependent variable at the next stage. But this is not easy when many of the variables are categorical, and does not always seem to be a realistic model of the real world. We are left with the possibility of several stage residual analysis.

Complex Dependent Variables, or Joint Decisions: We pointed out earlier that sometimes when a dependent variable seems badly distributed, such as an expenditure when many people spend nothing, it can be decomposed into two parts, each with a more tractable distribution: whether the individual spent anything, and for those who did, the amount of the expenditure. The two alternatives, elaborate statistical procedures to deal with limited dependent variables, or grouping subsets of individuals to average over time by averaging over people, both have their drawbacks. From a purely statistical point of view, the probability of two things happening, such as a man buying a car, and buying it on credit, can be expressed as the product of two probabilities, without loss of information:

$$P(ab) = P(a|b) \cdot Pb = P(b|a)Pa$$

In a true joint decision, of course, one cannot say which decision came first, they may really have been made jointly. For instance, having once decided to buy a car, a man has to decide whether to buy a new one or a used one, and whether to pay cash or use credit, but the two decisions are not independent, since the greater price of a new car may make it more imperative to use credit. In practice, however, we can either analyze the new-used decision, and then analyze the cash-credit decision with the new-used decision as one of the explanatory variables, or we can reverse it and analyze the cash-credit decision regardless of new-used, and then analyze the decision whether to buy new or used, with the credit decision as part of the explanation.

These are examples of recursive systems, of course, applied to dichotomous dependent variables. In fact there are many consumer behavior areas where whole sets of decisions are involved, and a variety of analytical models can be applied. Let us take the car purchase decision and show some alternative models:

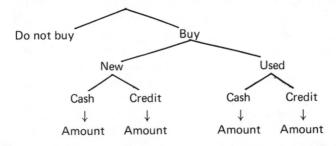

Here we analyze first the decision to buy, then the new-used decision for the buyers, then the cash-credit choice (for buyers) separately for new-used, or with new-used as one explanatory variable (preferably in a non-additive model). Finally we analyze the amount, either separately for the four groups, or with the new-used, and cash-credit decisions as part of the explanation (again preferably in an analysis which does not assume additivity).

But one could equally well have varied the order of the three decisions of buyers' new-used, cash-credit, and amount spent.

Indeed, one could produce a totally sequential line of decisions:

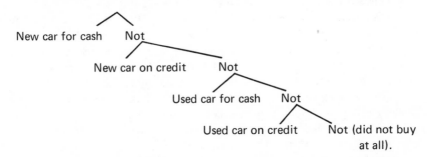

It can be shown that from the point of view of prediction, it does not make much difference which way one decomposes joint probabilities. But the interpretation of the behavior patterns is different, and one certainly would like a pattern of analysis which made intuitive sense. In the analysis of determinants of family income, we built up components starting with the head's hourly earnings, his work hours, moving to the wife's work, and then to other sources of income, and ending with an analysis of who moved in with relatives, or provided housing for relatives.[76]

Canonical Correlation: A totally different approach is possible if one is willing to impose several more assumptions: If one has a set of dependent variables, and a set of independent variables, one can ask what linear function of the first set and what linear function of the second set could be developed so that the correlation between the two functions would be a maximum. This is technically known as canonical correlation: It assumes that it is an appropriate model of the real world to create a weighted sum of the dependent variables with fixed weights, and to relate this to a weighted sum of the explanatory variables.

There has been some limited use of canonical correlations in the analysis of economic surveys and there may be further applications of the methods in the future.[77]

The purpose of canonical correlation is to exhibit the correlations between two sets of variates. It is useful to think of the analyst as starting with a single set of variates and the covariance matrix which shows the relationships between all possible pairs of these variates. He then partitions the list of variates into two parts, one of which he may wish to consider as a group of dependent variables, and the other, as independent variables. The statistical procedure is designed to reveal linear additive combinations of each of the two sets of variates. The desired linear combination of the dependent variates is that linear additive combination which can best be predicted; the desired linear additive combination of the independent variates is that combination which is the best predictor.

It is also possible to go on to find other pairs of linear combinations uncorrelated with the first pair which exhibit any further relationships which may exist between the two sets of variates. This extension of the calculations, however, has not yet been found useful in survey work. We may note, however, that there may be little to choose empirically between the first pair of combinations and the second or later pairs. Caution would suggest the extension of the calculations to check on this possibility. It is preferable to establish rather than to assume that little can be added to the initial results by the added calculations.

The development of canonical correlation, like the development of factor analysis, is due to Hotelling. A brief comparison of the techniques may be helpful. For both, the basic raw material is the covariance matrix. For both, the purpose is to "boil down" the data, to identify a limited number of factors which can account for what is observed. Both are most likely to be useful in fields of inquiry where the theory is poorly developed. Later on, presumably one knows what the basic variables are, and can develop measures of them.

There is, however, a basic difference between the two procedures. The criterion in canonical correlation is essentially a correlation coefficient. The magnitude of a correlation coefficient is not affected by the units of measurement employed. Factor analysis is so affected. In a canonical correlation, just as in any regression problem, it is possible to multiply any variate by an arbitrary constant without changing the final results of the analysis. In factor analysis the results would be changed by such a procedure.

Canonical correlation with dummy variables might be used in any problem in which the dependent variable is a nominal scale. In effect, the canonical correlation provides a method for scaling the dependent variable. This approach has been used in a problem in which the dependent variable was type of housing preferred, and respondents could select one of several possibilities.[78] Predictors included income and stage in the family life cycle.

An example of a problem to which the method might be applied is the prediction of interviewer performance. There are a number of possible measures of performance, as discussed in Chapter III, including completion rate, measures of response error, and reports from respondents about their reactions to the interview. There are also a variety of possible measures of interviewer characteristics, including performance on psychological tests, years of experience, age, sex, education, and so forth. Both sets could be handled in one canonical correlation.

Another example of a problem is the assessment of consumers' characteristics. A set of measures of behavior might be explained by a set of measures of psychological characteristics, with a view to developing a typology of consumers. In this problem, as in others mentioned, the statistical procedure becomes a method of developing scales. Thus, it is an alternative in some circumstances to the use of other procedures which develop scales. Canonical correlation, however, provides a measure of relationship as well as two scales.

It should be kept in mind that canonical correlation is subject to the same basic assumptions as ordinary regression, applied to *both* sides of the equation.

These assumptions are least restrictive when the variables on both sides are dummy variables, i.e. when linearity in the sets of variables is actually not assumed. Indeed, perhaps the most useful application of canonical correlation is as a measure of association in cross-classification. One thinks of each category of one class as a dummy variable predictor and each category of the other classification as a dummy variable dependent variable, and computes the canonical correlation, the *size* of the coefficient indicating the extent to which one can predict the distribution of one knowing the distribution of the other. As was pointed out earlier, when most or all of the predictors in some multivariate analysis are classifications (ordinal scales), then this becomes an effective way of displaying the pattern of intercorrelations among the predictors, in the form of the canonical correlations among the sets (age, occupation, sex, etc.), though Cramer's V is equivalent and easier to compute, being based on chi-square.[25]

Structural Models: As analysts attempt to develop models of situations in which large numbers of variables are relevant, it frequently becomes inappropriate or impossible to describe the model in a single equation or even focus on one dependent variable at a time. The variables may be regarded on theoretical grounds as subject to a system of relationships. In the development of econometric theory Frisch and Haavelmo criticized the single equation approach of Moore and Working on the ground that it would lead to biased estimates when the appropriate model is a system of simultaneous equations.[79]

In much econometric work the method of working with sets of simultaneous equations has been used. This approach is commonly used, for example, in aggregative models of the American economy, such as that initiated by Klein and Goldberger and revised by Suits.[80] In the analysis of survey data, the reliance has mostly been on a special type of simultaneous system, the recursive system.

In recursive systems development up to time t-1 determines values at time t. Also, the variables at time t are obtained one by one. A recursive system may have the following form:

$$X_1 = e_1$$

$$X_2 = b_{21} \; X_1 + e_2$$

$$X_3 = b_{31} \; X_1 + b_{32} \; X_2 + e_3$$

$$X_k = b_{k1} \; X_1 + b_{k2} \; X_2 + \ldots + b_{k, \, k-1} \; X_{k-1} + e_k$$

Thus X_1 is endogenous; X_2 is a function of X_1 plus an error term; X_3 is a function of X_1, X_2 and an error term; and so forth. It should be understood that the relationships in a recursive system need not be linear and additive as in the above example. What is required is that the variables appear in successive equations as shown. For example, X_3 might depend upon the product of X_1 and X_2. Recursive systems can be fitted by ordinary least squares. They can exploit the flexibility of the survey method in using information about timing to assist in the analysis of causal patterns.

In setting up recursive systems economists tend to rely to a considerable extent upon *a priori* reasoning concerning the relationships. There has been work recently by Blalock on the problem of how to use correlation coefficients to discover the nature of recursive systems.[81] Blalock argues that the correlation coefficients can be used in such analysis rather than regression coefficient since what is at issue is whether or not a variable belongs in a certain equation. If the correlation coefficient is zero, the regression coefficient is also zero, and vice versa. Blalock develops each equation by testing to see whether the data are consistent with a model in which certain variables do appear in that equation while others drop out. In other contexts, however, Blalock argues that regression coefficients are better for making comparisons across populations.

The great contribution of econometrics to aggregate analysis was to point out that in a system where there were feedback loops, one could not derive unbiased estimates of any of the parameters without estimating the whole structural model. To what extent do these same problems arise with survey data?

Clearly if we had sufficiently dynamic data about individual households over time, such problems arise. Much survey analysis to date, however, has been dynamic only in a limited sense, incorporating all the past in certain measures of initial state (beginning of year assets, debts, housing and location, durable stocks) and certain "demographic" data such as age, education, where grew up, past mobility, etc. Even here there are feedback problems. For example, one may use initial assets to help explain saving behavior, but the accumulation of those assets resulted from past saving behavior and their stock reflects both a current influence and a representation of "personality" or past behavior which should also continue to affect current behavior. Clearly we do not have the data to untangle this, until we secure long-run data on individual families. We might, however, do better if we knew more about how the assets were accumulated, i.e. if we had even a retrospective history of income and asset accumulations from memory.

It is not surprising then, that there have been no instances where a realistic structural model has been fitted to actual survey data. More static models of causal inference have been attempted, mostly with recursive systems, where at each stage any or all of the variables of the preceding stage can have an effect, but the reverse is not true. These are particularly easy models to deal with, essentially because they do not really have dynamic feed-back loops, but are decompositions of chains of causation. And if one is willing to select some particular model, assume that the effects are linear and additive, then it is possible to estimate path coefficients which allocate the explanation of any variable in the system among the variables that precede it in the system.[82]

One must also assume that the laws governing the system specify the causal priorities in an undebatable way, that the disturbances of the dependent variables are all uncorrelated (i.e., that all system inputs are entered explicitly into the analysis), and that the usual assumptions of multiple correlation are met: independent units, homogeneous variances, additivity, linearity and no serious multicollinearity). If a theory happens to come closer to being a complete recursive system (each variable used in all the following stages) it will usually do a better job of reproducing the correlation matrix, even though it may be further from the truth. And the more paths one adds in the model, the more likely that the modified theory will reproduce the empirical correlations regardless whether the redefined model is more nearly valid.

Hence, one pays for the elegant analysis by being forced to specify the structure of the real world, when for most researchers, that is the prime question—what that structure really looks like. When one admits the possibility of interaction effects, the number of possible causal models explodes.

Are we left then with the policy of shaking the data to see what the structure looks like, with the intention of selecting a model out of the data? If so, we
are left with little or no evidence of the reliability of our conclusions. One cannot develop a hypothesis from a set of data and test it with the same data. The
problem is, do we have hypotheses worth testing, i.e. such that the suggestion
that an alternative hypothesis would fit the data better would not upset us? In
most of the social sciences, economics being no exception, we doubt that our
theoretical structures and our substantive knowledge are good enough to move
us from the data searching stage to the hypothesis testing stage.

Simulation: There is, however, a possible approach for dealing with structural and feedback problems, and for using the results of survey data in dynamic
models which tell us something about the dynamic properties of the economic
system. It relies on simulation with a model where the time periods used are so
short that one can ignore the possible feed-back problems. If one can also assume
that the relationships between initial states and subsequent actions (during a
month, for instance) are stable, then the system is a set of Markov processes. The
inputs are the kind of micro-data easily derivable from surveys, and the computer can, each "month" add up subtotals, to provide an output describing aggregate dynamic changes in the simulated system.[83] It is not necessary for the computer to keep track of each one of sixty million households and many firms. The
system can be aggregated to the extent of having a thousand or so "representative" types of families, and similarly with firms. And where not all do something,
the computer can use a built-in random number table or "jiffy randomizer" to
assign the right proportions.

The procedure requires the initial specification of a set of households with
the characteristics of the individual households specified in such a manner that
the households represent the population. For example, the proportion of households with head within a certain age range should agree with the proportion for
the population. The income distribution of households with head of that age
should agree with the population distribution etc. (Note that representativeness
is needed at this stage even though relationships may have been estimated using
experimental designs.)

During each pass-through, the assigned relations impinge on individual
households in the sample. The characteristics of the household to be affected in
different ways are determined by relationships built into the model; which
specific units in the representative sample are affected are determined by random
numbers. For example, a relationship may be built in that a certain proportion
of households containing married women of certain ages will add members
through births. Individual households, randomly selected, each will have their
numbers increased by one infant. How many births are to occur will depend on
the length of time represented by a pass—Orcutt chose a period of one month. A
complete demographic model obviously requires other events in addition to

births—deaths, marriages, divorces. A complete economic model of household behavior must also contain relationships to determine income, expenditure, saving etc. Orcutt reports in his book actual development only of a demographic model, but the methods set forth are designed for economic relationships as well.

The first test of the model is whether the dynamic output is reasonable. Basic uses of the method are for prediction and analysis. It makes possible the working out over an indefinite number of passes, i.e. an indefinitely long period of time, of the implications of the initial conditions plus the relationships specified. Thus, in principle, a demographic model can be used to simulate the demographic processes affecting the population of the country.

A related use of the model is for the assessment of the effects of choice of policy. Alternative assumptions can be made about policy decisions, and runs of the model can trace the probable course of events which may be expected to follow. And, in the same way, simulation can explain outcomes in the sense of demonstrating how they can result from the inputs of the model.

A basic limitation on the possible uses of this method is that the requirements for data can be formidable. The quality of the inputs, including especially the inputs of estimated relationships, will be reflected in the results. It is further necessary for good results that the inputs be mutually consistent even when they come from diverse sources. There is the possibility that the random elements in the simulation may by chance lead to peculiar results especially if the number of households included in the simulation is limited—as it may be limited by the capacity of the computer being used. Yet it remains true that this method is at present the only technique which anyone has seriously attempted to develop for handling anything like the full complexity of the relationships which are appropriate to analysis of household behavior.

Actually the use of simulation models has proceeded most rapidly in subareas such as population models, for people or livestock. For instance, one can start with a model which assumes that people's output depends on their level of education, that taxes depend on output, and that a fraction of taxes will support the school system and determine the level of tuition fees to cover the rest of education costs. Such simulation models are actually complex to implement. One simple livestock model set up by the staff at the World Bank requires some 2500 computer cards of instructions merely to instruct the computer on the relations.

Summary on Analysis

It may be useful to summarize the main steps in analysis, since we have brought in so many special problems and possibilities:

First, one must look carefully at the dependent variable or variables. Extreme cases may be actual errors, or reveal conceptual problems. If they must be left in, they can be truncated to avoid undue distortions of least squares procedures, or the whole distribution can be transformed by taking logs or square roots (provided there are no zero or negative numbers).

If the dependent variable is a yes-no dichotomy, or has little variance one may want to consider building a more complex dependent variable with more variance to be explained. If it is a joint decision, one may want to transform it into a series of sequential or conditional decisions, such recursive models being easier to handle than complete systems of structural equations. Finally, one may want to analyze separately the forces pushing people into the top third of the dependent variable, and those pushing them into the bottom third, since the second set may not be the mirror image of the first.

As for the explanatory variables, one may want to compress them by building indexes, even arbitrary additive indexes. This provides a speedy way of getting rid of a lot of hypotheses at once, or else an indication in which set to search further. And if an additive index has a linear effect, one can rest with the additivity, but if not one knows to look for interactions. Where intercorrelations are too high, one may also want to build indexes, or orthogonal components, such as the average age of husband and wife, and the difference in their ages.

One may want to test whether the very economical assumption of additivity of effects is justified, by comparing an additive regression with the variance explained by subcells of a k-dimensioned table where there are k sets of predictors. Or one may prefer to proceed to some search process which does not assume additivity.

And if there is one variable, dominant because of its power, or its theoretical importance, or its likelihood of changing in the future, then one may want to move to a covariance search process, looking for subsets of the population which differ in their response to it.

Once one has a clear view of the structure that seems to fit the data, it can always be written as a linear model in a new set of complex variables, and one may want to fit the data to such a model, in preparation for fitting the same model to some other set of data, in more of a hypothesis testing operation.

In all this, one must steer a middle course between too little theory and structure on one hand, and too much on the other. What is needed is a working theory which indicates the kinds of variables to be tried, and reasonable ways they might fit together. This guides the selection of variables and the analytical approach without binding it, or binding it to alternative interpretations of the same data. The fact is that none of the social sciences, certainly not economics, have theories so well based that one would be comfortable testing them against the data without ever asking whether some other theory might explain the world better.

Finally, one must move to more complex models than the single-stage analysis of one dependent variable at a time. There are, first, stages in the causal process, and secondly, feedback problems, and the need for some more complete structure. It is simpler if the model can be made recursive. Even if the full model cannot be investigated, it may be useful to work it out as a guide to what analysis can fruitfully be done.

The authors feel that many of the mathematically elegant procedures attack the wrong problems, e.g., spelling out the implications of a model rather than selecting among several different ones, and place much too heavy a load of assumptions on the nature and quality of the data and the relationships. At the same time, the power of computers can seduce us into rank empiricism—trying everything and running everything, without imposing any judgment, limitations, or theoretical structure. Throwing all the variables into one big multiple regression often leads the analyst into embarrassing problems of interpreting the results. The middle course seems best: Some general theoretical structure, attention to what causal directions can be specified, but within those limits, a focus on the most powerful variables and models using them, in order to select the most promising explanatory structure.

Organizational Aspects and Practical Problems of Analysis

A parody of the *New York Times* once changed its famous motto to "All the News, Printed to Fit." Even a casual glance at the kinds of analysis done with survey data over the past twenty years will reveal a certain domination by the computer technology available at the time. This meant not only avoiding things that were difficult or impossible to do, but overdoing things that were easy to do. Once an efficient program is available for turning out tables, particularly percentagized tables, there is a temptation to run "everything by everything." And the availability of multiple regression programs subsequently led to an over-enthusiastic use of that. The problem is accentuated by our temptation to overlook the hidden costs of something whose direct costs look cheap. It may seem easy to turn out a lot of tables, but analyzing them, keeping track of them, and avoiding duplication, are not easy.

If the most common practical problem of analysis is the proper balance between selectivity and allowing a little serendipity, the next most common is documentation. Particularly when many people are working, or will be working, on a set of data, it would seem elemental that proper documentation was essential. It often happens that errors are discovered and corrections made after some new variables have been generated, and even some analysis tabulations done. Unless every step has been carefully dated, when completed, not when ordered, it may prove difficult to know whether some variable was created with components before certain errors were found in them, or whether some analysis run was done before or after certain corrections were made. With modern technology, it is easy to re-do certain steps, but careful attention to the disposal of the early output and referring the later searcher to its replacement, is less certain. What is even more likely, if tables have been made from the earlier output, without careful notation *on the table* as to the tabulation request which was its source, more trouble will ensue.

As tables and other analysis results go through many drafts, their connection to the basic data will become even more difficult to maintain unless there is preserved at the bottom of every one the serial number of the computer run and perhaps also the original code numbers of the main variables involved.

It may seem a trivial point, but the ability to go from a table back to the original code definition of the variables in that table and the computer instructions that produced it, is important. When work decks of computer cards tended to multiply, it was necessary to produce full code descriptions of each of them, rather than attempt to work back through a series of translations to the original (col. 75 came from col. 63 of card 15, which came from col. 59 of card 10, which came from col. 40 of card 7, where it was created by combining columns 5 and 23). With data tapes, it is not even possible to keep most of the material in the same positions, the tape locations change, and we have found it expedient to have a dictionary of variables on each tape which is automatically transferred when a new tape is built, and which, in naming each variable, also gives its original variable number on the first tape where it appeared, so that all variables can be referred back to a single master code, made up of the originally coded material, and any subsequently added variables.

The names given to variables are themselves a problem, together with a natural but lamentable habit of resorting to abbreviations and even acronyms which are utterly confusing to anyone but their creator, and often after a few months even to him. The only true definition of a variable is a reference to its detailed code which should include a frequency distribution (or mean and list of extreme cases), and a clear description of whatever process generated it, if it was a variable created from others (for instance, what was done with missing information, or extreme cases, or negatives). The labeling problem becomes even more difficult with panel studies, doubly so when the same "fact" may be asked more than once, in different waves of interviewing.

We have already pointed out that after a process of locating and correcting errors, new variables are often created, by recoding, combining, or simply bracketing variables into classifications. Checks on the distribution of these new variables are extremely important, not only to make sure the creation was properly done, but also to provide basic information about the distributions and to uncover additional errors. Even if one decided that missing information did not need to be assigned—on the argument that it was illegitimate to assign dependent variables, using later variables to explain them, and that it was unnecessary to assign explanatory variables since a separate dummy variable for "Not Ascertained" can handle them—one has to know what to do with such cases when combinations of variables are desired.

In the rush to get data ready for analysis, the question of whether weights are necessary, and how they should be developed, requires a tight strategy. Commonly when only varying non-response is at issue, weights turn out to make so little difference as to be disposable, particularly if the main purpose is analysis, not national estimates. But if and when weights are required, it is a strategy problem whether to make them internal (the inverse of the sampling-times-response rates) or external (blowing up to outside proportions in one or more dimensions so that all weighted data are ratio estimates). If the latter is envisaged, then preparatory work preparing outside estimates of the number of families or individuals in each of several subclassifications and preparing the analysis sheets for calculating the weights, will avoid delays.

In keeping track of computer work, one can number every request serially, or have ranges of numbers for various kinds of operations. The latter is sometimes used as an accounting device in order to estimate the costs of the separate steps.

In handling large masses of data, one always has the basic questionnaires, editing worksheets, and coding sheets, but as each step in the cleaning and manufacturing of the data progresses, the costs of having to go back to the original documents increase. Hence a strategy of back-up files has to be developed.

Finally, when the main analysis is done, and the data are to be made available to any potential user, proper documentation of the codes, the editing process, the basic data source, and the way the data are physically on the data tape, are essential. Since the research staff is often unfamiliar with computer differences in tape handling: header labels, bits or bytes per inch, seven or nine channel tape, etc., they frequently find difficulties in sharing data. And potential users are frequently unaware of the costs of answering the questions.

But transferring data from one computer to another is simple compared with the problems of transferring computer programs. The modern computer is usually a constellation of components which differ from one installation to another, and each one has its own internal control mechanisms and executive languages. The rules of getting on and off are likely to be idiosyncratic, as well as the list of special subroutines that are kept available and can be called and used. The net result is that programmers can usually do better if they start from scratch and rewrite a program than if they try to adapt it. This is partly because most computer programs are inadequately documented. If they provide a logical flow-diagram, it was made before many of the bugs were found and eliminated, some by changing the design. Often the capacity limits have not really been explored, nor have the speed and costs of tasks supposedly within the capacity but never really tried.

Another basic problem is that many statistical "package" programs, are written with so many options that the "set-up" instructions for using them become cumbersome and error-prone. A reference back to Chapter VI on data analysis shows that with a numerical dependent variable, the basic elements are the total variance of the variable, and the means and number of cases for variously defined subgroups—all that is necessary for one-way analyses of variance. Yet it is hard to find a fast, efficient, flexible program that will provide means for sample subgroups. Table-making programs are better, but even they are frequently inflexible when it comes to procedures for eliminating the irrelevant cases before percentagizing.

A final difficulty is the delay in billing so that the analyst may find his analysis costs exploding beyond his budget before he is aware of the problem. Interim checks on actual computer times help, provided one takes account of the aborted runs as well.

In sum, a great deal of complex administrative foresight is necessary in order to avoid errors, or at least to correct them before they get compounded through a series of subsequent steps. And some economy in using computers is essential, they are not free.

With card-programmed computers, there is a new problem of documentation: The instructions for building data files, creating new variables, selecting subgroups, and doing analysis, may not always be printed so that they can be saved. And the cards with the instructions on them are difficult to save, and to read. Someone searching back to check just how something was done may find it difficult to reconstruct. The moral is, any program cards used in file building or analysis should be printed and those listings kept filed by the tabulation request number as though it were the output, or together with the output if there was some. The cards should also be kept for a while, in case the task needs to be redone, but they are a kind of expendable back-up. It may also be useful to have a system for entering on this same paper the numbers of the tape decks (input and output if they are different).

In the haste of getting things done, and particularly in the frantic process of redoing things when the first pass was wrong, it is easy to forget the need for keeping records. This is one of the reasons why errors seem to compound themselves at times. It is also possible to overdo record keeping. More than two copies of the master code lead to situations where marginal notes do not get added to all copies. Attempts to keep track of every time a variable has been used, transferred, etc., tend to get cumbersome and break down of their own weight.

In view of the difficulties of keeping track of data, and the speed and ease with which new variables can be built, it is increasingly appropriate not to save anything but the original data, plus copies of the programs that generate other variables. In other words, it may be more efficient to generate a variable every time you use it than to store it. One stores the instructions necessary to generate it, rather than the secondary data themselves.

Examples of Analysis

It would require far too much space to provide detailed descriptions and evaluations of even a small sample of survey analyses. The reader who wishes to make use of what he has read in this book, however, is urged to select one or two reports of surveys, perhaps starting with a brief one in one of the journals, and to make his own assessment. Indeed, it would be a useful exercise to assess the whole survey design at the same time. The following cursory outline of questions might be helpful:

1. Is there a probability sample, from some reasonably adequate frame, and with good coverage?
2. Was the response rate sufficient, along with the treatment of missing information, to hold down biases?
3. What about the actual stimulus questions, and their order? Were they calculated to secure the right information?
4. Who was the respondent (in theory and in practice)?
5. What were the things being explained, the behaviors or situations, or attitudes?
6. Was there some operational model into which various sets of variables fit? How was the possibility of causal sequences treated? What about the possibility of alternative models?
7. How were the following statistical problems treated:
    a. Effects of differential errors or extreme cases on the selection of variables that "work," and on estimation of effects.
    b. Intercorrelations among predictors, and spurious correlation.
    c. Interaction effects (relations that differ from some, or do not exist everywhere).
8. Do the conclusions follow directly from the data, or require the author to bring in other information or value judgements? If other information is added, is it documented?
9. Is the study related to previous research, and are its implications for future research spelled out?

A warning is in order: It is often the better studies which provide enough documentation so that the reader can spot flaws in the design or analysis. The authors may even spell out their errors as a warning to others. It is unfair to compare such well-described studies with others where one cannot tell just what happened.

It is common for an analysis of survey data to be preceded by an elaborate theoretical model containing terms with no operational measures. The "assumptions and implications" of that model are then subjected to "test" in a subsequent analysis. But the analysis design bears little resemblance to the original model, and frequently what is tested is mostly the assumptions of the model, rather than its "implications." (Or those implications are themselves any reasonable man's assumptions.) Hence the original model served largely as window dressing. If the model served to direct attention to the particular behavioral parameters of greatest importance (because important economic implications would be sensitively altered in the model system when those parameters changed), then it would serve a useful purpose. Or if there were competing models (hypotheses) the choice between which required a particular statistical analysis, again the theoretical discussion would serve a useful purpose. But too much of the time unbelievable assumptions (requiring foresight or insight that people are unlikely to have) are tested rather than asking more broadly what really did determine behavior.

Summary

We have touched on a wide variety of problems and techniques in this chapter. Where does all this leave the economist desiring to analyze his survey data? Should he feel guilty if he has not worked out a formal structural model, hopefully just identified? Should he feel compelled to conduct factor analysis or least space analysis or some other procedure in developing a reduced set of explanatory variables? Our feeling is no. What is needed is a more flexible general statement of the behaviors or statuses to be explained, and their relation to one another, a listing of the explanatory factors that are to be examined, and a discussion of the relation of the things measured to those explanatory factors. Some attention must be paid to the relative accuracy of different variables, since one may refuse to throw out a variable with weak influence, if that weakness may be due to poor measurement, not lack of effect. And for economists, one needs to ask which of the explanatory variables are of significance in dynamic economics, i.e. are likely to change for substantial groups at the same time in the same direction, or at least to influence the effects of things that do change.

Economists are unlikely to be unaware of problems of spurious correlation, or the necessity for multivariate analysis. We are perhaps less likely to be aware of the possibility of important relations (effects) existing only for a subgroup of the population, even though that is exactly what marginal analysis would predict. But most important of all, the tradition of multiple regression has made us under-sensitive to interaction effects of all kinds. We carry over the truth that non-linear relations can be treated as linear to a first approximation, especially for small changes, into the non-truth that non-additivity can be treated with additive approximations.

Finally, and perhaps most important, we are all too casual about the relationship of what we measure to our theoretical constructs, and about the possibility of many alternative hypotheses. The basic problem of behavioral science is not the testing of elaborate deductive hypotheses, but the selection among competing hypotheses. The final test of analysis, then, is whether it really allows one to select among the competing hypotheses, by selecting among competing explanatory variables, perhaps in different structural forms.

Footnotes to Chapter VI

1. See on this point the discussion in Hubert M. Blalock, Jr., *Causal Inference in Nonexperimental Research,* The University of North Carolina Press, Chapel Hill, 1964, Ch. 1, "Introduction," pp. 3-26. See also H. M. Blalock, Jr., "The Measurement Problem: A Gap Between the Languages of Theory and Research" in H. M. Blalock, Jr. and A. B. Blalock, Eds., *Methodology in Social Research,* McGraw Hill, N.Y., 1968, pp. 5-27. See also Herbert L. Costner, "Theory, Deduction, and Rules of Correspondence," *American Journal of Sociology* 75 (Sept. 1969), pp. 245-263.

2. Milton Friedman, *A Theory of the Consumption Function,* Princeton Univ. Press, 1957.

3. J. Lansing and E. S. Maynes, "Inflation and Saving by Consumers," *Journal of Political Economy,* Vol. IX, No. 5, Oct. 1952, pp. 383-391.

4. The following discussion draws upon "Theory and Methods of Social Measurement" by Clyde H. Coombs, in *Research Methods in the Behavioral Sciences,* edited by Leon Festinger and Daniel Katz, Holt, Rinehart, and Winston, New York, 1953, pp. 471-535. See also *A Theory of Data* by Clyde H. Coombs, John Wiley and Sons, New York, 1964; and Henry S. Uphsaw, "Attitude Measurement" in H. M. and A. B. Blalock, Eds., *Methodology in Social Research,* McGraw Hill, New York, 1968, pp. 60-111.

5. For a discussion of non-parametric statistics see H. M. Blalock, *Social Statistics,* McGraw-Hill, New York, 1960. See also Sidney Siegel, *Non-Parametric Statistics,* McGraw-Hill, New York, 1956.

6. Daniel B. Suits, "The Use of Dummy Variables in Regression Equations," *J.A.S.A.,* 52 (Dec. 1957), pp. 548-551.

Arthur S. Goldberger, *Econometric Theory,* John Wiley & Sons, 1964, pp. 218-227.

For one of the first uses in economic analysis, see T. P. Hill, "Analysis of the Distribution of Wages and Salaries in Great Britain," *Econometrica,* 27 (July 1959), pp. 355-381.

7. See Graham Kalton, *A Technique for Choosing the Number of Alternative Response Categories to Provide in Order to Locate an Individual's Position on a Continuum,* 3 memos dated Nov. 7, 1966; Feb. 10, 1967 and Mar. 10, 1967, Sampling Section, Survey Research Center, Ann Arbor, Michigan.

8. For an example see Daniel C. Rogers, "Private Rates of Return to Education in the United States: A Case Study," *Yale Economic Essays* (Spring, 1969), pp. 89-136.

9. H. S. Houthakker and John Haldi, "Household Investment in Automobiles: An Intertemporal Cross-Section Analysis," in I. Friend and R. Jones, Eds., *Consumption and Saving,* Vol. I, Univ. of Penna., 1960, pp. 175-224.

10. There are many introductory discussions of the subject. For example, see Chapter 6 of A. N. Oppenheim, *Questionnaire Design and Attitude Measurement,* Heinemann, London, 1966, or H. S. Upshaw, *op. cit.* For an intermediate level discussion prepared some years ago, see Helen Peak, "Problems of Objective Observation," pp. 243-299, in L. Festinger and D. Katz, editors, *Research Methods in the Behavioral Sciences,* Dryden, New York, 1953. For advanced treatments see W. S. Torgerson, Theory and Method of Scaling, John Wiley & Sons, Inc., 1958, and Clyde H. Coombs, *A Theory of Data,* John Wiley & Sons, Inc., New York, 1964.

11. See the discussion by Helen Peak, "Problems of Objective Observation," pp. 243-299, in Festinger and Katz, *op. cit.*

12. See Peak, *op. cit.,* p. 252. See also Rensis Likert, "A Technique for the Measurement of Attitudes," *Archives of Psychology,* 140 (1932), pp. 1-55.

13. For a clear description, see Oppenheim, *Questionnaire Design and Attitude Measurement,* Heinemann, London, 1966, Ch. 6. For careful assessment, see P. C. Sagi, "A Statistical Test for the Significance of a Coefficient of Reproducibility," *Psychometrika* 2 (1959), pp. 19-27 and L. A. Goodman, "Simple Statistical Methods for Scalogram Analysis," *Psychometrika* 2 (1959), pp. 29-43.

14. The account which follows is based on Clyde H. Coombs, "Theory and Methods of Social Measurements," pp. 471-535 in Festinger and Katz, *op. cit.* For a more elaborate treatment see his *A Theory of Data, op. cit.*

15. Coombs, *op. cit.,* pp. 515-516.

16. Alan C. Kerckhoff, "Nuclear and Extended Family Relationships: A Normative and Behavioral Analysis," in Ethel Shanas and Gordon Streib, Eds., *Social Structure and The Family: Generational Relations.* Prentice Hall, N.Y., 1965.

17. Harold Hotelling, "Analysis of a Complex of Statistical Variables into Principal Components," *Journal of Educational Psychology,* 24, pp. 417-441, 498-520 (1933).

18. See T. W. Anderson, *An Introduction to Multivariate Statistical Analysis,* New York, John Wiley & Sons Inc., London, Chapman & Hall Ltd., 1958; and Richard Stone, "On the Interdependence of Blocks of Transactions," *Journal of Royal Statistical Society,* Vol. IX, No. 1 (1947), *Supplement,* pp. 1-45.

19. Eva Mueller, "A Study of Purchase Decisions," in Clark, Ed., *Consumer Behavior,* New York University Press, New York, 1954.

20. See James Morgan, Ismail Sirageldin and Nancy Baerwaldt, *Productive Americans,* Survey Research Center, Ann Arbor, Michigan, 1966.

21. G. E. P. Box, "Non-Normality and Tests on Variances," *Biometrika,* 40, (Dec. 1953), pp. 318-444.

22. See any text on non-parametric statistics, e.g., William Hays, *Statistics for Psychologists,* Holt, Rinehart and Winston, New York, 1963; or Sidney Siegel, *Nonparametric Statistics,* McGraw Hill, New York, 1956.

23. M. Kendall and Stuart, *The Advanced Theory of Statistics,* 2 Vols. See also W. H. Kruskal, "Ordinal Measures of Association," *Journal of the American Statistical Association,* 63 (December, 1958), pp. 814-861; and for a brief exploration and proposed asymmetric measures, see Robert H. Somers, "A New Asymmetric Measure of Association for Ordinal Variables," *American Sociological Review,* 27 (December 1962), pp. 799-811.

24. See L. A. Goodman and W. H. Kruskal, "Measures of Association for Cross Classifications," *Journal of the American Statistical Association,* 49 (Dec. 1954), pp. 732-764; and Frederick Mosteller, "Association and Estimation in Contingency Tables," *Journal of the American Statistical Association,* 63 (March, 1968), pp. 1-28, who points out that correlations are affected by the actual frequencies, but that you may *want* a measure of importance in prediction which does that, rather than a pure measure of association. See also H. M. Blalock, *Social Statistics,* McGraw Hill, New York, 1960.

25. Orley Ashenfelter and Joseph Mooney, "Graduate Education, Ability, and Earnings," *Review of Economics and Statistics,* 50 (Feb. 1968), pp. 78-86; and K. S. Srikantan, "Canonical Association between Nominal Measurements," *Journal of the American Statistical Association,* 65 (March 1970), pp. 284-292.

26. See the discussion in A. S. Goldberger, *Econometric Theory,* John Wiley & Sons, Inc., New York, London, Sydney, 1964, Chapter 5, "Expansions of Linear Regression."

27. Guy H. Orcutt, et al., *Microanalysis of Socioeconomic Systems,* Harper and Brothers, New York, 1961. See Chapter 11, especially pp. 224-231.

28. D. J. Finney, *Probit Analysis,* 1952 (second edition), Cambridge, at the University Press.

29. Joseph Berkson, "Application of the Logistic Function to Bio-Assay," *Journal of the American Statistical Association* 39 (Sept., 1944), pp. 357-365.

30. Stanley L. Warner, *Stochastic Choice of Mode in Urban Travel: A Study in Binary Choice,* Northwestern University Press, Evanston, Illinois, 1962; Henri Theil, *Logit Specifications in the Multivariate Analysis of Qualitative Data,* Report 6944; *Conditional Logit Specifications for the Multivariate Analysis of Qualitative Data in the Multiple Response Case,* Report 6956; and *The Explanatory Power of Determining Factors in the Multivariate Analysis of Qualitative Data,* Report 6946, all October 1969, Center for Mathematical Studies of Business and Economics, University of Chicago.

31. James Tobin, "Estimation of Relationships for Limited Dependent Variables," *Econometrica,* 26 (January, 1958), pp. 24-36.

32. See the discussion in T. W. Anderson, *An Introduction to Multivariate Statistical Analysis,* New York, John Wiley & Sons, Inc., 1958, Chapter 6, "Classification of Observation."

33. George W. Ladd, "Linear Probability Functions and Discriminant Functions," *Econometrica,* 34 (Oct. 1966), pp. 873-885.

34. C. Radhakrishna Rao, *Advanced Statistical Methods in Biometric Research,* Wiley, 1952, especially Chapter 8.

35. Eva Mueller, "The Savings Account as a Source for Financing Large Expenditures," *Journal of Finance* 22 (Sept. 1967) 375-393.

36. For examples of criticisms based on considerations of these types, see *Consumption and Saving,* edited by Irvin Friend and Robert Jones, Philadelphia, University of Penna. Press, 1960, 2 vols.; comments by Guy Orcutt, Vol. I, pp. 155-519, and by Milton Friedman, Vol. II, p. 192.

37. M. Ganguli, "A Note on Nested Sampling," *Sankya,* 5 (1941), pp. 449-452. See also, George W. Snedecor and William A. Cochran, *Statistical Methods,* Iowa State University Press, Ames, Iowa, 1956, p. 274; and R. L. Anderson and T. A. Bancroft, *Statistical Theory in Research,* McGraw Hill, New York, 1952, p. 327.

38. S. J. Prais and H. S. Houthakker, *The Analysis of Family Budgets,* Cambridge, University Press, 1955. See Chapter 5. See also J. Durbin and G. S. Watson, "Testing for Serial Correlation in Least-squares Regression," *Biometrika,* 37, 409 and 38, 159 (1950 and 1951).

39. For a discussion of alternatives and results with actual data, see Lawrence R. Klein and James Morgan, "Results of Alternative Statistical Treatments of Sample Survey Data," *Journal of the American Statistical Association,* 51 (December 1951), pp. 442-460. For an example of three different ways of estimating the wealth-elasticities of components of wealth, see Dorothy Projector and Gertrude Weiss, *A Survey of Financial Characteristics of Consumers,* Board of Governors of the Federal Reserve System, Washington, D.C., 1966.

40. Harold Guthrie, "Propensities to Hold Liquid Assets," *Journal of the American Statistical Association* 55, (Sept. 1960), pp. 469-490.

41. J. Johnston, *Econometric Methods,* McGraw-Hill, New York, 1963. See Chapter 6. See also, M. Kendall and Stuart, *The Advanced Theory of Statistics,* Vol. 11, Chapter 29, "Functional and Structural Relationship."

42. Hans Theil, Economic Forecasts and Policy, 2nd revised edition, North Holland Publishing Co., 1961, pp. 225-231, 334-344; see also R. L. Bassmann, "A Generalized Classical Method of Linear Estimation of Coefficients in a Structural Equation," *Econometrica,* 25 (Jan. 1957), pp. 77-83. See also A. Goldberger, *Econometric Theory,* John Wiley, New York, 1964, who proves that two-stage least squares is identical with an instrumental variable estimation, p. 332.

43. See Louis H. Bean, "Simplified Method of Graphic Curvilinear Correlation," *Journal of the American Statistical Association,* 24 (Dec. 1929), pp. 386-397.

44. For a detailed discussion of multiple regression using categorical or dummy variables, see Frank Andrews, James Morgan and John Sonquist, *Multiple Classification Analysis,* Survey Research Center, Ann Arbor, Michigan, 1966. See also Daniel Suits, "The Use of Dummy Variables in Regression Equations," *Journal of the American Statistical Association,* 52 (Dec. 1957), pp. 548-551.

45. See Eva Mueller, "The Savings Account as a Source for Financing Large Expenditures," *Journal of Finance* 22 (Sept. 1967), pp. 375-393, cited earlier, where the forces leading to large decreases in savings accounts were not the mirror image of those leading to above average increases.

46. Richard Barfield and James Morgan, *Early Retirement,* Survey Research Center, The University of Michigan, Ann Arbor, Michigan, 1969, pp. 25ff.

47. See Morgan, Sirageldin and, Baerwaldt, *Productive Americans,* Survey Research Center, Ann Arbor, Michigan, 1966, p. 128.

48. See John Sonquist and James Morgan, *The Detection of Interaction Effects,* Survey Research Center, The University of Michigan, Ann Arbor, Michigan, 1964.

49. James N. Morgan, "The Achievement Motive and Economic Behavior," *Economic Development and Cultural Change,* 12 (April, 1964), 243-267.

50. Grover C. Wirick, James N. Morgan and Robin Barlow, "Population Survey: Health Care and Its Financing," in Walter J. McNerney, Ed., *Hospital and Medical Economics,* Vol. 1, Hospital Research and Educational Trust, Chicago, 1962, pp. 61-357, and James Morgan and John Sonquist, "Some Results from a Non-symmetrical Branching Process that Looks for Interaction Effects," *Proceedings of the Social Statistics Section.*

51. James Morgan, Ismail Sirageldin, and Nancy Baerwaldt, *op. cit.,* p. 128.

52. Robert Hermann, "Interaction Effects and the Analysis of Household Food Expenditures," *Journal of Farm Economics,* 49 (November 1967), pp. 821-832.

53. See the discussion in S. J. Prais and H. S. Houthakker, *The Analysis of Family Budgets,* Cambridge Univ. Press, Cambridge, 1955, Chapter 7.

54. Prais and Houthakker, *op. cit.,* Chapter 9.

55. Martin David, *Family Composition and Consumption,* North Holland Publishing Co., Amsterdam, 1962. As we noted earlier Hermann has found that not only are there different income elasticities of food expenditure according to family size, but that these differences differ depending on whether the families live in rural areas or not. Hermann, *op. cit.*

56. Compare Eisner's comments on Crockett and Friend, in Friend and Jones, ed., *Consumption and Saving,* Vol. I, *op. cit.,* p. 162.

57. Edwin Kuh and John R. Meyer, "How Extraneous Are Extraneous Estimates?" *Review of Economics and Statistics,* 39 (November 1957), pp. 380-393.

58. Gerry Miner, "Consumer Personal Debt: An Intertemporal Cross-section Analysis," in Friend and Jones, eds., *Conference on Consumption and Saving,* University of Penna. Press, Philadelphia, Penna., 1960, Vol. II, pp. 400-461. See also James Morgan, "Analysis and Interpretation of Cross-National Surveys," in *Interdisciplinary Topics in Gerontology,* 2 (1968), pp. 106-110, where the problem is the same.

59. For additional comparisons over time see John B. Lansing and Dwight M. Blood, *The Changing Travel Market,* Institute for Social Research, University

of Michigan, Ann Arbor, Michigan, 1964; and John Lansing and Gary Hendricks, *Automobile Ownership and Residential Density,* Survey Research Center, University of Michigan, Ann Arbor, Michigan, 1967.

60. Lewis Shipper, *Consumer Discretionary Behavior,* North Holland Publishing Co., Amsterdam, 1964.

61. See H. S. Houthakker and John Haldi, "Household Investments in Automobiles: An Inter-Temporal Cross-Section Analysis," in I. Friend and R. Jones, eds., *Consumption and Saving,* Vol. I, University of Penna., 1960, pp. 175-224.

62. Philip Cagan, "The Use of Wealth to Compare Household's Average Saving," *Journal of the American Statistical Association,* 59, Sept. 1964, pp. 737-745.

63. See James Coleman, "The Mathematical Study of Change," in H. B. Blalock, Jr. and A. B. Blalock, eds., *Methodology in Social Research,* McGraw Hill, New York, 1968, pp. 428-478, especially pp. 441-444.

64. "1948 Survey of Consumer Finances, Part I, Expenditure for Durable Goods," *Federal Reserve Bulletin,* June 1948, pp. 634-643.

65. Ronald Bodkin, "Windfall Income and Consumption," in Friend and Jones, *op. cit.,* pp. 175-187.

66. George Katona, *Private Pensions and Individual Saving,* Institute for Social Research, University of Michigan, Ann Arbor, Michigan, 1965; Philip Cagan, *The Effect of Pension Plans on Aggregate Saving,* Columbia Univ. Press, New York, 1965.

67. This point is strongly made by Robert Eisner, *Determinants of Capital Expenditures: An Interview Study,* Bureau of Economic and Business Research, University of Illinois, Urbana, Illinois, 1956.

68. For a good treatment of this, see Hubert M. Blalock, Jr., *Causal Influences in Nonexperimental Research,* University of North Carolina Press, Chapel Hill, 1961.

69. J. G. Kemeny and J. L. Snell, *Mathematical Models in the Social Sciences,* Ginn, New York, 1962; and Patrick Billingsley, *Statistical Inference for Markov Processes,* Univ. of Chicago Press, Chicago, 1961.

70. J. Morgan, M. David, W. Cohen and H. Brazer, *Income and Welfare in the U.S.,* McGraw Hill, New York, 1962.

71. Sherman J. Maisel, "Rates of Ownership, Mobility and Purchase," *Essays in Urban Land Economics,* pp. 76-108, in honour of the 65th birthday of Leo Grebler, University of California, Real Estate Research Program, L.A., 1966.

72. See Arthur Goldberger, "Stepwise Least Squares: Residual Analysis and Specification Effort," *Journal of the American Statistical Association,* 56 (December, 1961), pp. 998-1000, and Arthur Goldberger and D. B. Jochem, "A Note on Stepwise Least Squares," *Journal of the American Statistical Association,* 56 (March, 1961), pp. 105-110.

73. For the best statement, see David R. Heise, "Problems in Path Analysis and Causal Inference," in Edgar F. Borgatta, ed., *Sociological Methodology,* Jossey-Bass, San Francisco, 1969, pp. 38-73. For a discussion of the impact of errors in measurement (or imperfect proxy variables) on the interpretation of causal structures, see Herbert Costner, "Theory Deduction, and Rules of Correspondence," *American Journal of Sociology,* 75 (Sept. 1969), pp. 245-263.

74. Herbert Simon, "Spurious Correlation: A Causal Interpretation," *Journal of the American Statistical Association,* 49 (Sept. 1954), pp. 467-479.

75. See A. Goldberger, *op. cit.* For examples of residuals analysis, see J. Morgan, I. Sirageldin, and N. Baerwaldt, *Productive Americans,* Survey Research Center, University of Michigan, Ann Arbor, Michigan, 1966.

76. J. Morgan, M. David, W. Cohen and H. Brazer, *Income and Welfare in the United States,* McGraw Hill, New York, 1962.

77. For a systematic discussion, see T. W. Anderson, *op. cit.,* Chapter 12. The subject is also treated in M. H. Quenouille, *Associated Measurements,* London, Butterworths Scientific Publications, 1952, pp. 203 ff. Canonical correlation is not usually discussed in introductory textbooks on statistics.

78. John B. Lansing and Nancy Barth, *Residential Location and Urban Mobility: A Multivariate Analysis,* Institute for Social Research, University of Michigan, Ann Arbor, Michigan, December 1964.

79. See the discussion by Herman Wold and Lars Jureen, *Demand Analysis,* Wiley and Sons, New York, 1953.

80. Daniel Suits, "Forecasting and Analysis with an Econometric Model," *American Economic Review,* 52 (March 1962), pp. 104-132. See also J. Johnston, *Econometric Methods,* McGraw Hill, New York, 1963; and Lawrence R. Klein, *A Textbook of Econometrics,* Harper and Row, New York, 1953.

81. H. B. Blalock, Jr., *Causal Inferences in Nonexperimental Research,* The University of North Carolina Press, Chapel Hill, 1961, 1964, and his "Theory Building and Causal Influences," in H. M. Blalock, Jr. and A. B. Blalock, eds., *Methodology in Social Research,* McGraw Hill, New York, 1968, pp. 155-198.

82. For a clear explanation, see Otis Dudley Duncan, "Path Analysis: Sociological Examples," *American Journal of Sociology,* 72 (July, 1966), pp. 1-16. For a clear statement of the restrictions and limitations, see David R. Heise, "Problems in Path Analysis and Causal Inference," in *Sociological Methodology,* Edgar F. Borgatta, ed., Jossey-Bass, San Francisco, 1969, pp. 38-73.

83. Guy H. Orcutt, et al., *Microanalysis of Socioeconomic Systems,* Harper and Brothers, New York, 1961.

Chapter VII

THE FINANCING, ORGANIZATION, AND UTILIZATION OF SURVEY RESEARCH

Introduction

Survey research is expensive, particularly if it is well done. Since knowledge is a "social good" not really salable in the market place, the problem of how an optimal quantity of survey research focused on the right topics is to be financed is a difficult one. Given some level of financing and general focus there is a problem of how to select individual projects and organize them so as to keep the information/cost ratio high. And finally, given some information, there is a problem of how to achieve an effective diffusion of the results so that the social benefits/information ratio is high, and hence the social benefits/costs information as well. We shall discuss these three topics—financing, efficient organization, and effective diffusion of the results, in order.

Financing of Survey Research

All research output is not marketable at its full value, hence its financing must be based on social rather than market criteria. But surveys are expensive, particularly as compared with dissertation fellowships, or small-scale projects using aggregate data or micro-data that are already collected. Nor can they compete for national funds now devoted to the collections of large scale data sets by government, because there the pressures for information about local areas or individual industries require censuses or huge samples, and put severe limits on the type and amount of information that can be collected on each unit.

The financing of survey research comes largely from private foundations and from government agencies which have provisions for research funding, like the National Institutes of Health, the Department of Health, Education, and Welfare, the Office of Economic Opportunity, and the National Science Foundation. Occasionally financing comes from business corporations or trade associations or non-profit organizations.

Since funding is on a project basis, it is impossible to separate the problem of total funding from the problem of the selection of projects. It is common to ask whether the dependence on financing by "clients" does not make the researcher the handmaiden of whoever has money. A counter charge is sometimes made that researchers insist on tackling trivial projects that intrigue them or build their reputation with their professional colleagues, ignoring the great social needs of the day.

The real situation, of course, is more complex and less extreme than either of these views. Following are the sequences by which survey research projects get developed, financed, and reported:

Foundations or government agencies may initiate the process by announcing the availability of funds, describing the research areas for which they stand ready to fund proposals, or even issuing requests for proposals in rather narrowly described areas. They may, if they have their own research staff, design a study and look for a survey organization to do the field work.

In general, however, the research groups have rather wide latitude in formulating proposals, interpreting, altering, or implementing the concerns of the fund sources. There have been occasions when offers of research funds for research projects in specific areas, have had such little interest that the funds could not be used, presumably because no one thought the research was feasible, or worth doing. And, of course, researchers find some of the research they think most crucial is not fundable.

There is often some mutual adaptation, so that the ultimate question of who initiated the design, or who really had the power to decide what was to be done, has no simple answer. It is not true that the researcher has more flexibility and freedom with research *grants* than with research *contracts,* it all depends on the particular situation. Some foundations have quite firm notions what they will support, and quite actively coerce researchers into redesigning their projects. Government mission-oriented agencies, and even private corporations, on the other hand, sometimes make grants or contracts for very broadly specified research which the researcher is free to design, analyze, and publish without restraints.

The complex process does not end with the submission of a formal proposal, since the proposal must then be evaluated and compete with other proposals. Frequently this involves formal committees set up by, but somewhat independent of, the source of funds. These committees may merely rank and evaluate, or they may make the final decision. There are problems of conflict of interest here, of course, since the more the evaluators know about the research area in question, the more likely they are to have strong feelings about what should be done and who should do it. On the other hand, those with no research experience may not be able to provide adequate evaluations.

The practice has been much better than the suspicious might think, though it leaves much to be desired. Perhaps the best procedures have been those of the National Institutes of Health, whose evaluation teams are encouraged to make site visits, and actually communicate with the researchers who may even respond by altering a research design. In other fields, it has often been difficult for the researcher even to know about and respond to the criticisms and comments of an evaluating committee or their consultants. In fact, this lack of two-way-communication can lead to uncorrected misunderstandings of the purpose or method of a project, since writing out a study design unambiguously and clearly is not easy.

One criterion for evaluating any research proposal is, of course, the past performance of the principal researchers. This implies that there should be not only prior evaluation of proposals, but later evaluation of what came out of each research project. There is little evidence that this evaluation is being systematically done either by the sources of research funds, or by the professional associations. There is a relatively high turnover in the staffs of fund-giving organizations, and so much pressure to allocate the new grants, that little time seems left for asking what happened to the old ones. The professional associations have not been very active in attempting any systematic assessment of survey research projects, particularly in economics, perhaps because they are often so large and complex, but partly because survey research in economics is relatively new and alien to the main traditions of analytic analysis and macro-dynamic research.

In spite of everything, however, there is some selective process, and some feedback from past results to future capacity to secure research funds. The total support for survey research is partly the result of the total support for social science research, and partly the result of the proportion of those funds allocated to survey research in economics, presumably based on the quality and relevance of the research proposals advanced.

The total research support for the social and behavioral sciences is not determined on any broad national basis, particularly since it comes from many sources. Presumably it should bear some relation to the total social benefits likely from such research, which, as any economist knows, requires adding utilities (themselves not usually quantifiable) vertically, not horizontally. The more people there are who use the results, the more the total social benefit. And the benefits are partly contributions to better decisions by government agencies, legislators, businessmen, private organizations, or individuals, and partly contributions to a body of scientific knowledge of human behavior, or of research methods. Those of us engaged in economic survey research are convinced that an increase in such research of several orders of magnitude would be clearly justified. But it is difficult to prove it.[1]

Financing on a project basis has developed out of the desire to see to it that the allocation of funds was effective, and the desire to achieve accountability, not just of the expenditures, but of the results. Such financing does introduce some uncertainty, and some costs, not so much because of the need to justify each project, even if it is part of a sequence of studies, but because of the short duration of most grants and the inability of researchers because of this to make long-term plans. We shall see shortly that there are not only economies of scale for a survey research organization, and for each project, but also economies from a steady flow of work and a long planning horizon.

It seems unlikely that these problems would be reduced by institutional grants. What is needed is a much longer time period for grants for survey research, realizing that it takes two to three years to design, conduct, analyze and report, a piece of survey research. Hence, studies need to overlap, too. One of the problems is that the gestation period for other kinds of economic or social research may be shorter, but a more important reason is that Congress in its desire to keep control of the budget, does not allow its agencies to make long-term commitments, unless the funds have already been appropriated. (And the agencies hesitate to set aside their present funds for such future commitments, restricting the number of things they can start this year.)

It seems likely that the future will not differ much from the past. That is, there is likely to remain a number of different and hopefully competing sources of research funds available for economic survey research, a balancing of interests in the design of projects, a selection process among competing proposals, and ultimately some evaluation of the outcome. Perhaps the major long run improvement will come from better evaluation of the results, which will in itself improve the selection of new projects.

Institutional grants may increase the total funds available, but they raise problems of evaluation, since there is no explicit research attached, as with project grants. There will also be problems of accounting, with the change in overhead versus direct costs.

If there were to be some major increase in the support for behavioral science research at the National Science Foundation, or with a new Social Science Foundation, the decisions about the allocation of those funds might well require some new procedures which would represent the interests not just of the professions, but also of the potential users of the results—Congress, mission agencies, etc.

The main sources of funds for economic surveys have been:

The Ford Foundation
The Carnegie Corporation
The Rockefeller Foundation
The Board of Governors of the Federal Reserve System (mostly 1947-60 and 1963-65)
The National Science Foundation
The Social Security Administration
United States Office of Experiment Stations.

Given the difficult problem of assessing research needs in the social sciences, and the embarrassing position of those who want to do research and must tout their own product, some intermediaries have sprung up:

The Social Science Research Council, while it has some funds of its own, often serves as an allocating channel for funds from other foundations or the government. Its Board has representatives of the various professional societies, plus some "at large" members.

The Behavioral Science Division of the National Research Council, whose original and main purpose was to provide unbiased (unpaid) technical advice to government agencies, occasionally serves to allocate small research grants, and, more important, sets up ad hoc advisory committees which recommend directions in which research support should go. It also is made up of official representatives of the various professional societies and some others "at large."

The Russell Sage Foundation also, while having some funds of its own, often secures funds from other foundations for projects which it deems worthy.

Foundations are understandably reluctant to support research which seems fundable by government agencies. Yet occasionally an agency without funding capacity, such as the Council of Economic Advisers, will induce a foundation to support some timely research project. And the Ford Foundation made large grants to the Brookings Institution for a program of studies in public finance, some of which supported survey research.

From a more historic point of view, the various sources of funds, the kinds of things they would support, and the various rules for applying, have been subject to a great deal of change, some of it rather sudden. Foundation boards will decide to change the whole focus of their interests, or Congress will make dramatic shifts in the amount of financial support in the budgets of agencies or for the National Science Foundation.

The variety of accounting rules, and demands for "local participation" increase the complexity and the real cost of securing research funds. The allowable "indirect cost" charges vary from ten percent of total costs with some foundations, to fifty-five percent of wages and salaries with some government agencies. Requirements to prove that the university, for instance, is providing part of the costs of a research project are good in theory, but clearly no university could engage in much research if each project was really a net burden on the university's teaching budget. And a state legislature providing research money for a university might resent having it supplement the funds of some Federal agency which was deciding what research should be supported.

Basically, however, all these confusions and costs of securing research funds would not be so bad if the process had to be endured only at infrequent intervals. When it must be done annually for each project, the sheer accounting burden and the burden on the time and energy of the researchers is formidable.

When research *contracts* are used, there is a general problem as to who "owns" the results of the research.[2] Clearly the survey organization must keep control of the sample books and, if there is any possibility of revealing individual responses, of the questionnaires as well. There is also a question about "clearance" of results before publication, and, in the case of research where the results relate to controversial reform proposals, the secrecy until a report is cleared. Actually the problem has existed more in prospect than in actuality, but the legalistic wording used in some federal contracts is enough to give a researcher pause.

For surveys conducted with federal funds, there is also a requirement that the questionnaires be cleared through the Bureau of the Budget.* Given the tight time schedules of many surveys, and the understandable reluctance to freeze the questionnaire until the last minute (and a desire not to change it after the last pretest), it is difficult for this process to avoid irritating and expensive delays. There have been instances of questionnaires taking long periods to clear, of demands for changes that implied real alterations in the research design, and of objections on minor and irrelevant points. Since there is no appeals procedure, a project can be held up so long that it has to be canceled. The original purpose was to avoid subjecting people to redundant questionnaires from different government agencies, or questions irrelevant and unnecessary for the legitimate purposes of the project, or to badly designed instruments. And this seems justified.

A recent ruling that questionnaires designed for research only, not for descriptive data, need not go through the Bureau of the Budget clearing process, remains to be interpreted. For those not exempted, the ruling that whenever more than six people are to be given the same questionnaire, it must be cleared, makes it difficult even to do pretesting legally, except by making minor changes in each set of six.

It is often argued that "applied" research directed to current social problems, does not provide any lasting basic findings. Our contention is that the distinction between "basic" and "applied" research in the social sciences is a false one. There are many real problems whose answers would be of real utility to people in making decisions, but which would also contribute to the basic body of knowledge in the behavioral sciences. Indeed, many economists have now come to the conclusion that further progress will require a much better data base, and better information about behavioral parameters, before the implications of the econometric models will be of real use in national policy.[3]

A more cooperative working relationship is required between the analytical economists working out the implications of systems of behavioral relationships, and the behavioral economists attempting to make the behavioral parameters in those relationships more realistic.

*Now Office of Management and Budget.

The Organization of Survey Research and the Search for High Information/Cost Ratios

In the true tradition of economic analysis, we can approach the problem of efficient organization of survey research both as a problem of maximizing the output of information per dollar spent, and as a problem of minimizing the costs of providing a given set of information. And we must also look at the total cost curve, that is, the economies of scale. There are also costs associated with instability or with short planning horizons.

Survey research, particularly good survey research, is expensive, particularly in comparison with the costs of econometric analysis of aggregate time series. The difference is several orders of magnitude. In addition it is labor-intensive, using large amounts of time of many highly trained specialists, and providing very little hope for mechanization or automation. But there *are* advantages and economies in specialization and division of labor, and there are heavy overhead costs (again mostly labor) so that there are economies of scale. The costs of survey research, per bit of information, start reaching their lowest possible levels only when the survey organization is regularly doing several million dollars worth of research each year. It may be worthwhile to provide some of the reasons in more detail.

Much of the overhead cost is in the training of specialists and coordinating their efforts. In addition to the researcher who is generally responsible for the design and the analysis of the substantive findings, there must be highly trained professional specialists in:

Field operations—the hiring, training, and supervision of interviewers and the improvement of procedures and continual research on methodology.

Content analysis—the hiring, training, and supervision of editors and coders and the improvement of procedures and research on coding error, coding drift, etc.

Sampling—the design of multi-purpose and special samples, the supervision of collection and processing of sample materials, the development of specific and general purpose approximate sampling errors.

Computer services—file management, data processing, statistical analysis, and improvement of archival and retrieval systems.

Bookkeeping, business management—the rapid provision of cost data required by sponsors and by the organization to avoid cumulative disasters, and the efficient procurement of printing and other services and supplies.

Editing and library—the conversion of reports into readable documents, the collection of relevant outside data, maintenance of archives and files, etc.

If people are assembled for a single limited project, they have neither the time nor the incentive to learn to work together, nor to cooperate. The difference is like the response of a plumbing firm to an individual who is building a single house and their response to a contractor who is building many houses. In the second case they have a long-term concern that the latter be satisfied, for he is a source of future business as well. It is for this reason that the authors have serious doubts about the viability of a survey facility available purely as a service to a rotating series of outside researchers for whom it collects data. Some collaboration between a specialist in methodology and a specialist in a substantive area of behavior is called for.

Not only does the training and assembly of staff represent a kind of fixed cost that needs to be spread over many surveys—and this includes hiring and training of interviewers—but since most of the capital is human capital, it deteriorates through non-use even faster than through use. The sampling materials get out of date, interviewers drift off to other jobs, computer software does not fit the newer generation of computers that come along, etc. This means that both a substantial flow *and* some regularity in its rate is required for efficiency.

Furthermore, given sources of financing which do not like indirect or overhead costs and put arbitrary limits on them, it is necessary to have cost systems which make as many things as possible into variable costs, chargeable to specific surveys. This is much easier with a continuous stream of work where, for instance, each survey can pay for some of the costs of updating the sampling materials in the field. The preparation of manuals, procedures, etc. also represents a cost which can be spread over many surveys, and indeed the development of conventions, standard procedures, etc. makes the work easier all along the line.

In order to achieve these economies of scale, it may be necessary for a survey research center to engage in a rather wide range of surveys in several fields. It is an interesting question just how much variety can be covered without difficulties. Interviewers trained to fixed-question open-answer interviews with heads of families may find it difficult to shift to other techniques. Very small samples have different computing problems from larger ones or panel studies. But the range can be rather wide, and indeed people who start out with rather widely different notions may converge somewhat as they learn from one another.

Problems arise as to the evaluation of individual performance necessary for the proper rewards and career development of the various individuals involved. The principal researcher can follow the usual path of articles and authorship, though even here the growing necessity for multiple authorship demanded by the staff needs of surveys, makes individual evaluation and recognition difficult.

More serious problems arise with the more specialized methodological skills involved, and with the sub-professional specialties. The heads of the specialized service sections such as sampling, field, etc., may have their own programs of methodological research and teaching, but still the demands of the organization take their time and provide little recognition from their profession-al colleagues. The most dramatic case has been computer programming, a highly specialized and demanding occupation. But a competent programmer finds him-self solving other people's problems and seeing them get the glory. This, coupled with the unwillingness or inability of many universities to provide monetary re-wards, titles, or tenure for such people, has left many a magnificent computer almost bereft of adequate software, or of programming service for those who want to use the computer. Some professors have become programmers, or con-vinced graduate students to do so, in clear violation of the economist's law of comparative advantage and the principle of specialization.

One major advantage of large, on going survey organizations, is that they can provide tenure, titles, recognition, and evaluation of their own staff. They can also provide career lines and promotions within the organization, allowing people to upgrade their skills. The status of the specialists can also be enhanced by their gradual "professionalization" and by separate authorship in study re-ports of methodological chapters by the specialists in sampling, interviewing, coding, and data processing.

There is another way in which the scale of a survey operation affects its efficiency or information/cost ratio. There is transfer of learning enthusiasm, and criticism across different substantive programs. People studying one kind of economic behavior learn from those studying another kind, and also from those studying political behavior. Frequently one group borrows from the other, par-ticularly in the development of measures of the explanatory variables which are often interdisciplinary.

Effective survey research often requires cooperation with specialists in more than one field. Economic surveys may require active participation by ex-perts in law, medicine, public health, religion or philanthropy, city planning, outdoor recreation, air transport, etc. And this cooperation should begin in the early design stages and continue through the writing of the results.

In practice, securing funds for a piece of survey research involves working out a design, getting cost estimates from the various specialists (sampling, field, data processing, content analysis) estimating a total budget of time and money, and summarizing all this in a research proposal. We now turn to some explicit es-timates of components of survey costs.

We have already seen that there is another resource allocation problem in designing each survey. It is usually stated in the form of maximizing the incre-ment to knowledge from the utilization of a fixed total budget. The most com-mon error is to invest so much in collecting data that there are insufficient funds for analyzing and writing. The second most common is to devote so little to de-sign and pretesting work that the data are not worth analyzing.

Within a topic there is a question whether to focus on a more limited area and spend more time on it, or to cover several areas (usually on the grounds that they are related anyway and hence must be studied together—like the components of saving).

And in the explanatory variables, again one has a choice of spending much time measuring a few very carefully, or whether to expand the range of explanatory variables with less attention to each.

There are also economies of scale in conducting a single survey, even in an organization doing surveys continually. The costs of many components are almost independent of the number of interviews: original design, pretesting, interviewers instructions, editing and coding procedures, programming the file building and cleaning of data on the computer, and writing the results. And other costs are less than proportionate to the number of interviews: printing, computer runs, interviewing. Hence, there are sample sizes below which it does not seem worth the investment for the little information that comes out. If a sample is designed with 50-100 primary sampling areas, and it is very costly for a single interviewer to take fewer than 10-20 interviews in any one study, this becomes a kind of restriction, unless there is a probability subsample which uses only half of the primary sampling areas (except for the self-representing ones). But the most important overhead cost is probably in design and development of the questionnaire and materials.

A Preliminary Analysis of Survey Costs

The purpose of this section is to present an elementary analysis of the determinants of survey cost as a contribution to the rational planning of sample surveys. In the design of a sample survey there are a large number of choices to be made about what is to be done. Comparisons of two surveys in which different options were selected can be of doubtful meaning, or, in the extreme, completely meaningless. Nobody would conclude that Fords cost more than Chevrolets from the comparison of two cars without taking into account the detailed characteristics of the particular vehicles. Surveys are, if anything, more heterogeneous than automobiles. It is important, therefore, to know the cost of the options.

A few general observations may be made at the start. Surveys are labor intensive. Hence, costs tend to move with wages and salaries, especially, for academic personnel, with university salary rates. In most aspects of survey work gains in productivity are not easy to achieve. In this respect surveys are more like live theatrical performances than they are like the manufacture of durable goods. The principal technological innovation now in process is the introduction of new and improved computers. The gain has been primarily in more and better tabulations for the same expenditure rather than in a reduction of cost for a given quantity and quality of tabulations. Even when the gain is taken in cost reduction, tabulating costs represent a comparatively minor part of the total cost of a typical survey. They may be ten percent of total costs, or less. Even cutting tabulating costs in half would not reduce total costs very much. In other aspects of survey work technical gains have been limited. Hence, there is a tendency toward upward pressure on survey costs over time.

Here we merely assemble information readily available at the Survey Research Center, primarily from the heads of the sections of the Center. The starting point is existing practice and observed costs on current financial surveys. In general, the greater the departure from existing practice at the Survey Research Center, the less certain the cost estimates. No attempt has been made to develop new knowledge of costs.

Table 1 presents estimates of the approximate total data collection cost for a recent financial survey conducted for the Office of Economic Opportunity.

This was an unusually large survey for the Survey Research Center, with a total of 4800 interviews taken in 1968. As Table 1 indicates, total direct costs were $47.60 per interview, the largest items being field salaries at $21.88 and field travel at $8.12, or $30.00 per interview for total field costs. On this study sampling, coding, supplies, and tabulating were all in the range of $3.50 to $5.00 per interview. Each of these components of the cost of data collection will be considered below. Information on research salaries will be presented separately in a concluding section.

Field Costs: It is possible to prepare tables showing long-run trends in direct field costs. Table 2 shows such a trend for selected "Omnibus" surveys conducted by the Survey Research Center in the period 1951-1952 to 1968. Note that this tabulation includes only interviewers' salaries and interviewers' travel, and excludes field supervisors' salaries and travel and costs in the Ann Arbor office of the field staff. Note, first, that there has been a major upward trend in cost per interview for interviewers' salaries and travel, from about $6-$7 in 1951-1953 to $16-$21 in 1967-1968. Note also that there has been variation from survey to survey in these costs. For example, the costs per interview fell from $20.05 in the fall of 1966 to $16.07 in the spring of 1967 but returned to $20.81 a year later.

The basic trend can be explained in considerable part by changes in hourly wage rates. Data on minimum and maximum hourly rates are available for the period, but weighted average hourly salaries are available only for the last year or two. They are shown in the lower part of Table 2. Since in 1952-1953 the spread between the minimum and maximum rates was only 20¢, we can assume that the average was about the mid-point, that is, $1.25 per hour. The average of $2.43 in 1968-1969 then is about double the rate paid in 1952-1953 for an hour of interviewer's time. Strictly speaking, the comparison of total costs should consider separately the shifts in reimbursement rates per mile of interviewers' travel, but they increased more or less in the same manner as salary rates over this period. If

TABLE 1

Approximate Data Collection Cost of a Financial Survey,

Based on First Wave of Interviews for

Study of Income Dynamics

(1968, n = 4800)

		Total	Per Interview
1.	Field salaries (interviewers and supervisors)	$105,000	$21.88
2.	Field travel (by interviewers and supervisors)	39,000	8.12
3.	Sampling	17,000	3.54
4.	Coding	21,000	4.38
5.	Supplies	23,000	4.79
6.	Tabulating	23,500	4.90
	Subtotal	$228,500	$47.60
7.	Fringe benefits, service personnel, at 10% of lines 1, 3, 4	$ 14,300	$ 2.98
8.	Indirect costs at 47% of lines 1, 3, 4, 7	$ 73,931	$15.40
		$316,731	$65.98

Note: This table includes no entry for payments to respondents
which were made between the first and second waves of
interviews on this study. This study was also unusual
in using additional sample points and in these and the
regular sample points in reinterviewing families previously
interviewed once or twice by the United States Census
Bureau.

TABLE 2

Long Run Trends in Direct Field Costs Per Interview

for "Omnibus" Surveys

Year	Interviewers' Salaries	Interviewers' Travel	Total
Fiscal 1951-1952 #601	$4.46	$1.16	$5.62
Fiscal 1952-1953 #607	6.26	1.52	7.78
Fiscal 1956-1957 #649	7.30	2.17	9.47
Fall 1962	10.02	3.97	13.99
Summer 1963	11.93	4.91	16.84
Fall 1963	11.08	3.47	14.55
Spring 1964	10.28	3.17	13.45
Fall 1965	11.45	3.73	15.18
Summer 1966	12.29	3.49	15.78
Fall 1966	15.99	4.06	20.05
Spring 1967	13.00	3.07	16.07
Summer 1968	15.02	5.79	20.81

Hourly Rates:	1952-53	1968-69
Minimum hourly rate	$1.15	$2.00
Maximum hourly rate	1.35	2.80

	1967	1968-69
Weighted average hourly salary	$2.16	$2.43

we take Study 607 in 1952-1953 as a starting point for a comparison, then that study would have cost not $7.78 per interview but a little under $16 at wage and mileage rates in 1968-1969. Actual surveys in 1967-1968 cost $16.07 to $20.81. If we consider interviewers' salaries alone, then we may take $6.26, roughly double it, to about $13-$14, and compare that figure with the observed $15.02 in the summer of 1968. It is clear that costs per interview have increased slightly more than can be accounted for by changes in hourly wage rates.

What is lacking in this comparison are data on the characteristics of the interviews. It is entirely possible that the interviews have become longer and more complex over this period. One way to reduce cost per unit of information collected is to collect more items of information in a single interview. Thus, cost per unit information may have been constant while costs per interview increased. Another difference between interviewing in 1968 and in 1952-1953 is that the geographic distribution of the population in the country has changed. In general, people have tended to shift into metro areas, where costs are higher, and also to shift into spread-out suburban areas where travel costs are higher. Such changes may have increased the amount of time interviewers spend in locating their respondents, thus increasing both the mileage costs for travel, and salaries while traveling. We can only speculate as to the importance of these factors with the data at hand.

Determinants of Cost Per Interview: In view of the importance of field costs as a proportion of total survey cost it is not surprising that considerable attention has been given to the determinants of cost per interview. Information on four factors has been assembled in Table 3 and additional historical data appear in Table 4.

First, cost per interview depends upon the number of interviews taken by a given interviewer employed on a survey. As shown in part I of Table 3, the average cost per interview on a project for a given interviewer falls at a decreasing rate as the number of interviews taken increases. The shape of the relationship suggests the existence of some initial fixed cost which is being distributed over an increasing number of interviews. This cost presumably is the time taken by an interviewer to become familiar with the questionnaire and instruction book for a particular project. There may also be some efficiency in actual data collection in calling on different addresses if one has more addresses to cover and, hence, more options open on a given trip into the field. In any event the data show quite clearly that it costs more for interviewers to take less than ten interviews on a given project. Yet, on comparatively small surveys, such as Study #504, as many as thirty-six percent of the interviews were in fact taken by interviewers who took one to nine interviews. On Study 763, the 1967 Survey of Consumer Finances, with a total of 3102 interviews, only four percent of the interviews were taken by interviewers who took less than ten interviews a

TABLE 3

Four Determinants of Cost Per Interview for

Interviewers' Salaries and Travel

I. Size of sample and number of interviews per interviewer employed

Number of interviews taken per interviewer	Average cost per interview		Percent of interviews taken by interviewers with each "take"	
	#763	#504	#763	#504
1-9	$27.50	$24.28	4	36
10-14	19.70	18.79	17	37
15-19	18.98	15.08	18	12
20-29	17.40 ⎰	14.29	36	15
30+	16.09 ⎱		25	
			100	100
overall	$18.13	$19.68	N= 3102	1496

Based on #763, 1967 S.C.F., and #504

II. Type of place--large cities versus medium sized cities and other areas

Size	Interviewers' Salaries		Interviewers' Travel		Total	
	#763	#750	#763	#750	#763	#750
Small towns, rural	$12.12	$ 9.87	$ 3.14	$ 3.20	$15.26	$13.07
Metro areas, not including 12 largest	13.20	10.85	3.96	3.42	17.16	14.27
12 largest cities	18.34	14.55	5.37	4.91	23.71	19.46

TABLE 3 - continued

III. Local vs. national surveys

A.   "Time Use" Study

	Jackson, Mich. (n = 792)	National metropolitan sample
	#471	#491
Interviewers' salaries	$ 8.94	$14.62
Interviewers' travel	2.46	4.90
Total	$11.40	$19.52

"Extra" 96 interviews taken at the end of the study in Jackson

Interviewers' salaries	$ 6.70
Interviewers' travel	3.14
Total	$ 9.84

B. #755 Living Patterns and Attitudes in Detroit, Data for Detroit
    Interviewers' work only (n = 1008)

	#755 (Spring 1966)
Interviewers' salaries	$ 7.52
Interviewers' travel	1.76
Total	$ 9.28

C. Comparison between Detroit and Other Large Metro Areas (#763)

	Interviewers' Salaries	Interviewers' Travel	Total
Detroit	$15.93	$ 4.66	$20.59
All large metro areas	18.34	5.37	23.71

D. Study of Young Drivers (Pelz), Detroit area, n = 669 (Required
    screening at 6 addresses per 1 final selection included. Also,
    badly located for Detroit staff in western Wayne, Washtenaw, etc.)

Interviewers' salaries	$13.48
Interviewers' travel	$ 4.45
Total	$17.93

IV. Cost of telephone interviews ("Omnibus," brief interview by phone)
     #757, telephone reinterviews, with personal interviews where
     no telephone

Interviewers' salaries	$ 2.84
Interviewers' travel	.63
Total	$ 3.47

TABLE 4

Historical Data on Interviewers' Salaries as a Function of

Length of Interview and a Breakdown of Interviewers' Time

I. Relation between length of questionnaire and costs:
costs of interviewers' salaries, for omnibus studies,
1957-58 through 1962-63: I = $2.50 plus $.11 L,
where L = length of interview in minutes
I = interviewers' salaries per interview

II. Breakdown of time spent:

	Metro	Urban	Rural
Interviewing	17%	23%	23%
Calling	17	13	12
Editing	12	15	16
Training	5	7	9
Administration	7	10	7
Travel	35	22	19
Sampling*	7	10	14
Total	100%	100%	100%

*Estimated.

This table is based on data from day-by-day records
kept by interviewers as tabulated for a sample of
counties on one "omnibus" survey, #685, in 1960.

piece. It is not surprising, therefore, that the average cost per interview was $1.50 cheaper on Study 763 than Study 504.

While it is possible to consider this relationship in terms of administrative practices in the field, it is also possible to think of it in terms of sampling. If the number of primary sampling units in which interviews were taken on Study 504 had been reduced, no doubt the number of interviews taken per interviewer could have been kept at the level of the larger survey. There would have been a loss, however, in the form of increased sampling error.

A second determinant of field cost per interview is the type of place in which the interviews are taken. Data on cost per interview by type of place are shown in part II of Table 3 for Study 763 and Study 750. These results are typical. On Study 763, for example, costs per interview in small towns and rural areas were $15.26, and in the 12 largest cities, $23.71. The difference was $8.45 per interview. On Study 750 it was $6.39.

There are at least four underlying factors at work. First, wage rates are higher in large cities, and on the average interviewers must be paid more per hour. Second, interviewers in large cities spend more time traveling and less time interviewing than those in smaller cities and rural areas, as is indicated by Table 4.

Third, there is a substantial difference in costs between local and national surveys as shown in part III of Table 3. A direct comparison can be made in connection with the study of time use undertaken by Converse and his colleagues in which a national sample of people in metropolitan areas was interviewed on the same schedule as a cross-section of a small metropolitan area, Jackson, Michigan. Costs per interview for interviewers' salaries and travel were $11.40 in Jackson compared to $19.52 in the national sample, a difference of about $8. This comparison is complicated by the fact that some of the interviews in the national sample were taken in large metropolitan areas where as just noted, costs tend to be $5-$6 higher. There is still a cost advantage of $4 or so for the local study.

It is also of some interest to note the results of a special situation in the Jackson sample. At the end of the study an extra 96 interviews were taken which had not been planned for in advance, and the cost information about these interviews was kept separate. The cost per interview was $9.84, or $1.56 less than the average for the project in Jackson. This result is consistent with what was observed above about the effect of increasing the number of interviews per interviewer.

A second example of a study in a single area is Study 765, Living Patterns and Attitudes in Detroit, in which 1008 interviews were taken by Detroit interviewers in the Detroit metropolitan region. (We exclude a few interviews by non-Detroit staff.) Cost per interview was $9.28 for interviewers' salaries and travel. These results may be compared with the experience on Study 763, a national survey involving 93 interviews in Detroit, in which the total costs were $20.59

in Detroit. Note, however, that Detroit is a low cost city for interviewing by the Survey Research Center. On Study 763, in all large metropolitan areas combined average cost per interview was $23.71. Another recent local project in the Detroit area was a study of young drivers under the direction of Donald Pelz with 669 interviews. This project was unusually difficult in that it required screening interviews to locate people in the appropriate demographic group with about six screening interviews for one final-selection. Nevertheless, interviewers' salary and travel per final interview cost only $17.93.

Fourth, costs per interview can be drastically affected by changing from personal interviews to telephone interviews. The cost of telephone interviewing depends heavily on the length of the interview and on the procedures used to deal with people who do not have telephones. On Study 757, a brief telephone reinterview on an "Omnibus" survey, personal interviews were taken where no telephone was available. Even including the cost of these personal interviews, the total interviewers' salaries plus travel was only $3.47 per interview.

Information was collected about the length of interview on the average in the field as well as on costs for Omnibus surveys in the period of 1957-1958 through 1962-1963. Results are summarized in a simple equation shown in Table 4 part I. In effect, this equation assumes that all of the variation from one Omnibus survey to another is the result of differences in length of interview. The marginal cost shown of eleven cents per minute reflects cost levels in the period around 1960, and would have to be substantially increased for 1968-1969. It should be pointed out that the length of an interview influences the time actually spent interviewing and editing plus the number of interviews that an interviewer may be able to complete successfully on a single excursion into the field. If the interview is reasonably short, the chances are better that she can complete more than one interview on a given visit to a cluster of sample addresses. It may also affect the amount of non-response, the costs of which are spread over the other interviews.

The second part of Table 4 shows data from 1960 breaking down the amount of time spent in different activities by interviewers working in different types of areas. Note that in metropolitan areas on that study only seventeen percent of the hours of the interviewers were actually spent in interviewing, compared to thirty-five percent spent in travel. The reference to sampling is to work done in assembling information for sampling purposes by interviewers in the field.

Sampling Costs: The selection of the sample involves two stages, the development of a sampling frame, and then the selection of elements from that frame. A given frame may be usable for selection of several specific samples. The first question, therefore, in considering the cost of selecting a sample for a particular study is whether there is an existing sampling frame which is appropriate for this survey. If there is, a sample can be drawn quickly and economically.

In general, the sampling section has a well developed frame for national samples which makes use of a specific selection of primary sampling units. To include additional primary sampling units would involve an extension of the frame, but this expansion is not likely to be necessary except in the event that the one wishes to use a very large national sample for some purpose. Local surveys also require frames, and, in general, the sampling section does not have such frames available for most metropolitan areas in the country. There are a few exceptions: Detroit, Philadelphia, and a few other areas.

For a national sample using the existing frame the cost is a function primarily of the number of interviews. Some costs, such as the cost of selecting individual segments, are proportional to the size of the sample. Other aspects of sample selection do not increase very much as the size of the sample increases. For a sample of about 1500 interviews, expense for sampling salaries is about $6000-$7000, that is, about $4.00-$4.66 per interview. Doubling the size of the sample to 3000 interviews would roughly increase the cost by fifty to sixty percent, that is, to $9000-$11,000. Cost per interview would fall to about $3 to $3.66. For particular projects additional expense may be incurred if, for example, there are extensive calculations of sampling errors, or if there are special problems such as splicing two samples.

Samples located in a single metropolitan area are somewhat less complicated, and, therefore, somewhat more economical for a given number of interviews. In 1967 the sampling section drew a sample of about 1000 in the Cleveland metropolitan area. A total cost of $3,250 covered both these selections and a sample of union locals which was needed at the time. If roughly $650 of the total is allocated to the sample of union locals, and about $2600 to the area sample of the metropolitan area, then the cost per selection was about $2.60. (Cost per interview would be slightly higher owing to the usual losses from non-response and non-sample addresses.)

A sample is now being drawn for the Boston metropolitan area. Including the setting up of a frame with a capability for future use and actual selection of 800 addresses the total cost is estimated at $3,950 in sampling salaries. If the total amount is allocated to these 800, then the cost is nearly $5 per selection. The work has been done in such a manner, however, that an extra 2400 selections could be made at a very small additional cost, implying a cost per selection well under $2.00. The experience in Boston clearly illustrates both the economies in the full exploitation of a given sampling frame, and the difference in cost between a local and a national frame.

A final comment about sampling costs may be made for panel studies. There is little additional sampling work required on a "pure" panel survey after initial selection. If, however, the panel is to be used also as a cross-section of the population of dwelling units existing in the future, there is additional sampling work. It becomes necessary to develop and apply checking procedures designed to pick up the new dwelling units which may be created after the initial selections have been made.

Coding Costs: The estimation of the cost to code an interview may be described in a series of steps:

a) *Time to code a standard interview.* An interview from a study takes one hour to code and requires six to eight cards. A rule of thumb is to estimate the length of time an average interview takes in the field and estimate that the time to code will be the same. This rule applies to "standard" economic interviews, which contain twenty-five percent or less open-ended questions.

b) *Additional time.* Adding twenty-five percent to the time to code an interview to allow for training, check coding, and miscellaneous time. Thus, the result of these two steps is an estimate of time per interview in man-hours.

c) *Apply an average rate.* The average rate is now about $2.40 per hour. It varies depending on the rates for the coders assigned to a project. Currently the range is $1.90-$2.65, the latter level being that paid to people who have been coding for 1 1/2 years or more. Multiply the average rate by the number of interviews.

d) *Office time and supervision.* The cost of office time and supervision is now about $150 per week for a typical study, assuming that there are two studies in coding at the same time, which is typical. The length of time in coding is ordinarily comparable to the length of time a study is in the field.

In addition, although many surveys need no editing, a separate editing operation is required on complex surveys such as the Surveys of Consumer Finances. The cost may be estimated on the same basis as for coding, but obviously must depend on the complexity of the work to be done by the editors. On the 1968 Survey of Consumer Finances editing required an average of 0.8 hours per interview while coding required 1.1 hours.

Coding costs may be expected to vary depending upon the number of open-end questions. Elimination of open-end questions will cut coding time to roughly half of field time instead of the same as field time. Increasing to fifty percent open questions will increase coding time roughly to 1 1/2 times interviewing time. It should be understood that these estimates are approximate and depend on the complexity of the code for the open-ended questions.

Tabulating Costs: Tabulating and computing costs have two basic characteristics. First the technology is shifting very rapidly. Second, there is a close and complex interaction between the computing staff and the research staff. Functions may be shifted back and forth between these two groups of people. In addition, there is a tendency for the detailed knowledge of the computing facility by the analysis staff to become obsolete very quickly. Between the analysis of one study and the analysis of the next there may be major changes in the computer software. There are also important trade-offs between computing costs and research salary costs. An organization of the flow of work which is efficient from the point of view of minimizing tabulating costs may not be an organization which is efficient from the point of view of the utilization of the research staff. Compromises may be necessary.

The computing section at present is working with an organization of costs for their services into eight types of operation. As one proceeds down the list these costs become increasingly difficult to estimate. The available information may be summarized as follows. (Remember, however, that they depend heavily on the computer software available and require a heavy input of research staff time.)

1. *Transcription.* The cost of punching and verifying is now about ten cents per card. This figure is based on the rate of $5.50 per hour for the machine plus the operator. That rate, like other rates to be cited below, includes an allowance for the overhead costs of the data processing section. If we think of a hypothetical standard survey with a sample of 1500 and five IBM cards per interview, the cost of transcription works out to $750.

2. *File construction.* The data processing charges involved in file construction for a typical survey are $25 plus $15 per 100 cases. For the standard survey used as an example here the total amount would be $250. This process involves certain checking and matching operations as well as the conversion from card to tape.

3. *Cleaning.* This step involves the internal checking of the data for consistency and correction of any errors which are found. The amount spent will depend on the extent of the checking. A typical figure is thirty-five cents per interview, or, for the hypothetical standard survey, $525.

4. *Variable generation.* On an average in a typical survey 50 variables will be generated per 100 variables coded. The cost of the operation is thirty cents to fifty cents per interview depending upon the number of variables, their complexity, any errors detected in the process, and the number of passes through the computer which are required. The total cost for the hypothetical survey thus would be in the range of $450 to $750.

5. *Univariate analysis.* The typical first step in actual analysis is the preparation of univariate distributions. The cost is in the range five cents to fifteen cents per variable per 1000 cases. For the standard survey, it would be in the range of $33 to $100.

6. *Bivariate analysis.* The cost of bivariate distributions ranges from ten cents to twenty-five cents per table per 1000 cases. If we assume 1500 cases and 450 tables, which would not be unusual, the range would be $60 to $150.

Up to this stage in the analysis the standard survey has cost $1525 for steps 1, 2, and 3, plus $550 to $1000 for steps 4, 5, and 6, for a grand total of about $2000-$2500. Roughly speaking, the costs are in direct proportion to the number of variables coded and the number of interviews for a given level of effort in cleaning and variable generation. From this stage on costs depend on the complexity of the analysis which is undertaken.

7. *Analysis of interrelations.* Costs of this type of analysis depend on what is being done, whether it is missing data correlations, factor analysis, scaling, or whatever. Minimum costs are about $50 to $100 per run per 1000 cases with a limited number of variables, that is, 60 to 100 variables. Costs may be higher depending on what is required.

8. *Multivariate analysis.* The cost of multivariate analysis depends directly on the program and the complexity of the analysis.

It is prudent practice to add a safety factor to the above estimates. Unexpected developments and errors can add to costs, but they cannot reduce them. Experience with previous studies is often a better guide than estimates built from components, where errors can cumulate.

One approach has been suggested for handling the problem of how to estimate costs for the later, more complicated analysis of (7) and (8). Sonquist suggests using a rough estimate of $1000 per man-month of analysts' time. He has in mind estimating tabulating costs on the basis of the number of man-months of time of professional staff who will be making use of the computer in this phase of a project. All these estimates assume continuous operations and a lot of previous investment in human and physical capital.

Research Salaries: There are two broad choices to be made in planning or estimating research salaries: first, how large a total staff in man-years of different types of personnel should be assigned to a project? Second, how should the time of the research staff be distributed among the different phases of a project? It may be useful to distinguish five stages as follows:

1. *Planning.* This period extends from the initial conception of a project up to the time when data collection actually begins. Several months are ordinarily required, depending on the novelty of the project.

2. *Supervision of data collection.* This period extends from the data when materials are mailed to interviewers to the date when coding is completed and the cards have been keypunched. The lag between the completion of coding and the completion of keypunching is ordinarily negligible. It is standard practice for interviewing, coding, and keypunching to proceed simultaneously, so that the total length of time for data collection exceeds by only a few weeks the total time in the field.

3. *Supervision of data preparation.* The next phase is the supervision of data preparation, that is stages 2, 3, and 4 above: file construction, cleaning and correction, and variable generation. File construction ordinarily requires about

one week, and cleaning and correction and variable generation may proceed
more or less at the same time. The total period required for the cleaning and correction (only) of the 1968 Survey of Consumer Finances was about two months.
For the OEO study the total period was approximately three months for the
Survey Research Center part of the study for the three steps. Of course, if little
or no cleaning or variable generation is needed, these two steps can be reduced
or omitted.

4. *Computing.* The next phase is analysis proper, in which computing proceeds through steps five-eight above, the statistical manipulation of the data.
Some overlap is possible both with the preceding and following phases of the
work.

5. *Report preparation.* Report preparation may well be commenced while
computing is still going on. The usual experience is that computing gradually
tapers off as the report is going through its final phases of preparation. This
phase may be regarded as completed with the delivery of the final published report. This phase is the one most usually under-budgeted, and the part of the
budget most often robbed by over-doing other things.

Supplies: The category "supplies" used at the Institute for Social Research
includes four main components: duplicating and printing, postage, communications (toll calls), and general office supplies, including maps and other materials
needed for sample selection. It is sufficiently heterogeneous so that it is custom-
arily estimated simply as a percentage of total costs. That approach seems appropriate, for example, to handle variations in duplicating, which includes duplicating of drafts as well as final copies of memoranda, questionnaires, codes,
worksheets, instructions, tables, reports, and so forth. Field work requires expenses for postage on completed interviews and toll calls to interviewers which
are roughly proportional to the total volume of work.

An exception is the preparation of the final report or reports. The length
of these documents, the number of copies, the use of graphic displays, and the
type of reproduction vary substantially. Costs vary accordingly from small sums
for mimeographed reports to several thousand dollars. However, for more than
one hundred copies, printing (photo-offset) is cheaper than mimeographing or
multilithing, because the paper is so much cheaper and the actual printing so
much faster.

Concluding Comments: The preceding discussion has been based on the
assumption that the basic research techniques required for a particular inquiry
have been developed. Allowance is made only for a planning period and a standard type of pretest. It may be true, however, that the techniques needed for a
particular project do not exist. If innovations are needed in sample design, questionnaire design, or analysis, appropriate allowance should be made in the budget.
A pilot study may be required, particular measures may need development or

validation, new computer programs may need to be developed, or some other special effort may be called for. This work may be thought of as "extra" in the sense that it is in addition to the basic costs of a standard survey, but it may be fundamental to the success of the research. The estimates also probably understate the amount of research salaries that ought to be provided if more attention is to be given to dissemination of the results, increasing their social benefits. The difficulties in financing and the natural tendency to collect adequate data in a historic context where they could not be improved later, have led to underspending on careful writing of separate interpretations for different audiences.

Although the previous estimates have looked at separate components, and to some extent built them up from subparts, it is often quite misleading to estimate the costs of a new survey in this manner. It is easy to omit things, and underestimate the total.

For example one might estimate the time an interview would take, multiply by the average interviewers' salary, and add some travel costs. But the interviewing costs also include the interviewer's salary while she is:

> travelling
> being trained
> reading instruction books
> doing pretesting of earlier questionnaires
> doing preliminary sampling work (listing addresses, checking for new
>   construction, etc.)
> calling on not-at-homes
> making call-backs
> chatting with respondents during or after the interview to assure com-
>   pletion and satisfied respondents (interviews often take longer
>   than pretests)
> writing afterwards to fill out shorthand and abbreviations, and adding a
>   description of the situation
> filling out forms for non-response, for financial accounting, etc.

Furthermore, the total field budget may be expected to include the salaries and expenses of supervisors who hire, train, and supervise the interviewers, the salaries of office contact persons, typists and mailers, the salaries of the head of the field section and others who aided in designing the questionnaire, pretesting, etc. Someone has to check the sample books, and there are bills for telephone, mail, paper and printing.

Some functions fall between sections, so that the budget may inadvertently omit them because each section assumes the other will handle it, when that section is asked for an estimate of its costs for a survey. This is particularly true of sample book controls which may be done by the field section, the sampling section, or the analysis section, or of supervision of editing and coding which is often divided between the analysis section and the supervisors in the coding section.

It is also common to estimate how much each subcomponent would cost if little went wrong, multiply by the number of such components, and leave insufficient margin for errors and breakdowns. The tendency for building contractors to underestimate, year after year and house after house, how long it will take to finish the job, illustrates the kind of perceptual bias involved.

A major cost often overlooked is the cost of delay, since salaries are a major part of the cost, and many of them are paid even if the people cannot do their job because they are waiting for something. Hence proper scheduling and meshing of the parts are critical. This is true for each survey, and for a series of surveys. For instance, it is efficient to have interviewers starting their calls on a new survey while still attempting to find a few "not-at-homes" left from the previous one, particularly since the final sample clusters are located close together. For each survey some common instances of delays that keep staff "standing on their own shoelaces" are:

> Assembling and training editors before there is a sufficient supply of interviews to edit.
> Assembling and training coders before there is a sufficient backlog of interviews edited to assure a steady flow of work.
> Starting either editing or coding too late, so that problems in field interviewing or editing are not caught until a large number of errors have already been made.
> Failure to plan for the analysis, so that things stop while additional variables are generated, etc.
> Failure to enforce a deadline in the field, so that interviews keep trickling in.

Another cost-raising error is unnecessary complexity in the questionnaire, in sample design, in editing procedures, in codes, etc. Interviewers make costly mistakes if the instrument is too complex. Complex samples cause problems in the field, in weighting the data, in computation of sampling errors. Complex codes slow down coders and multiply the error rate. The use of several different questionnaires makes codes complex, exacerbates analysis problems, and often leads either to no differences in results, or unexplained differences. If some questions are asked of only half the sample and a different set from the other half, again the analysis and the data file management is more complicated. Combining samples and splicing them together is another example, though it may sometimes be necessary.

A major source of difficulty is that time and money budgeted run out before the study is finally cleaned up, archived, etc. Some procedure for reserving funds to be used for final editorial work, cleaning up files, providing a proper final documentation and lending library of data tapes, would vastly improve the archives of the future. Even the final costs of printing or typing derivative articles often come in long after the study budget is closed.

The implications of all this discussion on maximizing the information cost ratio is that what is required is a large, steady, well-planned program of surveys, efficiently organized with attention to costs as well as to amount of information. There are economies of scale for survey organizations, for each individual survey, and for sequences of surveys on one general topic area.

Diffusion of Results; the Social Benefits/Information Ratio

The benefits of research are a function of the extent to which the information is utilized. In so far as the responsibility for interpreting the research findings to a variety of audiences falls upon the researcher, the previously discussed problems in financing research are relevant. In the current state of short-run project financing, a survey research specialist must be simultaneously writing proposals, designing other studies, supervising the implementation of still others, and writing up the findings of earlier studies. Once the main report of a study is written, there is tremendous pressure to move on to the other projects at various stages of their development. This pressure is intensified by the overall underfinancing of economic surveys, and the large number of things that need to be done. It is also made dramatic by the fact that research is in a historical context, and findings relate to major events in the economy. Data not collected at a point in time cannot be collected later, and every economic event whose impact on the economic actors is unstudied, is one more chance lost forever. The mere calendar limitations on budgets also make it difficult for a researcher to continue writing and speaking on past studies, while charging his time to a budget supporting other, later studies.

Excuses aside, it is worth looking at the problem of how the results of economic survey research might be put to use more effectively, making their potential social benefits a reality. Any presentation, the communications experts tell us, must know its audience. There are several audiences: respondents, interviewers, the general public, professional colleagues, and perhaps most important the various groups whose decisions may be affected by the information: sponsors, legislators, government agencies, private organizations.

Whatever the audience, there is a real problem how the results should be presented—with precision or with passion. All the professional training of academic researchers stresses precision, detailed care as to the accuracy of the results, presentation of the methodology, and not making statements that cannot be backed up by the data. This makes for dull reports and difficulty in finding what really matters. On the other hand, colorful writing is frequently inaccurate, or at least misleading, and may well combine the survey results with (a) other knowledge and (b) value judgements, explicitly or implicitly.

A few examples may be useful. Peter Townsend wrote a book on his studies of old people's homes in Britain, so dramatizing the plight of the people in them that the book led to Parliamentary action. Is it unscientific to put photographs of desolate looking old people in a report supposedly based on probability sampling?

A reverse example was a study in Michigan of the outcome of lump-sum settlements under the Workmen's Compensation law. An injured worker receiving medical care and weekly subsistence payments could settle his total future claim against his employer for a lump sum, if the hearing examiner approved. Some argued that this merely took the insurance company and the employer off the hook, let the man pay his back debts (including welfare, which demanded repayment), and that he would end up on welfare again. Others argued that the end of the gravy train and any future claims would miraculously cure bad backs and get people back to work. The study showed conclusively that people who settled for a lump sum payment were mostly not back at work, even the cases of injured backs, but the report did not go into the whole issue of reform of the workmen's compensation law. The immediate result was that the examiners made it very difficult for workers to get settlements, but inflation had so eroded the value of the weekly payments that they could hardly live on them. It was a number of years before the schedule of payments was raised so that the situation was genuinely improved.

A similar example occurred with studies of auto accident costs and compensation where studies show gross inequities, but a series of alternative reforms have been proposed. What obligation does the survey researcher, whose expertise is in research and perhaps also economics (but not law or insurance) have to enter that battle?

In between the active support of particular policies, and the refusal to go beyond the survey findings, there may well be a broad no-man's land of opportunities for making clear the implications of findings. Consumers' ignorance of effective interest rates, or their inefficient purchasing practices have relatively obvious importance to the effective operation of a market economy, and should not be buried in dull complicated reports.

To some extent the problem reflects a general tendency for researchers to allocate too little time and funds to both ends of the process. The design, pretesting, and development are often skimped in the haste to get into the field, and then the careful writing, and development of alternate presentations for different audiences, are skimped in the desire to get at the next piece of research. Most people dislike giving up the chance for more statistical analysis and finally putting a finished report on paper, until they are about to run out of time and money.

As the complexity of the analysis and of other survey procedures increase, the problem of reporting *simply* what the results were also increases. One interesting exercise is to see whether one can state in one sentence what a table shows and, if so, whether it is necessary to produce the whole table to show it. Another main issue in presentation is whether to present in detail all the negative findings—the variables that did *not* explain behavior and, if so, whether to first give the positive findings, and then separately the negative ones, so as to make the presentation simpler.

We discussed in the previous chapter some of the problems of presenting data. Even the titles given to variables can cause difficulty for readers, if they do not clearly indicate the operation that developed them. It is useful for the reader to have easy access to the actual question which elicited the information. Where a great deal of complex analysis is done, it is a great help to the reader to have, perhaps in an appendix, a complete list of questions, with numerical distributions of the answers by categories. Where many additional variables are created, their definitions and distributions (or means and variances) should also be easily accessible. In addition, where many complex terms are involved, for variables or procedures or units of analysis, a glossary of terms is frequently useful. Most United States Census Bureau publications are models in this respect.

When complex analyses are done, particularly such multivariate analyses as multiple regression, it is important to give the reader the univariate relations as well. When dummy or dichotomous variables are used, this means that the reader should have the unadjusted mean of the dependent variable for each subgroup (for whom some dummy variable is 1 rather than 0).

In addition it is extremely useful for the reader to know the degree of intercorrelation among the pairs of predictors used in a multivariate analysis. When they are numerical, this implies a table of simple correlation coefficients. When they are categorical, it is the association among sets of them which matters (age and education, for instance). The two-way tables would help and, if computers allow, Kendall's Tau Beta or even the canonical correlations between the sets of dummy variables, or Cramer's V.

Finally, and perhaps most important, the number of cases on which any estimate is based, together with some general procedures for approximating sampling errors, need to be provided, even if the analysis carefully discusses only results which are clearly statistically significant.

Research on communication (and persuasion) seems to indicate that written word is much less effective than personal communication, particularly if the latter allows two-way communication. While most people can read much faster than they can listen, they prefer to listen, and can often save a lot of time if they can ask a question. The questions also reveal problems in communication. Hence verbal communication, particularly with concerned people, may vastly improve the quality of a written report. It may also reveal complexities with policy implications, or new policy implications, that would not have occurred to the researcher.

In a broader perspective, one can think of the output of a survey research project as a lot of printed paper, plus some verbal presentations. The output serves many audiences, however, and must be tailored for them: They have some vested interest and a right to information. Most of them will be asked for further cooperation in the future, too.

1) *Respondents.* They may not be called on for reinterviews, but their neighbors will be interviewed in future studies. They gave time and energy and deserve some expression of thanks. They do not want the complex details, but may be interested in very simple things such as how many other people use their seat belts, or approve of installment credit. They need a report rapidly, before they forget all about the interview, and most such reports are based on the straight runs of questions likely to interest them, with perhaps a few comparisons among regions, or people of different ages.

2) *Interviewers.* They like to know not just some of the overall answers but reports on how the field work went, stories of unusual cases, and perhaps some notion what difference the study will make on issues of public policy. They also like to know a little about how the data get processed and how one goes from a series of questions to an index of, say, "risk avoidance."

3) *Specialists in the survey center itself.* They are most likely to be interested in a broader picture of the whole process, of which their work is a part, and in the implications of the study for science and for public policy. They usually get their feed-back personally, or in meetings which include the next group:

4) *Professional colleagues in the center and in the university.* These are busy people, often not much interested in the technical details (unless they suspect deficiencies) but concerned with how the material relates to a larger picture both of research and theory. They usually serve as a trial audience for papers and presentations designed for a larger national or international audience of professionals. But they are more crucial, in the sense that it is important that other parts of a university are sufficiently well informed to be reassured as to the quality and the importance of the work. Even if there is a national advisory committee, there needs also to be a local university committee which is kept well informed about the findings and the new research plans of a survey center.

5) *Colleagues in the professional associations.* This is the traditional audience, the one to which most research reports are directed, and the least interested in many cases. They have learned that it is necessary to be very selective about additions to the body of knowledge for which they are responsible, and those whose main interest is theory tend to be impatient with empirical findings

unless they are directly related to a particular theoretical structure. In economics, for instance, it is mainly income and price elasticities that are of interest to the profession. Reports which show the importance of other variables are not very interesting, unless it turns out that they actually account for differences (over time or between groups) in their dynamic responses to changes in income or prices. In the process of developing such information, the researcher must also generate a lot of other information, if only to remove "noise" in the estimates of interest to economists. And there is a great temptation to present all the ancillary information, to the distress of the readers. Some of it belongs in the professional journals of sociology or psychology, or statistics and methodology. The difficulty, of course, is that it is not easy to present only the findings of interest to one audience, without describing the whole study. Hence, there must be a full report available which gives the full methodology and most of the findings. The difficulty is that this main report usually exhausts the staff and the budget, leaving most of the audiences unsatisfied.

6) *Legislators and administrators.* People responsible for making or implementing public policy are again selective in what they want from a survey. They want the findings relevant for their decisions, and yet they do not want the researcher to try to make their decisions for them. For one thing, he often does not know a lot of other things essential for wise decisions. For another, it is not his responsibility, nor will he be called to task for the results. This puts the researcher in the position of trying to find out what the connection is between his findings and the problems of legislators or administrators, and making clear the relation of his findings to those problems, without attempting to go on to the next logical step (and an attractive one to anyone interested in problem solving) of working out the implications for action.

In underdeveloped countries this temptation is even stronger, and research experts frequently give advice (often bad) without realizing the extent of their ignorance about problems of implementing it, or other considerations. The more restricted contribution of providing continuous feedback on how programs are going and why (by interviewing people whose actions the government is trying to influence) would be far more useful.

7) *Reform groups.* Perhaps we should think of reform groups as another audience, and make a special effort to see that they understand the research findings in designing their reforms.

8) *The general public.* They indirectly support survey research and may be affected by the influence of its findings, so they deserve to know what is going on. Popularization of research findings is perhaps the most difficult of all, and often done by professional writers who may put too much emphasis on what is sensational or sexy, or jump too fast to generalize or draw policy implications. Press releases, issued by the survey center itself, can go a long way to close the gap and, when they are really well written, tend to be published almost verbatim

by newspapers. Once again, this obligation tends to be forgotten or delegated to someone with many other duties or little knowledge of the study or both.

Relation of Survey Research to the Universities

We have already argued that survey research can attack important current problems and still be contributing to the permanent body of scientific knowledge about human behavior. There is the danger, of course, of pressure to attack very much ad-hoc problems with little basic scientific interest. Another danger is that even if basic knowledge is created, it is a long time getting into the body of material being transmitted in the educational system. For this reason it seems important that survey research centers be closely attached to teaching institutions and that the researchers themselves do some teaching. It is not that status and titles still go with teaching, but that there is a symbiotic relation between teaching and research. Teaching material forces one to organize it, be prepared to defend it against criticism, and relate it to larger bodies of knowledge. The inevitable criticism from students and colleagues often points up the optimal next steps in a program of research. At the same time, a university is then teaching the best new knowledge, not material that is well-organized but out of date (or even wrong).

This, of course, benefits the individual university where there happens to be a survey center. National advisory committees can serve the function on a broader scale of alerting professionals all over the country of the available findings, and of data sets that can be used for further analysis. Such a committee also gives the survey center advice and counsel about the direction of research and even about specific research designs.

The other alternative, panels of readers and critics asked to judge designs and manuscripts, has not worked well, perhaps because it expects too much work and involvement from people who may be interested in the results and in future designs, but not in details.

In general the history of independent, isolated research groups or groups totally imbedded in administrative or action agencies has not been good. It is interesting to note that two national commissions have recently come out in favor of a number of university-based multi-disciplinary research organizations on a relatively permanent basis.[41] The advantages of such an arrangement seem clear, including some competition among them. What is not clear is how to assure that they will be responsible to the really important problems of the day and see to it that both legislators and administrators receive feed-back as to the implications of the research.

There are two main problems of large scale research organizations within universities, including survey research organizations. They are: titles, accreditation, and the maintenance of standards on the one hand, and financing, tenure, perquisites, and reserve funds on the other.

A university depends on its teaching departments for awarding titles and promotions, and maintaining standards of academic excellence. Professors see the results of their colleagues' teaching, and of their published scholarship, and are competent to judge it. It is not so easy for them to judge the competence of those engaged largely in research of a new, interdisciplinary, large-scale kind. Yet there is reluctance to see the title "Professor" awarded without some systematic accreditation and judging process, even if it is a title like Research Professor. One consequence is a second-class status for all but a few top staff in a research institute in terms of titles and some non-economic perquisites. "Teaching" titles also imply voting rights in the department on curricular matters, new staffing, etc. on which a department might justifiably feel that it would not want to be outvoted by a large group of part-time teachers. When it comes to maintaining the quality of the research, that monitoring is actually done within the research institute itself, but it has been found salutary to have an executive committee widely representative of interested segments of the university, approving the general policies and even each new proposal of the research institute. Not only can such a group warn against slipping standards, or unwise shifts in emphasis, but it can also communicate to the university a better sense of what is going on.

The issue of titles and standards is usually included in the discussions with the other, financial, issues. Joint appointments always raise questions of equity in the distribution of time and payments. More important, universities generally provide tenure to their senior faculty, in order to assure academic freedom. But they wince at the thought of providing such guarantees to personnel engaged in research with outside funds, outside the teaching budgets that is, which are seen as capable of withering any time. The history of oscillations in government and foundation support, particularly if one looks at individual areas of research, makes such fears credible. Since professional titles usually imply tenure, the two issues easily get mixed up.

Another economic issue has to do with indirect costs, and the extent to which there are hidden subsidies, in either direction. Foundation grants with limited "indirect costs" allowed, may be charged with adding to the university's general budget some of the total real costs of the research they support. After all, the university administration has to spend some part of its energies on these matters, and the university may be providing buildings, library services, etc. On the other hand, if a university takes all the indirect cost allocations in research contracts, it can easily use the funds to support other research or even some of its teaching functions.

One sensible solution to both these financial problems is to allow the research institute to keep nominal control of its own reserve funds, accumulated out of indirect charges on grants and contracts. With such funds it can provide tenure for its own staff. It can also take care of many of its own administrative functions and cost accounting. Perhaps more important, the research institute is then vitally concerned with its economic efficiency, since that builds its own security and capability for pioneering in areas otherwise unfinanced.

Conclusion

The future of economic survey research depends on adequate financing with long time horizons, judicious selection of the important areas of research, adequate evaluation of the benefits of past projects, efficient organization of research centers to maximize the information per dollar spent, and the wide diffusion of the results. A group of writers capable of interpreting the results of economic survey research, or a system of cooperating with specialists in producing separate statements of the action implications of studies needs to be developed. In the meantime, a major increase in the social benefits from economic surveys could come from clearer, and perhaps more specialized, reporting of the findings.

Not only is there need for greater total support for economic survey research, but a need for several research centers which can compete with one another and for an accompanying expansion of support for methodological research and for training of personnel. It has been difficult to convince people to learn economic survey methods when the total support for, and jobs in, the field were limited. It has been difficult to finance methodological research, when its benefits would be too late to help the current sponsors of individual substantive studies. And potential rates of expansion of economic surveys are hampered by shortages of personnel and inadequate development of methodology.

Hopefully, we are on the threshold of an era when analytical economists will be explicit but reasonable in their needs for behavioral information, and when the behavioral economists will focus survey research on these needs, so that the gap between what we hypothesize about behavior and what we seek to know, is narrowed.

Footnotes to Chapter VII

1. See the 1969 Budget Hearings and Testimony on the National Science Foundation, for example.

2. For a dramatic history of supression of research findings in another area (forestry) see Ashley Schiff, *Fire and Water,* Harvard University Press, Cambridge, Mass., 1962. Classified research supported by the government has usually not been survey research, except for some state department studies some years ago.

3. Guy Orcutt, "Data, Research, and Government," *American Economic Review,* 60 (May 1970), pp. 132-137.

4. Behavioral and Social Sciences Survey Committee, *The Behavioral and Social Sciences, Outlook and Needs,* National Academy of Sciences, Washington, D.C., 1969. (Committee under the auspices of the Committee on Science and Public Policy of the National Academy of Sciences and the Committee on Problems and Policy, of the Social Science Research Council; and Special Commission on the Social Sciences of the National Science Board, *Knowledge into Action: Improving the Nation's Use of the Social Sciences.* National Science Foundation, Washington, D.C., 1969.

   See also Gene M. Lyons, *The Uneasy Partnership,* Social Science and the Federal Government in the Twentieth Century, Russell Sage Foundation, New York, 1969.

INDEX